THE
GOOD
DEAL
DIRECTORY
2000

NOELLE WALSH

First published in 1996 by
The Good Deal Directory Company Limited
P.O. Box 4, Lechlade, Glos GL7 3YB
Telephone 01367 860016

ISBN 0-9526529-4-3

Typeset by Neon, 87-89 Saffron Hill, London EC1N 8QU.
Research team: Tracy Cambell, Jane Stevens,
Antoinette Brooke, Tessa Milne-Day, Rosie Gorman with special thanks to Alison
Goldingham.

DEAR READER

We hope you enjoy reading this book,
the definitive guide to value for money shopping
in Britain.

We also run a series of discount designer fashion
Sales at the elegant Pavilion at Ascot Racecourse in
Berkshire every November and May/June; at Ripley
Castle, Ripley, near Harrogate, Yorkshire, in April; in
Edinburgh in September, and at Sudeley Castle near
Cheltenham and Tatton Park, Cheshire, in October.
These Sales feature up to 100 top fashion and acces-
sory companies selling ends of lines, last season's
stock and over-runs at fantastically reduced prices.

If you'd like to know more about how to apply
for a ticket, send us a card with your name address
to the FREEPOST address below and we will send
you the information you require.

WRITE TO:
The Good Deal Directory's Fashion Sales,
FREEPOST SW 6037, London SW10 9YY.

You do not need to affix a stamp.

CONTENTS

Welcome to the seventh edition of The Good Deal Directory, packed with even more bargain outlets than ever before as befits a book that will see us all into the next century.

Who knows what the Millennium will bring in terms of new shopping habits?

Certainly, the Internet will be a big influence. And shopping on television. On a more basic level, I predict that value for money will be the mantra of the millennium. The Government has already started down this road as it launches investigations into the high prices charged by British retailers and manufacturers compared with their European counterparts. Meanwhile, value for money US-style has come to the UK in the form of American supermarket giant Wal-Mart teaming up with Asda.

None of this will be news to regular readers of The Good Deal Directory. As canny consumers, they appreciate that buying wisely is all about trading up - opting for labels and brand names that are out of reach on the full-price high street. They know that value for money isn't about cheapness but about quality at an affordable price. That cloth and cut, design and originality, are worth paying for. But you don't have to pay the prices touted in department stores and glossy magazine advertisements if you know where to look!

The biggest change since the last edition of this book is the number of top end of the market retailers and manufacturers who are either going into factory shopping or expanding their number of sites. Names such as Armani, Donna Karan, Paul Smith, Dunhill, Margaret Howell, Gianfranco Ferre and Polo Ralph Lauren. They've discovered that a well-chosen site, away from the retailers who stock them in quantity, can enhance the bottom line while not harming their core, full-price business.

As one designer explained to me, if you know that you can clear some of your excess stock, it means you can be more adventurous with your designs and you can make more of each size - particularly the smaller and larger sizes. For example, say a designer normally makes ten size 8s, ten size 10s, ten size 12s and ten size 14s and sells seven of each size at the full price of £600, cost price £200.

If she decided to add four more size 8s and four more size 14s and a couple each to the in-between sizes, because she was offering more choice she could sell more. Thus she sells eleven size 8s and eleven size 14s at full price and another one each of the in-between sizes. So she's sold ten more outfits at the full price of £600 each and is fairly certain of selling most of her overstock of fourteen outfits at half price. That's, say, 10 of the 14 at £300 each. Remember, she's still making a profit of £100 each on her half-price outfits. So instead of making £12,000 gross from her original production, she makes £18,000, and there's the bonus from both methods of another £3,000 from her factory shop.

Smaller designers who don't have sufficient stock to fill a factory shop on their own are turning more and more either to Designer Sales or to their own showroom sales, using a mailing list of their best customers. This can have its drawbacks, though. I was frantically trying on clothes at a Tomasz Starzewski showroom sale when a wail went up from the lady next to me. She had just that day bought exactly the same trousers I was trying on in Tomasz's shop - at twice the price! Technically, this shouldn't happen as the clothes in the Sale should be last season's stock.

Last year, I wrote about the growth of factory shopping centres countrywide. This has continued and will do so until mid-way into the year 2000 when it will slow down as activity moves to the Continent. In the next century, you will be inundated with information on factory shopping while you're skiing in Austria, quaffing wine in France or soaking up the sun in Spain! There are even plans for factory shops at Disneyland in France! You'll find a full list of factory shopping villages in the UK, together with projected centres still to open, further on in the Introduction.

At the other end of the scale from the top designers, shops such as Matalan and T K Maxx are thriving. Both stock fashion for all the family, homewares and an ever-changing mixed merchandise of perfumes, tights, accessories, gifts, beauty products or whatever they can buy in sufficient quantity and at very good prices. Matalan has strong brand names rather than top designer names; T K Maxx has both, although you have to be a real bargain hunter as their layout doesn't make it easy to find hot items. You can find some fabulous names at T K Maxx, though, if you're prepared to spend time and energy. There will be fifty T K Maxx stores countrywide by January 2000 so you should be able to find one near you.

The massive amount of overstock in the world of fashion has also permeated down to permanent discount outlets and designer sales. End of line retailers are able to go over to the Continental factories where top designer labels are manufactured and buy merchandise that hasn't been bought by the big department store buyers at knockdown prices early in the selling season, bring it back to the UK and sell it at discounted prices only weeks after it has first appeared in our top boutiques and stores.

Dress agencies, those places where gently worn clothes go after their owners have tired of them, also benefit from this. The cognoscenti buy their top designer labels at discount prices and then, if they discover they've made a mistake or have only worn it once, sell it on to dress agencies. Because they got it so cheap, the mistakes don't matter so much. The growing number of dress agencies is testimony to the knock-on effect when fashion is widely discounted.

Meanwhile, in the homes arena, your home, after all, is as much a victim of fashion trends as your wardrobe. Bad news if you like being a style leader but good news if you want to save money. Why? Because shops make it their business to sell the newest fabrics, the latest sofa shape, the most technologically advanced piece of kitchen equipment. When, the following season, the next new designs are ready to take their place on the shop floor, the only-just-arriveds have to depart.

For example, white goods manufacturers (fridges, freezers, washing machines etc) often bring out new models which are only the tiniest bit different to the old model. A washing machine may have a top spin speed of 1100 rpm instead of 1000. This is so that the shops have something new to sell and something new to say to customers. But it makes very little difference to you, the consumer. Unless you want a bargain - in which case, you opt for the old model and get it cheaper!

Some of the unsold stock is held over in the shop's limited storage space until the twice-yearly sale; the remainder makes it way to a wide variety of disposal channels ranging from warehouse sales to factory shops. If you don't mind buying last year's trend-setting fabric to cover your Ottoman, you can pick up some exciting bargains. The same is true for almost everything you find in the home from carpets to curtains, fridges to furniture, bedlinen to breadmakers, and cutlery to ceramics.

Fabrics
Some companies such as Osborne & Little, Colefax & Fowler, Sanderson and Designers Guild hold their own "warehouse" sales, reducing stock significantly to clear it to existing customers whom they mail. If you want to find out about these clearance sales, write to the company and ask for your name to be put on the mailing list (the addresses are in the book under London, Designer Sales).

There are hundreds of fabric discount shops countrywide: shops such as Knickerbean, which has five outlets selling Designers Guild, Anna French, Jane Churchill, Colefax & Fowler and Osborne & Little, among the scores of different fabrics. Some are discontinued lines, ends of ranges or off-shade lots, but a growing number come in directly from mills and manufacturers overseas. Their fast-moving selection of more than 200,000 metres from £5.95 a metre includes glazed chintzes, cotton prints, stripes and checks as well as a huge selection of luxurious upholstery fabrics, Italian damasks and tapestries.

If you're looking for curtain fabric, try one of the many secondhand curtains businesses countrywide first. They stock a wide range of curtains, many of which are from show houses or interior designers' mistakes or simply bought by people who didn't like them once they hung them! Others are made from incredibly expensive fabric, lined, interlined and weighted and in almost-perfect condition and sold at between one third and one half of the as-new price. Most secondhand curtain shops let you take the curtains home and try them out against your windows before they cash your cheque so you, too, won't make a costly mistake.

Kitchen and dining room
Brand names such as Remington, Pifco, Moulinex and Swan are all available in factory shops where you can also buy Oneida cutlery, Swan fryers, Kenwood food mixers, kitchen knives, Russell Hobbs kettles, Tower pans, Krups kitchen applicances at discounts of at least 25%. If a new food processor comes out, shops again no longer want to sell the old one so it goes back to the factory for selling in the factory shop. Occasionally, items are returned because of damaged packaging when they are re-checked by factory technicians and then sold at discount prices.

The result of all this is that for you, the customer, there is greater choice than ever before. As long as you are prepared to wait - not to buy when an item is first on the market - you can get some great bargains. With shop rents rising, there is more and more pressure on them to change stock regularly, keep bringing in new lines - which means they have to clear out unsold stock very quickly. It's madness to try and clear old stock at discount prices in the same high-rent shop as you are also trying to sell new stock at full price - hence the increase in factory shops and discount shops.

What's New
Soon, there will be a factory shopping village within reasonable driving distance of most of us - apart from the geographical extremes of the country. By the end of 2000, there will be 30 factory shopping centres and many smaller centres linked to already-existing leisure facilities such as garden centres. As John Drummond, chief executive of the company which developed the Clacton Common centre, says, "Four or five years ago, there was not much competition in the outlet market, but now things have moved on. People now have a choice of factory outlets to visit within a two-hour drive time and, in

terms of the shops themselves, a Bed & Bath Works here is the same as a Bed & Bath Works in Cheshire Oaks. The only way to differentiate and attract real shoppers is to make sure the experience of the visit is enjoyable and memorable."

Most of the villages open in phases, so they are constantly changing as well as bringing in new shops. Even when they are completely full, some tenants may find they have taken on too large an outlet and decide to split it in two, in which case this makes room for another new tenant. Occasionally, tenants find that factory shopping doesn't work for them and close down their operations, but this is rare.

Factory shopping centres

Factory shopping centres - the smallest has 10 shops, the largest more than 160 - are for a different type of bargain shopper than the traditional stand-alone factory outlet. The latter attracts those who take pleasure in the hunt: in finding an out-of-the-way, sometimes unattractive shed on an industrial estate miles off the beaten track. The level of attractiveness of the site is usually directly related to the price of the goods on sale - the more unattractive the actual factory outlet is, the lower the prices. However, you can't go shopping with a list at these individual outlets.

Factory shopping centres, on the other hand, offer a higher level of certainty. If there are 120-plus shops - as at the McArthurGlen Designer Outlet in York - you'd have to be pretty picky not to find something you like and can afford. The choice is usually enormous - most of the shops are fashion oriented although they now offer a growing selection of children's goods, luggage, jewellery, shoes, cookware, toys, glassware and electrical goods. But the choice comes at a price. On the whole, prices are higher at the factory shopping centres than at stand-alone factory shops - except at traditional sale times when the village shops also slash prices in order to clear stock.

Factory shopping centres here began with the Freeport Leisure Village in Hornsea on the East Yorkshire coast in the late Eighties, early Nineties. This was followed by the first purpose-built factory shopping centre, Clarks Village in Street, Somerset, built around an already-existing shoe museum and shoe discount town. In the early Eighties, the American developers came over here, factory shopping centres in the US having reached a plateau. Many of them tied up with an existing British company in joint ventures. Being American, they thought BIG. Their centres tended to be much much bigger than the traditional British ones with twice the number of shops. Now that they have reached a plateau here, too, they have moved onto the Continent.

OUTLET VILLAGES

Bicester Outlet Shopping Village, junction 9 of M40, Pingle Drive, Bicester, Oxfordshire OX6 7WD
☎ 01869 323200   approx 60 shops

Cheshire Oaks Designer Outlet Village, junction 10 of M53, Kinsey Road, near Ellesmere Port, South Wirral CH65 9JJ
☎ 0151 356 7932   120-166 shops

Jacksons Landing, The Highlight, Hartlepool Marina, Hartlepool, Cleveland TS24 OXN
☎ 01429 866989   24 shops

K Village, Kendal junction 36 of M6, Cumbria
☎ 01539 734347   12 shops

Clarks Village, Farm Road, Street, Somerset BA16 OBB
☎ 01458 840064 approx 56 shops

Galleria Outlet Centre, Comet Way, Hatfield, Herts. AL10 OXR
☎ 01707 278301   70   shops

Hornsea Freeport Shopping Village, Rolston Road, Hornsea, East Yorkshire HU18 1UT
☎ 01964 534211   approx 50 shops

Freeport Shopping Village, Anchorage Road, Fleetwood, junction 3 of M55, Lancashire FY7 6AE
☎ 01253 877377   approx 50 shops

Freeport Scotland, West Calder, West Lothian EH55 8QB
☎ 0151 763488   40 shops

Royal Quays Factory Outlet Centre, North Shields, Newcastle-upon-Tyne; 0191 296 3743   will have 60 shops eventually

The Yorkshire Outlet, White Rose Way, junction 3 of M18, Doncaster, South Yorks. DN4 5JH
☎ 01302 367021   44 shops

Village Square, Brighton Marina Village, Brighton, East Sussex BN2 5WB
☎ 01273 693636.   12 shops with more planned

Great Western Designer Outlet Village, Kemble Drive, Churchward Village, junction 16 of M4, Swindon, Wilts SN2 2DY
☎ 01793 507600   108 shops, with more planned

Festival Park Factory Outlet Shopping, Festival Park, Victoria, Ebbw Vale, South Wales
☎ 01495 350010.   38 shops

Loch Lomond Factory Outlets, Main Street, Alexandria, on the A82, Loch Lomond, near Glasgow, Scotland G83 OUG
☎ 01389 710077   approx 21   shops

Designer Outlet Wales, The Derwen, Bridgend, South Wales CF32 9SU
☎ 01656 665700   approx 94 shops

Clacton Common Factory Outlet Village, Clacton, Essex
☎ 01255 479595   approx 50 shops

McArthurGlen Designer Outlet York, St Nicholas Avenue, Fulford, Junction A19 and A64, York, North Yorkshire YO19 4TA
☎ 01904 682700   150 factory shops planned
McArthurGlen Designer Outlet Derbyshire, Mansfield Road, South Normanton, Alfreton, junction 28 of M1,Derbyshire DE55 2JW
☎ 01773 545000   four themed areas: fashion, home, sport/leisure and accessories
Peak Village, Chatsworth Road, Rowsley, on the A6 between Bakewell and Matlock, Derbyshire DE4 2JE
☎ 01629 735326   15 factory shops and leisure facilities
Evesham Country Park, Country Park Management, Evesham, at northern end of the Evesham by-pass at its junction with Stratford Road, Worcestershire WR11 4TP
☎ 01386 41661   factory shops, garden centre, leisure facilities
Sterling Mill Designer Outlet Village, Tillicoultry, near Stirling, midway between M9 and M90, Scotland FK13 6HQ
☎ 01259 752100   22 outlets with more planned
Gretna Gateway, Glasgow Road, Gretna DG16 6GG
☎ 07771 658343.   60 factory shops planned
Freeport Talke Outlet Mall, Pit Lane, Talke Pits, Stoke-on-Trent, Staffordshire ST7 1XD
☎ 01782 774113.   approx 30 factory shops
Wilton Factory Shopping Village, Minster Street, Wilton, near Salisbury, Wiltshire SP2 ORS
☎ 01722 741 211   approx 11 factory shops

TO OPEN
Whiteley Village, off M27 between Southampton and Portsmouth, Hampshire   opening autumn 1999
Europoort Harwich Ltd, Harwich, Essex   46 shops planned
due to open in summer 1999 as we went to press
Freeport Essex Village, Braintree, Essex   opening autumn 1999
Gunwharf Quays, Portsmouth, Hampshire   85 factory shops, restaurants, craft market, leisure complex, cinema   opening 2000
Freeport Castleford, Castleford, near junction 32 of M62, West Yorkshire opening summer/autumn 1999
McArthurGlen Designer Outlet Scotland, Almondvale Boulevard, Livingston, West Lothian   100 factory shops, Ferris wheel, cinema
opening summer 2000

What are factory shops?
Factory shops sell manufacturer's surplus stock - cancelled orders, returned merchandise from the store, over-production, seconds or discontinued lines - at

prices which are much lower than those in the high street shops which the factory supplies. Discounts vary but in general they are higher in the fashion sector where an outfit can be out of date very quickly and where markups can be as high as 280%, and lower in ceramics and glassware. There are far fewer homeware factory shops than fashion ones because for a housewares retailer whose mark-up is not very high, half-price is not profitable whereas if you're a fashion manufacturer with a high mark-up, half-price still leaves a significant profit margin. The older the item is, the cheaper the price. As a general rule, you can expect at least 30% off, and up to 80%.

GETTING THE BEST OUT OF FACTORY SHOPPING

1. Eighty percent of factory shopping village customers visit on a weekend, leaving you with queues at the tills, parking problems and less chance of getting a table at the centre's restaurants. If you can, shop at villages during the week when they are usually quiet and where there may be extra discounts available to weekday shoppers.

2. Although they don't advertise the fact, most factory shopping villages discount their products even further at traditional high street sale times (January and June). So if you only visit villages twice a year, ring and check the sale times before you go. The disadvantage, however, is that you will be getting the last of the line in stock so colour and size choices will be limited. This is offset by the really good bargains.

3. Keep your eyes and ears open all the time. On a day trip, watch out for signs for out-of-the-way factory shops; scour the small ads of your local papers for one-day factory shop sales.

4. Put your name down on the mailing list of factory shops you visit. Fabric factory shops, for instance, often hold twice-yearly sales at their warehouses to which they invite customers and sell last year's stock at greatly reduced prices. Many fashion factory shops have one or two-day sales when even the reductions are reduced.

5. Tourist information centres are useful sources of free information on factory shops in their area.

6. If it's a particular brand name you're after, such as Jaeger, Burberry or Aquascutum, and you want a specific item (a raincoat or blazer) ring first and check their stock. There are certain times of year when it is very low. The staff are usually very helpful.

7. Check if the item is a second - usually there is a label on the garment stating why it is so. For example, Aquascutum label their seconds "Slightly Imperfect" and mark on an illustration of the garment where the imperfection lies. You cannot return a second if it says what's wrong with it - although all your statutory rights are in place at factory shops.

8. Never travel a long way without phoning first to check opening hours and stock levels. It's also a good idea to phone to get directions as many of the individual factory shops are in out-of-the-way, hard to find places.

9. If you're looking to be the height of fashion, factory shopping isn't for you - unless you're a natural stylist and can mix looks to modernise. Fashion factory shopping is great for children's clothes, jeans, leisure wear, sweaters, underwear and classic items such as blazers, coats and raincoats.

10. If you see something you like, buy it. You won't find it again.

11. If you want to pay by credit card, check first that some of the smaller, individual factory shops accept them.

12. If you're looking for small electrical appliances for the kitchen, it's unlikely that you will find the latest gadget, but there will be good bargains in ends of lines.

13. Whatever the condition of the outlet, your rights are just the same as if you were shopping in the mainstream. You are covered by the Sale of Goods Act and the Consumer Protection Act.

14. Factory outlets sell limited ranges, colours and sizes so don't expect either co-ordinated ranges or to be able to exchange an item for the same thing but bigger/smaller a few days later.

15. Some of the major high street stores insist on the manufacturer cutting out their label before selling in the factory outlet, so some of the goods may be unbranded. This applies even to the washing instructions in some cases.

16. If there isn't a double price on the price tag (ie the original selling price crossed out and replaced with the reduced one), it may be that this item has been specially made for the factory shop from leftover fabric used in the manufacture of the original garment. Sometimes, factories are left with hundreds of a particular skirt left but very few of the matching blouses, so they make up more blouses from the same fabric. Watch out that the colours match exactly. Or it may be that the item was originally made for export and has never been on sale in the UK.

17. Don't always believe what the size tag tells you - some items are seconds because they are incorrectly marked up.

18. Before you travel, sit down with a map book and plot your journey. Often, there are three or four factory shops within a few miles of each other or on your route so you can make the most of your trip.

19. Carry room and window measurements with you if visiting carpet or fabric factory shops and children's ages and sizes with you if visiting toy or clothing outlets. What you see when you visit is all there usually is of that item.

20. In the more traditional factory shops, you may not find items as flatteringly presented as they are in department and high street stores. Be prepared to rummage.

DEFINITION OF TERMS
Factory shop
Run by the manufacturer or a representative of the manufacturer (who may also be a retailer) selling last season's stock as well as ends of lines, slow-selling items, returned merchandise. A few global manufacturers bring in stock from other countries which may not have been on sale here before. A few others make up clothes from the same fabric which was used to make the clothes originally on sale in high street shops. Thus, if they have hundreds of a particular skirt left over but only a few dozen of its matching jackets, but plenty of the fabric, they will make up jackets to match. They will then not be able to give two prices - an original and a discounted price - for these items.

Permanent discount outlets
Run by entrepreneurs who buy in stock from a variety of sources: overseas manufacturers clearance lines; bankrupt stock; fortuitous purchasing (perhaps from a designer who needs cash quickly); other full-price shops' slower-selling lines; returns from department stores; overstocks from the chain stores (although these usually have the labels removed). Those outlets selling clothes from Marks & Spencer have to agree to remove the St Michael label and any other identifying label such as the care label.

Permanent discount outlets also include all the shops run by mail order companies (Scoops, M C Hitchen, Next to Nothing, Choice), clearing their old catalogue stock. These are often very good value for large electrical equipment, although these items sell out so quickly that you almost have to visit the shop every day in order to buy one. Many mail order companies now also sell designer-led merchandise and some of this makes its way into these clearance shops but you have to be willing to scour the rails. Remember that half price in these shops isn't necessarily half price in that up to 11% is added to the cost of items to cover direct marketing costs and mailing of catalogues. So half price is actually a discount of 39%.

Dress Agencies
Have you ever wondered how some women always manage to look smartly dressed? Have they just got lashings of natural style, a family member who owns a dress shop or simply money to burn? It's just as likely that they have discovered the secret of of secondhand clothes shopping.

Now called dress agencies by those anxious to dispel visions of jumble sale leftovers, these recession-spawned shops are a boon both to those wishing to spend money and those wanting to earn some. As a customer, you have the opportunity to buy good quality clothes at very reasonable prices and you can also clear out your own "mistakes" and make a bit of money.

Dress agency owners are very particular about which clothes they choose to sell. They have to be - the quality of their merchandise reflects how successful they - and ultimately, you if you're a seller - will be. If you're looking for designer labels, choose the best areas of town to shop in. For example if the dress agency is in London's Beauchamp Place or Hampstead, the labels will be the best: Armani, DKNY, Valentino, Bruce Oldfield. If it's the high street, Suburbia, there will probably be a good mix of labels such as Jaeger and Country Casuals as well as a sprinkling of high street favourites: Next, Principles, Marks & Spencer. But dress agency owners rely on the clients who bring them in clothes to sell so one visit may yield a goldmine of covetable clothes; another just fool's gold.

Dress agencies only accept cleaned, pressed clothes in mint condition. A price is agreed, of which most agencies take 40%-50% as their commission. The clothes are put on the rails for a set period of time - usually 6-12 weeks. If, after that time, an item hasn't sold, some proprietors will talk to the owner about reducing the price. If it still doesn't sell, it will be returned to the owner. Uncollected items are usually sent to charity shops.

Dress agencies are usually friendly places - many offer coffee or tea and some even have small coffee rooms where you can relax and read a paper. The best ones build up a rapport with their regular customers, letting them know if something comes in which might be of interest.

Tips for getting the best out of dress agencies

1. If you're looking for top designer labels, choose a dress agency in an expensive neighbourhood. They're most likely to have the sort of clientele who dress in the best and then sell it on.

2. If your child is about to start a new school with all the expense of a uniform, find out if there is a dress agency dealing in childrenswear in the vicinity of the school - there's bound to be some secondhand uniforms there.

3. Clearing out your own wardrobe is a good way to find out if a dress agency is right for you. If they sift carefully through your clothes insisting on a certain quality and on the garments being dry cleaned then you know they're good enough to buy from. It's also a way of making money for yourself from clothes which you no longer wear or which were mistakes.

4. Instead of spending money hiring an evening outfit for that once-a-year special occasion, buy your evening gown/cocktail dress from a dress agency. Whether you hire or buy, you'll still be wearing a garment that's already been worn, and you might as well have use of it for another occasion!

5. Dress agencies are great places to buy almost brand new ski wear and horse riding gear, which are sold there by people who tried skiing and didn't like it or who had a short-lived passion for horses.

6. If the garment or accessory you're buying is a top designer label and that's the main reason you're buying it, insist on that fact being written on your receipt. If it turns out to be a fake, you will then have evidence that you bought what you were told was the real thing.

Architectural salvage

Someone else's rubbish could be your treasure. Architectural salvage business-es deal in reclaimed items from homes and gardens. Some specialise in, say, gar-den statuary or fireplaces or floorboards. They tend to be vast caverns and you need to have a keen eye.

Showroom sales

Like any business, the fashion trade has surplus stock and precisely because it is a fashion business, they can't hang on to it for too long before it becomes unsellable. Showroom sales are held by a variety of different people: whole-salers who haven't sold in to shops all the stock they bought; agents who have lots of last season's samples which they use to show buyers (remember last sea-son in fashion language is usually this season in yours - thus, by May summer stock may be last season's just as the weather is hotting up sufficiently for you to buy it for this); designers who control the design, manufacture and whole-saling of their clothes who may have a mixture of samples, unsold items, returned goods and overstock; individuals who gather together surplus stock from a variety of different sources, hire a venue and sell it to the general pub-lic, taking a cut of the total sales.

The majority of these sales take place in London and many are advertised in the days preceding the sale in the Evening Standard newspaper. They're well worth visiting - if you don't mind a scrum and aren't over-modest as most don't boast changing rooms. (There is a list of Designer Showroom Sales in the book in the London section under Designer Sales.) Showroom sales at venues usual-ly charge a small fee to cover their mailing costs. They keep a list of everyone who has visited their Sales and mail them with the date of the next one.

Some Sale organisers also run sales outside London, including The Good Deal Directory, which runs the Really Good Deal Fashion Sales at six venues around the country. November and late May/early June at the elegant Pavilion at Ascot Racecourse; every April at Ripley Castle, Ripley, near Harrogate, Yorkshire; every September in Edinburgh at the Assembly Rooms and every October at Tatten Park, Cheshire and Sudeley Castle, near Cheltenham, Glos. These Sales were inspired by the book, The Good Deal Directory, and offer a huge range of designer and top brand-name fashion and accessories at end of the line prices.

Live Well on Less

When I first started The Good Deal Directory, I used to include tips for sav-ing money which didn't really fall into any category. They might be things like Entertainment Guides which gave you 25% off meals at hundreds of restau-rants or where lost property ends up and how you can buy some amazing bar-gains at the lost property auctions. Almost all of these have either been tried out by me or recommended to me by readers, so they're not just money-making schemes by some unscrupulous individual. For the Millennium Edition, I have decided to bring back these helpful hints in a big way and drop them in throughout the book.

MORE BARGAIN HUNTING TIPS

1. Discount shopping isn't all about factory shops. There are lots of permanent discount shops all over the country, run by people who know how to find a bargain. Many of these are selling items left over from the big catalogue companies - anything from babygros to television sets, jewellery to hi-fis. Others sell Continental designers obtained direct from the manufacturers abroad.

2. Don't ignore dress agencies as a way of saving - and making - money. You can buy clothes you couldn't otherwise afford in these nearly-new shops which are springing up all over the country. Or sell off your mistakes or items you no longer like wearing and make a bit of cash yourself.

3. Someone else's rubbish may be your treasure. If you're doing up your house and want to, for example, put floorboards down instead of carpets, check out the architectural salvage experts first. They may have floors taken out of old school rooms or manor houses at very reasonable prices.

4. Visit large exhibitions such as Gardener's World or The Clothes Show Live on the afternoon of the last day. Exhibitors don't always want to take the stock on their stand home so will often sell it off at rock-bottom prices, making the entrance ticket price well worthwhile.

5. If you buy women's magazines, always check out the small ads at the back where lots of companies advertise end of line fabrics, direct-from-the-factory spiral staircases, factory shop sofas, architectural reclamation services and the like.

6. Free information - and sometimes even samples - is widely available from supermarkets (recipe suggestions for a new vegetable they're stocking), large food companies, perfume and cosmetic companies launching new products.

7. If you're trying to buy curtain fabric to match sofa upholstery, bring a cushion from the sofa with you if you can. If you're trying to match curtains with your walls, paint a piece of wood with your wall colour and bring that with you.

8. The best buys at discount shops are always the most expensive items. Thus, large items such as sofas, beds and carpets offer the best bargains.

9. White goods such as fridges, washing machines and vacuum cleaners have quite small markups anyway - 20-28% compared with 110% for furniture and up to 280% for clothes - so don't expect huge discounts on these items.

10. Anything that shouts out the season will always be the better bargain: dates on T-shirts, for example. Bear in mind, though, that everyone will know what year you bought it.

11. The advice for clever bargain home buys is the same as for fashion: buy classics. The classic tin of white or cream paint; cream fabric; white tiles...you can always buy in some splashes of colour later to add interest and excitement.

12. Buy items such as evening wear. Because they're expensive to start with, you will save more. Even if you have no particular event in mind, it's much better to have that half-price bargain in your wardrobe in six months time when an unexpected invitation arrives than rush out the Saturday before and buy something expensive just to have something different to wear.

13. If you're buying shoes, trade up - buy top brand shoes at the sort of price you would normally pay for your full-price cheaper brands. Good shoes do last much longer than cheap ones. Invest in shoe trees and shoe brushes and vow to maintain them.

14. If you're trying to create a designer wardrobe from scratch, start with an anchor piece. If you've got a good coat or jacket, you will always look well dressed. Or buy a classic suit that can also be worn as separates. Go for classic colours which will stand the test of time and inject the "now" colours from the full-price high street.

15. If you need a flat pair of shoes or a handbag or a scarf in order to stretch your wardrobe and wear things that you haven't been able to, look out for that one buy which will give you a total new outfit when added to what you already have in your wardrobe.

16. Remember, the price of things can be divided by the number of times you wear it so if you can see yourself getting a lot of wear out of something that's still a bit more than you would normally pay for an item, it's probably worth it.

17. Don't buy something that looks wonderful but just doesn't go with your lifestyle.

18. Don't leave gift buying until the last minute when you're tempted to pay anything just to turn up with something. Keep a list of everyone on your birthday/Christmas/wedding anniversary list and take it with you whenever you go shopping. Look over it quickly before you shop in case you find something that suits someone on your list. The right gift at the right price may not be around the week before a birthday, but it might be there six months before. Remember to keep a note of what you've bought and when it has been given.

19. When factory shopping for clothes if you haven't got a definite must-buy in mind, find replacements for your old favourites which are beginning to look a bit shoddy. If you've got a jacket or a pair of trousers that you wear almost every day, look out for something that fulfils the same purpose. Of if you've got a jacket in your wardrobe that you haven't worn this season because you never had the right thing to go with it, now is the time to fill in that gap.

20. Avoid outrageous outfits that people will remember you in as you won't be able to wear them more than once.

The Good Deal Directory isn't about where to find items cheaply. If it was, it would be full of details of markets and car boot sales. What it is about is buying quality goods at prices which are lower than they were originally. Most of the information has been gathered by myself and my team of researchers over the past eight or more years; now, a lot of it is also supplied by readers of The Good Deal Directory. I pay for tips: places which readers have visited and believe are good value and which I don't already know about. My readers tell me what they bought, what else was for sale there, what the discounts were and what the service was like. I couldn't ask for a better team of researchers, and all those who contributed to this book are thanked at the back of the book. If you know of somewhere that isn't in this book and which I subsequently publish, remember, I pay £10 for tips. So you could end up enjoying a free book. There are pages at the back of the book which you can fill in and send to me or if you don't want to tear pages out, simply photocopy a page and send it to me or write a letter. The address is on the pages at the back of the book.

Happy bargain hunting! Noelle Walsh

Geographical breakdown of Book

Unlike previous years where shops are gathered into ten areas of the country, for the first time shops are broken down by county. For example if you are looking for glassware in Stoke-on-Trent, you will find a list of all household shops at the beginning of the Staffordshire chapter and can then flick through picking out just the glassware shops alphabetically.

Each shop now has a symbol denoting whether it sells clothes or curtains, sportswear or books. For a definition of what these symbols mean, please turn over.

All factory shops within factory villages are categorised under the village and not the individual factory shop.

Womenswear

Menswear

Childrenswear

Household

DIY Renovation

Electrical Equipment

Sportswear

Leisure

Soft furnishings

ENGLAND

BY COUNTY
(including West Midlands & Greater Manchester)

Bedfordshire

WOMENSWEAR ONLY   🏵 Gossard, *Leighton Buzzard*.   The Changing Room, *Leighton Buzzard*. The Vanity Box, *Dunstable*.

WOMENSWEAR & MENSWEAR   🏵 🏵 Matalan, *Bedford*. Walter Wright Factory Shop, *Luton*.

CHILDREN   🏵 Matalan, *Bedford*.

HOUSEHOLD AND GIFTWARE   🏠 Including china, glass, cutlery, towels, bedding, sheets, linen Freelance Fabrics, *Luton*.   Matalan, *Bedford*.

ARCHITECTURAL SALVAGE   🏠 Architectural Antiques, *Bedford*. D.S. & A.G. Prigmore & Son, *Colmworth*.

FURNITURE/SOFT FURNISHINGS   🏠 Boynett Fabrics Co Ltd, *Bedford*. Freelance Fabrics, *Luton*.

ARCHITECTURAL ANTIQUES

70 PEMBROKE STREET, BEDFORD, BEDFORDSHIRE MK40 3RQ
☎ (01234) 213131. OPEN 12 - 5 MON - FRI, 9 - 5 SAT.
Buy and sell antiques, good quality furniture, original fireplaces and all archi-tectural salvage. They have a large selection of original Georgian, Victorian and Edwardian fireplaces in marble, slate, cast iron, mahogany, oak and pine, and provide a restoration and installation service. All types and sizes of inter-nal and external doors and cupboards, glazed doors and bookshelves; rolltop baths, basins, glazed and stone sinks, brass taps, radiators and towel rails, stone flooring, tiles, bricks, floorboards, moulded skirting and architrave. Balustrades, chimney pots, garden edging, grates and timber; good quality antique chests of drawers, wardrobes, dressing tables, dining chairs, dressers, bookcases, mirrors, clocks, lamps radios and other unusual items.
Architectural Salvage

Live Well On Less Tips
If you're pregnant, don't forget that you are eligible for free dental treatment and prescriptions during your pregnancy and for up to one year after the birth of your baby.

BOYNETT FABRICS CO LTD

2 ASTON ROAD, CAMBRIDGE ROAD, BEDFORD, BEDFORDSHIRE
MK42 OJN

☎ (01234) 217788. OPEN 8.30 - 5 MON - FRI, 10 - 3 SAT.

Curtain and upholstery fabrics manufactured by Boynett, who are wholesalers
and distributors to the interior design market, are sold in this factory shop at
discount prices for seconds and over-runs. Prices start at £1 per metre.
Factory Shop

D.S. & A.G. PRIGMORE & SON

MILL COTTAGE, MILL ROAD, COLMWORTH, BEDFORDSHIRE
MK44 2NU

☎ (01234) 376264. OPEN 8 - 4 MON - FRI, 8 - 12 SAT.

Reclaimed building materials, oak and pine beams, slates, tiles, bricks, woodblock flooring, doors and other quality items including a good selection of 2-
inch Tudor-style bricks. Also RSJs. *Architectural Salvage*

FREELANCE FABRICS

1-3 HANCOCK PARADE, BUSHMEADS, LUTON, BEDFORDSHIRE
L42 7SF

☎ (01582) 411522. OPEN 9.30 - 5.30 MON - FRI, 9 - 5 SAT, 10 - 4 SUN.

Part of a chain of shops selling well-known fabrics, curtain and upholstery
weights, tracks, ready-made nets. Current fabrics are sold at reduced prices and
there is a small range of end of line fabrics. For details of your local branch
phone 01582 411522. *Permanent Discount Outlet*

GOSSARD FACTORY SHOP

GROVEBURY ROAD, LEIGHTON BUZZARD, BEDFORDSHIRE LU7 8SN

☎ (01525) 851122/850088. OPEN 9.30 - 5.30 MON - SAT.

Factory shop sells seconds and discontinued ranges of Gossard and Berlei
underwear including bras, briefs, suspender belts and bodies at discounted
prices (no nightwear or long-line slips). Most of the stock is last year's trade
catalogue styles at discounts of between 25%-75%. Large car park at rear of
building; wheelchair ramp. *Factory Shop*

MATALAN

UNIT C, INTERCHANGE RETAIL PARK, AMPTHILL ROAD, BEDFORD,
BEDFORDSHIRE MK42 7AZ

☎ (01234) 365077. OPEN 10 - 8 MON - FRI, 9 - 6 SAT, 11 - 5 SUN.

Matalan is a fashion and homewares shop giving customers what they claim to
be unbeatable value for money with huge savings on a wide range of products

including high quality fashionable clothing for women, women and children at up to 50% off high street prices. Matalan is situated out of town and stores are open seven days a week all year round. *Permanent Discount Outlet*

THE CHANGING ROOM

1 PEACOCK MEWS, LEIGHTON BUZZARD, BEDFORDSHIRE
☎ (0402) 809941. OPEN 9.30 - 4 TUE - SAT.
Nearly-new designer shop selling Armani, Kenzo and Jaeger, as well as shoes and costume jewellery. *Dress Agency*

THE VANITY BOX

16 CHURCH STREET, DUNSTABLE, BEDFORDSHIRE LU5 4RU
☎ (01582) 600969. OPEN 9.30 - 5 MON - WED, FRI, SAT,
10 - 4 THUR.
Large shop on two levels which has been in operation for 21 years selling good as new seasonal ladies wear. Only items up to two years old accepted and 50% of stock is designer wear such as Jaeger, Mondi, Bianca, Frank Usher, Ted Lapidus and Windsmoor in sizes 10 - 26. Both day and evening wear are available. The owner also buys in Danish designer samples and sells them at half price. Hats, shoes, jewellery and bags are also stocked. Twice yearly sales usually in July and January. *Dress Agency*

WALTER WRIGHT FACTORY SHOP

29 ALBION ROAD, LUTON, BEDFORDSHIRE LU2 0DS
☎ (01582) 721616. OPEN 9 - 7 MON - FRI.
Walter Wright, family hat manufacturer since 1889, makes headwear for a variety of national and international couture milliners and dress houses, as well as one high quality partnership department store. If you are lucky, you may be able to purchase a hat from stock at a fraction of the retail price. The factory also serves the public with their own one-off couture service, normally reserved for the trade, at far less cost than normal designer outlets. *Factory Shop*

Live Well On Less Tips

About to wean your baby? Test her taste buds without opening your purse. Write to Milupa, who produce baby foods, with the date of birth of your infant and they will send you free samples at a time that is appropriate to your baby's age. Milupa Babyfood, Scientific Department, Milupa House, Uxbridge Road, Hillingdon, Middx UB10 0NE; 081 573 9966.

Berkshire

WOMENSWEAR ONLY 🎗 Lavender House, *Windsor.* Seconds Out, *Cookham.*
Switchgear, *Windsor.*

WOMENSWEAR & MENSWEAR 🎗 🎗 Matalan, *Reading.* Matalan, *Slough.*
The Stock Exchange, *Ascot.* TK Maxx, *Reading.* TK Maxx, *Slough.*

CHILDREN ⚜ Kid2Kid, *Cookham.* Matalan, *Reading.* Matalan, *Slough.*
The Stock Exchange, *Ascot.* TK Maxx, *Reading.* TK Maxx, *Slough.*

HOUSEHOLD AND GIFTWARE 🏠 Matalan, *Reading.* Matalan, *Slough.*
TK Maxx, *Reading.* TK Maxx, *Slough.*

DIY/RENOVATION 🪓 GD Evans, *Slough.* Marlborough Tiles, *Madenhead.*
Bathroom World, *Ascot.*

ELECTRICAL EQUIPMENT 🔌 GD Evans, *Slough.*

FURNITURE/SOFT FURNISHINGS 🛏 Knickerbean, *Newbury.* RA Pickering, *Windsor.*

BATHROOM WORLD
ASCOT LTD, THE HIGH STREET, ASCOT, BERKSHIRE SL5 7HG
☎ (01344) 873366. FAX 626688. OPEN 9 - 6 MON - SAT, UNTIL 8 WED.
Fantastic, extensive bathroom showrooms pandering to any taste or budget.
Many products are exclusive to the Group who are continually expanding their
already large product portfolio. The buying power of the Group ensures that
prices are always extremely competitive. Experienced staff and designers guide
customers through styles, choices and specifications as part of a free service.
Permanent Discount Outlet

GD EVANS 🔌
331-333 HIGH STREET, SLOUGH, BERKSHIRE SL1 1TX
☎ (01753) 524188/535138. OPEN 9 - 5.30 MON - SAT.
Established for over 40 years, this is the place to come for built-in appliances.
Great discounts on new boxed, ex-display and discontinued models of up to
50%. Former exhibition Bosch, Neff and Siemens appliances. Phone for free
brochure. *Permanent Discount Outlet*

KID2KID
HIGH STREET, COOKHAM, BERKSHIRE SL6 9SH
☎ (01628) 531804. OPEN 10 - 5 MON - SAT.
Nearly-new designer clothes for children 0-10 years. Some of the most popular designer labels include Oilily, Cacherel, Ozona, Jean Bourget, Poivre Blanc,

and Oshkosh, although quality items from Next, Marks & Spencer and Laura Ashley are also on sale. Prices range from £3 to £30, normally at least one-third of the original price. Own range of new children's clothes also available, as well as made-to-order bridesmaids dresses and they now also sell nearly-new baby equipment and maternity clothes. There is a play area for children. *Dress Agency*

KNICKERBEAN

8 BARTHOLOMEW STREET, NEWBURY, BERKSHIRE RG14 5LL
☎ (01635) 529016. OPEN 9 - 5.30 MON - SAT.
Knickerbean is one of the few companies that continue to offer genuine top-name designer fabric bargains...the kind of curtain and upholstery fabrics that are found at Decorex and the Chelsea Harbour Design Centre. Their rapidly-changing stock often includes excess inventory and discontinued lines from these kinds of designers, as well as occasional slight seconds, with many sold at between 20%-50% off the regular price. They also carry a large range of top-quality fabrics in the latest styles which they buy directly from mills and manufacturers in the UK, Europe and North America, offering similar top quality, but at vastly reduced prices. Their attractively laid-out shops feature a vast range of different selections of curtain and upholstery fabrics. These include classic country house glazed chintzes, fresh stripes and checks, fashionable toiles de jouy, bright cotton prints and PVC-coated fabrics, a wide range of damasks and natural fabrics, sumptuous chenilles, rich kilim patterns, self-patterned dobby weaves and a fabulous selection of upholstery brocades and tapestries. Prices start from £4.95 for plain cottons and prints to £19.95 and occasionally more for chenilles and tapestries. Customers are encouraged to pop in regularly to check out the latest arrivals in their stock. The benefit here is that they are able to see entire rolls rather than just a small sample book of swatches. Their professionally trained staff are ready to advise on quality and quantity for any type of furnishing project. They extend their service to measure and quote, as they offer a complete making up service for all soft furnishings, including loose covers and upholstery. They are even prepared to bring along a few rolls to try out against a customer's own colour scheme. Twice-yearly sales are held in January and June to enable customers to snap up even bigger bargains. *Permanent Discount Outlet*

LAVENDER HOUSE OF OLD WINDSOR

42 ST LUKE'S ROAD, OLD WINDSOR, WINDSOR, BERKSHIRE SL4 2QQ
☎ (01753) 841194. OPEN 10 - 5.30 TUE - FRI, 9 - 4 SAT, OR BY APPOINTMENT.
Opened in 1999, this dress agency can provide a working wardrobe, special occasion outfits, evening gowns or accessories. Designers stocked include Giorgio Armani, Chanel, Moschino, Valentino, Jean Paul Gaultier, Karen Millen, Frank Usher, Betty Barclay, Escada and Jaeger. An elegant shop, with a relaxed feel, the clothes are arranged in colour co-ordinated groups, regardless of designer. *Dress Agency*

MARLBOROUGH TILES

BISHOP CENTRE, TAPLOW, MAIDENHEAD, BERKSHIRE SL6 ONY
☎ (01628) 667456. OPEN 10 - 5.30 MON - FRI, 9.30 - 5 SAT,
10.30 - 4.30 SUN.
Wall and floor tiles from Marlborough and other top quality, specialist
manufacturers. Seconds come mostly from Marlborough's own factory with
discounts of up to 50% on first quality prices. *Permanent Discount Outlet*

MATALAN

ROSE KILN LANE, READING, BERKSHIRE RG2 OSN
☎ (01189) 391958. OPEN 10 - 8 MON - FRI, 9 - 6 SAT, 11 - 5 SUN.
217 BATH ROAD, SLOUGH, BERKSHIRE SL1 4AA
☎ (01753) 487900. PHONE FOR OPENING TIMES.
Matalan is a fashion and homewares shop giving customers what they claim
to be unbeatable value for money with huge savings on a wide range of products including high quality fashionable clothing for men, women and children
at up to 50% off high street prices. Matalan is situated out of town and stores
are open seven days a week all year round. *Permanent Discount Outlet*

R A PICKERING

WILLOWSIDE, DEDWORTH ROAD, OAKLEY GREEN, WINDSOR,
BERKSHIRE SL4 4LN
☎ (01753) 833855. OPEN 9 - 6 SEVEN DAYS A WEEK. PHONE FIRST.
A clearing house for major manufacturers selling perfect suites for a fraction
of their retail value, they claim to beat any price and offer three-piece suites at
wholesale prices from £199. Local delivery £30; elsewhere in the country at
small extra cost. *Permanent Discount Outlet*

SECONDS OUT DESIGNER COLLECTION

PEPPER MILL COURT, HIGH STREET, COOKHAM, BERKSHIRE SL6 9SQ
☎ (01628) 850371. OPEN 9.30 - 5 MON - SAT, 9.30 - 9 ON THUR.
This shop, situated in a large timbered building in the riverside village of
Cookham, has been in operation for 14 years, offering middle to upper range
designer labels, including Laurel, Armani, Gucci, Prada, Versace and Chanel.
There's casual wear and smart Ascot and wedding outfits, as well as evening
wear displayed in spacious surroundings. All the clothes are colour coded by
hangers. There is also a selection of brand new clearance stock and never-worn
outfits and accessories including up to 80 hats at any one time, shoes and new
stock handbags at unbelievable prices. Recently voted the best nearly-new in
the Thames Valley.*Dress Agency*

SWITCHGEAR

20 ST LEONARD'S ROAD, WINDSOR, BERKSHIRE SL4 3BU

☎ (01753) 867438. OPEN 9.30 - 5 MON - SAT.

Established since 1970, this dress agency offers a selection of Escada, Frank Usher, Jaeger and Betty Barclay among other designer names. Merchandise is general wear with some evening outfits. There's also leisure wear, hats, shoes, handbags and belts, with a continuous flow of reductions to two-thirds of the original price. *Dress Agency*

THE STOCK EXCHANGE

1 HIGH STREET, SUNNINGHILL, ASCOT, BERKSHIRE SL5 5NQ

☎ (01344) 25420 . OPEN 9 - 5.30 MON - FRI, 9 - 4.30 SAT.

Excellent selection of nearly-new designer and high street labels for ladies, men and children including Calvin Klein, Boss and Yves St Laurent. Rapid turnover of clothes, all very well presented, in this very busy shop with cheerful, helpful staff. Clothes are sold in season and all items are clean and up-to-date. Garments are displayed for four weeks at full price and then one week at half price. *Dress Agency*

TK MAXX

BROAD STREET MALL, BROAD STREET, READING, BERKSHIRE RG1 7QE

☎ (01189) 511117. OPEN 9 - 5.30 MON - FRI, 9 - 6 SAT.

THE OBSERVATORY SHOPPING CENTRE, SLOUGH, BERKSHIRE

☎ (01753) 572550. OPEN 9 - 5.30 MON - FRI, 8 ON THUR, 9 - 6 SAT, 10.30 - 4.30 SUN.

Based on an American concept, TK Maxx is situated in easily accessible, often centrally located stores and offers famous label goods with up to 60% savings off recommended retail prices. TK Maxx has fashion for the whole family - women's, men's and childrenswear - accessories, shoes, gifts, kitchenware and home goods. Everything in the store is branded with a choice of well-known high street names to designer labels, and while a small percentage might be clearly marked past season, the great majority of items in store are current season, current stock and still with phenomenal savings. There is a huge choice with 50,000 pieces in store and up to 10,000 new items arriving a week. The stores are simple and unfussy with wide aisles, shopping trolleys and baskets, and a spacious, functional feel to them but there are individual changing rooms, ramps for buggies and wheelchairs and plenty of staff on the shop floor. Every branch accepts all major credit and debit cards and has a liberal refund and return policy. *Permanent Discount Outlet*

Buckinghamshire

WOMENSWEAR ONLY   Alexon Sale Shop, *High Wycombe.*
Bumpsadaisy Maternity Style, *Marlow.*   Encore, *Little Chalfont.*   Hang-ups, *Near Thame.*
Number Twenty, *Old Amersham.*   Revival, *Gerrards Cross.*   The Changing Room, *Chalfont St Giles*
The Go-Between, *Olney.*

WOMENSWEAR & MENSWEAR   Imps, *High Wycombe.*   Matalan, *Milton Keynes.*
Rohan Designs Plc, *Milton Keynes.*   TK Maxx, *Slough.*

CHILDREN   Imps, *High Wycombe.*   Matalan, *Milton Keynes.*   Nippers, *Milton Keynes.*
TK Maxx, *Slough.*

HOUSEHOLD AND GIFTWARE   Imps, *High Wycombe.*   Matalan, *Milton Keynes.*   Silver
Edition, *Chalfont St Giles.*   TK Maxx, *Slough.*

FURNITURE/SOFT FURNISHINGS   World of Wood, *Buckingham.*

FOOD AND LEISURE   The Go-Between, *Olney.*   Bookends, *Marlow.*   The Chiltern
Brewery, *Aylesbury.*

SPORTSWEAR AND EQUIPMENT   Rohan Designs Plc, *Milton Keynes.*

ALEXON SALE SHOP
UNIT 17, CHILTERNS SHOPPING CENTRE, FROGMORE, HIGH
WYCOMBE, BUCKINGHAMSHIRE HP13 5ES
☎   (01494) 464214. OPEN 9 - 5.30 MON - SAT.
Alexon, Eastex, Ann Harvey and Calico from previous seasons at 40%-70%
less than the original price; during sale time in January and June, the reductions are up to 70%. Stock includes separates, skirts, jackets, blouses. Current
stock at 10%-40% discounts. *Permanent Discount Outlet*

BOOKENDS
22 HIGH STREET, MARLOW, BUCKINGHAMSHIRE SL7 1A,
☎   (01628) 850 007. OPEN 9.30 - 6.30 MON - SAT.
Secondhand and damaged books and publishers' returns, as well as new and
review copies, including recently published books, usually one-third off and
sometimes half price. *Secondhand Shops, Hre Shop*

BUMPSADAISY MATERNITY STYLE
33 WEST STREET, MARLOW, BUCKINGHAMSHIRE SL7 2LS
☎   (01628) 478487. OPEN 10 - 5.30 MON - SAT.
Franchised shops and home-based branches with large range of specialist
maternity wear, from wedding outfits to ball gowns, to hire and to buy. Hire
costs range from £30 to £100 for special occasion wear. To buy are lots of casual and business wear in sizes 8 - 18. For example, skirts £20-£70; dresses £40-
£100. Phone ☎   0181-789 0329 for details of your local stockist. *Hire Shop*

ENCORE

NIGHTINGALES CORNER, LITTLE CHALFONT, BUCKINGHAMSHIRE
HP7 9PY

☎ (01494) 764174. OPEN 9.30 - 5.30 MON - SAT.

Good quality stylish but wearable ladies clothes and accessories at sensible
prices. The shop is welcoming and friendly and of a high standard. Clothes
arrive every day so frequent visits are essential. *Dress Agency*

HANG-UPS

1A THE SQUARE, LONG CRENDON, NEAR THAME,
BUCKINGHAMSHIRE HP18 9DA

☎ (01844) 201237. OPEN 9.30 - 5.30 TUE, FRI, 10 - 5 SAT.

Nearly new top designer labels offered at a fraction of their original price in
sizes 8-22. For example, Nicole Farhi suit, worth about £350 would sell for
£65. Larger sizes of Elvi clothes available. Free parking. *Dress Agency*

IMPS

35-39 FROGMOOR, HIGH WYCOMBE, BUCKINGHAMSHIRE

☎ (01494) 524924. OPEN 9 - 5 MON - SAT.

High street shops selling popular chainstore seconds fashion for all the family
as well as towels, china, trays and flower cachepots. For women, there are
jeans, £12.99, dressing gowns, £20. For men, shirts, £8-£12, Y-fronts, £1.65,
boxer shorts, £2.99, socks, 90p, pyjamas, £11.99, four-button collar T-shirts,
£6.99. For children, vests and knickers, 75p, socks, 75p, jeans, £6.99, pyjamas, £6.99, smocked dresses, £6.99. There are also hand towels, £2.99, bath
towels, £5.99, bath sheets, £9.99, plates, £3.50. Stock changes constantly.
Permanent Discount Outlet

MATALAN

BILTON ROAD, BLETCHLEY, MILTON KEYNES, BUCKINGHAMSHIRE
MK1 1HS

☎ (01908) 373735. OPEN 10 - 8 MON - FRI, 9 - 6 SAT, 11 - 5 SUN.

Matalan is a fashion and homewares shop giving customers what they claim
to be unbeatable value for money with huge savings on a wide range of products including high quality fashionable clothing for women, women and children at up to 50% off high street prices. Matalan is situated out of town and
stores are open seven days a week all year round. *Permanent Discount
Outlet*

NIPPERS

CODDIMOOR FARM, WHADDON, MILTON KEYNES,
BUCKINGHAMSHIRE MK17 OIR

☎ (01908) 504506. FAX ☎ (01908) 505636.

Nippers, the nursery equipment and toy specialists, operate from previously
redundant buildings in rural areas around the country. They offer easy parking, no queues and personal service. This is on top of competitive prices on
prams, cots, pushchairs, car seats, outdoor play equipment and toys, some of
which are new, some seconds or secondhand and some ends of lines. Prices are
low because they avoid the high overheads of traditional retail outlets and also
because the successful growth of a number of branches means they can now
buy in bulk and negotiate good deals. Customers are invited to try out the
merchandise while the children look at the animals, mostly sheep, chicken and
pigs. Familiar brand names are on sale at all the branches, including Mamas
& Papas, Britax, Maclaren and Bebe Confort, plus Fisher-Price and Little
Tikes. You can try out the car seats in your car and there is usually a
pram/pushchair repair service on site. *Permanent Discount Outlet*

NUMBER TWENTY

20 HIGH STREET, OLD AMERSHAM, BUCKINGHAMSHIRE HP8 ODJ

☎ (01494) 432043. OPEN 9.30 - 5.30 TUE - SAT.

Spacious shop in historic market town of Old Amersham which works in
partnership with a Knightsbridge dress agency. Labels stocked include
Chanel, Caroline Charles, Cerruti, Mondi, MaxMara, Mulberry, Joseph,
Jaeger, Jasper Conran, Betty Barclay, Burberry, Episode, Escada and Armani.
Dress Agency

REVIVAL

8 - 10 STATION APPROACH, GERRARDS CROSS, BUCKINGHAMSHIRE
SL9 8PP

☎ (01753) 891130. OPEN 9.30 - 5 TUE - SAT.

Quality chainstore and designer labels mix here in this dress agency. Labels
include Mondi and Escada, which join the handbags, belts, scarves and costume jewellery on sale here. *Dress Agency*

ROHAN DESIGNS PLC

1 - 3 KNEBWORTH GATE, GIFFORD PARK, MILTON KEYNES,
BUCKINGHAMSHIRE MK14 5QD

☎ (01908) 615407.

OPEN 9.30 - 5.30 MON - SAT.

High performance fabrics with unique design features ranging from waterproof jackets to the famous Rohan 'bags'. Seconds and discontinued items
available at discount prices. Also sells shirts, trousers, T-shirts and fleeces.
Factory Shop

Live Well On Less Tips
Any mum who's staggered home with the weekly shopping and the nappies will jump at the chance to have them delivered free. Boots the Chemist will transport nappies to your home as long as you buy £50-worth of goods from the Mother & Baby at Home catalogue, which includes everything from nipple shields to prams. You can order the catalogue on 0845 840 200 (a local rate phone call).

SILVER EDITIONS

PO BOX 16, CHALFONT ST GILES, BUCKINGHAMSHIRE HP8 4AU
☎ (01753) 888810/888830 FAX. MAIL ORDER
Specialises in selling fine English sterling silver and silver-plated gifts and cutlery at wholesale prices, often half the sum for the same items in high street shops. Their catalogue features an exceptionally wide range of gifts and cutlery at prices from £2.50 to several thousand pounds. Canteens of cutlery, photo frames, desk sets, serving pieces and children's christening gifts are just a few of the categories on offer. The catalogue also carries the complete range of Hagerty silver cleaning products. Write to the address above for a copy of the catalogue. *Permanent Discount Outlet*

THE CHANGING ROOM

50 HIGH STREET, CHALFONT ST GILES, BUCKINGHAMSHIRE HP8 4QQ
☎ (01494) 875933. OPEN 10 -5 TUE - SAT.
Nearly-new fashions ranging from names such as Gerry Weber and Basler to Paul Costelloe and Armani. Generally caters to the upper end of the market. Clothes sold at one-third of the original price and bargains can always be found. Clothing tends to be very seasonal with a swift turnover of stock. Wonderful selection of hats and a wide range of special occasion wear in all sizes. A fascinating little shop - not to be missed if you like hunting for bargains. *Dress Agency*

THE CHILTERN BREWERY

NASH LEE ROAD, TERRICK, AYLESBURY, BUCKINGHAMSHIRE HP17 0TQ
☎ (01296) 613647. OPEN 9 - 5 MON - SAT.
Three different types of bitter are manufactured here: Chiltern and Beechwood bitters, and Three Hundreds Old Ale. Or take your own pint container and fill with beer for £1.35 per pint. All the beers are draught except for John Hampdens Ale and Three Hundreds, which is both bottled and draught. Also stocks mustards and chutney with beer, marmalade with malt, pickled onions with hops and fruit cake with barley wine. Also three new beer sausages and beer shampoo. Free parking; museum; conducted tours on Saturdays - phone first. *Food and Drink Discounter*

THE GO BETWEEN

34B THE MARKET PLACE, OLNEY, BUCKINGHAMSHIRE MK46 4AJ
☎ (01234) 241193. OPEN 10 - 4.30 MON - SAT.
Designer labels from Escada and Mondi to Nicole Farhi, Betty Barclay and
Jaeger. Also stocks modern high street chainstore garments from Laura Ashley,
Marks & Spencer and Wallis. There is a full range of accessories, jewellery and
bric a brac and a recent addition, maternity wear. *Dress Agency*

TK MAXX

THE OBSERVATORY CENTRE, SLOUGH, BUCKINGHAMSHIRE
☎ (01753) 572550. OPEN 9 - 5.30 MON - FRI, 9 - 8 THUR, 9 - 6 SAT,
10.30 - 4.30 SUN.
Based on an American concept, TK Maxx is situated in easily accessible, often
centrally located stores and offers famous label goods with up to 60% savings
off recommended retail prices. TK Maxx has fashion for the whole family -
women's, men's and childrenswear - accessories, shoes, gifts, kitchenware and
home goods. Everything in the store is branded with a choice of well-known
high street names to designer labels, and while a small percentage might be
clearly marked past season, the great majority of items in store are current season, current stock and still with phenomenal savings. There is a huge choice
with 50,000 pieces in store and up to 10,000 new items arriving a week. The
stores are simple and unfussy with wide aisles, shopping trolleys and baskets,
and a spacious, functional feel to them but there are individual changing
rooms, ramps for buggies and wheelchairs and plenty of staff on the shop
floor. Every branch accepts all major credit and debit cards and has a liberal
refund and return policy. *Permanent Discount Outlet*

WORLD OF WOOD

7 CORNWALL PLACE, BUCKINGHAM, BUCKINGHAMSHIRE MK18 1SB
☎ (01280) 822003. OPEN 9 - 5.30 M ON - SAT.
Furniture for the home which offers everything except the bath! All the furniture is designed by craftsmen in Italy and much of it is made from original
wood reclaimed from houses in Italy, mainly Verona, and made by small
Italian manufacturers. If you're looking for modern glass-topped tables to massive semi-distressed sideboards, World of Wood has something to offer at
prices which are very competitive. *Permanent Discount Outlet*

Live Well On Less Tips

Entertain your children in the car with cassette tapes of their favourite sto-
ries recorded by you. Or they can follow the words while listening to you.
But don't forget to say "turn the page" when recording.

Cambridgeshire

WOMENSWEAR ONLY   Circles of Yaxley, *Peterborough*.   Pretty Brides, *Wisbech*. Rotations, *Peterborough*.   Second Glance, *Cambridge*.   The Frock Exchange, *Huntingdon*.

WOMENSWEAR & MENSWEAR   Barneys Factory Outlets, *Cambridge*. Catalogue Bargain Shop, *Wisbech*.   Cobblers, *Peterborough*. Matalan, *Peterborough*.   QD Stores, *Cambridge*.   Stage 2, *Peterborough*. The Factory Shoe Shop, *Great Shelfords*.   The Frock Exchange, *Fenstanton*. Vandel Factory Shoes Shop, *Great Shelford*.

CHILDREN   Catalogue Bargain Shop, *Wisbech*.   Circles of Yaxley, *Peterborough*. Matalan, *Peterborough*.   QD Stores, *Cambridge*.   Stage 2, *Peterborough*.

HOUSEHOLD AND GIFTWARE   Catalogue Bargain Shop, *Wisbech*.   Dunelm Fabric Shop, *Huntingdon*.   Jane Barrett Ltd, *Cambridge*.   Matalan, *Peterborough*.   QD Store, *Cambridge*. Spoils, *Cambridge*.   Stage 2, *Peterborough*.

ELECTRICAL EQUIPMENT   Catalogue Bargain Shop, *Wisbech*.   Stage 2, *Peterborough*.

DIY/RENOVATION   Charlton Recycled Autoparts Ltd, *Waterbeach*. Ramsey Paint Company, *St Ives*.   Solopark Plc, *Nr Pampisford*.   St Ives Tiles, *Huntingdon*.

ARCHITECTURAL SALVAGE   Solopark Plc, *Nr Pampisford*.

FURNITURE/SOFT FURNISHINGS   Chelford Fabrics, *Gamlingay*. Countrywide Discount Club, *Huntingdon*.   Dunelm Fabric Shop, *Huntingdon*. Fabric Warehouse, *Sawston*.   The Window Scene, *Wisbech*.

FOOD AND LEISURE   Booksale, *Peterborough*.   Galloway & Porter Ltd, *Cambridge*. The Works, *Peterborough*.

BARNEYS FACTORY OUTLETS

38-42 MILL ROAD, CAMBRIDGE, CAMBRIDGESHIRE CB1 2AD
☎ (01223) 369596. OPEN 9.30 - 5.30 MON, TUE, WED, FRI, 9.30 - 7 THUR, 10 - 6 SAT, 11 - 5 SUN.
Up to 60% off designer labels such as Calvin Klein, Ralph Lauren, Yves St Laurent, Marco Polo for both men and women. Mostly end of line and end of season stock. ***Permanent Discount Outlet***

BOOKSALE

BROADWAY, PETERBOROUGH, CAMBRIDGESHIRE
☎ (01733) 562566. OPEN 9 - 6 MON - FRI, 9 - 6 SAT.
Founded 15 years ago, Booksale now boasts more than 100 shops throughout the UK. It sells books, stationery, paints, tapes, videos, all at enormously discounted prices. Paperbacks from 99p, hardbacks, £2.99; story tapes, £1.99; children's books, 75p; videos 99p - £2.99; prints in clip frames, 99p - £19.95; posters, £1.50 - £6.99, and classical CDs from £2.99. ***Food and Leisure***

CATALOGUE BARGAIN SHOP

51 WEST STREET, WISBECH, CAMBRIDGESHIRE PE13 2LY

☎ (01945) 584327. OPEN 9 - 4.30 MON - SAT, 10.30 - 4.30 SUN.

Catalogue Bargain Shop is a growing national chain of stores which obtains the majority of its goods from mail order giants Great Universal and Kays, and offers a range of clothing for all the family, a wide selection of shoes, bed linen, household goods, electrical equipment and hundreds of other catalogue items at very competitive prices. The merchandise consists of ends of ranges and previous season's stock for which there is no longer storage space when the catalogues change. *Permanent Discount Outlet*

CHARLTON RECYCLED AUTOPARTS LTD

VEHICLE RECYCLING CENTRE, ELY ROAD, WATERBEACH, CAMBRIDGESHIRE CB5 9PG

☎ (01223) 863386. OPEN 8.30 - 6 MON - FRI, 8.30 - 5 SAT.

Sells car spares and accessories, but it's not like any usual spares or salvage yard! All parts have been checked, tagged and stored in a warehouse on a computer-controlled inventory. Examples of prices include new Nissan branded hub caps for a Micra model, £20. The shop is clean, efficient and all parts have a 101-day guarantee. Although the main business is used car parts, they also often stock brand new parts, either from bankrupt or flood damaged stock. Stock spare parts for vehicles from a Mini to a Mercedes. *Permanent Discount Outlet*

CHELFORD FABRICS

CHELFORD HOUSE, STATION ROAD, GAMLINGAY, CAMBRIDGESHIRE SG19 3HQ

☎ (01767) 651888. OPEN 9.30 - 5.30 MON - SAT.

A large, out-of-town showroom selling only perfect regular curtain and upholstery fabrics at greatly reduced prices, ranging from £2.99 a yard to £11.99 a yard and including everything from glazed cotton chintzes to prints, tapestries and damasks from all leading manufacturers. Choose from more than 4,000 rolls, order from the extensive range of manufacturers pattern books or buy own-brand fabrics which are one-third less expensive than branded material. A full high quality making-up service is available. Curtain accessories, rails, tapes and hooks are also on sale at reduced prices. There is also a huge selection of towels, cushions, pillows and duvets. There is another branch in Harpenden, Hertfordshire. *Permanent Discount Outlet*

CIRCLES OF YAXLEY

CHAPEL STUDIO, CHAPEL STREET, YAXLEY, PETERBOROUGH, CAMBRIDGESHIRE PE7 3LN

☎ (01733) 242539. OPEN 10 - 4 MON - SAT.

Circles sells ladies and children's wear. For example, a Basler blouse and matching skirt, size 16, £65; Robina striped and checked outfit, £75, originally £375. Eveningwear is stocked all year round, as are accessories such as hats, handbags and belts. Sizes range from 8 to 22. For children, labels include Marks & Spencer, Laura Ashley and Next. There are sales in January and July, during which everything except evening wear is reduced by 25%, with 40% off promotions for adult clothes during February and August. *Dress Agency*

COBBLERS

41 BRIDGE STREET, PETERBOROUGH, CAMBRIDGESHIRE PE1 1HA
☎ (01733) 891640. OPEN 9 - 5.30 MON - SAT.
Shoes from Evan Picone, Nickles, Doc Martens, Cobblers. Doc Martens Youths, sizes 2-6, £42.99; adults, £44.99; Trickers soft leather bootees, £49.99 from £63.99. Also half-price sample shoes. Ladies sizes range from three and a half to nine. For example Trickers gold leather flatties, £39.99, reduced from £53.99; Bandonino black suede shoes with buckle, £24.99 from £49.99. Leather handbags, £68.99 reduced from £91.99. *Factory Shop*

COUNTRYWIDE DISCOUNT CLUB

8 TOWER CLOSE, HUNTINGDON,CAMBRIDGESHIRE PE18 7DT
☎ (01480) 52440. OPEN 9.30 - 5 MON - SAT, CLOSED WED, PHONE FOR SUN OPENINGS.
Furniture including beds, carpets and three-piece suites at discounts of up to 50% once you pay your £1 joining fee. For example, single divan bed, £79.90; double pine bed, £99.90. Fifty percent off bedroom, lounge and dining room and cane furniture. We've been told that you can carpet a whole house in stain-free twist for less than £599; or in 80/20 wool twist for £1,100. Underlay is £2.40 a square yard. *Permanent Discount Outlet*

DUNELM FABRIC SHOP

UNIT 7, STUKELEY MEADOWS TRADING ESTATE, STUKELEY ROAD, HUNTINGDON, CAMBRIDGESHIRE PE18 6EB
☎ (01480) 417807. OPEN 9 - 5.30 MON - THUR, SAT, 9 - 8 FRI, 10 - 4 SUN.
35 WESTGATE, PETERBOROUGH, CAMBRIDGESHIRE PE1 1PZ
☎ (01733) 349848. OPEN 9 - 5.30 MON - SAT.
Part of a chain of shops based in the Midlands selling brand-name and chain-store curtains, masses of bedlinen, towels, wickerware, pictures and frames, all at competitive prices. *Permanent Discount Outlet*

FABRIC WAREHOUSE

UNIT 15, LONDON ROAD INDUSTRIAL ESTATE, SAWSTON, CAMBRIDGESHIRE CB2 4EG
☎ (01223) 832810. OPEN 9 - 5.30 MON - FRI, 9 - 5 SAT, 10 - 4 SUN.
Furnishing fabric, cushions and foam. Good range of printed furnishing fabrics from £4.99, with a bargain selection from £2.50; Jeff Banks prints, £8.99 instead of £16.99; wonderful Italian damasks, £13.99, usual price £18; cotton damask half price at £10.99; cotton muslins, £4.99 instead of £6.99;

Belgian flat weaves and tapestries, £10.99; polycotton lining, £2.50 for 54 width. They also sell curtain rails, tiebacks, fringing, braid, chunky tassel tie backs and have their own in-house curtain making service at competitive prices. *Permanent Discount Outlet*

GALLOWAY & PORTER LTD

THE PADDOCKS, CHERRYHINTON ROAD, CAMBRIDGE, CAMBRIDGESHIRE

☎ (01223) 367876. RING FOR SALE DATES.

MAIN BRANCH: 30 SIDNEY STREET, CAMBRIDGE CB2 3HS

☎ (01223) 367876. OPEN 8.45 - 5.30 MON - FRI, 9 - 5.15 SAT.

3 GREEN STREET, CAMBRIDGE,

☎ (01223) 367876. OPEN 9 - 5 MON - SAT.

Regular book warehouse sales are held at the Cherryhinton outlet about once a month on a Saturday from 9 - 5 at which most books cost £1, regardless of the original price. There are new hardback copies in the huge variety of tomes, covering many subjects including children's. Free parking. The other two branches stock secondhand as well as new, discounted books, the Green Street branch specialising in antiquarian and secondhand books. *Permanent Discount Outlet*

JANE BARRETT LTD

THE MALL, BAR HILL, CAMBRIDGE, CAMBRIDGESHIRE CB3 8DZ

☎ (01954) 782171. OPEN 9 - 5.30 MON - SAT.

Seconds and special purchases of Royal Doulton, Royal Albert, Minton, crystal and china, discounted by up to 60% against the normal retail price. Free parking. *Permanent Discount Outlet*

MATALAN

EAST STATION ROAD, PETERBOROUGH, CAMBRIDGESHIRE PE2 8AA

☎ (01733) 341229. OPEN 10 - 8 MON - FRI, 9 - 6 SAT, 11 - 5 SUN.

Matalan is a fashion and homewares shop giving customers what they claim to be unbeatable value for money with huge savings on a wide range of products including high quality fashionable clothing for women, women and children at up to 50% off high street prices. Matalan is situated out of town and stores are open seven days a week all year round. *Permanent Discount Outlet*

PRETTY BRIDES

TOWN STREET, UPWELL, WISBECH, CAMBRIDGESHIRE PE14 9DA

☎ (01945) 772592. OPEN 10 - 8 MON AND THUR, 10 - 5 TUE, FRI, SAT.

Wedding dress shop which offers discounts on styles which have been discontinued by the manufacturer and therefore cannot be ordered in again. Also offers a limited amount of hire. *Permanent Discount Outlet*

QD STORES

62 BURLEIGH STREET, CAMBRIDGE, CAMBRIDGESHIRE CB1 1DG

☎ (01223) 323174. OPEN 9 - 5.30 MON - SAT, 11 - 5 SUN.

Discount shop selling a mixture of clothes, household textiles, ceramics, kitchenware, knitting wool, garden tools, curtains, toys, stationery, dusters, Christmas decorations, masking tape, lingerie and a host of other items. Stock changes regularly because the low prices mean a quick turnover. Some items are seconds or end of season stock from the major chain stores. *Permanent Discount Outlet*

RAMSEY PAINT COMPANY

EAST STREET, ST IVES, CAMBRIDGESHIRE PE17 2NE

☎ (01480) 465002. OPEN 8 - 5 MON - FRI, 9 - 12 SAT.

LITTLE WHYTE, RAMSEY, CAMBRIDGESHIRE PE17 1DS

☎ (01487) 710876. OPEN 8 - 5 MON - FRI, 9 - 12 SAT.

Paints, paint accessories and wallpapers at discounted prices. Stocks most major paint brands including Crown and holds 100 wallpaper books from which you can order at discounts of 20%. Mainly caters for the trade, but will serve the public, too. More than 6,000 colours from which to choose. *Permanent Discount Outlet*

ROTATIONS

33 ELM ROAD, FOLKSWORTH, NEAR STILTON, PETERBOROUGH, CAMBRIDGESHIRE PE7 3SX

☎ (01733) 241100. OPEN 9.30 - 4.30 TUE - SAT.

Nearly-new garments from Marks & Spencer, Next, Principles, Laurel, Escada and Mondi. sizes range from 8-20 and there is also a selection of wedding dresses, bridesmaids dresses and accessories, hats, belts, handbags, jewellery and scarves. *Dress Agency*

Live Well On Less Tips

Lots of supermarkets now produce free recipe leaflets. Watch out for them at the fresh foods departments where the shop may be trying out a new type of exotic fruit or vegetable and offers meal suggestions in order to encourage you to buy it for the first time. Many supermarkets also offer a free advice service when you can write in with a query regarding their products and how to use them. Sainsbury's has a freephone student line, which is particularly useful for those doing projects; phone 0800 387504; and a Customer Service Line on 0800 626262. Tesco run a Careline on 0800 505555 and a Baby Club which sends out useful booklets and money off coupons - phone 0800 591688.

SECOND GLANCE

4 BAR LANE, STAPLEFORD, CAMBRIDGE, CAMBRIDGESHIRE CB2 5BJ

☎ (01223) 844677. OPEN 10 - 5 MON - SAT.

Sells a range of nearly-new labels from Next, Laura Ashley and M&S to Jaeger and Escada with a wide variety of dresses, ballgowns, suits, separates. A small selection of hats also available. *Dress Agency*

SOLOPARK PLC

STATION ROAD, NR PAMPISFORD, CAMBRIDGESHIRE CB2 4HB

☎ (01223) 834663. OPEN 8 - 5 MON - THUR, 8 - 4 FRI, SAT, 9 - 1 SUN.

Reclaimed bricks including soft reds, Suffolk whites, Cambridge stocks, Tudors, roofing tiles, slates, timbers, oak beams, doors, wood block, flooring, railway sleepers, chimney pots, York stone, granite setts, gates, fireplaces, statuary, garden furniture, etc. *Architectural Salvage*

SPOILS

5-7 SUSSEX STREET, CAMBRIDGE, CAMBRIDGESHIRE CB1 1PA

☎ (01223) 316518. OPEN 9 - 5.30 MON - SAT.

General domestic glassware, non-stick bakeware, kitchen gadgets, ceramic oven-to-tableware, textiles, cutting boards, aluminium non-stick cookware, bakeware, plastic kitchenware, plastic storage, woodware, coffee pots/makers, furniture, mirrors and picture frames. Rather than being discounted, all the merchandise is very competitively priced - in fact, the company carry out competitors' checks frequently in order to monitor pricing. With 38 branches, the company is able to buy in bulk and thus negotiate very good prices. *Permanent Discount Outlet*

ST IVES TILES

HIGH STREET, BLUNTISHAM, ST IVES, HUNTINGDON, CAMBRIDGESHIRE PE17 3LD

☎ (01487) 840471. OPEN 8.30 - 5.30 MON - FRI, 9 - 4 SAT, 10 - 1 SUN.

Importers of top quality floor and wall tiles, mainly Italian and Spanish terracotta and quarry style and sold at discounts of one third on selected lines. Warehouse-type shop with a wide selection of tiles displayed and laid to give you some idea of what they look like. One reader saved 50% on their floor tiles here, having been quoted £600 elsewhere. *Permanent Discount Outlet*

STAGE 2

SAVILLE ROAD, PETERBOROUGH, CAMBRIDGESHIRE PE3 6PR

☎ (01733) 263308. OPEN 10 - 8 MON - FRI, 9 - 6 SAT, 10 - 4 SUN, BANK HOLIDAYS.

Sells discontinued lines from Freeman's Catalogues. The full range is carried, but stock depends on what has not been sold at full price from the catalogue itself, or has been returned or the packaging is damaged or soiled. Clothing discounts range from about 50% - 65%. There are also household items and electrical equipment. *Permanent Discount Outlet*

THE FACTORY SHOE SHOP

48 WOOLLARDS LANE, GREAT SHELFORDS, CAMBRIDGESHIRE CB2 5LZ

☎ (01223) 846723. OPEN 9.30 - 5.30 MON - FRI, 9.30 - 5 SAT.

Slight seconds and clearance lines of Van-Dal and Holmes shoes, as well as other makes. Typical discounts include shoes which would normally cost £54.99 reduced to £32.50. *Permanent Discount Outlet*

THE FROCK EXCHANGE

7 HIGH STREET, FENSTANTON, CAMBRIDGESHIRE PE18 9LQ

☎ (01480) 461187. OPEN 9 - 5 TUE - SAT.

The Frock Exchange opened its doors in 1981, the first dress agency in East Anglia. 1983 saw the introduction of ballgown hire, again a first for the area. Esquire, a men's formal occasion wear business to buy or to hire, was opened in 1984. Originally in premises facing the ladies shop, Esquire has now moved above the Frock Exchange and complements the evening and special occasion wear which is such a feature of this popular and busy shop. Hat hire completes the services on offer. The Frock Exchange has been featured on The Clothes Show, Look East and About Anglia. *Dress Agencies, Hire Shop*

THE FROCK EXCHANGE

2 BAKERS MEWS, EAST STREET, KIMBOLTON, HUNTINGDON, CAMBRIDGESHIRE PE18 OHJ

☎ (01480) 860920. OPEN 10 - 5 TUE - FRI, 10 - 4 SAT.

Located in the charming Cambridgeshire village of Kimbolton, they stock very good quality ladies wear and accessories and hire out evening wear upstairs. Mostly German designer labels such as Bianca, Ara Fink but also includes Nicole Farhi and Paul Costelloe. *Dress Agency*

THE WINDOW SCENE

105 NORFOLK STREET, WISBECH, CAMBRIDGESHIRE PE13 2LD

☎ (01945) 474335. OPEN 10 - 5 MON - FRI, CLOSED WED, 10 - 4 SAT.

Tiny, back-street shop crammed with everything to do with soft furnishings including curtain fabrics, velvets, chintzes, nets, blind tapes, linings, heading tapes, foam, track, upholstery fabrics, at very competitive prices. Brands sold include Moygashel, Nouveau, Acorn, Corniche, Harmony, Prestigious and S.N.O. Textiles. *Permanent Discount Outlet*

THE WORKS

BRIDGE STREET, PETERBOROUGH, CAMBRIDGESHIRE PE1 1DW

☎ (01733) 358496. OPEN 9 - 6 MON - SAT, 8 ON THUR, 10 - 4 SUN.

One of 98 branches of this remainders company for books, particularly travel guides and glossy hardbacks, cards, gifts, toys, ornaments, gift wrap, stationery, videos and CDs, all discounted by at least 50%. For example, AA road maps, £2.99p, usually £6.99; Star Wars Essential Guide to Characters, £6.99, usually £14.99; Hutchinson's Encyclopaedia 1998 edition, £5.99, usually £40; double music cassettes, £1.99; greetings cards, 4 for 99p. Phone 0121 355 3601 for your local branch. *Permanent Discount Outlet*

VANDEL FACTORY SHOE SHOP

48 WOOLLARD'S LANE, GREAT SHELFORD, CAMBRIDGE, CAMBRIDGESHIRE CB2 5LZ

☎ (01223) 846723. OPEN 9.30 - 5.30 MON - FRI, 9.30 - 5 SAT.

Leather shoes for men and women, all of which are discounted by at least one third. The men's shoes are perfects while the women's selection includes some slight seconds and ends of ranges. Vandel Shoes are known for their wide fit, while the shop also sells Holmes shoes which are known for their narrow (double A) fit. A bonus scheme operates whereby if you buy five pairs of shoes in one year, you get an extra £10 discount off your sixth pair. *Factory Shop*

Live Well On Less Tips

Many of the big food companies produce free recipe booklets. John West, well-known for their tinned fish, publish recipe booklets for free tuna, salmon, spices and tinned fruits. Write to the Marketing Department, John West Foods Ltd, West House, Bixteth St, Liverpool L3 9SR or phone 0151 236 8771. Batchelors Foods also produce helpful leaflets on meals using their packet soups or rice, noodles or pasta. Send a stamped, self-addressed envelope to Brooke Bond Foods, Brooke House, Manor Royal, Crawley, West Sussex OH10 2RQ. Tel: 0845 601 0222.

Cheshire

WOMENSWEAR ONLY 🏷 Delia Metcalfe, *Congleton.* Designers Clearance, *Wallasey.*
Discount Clothing, *Bramhall.* Evans, *Nr Ellesmere Port.* Jane Shilton, *Ellesmere Port.*
Jeffrey Rogers, *Nr Ellesmere Port.* Just One Night, *Knutsford.* Liz Clairborne, *Nr Ellesmere Port.*
One-Night Affair, *Altrincham.* Paco Life in Colour, *Nr Ellesmere Port.* Pilot, *Ellesmere Port.*
Richards, *Nr Ellesmere Port.* Something Different, *Chester.* Special Event, *Chester.*
The Designer Warehouse, *Macclesfield.* The Really Good Deal Fashion Sale, *Tatton Park.*
Top Notch, *Nantwich.* Velmore, *Ellesmere Port.* Vogue Eleven, *Macclesfield.*
Wallis, *Nr Ellesmere Port.* Warehouse, *Nr Ellesmere Port.* Yes Stores, *Birkenhead*
Yes Stores, *Ellesmere Port.*

MENSWEAR ONLY 🏷 Fairway Menswear, *Nantwich.* James Barry Menswear, *Nr Ellesmere Port.*
Suits You, *Nr Ellesmere Port.* The Suit Company, *Ellesmere Port.* Tie Rack, *Nr Ellesmere Port.*

WOMENSWEAR & MENSWEAR 🏷 🏷 Banner Ltd, *Stockport.* Benetton, *Nr Ellesmere Port.*
Big Factory Outlet, *Nr Ellesmere Port.* Burberry, *Nr Ellesmere Port.* Chester Barrie, *Crewe.*
Ciro, *Nr Ellesmere Port.* Clark's, *Ellesmere Port.* Country Store, *Nr Ellesmere Port.*
Daks Simpson, *Ellesmere Port..* Designer Warehouse, *Bromborough.* Diesel, *Nr Ellesmere Port.*
Ecco, *Ellesmere Port.* Elite Dress Agency, *Altrincham.* Emporium, *Nantwich.*
Famous Footwear, *Nr Ellesmere Port.* Fruit of the Loom, *Nr Ellesmere Port.*
Jaeger Factory Shop, *Ellesmere Port.* Joe Bloggs, *Ellesmere Port.*
Jumper, *Ellesmere Port.* Kurt Geiger, *Nr Ellesmere Port.* Lee Cooper, *Ellesmere Port*
Littlewoods Catalogue Discount Store, *Nr Ellesmere Port.* Matalan, *Cheste.* Matalan, *Bromborough.*
Matalan, *Warrington.* McArthurglen Designer Outlet, *Nr Ellesmere Port.*
Mexx International, *Ellesmere Port.* Next to Nothing, *Ellesmere Port.* Principles, *Nr Ellesmere Port.*
QS Fashion, *Sale* Russell Athletic, *Ellesmere Port.* The Gap, *Nr Ellesmere Port.*
Timberland, *Nr Ellesmere Port.* Tog 24, *Ellesmere Port.* Viyella, *Nr Ellesmere Port.*
Wynsors World of Shoes, *Stockport.*

CHILDREN 🏷 Banner Ltd, *Stockport.* Benetton, *Nr Ellesmere Port.* Burberry, *Nr Ellesmere Port.*
Colour Me Crayons, *Near Elworth.* Country Store, *Nr Ellesmere Port.* Delia Metcalfe, *Congleton.*
Ecco, *Ellesmere Port.* Joe Bloggs, *Ellesmere Port* Jokids Ltd, *Nr Ellesmere Port.*
Lee Cooper, *Nr Ellesmere Port.* Littlewoods, *Nr Ellesmere Port.* Matalan, *Chester.*
Matalan, *Bromborough.* Matalan, *Warrington.* McArthurglen Designer Outlet, *Nr Ellesmere Port.*
Mexx International, *Ellesmere Port.* Molly Mumbles, *Nr Holmes Chapel.*
Next to Nothing, *Ellesmere Port.* North West Baby Hire, *Altrincham.*
Paco Life in Colour, *Nr Ellesmere Port.* QS Fashion, *Sale.* Russell Athletic, *Ellesmere Port.*
The Gap, *Nr Ellesmere Port.* Tog 24, *Ellesmere Port.* Toyworld Factory Outlets Ltd, *Ellesmere Port.*
Wynsors World of Shoes, *Stockport.*

HOUSEHOLD AND GIFTWARE 🏷 Allweis China & Crystal, *Altrincham.*
Bed & Bath Works, *Nr Ellesmere Port.* Birthdays, *Nr Ellesmere Port.* Cheshire Workshops, *Chester.*
Denby Factory Shop, *Ellesmere Port.* Edinburgh Crystal, *Ellesmere Port.* Florakits Ltd, *Congleton.*
Matalan, *Chester.* Matalan, *Bromborough.* Matalan, *Warrington.*
McArthurglen Designer Outlet, *Nr Ellesmere Port.* Oneida, *Ellesmere Port.*
Ponden Mill Linens, *Ellesmere Port.* Price's Candles, *Ellesmere Port.*
Royal Worcester & Spode Factory Shop, *Ellesmere Port.* Spoils, *Birkenhead.* The Cape, *Chester.*
Villeroy & Boch (UK) Ltd, *Ellesmere Port.* Woods of Windsor, *Ellesmere Port.*

ELECTRICAL EQUIPMENT 🏷 Hamlet's Famous Names, *Stockport.*
Littlewoods Catalogue Discount Store, *Nr Ellesmere Port.*
McArthurglen Designer Outlet, *Nr Ellesmere Port.* Remington, *Nr Ellesmere Port.*

DIY/RENOVATION ⚒ Cheshire Brick & Slate Co, *Nr Chester.* Glynn Webb, *Chester.* Great Northern Architectural Antiques, *Tattenhall.* Nostalgia Antique Fireplace, *Stockport.* Tile Clearing House, *Stockport.*

ARCHITECTURAL SALVAGE ⚒ Cheshire Brick & Slate Co, *Nr Chester.* Great Northern Architectural Antiques, *Tattenhall.* Nostalgia Antique Fireplace, *Stockport.*

FURNITURE/SOFT FURNISHINGS 🗄 Bramwell Interior Design, *Stockport.* Material Things, *Macclesfield.* Sunridge Upholstery, *Warrington.* The Curtain Exchange, *Wilmslow.* The Fabric Emporium, *Crewe.* The Old Sofa Warehouse, *Wilmslow.* Victoria Lighting Factory Shop, *Congleton.*

FOOD AND LEISURE 🍴 Denby Factory, *Ellesmere Port.* E Simpson Ltd, *Stockport.* Homefreeze Frozen Foods, *Poynton.* Homefreeze Frozen Foods, *Cheadle.* McArthurglen Designer Outlet, *Nr Ellesmere Port.* Thorntons, *Ellesmere Port.* Travel Accessory Outlet, *Nr Ellesmere Port.*

SPORTSWEAR AND EQUIPMENT 🏸 Abris Outdoor Clothing Factory Shop, *Wilmslow.* Allsports, *Stockport.* Calange, *Stockport.* Fred Perry UK Ltd, *Nr Ellesmere Port.* McArthurglen Designer Outlet, *Nr Ellesmere Port.* Nike Factory Store, *Nr Ellesmere Port.* Paco Life in Colour, *Nr Ellesmere Port.* Russell Athletic, *Ellesmere Port.*

ABRIS OUTDOOR CLOTHING FACTORY SHOP 🏸

60 WATER LANE, WILMSLOW, CHESHIRE SK9 5AP
FAX 01625 539948. OPEN 10 - 5 MON - SAT.
Outdoor clothing for hillwalkers and backpackers and tops suitable for snowboarders sold at prices which are up to 60% off normal retail prices. For example, walking trousers, £24.99 which would normally sell for £39.99 in the high street; breathable waterproofs from £69.99, fleece jackets from £49.99. Sizes range from extra small to double extra large; ladies from 10 - 18; men's trousers from 28-inch to 40-inch waist. *Factory Shop*

ALLSPORTS 🏸

98 PRINCES STREET, STOCKPORT, CHESHIRE SK1 1RJ
☎ (0161) 480 6278. OPEN 9 - 5.30 MON - SAT, 10 - 4 SUN.
Allsports is a standard shop but at the rear, it has a dedicated area of marked-down goods. These are all damaged or end of season and there are great bargains to be had. Goods can be one-offs to particular items in various sizes. Stock varies from day to day so you could be delighted one day and disappointed the next. Typical bargains are British and foreign football shirts at between one quarter and one half of the normal perfect price. There are also trainers, sports goods, clothing, football boots, including some Man. United merchandise. There are fresh deliveries every day. *Permanent Discount Outlet*

ALLWEIS CHINA AND CRYSTAL

51 STAMFORD NEW ROAD, ALTRINCHAM, CHESHIRE WA14 1DS

☎ (0161) 941 6431. OPEN 9 - 5.30 MON - SAT.

84 HIGH STREET, CHEADLE, CHESHIRE

☎ (0161) 428 7571. OPEN 9 - 5.30 MON - SAT

Branded china and cutlery at discount including Waterford, Wedgwood, Royal Doulton, Royal Worcester and many others. None of the stock is seconds and discounts start at 10%. *Permanent Discount Outlet*

BANNER LTD

BANNER HOUSE, GREG STREET, REDDISH, STOCKPORT, CHESHIRE SK5 7BT

☎ (0161) 474 7600. OPEN 10 - 4 MON - THUR, 10 - 3 FRI.

Manufactures clothes for all the family destined for top high street department stores. Seconds, overmakes and returns are sold here at discount prices, although only about 20% of the stock consists of seconds. About 80% of the merchandise sold here is made by the factory, with a further 20% manufactured within the company. Large selection of schoolwear. *Factory Shop*

BED & BATH WORKS

CHESHIRE OAKS DESIGNER OUTLET VILLAGE, JUNCTION 10 OF M53, KINSEY ROAD, NEAR ELLESMERE PORT, CHESHIRE CH65 9JJ

☎ (0151) 356 7377. OPEN 10 - 6 MON - SAT, 8 ON THUR, 11 - 5 SUNS AND BANK HOLS.

Bed & Bath Works sells bedlinen and towels from famous-name companies. Bedding companies include Vantona, Horrocks, Janet Reger, Broomhill and Coloroll; towels are by Christys; duvets and pillows by Fogarty and Trendsetter. There are also duvet covers, soaps, brushes, sponges, bath mitts, bath mats, flannels, cushions and throws by Opalcraft as well as lighting by Shades Unlimited. Discounts range from 30% upwards. *Factory Shopping Village*

BENETTON

CHESHIRE OAKS OUTLET VILLAGE, KINSEY ROAD, NEAR ELLESMERE PORT, CHESHIRE CH65 9JJ

☎ (0151) 357 3131. OPEN 10 - 6 MON - SAT, 11 - 5 SUN AND BANK HOLIDAYS.

The usual well-known range of Benetton clothes for women and children at discounts of up to 50%. Most are ends of lines, end of season and samples, with a few seconds. *Factory Shopping Village*

BIG L FACTORY OUTLET

UNIT 6, CHESHIRE OAKS OUTLET VILLAGE, KINSEY ROAD, NEAR ELLESMERE PORT, JUNCTION 10 OF M53, SOUTH WIRRAL, CHESHIRE L65 9HN

☎ (0151) 356 8484. OPEN 10 - 6 MON - SAT, UNTIL 8 ON THUR, 11 - 5 SUN.

Men's and women's Levi jeans, jackets, cord and Sherpa fleece jackets, T-shirts and shirts but no children's, all at discount prices. *Factory Shopping Village*

BIRTHDAYS

MCARTHURGLEN DESIGNER OUTLET VILLAGE CHESHIRE OAKS, JUNCTION 10 OF M53, ELLESMERE PORT, CHESHIRE CH65 9JJ

☎ (0151) 356 7393. OPEN 10 - 6 MON - SAT, UNTIL 8 ON THUR, 11 - 5 SUN AND BANK HOLIDAYS.

Cards, notelets, stationery sets, colouring books, stuffed toys, photo albums, picture frames, gifts, giftwrap, tissue paper, party packs, candlesticks, Christmas crackers, string puppets, fairy lights all at discounts of up to 30%. Some are special purchases, some seconds. *Factory Shopping Village*

BRAMHALL INTERIOR DESIGN

10 BUXTON ROAD, STOCKPORT, CHESHIRE SK2 6NU

☎ (0161) 477 7173. OPEN 9 - 5 MON - SAT.

Sells fabrics and wallpapers at discounts of 20%. As agents for most leading makes, you can find almost anything you want here. If you pay full price for the fabric you choose, curtains will be made free of charge. *Permanent Discount Outlet*

BURBERRY

CHESHIRE OAKS OUTLET VILLAGE, KINSEY ROAD, NEAR ELLESMERE PORT, CHESHIRE CH65 9JJ

☎ (0151) 357 3203. OPEN 10 - 6 MON - SAT, UNTIL 8 ON THUR, 11 - 5 SUN.

These Burberry factory shops sell seconds and overmakes of the famous name raincoats and duffle coats as well as accessories such as the distinctive umbrellas, scarves and handbags. They also sell children's duffle coats, knitwear and shirts, as well as some of the Burberry range of food: jams, biscuits, tea and chocolate. All carry the Burberry label and are about one third of the normal retail price. *Factory Shopping Village*

CALANGE

PO BOX 61, STOCKPORT, CHESHIRE SK3 OAP

☎ (0161) 474 7097. OPEN 9 - 5 MON - FRI.

Twice-yearly sales of adults and childrens' leisure and outdoor gear such as cycling shorts, waterproof jackets, warm hats, fleeces at incredibly cheap prices. On sale are ends of lines, imperfects and some design samples which they haven't pursued into full manufacturing. Phone or write to be put on the mailing list. *Designer Sale*

CHESHIRE BRICK & SLATE COMPANY

BROOK HOUSE FARM, SALTERS BRIDGE, TARVIN SANDS, NR CHESTER, CHESHIRE CH3 8HL

☎ (01829) 740883.☎ (01829) 740481 (FAX). OPEN 8 - 5.30 MON - FRI, 8 - 4.30 SAT, 10 - 4 SUN.

Reclaimed bricks, slates, setts, tiles, lamposts, doors, Victorian bathroom suites, fireplaces, ranges, garden ornaments, beams, Yorkshire paving and brass door furniture. *Architectural Salvage*

CHESHIRE WORKSHOPS

BURWARDSLEY, NEAR CHESTER, CHESHIRE CH3 9PF

☎ (01829) 770401. OPEN 10 - 5 SEVEN DAYS A WEEK.

Cheshire Workshops offer a day out for all the family as well as the opportunity to choose from a large range of candles at factory shop prices. You can watch skilled craftspeople carving candles by hand, and see the unique candle dipping Ferris wheel, standing over thirty feet high. Most of the candles made here are exported throughout the world. There are also hundreds of other gift ideas in the shop. Candles start from 15p, much cheaper than the equivalent quality in the high street, and are available in a wide range of colours, shapes and sizes. There is free parking, a play area for children and a restaurant. *Factory Shop*

CHESTER BARRIE

WESTON ROAD, CREWE, CHESHIRE, CW1 6BA,

☎ (01270) 253865. OPEN 10 - 4.30 MON - FRI, 9 - 3.30 SAT.

Now well established in Crewe this shop is just 1/4 mile from the railway station. The outlet has an ever-increasing customer base who recognise and value top quality ladies and gents tailored clothing at reasonable prices. The shop has recently doubled in size and has been completely refurbished with excellent access, free parking and generously sized changing rooms. A recent development has seen the introduction of a bespoke tailoring service of Savile Row quality for Chester Barrie suits, jackets and coats for men. An extensive range and selection of Chester Barrie ready to wear garments is always held in stock. Chester Barrie has now launched into the ladies' tailored clothing market, a selection of which is always available. Regular special offers, sales and shopping evenings are held and a mailing list is maintained to notify regular customers of times and dates of promotions. Friendly and helpful staff will help you not only with Chester Barrie but other famous brands including Austin Reed tailored wear for men and women, Stephen Brothers shirts of the finest quality, silk ties, caps, cashmere and wool knitwear. Grenson shoes have been added to complement the high quality hand tailored merchandise on sale. Bladen country wear is available as well as weatherproof shooting clothes and rainwear. All items on display are of the finest quality and made to exact standards with the emphasis on traditional hand tailoring skills. Cloths used for manufacture are selected from the finest mills. The shop also specialises in coats and jackets made from cashmere. *Factory Shop*

CIRO

CHESHIRE OAKS DESIGNER OUTLET VILLAGE, JUNCTION 10 OF THE M53, NEAR ELLESMERE PORT, CHESHIRE CH65 9JJ
☎ (0151) 355 4037. OPEN 10 - 6 MON - SAT, UNTIL 8 ON THUR, 11 - 5 SUN AND BANK HOLIDAYS.
One of more than 120 outlets, all selling brand name merchandise at discounted prices, with more outlets in the pipeline. Internationally famous jewellers Ciro sell a range of jewellery. There is a children's play area, a Garfunkels restaurant and free car parking. *Factory Shopping Village*

CLARK'S

CHESHIRE OAKS DESIGNER OUTLET VILLAGE, KINSEY ROAD, ELLESMERE PORT, JUCNTION 10 OF M53, CHESHIRE CH65 9JJ
☎ (0151) 356 7492. OPEN 10 - 6 MON - SAT, UNTIL 8 ON THUR, 11 - 5 SUN AND BANK HOLIDAYS.
Shoes for men and women, handbags and evening bags at discounts of at least 25%. Also luggage and coats - fleeces and waterproofs. *Factory Shopping Village*

COLOUR ME CRAYONS

ABBEYFIELDS, LODGE ROAD, NEAR ELWORTH, CHESHIRE
☎ (01270) 753030. OPEN 8.30 - 5 MON - FRI.
Manufacturer of crayons, chalks, face paints, glitter, sugar paper etc, overstock of which is sold here at discounted prices. Also on sale are card, drawing paper, sand, paint brushes, poster paints, masks, glue for papier mache, sequins, bean bags, erasers, pencils, play dough, jigsaws and bracelet kits. *Factory Shop*

COUNTRY STORE (JOHN PARTRIDGE)

CHESHIRE OAKS OUTLET VILLAGE, KINSEY ROAD, NEAR ELLESMERE PORT, CHESHIRE CH65 9JJ
☎ (0151) 357 1729. OPEN 10 - 6 MON - SAT, 11 - 5 SUN, UNTIL 8 ON THUR.
John Partridge specialises in hardwearing outdoor clothes. Ranges include waxed cotton jackets, trench coats and waistcoats; showerproof classic town

coats; Gore-tex coats and tweed coats; quilted jackets and waistcoats; children's waxed jackets and puffa jackets, quilted jackets and waistcoats; hats and caps; moleskin and cord trousers; knitwear and shirts. Discontinued lines and seconds are on sale at discounted prices - a minimum of 30% and up to 70% off during promotions. *Factory Shopping Village*

DAKS SIMPSON

MACARTHUR GLEN DESIGNER OUTLET VILLAGE CHESHIRE OAKS, JUNCTION 10 OF M53, ELLESMERE PORT, SOUTH WIRRAL, CHESHIRE CH65 9JJ

☎ (0151) 3558703. OPEN 10 - 6 MON - SAT, UNTIL 8 ON THUR, 11 - 5 SUNS AND BANK HOLS.

Sells previous season's stock for women and men as well as any returned merchandise and overmakes in duffle coats, belts, gloves, handbags, sweaters, men's suits, Simpson shirts, socks, silk ties and scarves. There are good bargains to be had, but stock is very much dependent on what has not sold in the shops. Sizes vary but tend towards the two extremes: 6s, 8s and 10s on the one hand, and 20s and 22s on the other. Ladies jackets, £99, originally £279. Daks Simpson was founded in 1894 by Simeon Simpson and produced quality English tailoring for more than 100 years. *Factory Shopping Village*

DELIA METCALFE

15A BRIDGE STREET, CONGLETON, CHESHIRE CW12 1AS

☎ (01260) 297521. OPEN 9.30 - 5 MON - THUR, 9 - 5.30 FRI, SAT.

Chainstore and designer surplus stock are sold in this small town centre shop. The children's clothes are aged from 6 months to 12 years; ladies sizes from 8 to 30. Marks & Spencer merchandise is discounted by 50%, and there are many German designer labels such as Verse and Bianca. *Permanent Discount Outlet*

DENBY FACTORY SHOP

CHESHIRE OAKS, ELLESMERE PORT, SOUTH WIRRAL, CHESHIRE L65 9JJ

☎ (0151) 356 4949 . OPEN 10 - 6 MON, TUE, WED, FRI, SAT, 10 - 8 THUR, 11 - 5 SUN.

Denby is renowned for its striking colours and glaze effects. This outlet stocks seconds quality Denby cookware and mugs with prices starting at 20% off the recommended retail price. There are regular special offers throughout the year. *Factory Shop*

DESIGNER CLEARANCE

LISCARD WAY (NEXT TO CAPITAL BINGO HALL), WALLASEY, CHESHIRE

☎ (0151) 653 0780. OPEN 9 - 5.30 MON - SAT.

Fashion clearance house for many well-known high street names such as Etam, Dorothy Perkins and Tesco. Most of the labels are cut out. Stock turns over quickly and so changes constantly. There is another branch at Whitechapel in Liverpool. *Permanent Discount Outlet*

DESIGNER WAREHOUSE

UNIT 7, DINSDALE ROAD, CROFT BUSINESS PARK, BROMBOROUGH,
WIRRAL, CHESHIRE

☎ (0151) 343 9957. OPEN 10 - 5.30 MON - SAT, 11 - 4 SUN.

Men's and women's discounted fashion items from Morgan, DKNY, Dolce &
Gabanna, Moschino, Ralph Lauren, Armani, Hugo Boss and Versace Jeans.
Permanent Discount Outlet

DIESEL

CHESHIRE OAKS DESIGNER OUTLET VILLAGE, JUNCTION 10 OF THE
M53, NEAR ELLESMERE PORT, CHESHIRE CH65 9JJ

☎ (0151) 355 1478. OPEN 10 - 6 MON - SAT, UNTIL 8 ON THUR, 11 - 5
SUN AND BANK HOLIDAYS.

Diesel, which claims to be the fastest growing jeans label in the world, sells
Modern Basic in addition to Diesel Spare Part accessories. Based in Molvena,
Italy, Diesel now distributes to 72 countries worldwide, though this is its only
outlet store in the UK. Jeans seconds costs from £28 a pair or £45 for two
pairs. *Factory Shopping Village*

DISCOUNT CLOTHING

11 WOODFORD ROAD, BRAMHALL, CHESHIRE

☎ (0161) 439 0430. OPEN 9.30 - 5.30 MON - SAT.

19 PARK LANE, POYNTON, CHESHIRE

☎ (01625) 871571. OPEN 9.30 - 5.30 MON - SAT.

Sell perfects and seconds of chainstore and German manufacturers clothes for
women, mostly made up of mix and match separates, including evening wear
at Christmas time only. The Poynton branch also sells childrenswear.
Permanent Discount Outlet

E SIMPSON LTD

BUXTON ROAD, HAZEL GROVE, STOCKPORT, CHESHIRE SK7 6LZ

☎ (0161) 483 1241. OPEN 5 - 3.45 MON - FRI, 6 - 10.45 SAT.

Pork butchers who make sausages and cure hams. They supply top quality
sausages, ham, bacon and other meats to wholesalers and supermarket chains
countrywide. Overstocks sold here at greatly reduced prices. *Factory Shop*

ECCO

CHESHIRE OAKS DESIGNER OUTLET VILLAGE, KINSEY ROAD,
ELLESMERE PORT, JUNCTION 10 OF M53, CHESHIRE CH65 9JJ

☎ (0151) 356 3045. OPEN 10 - 6 MON - FRI, 8 ON THUR, 11 - 5 SUN,
BANK HOLS.

Ladies', men's and children's shoes, all discounted by at least 25%. Phone 0800
387368 for a catalogue. Other outlets in South Wales, Hertfordshire,
Somerset and Wiltshire. *Factory Shopping Village*

EDINBURGH CRYSTAL

CHESHIRE OAKS OUTLET VILLAGE, ELLESMERE PORT, JUNCTION 10
OF M53, CHESHIRE CH65 9JJ
☎ (0151) 357 3661. OPEN 10 - 6 MON - SAT, UNTIL 8 ON THUR,
11 - 5 SUN.
Wide range of crystalware from glasses and vases to tumblers and bowls at discounts of between 33% - 40%. The shop sells firsts and seconds of crystal
from one third off the normal price. There are also special promotional lines
at discount prices up to 70% off seconds. *Factory Shopping Village*

ELITE DRESS AGENCY

1 MARKET STREET, ALTRINCHAM, CHESHIRE WA14 1QE
☎ (0161) 928 5424. OPEN 10 - 5 MON - SAT.
Established since 1964, this shop sells mainly ladies wear which is less than
two years old, with a small but comprehensive selection of menswear. Wide
range of clothing includes some sports wear. Labels range from high street to
designer and includes names such as Genny, Guy Laroche, Hardy Amies, YSL,
Dior, Valentino, Ungaro, Thierry Mugler, Sonia Rykiel, Mondi, KooKai,
Morgan and Ralph Lauren for women, and Boss, Versace, Armani, YSL,
Cerruti and Ralph Lauren for men. Twice yearly sales at the end of June and
December. A dress hire section stocks a wide selection of brand new dresses,
updated twice a year (see One-Night Affair). *Dress Agency*

EMPORIUM

17 PILLORY STREET, NANTWICH, CHESHIRE CW5 5BZ
☎ (01270) 610144. OPEN 9.30 - 5.30 MON - SAT.
Range of designer clothes for men and women including Moschino, Dolce
and Gabbana, Armani, Lambretta, Boss, Firetrap, Chipy and Morgan and
Hush Puppy at competitive prices. *Permanent Discount Outlet*

EVANS

CHESHIRE OAKS OUTLET VILLAGE, KINSEY ROAD, JUNCTION 10 OF
M53, NEAR ELLESMERE PORT, CHESHIRE CH65 9JJ
☎ (01513) 554334. OPEN 10 - 6 MON - SAT, 8 ON THUR, 11 - 5 SUN.
End of season lines at discounts of between 25% and 50%, all with the normal Evans refund guarantee. The range includes tailoring, soft dressing, dresses, Profile, knitwear, East Coast (denim/jeans), lingerie/nightwear, blouses,
coats, outerwear and accessories. *Factory Shopping Village*

FAIRWAY MENSWEAR

BEAM HEATH WAY, MIDDLEWICH ROAD, NANTWICH,
CHESHIRE CW5 6PQ

☎ (01270) 625900. OPEN 9 - 5 MON - SAT. OPEN BANK HOLIDAYS 10 - 4.
Men's suits, jackets, trousers and coats which are either own brand or made
for chainstores such as Next and C & A but sold here under the Fairway
name. Good selection in most sizes with larger sizes up to 52 now available.
Suits all £89.95. Changing rooms and car park. *Factory Shop*

FAMOUS FOOTWEAR

CHESHIRE OAKS OUTLET VILLAGE, KINSEY ROAD, NEAR ELLESMERE
PORT, JUNCTION 10 OF M53, CHESHIRE CH65 9JJ

☎ (0151) 357 1512. OPEN 10 - 6 MON - SAT, UNTIL 8 ON THUR, 11 - 5
SUN.
Wide range of brand names including Stead & Simpson, Lilley & Skinner,
Hobos, Hush Puppies, Lotus, Sterling & Hunt, Richleigh, Scholl, Red Tape,
Flexi Country, Padders, Canaletto, Bronx, Frank Wright, Brevitt, Romba
Wallace, Rieker, all at discount prices of up to 50%. *Factory Shopping
Village*

FLORAKITS LIMITED

WORRAL STREET, CONGLETON, CHESHIRE CW12 1DT

☎ (01260) 271371. OPEN 8 - 5 MON - FRI, 8 - 6 THUR, 9 - 5 SAT, 10 - 4
SUN.
Importers and distributors of dried flowers and artificial flowers, trees, plants,
baskets, pottery and glass, they have a constant stock of dried and artificial
flower arrangements at wholesale prices, as well as everything for the flower
arranger from ribbons and wires to floral foam and wrought iron pedestals.
Also now stocking craft supplies for decoupage, stencilling, candle making,
quilling and glass engraving etc, together with a full range of artists' materials.
Examples of prices include flower arrangements from £3.50, headresses from
£1-£12; posies from £1.25; stencils from 49p; wooden picture frames from
£2.45; and Anton Piek decoupage prints from 25p (VAT must be added to all
prices). *Permanent Discount Outlet*

FRED PERRY UK LTD

CHESHIRE OAKS OUTLET VILLAGE, KINSEY ROAD, NEAR ELLESMERE
PORT, JUNCTION 10 OF M53, CHESHIRE CH65 9JJ

☎ (0151) 357 1383. OPEN 10 - 6 MON - SAT, UNTIL 8 ON THUR, 11 - 5
SUN AND BANK HOLIDAYS.
Men's and women's ranges of the famous Fred Perry active performance
clothing: shorts, tennis tops, tracksuits, T-shirts. All price labels show the
original and the reduced price, which usually amount to a 30% discount.
Factory Shopping Village

FRUIT OF THE LOOM

CHESHIRE OAKS OUTLET VILLAGE, KINSEY ROAD, NEAR ELLESMERE PORT, JUNCTION 10 OF M53, CHESHIRE CH65 9JJ

☎ (0151) 355 6169. OPEN 10 - 6 MON - SAT, UNTIL 8 ON THUR, 11 - 5 SUN.

Men's, women's and children's (ages 3-14) casual wear in the form of T-shirt, sweatshirts, shorts and tracksuits with the distinctive Fruit of the Loom logo at discounts starting at 25%. *Factory Shopping Village*

GLYNN WEBB

UNIT 1C, THE BOUGHTON CENTRE, BOUGHTON, CHESTER, CHESHIRE CH3 5AF

☎ (01244) 344 144. OPEN 9 - 8 MON - SAT, 10 - 4 SUN AND BANK HOLIDAYS.

Stockists of all your home improvement needs from wallpaper to paint, furniture to flooring, tiles to textiles, housewares to lighting - in fact, almost everything for your home, with 24 branches in the North-West, Midlands and Yorkshire. Specialists in discontinued mail order, slightly imperfect branded stocks as well as perfect quality superior products. They carry top brands such as Dulux, Crown Paints and Vymura and Coloroll wall coverings, Rectella and Norwood textiles and much more in store. Different branches carry different lines so if you want something specific, phone first. To find your nearest branch, phone 0161 621 4500. *Permanent Discount Outlet*

GREAT NORTHERN
ARCHITECTURAL ANTIQUES

NEW RUSSIA HALL, CHESTER ROAD, TATTENHALL, CHESHIRE CH3 9AH

☎ (01829) 770796. FAX ☎ (01829) 770971. OPEN 9.30 - 5 SEVEN DAYS A WEEK.

Doors, panelled rooms, sanitary fittings, stained glass, garden furniture, York stone sets and pews, gates, railings, curios, bric a brac. *Architectural Salvage*

HAMLET'S FAMOUS NAMES

65-69 PRINCE'S STREET, STOCKPORT, CHESHIRE, SK1 1RW,

☎ (0161) 476 3500. OPEN 9 - 5.30 MON - SAT, 10 - 4 SUN.

THE RIDGEDALE CENTRE, HOLLINS LANE, MARPLE, CHESHIRE SK6 6AW

☎ (0161) 449 0461. OPEN 9 - 5.30 MON - SAT, CLOSED WED.

Sells ends of lines and A-grade manufacturers' returns of electrical goods which dealers have sent back to suppliers as faulty and which have then been repaired to the original specification at discounts of up to 50%. These include Panasonic, Toshiba, JVC, Philips, Sharp and Aiwa television sets, videos, hi-fis and camcorders. *Permanent Discount Outlet*

HOMEFREEZE FROZEN FOODS

PARK LANE, POYNTON, CHESHIRE SK12 1RE

☎   (01625) 871322. OPEN 9 - 5.30 MON - THUR, 9 - 6 FRI, 9 - 5 SAT.

28 HIGH STREET, CHEADLE, CHESHIRE SK8 5JD

☎   (0161) 428 2626. OPEN 9 - 5.30 MON - THUR, 9 - 6 FRI, 9 - 5.15 SAT.

Sell a range of brand name and low calorie ready-made meals at discounts of, on average, about one third off the normal retail price. The meals have usually been created for famous high street stores and include Marks & Spencer oven chips, individual chicken or steak pies, wholemeal quiches and pizzas. Also Romantica ice cream and Sainsbury and Tesco ready-meals, when in stock, and hundreds of other lines as and when available. *Food and Drink Discounter*

JAEGER FACTORY SHOP

UNIT 48, CHESHIRE OAKS DESIGNER OUTLET VILLAGE, KINSEY ROAD, ELLESMERE PORT, JUNCTION 10 OF M53, CHESHIRE CH65 9JJ

☎   (0151) 355 0022. OPEN 10 - 6 MON - SAT, UNTIL 8 ON THUR,

11 - 5 SUN AND BANK HOLIDAYS.

Contemporary classics from Jaeger at excellent prices. Most of the merchandise is previous seasons' stock, but you might also find some special makes. *Factory Shopping Village*

JAMES BARRY MENSWEAR

CHESHIRE OAKS OUTLET VILLAGE, KINSEY ROAD, NEAR ELLESMERE PORT, CHESHIRE CH65 4AW

☎   (0151) 357 1416. OPEN 10 - 6 MON - SAT, UNTIL 8 ON THUR, 11 - 5 SUN.

Range of men's suits, jackets, trousers, socks, belts, briefs, shirts and casual wear from James Barry and Wolsey. Some of the factory shops also stock the Double Two range of brand names. Suits from £120; casual shirts, £11.95 or two for £20; trousers reduced from £44.95 to £29.95; Pierre Cardin casual and business shirts, knitwear and trouser are available, too. *Factory Shopping Village*

JANE SHILTON

CHESHIRE OAKS DESIGNER OUTLET VILLAGE, JUNCTION 10 OF M53, ELLESMERE PORT, CHESHIRE CH65 9JJ

☎   (0151) 355 8266. OPEN 10 - 6 MON - SAT, UNTIL 8 THUR, 11 - 5 SUN, BANK HOLIDAYS.

Merchandise from past seasons' collections or factory seconds at discounts of at least 30% off the original price. There is a wide range of handbags, suitcases, women's shoes, luggage, briefcases, umbrellas, scarves and travel bags. *Factory Shopping Village*

JEFFREY ROGERS

CHESHIRE OAKS OUTLET VILLAGE, KINSEY ROAD, NEAR ELLESMERE
PORT, JUNCTION 10 OF M53, CHESHIRE CH65 9JJ

☎ (0151) 355 6797. OPEN 10 - 6 MON - SAT, UNTIL 8 ON THUR, 11 - 5
SUN.

Factory outlet with the emphasis on young street style: from sleeveless mini
dresses to drawstring waist trousers, T-shirts, sweaters and skirts though there
is also the Roger Plus range for sizes 16-24. Twenty-five percent of the stock
is sold at a discount of 75%. *Factory Shopping Village*

JOE BLOGGS

CHESHIRE OAKS DESIGNER OUTLET VILLAGE, JUNCTION 10 OF M53,
ELLESMERE PORT, CHESHIRE CH65 9JJ

☎ (0151) 356 7417. OPEN 10 - 6 MON - SAT, UNTIL 8 ON THUR,
11 - 5 SUN AND BANK HOLIDAYS.

Range of casual clothing for men, women, children and babies which are ends
of lines, imperfects or surplus ranges. Jeans, tops, long sleeved shirts and jackets at discounts of between 30% and70%. *Factory Shopping Village*

JOKIDS LTD

CHESHIRE OAKS OUTLET VILLAGE, KINSEY ROAD, NEAR ELLESMERE
PORT, CHESHIRE CH65 9JJ

☎ (0151) 357 1404. OPEN 10 - 6 MON - SAT, 11 - 5 SUN, UNTIL 8 THUR.

JoKids is the factory shop trading name for Jeffrey Ohrenstein which sells
unusual and attractive clothes for children aged from birth to ten years. This
includes pretty party dresses for girls at reductions of up to 40%, all-in-one
smocked playsuits, T-shirts, denim shirts, denim dresses, sunhats, shorts, and
accessories. *Factory Shopping Village*

JUMPER

CHESHIRE OAKS DESIGNER OUTLET VILLAGE, KINSEY ROAD,
ELLESMERE PORT, CHESHIRE CH65 9JJ

☎ (0151) 356 7414. OPEN 10 - 6 MON - SAT, UNTIL 8 ON THUR,
11 - 5 SUN.

A wide range of Jumper label sweaters, gloves, scarves, shirts and cardigans for
men and women all at discount prices of up to 50% off. Prices start at £2.
Factory Shopping Village

Live Well On Less Tips

Saturday mornings take on a whole new look when you realise you can spend
them drinking wine free. Oddbins, the wine merchants, have free wine tasting most weekends. Check out your local Oddbins for details.

JUST ONE NIGHT

11 BROOK ST, KNUTSFORD, CHESHIRE WA16 8EB

☎ (01565) 633059. OPEN 10 - 8 TUE & THUR, 10 - 6 MON, FRI, 10 - 4 SAT, 10 - 3 WED.

More than 350 designer dresses and gowns to choose from in sizes 8-22, many of which are exclusive to Just One Night. Also an extensive collection of jewellery, evening bags and gloves to hire. Minor alterations can be undertaken for a small extra charge. Garments are available to hire from £50 - £125 or to buy from £120 - £850. Collection changes twice a year. Shop has its own car park. *Hire Shop*

KURT GEIGER

CHESHIRE OAKS OUTLET VILLAGE, KINSEY ROAD, NEAR ELLESMERE PORT, CHESHIRE CH65 9JJ

☎ (0151) 357 1794. OPEN 10 - 6 MON - FRI, 10 - 6 SAT, 11 - 5 SUN, UNTIL 8 ON THUR.

Shoe shop for men and women which sells Kurt Geiger, Van Dal and Carvela ranges. Shoes are laid out by gender and in sizes, so it's easy to find your way round. New ranges are arranged separately. Examples of prices include a pair of Carvela shoes reduced from £49 to £25 and another blue suede pair from £65 to £35. *Factory Shopping Village*

LEE COOPER

UNIT 60, CHESHIRE OAKS DESIGNER OUTLET VILLAGE, JUNCTION 10 OF M53, ELLESMERE PORT, CHESHIRE CH65 9JJ

☎ (0151) 355 8808. OPEN 10 - 6 MON - SAT, UNTIL 8 ON THUR, 11 - 5 SUN AND BANK HOLIDAYS.

Rack upon rack of denim jeans, interspersed with rails of jackets and shirts, each ranked by size and gender at discounts of up to 30%. Casual shirts from £9.99, jeans from £14.99, T-shirts and ladieswear. Lee Cooper was founded in 1908 as a workwear manufacturer before becoming a supplier to the armed forces. Most of the stock here is current, discontinued and irregular merchandise, all of which comes straight from Lee Cooper's factories in Europe. *Factory Shopping Village*

LITTLEWOODS
CATALOGUE DISCOUNT STORE

MCARTHURGLEN OUTLET CENTRE CHESHIRE OAKS, KINSEY ROAD, NEAR ELLESMERE PORT, JUNCTION 10 OF M53, SOUTH WIRRAL, CHESHIRE CH65 9JJ

OPEN 10 - 6 MON - SAT, 8 ON THUR, 11 - 5 SUN, BANK HOLIDAYS.

Littlewoods clearance shops offering up to 50% off the catalogue price for clothing and between 50% and 60% off for electrical goods. Stock changes constantly and varies from day to day but can include well-known brand names such as Berlei and Gossard lingerie, Vivienne Westwood, Pamplemousse leisure wear, Nike and Adidas sports shoes, Workers For Freedom, and Timberland and Caterpillar footwear. Stock depends on the size and location of the shop, so larger shops will get the longer discontinued runs and smaller shops over-runs with only a small amount of colour and size variations left. Littlewoods also run a mobile shop which operates in cities where they don't have a sale shop. For details of further venues for the sales, which usually take place once a month, contact Melanie Lamb, c/o Crosby DC, Kershaw Avenue, Endbutt Lane, Crosby, Merseyside L70 1AH. *Factory Shop*

LIZ CLAIBORNE

CHESHIRE OAKS OUTLET VILLAGE, KINSEY ROAD, NEAR ELLESMERE PORT, CHESHIRE CH65 9JJ

☎ (0151) 355 9183. OPEN 10 - 6 MON - SAT, UNTIL 8 ON THUR, 11 - 5 SUN.

An American designer, Liz Claiborne offers mid market priced smart clothes for work and casual wear. All are ends of lines or styles which are at least one year old. Comfortable, fitting denims are reduced from £49 to £24.50 and under; plus there is a full range of co-ordinating tops from £14. Classic silk blouses cost from £35; and casual suited jackets start from £45. There is a range available in petite sizing and a wide choice of accessories, with belts from £3, and summer handbags in a large choice of colours. *Factory Shopping Village*

MATALAN

UNIT 29, GREYHOUND RETAIL PARK, SEALAND ROAD, CHESTER, CHESHIRE CH1 1QG

☎ (01244) 380877. OPEN 10 - 8 MON - FRI, 9 - 6 SAT, 11 - 5 SUN.

NEW CHESTER ROAD, BROMBOROUGH, SOUTH WIRRAL, L62 7EK

☎ (0151) 343 9494. OPEN 10 - 8 MON - FRI, 9 - 6 SAT, 11 - 5 SUN.

WINWICK ROAD, WARRINGTON, CHESHIRE WA2 8NU

☎ (01925) 235365. OPEN 10 - 8 MON - FRI, 9 - 6 SAT, 11 - 5 SUN.

Matalan is a fashion and homewares shop giving customers what they claim to be unbeatable value for money with huge savings on a wide range of prod-ucts including high quality fashionable clothing for women, women and chil-dren at up to 50% off high street prices. Matalan is situated out of town and stores are open seven days a week all year round. *Permanent Discount Outlet*

MATERIAL THINGS

38 CHARLOTTE STREET, MACCLESFIELD, CHESHIRE SK11 6JB
☎ (01625) 613955. OPEN 9.30 - 5 MON, TUE, 10 - 5 WED, 9.30 - 5.30
THUR, FRI, SAT.
Sells seconds, fents (small sections of 2 yards in length), roll stock and perfect ends of lines of furnishing and upholstery fabrics from top designers at very cheap prices. The material from which the fents come would normally cost about £15-£25 a metre; here, fents are sold from £4 each. Upholstery fabric costs from £10 a metre, about one third of the normal price. Also seconds of lace, muslins, calico and top designer trimmings from £2.50 a metre. Making-up service available. *Permanent Discount Outlet*

MCARTHURGLEN DESIGNER OUTLET

CHESHIRE OAKS, JUNCTION 10 OF THE M53, KINSEY ROAD, NEAR
ELLESMERE PORT, CHESHIRE CH65 9JJ
☎ (0151) 357 3633. OPEN 10 - 6 MON - SAT, UNTIL 8 ON THUR,
11 - 5 SUN AND BANK HOLIDAYS.
More than 120 outlets, with 46 more planned, selling brand name merchandise at discounted prices. Fashion labels for women include Austin Reed, Benetton, Big L Levi's, Burberrys, Cap It All, Cartoon Fashion, Ciro Pearls, Claire's Accessories, Cotton Traders, Cross Creek, Daks Simpson, Diesel, DKNY, Donna Karan (for men and women as well as DKNY Active diffusion ranges), Donnay sportswear, Ecco, Episode, Evans, Falmer Jeans, Famous Footwear, Fred Perry, Fruit of the Loom casualwear, Gap, Helly Hansen, Jaeger, Jeffrey Rogers, Jesire, Joe Bloggs, Jane Shilton, John Partridge, Jumper, Karrimor Store, Kurt Geiger, La Senza, Lee Cooper, Lingerie Shop, Liz Claiborne, Mexx, Monet jewellery, Next to Nothing, Nike, Paco, Pied a Terre, Pilot, Principles, Proibito (ends of lines from Moschino, Versace, Fendi, Gianfrance Ferre, Byblos, Armani), Ravel, Red/Green, Reebok, Richards, Russell Athletic, Shoe Studio, Soled Out, Sportsystem, The Designer Room, The Sweater Shop, Timberland, Tog 24 outdoorwear, U Wear I Wear, Vans footwear, Viyella, Walker and Hall jewellery and watches, Wallis, Warehouse, Warners, Winning Line. For men, Austin Reed, Baron Jon, Benetton, Ben Sherman, Blazer, Big L Levis', Burberrys, Cap It All, Cecil Gee, Cotton Traders, Cross Creek, Daks Simpson, Diesel, Donnay sportswear, Ecco, Eddie Bauer, Falmer Jeans, Famous Footwear, Fosters, Fred Perry, Fruit of the Loom casualwear, Gap, Helly Hansen, Jaeger, James Barry, Joe Bloggs, John Partridge, Jumper, Karrimor Store, Kurt Geiger, Lee Cooper, Mexx, Next to Nothing, Nike, Paco, Principles, Red/Green, Reebok, Russell Athletic, Shoe Studio, Soled Out, Sportsystem, Suits You, The Suit Company, The Sweater Shop, Tie Rack, Timberland, Tog 24 outdoorwear, Van Heusen, Vans footwear, Viyella, Walker and Hall watches, Woodhouse. Shops for children include Benetton, Big L Levis', Cap It All, Cartoon Fashion, Donnay

sportswear, Ecco, Falmer Jeans, Famous Footwear, Fruit of the Loom casualwear, Gap, Joe Bloggs, Jo Kids, Lee Cooper, Mexx, Mothercare, Next to Nothing, Nike, Paco, Principles, Reebok, Russell Athletic, Shoe Studio, Soled Out, Sportsystem, Thorntons, Tog 24 outdoorwear, Toyworld and Vans footwear. Shops for the home include Bed & Bath Works towels and bedlinen; Clover House tablemats and kitchenware; Denby; Edinburgh Crystal; Kitchen Store; Onieda cutlery; Ponden Mill bedlinen, duvets and towels; Price's Candles; Royal Doulton; Royal Worcester; Villeroy & Boch; Whittard of Chelsea cafetieres, china and kitchen containers; Woods of Windsor fragrances, and XS Music and Video. Electrical shops include Remington which sells everything from knives and saucepans to hairdryers and shavers and Thorn which sells TVs, videos, CD players, and small electrical equipment. Leisure shops include Antler luggage; Bookends; Card & Gift cards and small gifts; Carphone Warehouse; Thorntons and Travel Accessory Outlet which sells a range of brand name luggage, handbags and travel accessories. Sports and outdoor wear labels include Donnay sportswear, Fred Perry, Helly Hansen, John Partridge, Karrimor Store, Nike, Red/Green, Reebok, Russell Athletic, Sportsystem, Timberland, Tog 24 outdoorwear. There is a children's play area and a variety of different restaurants from pizzas to McDonalds. *Factory Shopping Village*

MEXX INTERNATIONAL

CHESHIRE OAKS DESIGNER OUTLET VILLAGE, ELLESMERE PORT, JUNCTION 10 OF M53, CHESHIRE CH65 9JJ

☎ (0151) 355 8238. OPEN 10 - 6 MON - SAT, UNTIL 8 ON THUR, 11 - 5 SUN AND BANK HOLIDAYS.

High street fashion at factory outlet prices for men, women, babies, children and teenagers, all of which are heavily discounted by more than 30% *Factory Shopping Village*.

MOLLY MUMBLES

I BOOTHBED LANE, NEAR HOLMES CHAPEL, CHESHIRE CW4 8JP

☎ (01477) 532234. OPEN 9.30 - 3 MON - FRI, 9.30 - 12 WED, 9.30 - 3 SAT.

Huge selection of top quality secondhand childrenswear and equipment at bargain prices. Labels include Mothercare, Miniman, Gap, OshKosh, Jean Bourget, Oilily, Mamas & Papas, Fisher Price Maclaren, Playmobil and Duplo. Also hires out buggies, high chairs, prams, travel cots, car seats by the day, week or month. *Dress Agencies, Hire Shop*

Live Well On Less Tips

Many art galleries and museums offer free workshops during the school holidays and at half term. Check if your local galleries and museums do, but remember, they're very popular so book up well in advance.

NEXT TO NOTHING

CHESHIRE OAKS DESIGNER OUTLET VILLAGE, JUNCTION 10 OF M53, ELLESMERE PORT, CHESHIRE CH65 9JJ

☎ (0151) 356 7404. OPEN 10 - 6 MON - SAT, 8 ON THUR, 11 - 5 SUN AND BANK HOLIDAYS.

Sells perfect surplus stock from Next stores and the Next Directory catalogue at discounts of 50% or more. The ranges are usually last season's and overruns but there is the odd current item if you look carefully. There are shoes, lingerie, swimwear, and clothes for men, women and children. *Factory Shopping Village*

NIKE FACTORY STORE

CHESHIRE OAKS OUTLET VILLAGE, KINSEY ROAD, NEAR ELLESMERE PORT, CHESHIRE CH65 9JJ

☎ (0151) 357 1252. OPEN 10 - 6 MON - SAT, UNTIL 8 ON THUR, 11 - 5 SUN.

Men's, women's and children's trainers, jackets, T-shirts, sports shirts, shorts, sleeveless T-shirts and tracksuits. Nike has been making clothes for people who live and play outdoors since 1972. This factory shop sells unsold items from previous seasons. The selection represents their worldwide collection, which means that some garments may not have been offered for sale in the UK. As ranges tend to be incomplete, they are offered at up to 30% off the recommended retail price or the price they would have commanded in the UK. Occasionally, there are some slight seconds on sale, which are always marked as such. There is another factory shop in Swindon in Wiltshire. *Factory Shopping Village*

NORTH WEST BABY HIRE

1 SIDE AVENUE, HALL ROAD, BOWDON, ALTRINCHAM, CHESHIRE WA14 3AP

☎ (0161) 941 4916.

Quality baby equipment hire from high chairs, cots and travel cots to baby car seats and buggies. Also specialises in altering push chairs for sale and hire. *Hire Shop*

NORTH WEST BABYHIRE

1 SIDE AVENUE, HALL ROAD, BOWDON, ALTRINCHAM, CHESHIRE WA14 3AP

☎ (0161) 941 4916, KIDDICARE, 33 THE RIDINGS, SAUGHALL, CHESTER, CHESHIRE CH1 6AX,

☎ (01244) 880690.

Part of the Baby Equipment Hirers Association (BEHA), which has more than 100 members countrywide. A range of equipment can be hired from high chairs, cots and travel cots to baby car seats and buggies. Some members also hire out party equipment including child-sized tables and chairs. BEHA run an advice line which will try and answer any queries you have regarding hiring services for children. Phone the Babyline on 0831 310355. *Hire Shop*

NOSTALGIA ANTIQUE FIREPLACE

61 SHAW HEATH, STOCKPORT, CHESHIRE SK3 8BH

☎ (0161) 477 7706. FAX ☎ (0161) 477 2267. OPEN 10 - 6 TUE - FRI, 10 - 5 SAT.

A constant stock of more than 1,200 genuine antique fireplace of all descriptions and materials dating from 1750-1920. Also lots of Victorian and Edwardian washbasins and loos. Expert restoration is carried out on this extensive stock and a wealth of advice is available. *Architectural Salvage*

ONE-NIGHT AFFAIR

1 MARKET STREET, ALTRINCHAM, CHESHIRE WA14 1QE

☎ (0161) 928 8477. OPEN 10 - 5 MON - SAT.

Situated within the Elite Dress Agency, you can choose from more than 350 outfits, including cocktail wear, ball gowns, party gear and accessories to hire or to buy. Stock changes frequently. Hire costs £65-£85. No appointment necessary. *Hire Shop*

ONEIDA

CHESHIRE OAKS OUTLET VILLAGE, KINSEY ROAD, ELLESMERE PORT, JUNCTION 10 OF M53 CHESHIRE CH65 9LA

☎ (0151) 356 1024. OPEN 10 - 6 MON - SAT, 8 ON THUR, 11 - 5 SUN.

Oneida is one of the world's largest cutlery companies and originates from the United States of America. In addition to cutlery, it sells silver and silver plate at discounts of between 30% and 50%, plus frames, candlesticks and trays. They now also have their own range of chinaware and glass, also sold here at discounts of 30%-50%. *Factory Shopping Village*

PACO LIFE IN COLOUR

UNIT 25, CHESHIRE OAKS OUTLET VILLAGE, KINSEY ROAD, NEAR ELLESMERE PORT, JUNCTION 10 OF M53, SOUTH WIRRAL, CHESHIRE L65 9JJ

☎ (0151) 3573722. OPEN 10 - 6 MON - SAT, 11 - 5 SUN, UNTIL 8 ON THUR.

Comprehensive range of casualwear clothing and accessories for women in a wide variety of colours. End-of-season lines are on sale at discounts of around 30%. Included in the range are T-shirts, sweatshirts, wool sweaters and cardigans, jeans, leggings, shorts, bags and socks, all offering outstanding value for money. *Factory Shopping Village*

PILOT

CHESHIRE OAKS DESIGNER OUTLET VILLAGE, JUNCTION 10 OF M53, ELLESMERE PORT, CHESHIRE CH65 9JJ

☎ (0151) 355 8082. OPEN 10 - 6 MON - SAT, 8 ON THUR, 11 - 5 SUN AND BANK HOLIDAYS.

Mainly younger-style clothes for women only. Some are seconds but most are end of season and end of line. Reductions are about 30%, e.g. in the summer of 1999: pedal pushers, £23 reduced to £17, short strap top £17 reduced to £10. *Factory Shopping Village*

PONDEN MILL LINENS

MCARTHURGLEN DEISNGER OUTLET VILLAGE, KINSEY ROAD, ELLESMERE PORT, SOUTH WIRRAL, CHESHIRE CH65 9LA

☎ (0151) 356 4411. OPEN 10 - 6 MON - SAT, 8 ON THUR, 11 - 5 SUN.

Famous branded products at direct from the mill prices. Towels, co-ordinated bedlinen, duvets, pillows and curtains from Crown, Coloroll, Chortex, Rectella together with bathroom and kitchen accessories. *Factory Shopping Village*

PRICE'S CANDLES

CHESHIRE OAKS DESIGNER OUTLET VILLAGE, JUNTION 10 OF M53, SOUTH WIRRAL, CHESHIRE CH65 9LA

☎ (0151) 356 0248. OPEN 10 - 6 MON - SAT, 8 ON THUR, 11 - 5 SUN.

Everything sold in this shop are seconds, which may be discoloured or have a damaged pattern; discontinued sizes not available elsewhere; over-runs from the garden selection or dinner candles in old packaging that has now been replaced. There are church candles, lanterns, candles in pots and glass jars, star-shaped candles, floating candles, candlestick holders, serviettes, scented candles and garden torches. Some of the ceramic items are bought in. *Factory Shopping Village*

PRINCIPLES

CHESHIRE OAKS OUTLET VILLAGE, KINSEY ROAD, NEAR ELLESMERE PORT, JUNCTION 10 OF M53, CHESHIRE CH65 9JJ

☎ (0151) 357 1033. OPEN 10 - 6 MON - SAT, 8 ON THUR, 11 - 5 SUN.

End of season lines with the normal Principles refund guarantee. The range includes, for women, dresses, blouses, coats, outerwear, knitwear, casualwear and a selection of Petite clothing for women who are 5ft 3ins and under. Also stocks Amanda Wakeley's special ranges for Principles at up to 50% discount. For men, there is formalwear, smart casualwear, knitwear, outerwear, PFM Sport, jeanswear and casualwear. *Factory Shopping Village*

QS FASHION

1-5 BROAD ROAD, SALE, CHESHIRE

☎ (0161) 976 2747. OPEN 9 - 8 MON - FRI, 9 - 5.30 SAT, 11 - 5 SUN.

Although not a discount shop as such, most of the stock on sale here is cheaper than it could be found elsewhere. Fashion for all the family includes brands such as Lee Cooper, Timberland, Joe Bloggs, Fila, Nike, Reebok, Ralph Lauren. *Permanent Discount Outlet*

REMINGTON

MCARTHURGLEN DESIGNER OUTLET, JUNCTION 10 OF THE M53, KINSEY ROAD, NEAR ELLESMERE PORT, CHESHIRE CH65 9JJ

☎ (0151) 357 2477. OPEN 10 - 6 MON - SAT, UNTIL 8 ON THUR, 11 - 5 SUN.

Lots of famous names here from Oneida and Monogram cutlery to Braun, Philips, Remington, Clairol, Wahl, Krups, Swan and Kenwood small kitchen equipment as well as a wide range of hair, beauty and male grooming accessories, all at reduced prices. It's a great place to buy gifts or replenish the kitchen equipment with combi stylers, turbo travel plus hairdryers, air purifiers, liquidisers; food processors; batteries; clocks; and cutlery. Some of the packaging may be damaged but the products are in perfect working order *Factory Shopping Village*

RICHARDS

CHESHIRE OAKS OUTLET VILLAGE, KINSEY ROAD, NEAR ELLESMERE PORT, CHESHIRE CH65 9JJ

☎ (0151) 357 1159. OPEN 10 - 6 MON - SAT, UNTIL 8 ON THUR, 11 - 5 SUN.

Wide range of clothes from summerwear to coats, all at discount prices of up to 30%. *Factory Shopping Village*

ROYAL WORCESTER & SPODE FACTORY SHOP

MCARTHUR GLEN DESIGNER OUTLET VILLAGE, CHESHIRE OAKS, KINSEY ROAD, ELLESMERE PORT, CHESHIRE CH65 9JJ

☎ (0151) 3569199. OPEN 10 - 6 MON - SAT, 8 ON THUR, 11 - 5 SUN.

Infinitesimally flawed porcelain and china seconds at 25% less than perfect prices. This outlet stocks Royal Brierley, Gleneagles, Langham Glass, Country Artists, Paw Prints, Bowbrook, Ornamenal Studio, Collectable World, Fo-Frame, Six Trees, Pimpernel table mats and Lakeland Plaques. There is a vast range with special offers throughout the year on anything from crystal decanters and bowls to figurines, cookware and dinner sets. Shipping arrangements worldwide can be organised. *Factory Shopping Village*

RUSSELL ATHLETIC

CHESHIRE OAKS DESIGNER OUTLET VILLAGE, ELLESMERE PORT,
JUNCTION 10 OF M53, CHESHIRE CH65 9JJ

☎ (0151) 356 7440. OPEN 10 - 6 MON - SAT, UNTIL 8 ON THUR,
11 - 5 SUN AND BANK HOLIDAYS,

For more than 50 years, Russell Athletic has been a major supplier to American
sports teams. Here they sell jogging pants, sweat tops, sports bags and T-shirts
which are either discontinued or imperfects at discounts of up to 50%.
Factory Shopping Village

SOMETHING DIFFERENT

44 LOWER BRIDGE STREET, CHESTER, CHESHIRE CH1 1RS

☎ (01244) 317484. OPEN 9.30 - 5 MON - SAT.

Upmarket ladies clothes, with a lot of day wear from the top end of the high
street names such as Alexon, Louis Feraud, Liberty and Jaeger, amongst others. There is a special events room, a hire section for ballgowns and cocktail
dresses. Casual wear is also available with some sports wear including ski
clothing. There are no annual sales but there is a special couture designer rail.
The shop also runs charity shows at hotels. They also sell a varied range of new
clothes including German designer wear. *Hire shop*

SPECIAL EVENT

44 LOWER BRIDGE STREET, CHESTER, CHESHIRE CH1 1RS

☎ (01244) 340757. OPEN 9.30 - 5 MON - SAT, 11 - 4 SUN (MAR - DEC),

Nearly-new ball gowns and cocktail wear, with a large selection of designer
dresses from sizes 8-24. Owned by the proprietor of the dress agency called
Something Different which specialises in mother of the bride outfits from
Armani and Laurel to Mondi and Jaeger. Also sells new clothing by Indian
summer wear label, Phool, at competitive prices. *Dress Agency*

SPOILS

UNIT MSU4, THE PYRAMIDS CENTRE, BIRKENHEAD, CHESHIRE
CH41 2RA

☎ (0151) 647 5753. OPEN 9 - 5.30 MON - SAT, 10.30 - 4 SUN.

General domestic glassware, non-stick bakeware, non-electrical kitchen gadgets, ceramic oven-to-tableware, textiles, cutting boards, aluminium non-stick
cookware, bakeware, plastic kitchenware, plastic storage, woodware, coffee
pots/makers, furniture, mirrors and picture frames. Rather than being discounted, all the merchandise is very competitively priced - in fact, the company carry out competitors' checks frequently in order to monitor pricing.
With 38 branches, the company is able to buy in bulk and thus negotiate very
good prices. *Permanent Discount Outlet*

SUITS YOU

UNIT 58, CHESHIRE OAKS OUTLET VILLAGE, KINSEY ROAD, NEAR ELLESMERE PORT, CHESHIRE CH65 9JJ

☎ (0151) 355 6701. OPEN 10 - 6 MON - SAT UNTIL 8 ON THUR, 11 - 5 SUN.

Most of the suits and jackets here are sold under the Suits You label, although there are some Van Kollen jackets and Pierre Cardin suits, as well as suits by Cezar, Dylo, Statz, Benvenuto and Pierre Balmain. A large sign at the door tells you the sorts of discounts you can expect. For example, you can buy two £100 suits for £180 or two £130 suits for £235. There are also cuff links shirts, two for £26; trousers, two for £50; braces, ties and casual shirts. *Factory Shopping Village*

SUNRIDGE UPHOLSTERY

19 FARNWORTH ROAD, PENKETH, WARRINGTON, CHESHIRE WA5 2RZ

☎ (01925) 727610. OPEN 8 - 4 MON - FRI.

A small factory with a showroom, principally making sofas and suites for showhouses. It sells three-piece suites, sofas and upholstery fabrics. Sunridge are willing to customise the sofa design based on the half dozen or so sofas they have on display. Two-seater sofas cost from £600; armchairs from £350 and foot stools from £130. There are hundreds of upholstery fabrics to choose from including Monkwell, Crowsons, Romo and John Wilman. Delivery, which is free in the northwest only, takes six weeks. They also offer a 12 months interest free credit service after paying a 10% deposit. *Factory Shop*

THE CAPE

114 FOREGATE STREET, CHESTER, CHESHIRE CH1 1HB

☎ (01244) 329880. OPEN 10 - 5 SEVEN DAYS A WEEK.

High quality, high density pine furniture made in South Africa from trees grown in managed forests, is sold at factory direct prices with home delivery through-out the UK. The range includes beds, wardrobes, blanket boxes, chests of draw-ers, tallboys, dressing tables, cheval mirrors, headboards, mattresses, a kitchen range, dining room tables, Welsh dressers, hi-fi units, bookcases. Also on sale in this shops is a range of African accessories and artefacts from Zimbabwe encom-passing mirrors, prints, serpentine (stone) ornaments, recylced stationery, hand-made wirework, candles and other ethnic and traditional gifts. Colour brochure and price list available on 01535 600483. *Factory Shop*

Live Well On Less Tips

For ideas about places to visit on family outings, visit your local tourist board where there are scores of leaflets and booklets about your area. They are often useful educational tools, too, as they offer historical information which you can pass on to your children on the spot.

THE CURTAIN EXCHANGE

3 HAWTHORN LANE, WILMSLOW, CHESHIRE SK9 1AQ

☎ (01625) 536060 OPEN 10 - 5 MON - SAT.

The Curtain Exchange is a franchised group of shops selling beautiful top quality secondhand curtains, blinds, pelmets, etc at between one-third and one half of the brand new price. Their stock comes from a variety of sources: people who are moving house and dislike the drapes in their new home; people who are moving house and want to sell their old curtains to help with the bills; show houses, where the builder wants to recoup some of his outgoings; interior designers' mistakes. Stock changes constantly and ranges from rich brocades, damasks and velvets to chintzes, linens and cottons. Designer names include Colefax & Fowler, Designers Guild, Laura Ashley, Warner, Sanderson, Osborne & Little, Fortuny and Bennison. A team of fitters and alteration experts are available if required. They offer a 24-hour availability. The Curtain Exchange also supply bespoke ranges with samples of curtains hanging. These fabrics are chosen from suppliers all over the world and are an excellent buy. *Secondhand Shop*

THE DESIGNER WAREHOUSE

PARADISE MILL, PARK LANE, MACCLESFIELD, CHESHIRE SK11 6TL

☎ (01625) 511169. OPEN 9.30 - 5.30 MON - SAT.

Designer warehouse selling a wide range of top quality Continental designer labels at discounts of up to 50% and more. Stock changes constantly. For example, Klassic Kemper dresses, suits and co-ordinates all at a saving of 50% so that dresses are £89 instead of £195 and suits £149 instead of £325. There is also Hirsch, Elinette, Joyce Ridings dresses, £89 instead of £250 and jackets £125 instead of £299; and Joseph Janard at great savings. There are lots more top labels, all of which represent up-to-the-minute fashion. *Permanent Discount Outlet*

THE FABRIC EMPORIUM

BON MARCHE, UNIT A, VICTORIA CENTRE, CREWE, CHESHIRE CW1 2PU

☎ (01270) 255455. OPEN 9 - 5.30 MON - SAT.

Curtain and upholstery own brand fabrics and those from many well-known high street brands such as Laura Ashley, Next and Marks & Spencer. Because they buy job lots from the USA, Europe and the UK, prices range from £2.99 a metre to £12.99 a metre although the normal recommended retail price of many items ranges from £16 to £30 a metre. Most goods are first quality. The majority of goods are priced in the range of £3.99 to £7.99 a metre. Stock is continually changing and brands include Crowson, Blendworth, Moggashel, Monkwell, and Matthew Stevens. *Permanent Discount Outlet*

THE GAP

CHESHIRE OAKS DESIGNER OUTLET VILLAGE, JUNCTION 10 OF THE M53, NEAR ELLESMERE PORT, CHESHIRE CH65 9JJ

☎ (0151) 355 2922. OPEN 10 - 6 MON - SAT, UNTIL 8 ON THUR, 11 - 5 SUN AND BANK HOLIDAYS.

The Gap sells casual clothes for men, women and children of all ages. *Factory Shopping Village*

THE OLD SOFA WAREHOUSE

UNIT 1, 3 HAWTHORN LANE, WILMSLOW, CHESHIRE SK9 1AA

☎ (01625) 536397/(07803) 497938. OPEN 10 - 5 THUR, FRI, 10.30 - 5 SAT. OTHER TIMES BY APPOINTMENT ONLY.

The Old Sofa Warehouse buys Victorian, Edwardian and later furniture, drop-end sofas, chaise longues, winged-back armchairs or the odd dining chair in their original condition, which are all sold at very reasonable prices. They stock a selection of designer fabrics and swatches - for example, from Thomas Dare, Andrew Martin, Titley and Marr, Brown & Rowan, Hill & Knowles, Ian Sanderson, Linwood and Leon Brunswick. They offer an upholstery service with customers either choosing their own fabric or the Sofa Warehouse's. *Secondhand Shop*

THE REALLY GOOD DEAL FASHION SALE

TATTON PARK, CHESHIRE

☎ (01367) 860017 TICKET ENQUIRIES. OPEN 10 - 6, FRI 6TH & SAT 7TH OCTOBER 2000.

One of six countrywide fashion sales run by the team behind The Good Deal Directory. Each one features between 50 and 90 top quality fashion houses and well-known brand names selling their ends of lines, discounted stock and last season's merchandise at discount prices. Exhibitors usually include top catwalk names, middle market companies, some retailers clearing excess stock, a few manufacturers and agents selling samples and some entrepreneurs selling top Continental designer names. There are clothes for all occasions, knitwear, scarves, shawls, pashmina, shoes, jewellery, some gifts, a few childrenswear companies, and some men's gift fashion lines such as ties and shirts. Quality is middle to upper market, aimed at 25-50 year olds. *Designer Sale*

THE SUIT COMPANY

CHESHIRE OAKS OUTLET VILLAGE, KINSEY ROAD, ELLESMERE PORT, SOUTH WIRRAL, CHESHIRE CH65 9JJ

☎ (0151) 355 7473. OPEN 10 - 6 MON - SAT, 11 - 5 SUN, UNTIL 8 ON THUR.

This shop is part of the Moss Bros group and includes labels such as YSL, Pierre Cardin, Wolsey and Jockey underwear, as well as leather gloves, belts, ties, work shirts, suits, jackets. *Factory Shopping Village*

THORNTONS

CHESHIRE OAKS OUTLET VILLAGE, KINSEY ROAD, ELLESMERE PORT, SOUTH WIRRAL, CHESHIRE CH65 9JJ

☎ (0151) 355 5637. OPEN 10 - 6 MON - SAT, 8 ON THUR, 11 - 5 SUN.

The UK's leading specialist confectionery retailer has more than 500 shops and franchises nationwide selling a wide range of boxed and loose, chocolate and sugar confectionery. The factory outlets sell three different categories: misshapes. discounted lines and standard lines. Misshapes are loose chocolates which are the result of new product development, product trials or end of production runs which cannot be packed as Thorntons standard lines. They are packed into assorted bags and offer a saving of 35%-55% over the recommended retail price of standard loose line products. Discounted lines are excess to Thorntons' normal retail requirements and can be as a result of excess seasonal or export stock, discontinued lines or packaging changes. These products, when available, are offered at a discount of 25%-50% over the standard retail price. Standard lines from the full Thorntons range are also on sale at normal prices. *Factory Shopping Village*

TIE RACK

CHESHIRE OAKS OUTLET VILLAGE, KINSEY ROAD, NEAR ELLESMERE PORT, CHESHIRE CH65 9JJ

☎ (0151) 355 6166. OPEN 10 - 6 MON - SAT, 10 - 8 THUR, 11 - 5 SUN.

Usual range of Tie Rack items including boxer shorts, silk ties, socks, silk scarves and waistcoats, all at 50% reductions. Customer Careline: 0181 230 2333. *Factory Shopping Village*

TILE CLEARING HOUSE

MALBERN INDUSTRIAL ESTATE, GREF STREET, REDDISH, STOCKPORT, CHESHIRE

☎ (0161) 476 4355. OPEN 8 - 6 MON - FRI, 9 - 6 SAT, 10 - 4 SUN.

Over 500 ranges of top quality ceramic wall and floor tiles permanently in stock, plus a comprehensive range of grouts, adhesives, tools and accessories to complete the job. Save up to 75% on manufacturers' recommended selling prices. *Permanent Discount Outlet*

TIMBERLAND

CHESHIRE OAKS OUTLET VILLAGE, KINSEY ROAD, NEAR ELLESMERE PORT, JUNCTION 10 OF M53, CHESHIRE CH65 9JJ

☎ (0151) 357 1359. OPEN 10 - 6 MON - SAT, 11 - 5 SUN, UNTIL 8 ON THUR.

Footwear, clothing and outdoor gear from the well-known Timberland range at discounts of 30% or more. All stock is last season's excess stock in limited ranges and sizes. As most of Timberland's stock is from a core range which rarely changes, there are few discontinued lines. *Factory Shopping Village*

TOG 24

CHESHIRE OAKS DESIGNER OUTLET VILLAGE, KINSEY ROAD,
ELLESMERE PORT, CHESHIRE CH65 9JJ

☎ (01513) 567477. OPEN 10 - 6 MON - SAT, UNTIL 8 ON THUR,
11 - 5 SUN AND BANK HOLIDAYS.

Tog 24 are the UK's fastest growing brand name in outdoor clothing and leisurewear, with a total of three UK factories and 36 stores nationwide. They utilise the world's finest performance fabrics including Gore-Tex, Polartec and Burlington macs. Catering for all the family for all seasons, with cosy fleeces and waterproofs for the winter, and trekking ranges, shorts and T-shirts for the summer. With all prices at least 30% below the recommended retail price you can afford to enter the Tog comfort zone. *Factory Shopping Village*

TOP NOTCH

54 HOSPITAL STREET, NANTWICH, CHESHIRE

☎ (01270) 623334. OPEN 9 - 4.30 MON - FRI, 9 - 5 SAT.

Dress agency selling names such as Betty Jackson, Louis Feraud and Paul Costelloe, as well as shoes, accessories and handbags. Specialises upstairs in a new Danish range of larger sizes from 16-26. *Dress Agency*

TOYWORLD FACTORY OUTLETS LTD

MCARTHURGLEN DESIGNER VILLAGE, CHESHIRE OAKS, KINSEY
ROAD, ELLESMERE PORT, SOUTH WIRRAL, CHESHIRE CH65 9JJ

☎ (0151) 355 9998. OPEN 10 - 6 MON - SAT, UNTIL 8 ON THUR,
11 - 5 SUN AND BANK HOLIDAYS.

Brand name toys at discounted prices makes this a great place for Christmas and birthday presents. Items range from small plastic toys to jeeps and plastic houses. Recognisable names include Barbie, Disney, Mattel, Playskool, Lego, Duplo, Sylvanian Families, Fisher-Price, Tomy, Tyco, Waddington, M&B Games and Safe & Sound. Discounts can be as much as 75%. There are other factory shops at Jacksons Landing and Royal Quays Outlet Centre (see North East). *Factory Shopping Village*

TRAVEL ACCESSORY OUTLET

UNIT 28, CHESHIRE OAKS OUTLET VILLAGE, KINSEY ROAD,
NEAR ELLESMERE PORT, CHESHIRE CH65 9JJ

☎ (0151) 357 3248. OPEN 10 - 6 MON - SAT, UNTIL 8 ON THUR,
11 - 5 SUN.

Luggage and travel-related products including executive cases, handbags, umbrellas and accessories available in leading brands such as Samsonite, Brics, Hidesign, Globe Trotter and Tula. The products also include couture and high fashion brands such as YSl and Moschino. All products are offered at a considerably reduced price due to their being production over-runs, last season's stock of slight seconds (ie they have minor aesthetic blemishes). *Factory Shopping Village*

VELMORE LTD

UNIT 14, TELFORD ROAD, THORNTON ROAD INDUSTRIAL ESTATE, ELLESMERE PORT, CHESHIRE CH65 5EP

☎ (0151) 357 1212. OPEN 10.30 - 3 TUE, WED, THUR, 10.30 - 2 FRI, 9 - 1 SAT.

PICOW FARM ROAD, RUNCORN CHESHIRE WA7 4UJ

☎ (01928) 560169. OPEN 10.30 - 3 TUE, THUR, FRI.

UNIT 52, APPIN WAY, ARGYLE INDUSTRIAL ESTATE, BIRKENHEAD

☎ (0151) 666 1579. OPEN 10.30 - 3 MON - THUR.

Overmakes and seconds of skirts, dresses, suits, shorts, jackets and trousers originally made for the most famous high street name at very cheap prices. *Factory Shop*

VICTORIA LIGHTING FACTORY SHOP

FOUNDRY BANK, CONGLETON, CHESHIRE CW12 1EE

☎ (01260) 281071. OPEN 10 - 5 MON - SAT.

Factory shop situated in an old mill selling literally thousands of lamps - bases and shades, patterned and plain. Most of the stock is seconds and reduced by about one-third. In another part of the building, bedding, curtains and clothes are sold including Dorma, Sheridan, Fogarty and Horrick's. Hand towels from £3.99, fitted single sheets from £9.99, ready-made curtains £19.99, with matching duvet sets, £20.99. A made-to-measure curtain service is available. On the ground floor is a new furniture department which although not part of the factory shop, has settees, beds, suites and cabinet furniture at competitive prices. Recently opened top floor has a huge stock of cane furniture and giftware. There is also a coffee shop. *Factory Shop*

VILLEROY & BOCH (UK) LIMITED

UNIT 44, CHESHIRE OAKS OUTLET VILLAGE, KINSEY ROAD, ELLESMERE PORT, CHESHIRE CH65 9JJ

☎ (0151) 355 7771. OPEN 10 - 6 MON, TUE, SAT, 10 - 8 WED, THUR, FRI, 11 - 5 SUN.

An exclusive range of tableware, crystal and cutlery from Europe's largest tableware manufacturer. A varied and constantly changing stock, including seconds, hotelware and discontinued lines, on sale at excellent reductions, always makes for a worthwhile visit. *Factory Shopping Village*

VIYELLA

CHESHIRE OAKS OUTLET VILLAGE, KINSEY ROAD, NEAR ELLESMERE PORT, CHESHIRE CH65 9JJ

☎ (0151) 357 2627. OPEN 10 - 6 MON - SAT, UNTIL 8 ON THUR, 11 - 5 SUN.

Wide range of Viyella ladieswear at discount prices of 30% from jackets and blouses to sweaters and hats. *Factory Shopping Village*

VOGUE ELEVEN

11 PARK LANE, MACCLESFIELD, CHESHIRE SK11 6TJ
☎ (01625) 427031. FAX ☎ (01625) 427031. OPEN 10 - 4 MON - FRI,
10 - 1 WED, 10 - 4 SAT.
Small shop in 200-year old building run by the irrepressible Marjorie Potts,
who dispenses advice cheerfully and knowledgeably. Marjorie wouldn't have
been running the business so successfully for 20 years without being extremely good at it and the quality of the clothes and the labels prove that. There's
Mondi, Emanuel, Workers for Freedom, Jasper Conran, Diane Fres, Jaeger,
Escada, Basler, Louis Feraud, Ralph Lauren and Country Casuals. There are
also some brand new samples. Prices range from £5 to £200. *Dress Agency*

WALLIS

CHESHIRE OAKS OUTLET VILLAGE, KINSEY ROAD, NEAR ELLESMERE
PORT, CHESHIRE CH65 9JJ
☎ (0151) 356 9297. OPEN 10 - 6 MON - SAT, UNTIL 8 ON THUR,
11 - 5 SUN.
Wide range of clothes from summerwear to coats, all at discount prices of up
to 30%. *Factory Shopping Village*

WAREHOUSE

CHESHIRE OAKS OUTLET VILLAGE, KINSEY ROAD, NEAR ELLESMERE
PORT, CHESHIRE CH65 9JJ
☎ (0151) 357 3168. OPEN 10 - 6 MON - SAT, UNTIL 8 ON THUR, 11 - 5
SUN.
Wide range of clothes from summerwear to coats, all at discount prices of up
to 30%. *Factory Shopping Village*

WOODS OF WINDSOR

UNIT 54, CHESHIRE OAKS DESIGNER OUTLET VILLAGE, KINSEY ROAD,
ELLESMERE PORT, JUNCTION 10 OF M53, CHESHIRE CH65 9JJ
☎ (0151) 355 8170. OPEN 10 - 6 MON - SAT, UNTIL 8 ON THUR, 11 - 5
SUN AND BANK HOLIDAYS.
This shop sells gift sets, soaps, perfume, bath gel, room fragrance sprays, hand
and body lotions and talc at discounts of 30% for standard ranges and 50%
for discounted ranges. *Factory Shopping Village*

Live Well On Less Tips

Visit the library once a week and read through the newspapers and magazines. You'll be surprised at the number of companies offering free information on a range of subjects from pensions to haircare. And the fashion pages,
for example, often have details of free store events such as fashion shows
which would be fun to attend.

WYNSORS WORLD OF SHOES

LONDON ROAD, HAZEL GROVE, STOCKPORT, CHESHIRE SK7 4AX

☎ (0161) 456 2632. OPEN 9 - 5.30 MON, TUE, WED, SAT, 9 - 8 THUR, FRI, 10 - 4 SUN AND BANK HOLIDAYS.

Stocks top brand-name shoes at less than half price. Special monthly offers always available. There are shoes, trainers, slippers, sandals and boots for all the family, with a selection of bags, cleaners and polishes available.
Permanent Discount Outlet

YES STORES

207 GRANGE ROAD, BIRKENHEAD, CHESHIRE CH41 2PH

☎ (0151) 647 3050. OPEN 9 - 5.30 MON - SAT.

UNIT 11, PORT ARCADES, MERCER WALK, ELLESMERE PORT, SOUTH WIRRAL, CHESHIRE CH65 OAP

☎ (0151) 357 3782. OPEN 9 - 5.30 MON - SAT.

Mainly former catalogue clothes for women, with a small selection for men and children, as well as some high street store names, although the labels are often cut out. Stock changes twice-weekly as turnover is quick.*Permanent Discount Outlet*

Live Well On Less Tips

Sewing enthusiasts can find plenty of material for their hobby by asking for free fabric swatches in soft furnishings departments of big stores and interior design shops. Some businesses limit the number of swatches you can have but if you collect sufficient, they could be used to make patchwork quilts or dolls' clothes. Another rich source of small pieces of material can be found in the small ads at the back of magazines devoted to home decorations. There, mail order companies advertise their fabric service and you can send off for swatches.

Co Durham

WOMENSWEAR ONLY Best Dress Club, *Crook.* Classy Clothes, *Hartlepool.*
Coco, *Darlington.* Designer, *Newcastle-upon-Tyne.* Encore, *Sunderland.* Honey, *Hartlepool.*
Next Encounter, *Darlington.* Praxis Tailoring, *Ferryhill.*

MENSWEAR ONLY Baird Menswear Brands, *Hartlepool.* Tom Sayer Clothing Co, *Hartlepool.*

WOMENSWEAR & MENSWEAR Claremont Garments, *Bishops Auckland.*
Claremont Garments, *Peterlee.* Clinkard Group, *Hartlepool.*
Dewhirst Clothing Factory Shop, *Peterlee.* Discount Clothing Store, *Ashington.*
Jacksons Landing Factory Shops, *Cleveland.* Jockey Underwear Factory Shop, *Gateshead.*
Labels of Barnard Castle, *Barnard Castle.* Littlewoods Catalogue Discount Store, *Sunderland.*
Matalan, *Stockton-on-Tees.* Matalan, *Hartlepool.* Matalan, *Sunderland.* Matalan, *Gateshead.*
The Factory Shop, *Crook.* Tog 24, *Hartlepool.* Warners UK Ltd, *Hartlepool.*
Windsmoor Distribution Centre, *Bowburn.* Wynsors World of Shoes, *Stockton-on-Tees.*

CHILDREN Claremont Garments, *Bishops Auckland.* Clinkard Group, *Hartlepool.*
Dewhirst Clothing Factory Shop, *Peterlee.* Discount Clothing Unit, *Ashington.*
Jacksons Landing Factory Shops, *Hartlepool.* Littlewoods Catalogue Discount Store, *Sunderland.*
Matalan, *Stockton-on-Tees.* Matalan, *Gateshead.* Rock-a-Bye Baby, *Stockton-on-Tees.*
Seymour's of Darlington, *Darlington.* Tensor Marketing Ltd, *Darlington.* The Factory Shop, *Crook.*
Tog 24, *Hartlepool.* Toy world Factory Outlets Ltd, *Hartlepool.*
Wynsors World of Shoes, *Stockton-on-Tees.*

HOUSEHOLD AND GIFTWARE Discount Clothing Store, *Ashington.*
Edinburgh Crystal, *Hartlepool.* Jacksons Landing Factory Shops, *Hartlepool.*
Matalan, *Stockton-on-Tees.* Matalan, *Hartlepool.* Matalan, *Gateshead.*
McIntosh's Factory Shop, *Gateshead.* Newhall Company Shop, *Sunderland.*
Ponden Mill Linens, *Durham.* Jacksons Landing, *Hartlepool.* Royal Brierley Crystal, *Hartlepool.*
Seymour's of Darlington, *Darlington.* Tensor Marketing Ltd, *Darlington.* The Cape, *Gateshead.*
The Factory Shop, *Crook.*

ELECTRICAL EQUIPMENT Ebac, *Bishop Auckland.*
Littlewoods Catalogue Discount Store, *Sunderland.*

DIY/RENOVATION BMJ Power, *Spennymoor.*

FURNITURE/SOFT FURNISHINGS Seymour's of darlington, *darlington.*
Tecaz, *North Shields.* The Cape, *Gateshead.* The Factory Shop, *Washington.*

FOOD AND LEISURE Baggage Depot, *Hartlepool.* Hallmark, *Hartlepool.*
Northumbrian Fine Foods Plc, *Gateshead.* Saga Bargain Books, *Hartlepool.*

SPORTSWEAR AND EQUIPMENT Jacksons Landing Factory Shops, *Hartlepool.*
Tensor Marketing Ltd, *Darlington.*

BAGGAGE DEPOT
UNIT 22, JACKSONS LANDING, HARTLEPOOL FACTORY OUTLET SHOPPING MALL, THE HIGHLIGHT, HARTLEPOOL MARINA, HARTLEPOOL, CO DURHAM TS24 OXN
☎ (01429) 235998. OPEN 10 -6 MON - SAT, 11 - 5 SUN.
Luggage and travel-related products including executive cases, handbags, umbrellas and accessories available in leading brands such as Samsonite, Brics, Hidesign, Globe Trotter and Tula. The products also include couture and high fashion brands such as YSl and Moschino. All products are offered at a considerably reduced price due to their being production over-runs, last season's stock of slight seconds (ie they have minor aesthetic blemishes). *Factory Shopping Village*

BAIRD MENSWEAR BRANDS
POWLETT ROAD, HARTLEPOOL, CLEVELAND TS24 8LY, CO DURHAM TS24 8LY
☎ (01429) 891740. OPEN 9.30 - 4.30 MON - SAT, 10 - 4 BANK HOLIDAYS.
Manufactures men's suits, jackets and trousers for a well-known high street chain store, the factory shops sell seconds and overmakes at as little as one-third of their normal retail price. About 40% percent of the merchandise sold here is made by the factory, with a further 60% percent manufactured within the company. *Factory Shop*

BEST DRESS CLUB
NEW ROAD, CROOK, CO DURHAM
☎ (01388) 764900. OPEN 10 - 5 MON - FRI, 10 - 4 SAT.
Ladies daywear from well-known high street names such as Dorothy Perkins, Next and Etam reduced by at least 50%. Prices for the dresses, skirts, tops, jumpers and trousers range from £7.50 to £24.95. *Permanent Discount Outlet*

BMJ POWER
SERVICE STATION, GREEN LANE, SPENNYMOOR, CO DURHAM DL16 6JG
☎ (01388) 422429. OPEN 8.30 - 5 MON, TUE, THUR, FRI, 9.30 - 5 WED, 8.30 - 4 SAT, 10 - 4 SUN.
Predominantly an after-sales service with retail added on, this outlet sells reconditioned tools and acccessories from the famous Black & Decker range, as well as other power tools, circle saws, lawnmowers, staple guns and drills, all with full manufacturer's warranty and at discounts of about 25%. Often, stock consists of goods returned from the shops because of damaged packaging or part of a line which is being discontinued. Lots of seasonal special offers. There are more than three dozen BMJ outlets countrywide. Phone 0345 230230 and you can find out where your nearest outlet is. *Factory Shop*

CLAREMONT GARMENTS

GREENFIELDS ESTATE, TINDALE CRESCENT, BISHOPS AUCKLAND, CO
DURHAM DL14 9TF

☎ (01388) 661703. OPEN 10 - 4.30 MON - FRI, 10 - 5 SAT.

Manufacturers for Marks & Spencers, this factory shop sells mostly women's
clothes, leisurewear, swimwear in season, outerwear in season, and underwear
and children's clothes including a small range of schoolwear. *Factory Shop*

CLAREMONT GARMENTS

2 DOXFORD DRIVE, S/W INDUSTRIAL ESTATE, PETERLEE,
CO DURHAM S60 2RL

☎ (0191) 518 3026. OPEN 10 - 5 MON - SAT, 10.30 - 4.30 SUN.

Claremont manufacture for Marks & Spencer and sell overmakes and ends of
lines here at about half price. Most of the stock is for ladies and men. *Factory
Shop*

CLASSY CLOTHES

USWORTH ROAD, HARTLEPOOL, CO DURHAM TS25 1YA

☎ (01429) 868553. OPEN 9 - 5 MON - FRI, 9 - 5.30 SAT.

Deals mostly in brand new, well-known high street names such as Wallis,
Principles, Richard, BhS and Ann Harvey. All are on sale at savings of at least
40% in sizes 8 - 24. For example, trousers reduced from £28.99 to £15;
jackets; £29.99 from £59.99; dresses, £15 from £49.99; bodies from £8.99;
sweaters from £9.99 to £55. *Permanent Discount Outlet*

CLINKARD GROUP

JACKSONS LANDING, HARTLEPOOL FACTORY OUTLET SHOPPING
MALL, HARTLEPOOL MARINA, HARTLEPOOL, CO DURHAM TS24 OXN

☎ (01429) 866939. OPEN 10 - 6 MON - SAT, 11 - 5 SUN,
10 -6 BANK HOLIDAYS.

Labels on sale here include Rockport, Loake, Camel, Bally, Church's, Ecco,
Gabor, Rohde, Van-Dal, Kickers, Clarks, Dr Martens, K Shoes, Lotus and
Renata plus handbags by Jane Shilton. *Factory Shopping Village*

COCO

11 GRANGE ROAD, DARLINGTON, CO DURHAM DL1 5NA

☎ (01325) 383720. OPEN 10 - 5 MON - SAT.

Small shop packed with daywear, evening wear and accessories from every
kind of label - Wallis, Next and Laura Ashley to Basler, Escada and Nicole
Farhi. Clothes are immaculate and often mistaken for new by window shoppers. Sizes are mostly 10-14 with some 16s, and prices range from £5 to £200
Dress Agency

DESIGNER

15A CLAYTON ROAD, JESMOND, NEWCASTLE-UPON-TYNE,
CO DURHAM

☎ (0191) 281 5351. OPEN 10 - 5 MON - FRI, 10 - 4 SAT.

Brand new fashion, most of which is last season's stock, from Frank Usher, Jeff Banks, Paul Costelloe, Gerry Weber, Mansfield, Fink, Yarell and Ravens. Some costume jewellery and the odd pair of shoes. *Permanent Discount Outlet*

DEWHIRST
CLOTHING FACTORY SHOP

NORTH WEST INDUSTRIAL ESTATE, PETERLEE, CO DURHAM
SR8 2HR

☎ (0191) 586 4525. OPEN 9 - 5.30 MON, TUE, WED, SAT, 9 - 7 THUR,
9 - 6 FRI, 11 - 5 SUN.

PENNYWELL INDUSTRIAL ESTATE, PENNYWELL, SUNDERLAND
SR4 9EN

☎ (0191) 534 7928. OPEN 9 - 5.30 MON - SAT, 11 - 5 SUN.

WEST COTHAM LANE, DORMANSTOWN INDUSTRIAL ESTATE,
DORMANSTOWN, REDCAR TS10 5QD

☎ (01642) 474210. OPEN 9 - 5.30 MON - SAT, 10.30 - 4.30 SUN.

Dewhirst Clothing Factory Shops sell garments from the manufacturing side of the business direct to the public and are part of the Dewhirst Group plc which manufactures ladies, men's and childrenswear for a leading high street retailer. You can choose from a huge selection of surplus production and slight seconds at bargain prices, making savings of more than 50% of the normal retail cost. For men there is a wide range of suits, formal shirts and casual wear. For example, wool suits from £60, formal and casual shirts from £7. For ladies there's a selection of blouses, smart tailoring and casual wear that includes a denim range. You can find ladies jackets from £50, skirts, trousers and blouses from £8. Children's clothes start at £3. High street quality and style at wholesale prices. *Factory Shop*

DISCOUNT CLOTHING STORE

UNIT 1, MORPETH ROAD, ASHINGTON, CO DURHAM

☎ (01670) 858300. OPEN 10 - 5.30 MON - SAT, 10 - 4 SUN.

Wide range of clothes for all the family and some bedlinen and towels, most of which is from Next but also some from Marks & Spencer, Principles, Top Shop and Dorothy Perkins. *Permanent Discount Outlet*

EBAC

ST HELENS TRADING ESTATE, BISHOP AUCKLAND, CO DURHAM
☎ 0800 591991. OPEN 9.30 - 3.30 SEPT - END APRIL.
Quality end of range dehumidifiers at discount prices, plus graded ex-display models which are in perfect working order. The shop itself is only open from September to the end of April but at other times you can go to reception and they will open it up for you. *Factory Shop*

EDINBURGH CRYSTAL

JACKSONS LANDING, HARTLEPOOL FACTORY OUTLET SHOPPING MALL, HARTLEPOOL MARINA, HARTLEPOOL, CO DURHAM TS24 OXN
☎ (01429) 234335. OPEN 10 - 6 MON - SAT, 11 - 5 SUN AND BANK HOLIDAYS.
This shop has displays all round packed with glasses, decanters, gifts, glass picture frames, coloured glass, vases, bowls and jugs. Examples of prices include decanters reduced from £80 to £55.99; large tumblers from £14 to £9.75 for perfects; seconds wine glasses from £21 to £10.50; seconds decanters from £84.95 to £42.50; glass bowls from £50 to £19.99; and Caithness handmade glass vases from £9.95 to £5.99. Also when we visited, there were Royal Worcester special offer table mats and oven gloves, 20% off Arthur Price cutlery and 50% off George Butler cutlery. *Factory Shopping Village*

ENCORE

20 FREDERICK ST, SUNDERLAND, CO DURHAM SR1 1LT
☎ (0191) 564 2227. OPEN 10- 4 MON - SAT.
Sells designer labels, smart day wear, evening wear, special occasion wear, wedding outfits, hats and accessories. Labels stocked include various German labels, Escada, Louis Feraud, Frank Usher, Betty Barclay, Windsmoor, Planet, Wallis and Next. One of the two rooms in this outlet specialises in special occasion wear, the other in smart daywear. There is also a hire service for evening wear only, which costs from £60-£95 a weekend. For example, a £300 dress would cost £60 to hire. *Dress Agencies, Hire Shop*

HALLMARK

JACKSONS LANDING, HARTLEPOOL FACTORY OUTLET SHOPPING MALL, HARTLEPOOL MARINA, HARTLEPOOL, CO DURHAM TS24 OXN
☎ (01429) 275680. OPEN 10 - 6 MON - SAT, 11 - 5 SUN, BANK HOLIDAYS.
Wverything you need for celebrations. Most of the stock here is discounted by 50% including Noddy party packs, stuffed toys, cards, wrapping paper, gift rosettes, Sellotape, crepe paper, souvenir mugs. Gift wrap, 25p or ten sheets for £2; wedding day albums, £2.99 reduced from £6.99; Christmas cards in boxed sets of 10 with envelopes, £1.99 reduced from £3.99; 20 napkins, 50p reduced from 90p. All the cards are half price and include the usual range of celebratory valedictions. *Factory Shopping Village*

HONEY

JACKSONS LANDING, HARTLEPOOL FACTORY OUTLET SHOPPING MALL, HARTLEPOOL MARINA, HARTLEPOOL, CO DURHAM TS24 OXN
☎ (01429) 260488. OPEN 10 - 6 MON - FRI, 11 - 5 SUN, 10 - 6 BANK HOLIDAYS.
Leisure-oriented women's T-shirts, leggings and sweaters at discounts of mostly 30% or more. *Factory Shopping Village*

JACKSONS LANDING FACTORY SHOPS

THE HIGHLIGHT, HARTLEPOOL MARINA, HARTLEPOOL, CLEVELAND, CO DURHAM TS24 OXN
☎ (01429) 866989 INFORMATION LINE. OPEN 10 - 6 MON - SAT, 11 - 5 SUN, 10 - 6 BANK HOLIDAYS.
There is now more than ever before at the Jacksons Landing Factory Outlets. The Designer Room now has two large sales floors packed with designer labels and is the biggest Designer Room in the UK with savings of up to 70%. Jacksons Landing is a purpose-built shopping centre situated on the prestigious Hartlepool Marina next to the Historic Quay and HMS Trincomalee. Around one million people visit the centre each year to take advantage of the bargains on offer. The shops sell goods direct from the factory or as excess stock and end of lines from the high street, but wherever the goods come from you will find tremendous discounts. The twenty-four shops include famous brands such as Benetton, Windsmoor Sale Shop, Edinburgh Crystal, Royal Brierley and Ponden Mill. The Designer Room stocks a tremendous range of men's, ladies and children's designer clothing from names such as Calvin Klein, Moschino, Versace, Cerutti 1881 and The Suit Company, again with up to 70% off normal high street prices. The Designer Room also stocks perfumes and accessories to complete the range but still with those discount price tags attached. The Designer Room Cafe on the first floor provides a wide selection of hot and cold food and drinks, making the ideal resting place between shopping for bargains. Jacksons Landing has 400 free car parking spaces and is situated in the fabulous Hartlepool Marina. The centre is 15 minutes from the A19. Follow the signs for the Hartlepool Marina on the A689 or A179 and sail away with a bargain every day. Purpose-built, all-weather factory outlet selling quality goods at prices reduced by up to 60% off high street prices. Well-respected retailers including fashion names such as Windsmoor and Planet for women; Benetton for women, men and children; Charisma Leather selling own-label jackets and jeans; Joe Bloggs for men and youths; Warners lingerie; Tom Sayers menswear are represented in the centre, as are Edinburgh Crystal; Tog 24; Hallmark; luggage; Ponden Mills duvets and bedlinen; and Royal Brierley. Footwear brands including Bally, Clarks, Kickers and Doc Marten are available from Charles Clinkard. Nike, Reebok and Adidas are just a few of the major sporting brands stocked in Freetime Sports. For children, there is

Toyworld, selling brand name toys and games; for women, Honey fashion selling everydaywear; and for everyone, Bookscene. The centre is also located within walking distance of visitor attractions including Historic Quay, HMS Trincomalee and the Museum of Hartlepool. *Factory Shop*

JOCKEY UNDERWEAR FACTORY SHOP
EASTERN AVENUE, TEAM VALLEY TRADING ESTATE, GATESHEAD, CO DURHAM NE11 0PB
☎ (0191) 491 0088. OPEN 9 - 4 MON - FRI.
Up to 17 different types of men's underwear from Y-fronts and boxers to tangas and hipsters. Also ladies underwear: briefs, ribbed vests, cami-tops, bodies. Although well known for underwear, the factory shop also sells Wolsey socks, Christy towels, Zorbit babywear, pillows and duvets with up to 50% discount. *Factory Shop*

LABELS OF BARNARD CASTLE
8 THE BANK, BARNARD CASTLE, CO DURHAM DL12 8PQ
☎ (01833) 6905481. OPEN 10.30 - 5 MON - SAT.
Located in a historic market town with easy parking, labels here range from top end Chanel and Moschino Couture to Nicole Farhi, Paul Costelloe and MaxMara with a good measure of quality German designer labels as well. Popular men's ranges include Hugo Boss, Armani and Cerruti suits as well as casual wear. As-new clothes sell for about one third of the brand new price. New end of range clothes are sometimes available - telephone for details. *Dress Agency*

LITTLEWOODS
CATALOGUE DISCOUNT STORE
19 FAWCETT STREET, SUNDERLAND, CO DURHAM SR1 1RH
☎ (0191) 564 0684. OPEN 9.30 - 5.30 MON - THUR, 9 - 5.30 FRI, SAT.
Littlewoods clearance shops offering up to 50% off the catalogue price for clothing and between 50% and 60% off for electrical goods. Stock changes constantly and varies from day to day but can include well-known brand names such as Berlei and Gossard lingerie, Vivienne Westwood, Pamplemousse leisure wear, Nike and Adidas sports shoes, Workers For Freedom, and Timberland and Caterpillar footwear. Stock depends on the size and location of the shop, so larger shops will get the longer discontinued runs and smaller shops over-runs with only a small amount of colour and size variations left. Littlewoods also run a mobile shop which operates in cities where they don't have a sale shop. For details of further venues for the sales, which usually take place once a month, contact Melanie Lamb, c/o Crosby DC, Kershaw Avenue, Endbutt Lane, Crosby, Merseyside L70 1AH. *Factory Shop*

MATALAN

16 GOODWIN SQUARE, TEESSIDE RETAIL PARK, THORNABY,
STOCKTON-ON-TEES, CO DURHAM TS17 7BW
☎ (01642) 633204. OPEN 10 - 8 MON - FRI, 9 - 6 SAT, 11 - 5 SUN.
ANCHOR RETAIL PARK, MARINA WAY, HARTLEPOOL, CO DURHAM
TS24 0XR
☎ (01429) 855960. OPEN 10 - 8 MON - FRI, 9 - 6 SAT, 11 - 5 SUN.
UNIT 1, HYLTON RIVERSIDE RETAIL PARK, SUNDERLAND, DURHAM
SR5 3XG
☎ (0191) 516 0141. OPEN 10 - 8 MON - FRI, 9 - 6 SAT, 11 - 5 SUN.
UNIT 4B, METRO RETAIL PARK, GATESHEAD, CO DURHAM NE11 4YD
☎ (0191) 461 0880. OPEN 10 - 8 MON - FRI, 9 - 6 SAT, 11 - 5 SUN.
Matalan is a fashion and homewares shop giving customers what they claim
to be unbeatable value for money with huge savings on a wide range of products including high quality fashionable clothing for women, women and children at up to 50% off high street prices. Matalan is situated out of town and
stores are open seven days a week all year round *Permanent Discount
Outlet*

MCINTOSH'S FACTORY SHOP

UNIT 1, THE FACTORY SHOP CENTRE, TUNDRY WAY, CHAINBRIDGE
INDUSTRIAL ESTATE, BLAYDON ON TYNE, GATESHEAD, CO DURHAM
NE21 5SJ
☎ (0191) 414 8598. OPEN 9.30 - 5 MON - FRI, 7 ON THUR, 9 - 5 SAT,
10 - 4 SUN.
Quilts, duvet covers, towels, beach towels, bedlinen, dusters and bath mat sets
at bargain prices. Most of the household textiles are perfect with some seconds. Parking is easy and there is a coffee shop. *Factory Shop*

NEWELL COMPANY SHOP

WEAR GLASS WORKS, OFF TRINDON STREET, MILLFIELD,
SUNDERLAND, CO DURHAM SR4 6EB
☎ (0191) 515 6500. OPEN BUS TRIPS ONLY: 10.30 - 5.30 WED,
11 - 3 THUR, PUBLIC: 9.30 - 3.30 SAT.
Heat-resistant dishes for the kitchen including Pyrex cookware, bakeware and
oven to tableware and Pyroflam white casserole dishes which are safe to use in
the microwave, dishwasher, freezer or oven top. Also glasses, jugs, vases, lunch
boxes and plastic containers. Current perfect lines are sold her at full price, but
there are lots of end of line ranges, as well as surplus orders, sold at factory
shop prices. *Factory Shop*

NEXT ENCOUNTER

3B HOUNDGATE, DARLINGTON, CO DURHAM DL1 1RL

☎ (01325) 255033. OPEN 10 - 5 MON - FRI, 11 - 4 WED, 10 - 5 SAT.

Mostly high street labels such as Next, Principles, Laura Ashley and Marks & Spencer. Also sells shoes, handbags and other accessories. *Dress Agency*

NORTHUMBRIAN FINE FOODS PLC

DUKESWAY, TEAM VALLEY INDUSTRIAL ESTATE, GATESHEAD, CO DURHAM NE11 0QP

☎ (0191) 487 0070. OPEN 9.30 - 3 MON - FRI.

Value-for-money cakes, biscuits and snack foods from this north-east based company which manufactures biscuits and cakes under its own brand name, such as Cake Break, Sunwheel, Knightsbridge, Bronte, and Cakes for the Connoisseur. They also produce a selection of private label goods for many of the high street supermarkets. The factory shop sells overruns of its entire range at very reasonable prices. Availability varies but typically includes plain and chocolate biscuits, flapjacks, cookies, confectionery and cakes. *Food and Drink Discounter*

PONDEN MILL LINENS

UNITS 13-14 MLBURNGATE SHOPPING CENTRE, CO DURHAM DH1 4SL

☎ (0191) 383 1783.

JACKSONS LANDING, THE HIGHLIGHTS, HARTLEPOOL TS24 0XN

☎ (01429) 266935. OPEN 10 - 6 MON - SAT, 11 - 5 SUN.

Famous branded products at direct from the mill prices. Towels, co-ordinated bedlinen, duvets, pillows and curtains from Crown, Coloroll, Chortex, Rectella together with bathroom and kitchen accessories. *Factory Shopping Village*

PRAXIS TAILORING

DEANBANK, FERRYHILL, CO DURHAM DL17 8NP

☎ (01740) 651284. OPEN 9.30 - 6 MON - FRI, 9.30 - 4 SAT.

Sells high quality high street brand name clothes (Next, Laura Ashley, BHS, Active Sportswear) for women. There are jackets, skirts, trousers and suits, tailored trousers, perfect blazers at half the retail price; jackets, kilts. Sizes range from 8-20. *Factory Shop*

ROCK-A-BYE BABY

65 THE LARUM BEAT, YARM, STOCKTON-ON-TEES, CO DURHAM TS15 9MR

☎ (01642) 898537. PHONE FIRST. *Hire Shop*

ROYAL BRIERLEY CRYSTAL

JACKSONS LANDING, THE HIGHLIGHT, HARTLEPOOL MARINA,
HARTLEPOOL, CLEVELAND, CO DURHAM TS24 OXN

☎ (01429) 865600. OPEN 10 - 6 MON - SAT, 11 - 5 SUN.

Royal Brierley crystal seconds and Spiegelau glassware at very good prices,
with a minimum of 30% off retail. *Factory Shopping Village*

SAGA BARGAIN BOOKS

JACKSONS LANDING, HARTLEPOOL FACTORY OUTLET SHOPPING
MALL, HARTLEPOOL MARINA, CLEVELAND, HARTLEPOOL,
CO DURHAM TS24 OXN

☎ (01429) 861223. OPEN 10 - 6 MON - SAT, 11 - 5 SUN AND BANK
HOLIDAYS.

A wide range of books from fiction to health, sport to children, cookbooks to
biographies. Price reductions include cookbooks reduced from £16.99 to £6.99.
Factory Shopping Village

SEYMOUR'S OF DARLINGTON

1-3 EAST ROW, DARLINGTON, CO DURHAM DL1 5PZ,

☎ (01325) 355272. OPEN 9 - 5 MON - SAT.

Seymour's of Darlington is the longest-established household linen retailer in
the area and has recently increased its trading area by 300%. This unique
family-owned business combines old-fashioned quality and service with the
newest designs and keenest prices. There is a constantly changing, stunning
variety of stock from tea towels to velvet throws. Customers of all ages will
find trendy to traditional items at prices to suit all pockets. There are always
special offers giving extra value and there is a full range of duvets, pillows,
throws, cushion covers, duvet covers and curtains (ready-made and made-to-
measure), and bathroom fittings include shower curtains. Seymour's have their
own high quality brand of polycotton sheets, valances and pillowcases, also
available in percale. More unusual items include flannelette sheets, super king-
size bedding and candlewick bedspreads. Makes include current perfect ranges
from Sanderson, Dorma, Nimbus, Snuggledown, Christy, Coloroll and
Miller, plus economy lines and seconds. Chainstore seconds are often on offer
and all prices are extremely competitive. Staff are friendly and obliging and
will advise if required, and many items can be ordered if not in stock. Short-
term parking is available right outside from Tuesday to Friday and there is
wheelchair access. Debit and credit cards are accepted. *Permanent Discount
Outlet*

TECAZ

NORHAM ROAD, NORTH SHIELDS, CO DURHAM

☎ (0191) 257 6511. OPEN 9 - 6 MON - FRI, 9 - 5 SAT, 10 - 4 SUN.

Vast area with lots of dispalys of bathroom suites from Heritage, Armitage Shanks as well as kitchens, including the electrical equipment to go in them, which are all Whirlpool brands. There are baths, sinks, taps, shower trays, showers, soap dishes, toilets, loo roll holders, mirrors as well as a wide range of kitchens. Because Tecaz buy in large numbers, they can get better discounts from the manufacturer, some of which they pass on to the customer. *Factory Shop*

TENSOR MARKETING LTD

LINGFIELD WAY, YARM ROAD INDUSTRIAL ESTATE, DARLINGTON, CO DURHAM DL1 4XX

☎ (01325) 469 181. OPEN 9 - 5 MON - FRI, 10 - 4.30 SAT.

A marketing company specialising in innovative products with a huge range of goods covering home and garden, office, motoring, gifts, novelties, pets, pest control systems, security, health and fitness, sport and leisure. www.tensormarketing.co.uk. E-mail: TensorLimited @aol.com. *Factory Shop*

THE CAPE

METROCENTRE, GATESHEAD, CO DURHAM, OPENING EARLY 2000. NO MORE DETAILS AS WE WENT TO PRESS.

High quality, high density pine furniture made in South Africa from trees grown in managed forests, is sold at factory direct prices with home delivery throughout the UK. The range includes beds, wardrobes, blanket boxes, chests of drawers, tallboys, dressing tables, cheval mirrors, headboards, mattresses, a kitchen range, dining room tables, Welsh dressers, hi-fi units, bookcases. Also on sale in this shops is a range of African accessories and artefacts from Zimbabwe encompassing mirrors, prints, serpentine (stone) ornaments, recylced stationery, handmade wirework, candles and other ethnic and traditional gifts. Colour brochure and price list available on 01535 600483. *Factory Shop*

THE FACTORY SHOP

UNIT 5, SPOUT LANE, CONCORDE, WASHINGTON, CO DURHAM NE37 2AH

☎ (0191) 416 0422. OPEN 9 - 5 MON - SAT.

Carpets, beds and own-brand furniture at discount due to the comany's bulk buying power. Carpets are by Merdew, Wilkies and Solmere; the beds are Sleepking. They also sell secondhand furniture. *Factory Shop and Secondhand Shop*

THE FACTORY SHOP

2 - 4 COMMERCIAL STREET, CROOK, CO DURHAM DL15 9HP
☎ (01388) 763211. OPEN 9 - 5.30 MON - SAT, 10.30 - 4.30 SUN.
Wide range on sale includes men's, ladies and children's clothing and footwear; household textiles; toiletries; hardware; luggage; lighting and bedding, most of which are chainstore and high street brands at discounts of approximately 30%-50%. There are weekly deliveries and brands include many major stars such as Adidas, Nike, Wrangler and Dartington, to name just a few. Now has kitchen and furniture displays with a line of Cape Country furniture on sale. Ranges are continually changing and few factory shops offer such a variety under one roof. Most of the shops have their own car parks or there are near-by car parking facilities. *Factory Shop*

TOG 24

UNIT 21, THE HIGHLIGHT, JACKSONS LANDING, HARTLEPOOL FACTORY OUTLET SHOPPING MALL, HARTLEPOOL MARINA, HARTLEPOOL, CLEVELAND, CO DURHAM TS24 0NX
☎ (01429) 866103. OPEN 10 - 6 MON - SAT, 11 - 5 SUN AND BANK HOLIDAYS.
Tog 24 are the UK's fastest growing brand name in outdoor clothing and leisurewear, with a total of three UK factories and 36 stores nationwide. They utilise the world's finest performance fabrics including Gore-Tex, Polartec and Burlington macs. Catering for all the family for all seasons, with cosy fleeces and waterproofs for the winter, and trekking ranges, shorts and t-shirts for the summer. With all prices at least 30% below the recommended retail price you can afford to enter the Tog comfort zone. *Factory Shopping Village*

TOM SAYERS CLOTHING CO

JACKSONS LANDING, THE HIGHLIGHT, HARTLEPOOL, CO DURHAM TS24 0RU
☎ (01429) 861439. OPEN 10 - 6 MON - SAT, 11 - 5 SUN.
Tom Sayers make sweaters for some of the top high street department stores. Unusually for a factory shop, if they don't stock your size, they will try and order it for you from their factory or one of their other factory outlets and send it to you. Most of the stock here is overstock, cancelled orders or last season's and includes jumpers, trousers and shirts at discounts of 30%. The trousers and shirts are bought in to complement the sweaters which they make. *Factory Shop*

Live Well On Less Tips
Free sight tests are available to children under 16, students under 19, and those on income support or family credit, as well as those with a history of glaucoma in their family.

TOYWORLD FACTORY OUTLETS LTD

JACKSONS LANDING, HARTLEPOOL FACTORY OUTLET SHOPPING
MALL, THE HIGHLIGHT, HARTLEPOOL MARINA, HARTLEPOOL, CO
DURHAM TS24 OXN

☎ (01429) 866606. OPEN 10 - 6 MON - SAT, 11 - 5 SUN, 10 - 6 BANK
HOLIDAYS.

Toy World sells brand name items including a wide range of toys from names
such as, Barbie (Mattel), Disney, Playskool, Lego, Sylvanian Families, Fisher-
Price, Tyco, Tomy, Waddington, M&B Games, Safe & Sound, Matchbox, and
many others at very low prices. *Factory Shopping Village*

WARNERS UK LTD

JACKSONS LANDING, THE HIGHLIGHT, HARTLEPOOL MARINA,
HARTLEPOOL, CLEVELAND, CO DURHAM TS24 OXN

☎ (01429) 890134. OPEN 10 - 6 MON - SAT, 11 - 5 SUN.

This shop sells a wide range of women's lingerie from Lejaby, Valentino,
Warners, with bras, slips, thongs, bodies and briefs at discounts from 25% to
70%. Each item is labelled with both the rrp and the discounted prices. For
example, bikini brief, £6.99 reduced from £17; underwire bra, £14.99
reduced from £33; body, £24.99 reduced from £65. Slightly imperfect stock
as well as perfect quality, end of season and discontinued merchandise and
swimwear are also stocked. Underwear for men, including Calvin Klein briefs
for £2.99, is on offer too. *Factory Shopping Village*

WINDSMOOR DISTRIBUTION CENTRE

UNIT 1, NORTHERN INDUSTRIAL ESTATE, BOWBURN, DURHAM,
CO DURHAM DH6 5AT

☎ (0191) 377 9897.

Regular sales are held here (usually five or six times a year) during which first
quality fashion from the Windsmoor, Planet and Precis Petite ranges are sold
at discounts starting at 50%. Sometimes, there is also Dannimac rainwear for
men and women. Phone or write to be put on the mailing list. *Designer Sale*

WYNSORS WORLD OF SHOES

PARKFIELD ROAD, OFF BRIDGE ROAD, STOCKTON-ON-TEES,
CLEVELAND, CO DURHAM

☎ (01642) 672525. OPEN 9 - 5.30 MON, TUE, WED, SAT, 9 - 8 THUR, FRI,
10 - 4 SUN AND BANK HOLIDAYS.

Stocks a wide range of seconds footwear for children as well as adults. There
are slippers, sandals, boots, leather and vinyl handbags and purses, shoe cleaners and polishes. Ladies fashion shoes start from £6 a pair. There are some well
known brands, all at substantial savings on high street prices. *Permanent
Discount Outlet*

Cornwall

WOMENSWEAR ONLY   Fine Feathers, *Kendal.*   Linton Tweeds Ltd, *Carlisle.*
New To You, *Carlisle.*

WOMENSWEAR & MENSWEAR   Selections, *Launceston.*   Silken Ladder, *Nr Roche.*
The Factory Shop, *Redruth.*   The Factory Shop, *Bodmin.*   Trago Mills, *Falmouth.* and *Liskeard.*

CHILDREN   The Factory Shop, *Redruth.*   The Factory Shop, *Bodmin.*   Trago Mills, *Falmouth.*
Trago Mills, *Liskeard.*

HOUSEHOLD AND GIFTWARE   Art Candles, *Bodmin.*
Dartington Crystal, *Treryulefoot, Nr Saltash.*   The Factory Shop, *Redruth.*
The Factory Shop, *Bodmin.*   Trago Mills, *Falmouth.*   Trago Mills, *Liskeard.*

ELECTRICAL EQUIPMENT   Littlewoods Catalogue Discount Store, *Barrow-in-Furness.*

DIY/RENOVATION   Trago Mills, *Falmouth.*   Trago Mills, *Liskeard.*

FURNITURE/SOFT FURNISHINGS   Just Fabrics, *Launceston.*   The Factory Shop, *Redruth.*
The Factory Shop, *Bodmin.*

ART CANDLES

DUNMERE ROAD, BODMIN, CORNWALL PL31 2QN
☎ (01208) 73258. OPEN 10 - 6 MON - FRI, EASTER TO SEPTEMBER:10 - 5
SAT, 11 - 6 SUN, SEPTEMBER TO CHRISTMAS: 10 - 2 SAT.
A family business with a factory outlet selling candles and candleholders of
every shape and design from beeswax to scented, figurative holders to pottery.
They specialise in marbled candles, and there are also 3ft high stalagmite candles, owl, tortoise and Buddha-shaped candles. There are tubs of seconds at
even cheaper prices. They also sell candle making materials, joss sticks and oil
burners, boxes or kilos of wax, moulds, colours and wicks, and pottery.
Factory Shop

DARTINGTON CRYSTAL

KERNOW MILL, TRERYULEFOOT, NEAR SALTASH, CORNWALL PL12 5BL
☎ (01752) 851161. OPEN 9.30 - 5.30 MON - SAT, 11 - 5 SUN.
Range of Dartington Crystal seconds at greatly reduced prices. Shopping
opportunities include a kitchen giftware shop selling Portmeirion and Denby,
locally produced quality foods, gifts and candles as well as The Edinburgh
Woollen Mill with a large selection of classic knitwear and co-ordinated clothing. There is a coffee shop serving hot and cold meals. Other outlets sell crystal first and second quality, and also some discounted items. *Factory Shop*

JUST FABRICS

THE BRIDEWELL, DOCKACRE ROAD, LAUNCESTON, CORNWALL PL15 8YY

☎ (01566) 776279. OPEN 9 - 5 MON - SAT. MAIL ORDER ALSO.

Based in a large showroom in a very attractive converted stone-built warehouse, Just Fabrics hold the largest sample library in the country for all types of furnishing fabrics and wallpapers. Most top brand names are represented and there is a discount of up to 20% off the recommended retail prices of most items. The company undertakes to despatch the goods to customers on receipt of the order, and says that distance is no object. The showroom carries extensive stock from the very best designer fabrics plus all making-up accessories at unbeatable prices. They have also recently installed the Stylepoint computer aided design system which helps customers to see what fabrics look like in situ. *Permanent Discount Outlet*

SELECTIONS

4 RACE HILL, LAUNCESTON, CORNWALL PL15 9BB

☎ (01566) 775471. OPEN 9.30 - 4.30 MON - SAT.

Selections nearly-new shop sells quality high street and designer label nearly-new garments. There is always a wide selection of day clothes, as well as separates, jackets and an excellent choice of evening wear and special occasion outfits. For example, there are usually at least fifty different mother of the bride outfits, some with matching hats. In fact, hats are a minor speciality, with more than three dozen usually in stock, some new and some nearly-new. Prices range from £12-£25. Labels include Planet, Jacques Vert, Ultima, Wallis, Jaeger, Betty Barclay, Berkertex, Next and Marks & Spencer. New and nearly-new costume jewellery is also on sale here at prices ranging from £2.50 to £12. There is a good selection of sizes up to 24 and above. Also stocks men's formal and evening wear as well as a full range of men's shoes, separates and jackets. *Dress Agency*

Live Well On Less Tips

If the wedding bells are ringing but you don't know where to start looking for the dress, the cake, the venue...help is at hand from The National Wedding Information Service. This offers free information on a range of facilities in your area from car hire to bridal wear, florists to discos, hall decoration to marquee hire. Phone and tell them where your wedding is taking place and they will send you, free, a list of services local to you. Rather like Talking Pages, the quality of the companies they refer you to depends on who has registered with them, but you've got to start somewhere. Freephone 0800 783 7452.

SILKEN LADDER

VICTORIA SQUARE, NEAR ROCHE, CORNWALL PL26 8LX,
☎ (01726) 891092. OPEN 9.30 - 5.30 MON - SAT, 10 - 5 SUN, BANK HOLIDAYS.

Silken Ladder originally specialised in the design, manufacture and wholesale of ladies' blouses in a myriad of options, both pretty and classic. Now their ranges extend to four labels. They still produce two new complete ranges of blouses annually and La Scala di Sieta is their upmarket label. Newly on the market are Sanderson Hall, tailored and casual men's shirts, and the exciting new ladieswear range for women on the fast track, Victoria Roche. The factory shop sells prototypes, samples, ends of lines, overmakes, less-than-perfects and mistakes at appropriately reduced prices. There is an enormous spread of ladies' blouses from under £3 to £100; plain polycotton tops, cut-work, Broderie Anglaise and hand-embroidered in polyester, polycotton, cotton, silk and man-made fabrics. Sizes range from 10-30. There are also Silken Ladder's own jackets, skirts, trousers and shorts available and a supporting range of accessories, giftware, costume jewellery, lingerie and hosiery. The shop also sells excess stock from other companies such as Kinloch Anderson, who are kilt makers to the Queen and the Prince of Wales (as well as Sean Connery) and Hourihan's of Ireland, tailors of ladies' jackets and skirts. Knitwear is supplied by Ireland's Eye and Balmoral of Scotland. Also stocked are their own ties for men as well as a selection from Frank Theak and Roskilly Ltd in Wales. Finishing touches are supplied with a good selection of accessories and jewellery, all at greatly reduced prices. Find it on Cornwall's main arterial road, the A30, six miles west of Bodmin and six miles north of St Austell, next to a BP petrol station, opposite Victoria Business Park. *Factory Shop*

THE FACTORY SHOP

MOUNT AMBROSE, SCORRIER, REDRUTH, CORNWALL TR15 1QT
☎ (01209) 219116. OPEN 9.30 - 5.30 MON - FRI, 9 - 5.30 SAT, 10 - 4 SUN.
OLD STATION YARD, BERRYCOMBE ROAD, BODMIN, CORNWALL PL31 2NF
☎ (01208) 78492. OPEN 9 - 5.30 MON - SAT, 10.30 - 4.30 SUN.

Wide range on sale includes men's, ladies and children's clothing and footwear; household textiles; toiletries; hardware; luggage; lighting and bedding, most of which are chainstore and high street brands at discounts of approximately 30%-50%. There are weekly deliveries and brands include many major stars such as Adidas, Nike, Wrangler and Dartington, to name just a few. Now has kitchen and furniture displays with a line of Cape Country furniture on sale. Ranges are continually changing and few factory shops offer such a variety under one roof. Most of the shops have their own car parks or there are nearby car parking facilities. *Factory Shop*

TRAGO MILLS

ARWENACK STREET, FALMOUTH, CORNWALL TR11 3LF
☎ (01326) 315738. OPEN 9 - 5.30 MON - SAT, 10.45 - 4.45 SUN.
2 WATERSFOOT, LISKEARD, CORNWALL PL14 6HY
☎ (01579) 320584. OPEN 9 - 5.30 MON - SAT, 10.45- 4.45 SUN.

A vast outlet which takes the whole day to do justice to. Sells virtually everything from men's, women's and children's wear, gardening equipment and cookware to wallpaper, carpets and fitted kitchens. Most are branded goods and there is a cafe, pizza bar and petrol station. The women's fashion has a reasonable amount coming from high street multiples. The menswear offers Lee Cooper jeans, Joe Bloggs jeans, Farah trousers, Pierre Cardin, all-leather classic brogues and Oxford shoes, and Doc Martens. Vast car parking areas, lots of outdoor picnic spots. For the home, there are Black & Decker Dustbusters, Hotpoint dryers and washing machines with cosmetic blemishes; curtain fabrics by the metre from Monkwell, Sekers, Filigree, Laura Ashley as well as Janet Reger for Vantona double quilt covers, with matching sheets, pillow cases and valances. There is a vast range of tiles including Pilkington seconds. A separate building houses garden equipment and plant life while the home decorating department has a vast selection of paint, brushes and wallpapers. For example, Crown vinyl emulsion, Magicoat non-drip gloss. An excellent leisure section offers bicycles and accessories, golf gear, keep-fit systems, fishing rods and flies. A separate building houses garden equipment and plant life while the home decorating department has a vast selection of paint, brushes and wallpapers. Comparison prices are not given here, although staff say most items are discounted by up to 50%, so if you're looking for a bargain, make sure you've done your homework on the high street first. The best deals are in fabrics, carpets, tiles and diy. There is a Leisure park with a giant free fall slide, Supakart go-Kart circuit, model railway, miniature steam railway, nature reserve, coarse fishing and Edwardian Penny Arcade. ***Permanent Discount Outlet***

Live Well On Less Tips

How do hairdressers learn their craft? They've got to practise on someone and volunteers can often have a haircut for nothing and more sophisticated treatments, such as perms or colour, for the price of the products used. There are always trained staff on hand to watch over the trainees. Ask at your local hairdresser or hair and beauty department of the nearest further education college. There, you may also be able to enjoy a wide range of free beauty treaments from foot massage and aromatherapy to waxing and a manicure from the students.

Cumbria

MENSWEAR ONLY   Farah Menswear, *Kendal.*

WOMENSWEAR & MENSWEAR   Briggs Shoes, *Penrith.*
Furness Footwear, *Dalton-in-Furness.*   K Shoes, *Kendal.*
K Village Factory Shopping, *Kendal.*   Kit4Kids, *Kendal.*
Littlewoods Catalogue Discount Store, *Barrow-in-Furness.*   Matalan, *Workington.*   Matalan, *Barrow.*
The Factory Shop, *Egremont.*   The Sports Factory, *Kendal.*   Tog 24, *Ambleside.*
Wynsors World of Shoes, *Dalton-in-Furness.*

CHILDREN   Briggs Shoes, *Penrith.*   Fitness Footwear, *Dalton-in-Furness.*   Jumper, *Kendal.*
K Shoes, *Kendal.*   K Village Factory Shopping, *Kendal.*   Kangol Factory Shop, *Cleator.*
Littlewoods Catalogue Discount Store, *Barrow-in-Furness.*   Matalan, *Workington.*   Matalan, *Barrow.*
The Factory Shop, *Egremont.*   The Sports Factory, *Kendal.*   Tog 24, *Ambleside.*
Wynsors World of Shoes, *Dalton-in-Furness.*

HOUSEHOLD AND GIFTWARE   Dartington Crystal, *Kendal.*
Denby Factory Shop, *Kendal.*   Factory Bedding Shop, *Carlisle.*
K Village Factory Shopping, *Kendal.*   Matalan, *Workington.*   Matalan, *Barrow.*
Ponden Mill Linens, *Kendal.*   Price's Candles, *Kendal.*   The Colony Country Store, *Ulverston.*
The Factory Shop, *Egremont.*   The Tea Pottery, *Keswick.*

DIY/RENOVATION   Cumbria Architectural Salvage, *Carlisle.*
Wilson Reclamation Services, *Grange-over-Sands.*

ARCHITECTURAL SALVAGE   Cumbria Architectural Salvage, *Carlisle.*
Wilson Reclamation Services, *Grange-over-Sands.*

FURNITURE/SOFT FURNISHINGS   Factory Bedding Shop, *Carlisle.*
Sekers Fabrics, *Whitehaven.*   Stead McAlpin & Co Ltd, *Carlisle.*
The Factory Shop, *Egremont.*

SPORTSWEAR AND EQUIPMENT   Hi-Pennine Outdoor Shop, *Alston.*
The Sports Factory, *Kendal.*

BRIGGS SHOES
SOUTHEND ROAD, PENRITH, CUMBRIA
☎ (01768) 899001. OPEN 9.30 - 5.30 MON - SAT.
Vast selection of well-known brands of shoes with permanent clearance lines
always on display. Some of the brands stocked include Van-Del, Gabor and
the wider-fitting Elmdale range. *Permanent Discount Outlet*

CUMBRIA ARCHITECTURAL SALVAGE
BIRKS HILL, RAUGHTON HEAD, CARLISLE, CUMBRIA CA5 7DH
☎ (01697) 476420. OPEN 9 - 5 MON - FRI, 9 - 12 SAT.
Period fireplaces, ranges, old free-standing baths, re-claimed doors, oak beams,
building materials and general fittings from old houses. *Architectural
Salvage*

DARTINGTON CRYSTAL
WESTMORELAND SHOPPING CENTRE, KENDAL, CUMBRIA LA9 4LR
☎ (01539) 734263. OPEN 9.30 - 5.30 MON - SAT.
An extensive range of Dartington Crystal seconds at greatly reduced prices as well as some perfect crystal at full price. Range includes wine suites, sherry glasses, tankards, decanters, rippled glass, fruit and salad bowls. Cloverleaf pottery is also available. *Factory Shop*

DENBY FACTORY SHOP
K VILLAGE, KENDAL, CUMBRIA LA9 7DA
☎ (01539) 735418. OPEN 9.30 - 5.30 MON - FRI (WINTER), 9.30 - 6 MON, TUE, WED, FRI (SUMMER), 9.30 - 8 THUR (SUMMER) 9 -6 SAT, 11 - 5 SUN.
Denby is renowned for its striking colours and glaze effects. The Factory Shops stock first and second quality with seconds discounts starting at 20% off RRP. There are regular mega bargains with up to 75% off throughout the year. *Factory Shopping Village*

FACTORY BEDDING SHOP
ATLAS HOUSE, NELSON STREET, DENTON HOLME, CARLISLE, CUMBRIA CA2 5NB
☎ (01228) 514703. OPEN 10 - 5.30 MON - FRI, 9 - 5 SAT.
Bedding, curtains, duvets, duvet covers, pillows, towels, cushions, and curtain fabrics bought in direct from the manufacturer at factory shop prices. No brand names, but all sold in high street department stores. Pillows from £1.99; quilts from £5.99; curtains from £10.99; double fitted sheet from £6.49; double duvet cover, £12.99; double valances, £8.99. Wide range of curtain fabrics from £1.99 a metre and a curtain making service. *Factory Shop*

FARAH MENSWEAR
K VILLAGE, KENDAL, CUMBRIA
☎ (01539) 721892. OPEN 9.30 -6 MON - FRI, 9 - 6 SAT AND BANK HOLIDAYS, 11 - 5 SUN.
A wide range of men's clothes - sweaters, sweatshirts and trousers - all at reduced prices. *Factory Shopping Village*

FINE FEATHERS
6 LIBRARY ROAD, KENDAL, CUMBRIA LA9 4QB
☎ (01539) 727241. OPEN 10 - 5 MON - SAT.
Wide range of middle of the market names such as Country Casuals and Lakelands, with mix of in-season styles. Also Jacques Vert, Principles, Next, and Jaeger. More than 6,000 clients sell their as-new clothes here. *Dress Agency*

FURNESS FOOTWEAR

LONG LANE, DALTON-IN-FURNESS, CUMBRIA

☎ (01229) 468837. OPEN 9 - 5.30 MON - SAT, 8 ON FRI, 10 - 4 SUN.

Stocks a wide range of branded footwear for children as well as adults and a few seconds. There are slippers, sandals, boots, leather and vinyl handbags, shoe cleaners and polishes. Ladies fashion shoes start from £6 a pair. There are some well known brands, all at substantial savings on high street prices. Free parking. *Permanent Discount Outlet*

HI-PENNINE OUTDOOR SHOP

MARKET SQUARE, ALSTON, CUMBRIA CA9 3QN

☎ (01434) 381389. OPEN 9.30 - 4.30 MON - FRI, 9 - 5 SAT.

Permanent discount outlet selling Gore-tex and Polartec fleece clothing including jackets, windproof trousers, mitts, gaitors, scarves, headbands and hats all manufactured under the Mountain Range label. The Outdoor Shop acts as a factory shop on behalf of the Mountain Range factory, selling seconds and ends of lines at discounts of up to 25%. There is a mail order service. For details call 01453 381389. *Permanent Discount Outlet*

JUMPER

UNIT 2, K VILLAGE, NETHERFIELD, KENDAL, CUMBRIA LA9 7BT

☎ (01539) 720437. OPEN 9.30 - 6 MON - FRI, 9 - 6 SAT AND BANK HOLIDAYS, 11 - 5 SUN, UNTIL 8 ON THUR. (WINTER: 9.30 - 5.30 MON - FRI.)

A wide range of Jumper label sweaters, gloves, scarves, shirts and cardigans for men and women all at discount prices of up to 50% off. Prices start at £2. *Factory Shopping Village*

K SHOES

K VILLAGE, NETHERFIELD, KENDAL, CUMBRIA LA9 7BT

☎ (01539) 734347. OPEN 9.30 - 6 MON - SAT, 8 ON THUR, 11 - 5 SUN.

Clarks International operate a chain of factory shops nationally which specialise in selling discontinued lines and slight sub-standards for children, women and men from Clarks, K Shoes and other famous brands. These shops trade under the name of Crockers, K Shoes Factory shop or Clarks Factory Shop and while not all are physically attached to a shoe factory, these shops are treated as factory shops by the company. Customers can expect to find an extensive range of quality shoes, sandals, walking boots, slippers, trainers, handbags, accessories and gifts, while their major outlets also offer luggage, sports clothing, sports equipment and outdoor clothing. Brands stocked include Clarks, K Shoes, Springer, CICA, Hi-Tec, Puma, Mercury, Fila, Mizuno, Slazenger, Samsonite, Delsey, Antler and Carlton, although not all are sold in every outlet. Discounts are on average 30% off the normal high street price for perfect stock. *Factory Shop*

K VILLAGE
FACTORY SHOPPING
KENDAL, NEAR JUNCTION 36 OF M6, CUMBRIA LA9 7DA
☎ (01539) 732363. OPEN 9.30 - 6 MON - FRI, 9 - 6 SAT, 11 - 5 SUN, 9 - 6
BANK HOLIDAYS (END OCT-EASTER OPEN 9.30 - 5.30 MON - FRI).
Eleven outlets including Crabtree & Evelyn, Van Heusen, Denby Pottery,
Jumper, The Baggage Factory, The Sports Factory, Ponden Mill, Price's
Candles, Tog 24, National Trust Gift Shop and a giant K Shoes factory shop
selling a wide range of labels from K Shoes, Clarks, Cica, Delsey, and Antler,
as well as a full-price K shop. There is also a heritage centre, a 150-seater
restaurant, a coffee shop, childrens play area, baby changing facilities, a picnic
area next to a river, disabled facilities and free parking. Take the South Kendal
exit and follow the signs for K Village. *Factory Shop*

KANGOL FACTORY SHOP
CLEATOR, CUMBRIA CA23 3DJ
☎ (01946) 810312. OPEN 9 - 5 MON - SAT.
Europe's largest manufacturer of headwear has a factory shop selling hats,
scarves, bags and caps as well as Jane Shilton bags, scarves and belts at about
half the shop price. Some are seconds, others obsolete shades, yet others shop
returns. Kangol branded clothing includes jackets, shirts, T-shirts, sweaters,
streetwise clothing for teenagers, ladies underwear and towels. *Factory Shop*

KIT4KIDS
99 SERPENTINE ROAD, KENDAL, CUMBRIA LA9 4PD
☎ (01539) 724920.
Part of the Baby Equipment Hirers Association (BEHA), which has more than
100 members countrywide. A range of equipment can be hired from high
chairs, cots and travel cots to baby car seats and buggies. Short or long term
hire can be arranged. They also sell three wheel all-terrain Land Rover
pushchairs and buggies. BEHA run an advice line which will try and answer
any queries you have regarding hiring services for children. Phone the
Babyline on 0831 310355. *Hire Shop*

LINTON TWEEDS LTD
SHADDON MILLS, CARLISLE, CUMBRIA CA2 5TZ
☎ (01228) 527569. OPEN 9.30 - 5 MON - SAT. MAIL ORDER.
Eighty percent of Linton Tweeds Ltd's business is for the couture trade for
export and includes exclusive fabrics for Chanel, Ann Klein, Ungaro,
Courreges, Bill Blass and Escada. British designers to whom it supplies fabrics
include Jean Muir, Windsmoor, Aquascutum, Jaeger and Liberty, and ranges
from fancy yarns to silk and wool crepes. The mill shop has a large selection
of ends of lines and remnants at prices ranging from £15-£25 per metre. You
have to buy the fabric when you see it as there are no repeat orders. Also offer

an exclusive designer knitwear section sold at discounted prices. There is an exhibition section, small museum and restaurant on site with hands-on display for adults and children. The site also has its own car park. *Factory Shop*

LITTLEWOODS
CATALOGUE DISCOUNT STORE

RAWLINSON STREET, BARROW-IN-FURNESS, CUMBRIA LA14 1BS
☎ (01229) 870668. OPEN 8.45 - 5.30 MON - SAT, 11 - 5 SUN.
Littlewoods clearance shops offering up to 50% off the catalogue price for clothing and between 50% and 60% off for electrical goods. Stock changes constantly and varies from day to day but can include well-known brand names such as Berlei and Gossard lingerie, Vivienne Westwood, Pamplemousse leisure wear, Nike and Adidas sports shoes, Workers For Freedom, and Timberland and Caterpillar footwear. Stock depends on the size and location of the shop, so larger shops will get the longer discontinued runs and smaller shops over-runs with only a small amount of colour and size variations left. Littlewoods also run a mobile shop which operates in cities where they don't have a sale shop. For details of further venues for the sales, which usually take place once a month, contact Melanie Lamb, c/o Crosby DC, Kershaw Avenue, Endbutt Lane, Crosby, Merseyside L70 1AH. *Permanent Discount Outlet*

MATALAN

PLOT 12, DERWENT HOUSE, SOLWAY ROAD, WORKINGTON, CUMBRIA CA14 3YA
☎ (01900) 870966. OPEN 9.30 - 8 MON - FRI, 9 - 6 SAT, 11 - 5 SUN.
WALNEY ROAD, BARROW LA14 5UN
☎ (01229) 430899. OPEN 10 - 8 MON - FRI, 9 - 6 SAT, 11 - 5 SUN.
Matalan is a fashion and homewares shop giving customers what they claim to be unbeatable value for money with huge savings on a wide range of products including high quality fashionable clothing for women, women and children at up to 50% off high street prices. Matalan is situated out of town and stores are open seven days a week all year round. *Permanent Discount Outlet*

NEW TO YOU

1 BOUNDARY ROAD, CURROCK, CARLISLE, CUMBRIA CA2 4HH
☎ (01228) 592669. OPEN 9.30 - 5 MON - FRI, 10 - 4 SAT
Classic clothing from Louis Feraud, Mansfield, Frank Usher and Mondi to Kanga, Next and Laura Ashley at anything from one half to one quarter of the original price. Sizes range from 10 - 20. Also sells and hires hats from a range of about forty for £12 with a refundable £2. *Dress Agency and Hire Shop*

PONDEN MILL LINENS

K VILLAGE, LOUND ROAD, KENDAL, CUMBRIA LA9 7DA
☎ (01539) 737116. OPEN 9.30 - 6 MON - FRI, 9 - 6 SAT, 11 - 5 SUN.
Famous branded products at direct from the mill prices. Towels, co-ordinated
bedlinen, duvets, pillows and curtains from Crown, Coloroll, Chortex, Rectella
together with bathroom and kitchen accessories. *Factory Shopping Village*

PRICE'S CANDLES

K VILLAGE, KENDAL, NEAR JUNCTION 36 OF M6, CUMBRIA LA9 7DA
☎ (01539) 733736. OPEN 9.30 - 6 MON - FRI, 9 - 6 SAT, 11 - 5 SUN, 9 - 6
BANK HOLIDAYS (END OCT-EASTER OPEN 9.30 - 5.30 MON - FRI).
Everything sold in this shop are seconds, which may be discoloured or have a
damaged pattern; discontinued sizes not available elsewhere; over-runs from
the garden selection or dinner candles in old packaging that has now been
replaced. There are church candles, lanterns, candles and glass jars, star-shaped
candles, floating candles, candlestick holders, scented candles and garden
torches. Some of the ceramic items are bought in. *Factory Shopping Village*

SEKERS FABRICS

HENSINGHAM, WHITEHAVEN, CUMBRIA CA28 8TR
☎ (01946) 692691. OPEN 9 - 7 THUR, 9 - 3 FRI, 9 - 1 SAT ONCE A
MONTH ONLY.
Discontinued curtain and upholstery fabrics and braiding sold off at monthly sales, usually held on the second Thursday, Friday and Saturday of each
month. There are 5,000-6,000 metres to choose from at discounts of up to
75% off normal retail prices. Please phone for sale times before travelling.
Factory Shop

STEAD McALPIN & CO LTD

CUMMERSDALE PRINT WORKS, CARLISLE, CUMBRIA CA2 6BT
☎ (01228) 599589. OPEN 9 - 4 MON - FRI, 10 - 4 SAT AND BANK
HOLIDAY MONDAY.
This genuine factory shop has been refurbished and expanded recently. There
is a wide variety of prints in traditional and modern designs at £6.50/metre
produced in the factory, together with plain dyed fabrics and upholstery
weaves from a sister company in Lancashire, priced from £7.50. The mill
prints fabric for the top end of the furnishing trade and sells seconds that are
checked for suitability before sale. The staff are always pleased to help you
with calculations for making up. Accessories include haberdashery, pillows
and cushions, duvets, bed linen and occasional specials such as wallpaper or
ready-made curtains; wooden curtain poles have recently been added. The
stock varies according to factory production, so ring before travelling if there
is something special you are looking for. *Factory Shop*

THE COLONY COUNTRY STORE

LINDAL-IN-FURNESS, ULVERSTON, CUMBRIA LA12 OLL

☎ (01229) 461102. OPEN 9 - 5 MON - SAT, 12 - 5 SUN.

This is one of the biggest outlets for factory price candles, scented candles, candle holders and lamps in Britain, with stock selling at between 10% and 50% of the normal retail price. There are normally 3,000 candles on display, both perfect and seconds. Waxworks is the name of the special section offering goods at a fracton of their usual retail price. The store also sells dining room textiles, pot pourri and gift soaps. There is a special all-year-round Christmas shop with Santa's grotto on site. You can watch the candles being made from a viewing gallery. *Factory Shop*

THE FACTORY SHOP

EMPIRE BUILDINGS, MAIN STREET, EGREMONT, CUMBRIA CA22 2BD

☎ (01946) 820434. OPEN 9 - 5 MON - SAT. 10 - 4 SUN.

Wide range on sale includes men's, ladies and children's clothing and footwear; household textiles; toiletries; hardware; luggage; lighting and bedding, most of which are chainstore and high street brands at discounts of approximately 30%-50%. There are weekly deliveries and brands include many major stars such as Adidas, Nike, Wrangler and Dartington, to name just a few. Now has kitchen and furniture displays with a line of Cape Country furniture on sale. Ranges are continually changing and few factory shops offer such a variety under one roof. Most of the shops have their own car parks or there are nearby car parking facilities. *Factory Shop*

THE SPORTS FACTORY

K SHOE FACTORY SHOP, K VILLAGE, KENDAL, JUNCTION 36 OF M6, CUMBRIA LA9 6DA

☎ (01539) 721892. OPEN 9.30 - 6 MON - FRI, 9 - 6 SAT, 11 - 5 SUN.

Wide range of sports clothes, equipment and accessories, some of which are only stocked in season (for example, cricket bats and tennis rackets in summer only). Golf equipment includes clubs, shoes, balls, bags, putters, and brands on sale include Phoenix, Howson, Slazenger, Second Chance golf balls, Mizuno and Wilsons. There are also tennis rackets and cricket gear. All are discontinued lines and are cheaper than in the high street by between 10%-40%. *Factory Shopping Village*

THE TEA POTTERY

CENTRAL CAR PARK ROAD, KESWICK, CUMBRIA CA12 5DF

☎ (017687) 73983. OPEN 9 - 5 SEVEN DAYS A WEEK.

Paradise for collectors of novelty teapots, all of which are manufactured on site in up to 50 different designs and in sizes from one cup to five cups. Designs include Welsh dressers, caravans, Agas, cookers, bellboys with luggage, can-can girls, washbasins and a host of others, many of which are collectors' items. Prices range from £9.95 - £45 for perfects, which represents a 10% - 20% savings on retail prices, and up to 50% discounts on seconds. This factory shop is smaller than its sister shop in Leyburn and has no refreshments. *Factory Shop*

TOG 24

UNIT 4, MARKET CROSS, AMBLESIDE, CUMBRIA LA22 9BT
☎ (01539) 433913. OPEN 9.30 - 6.30 MON - SAT, 10 - 6 SUN.
CRAG BOW, BOWNESS, CUMBRIA LA23 3BX
☎ (01539) 488656. OPEN 9.30 - 6 MON - SAT, 10 - 6 SUN.
UNIT 5, FACTORY SHOP SCHEME, K VILLAGE, LOUND ROAD, KENDAL, CUMBRIA LA9 7DA
☎ (01539) 721555. OPEN 9.30 - 6 MON - FRI, 9 - 6 SAT, 11 - 5 SUN.
Tog 24 are the UK's fastest growing brand name in outdoor clothing and leisurewear, with a total of three UK factories and 36 stores nationwide. They utilise the world's finest performance fabrics including Gore-Tex, Polartec and Burlington macs. Catering for all the family for all seasons, with cosy fleeces and waterproofs for the winter, and trekking ranges, shorts and t-shirts for the summer. With all prices at least 30% below the recommended retail price you can afford to enter the Tog comfort zone. *Factory Shop*

WILSON RECLAMATION SERVICES

YEW TREE BARN, LOW NEWTON IN CARTMEL, GRANGE-OVER-SANDS, CUMBRIA LA11 6JP
☎ (0153 95) 31498. OPEN 10 - 5 MON - SAT, 12 - 5 SUN.
Fireplaces, oak beams, doors, bathroom fittings, flagstones, chimney pots, quoins and antiques. There's also a soft furnishing department, antique restoration and upholstery service and cafe. *Architectural Salvage*

WYNSORS WORLD OF SHOES

FURNESS FOOTWEAR, LONG LANE, DALTON-IN-FURNESS, CUMBRIA LA15 8PB
☎ (01229) 468837. OPEN 9 - 5.30 MON, TUE, WED, SAT, 9 - 8 THUR, FRI, 10 - 4 SUN AND BANK HOLIDAYS.
Stocks top brand-name shoes at less than half price. Special monthly offers always available. There are shoes, trainers, slippers, sandals and boots for all the family, with a selection of bags, cleaners and polishes available. *Permanent Discount Outlet*

Live Well On Less Tips
Have your makeup done for nothing in the cosmetics departments of most big department stores. Choose a quiet day, preferably a Monday, and avoid lunchtimes and Saturdays. Then say you want to live with the new look before you decide to buy.

Derbyshire

WOMENSWEAR ONLY   David Nieper, *Alfreton*.   Discount Dressing, *Rowsley*.

MENSWEAR ONLY   Armstrong's Mill, *Ilkeston*.   James Barry Menswear, *Ilkeston*.

WOMENSWEAR & MENSWEAR   Big L Factory Outlet, *South Normanton*.
Broughton Shoe Warehouse, *Matlock*.   Charnos, *Ilkeston*.   Claremont Garments, *Allenton*.
Factory Shop Outlet, *Ambergate*.   Gillivers Footwear and Clothing Warehouse, *Swadincote*.
Jaeger factory Shop, *Somercotes*.   John Smedley Ltd, *Matlock*.   Jumper, *South Normanton*.
Labels of Baslow, *Matlock*.   Littlewoods Catalogue Discount Store, *South Normanton*.
Massons Mill, *Nr Matlock*.   Matlock Shoe Sales, *Matlock*.
McArthurglen Designer Outlet, *South Normanton*.   Peak Village, *Rowsley*.
RS Sports & Leisurewear, *Ilkeston*.   Slenderella Factory Shop, *Belper*.
Stevenson's of Ambergate, *Ambergate*.   TDP Factory Shop, *Swadlincote*.
The Courtaulds Textiles Factory Shop, *Alfreton*.   The Shoe Factory Shop, *Derby*.
Tog 24, *South Normanton*.   Trade Prices, *Ripley*.   Tweedies Trade Prices, *Ripley*.
Webb Ivory Ltd, *Swadincote*.   Wirksworth Factory Shop, *Wirksworth*.
Wynsors World of Shoes, *Chesterfield*.

CHILDREN   Broughton Shoe Warehouse, *Matlock*.   Charnos, *Ilkeston*.
Claremont Garments, *Allenton*.   Factory Shop Outlet, *Ambergate*.   Jokids Ltd, *South Normanton*.
Littlewoods Catalogue Discount Store, *South Normanton*.   Massons Mill, *Nr Matlock*.
McArthurglen Designer Outlet, *South Normanton*.   Peak Village, *Rowsley*.
RS Sports & Leisurewear, *Ilkeston*.   Stevenson's of Ambergate, *Ambergate*.
TDP Factory Shop, *Swadlincote*.   The Courtaulds Textiles Factory Shop, *Alfreton*.
The Shoe Factory Shop, *Derby*.   Tog 24, *South Normanton*.   Toy world Factory Outlets Ltd,
Alfreton.
Trade Prices, *Ripley*.   Tweedies Trade Prices, *Ripley*.   Webb Ivory Ltd, *Swadlincote*.
Wirksworth Factory Shop, *Wirksworth*.   Wynsors World of Shoes, *Chesterfield*.

HOUSEHOLD AND GIFTWARE   Charnos, *Ilkeston*.
Demaglass Factory Shop, *Chesterfield*.   Denby Pottery Visitor Centre, *Denby, Nr Ripley*.
Derwent Crystal Ltd, *Ashbourne*.   Massons Mill, *Nr Matlock*.
McArthurglen Designer Outlet, *South Normanton*.   Oneida, *South Normanton*.   Peak Village, *Rowsley*.
Ponden Mill Factory Shop, *Rowsley*.   Price's candles, *South Normanton*.   Royal Crown Derby, *Derby*.
TG Green, *Swadlincote*.   The Courtaulds Textiles Factory Shop, *Alfreton*.   Trade Prices, *Ripley*.
Tweedies Trade Prices, *Ripley*.   Webb Ivory Ltd, *Swadlincote*.
Wirksworth Factory Shop, *Wirksworth*.

ELECTRICAL EQUIPMENT   Littlewoods Catalogue Discount Store, *South Normanton*.
Remington, *South Normanton*.

DIY/RENOVATION   Glynn Webb, *Derby*.

FURNITURE/SOFT FURNISHINGS   Fabric Design, *Matlock Bath*.
Filigree, *South Normanton*.   Langley Furniture, *Heanor*.   Peak Village, *Rowsley*.
The Fabric Factory, *Heanor*.

FOOD AND LEISURE   Book Thrift, *Derby*.   Denby Pottery, *Denby, Nr Ripley*.
Luggage & Baggage, *Rowsley*.   Luggage & Bags, *Rowsley*.
McArthurglen Designer Outlet, *South Normanton*.   Peak Village, *Rowsley*.
Thorntons, *South Normanton*.   Travel Accessory Outlet, *South Normanton*

SPORTSWEAR AND EQUIPMENT   Abris Outdoor Clothing Factory Shop, *Glossop*.
Massons Mill, *Nr Matlock*.   McArthurglen Designer Outlet, *South Normanton*.   Peak Village, *Rowsley*.
RS Sports & Leisurewear, *Ilkeston*.   Trade Prices, *Ripley*.

ABRIS OUTDOOR
CLOTHING FACTORY SHOP

3 WREN'S NEST, BEHIND TELEGRAPH PETROL STATION, HIGH
STREET, WEST, GLOSSOP, DERBYSHIRE SK13 8EX

☎ (01457) 863966. FAX 854712. OPEN 10 - 5 MON - THUR, 10 - 3 FRI, SAT.
Outdoor clothing for hillwalkers and backpackers and tops suitable for snowboarders, all of which are made in the on-site factory and sold at prices which
are up to 60% cheaper than in the high street. For example, walking trousers,
£24.99 which would normally sell for £39.99 in the high street; breathable
waterproofs from £69.99, fleece jackets from £49.99. Sizes range from extra
small to double extra large; ladies from 10 - 18; men's trousers from 28-inch
to 40-inch waist. *Factory Shop*

ARMSTRONG'S MILL

MIDDLETON STREET, OFF STATION ROAD, ILKESTON, DERBYSHIRE
DE7 5TT

☎ (0115) 932 4913. OPEN 9.15 - 5 MON, TUE, THUR, FRI, 9.15 - 6 WED,
9.30 - 5.30 SAT, 10.30 - 4.30 SUN.

Just 10 mins from M1 Junction 26, follow signs for Ilkeston A610, carry on
over railway bridge and turn immediately sharp left, the mill car park is
straight ahead. Armstrong's manufactures high quality men's suits, jackets and
trousers. You can also find offers from Wolsey, Pierre Cardin and Double Two,
all at factory prices. *Factory Shop*

BIG L FACTORY OUTLET

BUILDING 3, DERBYSHIRE DESIGNER OUTLET, MANSFIELD ROAD,
SOUTH NORMANTON, DERBYSHIRE DE55 2ER

☎ (01773) 545000. OPEN 10 - 6 MON, TUE, WED, FRI, 10 - 8 THUR,
9 - 6 SAT, 11 - 5 SUN.

Men's and women's Levi jeans, jackets, cord and Sherpa fleece jackets, T-shirts
and shirts but no children's, all at discount prices. *Factory Shopping Village*

BOOK THRIFT

44 SADDLEGATE, DERBY, DERBYSHIRE DE1 3NQ
☎ (01332) 290912.
OPEN 9.30 - 5.30 MON - SAT.

One of many outlets supplied by a central warehouse with remaindered books,
all first hand, sold at around half price. Most are the result of over buying on
the part of bookshops and overprints by publishers and they include hard and
soft backs, fiction, fact, reference and academic. They also sell some stationery
and local ordnance maps at full price. Phone 01625 576890 for details of your
nearest outlet. *Permanent Discount Outlet*

BROUGHTON SHOE WAREHOUSE

7 CROWN SQUARE, MATLOCK, DERBYSHIRE DE4 3AT

☎ (01629) 55616. OPEN 9 - 5.30 MON - SAT, 10 - 4 SUN.

Sells ladies boots, shoes, sandals and slippers as well as men's and children's footwear. Savings can be between 20% and 50% here. Some of the boots are by Mondi, and there are shoes by Kappa, Timberalnd, Hi-Tec, Trickers, Caterpillar, Kickers and some Italian and Spanish designers. Deliveries are made every Tuesday. *Permanent Discount Outlet*

CHARNOS

CORPORATION ROAD, ILKESTON, DERBYSHIRE

☎ (0115) 9440301. OPEN 10 - 4 TUE - FRI, 9.30 - 1 SAT.

About 25% of the shop is given over to discontinued perfects of the famous Charnos lingerie at discounts of 25%-50%. Current ladies lingerie is discounted by 25%, discontinued lingerie by 50%. The rest of the shop stocks wool, acrylic and cotton knitwear for women and men at factory shop prices, and babywear, cards and giftwrap at very competitive prices. Some stock is grade B quality. *Factory Shop*

CLAREMONT GARMENTS

399 BOULTON LANE, ALLENTON, DERBYSHIRE DE24 9TA

☎ (01332) 691909. OPEN 9 - 4.30 MON - SAT.

Sells a wide range of ladies, men's and childrens high street fashions at up to 50% below high street prices. *Factory Shop*

DAVID NIEPER

NOTTINGHAM ROAD, ALFRETON, DERBYSHIRE DE55 7LE

☎ (01773) 833335. OPEN 9 - 5 MON - SAT AND BANK HOLIDAYS.

Classic ladies clothing and specialists in nightwear/lingerie. David Nieper is an internationally acclaimed designer and from this factory in Alfreton private customers order directly from all over the world. The factory shop has design room samples including beautiful silk fabrics and laces; pure cotton nightdresses; silk/satin slips; luxury velvet housegowns; Liberty blouses and skirts. There is also an amazing range of lingerie from well-known designers. Free car park. *Factory Shop*

DE BRADELEI MILL SHOPS LTD

DE BRADELEI HOUSE, CHAPEL STREET, BELPER, DERBYSHIRE DE56 1AR

☎ (01773) 829830. OPEN 9.30 - 5.30 MON - FRI, 9.30 - 6 SAT, 11 - 5 SUN.

A delightful Mill centre with individual shops based round a central courtyard, each one selling top brand names in fashions and footwear for men and women, along with soft furnishings and giftware. The ladieswear includes such names as Windsmoor, Planet, Precis Petite, Jaeger Knitwear Shop, French Connection, Elle, Virgin, Jackpot, Phase Eight, Country Casuals, Elvi, top American and German designer labels, plus many more. The menswear range includes underwear, socks, sweaters, trousers, jackets, coats and suits from labels such as Wolsey, French Connection, Virgin, Jaeger Knitwear Shop and Glenmuir. Robert Leonard's Menswear provides Pierre Cardin, Gabicci, Gurteen, Oakman and many more. There is a large shoe department with a superb range of shoes and accessories for men and women. Soft Furnishings from Ponden Mill includes duvets, bedlinen, pillows, towels and much more. The giftware department offers a superb collection of Liberty giftware with scented candles, Dart Valley Foods and chocolates from Italo Suisse. Chevin Coffee Shop serves delicious home-cooked food throughout the day. De Bradelei Mill Shop has its own car park with alternative parking nearby; coach parties are always welcome though booking is preferred. *Permanent Discount Outlet*

DEMAGLASS FACTORY SHOP

POTTERY LANE WEST, CHESTERFIELD, DERBYSHIRE S41 9BN
☎ (01246) 545193. OPEN 9.30 - 4.15 MON - FRI, UNTIL 8 ON THUR, 9.30 - 1 SAT.

Sells glassware, giftware and some pottery at its seconds factory shop at the rear of the building. Glasses start at around 30p each to 95p. Crystal d'arque modern flutes and tumblers in boxes of 6 sell for £21.99 for flutes, £23.99 for tumblers. The factory shop also sells Royal Scot Crystal, Crystal D'Arque, Caithness Crystal and Edinburgh Crystal seconds. There are also gifts, china, crockery, tablemats, candles, silverplated gifts, photoframes and christening presents and Caithness Crystal paperweights. Three main sales a year are held - usually over the Easter weekend, August and November - at which prices are discounted still further. *Factory Shop*

DENBY POTTERY VISITOR CENTRE

DERBY ROAD, DENBY, NR RIPLEY, DERBYSHIRE DE5 8NX
☎ (01773) 740 799. OPEN 9.30 - 5 MON - SAT, 10 - 5 SUN (CENTRE), 11 - 5 SUN (FACTORY SHOP).

Renowned for its striking colours and glaze effects, Denby has been inviting people to tour and visit the pottery for more than thirty years. Their own factory shop warehouse sells both seconds and best quality products. Second discounts start at 20% off RRP. There are regular mega bargains with up to 75% off individual items, plus mid season and main sales throughout the year. The attractive Visitor Centre also features a Dartington Factory shop and an excellent Cookery Emporium which stocks over 3,000 pots, pans and gadgets. In the adjacent Demonstration Theatre you can see the latest equipment put to the test - then taste the results! Demonstrations are held twice daily (normally 1pm and 2.30pm) and are free of charge. The centre also includes Goodalls

Restaurant, ample parking facilities and a children's play area. Full guided factory tours are offered from Monday to Thursday. You can also 'have a go' yourself - paint a plate and make a Denby Frog any day of the week. *Factory Shop*

DERWENT CRYSTAL LTD

SHAWCROFT, ASHBOURNE, DERBYSHIRE DE6 1GH
☎ (01335) 345219. OPEN 9 - 5 MON - SAT.
LITTLE BRIDGE STREET, DERBY, DERBYSHIRE DE1 3LE
☎ (01332) 360186. OPEN 9 - 5 MON - SAT.
A wide selection of glassware and fancy items at factory shop prices. Full English lead crystal from liqueur glasses to vases and bowls, ringstands and dressing-table novelties. More than 200 different items on sale. Gift wrap service available. *Factory Shop*

DISCOUNT DRESSING

PEAK VILLAGE, CHATSWORTH ROAD, ROWSLEY, DERBYSHIRE
☎ (01629) 733000. OPEN 9.30 - 5.30 MON - SAT, 10 - 5 SUN.
A veritable Aladdin's Cave of designer bargains, Discount Dressing sells mostly German, Italian and French designer labels at prices at least 50% and up to 90% below those in normal retail outlets. All items are brand new and perfect. A team of buyers all over Europe purchase stock directly from the manufacturer for this growing chain of discount shops. This enables Discount Dressing to by-pass the importers and wholesalers and, of course, their mark-up. They also buy bankrupt stock in this country. Their agreement with their suppliers means that they are not able to advertise brand names for obvious reasons, but they are all well-known for their top quality and style. So confident is Discount Dressing that you will be unable to find the same item cheaper elsewhere, that they guarantee to give the outfit to you free of charge should you perform this miracle. Merchandise includes raincoats, dresses, suits, trousers, blouses, evening wear, special occasion outfits and jackets, in sizes 6-24 and in some cases larger. GDD readers can obtain a further 10% discount if they visit the shop taking a copy of this book with them. There are other branches in Lincolnshire, Northern Ireland, Hertfordshire, East Yorkshire and London. *Permanent Discount Outlet*

FABRIC DESIGN

10-12 NORTH PARADE, MATLOCK BATH, DERBYSHIRE DE4 3NS
☎ (01629) 584747. OPEN 1.30 - 5 MON, THUR, SUN, 11 - 5 TUE, WED, FRI, SAT.
Situated in a beautiful spa town, the Matlock Bath outlet is a busy, exciting Victorian shop on the parade by the river, which carries a huge range of designer clearance fabrics from £4.25 per metre, heavy linens from £5.99 per metre and an ever-changing range of bargain one-off buys such as £42 per metre fabric reduced to £9.99 per metre. Fabrics sold in the shop include such

names as Sanderson, Monkwell, Jane Churchill, Warner, Anna French and Liberty, but there is also available a range of natural fabrics - calico, twills and cream weaves. Those looking for good quality fabric for upholstery and curtaining should be prepared to buy on the day as the good deals don't stay in the shop for long. Huge range of discounted one-off end of lines and a discount is also offered on perfect fabrics and wallpapers ordered from pattern books in store. *Permanent Discount Outlet*

FACTORY SHOP OUTLET

STEVENSONS, DROVERS WAY, BULLBRIDGE, AMBERGATE, DERBYSHIRE DE5 2EX

☎ (01773) 853473. OPEN 10 - 5.30 MON - FRI, 10 - 5 SAT, SUN AND BANK HOLIDAYS, 10 - 4

Part of the Coats Viyella group, which makes quality clothing for many of the major high street stores, overstocks and clearance lines are sold through more than 30 of the group's factory shops. Many of you will recognise the garments on sale, despite the lack of well-known labels. Ladieswear includes dresses, blouses, jumpers, cardigans, trousers, nightwear, underwear, lingerie, hosiery, coats and swimwear. Menswear includes trousers, belts, shirts, ties, pullovers, cardigans, T-shirts, underwear, nightwear, hosiery and jackets. Childrenswear includes jackets, trousers, T-shirts, underwear, hosiery, jumpers and babywear. There are regular deliveries to constantly update the range. *Factory Shop*

FILIGREE

CARTER LANE EAST, SOUTH NORMANTON, (JCT 28 OF M1), DERBYSHIRE DE55 2EG

☎ (01773) 811630 EXT 296. OPEN 9 - 4.30 MON - THUR, 9 - 5 FRI, 9 - 1.30 SAT, 10 - 2 SUN.

Real factory shop behind factory makes filigree and Stiebel of Nottingham lace curtain and printed curtains. Makes net curtains on the premises for well-known high street department stores and mail order companies and sells them at reduced prices. Nets range from 50p a metre to £6 with fabric from £2.99 a yard to £5.99 a yard and remnants from 50p. Also readymade curtains, curtain accessories and bedding. *Factory Shop*

GILLIVERS FOOTWEAR
AND CLOTHING WAREHOUSE

1-3 ASHBY ROAD, MOIRA, SWADLINCOTE, DERBYSHIRE DE12 6DJ

☎ (01283) 214255. OPEN 9 - 8 MON - FRI, 9 - 5.30 SAT, 10 - 5 SUN.

Shoes from £1.99 to £40, at much reduced prices. The clothes are mainly from BhS and Marks & Spencer, although the labels are removed, and are discounted by between 25% and 50%. There are also bags, accessories and jewellery. Refreshments available. *Permanent Discount Outlet*

GLYNN WEBB

ASCOT DRIVE, DERBY, DERBYSHIRE DE24 8QZ
☎ (01332) 204282. OPEN 9 - 8 MON - SAT, 10 - 4 SUN AND BANK HOLIDAYS.
Stockists of all your home improvement needs from wallpaper to paint, furniture to flooring, tiles to textiles, housewares to lighting - in fact, almost everything for your home, with 24 branches in the North-West, Midlands and Yorkshire. Specialists in discontinued mail order, slightly imperfect branded stocks as well as perfect quality superior products. They carry top brands such as Dulux, Crown Paints and Vymura and Coloroll wall coverings, Rectella and Norwood textiles and much more in store. Different branches carry different lines so if you want something specific, phone first. To find your nearest branch, phone 0161 621 4500. *Permanent Discount Outlet*

JAEGER FACTORY SHOP

JAEGER DEPT, VIYELLA HOUSE, NOTTINGHAM ROAD, SOMERCOTES, DERBYSHIRE DE55 4SB
☎ (01773) 541183. OPEN 9 - 5 MON - SAT.
Contemporary classics from Jaeger at excellent prices. Most of the merchandise is previous seasons' stock, but you might also find some special makes. *Factory Shop*

JAMES BARRY MENSWEAR

ARMSTRONG'S MILL, MIDDLETON STREET, OFF STATION ROAD, ILKESTON, DERBYSHIRE DE7 5TT
☎ (0115) 932 4913. OPEN 9.15 - 5 MON - FRI, UNTIL 6 WED, 9.15 - 5.30 SAT, 10.30 - 4 SUN.
Designer menswear and ladieswear available at discount of up to 50% off rrp. Join the mailing list at any of the James Barry outlets which will give you advanced warning of any promotions (your details will not be passed on to anyone else). *Factory Shop*

JOHN SMEDLEY LTD

LEA MILLS, LEA BRIDGE, MATLOCK, DERBYSHIRE DE4 5AG
☎ (01629) 534571. OPEN 10 - 4 SEVEN DAYS A WEEK AND MOST BANK HOLIDAYS.
Sells John Smedley high quality knitwear which are ends of ranges or seconds, as well as some perfects, all at substantial discounts. There are more than 5,000 garments to choose from in cotton and wool, including cardigans and sweaters for ladies and men; own range underwear called Second Skin which includes cropped tops and bodies, and an assortment of accessories. Childrenswear is not stocked. There is another outlet in Doncaster. *Factory Shop*

JOKIDS LTD

MCARTHURGLEN DESIGNER OUTLET STORE, SOUTH NORMANTON,
DERBY, DERBYSHIRE DE55 2ER

☎ (01773) 545209. OPEN 10 - 6 MON - SAT, 10 - 8 THUR, 11 - 5 SUN.

JoKids is the factory shop trading name for Jeffrey Ohrenstein which sells
unusual and attractive clothes for children aged from birth to ten years. This
includes pretty party dresses for girls at reductions of up to 40%, all-in-one
smocked playsuits, T-shirts, denim shirts, denim dresses, sunhats, shorts, and
accessories. *Factory Shopping Village*

JUMPER

DERBYSHIRE DESIGNER OUTLET VILLAGE, MANSFIELD ROAD, SOUTH
NORMANTON, DERBYSHIRE DE55 2EF

☎ (01773) 545251. OPEN 9.30 - 5.30 MON - SAT, 11 - 5 SUN.

A wide range of Jumper label sweaters, gloves, scarves, shirts and cardigans for
men and women all at discount prices of up to 50% off. Prices start at £2.
Factory Shopping Village

LANGLEY FURNITURE

DELVES ROAD, HEANOR GATE INDUSTRIAL ESTATE, HEANOR,
DERBYSHIRE DE75 7SJ

☎ (01773) 765544. FAX ☎ (01773) 531322. OPEN 9 - 6 MON - FRI,
9 - 5 SAT, 10.30 - 4 SUN AND BANK HOLIDAYS.

A comprehensive and distinctive range of furniture individually manufactured
by craftsmen in Langley's own factories using selected quality pine and traditional carpentry methods. Each piece of furniture is stained to customers'
choice of colour using exclusive mixes of natural pigments and then finished
with dressings of high quality wax polish. The Langley collection offers a complete range of bedroom, lounge and dining-room furniture, and individually
designed kitchen units, fitted or free standing. In addition, Langely offer a
made-to-measure service, producing items to customers' own designs and
dimensions. For commercial customers, Langely design, manufacture and
supply stand-alone display and merchandiser units and other specialist shop
fixtures. Free brochure and price list available on request. *Factory Shop*

Live Well On Less Tips

Some museums offer free entrance after a certain time of day, usually an hour
or two before closing. The Imperial War Museum in Lambeth Road, London,
for example, is free after 4.30pm on weekdays and weekends, leaving you one
and a half hours to enjoy the exhibitions. Check out your local museums.

LITTLEWOODS
CATALOGUE DISCOUNT STORE

MANSFIELD ROAD, SOUTH NORMANTON, ALFRETON, JUNCTION 28
OF M1, DERBYSHIRE DE55 2ER

☎ (01773) 545105. OPEN 10 - 6 MON - FRI, 8 ON THUR, 9 - 6 SAT,
11 - 5 SUN.

Littlewoods clearance shops offering up to 50% off the catalogue price for
clothing and between 50% and 60% off for electrical goods. Stock changes
constantly and varies from day to day but can include well-known brand names
such as Berlei and Gossard lingerie, Vivienne Westwood, Pamplemousse leisure
wear, Nike and Adidas sports shoes, Workers For Freedom, and Timberland
and Caterpillar footwear. Stock depends on the size and location of the shop,
so larger shops will get the longer discontinued runs and smaller shops over-
runs with only a small amount of colour and size variations left. Littlewoods
also run a mobile shop which operates in cities where they don't have a sale
shop. For details of further venues for the sales, which usually take place once
a month, contact Melanie Lamb, c/o Crosby DC, Kershaw Avenue, Endbutt
Lane, Crosby, Merseyside L70 1AH. *Factory Shop*

LUGGAGE & BAGGAGE

UNIT 1, THE PEAK VILLAGE, CHATSWORTH ROAD, ROWSLEY,
DERBYSHIRE DE4 2JE

☎ (01629) 732 883. OPEN 9.30 - 5.30 MON - SAT, 10 - 5 SUN.

Luggage and travel-related products including executive cases, handbags,
umbrellas and accessories available in leading brands such as Samsonite, Brics,
Hidesign, Globe Trotter and Tula. The products also include couture and high
fashion brands such as YSL and Moschino. All products are offered at a considerably reduced price due to their being production over-runs, last season's
stock of slight seconds (ie they have minor aesthetic blemishes). *Factory
Shopping Village*

MASSONS MILL

NEAR MATLOCK, PEAK DISTRICT, DERBYSHIRE
DUE TO OPEN IN SUMMER 1999.

Anchored by Edinburgh Woollen Mills, this shopping village will also have a
heritage attraction in the setting of this regenerated 18th century mill building. Other shops will sell fashion, golfwear and equipment, gifts, speciality
foods and country goods. *Factory Shopping Village*

MATLOCK SHOE SALES

PAXTON WAREHOUSE, MATLOCK GREEN, MATLOCK, DERBYSHIRE
DE4 3BX

☎ (01629) 583105. OPEN 9 - 6 MON - SAT, 10 - 5 SUN.

Sells discounted men's and women's shoes in sizes 3 - 8 for women and 5 - 12
for men. The shoes range from ladies Italian leather shoes and wide fitting

lines from Equity, Jenny and Elmdale, to Hi-Tec trainers, Ecco, walking boots, leather boots and a range of Rombah Wallace shoes. *Permanent Discount Outlet*

MCARTHURGLEN DESIGNER OUTLET DERBYSHIRE

MANSFIELD ROAD, SOUTH NORMANTON, ALFRETON, JUNCTION 28 OF M1, DERBYSHIRE DE55 2JW

☎ (01773) 545000. OPEN 10 - 6 MON - FRI, 8 ON THUR, 9 - 6 SAT, 11 - 5 SUN.

Unusually, this outlet centre is set out in department store format with four distinct merchandise areas: fashion, homewares, sport/leisure and accessories. Sited 400 metres from the M1, there are about 70 different companies selling a variety of brand names at discount prices, a Sherwood Forest themed food court, a children's play area and free parking for 1,200 cars. The House & Home building houses Oven2Table selling Cole & Mason condiments, glasses and trays; Whittards selling bowls, plates, teapots, kitchen utensils, saucepans and mugs; Churchill selling china and dinner servcies; Denby; Portmeirion; Dartington Crystal; Spode; Royal Worcester with glasses, glass bowls and dinner services; Oneida with cutlery and Schott Zwiesel glasses; Royal Doulton; Bed & Bath Works selling cushions, blankets, sheets and lamps; Spiegelau glass and Coloroll bedlinen and curtains. The Women's and Men's Fashion building houses Ciro jewellery; Jaeger/Viyella/Van Heusen; Marilyn Moore knitwear for women; Baird menswear (casual jackets, suits); Double Two men's shirts; Haggar Clothing Co (shorts, jeans, casual trousers, shirts for men and women); Tom Sayers men's sweaters and trousers; Jacques Vert womenswear; Roman Originals coats, blouses and jackets for women; Suits You for men; Winning Line womenswear; The Brand Store - Labels for Less (Kangol, Pringle, Hide Park Leathers, Moorcroft, Glenmuir, Gabicci, Tootal, Wolsey, Alexara, Kushi, Chilli Pepper, Cote a Cote); Camille lingerie and nightwear for women; the Watch Store selling men's and women's watches; Antler luggage; Travel Accessory Outlet selling Samsonite, Equator, Head; Ak-ses-a-re bags, scarves and jewellery; Pilot teenage wear; Ton Sur Ton casual sweats, trousers and jackets for men and women; Claire's jewellery, hair accessories, hats and small gifts; Littlewoods Catalogue outlet selling brand name casual clothes and shoes for men, women and children including Adidas, Fila, Reebok, Umbra, Timberland; Nickleby's selling a range of clothes for men and women; The Shoe Company by Pavers with shoes for both sexes. The Sport & Leisure building caters for both sexes with some childrenswear at Fruit of the Loom and Tog 24 and houses Falmer; Fruit of the Loom; Cotton Traders; Lee Cooper; Tog 24; Speedo (goggles, T-shirts, swimming trunks and costumers, shorts); View From selling fleeces, sports shorts and outdoor jackets; Karrimor outdoorwear (including Timberland, Caterpillar, Kickers and Adidas). The Lifestyle/Children building houses Toyworld; XS

Music and Video; The Christmas Shop; The Garden Centre (spring/summer) Remington; Interior Selections selling a range of colonial heavy wooden furniture, throws, candles and picture frames; The Fabric Corner selling tiebacks and material (Sandown & Bourne, Warwick, Prestigious); JoKids childrenswear; Guru Retail selling metal furniture, mirrors, baskets, picture frames, cushions (eg large metal mirror, £108 reduced from £155; metal soap dish, £12 from £15; wooden nest of tables, £175 from £255); Banana Bookshop; Julian Graves selling spices and herbs, nuts and dried fruit (eg allspice, £1,20 for 100g; caraway seeds, 94p for 150g; marjoram, 50p for 30g; penne pasta, 58p for 500g; dessert dates, 60p for one tray); Price's Candles; Birthdays selling cards, gifts, gift tags, wrapping paper. There is also a Thornton's factory shop alongside the food court. *Factory Shopping Village*

ONEIDA

MCARTHURGLEN DESIGNER OUTLET CENTRE, MANSFIELD ROAD, SOUTH NORMANTON, ALFRETON, DERBYSHIRE DE55 OER

☎ (01773) 545130. OPEN 10 - 6 MON - FRI, 8 ON THUR, 9 - 6 SAT, 11 - 5 SUN.

Oneida is one of the world's largest cutlery companies and originates from the United States of America. In addition to cutlery, it sells silver and silver plate at discounts of between 30% and 50%, plus frames, candlesticks and trays. They now also have their own range of chinaware and glass, also sold here at discounts of 30%-50%. *Factory Shopping Village*

PEAK VILLAGE

CHATSWORTH ROAD, ROWSLEY, (ON THE A6 BETWEEN BAKEWELL AND MATLOCK), DERBYSHIRE DE4 2JE

☎ (01629) 735326. OPEN 9.30 - 5.30 MON - SAT, 10 - 5 SUN, EXCEPT CHRISTMAS DAY.

Fifteen factory outlets including Leading Labels, Discount Dressing, Winning Line, Luggage & Bags, The Book Depot, Because It's There, Yeoman Outdoors, Famous Shoes 4U, Staffordshire Pottery, Ponden Mill and Hornsea Pottery just 30 minutes from the M1 at the entrance to the Peak National Park. Peak village also features a Craft Courtyard with local craft businesses offering a range of original gifts including candles, soaps, healthfoods, exotic snacks, prints and paintings, basketware and dried flowers. On-site catering includes a choice of the Gold Restaurant, Coffee House and Ice Cream Parlour which offer everything from an ice cream sundae to a traditional Sunday roast and fast-food treats from Peak Express. The Wind in the Willows Attraction is a magical journey through the world of Ratty, Badger, Mole and of course the irrepressible Mr Toad. The latest sound and lighting effects bring Kenneth Grahame's classic tale to life in an enchanting recreation that's not just for kids! Free parking for up to 400 cars. *Factory Shopping Village*

PONDEN MILL

PEAK VILLAGE, ROWSEY, DERBYSHIRE DE4 2JE
☎ (01629) 733857. OPEN 9.30 - 5.30 MON - SAT, 10 - 5 SUN.
DE BRADELEI MILL SHOPS, DE BRADELEI HOUSE, CHAPEL STREET,
BELPER DE56 1AR
☎ (01773) 882815. OPEN 9.30 - 5.30 MON - FRI, 9 - 6 SAT, 11 - 5 SUN.
Famous branded products at direct from the mill prices. Towels, co-ordinated
bedlinen, duvets, pillows and curtains from Crown, Coloroll, Chortex,
Rectella together with bathroom and kitchen accessories. *Factory Shopping
Village*

PRICE'S CANDLES

MCARTHURGLEN DESIGNER OUTLET DERBYSHIRE, MANSFIELD
ROAD, SOUTH NORMANTON, ALFRETON, JUNCTION 28 OF M1,
DERBYSHIRE DE55 2JW
☎ (01773) 545202. OPEN 10 - 6 MON - FRI, 8 ON THUR, 9 - 6 SAT,
11 - 5 SUN.
Everything sold in this shop are seconds, which may be discoloured or have a
damaged pattern; discontinued sizes not available elsewhere; over-runs from
the garden selection or dinner candles in old packaging that has now been
replaced. There are church candles, lanterns, candles in pots and glass jars,
star-shaped candles, floating candles, candlestick holders, serviettes, scented
candles and garden torches. Some of the ceramic items are bought in. *Factory
Shopping Village*

R S SPORTS & LEISUREWEAR

192-194 NORMAN STREET, COTMANHAY, ILKESTON, DERBYSHIRE
DE7 8NR
☎ (0115) 932 3865. FAX ☎ (0115) 930 1919. OPEN 9.30 - 3.30 MON - FRI.
SAT: PHONE TO CONFIRM.
Sports, leisurewear and sweatshirts and cardigans for schoolwear in sizes from
1 year to XXXXL (60 waist) at discounts of up to 50%. Ladies cardigans,
sweatshirts and ski pants plus a variety of clothes, but no shoes, ranging from
£1 to £12. All the merchandise is made up of overmakes, slight imperfects and
end of season lines. There is a permanent sale rail. E-mail: RSCMT@aol.com.
Permanent Discount Outlets

REMINGTON

MCARTHURGLEN OUTLET CENTRE, MANSFIELD ROAD, SOUTH NORMANTON, ALFRETON, JUNCTION 28 OF M1, DERBYSHIRE DE55 2JW

☎ (01773) 545062. OPEN 10 - 6 MON - FRI, UNTIL 8 ON THUR, 9 - 6 SAT, 11 - 5 SUN.

Lots of famous names here from Oneida and Monogram cutlery to Braun, Philips, Remington, Clairol, Wahl, Krups and Kenwood small kitchen equipment. There are usually hair, beauty and male grooming accessories as well as kitchen equipment, all at reduced prices. It's a great place to buy gifts or replenish the kitchen equipment with combi stylers, turbo travel plus hairdryers, air purifiers, liquidisers; food processors; batteries; clocks; and cutlery. Some of the packaging may be damaged but the products are in perfect working order. For example, Silencio 1200 hairdryer, £11.99; Remington beard and moustache trimmer, £12.99; Oneida cutlery 44-piece set, £39.99; Braun Multi-mix, £42.99; Remington deep heat massager with infra red, £14.49; Wahl Compact comfort massager, £17.99. *Factory Shopping Village*

ROYAL CROWN DERBY

194 OSMASTON ROAD, DERBY, DERBYSHIRE DE23 8JZ

☎ (01332) 712833. OPEN 9 - 5 MON - SAT, 11 - 5 SUN,

One third of the stock in this shop is made up of seconds of bone china at discount prices of about one third off normal retail. This includes giftware, tableware and paperweights. Factory tours can be arranged on weekdays, while a new seven-day-a-week visitor centre allows you to see Royal Crown Derby being made and have a go at it yourself. *Factory Shop*

SLENDERELLA FACTORY SHOP

65 KINGS STREET, BELPER, DERBYSHIRE DE56 1QA

☎ (01773) 821532. OPEN 9 - 4 MON - SAT.

Sells ladies clothes, Slenderella nightwear, menswear and bed linen and towels. In the ladies department are ladies underwear and panti girdles, from £6.45; Brettle ladies vests, from £4.25; knee-length slips, from £3.99; bras, from £5.50; Brettles stockings, 55p; opaque tights, 99p; swimming costumes, £8.99 to £25.99; Fabrizio T-shirts, £10.99; dresses, from £11.25 to £39; silk scarves from £2.99; and nightdresses, from £4.50. There are also cushion covers, Dorma bedlinen, quilt covers, Horrockses bedlinen, beach towels for £9.99. The men's department has men's socks by H J of Leicester; Champion winter shirts; Storm Rebels outdoor jackets; sleeveless quilted gilets; Tootal dressing gowns; Peter England shirts; sweaters; underwear; boxers, Wolsey sweaters and David Jones pyjamas. Stock changes regularly but you can expect to find discounts of up to 60% on retail. Many lines are overmakes and high street brands with labels removed, but can be easily identified. *Factory Shop*

STEVENSON'S OF AMBERGATE

BULLBRIDGE, AMBERGATE, DERBYSHIRE DE56 2HH

☎ (01773) 853473. OPEN 10 - 5.30 MON - FRI, 10 - 5 SAT, 10 - 4 SUN AND BANK HOLIDAYS.

Sells a wide range of ladies knitwear, blouses, skirts, dresses, underwear, night-dresses, hosiery, men's trousers, outerwear, knitwear and childrenswear, as well as towels, face cloths and tea towels. Ladies clothes range from 8-26 in size, men's from 28 waist to 44 in season. There is a huge range of underwear, as well as wool coats, macs and anoraks in the outerwear. Childrenswear ranges from babies to teenwear, although there is more choice for girls than for boys. *Factory Shop*

T G GREEN

POOL STREET, CHURCH GRESLEY, SWADLINCOTE, DERBYSHIRE DE11 8EF

☎ (01283) 226696. OPEN 9.30 - 4.30 MON - FRI, 9.30 - 4 SAT, 10 - 3.30 SUN.

Part of the Clover Leaf group, this factory shop sells table mats, dinner sets, clocks, linen, towels, tablecloths, pottery and aprons, most of which are either discontinued lines or seconds of ongoing ranges. Many items are half the normal retail price. They will send you a catalogue and you can order by phone, although a price list won't be included - you will have to ring for prices. *Factory Shop*

TDP FACTORY SHOP F

TDP HOUSE, RAWDON ROAD, MOIRA, SWADLINCOTE, DERBYSHIRE DE12 6DT

☎ (01283) 550400. OPEN 9.30 - 5.30 MON - FRI, 10 - 4 SAT, SUN.

Disney character clothes for children, mainly nightwear and underwear, at good discounts. Also ladies and menswear at reasonable prices. *Factory Shop*

THE COURTAULDS
TEXTILES FACTORY SHOP

NIX HILL INDUSTRIAL ESTATE, ALFRETON, DERBYSHIRE DE55 7FQ

☎ (01773) 831035. OPEN 9 - 5.30 MON - SAT, 10.30 - 4.30 SUN.

Sells a wide range of ladies, men's and childrens high street fashions at between 30% and 50% below high street prices. Also stocks a wide range of household textiles, shoes and accessories. *Factory Shop*

THE FABRIC FACTORY

LOSCOE ROAD, HEANOR, DERBYSHIRE DE75 7FF

☎ (01773) 718911. OPEN 9.30 - 5.30 MON - SAT, 10 - 2 SUN.

Furnishing and dress fabrics at prices from £1.99 to £9.99 a metre. Furnishing fabrics include Prestigious, SMD, Fairfield Mills, Claremont and Villa Nova. Dress fabrics include Derby House and Rose & Hubble clearance lines. *Factory Shop*

THE SHOE FACTORY SHOP

UNIT 6, TRAFFIC STREET, EAGLE CENTRE, DERBY, DERBYSHIRE DE1 2NL

☎ (01332) 372823. OPEN 9 - 5 MON - SAT, 10.30 - 4.30 SUN.

Men's, women's and children's shoes and accessories which are bought in from other manufacturers including Spanish, Portuguese and Italian companies. All are unbranded. The range covers from mocassins to dressy shoes. Ladies shoes which would cost £35 retail are £29. Children's shoes from size 6 to adult size 5 from £10 upwards. Slippers start at baby size 4 to junior size 2 from £3.50 - £6.50. *Factory Shop*

THORNTONS

MCARTHURGLEN DESIGNER OUTLET VILLAGE, MANSFIELD ROAD, SOUTH NORMANTON, ALFRETON, DERBYSHIRE DE55 2JW

☎ (01773) 545289. OPEN 10 - 6 MON - FRI, 8 ON THUR, 9 - 6 SAT, 11 - 5 SUN.

The UK's leading specialist confectionery retailer has more than 500 shops and franchises nationwide selling a wide range of boxed and loose, chocolate and sugar confectionery. The factory outlets sell three different categories: misshapes. discounted lines and standard lines. Misshapes are loose chocolates which are the result of new product development, product trials or end of production runs which cannot be packed as Thorntons standard lines. They are packed into assorted bags and offer a saving of 35%-55% over the recommended retail price of standard loose line products. Discounted lines are excess to Thorntons' normal retail requirements and can be as a result of excess seasonal or export stock, discontinued lines or packaging changes. These products, when available, are offered at a discount of 25%-50% over the standard retail price. Standard lines from the full Thorntons range are also on sale at normal prices. *Factory Shopping Village*

TOG 24

BUILDING 3, DERBYSHIRE DESIGNER OUTLET VILLAGE, MANSFIELD ROAD, SOUTH NORMANTON, DERBYSHIRE DE55 2ER

☎ (01773) 545206. OPEN 10 - 6 MON, TUE, WED, FRI, 10 - 8 THUR, 9 - 6 SAT, 11 - 5 SUN.

Tog 24 are the UK's fastest growing brand name in outdoor clothing and leisurewear, with a total of three UK factories and 36 stores nationwide. They utilise the world's finest performance fabrics including Gore-Tex, Polartec and Burlington macs. Catering for all the family for all seasons, with cosy fleeces and waterproofs for the winter, and trekking ranges, shorts and t-shirts for the summer. With all prices at least 30% below the recommended retail price you can afford to enter the Tog comfort zone. *Factory Shopping Village*

TOYWORLD FACTORY OUTLETS LTD

MCARTHURGLEN DESIGNER OUTLET, DERBYSHIRE OUTLET STORE, MANSFIELD ROAD, SOUTH NORMANTON, ALFRETON, DERBYSHIRE DE55 2JH

☎ (01773) 545 333. OPEN SEVEN DAYS A WEEK, 10 -6 MON, TUE, WED, FRI, TILL 8 THUR, 9 - 6 SAT, 11 - 5 SUN.

Toy World sells brand name items including a wide range of toys with well-known brand names. For example, Barbie (Mattel), Disney, Playskool, Lego, Sylvanian Families, Fisher-Price, Tyco, Tomy, Waddington, M&B Games, Safe & Sound, Matchbox, and many others at very low prices. *Factory Shopping Village*

TRADE PRICES

3 NOTTINGHAM ROAD, RIPLEY, DERBYSHIRE DE5 3DJ

☎ (01773) 513483. OPEN 9 - 5.30 MON - FRI, 9 - 5 SAT, 10 - 4 SUN.

Men's, women's and children's clothes as well as household goods and giftware. Two floors of brand name perfects and chainstore items, the latter consisting of factory over-runs, ends of lines and slight seconds, with up to 50% off high street prices. Brand names include Farah, Wrangler, Lyle & Scott, Wolsey, Naturana, Adidas, Reebok, Nike and Fruit of the Loom. Chainstore clothes have the labels cut out, but many are still recognisable as current high street stock. Names such as Marks & Spencer, BhS, Principles, Etam, Dorothy Perkins, New Look, Richards and Mothercare are available, to name just a few. There is a lift available for pushchairs and disabled customers. *Permanent Discount Outlet*

TRAVEL ACCESSORY OUTLET

BUILDING NO 4, MACARTHURGLEN DESIGNER OUTLET VILLAGE, MANSFIELD ROAD, SOUTH NORMANTON, DERBYSHIRE DE55 2ER

☎ (01773) 545255. OPEN 10 - 6 MON - WED, 10 - 8 THUR, 10 - 6 FRI, 9 - 6 SAT, 11 - 5 SUN.

Luggage and travel-related products including executive cases, handbags, umbrellas and accessories available in leading brands such as Samsonite, Brics, Hidesign, Globe Trotter and Tula. The products also include couture and high fashion brands such as YSl and Moschino. All products are offered at a considerably reduced price due to their being production over-runs, last season's stock of slight seconds (ie they have minor aesthetic blemishes). *Factory Shopping Village*

TWEEDIES TRADE PRICES

3 NOTTINGHAM ROAD, RIPLEY, DERBYSHIRE DE5 3DJ

☎ (01773) 513483. OPEN 9 - 5 MON - SAT, 10 - 4 SUN.

Clothes for all the family as well as household goods and giftware. Two floors of brand name perfects and chainstore items, the latter consisting of factory over-run, ends of lines and slight seconds, with up to 50% off high street prices. Brand names include Farah, Wrangler, Lyle & Scott, Wolsey, Naturana, Adidas, Reebok, Nike and Fruit of the Loom. Chainstore clothes have the labels cut out, but many are still recognisable as current high street stock. Names such as Marks & Spencers, BhS, Principles, Etam, Dorothy Perkins, New Look, Richards and Mothercare, to name just a few. There is a lift available to help those with pushchairs and disabled customers. *Permanent Discount Outlet*

WEBB IVORY LTD

36 HIGH STREET, SWADLINCOTE, DERBYSHIRE DE11 8HY

☎ (01283) 226700. OPEN 9 - 5 MON - SAT.

38 MAIN CENTRE, DERBY, DERBYSHIRE DE1 2DE

☎ (01332) 204078. OPEN 9 - 5 MON - SAT.

Items from the Webb Ivory catalogue at reduced prices including cards, gifts, soft toys, books, pens, lamps, kitchenware, garden furniture and clothes. Discounts range from at least 50%. *Factory Shop*

WIRKSWORTH FACTORY SHOP

BENCO HOSIERY, NORTH END MILLS, WIRKSWORTH, DERBYSHIRE DE4 4FG

☎ (01629) 824731. OPEN 9 - 5 SEVEN DAYS A WEEK, 8,30 ON THUR.

Wide selection of clothes for the family, household goods, giftware and linen. There are T-shirts, shorts, sun vests, skirts, blouses, shirts, sweatshirts, jeans, trousers, dresses, work shirts, swimwear, jog suits, underwear, babywear, socks, tea towels, pillows, duvets and towels. There is a children's play area and snacks facility. Men's shirts are up to 19 inch collar. For women, the stockings are less than half the shop prices and there is cotton, thermal and woollen underwear. Car park. *Factory Shop*

WYNSORS WORLD OF SHOES

SHEFFIELD ROAD, CHESTERFIELD, DERBYSHIRE

☎ (01246) 276690. OPEN 9 - 5.30 MON, TUE, WED, SAT, 9 - 8 THUR, FRI, 10 - 4 SUN AND BANK HOLIDAYS.

Stocks a wide range of footwear for children as well as adults, including some seconds. There are slippers, sandals, boots, leather and vinyl handbags and purses, shoe cleaners and polishes. Ladies fashion shoes start from £6 a pair. There are some well known brands, all at substantial savings on high street prices. *Permanent Discount Outlet*

Devon

WOMENSWEAR ONLY 🎀 Bairdwear Clothing, *Barnstaple*.   Origin, Bampton, *Nr Tiverton*. Windsmoor Sale Shop, *Torquay*.

WOMENSWEAR & MENSWEAR 🎀 🎩 Clarks Shoes, *Paignton*.   Matalan, *Exeter*. Matalan, *Plymouth*.   The Frock Exchange, *Paignton*.   The Shoe Shed, *Exmouth*.   TK Maxx, *Plymouth*. Trago Mills, *Newton Abbot* .

CHILDREN 🧸 Babe-Equip, *Tiverton*.   Child's Play, *Tiverton*.   Clarks Shoes, *Paignton*. Matalan, *Exeter* and *Plymouth*.   The Shoe Shed, *Exmouth*.   TK Maxx, *Plymouth*. Trago Mills, *Newton Abbot*.

HOUSEHOLD AND GIFTWARE 🧸 CH Brannam, *Barnstaple*. Croydex Factory Shop, *Barnstaple*.   Dartington Crystal, *Great Torrington*. Dartmouth Pottery, *Dartmouth*.   Exeter Surplus, *Exeter*.   House of Marbles, *Bovey Tracey*. Matalan, *Exeter*.   Matalan, *Plymouth*.   Sheridan Seconds Shop, *Tiverton*. The Cardew Teapot Pottery, *Bovey Tracey*.   TK Maxx, *Plymouth*.   Trago Mills, *Newton Abbot*

DIY/RENOVATION 🔨 Ashburton Marbles, *Ashburton*.   CMS Country Ranges, *Dartington*. Colin Baker, *Tiverton*.   MC Slates, Bow, *Nr Crediton*.   Tobys, *Exeter*.   Trago Mills, *Newton Abbot*. Winkleigh Timber, *Winkleigh*.

ARCHITECTURAL SALVAGE 🔨 Ashburton Marbles, *Ashburton*.   Colin Baker, *Tiverton*. MC Slates, Bow, *Nr Crediton*.   Tobys, *Exeter*.   Winkleigh Timber, *Winkleigh*.

FURNITURE/SOFT FURNISHINGS 🛋 Curtain Trader, *Honiton*.   Harvey Baker, *Paignton*. Exeter Surplus, *Exeter*.   Honiton Remnant Shop, *Honiton*.   The Factory Fabric Warehouse, *Exeter*. Winkleigh Timber, *Winkleigh*.

FOOD AND LEISURE 🍴 Exeter Surplus, *Exeter*.

SPORTSWEAR AND EQUIPMENT 🎿 Exeter Surplus, *Exeter*.

ASHBURTON MARBLES 🔨

GREAT HALL, NORTH STREET, ASHBURTON, DEVON TQ13 7QD
☎ (01364) 653189. OPEN 8 - 5 MON - FRI, 10 - 1 SAT.
Ashburton Marbles offers an extensive array of items at their 18th century showrooms including period marble and wood chimney pieces, cast iron inserts, fire baskets, fenders, guards, etc and anything related to your fireplace spanning 250 years. There is also a varied selection of furnishings, including Art Deco suites, Victorian chaise longues, comfortable Victorian sofas, gilt overmantels and mirrors, chandeliers and wall lights from country-made cast iron to French ormolu. For the garden, there are cast iron fountains, stone bird baths, sun dials, staddle stones, Moroccan pots, reconstituted stone bird baths, stone sundial stands, lead planters, massive olive jars, planters, garden statuary and furniture. Delivery can be arranged throughout the UK. *Architectural Salvage*

BABE-EQUIP
9 LEAT STREET, TIVERTON, DEVON EX16 5LG
☎ (01884) 257938.

HUSH-A-BYE-HIRE
16 WHITCHURCH AVENUE, EXETER, DEVON EX2 5NU
☎ (01392) 257636.

BABY EQUIPMENT HIRE
HEATHERTON, FIR HILL, WOODBURY, EXETER, DEVON EX5 1JX
☎ (01395) 233057.

BABE-EQUIP
27 JOHN STREET, TIVERTON, DEVON EX16 5JP
☎ (01884) 259042.
Bouncy castles for children's parties; storks accouncement boards and party
signs. Cots, highchairs, buggies, car seats, safety gates and toys. All items are
bought new specially for hire. All these businesses are members of the BEHA,
which has more than 100 members countrywide who can provide you with a
travel cot, high chair, buggy, back pack or almost anything a parent of young
children might want. Phone 0831 310355 to find your nearest BEHA member. *Hire Shop*

BAIRDWEAR CLOTHING
HOWARD AVENUE, WHIDDON VALLEY, BARNSTAPLE, DEVON
EX32 8LA
☎ (01271) 321337. OPEN 9.30 - 4.30 MON - SAT.
SHOWGROUND ROAD, BRIDGWATER, SOMERSET
☎ (01278) 431465. OPEN 9.30 - 4.30 MON - SAT.
Manufactures lingerie for a well-known department store, seconds, overmakes
and returns of which are sold in the factory shop at discount prices. About
80% of the merchandise sold here is made by the factory, with a further 20%
manufactured within the company. *Factory Shop*

C H BRANNAM
ROUNDSWELL INDUSTRIAL ESTATE, BARNSTAPLE, DEVON EX31 3NJ
☎ (01271) 376853. OPEN 9 - 5 MON - SAT,
10 - 4 SUN FROM MAY - SEPT ONLY.
On-site factory shop selling terracotta gardening and cookware, including many
different forms of pots, especially glazed pots. Seconds are usually available.
Factory Shop

CHILD'S PLAY

28 ALBION STREET, EXMOUTH, DEVON EX8 1JJ
☎ (01395) 276975. OPEN 10 - 4 MON, TUE, THUR-SAT, 10 - 1 WED,
CLOSED 1 - 2 DAILY.
Secondhand and new baby equipment and clothes for ages 0 - 6 years.
Babygros cost from 50p to £3; prams from £5 to £100. Also offers hire service. For example, cot or buggy, £1.50 a day or £10 a week per item. *Dress Agency*

CLARKS SHOES

SHOE VALUE, 22 THE CROSSWAYS, HYDE ROAD, PAIGNTON, DEVON
TQ4 5BL
☎ (01803) 553444. OPEN 9 - 5.30 MON - SAT, 10 - 4 BANK HOLIDAYS.
Clarks International operate a chain of factory shops nationally which specialise in selling discontinued lines and slight sub-standards for men, women and children from Clarks, K Shoes and other famous brands. These shops trade under the name of Crockers, K Shoes Factory shop or Clarks Factory Shop and while not all are physically attached to a shoe factory, these shops are treated as factory shops by the company. Customers can expect to find an extensive range of quality shoes, sandals, walking boots, slippers, trainers, handbags, accessories and gifts, while their major outlets also offer luggage, sports clothing, sports equipment and outdoor clothing. Brands stocked include Clarks, K Shoes, Springer, CICA, Hi-Tec, Puma, Mercury, Fila, Mizuno, Slazenger, Samsonite, Delsey, Antler and Carlton, although not all are sold in every outlet. Discounts are from 30% to 60% off the normal high street price for perfect stock. The Swindon branch is also a sports factory shop and baggage factory shop. *Factory Shop*

CMS COUNTRY RANGES LTD

4 WEBBERS YARD, DARTINGTON, NR TOTNES, DEVON TQ9 6JY
☎ (01803) 865555/867267. OPEN 9 - 5 MON - FRI, 8 - 12.30 SAT.
Specialist suppliers of factory renovated Aga and Rayburn cookers, plus a range of new appliances for cooking or central heating, all at very competitive prices. Also stock refurbished cast iron baths and radiators. Main agent for Nobel and Sandyford products, spares and discount heating materials especially flue products. Installations undertaken at competitive prices. *Secondhand Shop*

COLIN BAKER

CROWN HILL, HALBERTON, TIVERTON, DEVON EX16 7AY
☎ (01884) 820152. BY APPOINTMENT ONLY.
Reclaimed oak beams and joists, oak, green oak and pine floorboards and period joinery. Quality timber for furniture making and flooring, doors, mullioned windows. *Architectural Salvage*

CROYDEX FACTORY SHOP

ROUNDSWELL INDUSTRIAL ESTATE, BARNSTAPLE, DEVON

☎ (01271) 375589. OPEN 9 - 4 MON - FRI.

Bathroom fittings, showers, medicine cabinets, towel rails, loo brushes, soap dishes, bathroom roller blinds, shower curtains, waterproof window curtains, all at discounted prices. The shop has recently moved to this new address so telephone number may change as may opening hours. Do check first. *Factory Shop*

CURTAIN TRADER

187 HIGH STREET, HONITON, DEVON EX14 8LQ

☎ (01404) 45451. OPEN 9.30 - 4.30 TUE - SAT, 9.30 - 1 THUR.

Secondhand curtain agency, they are also specialists in discontinued and seconds designer fabrics and sale stock from £2 to £20 a metre, selling curtain fabrics, linings and accessories from many different labels.*Secondhand Shop*

DARTINGTON CRYSTAL

LINDEN CLOSE, SCHOOL LANE, GREAT TORRINGTON, DEVON
EX38 7AN

☎ (01805) 626262. OPEN 9.30 - 5 MON - SAT, 10.30 - 4.30 SUN.
MAIL ORDER.

BARBICAN GLASSWORKS, THE OLD FISH MARKET, THE BARBICAN,
PLYMOUTH, DEVON PL1 2LT

☎ (01752) 224777. OPEN 9.30 - 6 MON - SAT, 11 - 5 SUN.

The factory shop at Torrington has an extensive range of Dartington Crystal seconds at greatly reduced prices. Shopping opportunities include a kitchen giftware shop selling Portmeirion and Denby, locally produced quality foods, gifts and candles as well as The Edinburgh Woollen Mill with a large selection of classic knitwear and co-ordinated clothing. For a small charge, there are factory tours where you can watch skilled craftsmen blowing and shaping beautiful crystal. In the Visitor Centre, you can try your hand at Glass Art, paint or engrave your own designs on a piece of glass. There is a restaurant serving hot and cold means. *Factory Shop*

DARTMOUTH POTTERY

WARFLEET, DARTMOUTH, DEVON TQ6 9BY

☎ (01803) 832258. OPEN 10 - 5 SEVEN DAYS A WEEK IN SUMMER;
WINTER: 10 - 5 MON - FRI.

Discontinued lines and some perfects of Dartmouth Pottery at varied discounts. Always some special offers on; prices range from 50p to £15. Cafe on site. *Factory Shop*

EXETER SURPLUS, BAKERS YARD

ALPHINBROOK ROAD, MARSH BARTON INDUSTRIAL ESTATE, EXETER, DEVON EX2 8SS

☎ (01392) 427508. OPEN 8.30 - 5 MON - SAT, 10 - 4 SUN.

Operates from a 4,000 sq ft retail unit and a 10,000 sq ft trade site half a mile away on Christow Road, the latter specialising in quality office furniture and shelving. In the past, most of their stock came through buying good quality, used goods from government departments, schools and the armed forces, among others, though this is dropping off and more of it is now new, though still very competitively priced. Expanding rapidly is the budget hand tool section, where they claim they can't be beaten on price. There is also a lot of hardware, some bedding, ex-MOD saucepans and cutlery - some new, some used - garden tools from shovels and spades to axes and pickaxes, both new and ex-MOD; ex-MOD furniture, chandlery and clothes, as well as big and smaller tents. The outdoor leisure market is their new specialisation. For example, ex-government Conquest three-man tents that usually retail for nearly £300 for £85, high quality rucksacks, sleeping bags and other equipment. *Permanent Discount Outlet*

HARVEY BAKER DESIGNS

RODGERS INDUSTRIAL ESTATE, YALBERTON ROAD, PAIGNTON, DEVON TQ4 7PJ

☎ (01803) 521515. PHONE BEFORE VISITING.

Studio/showroom where you can buy both unpainted MDF furniture and gift items to decorate yourself and finished painted versions. There are chests of drawers, wardrobes, beds and bedheads, cabinets as well as unusual items such as Gothic chairs made for clients. Hands-on instruction is given on the spot and there is a telephone advice service from the owners who run courses and do demonstrations for the BBC Good Homes Show. Also available are paints, glazes, varnishes, brushes, stencils and mosaics. *Factory Shop*

HOUSE OF MARBLES & TEIGN VALLEY GLASS

POTTERY ROAD, BOVEY TRACEY, DEVON TQ13 9DS

☎ (01626) 835358. OPEN 9 - 5 SEVEN DAYS A WEEK.

Stocks a large range of pottery on site plus gifts for all occasions, with lots of discounted seconds at up to 50% off. There are museums of pottery, glass marbles and games and a coffee shop and licensed restaurant. Glass blowing can be viewed from 9am - 4.30pm Monday to Friday and from 10am - 3pm on Sundays all year round. No entrance charge and free parking. *Factory Shop*

HONITON REMNANT SHOP

52 HIGH STREET, HONITON, DEVON EX14 9PW

☎ (01404) 43004. OPEN 9 - 5 MON - SAT.

Packed full of ends of lines and seconds from famous name furnishing manufacturers. Lining, £2.20 a metre, upholstery fabrics, velvet, from £3.99 a metre for seconds. Curtain fabrics stocked include those from famous names such as Hardy, Sanderson, Derby House, Prestigious, Curtaina, Crowsons and many others. Fabrics start at £2.99 a yard or £3.20 a metre. *Permanent Discount Outlet*

M C SLATES

BOW STATION YARD, BOW, NEAR CREDITON, DEVON EX17 6JD

☎ (01363) 82598. OPEN 8 - 4.30 MON - FRI, 9 - 12 SAT.

Reclaimed roofing slates and new terracotta flooring - natural not ceramic. *Architectural Salvage*

MATALAN, UNIT 2

HAVEN BANKS, WATER LANE, EXETER, DEVON EX2 8DW

☎ (01392) 413375. OPEN 10 - 8 MON - FRI, 9 - 6 SAT, 11 - 5 SUN.

TRANSIT WAY, PLYMOUTH, DEVON PL5 3TW

☎ (01752) 772313. OPEN 10 - 8 MON - FRI, 9 - 6 SAT, 11 - 4 SUN.

Matalan is a fashion and homewares shop giving customers what they claim to be unbeatable value for money with huge savings on a wide range of products including high quality fashionable clothing for women, women and children at up to 50% off high street prices. Matalan is situated out of town and stores are open seven days a week all year round. *Permanent Discount Outlet*

ORIGIN

STATION ROAD INDUSTRIAL ESTATE, BAMPTON, NEAR TIVERTON, DEVON EX16 9NG

☎ (01398) 331704. OPEN 9 - 5 MON - FRI, 9 - 1 SAT.

The Origin factory shop offers a large range of womenswear (dresses, soft suits and separates) suitable for casual and special occasions at approximately 50% less than the recommended retail price. The fabrics used are of a high quality, predominantly natural fibres, including Liberty of London and Rose & Hubble. Situated in the attractive town of Bampton on the edge of Exmoor, the factory offers parking, wheelchair access and a friendly, relaxed atmosphere. Dresses and skirts can be shortened free of charge. *Factory Shop*

SHERIDAN SECONDS SHOP

KENNEDY WAY INDUSTRIAL ESTATE, MOUNTBATTEN ROAD,
TIVERTON, DEVON EX16 6SW

☎ (01884) 255997. OPEN 10 - 5 MON - SAT.

Sells bed linen from Australia, which is superb quality. Fitted and flat sheets,
bath towels, valances and quilt covers. The shop is sited behind Safeways store
(second exit off Devon Link Road North). *Permanent Discount Outlet*

THE CARDEW TEAPOT POTTERY

NEWTON ROAD, BOVEY TRACEY, DEVON TQ13 9DX

☎ (01626) 832172. OPEN 9.30 - 5.30 SEVEN DAYS A WEEK.

It's said that Josiah Wedgwood used to personally smash any pottery which
didn't come up to his exacting standards - Paul Cardew has much the same
philosophy. As Cardew don't sell anything other than first quality perfect
goods to retailers, here in Bovey Tracey they can sell a selected range of slightly imperfect teapots, miniature teapots and other ceramics at up to 50% less
than half the normal price. Their shop is also a Mecca for all other things to
do with tea - from tea itself to teatowels, books about tea, tea cosies etc. There
are free tours when you can see these collectable teapots being made. Large
free car park and tea room. *Factory Shop*

THE FACTORY FABRIC WAREHOUSE

UNIT 1, MERRIOTT HOUSE, HENNOCK ROAD, MARSH BARTON
TRADING ESTATE, EXETER, DEVON EX2 8NJ

☎ (01392) 422881. OPEN 9 - 5.30 MON - SAT, 10 - 4 SUN.

7/9 FARADAY MILL, PRINCE ROCK, PLYMOUTH PL4 0ST

☎ (01752) 253351. OPEN 9 - 5 MON - SAT, 10 - 4 SUN.

By buying vast quantities of fabric direct from the factory, they are able to sell
the material at discounts averaging 25%. There is a large selection of fabrics
from £2.99 a metre for curtaining to £16.99 for upholstery. They also sell zips,
brass hooks, curtain tracks and accessories, Velcro, pillow and cushion covering, pelmets, foam, nets and bean bags. Competitive curtain making service.
Permanent Discount Outlet

THE FROCK EXCHANGE

9 SEAWAY ROAD, PRESTON, PAIGNTON, DEVON TQ3 2NX

☎ (01803) 522951. OPEN 10 - 4.30 TUE - SAT. CLOSED 1 - 2.

Women's and menswear with a cross section of clothes from designer labels to
high street names and chain stores: Jacques Vert, Louis Feraud, YSL, Christian
Dior, Hodges and Dunns. Suits range from £18-£60, and there are hundreds
of ties, some shoes from Barkers and Church's, morning suits, blazers, flannels
and grey suits. One-third of the shop is taken up with menswear; two thirds
with women's. Also jewellery, unwanted gifts, curtains. *Dress Agency*

THE SHOE SHED

UNITS 1 AND 2, ROLLE HOUSE, ROLLE STREET, EXMOUTH, DEVON
EX8 2SM

☎ (01395) 223343. OPEN 9 - 5.30 MON - SAT, 10 - 4 SUN.

Large factory shop selling a vast range of all types of children's, men's and women's shoes, all of which are perfects, at up to 30% below normal high street prices. Ladies sandals cost from £5; ladies shoes from £7.50. Men's shoes from £10; sports shoes from £10. *Factory Shop*

TK MAXX

YEO BUILDING, 28 ROYAL PARADE, PLYMOUTH, DEVON PL1 1SA

☎ (01752) 255081. OPEN 9 - 5.30 MON FRI, UNTIL 8 THUR, 9 - 6 SAT,
11 - 5 SUN.

Based on an American concept, TK Maxx is situated in easily accessible, often centrally located stores and offers famous label goods with up to 60% savings off recommended retail prices. TK Maxx has fashion for the whole family - women's, men's and childrenswear - accessories, shoes, gifts, kitchenware and home goods. Everything in the store is branded with a choice of well-known high street names to designer labels, and while a small percentage might be clearly marked past season, the great majority of items in store are current season, current stock and still with phenomenal savings. There is a huge choice with 50,000 pieces in store and up to 10,000 new items arriving a week. The stores are simple and unfussy with wide aisles, shopping trolleys and baskets, and a spacious, functional feel to them but there are individual changing rooms, ramps for buggies and wheelchairs and plenty of staff on the shop floor. Every branch accepts all major credit and debit cards and has a liberal refund and return policy. *Permanent Discount Outlet*

Live Well On Less Tips

Real nappies are much cheaper than disposable ones. Plus, the Real Nappy Association argue, your baby stays comfortable and healthy and you save resources and minimise pollution. Write to the Real Nappy Association, PO Box 3704, London SE26 4RX (enclosing large SAE) for free information pack or phone 0181 299 4519.

TOBYS

(THE OLD BUILDERS YARD AND STORE), EXMINSTER STATION,
EXMINSTER, EXETER, DEVON EX6 8DZ

☎ (01392) 833499. OPEN 9 - 5 MON - FRI, 9.30 - 4 SAT, 11 - 3 SUN.
BRUNEL ROAD INDUSTRIAL ESTATE, NEWTON ABBOT, DEVON
TQ12 4PB

☎ (01626) 351767. OPEN 8.30 - 4.30 MON - FRI, 9.30 - 4.30 SAT.
TORRE STATION, TORQUAY ROAD, TORQUAY, DEVON

☎ (01803) 212222. OPEN 10 - 5 MON - SAT, 10.30 - 4.30 SUN, BANK
HOLIDAYS.

Ten thousand square feet of reclaimed doors, windows, slates, sanitaryware,
bricks, chimney pots, roof tiles, timber, pine stripping and much more.
Architectural Salvage

TRAGO MILLS

REGIONAL SHOPPING CENTRE, NEWTON ABBOT, DEVON TQ12 6JD
☎ (01626) 821111. OPEN 9 - 5.30 MON - SAT, 10.30 - 4.30 SUN.

A vast outlet which takes the whole day to do justice to. Sells virtually everything from men's, women's and children's wear, gardening equipment and
cookware to wallpaper, carpets and fitted kitchens. Most are branded goods
and there is a cafe, pizza bar and petrol station. The women's fashion has a reasonable amount coming from high street multiples. The menswear offers Lee
Cooper jeans, Joe Bloggs jeans, Farah trousers, Pierre Cardin, all-leather classic brogues and Oxford shoes, and Doc Martens. Vast car parking areas, lots
of outdoor picnic spots. For the home, there are Black & Decker Dustbusters,
Hotpoint dryers and washing machines with cosmetic blemishes; curtain fabrics by the metre from Monkwell, Sekers, Filigree, Laura Ashley as well as
Janet Reger for Vantona double quilt covers, with matching sheets, pillow
cases and valances. There is a vast range of tiles including Pilkington seconds.
A separate building houses garden equipment and plant life while the home
decorating department has a vast selection of paint, brushes and wallpapers.
For example, Crown vinyl emulsion, Magicoat non-drip gloss. An excellent
leisure section offers bicycles and accessories, golf gear, keep-fit systems, fishing rods and flies. A separate building houses garden equipment and plant life
while the home decorating department has a vast selection of paint, brushes
and wallpapers. Comparison prices are not given here, although staff say most
items are discounted by up to 50%, so if you're looking for a bargain, make
sure you've done your homework on the high street first. The best deals are in
fabrics, carpets, tiles and diy. There is a Leisure park with a giant free fall slide,
Supakart go-Kart circuit, model railway, miniature steam railway, nature
reserve, coarse fishing and Edwardian Penny Arcade. *Permanent Discount
Outlet*

Live Well On Less Tips

If you're put off buying secondhand clothes and equipment for your new-born, remember: this is the one time when secondhand probably means brand new. New babies receive so many clothes that they never wear. These find their way into secondhand shops where you can buy them at half price. However, never buy a secondhand car seat - even the slightest shunt in a car can damage a baby car seat.

WINDSMOOR SALE SHOP

34 FLEET STREET, TORQUAY, DEVON TQ2 5DJ

☎ (01803) 201081. OPEN 9 - 5.30 MON - SAT.

Previous season's stock as well as any returned merchandise and overmakes from the Windsmoor, Planet and Precis Petite ranges at discounts averaging about 50% off the original price. *Permanent Discount Outlet*

WINKLEIGH TIMBER

SECKINGTON CROSS, INDUSTRIAL ESTATE, WINKLEIGH, DEVON EX19 8DQ

☎ (01837) 83573. OPEN 9 - 5 MON - FRI, 9 - 12.30 SAT.

SHOWROOM

☎ (01837) 83832. OPEN 8 - 5 MON - FRI, 8 - 12.30 SAT.

Largest source of reclaimed timber in the South of England, including pine, oak and pitch pine planks. Parquet flooring in oak, mahogany, maple, meranti; strip flooring in maple, mahogany, oak and pitch pine. Joinery grade timber, beams and new random width oak and elm. Large stocks of handmade furniture in reclaimed timber always on display in showroom. *Architectural Salvage*

Live Well On Less Tips

If you're planning a fund-raising event, your local branch of McDonalds will supply free orange juice on a stand manned by a staff member as long as it is a participating "Orange Bowl" member. This can be used either as free refreshment or sold to raise cash. Contact your local branch manager for details and booking.

Dorset

WOMENSWEAR ONLY   Browsers, *Sherborne.*   Gemma, *Christchurch.*
Lori's Boutique, *Wimborne.*

WOMENSWEAR & MENSWEAR   Damart, *Bournemouth.*   Matalan, *Poole.*
Matalan *Weymouth.*   The Catalogue Shop, *Highcliffe.*   TK Maxx, *Bournemouth.*

CHILDREN   Gemma, *Christchurch.*   Matalan, *Poole.*   Matalan, *Weymouth.*
The Catalogue Shop, *Highcliffe.*   TK Maxx, *Bournemouth.*

HOUSEHOLD AND GIFTWARE   Highbury China, *Sherborne.*   Matalan, *Poole.*
Matalan, *Weymouth.*   Poole Pottery, *Poole.*   The Catalogue Shop, *Highcliffe.*   TK Maxx, *Bournemouth.*

DIY/RENOVATION   Dorset Reclamation, *Wareham.*   Pilkington's Tiles Factory, *Poole.*

ARCHITECTURAL SALVAGE   Dorset Reclamation, *Wareham.*

FURNITURE/SOFT FURNISHINGS   Balmain & Balmain, *Dorset.*
Curtains Encore, *Blandford Forum.*   Fabric Warehouse, *Poole.*
Hansons Fabrics, *Sturminster Newton.*   Lyme Regis Remnant Shop, *Lyme Regis.*
The Catalogue Shop, *Highcliffe.*   The Old Mill Factory Shop, *Bridport.*

FOOD AND LEISURE   CD & Book & Video Selections, *Dorset.*
Moores Biscuits, Morocombelake, *Nr Bridport.*   Poole Pottery Ltd, *Poole.*

BALMAIN & BALMAIN

DORSET DT9 4SB
☎ (01963) 220247. PHONE FOR APPOINTMENT.
Buying a sofa is one of the biggest home purchases you make, particularly for good quality. Balmain & Balmain offer traditional handmade furniture which is custom made and can be delivered throughout the country at workshop direct prices. The sofas and chairs are built on best beechwood frames, with coil-sprung seats and feather cushions and carry a ten-year guarantee. Prices are 20%-30% less than the equivalent quality in the high street. *Factory Shop*

BROWSERS

35 CHEAP STREET, SHERBORNE, DORSET DT9 3PU
☎ (01935) 813326. OPEN 10 - 5 MON - SAT.
THE BOROUGH, WEDMORE, SOMERSET BS28 4EB
☎ (01934) 713663. OPEN 10 - 5 MON - SAT.
An upmarket dress agency selling nearly-new labels from Jaeger to Mondi, Viyella to Valentino. Whilst most of their range consists of designer labels, some better quality high street names are also available. This shop is renowned for brand new clearance stock, overmakes and sample sales. It has a large stock which turns over very quickly. They also stock belts, hats, handbags, jewellery and accessories. *Dress Agency*

CD & BOOK & VIDEO SELECTIONS
DORCHESTER, DORSET DT2 7YG

☎ (01305) 848725. MAIL ORDER ONLY.

CD, Book & Video Selections publishes their bargain selection of CDs, tapes, books and videos five times a year. Two editions are 56 or more pages; three editions are sale supplements. These full-colour guides offer a remarkable range of classical, opera, jazz, easy listening and popular CDs with prices starting at 99p. Overstocks, deletions and ongoing titles are selected for value for money. All sales are backed by a full refund guarantee. CD, Book & Video Selections also sells popular and general interest videos, and bargain books. They publish specialist catalogues for opera and jazz. All stock is now available at the internet site at www.cdselections.com. *Permanent Discount Outlet*

CURTAINS ENCORE
62 SALISBURY STREET, BLANDFORD FORUM, DORSET DT11 7PR

☎ (01258) 458871. OPEN 9.30 - 1.30 MON - SAT OR BY APPOINTMENT.

Quality new and secondhand curtains, lined and interlined, as well as headboards, tablecloths, bedspreads, stencils, blanks and decoupage materials. Also sells lined and interlined calico curtains for DIY patterning. Alteration service also available. *Secondhand Shop*

DAMART
ADELINE ROAD, OFF CHRISTCHURCH ROAD, BOSCOMBE, BOURNEMOUTH, DORSET

☎ (01202) 301627. OPEN 9 - 5 MON - SAT.

Damart underwear and merchandise - anything from tights, socks and gloves to dresses, coats, cardigans and jumpers - some of which is current stock sold at full price, some discontinued and ends of lines sold at discount. There several shops selling some discounted stock from the Damart range, known as Damart Extra. *Factory Shop*

DORSET RECLAMATION
COW DROVE, BERE REGIS, WAREHAM, DORSET BH20 7JZ

☎ (01929) 472200. OPEN 8 - 5 MON - FRI, 9 - 4 SAT

Bathroom fittings, fireplaces, stained glass, Dorset bricks, flagstones, quarry tiles, clay Peg and ridge tiles, doors, oak beams, reclaimed wood flooring, garden ornaments, chimney pots, and lead garden figures. Take business park exit off A31/A35 roundabout at Bere Regis. *Architectural Salvage*

FABRIC WAREHOUSE

50-52 COMMERCIAL ROAD, POOLE, DORSET BH14 OJT
☎ (01202) 740459. OPEN 9.30 - 5.30 MON - SAT.
58-60 BRIDGE STREET, CHRISTCHURCH, DORSET BH23 1EB
☎ (01202) 481188. OPEN 9.30 - 5.30 MON - SAT.
89 COMMERCIAL ROAD, POOLE, DORSET BH14 OJD
☎ (01202) 723544. OPEN 9.30 - 2 MON - SAT.
More than 900 different rolls of curtaining fabrics, all well-known brand names, from £4.50 to £14.50 a metre. Expert and friendly curtain making service using traditional methods. Foam and upholstery centre at 89 Commercial Road, Poole. *Permanent Discount Outlet*

GEMMA

422 LYMINGTON ROAD, HIGHCLIFFE, CHRISTCHURCH, DORSET BH23 5HE
☎ (01425) 276928. OPEN 10 -5 MON - SAT, 10 - 1 WED.
Stocks anything from Marks & Spencer to Ralph Lauren in sizes 8-20, with a wide range of shoes available. Childrenswear is also stocked up to the age of 8 and there is a separate play area for kids. Bargain rail of older stock sold at half-price; sales in the summer and after Christmas. Large range of hats, handbags, scarves and jewellery. *Dress Agency*

HANSONS FABRICS

STATION ROAD, STURMINSTER NEWTON, DORSET DT10 1BD
☎ (01258) 472698. OPEN 9 - 5.30 MON - SAT.
Fashion and curtaining fabric specialist which also sells sewing machines, haberdashery, craft items, patterns and knitting wools. It stocks all the well-known names and the full range of fabric weights. Lots of choice for wedding dress fabric: polyester, satin, silk dupion, taffeta, tulles, veiling and lining and plenty of bridal pattern books available. If you spend more than £25, you get a 5% discount; more than £125 and you receive a seven and a half percent discount; more than £250 and your discount is 10%. All leading makes of sewing machines, including Bernina and Brother, are very competitively priced and machines can also be repaired. Stocks specialist craft books and sells seasonal fabrics out of season. Sewing and craft workshops throughout the year - send for brochure. *Permanent Discount Outlet*

HYBURY CHINA

HIGHER FARM BARN, MILBORNE WICK, SHERBORNE, DORSET DT9 4PW
☎ (01963) 250500. FAX ☎ (01963) 250335. MAIL ORDER ONLY.
Sells pure white English bone china seconds, all from famous manufacturers. Brilliant value at very competitive prices. All items are dishwasher safe and

available delivered to your door by mail order. All the china is ideal for hand painting. There are several ranges which offer a wide selection of cups and saucers, plates, vegetable dishes, teapots, tureens etc.The china comes from major English companies prior to being stamped by the manufacturer. A perfect bone china dinner plate would normally cost £17-£35; Hybury offer their dinner plates from £4.50. The china is ideal for use at home or in restaurants, rented properties, B&Bs, boardrooms and offices. Call for a free brochure. *Permanent Discount Outlet*

LORI'S BOUTIQUE

MILLSTREAM CLOSE, EAST STREET, WIMBORNE, DORSET BH21 1DX
☎ (01202) 889575. open 10 - 5 MON, TUE, THUR, FRI, 10 - 1 WED, 10 - 4 SAT.
Quality high street names such as Country Casuals, Windsmoor, Jaeger as well as designer names, mostly German, such as Gerry Weber and Bianca. Also sell hats from £10 - £60 and competitively priced shoes, handbags and accessories. *Dress Agency*

LYME REGIS REMNANT SHOP

16 MARINE PARADE, THE COB, LYME REGIS, DORSET DT7 3JF
☎ (01297) 442706. OPEN 10 - 5 SEVEN DAYS A WEEK.
Packed full of ends of lines and seconds from famous name furnishing manufacturers. Lining, £2.20 a metre, upholstery fabrics, velvet, from £3.99 a metre for seconds. Curtain fabrics stocked include those from famous names such as Hardy, Sanderson, Derby House, Prestigious, Curtaina, Crowsons and many others. Fabrics start at £2.99 a yard or £3.20 a metre. *Permanent Discount Outlet*

MATALAN

UNITS 2/3, TURBARY RETAIL PARK, RINGWOOD ROAD, POOLE, DORSET BH12 3JJ
☎ (01202) 590686. OPEN 10 - 8 MON - FRI, 9 - 6 SAT, 10 - 4 SUN.
UNIT 2, JUBILEE RETAIL PARK, RADIPOLE DRIVE, WEYMOUTH DT4 7BG
☎ (01305) 331300. PHONE FOR OPENING TIMES.
Matalan is a fashion and homewares shop giving customers what they claim to be unbeatable value for money with huge savings on a wide range of products including high quality fashionable clothing for women, women and children at up to 50% off high street prices. Matalan is situated out of town and stores are open seven days a week all year round. *Permanent Discount Outlet*

MOORES BISCUITS FACTORY SHOP

MORCOMBELAKE, NEAR BRIDPORT, DORSET DT6 6ES

☎ (01297) 489253. OPEN 9 - 5 MON - FRI, 9 - 1 SAT (SUMMER ONLY).

Broken biscuits including shortbreads, walnut crunch, chocolate chip and ginger biscuits sold in 800 gram bags at 30% saving. Tend to sell out very early in the day, so don't leave your visit until late in the afternoon. There is also a small gallery of West Country paintings and bakery bygones. *Food and Drink Discounter*

PILKINGTON'S TILES FACTORY SHOP

BLANDFORD ROAD, HAMWORTHY, POOLE, DORSET BH15 4AR

☎ (01202) 675200. OPEN 8.30 - 5.30 MON -FRI, 8 ON THUR, 9 - 5 SAT, 10 - 4 SUN.

Sells seconds of the well-known Pilkington's bathroom and kitchen wall and floor tiles and DIY tiling equipment at discount prices of up to 75% off manufacturers' prices. Two hundred and fifty ranges of wall and floor tiles from which to choose. *Factory Shop*

POOLE POTTERY LTD

THE QUAY, POOLE, DORSET BH15 1RF

☎ (01202) 666200. FAX ☎ (01202) 682894. OPEN 9 - 5.30 MON - SAT, 10 - 5 SUN. PHONE FOR LATE OPENING SEASONAL TIMES.

The Poole Factory Shop is still the cheapest place to buy the widest selection of Poole Pottery. All the old favourite ranges such as Dorset Fruit, Vincent and Vineyard are joined by new exciting ranges like Fresco. The critically acclaimed new Living Glaze gift range which uses a glazing method pioneered at Poole nearly forty years ago is now also available. However, it has long since ceased to be just an outlet for Poole Pottery firsts and seconds, it now boasts some of the top brands in giftware such as Dartington and Stuart Crystal, Colony, Spiegelau, Candles and Edinburgh Woollen Mill and more recently, Julian Graves, Book Ends, Nauticalia, Nachtmann, Sia Parlane and home-made fudge. All these plus the new cook shop makes it the perfect place for the first-time housebuyer to buy practically all their home essentials - it is fast becoming the biggest gift shop in the South. Poole Pottery has recently undertaken an extensive site re-development responding to their own research which suggested that both parents and children prefer a separate area to paint plates, throw pots and learn the ancient skills of the potter. The activity area can now be found on a floor of its own offering more freedom and security. The Have-A-Go area has also increased in size from 3,000 sq ft to 6,000 sq ft. Glass blowing demonstrations are regularly held, and a tour of the superb museum together with the factory provides a stimulating and interesting experience. In addition you can enjoy an a la carte, table d'hote meal with fine wines and with unique harbour views at Carters restaurant, or opt for a light snack in the tea room or self-service area. *Factory Shop*

THE CATALOGUE SHOP

401 LYMINGTON ROAD, HIGHCLIFFE, DORSET BH25 5HE
☎ (01425) 271202. OPEN 9 - 5 MON - SAT, 10 - 5 SUN.

Returns, damaged and worn goods as well as clearance lines and ends of lines of branded merchandise from mail order catalogues. This includes men's, women's and children's wear, footwear, bedding, curtains, furniture, exercise equipment and leather coats. These items are always in stock in all four shops but each outlet also has an ever-changing range of items as well. Turnover is very fast with new deliveries every day. All items are sold at less than 50% of the catalogue price, starting at 99p. *Permanent Discount Outlet*

THE OLD MILL FACTORY SHOP

PYMORE MILLS, BRIDPORT, DORSET DT6 5PJ
☎ (01308) 420969. OPEN 9.30 - 4.30 TUE, WED, THUR, 9.30 - 6.30 FRI, 10 - 4 SAT. CLOSED BANK HOLIDAYS.

Traditional-style headboards and bedsteads, top quality handmade sofa beds and mattresses, designer fabric and period wooden furniture, slight seconds and discontinued lines of which are on sale at huge discounts. For example, French pine bed, £3,500 normally; on sale here at £700. The beds are a very well-known brand name, made for top quality stores. *Factory Shop*

TK MAXX

QUADRANT ARCADE, OLD CHRISTCHURCH ROAD, BOURNEMOUTH, DORSET BH1 2BX
☎ (01202) 316367. OPEN 9 - 5.30 MON - FRI, 9 - 6 SAT, 10 - 4 SUN, UNTIL 8 ON THUR.

Based on an American concept, TK Maxx is situated in easily accessible, often centrally located stores and offers famous label goods with up to 60% savings off recommended retail prices. TK Maxx has fashion for the whole family - women's, men's and childrenswear - accessories, shoes, gifts, kitchenware and home goods. Everything in the store is branded with a choice of well-known high street names to designer labels, and while a small percentage might be clearly marked past season, the great majority of items in store are current season, current stock and still with phenomenal savings. There is a huge choice with 50,000 pieces in store and up to 10,000 new items arriving a week. The stores are simple and unfussy with wide aisles, shopping trolleys and baskets, and a spacious, functional feel to them but there are individual changing rooms, ramps for buggies and wheelchairs and plenty of staff on the shop floor. Every branch accepts all major credit and debit cards and has a liberal refund and return policy. *Permanent Discount Outlet*

Essex

WOMENSWEAR ONLY ⌂ Leather for Less, *Saffron Waldon*. Switch Gear, *Buckhurst Hill*. The Z Collection, *Leigh-on-Sea*. Valrose, *Woodford Bridge*.

WOMENSWEAR & MENSWEAR ⌂ ⌂ Branded Stocks, *Laindon*. Charles Clinkard, *Clacton-on-Sea*. Choice Discount Stores Ltd, *Benfleet*. Clacton Common Factory Shopping Village, *Clacton-on-Sea*. Freeport Baintree Designer Outlet Village, *Essex*. Harwich factory Outlet Centre, *Harwich*. Matalan, *West Thurrock*. Matalan, *Chelmsford*. Matalan, *Colchester*. Matalan, *Crayford*. Matalan, *Southend*. Swaine, *Chesterford*. The Factory Shop, *Basildon*. The Factory Shop, *Rockford*. The Factory Shop Ltd, *Tiptree*. TK Maxx, *Ilford*. Tog 24, *Clacton-on-Sea*.

CHILDREN ⌂ Baby Direct Discount Warehouse, *Barking*. Charles Clinkard, *Clacton-on-Sea*. Choice Discount Stores Ltd, *Benfleet*. Clacton Common Factory Shopping Village, *Clacton-on-Sea*. Freeport Baintree Designer Outlet Village, *Essex*. Jokids, *Clacton-on-Sea*. Kids Collections, *Buckhurst Hill*. Kids Play Factory, *Clacton-on-Sea*. Matalan, *West Thurrock*. Matalan, *Chelmsford*. Matalan, *Colchester*. Matalan, *Crayford*. Matalan, *Southend*. Nippers, *Colchester*. The Factory Shop, *Basildon*. The Factory Shop, *Rockford*. The Factory Shop Ltd, *Tiptree*. TK Maxx, *Ilford*. Tog 24, *Clacton-on-Sea*. Valrose, *Woodford Bridge*.

HOUSEHOLD AND GIFTWARE ⌂ Clacton Common Factory Shopping Village, *Clacton-on-Sea*. Fairheads, *Ilford*. Freeport Baintree Designer Outlet Village, *Essex*. Matalan, *West Thurrock*. Matalan, *Chelmsford*. Matalan, *Colchester*. Matalan, *Crayford*. Matalan, *Southend*. Price's Candles, *Clacton-on-Sea*. Spoils, *West Thurrock*. Spoils, *Colchester*. Spoils, *Southend*. Spoils, *Romford*. Spoils, *Ilford*. Spoils, *Basildon*. Swaine, *Chesterford*. The Factory Shop, *Basildon*. The Factory Shop, *Rockford*. The Factory Shop Ltd, *Tiptree*. TK Maxx, *Ilford*.

ELECTRICAL EQUIPMENT ⌂ Clacton Common Factory Shopping Village, *Clacton-on-Sea*. Freeport Baintree Designer Outlet Village, *Essex*. Leigh Lighting Company, *Leigh-on-Sea*. Remington, *Clacton-on-Sea*. Stellisons Ltd, *Colchester*.

DIY/RENOVATION ⌂ Glynn Webb, *Colchester*.

FURNITURE/SOFT FURNISHINGS ⌂ Freeport Baintree Designer Outlet Village, *Essex*. Hubbinet Reproductions, *Romford*. Just Fabrics, *Maldon*. The Curtain Exchange, *Coggeshall*. The Fabric Factory, *Basildon*. The Factory Shop, *Basildon*. The Factory Shop, *Rockford*. The Lighting and Furniture Factory Shop, *Hastingwood, Nr Harlow*. The Remnant Shop, *Colchester*.

FOOD AND LEISURE ⌂ Baggage Depot, *Barking*. Brandler Galleries, *Brentwood*. Clacton Common Factory Shopping Village, *Clacton-on-Sea*. Freeport Baintree Designer Outlet Village, *Essex*. New Hall Vineyards, *Chelmsford*. Papworth Travel Goods Ltd, *Great Chesterford*. The Warehouse (Booksale) Co, *Maldon*. Thorntons, *Clacton-on-Sea*. Travel Accessory Outlet, *Clacton-on-Sea*.

SPORTSWEAR AND EQUIPMENT ⌂ Freeport Baintree Designer Outlet Village, *Essex*.

BABY DIRECT DISCOUNT WAREHOUSE
BABY DIRECT, CROMWELL CENTRE, RIVER ROAD, BARKING, ESSEX
☎ 0181-507 0572. OPEN 9.30 - 5.30 MON - SAT, 10 - 2 SUN.

Recently opened to the general public, having been trade only for several years, it sells baby goods including cots from £49.95; high chairs from £19.95; walkers from £19.95; gates from £16.95; playpens from £39.95; quilt sets from £9.95; cot beds from £139.95; travel cots from £54.95. All cots come with free mattresses. Baby Direct is a Mamas & Papas main stockist and offers sales, service and spares. Items can be paid in instalments *Permanent Discount Outlet*

BAGGAGE DEPOT
UNIT 32, VICARAGE FIELDS SHOPPING CENTRE, BARKING, ESSEX
lG11 8DH
☎ 0181-591 1961. OPEN 9 - 5.30 MON - SAT.

Luggage and travel-related products including executive cases, handbags, umbrellas and accessories available in leading brands such as Samsonite, Brics, Hidesign, Globe Trotter and Tula. The products also include couture and high fashion brands such as YSL and Moschino. All products are offered at a considerably reduced price due to their being production over-runs, last season's stock of slight seconds (ie they have minor aesthetic blemishes). *Permanent Discount Outlet*

BRANDED STOCKS
SHARP HOUSE, 2 3 ARTERIAL ROAD, LAINDON, ESSEX SS15 6DR
☎ (01268) 418000. OPEN 9 - 4.30 MON - SAT.

Men's and ladies casual wear from Thomas Burberry, Burberry, Versace, Armani, Ralph Lauren, Romeo Gigli, Diesel, Aquascutum, Moschino, Gucci, MaxMara Weekend, Jean Paul Gaultier, Iceberg and Calvin Klein.
Permanent Discount Outlet

BRANDLER GALLERIES
1 COPTFOLD ROAD, BRENTWOOD, ESSEX CM14 4BM
☎ (01277) 222269. OPEN 10 - 5.30 TUE - SAT. PHONE FIRST IF LOOKING FOR A PARTICULAR ITEM.

Prints, sculptures and paintings of a high standard at prices which reflect the low overheads outside London. Works by Diana Armfield, Bill Bowyer, Fred Cuming, Bernard Dunstan, Mary Fedden, David Tindle, Carel Weight, Andy Warhol, David Hockney, Picasso and others of a similar calibre. Prices range from £45-£20,000. A Turner watercolour was sold for £18,500 which would have cost as much as £75,000 in Bond Street. Also offer mirror frames and a mirror framing service; original book illustrations for Noddy, Postman Pat, Pugwash, Rupert etc. Can be found on the Internet at WWW.BRANDLER-GALLERIES.COM. E-mail is ArtBritish@Dial. Pipex.Com. Free car park. *Permanent Discount Outlet*

CHARLES CLINKARD

CLACTON COMMON FACTORY SHOPPING VILLAGE, STEPHENSON ROAD WEST, CLACTON ON SEA, ESSEX CO15 4TL
☎ (01255) 220384. OPEN 10 - 6 MON - SAT, 11 - 5 SUN.
Footwear for the family at discounts of between 20% and 50%. Labels on sale here include Rockport, Loake, Camel, Bally, Church's, Ecco, Gabor, Rohde, Van-Dal, Kickers, Clarks, Dr Martens, K Shoes, Lotus and Renata. *Factory Shopping Village*

CHOICE DISCOUNT STORES LIMITED

14-20 RECTORY ROAD, HADLEIGH, BENFLEET, ESSEX SS7 2ND
☎ (01702) 555245. OPEN 9 - 5.30 MON - THUR, 9 - 6 FRI, SAT.
26-28 HIGH STREET, BARKINGSIDE, ILFORD, ESSEX IG6 2DO
☎ 0181-551 2125. OPEN 9 - 5.30 MON - FRI, 9 - 6 SAT, 10 - 4 SUN.
10-11 LADYGATE CENTRE, HIGH STREET, WICKFORD, ESSEX SS12 9AK
☎ (01268) 764893. OPEN 9 - 5.30 MON - FRI, 9 - 6 SAT.
UNIT 6A, MAYFLOWER RETAIL PARK, GARDINERS LINK, BASILDON, ESSEX SS14 3AR
☎ (01268) 288331. OPEN 9 - 6 MON - SAT, 7 ON THUR, FRI, 11 - 5 SUN.
14-16 HIGH STREET, GRAYS, ESSEX RM17 6LV
☎ (01375) 385780. OPEN 9 - 5.30 MON - SAT.
CLACTON COMMON FACTORYSHOPPING VILLAGE
STEPHENSON ROAD WEST, CLACTON-ON-SEA, ESSEX CO15 4TL
☎ (01255) 430777
OPEN 10 - 6 MON - SAT, 11 - 5 SUN.
Surplus stock including women's, men's and children's fashions from Next plc, Next Directory and other high street fashion houses, Next Interiors and footwear. You can save up to 50% off normal retail prices for first quality; up to two thirds for seconds. There are no changing rooms but the shop offers refunds if goods are returned in perfect condition within 28 days. There are special sales each January and September. Easy access for wheelchairs and pushchairs. The Wickford store is known as Next 2 Choice. The telephone number for the Clacton Common outlet is for the centre, not the shop. *Permanent Discount Outlet*

Live Well On Less Tips
Don't pay for a professional babysitter. Organise a baby sitting circle with other parents instead. Exchange tokens according to the number of hours worked.

CLACTON COMMON FACTORY SHOPPING VILLAGE

STEPHENSON ROAD WEST, CLACTON-ON-SEA, ESSEX CO15 4TL

☎ (01255) 479595 INFORMATION OR

☎ (01255) 430777. OPEN 10 - 6 MON - SAT, 11 - 5 SUN.

Fifty units centred around a Victorian winter garden comprising the following: Bed & Bath Works, a homeware outlet with discounted branded linens and housewares from Janet Reger, Sheridan, Christy and Kingsley; Benetton selling men's, women's and children's casual wear; Jean Scene for men, women and children; Stefanel for younger women's fashion; Cotton Traders casual wear; Eye Zone fashion sunglasses and accessories; Braveoffer; Birthdays, stocking mainstream cards and gifts from manufacturers such as Andrew Brownsword, Disney, Parker, Galt and Warner Brothers; Catwalk Footwear; Choice, which sells family clothing from Next; Clinkards family footwear from Church's, Gabor, Bally and Loake; Cook & Dine kitchenware, glass and ceramics; Designer Room selling designer fashion from Christian Lacroix and Louis Feraud; Event fashion costume jewellery and watches from Accurist, Timberland, Seiko and Timex; Claire's Accessories; Greenwich Group (formerly known as Equator) with travel goods from Delsey and Samsonite; Jacques Vert selling ladies dresses, skirts, suits, blouses, hats, belts and scarves; Julian Graves foods and nut mixes; Honey, a manufacturer which supplies the major high street stores with women's knitwear and co-ordinated separates; Jane Shilton handbags, shoes, scarves and leathergoods; JD Sports selling branded sports merchandise from Adidas, Nike, Reebok, Ellesse and Le Coq Sportif; Joe Bloggs jeans and casualwear for men, women and children; Kids Play Factory with toys from ranges such as Fisher-Price and Lego; Leading Labels, with men's and women's fashions from Bruna Fashions, Gemini, Cote a Cote, Ben Sherman, Farah and Double Two; Massarella; Pilot, a young women's fashion outlet; Remington electrical and housewares; Suits You men's shirts, suits, and casual separates; Tog 24 outdoor and activity wear; Tom Sayer men's knitwear and co-ordinated separates; Thorntons; Windsmoor; and Woods of Windsor toiletries and gift items; XS Music CDs and videos. There are also be two restaurants, a tourist information centre, parking for 1,000 cars and a bus service link to Clacton town centre and railway station. *Factory Shopping Village*

FAIRHEADS

60-64 CRANBROOK ROAD, ILFORD, ESSEX IG1 4NQ

☎ 0181-4780328. OPEN 9 - 5.30 MON - SAT.

There are thirteen different departments at Fairheads, including household, linen, soft furnishings, lingerie, fashion, hosiery, craft and haberdashery. There are often 'blue ticket' specials where if, for example, you bought three pairs of

Sloggi briefs you get the fourth for free. Best quality stock at the lowest price possible and always special offers and reduced lines throughout the store. At sale time stock is half price or less. There are two genuine sales a year: after Christmas and at the end of June, telephone for details. *Permanent Discount Outlet*

FREEPORT BRAINTREE

DESIGNER OUTLET VILLAGE, ESSEX, FACTORY SHOPPING VILLAGE
OPENING OCTOBER 1999
With a direct rail link to London's Liverpool Street station and its own station, this new centre will have 70 different shops at the top end of the market including Versace. *Factory Shopping Village*

GLYNN WEBB

ST ANDREW AVENUE, COLCHESTER, ESSEX CO4 3BQ
☎ (01206) 798407. OPEN 9 - 8 MON - SAT, 10 - 4 SUN AND BANK HOLIDAYS.
Stockists of all your home improvement needs from wallpaper to paint, furniture to flooring, tiles to textiles, housewares to lighting - in fact, almost everything for your home, with 24 branches in the North-West, Midlands and Yorkshire. Specialists in discontinued mail order, slightly imperfect branded stocks as well as perfect quality superior products. They carry top brands such as Dulux, Crown Paints and Vymura and Coloroll wall coverings, Rectella and Norwood textiles and much more in store. Different branches carry different lines so if you want something specific, phone first. To find your nearest branch, phone 0161 621 4500. *Permanent Discount Outlet*

HARWICH FACTORY OUTLET CENTRE

HARWICH, ESSEX, DUE TO OPEN IN EASTER 2000.
Planned to open in Easter 2000, there will be forty-six factory shops offering end of season lines and overstock at discount prices. If you live locally, watch out for opening notices in the local press. *Factory Shopping Village*

HUBBINET REPRODUCTIONS

UNIT 7, HUBBINET INDUSTRIAL ESTATE, EASTERN AVENUE WEST, HAINAULT ROAD, ROMFORD, ESSEX RM7 7NU
☎ (01708) 762212. OPEN 9 - 5 MON - FRI, 10 - 4 SAT.
Manufacturers of reproduction furniture in mahogany and yew, all of which are sold in the factory shop at discounts of about 20%. Seconds in dining room suites, bookcases, video cabinets, display cabinets, desks, computer desks and cupboards at factory shop prices. Free parking and refreshments available. Staff are willing to take customers round the factory. *Factory Shop*

JOKIDS LTD

UNIT 37, CLACTON COMMON FACTORY SHOPPING VILLAGE,
CLACTON ON SEA, ESSEX CO16 9HB

☎ (01255) 421311. OPEN 10 - 6 MON - SAT, 11 - 5 SUN.

JoKids is the factory shop trading name for Jeffrey Ohrenstein which sells unusual and attractive clothes for children aged from birth to ten years. This includes pretty party dresses for girls at reductions of up to 40%, all-in-one smocked playsuits, T-shirts, denim shirts, denim dresses, sunhats, shorts, and accessories. *Factory Shopping Village*

JUST FABRICS

102 HIGH STREET, MALDON, ESSEX

☎ (01621) 852552. OPEN 9 - 5.30 MON - SAT.

Small fabric shop selling discounted fabric from dress material to net curtains, fleece, tapestry, curtaining, voile, cushion covers, toy making fabric, buttons, zips, tapes and a full range of haberdashery. If it's not end of line, it's always reasonably priced. For example, at time of writing, they had Sanderson fabric at £2.99 a sq yard, cotton satine at £1.99 a yard and fabric which would normally cost between £8 and £17.99 costs £2.99 here. *Dress Agency*

KIDS COLLECTIONS

176C QUEEN ROAD, BUCKHURST HILL, ESSEX IG9 5BD

☎ 0181-502 9600. OPEN 10 - 5.30 MON - SAT.

Nearly-new children's clothes. Labels on sale at about one third of the retail price include Kenzo, Portofino, Oilily, Chipie and Levi's and all are in excellent condition. There are also new shoes, high chairs and a range of First Holy Communion accessories for sale. *Dress Agency*

KIDS PLAY FACTORY

CLACTON COMMON FACTORY SHOPPING VILLAGE, STEPHENSON
ROAD WEST, CLACTON ON SEA, ESSEX CO15 4TL

☎ (01255) 222219. OPEN 10 - 6 MON - SAT, TILL 8 ON THUR, 11 - 5 SUN.

This shop sells a wide range of well-known children's brand names: Tomy, Matchbox, Lego, The First Years, Hasbro, Disney, Playskool, Mattel and Fisher-Price at discounts of up to 50%. They also stock a wide range of soft toys including TY Beanie Babies. *Factory Shopping Village*

LABELS FOR LESS

THE COCKPIT, EMSON CLOSE, SAFFRON WALDEN, ESSEX CB10 1H,

☎ (01799) 523533. OPEN 10 - 5.30 MON - FRI, 9.30 - 5.30 SAT.

Designer ladieswear, menswear and footwear including labels such as Calvin Klein, Ralph Lauren, Moschino, Versace, YSL, Timberland, Ton Sur Ton, Lacoste and Armani at discount prices. *Permanent Discount Outlet*

LEATHER FOR LESS

7 MARKET ROW, SAFFRON WALDEN, ESSEX

☎ (01799) 516711. OPEN 10 - 5.30 MON - SAT.

Leather bags, shoes, belts and hats at discount prices. *Factory Shop*

LEIGH LIGHTING COMPANY

1593 LONDON ROAD, LEIGH-ON-SEA, ESSEX SS9 2SG

☎ (01702) 477633/470112 FAX. OPEN 9 - 5 MON - FRI, 9 - 5.30 SAT.
MAIL ORDER.

Thousands of lighting fixtures at between 20-50% below normal retail prices. Selling to both the commercial and domestic market, they offer recessed lights, table lamps, chandeliers, wall lights and outdoor security lighting, all of which are bought direct from the manufacturer. They can supply virtually any lighting seen elsewhere at very competitive prices. Catalogues available for mail order. *Factory Shop*

MATALAN

UNIT 4B, THE TUNNEL ESTATE, WESTERN AVENUE, LAKESIDE RETAIL PARK, WEST THURROCK, ESSEX RM16 1HH

☎ (01708) 864350. OPEN 10 - 8 MON - FRI, 9.30 - 6 SAT, 11 - 5 SUN.

UNIT 4, RIVERSIDE RETAIL PARK, VICTORIA ROAD, CHELMSFORD, ESSEX EM2 6LL

☎ (01245) 348787. OPEN 10 - 8 MON - FRI, 9 - 6 SAT, 11 - 5 SUN.

UNIT E, COLCHESTER RETAIL PARK, SHEEPHEN ROAD, COLCHESTER CO3 3LE

NO TELEPHONE NUMBER AS WE WENT TO PRESS.

UNIT 3, TOWER RETAIL PARK, CRAYFORD, ESSEX

☎ (01322) 552140. PHONE FOR OPENING TIMES.

THE GREYHOUND RETAIL PARK, SUTTON ROAD, SOUTHEND, ESSEX SS2 5PY

☎ (01702) 466248. PHONE FOR OPENING TIMES.

Matalan is a fashion and homewares shop giving customers what they claim to be unbeatable value for money with huge savings on a wide range of products including high quality fashionable clothing for women, women and children at up to 50% off high street prices. Matalan is situated out of town and stores are open seven days a week all year round. *Permanent Discount Outlet*

NEW HALL VINEYARDS

CHELMSFORD ROAD, PURLEIGH, CHELMSFORD, ESSEX CM3 6PN

☎ (01621) 828343. OPEN 10 - 5 MON - FRI, 10 - 1.30 SAT, SUN.

Specialises in white wine - Muller, Bacchus, Huxelrebe and Chardonnay - on which it offers discounts of up to 10% depending on the quantities you buy.

There is an annual English wine festival on the weekend before August Bank Holiday and guided tours are available from May to September. Book in advance - phone for details. *Food and Drink Discounter*

NIPPERS

WHITES FARM, BURES ROAD, WHITE COLNE, COLCHESTER, ESSEX CO6 2QF

☎ (01787) 228000. FAX ☎ (01787) 228560.

Nippers, the nursery equipment and toy specialists, operate from previously redundant buildings in rural areas around the country. They offer easy parking, no queues and personal service. This is on top of competitive prices on prams, cots, pushchairs, car seats, outdoor play equipment and toys, some of which are new, some seconds or secondhand and some ends of lines. Prices are low because they avoid the high overheads of traditional retail outlets and also because the successful growth of a number of branches means they can now buy in bulk and negotiate good deals. Customers are invited to try out the merchandise while the children look at the animals, mostly sheep, chicken and pigs. Familiar brand names are on sale at all the branches, including Mamas & Papas, Britax, Maclaren and Bebe Confort, plus Fisher-Price and Little Tikes. You can try out the car seats in your car and there is usually a pram/pushchair repair service on site. *Permanent Discount Outlet*

PAPWORTH TRAVEL GOODS LTD

NURSERY ROAD, GREAT CHESTERFORD, ESSEX CB10 1QW

☎ (01799) 530 521. OPEN 10 - 5 MON, TUE, WED, FRI, SAT, 10 - 6 THUR.

Handmade business cases and luggage in leather and leather trim, all manufactured in their own factory. Goods offered for sale here are discontinued lines or seconds in briefcases, executive cases, folios, document cases, attache cases, suitcases, suit cariers, travel bags, holdalls, and small leather goods *Permanent Discount Outlet*

PRICE'S CANDLES

CLACTON COMMON OUTLET VILLAGE, CLACTON ON SEA, ESSEX

☎ (01255) 479595 (CENTRE INFORMATION LINE).

OPEN 10 - 6 MON - SAT, 11 - 5 SUN.

Everything sold in this shop are seconds, which may be discoloured or have a damaged pattern; discontinued sizes not available elsewhere; over-runs from the garden selection or dinner candles in old packaging that has now been replaced. There are church candles, lanterns, candles in pots and glass jars, star-shaped candles, floating candles, candlestick holders, serviettes, scented candles and garden torches. Some of the ceramic items are bought in. *Factory Shopping Village*

REMINGTON

CLACTON COMMON FACTORY SHOPPING VILLAGE, STEPHENSON
ROAD WEST, CLACTON-ON-SEA, ESSEX CO15 4TL
☎ (01255) 479922. OPEN 10 - 6 MON - SAT, 11 - 5 SUN.

Lots of famous names here from Oneida and Monogram cutlery to Braun,
Philips, Remington, Clairol, Wahl, Krups and Kenwood small kitchen equipment. There are usually hair, beauty and male grooming accessories as well as
kitchen equipment, all at reduced prices. A great place to buy gifts or replenish the kitchen equipment with combi stylers, turbo travel plus hairdryers, air
purifiers, liquidisers; food processors; batteries; clocks; and cutlery. Some of
the packaging may be damaged but the products are in perfect working order.
Factory Shopping Village

SPOILS

253-254 LAKESIDE SHOPPING CENTRE, WEST THURROCK, GRAYS,
ESSEX RM16 1ZQ
☎ (01708) 890298. OPEN 10 - 10 MON - FRI, 9 - 7.30 SAT, 11 - 5 SUN.
UNIT 21/22 CULVER STREET WEST, CULVER SQUARE, COLCHESTER,
ESSEX CO1 1PB
☎ (01206) 763411. OPEN 9 - 5.30 MON - SAT, 11 - 4 SUN.
145 HIGH STREET, SOUTHEND, ESSEX SS1 1LL
☎ (01702) 352733. OPEN 9 - 5.30 MON - SAT.
UNIT 22, LIBERTY 2, ROMFORD, ESSEX RM1 3EE
☎ (01708) 751413. OPEN 9 - 5.30 MON - SAT.
UNITS 85, 86 AND 87, THE EXCHANGE SHOPPING CENTRE, ILFORD,
ESSEX IG1 1AT
☎ 0181-514 5894. OPEN 9.30 - 6 MON - FRI, 8 ON WED, 9 - 6 SAT, 11 - 5
SUN.
82/84 EASTGATE CENTRE, BASILDON, ESSEX
☎ (01268) 520827. OPEN 9 - 5.30 MON - FRI, 9 - 6 SAT, 11 - 4.30 SUN.

General domestic glassware, non-stick bakeware, kitchen gadgets, ceramic
oven-to-tableware, textiles, cutting boards, aluminium non-stick cookware,
bakeware, plastic kitchenware, plastic storage, woodware, coffee pots/makers,
furniture, mirrors and picture frames. Rather than being discounted, all the
merchandise is very competitively priced - in fact, the company carry out
competitors' checks frequently in order to monitor pricing. With 38 branches, the company is able to buy in bulk and thus negotiate very good prices.
Factory Shopping Village

STELLISONS LTD

350 HARWICH ROAD, COLCHESTER, ESSEX

☎ (01206) 870674. OPEN 9 - 6 MON - SAT, 10 - 4 SUN.

Excellent display of electrical goods from television sets and videos to cookers, fridges, freezers, washing machines, tumble dryers which they claim to sell at prices which are lower than any other shop in Essex. Sell only mainstream brands. *Permanent Discount Outlet*

SWAINE ADENEY BRIGG

NURSERY ROAD, GREAT CHESTERFORD, ESSEX
CB10 1QW

☎ (01799) 531522. OPEN 10 - 5 MON - SAT, 10 - 6 THUR.

Clearance outlet for the main London shop at discounts of 30%-50%. Having recently doubled its size, it provides excellent value, selling men's and women's clothes, shirts, waistcoats, trousers, jackets, shoes, wallets, ties, leather goods, including Papworth leather goods, luggage and small gifts. The clothes ranges are a season behind the St James' Street shop and include samples, clothes which have been used in photo shoots and therefore cannot be sold as brand new, waxed coats and smart casual country clothing. Golfing umbrellas cost from £15 (there is also an umbrella repair service); cord trousers; wool sports jackets, £175 which normally retail at £315; briefcases from £195; Herbert Johnson hats; Grenson leather shoes; ladies linen jackets, £79, usually £225; waxed coats; wool and cashmere hooded cloaks; men's waistcoats, shooting jackets, leather wallets, walking sticks, shirts, trousers, sports jackets, and overnight bags, filofaxes, purses, photo frames, belts and walking sticks. There is plenty of parking. *Factory Shop*

SWITCH GEAR

160A QUEENS ROAD, BUCKHURST HILL, ESSEX IG9 5BD

☎ 0181-505 3113. OPEN 10 - 5 MON - SAT, CLOSED WED AND
1 - 2.15 DAILY.

Established for more than 20 years, the range covers nearly-new designer wear by Escada, Mondi, Ara and Lucia through to less high profile labels. Also shoes and an excellent range of hats. *Dress Agency*

THE CURTAIN EXCHANGE

11 MARKET HILL, COGGESHALL, ESSEX CO6 1TS

☎ (01376) 561199. OPEN 10 - 5 MON - SAT.

The Curtain Exchange is a franchised group of shops selling beautiful top quality secondhand curtains, blinds, pelmets, etc at between one-third and one half of the brand new price. Their stock comes from a variety of sources: people who are moving house and dislike the drapes in their new home; people who are moving house and want to sell their old curtains to help with the bills; show houses, where the builder wants to recoup some of his outgoings;

interior designers' mistakes. Stock changes constantly and ranges from rich brocades, damasks and velvets to chintzes, linens and cottons. Designer names include Colefax & Fowler, Designers Guild, Laura Ashley, Warner, Sanderson, Osborne & Little, Fortuny and Bennison. A team of fitters and alteration experts are available if required. They offer a 24-hour availability. The Curtain Exchange also supply bespoke ranges with samples of curtains hanging. These fabrics are chosen from suppliers all over the world and are an excellent buy. *Secondhand Shop*

THE FABRIC FACTORY

33-35 EAST WALK, BASILDON, ESSEX CM9 5ET

☎ (01268) 521887. OPEN 9 - 5.30 MON - SAT.

The Fabric Factory sells dress and furnishing fabrics at discounted prices. All stock is regular, not ends of lines, and they also sell tracks, poles, and offer a made-to-measure service. *Permanent Discount Outlet*

THE FACTORY SHOP (ESSEX) LTD

THE GLOUCESTERS, LUCKYN LANE, PIPPS HILL INDUSTRIAL ESTATE, BASILDON, ESSEX SS14 3AX

☎ (01268) 520446. OPEN 9 - 5.30 MON - SAT, 10 - 5 SUN.

PURDEY'S INDUSTRIAL ESTATE, 1 MAGNOLIA WAY, ROCKFORD, ESSEX SS4 1ND

☎ (01702) 531153. OPEN 9 - 6 MON - SAT, 10 - 5 SUN.

No-frills factory shop selling seconds, discontinued lines and some perfect current stock from department and chain store high street names, as well as direct from the manufacturer. This is not the place to look for high fashion, but it has an enormous amount of middle-of-the-range men's, women's and children's clothes, as well as bedlinen, towels, toys, food, kitchen utensils, disposable cutlery and partyware, short-dated food, garden furniture, tools, sportswear, china, glass and barbecues within its 8,000 square feet of selling space. Everything is sold at between 30% and 50% of the retail price. Parking is easy, the M25 is near and there's good wheelchair/pushchair access. *Factory Shop*

THE FACTORY SHOP LTD

THE CROSS ROADS, KELVEDON ROAD, TIPTREE, ESSEX CO5 OLJ

☎ (01621) 817662. OPEN 9 - 5.30 MON - SAT, 10 - 4 SUN.

High street chainstore seconds and ends of ranges from clothes for all the family, bedding, toiletries, kitchenware, glassware, footwear, lighting, cosmetics, jewellery, and luggage at discounts of approximately 30%-50%. There are weekly deliveries and brands include many major stars: Wrangler, Nike, Adidas and Dartington, to name just four. Lines are continually changing and few factory shops offer such a variety under one roof. There are furniture displays and a new line of Cape Country Furniture is now on sale. This high quality pine furniture made exclusively for The Factory Shop in South Africa is sold at factory direct prices with home delivery throughout the UK. Colour brochure and price list available. This branch has its own free car park. *Factory Shop*

THE LIGHTING AND
FURNITURE FACTORY SHOP

UNIT 1, HASTINGWOOD ROAD, HASTINGWOOD, NEAR HARLOW, ESSEX CM17 9JH
☎ (01279) 413466. OPEN 10 - 4 MON, TUE, FRI, SAT, SUN.
FURNITURE ☎ (01279) 431152. OPEN 10 - 1 FRI, 10 - 4 SAT, SUN.

Outdoor lights, lamps, chandeliers, bulbs, lamp bases, shades, all at factory shop prices. Also makes lamp bases and fabric shades. Next door is a factory manufacturing furniture, so this factory shop also sells reproduction and pine furniture from its neighbour. The next door shop makes and sells small reproduction pieces in mahogany and beech including magazine rack tables, hall tables, desks, computer desks, small bookcases, hi-fi and video units, and bureaux. It also buys in larger repro pieces. *Factory Shop*

THE REMNANT SHOP

12 - 14 HEAD STREET, COLCHESTER, ESSEX CO1 1NY
☎ (01206) 763432. OPEN 9 - 5.30 MON - SAT.
Although not strictly a discount fabric shop, they sell cut-price ends of rolls and remnants in curtain materials, dressmaking fabrics (satins, silks, dupions, polyesters) and patterns. They always have a good range of curtain fabrics and hold thousands of rolls of fabric in stock. But lines change constantly so you might not always find something to suit. *Permanent Discount Outlet* .

THE WAREHOUSE (BOOKSALE) COMPANY

EDWARD'S WALK, MALDON, ESSEX
☎ (01621) 841292. OPEN 9 - 5 MON - SAT, CLOSES 1 ON WED.
Hardback books at exceedingly cheap prices. For example, novels that normally cost £17 at £2; big format gardening books that normally cost £30 at £5. Most of the stock is priced at £2. *Permanent Discount Outlet*

THE Z COLLECTION

120 ELM ROAD, LEIGH-ON-SEA, ESSEX SS9 1SQ
☎ (01702) 480505. OPEN 9.30 - 1 WED - SAT.
As manufacturers of top quality ladies clothes, which are sold only in this retail showroom, prices are extremely competitive as there is no wholesaler to add his margin. Wide range of womenswear from dresses, jackets and tops to skirts, shorts and blouses - everything except swimwear, nightwear and coats. The garments tend to be more dressy than casual. *Factory Shop*

THORNTONS

CLACTON COMMON FACTORY VILLAGE, CLACTON ON SEA, ESSEX
CO16 9HB

☎ (01255) 220527. OPEN 10 - 6 MON - SAT, 11 - 5 SUN.

The UK's leading specialist confectionery retailer has more than 500 shops
and franchises nationwide selling a wide range of boxed and loose, chocolate
and sugar confectionery. The factory outlets sell three different categories:
misshapes. discounted lines and standard lines. Misshapes are loose chocolates
which are the result of new product development, product trials or end of production runs which cannot be packed as Thorntons standard lines. They are
packed into assorted bags and offer a saving of 35%-55% over the recommended retail price of standard loose line products. Discounted lines are
excess to Thorntons' normal retail requirements and can be as a result of excess
seasonal or export stock, discontinued lines or packaging changes. These products, when available, are offered at a discount of 25%-50% over the standard
retail price. Standard lines from the full Thorntons range are also on sale at
normal prices. *Factory Shopping Village*

TK MAXX

THE EXCHANGE, ILFORD, ESSEX

☎ 0181-514 1288. OPEN 9.30 - 6 MON - FRI, 8 ON WED, 9 - 6 SAT,
11 - 5 SUN.

EASTGATE SHOPPING CENTRE, BASILDON, ESSEX

☎ (01268) 273604. OPEN 9 - 5.30 MON - FRI, 9 - 6 SAT, 11 - 5 SUN.

Based on an American concept, TK Maxx is situated in easily accessible, often
centrally located stores and offers famous label goods with up to 60% savings
off recommended retail prices. TK Maxx has fashion for the whole family -
women's, men's and childrenswear - accessories, shoes, gifts, kitchenware and
home goods. Everything in the store is branded with a choice of well-known
high street names to designer labels, and while a small percentage might be
clearly marked past season, the great majority of items in store are current season, current stock and still with phenomenal savings. There is a huge choice
with 50,000 pieces in store and up to 10,000 new items arriving a week. The
stores are simple and unfussy with wide aisles, shopping trolleys and baskets,
and a spacious, functional feel to them but there are individual changing
rooms, ramps for buggies and wheelchairs and plenty of staff on the shop
floor. Every branch accepts all major credit and debit cards and has a liberal
refund and return policy. *Permanent Discount Outlet*

TOG 24

UNIT 20, CLACTON COMMON FACTORY OUTLET, STEPHENSON
ROAD, CLACTON ON SEA, ESSEX CO15 4T1

☎ (01255) 435035. OPEN 10 - 6 MON - SAT, 11 - 5 SUN.

Tog 24 are the UK's fastest growing brand name in outdoor clothing and
leisurewear, with a total of three UK factories and 36 stores nationwide. They
utilise the world's finest performance fabrics including Gore-Tex, Polartec and
Burlington macs. Catering for all the family for all seasons, with cosy fleeces
and waterproofs for the winter, and trekking ranges, shorts and t-shirts for the
summer. With all prices at least 30% below the recommended retail price you
can afford to enter the Tog comfort zone. *Factory Shopping Village*

TRAVEL ACCESSORY OUTLET

UNIT 16, CLACTON COMMON OUTLET, STEVENSON ROAD,
CLACTON-ON-SEA, ESSEX CO15 4TL

☎ (01255) 221500. OPEN 10 -6 MON - SAT, 11 - 5 SUN.

Luggage and travel-related products including executive cases, handbags,
umbrellas and accessories available in leading brands such as Samsonite, Brics,
Hidesign, Globe Trotter and Tula. The products also include couture and high
fashion brands such as YSl and Moschino. All products are offered at a considerably reduced price due to their being production over-runs, last season's
stock of slight seconds (ie they have minor aesthetic blemishes). *Factory
Shopping Village*

VALROSE

610 CHIGWELL ROAD, WOODFORD BRIDGE, ESSEX 1G8 8AA

☎ 0181-506 1667. OPEN 9.30 - 5 TUE - SAT.

Valrose is a well-established dress agency dealing in women's and secondhand
children's clothes. Labels in the adult section include anything from high street
chainstore makes to Laura Ashley, Ouiset, Windsmoor, Next, Jaeger, Escada,
Valentino, Calvin Klein, Betty Barclay and Moschino. Labels in the children's
section include Oilily, Next and Gap. There is always plenty of stock available
and friendly, helpful staff. Clothing is sectioned into skirts, trousers, blouses,
jumpers, coats, swimwear, suits, bags, hats and shoes and then divided into
sizes. *Dress Agency*

Gloucestershire

WOMENSWEAR ONLY ⚘ Ancilla, *Cheltenham*. Castaway, *Moreton-in-Marsh*.
Chantilly, *Cheltenham*. Encore, *Cirencester*. Graceful Gowns, *Bristol*. Just Thoughts, *Tewkesbury*.
Magpie, *Cheltenham*. Penny Plain, *Cheltenham*. Rags to Riches, *Cirencester*. Revival, *Lechlade*.
Sequels, *Stow-on-the-Wold*. Stock Exchange, *Gloucester*. Toad Hall, *Cheltenham*.

MENSWEAR ONLY ⚘ Fox & Chave, *Bath*.

WOMENSWEAR & MENSWEAR ⚘ ⚘ Catalogue Bargain Shop, *Gloucester*.
Courtaulds, *Bristol*. Damart, *Gloucester*. Gerald Anthony Fashions, *Cirencester*.
Glenmatch, *Stow-on-the-Wold*. Just-In Ltd, *Winchcombe*. Matalan, *Bristol*. Matalan, *Cheltenham*.
Outlet Direct Ltd, *Cheltenham*. Primark, *Gloucester*. Second to None, *Bristol*.
The Continental Wardrobe, *Bristol*. The Edinburgh Woollen Mill, *Gloucester*.
The Factory Shop Ltd, *Stroud*. TK Maxx, *Bristol*. Top Marks, *Moreton-on-Marsh*. Woosters, *Cheltenham*.

CHILDREN ⚘ Catalogue Bargain Shop, *Gloucester*. Kids Stuff Mail Order, *Bristol*.
Matalan, *Bristol*. Matalan, *Cheltenham*. Outlet Direct Ltd, *Cheltenham*. Primark, *Gloucester*.
Second to None, *Bristol*. Small Talk Equipment Hire, *Cheltenham*. Stock Exchange, *Newent*.
The Factory Shop Ltd, *Stroud*. TK Maxx, *Bristol*. Top Marks, *Moreton-on-Marsh*.

HOUSEHOLD AND GIFTWARE ⚘ Catalogue Bargain Shop, *Gloucester*.
Crock Shop, *Stow-on-the-Wold*. Discount China, *Bourton-on-the-Water*.
Dunelm Mills Shop Ltd, *Gloucester*. English Country Pottery, *Wotton-under-Edge*.
Homes & Gardens Magazine, Spring Grand Sale, *Winchcombe*. Index, *Cheltenham*.
Kelsey Giftware Ltd, *Stonehouse*. Matalan, *Bristol*. Matalan, *Cheltenham*.
The Factory Shop Ltd, *Stroud*. TK Maxx, *Bristol*.

ELECTRICAL EQUIPMENT ⚘ Index, *Cheltenham*. Index, *Gloucester*.

DIY/RENOVATION ⚘ Au Temps Perdu, *Bristol*. Cox's Yard, *Moreton-in-Marsh*.
Marlborough Tiles, *Cheltenham*. Reclamation Services Ltd, *Painswick, Nr Stroud*.
The Original Architectural Antiques Co Ltd, *Cirencester*. Walcot Reclamation, *Bath*

ARCHITECTURAL SALVAGE ⚘ Au Temps Perdu, *Bristol*. Cox's Yard, *Moreton-in-Marsh*.
Reclamation Services Ltd, Painswick, *Nr Stroud*.
The Original Architectural Antiques Co Ltd, *Cirencester*. Walcot Reclamation, *Bath*.

FURNITURE/SOFT FURNISHINGS ⚘ Carpets of Worth Ltd, *Stroud*.
Cotswold Fabric Warehouse, *Cheltenham*. James Gaunt, *Gloucester*.
The Cape, *Cheltenham*. The Factory Shop Ltd, *Stroud*.

SPORTSWEAR AND EQUIPMENT ⚘ Mash, *Gloucester*. Outlet Direct Ltd, *Cheltenham*.

ANCILLA

15 LECKHAMPTON ROAD, CHELTENHAM, GLOUCESTERSHIRE

☎ (01242) 242799. OPEN 10 - 5 TUE, THUR, FRI, 10 - 1 WED, 10 - 1 SAT.
Wide selection of womenswear from casual to occasion wear; good range of
separates and acessories. Caters for ages 18-80 in sizes 8 - 20. Examples of
labels sold inclue Windsmoor, Planet, Paul Costelloe and Louis Feraud,
Armani, Jaeger. *Dress Agency*

AU TEMPS PERDU

28 - 30 MIDLAND ROAD, ST PHILIPS, BRISTOL, GLOUCESTERSHIRE
BS2 OYJ

☎ (0117) 9299143. OPEN 10 - 5 TUE - SAT.
General architectural salvage with French and English stock: bathroom fittings, fire surrounds, cooking ranges, door and furniture stripping, landscaping materials, paving, flagstones and Victorian fireplaces. *Architectural
Salvage*

CARPETS OF WORTH LTD

HAM MILLS, THRUPP, STROUD, GLOUCESTERSHIRE GL5 2BE

☎ (01453) 882421. OPEN 9.30 - 4.30 MON - FRI, CLOSED 1 - 2 DAILY, 9 -
1 SAT.
Manufactures Axminster weave carpets, ends of lines and slight seconds of
which are sold in their on-site factory shop at discounts of half price. They can
recommend a fitter and sell underlay at full price. *Factory Shop*

CASTAWAY

HIGH STREET, MORETON-IN-MARSH, GLOUCESTERSHIRE GL56 OAD

☎ (01608) 652683. OPEN 9.30 - 5.30 MON - SAT.
Sells suits, separates, evening wear, shoes and accessories by names such as
Monsoon and Laura Ashley, with some designer wear from labels such as
Mondi, Louis Feraud, Christian Dior and Mulberry. A rocking horse and a
selection of newspapers keeps the rest of the family entertained. *Dress
Agencies*

CATALOGUE BARGAIN SHOP

4-6 GROSVENOR HOUSE, STATION ROAD, GLOUCESTER,
GLOUCESTERSHIRE

☎ (01452) 308779. OPEN 9 - 5.30 MON - SAT, 10.30 - 4.30 SUN.
Catalogue Bargain Shop is a growing national chain of stores which obtains
the majority of its goods from mail order giants Great Universal and Kays, and
offers a range of clothing for all the family, a wide selection of shoes, bed linen,
beds, household goods, electrical equipment and hundreds of other catalogue
items at very competitive prices. For example, double bed, £99.99, wardrobes

and three-piece suites. The merchandise consists of ends of ranges and previous season's stock for which there is no longer storage space when the catalogues change. *Permanent Discount Outlet*

CHANTILLY

65 GREAT NORWOOD STREET, CHELTENHAM, GLOUCESTERSHIRE GL50 2BQ
☎ (01242) 512639. OPEN 10 - 4.45 TUE - SAT.
Medium-sized shop with up to 3,000 items on two floors including a selection of clothes perfect for a working wardrobe from Marks & Spencer, Next and Wallis to Monsoon and Jigsaw with some designer labels such as Windsmoor, Eastex and MaxMara. There are also shoes, handbags and jewellery. Examples of average prices include blouses, £12.99; jackets £28; skirts from £12-£14. Free parking. *Dress Agency*

COTSWOLD FABRIC WAREHOUSE

TEWKESBURY ROAD, CHELTENHAM, GLOUCESTERSHIRE GL51 9AH
☎ (01242) 255959. OPEN 9 - 5 MON - SAT, 10 - 4 SUN.
Huge range of well-known designer label furnishing fabric in very large premises. Fabrics start at £1.99 per metre. Beautiful Indian linen checks, bargain remnants at £1 per metre; as well as a selection of dress fabrics, curtain poles and accessories. Stock changes constantly so buy when you see.
Permanent Discount Outlet

COURTAULDS
BODYWEAR FACTORY SHOP

THE GARDEN FACTORY, SIGNAL ROAD, STAPLE HILL, BRISTOL, GLOUCESTERSHIRE BS16 5PG
☎ (0117) 975 5599. OPEN 1.15 - 3 FRI ONLY.
Lingerie seconds from the factory, mainly for women but with some men's underwear and a small children's selection. Briefs, camisoles, bodyshapers, swimwear, Y-front and vests. *Factory Shop*

COX'S YARD

10 FOSSE WAY BUSINESS CENTRE, MORETON IN MARSH, GLOUCESTERSHIRE GL56 9NQ
☎ (01608) 652505. OPEN 8.30 - 6 MON - SAT.
Architectural antiques, reclamation oak, pine, elm and pitch beams and boards. Can make traditional oak doors from reclaimed oak to your dimensions.
Architectural Salvage

CROCK SHOP

FOUNTAIN COURT, DIGBETH STREET, STOW ON THE WOLD,
GLOUCESTERSHIRE GL54 1BN

☎ (01451) 870340. OPEN 9.30 - 6 SEVEN DAYS A WEEK.

China, glass and cookware direct from the factories of the manufacturers of
Churchill, BhS, Wood and Sons and Portmeirion at discounts of up to 50%.
Permanent Discount Outlet

DAMART

LISTER BUILDINGS STATION ROAD, GLOUCESTER,
GLOUCESTERSHIRE

☎ (01452) 526510. OPEN 9.30 - 5 MON - SAT.

Damart underwear and merchandise - anything from tights, socks and gloves
to dresses, coats, cardigans and jumpers - some of which is current stock sold
at full price, some discontinued and ends of lines sold at discount. There are
several shops selling some discounted stock from the Damart range, known as
Damart Extra. *Factory Shop*

DISCOUNT CHINA

HIGH STREET, BOURTON-ON-THE-WATER, NEAR CHELTENHAM,
GLOUCESTERSHIRE GL54 2AP

☎ (01451) 820662. OPEN 10 - 5 SEVEN DAYS A WEEK.

Retailers of china and cookware direct from the factories of Staffordshire.
Supplies are sourced from different manufacturers so varies according to what
is available at the time, but includes china fancies, beakers, cookware, planters,
Portmerion cookware and dinner sets. *Permanent Discount Outlet*

DUNELM MILL SHOPS LTD

CARRIAGE BUILDINGS, BRUTON WAY, GLOUCESTER,
GLOUCESTERSHIRE GL1 1BZ

☎ (01452) 385063. OPEN 9 - 5 MON - SAT, 10.30 - 4.30 SUN,
UNTIL 5.30 ON FRI.

Part of a chain of shops based in the Midlands selling brand-name and chainstore curtains, masses of bedlinen, towels, wickerware, pictures and frames, all
at competitive prices. *Permanent Discount Outlet*

ENCORE

8 SWAN YARD, WEST MARKET PLACE, CIRENCESTER,
GLOUCESTERSHIRE GL7 2NH

☎ (01285) 885223. OPEN 10 - 4 MON - FRI, 10 - 5 SAT.

Using their celebrity and TV presenter contacts, the owners of this relatively
new dress agency sell top-name, up-to-date, hardly worn clothes at very reasonable prices. Current stock usually includes Armani, Alexon, Escada,
Maxmara, Joseph, Jaeger, Planet, Valentino, Amanda Wakeley as well as items

from smaller fashion chains such as Karen Millen, Jigsaw, Kookai, Hobbs, Warehouse, etc. *Dress Agency*

ENGLISH COUNTRY POTTERY

STATION ROAD, WICKWAR, WOTTON-UNDER-EDGE,
GLOUCESTERSHIRE GL12 8NB
☎ (01454) 299100. OPEN 9 - 4 MON - FRI. MAIL ORDER.
English Country Pottery has a factory shop on site just down the stairs from where the large range of pottery is made. Each pot is taken through eight traditional processes, before being handpainted and signed by the painters. Finally, the pattern is sealed under the glaze and fired, making it very durable: oven, dishwasher, microwave and freezer proof. Here, seconds and discontinued pottery from their own ranges are sold at half price or less. Some of the pottery has been made by special commission for department stores, galleries and mail order companies, some is wholesaled to the independent gift trade. Because of this, and the fact that they design and manufacture their own pottery, the variety of styles is very wide, resulting in a vibrant, individualistic and very English style of pottery. The designs include: Cats, New England which features farmyard animals, Home Sweet Home, Wild Olives, Zanzibar (featuring brightly coloured elephants), Cote d'Azur (a mediterranean pattern), Abstract, Dolby Cat, Fruit Tree Topiary, White House Farm and Cockerel. The range includes tableware, children's items, giftware and bathroom accessories. Crafts, in Bath, also sells seconds at discounted prices. Write or phone for a free brochure. *Factory Shop*

FOX & CHAVE

12 ROYAL CRESCENT, BATH, GLOUCESTERSHIRE BA1 2LR
(0800) 3897580. BY APPOINTMENT ONLY.
Fox & Chave, who are wholesalers of the largest Italian silk tie collection in the UK, have a showroom where the public can purchase from their complete range and receive a 50% discount on the recommended retail price. Phone for an appointment and a chance to pay just £10 for a hand-made Italian silk tie. *Factory Shop*

GERALD ANTHONY FASHIONS

1 WEST WAY, OFF CRICKLADE STREET, CIRENCESTER,
GLOUCESTERSHIRE GL7 1JA
☎ (01285) 656100. OPEN 9.30 - 5 MON - SAT.
Chainstore clothes for ladies and men at reduced prices. Discontinued lines and Grade A garments are reduced by about one third. There are skirts, trousers, socks, underwear, nightwear, sweaters, blouses, dressing gowns, shorts, T-shirts and swimwear. Primarily Marks & Spencers' merchandise (with labels removed), Principles, Next, BHS and well known brands. *Permanent Discount Outlet*

GLENMATCH

2 BREWERY YARD, SHEEP STREET, STOW-ON-THE-WOLD,
COTSWOLDS, GLOUCESTERSHIRE GL54 1AA

☎ (01451) 870840. OPEN 9.30 - 5.30 MON - SAT.

Glenmatch offers you the luxury of Scottish knitwear direct from the Scottish
Borders at prices which are approximately 30%-40% below normal retail
prices. You can choose from cashmere, cashmere/silk, merino and lambswool
for men and women. Also some trousers, gloves, scarves and handbags.
Factory Shop

GRACEFUL GOWNS

69 BELL HILL ROAD, ST GEORGE, BRISTOL, GLOUCESTERSHIRE BS5 7LY

☎ (0117) 9557166. OPEN 10.30 - 5 THUR, FRI, SAT OR BY
APPOINTMENT SEVEN DAYS A WEEK.

Wedding dresses, shoes, veils, head-dresses - dresses from £50 - £1,000; bridesmaids' dresses from £20-£150. Labels include Alfred Angelo, Dreammaker
and Moira Lee. Large selection of bridal headdresses and veils including Trudy
Lee and Richards. Nicholas House handmade veils made to order and alterations by hand. *Permanent Discount Outlet*

GRAND SALE

SUDELEY CASTLE, WINCHCOMBE, NEAR CHELTENHAM,
GLOUCESTERSHIRE, ORGANISER: ROBERT TORRANCE, PO BOX 427,
LONDON SW10 9QE.

☎ 0171-351 3088.

There are now three annual Grand Sales taking place countrywide selling middle and top end of the market items for the home and decorative accessories.
The Christmas Grand Sale in London, with over 120 different small companies selling their merchandise to the public, is the largest. This takes place in
mid-November each year. Quality is high and covers everything from dried
flowers to bath accessories, Amish quilts to silverware, wooden toys to hand-
painted kitchenware, often at discount because they are ends of lines. There is
a Spring Grand Sale at Sudeley Castle, Winchcombe, near Cheltenham, Glos,
usually at the end of April, beginning of May, and a Summer Grand Sale at
Ripley Castle, near Harrogate, North Yorkshire, in June, both of which feature
gardening equipment as well as decorative homes accessories. Write for more
information on booking tickets. *Designer Sale*

Live Well On Less Tips

Many women's magazines now have pages of freebies. Nip into a large
newsagents where you won't be spotted noting down the details, and then
send in your name and address and hope you strike lucky. The winners are
usually picked at random after a set closing date.

INDEX

THE PROMENADE, CHELTENHAM, GLOUCESTERSHIRE GL50 1LN
☎ (01242) 226674. OPEN 9 - 5.30 MON - SAT.
31-33 NORTHGATE STREET, GLOUCESTER
☎ (01452) 300357. OPEN 9 - 5.30 MON - SAT.
There are 12 'bargain zones' within Index stores countrywide selling catalogue clearance items from toys to electrical goods at discounts of 30%-70%. Ring 01242 226674 to find for your nearest department. *Permanent Discount Outlet*

JAMES GAUNT

33 SOUTHGATE STREET, GLOUCESTER, GLOUCESTERSHIRE GL1 1TX
☎ (01452) 311 709. OPEN 9 - 5.30 MON - SAT.
Specialist interior designers James Gaunt have a clearance fabric shop which also sells regular lines. It stocks labels such as Crowsons and Malabar. Curtain material costs from £1.99 to £30 per metre. A large selection of cotton and damask fabrics. Half price is the average discount but fabrics sold for, say £6 or £7, may well have been originally priced at £30. The emphasis is on designer stock at bargain prices. *Permanent Discount Outlet*

JUST THOUGHTS

56 CHURCH STREET, TEWKESBURY, GLOUCESTERSHIRE GL20 5RZ
☎ (01684) 293037. OPEN 10 - 5 TUE - FRI, 10 - 4 SAT, CLOSED 1.30 - 2.30 DAILY.
Wide selection of labels, mostly middle to upmarket with some high street and designer names. For example, Escada, Paul Costelloe, Frank Usher and Betty Barclay. A Jean Paul Gaultier worth £1,000 was sold for £350 and Escada normally sells for £50 - £75. Situated opposite Tewkesbury Abbey, it's a small shop on one level. *Dress Agency*

JUST-IN LIMITED

2 HAILES STREET, WINCHCOMBE, GLOUCESTERSHIRE GL54 5HU
☎ (01242) 603204. OPEN 10 - 5.30 MON - SAT, 12 - 5 SUN.
21 ST JOHNS AVENUE, CHURCHDOWN, GLOUCESTERSHIRE GL3 2DG
☎ (01452) 530530. OPEN 10 - 5 MON - SAT.
Both branches sell quality fashion seconds, continental designer wear, a range of nearly-new clothes and incorporate Nightingales Ltd. The Churchdown shop is small but well stocked with a large car park. The Winchcombe branch is made up of three shops and also carries a large stock. The latter consists of anything from Marks & Spencer to designer labels and there is a new section of designer clothes, mostly German makes, in sizes 8-30. Alterations can be carried out on the premises. Wax jackets are sold from the Oxford range from £25-£85 and there is an evening dress hire service for men and women. Accessories such as handbags, jewellery, scarves and hats are also stocked *Dress Agency and Hire Shops*

KELSEY GIFTWARE LTD

OLDENDS LANE INDUSTRIAL ESTATE, STONEHOUSE,
GLOUCESTERSHIRE GL10 3RQ

☎ (01453) 824482. OPEN 9 - 4 MON - THUR, 9 - 3 FRI.

Tiny shop attached to the factory that makes the placemats, trays, coasters, glass boards and chopping boards. Stock varies, depending on whether there are any overmakes, cancelled orders, seconds or discontinued lines. Prices are extremely good: from 50p for small chopping boards with slight mistakes; £4.99 for huge chopping boards. Most items are under £5. *Factory Shop*

KIDS' STUFF MAIL ORDER LTD

10 HENSMANS HILL, CLIFTON, BRISTOL, GLOUCESTERSHIRE BS8 4PE

☎ (0117) 970 6095. OPEN 9 - 5 MON - FRI, 9.30 - 5.30 SAT.

In operation for over 20 years, Kids' Stuff sells high quality children's clothes (no coats), almost all of which are 100% cotton, for ages one to 12-years. Sited under the factory where the clothes are made, the factory shop sells over-runs, discontinued lines and ex-catalogue items at up to 50% discount, also clothing from current ranges. Phone for a mail order catalogue. *Factory Shop*

MAGPIE

41 LYFIELD ROAD WEST, CHARLTON KINGS, CHELTENHAM,
GLOUCESTERSHIRE GL53 AT2

☎ (01242) 573909. OPEN 10 - 5 MON - FRI AND 10 - 3 SAT.

A dress agency with three rooms selling a good selection of designer wear and high street names. A good selection of handbags, hats and shoes. *Dress Agency*

MARLBOROUGH TILES

14 MONTPELLIER STREET, CHELTENHAM, GLOUCESTERSHIRE
GL50 1SX

☎ (01242) 224870. OPEN 9.30 - 5, MON - SAT.

Wall and floor tiles from Marlborough and other top quality, specialist manufacturers. Seconds come mostly from Marlborough's own factory with discounts of up to 50% on first quality prices. *Permanent Discount Outlet*

Live Well On Less Tips

When having your first baby, don't buy anything until after the birth when your friends have all visited. They're bound to bring presents of clothes which will simply duplicate those you would already have bought.

MASH

INNSWORTH TECHNOLOGY PARK, INNSWORTH LANE, GLOUCESTER, GLOUCESTERSHIRE GL3 1DL

☎ (01452) 730577. OPEN 8.30 - 5.30 MON - FRI, 8.30 - 5 SAT, 10 - 4 SUN, BANK HOLIDAYS.

Warehouse/shop carrying an extensive range of backpacking and camping equipment, outdoor clothing, tools and government surplus stock at discount prices. *Secondhand Shop*

MATALAN

UNIT 1, ALDERMOOR WAY, LONGWELL GREEN, BRISTOL, GLOUCESTERSHIRE BS15 7AD

☎ (0117) 935 2828. OPEN 10 - 8 MON - FRI, 9 - 6 SAT, 11 - 5 SUN.

UNITS A1/A2, GALLAGHER RETAIL PARK, TEWKESBURY ROAD, CHELTENHAM, GLOUCESTERSHIRE GL51 9RR

☎ (01242) 254001. OPEN 10 - 8 MON - FRI, 9 - 6 SAT, 11 - 5 SUN.

UNIT 1, ABBEY RETAIL PARK, STATION ROAD, FILTON, BRISTOL BS12 7JW

☎ (0117) 974 8000. OPEN 10 - 8 MON - FRI, 9 - 6 SAT, 11 - 5 SUN.

Matalan is a fashion and homewares shop giving customers what they claim to be unbeatable value for money with huge savings on a wide range of products including high quality fashionable clothing for women, women and children at up to 50% off high street prices. Matalan is situated out of town and stores are open seven days a week all year round. *Permanent Discount Outlet*

OUTLET DIRECT LTD

ADMAIL 2116, CHELTENHAM, GLOUCESTERSHIRE G;50 4BB

0845 12 688538 ORDER LINE. MAIL ORDER ONLY.

Discount sports and designer wear catalogue selling names such as Umbro, Timberland, Tommy Hilfiger, Adidas, Calvin Klein, Kappa for men, women and children. The range is all casual and sports wear and includes T-shirts, sweatshirts, tracksuits, trainers, shorts, sports watches, caps, holdalls, rucksacks, socks, swimming costumes, casual shoes, golf bags, all at discount prices. All items are marked with the recommended retail price and the discounted price. Free delivery on orders over £75, otherwise, £3.50. *Permanent Discount Outlet*

PENNY PLAIN

2 QUEENS CIRCUS, MONTPELLIER, CHELTENHAM, GLOUCESTERSHIRE GL50 1RX

☎ (01242) 571901. OPEN 9 - 5 MON - SAT.

Permanent sale shop in the lower ground floor of their full-price shop selling overstock from previous seasons' collections along with some designer samples and slight seconds. *Permanent Discount Outlet*

PRIMARK
53 EASTGATE STREET, GLOUCESTER, GLOUCESTERSHIRE GL1 1NN
☎ (01452) 424 174. OPEN 9 - 5.30 MON - SAT, 10 - 4 SUN.
Not a discount shop as such, but with extremely low prices, Primark sells women's, men's and childrenswear, eveningwear, swimwear, lingerie, hosiery, shoes and accessories. *Permanent Discount Outlet*

RAGS TO RICHES
7 GOSDITCH STREET, CIRENCESTER, GLOUCESTERSHIRE GL7 2AG
☎ (01285) 656864. OPEN 10 - 5 MON - SAT.
Sells a mixture of high street and designer labels; featuring Paul Costelloe, MaxMara and Nicole Farhi, among other leading labels. Also sells accessories. *Dress Agency*

RECLAMATION SERVICES LTD
CATBRAIN QUARRY, PAINSWICK BEACON, PAINSWICK, NEAR STROUD, GLOUCESTERSHIRE GL6 6SU
☎ (01452) 814064. FAX ☎ (01452) 813634. OPEN 8 - 5 MON - FRI, 8.30 - 3 SAT.
Antique statuary, chimney pieces, fireplaces, oak panelled rooms doors, columns, arches, cornice, pediments, porches, mullions, capitals, gargoyles, sundials, troughs, staddlestones, coping, ridge, stone tiles, quarry tiles, stone walling, flagstones, setts, bricks, floorboards, building stone, woodstrip, pine beams, boarding, baths, basins and taps. Specialists in hardwood floors. *Architectural Salvage*

REVIVAL
BURFORD STREET, LECHLADE, GLOUCESTERSHIRE GL7 3AP
☎ (01367) 253803. OPEN 10 - 5 MON - SAT, CLOSED 1 - 2 DAILY.
Revival sells blouses, dresses, trousers, skirts, shoes, wedding outfits, some evening wear, and jewellery. Sizes range from 8-20. There are also hats, shoes, scarves, handbags. Labels include MaxMara, Jaeger, Jacques Vert and Marks & Spencer. *Dress Agency*

SECOND TO NONE
61 HENLEAZE ROAD, HENLEAZE, BRISTOL, GLOUCESTERSHIRE BS9 3AW
☎ (0117) 962 1365. OPEN 9 - 5 MON - SAT.
792 FISHPONDS ROAD, FISHPONDS, BRISTOL BS16 3TE
☎ (0117) 965 9852. OPEN 9 - 5 MON - SAT.
2 SOMERSET SQUARE, NAILSEA, BRISTOL BS9 2EU
☎ (01275) 851333. OPEN 9 - 5 MON - SAT, SOME BANK HOLS.
42A HIGH STREET, KEYNSHAM, BRISTOL BS18 1DX

☎ (0117) 986 8627. OPEN 9 - 5 MON - SAT.
95 HENLEAZE ROAD, HENLEAZE, BRISTOL BS9
☎ (0117) 962 8354. OPEN 9 - 5 MON - SAT
Established in the South West for twenty-six years, this company has built a reputation for giving excellent customer service and for selling goods which are of a quality and value that are Second to None! This chain of shops specialise in selling famous chainstore and branded clearing lines, which includes surplus stocks of branded goods such as Gossard, Berlei, Zorbit, Naturana and many more. They stock a large range of ladies and children's and baby wear (including baby bedding and accessories), some menswear, and an extensive range of underwear and nightwear for all the family. You can save up to 75% off recommended retail prices and they offer a seven-day money back guarantee. The shop at 95 Henleaze Road caters for children only. *Permanent Discount Outlet*

SEQUELS

DIGBETH STREET, STOW ON THE WOLD, GLOUCESTERSHIRE GL54 1BN
☎ (01451) 870041. OPEN 10 - 5 MON - SAT, CLOSED 1 - 2 DAILY.
Designer clothes for day and evening from Marks & Spencer to Yves St Laurent. *Dress Agency*

SMALL TALK EQUIPMENT HIRE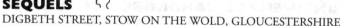

24 OLD BATH ROAD, CHELTENHAM, GLOUCESTERSHIRE GL53 9EQ
☎ (01242) 231231. FAX ☎ (01242) 231902.
Exciting inflatable play structures for parties and special events. New shapes include Nessie the Sea Monster - 40 feet of adventure - the first in the UK. Also Balloon Typhoons and Bouncy Castles. Cots, car seats, highchairs, buggies etc. In fact everything you need for kids. E-mail sheathers@zoo.co.uk. *Hire Shop*

STOCK EXCHANGE

14 CHURCH STREET, NEWENT, GLOUCESTER, GLOUCESTERSHIRE GL18 1PP
☎ (01531) 821681. OPEN 9 - 1 AND 2 - 5 MON, TUE, THUR, FRI, SAT, 9 - 1 WED.
Nearly-new shop stocking labels from Mondi to Marks & Spencer, Laura Ashley, Next, Wallis and Principles. Also childrenswear from babygros to clothes for 14-year-olds, family videos and books, curtains and jewellery. *Dress Agency*

Live Well On Less Tips
Make hand puppets from old socks. Sew on buttons and bits of wool for eyes and hair.

THE CAPE

25 REGENT ARCADE, CHELTENHAM, GLOUCESTERSHIRE GL50 1JZ

☎ (01242) 519021. OPEN 9 - 5.30 MON - FRI, 9 - 6 SAT, 11 - 5 SUN.

High quality, high density pine furniture made in South Africa from trees grown in managed forests, is sold at factory direct prices with home delivery throughout the UK. The range includes beds, wardrobes, blanket boxes, chests of drawers, tallboys, dressing tables, cheval mirrors, headboards, mattresses, a kitchen range, dining room tables, Welsh dressers, hi-fi units, bookcases. Also on sale in this shops is a range of African accessories and artefacts from Zimbabwe encompassing mirrors, prints, serpentine (stone) ornaments, recylced stationery, handmade wirework, candles and other ethnic and traditional gifts. Colour brochure and price list available on 01535 600483. *Factory Shop*

THE CONTINENTAL WARDROBE

13 REGENT STREET, CLIFTON VILLAGE, BRISTOL, GLOUCESTERSHIRE BS8 4HW

☎ (0468) 738116. OPEN 10 - 5.30 TUE - SAT.

Unusual dress agency in that the stock is sourced from the Continent, mainly from Germany. Labels such as Betty Barclay, Jil Sander and Gil Brett feature constantly and there is a good men's range of linen jackets, shirts and trousers as well as wonderful winter coats and raincoats. Also new evening wear and 50s, 60s, 70s as new evening wear. *Dress Agency*

THE EDINBURGH WOOLLEN MILL

MERCHANTS QUAY, DOCKYARD, GLOUCESTER, GLOUCESTERSHIRE GL1 2EH

☎ (01452) 300983. OPEN 10 - 5.30 MON - SAT, 11 - 5 SUN (10 - 5 MON - SAT, WINTER)

Edinburgh Woollen Mill factory outlet where overmakes and clearance stock are sold off. Wool sweaters and cardigans, two for £30; cotton sweaters, £12.95; waxed jackets, £34.95; Arran cardigans, £19.99. Follow signs for Historic Dockyard. *Permanent Discount Outlet*

THE FACTORY SHOP LTD

WESTWARD ROAD, CAINSCROSS, STROUD, GLOUCESTERSHIRE GL5 4JE

☎ (01453) 756655. OPEN 9 - 5 MON - THUR, SAT, 9 - 6 FRI, 10 - 4 SUN.

Wide range on sale includes men's, ladies and children's clothing and footwear; household textiles, toiletries, hardware, luggage, lighting and bedding, most of which are chainstore and high street brands at discounts of approximately 30%-50%. There are weekly deliveries and brands include many major stars such as Adidas, Nike, Wrangler and Dartington, to name just four. Lines are continually changing and few factory shops offer such a variety under one roof. This branch also displays furniture and sells the Cape Country Furniture range. This high quality pine furniture made exclusively for The Factory Shop in South Africa is sold at factory direct prices with home delivery throughout the UK. Colour brochure and price list available. It also has its own free car park. *Factory Shop*

THE ORIGINAL
ARCHITECTURAL ANTIQUES CO LTD

22 ELLIOT ROAD, LOVE LANE INDUSTRIAL ESTATE, CIRENCESTER, GLOUCESTERSHIRE GL7 1YS

☎ (01285) 653532. OPEN 9 - 5 MON - SAT, 10 - 4 SUN.

Internal architectural reclamation including period fireplaces and doors, floor tiles, chairs, doors, baths, beams, beds, busts, fire surrounds, kitchen ranges, marble fireplaces, mirrors, oak floorboards, objets d'art, painting, pews, prints, radiators, shutters, sinks, stained glass, taps, towel rails. Also gardenware, including stone troughs, flagstones, stone artefacts, sundials, terracotta pots, weather vanes, windowns, wrought ironwork, gates, lead cisterns and many other one-off architectural features. *Architectural Salvage*

THE REALLY GOOD DEAL FASHION SALE

SUDELEY CASTLE, WINCHCOMBE, NEAR CHELTENHAM, GLOUCESTERSHIRE

☎ (01367) 860017 TICKET ENQUIRIES. OPEN 10 - 6, FRI 13TH & SAT 14TH OCTOBER 2000.

One of six countrywide fashion sales run by the team behind The Good Deal Directory. Each one features between 50 and 90 top quality fashion houses and well-known brand names selling their ends of lines, discounted stock and last season's merchandise at discount prices. Exhibitors usually include top catwalk names, middle market companies, some retailers clearing excess stock, a few manufacturers and and some entrepreneurs selling top Continental designer names. There are clothes for all occasions, knitwear, scarves, shawls, pashmina, shoes, jewellery, some gifts, a few childrenswear companies, and some men's gift fashion lines such as ties and shirts. Quality is middle to upper market, aimed at 25-50 year olds. *Designer Sale*

TK MAXX

THIRD FLOOR, THE GALLERIES, BRISTOL, GLOUCESTERSHIRE
BS1 3XE
☎ (0117) 930 4404. OPEN 9 - 5.30 MON - SAT, 11 - 5 SUN,
UNTIL 7 ON THUR.
REGENT ARCADE SHOPPING CENTRE, CHELTENHAM
☎ (01242) 513848. OPEN 9 - 5.30 MON - WED, 9 - 8 THUR, 9 - 6 FRI, SAT,
11 - 5 SUN.
Based on an American concept, TK Maxx is situated in easily accessible, often centrally located stores and offers famous label goods with up to 60% savings off recommended retail prices. TK Maxx has fashion for the whole family - women's, men's and childrenswear - accessories, shoes, gifts, kitchenware and home goods. Everything in the store is branded with a choice of well-known high street names to designer labels, and while a small percentage might be clearly marked past season, the great majority of items in store are current season, current stock and still with phenomenal savings. There is a huge choice with 50,000 pieces in store and up to 10,000 new items arriving a week. The stores are simple and unfussy with wide aisles, shopping trolleys and baskets, and a spacious, functional feel to them but there are individual changing rooms, ramps for buggies and wheelchairs and plenty of staff on the shop floor. Every branch accepts all major credit and debit cards and has a liberal refund and return policy. *Permanent Discount Outlet*

TOAD HALL: THE DRESS AGENCY

7 ROTUNDA TERRACE, MONTPELLIER, CHELTENHAM,
GLOUCESTERSHIRE GL50 1SW
☎ (01242) 255214. OPEN 9 - 5.30 MON - SAT.
Large shop with two floors, almost exclusively filled with designer names. This is a top quality shop: Emporio Armani, MaxMara, Chanel, Givenchy, Caroline Charles, Escada and Nicole Farhi. The ground floor is devoted to daywear and there's lots of it well set out and presented. Suits, jackets, trousers, blouses, bags, hats, sweaters, cardigans. Downstairs is an extensive range of evening wear including evening wraps and coats, plus day coats and jackets and a good range of shoes. Toad Hall has recently been extensively refurbished, adding extra changing rooms and display areas. Situated in fashionable Montpellier, it has free parking facilities. *Dress Agency*

TOP MARKS

23 HIGH STREET, MORETON-IN-MARSH, GLOUCESTERSHIRE
GL56 0AF
☎ (01608) 651272. OPEN 9 - 5.30 MON - FRI, 9 - 5 SAT.
Sells seconds from leading chain stores for all the family. Most of the stock is made up of men's and women's wear, with some childrenswear. The clothes are mainly Marks & Spencer seconds, sold at about one third cheaper than in the

high street. wide range of stock in various sizes with new stock arriving twice a week. They also stock Debenhams' and Richards' stock when available. There are other branches at Banbury and Chipping Norton in Oxfordshire. *Permanent Discount Outlet*

WALCOT RECLAMATION

108 WALCOT STREET, BATH, GLOUCESTERSHIRE BA1 5BG

☎ (01225) 444404. OPEN 8.30 - 5.30 MON - FRI, 9 - 5 SAT.

Ideas and advice for the period house owner. Everything from panelling to paving, doors, flagstones, flooring, bathroom fittings, fireplaces, radiators, garden ornaments, railings and gates. High quality replicas also available from The Repro Shop. Stone carving, wood and metal-working restoration workshops on site. *Architectural Salvage*

WOOSTERS & CO

2 BATH ROAD, OFF HIGH STREET, CHELTENHAM, GLOUCESTERSHIRE GL53 7HA

☎ (01242) 256855. OPEN 10 - 5 MON - SAT.

Busy shop in town centre location with a brisk turnover so there's always something new to see. One of the very few in the area which also sells men's nearly-new, which has resulted in Woosters cornering the market in the good quality clothes. Ground level packed with very stylish ladieswear, with an excellent selection of designer labels such as Nicole Farhi, Armani, Mulberry etc, plus accessories to complement any outfit. The lower ground floor houses good quality menswear, country tweeds, business and dinner suits with designer labels such as Boss, Paul Smith and many more. Friendly atmosphere in which to browse, with expert advice if needed. *Dress Agency*

Live Well On Less Tips

Buy baby equipment such as prams, pushchairs and car seats in late October. These are all fashion items. That means the cover fabric design gets replaced every year. The big trade baby show with the new designs and colours happens at the beginning of October - after that, shops drop their prices on last year's ranges.

Hampshire

WOMENSWEAR ONLY Alexon Sale Shop, *Fleet.* Ancora Dress Agency, *Bournemouth.* Artigiano, *Isle of Wight.* Private Collection, *Fareham.* The Clothes Line, *Winchester.*

WOMENSWEAR & MENSWEAR Cameo of Cowes, *Isle of Wight.*
Gieves & Hawkes, *Portsmouth.* Gunwharf Quays, *Portsmouth.* James Meade Ltd, *Andover.*
Matalan, *Portsmouth.* Pret a Porter, *Ringwood.* The Catalogue Shop, *New Milton.*
The Catalogue Shop, *Romsey.* The Shoe Shed, *Bournemouth.* TK Maxx, *Southampton.*
Tog 24, *Southampton.* Whiteley Village, *Between Portsmouth and Southampton*

CHILDREN Gunwharf Quays, *Portsmouth.* Kids Play Factory, *Southampton.*
Matalan, *Portsmouth.* Pret a Porter, *Ringwood.* The Catalogue Shop, *New Milton.*
The Catalogue Shop, *Romsey.* The Shoe Shed, *Bournemouth.* TK Maxx, *Southampton.*
Tog 24, *Southampton.*

HOUSEHOLD AND GIFTWARE John Jenkins & Son Ltd, *Petersfield.*
Kenwood Services, *Havant.* Matalan, *Portsmouth.* Mountjoy Picture Frames, *Alton.*
Spoils, *Southampton.* The Catalogue Shop, *Romsey.* The Catalogue Shop, *New Milton.*
TK Maxx, *Southampton.*

ELECTRICAL EQUIPMENT Direct Electrical, *Fareham.*
Southern Domestic Electrical Services, *Southampton.*

DIY/RENOVATION Botley Bathroom Centre, *Botley.*
CJ Rogers Demolition & Salvage, *Southampton.* Romsey Reclamation, *Romsey.*
The Bathroom Warehouse Winchester Ltd, *Winnall.* The Malthouse, *Botley.*

ARCHITECTURAL SALVAGE CJ Rogers Demolition & Salvage, *Southampton.*
Romsey Reclamation, *Romsey.*

FURNITURE/SOFT FURNISHINGS Curtains Up, *Stockbridge.*
Freelance Fabrics, *Southampton.* Grandford Carpet Mills, *Fareham.*
Sue Foster Fabrics, *Emsworth.* The Catalogue Shop, *Romsey.* The Catalogue Shop, *New Milton.*
Westhouse Textiles, *Portsmouth.*

SPORTSWEAR AND EQUIPMENT Cameo, *Isle of Wight.* Pret a Porter, *Ringwood.*

ALDERSHOT GALLERIES

ALDERSHOT TOWN CENTRE, HAMPSHIRE
NO TELEPHONE NUMBER AS WE WENT TO PRESS.
Formerly a full-price town centre shopping mall, the Wellington Shopping Centre relaunches in October 1999 as a discount centre with shops such as TK Maxx, Bed & Bath Works, Suits You and Jeans Scene opening up outlets there. There will eventually be two levels, linked by a pedestrian bridge, with up to 31 discount shops and a cafe. ***Permanent Discount Outlet***

ALEXON SALE SHOP

HART SHOPPING CENTRE, FLEET, HAMPSHIRE

☎ (01252) 815055. OPEN 9 - 5.30 MON - SAT.

Alexon, Eastex, Ann Harvey and Calico from previous seasons at 40%-70% less than the original price; during sale time in January and June, the reductions are up to 70%. Stock includes separates, skirts, jackets, blouses. Current stock at 10%-40% discounts. *Permanent Discount Outlet*

ANCORA DRESS AGENCY

275 CHARMINSTER ROAD, BOURNEMOUTH, HAMPSHIRE BH8 9QJ

☎ (01202) 523848. OPEN 10 - 5.30 MON - SAT.

Top designer labels including Armani, Escada, Caroline Charles, Christian Dior, Versace, Christian Le Croix, Jaeger, Country Casuals, Viyella, Louis Feraud *Dress Agency*

ARTIGIANO

49 HIGH STREET, COWES, ISLE OF WIGHT, HAMPSHIRE PO31 7RR

☎ (01983) 297773. OPEN 10 - 4 MON - SAT, 10 - 1 WED.

Artigiano, the mail order company, has a shop which sells overstocks from the previous catalogues at discounted prices. Artigiano is known for its ladies fashion exclusively made in Italy. The beautiful and elegant outfits range from cool wool suits to angora sweaters and silk scarves. Available in sizes 10 - 26. *Permanent Discount Outlet*

BOTLEY BATHROOM CENTRE

THE MALTHOUSE, CHURCH LANE, BOTLEY, HAMPSHIRE SO30 2EJ

☎ (01489) 786272. OPEN 8.30 - 4.45 MON - SAT.

The ground floor houses a discontinued stock section, all at reduced prices, while the second floor houses the Botley Bathroom Centre, with more than 3,000 pieces of bathroom china, two-thirds of which are discontinued styles or colour. Most are well-known brand names: Shanks, Twyfords, Ideal Standard. Discontinued suites are sold at half price. Supplies come from Allders, B&Q and Wimpey house builders. The first floor is stacked high with household goods from floor polish to cups while another section at the side of the building sells diy equipment, screws, nails, worktops and bric a brac. *Permanent Discount Outlet*

CAMEO OF COWES

16 BATH ROAD, THE PARADE, COWES, ISLE OF WIGHT, HAMPSHIRE PO31 7QN

☎ (01983) 297907. OPEN 10 - 5 SEVEN DAYS A WEEK.

Buy and sell unclaimed lost property from British Airways, Royal Mail, London Transport and police departments. This can include anything from clothes and shoes to umbrellas and jewellery; make-up and perfume to purses and designer items. *Secondhand Shop*

CAMEO SPORT AND LEISURE

92 HIGH STREET, COWES, ISLE OF WIGHT, HAMPSHIRE PO31 7AW

☎ (01983) 297219. OPEN 10 - 5 SEVEN DAYS A WEEK.

Run by the son of the owner of Cameo of Cowes, this shop also specialises in buying and selling unclaimed lost property and bankrupt stock but with the emphasis on sportswear: tennis rackets, wet suits, surf boards and anything to do with sports generally. *Secondhand Shop*

C J ROGERS DEMOLITION AND SALVAGE

33 - 43 EMPRESS ROAD, BEVOIS VALLEY, PORTSWOOD, SOUTHAMPTON, HAMPSHIRE SO14 OJU

☎ (01703) 235777. OPEN 8 - 5.45 MON - FRI, 8 - 4 SAT.

Literally anything that can be salvaged from architectural demolition, including sheds, barns, gates and railings. Huge selection of timber as well as fireplaces, bricks and tiles. *Architectural Salvage*

CURTAIN UP

STONEFIELD PARK, MARTINS LANE, CHILBOLTON, STOCKBRIDGE, HAMPSHIRE SO20 6BL

☎ (01794) 341893. OPEN 2 - 5 MON, WED, THUR, 10 - 1 SAT, AND BY APPOINTMENT.

Now in its ninth year and in larger premises, this shops stocks an even greater choice of top quality and designer secondhand curtains at a fraction of their original cost. Names such as Colefax & Fowler, Designers Guild, GP & J Baker, Warners and Sanderson feature prominently. Stock changes constantly and there is a huge range of sizes and prices, from £20 for a small pair through to £400 for large, grand drapes. Alteration and making-up services are also available, as are a selection of bedspreads, cushions, circular cloths, lamps and tie-backs. Just off the A30, close to the village of Stockbridge; do phone for directions. *Secondhand Shop*

DIRECT ELECTRICAL

UNIT 2, FAREHAM ENTERPRISE CENTRE, NEWGATE LANE, FAREHAM, HAMPSHIRE

☎ (01329) 319999. OPEN 10 - 4 MON - THUR.

Small warehouse specialising in very competitively priced telephones, answerphones, mobile phones, television sets, music centres and faxes. For example, pay as you go Orange mobile phone £59 instead of £69; 28 inch Nicam stereo TV, £199; Philips 20 inch TV, £119. *Permanent Discount Outlet*

Live Well On Less Tips
Buy a universal child's car seat from Kwik Fit and if returned in good condition, £20 will be refunded in Kwik Fit vouchers (to be used within one year). Check Yellow Pages for your local supplier.

FREELANCE FABRICS
WEST KEY ROAD, (ADJACENT HONDA GARAGE), SOUTHAMPTON, HAMPSHIRE SO15 1GZ
☎ (01703) 336410. OPEN 9.30 - 5 MON - SAT, 10 - 4 SUN.
Part of a chain of shops selling well-known fabrics, curtain and upholstery weights, tracks, ready-made nets. Current fabrics are sold at reduced prices and there is a small range of end of line fabrics. For details of your local branch phone 01703 336410. *Permanent Discount Outlet*

GIEVES & HAWKES
22 THE HARD, PORTSMOUTH, HAMPSHIRE PO1 3DY
☎ (01705) 826648. OPEN 9.30 - 5 MON - FRI, 9 - 5 SAT.
This Savile Row retailer's clearance shop sells Gieves & Hawkes menswear at discounts of 60% - 70%. The shop also stocks new Gieves & Hawkes outfits at full price. For men, there is countrywear, suits, shirts, coats, socks, ties, shorts, pajamas and trilbys. Suits range from £195 upwards, depending on the season in which they originated; trousers from £30 - £49 for those normally costing £125; woollen blazers, £195, ties from £5, usually £30. Wide selection of sports jackets from £49, coats from £195, business shirts, £29, originally £69, raincoats from £195. The women's labels vary but have included in the past Austin Reed, Daks and Yarell and Aquascutum. *Factory Shop*

GRANDFORD CARPET MILLS
UNIT 11, BRIDGE INDUSTRIES, BROAD CUT, FAREHAM, HAMPSHIRE PO16 8ST
☎ (01329) 289612. FREEPHONE 0500 717124. OPEN 9 - 5 MON - FRI, 10 - 4 SAT.
Family-run factory shop which sells the majority of their carpets direct to the consumer. Good quality carpets at half the price you would pay in high street shops. The top price is £15.95 a square yard for carpet which you would pay at least £30 for in the high street. Seconds, which may be due to uneven dyeing, are £6.50 per square yard. Carpets can be dyed and made to customer's own colour requirements in 80/20 twist, minimum order 50 square yards. Measuring and fitting can be undertaken and underlay and accessories are available. *Factory Shop*

GUNWHARF QUAYS

PORTSMOUTH, HAMPSHIRE
NO TELEPHONE NUMBER OR OPENING HOURS AS WE WENT
TO PRESS.
Due to open in 2000, there are plans for 85 factory shops on this site next to
historic Portsmouth harbour, home to HMS Victory and the Mary Rose. As
well as the factory shops, there will be 20 restaurants, a craft market, a leisure
complex, a 14-screen cinema, bowling centre, comedy club, casino and 300
Berkeley homes. *Factory Shopping Village*

JAMES MEADE LTD

48 CHARLTON ROAD, ANDOVER, HAMPSHIRE SP10 3JL
☎ (01264) 387700. OPEN 9 - 5.30 MON - FRI.
Discontinued lines from the well-known mail order catalogues, James Meade
Ltd, Jake and Cashmere by James Meade, are available at discounted prices at
this factory shop. Classic clothing for men and women on display including
shirts, jackets, skirts, trousers, ties and knitwear. Items in the current catalogues can also be bought at normal prices - including Cashmere. Displays are
good and there are facilities for trying on clothes. Mention The Good Deal
Directory when shopping here. *Factory Shop*

JOHN JENKINS & SON LTD

NYEWOOD, ROGATE, PETERSFIELD, HAMPSHIRE GU31 5HZ
☎ (01730) 821811. OPEN 9.30 - 5 MON - SAT.
Factory shop situated next door to the factory selling cut crystal, plain glass
and porcelain. *Factory Shop*

KENWOOD SERVICE SHOP

NEW LANE, HAVANT, HAMPSHIRE PO9 2NH
☎ (01705) 476000. OPEN 9.15 - 3.45 MON - THUR, 9.15 - 11.45 FRI.
Wide range of Kenwood items from food processors, coffee makers and deep
fryers to kitchen scales, irons, can openers, water filters, juice extractors and
toasters at factory prices. This usually means 20%-25% off the normal retail
price. They are in perfect working order, but may be cosmetically slightly
imperfect or box damaged. All come with a one year's guarantee. On-site parking available. *Factory Shop*

KIDS PLAY FACTORY

WHITELEY VILLAGE, JUNCTION 10 OFF M27, SOUTHAMPTON,
HAMPSHIRE.
NO PHONE NUMBER AS WE WENT TO PRESS.
This shop sells a wide range of well-known children's brand names: Tomy,
Matchbox, Lego, The First Years, Hasbro, Disney, Playskool, Mattel and

Fisher-Price at discounts of up to 50%. They also stock a wide range of soft toys including TY Beanie Babies. *Factory Shopping Village*

MATALAN

STATION STREET, PORTSMOUTH, HAMPSHIRE PO1 1BE
☎ (01705) 851967. OPEN 9 - 7 MON - WED, FRI, 9 - 8 THUR, 9 - 6 SAT, 11 - 5 SUN.
Matalan is a fashion and homewares shop giving customers what they claim to be unbeatable value for money with huge savings on a wide range of products including high quality fashionable clothing for women, women and children at up to 50% off high street prices. Matalan is situated out of town and stores are open seven days a week all year round. *Permanent Discount Outlet*

MOUNTJOY PICTURE FRAMES

61 WINCHESTER ROAD, FOUR MARKS, ALTON, HAMPSHIRE GU34 5HR
☎ (01420) 561220. OPEN 9 - 5 TUE - SAT.
Sells ready-made picture frames, framed chalkboards and letter boards, manufactured on the premises, at about 20% less than high street retail. Also a growing range of lap-trays starting at £15.75, which are available by mail order. *Factory Shop*

PRET A PORTER

SHOP ONE, 18-20 HIGH STREET, RINGWOOD, HAMPSHIRE BH24 1AF
☎ (01425) 476090. OPEN 10 - 5 MON - SAT.
Sells nearly new designer ladies and menswear. Labels include Oscar de la Renta, Frank Usher, Jacques Vert, Zandra Rhodes, Betty Barclay, Escada, Eastex and Alexon. Examples of prices include Frank Usher ballgown, £80; Jacques Vert suits, £34. Also, from January to Easter, a huge selection of ski wear for women and children is kept. They specialise in cruise wear and bridal wear and hats, a wedding dress from Harrods originally £3000 selling for £450. *Dress Agency*

PRIVATE COLLECTION

SHOEMAKERS COTTAGE, 7 UNION STREET, FAREHAM, HAMPSHIRE PO16 7XX
☎ (01329) 826123. OPEN 10 - 5 MON - SAT.
Exclusive dress agency with no chainstore items. Sells wedding outfits, evening dresses, day wear, casualwear, hats, belts and bags. Labels include MaxMara, Gerry Weber and Jaeger. *Dress Agency*

ROMSEY RECLAMATION

STATION APPROACH, RAILWAY STATION, ROMSEY, HAMPSHIRE
SO51 8DU

☎ (01794) 524174/515486. OPEN 8 - 5 MON - FRI, 8.30 - 12 SAT.

Reclaimed slates, railway sleepers, bricks, tiles and oak beams, Yorkshire flags, quarry tiles, and telegraph poles and other reclaimed materials. *Architectural Salvage*

SOUTHERN DOMESTIC ELECTRICAL

SERVICES, 4-6 BRIDGE ROAD, WOOLSTON, SOUTHAMPTON,
HAMPSHIRE SO19 7GQ

☎ (01703) 421021. WAREHOUSE: ☎ (01703) 328428.
OPEN 8.30 - 6 MON - FRI, 9 - 5 SAT.

Domestic electrical kitchen goods - washing machines, fridges, cookers, tumble dryers, freezers - sold at prices which are usually 10%-25% below competitors. Also sell goods that are slight seconds with damaged boxes or a small scratch, which are priced even lower. Makes sold include Bosch, Neff, Siemens, Creda, Zanussi, AEG, Stoves, Lacanche, Amana, White Knight, Baumatic, Cannon, Belling, Hotpoint, Flavel Leisure, Miele, Zanussi, AEG, Stoves, Electrolux, Panasonic and all other leading brands. Free delivery. *Permanent Discount Outlet*

SPOILS

UNIT F7-11, THE MARLANDS, SOUTHAMPTON, HAMPSHIRE SO14 7SJ
☎ (01703) 332019. OPEN 9 - 5.30 MON - SAT.

General domestic glassware, non-stick bakeware, kitchen gadgets, ceramic oven-to-tableware, textiles, cutting boards, aluminium non-stick cookware, bakeware, plastic kitchenware, plastic storage, woodware, coffee pots/makers, furniture, mirrors and picture frames. Rather than being discounted, all the merchandise is very competitively priced - in fact, the company carry out competitors' checks frequently in order to monitor pricing. With 38 branches, the company is able to buy in bulk and thus negotiate very good prices. *Permanent Discount Outlet*

SUE FOSTER FABRICS

57 HIGH STREET, EMSWORTH, HAMPSHIRE PO10 7YA
☎ (01243) 378831. OPEN 9.30 - 5 MON - FRI, 9.30 - 1 WED, 9.30 - 4 SAT.

Supplies top name furnishing fabrics at discounts. Her showroom has one of the widest ranges of pattern books outside London, where customers can choose perfect fabrics and wallpapers, usually 15%-20% below retail price and where they can also find trimmings, cushions, sofas and chairs. Also takes orders over the phone and sends out samples and undertakes sample searches - send for the questionnaire. E-mail: Suefoster@cwcom.net. *Permanent Discount Outlet*

> *Live Well On Less Tips*
> Swap a box of toys with a friend or neighbour for a week rather than go out
> and buy lots of new toys for your children....
> ...Or join the local toy library

THE BATHROOM
WAREHOUSE WINCHESTER LTD

UNIT 3, WYKEHAM ESTATE, MOORSIDE ROAD, WINNALL, NEAR
WINCHESTER, HAMPSHIRE SO23 7RX
☎ (01962) 862554.
FAX ☎ (01962) 840927. OPEN 9 - 6 MON - SAT, UNTIL 8 WED.
BATHROOM WORLD, 9 SOLARTRON ROAD, FARNBOROUGH,
HAMPSHIRE GU14 7QL
☎ (01252) 373366. FAX ☎ (01252) 370333. OPEN 9 - 6 MON - SAT,
UNTIL 8 WED.
Fantastic, extensive bathroom showrooms pandering to any taste or budget.
Many products are exclusive to the Group who are continually expanding their
already large product portfolio. The buying power of the Group ensures that
prices are always extremely competitive. Experienced staff and designers guide
customers through styles, choices and specifications as part of a free service.
Permanent Discount Outlet

THE CATALOGUE SHOP

6 CHURCH STREET, ROMSEY, HAMPSHIRE SO51 8BU
☎ (01794) 518522. OPEN 9 - 5 MON - SAT.
49 OLD MILTON ROAD, NEW MILTON, HAMPSHIRE BH5 6DJ
☎ (01425) 629697. OPEN 9 - 5 MON - SAT, 10 - 5 SUN.
Returns, damaged and worn goods as well as clearance lines and ends of lines
of branded merchandise from mail order catalogues. This includes men's,
women's and children's wear, footwear, bedding, curtains, furniture, exercise
equipment and leather coats. Turnover is very fast with new deliveries every
day. All items are sold at less than 50% of the catalogue price, starting at 99p.
Permanent Discount Outlet

THE CLOTHES LINE

171 HIGH STREET, WINCHESTER, HAMPSHIRE SO23 9BQ
☎ (01962) 868892. OPEN 10 - 4 MON - SAT, CLOSED 1 ON WED.
Designer and high street labels from Next and Laura Ashley to Frank Usher,
Laurel, YSL, Marella and Jacques Vert, Ramsay of Dublin, Yarell, Paul
Costelloe, Nicole Farhi, Moschino and Max Mara, plus accessories: hats, cos-
tume jewellery and shoes. The shop is situated near King Alfred's statue. *Dress
Agency*

THE MALTHOUSE

CHURCH LANE, BOTLEY, HAMPSHIRE SO30 2EJ

☎ (01489) 786272. OPEN 9 - 5 MON - SAT.

On the ground floor, the Malthouse, which incorporates the Botley Bathroom Centre, sells discontinued taps, DIY materials, screws, nails, worktops, bric-a-brac; on the first floor, there are 50 displays of bathroom furniture including everything from toilet roll holders to Jacuzzis, some of which are discontinued lines. They can match up, for example, windows to a Wimpey house or replace parts of a broken avocado suite. *Permanent Discount Outlet*

THE SHOE SHED

UNIT 9, QUADRANT CENTRE, HINTON ROAD, BOURNEMOUTH, HAMPSHIRE BH1 2AD

☎ (01202) 292992. OPEN 9 - 5.30 MON - SAT, 10 - 4 SUN.

Large factory shop selling a vast range of all types of men's, women's and children's shoes, all of which are perfects, at up to 30% below normal high street prices. Men's shoes from £10; sports shoes from £10. Ladies sandals cost from £5; ladies shoes from £7.50. *Factory Shop*

TK MAXX

173-178 HIGH STREET (BELOW BAR), SOUTHAMPTON, HAMPSHIRE SO14 2BY

☎ (01703) 631600. OPEN 9 - 5.30 MON - FRI, 9 - 6 SAT, 11 - 5 SUN, UNTIL 7 ON THUR.

Based on an American concept, TK Maxx is situated in easily accessible, often centrally located stores and offers famous label goods with up to 60% savings off recommended retail prices. TK Maxx has fashion for the whole family - women's, men's and childrenswear - accessories, shoes, gifts, kitchenware and home goods. Everything in the store is branded with a choice of well-known high street names to designer labels, and while a small percentage might be clearly marked past season, the great majority of items in store are current season, current stock and still with phenomenal savings. There is a huge choice with 50,000 pieces in store and up to 10,000 new items arriving a week. The stores are simple and unfussy with wide aisles, shopping trolleys and baskets, and a spacious, functional feel to them but there are individual changing rooms, ramps for buggies and wheelchairs and plenty of staff on the shop floor. Every branch accepts all major credit and debit cards and has a liberal refund and return policy. *Permanent Discount Outlet*

TOG 24

UNIT D, CANUTE PAVILION, OCEAN VILLAGE, SOUTHAMPTON, HAMPSHIRE SO14 3JS

☎ (01703) 337383. OPEN 9.45 - 5.45 SEVEN DAYS A WEEK.

Tog 24 are the UK's fastest growing brand name in outdoor clothing and leisurewear, with a total of three UK factories and 36 stores nationwide. They utilise the world's finest performance fabrics including Gore-Tex, Polartec and Burlington macs. Catering for all the family for all seasons, with cosy fleeces and waterproofs for the winter, and trekking ranges, shorts and t-shirts for the summer. With all prices at least 30% below the recommended retail price you can afford to enter the Tog comfort zone. *Factory Shop*

WESTHOUSE TEXTILES

CORNWALL ROAD, FRATTON, PORTSMOUTH, HAMPSHIRE PO1 5AA
☎ (01705) 851275. OPEN 9 - 5 MON - SAT.
103-105 LYNCHFORD ROAD, NORTH CAMP, FARNBOROUGH, HAMPSHIRE GU14 6ET

☎ (01252) 372701. OPEN 9 - 5 MON - SAT.

Sells quality fabrics, curtaining, sheeting, dress fabrics, haberdashery and houses one of the biggest ranges of craft fabrics in the South. Most of the major fabric names are sold here. Half the stock is clearance, ends of lines and seconds sold at discounts of 50%; half is perfect stock sold at discounts of about 20%. Also offers a curtain making service. *Permanent Discount Outlet*

WHITELEY VILLAGE
DESIGNER OUTLET CENTRE

OFF THE M27 BETWEEN SOUTHAMPTON AND PORTSMOUTH, JUNCTION 9 OF M27, HAMPSHIRE.
NO TELEPHONE NUMBER AS WE WENT TO PRESS.

Planned to open in November 1999, look out for opening details in the local press. There are plans for 50 factory shops, cafes, and car parking for 1,400 cars with a Tesco food store next door. *Factory Shopping Village*

Live Well On Less Tips

Buy equipment as the baby needs it. By then you'll have at least a smidgeon of practical experience plus you'll probably be friends with other new mothers who may be a bit ahead of you in the purchasing game and you can learn from their mistakes and perhaps even be given their surplus.

Herefordshire

WOMENSWEAR ONLY   Chameleon Dress Agency, *Hereford.*
Designer Discount Club, *Ross-on-Wye.*

WOMENSWEAR & MENSWEAR   M & M Sports, *Leominster.*
Ross Labels, *Ross-on-Wye.*   Stewart Seconds, *Ross-on-Wye.*

CHILDREN   E Walters Factory Shop, *Leominster.*   M & M Sports, *Leominster.*
Ross Labels, *Ross-on-Wye.*   Stewart Seconds, *Ross-on-Wye.*

HOUSEHOLD AND GIFTWARE   Dunelm Mill Shops Ltd, *Hereford.*
Ponden Mill Linens, *Ross-on-Wye.*   Ross Labels, *Ross-on-Wye.*   Stewart Seconds, *Ross-on-Wye.*

DIY/RENOVATION   Baileys Home & Garden, *Ross-on-Wye.*

ARCHITECTURAL SALVAGE   Baileys Home & Garden, *Ross-on-Wye.*

FURNITURE/SOFT FURNISHINGS   Affordable Fabrics, *Hay-on-Wye.*
Twyford Cookers, *Hereford.*

FOOD AND LEISURE   Bookends, *Hay-on-Wye.*

SPORTSWEAR AND EQUIPMENT   M & M Sports, *Leominster.*

AFFORDABLE FABRICS

THE GRANARY, LOWER COURT, CLIFFORD, HAY-ON-WYE,
HEREFORDSHIRE HR3 5ER
(01497) 831309. OPEN 10 - 5 MON - SAT.
Ends of lines and overstocks of designer fabrics from names such as Zoffany,
Monkwell, Malibar and G P & J Baker at discounted prices. Also crewel work
imported direct from India at affordable prices. They provide a full curtain
making and design service. ***Permanent Discount Outlet***

BAILEYS HOME & GARDEN

THE ENGINE SHED, STATION APPROACH, ROSS-ON-WYE,
HEREFORDSHIRE HR9 7BW
(01989) 563015. OPEN 9 - 5 MON - SAT.
Bathroom fittings, fireplaces, statuary, stonework, garden furniture, gates
ironwork, lighting, Belfast sinks and dressers. They also sell a range of garden
statuary and items made from reconstituted stone as well as original troughts,
staddles stones, original oak benches, repro Regency-style distressed metal
benches with Gothic arched backs, French folding chairs, and lots of terracotta plant pots. This company specialise in antique garden tools and horticultural antiques. ***Architectural Salvage***

BOOKENDS

THE PAVEMENT, HAY-ON-WYE, HEREFORDSHIRE HR3 5BU
☎ (01497) 821341. OPEN 9 - 8 MON - SAT, 11 - 5 SUN.
9-13 PUMP STREET, WORCESTER WR1 2QX
☎ (01905) 24389. OPEN 9 - 5.30 MON - SAT.
9 CASTLE STREET, HAY-ON-WYE, HEREFORDSHIRE HR3 5BU
☎ (01497) 821572. OPEN 9 - 5.30 SEVEN DAYS A WEEK.
Secondhand and damaged books and publishers' returns, as well as new and
review copies, including recently published books, usually one-third off and
sometimes half price. *Secondhand Shop*

CHAMELEON DRESS AGENCY

123 EIGN STREET, HEREFORD, HEREFORDSHIRE HR4 ORJ
☎ (01432) 353436. OPEN 10 - 5 MON - SAT.
Very friendly shop, which is light and well stocked. Customers are encouraged
to exchange views - if it doesn't suit, the owner says they don't sell it to you.
Sited near Sainsbury's, it stocks a wide range of clothes, from Marks &
Spencer, Jaeger, Country Casuals, Alexon, Berkertex and Eastex to Yarrell,
Nicole Farhi, Bianca, Ralph Lauren and Joseph. There is plenty of day wear,
wedding outfits and evening wear, as well as accessories. Prices range from £10
upwards to about £100. A Bianca jacket would sell for about £45, Jaeger jacket, £55, Nicole Farhi two-piece, £75, Joseph leggings, £30. There is also a
huge selection of hats. *Dress Agency*

DESIGNER DISCOUNT CLUB

UNIT E, ASHBURTON ESTATE, ROSS-ON-WYE,
HEREFORDSHIRE HR9 7BW
☎ (01989) 564357. OPEN 9.30 - 5 MON - FRI, 10 - 5 SAT.
This designer discount business has a retail outlet in Ross-on-Wye where
members can come and purchase top quality German clothes at wholesale
prices. Provides classic, smart clothes for work or day wear and plenty of special occasion wear and evening clothes. Members are kept up-to-date by post
of special offers. You can join during your first visit when you will be issued
with your own card and membership number at a cost of £5. *Permanent
Discount Outlet*

DUNELM MILL SHOPS LTD

2/3A UNION WALK, HEREFORD, HEREFORDSHIRE HR1 2EP
☎ (01432) 266466. OPEN 9 - 5 MON - THUR, 9 - 5.30 FRI, SAT,
10.30 - 4.30 SUN.
Part of a chain of shops based in the Midlands selling brand-name and chainstore curtains, masses of bedlinen, towels, wickerware, pictures and frames, all
at competitive prices. *Permanent Discount Outlet*

Live Well On Less Tips

Don't throw out that comfortable old country jacket that needs a new wax coating. A new coat will set you back more than £100 but re-waxing only costs about one quarter (from £27.50) of that for a three-quarter length jacket. Waxmaster of Rotherham, South Yorkshire, will collect your jacket and deliver it back. Phone 0800 590978 to arrange.

E WALTERS FACTORY SHOP

STATION YARD, LEOMINSTER, HEREFORDSHIRE HR6 8TW

☎ (01568) 616127. OPEN 9 - 5 MON - FRI, 9 - 4 SAT.

Europe's largest trouser manufacturer sells ends of lines, cancelled orders and samples of jeans, trousers and shorts for all the family at factory direct prices. Also available ancillary lines of casual wear at bargain prices. *Factory Shop*

M & M SPORTS

CLINTON ROAD, LEOMINSTER, HEREFORDSHIRE HR6 OSP

☎ (01568) 616161. FAX ☎ (01568) 619555. 9 - 10 MON - FRI, 9 - 7 SAT, SUN. MAIL ORDER ONLY.

M and M Sports are the UK's largest sports mail order company, offering quality branded sportswear for all the family at greatly discounted prices. Five catalogues are issued each year, featuring seasonal merchandise from all the major names such as Nike, Adidas, Reebok, Fila, Ellesse and Caterpillar. The range on offer includes cross-trainers, running shoes, football boots, walking boots, all types of sports clothing, rackets, eyewear, watches, footballs, casual clothing and fleeces. In addition there is now an excellent value for money range of M & M branded clothing. M & M can offer discounted prices because they buy up end of line ranges in huge quantities. A factory shop is now being planned. To order a catalogue, phone or fax the above numbers or visit their website on: www.mmsports.co.uk/. *Permanent Discount Outlet*

PONDEN MILL LINENS

ROSS LABELS LTD, OVEROSS, ROSS-ON-WYE, HEREFORDSHIRE HR9 7AS

☎ (01989) 564348. OPEN 10 - 6 MON - SAT, 11 - 5 SUN.

Famous branded products at direct from the mill prices. Towels, co-ordinated bedlinen, duvets, pillows and curtains from Crown, Coloroll, Chortex, Rectella together with bathroom and kitchen accessories. *Factory Shopping Village*

ROSS LABELS LTD

OVERROSS HOUSE, ROSS ON WYE, HEREFORDSHIRE HR9 7QJ
☎ (01989) 769000. OPEN 10 - 6 MON - SAT, 11 - 5 SUN.

Recently refurbished, there is now double the selling space here at forty thousand square feet, with women's, mens and children's wear from underwear and jeans to good, middle-of-the-road brand name outfits and suits bought direct from the manufacturer. Some of the labels on sale include Aquascutum, Lee Cooper, Wolsey, Double Two, Telemac and Lyle & Scott. Stock is usually one year old, while current merchandise consists of overmakes. Discounts range from 20% to 50%. There is also a Lee Cooper and big kids wear department and Aquascutum clothes are sold at less than normal high street prices.
Permanent Discount Outlet

STEWART SECONDS

33 HIGH STREET, ROSS-ON-WYE, HEREFORDSHIRE HR9 5HD
☎ (01989) 762403. OPEN 9.30 - 5.30 MON - SAT.

Branded merchandise from most of the major UK chain stores, all well-known high street department store names, offered at a discount of 40%-70% off normal high street prices. The garments are selected with great care by experienced buyers direct from factories worldwide to bring customers top quality merchandise at highly competitive prices. *Factory Shop*

TWYFORD COOKERS

UNITS 4 - 6, LUGG VIEW INDUSTRIAL ESTATE, MORETON-ON-LUGG, HEREFORD, HEREFORDSHIRE HR4 8DP
☎ (01432) 761686. OPEN 9 - 5 MON - FRI.

Renovated Agas at prices which are very competitive with other similar outlets. They also supply Aga parts and re-fit lids with new chrome parts while you wait. Also supply gas CE-approved Agas and offer an installation service.
Secondhand Shop

Live Well On Less Tips

Instead of spending money hiring an evening outfit for that once-a-year special occasion, buy your evening gown/cocktail dress from a dress agency. Whether you hire or buy, you'll still be wearing a garment that's already been worn, and you might as well have use of it for another occasion!....you can even sell it on again to the dress agency.

Hertfordshire

WOMENSWEAR ONLY   🕊 Cameo, *Berkhamsted*.   Cara, *Watford*.   Central Park, *Barnet*.
Discount Dressing, *Hatfield*.   Dorothy Perkins, *Hatfield*.   Glasers factory Shop, *Watford*.
Just Between Us, *St Albans*.   Lawthers Factory & Sample Shop, *Hertford*.   Pilot, *Hatfield*.
Scent to You, *Watford*.

MENSWEAR ONLY   🕊 Burtons, *Hatfield*.   Tom Sayer Clothing Co Ltd, *Hatfield*.

WOMENSWEAR & MENSWEAR   🕊 🕊 A & D Hope, *Borehamwood*.
Aquascutum, *Hemel Hempstead*.   BHS for Less, *Hatfield*.   Catalogue Bargain Shop, *Hatfield*.
Catalogue Bargain Shop, *Faversham*.   Choice Discount Stores Ltd, *Hatfield*.
Choice Discount Stores Ltd, *Watford*.   Clinkard group, *Hatfield*.   Coutaulds Textiles, *Royston*.
Ecco, *Hatfield*.   First Impressions, *Hatfield*.   Littlewoods Catalogue Discount Store, *Hatfield*.
Matalan, *Stevenage*.   Millano, *Hatfield*.   R S Shoes, *Hatfield*.   Recollections, *Ware*.
The Galleria Outlet Centre, *Hatfield*.   The Shoe Shed, *Royston*.   TK Maxx, *Hatfield*.   Tog 24, *Hatfield*.
Walker & Hall, *Hatfield*.

CHILDREN   🐾 A & D Hope, *Borehamwood*.   BHS for Less, *Hatfield*.   Cameo, *Berkhamstead*.
Catalogue Bargain Shop, *Hatfield*.   Catalogue Bargain Shop, *Faversham*.
Choice Discount Stores Ltd, *Hatfield*.   Choice Discount Stores Ltd, *Watford*.
Clinkard group, *Hatfield*.   Coutaulds Textiles, *Royston*.   Ecco, *Hatfield*.   Kids Play Factory, *Hatfield*.
Littlewoods Catalogue Discount Store, *Hatfield*.   Matalan, *Stevenage*.   Millano, *Hatfield*.
Nippers, *Broxbourne*.   Outdoor Wear, *Bishops Stortford*.   The Galleria Outlet Centre, *Hatfield*.
The Shoe Shed, *Royston*.   TK Maxx, *Hatfield*.   Tog 24, *Hatfield*.

HOUSEHOLD AND GIFTWARE   🎁 BHS for Less, *Hatfield*.   Catalogue Bargain Shop,
Hatfield.   Catalogue Bargain Shop, *Faversham*.
Coutaulds Textiles, *Royston*.   Hornsea Pottery, *Hatfield*.   Matalan, *Stevenage*.
Nazeing Glass, *Broxbourne*.   Ponden Mill Linens, *Hatfield*.   Spoils, *Hemel Hempstead*.
The Galleria Outlet Centre, *Hatfield*.   TK Maxx, *Hatfield*.

ELECTRICAL EQUIPMENT   🔌 BHS for Less, *Hatfield*.   Catalogue Bargain Shop, *Hatfield*.

DIY/RENOVATION   🔧 Watford Bathrooms & Interiors, *Watford*.

FURNITURE/SOFT FURNISHINGS   🛋 Chelford Fabrics, *Harpenden*.
Direct Carpets of Hertford, *Hertford*.   Fabric warehouse, *New barnet*.
Knickerbean, *St Albans*.   The Curtain Connection Ltd, *St Albans*.   The Curtain Mill, *Watford*.

FOOD AND LEISURE   📖 Chamberlain, *Hatfield*.   The Baggage Factory, *Hatfield*.
Whittard, *Hatfield*.

SPORTSWEAR AND EQUIPMENT   🎿 Outdoor Trading Post, *Hatfield*.
Outdoor Wear, *Hatfield*.

A & D HOPE   🕊 🕊 🐾

EVELYN HOUSE, 3 ELSTREE WAY, BOREHAMWOOD, HERTFORDSHIRE
WD6 1RN

☎ 0181-953 7278. OPEN 8.30 - 5.30 MON - FRI.

Leather, suede and sheepskin manufacturers they make coats, jackets, trousers
and skirts for top name department stores. The factory shop sells samples,

ends of lines and excess stock. The shop caters for men, women and children with men's sizes up to 58 chest and ladies sizes 8-18, although the children's range does not include sheepskin. *Factory Shop*

AQUASCUTUM

CLEVELAND ROAD, MAYLANDS WOOD ESTATE, HEMEL HEMPSTEAD, HERTFORDSHIRE HP2 7EY

☎ (01442) 248333. OPEN 10 - 5 MON - SAT.

Previous season's stock and seconds for women and men at greatly reduced prices. For men, blazers, suits and silk ties. Examples include 20% off men's raincoats and half-price ladies silk blouses. Different promotions take place throughout the year with an average 50% reduction. *Factory Shop*

BHS FOR LESS

GALLERIA OUTLET CENTRE, COMET WAY, HATFIELD, HERTFORDSHIRE AL6 OXL

☎ (01707) 258351. OPEN 10 - 8 MON - FRI, 10 - 6 SAT, 11 - 5 SUN.

BhS for Less sells the Storehouse-owned chain's men's, women's and childrenswear ranges, plus selections from its home and lighting ranges, at discounts of at least thirty percent and up to seventy percent. *Factory Shopping Village*

BURTONS

GALLERIA OUTLET CENTRE, COMET WAY, HATFIELD, HERTFORDSHIRE AL10 0XR

☎ (01707) 251688. OPEN 10 - 8 MON - FRI, 10 - 6 SAT, 11 - 5 SUN.

Burton menswear end of season lines with the normal refund guarantee. The range includes suits, formal shirts, ties, trousers, jackets, casual shirts, T-shirts, sweatshirts, knitwear, shoes, jeans, socks and underwear. Other outlets can be found in Lancashire and Scotland. *Factory Shopping Village*

CAMEO

150 HIGH STREET, BERKHAMSTED, HERTFORDSHIRE HP4 3AT

☎ (01442) 865791. OPEN 9.30 - 5.15 MON - FRI, 9.30 - 5 SAT.

Cameo is a well-known shop in Berkhamsted High Street that sells ladies and children's nearly-new clothes and accessories with lots of designer wear. Famous makes include Osh Kosh, Oilily, Benetton, Absorba, Gap, Next, Windsmoor, Jacques Vert, Mondi, Bellino, Patsy Seddon, Benny Ong, Betty Barclay and many more. All clothes are in immaculate condition and are sold at very affordable prices. Cameo has been trading successfully for more than twenty years under the present owner and is well worth a visit. The shop is opposite the King's Arms. *Dress Agency*

CARA

GARSTON, WATFORD, HERTFORDSHIRE WD2 6PZ

☎ (01923) 670853. BY APPOINTMENT ONLY.

Cara is a home-based business selling a range of designers including Mondi, Betty Barclay, Krizia, Escada, Jacques Vert, Maxmara, Jaeger, Windsmoor and Planet as well as lots of French and Italian designers. Sizes range from 10-18. Evening wear is stocked all year round as well as accessories, bags, shoes, belts and hats. Prices range from £5 - £75. *Dress Agency*

CATALOGUE BARGAIN SHOP

GALLERIA OUTLET CENTRE, COMET WAY, HATFIELD, HERTFORDSHIRE AL10 OXR

☎ (01707) 278301. OPEN 10 - 8 MON - FRI, 10 - 6 SAT, 11 - 5 SUN.

19A PRESTON STREET, FAVERSHAM, KENT ME13 8NX

☎ (01795) 591203. OPEN 9 - 5.30 MON - SAT, 10 - 4 SUN.

Catalogue Bargain Shop is a growing national chain of stores which obtains the majority of its goods from mail order giants Great Universal and Kays, and offers a range of clothing for all the family, a wide selection of shoes, bed linen, household goods, electrical equipment and hundreds of other catalogue items at very competitive prices. The merchandise consists of ends of ranges and previous season's stock for which there is not longer storage space when the catalogues change. *Permanent Discount Outlet*

CENTRAL PARK

88 HIGH STREET BARNET, HERTFORDSHIRE EN5 5SN

☎ 0181-440 9950. OPEN 9.30 - 5.30 MON - SAT.

Large multiple group stocking cancelled orders and over runs for women, most of the clothes are de-labelled before they come here. There are dresses, suits, skirts, trousers and tops. Prices are very cheap. *Permanent Discount Outlet*

CHAMBERLAIN

GALERIA OUTLET CENTRE, COMET WAY, HATFIELD, HERTFORDSHIRE AL10 0XR

☎ (01707) 268433. OPEN 10 - 8 MON - FRI, 10 - 6 SAT, 11 - 5 SUN.

Sells GT, Dawes and Raleigh bikes for adults and children, helmets, baskets and tyres. Stock changes constantly and the owner says that their prices will not be beaten. *Factory Shopping Village*

CHELFORD FABRICS LTD

CHELFORD HOUSE, COLDHARBOUR LANE, HARPENDEN,
HERTFORDSHIRE AL5 4SR

☎ (01582) 763636. OPEN 9.30 - 5.30 MON - SAT.

A large, out-of-town showroom selling only perfect regular curtain and upholstery fabrics at greatly reduced prices, ranging from £2.99 a yard to £11.99 a
yard and including everything from glazed cotton chintzes to prints, tapestries
and damasks from all leading manufacturers. Choose from more than 4,000
rolls, order from the extensive range of manufacturers pattern books or buy
own-brand fabrics which are one-third less expensive than branded material. A
full high quality making-up service is available. Curtain accessories, rails, tapes
and hooks are also on sale at reduced prices. There is also a huge selection of
towels, cushions, pillows and duvets. This branch also sells high-quality three-
piece suites and occasional chairs at very reasonable prices. (There is another
branch in Gamlingay, Cambridgeshire.) *Permanent Discount Outlet*

CHOICE DISCOUNT STORES LIMITED

GALLERIA OUTLET CENTRE, COMET WAY, HATFIELD,
HERTFORDSHIRE

☎ (01707) 278301 (CENTRE TEL NO). OPEN 10 - 8 MON - FRI, 10 - 6 SAT,
11 - 5 SUN.

44-46 HIGH STREET, WATFORD, HERTFORDSHIRE WD1 2BR

☎ (01923) 233255. OPEN 9 - 5.30 MON - FRI, 9 - 6 SAT.

Surplus stock including women's, men's and children's fashions from Next plc,
Next Directory and other high street fashion houses, Next Interiors and
footwear. You can save up to 50% off normal retail prices for first quality; up to
two thirds for seconds. There are no changing rooms but the shop offers refunds
if goods are returned in perfect condition within 28 days. There are special sales
each January and September. Easy access for wheelchairs and pushchairs. The
Watford store is known as Next 2 Choice and specialises in ladies and menswear
only from Next plc and Next Directory. *Permanent Discount Outlet*

CLINKARD GROUP

25 THE GALLERIA, COMET WAY, HATFIELD, HERTFORDSHIRE
AL10 OXS

☎ (01707) 258653. OPEN 10 - 8 MON - FRI, 10 - 6 SAT, 11 - 5 SUN.

Footwear for the family at discounts of between 20% and 50%. Labels on sale
here include Rockport, Loake, Camel, Bally, Church's, Ecco, Gabor, Rohde,
Van-Dal, Kickers, Clarks, Dr Martens, K Shoes, Lotus and Renata. *Factory
Shopping Village*

COURTAULDS TEXTILES

ORCHARD ROAD, ROYSTON, HERTFORDSHIRE SG8 5HA

☎ (01763) 249941. OPEN 9 - 5.30 MON, TUE, WED, SAT, 9 - 6 THUR, FRI, 10 - 4 SUN.

Sells extensive range of casual wear for girls and boys from birth to twelve years, men's and women's clothes, as well as seconds and bought-in stock in bedding, towels, duvets and pillows, luggage, accessories and shoes at discounts of 30%-50%. About half the stock is perfect, the other half seconds. Childrenswear includes tights and underwear from 60p, cord trousers, knitwear, coats, socks, sweatshirts from £5.99, joggers from £3.99, and shirts, £3.99. For women, double-breasted ladies panel coat, £85 reduced from £140. Stocks Christian Marcos, Kushi, Wolsey, Lyle and Scott. *Factory Shop*

DIRECT CARPETS OF HERTFORD

9A CASTLE MEAD GARDENS, OFF HERTINGFORD BURY ROAD, HERTFORD, HERTFORDSHIRE SG14 1JZ

☎ (01992) 504944. OPEN 9 - 5.30 MON - SAT.

Beds and carpeting on the roll at 15%-20% cheaper than high street prices, plus remnants as large as 40 ft. Purchasers of carpets can also buy beds at discounts of 15%. Double bed, £99, single, £75. Free local delivery. *Permanent Discount Outlet*

DISCOUNT DRESSING

GALLERIA OUTLET CENTRE, COMET WAY, HATFIELD, HERTFORDSHIRE AL10 OXR

☎ (01707) 259925. OPEN 10 - 8 MON - FRI, 10 - 6 SAT, 11 - 5 SUN.

A veritable Aladdin's Cave of designer bargains, Discount Dressing sells mostly German, Italian and French designer labels at prices at least 50% and up to 90% below those in normal retail outlets. All items are brand new and perfect. A team of buyers all over Europe purchase stock directly from the manufacturer for this growing chain of discount shops. This enables Discount Dressing to by-pass the importers and wholesalers and, of course, their mark-up. They also buy bankrupt stock in this country. Their agreement with their suppliers means that they are not able to advertise brand names for obvious reasons, but they are all well-known for their top quality and style. So confident is Discount Dressing that you will be unable to find the same item cheaper elsewhere, that they guarantee to give the outfit to you free of charge should you perform this miracle. Merchandise includes raincoats, dresses, suits, trousers, blouses, evening wear, special occasion outfits and jackets, in sizes 6-24 and in some cases larger. GDD readers can obtain a further 10% discount if they visit the shop taking a copy of this book with them. There are other branches in Lincolnshire, Northern Ireland, London, East Yorkshire and Derbyshire. *Factory Shopping Village*

DOROTHY PERKINS

GALLERIA OUTLET CENTRE, COMET WAY, HATFIELD,
HERTFORDSHIRE AL10 0XR

☎ (01707) 263640. OPEN 10 - 8 MON - FRI, 10 - 6 SAT, 11 - 5 SUN.

End of season lines with the normal Dorothy Perkins refund guarantee. The range includes knickers, scarves, suits, blouses, sweaters, coats, jackets, dresses and jewellery. *Factory Shopping Village*

ECCO, GALLERIA OUTLET CENTRE

COMET WAY, HATFIELD, HERTFORDSHIRE AL10 0XR

☎ (01707) 258399. OPEN 10 - 8 MON - FRI, 10 - 6 SAT, 11 - 5 SUN.

Ladies', men's and children's shoes, all discounted by at least 25%. Phone 0800 387368 for a catalogue. Other outlets at South Wales, Wiltshire, Somerset and Cheshire. *Factory Shopping Village*

FABRIC WAREHOUSE

184 EAST BARNET ROAD, NEW BARNET, HERTFORDSHIRE EN4 8RD

☎ 0181-441 3114. OPEN 10 - 6 MON - SAT. ,

Furnishing fabric, cushions and foam. Good range of printed furnishing fabrics from £4.99, with a bargain selection from £2.50; Jeff Banks prints, £8.99 instead of £16.99; wonderful Italian damasks, £13.99, usual price £18; cotton damask half price at £10.99; cotton muslins, £4.99 instead of £6.99; Belgian flat weaves and tapestries, £10.99; polycotton lining, £2.50 for 54 width. They also sell curtain rails, tiebacks, fringing, braid, chunky tassel tie backs and have their own in-house curtain making service at competitive prices. *Factory Shopping Village*

FIRST IMPRESSIONS

UNIT 3, THE GALLERIA OUTLET CENTRE, HATFIELD,
HERTFORDSHIRE AL10 0XR

☎ (01707) 268755. OPEN 10 - 8 MON - FRI, 10 - 6 SAT, 11 - 5 SUN.

First Impressions, clothing direct from the factory, sells garments from the manufacturing side of the Dewhirst Group plc. The Dewhirst Group plc manufactures ladies, men's and childrenswear for a leading high street retailer. You can choose from a huge selection of surplus production and slight seconds at bargain prices, making savings of more than 50% of the normal retail cost. For men, there is a wide range of suits, formal shirts and casualwear. For example, suits from £60, formal and casual shirts from £7. For ladies, a selection of blouses, smart tailoring and casualwear that includes a denim range. For example ladies jackets from £50, skirts, trousers and blouses from £8. *Factory Shopping Village*

GLASERS FACTORY SHOP

REMBRANDT HOUSE, WHIPPENDELL ROAD, WATFORD,
HERTFORDSHIRE WD1 7QN

☎ (01923) 234067 FOR SALE DETAILS.

End of season sales of well-made ladies smart knitted suits, dresses and dress
and jacket sets. Skirts tend to be knee-length, although some suits also have
long skirts. *Factory Shopping Village*

HORNSEA POTTERY

GALLERIA OUTLET CENTRE, COMET WAY, HATFIELD,
HERTFORDSHIRE AL10 0XR

☎ (01707) 257877. OPEN 10 - 8 MON - FRI, 10 - 6 SAT, 11 - 5 SUN.

Sells table cloths, mugs, mug racks, aprons, bowls, cafetieres, storage jars and
plates at discount prices, with a minimum 30% discount on selected seconds
compared with the retail price. There are occasional special offers such as a 16-
plate set for £20 or a teapot, cream jug and sugar bowl for £15. *Factory
Shopping Village*

JUST BETWEEN US

29 HILLSIDE ROAD, ST ALBANS, HERTFORDSHIRE AL1 3QW

☎ (01727) 811172. BY APPOINTMENT ONLY.

Offers an enormous selection of evening wear from 150 long and zappy party
dresses to formal ballgowns and cocktail dresses in sizes 8-24. No accessories.
Cost: from £62 plus £50 deposit for a flexible number of days. By
appointment only, including evenings. The entire stock is changed every
season and brand new stock is introduced. The old stock is then put into
twice-yearly sales. Phone for dates. The sales are exceedingly popular as dresses
can go for less than £50. *Hire Shop*

KIDS PLAY FACTORY

GALLERIA OUTLET CENTRE, COMET WAY, HATFIELD,
HERTFORDSHIRE AL10 OXR

☎ (01707) 258720. OPEN 10 - 8 MON - FRI, 10 - 6 SAT, 11 - 5 SUN.

This shop sells a wide range of well-known children's brand names: Tomy,
Matchbox, Lego, The First Years, Hasbro, Disney, Playskool, Mattel and
Fisher-Price at discounts of up to 50%. They also stock a wide range of soft
toys including TY Beanie Babies. The centre has plenty to entertain children,
a cinema, dry ice rink, restaurants and parking. *Factory Shopping Village*

KNICKERBEAN

11 HOLYWELL HILL, ST ALBANS, HERTFORDSHIRE AL1 1EZ

☎ (01727) 866662. OPEN 9 - 5.30 MON - SAT.

Knickerbean is one of the few companies that continue to offer genuine top-
name designer fabric bargains . . . the kind of curtain and upholstery fabrics

that are found at Decorex and the Chelsea Harbour Design Centre. Their rapidly-changing stock often includes excess inventory and discontinued lines from these kinds of designers, as well as occasional slight seconds, with many sold at between 20%-50% off the regular price. They also carry a large range of top-quality fabrics in the latest styles which they buy directly from mills and manufacturers in the UK, Europe and North America, offering similar top quality, but at vastly reduced prices. Their attractively laid-out shops feature a vast range of different selections of curtain and upholstery fabrics. These include classic country house glazed chintzes, fresh stripes and checks, fashionable toiles de jouy, bright cotton prints and PVC-coated fabrics, a wide range of damasks and natural fabrics, sumptuous chenilles, rich kilim patterns, self-patterned dobby weaves and a fabulous selection of upholstery brocades and tapestries. Prices start from £4.95 for plain cottons and prints to £19.95 and occasionally more for chenilles and tapestries. Customers are encouraged to pop in regularly to check out the latest arrivals in their stock. The benefit here is that they are able to see entire rolls rather than just a small sample book of swatches. Their professionally trained staff are ready to advise on quality and quantity for any type of furnishing project. They extend their service to measure and quote, as they offer a complete making up service for all soft furnishings, including loose covers and upholstery. They are even prepared to bring along a few rolls to try out against a customer's own colour scheme. Twice-yearly sales are held in January and June to enable customers to snap up even bigger bargains. *Permanent Discount Outlet*

LAWTHER'S FACTORY & SAMPLE SHOP

21 ST ANDREWS STREET, HERTFORD, HERTFORDSHIRE SG14 3RY
☎ (01992) 504038. OPEN 10 - 5 TUE - SAT.
Small shop on two floors full of bargains from Azar, Domingo and Moonlight and including suits, dresses, separates, wool blazers at discounts of 50%. These are mostly keenly priced quality ladies samples and one-offs from stores such as Monsoon, all with the labels cut out, so you need to be able to recognise your favourite high street names. *Factory Shop*

LITTLEWOODS
CATALOGUE DISCOUNT STORE

GALLERIA OUTLET CENTRE, COMET WAY, HATFIELD,
HERTFORDSHIRE AL10 0XA
☎ (01707) 258536. OPEN 10 - 8 MON - FRI, 10 - 6 SAT, SUN.
Littlewoods clearance shops offering up to 50% off the catalogue price for clothing and between 50% and 60% off for electrical goods. Stock changes constantly and varies from day to day but can include well-known brand names such as Berlei and Gossard lingerie, Vivienne Westwood, Pamplemousse leisure wear, Nike and Adidas sports shoes, Workers For Freedom, and Timberland and Caterpillar footwear. Stock depends on the size

and location of the shop, so larger shops will get the longer discontinued runs and smaller shops over-runs with only a small amount of colour and size variations left. Littlewoods also run a mobile shop which operates in cities where they don't have a sale shop. For details of further venues for the sales, which usually take place once a month, contact Melanie Lamb, c/o Crosby DC, Kershaw Avenue, Endbutt Lane, Crosby, Merseyside L70 1AH. *Factory Shop*

MATALAN

UNITS B & C, DANESTRETE, STEVENAGE, HERTFORDSHIRE SG1 1NB
☎ (01438) 312433. OPEN 9 - 6 MON - FRI, 9 - 6 SAT, 11 - 4 SUN.
Matalan is a fashion and homewares shop giving customers what they claim to be unbeatable value for money with huge savings on a wide range of products including high quality fashionable clothing for women, women and children at up to 50% off high street prices. Matalan is situated out of town and stores are open seven days a week all year round. *Permanent Discount Outlet*

MILLANO

GALLERIA OUTLET CENTRE, COMET WAY, HATFIELD,
HERTFORDSHIRE AL10 OXR
☎ (01707) 259199. OPEN 10 - 8 MON - FRI, 10 - 6 SAT, 11 - 5 SUN.
This outlet sells designer suede, leather and sheepskin jackets, coats, trousers etc for men, women and children at discount prices. Larger than average sizes can sometimes be made on request. Prices can be up to 60% cheaper than in the high street, with samples, over-runs or slight seconds as well as a selection of last and current season's perfects. *Factory Shopping Village*

NAZEING GLASS

NAZEING NEW ROAD, BROXBOURNE, HERTFORDSHIRE EM10 6SU
☎ (01992) 464485. OPEN 9.30 - 4.30 MON - FRI, 9.30 - 3 SAT.
A large factory shop measuring almost 2,000 sq ft selling seconds, overmakes and ends of lines from a range of cut glass decanters, rose bowls, vases, jugs engraved to order, as well as champagne flutes, liqueur and cocktail glasses at factory shop prices, which in practice means 20%-40% off. There are 20 different suites of wine glass in seven different sizes. *Factory Shop*

NIPPERS

LEYHILL FARM, BRIDGE STREET, NR ROYSTON, HERTFORDSHIRE
SG8 5SQ
☎ (01223) 207071. FAX ☎ (01223) 208666.
Nippers, the nursery equipment and toy specialists, operate from previously redundant buildings in rural areas around the country. They offer easy parking, no queues and personal service. This is on top of competitive prices on

prams, cots, pushchairs, car seats, outdoor play equipment and toys, some of which are new, some seconds or secondhand and some ends of lines. Prices are low because they avoid the high overheads of traditional retail outlets and also because the successful growth of a number of branches means they can now buy in bulk and negotiate good deals. Customers are invited to try out the merchandise while the children look at the animals, mostly sheep, chicken and pigs. Familiar brand names are on sale at all the branches, including Mamas & Papas, Britax, Maclaren and Bebe Confort, plus Fisher-Price and Little Tikes. You can try out the car seats in your car and there is usually a pram/pushchair repair service on site. *Permanent Discount Outlet*

OUTDOOR TRADING POST

GALLERIA OUTLET CENTRE, COMET WAY, HATFIELD,
HERTFORDSHIRE AL10 OXR
☎ (01707) 256606. OPEN 10 - 8 MON - FRI, 10 - 6 SAT, 11 - 5 SUN.
Specialist outdoor sports factory shop for skiers and urban hikers selling top quality brands such as Patagonia, Salamon, SOS, Lowe Alpine and North Face at reductions which average 30%-40%. In the summer, they stock mostly outdoor and trekking gear and equipment with some lines in skiwear and equipment at final clearance prices. In the winter, from September to March, they carry the full range of premium brands in skiwear at the sort of prices you would pay for lower quality brands. Ski suits which would normally retail for £399 cost £249; ski boots which normally cost £200 are £129. *Factory Shopping Village*

OUTDOOR WEAR

10 - 14 POTTER STREET, BISHOPS STORTFORD, HERTFORDSHIRE
CM23 3UL
☎ (01279) 653694. OPEN 9 - 6 MON - SAT.
Ends of lines from Karrimor, Berghaus, Tenson, Barbour, Levi's, Rohan and Drizabone in shirts, jeans, hats, and skiwear. *Permanent Discount Outlet*

PILOT

GALLERIA OUTLET CENTRE, COMET WAY, HATFIELD,
HERTFORDSHIRE AL10 0XU
☎ (01707) 258144. OPEN 10 - 8 MON - FRI, 10 - 6 SAT, 11 - 5 SUN.
Mainly younger-style clothes for women only. Some are seconds but most are end of season and end of line at reductions of about 30%, e.g. in the summer of 1999: pedal pushers, £23 reduced to £17, short strap top £17 reduced to £10.

Live Well On Less Tips
Change buttons on an old jacket to update it.

PONDEN MILL LINENS

GALLERIA OUTLET CENTRE, COMET WAY, HATFIELD,
HERTFORDSHIRE AL10 OXS

☎ (01707) 270053. OPEN 10 - 8 MON - FRI, 10 - 6 SAT, 11 - 5 SUN.

Famous branded products at direct from the mill prices. Towels, co-ordinated
bedlinen, duvets, pillows and curtains from Crown, Coloroll, Chortex,
Rectella together with bathroom and kitchen accessories. *Factory Shopping
Village*

R S SHOES

GALLERIA OUTLET CENTRE, COMET WAY, HATFIELD,
HERTFORDSHIRE AL10 OXR

☎ (01707) 258021. OPEN 10 - 8 MON - FRI, 10 - 6 SAT, 11 - 5 SUN.

Sells men's, women's and children's shoes including Dr Martens, Kickers,
Wrangler, Levi's LSCO in this glass and steel factory shopping centre straddling the A1. *Factory Shopping Village*

RECOLLECTIONS

48 CHURCH STREET, WARE, HERTFORDSHIRE SG12 9EW

☎ (01920) 461188. OPEN 10 - 4 TUE - SAT.

On two floors, this pretty little shop in Ware's town centre specialises in once-
worn wedding gowns and holds about 150 gowns at any one time, together
with accessories. Labels include Benjamin Roberts, Stevie, Ellis, Mon Cherie,
with constantly changing stock. Prices from £100. Also offers formal wear hire
for men and boys as well as wedding dress hire. *Dress Agency*

SCENT TO YOU

UNIT 142A, HARLEQUIN CENTRE, WATFORD, HERTFORDSHIRE
WD1 2TL

☎ (01923) 225712. OPEN 9.30 - 5.30 MON - SAT.

Discounted perfume and accessories including body lotions and gels. The
company, which has two branches, buys in bulk and sells more cheaply, relying on a high turnover for profit. Discounts range from 5% to 60%, with
greater savings during their twice-yearly sales (phone for details). Most of the
leading brand names are stocked including Christian Lacroix, Armani,
Charlie, Givenchy, Anais Anais from Cacherel, Charlie from Revlon, Coco
Chanel, Christian Dior, Elizabeth Taylor, Blue Grass from Elizabeth Arden,
Aramis, Lagerfeld. Occasionally, they also buy in a limited range of skincare
lines. Stock varies greatly due to the fast turnover and varying supplies so more
than one visit may be necessary to obtain the scent of your choice. Or phone
first to avoid disappointment. *Permanent Discount Outlet*

SPOILS

UNIT D, THE MARLOWES CENTRE, HEMEL HEMPSTEAD,
HERTFORDSHIRE HP1 1DY

☎ (01442) 235018. OPEN 9 - 5.30 MON - SAT, UNTIL 8 ON THUR.

General domestic glassware, non-stick bakeware, kitchen gadgets, ceramic oven-to-tableware, textiles, cutting boards, aluminium non-stick cookware, bakeware, plastic kitchenware, plastic storage, woodware, coffee pots/makers, furniture, mirrors and picture frames. Rather than being discounted, all the merchandise is very competitively priced - in fact, the company carry out competitors' checks frequently in order to monitor pricing. With 38 branches, the company is able to buy in bulk and thus negotiate very good prices. *Permanent Discount Outlet*

THE BAGGAGE FACTORY

GALLERIA OUTLET CENTRE, COMET WAY, HATFIELD,
HERTFORDSHIRE AL10 0XR

☎ (01707) 257779. OPEN 10 - 8 MON - FRI, 10 - 6 SAT, 11 - 5 SUN.

Sells bags, cases and wallets, some well-known brand names such as Delsey and Samsonite, at discount prices. *Factory Shopping Village*

THE CURTAIN CONNECTION LTD

108 LONDON ROAD, ST ALBANS, HERTFORDSHIRE AL1 1NX

☎ (01727) 868368. FAX ☎ (01727) 758869. PLEASE TELEPHONE FOR OPENING HOURS.

A secondhand curtain shop with a well-deserved reputation for service and value for money. The shop is now in its sixth year and has recently been extended with currently over 450 pairs of good quality curtains, as well as a wide range of soft furnishings and accessories. Designer fabrics from all the main labels are represented here, including Liberty, Designers Guild, Anna French, Colefax & Fowler and Laura Ashley. Prices generally vary from £20 to £400 for a full-length pair of top-name interlined curtains complete with pelmet and tie-backs. The back of the shop has bee enlarged to accomodate a special section catering for the growing number of clients who are renting out properties. The curtains represented here, at the lower end of the price scale, are excellent value for money. The shop also sells secondhand furniture, mainly Victorian and early Twentieth century, and has started to specialise in one-off antique chairs. To get the best out of your visit, bring your measurements with you together with a sample of fabric, if possible. Find them also on the Internet on www.yell.co.uk/sites/curtain-connection/. *Secondhand Shop*

THE CURTAIN MILL

19 GREYCAINE ROAD, WATFORD, HERTFORDSHIRE WD2 4JP

☎ (01923) 220339. OPEN 9 - 5.30 SEVEN DAYS A WEEK. HOTLINE:

☎ 0171-375 1000.

Huge choice of fabrics at really low prices - from £1.99p a metre and including excellent discounts on many designer labels. A large warehouse, it stocks Ashley Wilde, Curtina and Swatchbox, among other leading names at discount prices. *Permanent Discount Outlet*

THE GALLERIA OUTLET CENTRE

COMET WAY, HATFIELD, HERTFORDSHIRE AL10 OXR

☎ (01707) 278301. OPEN 10 - 8 MON - FRI, 10 - 6 SAT, 11 - 5 SUN.

The outlet centre for London and the South East houses more than 70 outlets, including Bed & Bath Works selling bedlinen, towels and soaps; BhS for Less selling the Storehouse owned chain's men's, women's and childrenswear ranges, plus selections from its home and lighting ranges, at discounts of at least 30%; B52 for adult casualwear; Blazer selling men's clothes and accessories; Bow Bangles offering jewellery, hair accessories, sunglasses and bags; CBS selling a huge range of products synonymous with the UK's largest catalogue company, GUS; Chamberlaine's bicycles; Choice selling Next and other retailers' clothes for men, women and children; Ciro Citterio and City Menswear for vast selections of suits, shirts and leisure wear; Class Cosmetics who sell top name beauty and skincare products including Elizabeth Arden, Lancome, Revlon, Max Factor, L'Oreal, Almay, Cover Girl and Yardley at between 30%-75% off normal retail prices; Clubhaus golf outlet store; Cook Ware House; Cotton Traders, which specialises in sports and leisure wear; Designer Room ladieswear for Dolce & Gabbana, Calvin Klein, Maska and Versace; Designer Room Menswear for Cerruti 1881, Dolce & Gabbana, Valentino, Ralph Lauren, Nicole Farhi and Calvin Klein; Discount Dressing for designer womenswear; Dorothy Perkins; Ecco Shoes; Erdos Cashmere; Feet Street shoes; Hawkes Bay casualwear for adults and children; Hobby Horse childrenswear; Hornsea Pottery; Kidcraft childrenswear; Kids Play Factory for branded toys; Julian Graves which sells dried fruits and nuts; Littlewoods catalogue outlet selling a wide range of designer and non-designer label leisure wear and shoes; the Main Event selling continental and US bridalwear offering huge savings off retail prices; Outdoor Trading Post for famous-name fleeces, jackets, waterproofs and skiwear; Planet Hollywood Outlet Store, Europe's first, selling Planet Hollywood merchandise for highly discounted prices; Ponden Mill for bedlinen, duvets, towels, kitchen linen; RS Shoes for fashion footwear; Soled Out shoes; Suits You for menswear; The Baggage Factory stocking luggage, briefcases, handbags and accessories; TK Maxx for branded fashions, gifts and homewares; Tog 24 for outdoor wear; Tom Sayers knitwear and menswear; Tool Warehouse; Whittard of Chelsea; Winning Line fashions. There is a good range of stores for children: Team Spirit, Chamberlaine's bikes and Kids Play

Factory stock an enviable range of branded toys including Duplo, Lego, Raleigh and Scalextric. For clothes, Hobby Horse principally selling beautiful girls' clothes and Kidcraft selling branded fashion for 2-12-year-olds. Littlewoods, TK Maxx and Choice all offer a full range of childrenswear complimented by RS Shoes, Soled Out, Ecco and Feet Street selling branded footwear. For the home, TK Maxx always has an exciting array of decorative vases, cookware, glassware and crockery from famous manufacturers; BhS for Less sells the Storehouse-owned chain's men's, women's and childrenswear ranges, plus selections from its home and lighting ranges, at discounts of at least thirty percent; Chinacraft, Hornsea Pottery also sells cookware, table cloths, napkins and cutlery; Ponden Mill has bedlinen, towels, duvets and bathroom accessories, while Bed & Bath Works will compliment any home with a range of towels, duvets, pillows, bathroom accessories, lampshades and dried flowers, London China Shop offers brand-name glass and china at discounted prices and Cook Ware House. There are lots of restaurants and a multiplex cinema on site with masses of car parking. *Factory Shopping Village*

THE SHOE SHED

C/O CLOTHING WORLD, ORCHARD ROAD, ROYSTON, HERTFORDSHIRE SG8 5HA
☎ (01763) 241933. OPEN 9 - 5.30 MON - SAT, 10 - 4 SUN.
Large factory shop selling a vast range of all types of men's, women's and children's shoes, all of which are perfects, at up to 30% below normal high street prices. Men's shoes from £10; sports shoes from £10. Ladies sandals cost from £5; ladies shoes from £7.50. *Factory Shop*

TK MAXX

THE GALLERIA SHOPPING CENTRE, COMET WAY, JUNCTION 3 OFF THE A1, HATFIELD, HERTFORDSHIRE AL10 OXR
☎ (01707) 260066. OPEN 10 - 8 MON - FRI, 10 - 6 SAT, 11 - 5 SUN.
Based on an American concept, TK Maxx is situated in easily accessible, often centrally located stores and offers famous label goods with up to 60% savings off recommended retail prices. TK Maxx has fashion for the whole family - women's, men's and childrenswear - accessories, shoes, gifts, kitchenware and home goods. Everything in the store is branded with a choice of well-known high street names to designer labels, and while a small percentage might be clearly marked past season, the great majority of items in store are current season, current stock and still with phenomenal savings. There is a huge choice with 50,000 pieces in store and up to 10,000 new items arriving a week. The stores are simple and unfussy with wide aisles, shopping trolleys and baskets, and a spacious, functional feel to them but there are individual changing rooms, ramps for buggies and wheelchairs and plenty of staff on the shop floor. Every branch accepts all major credit and debit cards and has a liberal refund and return policy. *Permanent Discount Outlet*

TOG 24

UNIT 29B, GALLERIA OUTLET CENTRE, COMET WAY, HATFIELD, HERTFORDSHIRE AL10 OXR

☎ (01707) 258088. OPEN 10 - 8 MON - FRI, 10 - 6 SAT, 11 - 5 SUN.

Tog 24 are the UK's fastest growing brand name in outdoor clothing and leisurewear, with a total of three UK factories and 36 stores nationwide. They utilise the world's finest performance fabrics including Gore-Tex, Polartec and Burlington macs. Catering for all the family for all seasons, with cosy fleeces and waterproofs for the winter, and trekking ranges, shorts and t-shirts for the summer. With all prices at least 30% below the recommended retail price you can afford to enter the Tog comfort zone. *Factory Shopping Village*

TOM SAYERS CLOTHING CO

THE GALLERIA OUTLET CENTRE, COMET WAY, HATFIELD, HERTFORDSHIRE AL10 0XR

☎ (01707) 257729. OPEN 10 - 8 MON - FRI, 10 - 6 SAT, 11 - 5 SUN.

Tom Sayers make sweaters for some of the top high street department stores. Unusually for a factory shop, if they don't stock your size, they will try and order it for you from their factory or one of their other factory outlets and send it to you. Most of the stock here is overstock, cancelled orders or last season's and includes jumpers, trousers, jackets and shirts. The trousers and shirts are bought in to complement the sweaters which they make. *Factory Shopping Village*

WALKER & HALL

GALLERIA OUTLET CENTRE, COMET WAY, HATFIELD, HERTFORDSHIRE AL10 0XS

☎ (01707) 270121. OPEN 10 - 8 MON - FRI, 10 - 6 SAT, 11 - 5 SUN.

One of more than 70 shops in this glass and steel factory shopping centre straddling the A1. This outlet sells Raymond Weil watches, reduced from £550 to £385; Longines, Gucci, Maurice Lacroix and Tag Heuer. Some ranges reduced by 30%. *Factory Shopping Village*

WATFORD BATHROOMS AND INTERIORS

60-62 QUEEN'S ROAD, WATFORD, HERTFORDSHIRE WD1 2LA

☎ (01923) 442046. OPEN 9 - 5.30 MON - SAT, 10.30 - 4 SUN.

Good quality bathrooms at discounted prices including Sottini, Heritage, Daryl, Showerlux and Aqualisa. Discounts represents about 25% off normal retail prices. Bathrooms accessories are also discounted. Free parking. *Permanent Discount Outlet*

WHITTARD

GALLERIA OUTLET CENTRE, COMET WAY, HATFIELD, HERTS AL10 0YA

☎ (01707) 273930. OPEN 10 - 8 MON - FRI, 10 - 6 SAT, 11 - 5 SUN.

Sells tea, coffee, coffee-making equipment (cafetieres and stove-top espressos) and wide range of china at discount prices. *Factory Shopping Village*

Kent

WOMENSWEAR ONLY   Alexon sale Shop, *Ramsgate*. All Change, *Bexleyheath*.
Be-Wise, *Sidcup*. Bon Marche, *Canterbury*. Clothesline, *Maidstone*. Deja Vu, Seal, *Nr Sevenoaks*.
Frock Follies, *Beckenham*. McArthurglen Designer Outlet Centre, *Ashford*. Panache, *Tunbridge Wells*.
Phase Eight, *Canterbury*. Reflections, *Hythe*. Snips in Fashion, *Orpington*. The Dress Agency, *Bexley*.
The Frock Exchange, *Chislehurst*.

MENSWEAR ONLY   Michelsons, *Sittingbourne*.

WOMENSWEAR & MENSWEAR   Catalogue Bargain Shop, *Faversham*.
David Evans World of Silk, *Crayford*. De Bradelei Mill Shops, *Dover*. Hangers, *Beckenham*.
Matalan, *Maidstone*. Peter Newman Factory Shop, *Herne Bay*.
Ramsgate Boulevard Designer Outlet Village, *Ramsgate*. The Factory Shop Ltd, *Headcorn*.

CHILDREN   Catalogue Bargain Shop, *Faversham*. De Bradelei Mill Shops, *Dover*.
Deja Vu, Seal, *Nr Sevenoaks*. KiddieQuip, *Tunbridge Wells*. Matalan, *Maidstone*.
Nippers, *Hildenborough*. Nippers, *Bekesbourne*. Panache, *Tunbridge Wells*.
Peter Newman Factory Shop, *Herne Bay*. The Factory Shop Ltd, *Headcorn*. Toytime, *Hildenborough*.

HOUSEHOLD AND GIFTWARE   Clover Leaf, *Dover*. Catalogue Bargain Shop, *Faversham*.
David Evans World of Silk, *Crayford*. De Bradelei Wharf, *Dover*. Elite Lighting, *Beckenham*.
Matalan, *Maidstone*. Ponden Mill Linens, *Dover*. Spoils, *Maidstone*. The Factory Shop Ltd, *Headcorn*.

ELECTRICAL EQUIPMENT   Catalogue Bargain Shop, *Faversham*.

DIY/RENOVATION   Bromley Demolition, *Bromley*. In Doors, *Sevenoaks*.
Tile Clearing House, *Orpington*

ARCHITECTURAL SALVAGE   Bromley Demolition, *Bromley*. In Doors, *Sevenoaks*.

FURNITURE/SOFT FURNISHINGS   Bell House Fabrics, *Cranbrook*.
De Bradelei Wharf, *Dover*. Knickerbean, *Tunbridge Wells*. The Curtain Shop, *Tunbridge Wells*.
The Factory Shop Ltd, *Headcorn*. Tracks & Trimmings, *Tunbridge Wells*.

FOOD AND LEISURE   B & A Whelan, *Sheerness*. Baggins Books, *Rochester*.

ALEXON SALE SHOP
64 HIGH STREET, RAMSGATE, KENT CT11 9RS
☎ (01843) 589860. OPEN 9 - 5.30 MON - SAT.
Eastex, Dash and Alexon clothing at reduced prices. Stock is mostly last year's
and at least half the original price. ***Permanent Discount Outlet***

ALL CHANGE
228A BROADWAY, BEXLEYHEATH, KENT DA6 7AU
☎ 0181-303 3094. OPEN 9.15 - 4.30 MON - SAT.
Ladies clothing, including names such as Planet, Jacques Vert, John Charles, Next, Wallis and Marks & Spencer, as well as bridalwear and eveningwear sold at at least half of the original price. *Dress Agency*

B & A WHELAN
52 HIGH STREET, BLUE TOWN, SHEERNESS, KENT ME12 1RW
☎ (01795) 663879. OPEN 9 - 6 SEVEN DAYS A WEEK.
Manufacturers of concrete garden ornaments, they sell more than 1,300 different items including benches, gnomes, bird baths and sundials, all sold at prices which are about 75% less than those charged in most garden centres. Parking. *Permanent Discount Outlet*

BAGGINS BOOK BAZAAR
19 HIGH STREET, ROCHESTER, KENT ME1 1PY
☎ (01634) 811651. FAX 840591. OPEN 10 - 6 SEVEN DAYS A WEEK.
Largest secondhand bookshop in England with prices from 50p to £500. Deals in rare and secondhand books, but also sells some brand new review copies at substantial discounts. Prices of the older books depend on their condition. Book search service also offered. *Secondhand Shop*

BE-WISE
5 GLOUCESTER PARADE, BLACKFEN ROAD, SIDCUP, KENT DA15 8PS
☎ 0181-859 2658. OPEN 10 - 5 MON - SAT, CLOSED THUR.
Middle market names including Principles, Berkertex, Marks & Spencer and Next as well as the occasional designer label. *Dress Agency*

BELL HOUSE FABRICS
HIGH STREET, CRANBROOK, KENT TN17 3DN
☎ (01580) 712555. OPEN 9 - 5.30 MON - SAT.
Cranbrook is a two-storey shop which is a Sanderson specialist, but also offers an extensive range of beautiful fabrics from manufacturers such as Anne Swaffer, Jane Churchill, Monkwell and John Wilman, with 400 books to order from other well-known suppliers. Everything is sold at competitive prices, with current, seconds and discontinued lines at less than half price. Printed cottons from £6.99; upholstery fabrics - brocades, tapestries and damasks - from £13.99; Sanderson's linens from £10.99; dress fabrics from £2.99 and silks from £8. They also offer a quality design, makde-up and fitting service. Haberdashery, wallpapers and all soft furnishing accessories either in stock or to order. *Permanent Discount Outlet*

BON MARCHE
47 NORTHGATE, CANTERBURY, KENT CT1 1BE
☎ (01227) 764823. OPEN 9.30 - 5.30 MON - SAT
A large, well-established dress agency which offers across-the-board labels from Marks & Spencer up to YSL, with plenty of Jaeger, Maxmara, Mondi, Alexon and Caroline Charles. Prices range from £10 for an M&S top quality outfit to £150, though most items are in the £35-£75 price range. Day and evening wear as well as shoes, jewellery, bags, scarves and hats are stocked. The owner says that style is more important than the label and is as likely to stock Dorothy Perkins as Dior. After one month in the shop, stock is reduced by one third. *Dress Agency*

BROMLEY DEMOLITION
75 SIWARD ROAD, BROMLEY, KENT
☎ 0181-464 3610. OPEN 9 - 5 MON - FRI.
Bromley Demolition reclaim whatever is usable from demolished properties including doors, old bricks, assorted sizes of timbers, fireplaces. *Architectural Salvage*

CATALOGUE BARGAIN SHOP
19A PRESTON STREET, FAVERSHAM, KENT ME13 8NX
☎ (01795) 591203. OPEN 9 - 5.30 MON - SAT, 10 - 4 SUN.
Catalogue Bargain Shop is a growing national chain of stores which obtains the majority of its goods from mail order giants Great Universal and Kays, and offers a range of clothing for all the family, a wide selection of shoes, bed linen, household goods, electrical equipment and hundreds of other catalogue items at very competitive prices. The merchandise consists of ends of ranges and previous season's stock for which there is no longer storage space when the catalogues change. *Permanent Discount Outlet*

CLOTHESLINE
58 UNION STREET, MAIDSTONE, KENT ME14 1ED
☎ (01622) 758439. OPEN 9.30 - 5 TUE - SAT.
Designer labels of not more than two years in age in mint condition. Labels include Mondi, Jaeger, Laurel, Jacques Vert, Yarrell, Escada, Betty Barclay, Frank Usher, Tom Bowker and MaxMara. *Dress Agency*

CLOVER LEAF
DE BRADELEI WHARF,CAMBRIDGE ROAD, DOVER, KENT CT17 9BY
☎ (01304) 226616. OPEN 9.30 - 5.30 MON - FRI, 9.30 - 6 SAT, 11 - 5 SUN.
Part of the large household department at this large factory shopping complex, one section sells a range of melamine products, such as place mats, coasters and trays, oven to tableware and bathroom accessories. Seconds and discontinued lines are sold here at reduced prices. *Factory Shop*

DAVID EVANS WORLD OF SILK

BOURNE ROAD, CRAYFORD, KENT DA1 4BP

☎ (01322) 559401. OPEN 9.30 - 5 MON - FRI, 9.30 - 4 SAT.

Silk ties, silk fabric, purses, wallets, handbags, photo frames, silk cosmetic bags, seconds in scarves, silk dressing gowns, visitors books, silk waistcoats and cravats are all on sale here at what are described as real factory shop prices. Silk fabric sold by the metre. Occasional clearance sales make for even better bargains. Now also top fashion designer Paul Costelloe factory shop selling his ends of lines, seconds and samples at 50% off the usual shop prices. Museum and coffee shop, ample parking; also guided tours - please book. The shop is on the A223, five minutes from the A2 to London and 15 minutes from junction 2 of the M25. *Factory Shop*

DE BRADELEI WHARF

DE BRADELEI MILL SHOPS (DOVER) LTD, CAMBRIDGE ROAD, DOVER, KENT CT17 9BY

☎ (01304) 226616. OPEN 9.30 - 5.30 MON - FRI, 9.30 - 6 SAT, 11 - 5 SUN.

Large outlet in superb maritime setting just off the Dover Seafront, selling top brand names for all the family, including shoes. The ladieswear includes such names as Windsmoor, Planet, Precis Petite, Elle, French Connection, Virgin, Jackpot, Phase Eight, Gerard Pasquier, plus top American and German designer labels, handbags and much more. The menswear range includes underwear, socks, coats, sweaters, jackets, suits and trousers from labels such as Wolsey, Countrywear, French Connection, Virgin and Tog 24. Robert Leonard's Menswear provide Greiff, Pierre Cardin, Gabicci, Gurteen, Oakman, Saville Row, John Slim and many more. There is a large shoe department featuring international shoes for all the family and a wonderful Home Furnishings Department. The Interior Design shops sell bedding, towels, top-name furnishing fabric, cushions, throws, furniture and curtains. The Glass and China Department has an amazing selection from Waterford Wedgwood, Stuart Crystal, Royal Doulton, Arthur Price of England Silverware, Staffordshire Tableware, Churchill, Cloverleaf, Hornsea Pottery, Cristal d'Arques and much more. There is superb Liberty stock in the giftware department. Parking is easy with a large car park behind the store. The Waves Coffee Shop is open all day, serving delicious home-cooked food. Coach parties are welcome. *Permanent Discount Outlet*

Live Well On Less Tips

Nippers is a chain of 11 farm-based outlets which sell prams, pushchairs, car seats, cots, toys and books at discount prices. Most are end of lines or last season's designs with some secondhand items. Phone 01732 838333 for your nearest branch.

DEJA VU

OLD SEAL HOUSE, 19 CHURCH STREET, SEAL, NEAR SEVENOAKS, KENT TN15 0DA

☎ (01732) 762155. OPEN 10 - 4.30 TUE - SAT.

In this small, friendly shop, established in 1977, you will find British and European designers such as Paul Costelloe, Gerry Weber, Betty Barclay, Tomasz Starzewski, Valentino, Rodier, Yves St Laurent and Ouiset as well as old favourites such as Jaeger, Marks & Spencer and Laura Ashley. The price range is from £10 to £200. There is also a small range of children's dresses, and from September each year, ski wear for adults and children. After six to eight weeks, clothes which haven't sold are reduced. An alteration service is also offered for clothes purchased here. *Dress Agency*

ELITE LIGHTING

7 GOODWOOD PARADE, UPPER ELMERS END ROAD, BECKENHAM, KENT BR3 3QZ

☎ 0181-639 0050. OPEN 9.30 - 5.30 MON - SAT. ALSO MAIL ORDER.

Spectacular range of crystal chandeliers and wall brackets, all with 24 carat gold plate frames and dressed with Swarovski and brass crystal, according to one reader. Their prices are very competitive because they buy direct from leading importers. Also offers a mail order service. *Permanent Discount Outlet*

FROCK FOLLIES

49 HIGH STREET, BECKENHAM, KENT BR3 1DA

☎ 0181-650 9283. OPEN 9.30 - 5.30 MON - SAT.

Middle market labels from Marks & Spencer to Armani with some new samples. Specialises in hats, with more than 100 to choose from, as well as swimwear, shoes, hat pins, belts and scarves. The hats and jewellery are new. Plenty of evening wear, particularly ball gowns, especially from September to Christmas. *Dress Agency*

HANGERS

53 CROYDON ROAD, BECKENHAM, KENT BR4 4AB

☎ 0181-658 5386. OPEN 9.30 - 5.30 MON - SAT.

Mixture of high street and designer labels including Valentino, Boss, Windsmoor, Planet and Country Casuals. For men, there are suits, jackets, coats, shirts, trousers, ties and shoes. For women, day and evening wear, dresses, skirts, tops, hats, shoes and accessories. Prices range from £5 - £100. *Dress Agency*

IN DOORS

BEECHINWOOD FARM, BEECHINWOOD LANE, PLATT, SEVENOAKS, KENT TN15 8QN

☎ (01732) 887445. OPEN 9 - 5 MON - FRI, 9 - 12.30 SAT.

Reclaimed pine and some oak doors and new doors made from reclaimed wood for the kitchen, wardrobe or door frames. Reclaimed pine doors, £80, for small kitchen door; £60 for wardrobe door; £120 for large door. Free parking. *Architectural Salvage*

KIDDIEQUIP

36 NEWLANDS, LANGTON GREEN, TUNBRIDGE WELLS, KENT TN3 ODB

☎ (01892) 862369. PHONE FIRST.

Part of the Baby Equipment Hirers Association (BEHA), which has more than 100 members countrywide. A range of equipment can be hired from high chairs, cots and travel cots to baby car seats and buggies. Some members also hire out party equipment including child-sized tables and chairs. BEHA run an advice line which will try and answer any queries you have regarding hiring services for children. Phone the Babyline on 0831 310355. *Hire Shop*

KNICKERBEAN

87 HIGH STREET, TUNBRIDGE WELLS, KENT TN1 1XZ

☎ (01892) 520883. OPEN 9 - 5.30 MON - SAT.

Knickerbean is one of the few companies that continue to offer genuine top-name designer fabric bargains. . .the kind of curtain and upholstery fabrics that are found at Decorex and the Chelsea Harbour Design Centre. Their rapidly-changing stock often includes excess inventory and discontinued lines from these kinds of designers, as well as occasional slight seconds, with many sold at between 20%-50% off the regular price. They also carry a large range of top-quality fabrics in the latest styles which they buy directly from mills and manufacturers in the UK, Europe and North America, offering similar top quality, but at vastly reduced prices. Their attractively laid-out shops feature a vast range of different selections of curtain and upholstery fabrics. These include classic country house glazed chintzes, fresh stripes and checks, fashionable toiles de jouy, bright cotton prints and PVC-coated fabrics, a wide range of damasks and natural fabrics, sumptuous chenilles, rich kilim patterns, self-patterned dobby weaves and a fabulous selection of upholstery brocades and tapestries. Prices start from £4.95 for plain cottons and prints to £19.95 and occasionally more for chenilles and tapestries. Customers are encouraged to pop in regularly to check out the latest arrivals in their stock. The benefit here is that they are able to see entire rolls rather than just a small sample book of swatches. Their professionally trained staff are ready to advise on quality and quantity for any type of furnishing project. They extend their service to measure and quote, as they offer a complete making up service for all soft furnishings, including loose covers and upholstery. They are even prepared to bring along a few rolls to try out against a customer's own colour scheme. Twice-yearly sales are held in January and June to enable customers to snap up even bigger bargains. *Permanent Discount Outlet*

MATALAN

UNIT A, BROADWAY SHOPPING CENTRE, THE BROADWAY,
MAIDSTONE, KENT ME16 8PS

☎ (01622) 675153. OPEN 10 - 8 MON - FRI, 9 - 6 SAT, 11 - 4 SUN.

Matalan is a fashion and homewares shop giving customers what they claim to be unbeatable value for money with huge savings on a wide range of products including high quality fashionable clothing for women, women and children at up to 50% off high street prices. Matalan is situated out of town and stores are open seven days a week all year round. *Permanent Discount Outlet*

MCARTHURGLEN DESIGNER OUTLET CENTRE

ASHFORD, KENT

Due to open in March 2000, this centre will have 116 shops, a covered children's play area and parking for 1,500 cars. Designed by Lord Rogers, the centre takes the form of a leaf-shaped tented structure, one kilometre in circumference. Almost all of the parking takes place in the centre of the piazza so that shoppers can see all the shops immediately they leave their car. The Centre is located alongside the Ashford International Rail Station on the Channel Tunnel rail link. *Factory Shopping Village*

MICHELSONS

STAPLEHURST ROAD, SITTINGBOURNE, KENT ME10 2NH

☎ (01795) 426821. OPEN 9 - 12 FRI.

Michelsons, one of the largest tie manufacturers in Europe, has a small factory shop attached to the factory selling silk neckties, bowties, handkerchiefs, scarves and cravats. All the stock is current or last season's or ends of lines and is discounted by at least 30%. There is a choice of more than 1,000 ties in silk at maximum prices of £6. *Factory Shop*

Live Well On Less Tips

Save money on large items such as fireplaces, doors or garden statuary as well as household furniture, bought from the hundreds of architectural salvage yards countrywide which sell reclaimed items from old buildings. Find your local yard in the SALVO guide which costs £5.75 for a pack which includes your local outlet. SALVO!, Ford Village, Berwick-upon-Tweed TD15 2QG; 01890 820333.

NIPPERS

MANSERS, NIZELS LANE, HILDENBOROUGH, KENT TN11 8NX
☎ (01732) 832253. FAX ☎ (01732) 833658. OPENING HOURS VARY SO PHONE FIRST.
CHALKPIT FARM, SCHOOL LANE, BEKESBOURNE, CANTERBURY, KENT CT4 5EU
☎ (01227) 832008. FAX ☎ (01227) 831496.

Nippers, the nursery equipment and toy specialists, operate from previously redundant buildings in rural areas around the country. They offer easy parking, no queues and personal service. This is on top of competitive prices on prams, cots, pushchairs, car seats, outdoor play equipment and toys, some of which are new, some seconds or secondhand and some ends of lines. Prices are low because they avoid the high overheads of traditional retail outlets and also because the successful growth of a number of branches means they can now buy in bulk and negotiate good deals. Customers are invited to try out the merchandise while the children look at the animals, mostly sheep, chicken and pigs. Familiar brand names are on sale at all the branches, including Mamas & Papas, Britax, Maclaren and Bebe Confort, plus Fisher-Price and Little Tikes. You can try out the car seats in your car and there is usually a pram/pushchair repair service on site. *Permanent Discount Outlet*

PANACHE

90 - 92 HIGH STREET, ROYAL TUNBRIDGE WELLS, KENT TN1
☎ (01892) 522 883. OPEN 10 - 5 MON - SAT.

On two floors, Panache sells women's nearly-new at savings of up to 50% on high street prices. The agency stocks a wide range of labels from Marks and Spencer and Viyella to Jacques Vert, MaxMara and Escada. They also sell hats, a large selection of evening wear, coats, shoes, jackets, handbags and belts. *Dress Agency*

PETER NEWMAN FACTORY SHOP

UNIT IB, EDDINGTON BUSINESS PARK, THANET WAY, HERNE BAY, KENT CT6 5TT
☎ (01227) 741112. OPEN 9 - 5.30 MON - SAT, 10 - 4 SUN.

Discontinued styles, slight seconds and end of line adult and children's shoes. Clarks, Timberland, Lee, Pods, Lotus, Equity and Hi-Tec sportswear are typical names, available at up to 35% reductions. A GDD reader bought a pair of Clarks children's shoes for £20, usual price £29; and two pairs of sandals for £10 and £12, usual price, £29.95 and £34.95. Also sell bags. Small refreshment area, car parking and wheelchair accessible. *Factory Shop*

PHASE EIGHT

11 BUTCHERY LANE, CANTERBURY, KENT CT1 2JR
☎ (01227) 786581. OPEN 9 - 5.30 MON - SAT.
DE BRADELEI WHARF, CAMBRIDGE ROAD, DOVER, KENT CT17 9BY
☎ (01304) 226616. OPEN 9.30 - 5.30 MON - FRI, 9.30 - 6 SAT, 11 - 5 SUN.
Phase Eight, the 24-strong chain which sells smart workwear and wearable special occasion outfits, has a Sale Shop in Canterbury. Here, end of season merchandise, samples and seconds are sold at discount prices, including tailored trouser suits, dresses, skirts, knitwear and tops as well as more formal outfits for special occasions and casual weekend wear. *Permanent Discount Outlet*

PONDEN MILL LINENS

DE BRADELEI WHARF, CAMBRIDGE ROAD, DOVER, KENT CT17 9BY
☎ (01304) 225821. OPEN 9.30 - 5.30 MON - FRI, 9.30 - 6 SAT, 11 - 5 SUN.
Famous branded products at direct from the mill prices. Towels, co-ordinated bedlinen, duvets, pillows and curtains from Crown, Coloroll, Chortex, Rectella together with bathroom and kitchen accessories. *Factory Shopping Village*

RAMSGATE BOULEVARD DESIGNER OUTLET VILLAGE

RAMSGATE HARBOUR RAILWAY STATION, MARINE ESPLANADE,
RAMSGATE, KENT.
DUE TO OPEN SEPTEMBER 2000.
65,000 sq ft retail development set in the magnificent Victorian structure of the old Ramsgate Harbour Railways Station located on Marine Esplanade. *Factory Shopping Village*

REFLECTIONS

7-9 MARINE WALK STREET, HYTHE, KENT CT21 5NW
☎ (01303) 262233. OPEN 10 - 4 MON - SAT, CLOSED WED.
About fifty percent of Reflection's stock is second-hand, the other fifty percent are German and Italian designer samples. Nearly-new labels include Jaeger, Jobis, Ouiset, Windsmoor, Aquascutum, Country Casuals, Mondi and Betty Barclay. They also sell some manufacturers samples. They will buy on order if they know you, look out for particular requests in nearly-nearly new and phone you if anything suitable comes in, and are very helpful in choosing accessories. Large selection of hats for hire; also good selection of ballgowns. *Dress Agency and Hire Shop*

Live Well On Less Tips
Remove bows from old outfits to prettify a new plain cheap hat.

SNIPS IN FASHION

234 HIGH STREET, ORPINGTON, KENT BR6 OLS
☎ (01689) 828288. OPEN 9.30 - 5.30 MON - SAT.
Clearance outlet featuring labels such as Olsen, Fink, Michelle, Dolores and
Apsa at less than half the original price. Some are current stock, others samples from showrooms, yet others discontinued lines, seconds or late deliveries.
The whole range of clothing is stocked from ballgowns and coats to jeans and
beach wear, but no accessories. *Permanent Discount Outlet*

SPOILS

M323-324 CHEQUERS CENTRE, DUKES WALK, MAIDSTONE, KENT
ME15 6AS
☎ (01622) 678916. OPEN 9 - 5.30 MON - SAT, 9.30 - 5.30 TUE.
General domestic glassware, non-stick bakeware, kitchen gadgets, ceramic
oven-to-tableware, textiles, cutting boards, aluminium non-stick cookware,
bakeware, plastic kitchenware, plastic storage, woodware, coffee pots/makers,
furniture, mirrors and picture frames. Rather than being discounted, all the
merchandise is very competitively priced - in fact, the company carry out
competitors' checks frequently in order to monitor pricing. With 38 branches, the company is able to buy in bulk and thus negotiate very good prices.
Permanent Discount Outlet

THE CURTAIN SHOP

12 GOODS STATION ROAD, TUNBRIDGE WELLS, KENT TN1 2BL
☎ (01892) 527202. FAX ☎ (01892) 522682. OPEN 9.30 - 5.30 MON - SAT.
The seven show rooms are festooned with fine quality secondhand and new
curtains at reasonable prices. Designer fabrics are available on the roll at discount prices and the shop provides a making-up and track-fitting service.
Decorative pelmets are a speciality with the fringe and tassel room carrying an
extensive range of tassels, fringes and ropes of every sort for use in making pelmets. Prices range from £3 per metre for multi-coloured ropes through to a
rare piece of bullion fringe at £60 a metre. Curtain prices range from as little
as £30 for a pair of cottage curtains to more than £1,000 for a pair of antique
silk velvet curtains. Typically, a wide pair of long, lined and interlined damask
curtains covering nine feet of track would cost around £440, and a pair of curtains suitable for the spare room can cost as little as £185. On the other hand,
a gorgeous pair of white silk tassels threaded with silver and made for a sultan
will set you back £380. *Secondhand Shop*

THE DRESS AGENCY

5 BOURNE ROAD, BEXLEY, KENT DA5 1LG

☎ (01322) 523451. OPEN 10.30 - 5 TUE - SAT.

Chainstore clothes and secondhand designer wear plus a large selection of shoes and hats. Labels range from Richards to Rodier and Betty Barclay. *Dress Agency*

THE FACTORY SHOP LTD

THE FOREMAN CENTRE, HIGH STREET, HEADCORN, KENT TN27 9NE

☎ (01622) 891651. OPEN 9 - 5.30 MON - SAT, UNTIL 7 THUR, FRI, 11 - 5 SUN.

High street chainstore seconds and ends of ranges from clothes for all the family, bedding, toiletries, kitchenware, glassware, footwear, lighting, cosmetics, jewellery, and luggage at discounts of approximately 30%-50%. There are weekly deliveries and brands include many major stars: Wrangler, Nike, Adidas and Dartington, to name just four. Lines are continually changing and few factory shops offer such a variety under one roof, with at the Brighton branch, a large number of clothing concessions in addition to The Factory Shop range. On display is a new line of Cape Country Furniture has recently been introduced at all four South East branches. This high quality pine furniture made exclusively for The Factory Shop in South Africa is sold at factory direct prices with home delivery throughout the UK. Colour brochure and price list available. Free car park. *Factory Shop*

THE FROCK EXCHANGE

7 WALDEN PARADE, WALDEN ROAD, CHISLEHURST, KENT BR7 5DW

OPEN 9.30 - 4.30 MON - SAT, CLOSED WED.

Located less than one miles from Chislehurst high street, with easy free parking, the Frock Exchange sells an extensive range of nearly-new clothes from the high street chains, plus Mondi, Alexon, Mansfield, Betty Barclay and Jacques Vert. From time to time, there are also wonderful outifts from top houses such as Jean Muir, Bruce Oldfield, Escada and Valentino. Apart from frocks and separates, the shop also has a wide selection of bags, belts, jewellery (real diamonds as well as fakes), hats, scarves and footwear. Most clothing is no more than two years old and there is a rapid turnover with new stock constantly arriving each day. There is a small bric-a-brac area with pretty china, photo frames and ornaments, as well as secondhand curtain and other textiles. *Dress Agency*

Live Well On Less Tips

Don't let buttons pop off and have to be replaced - dab the cotton thread holding them with clear nail varnish.

TILE CLEARING HOUSE

UNIT A5, NUGENT INDUSTRIAL ESTATE, CRAY WAY, ST MARY CRAY, ORPINGTON, KENT BR5 3RP

☎ (01689) 890 511. OPEN 8 - 6 MON - FRI, 9 - 6 SAT, 10 - 4 SUN.

Over 500 ranges of top quality ceramic wall and floor tiles permanently in stock, plus a comprehensive range of grouts, adhesives, tools and accessories to complete the job. Save up to 75% on manufacturers' recommended selling prices. *Permanent Discount Outlet*

TOYTIME

MEOPHAM BANK FARM, LEIGH ROAD, HILDENBOROUGH, NEAR TONBRIDGE, KENT TN11 9AQ

☎ (01732) 833695/832416. OPEN 9 - 12 AND 7.30 - 8.30 TUE, 9 - 12 THUR, 9 - 4 SAT.

Sells both new and secondhand toys – anything from a rattle to a climbing frame. The stock is always changing as you can get immediate cash for your used toys in good condition. There is a huge selection in three barns including bikes, trikes, doll's prams, doll's houses, trampolines, slides, sandpits, to mention just a few. In addition, party bag fillers and baby toys abound. All the outdoor equipment (as well as Brio, Playmobil and Lego) is new and is sold at discounted prices. Climbing frames and swings are on display outside (and some animals) and advice is given, when required. *Permanent Discount Outlet*

TRACKS AND TRIMMINGS

50 THE PANTILES, TUNBRIDGE WELLS, KENT TN2 5TN

☎ (01892) 515288. OPEN 9.30 - 5.30 MON - SAT, 9.30 - 1 WED.

Tracks and trimmings, upholstery and curtains, cushions, tie-backs, from £3.95 each, compared with £18 in the high street; plaited and rope tie-backs, from £9.99; cushion covers, £3.95; pelmet boards and handmade lampshades. Extensive fabric and pole ranges. *Permanent Discount Outlet*

Live Well On Less Tips

If your dinner service is missing a few pieces, before you buy a new service, check out the china matching agencies who may be able to find you missing pieces and save you the cost of a new set. Some of them operate by matching up people wishing to buy one or two pieces with those wanting to sell; others actually buy in parts of services and then sell individual pieces.

Lancashire
(including Greater Manchester)

Greater Manchester

MENSWEAR ONLY 🐎 Chatleys, *Manchester.* Slaters Menswear, *Manchester.*

WOMENSWEAR & MENSWEAR   🐎 🐎 Affleck's Place, *Manchester.*
Baird Outwear Brands Ltd, *Oldham.* Barneys, *Manchester.* Catalogue Bargain Shop, *Manchester.*
K Shoes, *Eccles.* Littlewoods Catalogue Discount Store, *Bolton.* Matalan, *Bolton.*
Pumpkin Dress Hire, *Deansgate.* Scoops, *Manchester.* Terry's Stores Urmstone Ltd, *Urmstone.*
The Elite Dress Agency, *Manchester.* The Factory Shop, *Swinton.* Tog 24, *Manchester.*
Top Marks, *Manchester.*

CHILDREN 🐚 Bouncing Babes, *Manchester.* Catalogue Bargain Shop, *Manchester.*
K Shoes, *Eccles.* Littlewoods Catalogue Discount Store, *Bolton.* Matalan, *Bolton.*
Scoops, *Manchester.* Terry's Stores Urmstone Ltd, *Urmstone.* The Elite Dress Agency, *Manchester.*
The Factory Shop, *Swinton.* Tog 24, *Manchester.* Top Marks, *Manchester.*

HOUSEHOLD AND GIFTWARE 🏠 Allweis, *Manchester.* Catalogue Bargain Shop,
Manchester. Matalan, *Bolton.* Spoils, *Manchester.* Top Marks, *Manchester.*

ELECTRICAL EQUIPMENT 🔌 Catalogue Bargain Shop, *Manchester.*
Littlewoods Catalogue Discount Store, *Bolton.* Pifco group Factory Shop, *Manchester.*

DIY/RENOVATION 🖌 Bruce Kilner Architectural Salvage, *Worsley.* In Situ, *Hulme.*
Optiroc, *Manchester.* Pilkington's Tiles Factory Shop, *Manchester.*
Tile Clearing House, *Higher Openshaw.* Tile Wizard, *Walkden.*

ARCHITECTURAL SALVAGE 🖌 Bruce Kilner Architectural Salvage, *Worsley.*
In Situ, *Hulme.* Optiroc, *Manchester.*

FURNITURE/SOFT FURNISHINGS 🪑 Abakhan Fabrics, *Manchester.*
Sanderson Clearance Outlet Shop, *Ancoats.* Terry's Stores Urmstone Ltd, *Urmstone.*
Willsmart factory Shop, *Salford.*

SPORTSWEAR AND EQUIPMENT 🎿 Allsports, *Salford.*

ABAKHAN FABRICS 🪑
111-115 OLDHAM STREET, MANCHESTER
☎ (0161) 839 3229. OPEN 9.30 - 5.15 MON - SAT.
With five outlets in the North West, Abakhan Fabrics are as well known for
the emphasis they put on value for money as they are for the huge variety of
fabrics, needlecrafts, haberdashery, gifts and knitting yarns that they have

gathered from all around the world. There are baskets of remnant fabrics, wools, yarns and unrivalled selections of fabrics sold by the metre from evening wear, bridal wear and crepe de Chine to curtaining, nets and velvets all at mill shop prices. Abakhan is able to offer such bargains through bulk buying, or selling clearance lines, job lots and seconds. There are no free parking facilities or a coffee shop here. Free information pack available: ring 01745 562100.*Permanent Discount Outlet*

AFFLECK'S PALACE

52 CHURCH STREET, MANCHESTER M41 PW

☎ (0161) 834 2039. OPEN 10 - 5.30 MON - FRI, 10 - 6 SAT.

Indoor fashion market specialising in street fashion and alternative fashion. Seventies' fashion including platform shoes. Also jewellery, rubber clothes and hair extensions. Fifties and Sixties nostalgia, new designer clothes and clothes from the Twenties to the present day. Two cafes and two hairdressers, offering hair beading, on site. *Secondhand and Vintage Clothing*

ALLSPORTS

99 ALBANY WAY, SALFORD 6, GREATER MANCHESTER M6 5JA

☎ (0161) 736 8582. OPEN 9 - 5.30 MON - SAT.

Allsports is a standard shop but at the rear, it has a dedicated area of marked-down goods. These are all damaged or end of season and there are great bargains to be had. Goods can be one-offs to particular items in various sizes. Stock varies from day to day so you could be delighted one day and disappointed the next. Typical bargains are British and foreign football shirts at between one quarter and one half of the normal perfect price. There are also trainers, sports goods, clothing, football boots, including some Man. United merchandise. There are fresh deliveries every day. *Permanent Discount Outlet*

ALLWEIS CHINA AND CRYSTAL

GEORGE STREET, BURY OLD ROAD, CHEETHAM HILL VILLAGE, MANCHESTER M7 4PX

☎ (0161) 7402409. OPEN 9.15 - 5.30 MON - SAT, 11 - 2 SUN.

Branded china and cutlery at discount including Waterford, Wedgwood, Royal Doulton, Royal Worcester and many others. None of the stock is seconds and discounts start at 10%. *Permanent Discount Outlet*

Live Well On Less Tips

Turn your old clothes into cash by taking them to a dress agency. These nearly-new shops will sell your good quality clothes for you, giving you 40%-50% of the sale price.

BAIRD OUTERWEAR BRANDS LTD

LIME MILL, VICTOR STREET, OLDHAM, GREATER MANCHESTER
OL8 3QN

☎ (0161) 681 2060. OPEN 8.30 - 11 ALTERNATE SATS.
FLETCHER STREET, BOLTON, GREATER MANCHESTER BL3 6PR

☎ (01204) 371930. OPEN 10 - 4 MON - FRI, 9 - 3 SAT.
BROADSTONE HOUSE, BROADSTONE ROAD, REDDISH, STOCKPORT
SK5 7DL

☎ (0161) 953 4461. OPEN 9.30 - 4 MON - FRI, 9 - 1 SAT.
Sells mens and ladies famous-name raincoats, jackets, anoraks, trenchcoats,
and macs at factory shop prices. Labels include Dannimac, Cloud Nine,
Telemac and Thomas Marshall for women; Dannimac and Baracuta for men.
Jackets and coats range from £19 to £130. Most merchandise is either slight
seconds or discontinued lines and clearance items. Excellent quality lingerie is
also available at Oldham, Bolton and Stockport, but men's suits, jackets and
trousers are available at Bolton only. *Factory Shop*

BARNEYS

JULIA STREET, OFF DUTTON STREET, MANCHESTER, GREATER
MANCHESTER

☎ (0161) 833 0533. OPEN 9.30 - 5.30 MON, TUE, WED, FRI,
9.30 - 7 THUR, 10 - 6 SAT, 11 - 5 SUN.
Versace, Prada, Paul Smith, Armani, Boss, Diesel, Calvin Klein, Iceberg,
Moschino, Gianfranco Ferre and Gucci at around half their normal retail
value. Prices range from about £20 for a pair of designer sunglasses up to as
much as £500 for a Versace suit. *Permanent Discount Outlet*

BOUNCING BABES

NEWBROOKE COTTAGE, LANDSDOWN ROAD, ATHERTON,
MANCHESTER M46 9HL

☎ (01942) 894729.
Part of the Baby Equipment Hirers Association (BEHA), which has more than
100 members countrywide. A range of equipment can be hired from high
chairs, cots and travel cots to baby car seats and buggies. Some members also
hire out party equipment including child-sized tables and chairs. BEHA run
an advice line which will try and answer any queries you have regarding hiring services for children. Phone the Babyline on 0831 310355. *Hire Shop*

BRUCE KILNER
ARCHITECTURAL SALVAGE

ASHTON'S FIELD FARM, WINDMILL ROAD, WALKDEN, WORSLEY,
MANCHESTER M28 3RP

☎ (0161) 702 8604. OPEN EVERY DAY. RING FOR APPOINTMENT.

Original doors, baths, radiators, sinks, sash windows, Victorian stable fittings,
cart wheels, troughs. *Architectural Salvage*

CATALOGUE BARGAIN SHOP

2/4 UNITS EGARTON WALK, ELLESMERE CENTRE, WALKDEN,
MANCHESTER M28 3ZD

☎ (0161) 703 9311. OPEN 9 - 5.30 MON - SAT.

HALL BANK, WORSLEY, ECCLES, MANCHESTER M30 8NR

☎ (0161) 787 7726. OPEN 10 - 5.30 MON - FRI, 8 ON THUR. 9 - 4.45 SAT,
10.30 - 4.30 SUN.

Catalogue Bargain Shop is a growing national chain of stores which obtains
the majority of its goods from mail order giants Great Universal and Kays, and
offers a range of clothing for all the family, a wide selection of shoes, bed linen,
household goods, electrical equipment and hundreds of other catalogue items
at very competitive prices. The merchandise consists of ends of ranges and previous season's stock for which there is no longer storage space when the catalogues change. *Permanent Discount Outlet*

CHATLEYS

14 CHATLEY STREET, MANCHESTER, LANCASHIRE

☎ (0161) 833 3230. OPEN 10 - 6 MON - FRI, 7 ON THUR, 10 - 5 SAT, SUN.

Classic clothes for men from Gabicci, Oakman and Peter England. Shirts,
trouserers, ties, coats and shoes are all discounted by 20%. *Permanent
Discount Outlet*

IN SITU

WORSLEY STREET, ST GEORGE'S, HULME, MANCHESTER, GREATER
MANCHESTER M15 4LD

☎ (0161) 839 2010. OPEN 9 - 5.30 MON - SAT,
11 - 5 SUN.

Church interiors, period fireplaces, doors, joinery, leaded glass and French
polishing, antique bathrooms, garden ware, staircases, chimney pots, furniture, flooring. Deliver anywhere. Period fireplaces cost from £50 for a small
cast-iron bedroom fireplace; baths from £100; reclaimed maple strip flooring
from £12 per square yard. Possibly changing premises, phone first for address.
Architectural Salvage

Live Well On Less Tips

Sign on with mail order companies whose clothes you like and wait for their end-of-season sale catalogues and buy everything at reduced prices.

K SHOES

21 CHURCH STREET, ECCLES, GREATER MANCHESTER M30 OAF
☎ (0161) 788 7039. OPEN 9 - 5.30 MON - SAT, 10 - 3.30 WED.

Clarks International operate a chain of factory shops nationally which specialise in selling discontinued lines and slight sub-standards for children, women and men from Clarks, K Shoes and other famous brands. These shops trade under the name of Crockers, K Shoes Factory shop or Clarks Factory Shop and while not all are physically attached to a shoe factory, these shops are treated as factory shops by the company. Customers can expect to find an extensive range of quality shoes, sandals, walking boots, slippers, trainers, handbags, accessories and gifts, while their major outlets also offer luggage, sports clothing, sports equipment and outdoor clothing. Brands stocked include Clarks, K Shoes, Springer, CICA, Hi-Tec, Puma, Mercury, Fila, Mizuno, Slazenger, Samsonite, Delsey, Antler and Carlton, although not all are sold in every outlet. Discounts are on average 30% off the normal high street price for perfect stock. *Factory Shop*

LITTLEWOODS
CATALOGUE DISCOUNT STORE

102 DEANSGATE, BOLTON, GREATER MANCHESTER BL1 1 BD
☎ (01204) 527 669. OPEN 9.30 - 5.30 MON - WED, 9 - 5.30 THUR - SAT.
185 STAMFORD STREET, ASHTON-UNDER-LYME, GREATER
MANCHESTER OL6 7PY
☎ (0161) 339 0966. OPEN 9.30 - 5.30 MON - SAT.

Littlewoods clearance shops offering up to 50% off the catalogue price for clothing and between 50% and 60% off for electrical goods. Stock changes constantly and varies from day to day but can include well-known brand names such as Berlei and Gossard lingerie, Vivienne Westwood, Pamplemousse leisure wear, Nike and Adidas sports shoes, Workers For Freedom, and Timberland and Caterpillar footwear. Stock depends on the size and location of the shop, so larger shops will get the longer discontinued runs and smaller shops over-runs with only a small amount of colour and size variations left. Littlewoods also run a mobile shop which operates in cities where they don't have a sale shop. For details of further venues for the sales, which usually take place once a month, contact Melanie Lamb, c/o Crosby DC, Kershaw Avenue, Endbutt Lane, Crosby, Merseyside L70 1AH. *Permanent Discount Outlet*

MATALAN

TONGE MOOR ROAD, BOLTON, GREATER MANCHESTER BL2 2DJ

☎ (01204) 383733. OPEN 10 - 8 MON - FRI, 9 - 6 SAT, 11 - 5 SUN.

Matalan is a fashion and homewares shop giving customers what they claim to be unbeatable value for money with huge savings on a wide range of products including high quality fashionable clothing for women, women and children at up to 50% off high street prices. Matalan is situated out of town and stores are open seven days a week all year round. *Permanent Discount Outlet*

OPTIROC

NASH ROAD, TRAFFORD PARK, MANCHESTER

☎ (0161) 877 7294. OPEN 8.30 - 4.30 MON - FRI.

Reclaimed and new bricks, natural stone flagstones. *Architectural Salvage*

PIFCO GROUP FACTORY SHOP

PRINCESS STREET, FAILSWORTH, MANCHESTER M35 OHS

☎ (0161) 947 3000. OPEN 9 - 5 MON - FRI, 9 - 1 SAT, CLOSED TUE.

Discontinued lines and seconds of Pifco, Carmen, Salton, Russell Hobbs, Mountain Breeze and Tower, as well as some perfect lines. For example, kettles, haircare, saucepan sets, slow cookers, mini ovens, air cleaners, ionisers and aromatherapy products. Also Christmas tree lights in season. *Factory Shop*

PILKINGTON'S TILES FACTORY SHOP

RAKE LANE, CLIFTON JUNCTION, MANCHESTER M27 8LP

☎ (0161) 727 7088. OPEN 8.30 - 5.30 MON - FRI, 9 - 5 SAT, 10 - 4 SUN.

Sells seconds of the well-known Pilkington's bathroom and kitchen wall and floor tiles and DIY tiling equipment at discount prices of up to 75% off manufacturers' prices. Two hundred and fifty ranges of wall and floor tiles from which to choose. *Factory Shop*

PUMPKIN DRESS HIRE

22 THE FIRST BALCONY, 22 BARTON ARCADE, DEANSGATE, MANCHESTER M3 2BB

☎ (0161) 831 7610. OPEN 10 - 5 MON - SAT, UNTIL 7 ON THUR.

There are more than 2,000 outfits available at any one time at this shop which is well known to Granada TV, whose stars often make use of its hire service. The shop offers a choice of more than 450 garments in evening wear, cocktail wear, ballgowns, wedding outfits (for men only) and men's dinner suits. Costs range from £40 for up to one week to a maximum of £95. There is a discount for students of 15% as well as a discount for nurses and a corporate discount. Sizes range from 8-26 and there are also handbags and jewellery for hire. *Hire Shop*

SANDERSON CLEARANCE OUTLET SHOP

2 POLLARD STREET, ANCOATS, MANCHESTER M4 7DS

☎ (0161) 272 8705. OPEN 10 - 6 TUE - FRI, 10 - 5.30 SAT, UNTIL 7.30 ON THUR, 10 - 4 SUN.

Seconds in furnishing fabrics from discontinued patterns, lines and end of ranges; wallpapers and ready made curtains, duvet covers, most of which cost about half price. Lots of remnants and ends of ranges and slight seconds of bedding. Free parking. *Factory Shop*

SCOOPS

UNIT 56, ARNDALE CENTRE, MIDDLETON, MANCHESTER M24 4EL

☎ (0161) 653 5435. OPEN 9 - 5.30 MON - SAT.

2 BURY OLD ROAD, CHEETHAM HILL, MANCHESTER M8 7JN

☎ (0161) 795 9312. OPEN 9 - 5.30 MON - SAT.

984 STOCKPORT ROAD, LEVENSHULME, MANCHESTER M19 3NN

☎ (0161) 257 3515. OPEN 9 - 5.30 MON - SAT.

1318-1324 ASHTON OLD ROAD, OPENSHAW, MANCHESTER M11 1JG

☎ (0161) 371 8243. OPEN 9 - 5.30 MON - SAT.

Grattan catalogue shops. There is a selection of items from those featured in the catalogue, which can consist of anything from children's clothes and toys to bedding, electrical equipment and nursery accessories. Each shop sells a slightly different range, so always ring first to check they stock what you want. All items are discounted by up to 50%. *Permanent Discount Outlet*

SLATERS MENSWEAR

7 DALE STREET, MANCHESTER, GREATER MANCHESTER M1 1JA

☎ (0161) 228 6482. OPEN 8.30 - 5.30 MON - SAT, 7.30 ON THUR.

Full range of men's clothes from underwear and shoes to casualwear, suits and dresswear and including labels such as Odermark, Bulmer, Valentino, Charlie's Co, and Charlton Gray. Men's suits from £79. *Permanent Discount Outlet*

SPOILS

UNIT R10/17 VOYAGERS WALK, ARNDALE CENTRE, MANCHESTER M3 1AP

☎ (0161) 819 2633. OPEN 9 - 5.30 MON - SAT, 8 ON THUR.

UNIT L 36/37 TRAFFORD CENTRE, TRAFFORD, MANCHESTER

☎ (0161) 202 9364.

General domestic glassware, non-stick bakeware, non-electrical kitchen gadgets, ceramic oven-to-tableware, textiles, cutting boards, aluminium non-stick cookware, bakeware, plastic kitchenware, plastic storage, woodware, coffee pots/makers, furniture, mirrors and picture frames. Rather than being discounted, all the merchandise is very competitively priced - in fact, the company carry out competitors' checks frequently in order to monitor pricing. With 38 branches, the company is able to buy in bulk and thus negotiate very good prices. *Permanent Discount Outlet*

TERRY'S STORES URMSTONE LTD

47 STATION ROAD, URMSTONE, MANCHESTER, LANCASHIRE M41 9JG
☎ (0161) 748 6011. OPEN 9.30 - 5 MON - SAT, CLOSED WED.
The final resting-place for ex-catalogue stock, it sells everything that is normally available by catalogue at half price. This includes leather jackets, jeans, dress and curtaining fabric, watnot stands, nests of tables, dining table and chairs, bedlinen, curtains, electrical goods, wedding and bridesmaids dresses. Delivery is free locally. The company has been in operation for 45 years and is privately owned. ***Permanent Discount Outlet***

THE ELITE DRESS AGENCY

35 KINGS STREET WEST, MANCHESTER, LANCASHIRE M3 2PW
☎ (0161) 832 3670. OPEN 9.30 - 5.30 MON - SAT, 11 - 4 SUN.
Three floors of good quality men's, women's and children's clothing, many with a Continental flavour. Among womenswear can be found labels such as Moschino as well as Escada, Betty Barclay, Mondi, with lots of chainstore makes, too. For men, there are lots of Italian designer suits from £50-£150, including Boss and Armani. There are lots of hats from which to choose, from £8. There is also a selection of unwanted gifts for sale. ***Dress Agency***

THE FACTORY SHOP

DORMA, NEWTOWN MILLS, SWINTON, GREATER MANCHESTER
M27 2DD
☎ (01617) 285993. OPEN 12 - 2 MON - FRI.
Part of the Coats Viyella group, which makes quality clothing for many of the major high street stores, overstocks and clearance lines are sold through more than 30 of the group's factory shops. Many of you will recognise the garments on sale, despite the lack of well-known labels. Ladieswear includes dresses, blouses, jumpers, cardigans, trousers, nightwear, underwear, lingerie, hosiery, coats and swimwear. Menswear includes trousers, belts, shirts, ties, pullovers, cardigans, T-shirts, underwear, nightwear, hosiery and jackets. Childrenswear includes jackets, trousers, T-shirts, underwear, hosiery, jumpers and babywear. There are regular deliveries to constantly update the range. ***Factory Shop***

TILE CLEARING HOUSE

1326 ASHTON OLD ROAD, HIGHER OPENSHAW, MANCHESTER,
GREATER MANCHESTER M11 1LG
☎ (0161) 370 6449. OPEN 8 - 6 MON - FRI, 9 - 6 SAT, 10 - 4 SUN.
Over 500 ranges of top quality ceramic wall and floor tiles permanently in stock, plus a comprehensive range of grouts, adhesives, tools and accessories to complete the job. Save up to 75% on manufacturers' recommended selling prices. ***Permanent Discount Outlet***

TILE WIZARD

UNIT 39, ELLESMERE RETAIL PARK, WALKDEN, GREATER MANCHESTER
☎ (0161) 702 8886. OPEN 9 - 5.30 MON - SAT, 10 - 4 SUN.
English and Continental floor and wall tiles at discounted prices. There are
ten branches: Warrington, St Helen's, Northwich, Crewe, Chester, Southport,
Preston, Morecambe and Blackpool.*Permanent Discount Outlet*

TOG 24

UNIT L3, REGENCY CRESCENT, TRAFFORD CENTRE, MANCHESTER,
LANCASHIRE M41 7LW
☎ (01612) 029960. OPEN 10 - 9 MON - FRI, 9 - 7 SAT, 11 - 5 SUN.
Tog 24 are the UK's fastest growing brand name in outdoor clothing and
leisurewear, with a total of three UK factories and 36 stores nationwide. They
utilise the world's finest performance fabrics including Gore-Tex, Polartec and
Burlington macs. Catering for all the family for all seasons, with cosy fleeces
and waterproofs for the winter, and trekking ranges, shorts and t-shirts for the
summer. With all prices at least 30% below the recommended retail price you
can afford to enter the Tog comfort zone. *Factory Shopping Village*

TOP MARKS

149-151 HOLLAND STREET, DENTON, MANCHESTER, GREATER
MANCHESTER M34 3GE
☎ (0161) 336 1279. OPEN 9.30 - 5.30 MON - SAT, UNTIL 8 ON THUR, 10 -
4 SUN.
Sells grade A fashion seconds from high street stores, as well as end of season
and ends of lines in towels, homeware, handbags, shoes, underwear, hosiery,
jackets and evening wear. Hand towels, £3; bath towels, £6; bath sheets, £10;
face cloths, £1; tea towels, £1.50; half-price ladies sweaters; briefs, from £1.50;
bras, £8-£10; hosiery, from 75p; half price ladies shoes sizes 3-8. Ladies sizes
range from 8-18; men's from small to XXL, 30 -42 waist and 29 to 33 leg.
Evening wear is stocked from October until Christmas at one third off the
retail price. There are also branches at Walkden, Urmston and Monton.
Permanent Discount Outlet

WILLSMART FACTORY SHOP

LANGLEY MILL, LANGLEY ROAD, SALFORD, MANCHESTER, GREATER
MANCHESTER M6 6JP
☎ (0161) 737 9056. OPEN 9.30 - 5 MON - FRI, 10 - 4 SAT, SUN, BANK HOLS.
Willsmart manufactures bedding and curtains for high street stores and mail
order catalogues at its Lancashire mills. The Willsmart shops have a wide
range of bedding and curtains, quilts, pillows, cushions and nets. The vast
majority of the range is perfect with any seconds clearly marked. The shop is
ten minutes from Manchester city centre. *Factory Shop*

Lancashire

WOMENSWEAR ONLY 🎗 Alexon Sale Shop, *Southport*. Alexon Sale Shop, *Blackpool*.
Croft Mill, *Colne*. Evans, *Fleetwood*. Felicity Hat Hire, *Lancaster*. Four Seasons, *Liverpool*.
Honey, *Fleetwood*. Jane Shilton, *Fleetwood*. Laura Ashley, *Colne*. The Fashion Agency, *Blackpool*.
Windsmoor Sale Shop, *Wigan*.

MENSWEAR ONLY 🎗 Farah Menswear, *Fleetwood*. The Suit Company, *Fleetwood*.

WOMENSWEAR & MENSWEAR 🎗 🎗 Barden Mill, *Burnley*. Bargain Street, *Oldham*.
Bohemia Period Clothing, *Accrington*. Boundary Mill Stores, *Colne*. Catalogue Bargain Shop, *Burnley*.
Catalogue Bargain Shop, *Chorley*. Catalogue Bargain Shop, *Bolton*. CV Home Furnishings, *Bolton*.
CV Home Furnishings, *Burnley*. CV Home Furnishings, *Colne*.
Dale Mill Discounts, Milnrow, *Nr Rochdale*. Damart, *Bolton*. Double Two, *Fleetwood*.
Finsley Mill Shop, *Burnley*. Freeport Fleetwood Outlet Village, *Fleetwood*.
Gaghills Factory Shop, *Rossendale*. Jaeger factory Shop, *Colne*. Jumper, *Carnforth*.
K Shoes, *Blackpool*. Lambert Howarth Footwear, *Rossendale*.
Littlewoods Catalogue Discount Store, *Central Morecambe*.
Littlewoods Catalogue Discount Store, *Fleetwood*. Littlewoods Catalogue Discount Store, *Liverpool*.
Littlewoods Catalogue Discount Store, *Farnworth*. London Leathers Direct, *Fleetwood*.
Matalan, *Preston*. Matalan, *Oldham*. Matalan, *Blackpool*. Matalan, *Liverpool*. Matalan, *Wigan*.
Matalan, *Accrington*. Matalan, *Baughley*. Matalan, *Swinton*. Matalan, *Bootle*.
Next to Nothing, *Fleetwood*. Quiggins Centre, *Liverpool*. Regatta, *Fleetwood*. Revival, *Accrington*.
Scoops, *Failsworth*. Sports Unlimited, *Fleetwood*. Suttons Factory Shop, *Bacup*.
The Factory Shop, *Lancaster*. TJ Hughes, *Preston*. TK Maxx, *Liverpool*. TK Maxx, *Preston*.
TK Maxx, *Southport*. TK Maxx, *Bury*. Tog 24, *Bolton*. Tog 24, *Colne*. Tommy Balls, *Blackburn*.
VF Outlets, *Fleetwood*. Warners, *Fleetwood*. The Factory Shop, *Lancaster*.
The Lowry Centre, *Salford Quays*. The Salvage Shop, *Bolton*. Winfields, *Rossendale*.
Wynsors World of Shoes, *St Helens*. Wynsors World of Shoes, *Warrington*.
Wynsors World of Shoes, *Blackpool*. Wynsors World of Shoes, *Bacup*.

CHILDREN 🎗 Barden Mill, *Burnley*. Bargain Street, *Oldham*.
Bohemia Period Clothing, *Accrington*. Boundary Mill Stores, *Colne*. Catalogue Bargain Shop, *Burnley*.
Catalogue Bargain Shop, *Chorley*. Catalogue Bargain Shop, *Bolton*. CV Home Furnishings, *Bolton*.
CV Home Furnishings, *Burnley*. CV Home Furnishings, *Colne*.
Dale Mill Discounts, Milnrow, *Nr Rochdale*. Finsley Mill Shop, *Burnley*.
Freeport Fleetwood Outlet Village, *Fleetwood*. K Shoes, *Blackpool*.
Lambert Howarth Footwear, *Rossendale*.
Littlewoods Catalogue Discount Store, *Central Morecambe*.
Littlewoods Catalogue Discount Store, *Fleetwood*. Littlewoods Catalogue Discount Store, *Liverpool*.
Littlewoods Catalogue Discount Store, *Farnworth*. London Leathers Direct, *Fleetwood*.
Matalan, *Preston*. Matalan, *Oldham*. Matalan, *Blackpool*. Matalan, *Liverpool*. Matalan, *Wigan*.
Matalan, *Accrington*. Matalan, *Baughley*. Matalan, *Swinton*. Matalan, *Bootle*.
Next to Nothing, *Fleetwood*. Regatta, *Fleetwood*. Revival, *Accrington*. Scoops, *Failsworth*.
Sports Unlimited, *Fleetwood*. Suttons Factory Shop, *Bacup*. The Factory Shop, *Lancaster*.
TJ Hughes, *Preston*. TK Maxx, *Liverpool*. TK Maxx, *Preston*. TK Maxx, *Southport*. TK Maxx, *Bury*.
Tog 24, *Bolton*. Tog 24, *Colne*. Tommy Balls, *Blackburn*. Toyworld Factory Outlets, *Fleetwood*.
VF Outlets, *Fleetwood*. The Factory Shop, *Lancaster*. Wynsors World of Shoes, *St Helens*.
Wynsors World of Shoes, *Warrington*. Wynsors World of Shoes, *Blackpool*.
Wynsors World of Shoes, *Bacup*. Yews Farm Baby Equipment

HOUSEHOLD AND GIFTWARE   🖾 Abakhan Fabrics, *Liverpool.*
Abakhan Fabrics, *Birkenhead.*   Barden Mill, *Burnley.*   Bargain Street, *Oldham.*
Boundary Mill Stores, *Colne.*   Catalogue Bargain Shop, *Burnley.*
Catalogue Bargain Shop, *Chorley.*   Catalogue Bargain Shop, *Bolton.*   Churchill China, *Fleetwood.*
Dale Mill Discounts, Milnrow, *Nr Rochdale.*   Freeport Fleetwood Outlet Village, *Fleetwood.*
HL Linen Bazaars, *Liverpool.*   Hartleys Mail Order Ltd, *Colne.*
Lambert Howarth Footwear, *Rossendale.*   LBS Horticulture, *Colne.*   Matalan, *Preston.*
Matalan, *Oldham.*   Matalan, *Blackpool.*   Matalan, *Liverpool.*   Matalan, *Wigan.*   Matalan, *Accrington.*
Matalan, *Baughley.*   Matalan, *Swinton.*   Matalan, *Bootle.*   Musbury Fabrics Mill Shop, *Rossendale.*
Oneida, *Colne.*   Oswaldtwistle Mills, *Oswaldtwistle.*   Ponden Mill Linens, *Fleetwood.*
Royal Worcester & Spode Factory Shop, *Colne.*   Second Chance, *Southport.*   Spoils, *Bolton.*
Spoils, *Oldham.*   Spoils, *Liverpool.*   Tartleton Mill Factory Outlet, *Southport.*
The East Lancashire Towel Co, *Nelson.*   The Factory Shop, *Lancaster.*   The Salvage Shop, *Bolton.*
TK Maxx, *Liverpool.*   TK Maxx, *Preston.*   TK Maxx, *Southport.*   TK Maxx, *Bury.*   Winfields, *Rossendale.*

ELECTRICAL EQUIPMENT   🔌 Catalogue Bargain Shop, *Burnley.*
Catalogue Bargain Shop, *Chorley.*   Catalogue Bargain Shop, *Bolton.*
Dale Mill Discounts, Milnrow, *Nr Rochdale.*   Gorse Mill Lighting, *Chadderton.*
Hamlet's Famous Names, *Ashton.*   Littlewoods Catalogue Discount Store, *Central Morecambe.*
Littlewoods Catalogue Discount Store, *Fleetwood.*   Littlewoods Catalogue Discount Store, *Liverpool.*
Littlewoods Catalogue Discount Store, *Farnworth.*   Metro Domestic Appliances, *Ashton-under-Lyme.*
Wholesale Kitchen Appliances, *Stockport.*

DIY/RENOVATION   🏗 Architectural Wall & Floor Co, *Darwen.*   Glynn Webb, *Bolton.*
Glynn Webb, *Accrington.*   Glynn Webb, *Oldham.*   Glynn Webb, *Preston.*   Glynn Webb, *St Helens.*
Glynn Webb, *Liverpool.*   Glynn Webb, *Manchester.*   Glynn Webb, *Blackpool.*
Pilkington's Tiles Factory Shop, *Bury.*   Reclaimed Materials, *Morecambe.*
Reddish Demolition Ltd, Chadderton, *Nr Oldham.*   Tile Clearing House, *Preston.*

ARCHITECTURAL SALVAGE   🏗 Architectural Wall & Floor Co, *Darwen.*
Reclaimed Materials, *Morecambe.*   Reddish Demolition Ltd, Chadderton, *Nr Oldham.*

FURNITURE/SOFT FURNISHINGS   🛋 Abakhan Fabrics, *Liverpool.*
Abakhan fabrics, *Birkenhead.*   Barden Mill, *Burnley.*   Boundary Mill Stores, *Colne.*
Croft Mill, *Colne.*   Freeport Fleetwood Outlet Village, *Fleetwood.*   H L Linen Bazaars, *Liverpool.*
J B Carpets Ltd, *Bacup.*   Jorgus Carpets, Anderton, *Nr Chorley.*   Kitchenalia, Longridge, *Nr Preston.*
Laura Ashley, *Colne.*   Musbury Fabrics Mill Shop, *Rossendale.*
Standfast Factory Fabric Shop, *Lancaster.*   Staples, *Bolton.*   Thomas Witter Ltd, *Chorley.*
Willsmart Factory Shop, *Oswaldtwistle.*   Willsmart Factory Shop, *Bolton.*

FOOD AND LEISURE   🍴 Antler Ltd, *Bury.*   Freeport Fleetwood Outlet Village, *Fleetwood.*
Gardeners Choice Mill Shop, *Colne.*   Hallmark, *Fleetwood.*   Karrimor, *Accrington.*
Kippax Biscuits, *Colne.*   Luggage & Baggage, *Fleetwood.*   Luggage & Bags, *Colne.*
Luggage & Bags, *Fleetwood.*   The Book People Ltd, *St Helens.*   Thorntons, *Fleetwood.*

SPORTSWEAR AND EQUIPMENT   🎿 *Freeport Fleetwood Outlet Village, Fleetwood*
Karrimor, *Accrington.*   Pro Image, *Manchester.*   Regatta, *Fleetwood.*   Sports Unlimited, *Fleetwood.*

Live Well On Less Tips
A pile of old magazines and some child-proof scissors can keep kids occupied for hours.

ABAKHAN FABRICS,

34-44 STAFFORD STREET, LIVERPOOL

☎ (0151) 207 4029. OPEN 9.30 - 5 MON - SAT

8-12 GREENWAY ROAD, BIRKENHEAD, MERSEYSIDE

☎ (0151) 652 5195. OPEN 9 - 5 MON - SAT, UNTIL 8 ON THUR, 10 - 4 SUN.

65-67 CHURCH ROAD, BIRKENHEAD, MERSEYSIDE

☎ (0151) 647 6983. OPEN 9 - 5 MON - SAT.

With five outlets in the North West, Abakhan Fabrics are as well known for the emphasis they put on value for money as they are for the huge variety of fabrics, needlecrafts, haberdashery, gifts and knitting yarns that they have gathered from all around the world. Abakhan is able to offer such bargains through bulk buying, or selling clearance lines, job lots and seconds. The Liverpool outlets do not have free parking facilities or a coffee shop. The Greenway Road, Birkenhead, outlet has a bridal fabric and accessories shop, and the Church Road branch also supplies craft fabrics. Free information pack available: ring 01745 562100. *Factory Outlet*

ALEXON SALE SHOP

469 LORD STREET, SOUTHPORT, LANCASHIRE

☎ (01704) 531281. OPEN 9 - 5.15MON - SAT.

Alexon and Eastex from last season at 40% less than the original price; during sale time in January and June, the reductions are 70%. Stock includes separates, skirts, jackets, blouses; there is no underwear or night clothes. *Permanent Discount Outlet*

ALEXON SALE SHOP

71 BANK HEY STREET, BLACKPOOL, LANCASHIRE

☎ (01253) 622528. OPEN 9 - 5.30 MON - SAT.

Alexon, Dash and Eastex from last season at 40% less than the original price; during sale time in January and June, the reductions are 70%. Stock includes separates, skirts, jackets, blouses; there is no underwear or night clothes. *Permanent Discount Outlet*

ANTLER LTD

ALFRED STREET, BURY, LANCASHIRE BL9 9EF

☎ (0161) 764 5241. OPEN 10 - 4 TUE - SAT.

Two factory shops at either end of the factory site, one selling leather goods: handbags, business cases, wallets, purses, as well as travel aids and suitcases; the other selling soft luggage, tool cases and picnic baskets which tend not to be made out of leather. All the products are quality seconds and ends of lines. Free parking. *Factory Shop*

Live Well On Less Tips
Join two empty yogurt containers with string, knotted through holes in the bottoms. The kids will enjoy this walkie-talkie set if the string is kept tight.

ARCHITECTURAL WALL AND FLOOR CO

UNIT 3, PREMIER MILL, BEGONIA STREET, DARWEN, LANCASHIRE BB3 2DR,

☎ (01254) 873994. OPEN 9 - 5 MON - FRI, 9 - 2 SAT.

Ceramics, terracotta, floor coverings, traditional sanitaryware, glazed brick, Belfast sinks, architectural antiques, reclaimed building materials, timber, stone, slate, pine stripping. *Architectural Salvage*

BARDEN MILL

BARDEN LANE, BURNLEY, LANCASHIRE BB12 ODX

☎ (01282) 420333. OPEN 10 - 6 MON - FRI, 8 ON THUR APRIL - SEPT, 11 - 5 SUN.

A true working mill which operates a manufacturing and finishing plant handling all kinds of textiles, especially clothing. Prices are, they claim, unbeatable because the retailer is being cut out and you are buying direct. On offer is a full range of branded ladieswear, most of which is overmakes for chainstores. The menswear, ladieswear and childrenswear departments have a huge range of fashionable clothes and everyday wear at a fraction of high street prices. Some items are de-labelled but there are no seconds. Current and surplus high street stock arrives every week. Merchandise includes clothes for all the family; Musbury fabrics and curtains; Briggs Shoes department selling Clarks, K Shoes, Hotter, Sterling & Hunt; great gift ideas in the Hothouse Department, as well as books, luggage, wool, pictures, mirrors and furniture. Shopping takes place on one floor and there is free parking and excellent disabled access. *Factory Shop*

BARGAIN STREET

58-64 GEORGE STREET, OLDHAM, LANCASHIRE OL1 1LF

☎ (0161) 678 1778. OPEN 9.30 - 5.30 MON - SAT.

Offers a wide range of clothing for all the family, a large selection of footwear, household textiles, hardware, electrical equipment and hundreds of others items at very attractive prices. All the items are surplus stock from the Empire range of mail order catalogues, including famous brand names, and are offered with huge discounts from the original catalogue prices. Stock changes on a weekly basis and there are regular sales promotions offering even better value. *Permanent Discount Outlet*

BOHEMIA PERIOD CLOTHING

11 WARNER STREET, ACCRINGTON, LANCASHIRE
☎ (01254) 231119. OPEN 10.30 - 5 MON - SAT, CLOSED WED.
ECHOES, 650A HALIFAX ROAD, EASTWOOD, TODMORDEN,
LANCASHIRE OL14 6DW
OPEN 11 - 6 MON - SAT, CLOSED TUE, 12 - 5 SUN.
Specialises in Sixties and Seventies gear, although their clothing and accessories dates from the Forties. *Secondhand and Vintage Clothing*

BOUNDARY MILL STORES

BURNLEY ROAD, COLNE, LANCASHIRE BB8 8LS
☎ (01282) 865229. OPEN 10 - 6 MON - SAT, 8 ON THUR, 11 - 5 SUN, 10 - 5 BANK HOLS.
One of the largest clearance stores in Britain, it covers more than 70,000 sq ft. Some of the top end of the high street designer labels are on sale here for both women and men. The women and men's departments are very extensive - not to mention impressive - and cover the whole range from casual to evening wear, with reductions of between 30% and 70%. There is also a large shoe department; jeans and luggage sections; and a lingerie department. A 25,000 sq ft building next door to the fashion store sells brand-name home furnishings, glass and china, including Dartington Crystal. Four times a year there are special sales at which prices are discounted still further. Most of the stock is perfect clearance and ends of lines with the occasional marked seconds. There is a large coffee shop, TV lounge and restaurant, and free parking. A recent addition is an adjoining Polo Ralph Lauren factory shop on two storeys selling homeware, childrenswear and men's and women's fashions at discounted prices. *Permanent Discount Outlet*

BUILT-IN KITCHEN APPLIANCES

70 - 88 BRECK ROAD, LIVERPOOL, MERSEYSIDE, LANCASHIRE L4 3BU
☎ (0151) 263 8966. OPEN 9 - 5 MON - FRI, 9 - 4.30 SAT, 10 - 4 SUN.
Hobs, ovens, dishwashers, fridges, freezers, sinks from top brand names such as AEG, Neff, Bosch, Canon, Franke, all at prices which can be up to 30% off top department store prices. If you know the make and model number of the item you want, phone and find out their best price. *Permanent Discount Outlet*

Live Well On Less Tips
Make use of blobs of ketchup left in the bottle. Pour a small amount of hot water into the bottle and shake vigorously until the residue and the water combine. Pour liquid into ice cube trays and freeze for use in soups or casseroles later.

CATALOGUE BARGAIN SHOP

KINGSWAY, BURNLEY, LANCASHIRE BB11 1AB
☎ (01282) 420202. OPEN 9 - 5.15 MON - SAT, 10.30 - 4.30 SUN.
40-42 MARKET STREET, CHORLEY, LANCASHIRE BB11 1AA
☎ (012572) 68325. OPEN 9.30 - 5.30 MON - SAT, 10.30 - 4.30 SUN.
LORNE STREET, FARNWORTH, BOLTON, LANCASHIRE BL1 2DY
☎ (01204) 573511. OPEN 10 - 4.30 MON - FRI, 7 ON TUE, WED, THUR, 9
- 4.30 SAT, 10.30 - 4.30 SUN. ☎ (0161) 236 0005. OPEN 9 - 5 MON - FRI,
10.30 - 4.30 SUN.
THE BEEHIVE MILL, CRESCENT ROAD, GREAT WEAVER, BOLTON,
LANCASHIRE
☎ (01204) 361159. OPEN 10 - 5 MON - FRI, 9 - 4.30 SAT.
Catalogue Bargain Shop is a growing national chain of stores which obtains
the majority of its goods from mail order giants Great Universal and Kays, and
offers a range of clothing for all the family, a wide selection of shoes, bed linen,
household goods, electrical equipment and hundreds of other catalogue items
at very competitive prices. The merchandise consists of ends of ranges and previous season's stock for which there is no longer storage space when the catalogues change. *Permanent Discount Outlet*

CHURCHILL CHINA

FREEPORT SHOPPING VILLAGE, FLEETWOOD, LANCASHIRE FY7 6AE
☎ (01253) 773927. OPEN 10 - 6 SEVEN DAYS A WEEK, 8 ON THUR, FRI.
Top quality fine bone china, tableware and mugs from Queens and Churchill
at discount prices of up to 30%. All are seconds. *Factory Shopping Village*

CROFT MILL

LOWTHER LANE, FOULRIDGE, COLNE, LANCASHIRE BB8 7NG
☎ (01282) 869625. OPEN 10 - 4 SEVEN DAYS A WEEK. ALSO MAIL
ORDER.
Sells fabrics, dress and furnishing, haberdashery and sheeting material, both in
the shop and by mail order. Most of the fabrics are over-runs, samples, ends
of lines, bankrupt stock and some seconds. Nearly all, including the dress fabrics, are 60 (150cm) wide and range in price from £1.50 to £6.95 or so a
metre. They include cottons, jerseys, sweatshirting, drills, linings, anorak fabric, coatings, and suitings. They send out a catalogue describing their current
stock every two months or so and will supply samples up to ten items for £1;
up to 30 items for £2; up to 50 items for £5, all of which is refundable if you
make a purchase. Most have been manufactured for high street store clothes
for shops such as Marks & Spencer, BhS, Laura Ashley and for Dorma. The
range of fabrics available is not always very comprehensive, so if you're looking for something specific, you may not be lucky. There are also pillows, cushion pads, tea towels and quilts, all at factory shop prices. *Factory Shop*

CV HOME FURNISHINGS

CAWDOR STREET, FARNWORTH, BOLTON, LANCASHIRE BL4 7JA
☎ (01204) 578836. OPEN 10 - 4.30 MON - FRI, 9 - 11.45 SAT.
THE MILL SHOP, DORMA, OAK BANK MILL, CASTERTON AVENUE,
BURNLEY, LANCASHIRE BB10 2PG
☎ (01282) 425280. OPEN 9 - 5 MON - FRI, 10 - 2 SAT.
FACTORY SHOP OUTLET, ALBERT HARTLEY, CV HOME FURNISHINGS,
CROWNEST MILL, SKIPTON ROAD, BARNOLDSWICK, COLNE,
LANCASHIRE BB8 5RP
☎ (01282) 817993. OPEN 10 - 5 MON - SAT, 11 - 4 SUN.
Part of the Coats Viyella group, which makes quality clothing for many of the major high street stores, overstocks and clearance lines are sold through more than 30 of the group's factory shops. Many of you will recognise the garments on sale, despite the lack of well-known labels. Ladieswear includes dresses, blouses, jumpers, cardigans, trousers, nightwear, underwear, lingerie, hosiery, coats and swimwear. Menswear includes trousers, belts, shirts, ties, pullovers, cardigans, T-shirts, underwear, nightwear, hosiery and jackets. Childrenswear includes jackets, trousers, T-shirts, underwear, hosiery, jumpers and babywear. There are regular deliveries to constantly update the range. *Factory Shop*

DALE MILL DISCOUNTS

DALE STREET, MILNROW, NEAR ROCHDALE, LANCASHIRE
☎ (01706) 359737. OPEN 9 - 5.30 MON - WED, FRI, 9 - 8 THUR, 9 - 5.30 SAT, SUN.
A wide range of items from clothes and shoes for all the family to kitchenware, furniture, wallpaper, paints, tablecloths, beds and bedding, TVs and general electrical goods, all on sale at discounted prices. *Permanent Discount Outlet*

DAMART

85-87 DEANE ROAD, BOLTON, LANCASHIRE
☎ (0120 452 4608. OPEN 9.30 - 5 MON - SAT.
Damart underwear and merchandise - anything from tights, socks and gloves to dresses, coats, cardigans and jumpers - some of which is current stock sold at full price, some discontinued and ends of lines sold at discount. There are several shops selling some discounted stock from the Damart range, known as Damart Extra. *Factory Shop*

DOUBLE TWO

FREEPORT SHOPPING VILLAGE, FLEETWOOD, LANCASHIRE
☎ (01253) 777117. OPEN 10 - 6 SEVEN DAYS A WEEK,
UNTIL 8 THUR, FRI.
Men's shirts (both casual and formal), belts, ties, jeans and dress shirts and women's blouses, co-ordinates, dresses, trousers, skirts and waistcoats at discount prices of about 20%-50%. *Factory Shopping Village*

EVANS

FREEPORT VILLAGE FLEETWOOD, ANCHORAGE ROAD, JUNCTION 12
OF M55, LANCASHIRE FY7 6AE

☎ (01253) 878554. OPEN 10 - 6 SEVEN DAYS A WEEK, 8 ON THUR, FRI.
End of season lines with the normal Evans refund guarantee. The range
includes tailoring, soft dressing, dresses, Profile, knitwear, East Coast
(denim/jeans), lingerie/nightwear, blouses, coats, outerwear and accessories.
Factory Shopping Village

FARAH MENSWEAR

FREEPORT SHOPPING VILLAGE, ANCHORAGE ROAD, FLEETWOOD,
LANCASHIRE FY7 6AE

☎ (01253) 773767. OPEN 10 - 6 SEVEN DAYS A WEEK, 8 ON THUR, FRI.
A wide range of men's clothes - sweaters, sweatshirts and trousers - all at
reduced prices. *Factory Shop*

FELICITY HAT HIRE

22 THURNHAM STREET, LANCASTER, LANCASHIRE LA1 1XY
☎ (01524) 381822. OPEN 10 - 5 MON - SAT.
Elegant hats to hire from £15 - £40, including some by Frederick Fox. Ascot
hats and wedding hats a speciality. Also hires out unusual bags for the evening.
Hire Shop

FINSLEY MILL SHOP

FINSLEY GATE, BURNLEY, LANCASHIRE
☎ (01282) 471283. OPEN 9.30 - 5 MON - FRI, 9 - 4 SAT.
Sells high street brand name mens' ladies' and some children's shoes at discounts of up to 50% from toddlers' size upwards. Slippers, trainers,
Wellingtons, school and party shoes, as well as a small range of ladies clothes,
some pottery and towels, all this season's chainstore seconds, mostly made for
Marks & Spencer. *Permanent Discount Outlet*

FOUR SEASONS

154 COLLEGE ROAD, CROSBY, LIVERPOOL, LANCASHIRE L23 3DP
☎ (0151) 924 2863. OPEN 9.30 - 5.30 MON - SAT.
Specialists in hiring and selling hats, Four Seasons has been in business for 15
years and has more than 450 hats from which to choose. The main business is
in hiring hats for all occasions - customers can bring their outfit to find the
perfect match, and trimmings can be added from as little as £2.50. Hire fees
start from £10 up to £30 for a period of 4 days or longer by arrangement.
There are also accessories for sale, particularly jewellery, scarves, gloves and
handbags. Ex-hire hats are sold off at reasonable prices. *Hire Shop*

FREEPORTFLEETWOOD OUTLET VILLAGE

ANCHORAGE ROAD, FLEETWOOD, 12 MILES FROM JUNCTION 3 OF M55, LANCASHIRE FY7 6AE
☎ (01253) 877377. OPEN 10 - 6 SEVEN DAYS A WEEK, UNTIL 8 THUR, FRI.

Large, brightly-coloured seaside shopping village with retro US theme complete with Fat Al's Diner. There are more than 50 shops selling at up to 50% off high street prices, as well as restaurants, family attractions, free parking and free entry. Women's fashions include Next to Nothing, Honey, Planet, Double Two, Looks Impressive, Evans, Warner's, Jane Shilton, Woods of Windsor, the Sweater Shop. For men, there is Suit Company, Burtons, Lee Jeans, Rawhide, Ciro Citterio, Next to Nothing, London Leathers, Easy Jeans, VF Factory Outlet (Lee/Wrangler) and Double Two. Sportswear and outdoor wear shops include Regatta, Gibson Sports, Planet Outlet and Sports Unlimited while footwear outlets comprise Briggs & Shoe Mines and Shoe Sellers. Sweet-toothed visitors can sample from Thornton's factory shop. For electrics, there is Remingtons selling a range of kitchen and beauty products. Household outlets include Bed & Bath Works, Churchill China, Ponden Mill, Dartington Crystal, Mondian and Woods of Windsor selling, between them, homewares ranging from bedroom and bathroom accessories, linens, quilts, cushions, china and glass gift and tableware, cutlery, dried flowers, pot pourri, kitchenware and candles. Childrenswear stockists include Next to Nothing, Rawhide, VF Corp, Regatta and French childrenswear Vecopri, while teenage girls are catered for by Dorothy Perkins and boys by Burtons with music from XS Music outlet. Sporty children can look to Sports Unlimited for sports clothes, footwear and equipment for all ages, while for footwear, there's Shoe Sellers and Briggs and Shoe Mines. Present time is catered for with Toy World, Hallmark, Not Just Books and Thornton's. Sportswear shops include Russell Athletic, Gibson Sports and Sports Unlimited. *Factory Shopping Village*

GAGHILLS FACTORY SHOP

GAGHILLS ROAD, OFF BURNLEY ROAD EAST, WATERFOOT, ROSSENDALE, LANCASHIRE BB4 9AS
☎ (01706) 215417. OPEN 10.30 - 5 MON - THUR, 10 - 1 FRI, 9.30 - 3.30 SAT.

High street chainstore seconds specialising in footwear. Also sells ladies clothes, towels, handbags, pottery and a small selection of menswear. *Factory Shop*

GARDENERS CHOICE MILL SHOP

STANDROYD MILL, COTTONTREE, COLNE, LANCASHIRE BB8 7BW
☎ (01282) 873341. OPEN 9 - 5 MON - FRI, 9 - 4 SAT, 10 - 4 SUN.

Horticultural and garden sundries specialists covering all your needs also has a large gift section with varied and unusual gifts for all occasions, all at mill shop prices. Everything for the garden from terracotta pots and hosepipes to seeds, gardening gloves, weathervanes, chimes sold at very good prices as well as fancy goods which are cheap. *Factory Shop*

GLYNN WEBB

UNIT A, ORLANDO STREET, OFF MANCHESTER ROAD, BOLTON, LANCASHIRE BL2 1DY
☎ (01204) 365806. OPEN 9 - 8 MON - SAT, 10 - 4 SUN AND BANK HOLIDAYS.
144-146 BLACKBURN ROAD, ACCRINGTON, LANCASHIRE BB5 OAB
☎ (01254) 236831. OPEN 9 - 8 MON - SAT, 10 - 4 SUN AND BANK HOLIDAYS.
BRUNSWICK HOUSE, BRUNSWICK STREET, OLDHAM, LANCASHIRE OL1 1BU
☎ (0161) 620 4415. OPEN 9 - 8 MON - SAT, 10 - 4 SUN AND BANK HOLIDAYS.
126 RIBBLETON LANE, PRESTON, LANCASHIRE PR1 5LB
☎ (01772) 794373. OPEN 9 - 8 MON - SAT, 10 - 4 SUN AND BANK HOLIDAYS.
DENTONS GREEN LANE, DENTONS GREEN, ST HELENS, MERSEYSIDE WA10 2QB
☎ (01744) 454798. OPEN 9 - 8 MON - SAT, 10 - 4 SUN AND BANK HOLIDAYS.
BRIGHTON MILL, SPENCER STREET, OLDHAM, LANCASHIRE OL1 3QF
☎ (0161) 620 4415. OPEN 9 - 8 MON - SAT, 10 - 4 SUN AND BANK HOLIDAYS.
UNIT A, THE NEW MERSEY WAY RETAIL PARK, SPEKE ROAD, SPEKE, LIVERPOOL, LANCASHIRE L24 8QB
☎ (0151) 494 0421. OPEN 9 - 8 MON - SAT, 10 - 4 SUN AND BANK HOLIDAYS.
641 HYDE ROAD, BELLEVUE, MANCHESTER, LANCASHIRE M12 5PS
☎ (0161) 230 8099. OPEN 9 - 8 MON - SAT, 10 - 4 SUN AND BANK HOLIDAYS.
231 VICARAGE LANE, BLACKPOOL, LANCASHIRE FX4 4NG
☎ (01253) 692549. OPEN 9 - 8 MON - SAT, 10 - 4 SUN AND BANK HOLIDAYS.
Stockists of all your home improvement needs from wallpaper to paint, furniture to flooring, tiles to textiles, housewares to lighting - in fact, almost everything for your home, with 24 branches in the North-West, Midlands and Yorkshire. Specialists in discontinued mail order, slightly imperfect branded stocks as well as perfect quality superior products. They carry top brands such as Dulux, Crown Paints and Vymura and Coloroll wall coverings, Rectella and Norwood textiles and much more in store. Different branches carry different lines so if you want something specific, phone first. To find your nearest branch, phone 0161 621 4500. *Permanent Discount Outlet*

GORSE MILL LIGHTING

GORSE ST, BROADWAY, CHADDERTON, LANCASHIRE OL9 9RJ
☎ (0161) 628 4202. OPEN 9 - 4.30 MON - FRI, 10 - 4 SAT, SUN AND BANK
HOLIDAYS.
240,000 sq feet dedicated to lighting up your home. One of Britain's largest
decorative light manufacturers, this shop claims to house the biggest display
of lighting, halogen, garden and security lights as well as crystal fittings at
savings averaging 50% off high street prices. Lamp shades start at as little as
50p and also come in a variety of sizes, patterns and colours. A Gothic Light
costs £29. Gorse Mill supplies major chain stores and has vast ranges of
decorative lighting, outdoor lighting, crystal chandeliers, as well as Chinese
and Portuguese pottery. Coffee shop, parking for 300 cars, disabled facilities
Permanent Discount Outlet

H L LINEN BAZAARS

UNIT C2, PENNY LANE NEIGHBOURHOOD CENTRE, CHURCH ROAD,
WAVERTREE, LIVERPOOL, MERSEYSIDE, LANCASHIRE L15 9EB
☎ (0151) 734 2902. OPEN 9 - 6 SEVEN DAYS A WEEK, UNTIL 8 ON WED,
THUR, FRI.
The mail order catalogue of this company which sells bedlinen, duvets, towels and sheets is very busy and hides some of the gems which are on sale, ends
of lines of which can be found in their warehouse outlets both here and in the
West Midlands and Staffordshire. Hunt carefully at these outlets and you will
find many famous brand names such as Early's of Witney, Vantona and
Slumberdown. Their warehouses, some of which are the size of football pitch-
es, sell ends of lines, slight seconds and bulk purchases of duvets, pillows, cotton sheets (usually hotel over-orders) at discounts of up to 50%. There is free
parking here for 200 cars. *Permanent Discount Outlet*

HALLMARK

FREEPORT SHOPPING VILLAGE, ANCHORAGE ROAD, FLEETWOOD,
LANCASHIRE FY7 6AE
☎ (01253) 773854. OPEN 10 - 6 SEVEN DAYS A WEEK,
UNTIL 8 THUR, FRI.
A wide range of cards to suit every occasion, as well as stuffed toys, wrapping
paper, rosettes, gift cards from names such as Andrew Brownswood, Gordon
Fraser and Sharpe's Classics. Almost all the stock here is ends of lines as the
card business demands constant change and so there are always unsold lines.
Most of the items are half price. Cafes on site as well as children's play areas;
free parking. *Factory Shop*

Live Well On Less Tips

Squeeze about one inch of your new washing up liquid into an old empty washing up liquid bottle and fill with water. You'll be surprised how clean it gets the dishes.

HAMLET'S FAMOUS NAMES

32 STAVELEIGH WAY, LADYSMITH CENTRE, ASHTON, LANCASHIRE OL6 7JJ

☎ (0161) 343 5127. OPEN 9 - 5.30 MON - SAT.

Sells ends of lines and A-grade manufacturers' returns of electrical goods which dealers have sent back to suppliers as faulty and which have then been repaired to the original specification at discounts of up to 50%. These include Panasonic, Toshiba, JVC, Philips, Sharp and Aiwa television sets, videos, hi-fis and camcorders. *Permanent Discount Outlet*

HARTLEYS MAIL ORDER LTD

REGENT HOUSE, WHITEWALLS INDUSTRIAL ESTATE, COLNE, LANCASHIRE BB8 8LJ

☎ (01282) 861350. OPEN 9.30 - 4.30 MON - FRI, 9.30 - 12.30 SAT. MAIL ORDER.

By buying up clearance lines from manufacturers who supply well-known high street names, this company sells sheeting, pillows, dress fabric, towels, quilts and curtains, some of which are well-known brand names, as well as selected kitchenware and garden furniture. Examples of prices include 70 -110 sheeting from £2.75 to £5.25 a yard; goose down quilts from £78 for singles, £110 for doubles and £135 for king sizes; polyester quilt seconds, £10.75 for singles, £17.95 for doubles and £21.95 for king size. Curtaining is available from £2 to £20 a yard, dress fabrics from 99p a yard; plus a large stock of poly/cottons, cottons and wool and bridal silk. Curtaining can be ordered from the curtain range book in the shop which includes Crowson, Francis Price and Moygashel. Prices are the same whether you buy through the on-site shop or by mail order. Parking available. Send five 2nd class stamps for samples and a free copy of Hartleys' most recent offers. *Permanent Discount Outlet*

HONEY

FREEPORT SHOPPING VILLAGE, ANCHORAGE ROAD, FLEETWOOD, LANCASHIRE FY7 6AE

☎ (01253) 777123. OPEN 10 - 6 SEVEN DAYS A WEEK, 8 ON THUR, FRI.

Leisure-oriented women's T-shirts, leggings and sweaters at discounts of mostly 30% or more. *Factory Shopping Village*

J B CARPETS LTD
UNIT F2, TOLLBAR BUSINESS PARK, NEW CHURCH ROAD,
STACKSTEADS, BACUP, LANCASHIRE OL13 ONA
☎ (01706) 875709.
OPEN 9 - 5 MON - FRI, 9 - 4.30 SAT, 10 - 4 SUN.
Most of the stock here is clearance stock from middle of the road brand names
such as Berbers, Wilton, Saxony, at discounts of at least 50%. 80/20 twists and
50/50 wool twists from £4.99-£8.99, free delivery. Usually carries Axminster,
Wilton and Saxony in a wide range from shag piles to Berbers. Some
Axminster remnants are usually available in various sizes. The more you spend,
the bigger the discounts. *Permanent Discount Outlet*

JAEGER FACTORY SHOP
BOUNDARY MILLS, BURNLEY ROAD, COLNE, LANCASHIRE BB8 8LS
☎ (01282) 865229. OPEN 10 -6 MON - SAT, 11 - 5 SUN.
Contemporary classics from Jaeger at excellent prices. Most of the merchan-
dise is previous seasons' stock, but you might also find some special makes.
This shop stocks tailoring and knitwear for women only. *Factory Shop*

JANE SHILTON
FREEPORT SHOPPING VILLAGE, ANCHORAGE ROAD, FLEETWOOD,
LANCASHIRE FY7 6AE
☎ (01253) 773875. OPEN 10 - 6 SEVEN DAYS A WEEK, UNTIL 8 THUR, FRI.
Merchandise from past seasons' collections or factory seconds at discounts of
at least 30% and up to 50% off the original price. There is a wide range of
handbags, suitcases, women's shoes, luggage, briefcases, umbrellas, scarves and
travel bags. *Factory Shopping Village*

JORGUS CARPETS
GRIMEFORD MILL, GRIMEFORD LANE, ANDERTON, NEAR CHORLEY,
LANCASHIRE PR6 9HL
☎ (01257) 482636. OPEN 8 - 5 MON - FRI, 8.30 - 3 SAT, 11 - 3 SUN,
CLOSED 12 - 1 WEEKDAYS.
Manufacture twist, plain, tweed and wool carpets at discounted prices,
although most of the stock is plain. Bedroom quality carpets 80% wool/20%
nylon costs £7.99 a sq yd. Lounge quality carpet, 40 ounce twist pile, costs
£9.99 a sq yd, which represents a 50% discount. *Factory Shop*

JUMPER
BRIDGE MILL, COWAN BRIDGE, CARNFORTH, LANCASHIRE LA6 2HS
☎ (015242) 71071. OPEN 9.30 - 4.30 SEVEN DAYS A WEEK.
A wide range of Jumper label sweaters, gloves, scarves, shirts and cardigans for
men and women all at discount prices of up to 50% off. Prices start at £2.
Factory Shop

K SHOES

UNIT 3, CLIFTON ROAD RETAIL PARK, BLACKPOOL, LANCASHIRE
FY4 4RA
☎ (01253) 699380. OPEN 9.30 - 7.30 MON - FRI AND BANK HOLIDAYS, 9
- 5.30 SAT, 10 - 4 SUN, 9.30 - 6 BANK HOLIDAYS.
18/19 WILLIAMSON SQUARE, LIVERPOOL, MERSEYSIDE L1 1EJ
☎ (0151) 708 7564. OPEN 9 - 5.30 MON - SAT.
Clarks International operate a chain of factory shops nationally which specialise in selling discontinued lines and slight sub-standards for children,
women and men from Clarks, K Shoes and other famous brands. These shops
trade under the name of Crockers, K Shoes Factory shop or Clarks Factory
Shop and while not all are physically attached to a shoe factory, these shops
are treated as factory shops by the company. Customers can expect to find an
extensive range of quality shoes, sandals, walking boots, slippers, trainers,
handbags, accessories and gifts, while their major outlets also offer luggage,
sports clothing, sports equipment and outdoor clothing. Brands stocked
include Clarks, K Shoes, Springer, CICA, Hi-Tec, Puma, Mercury, Fila,
Mizuno, Slazenger, Samsonite, Delsey, Antler and Carlton, although not all
are sold in every outlet. Discounts are on average 30% off the normal high
street price for perfect stock. *Factory Shop*

KARRIMOR

PETRE ROAD, CLAYTON-LE-MOORS, ACCRINGTON, LANCASHIRE
BB5 5JZ
☎ (01254) 893134. OPEN 10 - 5 MON, TUE, WED, FRI, 10 - 7.30 THUR, 10
- 4 SAT, SUN.
Best known for their comprehensive range of rucksacks, Karrimor also make
an outstanding range of outdoor equipment for walkers, climbers and
campers. The factory shop sells seconds, former display items and clearance
stock at discounts of between 15% and 25% and always stocks the current
range for the season. *Factory Shop*

KIPPAX BISCUITS

FACTORY SHOP, KING STREET, COLNE, LANCASHIRE BB8 9HU
☎ (01282) 864 198. OPEN 10 - 3.45 MON, WED, FRI, SAT,
CLOSED 1 - 1.15.
More than 100 different types of biscuits from ginger wafers and shortbread
to plain assorted and chocolate sold in packets, tins or loose. Broken biscuits
also sold very cheaply. Coach parties welcome by prior appointment only.
Food and Drink Discounter

KITCHENALIA

36 INGLEWHITE ROAD, LONGRIDGE, NEAR PRESTON, LANCASHIRE
PR3 3JS

☎ (01772) 785411. OPEN 10 - 4 MON - SAT, CLOSED WED.

Freestanding furniture for the kitchen; sets of shelves made from the Bible
rests on the back of old church pews; dressers made from old wood; tables,
pottery; old church pews also for sale, as well as Belfast sinks and old brass
taps. *Architectural Salvage*

LAMBERT HOWARTH FOOTWEAR

GAGHILLS MILLS, BURNLEY ROAD EAST, WATERFOOT, ROSSENDALE,
LANCASHIRE BB4 9AS

☎ (01706) 215417. OPEN 10.30 - 5 MON - THUR, 10 - 1 FRI, 9.30 - 3.30
SAT.

A real mixture of seconds from the factory and perfects from other sources -
footwear, clothes, handbags and towels. The seconds in footwear are from
shoes made for major high street chainstores and all are at discounted prices.
These include slippers, walking boots, flat shoes and sandals for men, women
and children. The perfects in clothes, towels and bags are two-thirds of the
high street prices. *Factory Shop*

LAURA ASHLEY

BOUNDARY MILL STORES, BURNLEY ROAD, COLNE, LANCASHIRE
BB8 8LS

☎ (01282) 867511. OPEN 10 - 6 MON - FRI, 10 - 5 SAT AND BANK
HOLIDAYS, 11 - 5 SUN.

At Boundary Mill Stores, Laura Ashley is housed in a special homewares
building next to the huge high quality clearance warehouse for men and
women's clothes. Most of the merchandise is made up of perfect carry-overs
from the high street shops around the country, though there are also some discontinued lines. Stock reflects the normal high street variety, though at least
one season later and with less choice in colours and sizes. *Permanent
Discount Outlet*

LBS HORTICULTURE

COTTON TREE, NEAR TRAWDEN, COLNE, LANCASHIRE BB8 7BW

☎ (01282) 871777. OPEN 9 - 5 MON - FRI, 9 - 4 SAT, 10 - 4 SUN.

Suppliers of all gardening equipment from wheelbarrows to gardening gloves.
Sells grass seed, plant pots, furniture and trugs, plant labels and padded jackets. Prices are trade plus VAT. Car parking, disabled access. *Factory Shop*

LITTLEWOODS
CATALOGUE DISCOUNT STORE

160 MARINE ROAD, CENTRAL MORECAMBE, LANCASHIRE LA4 4BU
☎ (01524) 412074. OPEN 9.30 - 5.30 MON, 9 - 5.30 TUE - SAT,
10.30 - 4.30 SUN.
69-74 LORD STREET, FLEETWOOD, LANCASHIRE FY7 6DS
☎ (01253) 773418. OPEN 9 - 5.30 MON - SAT, 11 - 5 SUN.
UNIT 3, MONUMENT BUILDINGS, LONDON ROAD, LIVERPOOL L3 8JY
☎ (0151) 708 6118. OPEN 9 - 5.30 MON - SAT.
UNIT 2, KINGS STREET, FARNWORTH, LANCASHIRE BL4 7AZ
☎ (01204) 861464.

Littlewoods clearance shops offering up to 50% off the catalogue price for
clothing and between 50% and 60% off for electrical goods. Stock changes
constantly and varies from day to day but can include well-known brand
names such as Berlei and Gossard lingerie, Vivienne Westwood,
Pamplemousse leisure wear, Nike and Adidas sports shoes, Workers For
Freedom, and Timberland and Caterpillar footwear. Stock depends on the size
and location of the shop, so larger shops will get the longer discontinued runs
and smaller shops over-runs with only a small amount of colour and size variations left. Littlewoods also run a mobile shop which operates in cities where
they don't have a sale shop. For details of further venues for the sales, which
usually take place once a month, contact Melanie Lamb, c/o Crosby DC,
Kershaw Avenue, Endbutt Lane, Crosby, Merseyside L70 1AH. *Permanent
Discount Outlet*

LONDON LEATHERS DIRECT

FREEPORT VILLAGE, ANCHORAGE ROAD, FLEETWOOD, LANCASHIRE
FY7 6AE
☎ (01253) 779090. OPEN 10 - 6 SEVEN DAYS A WEEK, 8 THUR, FRI.
Very good quality leather and suede jackets and coats at discounts of at least
30%, with most at 50% off in this village which features lots of restaurants
and fun things for the family to take part in. *Factory Shopping Village*

LUGGAGE & BAGGAGE

UNIT V4 - V5, ANCHORAGE ROAD, FLEETWOOD, LANCASHIRE FY7 6AE
☎ (01253) 773548. OPEN 10 - 6 MON - SUN, UNTIL 8 THUR, FRI.
Luggage and travel-related products including executive cases, handbags,
umbrellas and accessories available in leading brands such as Samsonite, Brics,
Hidesign, Globe Trotter and Tula. The products also include couture and high
fashion brands such as YSL and Moschino. All products are offered at a considerably reduced price due to their being production over-runs, last season's
stock of slight seconds (ie they have minor aesthetic blemishes). *Permanent
Discount Outlet*

LUGGAGE & BAGS

BOUNDARY MILL STORES, BURNLEY ROAD, COLNE, LANCASHIRE
BB8 8LS

☎ (01282) 865 229. OPEN 10 - 6 MON - SAT, 8 ON THUR, 11 - 5 SUN,
10 - 5 BANK HOLS.

FREEPORT LEISURE SHOPPING VILLAGE, ANCHORAGE ROAD,
FLEETWOOD, LANCASHIRE FY7 6AE

☎ (01253) 773 548. OPEN 10 - 6 SEVEN DAYS A WEEK,
UNTIL 8 THUR, FRI.

A range of travel goods and accessories from recognisable brands and high
street names including Samsonite, Delsey, Head, Studio and Taurus. Each
product is offered at a substantially reduced prices to that found on the high
street due to their being production over-runs, last season's products or having
small cosmetic faults. Discounts range from 30% to 75% off high street
prices. *Factory Shopping Village*

MATALAN

HOLME ROAD, BAMBER BRIDGE, PRESTON, LANCASHIRE PR5 6BP

☎ (01772) 627365. OPEN 10 - 8 MON - FRI, 9 - 6 SAT, 11 - 5 SUN.

UNIT 3, ALEXANDRA CENTRE, PARK ROAD, OLDHAM, LANCASHIRE
OL4 1SG

☎ (0161) 620 6686. OPEN 10 - 8 MON - FRI, 9 - 6 SAT, 11 - 5 SUN.

UNIT 2, CLIFTON RETAIL PARK, CLIFTON ROAD, BLACKPOOL FY4 4UJ

☎ (01253) 697850. OPEN 10 - 8 MON - FRI, 9 - 6 SAT, 11 - 4 SUN.

UNITS G & H, THE TRIUMPH CENTRE, HUNTS CROSS, LIVERPOOL
L24 9GB

☎ (0151) 486 0325. OPEN 10 - 8 MON - FRI, 9 - 6 SAT, 11 - 4 SUN.

ROBIN RETAIL PARK, 35 LOIRE DRIVE, WIGAN WN5 00H

☎ (01942) 629500. OPEN 10 - 8 MON - FRI, 9 - 6 SAT, 11 - 5 SUN.

FOUNTAIN RETAIL PARK, HYNDBURN ROAD, ACCRINGTON BB5 4AA

☎ (01254) 356100. PHONE FOR OPENING HOURS.

BROOKWAY RETAIL PARK, ALTRINCHAM ROAD, BAUGHLEY,
MANCHESTER M23 9EL

☎ (0161) 902 2500. PHONE FOR OPENING TIMES.

WESTOVER STREET, OFF STATION ROAD, SWINTON M27 2AH

☎ (0161) 794 3441. OPEN 9.30 - 8 MON - FRI, 9.30 - 6 SAT, 11 - 5 SUN.

SEFTON RETAIL PARK, DUNNINGBRIDGE ROAD, BOOTLE, LIVERPOOL
L30 6UU

☎ (0151) 525 1190. OPEN 10 - 8 MON - FRI, 9 - 6 SAT, 11 - 5 SUN.

Matalan is a fashion and homewares shop giving customers what they claim
to be unbeatable value for money with huge savings on a wide range of products including high quality fashionable clothing for women, women and children at up to 50% off high street prices. Matalan is situated out of town and
stores are open seven days a week all year round. *Permanent Discount
Outlet*

> *Live Well On Less Tips*
> Re-use a soap-filled pad by popping it in the freezer after use. It will thaw quickly for the next use rather than sit rusting next to the sink.

METRO DOMESTIC APPLIANCES

PARK PARADE, ASHTON UNDER LYME, LANCASHIRE,
☎ (0161) 330 9090. OPEN 9 - 4.30 MON - FRI.
This cut-price warehouse specialises in ends of lines or slightly blemished ovens, hobs, hoods, fridges, freezers. Goods are branded names such as Zanussi, Hoover, Tricity, and New World, and a full warranty is provided.
Permanent Discount Outlet

MUSBURY FABRICS MILL SHOP

PARK MILL, HOLCOMBE ROAD, HELMSHORE, ROSSENDALE, LANCASHIRE BB4 4NP
☎ (01706) 221318. OPEN 9 - 4.30 MON - FRI, 9.30 - 4 SAT, 10 - 4 SUN.
Bedlinen by Dorma and Horrockses; fabric from Fairfield Mills, SMD and Ametex, all at discount prices. There are thousands of metres of fabric on sale here. Examples of prices include pillows, £1.50 reduced from £8; fitted sheet, £3.95 reduced from £17; single duvet cover, £7.95 reduced from £25.
Permanent Discount Outlet

NEXT TO NOTHING

FREEPORT SHOPPING VILLAGE, FLEETWOOD, LANCASHIRE L65 9JJ
☎ (01253) 779826. OPEN 10 - 6 MON - SAT, 8 ON THUR, FRI, 12 - 6 SUN.
Sells perfect surplus stock from Next stores and the Next Directory catalogue at discounts of 50% or more. The ranges are usually last season's and overruns but there is the odd current item if you look carefully. There are shoes, lingerie, swimwear, and clothes for men, women and children. *Factory Shopping Village*

ONEIDA

BOUNDARY MILL, BURNLEY ROAD, COLNE, LANCASHIRE
☎ (01282) 865 229. OPEN 10 - 6 MON - SAT, 8 ON THUR, 11 - 5 SUN, 10 - 5 BANK HOLS.
Oneida is one of the world's largest cutlery companies and originates from the United States of America. In addition to cutlery, it sells silver and silver plate at discounts of between 30% and 50%, plus frames, candlesticks and trays. Boundary Mill is one of the country's largest clearance stores for fashion and homewares. *Factory Shop*

OSWALDTWISTLE MILLS
MOSCOW MILL, COLLIER ST, OSWALDTWISTLE, LANCASHIRE
BB5 3DF
☎ (01254) 871025. OPEN 10 - 5 MON - SAT, 11 - 5 SUN,
UNTIL 8 ON THUR.
A working mill which manufactures for top hotels and restaurants within the UK, with lots of attractions for families, apart from the bargains on offer. There are landscaped grounds with mini golf, wendy house village, gnomeland, wildfowl reserve and picnic area. Musbery fabrics sell bedding, quilts, sheets and towels; hot house sell dried flowers, mirrors, ceramics, kitchenware and pictures. Also sells a selection of women's clothes plus cards and books. Craft House sell everything from salt dough to decoupage; Body shop sells shampoo and bathroom products; and there are other shops selling furniture, handicrafts, jewellery and sweets (made on the premises), all at competitive prices. There is also a weaver, silk painting, garden centre and a children's play area. Part of the Oswaldtwistle Mills complex sells everything from Egyptian cotton to household textiles, plus everything you need to keep the house clean, including brand-names such as JIF, Comfort and Flash. And you don't have to bulk buy. *Factory Shop*

PILKINGTON'S TILES FACTORY SHOP
BURY FACTORY SHOP, 1 DERBY STREET, ROCHDALE ROAD,
LANCASHIRE BL9 0NW
☎ (0161) 761 7771. OPEN 8.30 - 5.30 MON - FRI, UNTIL 8 THUR,
9 - 5 SAT, 10 - 4 SUN.
Sells seconds of the well-known Pilkington's bathroom and kitchen wall and floor tiles and DIY tiling equipment at discount prices of up to 75% off manufacturers' prices. Two hundred and fifty ranges of wall and floor tiles from which to choose. *Factory Shop*

PONDEN MILL LINENS
FREEPORT SHOPPING VILLAGE, ANCHORAGE ROAD, FLEETWOOD,
LANCASHIRE FY7 6AE
☎ (01253) 777252. OPEN 10 - 6 SEVEN DAYS A WEEK, 8 ON THUR, FRI.
Famous branded products at direct from the mill prices. Towels, co-ordinated bedlinen, duvets, pillows and curtains from Crown, Coloroll, Chortex, Rectella together with bathroom and kitchen accessories. *Factory Shopping Village*

PRO IMAGE LTD

20 BRIDDON STREET, STRANGEWAYS, MANCHESTER, LANCASHIRE
M3 1LS

☎ (0161) 839 2845. OPEN 9.30 - 7 MON - WED, 9.30 - 8 THUR, FRI, 9.30 - 5 SUN.

Discount designer golf wear and equipment from names such as Mizuno and Black Diamond. Clubs bags, shoes, track suits, sports shoes from Adidas and Nike. *Permanent Discount Outlet*

QUIGGINS CENTRE

12-16 SCHOOL LANE, LIVERPOOL, LANCASHIRE L1 3BT

☎ (0151) 709 2462. OPEN 10 - 6 MON - SAT.

There are 37 different shops at the Quiggins Centre, the second biggest market in Liverpool, selling a variety of goods including theatrical and period costumes, secondhand clothes, furniture, bric-a-brac, jewellery, antiques, a cafe and a music shop. *Secondhand and Vintage Clothing*

RECLAIMED MATERIALS

NORTHGATE, WHITE LUND INDUSTRIAL ESTATE, MORECAMBE, LANCASHIRE LA3 3AY

☎ (01524) 69094. 8.30 - 5 MON - FRI, 8.30 - 12 SAT.

Timber, roof tiles, pitch pine, hardwood flooring, chimney pots and flagstones, roofing, slates and felt. *Architectural Salvage*

REDDISH DEMOLITION LTD

ALBION HOUSE, UNDER LANE, CHADDERTON, NEAR OLDHAM, LANCASHIRE OL9 7PP

☎ (0161) 682 6660. OPEN 7.30 - 5 MON - FRI, 7.30 - 12 SAT.

Reclaimed bricks, slates, beams and Yorkshire flags. *Architectural Salvage*

REGATTA

FREEPORT SHOPPING VILLAGE, ANCHORAGE ROAD, FLEETWOOD, LANCASHIRE FY7 6AE

☎ (01253) 777705. OPEN 10 - 6 SEVEN DAYS A WEEK, 8 THUR, FRI.

Clothing for the great outdoors including fleece, waterproof and waxed jackets; quilted gilets, hiker shirts, rucksacks, socks, hats, scarves and balaclavas at discounts of at least 30%. *Factory Shopping Village*

Live Well On Less Tips

Damp cupboards can be helped by putting silver-backed foam insulation like wallpaper on the backs.

REVIVAL

36 WARNER STREET, ACCRINGTON, LANCASHIRE BB5 1HN

☎ (01254) 382316. OPEN 10.30 - 5 MON - SAT, CLOSED WED.

Vintage clothes from the beginning of the century to the Seventies including men and womens' flares, £8 - £12, tank tops and shirts from £4, cheesecloth tops, Biba trousers. Levi jeans, from £9 up to £18; Levi jackets, £10-£35; Adidas and Lacoste T-shirts from £5-£12; cocktail dresses from £14-£28; ball-gowns from £20-£75; Fifties-style shirts, £6-£12; dinner suits, £24. *Secondhand and Vintage Clothing*

ROYAL WORCESTER & SPODE FACTORY SHOP

BOUNDARY MILL, BURNLEY ROAD, COLNE, LANCASHIRE BB8 8LS

☎ (01282) 862793. OPEN 10 - 6 MON - SAT, 8 ON THUR, 11 - 5 SUN.

Infinitesimally flawed porcelain and china seconds at 25% less than perfect prices. Fo-Frame, Mayflower and Leeds Display also on sale here. There is a vast range with special offers throughout the year on anything from crystal decanters and bowls to figurines, cookware and dinner sets. Shipping arrangements worldwide can be organised. *Factory Shop*

SCOOPS

C/O DISCOUNT GIANT, SISSION STREET, OFF OLDHAM ROAD, FAILSWORTH, LANCASHIRE M35 OEJ

☎ (0161) 682 5684. OPEN 9 - 6 MON, TUE, SAT, 9 - 7 WED, 9 - 8 THUR, 10 - 4 SUN.

Grattan catalogue shops. There is a selection of items from those featured in the catalogue, which can consist of anything from children's clothes and toys to bedding, electrical equipment and nursery accessories. Each shop sells a slightly different range, so always ring first to check they stock what you want. All items are discounted by up to 50%. *Permanent Discount Outlet*

SECOND CHANCE

8 PORTLAND STREET, SOUTHPORT, LANCASHIRE PR8 1JU

☎ (01704) 538329. OPEN 9.30 - 5.30 MON - SAT.

Sells mostly good quality seconds in English bone china. For example, Queens cups and saucers, £3.99, list price approx £8.99; Queens mugs, £2.99, list price £5.99; Royal Stafford china 10 plate, £2.99, list price £7.26; teapot, £10, list price £30.70. also stocks Burgess & Leigh seconds at 30% discounts. *Permanent Discount Outlet*

SPOILS

48-50 UPPER MALL, MARKET PLACE, BOLTON, LANCASHIRE BL1 2AL
☎ (01204) 528860.
UNIT 16/17 THE SPINDLES, OLDHAM, LANCASHIRE OL1 1HE
☎ (0161) 628 6967. OPEN 9 - 5.30 MON - SAT, 8 ON THUR.
UNIT 1 WILLIAMSON SQUARE, LIVERPOOL
☎ (0151) 709 0075.
General domestic glassware, non-stick bakeware, non-electrical kitchen gadgets, ceramic oven-to-tableware, textiles, cutting boards, aluminium non-stick cookware, bakeware, plastic kitchenware, plastic storage, woodware, coffee pots/makers, furniture, mirrors and picture frames. Rather than being discounted, all the merchandise is very competitively priced - in fact, the company carry out competitors' checks frequently in order to monitor pricing. With 38 branches, the company is able to buy in bulk and thus negotiate very good prices. *Permanent Discount Outlet*

SPORTS UNLIMITED

FREEPORT SHOPPING VILLAGE, FLEETWOOD, LANCASHIRE FY7 6AE
☎ (01253) 773880. OPEN 10 - 6 SEVEN DAYS A WEEK,
UNTIL 8 THUR, FRI.
Sports shop, selling gear for men, women and children at 30% off high street prices. Stocks trainers, tracksuits, rucksacks, jackets, T-shirts, swimwear, shorts and sweatshirts. *Factory Shopping Village*

STANDFAST FACTORY FABRIC SHOP

CATON ROAD, LANCASTER, LANCASHIRE LA1 3PA
☎ (01524) 64334. OPEN 9.30 - 1 MON - FRI, 10 - 12.30 SAT.
Genuine factory shop selling a wide range of well-known designer named fabrics, which are suitable for all soft furnishings, at discounted prices. Stocks vary according to factory production and all fabrics are seconds. Prices range from £5 to £8 per metre. They always stock plenty of pieces for cushion covers and patchwork from 30p each to £3 for small sackful. Usually they also have some fabrics on special offer, ranging from £1.50 per metre to £7 a metre. None of the fabric is flame retardant but once treated, can be used for upholstery. *Factory Shop*

STAPLES

UNIT 4, TRINITY RETAIL PARK, BOLTON, LANCASHIRE BL2 1HY
☎ (01204) 365307. OPEN 8 - 8 MON - FRI, 9 - 6 SAT, 11 - 5 SUN.
Office equipment and furniture supplier which is aimed at businesses, but is also open to the public. The owner buys in bulk and so is able to sell at very competitive prices a range of goods from paper clips to personal computers. Customers do not have to buy in bulk to make savings. A mail order catalogue is available and delivery is free on purchases over £30 (area permitting). *Permanent Discount Outlet*

SUTTONS FACTORY SHOP

NEW CHURCH ROAD, BACUP, LANCASHIRE

☎ (01706) 875578. OPEN 10 - 5.30 MON - FRI, 9 - 5.30 SAT, 10 - 4 SUN.
Stocks a wide range of footwear for children as well as adults. There are slippers, sandals, boots, leather and vinyl handbags and shoe cleaners and polishes. Ladies fashion shoes start from £6 a pair. There are some well known brands, all at substantial savings on high street prices. *Permanent Discount Outlet*

T J HUGHES

FISHERGATE CENTRE, PRESTON, LANCASHIRE

☎ (01772) 887326. OPEN 9 - 5.30 MON - FRI, SAT, 8 ON WED, 11 - 5 SUN.
Expanding chain of shops offering, not discounts as such, but very competitively priced goods from clothes for all the family to china, towels, bedlinen, duvets, pots and pans, kettles, vacuum cleaners, television sets, CDs, toasters. There are branches around the contry, mostly in the Midlands and North West. Readers have found here and at other branches Dyson vacuum cleaner, £165; Kangol stationery, Waterman pens, Polo Ralph Lauren men's shirts, £19.99; Calvin Klein jeans, £25; Ultima cosmetics. *Permanent Discount Outlet*

TARLETON MILL FACTORY OUTLET

UNIT 8-10, CROWLAND STREET INDUSTRIAL ESTATE, CROWLAND STREET, SOUTHPORT, LANCASHIRE PR9 7RG

☎ (01704) 541543. OPEN 10 - 7 THUR, FRI, 10 - 5 SAT, 10 - 4 SUN. 10 - 5 BANK HOLIDAYS.
This factory shop sells only merchandise which is manufactured by Tarleton Mill who make household textiles for major high street stores, using only top quality fabrics. The shop sells duvet sets, throwovers, curtains (cotton, velvet), pelmets, tie-backs, Austrian blinds, cushion covers and pads, seat pads, bean bags, top-up beans, floor cushions, conservatory cushion and patchwork pieces. All stock is discontinued lines or surplus of current lines, so in some cases it is possible to purchase a whole matching range for a fraction of the high street price. They also hold factory sales here throughout the year - phone to get your name on the mailing list. *Factory Shop*

THE BOOK PEOPLE LTD

HALL WOOD AVENUE, HAYDOCK, ST HELEN, MERSEYSIDE, LANCASHIRE WA11 9UL

☎ (01942) 723333/721222 FAX. MAIL ORDER.
The catalogue promises no membership, no contract to sign, no further obligation, savings of up to 75% off high street prices, phone, fax or post ordering, guaranteed delivery within seven working days, and reduced price p&p for

pensioners. There are 13 pages of children's books, a variety of romantic novels; gardening and cookery titles; some sports books and contemporary autobiographies. Package and posting costs £2.95 regardless of the size of order. *Permanent Discount Outlet*

THE EAST LANCASHIRE TOWEL COMPANY
PARK MILL, BARROWFORD, NELSON, LANCASHIRE BB9 6HJ
☎ (01282) 612193. OPEN 8.30 - 5 MON - FRI. MAIL ORDER.
The East Lancashire Towel Company still produces towels by the traditional method - making them both highly absorbent and hard wearing - and are able to keep costs down by selling direct to the general public. They produce a wide variety of towels: bath sheets, jacquard woven with intricate floral patterns in a variety of designs, children's daisy duck bath towels, kitchen and terry roller towels, souvenir and promotional towels, football club towels, etc. Towels, dish cloths, tea towels, sheets, duvets, pillows, face cloths, dusters and hankies, all at about half price. Toilets and car parking. *Factory Shop*

THE FACTORY SHOP
LANCASTER LEISURE PARK, WYRESDALE ROAD, LANCASTER, LANCASHIRE LA1 3LA
☎ (01524) 846079. OPEN 10 - 5 MON - SAT, 11 - 5 SUN.
Wide range on sale includes men's, ladies and children's clothing and footwear; household textiles; toiletries; hardware; luggage; lighting and bedding, most of which are chainstore and high street brands at discounts of approximately 30%-50%. There are weekly deliveries and brands include many major stars such as Adidas, Nike, Wrangler and Dartington, to name just a few. There are furniture displays and a new line in Cape Country furniture is on sale. Ranges are continually changing and few factory shops offer such a variety under one roof. Most of the shops have their own car parks or there are nearby car parking facilities. This outlet is also part of the family Leisure Park with antique centres, restaurant, children's leisure facilities and other retail stores. It has its own free car park. *Factory Shop*

THE FASHION AGENCY, FIRST FLOOR
21 QUEEN STREET, BLACKPOOL, LANCASHIRE FY1 1LN
☎ (01253) 628679. OPEN 10.30 - 4.30 TUE - FRI, 10 - 4 SAT.
A spacious showroom above a fashion shop called Elizabeth Todd. In business for more than 20 years, it offers top end of the market nearly-new outfits and continental separates. A large and constantly-changing selection of labels such as YSL, Escada, Chanel, Morgan, Versace and Moschino make this a very popular shop. It caters for all ages and from casual to cocktail wear. It also sells shoes, handbags and jewellery; there is a permanent half-price sale rail. *Dress Agency*

THE LOWRY CENTRE

SALFORD QUAYS, NEAR MANCHESTER, LANCASHIRE
☎ (0161) 955 2028. RING FOR UP TO DATE INFORMATION.
Seventy shops in a site next to Manchester Ship Canal, this is due to open between spring and autumn 2000. The site will include a hotel, Warner Village, Millenium Multiplex cinema, 15 cafes/restaurants, health and fitness club, indoor activity centre for children and is built alongside the £127 million Lowry Millenium Project for the Arts. *Factory Shopping Village*

THE SALVAGE SHOP

71-77 NEWPORT STREET, BOLTON, LANCASHIRE
☎ (01204) 528528. OPEN 9 - 5.30 MON - SAT.
Sister shop to the Middlesex outlet which is an Aladdin's cave of salvaged stock for the avid bargain hunter, most of which has been the subject of bankruptcy, insurance claims, fire or flood. Regular visitors have found anything from half-price Kenwood Chefs, typewriters and telephones to furniture, kitchen items and designer clothes. Yves St Laurent, Ungaro, MaxMara, Chloe, Agnes B and Mondi are just some the labels (though they are often cut out) to appear. Discounts range from 50%-75%. *Permanent Discount Outlet*

THE SUIT COMPANY

FREEPORT SHOPPING VILLAGE, ANCHORAGE ROAD, FLEETWOOD, LANCASHIRE FY7 6AE
☎ (01253) 773998. OPEN 10 - 6 SEVEN DAYS A WEEK, 8 ON THUR, FRI.
This shop is part of the Moss Bros group and includes labels such as YSL, Pierre Cardin, Wolsey and Jockey underwear, as well as leather gloves, belts, ties, work shirts, suits, jackets. *Factory Shopping Village*

THOMAS WITTER LTD

PO BOX 16, FROOM STREET, CHORLEY, LANCASHIRE PR6 9AP
☎ (01257) 263031. OPEN 9 - 4.30 MON - FRI, 10 - 4 SAT.
Small outlet containing a lot of stock: quality and middle of the range carpets from £4.50 a sq metre. Only plain carpets are sold, either 50% wool/polyproplene and 80% wool/polyproplene. Nationwide delivery can be arranged. *Factory Shop*

Live Well On Less Tips

Re-use bread bags by cutting in half and using the bottom section as an alternative to sandwich bags. Use the original twist to close. Never re-use any plastic bag that has stored meat. Or pop one over your hand and wash by hand, drying by hanging over a kitchen utensil such as a large soup ladle.

THORNTONS

FREEPORT VILLAGE, ANCHORAGE ROAD, FLEETWOOD, LANCASHIRE FY7 6AE

☎ (01253) 770710. OPEN 10 - 6 SEVEN DAYS A WEEK, 8 ON THUR, FRI.

The UK's leading specialist confectionery retailer has more than 500 shops and franchises nationwide selling a wide range of boxed and loose, chocolate and sugar confectionery. The factory outlets sell three different categories: misshapes. discounted lines and standard lines. Misshapes are loose chocolates which are the result of new product development, product trials or end of production runs which cannot be packed as Thorntons standard lines. They are packed into assorted bags and offer a saving of 35%-55% over the recommended retail price of standard loose line products. Discounted lines are excess to Thorntons' normal retail requirements and can be as a result of excess seasonal or export stock, discontinued lines or packaging changes. These products, when available, are offered at a discount of 25%-50% over the standard retail price. Standard lines from the full Thorntons range are also on sale at normal prices. *Factory Shopping Village*

TILE CLEARING HOUSE

UNIT 2, RIBBLETON LANE, PRESTON, LANCASHIRE PR1 5LR

☎ (01772) 705 990. OPEN 8 - 6 MON - FRI, 9 - 6 SAT, 10 - 4 SUN.

UNIT 3 & 4, LAUREL TRADING ESTATE, HIGGINSHAW LANE, ROYTON, OLDHAM OL2 6LH

☎ (0161) 628 9462. OPEN 8 - 6 MON - FRI, 9 - 6 SAT, 10 - 4 SUN.

Over 500 ranges of top quality ceramic wall and floor tiles permanently in stock, plus a comprehensive range of grouts, adhesives, tools and accessories to complete the job. Save up to 75% on manufacturers' recommended selling prices. *Permanent Discount Outlet*

TK MAXX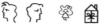

1ST FLOOR, 15 PARKER ST, OFF CLAYTON SQUARE, LIVERPOOL, LANCASHIRE L1 1DP

☎ (0151) 708 9919. OPEN 9 - 6 MON - SAT, 11 - 5 SUN.

FISHERGATE SHOPPING CENTRE, PRESTON, LANCASHIRE

☎ (01772) 253220. OPEN 9 - 5.30 MON - FRI, 9 - 8 WED, 9 - 6 SAT, 11 - 5 SUN.

MARBLE PLACE SHOPPING CENTRE, SOUTHPORT

☎ (01704) 501900. 9 - 5.30 MON - FRI, 9 - 6 SAT, 12 - 6 SUN.

ANGOULEME RETAIL PARK, BURY, LANCASHIRE

☎ (0161) 7611700. OPEN 9 - 5.30 MON - WED, SAT, 9 - 8 THUR, FRI, 10.30 - 4.30 SUN.

Based on an American concept, TK Maxx is situated in easily accessible, often centrally located stores and offers famous label goods with up to 60% savings off recommended retail prices. TK Maxx has fashion for the whole family - women's, men's and childrenswear - accessories, shoes, gifts, kitchenware and

home goods. Everything in the store is branded with a choice of well-known high street names to designer labels, and while a small percentage might be clearly marked past season, the great majority of items in store are current season, current stock and still with phenomenal savings. There is a huge choice with 50,000 pieces in store and up to 10,000 new items arriving a week. The stores are simple and unfussy with wide aisles, shopping trolleys and baskets, and a spacious, functional feel to them but there are individual changing rooms, ramps for buggies and wheelchairs and plenty of staff on the shop floor. Every branch accepts all major credit and debit cards and has a liberal refund and return policy. *Permanent Discount Outlet*

TOG 24

UNIT 7, THE LINKWAY, MIDDLEBROOK PARK, HORWICH, BOLTON, LANCASHIRE BL6 6JA
☎ (01204) 469899. OPEN 10 - 8 MON - FRI, 10 - 6 SAT, 11 - 5 SUN.
BOUNDARY MILLS STORE, BURNLEY ROAD, COLNE, LANCASHIRE
☎ (01282) 865229. OPEN 10 - 6 MON - SAT, 8 ON THUR, 11 - 5 SUN.

Tog 24 are the UK's fastest growing brand name in outdoor clothing and leisurewear, with a total of three UK factories and 36 stores nationwide. They utilise the world's finest performance fabrics including Gore-Tex, Polartec and Burlington macs. Catering for all the family for all seasons, with cosy fleeces and waterproofs for the winter, and trekking ranges, shorts and t-shirts for the summer. With all prices at least 30% below the recommended retail price you can afford to enter the Tog comfort zone. *Factory Shopping Village*

TOMMY BALLS

HART STREET MILL, BLACKBURN, LANCASHIRE BB11HW
☎ (01254) 261910. OPEN 10 - 5 MON - SAT, 11 - 5 SUN.
A large discount shoe warehouse selling quality shoes from leading British manufacturers for the whole family. Some are seconds, all are brand new. There is also a store at Eanam, which sells reconditioned footwear ☎ (01254) 261910. *Permanent Discount Outlet*

TOYWORLD FACTORY OUTLETS LTD

FREEPORT SHOPPING VILLAGE, ANCHORAGE ROAD, FLEETWOOD, FYLDE, LANCASHIRE FY7 6AE
☎ (01253) 773776. OPEN 10 - 6 SEVEN DAYS A WEEK,
UNTIL 8 THUR, FRI.
Brand name toys at discounted prices makes this a great place for Christmas and birthday presents. Items range from small plastic toys to jeeps and plastic houses. Recognisable names include Barbie, Disney, Mattel, Playskool, Lego, Duplo, Sylvanian Families, Fisher-Price, Tomy, Tyco, Waddington, M&B Games and Safe & Sound. Discounts can be as much as 75%. *Factory Shopping Village*

VF OUTLETS

FREEPORT SHOPPING VILLAGE, ANCHORAGE ROAD, FLEETWOOD, LANCASHIRE FY7 6AE

☎ (01253) 773988. OPEN 10 - 6 SEVEN DAYS A WEEK, 8 ON THUR, FRI, 11 - 5 SUN.

Men's, women's and children's denim jeans and jackets, cords, T-shirts, shirts, most of which are irregular (ie seconds). T-shirts and shirts are all perfects, as are some jeans. Discounts are about one-third off the normal price. Brand names on sale include Lee, Wrangler and Maverick. Children's range starts at two years. Also sells French underwear by Variance, Jan Sport bags, caps and hats. *Factory Shopping Village*

WARNERS

FREEPORT SHOPPING VILLAGE, ANCHORAGE ROAD, FLEETWOOD, LANCASHIRE FY7 6AE

☎ (01253) 773770. OPEN 10 - 6 SEVEN DAYS A WEEK, UNTIL 8 THUR, FRI.

This shop sells a wide range of women's lingerie from Leisureby, Valentino, Warners, with bras, slips, thongs, bodies and briefs at discounts from 25% to 70%. Each item is labelled with both the rrp and the discounted prices. For example, bikini brief, £6.99 reduced from £17; underwire bra, £14.99 reduced from £33; body, £24.99 reduced from £65. Slightly imperfect stock as well as perfect quality, end of season and discontinued merchandise and swimwear are also stocked. Underwear for men, including Calvin Klein briefs for £2.99, is on offer too. *Factory Shopping Village*

WHOLESALE KITCHEN APPLIANCES

142 -44 BUXTON ROAD, HEAVILEY, STOCKPORT, LANCASHIRE SK2 6PL

☎ (0161) 456 1187. OPEN 9.30 - 5.30 MON - FRI, 9 - 5 SAT, 11 - 2 SUN.

Specialists in Bosch, AEG, Neff and German appliances, there are discounts, particularly for cash purchasers. *Permanent Discount Outlet*

WILLSMART FACTORY SHOP

STONEBRIDGE MILL, SHED STREET, OSWALDTWISTLE, LANCASHIRE BB5 3HY

☎ (01254) 384289. OPEN 9.30 - 5 MON - FRI, 10 - 4 SAT, SUN, BANK HOLS.

ST PAULS MILL, CAROLINE STREET, BOLTON, LANCASHIRE BL3 6UQ

☎ (01204) 64215,

Willsmart manufactures bedding and curtains for high street stores and mail order catalogues at its Lancashire mills. The Willsmart shops have a wide range of bedding and curtains, quilts, pillows, cushions and nets. The vast majority of the range is perfect with any seconds clearly marked. The Oswaldtwistle shop is on the main street (phone for exact directions), the Bolton ship is five minutes from Bolton town centre. *Factory Shop*

WINDSMOOR SALE SHOP

21-23 MARKET PLACE, WIGAN, LANCASHIRE

☎ (01942) 820050. OPEN 9 - 5.30 MON - SAT.

Previous season's stock as well as any returned merchandise and overmakes from the Windsmoor, Planet and Precis ranges at discounts averaging about 50% off the original price. *Factory Shop*

WINFIELDS

HAZEL MILL, BLACKBURN ROAD, HASLINGDEN, ROSSENDALE, LANCASHIRE BB4 5DD

☎ (01706) 227916. OPEN 10 - 5.30 MON - WED, 10 - 8 THUR, FRI, 9 - 5.30 SAT, 11 - 5 SUN.

Clothing and housewares, some of which was made for Marks & Spencer, as well as catalogue seconds and surplus. Large car park. *Permanent Discount Outlet*

WYNSORS WORLD OF SHOES

BOUNDARY ROAD, ST HELENS, MERSEYSIDE, LANCASHIRE

☎ (01744) 454983. OPEN 9 - 5.30 MON, TUE, WED, SAT, 9 - 8 THUR, FRI, 10 - 4 SUN AND BANK HOLIDAYS.

WARRINGTON ROAD, PENKETH, NR WARRINGTON, MERSEYSIDE

☎ (01925) 727481. OPEN 9 - 5.30 MON, TUE, WED, SAT, 9 - 8 THUR, FRI, 10 - 4 SUN AND BANK HOLIDAYS.

DOCK STREET, FLEETWOOD, NR BLACKPOOL, LANCASHIRE

☎ (01253) 779871. OPEN 9 - 5.30 MON, TUE, WED, SAT, 9 - 8 THUR, FRI, 10 - 5 SUN AND BANK HOLIDAYS.OPEN 9 - 5.30 MON, TUE, WED, SAT, 9 - 8 THUR, FRI, 10 - 4 SUN AND BANK HOLIDAYS.

E. SUTTON & SON LTD, NEWCHURCH ROAD, BACUP, LANCASHIRE

☎ (01706) 875578.

Stocks top brand-name shoes at less than half price. Special monthly offers always available. There are shoes, trainers, slippers, sandals and boots for all the family, with a selection of bags, cleaners and polishes available.*Permanent Discount Outlet*

YEWS FARM BABY EQUIPMENT

47 STANLEY ROAD, BOOTLE, MERSEYSIDE, LANCASHIRE L20 7B2

☎ (0151) 933 4488. OPEN 9 - 5 MON - SAT.

Sells a wide variety of equipment for babies' needs including all leading makes of pushchairs, prams, cots, cot beds, and toys, all at much discounted prices. *Permanent Discount Outlet*

Leicestershire

WOMENSWEAR ONLY   Direct Cosmetics Ltd, *Oakham*.   Into Clothing, *Hinckley*.
Jilly's Dress Agency, *Near Market Harborough*.   The Dress Agency, *Enderby*.

MENSWEAR ONLY   Max Shoes, *Leicester*.

WOMENSWEAR & MENSWEAR   Beck Mill Factory Shop, *Melton Mowbray*.
Blunts, *Leicester*.   Charterhouse Holdings, *Loughborough*.   CV Clothing, *Loughborough*.
Factory Shop Outlet, *Leicester*.   Factory Shop Outlet, *Shepshed*.   Factory Shop Outlet, *Oakham*.
Gillivers Footwear And Clothing Warehouse, *Coalville*.
Good As New Clothes Sale, *Burley-On-The-Hill*.   Jaeger Factory Shop, *Coalville*.   Matalan, *Leicester*.
The Doc Shop, *Whetstone*.   The Factory Shop, *Hinckley*.   The Factory Shop Ltd, *Sileby*.
TK Maxx, *Leicester*.   Tweedies, *Coalville*.   Webb Ivory Ltd, *Hinckley*.

CHILDREN   A & J Carter Ltd, *Leicester*.   Charterhouse Holdings, *Loughborough*.
CV Clothing, *Loughborough*.   Factory Shop Outlet, *Leicester*.   Factory Shop Outlet, *Shepshed*.
Factory Shop Outlet, *Oakham*.   Geoff's Toys, *Coalville*.   The Doc Shop, *Whetstone*.
The Factory Shop, *Hinckley*.   The Factory Shop Ltd, *Sileby*.   TK Maxx, *Leicester*.
Tweedies, *Coalville*.   Webb Ivory Ltd, *Hinckley*.

HOUSEHOLD AND GIFTWARE   Charterhouse Holdings, *Shepshed*.
Dunelm Fabric Shop, *Leicester*.   Dunelm Fabric Shop, *Hinckley*.
Dunelm Fabric Shop, *Loughborough*.   Lady Clare Ltd, *Lutterworth*.   Matalan, *Leicester*.
Spoils, *Leicester*.   Standard Soap Company Ltd, *Ashby-De-La-Zouch*.   The Factory Shop Ltd, *Sileby*.
TK Maxx, *Leicester*.   Tweedies, *Coalville*.   Webb Ivory Ltd, *Hinckley*.

ELECTRICAL EQUIPMENT   Appliance Centre, *Leicester*.

DIY/RENOVATION   Glynn Webb, *Leicester*.

FURNITURE/SOFT FURNISHINGS   Creative Carpets Ltd, *Enderby*.
Curtains Complete, *Harborough*.   The Factory Shop Ltd, *Sileby*.

FOOD AND LEISURE   Bookends, *Leicester*.   Pic A Chic, *Ashby De La Zouch*.
Saga Bargain Books, *Market Harborough*.

SPORTSWEAR AND EQUIPMENT   Charterhouse Holdings, *Loughborough*.
Tweedies, *Coalville*.   Tweedies, *Melton Mowbray*.

BLUNTS

128-132 GRAMBY STREET, LEICESTER LE1 1DL
☎ (0116) 255 5959. OPEN 8.30 - 6 MON - SAT, 11 - 5 SUN.
Well-known brand name shoes for women and men at big discounts for discontinued stock, seconds and ends of ranges. Men's shoes, £5.99 - £79.99;
women's shoes from £2.99 - £45. *Permanent Discount Outlet*

> *Live Well On Less Tips*
> Swap comics with other families nearby.

DIRECT COSMETICS LTD

LONG ROW, OAKHAM, LEICESTER LE15 6LN

☎ (01572) 724477. MAIL ORDER.

This mail order business has been supplying discounted international, well-known brands of fragrances and cosmetics direct to the public since 1977. Products sold are from leading manufacturers such as Max Factor, Dior, Givenchy, YSL, Cacharel, Estee Lauder, Pantene, Oil of Olay, Piz Buin, Benetton, Cutex, Revlon, Old Spice, Brylcreem, Paco Rabanne, Kouros, etc. Products sold include fragrances, cosmetics, toiletries, skincare, sun preps and jewellery. Prices can be as much as 80% off the manufacturer's recommended retail price. New price lists are sent out every four weeks, each featuring more than 400 products. Further discounts are available on orders over £50. Phone for a current list to be sent to you free of charge and without obligation. *Permanent Discount Outlet*

A & J CARTER LTD

65A LONDON ROAD, OADBY, LEICESTER, LEICESTERSHIRE LE2 5DN

☎ (0116) 271 4962. OPEN 10 - 4 TUE - SUN, CLOSED MON.

Manufactures baby and children's clothes for Boots, Freemans catalogues and most of the good high street stores. The factory shop sells seconds and ends of lines. *Factory Shop*

APPLIANCE CENTRE

87 LOTHAIR ROAD, LEICESTER, LEICESTERSHIRE LE2 7QE

☎ (0116) 244 0150. OPEN 7.45 - 5.45 MON - FRI.

Small shop which holds brochures from most of the leading manufacturers of large white goods (cookers, ovens, hobs, washing machines, dishwashers, fridges, freezers, sinks, etc) from which you can order at very competitive prices. Deals mainly in seconds or graded products, these usually consist of slightly imperfect goods damaged in transit or ex-display. Other items are service or catalogue returns which have been in use for a very short period of time. All goods come with a full 12-month guarantee. All prices include home delivery (mainland GB only). Some typical examples are New World Image 1000 range gas cooker with two ovens, separate grill, four burners, griddle and fold-down lid, £800, as a current model the RRP was £1600; Bosch WFK2801GB 1400 spin, 'A' rated washing machine with delay timer etc, £460, current high street price, £600. Bosch KGU3102GB 6' 4 tall frost-free fridge freezer, £420, high street price £590. *Permanent Discount Outlet*

BECK MILL FACTORY SHOP

33 KINGS ROAD, MELTON MOWBRAY, LEICESTERSHIRE LE13 1QF
☎ (01664) 501105. OPEN 10 - 5 MON - SAT,
10 - 4 SUN.

Top high street women's and menswear at discounts of up to 70%. For women, there is Roman Originals, Dannimac, Legs and Co Swimwear, Double Two, Blast, Imogen, Spicy and Silhouette by Susan Jon. For men, there is Double Two, Dannimac, Barracuta, Wolsey, and David Andrews Ratcatcher Moleskins. Excellent selection of towels and giftware. There is easy parking at the side of the shop. *Factory Shop*

BOOKENDS

49 GALLOWTREE GATE, LEICESTER, LEICESTERSHIRE LE1 5AD
☎ (0116) 253 2093. OPEN 9 - 5.30 MON - SAT.

Secondhand and damaged books and publishers' returns, as well as new and review copies, including recently published books, usually one-third off and sometimes half price. *Secondhand Shop*

CHARTERHOUSE HOLDINGS

173 CHARNWOOD ROAD, SHEPSHED, LOUGHBOROUGH,
LEICESTERSHIRE LE12 9NN
☎ (01509) 505050. OPEN 10 - 5.30 MON - SAT, UNTIL 8 THUR, FRI,
11 - 5 SUN.
HELPLINE (01509) 600006.

The Charterhouse Retail Outlet was established 30 years ago and now enjoys its reputation as probably the largest of its kind in the UK. With over £1 million always in stock, Charterhouse offers family clothing, fashion, footwear, giftware, kitchenware, homeware and more - all ex chain and branded products at a fraction of high street prices. Ladieswear includes casual, evening, swimwear and lingerie - all styles and sizes. Childrenswear ranges from babies upwards with a special department for the early teens. Men will also find an excellent selection of sportswear, casual clothing and footwear. The recently expanded kitchenware and household department stocks a huge selection of present ideas. The outlet also offers a Reward Card scheme earning you free shopping vouchers on every average spend. There is free parking, a children's play area, parent and baby room, wheelchair access and cafe area. Open seven days a week, the outlet is only one mile from Juncion 23 of the MI. *Factory Shop*

CREATIVE CARPETS LTD

UNIT 8, MILL HILL INDUSTRIAL ESTATE, QUARRY LANE, ENDERBY, LEICESTERSHIRE LE9 5AU

☎ (0116) 2841455. OPEN 9 - 3 SAT, WEEKDAYS BY APPOINTMENT ONLY. CLOSED CHRISTMAS.

Genuine factory shop where carpets are manufactured on the premises. All carpets are quality heavy domestic, 80/20 wool, hessian backed. There is a large choice of colour including plain dyed, Berbers and heather tweeds. Savings of 50% can be made by buying direct from the factory. Prices for the perfects start at about £9.50 a sq yd; seconds also available. *Factory Shop*

CURTAINS COMPLETE

THE STABLES, EAST FARNDON HALL, MARKET HARBOROUGH, LEICESTERSHIRE LE16 9SE

☎ (01858) 466671. OPEN 9.30 - 3 TUE, OTHER TIMES BY APPOINTMENT.

Owner Caroline Everard spent a five-year apprenticeship in London making for most of the top interior decorators, and twenty years making top quality hand-made curtains and soft furnishings for private clients. Now, the stables at her home, East Farndon Hall, house more than 200 pairs of nearly-new curtains ranging in price from £35 to £800, many in top quality fabrics such as Colefax & Fowler, Jane Churchill and Designers Guild. A large number are in almost perfect condition, but for those needing repairs or alterations, these can be easily organised. Linings, interlinings, hooks and tapes are also available for those wishing to do their own alterations. She also sells new made-to-measure curtains from a wide range of fabrics. Curtains can also be taken home on approval. *Secondhand Shop*

DUNELM FABRIC SHOP

25 EAST STREET, LEICESTER, LEICESTERSHIRE LE1 6NB

☎ (0116) 247 1524. OPEN 9 - 5.30 MON, TUE, WED, THUR, SAT, 9 - 5 FRI, 10.30 - 4.30 SUN.

BRITANNIA CENTRE, HINCKLEY, LEICESTERSHIRE LE10 1RU

☎ (01455) 619044. OPEN 9 - 5 MON - SAT.

MILL SHOP, THE REX, MARLBOROUGH SQUARE, COALVILLE, LEICESTERSHIRE LE67 3LT

☎ (01530) 510004. OPEN 9 - 5 MON - SAT, 10.30 - 4.30 SUN, UNTIL 5.30 ON FRI.

40-44 CASTLE STREET, HINCKLEY, LEICESTERSHIRE LE10 1DD

☎ (01455) 234908. OPEN 9 - 5 MON - THUR, 9 - 5.30 FRI, 9 - 5.15 SAT.

MILL SHOP, 74 CHURCHGATE, LEICESTER LE1 4AL

☎ (0116) 253 7293. OPEN 9 - 5 MON - FRI, 9 - 5.30 SAT.

17-23 EAST STREET, LEICESTER LE1 6NB

☎ (0116) 247 0592/247 1524

(FABRIC SHOP). OPEN 9 - 5.30 MON - THUR, SAT, 9 - 5 FRI, 10.30 - 4.30 SUN.
3-6 THE RUSHES, LOUGHBOROUGH, LEICESTERSHIRE LE11 OBJ
☎ (01509) 234717. OPEN 9 - 5 MON - WED, SAT, 9 - 5.30 THUR, FRI.
Part of a chain of shops based in the Midlands selling brand-name and chain-store curtains, masses of bedlinen, towels, wickerware, pictures and frames, all at competitive prices. *Permanent Discount Outlet*

FACTORY SHOP OUTLET

COUNTERPART, PO BOX 63, ABBEY LANE, LEICESTER, LEICESTERSHIRE LE4 ODX
☎ (0116) 2611135. OPEN 9 - 5.30 MON - FRI, 9 - 5 SAT, 10 - 4 SUN.

CV CLOTHING KNITWEAR, FACTORY STREET, SHEPSHED, LEICESTERSHIRE LE12 9AQ
☎ (01509) 503068. OPEN 10 - 5 MON, 9 - 5 TUE - SAT, 10 - 4 SUN.

COUNTERPART HOSIERY, PO BOX 3, LOWER BOND STREET, HINCKLEY, LEICESTERSHIRE LE10 1QX
☎ (01455) 611991. OPEN 9.30 - 4.30 MON - FRI, 9 - 4 SAT.

CV CLOTHING MENSWEAR, COLD OVERTON ROAD, OAKHAM, LEICESTERSHIRE LE15 6NU
☎ (01572) 757955. OPEN 9 - 5.30 MON - SAT, 10 - 4 SUN, BANK HOLS.

MOIRA STREET, LOUGHBOROUGH, LEICESTERSHIRE LE11 1AX
☎ (01509) 240679. OPEN 10 - 5 MON - SAT, 10 - 4 SUN.

Part of the Coats Viyella group, which makes quality clothing for many of the major high street stores, overstocks and clearance lines are sold through more than 30 of the group's factory shops. Many of you will recognise the garments on sale, despite the lack of well-known labels. Ladieswear includes dresses, blouses, jumpers, cardigans, trousers, nightwear, underwear, lingerie, hosiery, coats and swimwear. Menswear includes trousers, belts, shirts, ties, pullovers, cardigans, T-shirts, underwear, nightwear, hosiery and jackets. Childrenswear includes jackets, trousers, T-shirts, underwear, hosiery, jumpers and babywear. There are regular deliveries to constantly update the range. *Factory Shop*

GEOFF'S TOYS

30 HIGH STREET, COALVILLE, LEICESTERSHIRE LE67 3ED
☎ (01530) 832795. OPEN 9 - 5 MON - SAT, 9- 12.45 WED.
20 HIGH STREEET, LOUGHBOROUGH, LEICESTERSHIRE LE11
☎ (01509) 216966. OPEN 9 - 5.30 MON - FRI, 9 - 5 SAT,
Vast array of toys at low prices. *Permanent Discount Outlet*

Live Well On Less Tips
Use half the amount of washing powder in your machine.

GILLIVERS FOOTWEAR AND CLOTHING WAREHOUSE

MARKET STREET, COALVILLE, LEICESTERSHIRE

☎ (01530) 811452. OPEN 9 - 5.30 MON - SAT.

Shoes from £1.99 to £40, at much reduced prices. The clothes are mainly from BhS and Marks & Spencer, although the labels are removed, and are discounted by between 25% and 50%. There are also bags, accessories and jewellery. Refreshments available. *Permanent Discount Outlet*

GLYNN WEBB

10A BURTON STREET, HUMBERSTONE GATE, LEICESTER, LEICESTERSHIRE LE1 1TE

☎ (0116) 251 6622. OPEN 9 - 8 MON - SAT, 10 - 4 SUN AND BANK HOLIDAYS.

Stockists of all your home improvement needs from wallpaper to paint, furniture to flooring, tiles to textiles, housewares to lighting - in fact, almost everything for your home, with 24 branches in the North-West, Midlands and Yorkshire. Specialists in discontinued mail order, slightly imperfect branded stocks as well as perfect quality superior products. They carry top brands such as Dulux, Crown Paints and Vymura and Coloroll wall coverings, Rectella and Norwood textiles and much more in store. Different branches carry different lines so if you want something specific, phone first. To find your nearest branch, phone 0161 621 4500. *Permanent Discount Outlet*

GOOD AS NEW CLOTHES SALE

RUTLAND COUNTY SHOW, BURLEY-ON-THE-HILL, LEICESTERSHIRE

One-day sale held annually on Sunday of spring bank holiday weekend in aid of Macmillan Cancer Relief. Usually featuring at least 8,000 items collected from around the country, there is a designer label section; a men's and women's section; a children's area' maternity wear, ski wear and riding wear. The designer section features names such as YSL, Chanel, Valentino, Dior, Armani, DKNY, Jasper Conran, Kenzo, Joseph; the men's and women's section outfits from Jaeger, MaxMara, Whistles, Jigsaw, Laura Ashley and Marks & Spencer; the children's section carries lines from Oilily, Jean Bourget and Osh Kosh as well as Mothercare and Next. Not only can you find your next designer ballgown, office suit and wedding outfit, but the hat, scarf, bag and shoes to finish the look, all at a fraction of the original cost. *Designer Sale*

INTO CLOTHING

45 CASTLE STREET, HINCKLEY, LEICESTERSHIRE

☎ (01455) 611558. OPEN 9 - 5.30 MON - SAT, AND BANK HOLIDAYS.

Sells ladies clothing, cotton knitwear, separates and jackets at factory direct prices, which can be as much as 70% off the normal retail prices. The shop is small but well stocked and organised to make the maximum use of the space. Most of the stock is leading chainstore makes and includes dresses, jackets, rainwear, shoes, underwear, tights, suits, blouses, sweaters, nightwear, leggings, trousers, jeans, anoraks, with dressing gowns and eveningwear at Christmas only. There is another branch in Leamington Spa, Warwickshire. *Permanent Discount Outlet*

JAEGER FACTORY SHOP

C/O R H N GRIEVE LTD, WOLSLEY ROAD, COALVILLE, LEICESTERSHIRE LE6 7ET

☎ (01530) 835506. OPEN 10 - 5 MON - SAT.

Contemporary classics from Jaeger at excellent prices. Most of the merchandise is previous seasons' stock, but you might also find some special makes. This shop stockswomenswear only. *Factory Shop*

JILLY'S DRESS AGENCY

THE SONDEES BARN, MAIN STREET, ROCKINGHAM, NEAR MARKET HARBOROUGH, LEICESTERSHIRE LE16 8TG

☎ (01536) 770352. OPEN 10.30 - 4 MON - SAT.

Designer dress agency and evening wear hire. Labels tend to be designer oriented - the high street names stocked regularly include Windsmoor, Wallis, Monsoon and Marks & Spencer. Hire costs from £35 - £75 for designer ballgowns. Also sells shoes, bags and jewellery and hat hire is now available from £20 to £55. *Dress Agency*

LADY CLARE LTD

LEICESTER ROAD, LUTTERWORTH, LEICESTERSHIRE LE17 4HF

☎ (01455) 552101. OPEN 9 - 4.45 MON - THUR, 9 - 3.45 FRI, CLOSED 1 - 1.30 DAILY.

Lady Clare supplies high class gift shops and top department stores with table mats, trays, coasters, wastepaper bins, picture frames and paper weights. Most of the stock in this small shop adjacent to the factory is seconds, cancelled orders or ends of lines with one third to one half off the normal price. Trays, bins and table mats are all hand lacquered, hand gilded and felt-backed with central designs. Perfect place mats which would cost £11, are about £5 here. *Factory Shop*

MATALAN

100 CHURCHGATE, VAUGHAN WAY, LEICESTER, LEICESTERSHIRE LE1 6AL

☎ (0116) 242 6700. PHONE FOR OPENING TIMES.

Matalan is a fashion and homewares shop giving customers what they claim to be unbeatable value for money with huge savings on a wide range of products including high quality fashionable clothing for men, women and children at up to 50% off high street prices. Matalan is situated out of town and stores are open seven days a week all year round. *Permanent Discount Outlet*

MAX SHOES

44-46 BELVOIR STREET, LEICESTERSHIRE

☎ (0116) 254 4394. OPEN 9 - 5.30 MON - SAT.

Large shop selling clearance lines of English and Italian top quality men's all-leather dress and leisure shoes. Often, there are brand names, but the shop will not divulge these beforehand. Shoes which cost £60 in high street retail outlets cost from £20-£40 here. Stocks sizes 6 - 11. *Permanent Discount Outlet*

PIC A CHIC

FACTORY SHOP, NOTTINGHAM ROAD INDUSTRIAL ESTATE, ASHBY DE LA ZOUCH, LEICESTERSHIRE LE6 51DR

☎ (01530) 413077. OPEN 9 - 4 MON - FRI, 9 - 12 SAT.

Frozen chicken pieces sold in packets of 40 (either legs, breasts or a mixture of both) at savings of 20%. Also 10% savings on steak and kidney pies sold in packs of 12. Frozen gateaux sells for an average of £3 a cake and has 18 portions. Many lines three for £1, e.g. tagliatelli ready meals, family-sized chicken and mushroom pies, fish in sauce, etc. Products always changing. *Food and Drink Discounter*

SAGA BARGAIN BOOKS

UNIT 7, ST MARY'S PLACE, MARKET HARBOROUGH, LEICESTERSHIRE LE16 7DR

☎ (01858) 461976. OPEN 9 - 5.30 MON - SAT.

34 DEVONSHIRE SQUARE, LOUGHBOROUGH, LEICESTERSHIRE LE11 3DW

☎ (01509) 238130. OPEN 9 - 5.30 MON - SAT.

A wide range of books from fiction to health, sport to children, cookbooks to biographies. Price reductions include cookbooks reduced from £16.99 to £6.99. *Food and Drink Discounter*

SPOILS

UNITS 11 AND 12, THE SHIRES, HIGH STREET, LEICESTER, LEICESTERSHIRE LE1 4FR

☎ (0116) 262 4002. OPEN 9 - 5.30 MON - FRI, UNTIL 8 ON WED, 9 - 6 SAT.

General domestic glassware, non-stick bakeware, kitchen gadgets, ceramic oven-to-tableware, textiles, cutting boards, aluminium non-stick cookware, bakeware, plastic kitchenware, plastic storage, woodware, coffee pots/makers, furniture, mirrors and picture frames. Rather than being discounted, all the merchandise is very competitively priced - in fact, the company carry out competitors' checks frequently in order to monitor pricing. With 38 branches, the company is able to buy in bulk and thus negotiate very good prices. *Permanent Discount Outlet*

STANDARD SOAP COMPANY LTD

DERBY RD, ASHBY-DE-LA-ZOUCH, LEICESTERSHIRE LE65 2HG
☎ (01530) 410000. OPEN 9 - 5 MON - THUR, 9 - 1 FRI.

Manufacturers to brand name retailers, they have factory shops selling seconds and ends of lines of well known soaps. Toiletry items include soaps from 50p per bag to £1.50 per bag, depending on the amount; shampoos, foam baths, talcs and various other toiletries which range from 25p to 99p. At certain times, there are other goods such as face cloths and gift baskets. *Factory Shop*

THE DOC SHOP

BRUCE WAY, CAMBRIDGE ROAD INDUSTRIAL ESTATE, WHETSTONE, LEICESTERSHIRE LE8 6HP
☎ (0116) 286 5958. OPEN 9 - 5.30 MON - FRI, 9 - 5 SAT.

Sells Doc Martens shoes and boots at discounted prices. For example, children's sizes at £15. *Permanent Discount Outlet*

THE DRESS AGENCY

THE SQUARE, CROSS STREET, ENDERBY, LEICESTERSHIRE LE9 5NJ
☎ (0116) 275 0501. OPEN 10.30 - 3 MON - FRI, 10 - 4 SAT.

Nearly-new shop selling mostly high street names such as Next, M&S, Richards, Debenhams, Wallis, with a small amount of menswear and childrenswear. Some of the designer labels stocked include Paul Costelloe, Betty Jackson and Yves St Laurent. They also sell accessories such as shoes and bags. *Dress Agency*

THE FACTORY SHOP LTD

NEWBOLD FOOTWEAR, BROOK STREET, SILEBY, LEICESTERSHIRE LE12 7RF
☎ (01509) 813514. OPEN 9 - 5 MON - SAT. CLOSED SUN.

Wide range on sale includes men's, ladies and children's clothing and footwear; household textiles; toiletries; hardware; luggage; lighting and bedding, most of which are chainstore and high street brands at discounts of approximately 30%-50% as well as the Cape Country Furniture range with free-standing kitchens, as well as living, bedroom and dining furniture. There are weekly deliveries and brands include many major stars such as Adidas, Nike, Wrangler and Dartington, to name just a few. Lines are continually changing and few factory shops offer such a variety under one roof. This outlet is sited adjacent to a factory. *Factory Shop*

Live Well On Less Tips
Store coffee in the freezer to prevent it from losing its flavour

TK MAXX, HAYMARKET CENTRE

LEICESTER, LEICESTERSHIRE LE1 3YD

☎ (0116) 251 0155. OPEN 9 - 5.30 MON - FRI, 9 - 6 SAT, 10 - 4 SUN.

Based on an American concept, TK Maxx is situated in easily accessible, often centrally located stores and offers famous label goods with up to 60% savings off recommended retail prices. TK Maxx has fashion for the whole family - women's, men's and childrenswear - accessories, shoes, gifts, kitchenware and home goods. Everything in the store is branded with a choice of well-known high street names to designer labels, and while a small percentage might be clearly marked past season, the great majority of items in store are current season, current stock and still with phenomenal savings. There is a huge choice with 50,000 pieces in store and up to 10,000 new items arriving a week. The stores are simple and unfussy with wide aisles, shopping trolleys and baskets, and a spacious, functional feel to them but there are individual changing rooms, ramps for buggies and wheelchairs and plenty of staff on the shop floor. Every branch accepts all major credit and debit cards and has a liberal refund and return policy. *Permanent Discount Outlet*

TWEEDIES

MARLBOROUGH SQUARE, COALVILLE, LEICESTERSHIRE LE67 2WD

☎ (01530) 510227. OPEN 9 - 5.30 MON - FRI, 9 - 5 SAT, 10 - 4 SUN.

NOTTINGHAM STREET, MELTON MOWBRAY, LEICESTERSHIRE

☎ (01664) 501072. OPEN 9 - 5 MON - SAT.

Three-storey building full of menswear, womenswear, children's clothes, luggage and gifts, which consist of a mixture of perfects, seconds and ends of lines, all sold at discounted prices. Top brand names and favourite high street labels are sold at up to 50% off. Brand names include Wrangler, Wolsey, Lyle & Scott, Nike, Adidas, Fruit of the Loom, Peter England, Farah and many more, plus high street names such as Marks & Spencer, Dorothy Perkins, Evans, Top Shop, BhS and Richards, to name just a few. A men's leisurewear department sells Burberry, Puma and much more. Plus on the first floor there's a European designerwear department with outfits for every occasion and a fabulous ladies golf department selling Lyle & Scott and Burberry golf accessories and luggage. *Permanent Discount Outlet*

WEBB IVORY LTD

BRITANNIA CENTRE, HINCKLEY, LEICESTERSHIRE LE10 1RU

☎ (01455) 891920. OPEN 9 - 5 MON - SAT.

Items from the Webb Ivory catalogue at reduced prices including cards, gifts, soft toys, books, pens, lamps, kitchenware, garden furniture and clothes. Discounts range from at least 50%. *Factory Shop*

Lincolnshire

WOMENSWEAR ONLY ⏀ Castaways, *Lincoln*. Alexon Sale Shop, *Lincoln*. Becoming Maternity Wear, *Lincoln*. Discount Dressing, *Lincoln*. Tallington Dress Agency, *Stamford*.

WOMENSWEAR & MENSWEAR ⏀ ⏀ Bedlam, *Lincoln*. Boundary Mill Stores, *A1 Grantham*. Catalogue Bargain Shop, *Gainsborough*. Cosalt International Ltd, *Grimsby*. Littlewoods Catalogue Discount Store, *Grantham*. Matalan, *Lincoln*. Matalan, *Scunthorpe*. Matalan, *Boston*. Matalan, *Grimsby*. Stage 2, *Lincoln*. Sundaes, *Spalding*. The Factory Shop, *Scunthorpe*. The Factory Shop, *Immingham*. The Factory Shop Ltd, *Barton On Humber*. The Factory Shop Ltd, *Spalding*. The Factory Shop Ltd, *Sleaford*. The Shoe Factory Shop, *Grimsby*. TK Maxx, *Lincoln*. Vogue Clothing Agency, *Louth*. Wynsors World Of Shoes, *Grimsby*.

CHILDREN ⏀ Boundary Mill Stores, *A1 Grantham*. Castaways, *Lincoln*. Catalogue Bargain Shop, *Gainsborough*. Davenport Stannard Knitwear Ltd, *Louth*. Littlewoods Catalogue Discount Store, *Grantham*. Matalan, *Lincoln*. Matalan, *Scunthorpe*. Matalan, *Boston*. Matalan, *Grimsby*. Stage 2, *Lincoln*. Sundaes Sandals, *Spalding*. The Factory Shop, *Scunthorpe*. The Factory Shop, *Immingham*. The Factory Shop Ltd, *Barton On Humber*. The Factory Shop Ltd, *Spalding*. The Factory Shop Ltd, *Sleaford*. The Shoe Factory Shop, *Grimsby*. TK Maxx, *Lincoln*. Wynsors World Of Shoes, *Grimsby*.

HOUSEHOLD AND GIFTWARE ⏀ Catalogue Bargain Shop, *Gainsborough*. Dunelm Fabric Shop, *Boston*. Dunelm Fabric Shop, *Lincoln*. Dunelm Fabric Shop, *Grantham*. Matalan, *Lincoln*. Matalan, *Scunthorpe*. Matalan, *Boston*. Matalan, *Grimsby*. Rutland Lighting, *Grantham*. Stage 2, *Lincoln*. The Factory Shop Ltd, *Barton On Humber*. The Factory Shop Ltd, *Spalding*. The Factory Shop Ltd, *Sleaford*. TK Maxx, *Lincoln*.

ELECTRICAL EQUIPMENT ⏀ Catalogue Bargain Shop, *Gainsborough*. Littlewoods Catalogue Discount Store, *Grantham*. Stage 2, *Lincoln*.

DIY/RENOVATION ⏀ Glynn Webb, *Lincoln*. Tile Cleaning House, *Doncaster*.

FURNITURE/SOFT FURNISHINGS ⏀ Cloth Market, *Stamford*. Designer Fabric Superstore, *Grantham*. Hemswell Cliff Antique And Crafts Centre, *Hemswell*. Magpie Fabrics, *Lincoln*. The Factory Shop Ltd, *Barton On Humber*. The Factory Shop Ltd, *Spalding*. The Factory Shop Ltd, *Sleaford*.

FOOD AND LEISURE ⏀ Jakemans, *Boston*.

SPORTSWEAR AND EQUIPMENT ⏀ Gymphlex Sportswear, *Horncastle*. Vogue Clothing Agency, *Louth*.

CASTAWAYS

10 BURTON ROAD, LINCOLN LN1 3LB

☎ (01522) 546035. OPEN 9.30 - 4.30 MON - SAT, CLOSED WEDS.

Cheery corner shop in up-hill Lincoln which specialises in almost-new children's clothing, nursery equipment and toys, all of which are housed downstairs, as well as ladies fashions (Next, Laura Ashley, Gap), accessories and maternity wear, which can be seen upstairs. *Dress Agency*

ALEXON SALE SHOP

ST BENEDICTS SQUARE, LINCOLN, LINCOLNSHIRE

☎ (01522) 545220. OPEN 9 - 5.30 MON - SAT.

Alexon and Eastex from last season at 40% less than the original price; during sale time in January and June, the reductions are as much as 70%. Stock includes separates, skirts, jackets, blouses; there is no underwear or night clothes. *Permanent Discount Outlet*

BECOMING MATERNITY WEAR

CHERRY WILLINGHAM, LINCOLN, LINCOLNSHIRE LN3 4AF

☎ (01522) 808310. BY APPOINTMENT ONLY.

One of a growing chain of home-based businesses hiring out practical, stylish and affordable outfits for expectant mothers for home, work or play. Separates cost from £10 to hire, with ballgowns at £50. Also offers made to order business wear. There are other outlets in Aberdeen, Barnsley, Basildon, Cheltenham, Enfield, Plymouth and South Lincolnshire. Phone the above number for further details. *Hire Shop*

BEDLAM

15 STEEP HILL, LINCOLN, LINCOLNSHIRE LN2 1LT

☎ (01522) 545498. OPEN 10 - 5 MON - SAT.

Secondhand period clothes from the Twenties to the Seventies, some of which are available to hire. Dresses cost from £8-£30, coats from £15-£25 and eveningwear, £20-£35, as well as some women's designer wear. Women's sizes range from 8-16. *Secondhand and Vintage Clothing*

BOUNDARY MILL STORES

WITHIN DOWNTOWN FURNITURE STORE, GONERBY MOOR,
GRANTHAM, LINCOLNSHIRE NG32 2AB

☎ (01476) 591001. OPEN 9.30 - 5.30 MON - SAT, 11 - 5 SUN.

Sister to the very large clearance store in Colne, Lancashire, it takes up 30,000 sq ft of the ground floor of this furniture store, selling ladies and men's top quality clothes, shoes and lingerie. Some of the top end of the high street designer labels are on sale here from casual to evening wear, with reductions of between 30% and 70%. Four times a year there are special sales at which prices are discounted still further. Most of the stock is perfect clearance and ends of lines with the occasional marked seconds. There is a coffee shop and free parking. ***Permanent Discount Outlet***

CATALOGUE BARGAIN SHOP

12-14 SILVER STREET, GAINSBOROUGH, LINCOLNSHIRE DN21 2DP
☎ (01427) 810604. OPEN 9 - 5.30 MON, THUR, FRI, 8.30 - 5 TUE, 9 - 5 WED, 8.30 - 5.30 SAT, 10 - 4 SUN.
29-31 THE STRAIT, LINCOLN LN1 1JD
☎ (01522) 527276. OPEN 9 - 5.30 MON - SAT, 10.30 - 4.30 SUN.
Catalogue Bargain Shop is a growing national chain of stores which obtains the majority of its goods from mail order giants Great Universal and Kays, and offers a range of clothing for all the family, a wide selection of shoes, bed linen, household goods, electrical equipment and hundreds of other catalogue items at very competitive prices. The merchandise consists of ends of ranges and previous season's stock for which there is no longer storage space when the catalogues change. ***Permanent Discount Outlet***

CLOTH MARKET

STAMFORD WALK, ST MARY'S STREET, STAMFORD, LINCOLNSHIRE PE9 2JE
☎ (01780) 753409. FAX 01780 753409. OPEN 9.30 - 5.30 MON - SAT, CLOSED THUR.
Small shop selling upholstery and furnishing fabric by Liberty, Sanderson, G P & J Baker, Monkwell and other good quality makes. Apart from offering a cut-length service on new collections, they specialise in discontinued designs and seconds in current designs, including undyed natural weaves and damasks, at prices starting at £3.90 a yard. Here, customers can see it all in stock, check out the good prices and walk away with it. Some even borrow a roll to look at against their home colours. There is also a marvellous stock of dress fabrics, with couture wools at a quarter of the regular price, starting at £10 a yard. Friendly, personal service. ***Permanent Discount Outlet***

COSALT INTERNATIONAL LTD

FISH DOCK ROAD, GRIMSBY, LINCOLNSHIRE DN31 3NW
☎ (01472) 504293 . OPEN 8.30 - 5 MON - FRI.
Specialises in workwear, safety clothing and marine wear but some of the merchandise is eminently wearable for everyday and is sold at very reasonable prices. There is plenty of stock on the shelves, but you can also order some lines from the catalogue. There is a wide selection of leisure and outdoor clothes from Doc Martens to padded jackets and denim shirts, dungarees and donkey jackets. VAT has to be added to prices. They also provide marine safety and life-raft servicing. ***Permanent Discount Outlet***

DAVENPORT STANNARD KNITWEAR LTD

NORTHOLME ROAD, LOUTH, LINCOLNSHIRE LN11 OHR

☎ (01507) 601951. OPEN 9 - 12 LAST SATURDAY OF
EACH MONTH ONLY.

Opens its factory shop to the public one morning a month only, selling brand name baby and toddler wear which is manufactured for well-known children's high street stores. The factory shop offers vast savings on high street prices for baby clothes up to the age of four years, and also on a small selection of ladies sweaters, which usually offer a better selection during the winter. Average discounts are 50%. In July and August, the factory shop opening times vary due to holidays. *Factory Shop*

DESIGNER FABRIC SUPERSTORE

UNIT 5, GREYFRIARS, GRANTHAM, LINCOLNSHIRE NG31 6PG

☎ (01476) 570022. OPEN 9.30 - 5.30 MON - SAT, 10 - 4 SUN.

HUCKNALL LANE, BULWELL, NOTTINGHAM

☎ (0115) 975 3311. OPEN 9.30 - 5.30 MON - SAT, 10 - 4 SUN.

Stocks up to 8,000 rolls of fabric from £2.99 a metre with remnants at £1 per metre. There are also made-up curtains, lampshades, cushions, pillows, net curtains, tassle tie-backs at £2.50 a pair, curtain poles, tracks, lining, braid, bean bags, upholstery and dress fabrics, some pottery and giftware. They will also take orders for fabric. There is a coffee shopat the Grantham branch, car parking and disabled facilities. In spring 1997, they introduced upholstery and dress fabrics. *Permanent Discount Outlet*

DISCOUNT DRESSING

45 STEEP HILL, LINCOLN, LINCOLNSHIRE LN2 1LU

☎ (01522) 532239. OPEN 10 - 6 MON - SAT.

A veritable Aladdin's Cave of designer bargains, Discount Dressing sells mostly German, Italian and French designer labels at prices at least 50% and up to 90% below those in normal retail outlets. All items are brand new and perfect. A team of buyers all over Europe purchase stock directly from the manufacturer for this growing chain of discount shops. This enables Discount Dressing to by-pass the importers and wholesalers and, of course, their mark-up. They also buy bankrupt stock in this country. Their agreement with their suppliers means that they are not able to advertise brand names for obvious reasons, but they are all well-known for their top quality and style. So confident is Discount Dressing that you will be unable to find the same item cheaper elsewhere, that they guarantee to give the outfit to you free of charge should you perform this miracle. Merchandise includes raincoats, dresses, suits, trousers, blouses, evening wear, special occasion outfits and jackets, in sizes 6-24 and in some cases larger. GDD readers can obtain a further 10% discount if they visit the shop taking a copy of this book with them. There are other branches in London, Northern Ireland, Hertfordshire, East Yorkshire and Derbyshire. *Permanent Discount Outlet*

Live Well On Less Tips
De-fur the kettle with a weak solution of vinegar. Always cover the element, boil the kettle and rinse it clean.

DUNELM FABRIC SHOP

LAWRENCE LANE, BOSTON, LINCOLNSHIRE PE21 8QD
☎ (01205) 353787. OPEN 9 - 5 MON, TUE, THUR, FRI, 9 - 5.30 WED, SAT, 10.30 - 4.30 SUN.
OUTER CIRCLE ROAD, PROCTERS ROAD, LINCOLN LN2 4LA
☎ (01522) 589737. OPEN 9 - 5 MON - THUR, 9 - 8 FRI, 9 - 6 SAT, 10.30 - 4.30 SUN.
6-8 WATERGATE, GRANTHAM, LINCOLNSHIRE NG31 6NS
☎ (01476) 574447. OPEN 9 - 5 MON - SAT.
Part of a chain of shops based in the Midlands selling brand-name and chain-store curtains, masses of bedlinen, towels, wickerware, pictures and frames, all at competitive prices. *Permanent Discount Outlet*

GLYNN WEBB

TRITTON ROAD, LINCOLN, LINCOLNSHIRE LN6 7QY
☎ (01522) 575252. OPEN 9 - 8 MON - SAT, 10 - 4 SUN AND BANK HOLIDAYS.
Stockists of all your home improvement needs from wallpaper to paint, furniture to flooring, tiles to textiles, housewares to lighting - in fact, almost everything for your home, with 24 branches in the North-West, Midlands and Yorkshire. Specialists in discontinued mail order, slightly imperfect branded stocks as well as perfect quality superior products. They carry top brands such as Dulux, Crown Paints and Vymura and Coloroll wall coverings, Rectella and Norwood textiles and much more in store. Different branches carry different lines so if you want something specific, phone first. To find your nearest branch, phone 0161 621 4500. *Permanent Discount Outlet*

GYMPHLEX SPORTSWEAR

BOSTON ROAD, HORNCASTLE, LINCOLNSHIRE LU9 6HU
☎ (01507) 523243.
Holds a one day factory shop sale just once a year, please phone 01507 523243 for details. Your chance to buy a huge range of sportswear for all the family: jogging pants, tracksuits, rugby and football shirts, rugby shorts, T-shirts, polo shirts, Lycra swimwear, leotards, tights, socks. Some of the stock is seconds, some overmakes. The rest is freshly-made stock which is specially reduced for the sale. *Designer Sale*

Live Well On Less Tips
Never replace anything in your kitchen cupboard until you have run out. Otherwise, you'll be tempted to open the new packet and never finish the old one.

HEMSWELL CLIFF
ANTIQUE AND CRAFTS CENTRE
NEAR CANEBY CORNER, HEMSWELL, LINCOLNSHIRE
☎ (01427) 668389. OPEN 10 - 5 SEVEN DAYS A WEEK.
Created from the former RAF Hemswell, it claims to be the largest centre for antiques, collectables and retro items in Europe, with about 300 stalls spread over five separate buildings. There is also a major craft centre, a wallpaper factory shop, pine and garden furniture manufacturers, pottery and a tools/diy centre. Many of the antiques are of high quality though the prices seem to be below most recognised major centres. Avoid Sundays when there is a very popular car boot sale/market when car parking is difficult. *Secondhand Shop*

JAKEMANS
46 WORMGATE, BOSTON, LINCOLNSHIRE PE21 6NS
☎ (01205) 362052. OPEN 9 - 5 MON - FRI, 9 - 4 SAT.
Sweets factory shop which sells way out sweets at discount prices from boiled sweets to chocolates and licquorice allsorts. Jakemans Throat and Chest cough sweet is a particular favourite. Discounted bulk £1 bags available. *Factory Shop*

LITTLEWOODS
CATALOGUE DISCOUNT STORE
7 HIGH STREET, GRANTHAM, LINCOLNSHIRE NG31 6PN
☎ (01476) 590552. OPEN 9.30 - 5.30 MON, 9 - 5.30 TUE - SAT.
Littlewoods clearance shops offering up to 50% off the catalogue price for clothing and between 50% and 60% off for electrical goods. Stock changes constantly and varies from day to day but can include well-known brand names such as Berlei and Gossard lingerie, Vivienne Westwood, Pamplemousse leisure wear, Nike and Adidas sports shoes, Workers For Freedom, and Timberland and Caterpillar footwear. Stock depends on the size and location of the shop, so larger shops will get the longer discontinued runs and smaller shops over-runs with only a small amount of colour and size variations left. Littlewoods also run a mobile shop which operates in cities where they don't have a sale shop. For details of further venues for the sales, which usually take place once a month, contact Melanie Lamb, c/o Crosby DC, Kershaw Avenue, Endbutt Lane, Crosby, Merseyside L70 1AH. *Permanent Discount Outlet*

MAGPIE FABRICS

22 BRIDGE STREET, SAXILBY, LINCOLN, LINCOLNSHIRE LN1 2PZ
☎ (01522) 702137. OPEN 10 - 1 MON, WED, 10 - 5 TUE, THUR,
FRI, 10 - 4 SAT.

Sells quality low-priced fabrics for curtaining and upholstery as well as fabrics and wallpapers to order from Blendworth, Malthouse, John Wilman, Nouveau, Wemyss, Sanderson, Dovedale and others at competitive prices. Curtaining from £7.50 per yard, upholstery from £8.50 per yard. Also stocks lining tapes, cording, haberdashery. Phone for the price of any of the fabrics you want. Making-up service available. The shop is five minutes out of Lincoln on the A57, with easy parking. *Permanent Discount Outlet*

MATALAN

LINDIS RETAIL PARK, TRITTON ROAD, LINCOLN
LINCOLNSHIRE LN6 7QY
☎ (01522) 696541. OPEN 10 - 8 MON - FRI, 9 - 6 SAT, 11 - 5 SUN.
DUDLEY ROAD, SCUNTHORPE DN16 1BA
☎ (01724) 270958. OPEN 9.30 - 8 MON - FRI, 9 - 6 SAT, 11 - 5 SUN.
JOHN ADAMS WAY, BOSTON PE21 6TY
☎ (01205) 312040. PHONE FOR OPENING TIMES.
UNIT 1, HEWITTS CIRCUS, CLEETHORPES, GRIMSBY DN35 9QH
☎ (01472) 200255. PHONE FOR OPENING TIMES.

Matalan is a fashion and homewares shop giving customers what they claim to be unbeatable value for money with huge savings on a wide range of products including high quality fashionable clothing for women, women and children at up to 50% off high street prices. Matalan is situated out of town and stores are open seven days a week all year round. *Permanent Discount Outlet*

RUTLAND LIGHTING

10-12 WATERGATE, GRANTHAM, LINCOLNSHIRE
☎ (01476) 591049. OPEN 9 - 5.30 MON - SAT.

Sells a full range of lampshades, table and floor lamps, chandeliers, bulbs, outdoor and indoor lights, plus other manufacturers' ends of lines and chainstore seconds. Most lines have genuine reductions on normal retail prices. This shop, unliked its sister shop in Market Overton, Leicestershire, is large and on the high street. *Permanent Discount Outlet*

Live Well On Less Tips
Cut new bread in thinner slices by dipping the knife in boiling water first.

STAGE 2

UNIT 3, TRITTON RETAIL PARK, TRITTON ROAD, LINCOLN, LINCOLNSHIRE LN6 7YA

☎ (01522) 560303. OPEN 10 - 8 MON - FRI, 9 - 6 SAT, 11 - 5 SUN AND BANK HOLIDAYS.

Sells discontinued lines from Freeman's Catalogues. The full range is carried, but stock depends on what has not been sold at full price from the catalogue itself, or has been returned or the packaging is damaged or soiled. Clothing discounts range from about 50% - 65%. There are also household items and electrical equipment. *Permanent Discount Outlet*

SUNDAES SANDALS

THE CHASE, 18 HIGH STREET, MOULTON, SPALDING, LINCOLNSHIRE PE12 6QB

☎ (01406) 371370. OPEN 9 - 3.30 MON - FRI, SAT BY APPOINTMENT.

Handmade shoes and sandals in bright summer colours, top quality materials, including leather uppers, insoles and linings. There are 35 styles for all the family, with some women's shoes up to size 9 and sandals to size 10, including an award-winning range of Ecco shoes and Hogl courts. Their small, informal factory shop sells the full range of sundaes made on the premises and usually has a selection of discontinued styles, colours and slight seconds at bargain prices. Visitors are always welcome, but do phone first. *Factory Shop*

TALLINGTON DRESS AGENCY

LODGE FARM, TALLINGTON, STAMFORD, LINCOLNSHIRE PE9 4RJ

☎ (01778) 342792. OPEN 10 - 5 SEVEN DAYS A WEEK.

Stocks everything from high street names such as Wallis to designer names such as Mondi, Escada, and Yarell. Sizes range up to 22. There is also a wedding dress hire service including veils and shoes. New shoes, hats and jewellery are also stocked. *Dress Agency*

THE FACTORY SHOP

CV CLOTHING LADIES AND CHILDRENSWEAR, SCOTTER ROAD, SCUNTHORPE, LINCOLNSHIRE DN15 8AT

☎ (01724) 270426. OPEN 9 - 5 MON - FRI, 9 - 4 SAT, 10 - 4 SUN.

WASHDYKE ROAD, IMMINGHAM, LINCOLNSHIRE DN40 2AA

☎ (01469) 574310. OPEN 9 - 5.30 MON - SAT, 10 - 4 SUN.

Part of the Coats Viyella group, which makes quality clothing for many of the major high street storres, overstocks and clearance lines are sold through more than 30 of the group's factory shops. Many of you will recognise the garments on sale, despite the lack of well-known labels. Ladieswear includes dresses, blouses, jumpers, cardigans, trousers, nightwear, underwear, lingerie, hosiery, coats and swimwear. Menswear includes trousers, belts, shirts, ties, pullovers, cardigans, T-shirts, underwear, nightwear, hosiery and jackets. Childrenswear includes jackets, trousers, T-shirts, underwear, hosiery, jumpers and babywear. There are regular deliveries to constantly update the range. *Factory Shop*

THE FACTORY SHOP LTD

MALT KILN ROAD, BARTON ON HUMBER, LINCOLNSHIRE DN18 5JT
☎ (01652) 636701. OPEN 9 - 7 MON, TUE, WED, 9 - 8 THUR, FRI, 8.30 - 7 SAT, 10 - 4 SUN.
51 FLEET STREET, HOLBEACH, SPALDING, LINCOLNSHIRE PE12 7AU
☎ (01406) 422180. OPEN 9 - 5 MON - SAT, 10 - 4 SUN.
CARRE STREET, SLEAFORD, LINCOLNSHIRE NG34 7TW
☎ (01529) 410155. OPEN 9 - 5.30 MON - SAT, 10 - 4 SUN.
Wide range on sale includes men's, ladies and children's clothing and footwear; household textiles; toiletries; hardware; luggage; lighting and bedding, most of which are chainstore and high street brands at discounts of approximately 30%-50%. Now has kitchen and furniture displays and the Cape Country Furniture range is on sale with free-standing kitchens, as well as living, bedroom and dining furniture. There are weekly deliveries and brands include many major stars such as Adidas, Nike, Wrangler and Dartington, to name just a few. Lines are continually changing and few factory shops offer such a variety under one roof. *Factory Shop*

THE SHOE FACTORY SHOP

21 WELLOWGATE, GRIMSBY, LINCOLNSHIRE DN32 ORA
☎ (01472) 342415. OPEN 9 - 5 MON - SAT, 9 - 7 THUR.
Men's, women's and children's shoes and accessories which are bought in from other manufacturers including Spanish, Portuguese and Italian companies. All are unbranded. The range covers from mocassins to dressy shoes. Ladies shoes which would cost £35 retail are £29. Children's shoes from size 6 to adult size 5 from £10 upwards. Slippers start at baby size 4 to junior size 2 from £3.50 - £6.50.
Factory Shop

TILE CLEARING HOUSE

UNIT 1, SPRONBROUGH ROAD, OFF YORK ROAD, DONCASTER, LINCOLNSHIRE DN5 8BN
☎ (01302) 787 000. OPEN 8 - 6 MON - FRI, 9 - 6 SAT, 10 - 4 SUN.
Over 500 ranges of top quality ceramic wall and floor tiles permanently in stock, plus a comprehensive range of grouts, adhesives, tools and accessories to complete the job. Save up to 75% on manufacturers' recommended selling prices.
Permanent Discount Outlet

TK MAXX

UNIT 16, ST MARK'S CENTRE, LINCOLN, LINCOLNSHIRE

☎ (01522) 530933. OPEN 9 - 6 MON - SAT, 8 ON THUR, 11 - 5 SUN.

Based on an American concept, TK Maxx is situated in easily accessible, often centrally located stores and offers famous label goods with up to 60% savings off recommended retail prices. TK Maxx has fashion for the whole family - women's, men's and childrenswear - accessories, shoes, gifts, kitchenware and home goods. Everything in the store is branded with a choice of well-known high street names to designer labels, and while a small percentage might be clearly marked past season, the great majority of items in store are current season, current stock and still with phenomenal savings. There is a huge choice with 50,000 pieces in store and up to 10,000 new items arriving a week. The stores are simple and unfussy with wide aisles, shopping trolleys and baskets, and a spacious, functional feel to them but there are individual changing rooms, ramps for buggies and wheelchairs and plenty of staff on the shop floor. Every branch accepts all major credit and debit cards and has a liberal refund and return policy. *Permanent Discount Outlet*

VOGUE CLOTHING AGENCY

94 EASTGATE, LOUTH, LINCOLNSHIRE LN11 9AA

☎ (01507) 604233. OPEN 10 - 5 MON - SAT, CLOSED THUR.

Trading for 25 years, this shop stocks a wide range of middle to high quality designer women's clothing. Consisting of two floors situated next to Curry's on the main street, it offers day wear, wedding and evening outfits with appropriate accessories including shoes and handbags. Labels include Escada, Jaeger, Laurel, Mondi and Wallis. There is a well-stocked hat hire department. Since 1996 a separate men's department has been established within the premises offering designer clothes such as Daks, Aquascutum, Armani and Hugo Boss plus casual wear separates. There is also a range of dinner suits and accessories. More recently the shop has diversified again, with a further department carrying a range of skiwear and motorcycle clothing, including one-piece and two-piece suits and boots. *Dress Agency*

WYNSORS WORLD OF SHOES

CROMWELL ROAD, GRIMSBY, LINCOLNSHIRE

☎ (01472) 251627. OPEN 9 - 5.30 MON, TUE, WED, SAT, 9 - 8 THUR, FRI, 10 - 4 SUN AND BANK HOLIDAYS.

Stocks top brand-name shoes at less than half price. Special monthly offers always available. There are shoes, trainers, slippers, sandals and boots for all the family, with a selection of bags, cleaners and polishes available. *Permanent Discount Outlet*

London

WOMENSWEAR ONLY ☆ Alexon Sale Shop, *Wood Green, N22* Annies, *Islington, N1*
Artwork, *Bermondsey, SE1* Bertie Golightly (UK) Ltd, *Nr Harrods, SW3*
Bumpsadaisy Maternity Style, *Covent Garden Market, WC2*
Bumpsadaisy Maternity Style, *Richmond, SW15* Butterfly, *Ponsonby Place, SW1*
Butterfly, *Old Bailey, EC4* Butterfly, *Putney Bridge, SW15* Caroline Charles, *St Johns' Wood, NW8*
Cassis, *Pimlico, SW1* Catherine Grosvenor Designs, *Chelsea Green, SW3*
Catwalk Nearly-New Designer Clothes, *Blandford Street, W1* Central Park, *Muswell Hill, N10*
Central Park, *Ealing, W5* Central Park, *Bond Street, W1* Central Park, *Oxford Circus, W1*
Central Park, *Hammersmith Broadway, W6* Central Park, *Baker Street Station, NW1*
Central Park, *Golders Green, NW11* Cerruti, *Old Bond Street W1X* Change Of Habit, *Clapham SW4*
Chiceria & The Wedding Studio, *Fulham SW6* Chloe Bromley Fashions Ltd, *Blackheath SE3*
Cornucopia, *Upper Tachbrook Street, SW1* Dash Sale Shop, *Wood Green, N22* Della Finch, *London*
Denner Cashmere, *SW11* Designer Bargains, *Kensington Church Street, W8*
Designs, *Rosslyn Hill, NW3* Discount Dressing, *Baker Street, W1* Dynasty, *Chiswick, W4*
Exclusivo, *Hampstead, NW3* Factory Direct, *Victoria, SW1* Frank Usher, *Noel Street, W1*
Frock Brokers, *Spitalfields, E1* Frock Follies, *Grange Park, N21* Frocks, *Barnes, SW13*
Gertrude Fashions, *Victoria, SW1V* Ghost Ltd, *Kensal Road, W10* Hang Ups, *Fulham Road, SW10*
I Kinn, *South Woodford, E18* Joel & Son Fabrics, *Church Street, NW8*
Joseph Clearance Shop, *King's Road, NW3* Labels, *Hampstead, NW3*
Laurel Herman, *Lambolle Place, NW3* Levy And Friend, *Sloane Avenue, SW3*
Louis Feraud, *Hortensia Road, SW10* Maxfield Parrish, *Congreve Street, SE17*
Nightingales Factory Shop, *Mill Hill, NW7* Oakville, *Great Portland Street, W1*
One Night Stand, *Pimlico Road, SW1* Pamela's, *Beauchamp Place, SW3* Pandora, *Cheval Place, SW7*
Proibito, *South Molton Street, W1* Sally Hair And Beauty Supplies, *Shaftesbury Avenue, W1V*
Salou, *Cheval Place, SW7* Screenface, *Powis Terrace, W11* Sheila Warren-Hill, *Highgate, N6*
Sign Of The Times, *Elystan Street, SW3* The Changing Room, *Wimbledon Park, SW19*
The Corridor, *King's Road, SW3* The Designer Store, *King's Road, SW3*
The Exchange Dress Agency, *Belgravia SW1* The Make-Up Centre, *Fulham, SW6*
Twentieth Century Frox, *Fulham, SW6* Upstairs Downstairs, *Hendon, NW4*
USA Fashion, *Fonthill Road, N4* Virginia, *Holland Park, W11* Wahl Fashions, *Great Portland Street, W1*

MENSWEAR ONLY ☆ Bertie Wooster, *Fulham Road, SW10*
Charles Tyrwhitt Shirts, *Silver Road, W12* City Menswear, *Cheapside, EC4*
Clothes Direct, *Finchley, N3* Designer Studio Man, *Covent Garden, WC2*
Designers For Less, *Uxbridge Road, W13* Dynasty Man, *Chiswick, W4*
L'Homme Designer Exchange, *Blandford Street, W1* Lipmans Hire Department, *Charing Cross Rd, WC2*
Moss Bros, *Covent Garden, WC2* Paul Smith Sale Shop, *Avery Row, W1* Stockhouse, *Goswell Road, EC1*
Surprise Surprise, *Golders Green Road, NW11*

WOMENSWEAR & MENSWEAR ☆ ☆ Angels And Bermans, *Shaftesbury Avenue, WC2*
Benny Dee (City) Ltd, *Middlesex Street, E1* Benny Dee (City) Ltd, *Walthamstow, E17*
Benny Dee (City) Ltd, *Kilburn High Road, NW6* Benny Dee (City) Ltd, *Wood Green, N22*
Blackout 11, *Covent Garden, WC2*
British Designers Sale For Women And Men, *Prince Of Wales Drive, SW11*
Browns Labels For Less, *South Molton Street, W1* Burberry, *Chatham Place, E9*
Butterfields 8, *Ravey Street, EC2* Catalogue Bargain Shop, *Peckham, SE15*
Cenci, *Monmouth Street, WC2* Change Of Heart, *Park Road, N8*
Choice Discount Stores Ltd, *Golders Green, NW11* Damart, *Lewisham, SE13*
Designer Sale UK, *Highbury Grange, N5* Dress Circle, *Leverton Place, NW5* Ellens Ltd, *Leyton, E10*
Emporium, *Greenwich, SE10* Fofo Club, *Old Bond Street, W1*
Gold's Factory Outlet, *Golders Green, NW11* In Wear Factory Outlet, *Wandsworth, SW18*
La Scala, *Elystan Street, SW3* Littlewoods Catalogue Discount Store, *Wandsworth, SW18*

Losners Dress Hire, *Stamford Hill, N16*   Matalan, *Cricklewood, NW2*   Matalan, *Beckton, E8*
Modern Age Vintage Clothing, *Chalk Farm Road, NW1*   Morry's, *Edmonton, N9*
Next To Nothing, *Ealing Broadway, W5*   Nicole Farhi Outlet Shop, *Bow, E3*
Not Quite New, *Hendon, NW4*   Notting Hill Housing Trust, *Fulham, SW10*
Oxfam Origin, *Ganton Street, W1*   Penguin Society, *West End Lane, NW6*
Philip Of King's Road, *King's Road, SW3*   Rainbow, *Highgate, N6*   Rokit, *Camden High Street, NW1*
Royal National Theatre, *Brixton, SW9*   Shipton & Heneage, *Queenstown, SW8*
Steinberg & Tolkien, *King's Road, SW3*   Swimgear, *Finchley, N3*   The Costume Studio, *Islington, N1*
The Designer Warehouse Sale For Women And Men, *Northampton Street, N1*
The Dress Box, *Cheval Place, SW7*   The Dresser, *Porchester Place, W2*
The Gallery Of Antique Costume & Textiles, *Marylebone, NW8*   The Loft, *Covent Garden, WC2*
The Observatory, *Greenwich, SE10*   TK Maxx, *Ealing, W5*   Tog 24, *Putney, SW15*
Wallers, *Charing Cross Road, WC2*   Wellingtons, *Wellington Place, NW8*
Windsmoor Warehouse, *Tottenham, N15*

CHILDREN   Benny Dee (City) Ltd, *Middlesex Street, E1*
Benny Dee (City) Ltd, *Walthamstow, E17*   Benny Dee (City) Ltd, *Kilburn, NW6*
Benny Dee (City) Ltd, *Wood Green, N22*   Burberry, *Chatham Place, E9*
Catalogue Bargain Shop, *Peckham, SE15*   Catalogue Bargain Shop, *Palmers Green, N13*
Change Of Habit, *Clapham, SW4*   David Charles, *Kings Cross Road, WC1*   Designs, *Rosslyn Hill, NW3*
Dress Circle, *Leverton Place, NW5*   Encore, *Stoke Newington, N16*   La Scala, *Elystan Street, SW3*
Letterbox Library, *Essex Road, N1*   Littlewoods Catalogue Discount Store, *Wandsworth, SW18*
Matalan, *Cricklewood, NW2*   Matalan, *Beckton, E8*   Morry's, *Edmonton, N9*
Next To Nothing, *Ealing Broadway, W5*   Rainbow, *Highgate, N6*   Rochelle, *NW7*
Scarecrow, *Moore Park Road, SW6*   Swallows & Amazons, *Nightingale Lane, SW12*
Swimgear, *Finchley, N3*   The Children's Warehouse, *Colville Road, W3*
The Nappy Express, *New Southgate, N11*   TK Maxx, *Ealing, SW5*   Tog 24, *Putney, SW15*
Totters, *Hornsey, N8*

HOUSEHOLD AND GIFTWARE   Aladdins, *Fulham, SW6*
Benny Dee (City) Ltd, *Middlesex Street, E1*
Benny Dee (City) Ltd, *Walthamstow, E17*   Benny Dee (City) Ltd, *Kilburn, NW6*
Benny Dee (City) Ltd, *Wood Green, N22*   Catalogue Bargain Shop, *Peckham, SE15*
Catalogue Bargain Shop, *Palmers Green, N13*   David Richards & Sons, *New Cavendish, Street W1M*
Hazle Ceramics, *Covent Garden Market, WC2*   Homes & Gardens Christmas Grand Sale, *Victoria, SW1*
Lunn Antiques Ltd, *Parsons Green, SW6*   Lunn Antiques Ltd, *Covent Garden, WC2*
Lunn Antiques Ltd, *Portobello Road, W11*   Matalan, *Cricklewood, NW2*   Matalan, *Beckton, E8*
Ocean Home Shopping, *Wandsworth, SW18*   Price's Patent Candle Co, *York Road, SW11*
Reject China Shop, *Golders Green, NW11*   Rococo Frames, *Fulham Road, SW6*
Rococo Frames, *Gloucester Road, SW7*   Rococo Frames, *Barnes High Street, SW13*
Roger Lascelles Clocks Ltd, *Carnwath Road, SW6*   S & B Evans & Sons, *Ezra Street, E2*
Soviet Carpet And Art Galleries, *Cricklewood Broadway, NW2*
The Candle Shop, *New King's Road, SW6*   The Fulham Factory Outlet, *Fulham Road, SW6*
TK Maxx, *Ealing, SW5*   Top Value Drugstore, *Finchley Road, NW11*
Villeroy & Boch (UK) Ltd, *Merton Road, SW18*   Zeon, *Waterloo Road, NW2*

ELECTRICAL EQUIPMENT   Appliance Direct, *Bayswater, W2*
Audio Gold, *Crouch End, N8*   Buyers & Sellers Ltd, *Ladbroke Grove, W10*
Catalogue Bargain Shop, *Peckham, SE15*   Catalogue Bargain Shop, *Palmers Green, N13*
Discount Cookers, *Catford, SE6*   Hot & Cold Inc, *Golborne Road, W10*
Littlewoods Catalogue Discount Store, *Wandsworth, SW18*   Morry's, *Edmonton, N9*
Sellcon Electrical Co Ltd, *Bethnal Green, E2*

DIY/RENOVATION   Brondesbury Architectural Reclamation, *Willesden Lane, NW6*
Chesney's Antique Fireplace Warehouse Ltd, *Battersea Park Road, SW11*   Dave's DIY, *Firs Lane, N13*
Discount Decorating, *Peckham, SE15*   Fens Restoration, *Chelsea, SW10*
G Thornfield Ltd, *Gray's Inn Road, WC1*   House Of Steel, *Caledonian Road, N1*
King's Cross Tiles, *King's Cross, NW1*   Lassco Flooring, *Maltby Street, SE1*   Lassco RBK, *Islington, N1*
Lassco Trade Warehouse, *Islington, N1*   Lassco St Michael's, *Mark Street, EC2*
Lazdan, *Bow Common Lane, E3*   Leyland SDM, *Edgware Road, W2*

Leyland SDM, *Upper Tachbrook Street, SW1*   Leyland SDM, *Finchley Road, NW2*
Leyland SDM, *Farringdon Road, EC1*   Leyland SDM, *Ealing, W5*   Leyland SDM, *King's Road, SW3*
Leyland SDM, *Kensington High Street, W14*   Leyland SDM, *Camden Road, NW1*
The Hardwood Flooring Co Ltd, *West Hampstead, NW6*   The House Hospital, *Wandsworth, SW18*
The Natural Wood Floor Company, *Wandsworth, SW18*
The Reject Tile Shop, *Wandsworth Bridge Road, SW6*   The Reject Tile Shop, *Englands Lane, NW3*
The Clearing House, *North Circular Road, NW10*
The Clearing House, *New Southgate Industrial Park, N11*
Tile Clearing House, *North Circular Road, NW10*   Tiles Galore, *Streatham, SW16*
Tiles Galore, *Addington, CR2*   Townsends, *Abbey Road, NW8*   Townsends, *Boundary Road, NW8*
Victorian Wood Works, *Temple Mills Lane, E15*   Ward & Stevens, *Manor Park, E12*

ARCHITECTURAL SALVAGE   Brondesbury Architectural Reclamation, *Willesden Lane, NW6*
Chesney's Antique Fireplace Warehouse Ltd, *Battersea Park Road, SW11*
Fens Restoration, *Chelsea, SW10*   House Of Steel, *Caledonian Road, N1*
Lassco Flooring, *Maltby Street, SE1*   Lassco RBK, *Islington, N1*   Lassco Trade Warehouse, *Islington, N1*
Lassco St Michael's, *Mark Street, EC2*   Lazdan, *Bow Common Lane, E3*
The Hardwood Flooring Co Ltd, *West Hampstead, NW6*   The House Hospital, *Wandsworth, SW18*
The Natural Wood Floor Company, *Wandsworth, SW18*   Townsends, *Abbey Road, NW8*
Townsends, *Boundary Road, NW8*   Victorian Wood Works, *Temple Mills Lane, E15*

FURNITURE/SOFT FURNISHINGS   A W Morris (Repro) Ltd, *West Road, N17*
Adam Richwood, *Garden Walk, EC2*   Alexander Furnishings, *Wigmore Street, W1*
Bucks, *Deptford, SE8*   Carpet Tile Centre, *North Finchley, N12*   Change Of Heart, *Park Road, N8*
Colefax & Fowler, *Grosvenor Hill, W1*   Curtain Trading Centre, *Baker Street, W1*
David J Wilkins, *Princess Road, NW1*   Designers For Less, *Uxbridge Road, W13*
Edward Symmons & Partners, *London Bridge, SE1*   Factory Shop At Poetstyle Ltd, *Hackney, E8*
Permanent Discount Shop Orient Expressions Ltd, *Michael Road, SW6*   Osborne & Little, *London.*
P N Jones, *Holly Grove, SE15*   Portobello Curtain Shop, *Portobello Road, W11*
Posners: The Floor Store, *Swiss Cottage, NW6*   Rainbow, *Highgate, N6*
Rococo Frames, *Fulham Road, SW6*   Rococo Frames, *Gloucester Road, SW7*
Rococo Frames, *Barnes High Street, SW13*   Russell & Chapple Ltd, *Monmouth Street, WC2*
S & M Myers Ltd, *Holloway, N7*   S & M Myers Ltd, *Finchley, N2*
Seers Antiques, *Battersea Park Rd, SW11*   Seers Antiques, *Greenwich, SE10*
Seers Antiques, *Norwood, SE27*   Seers Antiques, *Chelsea, SW6*
Sofa To Bed, *Bayford Street Industrial Centre, E8*   Sofa To Bed, *Mile End Road, E1*
Soviet Carpet And Art Galleries, *Cricklewood Broadway, NW2*   The Cloth Shop, *Portobello Road, W10*
The Curtain Exchange, *Stephendale Road, SW6*   The Curtain Exchange, *Ledbury Road, W11*
The Curtain Exchange, *Dulwich, SE21*   The Curtain Fabric Factory Shop, *North End Road, W14*
The Curtain Mill, *Fairfield Road, E3*   The Curtain Mill, *Acton, W3*   The Curtain Mill, *Colindale, NW9*
The Designer Warehouse Fabrics Sale, Roger Dack Ltd, *Northampton Street, N1*
The Fulham Factory Outlet, *Fulham Road, SW6*   The London Picture Centre, *Fulham Road, SW6*
The London Picture Centre, *Hackney Road, E2*   The London Picture Centre, *Leather Lane, EC1*
The London Picture Centre, *Crawford Street, W1*   The Old Cinema, *Tower Bridge Road, SE1*
The Old Cinema, *Chiswick High Road, W4*   Wall To Wall, *Battersea, SW11*

FOOD AND LEISURE   Bibliophile Books, *Thomas Road, E14*
Bookends, *Charing Cross Road, WC2*   Books For Amnesty, *Hammersmith, W6*
Gloucester Road Bookshop, *Gloucester Road, SW7*
Half-Price Pots, *Fulham Road, SW10*   Postscript, *Langroyd Road, SW17*
The Nappy Express, *New Southgate, N11*   Top Value Drugstore, *Finchley Road, NW11*
Travel Accessory Outlet, *Queensway, W2*

SPORTSWEAR AND EQUIPMENT   Catalogue Bargain Shop, *Peckham, SE15*
Catalogue Bargain Shop, *Palmers Green, N13*   Recycle, *Annerley, SE20*   Swimgear, *Finchley, N3*

A W MORRIS (REPRO) LTD

6 - 7 WEST MEWS, WEST ROAD, LONDON N17

☎ 0181-880 9191. OPEN 9 - 5 MON - FRI, 9 - 12 SAT.

Manufacturers of a wide variety of mirrors, including overmantels, for stores such as John Lewis and Selfridges. You can buy samples, seconds and overstock from the showroom as well as console tables, vanities and chevals at discounted prices. If you want something made specially, that can be arranged. *Factory Shop*

ADAM RICHWOOD

5 GARDEN WALK, LONDON EC2A 3EQ

☎ 0171-729 0976. OPEN 7 - 4 MON - FRI.

Makers of fine period furniture, Adam Richwood sells direct from their factory, top quality pieces at savings of between 75% and 100% on shop prices. (VAT is extra and delivery can be arranged at a nominal cost.) A 5ft mahogany sideboard with solid brass fittings costs £644; a 30in yew wood Regency bureau costs £473; a burr walnut Queen Anne 4ft by 2ft desk with solid brass handles costs £802. They also make chests, hi-fi and television cabinets, as well as open bookcases made to any size, the most popular being 6 ft by 3 ft and costing £260 in mahogany. Prices change in January each year. *Furniture/Soft Furnishing*

ALADDINS

47 FULHAM HIGH STREET, LONDON SW6

☎ 0171-731 2345. OPEN 10 - 6 MON - FRI, 10 - 5.30 SAT.

Clearing house for a whole range of household items from electrical equipment, gardening tools, binoculars, clothes, pots and pans to cast iron barbecues, fans, storage containers, brushes, air mattresses. Stock changes constantly so it's worth popping in regularly if you live nearby. *Permanent Discount Outlet*

ALEXANDER FURNISHINGS

51-61 WIGMORE STREET, LONDON W1H 9LF

☎ 0171-935 2624. OPEN 9 - 6 MON - SAT, UNTIL 7 ON THUR.

The largest independent curtain retailer in the UK, Alexander Furnishings has been operating from the same base for more than 40 years. Famous for curtaining, they also sell upholstery fabric and wallpapers and trimmings. There's always a discount on fabrics - for example Sanderson cotton chintz at just over one quarter of the original price. The biggest bargains are the discontinued lines which can be discounted by up to 50%. There is also a trimming shop on the premises and sofas and sofabeds are on sale. Fabrics start at £4.95 and there is a vast selection below £10. *Permanent Discount Outlet*

ALEXON SALE SHOP

UNIT 29, SHOPPING CITY, WOOD GREEN, LONDON N22

☎ 0181-889 9560. OPEN 9 - 5.30 MON - FRI, 9 - 6 SAT.

Alexon and Eastex from previous seasons at 40%-70% less than the original price; during sale time in January and June, the reductions are up to 70%. Stock includes separates, skirts, jackets, blouses. Current stock at 10%-40% discounts. *Permanent Discount Outlet*

ANGELS AND BERMANS

119 SHAFTESBURY AVENUE, LONDON WC2H 8AE

☎ 0171-836 5678. OPEN 9 - 5.30 MON - FRI,

LAST COSTUME FITTING 4.30.

This famous screen costumier has now devoted its Shaftesbury Avenue building to hiring out famous outfits to the public. You can choose from outfits worn in Four Weddings and a Funeral, Out Of Africa, Indiana Jones and the House of Eliott. Angels has been dressing the stars for over 150 years, storing a vast range of costumes from every age and many different nations. They have costumes from all over the world - from saris to sarongs, kilts to kimonos - as well as an extensive range of accessories, novelties, beards, masks and wigs - for hire from £70 a week with £100 deposit. *Hire Shop*

ANNIES

10 CAMDEN PASSAGE, ISLINGTON, LONDON N1 8DU

☎ 0171-359 0796. OPEN 11- 6 MON - SAT, WED, SAT: MARKET DAYS.

Mainly women's clothes from late Victorian times to the Forties, specialising in Twenties beaded garments, as well as ballgowns, silk lingerie, Forties suits and blouses, table linen, cushions, curtains, textiles and bed linen. *Secondhand and Vintage Clothing*

APPLIANCE DIRECT

66 WESTBOURNE GROVE, BAYSWATER, LONDON W2 5SH

☎ 0171-221 1144. OPEN 9.30 - 5.30 MON - FRI, TILL 7 TUE & THUR, 10 - 5.30 SAT.

Specialise in ex-display and graded white electrical goods. For example new, cosmetically damaged washing machines from £160. They also sell fridges, cookers, deep fat fryers, blenders, vacuum cleaners, toasters, irons, food processors and American fridges. *Permanent Discount Outlet*

ARTWORK

103 BERMONDSEY STREET, LONDON SE1 3XB

☎ 0171-403 6332. PHONE TO BE PUT ON MAILING LIST.

Twice-yearly showroom sales of these distinctive chunky knits, denim dresses, skirts, leggings and sweatshirts - all made from cotton and usually half price or less here. Sales are usually end of May and in November. Parking outside. Phone to put your name on the mailing list. *Designer Sale*

AUDIO GOLD

31 PARK ROAD, CROUCH END, LONDON N8 8TE

☎ 0181-341 9007. OPEN 11 - 6 MON - SAT, CLOSED THUR.

Small shop with friendly, unintimidating atmosphere where old, loved music machines get a second life. Catering for the run-of-the-mill end of the secondhand hi-fi market as well as the esoteric and expensive end. There aren't a lot of CD players as they are expensive to repair, but particular bargains can be found in the imposing speaker areas as most people trading in equipment tend to trade down, not up, in size. Most equipment is guaranteed for three months. One of the few places left in London where you can still get a good range of turntables. *Secondhand Shop*

BENNY DEE (CITY) LTD

74-80 MIDDLESEX STREET, LONDON E1

☎ 0171-377 9067. OPEN 9.30 - 6 MON, 8.30 - 6 TUE - FRI,
10 - 4 SAT, 9.30 - 4.30 SUN.

136-138 WALTHAMSTOW HIGH STREET, LONDON E17 1JS

☎ 0181-520 4637. OPEN 9 - 6 MON - SAT.

112-114 KILBURN HIGH ROAD, LONDON NW6 4HY

☎ 0171-624 2995. OPEN 9 - 6 MON - SAT, 10 - 4 SUN.

4-6 HIGH ROAD, WOOD GREEN, LONDON N22 6BX

☎ 0181-881 8101. OPEN 9 - 6 MON - SAT, 10 - 4 SUN.

The Middlesex Street branch is on two floors with children's clothes and baby bedding in the basement, most of which are end of lines or bankrupt stock with the labels cut out. Some of the brands there include Zorbit, Mothercare, Baby Gap, Baby Togs and Grasshopper. The ground floor contains predominantly ladies lingerie with masses of bras, all brand names such as Marks & Spencer, Berlei, Gossard, Triumph and Warner and some clothing. For men there are socks, ties, underwear shirts and occasionally suits. *Permanent Discount Outlet*

BERTIE GOLIGHTLY (UK) LTD

48 BEAUCHAMP PLACE, NEAR HARRODS, LONDON SW3 1NX

☎ 0171-584 7270. OPEN 10 - 6 MON - SAT.

Former stunt girl, Roberta Gibbs, opened Bertie Golightly in 1980 and sells a richly diverse selection of the world's most famous labels including Chanel, Valentino, Armani, Yves St Laurent. To complete your outfit, there are also hats, scarves, costume jewellery and shoes from Hermes, Philip Somerville and Gucci, etc. Ballgowns and evening wear are Bertie's speciality - a whole new floor full awaits you. Many samples are one-third of the normal price. All items are immaculate and in season. *Dress Agency*

BERTIE WOOSTER
284 FULHAM ROAD, LONDON SW10 9EW
☎ 0171-352 5662. OPEN 10 - 6 MON, WED, FRI, 10 - 7 TUE,
THUR, 10 - 5 SAT.
High street shop with two floors of the finest quality secondhand and new clothes and good luggage. New clothes are excellent quality at low prices - suits cost £320 made to measure. Secondhand clothes are of the quality rarely seen outside bespoke tailoring and includes suits, ties, blazers, waistcoats, and hankies at extremely attractive prices. The new and made-to-measure clothing including morning coats, morning coat trousers, full backed waistcoats, dinner and sports jackets. *Dress Agency*

BIBLIOPHILE BOOKS
5 THOMAS ROAD, LONDON E14 7BN
☎ 0171-515 9222/538 4115 FAX. OPERATES 8.30 - 5 MON - FRI.
MAIL ORDER ONLY.
Mail order books from biographies and art, to literature and general tomes at half price or less. Stock is brand new remainders, plus reprints, rare and sometimes signed editions. Send for free catalogue. *Permanent Discount Outlet*

BLACKOUT II
51 ENDELL STREET, COVENT GARDEN, LONDON WC2
☎ 0171-240 5006. OPEN 11 - 7 MON - FRI, 11.30 - 6.30 SAT.
Twenties and upwards gear, plus accessories, for sale and to hire at reasonable prices. Specialises in Sixties and Seventies gear. *Secondhand and Vintage Clothing*

BOOKENDS
108 CHARING CROSS ROAD, LONDON WC2H OBP
☎ 0171-836 3457. OPEN 9 - 8 MON - SAT.
Secondhand and damaged books and publishers' returns, as well as new and review copies, including recently published books, usually one-third off and sometimes half price. *Secondhand Shop*

BOOKS FOR AMNESTY
139 KING STREET, HAMMERSMITH, LONDON W6
☎ 0181-746 3172. OPEN 10 - 6 MON - FRI, 10 - 4 SAT.
New books hot off the presses, many of which are critics' copies, at reductions of 25%-30%. Also remainders, secondhand and some antiquarian books, secondhand CDs, records and videos and a small range of Amnesty products. *Secondhand Shop*

BRITISH DESIGNERS SALE FOR WOMEN AND MEN

42 YORK MANSIONS, PRINCE OF WALES DRIVE, LONDON SW11 4BP
☎ 0171-228 5314. OPEN 10 - 4 MON - FRI.

The first top end of the market designer sale - now a booming industry - the British Designers Sale was started by Deborah Hodges, a former PR, more than eighteen years ago. Because of her contacts, it offers top British, Italian, German and French labels you won't find at other designer sales - but no names mentioned or those publicity-shy designers would not be happy to let Debbie sell their overstocks. Labels are the sort you would expect to find in the designer rooms at Harrods or Harvey Nichols. The women's sales, held twice a year in Edinburgh and five times a year in London, are open to members only. Membership costs £32 per year. Please enclose an SAE when writing to Debbie or contact her at the above telephone number or by fax ☎ (0171 498 6956) for further information. There is no membership required for the Men's Sale, which takes place twice a year, also at Chelsea Town Hall. They also hold twice yearly sales in Edinburgh. *Designer Sale*

BRONDESBURY ARCHITECTURAL RECLAMATION

136 WILLESDEN LANE, LONDON NW6 7TE
☎ 0171-328 0820. OPEN 9 - 6 MON - SAT, 10 - 4 SUN.

Architectural salvage up to the Thirties including Art Deco, Victorian, Edwardian and Georgian with the occasional French piece. Lots of fireplaces, baths, sinks, taps, towel rails, kitchen ranges, marble surrounds, cast-iron. Garden department stocks garden tables, sun dials, bird baths, chimney pots. Everything you could want to convert a modernised house back to its former glory - all originals, no copies. *Architectural Salvage*

BROWNS LABELS FOR LESS

50 SOUTH MOLTON STREET, LONDON W1Y 1DA
☎ 0171-451 7833. OPEN 10 - 6 MON - SAT, UNTIL 7 ON THUR.

This designer sale shop supplies rails of clothes which, if you're a keen bargain hunter and don't mind rummaging, offers exciting names for bargain prices. Designers on sale here include most of those sold in the main, full-price shop including Rifat Ozbek, Issey Miyake, Missoni, Dolce & Gabbana, Comme des Garcons and Sonia Rykiel; prices are advertised as representing reductions of 50%-80%. *Permanent Discount Outlet*

Live Well On Less Tips
Save butter wrappers and use to line baking tins.

BUCKS

125 EVELYN STREET, DEPTFORD, LONDON SE8 5RJ

☎ 0181-692 4447. OPEN SEVEN DAYS A WEEK, 10 - 7 MON - FRI, 10 - 5 SAT, 10 - 4 SUN.

Warehouse selling cancelled orders, ex-display and ex-photo shoot furniture from famous department stores and other well-known brand names. Some of the department store furniture is from the current catalogue. Most of the three-piece suites are reduced by 40%-50% and the other items are all substantially discounted. Free car parking. *Permanent Discount Outlet*

BUMPSADAISY MATERNITY STYLE

43 COVENT GARDEN MARKET, LONDON WC2E 8HA

☎ 0171-379 9831. OPEN 10 - 6 MON - SAT, UNTIL 7.30 ON THUR.

157 LOWER RICHMOND ROAD, LONDON SW15 1HH

☎ 0181-789 0329. OPEN 9.30 - 5.30 MON, TUE, WED, FRI, SAT, 10 - 7 THUR.

Franchised shops and home-based branches with large range of specialist maternity wear, from wedding outfits to ball gowns, to hire and to buy. Hire costs range from £30 to £100 for special occasion wear. To buy are lots of casual and business wear in sizes 8 - 18. For example, skirts £20-£70; dresses £40-£100. Phone ☎ 0181-789 0329 for details of your local stockist. *Hire Shop*

BURBERRY

29-53 CHATHAM PLACE, LONDON E9 6LP

☎ 0181-985 3344. OPEN 11 - 6 MON - FRI, 9 - 3.30 SAT, 11 - 5 SUN.

This Burberry factory shop sells the full range of Burberry merchandise, none of which is current. It stocks seconds and overmakes of the famous name raincoats and duffle coats as well as accessories such as the distinctive umbrellas, scarves and handbags. All carry the Burberry label and are about one third of the normal retail price. Childrenswear tends to be thin on the ground, but there are plenty of gift items such as Burberry brand name teas, coffees and marmalade. A large warehouse with clothes set out on dozens of rails, surroundings are relatively spartan and the outlet is often full of tourists. *Factory Shop*

BUTTERFIELD 8

4 RAVEY STREET, LONDON EC2 4QP

☎ 0171-739 3026. RING FOR OPENING TIMES.

Period fancy dress for the party-goer from 1920s to the Sixties and Seventies. Cost from £40 - £65. Original vintage costumes from the twenties to the sixties. *Hire Shop*

Live Well On Less Tips
Milk jug rings can be used to keep socks together. Store in drawer with rings.

BUTTERFLY

28A PONSONBY PLACE, LONDON SW1
☎ 0171-821 1983. OPEN 12 - 6.30 WED, FRI, 12 - 7.30 THUR.
28 OLD BAILEY, LONDON EC4M 7HS
☎ 0171-489 8288. OPEN 11 - 6.30 MON, TUE, 11.30 - 4 WED, THUR, FRI.
Sells fashion samples obtained through extensive contacts in the industry at
wholesale price or less. Stock is from the current season and the following season so that you can be ahead of the fashion - but only if you are a size 10 or
12 as samples are mostly model-sizes with a few sizes 14 and 16. As well as
some British designers, the shop has a lot of French and Italian labels, many
of which can be seen in Harrods designer department. There's Dusk, Diana
Gee, Caroline Roumer, Character, August Silk, and Frank Usher, as well as silk
shirts and skirts from Fenn Wright & Manson and Soap Studio, and raincoats
and rain jackets from Savannah and Freetex, at less than half price.
Permanent Discount Outlet

BUTTERFLY

3 LOWER RICHMOND ROAD, PUTNEY BRIDGE, LONDON SW15
☎ 0181-788 8304. OPEN 10.30 - 6.30 MON - FRI, 10 - 5 SAT.
Selling middle to upper range nearly-new designer clothes, new samples and
end of ranges, this shop has been going since 1981. Selection includes Armani,
Rifat Ozbek, Chanel, Nicole Farhi, French Connection, Jigsaw and Hobbs.
Lots of linen, silks, cashmere, wool and natural fibres. Also some samples and
clothes used for modelling, handbags, scarves, new jewellery and purses. *Dress
Agency*

BUYERS & SELLERS LTD

120-122 LADBROKE GROVE, LONDON W10 5NE
☎ 0171-229 1947/8468. FAX 0171-221 4113.
OPEN 9.30 - 5.30 MON - FRI, 9.30 - 4.30 SAT, 10 - 5.30 WED.
Buyers & Sellers has been in business for more than 40 years, selling brand
name domestic equipment at bargain prices. Everything from fridges and
freezers, ovens and microwaves, hobs and vacuum cleaners, washing machines
and dishwashers, tumble dryers and cookers, all new and guaranteed and in
perfect working order. They stock and can obtain almost any make and model
currently available. Nationwide delivery service. Telephone orders taken.
Advice line and brochures are part of the service. Credit cards accepted.
Permanent Discount Outlet

CAROLINE CHARLES
9 ST JOHNS' WOOD HIGH STREET, LONDON NW8
☎ 0171-483 0080. OPEN 10 - 5.30 MON - SAT.
This shop has stock at full price and a sale basement for Caroline Charles merchandise. Here, end of season outfits, samples and one-offs which never made it into production are sold at discounts of at least 30%. Daywear to evening wear is covered as well as handbags, scarves and hats. *Permanent Discount Outlet*

CARPET TILE CENTRE
227-229 WOODHOUSE ROAD, NORTH FINCHLEY, LONDON N12 9BD
☎ 0181-361 1261. OPEN 9 - 5 MON - FRI, 9 - 1 SAT.
Offers a wide range of seconds as well as end of line carpet tiles, specials and non-standard colours of Heuga and Interface brands. Prices start at £1.95-£2.95 for tiles which normally cost £5. Even the perfect tiles are competitively priced.

CASSIS
21 UPPER TACHBROOK STREET, OFF WARWICK WAY, PIMLICO, LONDON SW1V 1SN
☎ 0171-976 5875. OPEN 11.30 - 6.30 THUR, 10 - 6.30 FRI, 10 - 5 SAT.
Designer label and good quality clothes such as Ralph Lauren, Nicole Farhi, Joseph, Moschino, Versace, Liberty, Jaeger, MaxMara, Alexon, Valentino, Next and Wallis. *Dress Agency*

CATALOGUE BARGAIN SHOP
103-113 RYE LANE, PECKHAM, LONDON SE15 4ST
☎ 0171- 358 1308. OPEN 9 - 5.30 MON - SAT, 10.30 - 4.30 SUN.
252 GREEN LANES, PALMERS GREEN, LONDON N13 5TU
☎ 0181-886 9532. OPEN 9 - 5.30 MON - SAT, 10 - 4 SUN.
Catalogue Bargain Shop is a growing national chain of stores which obtains the majority of its goods from mail order giants Great Universal and Kays, and offers a range of clothing for all the family, a wide selection of shoes, bed linen, household goods, electrical equipment (TVs, videos, hi-fis) and hundreds of other catalogue items at very competitive prices. The merchandise consists of ends of ranges and previous season's stock for which there is no longer storage space when the catalogues change. *Permanent Discount Outlet*

CATHERINE GROSVENOR DESIGNS

3 ELYSTAN STREET, CHELSEA GREEN, LONDON SW3 3NT

☎ 0171-584 2112. OPEN 10 - 5.30 MON - FRI, 10 - 4 SAT.

Own designer knitwear at competitive prices. There are pashminas, cottons, cashmere and merino wools, and linens, jumpers, cardigans, jackets, skirts, designer jewellery and accessories. Offers made-to-measure service. *Permanent Discount Outlet*

CATWALK NEARLY-NEW DESIGNER CLOTHES

52 BLANDFORD STREET, LONDON W1H 3HD

☎ 0171-935 1052. OPEN 12.30 - 6 MON, 11.15 - 6 TUE, WED, THUR, FRI, 11.15 - 5 SAT.

Nearly-new designer clothes from Chanel to Ghost, Gucci to Whistles and including Prada, Armani and Jil Sander. Always has a wide variety of jackets and separates as well as jewellery, hats, shoes, belts, scarves and handbags. For example, Gucci trousers, £50; Armani jacket, £80; Nicole Farhi silk blouse, £32. *Dress Agency*

CENCI

31 MONMOUTH STREET, LONDON WC2 HDD

☎ 0171-836 1400. OPEN 10.30 - 7 MON - FRI, 10.30 - 6.30 SAT.

Small shop selling vintage clothing from the Forties to the Seventies from America and Europe. There are about 10,000 items in the shop at any one time, many of which are bought from a factory in Italy devoted to the recycling of old style, quality clothing. As well as 1960s sweaters from £16 to £125, Forties' and Sixties' suits from £75 and a large selection of cashmere, there are also accessories such as luggage, watches, rings, cufflinks and glasses from the 1920s to the 1960s and a small selection of shoes. *Secondhand and Vintage Clothe*

CENTRAL PARK

152 MUSWELL HILL BROADWAY, MUSWELL HILL, LONDON N10

☎ 0181-883 9122. OPEN 9.30 - 6 MON - SAT, 1 - 5 SUN.

11 EALING BROADWAY, EALING. LONDON W5

☎ 0181-567 2250. OPEN 10 - 7 MON - SAT, 11 - 5 SUN.

WEST 1 SHOPPING CENTRE, LOWER GROUND FLOOR, BOND STREET STATION, LONDON W1

☎ 0171-495 5097. OPEN 10 -7 MON - SAT, 1 - 5 SUN.

5 ST CHRISTOPHER'S PLACE, OXFORD CIRCUS, LONDON W1

☎ 0171-487 3442. OPEN 10 - 6 MON - SAT.

HAMMERSMITH BROADWAY STATION, LONDON W6 9YE

☎ 0181-563 1700. OPEN 10 - 7 MON - SAT, 1 - 6 SUN.

UNIT B & C, BAKER STREET STATION, BAKERLOO TICKET HALL, LONDON NW1

☎ 0171-935 2820. OPEN 10 - 8 MON - SAT, 12 - 6 SUN.

54 GOLDERS GREEN ROAD, LONDON

☎ 0181-731 6200. OPEN 10 - 5.45 MON - SAT.

Large multiple group stocking cancelled orders and over runs for women, although most of the clothes are de-labelled before they come here. There are dresses, suits, skirts, trousers and tops. Prices are very cheap. Labels include Kookai, Morgan, Armani and Versace. A new store at 168 Muswell Hill Size Plus was opening as we went to press. It caters especially for more mature women and larger sizes. For more details phone ☎ 0181-883 9122. Formerly called The Outlet, the shops are now being changed to Central Park. *Permanent Discount Outlet*

CERRUTI 1881

23 OLD BOND STREET, LONDON W1X 3DA

☎ 0171-491 1881.

Phone or write to put your name down on the mailing list for an automatic invitation to the showroom sales at which prices are considerably reduced. *Designer Sale*

CHANGE OF HABIT

65 ABBEVILLE ROAD, CLAPHAM, LONDON SW4 9JW

☎ 0181-675 9475. OPEN 10 - 5.30 MON - SAT, UNTIL 6.30 WED.

Day and evening wear as good as new from high street to designer label. Also nearly-new clothes for babies and children up to the age of 8. Described by the owner as everyday clothes for everyday people at realistic prices . Very high turnover. Also has mothers-to-be wear and recently added a range of brand new clothes and accessories at very reasonable prices. *Dress Agency*

CHANGE OF HEART

59C PARK ROAD, LONDON N8 8DP

☎ 0181-341 1575. OPEN 10 - 6 MON - SAT.

Sells a mixture of designer and good high street labels for women, men and children including labels such as DKNY, Ghost, Betty Jackson, Armani, Jigsaw, Next, Whistles, Moschino, MaxMara, Oilily, Joseph and Paul Smith. Prices vary from £20 for a pair of Armani shorts to £50 for a Nicole Farhi silk two-piece suit. They now offer new and nearly new contemporary home furnishings. *Dress Agency*

Live Well On Less Tips
Buy coal at discounted prices during the summer months.

CHARLES TYRWHITT SHIRTS
UNIT 13, SILVER ROAD, LONDON W12 7RR
☎ 0181-735 1000. OPEN 8 - 8 MON - FRI, 10 - 4 SAT. MAIL ORDER ONLY.
Traditional, top quality Jermyn-Street shirts at high street prices. Selling through mail order, overheads are low and the price is kept down by a policy of high volume and low margins. The comparison with Jermyn Street comes not just from the cut of the shirts, but also from the fabric: longstaple Egyptian cotton, which produces a soft, silky finish which washes well and is hard-wearing. All shirts come with brass collar stiffeners. The mail order catalogue also includes cufflinks, £5-£60; a range of silk ties; and felt and many other accessories. Call for details of the introductory offer and for a free pair of collar stiffeners. *Permanent Discount Outlet*

CHESNEY'S ANTIQUE
FIREPLACE WAREHOUSE LTD
194-202 BATTERSEA PARK ROAD, LONDON SW11 4ND
☎ 0171-627 1410. OPEN 9 - 5.30 MON - FRI, 10 - 5 SAT.
Antique and reproduction fireplaces with at least 120 in stock at any one time. Full fitting service. marble fireplaces range from £450 to £6,000; stone from £495 to £3,000; pine from £230 to £900. *Architectural Salvage*

CHICERIA & THE WEDDING STUDIO
93 WANDSWORTH BRIDGE ROAD, FULHAM, LONDON SW6 4SW
☎ 0171-371 0697. OPEN 10 - 7 MON - SAT *Dress Agency and Hire Shop*

THE WEDDING STUDIO
☎ 0171-371 0900. OPEN BY APPOINTMENT ONLY.
Chiceria sells a wide range of new and nearly-new designer clothes and accessories ranging from Chanel, YSL, Valentino, Armani, Prada, Moschino and MaxMara, to high fashion high street names such as Joseph, Whistles, Hobbs, Jigsaw, Kookai and LK Bennet. New designer outfits are made available exclusively to Chiceria by leading London couturiers, as well as designer samples from fashion houses in Italy and France. Hat hire is also available for those special occasions, offering beautifully crafted and stylishly distinctive hats made by an exciting and up-and-coming milliner.

The Wedding Studio offers beautiful once-worn designer wedding gowns from such designers as Phillipa Lepley, Catherine Walker, Suzanne Neville, Tatters and many more. They will, take in once-worn gowns on a consignment basis. *Hire Shop*

CHLOE BROMLEY FASHIONS LTD
21 MONTPELLIER VALE, BLACKHEATH VILLAGE, LONDON SE3 OTJ
☎ 0181-318 4300. OPEN 9.30 - 6 MON - SAT, 11 - 5 SUN.
Chloe has been trading in top quality fashion for more than 30 years, specialising

in special occasion outfits in sizes 8-22. Chloe 2, on the lower ground floor, stocks thousands of samples and seconds from Chloe's usual suppliers, specialising in Frank Usher's and Joseph Ribkoff's factory rejects and seconds. This enables customers to buy top quality clothes at prices which range from 25%-75% off the usual retail price. There is always a batch clearance rail for under £40; hats at half price; jewellery from £6; but no shoes. *Permanent Discount Outlet*

CHOICE DISCOUNT STORES LIMITED

67 GOLDERS GREEN ROAD, GOLDERS GREEN, LONDON NW11 8EL
☎ 0181-458 8247. OPEN 9 - 6 MON - SAT, 11 - 5 SUN.
Surplus ladies and men's fashions and accessories from Next plc and the Next Directory. You can save up to 50% off normal retail prices for first quality; up to two thirds for seconds. There are no changing rooms but the shop offers refunds if goods are returned in perfect condition within 28 days. There are special sales each January and July. *Permanent Discount Outlet*

CITY MENSWEAR

1-5 BREAD STREET, CHEAPSIDE, LONDON EC4
☎ 0171-248 1809. OPEN 9 - 6 MON - FRI.
Part of the Moss Bros Group, this shop mostly hires out dinner and morning suits and sells at full price everything from suits, shirts, wedding suits and dinner suits to overcoats and ties from many different brands. From time to time, ex-hire wear from the other Moss Bros hire shops are sold off here at greatly reduced prices. For example, ex-hire morning tails - including jacket, trousers and waistcoat - which would normally cost £249 when new are sold here for £90. Ring first to check ex-hire availability. Remember when trying on that the ex-hire stock has been dry cleaned every time it's been hired out so there will be some shrinkage, so look out for sizes above your normal size.
Permanent Discount Outlet

CLOTHES DIRECT

48B HENDON LANE, FINCHLEY, LONDON NE 1TT
☎ 0181-343 4072. OPEN 10 - 6 TUES - SAT, 10 - 2 SUN.
Warehouse selling Italian brand name clothes for men at discount prices.
Permanent Discount Outlet

COLEFAX & FOWLER

19 - 23 GROSVENOR HILL, LONDON W1X 9HG
☎ 0171-493 2231.
Annual sales of Colefax & Fowler and Jane Churchill ranges, held at the Royal Horticultural Halls in London's SW1 usually in January. Ask for Trade and put your name on the mailing list. *Designer Sale*

CORNUCOPIA
12 UPPER TACHBROOK STREET, LONDON SW1
☎ 0171-828 5752. OPEN 11 - 6 SEVEN DAYS A WEEK.
Established for more than 28 years, Cornucopia specialises in glamorous evening wear for women from the Twenties to modern day. Huge selection of eveningwear, some evening shoes, some designer samples, silk suits and hats, shoes, accessories, handbags, jewellery. *Secondhand and Vintage Clothe*

CURTAIN TRADING CENTRE
24 BAKER STREET, LONDON W1M 1DF
☎ 0171-224 2006. OPEN 10 - 6 MON - SAT.
Superb quality nearly-new designer curtains at a fraction of the original cost. Stock includes roller, Austrian and Roman blinds, plus bedspreads, covered headboards, cushions and tie-backs. Colour photographs of the drapes in situ are pinned to lots of the samples. Downstairs, there are two additional rooms full of stock, including lined and interlined Roman and Austrian blinds from £40. *Secondhand Shop*

DAMART
45 LEWISHAM CENTRE, LEWISHAM, LONDON
☎ 0181-318 4274. OPEN 9.30 - 5 MON - THUR, 9 - 5 FRI, SAT.
Damart underwear and merchandise - anything from tights, socks and gloves to dresses, coats, cardigans and jumpers - some of which is current stock sold at full price, some discontinued and ends of lines sold at discount. There several shops selling some discounted stock from the Damart range, known as Damart Extra. *Factory Shop*

DASH SALE SHOP
WOOD GREEN SHOPPING CENTRE, LONDON N22 6VQ
☎ 0181-889 9560. OPEN 9 - 5.30 MON - FRI, 9 - 6 SAT.
Alexon and Eastex ends of ranges and seconds and some Dash sold here at discount. Jackets cost about £60 and skirts £30. Average discounts are about 50%. *Permanent Discount Outlet*

DAVE'S DIY
294 & 296 FIRS LANE, LONDON N13
☎ 0181-807 3539. OPEN 8.30 - 5 MON - FRI, UNTIL 7 FRI, 9 - 1 SAT.
Aimed at the trade, it will cater for members of the public who benefit from the discounts. Carries wallpaper brands from Kingfisher, Mayfair, Crown and Vymura, among others, from a range of 300 wallpaper books at discounts of up to 40%. Next day ordering for wallpapers. Also carries a large stock of paint, with a computerised mixing machine that offers thousands of combinations of colours. *Permanent Discount Outlet*

Live Well On Less Tips
Buy long-life milk

DAVID CHARLES

65 KINGS CROSS ROAD, LONDON WC1

☎ 0171-833 1166,

Phone or write to put your name down on the mailing list for an automatic invitation to the showroom sale of this children's range at which prices are considerably reduced. *Designer Sale*

DAVID J WILKINS

27 PRINCESS ROAD, LONDON NW1 8JR

☎ 0171-722 7608. OPEN BY APPOINTMENT.

Handmade rugs from Iran, Turkey, Afghanistan and Russia at what are claimed to be wholesale prices, giving members of the public average discounts of 25% compared with normal retail prices. Customers can spend the whole morning or afternoon looking at stock at this huge, bonded warehouse which specialises in large and unusual sizes. Car parking nearby. *Permanent Discount Outlet*

DAVID RICHARDS & SONS

12 NEW CAVENDISH STREET, LONDON W1M 7LJ

☎ 0171- 935 3206. OPEN 9.30 - 5.30 MON - FRI.

David Richards & Sons are really wholesalers, but they are pleased to help retail customers from their showroom. Their shop is stacked high with solid silver, silver plate and silver picture frames, christening presents, models of animals, candlesticks, salvers and silver jewellery. Also, they can provide wedding lists, personalised corporate gifts, customers repairs and valuations. Service is well informed and courteous, and prices are much more reasonable than comparable prices in the high street. This is due to the fact that because the shop wholesales in Britain and Europe, it buys enormous quantities and is thus able to pass on bulk-buying savings to customers. *Permanent Discount Outlet*

DELLA FINCH

LONDON

☎ 0171-834 9161.

Della organises designer sales, usually in London, selling top name clothes direct from the showroom at wholesale prices. Some are from next season's collections, some this season, and include top-name labels in evening wear, smart suits, blouses and swimwear. There's usually a special bargain rail from £5. Phone and leave your name and full address for the mailing list. *Designer Sale*

DENNER CASHMERE

PO BOX 8551, LONDON SW11 1ZP

☎ 0171-223 7754. OPEN 9 - 7 MON - SAT. MAIL ORDER ONLY.

Finest quality designer cashmere and silk/cashmere knitwear similar to TSE and N Peal, from as little as one third of shop prices. Because they only sell through mail order and occasional sales at well-known venues, overheads are low and profit margins can be kept to a minimum. Only the best quality yarns are used and the finishing is impeccable. They produce two collections a year: the spring/summer consists of garments made from silk/cashmere; the autumn/winter features items made of 100% cashmere. Styles include long cardigans, dresses, twinsets, cable knits, wraps, scarves, skinny ribs, tunics, classic V, round and polo neck sweaters. Each collection is designed so that pieces can be worn together to create a whole outfit or bought separately to mix and match with basics from a typical wardrobe. Prices from £39.90. Phone for the list of forthcoming sales, special offers and up-do-date brochure. *Permanent Discount Outlet*

DESIGNER BARGAINS

29 KENSINGTON CHURCH STREET, LONDON W8 4LL

☎ 0171-795 6777. OPEN 10 - 6.30 MON - SAT.

There are lots of top labels on sale here, as befits the catchment area, with hundreds of garments. Labels on sale include Thierry Mugler, Armani, Escada, Chanel, Dolce e Gabbana, Gucci, Moschino, Prada and Versace. *Dress Agency*

DESIGNER SALE UK

14, HIGHBURY GRANGE, LONDON N5 2PX

☎ 0171-226 7437.

During ten years in operation, Designer Sale UK has established itself as an increasingly popular way to buy desirable designer gear. Whether you're looking for something really offbeat or that classic item to complement any wardrobe, there are many bargains to be had with prices discounted by 80% to 90%. Ozbek jackets retailing at £350 can be bought for £90; an Armani men's shirt normally £115 is £39; a Burro shirt, £80 now priced at £20; a delicate bohemian Gharani Strok dress that sells in stores for £235 costs only £45; Duffer items start at £5 and Joe Caseley Hayford jackets go from a retail value of £290 to £55. There are many other bargains on names like Moschino, Versace, Mooks, D&G, Moni and Oswald Boateng. The venue is the Candid Arts Trust which offers a great location in the heart of fashionable Islington, behind Angel Tube, near many superb cafes, restaurants and pubs. There are four sales a year in London, in the last week of February, April, September and November. Each sale lasts four days from Thursday to Sunday and preview day (Wednesday) for mailing list customers. Plans for year 2000 may include a Road Show to Derby & Brighton. Phone the above number to join the mailing list and for information on upcoming sales. *Designer Sale*

DESIGNER STUDIO MAN

26 SOUTHAMPTON STREET, COVENT GARDEN, LONDON WC2
☎ 0171-240 9919. OPEN 11 - 7 MON - FRI, 11 - 6 SAT, 12 - 5 SUN.
Designerwear for men from Italian names such as Gucci and Prada as well as
Calvin Klein at discounts of up to 40%. *Permanent Discount Outlet*

DESIGNERS FOR LESS

203 UXBRIDGE ROAD, LONDON W13 9AA
☎ 0181-579 5954. OPEN 9.30 - 6 MON - SAT.
High street shop, established since 1973, which sells factory seconds, ends of
ranges, samples and previous season's stock in a range of men's clothes. Their
main attractions are suits from Germany, although the labels have to be
removed from their best contacts' merchandise. However, the normal retail
price for such suits is in the region of £350 while Designers for Less price is
£135 - recent best offers on Dior suits at half usual price due to late delivery.
Trousers are from Widax and Meyer at £27.50, normally £59.50. Factory seconds shirts from Kings Road and Helmold from £17.50. Top quality leather
Panelli shoes at £49.50. They have recently opened a king-size department -
up to size 60 jockey or giant, they promise to kit you out. There are two clearance sales a year - phone the shop to be put on the mailing list. There is also
an extensive dresswear hire department. *Permanent Discount Outlet*

DESIGNERS' GUILD

ARIEL WAY, WOOD LANE, LONDON W12
☎ 0171 351 5775 PHONE TO BE PUT ON MAILING LIST.
Twice-yearly warehouse clearance sale which is usually advertised in London
newspapers. Stock usually comprises some large furniture - sofas, chairs -
masses of rolls of fabric at greatly reduced prices, wallpaper borders, cushion
covers and upholstery fabrics. Come armed with measurements and exact
lengths required as it can be very busy. *Designer Sale*

DESIGNS

60 ROSSLYN HILL, LONDON NW3 1ND
☎ 0171-435 0100. OPEN 10 - 5.45 MON - SAT, UNTIL 6.30 ON THUR.
Designs has been established for more than seventeen years, selling ladies
designer clothes and accessories. Their most sought-after labels include
Hermes, Chanel, Donna Karan, Ralph Lauren, Giorgio Armani, Prada, Gucci,
Joseph and Valentino. They only accept perfect merchandise under two years
old, and are seasonal. They have a rapid turnover and regular customers talk
about the spacious, relaxed atmosphere. Prices remain keenly competitive and
the most exciting pieces come their way. Prices range from £5 to £500. They
have more than 6,000 clients and take in stock from the UK, America and Italy.
They also stock a range of girls' clothes from 0 - 8 years. *Dress Agency*

DISCOUNT COOKERS

97 RUSHEY GREEN, CATFORD, LONDON SE6 4AF

☎ 0181-461 5273. OPEN 9 - 6 MON - SAT.

New and reconditioned models from New World, Whirlpool, Canon with more than 2,000 new cookers in stock at any one time. Because they buy in bulk to supply their five south-east London shops, they can offer competitive prices - although they say that the more expensive the cooker you buy, the better the discount. They also stock between 400-500 reconditioned cookers at prices from £100 upwards - which works out at between 25%-50% cheaper than when new - as well as some new ex-display models. All the cookers come with a six month guarantee and there is free delivery within the M25 area. Countrywide delivery is by courier. *Permanent Discount Outlet*

DISCOUNT DECORATING

157-159 RYE LANE, PECKHAM, LONDON SE15 4TL

☎ 0171-732 3986. OPEN 8 - 5.30 MON - FRI, 9 - 5.30 SAT

Three thousand square foot warehouse selling top of the range wallpapers including Contour, Crown, Sanderson, Vymura, Hill & Knowles at between 10% and 50% discount. Also mainly Dulux paints and decorating equipment at low prices. All current, last season's or discontinued stock - no seconds sold. *Permanent Discount Outlet*

DISCOUNT DRESSING

58 BAKER STREET, LONDON W1

☎ 0171-486 7230. OPEN 10 - 6 SEVEN DAYS A WEEK.

16 SUSSEX RING, WOODSIDE PARK, LONDON N12

☎ 0181-343 8343. OPEN 10 - 6 SEVEN DAYS A WEEK.

A veritable Aladdin's Cave of designer bargains, Discount Dressing sells mostly German, Italian and French designer labels at prices at least 50% and up to 90% below those in normal retail outlets. All items are brand new and perfect. A team of buyers all over Europe purchase stock directly from the manufacturer for this growing chain of discount shops. This enables Discount Dressing to by-pass the importers and wholesalers and, of course, their mark-up. They also buy bankrupt stock in this country. Their agreement with their suppliers means that they are not able to advertise brand names for obvious reasons, but they are all well-known for their top quality and style. So confident is Discount Dressing that you will be unable to find the same item cheaper elsewhere, that they guarantee to give the outfit to you free of charge should you perform this miracle. Merchandise includes raincoats, dresses, suits, trousers, blouses, evening wear, special occasion outfits and jackets, in sizes 6-24 and in some cases larger. GDD readers can obtain a further 10% discount if they visit the shop taking a copy of this book with them. There are other branches in Lincolnshire, Northern Ireland, Hertfordshire, East Yorkshire and Derbyshire. *Permanent Discount Outlet*

DRESS CIRCLE

2 LEVERTON PLACE, LONDON NW5 2PL

☎ 0171-284 3967. OPEN 10 - 6 TUE, WED, FRI, SAT, 10 - 5 THUR.

Dress Circle is a nearly-new shop for adults which has a children's dress agency at the back called Boomerang. Dress Circle sells good quality secondhand clothing with strong emphasis on middle of the road high street names such as Next, Hobbs, Jigsaw and Gap. Prices range from £1-£100. There are also shoes, accessories, jewellery, hats and costume jewellery from £2-£30. Stock usually consists of wearable daywear; unusual, trendy separates; period dresses; evening clothes and special occasion outfits; and a good selection of Levi 501's for about £12. Menswear tends to be casual shirts, sweaters and jackets with the occasional Yves St Laurent suit, £75 and jacket £45. *Dress Agency*

DYNASTY

12A TURNHAM GREEN TERRACE, CHISWICK, LONDON W4

☎ 0181-995 3846. OPEN 10.30 - 5 MON - SAT.

Sells good quality secondhand clothes. Labels include Edina Ronay, Louis Feraud, Joseph, Moschino, as well as occasionally La Perla swimwear. Examples of outfits for sale include an Edina Ronay suit, £175, a Christian Lacroix dress, £99, and a Paul Costelloe dress, £49; La Perla swimsuits from £25-£39; Valentino three-piece, £220, originally £1,000. *Dress Agency*

DYNASTY MAN

12 TURNHAM GREEN TERRACE, CHISWICK, LONDON W4 1QP

☎ 0181-994 4450. OPEN 10.30 - 5.30 MON - SAT

Small dress agency which sells only labels from Jaeger upwards and including Boss suits and jackets, Yves St Laurent and Armani suits, Jean Paul Gautier, business shirts, pure silk ties, sweaters, leathers, Burberry raincoats and wool and cashmere coats. No separate trousers sold at all. Alterations can be undertaken *Dress Agency*

EDWARD SYMMONS & PARTNERS

2 SOUTHWARK STREET, LONDON BRIDGE, LONDON SE1 1RQ

☎ 0171-955 8454. OPEN 9.30 - 5.30 MON - FRI.

Auctioneers dealing mainly in plant and machine tools for liquidated companies but they have sold almost everything from aeroplanes to offices and restaurants. Some equipment is sold by private treaty or tender. Prices depend on how long they have available to market the sale; the shorter the time, the more your chances of picking up a bargain. *Permanent Discount Outlet*

Live Well On Less Tips
Fill the oven to capacity when it is on.

ELLENS LTD

46 CHURCH ROAD, LEYTON, LONDON E10 5JP

☎ 0181-539 6872. OPEN 10 - 4 MON - SAT.

Imports shoes from Italy, Spain and Portugal. Apart from their regular stock, they have some seconds and sample shoes in small sizes at amazingly low prices. They also stock boots and slippers. Most of the styles are described as upmarket daywear and glitzy eveningwear, and the choice is enormous, although the full range of sizes is not always available. Prices range from £5 to £40. *Permanent Discount Outlet*

EMPORIUM

330-332 CREEK ROAD, GREENWICH, LONDON SE10

☎ 0181-305 1670. OPEN 10.30 - 6 TUE - SUN.

Vintage clothes shop which supplies theatrical dress for sale and hire, also hires out ballgowns and evening wear for men. *Hire Shop*

ENCORE

53 STOKE NEWINGTON CHURCH STREET, LONDON N16 0AR

☎ 0171-254 5329. OPEN 10 - 5.30 MON -SAT.

Well-organised children's nearly-new clothes shop selling OshKosh, Oilily and other good quality clothes at about one-third of the original price. Also offers an exclusive range of new clothes and Start-Rite and Danish brand, Bundgaard, shoes. *Dress Agency*

EXCLUSIVO

24 HAMPSTEAD HIGH STREET, HAMPSTEAD, LONDON NW3

☎ 0171-431 8618. OPEN 11.30 - 6 SEVEN DAYS A WEEK.

A small shop stocked high with every kind of label from Jaeger and Windsmoor to YSL, Chanel, Donna Karan and Nicole Farhi. Prices range from £50-£500. For example, Alaia dress £120, as new £450. Specialise in accessories: for example Chanel handbags, £250 usually £750; Prada bags, from £85; Moschino bags, from £50. Good range of footwear such as Donna Karan shoes, £89, originally £200; Hermes scarves, £49; Chanel earrings, from £50; Donna Karan earrings, from £29. There are usually about 1,500 outfits from which to choose. *Dress Agency*

FACTORY DIRECT

17 STRUTTON GROUND, VICTORIA, LONDON SW1

☎ 0171-799 2651. OPEN 10.30 - 6 MON - FRI, 11 - 5 SAT.

Fashion for ladies which mostly consists of day and work wear: coats, suits, dresses, tops, skirts. Bought direct from a variety of different factories, there are no labels in any of these clothes. *Permanent Discount Outlet*

> *Live Well On Less Tips*
> Scour pots with wire wool

FACTORY SHOP AT POETSTYLE LTD

UNIT 1, BAYFORD STREET INDUSTRIAL CENTRE, MARE STREET, HACKNEY, LONDON E8 3SE

☎ 0181-533 0915. FAX ☎ 0181-985 2953.

E-MAIL WWW.UPHOLSTERERS.CO.UK/POETSTYLE

OPEN 8 - 5.30 MON - FRI, 10.30 - 50 SAT, 10.30 - 3 SUN AND BANK HOLIDAYS.

Sofas, sofa beds, chairs, curtains and divan sets sold direct to the public at factory prices. Also undertakes re-upholstering and refurbishing and sells brand-name fabrics including Sanderson, Liberty, Osborne & Little, Designers Guild, Monkwell and Parkertex and many more. Sofas can be seen being handmade by craftsmen and women on site. *Factory Shop*

FENS RESTORATION

46 LOTS ROAD, CHELSEA, LONDON SW10 0QF

☎ 0171-352 9883. OPEN 9 - 5 MON - FRI, BY APPOINTMENT SAT.

Sells reclaimed doors, bathroom fittings, fire surrounds and mouldings. Also sells furniture and carries out restoration work and repairs, French polishing and metal cleaning and (caustic) pine stripping. *Architectural Salvage*

FOFO CLUB

3 OLD BOND STREET, LONDON W1X 3DA

☎ 0171- 499 5132.

Regular sales of top designer names which in the past have included Mondi, Kasper, Maska and Louis Feraud at fantastically reduced prices. However, designers stocked do change regularly. Entrance by membership only with different degrees of membership at different prices. The top degree of membership, Gold, allows you to bring unlimited guests to the sales and gain entry to the preview day; Silver means you can bring two guests and gain entry on preview day; Basic means you can bring only one friend and only on general day. Contact Olivia Smart at FOFO at the above address for more details. *Designer Sale*

FRANK USHER

7 NOEL STREET, LONDON W1

☎ 0171-287 0800.

Phone or write to put your name down on the mailing list for an automatic invitation to the showroom sales at which prices are considerably reduced. *Designer Sale*

FROCK BROKERS

47 BRUSHFIELD STREET, SPITALFIELDS, LONDON E1 6AA

☎ 0171-247 4222. OPEN 11 - 6.30 TUE - FRI, 8 ON WED, 1 - 5.30 SUN.

A contemporary designer boutique with a difference. Ninety per cent of stock is end of season or sample pieces that either come directly from the designers or from independent shops. The remaining 10% is dress agency stock which can range from clothes used in photo shoots or catwalk shows, to unwanted presents or expensive mistakes. All designer labels are in perfect condition and absolute bargains! All staff offer personal shopping and free styling advice. Labels range from Gharani Stok and Ruti Danan to Gucci, Prada and Manolo Blahnik. Located in the heart of the city - two minutes from Liverpool Street station. *Dress Agency*

FROCK FOLLIES

18 THE GRANGEWAY, GRANGE PARK, LONDON N21 2HG

☎ 0181-360 3447. OPEN 9.30 - 5 TUE - SAT

Recommended by one of our readers who says that the owner is so helpful that shopping here is a pleasure. Double-fronted shop with more than 2,000 items in stock including costume jewellery, handbags, swimwear and shoes. Labels include Escade, Frank Usher, Karen Millen, Jacques Vert, Basler, Betty Barclay, Betty Jackson, Principles, Next and Monsoon - in other words, across the fashion spectrum. One of the cheapest second hand clothes shops you will find. *Dress Agency*

FROCKS

33 WESTFIELDS AVENUE, BARNES, LONDON SW13 0AT

☎ 0181-392 1123. OPEN 9 - 8 MON - FRI, 10 - 2 SAT.

BY APPOINTMENT ONLY.

Home-based business offering a wide range of evening wear to hire and for sale. Party frocks, cocktail dresses and ballgowns, in sizes 8-20, can be hired from £40 to £75 for up to five days. Jewellery, bags, stoles and capes are also available for hire or sale. *Hire Shop*

G THORNFIELD LTD

321 GRAY'S INN ROAD, LONDON WC1X 8PX

☎ 0171-837 2996. OPEN 10 - 6 MON - FRI, 9 - 2 SAT.

Offers from 20%-50% off wallcovering brands such as Sanderson and Kingfisher. The more you buy, the greater your discount. Also one-third off co-ordinating fabrics. Doesn't hold stocks of wallpapers and fabrics but you can order from their books. Next day delivery. Also sells frames, prints and posters at very low prices. Dulux paint colours mixed on the premises, with 1800 shades to choose from. *Permanent Discount Outlet*

GERTRUDE FASHIONS

84 WILTON ROAD, VICTORIA, LONDON SW1V 1DL

☎ 0171-834 6933. OPEN 10 - 5.30 MON - SAT.

Jackets, skirts, blouses, suits, dresses, trousers and coats. German designers as well as some Italian and French names at very competitive prices. Discounts from 35% on original prices. ***Permanent Discount Outlet***

GHOST LTD

263 KENSAL ROAD, LONDON W10 5DB

☎ 0181-960 3121.

Annual warehouse sale of famous Ghost label which consists of old stock, current season damaged stock, show pieces and one-off samples usually takes place in first or second week of December. Write to put your name down on the mailing list. ***Designer Sale***

GLOUCESTER ROAD BOOKSHOP

123 GLOUCESTER ROAD, LONDON SW7

☎ 0171-370 3503. OPEN 8.30 - 10.30 MON - FRI, 10.30 - 6.30 SAT, SUN.

Secondhand books including review copies, also catalogues in modern First Editions and rare antiquarian books. A reader who recommended this shop said they are strong on all areas: literature, arts, travel, gardening etc, all in good condition, well displayed and categorised. Book prices range from 20p - £200 and in the basement there is a bargain shelf with books at 50p each. ***Permanent Discount Outlet***

GOLD'S FACTORY OUTLET

108-114 GOLDERS GREEN ROAD, LONDON NW11 8HB

☎ 0181-905 5721. OPEN 10 - 6 MON- FRI, SUN, CLOSED SAT.

Men's pinstriped suits and cotton poplin shirts, mostly still in their original packaging, as well as women's suits, blouses and ballgowns, many with their brand names removed. There is a separate shoe shop. ***Permanent Discount Outlet***

HALF-PRICE POTS

340 FULHAM ROAD, LONDON SW10 9UH

☎ 0171-376 4808. OPEN 10 - 5.30 SEVEN DAYS A WEEK.

Terracotta pots from around the world at extremely competitive prices. The pots come in all shapes and sizes from China, Spain, Morocco, Mexico and Tunisia, Egypt, Turkey and India. Prices range from 20p to £1,000 and include antique pots and storage jars reclaimed from the desert. Stock changes constantly. ***Permanent Discount Outlet***

Live Well On Less Tips
If you're on a water meter and use a hot water bottle, reheat the same water
each night in an old kettle so your tea doesn't taste of rubber

HANG UPS

366 FULHAM ROAD, LONDON SW10 9UU

☎ 0171-351 0047. OPEN 11 - 6.45 MON - FRI, 10.30 - 6 SAT, 1 - 4 SOME
SUNS, PHONE FIRST.

High fashion designer labels plus vintage clothes, Seventies gear and accessories
for women. Designers include Azzedine Aliai, Ghost, Gaultier, Moschino,
Hobbs, Whistles. Prices range from £1 for a T-shirt to £500 for a Chanel suit.
Plenty of daywear, evening wear, casual clothes, shoes, handbags, as well as lin-
gerie and a selection of new designer clothing at discounted prices. *Dress
Agency*

HAZLE CERAMICS

JUBILEE HALL, COVENT GARDEN MARKET, LONDON WC2

☎ (01277) 220892. OPEN 10.30 - 5.

WORKSHOP: HAZLE CERAMICS, STALLIONS YARD, COOLHAM HALL,
GREAT WARLEY, BRENTWOOD ESSEX CM13 3JT.

☎ (01277) 220892. OPEN TO PUBLIC 11 - 5 FRI, SAT, SUN.

Covent Garden: Collectable Nation of Shopkeeper ceramic wall plaques in a
wide variety of different designs. Seconds are sold off here at weekends at one
third off the normal prices. Workshop: Tour available with tea, coffee, access
to gift shop and ceramics available at special workshop prices. *Permanent
Discount Outlet*

CHRISTMAS GRAND SALE

ROYAL HORTICULTURAL HALLS, VICTORIA, LONDON, SW1
ORGANISER: ROBERT TORRANCE, PO BOX 427, LONDON SW10 9QE.

☎ 0171-351 3088.

There are now three Grand Sales aimed at the home, garden and gift markets
taking place countrywide. The Christmas Grand Sale in London, with over
120 different small companies selling their merchandise to the public, is the
largest. This takes place in mid-November each year. Quality is high and covers everything from dried flowers to bath accessories, Amish quilts to silverware, wooden toys to hand-painted kitchenware, often at discount because
they are ends of lines. There is a Spring Grand Sale at Sudeley Castle,
Winchcombe, near Cheltenham, Glos every April/May and a Summer Grand
Sale at Ripley Castle, near Harrogate, North Yorkshire, in June, both of which
feature gardening equipment as well as decorative homes accessories. Phone tel
no. above for details of how to book tickets. *Designer Sale*

HOT & COLD INC

13-15 GOLBORNE ROAD, LONDON W10 5NY

☎ 0181-960 1200/1300. OPEN 10 - 6 MON - SAT.

Supplies domestic appliances from nearly one hundred brands. Range now includes American fridge freezers and range cookers. A total of about 10,000 different items - at prices which they claim will beat any genuine competitor's. In fact, they are so sure of this that they promise to refund the difference if you find you could have bought the same product elsewhere at the same time for a lower price, provided you give them proof of that within two weeks of purchase. All goods are brand new, perfect and guaranteed. Their strength is in built-in equipment, but they can also supply freestanding appliances. Also ends of lines, some at less than half the original price. Prices include VAT. Delivery can be arranged countrywide. *Permanent Discount Outlet*

HOUSE OF STEEL

400 CALEDONIAN ROAD, LONDON N1 1DN

☎ 0171-607 5889. OPEN 11.30 - 5 MON - FRI, BY APPOINTMENT ON SAT.

Five thousand square feet warehouse devoted to reclaimed metalwork of every kind including wrought-iron gates, old grilles, wrought-iron panels, arched gates, beds, staircases, balconies and lighting. Also designs and makes a range of steel furniture. Repairs and restoration undertaken. *Architectural Salvage*

I KINN

80 GEORGE LANE, SOUTH WOODFORD, LONDON E18 1JJ

☎ 0181-989 2927. OPEN 10 - 5.30 MON - FRI, 10 - 5 SAT, 10.30 - 1 SUN.

Large showroom selling classic store merchandise such as is found in Lewis and House of Fraser groups at bargain prices. There are plenty of ladies jackets, suits, dresses and skirts plus designer clothes from time to time at about half the normal retail price. *Permanent Discount Outlet*

IN WEAR FACTORY OUTLET

100 GARRATT LANE, WANDSWORTH, LONDON SW18 4DJ

☎ 0181-871 2155. OPEN 10 - 5.30 MON - SAT, 11 - 4 SUN.

In Wear for women and Matinique for men as well as Part Two for both men and women at discounts of between 30%-70% for last season's stock, ends of lines and seconds. All the stock is made up of separates and tends to be stylishly casual and includes blazers, jeans, trousers, dresses, knitwear, suits and outerwear. Twice-yearly designer sample sale is held here. Phone for details. *Factory Shop*

JOEL & SON FABRICS

75-81 CHURCH STREET, LONDON NW8 8EU

☎ 0171-724 6895. OPEN 8.30 - 5 MON - SAT.

London's foremost designer fabric store sells up-to-date fabrics used by the top catwalk designers and couturiers from St Laurent and Cerruti to Versace and Gianfranco Ferre. Prices are very competitive, and the fabric is exceptional. Also carries a wide range of supplies for bridal wear including embroidered laces, beaded fabrics, Jacquards, Duchess satins, as well as veils in silk and silk mixes. Good range of designer lookalike buttons. Mr Joel & Son have been in the business for 45 years and at the same premises for 15 years. Staff are always on hand to advise and are proud of their personal service. *Permanent Discount Outlet*

JOSEPH CLEARANCE SHOP

53 KING'S ROAD, LONDON SW3 1QN

☎ 0171-730 7562. OPEN 10.30 - 6.30 MON - SAT, UNTIL 7 ON WED, 12 - 5 SUN.

End of season and clearance lines from the Joseph label at reductions of up to 70%. Several concessions include Gucci and Helmut Lang. Samples of current stock are also available at discounts of 20%-30%. *Permanent Discount Outlet*

KING'S CROSS TILES

3-13 PANCRAS ROAD, KING'S CROSS, LONDON NW1 2QB

☎ 0171-833 3884. OPEN 8 - 7 MON - FRI, 9 - 5 SAT.

Wall tiles, floor tiles, mosaics, slates, borders, stick-ons and bathroom suites, all at very competitive prices. The tiles are imported directly from Spain so there is no middleman taking a cut, which is why prices are so good. The company don't produce glossy brochures so can offer the bathroom suites at prices lower than most of their competitors. Full range of exterior patio tiles also good value. *Permanent Discount Outlet*

L'HOMME DESIGNER EXCHANGE

50 BLANDFORD STREET, LONDON W1H 3HD

☎ 0171-224 3266. OPEN 11 - 6 MON - FRI, 11 - 7 THUR, 11 - 5 SAT.

This shop sells designer menswear from the outrageous to the classic for the beach, the office, the nightclub and special evenings out. Designers in stock vary, but usually include Versace (couture jackets from £180) and Armani (suits from £180), Boss (suits and coats from £140) and Prada, Gucci and Gaultier. All stock is less than two years old. Sales in July and December see the sell-off of hire stock. *Dress Agency*

> *Live Well On Less Tips*
> Use bicarbonate of soda to get rid of tea stains from cups...
> .....it works on oven grease, too - do it when the oven is still warm.

LA SCALA

39 ELYSTAN STREET, LONDON SW3 3NT
☎ 0171-589 2784. OPEN 10 - 5.30 MON - SAT.
La Scala sells women's nearly-new clothes, accessories, men's and children's clothes under the same roof. There is a separate room full of top designer men's clothes including Armani, Valentino and Boss, and plenty of cashmere. Owner Sandy Reid lived for 14 years in Northern Italy and uses her experience there in her shop behind the Conran Shop in Chelsea. There, she sells end of season Italian designer wear and current top designer nearly-new outfits from Armani, Mani, DKNY, Paddy Campbell, Valentino, MaxMara, Genny. Italian is spoken in the shop which has a large Italian clientele. There's an emphasis on younger lines and the price reductions are fantastic. ***Dress Agency***

LABELS

146 FLEET ROAD, HAMPSTEAD, LONDON NW3 2QX
☎ 0171-267 8521. OPEN 10 - 6 TUE - SAT.
A comprehensive selection of clothing from mid-market labels up to Nicole Farhi and including Escada, Ghost, Betty Barclay and Gap as well as Marks & Spencer, Options and French Connection. There are also accessories - shoes, handbags and costume jewellery - on sale. Prices range from £10-£150. ***Permanent Discount Outlet***

LASSCO FLOORING

41 MALTBY STREET, LONDON SE1 3PA
☎ 0171-237 4488. OPEN 10 - 5 MON - SAT.
Supplies over 150 lines of reclaimed, antique and new timber flooring in parquet strip and board. Superb gallery displaying finished samples of timbers with gallery 2 opening here soon. Mainland delivery service available and worldwide export can be arranged. Email: lasscoflo@zetnet.co.uk. ***Architectural Salvage***

> *Live Well On Less Tips*
> Clean copper pots with squeezed out lemon halves kept in cling film for this purpose after use

LASSCO RBK

BRITANNIA WALK, ISLINGTON, LONDON N1 7LU

☎ 0171-336 8221. OPEN 9.30 - 5.30 MON - SAT.

LASSCO TRADE WAREHOUSE, BRITANNIA WALK, ISLINGTON, LONDON N1 7LU

0171-490 1000.

Lassco RBK has an eclectic stocks of reclaimed cast iron radiators, many with decorative casting and unusual examples. Radiators restored and finished to order. Many finishes are available including burnishing, priming and powder coating. Continually changing and expanding stocks of bathtubs in enamel, porcelain, tin and copper; Art Deco suites, Edwardian shower units, original and antique taps, sinks, nauticalia plus much more. A colour brochure is available. E-mail: lasscorbk@aol.com. Lassco Trade Warehouse is a new company offering discounted architectural elements, door panelling, marine salvage counters, shop fittings, etc, many sourced from famous hotels, museums, theatres, department stores and public buildings. *Architectural Salvage*

LASSCO ST MICHAEL'S

ST MICHAEL'S CHURCH, MARK STREET, OFF PAUL STREET, LONDON, EC2M 4ER

☎ 0171-739 0448. OPEN 10 - 5 SEVEN DAYS A WEEK.

Fine architectural antiques, chimney pieces, panelled rooms, garden ornaments, lighting, door furniture and much more. Call for latest bulletin or email on www.lassco.co.uk. Their website is lassco@zetnet.co.uk. *Architectural Salvage*

LAUREL HERMAN

18A LAMBOLLE PLACE, LONDON NW3 4PG

☎ 0171-586 7925. FAX ☎ 0171 586 7926. BY APPOINTMENT ONLY.

Established for over 25 years, and with 2,000 regular clients, this is London's best-kept secret in order to maintain its exclusivity. Housed in a spacious, airy concealed Hampstead showroom is an ever-changing melange of 6,000 upmarket designer items (Armani, Escada, MaxMara, Donna Karan, Valentino, etc) at a fraction of their original price. Both brand new and gently-worn but sourced only from Laurel's own personal contacts who shop the world to answer all requirements for day or evening, casual or formal, business or leisure. This unique concept is ideal for those who normally hate shopping, need a new look, have figure problems - or just clothesaholics. Many clients work towards the ultimate wardrobe solution, ie Laurel Herman's Wardrobe That Works but all advice is totally objective, free of charge, and based on personal lifestyle, shape, personality and budget. (There is a brochure to explain the concept in more detail.) In order to maintain the peaceful, relaxed ambience, appointments are compulsory, from 10am Monday to Saturday, but extending to 11pm in the evening twice weekly for working women. Be warned, customers usually stay three or four hours! The collection is taken twice yearly to Southampton in June and November. Workshops and seminars are available for improving personal style and business image. Laurel Herman also creates women's events for the corporate market, professional organisations and groups such as golf clubs and charities. The sister company, Positive Presence, offers a wide range of consultancy for men, women and organisations, on all issues relating to appearance and presentation - including real life makeovers, metamorphosis, workshops, seminars and talks. *Permanent Discount Outlet*

LAZDAN

218 BOW COMMON LANE, LONDON E3 4HH
☎ 0181-981 4632. OPEN 8 - 5 MON - FRI, 8 - 12.30 SAT.
Secondhand bricks, reclaimed slates, sash weights and chimney pots.
Architectural Salvage

LETTERBOX LIBRARY

UNIT 2D, 2ND FLOOR, LEROY HOUSE, 436 ESSEX ROAD,
LONDON N1 3QP
☎ 0171-226 1633. FAX: ☎ 0171-226 1768. OPEN 10 - 5 MON, THUR, 10 - 4 FRI IN TERM TIME, OR BY APPOINTMENT IN SCHOOL HOLIDAYS.
MAIL ORDER.
Run by a co-operative, Letterbox offers non-sexist, non-racist, multi-cultural books, as well as those about the environment and disability for children of all ages. Books are sold at discounts of between 5% and 20%. Phone or fax for catalogue at the address above. *Permanent Discount Outlet*

LEVY AND FRIEND

47 SLOANE AVENUE, OFF KING'S ROAD, LONDON SW3 3DH
☎ 0171-589 9741. OPEN 11 - 5 TUE - SAT.
Well presented garments in pristine condition are sold in a relaxed atmosphere in this large ground floor shop. Specialising in day wear, the shop offers fashionable, functional, tailored clothing from labels such as MaxMara, Prada, Albera Ferretti, Joseph, Dolce e Gabbanna, Donna Karan, Margaret Howell and Ferragamo, as well as designer bags, belts, shoes and boots. Established for twelve years, the shop has a clientele from around the world and the owners are ready with advice, if needed. Prices range from £10 - £250 and credit cards - American Express, Visa, Mastercard and Diners - are taken. *Dress Agency*

Live Well On Less Tips
Keep a Thermos flask by the kettle and fill it each time you boil the kettle saving you having to boil it too often.

LEYLAND SDM

371-373 EDGWARE ROAD, LONDON, W2 1BS,
☎ 0171-723 8048. OPEN 7 - 7 MON - FRI, 7 - 6 SAT, 9 - 3 SUN.
6 UPPER TACHBROOK STREET, LONDON SW1
☎ 0171-828 8695. 7 - 6 MON - SAT.
683 FINCHLEY ROAD, LONDON NW2
☎ 0171-794 5927. 7 - 6 MON - SAT.
43-45 FARRINGDON ROAD, LONDON EC1
☎ 0171-242 5791. 7 - 6 MON - SAT.
9 THE WALL, EALING BROADWAY, EALING, LONDON W5
☎ 0181-566 0481. OPEN 7 - 6 MON - SAT.
335-337 KING'S ROAD, LONDON SW3 5EU
☎ 0171-352 4742. OPEN 7 - 6 MON - SAT, 9 - 3 SUN.
361-365 KENSINGTON HIGH STREET, LONDON W14 8QY
☎ 0171-602 9099. OPEN 7 - 6 MON - SAT.
7 - 15 CAMDEN ROAD, LONDON NW1
☎ 0171-284 4366. OPEN 7 - 6 MON - SAT, 9 - 3 SUN.

Everything the enthusiastic diy-er could require, from tools and equipment to wallpapers, cornicing, moulding, brace fittings and paint. In fact, there are four thousand colours from which to choose which can be mixed to match fabric or carpets, all at trade prices. Also special offers such as 40% off power tools. There are nine branches of Leyland SDM Londonwide; for details of your local branch, freephone 0800 454484. *Permanent Discount Outlet*

LIPMANS HIRE DEPARTMENT

22 CHARING CROSS RD, LONDON WC2
☎ 0171-240 2310. OPEN 9 -8 MON - FRI, 10 - 6 SAT, 10 - 5 SUN.

Hires and sells ex-hire outfits. For example, dinner suits which would normally cost £160 to buy are £110 while those which have seen more wear cost from £50. New business suits in pure wool cost from £149. They also hire out dinner suits and top and tails from £27.95 to £43. Separates, dinner jackets and trousers can be hired from £22.95.

LITTLEWOODS
CATALOGUE DISCOUNT STORE

THE ARNDALE CENTRE, WANDSWORTH, LONDON SW18 4BT
☎ 0181-874 1042. OPEN 9.30 - 5.30 MON - WED, 9 - 5.30 THUR - SAT.

Littlewoods clearance shops offering up to 50% off the catalogue price for clothing and between 50% and 60% off for electrical goods. Stock changes constantly and varies from day to day but can include well-known brand names such as Berlei and Gossard lingerie, Vivienne Westwood, Pamplemousse leisure wear, Nike and Adidas sports shoes, Workers For

Freedom, and Timberland and Caterpillar footwear. Stock depends on the size and location of the shop, so larger shops will get the longer discontinued runs and smaller shops over-runs with only a small amount of colour and size variations left. Littlewoods also run a mobile shop which operates in cities where they don't have a sale shop. For details of further venues for the sales, which usually take place once a month, contact Melanie Lamb, c/o Crosby DC, Kershaw Avenue, Endbutt Lane, Crosby, Merseyside L70 1AH. *Factory Shop*

LOSNERS DRESS HIRE

232 STAMFORD HILL, LONDON N16 6TT

☎ 0181-800 7466. OPEN 9 - 5.30 MON - SAT, UNTIL 7 ON WED, UNTIL 5 ON THUR.

Specialises in top end of the market wedding outfits to hire and to buy. Basic hire costs anything from £100 to £300; you can choose from a huge range that includes new and nearly-new bridal outfits. Labels include Ronald Joyce, Ellis, Alfred Angelo, Mori Lee. Can also make dresses to order. All the accessories are to buy only and they offer a shoe-dyeing service. There are also morning and dinner suits to hire from £40-£200. Other branches in Dunstable, Ilford, Edgware, Gants Hill, Enfield and St Albans, although the Dunstable and St Albans branches only stock menswear. *Hire Shop*

LOUIS FERAUD

REGENCY HOUSE, HORTENSIA ROAD, LONDON SW10

☎ 0171-351 3399.

Phone or write to put your name down on the mailing list for an automatic invitation to the showroom sales at which prices are considerably reduced. *Designer Sale*

Live Well On Less Tips

10 WAYS TO SAVE MONEY IN THE KITCHEN

1. Put lids on saucepans
2. Keep the flames under the base of the saucepans
3. Don't overfill kettles or pots
4. Think about using a pressure cooker to reduce cooking times
5. Turn the gas down as soon as the water boils
6. For most dishes, you do not need to pre-heat the oven
7. Don't wash up under running water - always use a bowl
8. Rinse in cool water
9. Always fully load your dishwasher or washing machine
10. A dripping tap can waste a huge amount of water. Replace the washer immediately.

LUNN ANTIQUES LTD

86 NEW KING'S ROAD, PARSONS GREEN, LONDON SW6 4LU

☎ 0171-736 4638. OPEN 10 - 6 MON - SAT.

22 CUCUMBER ALLEY, THOMAS NEAL'S, SHORTS GARDENS, COVENT
GARDEN, LONDON WC2 9LD

☎ 0171-379 1974. OPEN 10.30 - 6.30 MON - SAT.

UNIT 8, ADMIRAL VERNON ARCADE, PORTOBELLO ROAD,
LONDON W11 OPEN 7.30 - 3.30 SAT ONLY.

London's largest stockists of antique and modern linen and lace has its headquarters at the New King's Road shop where it specialises in antique and modern bedlinen, sheets, duvet covers and bedcovers. Here, they also sell top quality antique christening robes and modern reproductions and there is an expert laundry and restoration service for antique linen and lace. All wholesale and trade enquiries should be made here. The Cucumber Alley shop features Lunn Antique's most abundant selection of period clothing, including Victorian nightwear, Edwardian camisoles and blouses, 1920s beaded dresses, 1930s silk chiffon and 40s, 50s and 60s choice clothing. Also risque silk lingerie, luxurious lace and elaborate embroidery. A rich profusion of antique textiles. The Portobello Road shop is Lunn Antique's lace outlet with a good selection from four centuries: 17th century needlepoints: 18th century Brussels, Mechlin, Valenciennes and White work; 19th century Alencon, Point de Gaze, Chantilly, Honiton and Youghal, plus 20th century bed and table linen decorated with filet, cutwork, drawnwork, embroidery and needlepoint.

MATALAN

EDGWARE ROAD, CRICKLEWOOD BROADWAY, CRICKLEWOOD,
LONDON NW2 6PH

☎ 0181-450 5667. OPEN 10 - 8 MON - FRI, 9 - 6 SAT, 11 - 5 SUN.

UNIT 7 BECKTON RETAIL PARK, BECKTON, LONDON E8
NO TELEPHONE NUMBER AS WE WENT TO PRESS.

Matalan is a fashion and homewares shop giving customers what they claim to be unbeatable value for money with huge savings on a wide range of products including high quality fashionable clothing for women, women and children at up to 50% off high street prices. Matalan is situated out of town and stores are open seven days a week all year round. *Permanent Discount Outlet*

MAXFIELD PARRISH

5 CONGREVE STREET, LONDON SE17 ITJ

☎ 0171-252 5225.

Phone or write to put your name down on the mailing list for an automatic invitation to the showroom sales at which prices of these fabulous leather and suede jackets and coats are considerably reduced. Sales are normally three times a year. *Designer Sale*

MODERN AGE VINTAGE CLOTHING

65 CHALK FARM ROAD, LONDON NW1 8AN

☎ 0171-482 3787. OPEN 10.30 - 6 MON - FRI, 10 - 6 SAT, SUN.

American secondhand clothing, particularly from the Fifties, Sixties and Seventies to hire and to buy. Average price for any garment is £25; men's shirts from £8 - £50, dinner suits for hire at £25. Women's eveningwear for hire from £25.

MORRY'S

22 NORTH MALL, EDMONTON, LONDON N9 OEJ

☎ 0181-807 6747. OPEN 8.30 - 5 MON - SAT, CLOSED 1 ON THUR.

Liquidation stock which includes some famous makes and can comprise anything from gardening equipment (shovels, forks and hoses) and household items to electrical equipment (CDs, radios, TVs, radio alarms) and clothing for men, women and children. Everything is at least half the retail price. If you live nearby, drop in frequently. *Permanent Discount Outlet*

MOSS BROS

27 KING STREET, COVENT GARDEN, LONDON WC2E 8JD

☎ 0171-632 9700. OPEN 9 - 6 MON - SAT, UNTIL 7 ON THUR.

This Moss Bros London store has a permanent own-label ex-hire department. Morning suits from £205, black morning coats from £165, top hats from £40, dinner suits £79, trousers £30, kilts £199, white tuxedos £79. *Permanent Discount Outlet*

NEXT TO NOTHING

UNIT 11, ARCADIA CENTRE, EALING BROADWAY, LONDON W5 2ND

☎ 0181-567 2747. OPEN 9.30 - 6 MON - SAT.

Sells perfect surplus stock from Next stores and the Next Directory catalogue - from belts, jewellery and underwear to day and evening wear - at discounts of 50% or more. The ranges are usually last season's and overruns but there is the odd current item if you look carefully. Stock consists of men's, women's and children's clothing, and shoes. Stock is replenished three times a week and there is plenty of it. This branch does not stock a lot of homes items and has only a small amount of accessories. *Permanent Discount Outlet*

NICOLE FARHI OUTLET SHOP

75-83 FAIRFIELD ROAD, BOW, LONDON E3 2QR

☎ 0181-980 25681. OPEN 10-3 TUE, WED, SAT, 11-6.30 THUR, 10-5.30 FRI.

This tiny factory shop in London's East End sells previous season merchandise, samples and seconds from Nicole Farhi and French Connection for women and men. Stock varies so do phone first if you have a specific requirement. There is much more women's than menswear. There is also a Nicole Farhi/French Connection factory shop at Bicester Village designer outlet centre in Oxfordshire. *Factory Shop*

NIGHTINGALES FACTORY SHOP

MONTEREY PLACE, THE BROADWAY, MILL HILL, LONDON NW7 3DF

☎ 0181-906 4366. OPEN 10 - 4 MON - SAT.

The mail order company which sells smart but casual clothes for women - twill lined jackets in blazer stripes, button-through dresses, pinafore dresses, shirtwaisters, pure cotton blouses, lined short-sleeved jackets, polo neck sweaters, boucle jackets, blouses and skirt sets and cotton nightdresses - sells samples, ends of lines, seconds and material lengths here at discounted prices.
Permanent Discount Outlet

NOT QUITE NEW

159 BRENT STREET, HENDON, LONDON NW4 4DH

☎ 0181-203 4691. OPEN 10 - 4.30 MON - FRI, CLOSED WED, 10 - 1 SAT.

Personal service are the key words to this unique boutique which sells beautiful garments in pristine condition. In business for more than 20 years, Not Quite New sells top Italian, French and German designer names including Basler, Louis Feraud, Valentino, Yarell, Mondi, Betty Baclay and Jaeger, as well as shoes and bags of the highest quality. Sizes stocked range from 8-20 and most items cost less than £100. They now include menswear of the highest quality including Boss and Armani. *Dress Agency*

NOTTING HILL HOUSING TRUST

309 FULHAM ROAD, LONDON SW10 9QH

☎ 0171-352 7986. OPEN 10 - 6 MON - SAT, 12 - 4 SUN.

Charity shop featuring Betty Barclay, Mondi, Versace, Paul Costelloe and Moschino. Examples of prices include a Versus (Versace Diffusion) dress, unworn, for £75 and a Moschino jacket, slightly worn, £75. Men's clothes are also stocked including Ralph Lauren, Paul Smith and Conran. The shop accepts credit cards. *Dress Agency*

OAKVILLE

FIFTH FLOOR, 32-36 GREAT PORTLAND STREET, LONDON W1

☎ 0171-580 3686.

Phone or write to put your name down on the mailing list for an automatic invitation to the showroom sales at which prices are considerably reduced. Designers include Fendi and Ungaro and stock covers mother of the bride, evening and day wear. *Designer Sale*

OCEAN HOME SHOPPING

9 HARDWICKS WAY, WANDSWORTH, LONDON SW18 4AW

☎ 0171-670 1222. OPEN MON - SAT 10 - 6.

Based at the head office, this factory shop clears old stock from this catalogue company as well as selling imperfect returns. This could be anything from chrome soap dispensers or corkscrews to sofas and stainless steel laundry bins.
Permanent Discount Outlet

ONE NIGHT STAND

44 PIMLICO ROAD, LONDON SW1W 8LP

☎ 0171-730 8708. OPEN 10 - 6.30 MON - FRI, 10 - 5 SAT.

More than 500 designer dresses in stock, sizes 8-18. Also hires jewellery, evening bags, capes and jackets. Cost £70-£140 for four days with a small number of more expensive items. Retail section with lingerie to complement clothes. Appointments preferred. *Hire Shop*

ORIENT EXPRESSIONS LTD

ORIENT EXPRESSIONS LTD. STUDIO 3B2, COOPER HOUSE, 2 MICHAEL ROAD, LONDON SW6 2AD

☎ 0171-610 9311. PHONE FOR APPOINTMENT.

Specialises in buying genuine antiques from China. The majority of the stock is from the early to mid-19th century, although the rarer 18th century pieces are bought when possible. Shipments are regular but small. Each piece is hand-picked by the owners who both lived and worked in Hong Kong for years. They are chosen carefully for their appearance, character and practical potential. Pieces are left in their original condition as much as possible. If restoration is necessary, it is kept to a minimum to retain the character of the piece. The furniture comes mostly from the rural provinces of China and offers a variety of looks: simple, quite chunky, country pieces in elm and beech; more sophisticated pieces in huali or dark lacquer; highly decorative, lacquered and gilded items. Whether a piece is plain and simple or wild and whacky, the criteria for buying it remains the same - it must be beautiful, useful and genuine. Cupboards come with several internal drawers and sections, ideal for use in a bedroom, drawing room or study. The wedding cabinets are tailor-made as drinks cabinets or for hiding a television set and hi-fi. Other elegant and versatile items are tea tables which are the perfect size and height for sofa-side or bedside use and those with a middle shelf are specially useful. Narrow tables which can range in length from three to ten feet make excellent consoles for the smallest or largest hall. Music tables and half tables, often with attractive open work carving, look stunning as side tables or behind a sofa. Chairs come in many lovely shapes but are not for lolling in front of the fire. Small cabinets range from bedside size to TV-carrying dimensions; lacquered and leathered trunks and boxes can be used as coffee tables, blanket boxes, sofa side surfaces. The scope is immense before even mentioning the smaller items such as foot washing bowls, rice barrels, babies' baths, hand warmers, curtain hooks and food baskets. Orient Expressions has outlets in London and Hungerford, Berkshire. They can arrange a viewing or send photos of current stock. *Secondhand Shop*

OSBORNE & LITTLE

☎ 0171-352 1456

Annual sales of fabrics, wallpapers and accessories from O & L, Nina Campbell and Liberty ranges, usually held at London's Battersea Town Hall. Invitations are sent out to trade customers only but if you phone customer relations on the above telephone number, they will tell you the date of the next sale - normally in March. *Designer Sale*

OXFAM ORIGIN

26 GANTON STREET, LONDON W1

☎ 0171-437 7338. OPEN 11.30 - 6.30 MON - SAT.

Famous in the past for its one-off designs made up by fashion students using donated fabric from top designers, this shop sells trendy high-street clothes with a mixture of retro and funky fashion. Motto 'Original clothes for original people'.

P N JONES

18 HOLLY GROVE, LONDON SE15 5DF

☎ 0171-639 2113. OPEN 2 - 4 MON - THUR AND BY APPOINTMENT.

Packed with natural-fibre fabrics, all hand-woven Indian cotton and silks, at trade prices. More than fifty-two different colours in checks and stripes, and voiles as well as curtaining and upholstery fabrics. VAT extra. Ring for stock cuttings and prices. *Permanent Discount Outlet*

PAMELA'S

16 BEAUCHAMP PLACE, LONDON SW3 1MQ

☎ 0171-589 6852. OPEN 10- 5 MON - SAT.

Selection of mostly French and Italian designer labels – Chanel, Valentino – as well as middle range names such as Jaeger and Country Casuals. There is plenty to choose from for weddings and balls, as well as lots of accessories and a good selection of hats. *Dress Agency*

PANDORA

16-22 CHEVAL PLACE, LONDON SW7 1ES

☎ 0171-589 5289. OPEN 9 - 6 MON-SAT AND MOST BANK HOLIDAYS.

Based around the corner from Harrods, this large shop with more than 5,000 items in stock sells only the top, well-known designer names: Donna Karan, Emporio Armani, Thierry Mugler, Hardy Amies, Chanel, Bruce Oldfield, Valentino, Escada, Ghost. They sell everything to do with a woman's wardrobe but it has to be in good condition and sport a top label. Also stocks a range of size 16 plus, as well as handbags, belts, hats and shoes. shoes have to be mistakes (ie new) though bags can be older eg crocodile, Hermes, Gucci. Everything is categorised into daywear, evening wear, trousers, skirts, etc so it is easy to browse. December/January and July/August clear-out sales see everything reduced by 30% with a further 20% reduction in February and September of previous season items. *Agency*

PAUL SMITH SALE SHOP

23 AVERY ROW, LONDON W1

☎ 0171-493 1287. OPEN 10 - 6 MON - SAT, UNTIL 7 ON THUR.

Offers year-round seconds, ends of lines and sample stock in the heart of London's West End. This sale shop sells last season's stock from the main shop at discounts of 40%-50%, including R Newbold workwear range, jeans, shirts, knitwear, hats, gloves, suits, trousers and sportswear. There are lots of bargains with reductions of 75% off original retail price, and a wide selection of accessories from belts to cuff links. As with all permanent sale shops, stock varies, so more than one visit may be necessary *Permanent Discount Outlet*

PENGUIN SOCIETY

144 WEST END LANE, LONDON NW6 1SD

☎ 0171-625 7778. OPEN 11.OO - 7 MON - FRI, SAT 10.30 - 5.30

Gently worn designer ladies and mens wear. Designers range from Valentino and Ghost to Jigsaw and Warehouse in the womens' range and from Armani to John Richmond and Boss in the men's. The clothes stocked cover both casual working day and evening wear, though they tend towards the former. Prices range from £10 - £200. Twice yearly sales in summer and winter. Clothing styles range from current to classical. Quick turnover and deposits accepted on items of clothing. *Dress Agency*

PHLIP OF KING'S ROAD

191 KING'S ROAD, LONDON SW3 5ED

☎ 0171-352 4332. OPEN 10 - 6.30 MON - FRI, 10 - 7 SAT.

Specialises in American clothing, both new and secondhand, from baseball to army surplus, jeans, jackets, baseball boots and 501s. Full selection of American sports equipment and accessories including caps and baseball bats.

PORTOBELLO CURTAIN SHOP

245 PORTOBELLO ROAD, LONDON W11 1LT

☎ 0171-221 4277. OPEN 9.30 - 5.30 MON - SAT.

Quality upholstery and soft furnishing fabrics at very competitive prices, usually at least 25% cheaper than in the haberdashery and soft furnishings departments of stores. Also advises on curtains, fits tracks, makes blinds and curtains. Free estimates. Also makes up using customer's own fabric. *Permanent Discount Outlet*

POSNERS: THE FLOOR STORE

35A-37 FAIRFAX ROAD, SWISS COTTAGE, LONDON NW6 4EW
☎ 0171-625 8899. OPEN 9 - 6 MON - SAT.

Established in 1946, Posners is an independent family business specialising in fitted carpets and hardwood flooring. Customers are able to make a selection from more than 1,200 ranges either stocked, promotional lines at half the high street price or to order, getting amazing value for money together with unbiased professional advice, fitting within 48 hours if required, free cuttings and in-house skilled fitting staff to give peace of mind. The hardwood flooring section is the only showroom in London where all major brands can be viewed. Hardwood floors are supplied at trade prices. Posners is the recommended installer in central London for all major brands and the London stockist for Pergo - the high-pressure laminate floor that cannot be distinguished from real hardwood and is scratch and burn resistant. *Permanent Discount Outlet*

POSTSCRIPT

DEPT GDD20, 24 LANGROYD ROAD, LONDON SW17 7PL
☎ 0181-767 7421. FAX ☎ 0181-682 0280. MAIL ORDER ONLY 9 - 5.30 MON - FRI.

Specialises in high quality books by mail at greatly reduced prices. Unlike the big book clubs, you are under no obligation to buy any books at any time. The selection covers a huge range of interests from art, gardening, cookery, biography, travel and reference to history, philosophy, psychology and literature - from classic works to the frankly esoteric - many of which cannot be found in bookshops and all priced at a fraction of publishers' latest prices. Telephone for free catalogue. *Permanent Discount Outlet*

PRICE'S PATENT CANDLE CO

110 YORK ROAD, LONDON SW11 3RU
☎ 0171-228 3345. OPEN 9.30 - 5.30 MON - SAT, 11 - 5 SUN.

Factory shop selling the famous Price's candles at discounts of 10%-25% below the recommended retail price. Price's range now includes outdoor candles, church candles, a natural range, floating candles, brassware and decorative ranges. This shop is more of a showroom for Price's products, selling the complete range of merchandise at full price, but also carrying some seconds and over-runs. The Christmas factory shop sale with its decorations is legendary and well worth going to. *Factory Shop*

Live Well On Less Tips
Freeze leftover wine in ice cube trays for use another time.

PROIBITO

42 SOUTH MOLTON STREET, LONDON W1

☎ 0171-491 3244. OPEN 10 - 6.30 MON - FRI, UNTIL 7.30 THUR, 10 - 7 SAT, 10 - 4 SUN.

Sale outlet for the nearby full-price Proibito shop which carries end of season stock from designers such as Moschino, Fendi, Gianfranco Ferre, Armani, Versace, Christian Lacroix, Iceberg, Dolce & Gabbana and Byblos at much reduced prices. *Permanent Discount Outlet*

RAINBOW

249 & 253 ARCHWAY ROAD, HIGHGATE, LONDON N6 5BS

☎ 0181-340 8003. OPEN 10.30 - 5 MON, 10.30 - 5.30 TUE - SAT.

Number 249 sells secondhand items, while 253 is new merchandise. Nearly-new consists of a wide range of well-known baby and children's clothes - from Osh Kosh and Oilily to Baby Gap and Marks & Spencer - as well as good-condition baby equipment from cots and high chairs to car seats and playpens. Also good quality toys and adults clothes. The new shop at 253 sells a wide range of children's clothes, such as Osh Kosh, French Connection, IKKS, all discounted by at least twelve and a half percent. There are twice-yearly sales in January and July when prices are discounted further. They also sell new toys at reasonable prices, including Galt and a lot of traditional wooden toys such as Brio wooden trains, wood garages, dolls houses, furniture and books. Free parking in side streets weekdays and outside the shops on Saturdays. *Dress Agency*

RECYCLE

176-178 CROYDON ROAD, ANNERLEY, LONDON SE20 7YO

☎ 0181-676 0900. OPEN 10 - 5.30 MON - FRI, 9.30 - 5.30 SAT.

Recycle is based in two adjacent shops, one selling new bikes and equipment, the other selling good quality secondhand and reconditioned bikes, most of which are mountain bikes. Some of the secondhand bikes are actually test bikes which have been barely used. Prices are discounted, but there are some serious bikes here for the real enthusiast as well as some smaller ones for children. *Permanent Discount Outlet*

REJECT CHINA SHOP

23 GOLDERS GREEN ROAD, LONDON NW11 8EE

☎ 0181- 455 5609. OPEN 9 - 5.30 MON - FRI, 9 - 6 SAT, 11 - 5.30 SUN.

Sells china, crystal and some silverware. Formerly a Chinacraft branch, the shop sells overstocks and imperfect lines, mainly of well-known makes. Some of its larger branches also sell furniture. The majority of the stock in the Reject China Shop is first quality, but sold at discounted prices, and includes Crown Derby and Royal Doulton. Also seconds dinner sets from Spode, Royal

Doulton, Aynsley, and Royal Worcester at up to 50% off. For example, a Royal Doulton dinner service, £215, normally £430 when perfect; half a dozen Bohemian crystal glasses, £32.50, normally £63.00. Other manufacturers' available. *Permanent Discount Outlet*

ROCHELLE

☎ 0181-906 2158. PHONE FOR APPOINTMENT.
Home-based business in NW7 selling designer childrenswear at discount prices including Osh Kosh B'Gosh, Double Dutch and Coco. Dresses, jeans, tracksuits, pinafores, leggings for boys and girls aged 0-8. *Designer Sale*

ROCOCO FRAMES

19 JERDAN PLACE, ON FULHAM ROAD, LONDON SW6 1BE
☎ 0171-386 0506. OPEN 10 - 6 MON - SAT.
60 GLOUCESTER ROAD, OFF KENSINGTON HIGH STREET,
LONDON SW7
☎ 0171-581 9498. OPEN 10 - 6 MON - SAT.
3 BARNES HIGH STREET, LONDON SW13
☎ 0181-878 1279. OPEN 10 - 6 MON - SAT.
A fantastic sprawling shop with seven rooms decorated like a real house, near Fulham Broadway. One of the biggest ranges of gorgeous frames and mirrors in London in masses of styles from simple to ornate, in all standard sizes - at amazingly low prices. Everything is made by Rococo in London and sold direct to the public. Weekly delivery of offcut frames, seconds and bargain lines at clearance prices. Also sells prints, pictures, cards, furniture, interior accessories, gifts and has a highly experienced picture framing workshop for public, trade and artists. *Permanent Discount Outlet*

ROGER LASCELLES CLOCKS LTD

29 CARNWATH ROAD, LONDON SW6 3HR
☎ 0171-731 0072. FAX 0171- 384 1957, OPEN 11 - 4 MON - THUR,
Established for sixteen years, Mr Lascelles makes an inspiring selection of clocks from tickers in a tin to traditional styles which replicate covetable antiques. There are wall clocks, table clocks, kitchen ranges, mantel clocks and even tin clocks with nursery rhyme designs, all with quartz battery movement. At his factory in London, there are usually seconds and ends of lines available at about half the retail price and display items at discounts of up to 50%. For example, mantel clocks from £20. New for the millennium, the factory shop has just been extended to embrace a whole range of well-known, branded gift items including candles, tablemats, china, glassware, toys and games, at well below normal retail prices. Overlooking the Thames in Fulham, this factory shop is near a number of picturesque riverside pubs and is easily accessible. *Permanent Discount Outlet*

> *Live Well On Less Tips*
> Watch out for the special deals which most supermarkets offer and which
> change weekly, usually on a Monday. Many national newspapers now carry
> the supermarket "best buys" on a Friday. Local papers are also a good source
> of information, as are posters on the store windows.

ROKIT

225 CAMDEN HIGH STREET, LONDON NW1
☎ 0171-267 3046. OPEN 10.30 - 6.30 MON - FRI, 9.30 - 7 SAT, SUN.
A comprehensive range of Fifties to Eighties gear for mods, rockers etc.
including work shirts, shoes, hats and accessories, Vintage Capital E and
selvedge seam jeans.

ROYAL NATIONAL THEATRE

HIRE DEPARTMENT, CHICHESTER HOUSE, 1-3 BRIXTON ROAD,
LONDON SW9 6DE
☎ 0171-735 4774. OPEN 10 - 6 MON - FRI BY APPOINTMENT ONLY,
CLOSED 1-2 DAILY.
Stocks up to 100,000 theatrical costumes from Roman togas to leather biker
jackets which have been worn in past RNT productions. A warning note,
however: some of the costumes looked better on stage than they do in the full
glare of daylight. Also hires out props and furniture. *Hire Shop*

RUSSELL & CHAPPLE LTD

23 MONMOUTH STREET, LONDON WC2H 9DE
☎ 0171-836 7521. OPEN 8.30 - 5 MON - FRI, 10 - 5 SAT.
Specialists in artists' supplies, they also sell natural upholstery fabrics at rock
bottom prices for hessians, calicos and muslins. Prices from 97p per metre for
muslin to £20.64 a metre for linen which is 120 inches wide. The more you
buy, the bigger the discount. There are also flame retardant materials on sale.
Permanent Discount Outlet

S & B EVANS & SONS

7A EZRA STREET, LONDON E2 7RH
☎ 0171-729 6635. OPEN 9 - 1.30 FIRST SUN EACH MONTH.
Seconds from the kiln are half price on the first Sunday of each month. The
rest of the time, the shop is full-priced. Their stock is mostly for the garden
and ranges from flower pots to terracotta ware, mugs, jugs and bowls. Situated
near to Colombia Road Flower Market which is open from 8am-2pm every
Sunday. *Permanent Discount Outlet*

S & M MYERS LTD

100-106 MACKENZIE ROAD, HOLLOWAY, LONDON N7 8RG

☎ 0171-609 0091. OPEN 10 - 5.30 MON, WED, FRI, 10 - 5 TUE, THUR, 9.30 - 2 SAT.

81-85 EAST END ROAD, EAST FINCHLEY, LONDON N2 0ST

☎ 0181-444 3457. OPEN 9.30 - 5.30 TUE - SAT.

Specialists in plain wool carpets, this company, which was established in 1819, offers end of range carpets at discount prices, as well as value-for-money perfect quality carpets by buying direct from the manufacturer or selling liquidated stock. Mainly 80% wool twist carpets and English makes such as BMK, Westex, Wilton Royal and Berber with some ranges of wool blends and man-made velvet piles. *Permanent Discount Outlet*

SALLY HAIR AND BEAUTY SUPPLIES

81 SHAFTESBURY AVENUE, LONDON W1V 7AD

☎ 0171-434 0064. OPEN 9 - 8 MON - SAT, 11 -5 SUN.

Sells a huge range of hair products and hair styling and beauty equipment (including a wide range of nail products but no make-up) from cheap and cheerful curling tongs at around £4.95 to top-of-the-range professional hair driers at more than £100. You won't find any of the recognisable brands advertised on television here, but what you will find are products which professional hairdressers use - which means they're likely to last a long time and be well-priced. The curling tongs are sold with different barrel widths so you can give yourself a tight or a loose curl. All prices are exclusive of VAT in this shop which is primarily a wholesaler, but which does sell all but its chemical products to individual members of the public. There are 117 branches countrywide. Phone 0800 525118 for your nearest store. *Permanent Discount Outlet*

SALOU

6 CHEVAL PLACE, LONDON SW7 1ES

☎ 0171-581 2380. OPEN 10 - 5 MON - SAT

Two-storey shop which sells evening wear and separates downstairs, suits upstairs, as well as jewellery and accessories. Labels include Giorgio Armani, Valentino, Gucci, Prada, Christian Lacroix, Chanel and Jean Paul Gaultier. Prices from £10-£600 for a Chanel suit. The average price for a suit is between £60 and £120; the top end of the market averages £200-£400. *Dress Agency*

SCARECROW

131 WALHAM GREEN COURT, MOORE PARK ROAD, LONDON SW6 2DG

☎ 0171-381 1023. OPEN 10 - 5 TUE - FRI, 9.30 - 1 SAT.

London's biggest and probably best-known children's dress and equipment agency, Scarecrow offers two floors of hardly-worn clothes including popular designer labels which cater for all ages from babyhood to sixteen years. Also all types of equipment, including carriage prams. As well as the more traditional rompers, smocked dresses and velvet-collared coats, there are dinner jackets and party frocks alongside jeans, checked shirts and sweatshirts. There is also an extensive range of sports clothes which include karate suits, ski wear, riding and sailing gear, plus the appropriate footwear. When the cost of bringing up a child has been estimated at somewhere in the region of a staggering £140,000, it's no wonder that parents adept at judging quality and value have found their way to Scarecrow. *Dress Agency*

SCREENFACE

20 & 24 POWIS TERRACE, LONDON W11 1JH
☎ 0171-221 8289. OPEN 9 - 6 MON - SAT. MAIL ORDER.
48 MONMOUTH STREET, LONDON WC2 9EP
☎ 0171-836 3955. OPEN 10 - 7 MON - SAT, 12 - 5 SUN.
Stocks the largest selection of make-up in the UK and is open to individuals as well as professionals. The shop has collected together the very best from all over the world. In addition to everyday make-up, they stock body paints, eyelashes, temporary tattoos, camouflage products, shaders, highlighters, eye colours, glittering powders and a vast selection of accessory items. Their huge selection of brushes include retractable lip, eyeyline and mascara brushes, perfect for the handbag. They make bags from UV proof PVC that will not crack or split and stock a huge range of powder puffs and sponges. All the products are available by mail order using a credit card. Or you could have a make-up lesson, £45 for one hour. Screenface also runs a business renting out mirrors and make-up chairs for location shoots. *Permanent Discount Outlet*

SEERS ANTIQUES

THE CONSERVATORY, 238A BATTERSEA PARK ROAD,
LONDON SW11 4NG
☎ 0171-720 0263. OPEN 10 - 6 MON - SAT, 10 - 5 SUN.
THE BANK, 213 TRAFALGAR ROAD, GREENWICH SE10 9EQ
☎ 0181-293 0293. OPEN 10 - 6 TUE - SAT, 10 - 5 SUN.
119 KNIGHTS HILL, NORWOOD, LONDON SE27 0SP
☎ 0181-766 0466. OPEN 10 - 6 TUE - SAT, 10 - 5 SUN.
49 NEW KING'S ROAD, CHELSEA, LONDON SW6
☎ 0171-371 8999. OPEN 10 - 6 MON - SAT, 10 - 4 SUN.
Brimming with largely undiscovered bargains that you would never imagine were available in today's well-trodden market. The furniture is a mixture of antique and reproduction intermingling with a vast array of frames and mirrors and a selection of gifts all at bargain prices. Original bedroom fireplaces are priced from around £125 with reproduction dining tables varying between £75 and £175 and low-priced antiques such as Pembrokes starting at £95. Prices are competitive because they have a policy of quick turnover and low

profit margins. All the prices are clearly displayed and the friendly atmosphere, along with the bustle and bargains, is in stark contrast to the hush usually associated with antique shops. *Secondhand Shop*

SELLCON ELECTRICAL CO LTD

27 ROMAN ROAD, BETHNAL GREEN, LONDON E2 OHU

☎ 0181-980 2356. FAX ☎ 0181-980 0772. OPEN 9.30 - 5 MON - SAT.

Amazing prices for designer kettles and toasters, mixers, 60s lava lamps, retro radios, disco balls, low voltage and traditional lighting, sockets, cable and many other mundane electrical components. Round the corner from the Museum of Childhood in historic Bethnal Green, Sellcon are electrical contractors who, being NICEIC approved, provide electrical surveys and installation for homes, offices, commercial organisations etc. at keenly competitive prices. E-mail romajay@compuserve.com. *Permanent Discount Outlet*

SHEILA WARREN-HILL

THE GARDEN FLAT, 63 SHEPHERDS HILL, HIGHGATE, LONDON N6 5RE

☎ 0181-348 8282. BY APPOINTMENT ONLY.

Sheila is a lovely, lively character who operates from her garden flat in London's Highgate, offering open house on Sundays when lunch and drinks are served while customers try on couture outfits. Many of her outfits were originally owned by rich and famous personalities. Having worn a dress to a special event, they can't be seen wearing the same outfit twice and so pass it on to Sheila to dispose of discreetly and enable them to recoup some of the costs and buy another dazzling creation for the next outing. The labels are top range - Jasper Conran, Giorgio Armani, Yves St Laurent, Chanel, Tomasz Starzewski, Place Vendome, Gianfranco Ferre, Escada. The atmosphere is relaxed, with Sheila on hand to dispense advice if wanted. She also sells daywear, designer shoes, swimwear and jewellery. Sheila also has an arrangement with other nearly-new businesses around the country, who take some of her stock, which means that she always has a very good supply. Customers can also have clothes delivered to their home by chauffeur-driven Bentley. Phone her for details of her regular sales and for details of other shops taking her stock. *Dress Agency*

SHIPTON & HENEAGE

117 QUEENSTOWN ROAD, LONDON SW8 3RH

☎ 0171-738 8484. OPEN 9 - 6 MON - FRI, 10 - 2 SAT. MAIL ORDER.

Traditional men's and ladies shoes, loafers, half brogues, Oxfords, and Chelsea boots manufactured and supplied by the very best factories in Northampton, the traditional home of British footwear, and stocked typically by Savile Row outfitters and Jermyn Street tailors but sold here at discounts of up to 40% off shop prices. Their premium range is made from the finest hides from the best tanneries in Europe, while their grade range shoes are from sides of more mature hides. These are priced at £149 and £89 respectively. Additionally, they also sell a comprehensive range of deck shoes, plus a range of slippers equally discounted. Any style can be ordered from the catalogue and because there is no retail outlet, prices are low. ***Permanent Discount Outlet***

SIGN OF THE TIMES

17 ELYSTAN STREET, LONDON SW3 3NT
☎ 0171-589 4774. OPEN 10 - 6 MON - SAT, 7.30 ON WED.
Sells Prada, Gucci, Donna Karan, Voyage, Fendi, Louis Vuitton, Chanel and Armani among its range of nearly new bargains. Also lots of hats (Frederick Fox, Jilly Forge), handbags and shoes (eg Manolo Blahnik). ***Dress Agency***

SOFA TO BED

UNIT 1, BAYFORD STREET INDUSTRIAL CENTRE, LONDON E8 3SE
☎ 0181-533 0915. OPEN 7 - 6 MON - FRI, 10 - 5 SAT, 10 - 3 SUN.
1A CLEVELAND WAY, MILE END ROAD, LONDON E1 4TZ
☎ 0171-790 4233. OPEN 10-2.30 MON, THUR, SAT, SUN.
Established for more than 15 years, these shops sell ex-display model sofas and sofabeds at greatly reduced prices, as well as made to order sofas at reduced prices, upholstered using Sanderson, Liberty and Parkertex fabric. Also Ottomans, stools, armchairs. All goods sold here are manufactured on the premises using traditional methods. ***Permanent Discount Outlet***

SOVIET CARPET AND ART GALLERIES

303-305 CRICKLEWOOD BROADWAY, LONDON NW2 6PG
☎ 0181-452 2445. OPEN 10.30 - 5.30 SUN ONLY,
BY APPOINTMENT MON - FRI.
Sells Oriental rugs and Russian art at trade prices, giving savings of about 50% on high street prices. The company has only been open to the public since 1992 and then only on Sundays (established in 1983, it was exclusively a wholesale operation for the first nine years of its existence). It imports hand-made rugs directly from all the main rug-producing centres of the East (Persia, Turkey, Afghanistan, Pakistan, China) and is one of the principal world distributors of rugs from the former Soviet Union. This explains why the superb Caucasian and Turkmenian (Bukhara) rugs are a speciality. They also stock one of the largest collections of quality Russian art in Europe. Only a small fraction of this is displayed, the remaining thousands of paintings can be chosen from photographs, and will then be brought out from storage. All styles in Russian art are covered from museum-quality greatest names of the 19th century through propaganda art of the Stalin years to leading contemporary artists. All works are offered at prices well below retail/auction price levels, and in extreme cases paintings sold in West End galleries for thousands can be picked up here for a few hundred pounds. ***Permanent Discount Outlet***

STEINBERG & TOLKIEN

193 KING'S ROAD, LONDON SW3 5EQ

☎ 0171-376 3660. OPEN 10.30 - 7 MON - SAT, 12 - 6 SUN.

Situated on two floors, one floor is devoted totally to jewellery, the other floor to American vintage and European couture clothing from the Twenties and Thirties to the Seventies. Some of the more interesting items were worn by movie stars of the Thirties and Forties and the garment is often seen on the original wearer in photographs around the shop. Popular with those looking for something unusual for a theme evening or a gala event, it's also frequented by those searching for an individual look in a style and quality unmatched even by couture designers today. There is also a selection of men's clothes. *Permanent Discount Outlet*

STOCKHOUSE

101-105 GOSWELL ROAD, LONDON EC1V 7ER

☎ 0171-253 5761. OPEN 9 - 5 MON, TUE, FRI, 9 - 6 WED, THUR, 9 - 2 SUN, CLOSED SAT.

Formerly known as Goldsmith & Company, in late 1994 Stockhouse expanded from a purely wholesale warehouse into a trade discount centre for branded menswear that is also open to the public. It stocks more than 3,500 men's suits, from stylish business suits, formal dresswear and comfortable lounge suits to famous brand men's shirts, silk ties, blazers, sports jackets, casual jackets, overcoats, designer swimwear, underwear, socks and branded sportswear. Sizes range from 36 chest to 54. By purchasing cancelled orders and broken ranges from famous manufacturers at clearing prices, they are able to offer famous brands at greatly reduced prices without compromising on quality or style. Labels on sale include Christian Dior, Ben Sherman and Pierre Cardin shirts; and Rainman casual jackets; Pierre Balmain and Mario Barutti sports jackets; Hom swimwear, shorts and sportswear; Xen and Emilio Pucci silk ties. Suits include many famous labels and everything shows a considerable saving off normal shop prices. Stock is constantly changing. Well worth a visit *Permanent Discount Outlet*

SURPRISE SURPRISE

18 GOLDERS GREEN ROAD, LONDON NW11 9PU

☎ 0181-209 0003. OPEN 9 - 6.30 MON - SAT, 10 - 5 SUN.

Men's shirts, ties and socks at very reasonable prices. For example, polo shirts, £3.99 each or three for £10; silk ties, £3.99 or three for £10; socks from £3.99 to £6.99 for a pack of six. Ladies' mid range fashion. *Permanent Discount Outlet*

SWALLOWS & AMAZONS

91 NIGHTINGALE LANE, LONDON SW12 8NX

☎ 0181-673 0275. OPEN 10 - 5.30 MON - SAT.

Probably the largest good-as-new children's shop in London, S & A has a ground floor full of quality clothes for 0-12 year olds: OshKosh, Oilily, Jean Le Bourget, Mexx etc, as well as a large basement with toys, books and baby equipment. They carry some new playpens, high chairs and buggies due to demand, but at competitive prices. The stock is constantly changing and they pride themselves on keeping standards high, but prices low - from 90p to £99. There is also children's hairdressing (with videos) on most afternoons and on Saturdays (appointments necessary) and a play area. Friendly, helpful staff. *Dress Agency*

SWIMGEAR

11 STATION ROAD, FINCHLEY, LONDON N3 2SB

☎ 0181-346 6106. OPEN 9.30 - 5 MON - SAT. MAIL ORDER.

A mail order company which also operates via a retail outlet next to Finchley Central station. As well as selling their swimwear at less than the normal retail price by not putting the full markup on their products, they also sell discontinued and ends of line ranges of swimwear for men, women and children at between 20%-30% less than normal retail prices. They also stock goggles and flippers in adult sizes. Flippers normally cost about £18.50, but can be bought here for about £8 in black rubber; Lycra trunks, plain £7.35 up to £10 for patterned ones. Bikinis are on sale all year round, with women's swimwear ranging up to size 46. The catalogues are full colour and carry the names Adidas, Tyr, Moontide, Tweeka and Maru, as well as Swimgear's own brand full colour Mark One brochure. Prices are lower than would be offered at swim meets and retail shops. As part of their service, they do not cash your cheque until your full order has been completed. P&p extra. Orders over £20 are post free, excluding heavy items such as flippers and shampoo on which p&p is charged. *Permanent Discount Outlet*

THE CANDLE SHOP

50 NEW KING'S ROAD, LONDON SW6 4LS

☎ 0171-736 0740. OPEN 10 - 6 MON - SAT.

Warehouse outlet servicing the shop in Covent Garden's Piazza which sells candles at what they claim are the lowest prices in the country. You can buy anything from bulk boxes of two hundred 8 cream candles from £29.95 to church candles at wholesale prices, as well as floating, scented and novelty candles. Candle-making supplies are also available. Mail order catalogue on request. *Permanent Discount Outlet*

THE CHANGING ROOM

148 ARTHUR ROAD, WIMBLEDON PARK, LONDON SW19 8AQ

☎ 0181-947 1258. OPEN 10 - 6 TUES - FRI.

Fast-moving stock of designer samples and secondhand lables including: Ghost, Whistles, Jigsaw, Kenzo, Moschino, Armani, Resource, Romeo Gigli. Also shoes and accessories. Sample and second-hand childrenswear: Gap, Parsisal, Kenzo, Monsoon, Jigsaw, Petit Bateau, Armani. *Dress Agency*

THE CHILDREN'S WAREHOUSE

UNIT 4, 44 COLVILLE ROAD, LONDON W3 8BL

☎ 0181-752 1166. OPEN 10 -4 TUE - FRI, 10 - 2 SAT.

Designers and manufacturers of classic, casual, everyday clothes for children aged from 0 - 12 years. Sells designer samples, factory seconds and ends of lines all at trade price or less. Car parking. Phone for a catalogue. *Permanent Discount Outlet*

THE CLOTH SHOP

290 PORTOBELLO ROAD, LONDON W10 5TE

☎ 0181-968 6001. OPEN 10.30 - 6 MON - THUR, 10 - 6 FRI, SAT.

Discounted fabric from good tweeds and cottons, muslin and calico to Lycra, as well as brand name ends of rolls, sample lengths and former window drapes. There is also a large range of Indian furnishing fabrics at reduced prices and antique linen sheets and fabrics. Turnover is high and stock changes constantly. *Permanent Discount Outlet*

THE CORRIDOR

309A KING'S ROAD, LONDON SW3 5EP

☎ 0171-351 0772.

Small, personalised boutique providing nearly-new high quality designer clothing. Names include Chanel, Prada, Valentino, Ralph Lauren, Alberta Ferretti and Max Mara, sold seasonally. An alteration service is also available. *Dress Agency*

THE COSTUME STUDIO

MONTGOMERY HOUSE, 159-161 BALLS POND ROAD, ISLINGTON, LONDON N1 4BG

☎ 0171-388 4481/275 9614. OPEN 9.30 - 6 MON - FRI, 10 -5 SAT.

Twenty thousand costumes from medieval times to the 70s. Clients include TV and video companies. Individual hiring costs from £30-£75 for one week. There are plenty of accessories from shoes and hats to bags and gloves to complete an outfit. *Hire Shop*

THE CURTAIN EXCHANGE

133 STEPHENDALE ROAD, LONDON SW6 2PG
☎ 0171-731 8316/7. OPEN 10 - 5 MON - SAT.
56 LEDBURY ROAD, LONDON W11 2AJ
☎ 0171-229 4923. OPEN 10 - 5 MON - SAT.
80 PARK HALL ROAD, DULWICH, LONDON SE21 8BW
☎ 0181-670 5570. OPEN 10 - 5 MON - SAT.
The Curtain Exchange is a franchised group of shops selling beautiful top quality secondhand curtains, blinds, pelmets, etc at between one-third and one half of the brand new price. Their stock comes from a variety of sources: people who are moving house and dislike the drapes in their new home; people who are moving house and want to sell their old curtains to help with the bills; show houses, where the builder wants to recoup some of his outgoings; interior designers' mistakes. Stock changes constantly and ranges from rich brocades, damasks and velvets to chintzes, linens and cottons. Designer names include Colefax & Fowler, Designers Guild, Laura Ashley, Warner, Sanderson, Osborne & Little, Fortuny and Bennison. A team of fitters and alteration experts are available if required. They offer a 24-hour availability. The Curtain Exchange also supply bespoke ranges with samples of curtains hanging. These fabrics are chosen from suppliers all over the world and are an excellent buy. *Secondhand Shop*

THE CURTAIN FABRIC FACTORY SHOP

230-236 NORTH END ROAD, LONDON W14 9NU
☎ 0171-381 1777. FAX ☎ 0171-381 8879. OPEN 9.30 - 5.30 MON - SAT.
Genuine factory shop which prints curtain fabric on site and sells overstocks, seconds and cancelled orders at trade prices here - there are 1,000 rolls in stock. Makes for hundreds of shops countrywide and exports to twelve different countries. There are hundreds of different designs and qualities from which to choose at prices starting at £1.99 a metre. There are also quilted bedspreads available to match the fabrics, and a curtain making and track fitting service. This factory shop only opened in 1996 and has some very keen prices. *Factory Shop*

THE CURTAIN MILL

46-52 FAIRFIELD ROAD, LONDON E3 2QB
☎ 0181-980 9000. OPEN 9 - 5.30 SEVEN DAYS A WEEK.
2 THE VALE, ACTON, LONDON W3 75B
☎ 0181-743 2299. OPEN 9 - 5.30 SEVEN DAYS A WEEK.
UNIT 75, CAPITOL INDUSTRIAL PARK, CAPITOL WAY, COLINDALE, LONDON NW9 OEQ
(☎ 0181) 205 2220.
Huge choice of fabrics at really low prices - from £1.99p a metre and including excellent discounts on many designer labels. A large warehouse, it stocks Ashley Wilde, Curtina and Swatchbox, among other leading names at discount prices. *Permanent Discount Outlet*

THE DESIGNER STORE

289 KING'S ROAD, LONDON SW3 5EW

☎ 0171-351 0880. OPEN 10.30 - 6.30 MON - SAT, 12 - 5 SUN.

Light, airy shop about halfway down the King's Road with friendly atmosphere, stocking seven lines of Max Mara at discounted prices of 35%.
Permanent Discount Outlet

THE DESIGNER WAREHOUSE SALE FOR WOMEN AND MEN

ROGER DACK LTD, STUDIO 6, THE IVORIES, 6-8 NORTHAMPTON STREET, LONDON N1 2HY

☎ 0171-704 1064. FAX ☎ 0171-704 1379. SALES USUALLY OPEN 10 - 8 FRI, 10 - 6 SAT, 11 - 5 SUN.

The Designer Warehouse Sales stake claim to being the biggest and best sales to be found, offering clothes direct from the designers at around two thirds off the retail price as well as a totally unique fabric sale. Based in photographic studios in central London, there are five women's and five men's sales (and one combined sale at the Clothes Show Live in Birmingham) each year. The Designer Warehouse Sales pride themselves on stocking many of the 70+ contemporary labels exclusively. Established designers such as Nicole Farhi, John Rocha, Ally Capellino, Jasper Conran, Browns, Workers for Freedom, Jil Sander, Elspeth Gibson and Paul Smith are regular contributors. Samples, one-offs for the catwalk and current collections make up the rails of clothing which are displayed in the four studios at The Worx. The atmosphere is relaxed and casual. Communal changing rooms are not for the precious but add to the fun of the atmosphere. For further information and to put your name on the mailing list, please phone from 10am-5pm Monday to Friday or e-mail on dwslondon@aol.com. The Designer Warehouse Fabric Sale also takes place twice a year over three days, and offers sample lengths and ends of rolls from more than 40 of England's top designers who usually include Ally Capellino, Vivienne Westwood, Betty Jackson, Nicole Farhi, Neisha Crosland, Georgina von Etzdorf and Workers for Freedom. It's a great opportunity to buy exclusive fabrics not normally available to the public. Prices start at 50p per metre. Most of the lengths are dress and clothing fabrics, although the astute bargain hunter will find many are suitable (and cheaper) for soft furnishing. Admission to these sales is £2, students, £1. *Designer Sale*

THE DRESS BOX

8-10 CHEVAL PLACE, LONDON SW7 1ES

☎ 0171-589 2240. OPEN 10 - 6 MON - FRI, 10.30 - 6 SAT.

Operating for more than 50 years, the Dress Box caters for the top end of the market including new and nearly-new couture - YSL, Chanel, Gucci, Hermes, Valentino, Prada and Pierre Cardin. Those looking for special occasion wear, evening outfits or ball gowns are well catered for. among the 500 or so outfits in the shop at any one time are Chanel suits from £750 and Valentino and Ungaro suits from £450. Wonderful collection of YSL suits, some Chanel jackets and suits. Prices range from £150-£1,000 for suits though most outfits cost £200-£400. There is also a collection of hats from £45-£100 (Philip Somerville, Philip Treacy) and shoes from £25-£90. Alterations service available. There are also Chanel handbags, scarves from £95, costume jewellery, as well as a small selection of menswear. You can buy a whole wardrobe here from swimwear to coats. Also offers an in-house couture alteration service. *Dress Agency*

THE DRESSER

10 PORCHESTER PLACE, LONDON W2 2BS
☎ 0171-724 7212. OPEN 11 - 5.30 MON - FRI, 11 - 5 SAT.
Secondhand contemporary women's and men's clothes including Armani, Donna Karan, Jil Sander, Dolce & Gabanna, Gucci, Prada, Comme des Garcons, for women at the front of the shop, at prices ranging from £50-£400. The men's department is at the back of the shop with names such as Paul Smith, Yohji Yamamoto, Jasper Conran, Armani, Gaultier and Comme des Garcons at prices ranging from £30-£400. There is much more women's merchandise than men's, with lots of separates, some hats and shoes. *Dress Agency*

THE EXCHANGE DRESS AGENCY

30 ELIZABETH STREET, BELGRAVIA, LONDON SW1
☎ 0171-730 3334. OPEN 10 - 4 MON - SAT.
Set up in aid of The National Kidney Research Fund, to whom all the profits are donated, it stocks a range of women's clothing including Paul Costelloe, Valentino, Flyte Ostell, Moschino, Guy Laroche, Givenchy, Caroline Charles and Rifat Ozbek. Customers bringing in clothes to sell receive 50% of the selling price; the charity receives the other 50%. *Dress Agency*

THE FULHAM FACTORY OUTLET

793 FULHAM ROAD, LONDON SW6 5HD
☎ 0171-736 2387. OPEN 10 - 6 MON - SAT, 12 - 5 SUN.
Interior design accessories direct from the manufacturers at savings of up to 100% on retail prices. Items include antiqued reproduction oil paintings from £10 (usually £30) up to £400 for a 6ft x 4ft canvas; coffee tables at 40% savings; tapestry cushions from £25, representing a 40% saving; dummy books from £10, also a 40% saving; china vases; potted faux flowers from £10, a 50% saving; reproduction marble busts, console tables and many more items arriving each week. These ends of lines, overstocks, discontinued lines and slight seconds from some of the most well-recognised companies in interior accessories could have come straight out of the pages of House & Garden magazine. *Factory Shop*

THE GALLERY OF
ANTIQUE COSTUME & TEXTILES

2 CHURCH STREET, MARYLEBONE, LONDON NW8 8ED

☎ 0171-723 9981. OPEN 10 - 5.30 MON - SAT.

Original costumes from Victorian times to the 1940s and waistcoats and fabrics from the early textiles to mid nineteenth century. Cushions from £65-£500; table covers from £100-£400; curtains from £300; Edwardian tea dresses from £100; Twenties and Thirties evening wear from £75 upwards.

THE HARDWOOD FLOORING CO LTD

146-152 WEST END LANE, WEST HAMPSTEAD, LONDON NW6 1SD

☎ 0171-328 8481. OPEN 8.30 - 5.30 MON - FRI, UNTIL 8 ON THUR.

Situated in West Hampstead, this outlet has been established for more than 12 years. It has the largest showrooms with customer parking in London for over 200 different types of new hardwood floorings ranging from pre-finished strip and blocks to English oak wide board planking. full installation service is available, if required. *Architectural Salvage*

THE HOUSE HOSPITAL

UNIT 9, FERRIER STREET INDUSTRIAL ESTATE, WANDSWORTH, LONDON SW18 1SW

☎ 0181 870 8202. 10 - 5 MON - SAT.

Cast iron radiators, bathroom fittings, brass mixer taps, doors, door handles, fireplaces and stone flooring. *Architectural Salvage*

THE LOFT

35 MONMOUTH STREET, COVENT GARDEN, LONDON WC2H 9DD

☎ 0171-240 3807. OPEN 11 - 6 MON - SAT.

One-offs, ends of lines, nearly-new for men and women from the likes of Vivienne Westwood, Jean-Paul Gaultier, DKNY, Versace, Paul Smith, Gucci, Prada and Armani . A hire service is also available in this two-storey shop which is packed with bargains. Denise Van Outen, Bjork and George Michael have all been kitted out in The Loft's designer outfits at a fraction of their original price. Fed up with some of your own designer outfits? Take them here and turn them into cash. *Dress Agency*

THE LONDON PICTURE CENTRE

709 FULHAM ROAD, LONDON SW6 5UL

☎ 0171-371 5737. OPEN 9 - 5.30 MON - FRI, 10 - 6 SAT 11 - 3 SUN.

152 HACKNEY ROAD, LONDON E2 1QL

☎ 0171-729 0881. OPEN 9 - 5 MON - FRI, 10 - 2 SAT.

75 LEATHER LANE, LONDON EC1 7UJ. OPEN 9 - 4 MON - FRI.

☎ 0171-404 4110. OPEN 9.30 - 5.30 MON - FRI, 10 - 4 SAT.

18 CRAWFORD STREET, LONDON W1 1PF
☎ 0171-487 2895.
723 FULHAM ROAD, LONDON SW6 5HA
☎ 0171-371 5737. OPEN 9 - 5.30 MON - FRI, 10 - 6 SAT, 11 - 3 SUN.
287-9 HACKNEY ROAD, LONDON E2 8NA.
☎ 0171-729 1220. OPEN 8 - 5 MON - FRI, 10 - 4 SAT, 10 - 2 SUN.
Manufacturers and global importers of mirrors and frames with large whole-sale premises with own retail showroom offering an enormous selection of mirrors in all sizes and types from gilt frames to baroque style, as well as oil paintings and framed prints. Prices range from £2-£1,000. Framing is very reasonable, too, and the service is used regularly by local artists. The branch at 709 Fulham Road is a mirror gallery offering competitively priced mirrors to any specification. At 152 Hackney Road, there is a prints and posters show-room offering a huge selection of prints - flowers, impressionist, abstracts and many more - at unbeatable prices. ***Permanent Discount Outlet***

THE MAKE-UP CENTRE

52A WALHAM GROVE, FULHAM, LONDON SW6 1QR
☎ 0171-381 0213. OPEN 10 - 4 MON - FRI.
Sells own brands of matt eyeshadow, foundation, and blusher which are twice the size of ones you can buy in department stores. Also good sable brushes which are cheaper than those found in artists' shops. Also do makeovers and offer make-up lessons for £95 for one and a half hours. With more than thir-ty years experience in the business, they have not only trained the best make-up artists, but made up prime ministers, film stars and tv presenters. Full wed-ding makeovers from £95. ***Permanent Discount Outlet***

THE NAPPY EXPRESS

128 HIGH ROAD, NEW SOUTHGATE, LONDON N11 1PG
☎ 0181-361 4040. PHONE FIRST.
Part of the Baby Equipment Hirers Association (BEHA), which has more than 100 members countrywide. A range of equipment can be hired from high chairs, cots and travel cots to baby car seats and buggies. Some members also hire out party equipment including child-sized tables and chairs. BEHA run an advice line which will try and answer any queries you have regarding hir-ing services for children. Phone the Babyline on 0831 310355. There is also a free home delivery service aimed at new mothers in north, central and south London for Pampers and Huggies nappies, baby foods (including organic), baby toiletries, also large household items like washing powders, toilet rolls, bottled waters, fizzy drinks, beer etc, all at supermarket prices. ***Hire Shop***

Live Well On Less Tips
Freeze leftover gravy in ice cube trays for use another time.

THE NATURAL WOOD FLOOR

COMPANY, 20 SMUGGLERS WAY, WANDSWORTH, LONDON SW18 1EQ
☎ 0181-871 9771. OPEN 9 - 6 MON - FRI, 9 - 4 SAT.
Up to 170 different wood-flooring materials including reclaimed wooden floorboards: pine, douglas fir, woodblock and pitch pine. Pine floorboards cost from £21 sq metre; beechwood woodblock from £18, while oak starts at £57 a sq metre. Also sells new solid wood floors at prices which they claim are cheaper than anything offered in the same style. For example, 20 ml thick red-wood, £16.99 per square yard. *Architectural Salvage*

THE OBSERVATORY

20 GREENWICH CHURCH STREET, GREENWICH, LONDON SE10 9BJ
☎ 0181-305 1998. OPEN 10 - 6 EVERY DAY
Established for over ten years, this is a retrospective clothing shop selling turn-of-the-century fashion as well as Fifties, Sixties, Seventies and early Eighties gear. Women's frocks, shoes, hats and jewellery as well as lots of leather, suede and denim garments. Men's suits, jackets and trousers.

THE OLD CINEMA s

157 TOWER BRIDGE ROAD, LONDON SE1 3LW
☎ 0171-407 5371. OPEN 9.30 - 5.30 MON - SAT, 12 - 5 SUN.
160 CHISWICK HIGH ROAD, LONDON W4 1PR
☎ 0181-995 4166. OPEN 9.30 - 6 MON - SAT, 12 - 5 SUN.
The Tower Bridge branch is a thirty thousand square foot warehouse with antique furniture, some from pub fittings, garden furniture, and pine furniture. Periods include art deco, art nouveau, Victoriana and Americana. There's everything from kitchen sinks to veteran cars. Chairs start at £20, art deco dining room suites from £400 to £2,000, Victorian dining tables from £900. The Chiswick branch holds ten thousand square feet of antique furniture, some in complete room settings. Wide range of Victorian, Georgian, Edwardian and art nouveau. Items range from light fittings and mirrors to dining tables and room panelling. *Secondhand Shop*

THE REJECT TILE SHOP

178 WANDSWORTH BRIDGE ROAD, LONDON SW6 2UQ
☎ 0171-731 6098. OPEN 9.30 - 5.30 MON - FRI, 9.30 - 5 SAT.
2A ENGLANDS LANE, LONDON NW3 4TG
☎ 0171-483 2608. OPEN 10 - 6 MON - FRI, 10 - 5 SAT.
Specialises in second quality and low cost ceramic wall and floor tiles as well as terracotta and quarry tiles. Most tiles are sold at approximately half the cost of first quality equivalent products. Quality control is so tight nowadays that seconds are usually given this status due to minor glazing defects, barely per-

ceptible pinholing in the glaze or slightly off-standard colour shades. Many tiles are imported exclusively from Italy and there is also a wide selection of fine quality English and Victorian style decorated tiles, borders and dados, as well as a wide choice of discontinued and special purchase first quality tiles. *Permanent Discount Outlet*

TILE CLEARING HOUSE

ACE CORNER, STONEBRIDGE PARK, NORTH CIRCULAR ROAD, LONDON NW10 7UD

☎ 0181-965 8062. FAX ☎ 0181-453 0392. OPEN 8 - 6 MON - FRI, 9 - 6 SAT, 10 - 4 SUN.

6-9 LOWER PARK ROAD, NEW SOUTHGATE INDUSTRIAL PARK, LONDON N1 1HT

☎ 0181-361. OPEN 8 - 6 MON - FRI, 9 - 6 SAT, 10 - 4 SUN.

Over 500 ranges of top quality ceramic wall and floor tiles permanently in stock, plus a comprehensive range of grouts, adhesives, tools and accessories to complete the job. Save up to 75% on manufacturers' recommended selling prices. *Permanent Discount Outlet*

TILES GALORE

GRACEFIELD GARDENS, STREATHAM, LONDON SW16 2ST

☎ 0181-677 6068. OPEN 8 - 5.30 MON - SAT.

1 CROSS WAYS PARADE, SELSDON PARK ROAD, ADDINGTON, LONDON CR2 8JJ

☎ 0181-651 3782. OPEN 7.30 - 5 MON - SAT.

Sells perfect tiles from round the world at discount prices by buying direct from the factories, unlike the large department stores which buy from distributors. There are hundreds of designs to choose from. The Addington Shop is small, whereas the Streatham shop has 10,000 sq ft of tiles. *Permanent Discount Outlet*

Live Well On Less Tips

HOMELINK INTERNATIONAL LINFIELD HOUSE, GORSE HILL ROAD, VIRGINIA WATER, SURREY. GU25 4AS, (01344) 842642.

Home exchange is a great way to see the world, have a holiday and save money. You pay for travel, food and holiday spending only and you get to taste someone else's lifestyle! Homelink publishes a worldwide directory listing members interested in exchanging homes for holidays. £89 annual subscription brings five directories a year. Phone them for more details or try their website: www.homelink.org.

TK MAXX

THE ARCADIA CENTRE, EALING, LONDON

☎ 0181-566 0447. OPEN 9.30 - 6 MON - SAT, TILL 7 THUR, 11 - 5 SUN.

Based on an American concept, TK Maxx is situated in easily accessible, often centrally located stores and offers famous label goods with up to 60% savings off recommended retail prices. TK Maxx has fashion for the whole family - women's, men's and childrenswear - accessories, shoes, gifts, kitchenware and home goods. Everything in the store is branded with a choice of well-known high street names to designer labels, and while a small percentage might be clearly marked past season, the great majority of items in store are current season, current stock and still with phenomenal savings. There is a huge choice with 50,000 pieces in store and up to 10,000 new items arriving a week. The stores are simple and unfussy with wide aisles, shopping trolleys and baskets, and a spacious, functional feel to them but there are individual changing rooms, ramps for buggies and wheelchairs and plenty of staff on the shop floor. Every branch accepts all major credit and debit cards and has a liberal refund and return policy. *Permanent Discount Outlet*

TOG 24

UNIT SU28, THE EXCHANGE SHOPPING CENTRE, PUTNEY HIGH STREET, PUTNEY, LONDON SW15 1TW

(☎ 01817) 853565. OPEN 9 - 6 MON, TUE, WED, FRI, SAT, 9 - 7 THUR, 11 - 5 SUN.

Tog 24 are the UK's fastest growing brand name in outdoor clothing and leisurewear, with a total of three UK factories and 36 stores nationwide. They utilise the world's finest performance fabrics including Gore-Tex, Polartec and Burlington macs. Catering for all the family for all seasons, with cosy fleeces and waterproofs for the winter, and trekking ranges, shorts and t-shirts for the summer. With all prices at least 30% below the recommended retail price you can afford to enter the Tog comfort zone. *Factory Shopping Village*

TOP VALUE DRUGSTORE

23 TEMPLE FORTUNE PARADE, OPPOSITE MARKS & SPENCERS, FINCHLEY ROAD, LONDON NW11 0QS

☎ 0181-905 5448. OPEN 8.30 - 6 MON - SAT, 9.30 - 1.30 SUN.

One of those rare, family-run businesses which manages to undercut the competition, including with many items, Boots and Superdrug. Well-stocked shop which is divided into sections such as haircare, skincare, toiletries, baby equipment, household cleaning (Jif, Comfort, Pledge, Flash, Dettol, Ajax, Mr Muscle, Astonish etc.), bathroom cleaning products, oven cleaners, window cleaning products, polishes, scourers, brushes, cloths, sponges, air fresheners etc, bakeware, non-pharmaceutical drugs. The shop also stocks a selection of cards, toys and fancy goods and offers same-day developing for £2.99 for up to 40 prints with an extra set costing £1.99 if ordered at time of processing. Prices are generally 25%-30% cheaper than other chemist chains. You can phone your order through and there is a delivery service if you spend a minimum of £35. *Permanent Discount Outlet*

TOTTERS

57 TOTTENHAM LANE, CROUCH END, HORNSEY, LONDON N8 7DT
☎ 0181-341 0377. OPEN 10 - 5 MON - SAT, CLOSED WED.
Secondhand prams, baby equipment, clothes and toys which, according to one reader, are always of very high quality. Labels include everything from Mothercare to Joseph and Oilily. Always carries a stock of up-to-date toys, though there is a quick turnover. *Dress Agency*

TOWNSENDS

81 ABBEY ROAD, LONDON NW8 0AE
☎ 0171-624 4756. OPEN 10 - 6 MON - FRI, 10 - 5 SAT.
106 BOUNDARY ROAD, LONDON NW8 ORH
☎ 0171-372 4327. OPEN 10 - 6 MON - FRI, 10 - 5 SAT.
Antique fireplaces and related items, and antique stained glass at the Boundary Road branch just down the road. More than 200 fireplaces in stock at prices from £250 to £15,000 in wood, marble, cast-iron and natural stone. This business has been established for more than 20 years and offers a full survey and fitting service and free delivery in the London area. They also restore antique stained glass, acid-etched and sandblasted glass from £30 per square foot to £100. *Architectural Salvage*

TRAVEL ACCESSORY OUTLET

UNIT 109, IST FLOOR, WHITELEYS CENTRE,
QUEENSWAY, LONDON W24YH
☎ 0171-792 0691. OPEN 10 - 8 MON - FRI, 9 - 7 SAT, 11 - 5 SUN.
Luggage and travel-related products including executive cases, handbags, umbrellas and accessories available in leading brands such as Samsonite, Brics, Hidesign, Globe Trotter and Tula. The products also include couture and high fashion brands such as YSl and Moschino. All products are offered at a considerably reduced price due to their being production over-runs, last season's stock of slight seconds (ie they have minor aesthetic blemishes). *Permanent Discount Outlet*

Live Well On Less Tips
Fit reflective foil behind radiators (with the shiny side facing the radiator) to help keep heat indoors.

Live Well On Less Tips
Always fill in any gaps between the floor and the skirting boards using wood
moulding or a filler

TWENTIETH CENTURY FROX
614 FULHAM ROAD, LONDON SW6 5RP
☎ 0171-731 3242. OPEN 10 - 7 MON, WED, THUR, 10 - 6 TUE, FRI, SAT.
Two hundred dresses, mainly ballgowns and cocktail dresses, to hire or to buy.
Costs £65 - £120 for three days' hire. No appointment necessary. Also new
and ex-hire stock available to buy. *Hire Shop*

UPSTAIRS DOWNSTAIRS
8 MALCOLM COURT, MALCOLM CRESCENT,
HENDON, LONDON NW4 4PJ
☎ 0181-202 7720. BY APPOINTMENT ONLY.
Features top designer makes in perfect condition on uncluttered rails which
makes for unhurried browsing. Accessories are for sale as well as day clothes.
Customers come from all over the country and clothes from all over the world,
where they both enjoy personal attention. Designers include Louis Feraud,
Valentino, Jobis, Yarell, MaxMara and Cerruti. There is also an alterations service.
Dress Agency

USA FASHION
111 & 117 FONTHILL ROAD, LONDON N4 3HH
☎ 0171-272 3992. OPEN 9.30 - 5.30 MON - FRI, 9 - 4 SAT.
Specialises in a wide size-range in womenswear (8 to 26), including familiar
high street names and American designers, all at discount prices. For example,
a garment which would normally retail at £170 costs only £60 here. All the
stock is brand new. They also have a range of eveningwear in sizes 8 to 26, and
childrenswear aged 12 upwards. *Permanent Discount Outlet*

VICTORIAN WOOD WORKS
INTERNATIONAL HOUSE, LONDON INTERNATIONAL FREIGHT
TERMINAL, TEMPLE MILLS LANE, LONDON E15 2ES
☎ 0181-534 1000. OPEN 8.30 - 5.30 MON - FRI, 8 - 12 SAT.
Reclaimed or new oak, elm, jarrah, pitch pine beams, sawn and selected to
meet your needs. Also specialist suppliers of reclaimed wood floors, some up
to 500 years of age and up to 18 in width. Huge on-site stocks of woodblocks,
parquet, T&G strip, Versailles panels and inlaid parquetry. Also manufacture
staircases, bookcases, panelling, ledge and brace doors, window frames, skirting, architraves and dado as non-standard items. *Architectural Salvage*

VILLEROY & BOCH (UK) LIMITED

267 MERTON ROAD, LONDON SW18 5JS

☎ 0181-870 4168. OPEN 10 - 5 SEVEN DAYS A WEEK.

The UK's main factory outlet for Villeroy & Boch carries an exclusive range of tableware, crystal and cutlery from Europe's largest tableware manufacturer. Convenient parking and pleasant surroundings make for a pleasurable and unhurried shopping experience. A varied and constantly changing stock, including seconds, hotelware and discontinued lines, on sale at excellent reductions, always makes for a worthwhile visit. *Factory Shop*

VIRGINIA

98 PORTLAND ROAD, HOLLAND PARK, LONDON W11 4LQ

☎ 0171-727 9908. OPEN 11 - 6 MON - SAT.

Antique clothing from the turn of this century to the 1940s. Nightgowns, beaded dresses, chiffon, hats and accessories. Everything is a one-off and top quality.

VIVM (Value for Money)

70 NEW KINGS ROAD, LONDON SW6 4LT

☎ 0171-371 5412. OPEN 10 - 6 MON - SAT

Value for Mony offers designer labels for less with the emphasis on accessories. End of line stock and current samples from British and French designers with regular changes of merchandise make for a top quality mix of good quality clothes and accessories. *Permanent Discount Shop*

WAHL FASHIONS

4 GREAT PORTLAND STREET, LONDON W1N 5AA

☎ 0171-580 8050.

Agents for Blacky Dress, Beppi, Bondi, Pleinsud Jeans, Tuzzi, they hold showroom sales regularly. Write or phone to be put on the mailing list. *Designer Sale*

WALL TO WALL

549 BATTERSEA PARK ROAD, BATTERSEA, LONDON SW11 3BL

☎ 0171-585 3335. FAX ☎ 0171-228 5080. OPEN 10 - 6 MON - SAT.

Top name designer brand wallpaper, all at £7.95 a roll, with 450 different designs from which to choose. All their bargain lines are discontinued patterns, or ends of ranges so you have to buy the right quantity when you see it as there won't be any more. Names on sale include Anna French, Monkwell, Hill & Knowles and GP&J Baker. Also designer-name fabrics at clearance prices from £9.95 a metre - 10,000 metres always in stock. Full making-up and fitting service, which is particularly good for people who want to do places up quickly as there is a very fast operation free measuring and estimating service. There's also a free design service on the premises. *Permanent Discount Outlet*

> *Live Well On Less Tips*
> Make your fresh coffee last longer by re-using the grounds with half as much
> freshly ground coffee added to the old ones.

WALLERS

21-24 NEWPORT COURT, CHARING CROSS ROAD, LONDON WC2H 7JS
☎ 0171-437 1665. OPEN 9 - 5.30 MON - FRI, 9 - 4.30 SAT.
Wallers is a family firm established at the same address for more than 70 years.
They specialise in famous name suits, sports jackets, blazers, trousers, coats
and morning and evening dress wear at greatly reduced prices. Well known to
TV and film designers, who appreciate the value of choice, their Chinatown
shop looks small on the outside but inside is a rabbit warren, full to the brim.
Wallers clothes have been seen in Inspector Morse, Minder, Yes Minister, The
Bill, Between The Lines and even blockbuster Hollywood films such as
Mission Impossible. There are usually at least 5,000 items in stock at any one
time, in all sizes, most of which are ends of ranges, cancelled orders, seconds
(clearly marked as such) or bought as a result of liquidations. Examples of
prices include suits, £125, usual price £225; jackets, £79.50, usual price £125;
trousers, £25, usual price £59.50; raincoats and overcoats, from £79.50; dinner suits, from £110; three-piece morning suits, from £165. They also now
have a range of smart casual ladies wear designed by Elizabeth Emanuel at very
reasonable prices. *Permanent Discount Outlet*

WARD & STEVENS

248 HIGH STREET NORTH, MANOR PARK, LONDON E12 6SB
☎ 0181-472 4067. FAX ☎ 0181-470 9091. OPEN 9 - 5.30 MON - SAT.
Budget ranges of floor and wall tiles including standard quality and excellent
seconds. Specialise in low cost quarry floor tiles at prices starting from £6.80
per square metre plus VAT. Also 300x300 floors in a wide range available from
stock. Wall tiles from £2 per metre to £25 per metre. Budget range of wall-
coverings from stock. Full range of British Standard and NCS paints (5,000
plus colours) at less than trade prices. *Permanent Discount Outlet*

WELLINGTONS

1 WELLINGTON PLACE, LONDON NW8 7PE
☎ 0171-483 0688. OPEN 11 - 5 MON - SAT.
Stunning selection of Gucci, Prada, Chanel, MaxMara, Armani and Joseph.
Ladies suits from £48, jackets from £28. There's also a bargain basement full
of high street names such as Marks & Spencer and Karen Millen as well as
reduced designer clothing. Also sells menswear such as Armani, Boss, Kenzo,
Versace, Ralph Lauren. *Dress Agency*

WINDSMOOR WAREHOUSE

WINDSMOOR HOUSE, 83 LAWRENCE ROAD,
TOTTENHAM, LONDON N15 4EP

☎ 0181-800 8022.

Regular sales are held here (usually four times a year) during which first quality fashion from the Windsmoor, Planet and Precis Petite ranges are sold at discounts of up to 75%. Sometimes, there is also Dannimac rainwear for men and women. Phone or write to be put on the mailing list. *Designer Sale*

ZEON

39 WATERLOO ROAD, LONDON NW2 7TT

☎ 0181-208 1833. PHONE BEFORE VISITING.

Zeon is the UK's largest timepiece importer. Brands include Zeon, Ingersoll, Elle, Head, Speedo and Wrangler. Zeon is also a specialist in children's and young people's watches and clocks such as Disney, Barbie, Action Man, Furby, Power Rangers, Spiece Girls, MTV, Cleopatra, Five and B*witched. The products on sale here include watches of all types, clocks and executive gifts. *Factory Shop*

Live Well On Less Tips

CHINA MATCH EARLS COMMON HOUSE, EARLS COMMON, HIMBLETON, NEAR DROITWICH, WORCESTERSHIRE WR9 7LD. (01905) 391520/391520 FAX. MAIL ORDER.

Would you like to add to your dinner or tea service or replace breakages, but find the pattern is no longer available? Or perhaps you want to buy a new service but need to sell on your old service first. China Match registers your requirements and checks them constantly against existing and incoming stock: they stock most English manufacturers and Noritake. There are no registration fees. The company buys stock daily and only supplies pieces in new or little used condition. Most customers are supplied with their requirements from stock, but in those instances where stock is not available, every effort is made to find your particular need as quickly as possible, although success cannot be guaranteed. Established since 1980, this company prides itself on its pro-active, personal service. China Match can be found on the internet on: chinamatch_uk@compuserve.com

Middlesex

WOMENSWEAR ONLY   Ocean, *Harrow*.   Session, *Brentford*.   Sevals, *Enfield*.

WOMENSWEAR & MENSWEAR   Damart, *Hounslow*.
Gordons Connections, *West Drayton*.
The Salvage Shop, *Burnt Oak*.

CHILDREN   Children's Party Hire, *Stanmore*.   Little Stars, *Hatch End*.   Sevals, *Enfield*.
The Salvage Shop, *Burnt Oak*.

HOUSEHOLD AND GIFTWARE   The Salvage Shop, *Burnt Oak*.
Wheelhouse Ltd, *Hounslow*.

ELECTRICAL EQUIPMENT   Stewart & Young, *Hampton Hill*.

DIY/RENOVATION   Dave's DIY, *Enfield*.   Eurotiles, *Rugby Road*.
Just Tiles, *Harrow*.   Peco, *Hampton*.

ARCHITECTURAL SALVAGE   Peco, *Hampton*.

FURNITURE/SOFT FURNISHINGS   Arthur Sanderson & Sons Ltd, *Uxbridge*.
Kenton Warehouse Superstore, *Kenton*.   The Curtain Mill, *Enfield*.

ARTHUR SANDERSON & SONS LTD
100 ACRES, SANDERSON ROAD, UXBRIDGE, MIDDLESEX UB8 1DH
☎ (01895) 238244.
This world-renowned furnishing house holds an annual sale, on one of the
May bank holidays, at its factory shop in Uxbridge of seconds and discontinued fabrics and accessories at reduced prices. Whatever time the sale starts, get
there at least an hour earlier as there is usually a queue. Phone at the end of
April to find out the date. *Designer Sale*

CHILDREN'S PARTY HIRE
STANMORE, MIDDLESEX HA7 1AN
☎ 0181-952 8130. PHONE FOR DETAILS.
Small tables and chairs for hire for children's parties. Examples of prices
invlude three tables and chairs, £7; six tables and 26 chairs, £12. also offers
small-scale adult party hire. *Hire Shop*

Live Well On Less Tips
A carpet with good quality underlay will reduce the amount of heat loss
through ground floors.

DAMART

63-67 HIGH STREET, HOUNSLOW, MIDDLESEX

☎ 0181- 570 6796. OPEN 9 - 5 MON - SAT.

Damart underwear and merchandise - anything from tights, socks and gloves to dresses, coats, cardigans and jumpers - some of which is current stock sold at full price, some discontinued and ends of lines sold at discount. There several shops selling some discounted stock from the Damart range, known as Damart Extra. *Factory Shop*

DAVE'S DIY

4 ENFIELD ROAD, ENFIELD, MIDDLESEX

☎ 0181-363 1680. OPEN 8.30 - 5 MON - FRI, UNTIL 7 TUE, 9 - 5 SAT.

Aimed at the trade, it will cater for members of the public who benefit from the discounts. Carries wallpaper brands from Kingfisher, Mayfair, Crown and Vymura, among others, from a range of 300 wallpaper books at discounts of up to 40%. Next day ordering for wallpapers. Also carries a large stock of paint, with a computerised mixing machine that offers thousands of combinations of colours. *Permanent Discount Outlet*

EUROTILES

UNIT 2C, TWICKENHAM TRADING ESTATE, RUGBY ROAD, MIDDLESEX TW1 1DG

☎ 0181-744 0088. OPEN 8 - 5 MON - FRI, 9 - 4 SAT, 11 - 3 SUN.

Opposite the main entrance to Twickenham Rugby Ground, this showroom displays tiles and some bathroom suites. There are regular changes of merchandise which are good deals. *Permanent Discount Outlet*

GORDONS CONNECTIONS

92-100 HIGH STREET, YEWSLEY, WEST DRAYTON, MIDDLESEX UB7 7DU

☎ (01895) 441846. OPEN 9 - 6 TUE, WED, THUR, SAT, 9 - 7 FRI.

Well-known high street brands including Marks & Spencer and Principles, at discounts of up to 70%. Rapid turnover of stock. *Permanent Discount Outlet*

JUST TILES

142 KENTON ROAD, HARROW, MIDDLESEX HA3 8BL

☎ 0181-907 3020. OPEN 9 - 5.30 MON - SAT, 10 - 4 SUN AND BANK HOLIDAYS, CLOSED WED.

Specialise in discount tiles for both floor and wall. Trends are towards larger tiles and design printing can be carried out in house. Very large selection, including many Continental tiles, all at competitive prices. *Permanent Discount Outlet*

Live Well On Less Tips
Serve foods in the dish in which they are cooked, when possible.

KENTON WAREHOUSE SUPERSTORE

2A CHARLTON ROAD, KENTON, MIDDLESEX HA3 9HF
☎ 0181-732 2525. OPEN 9 - 5.30 MON - SAT.
Carpet and bed warehouse which sells Sealy beds up to 30% off the recommended retail price; Relyon beds up to 35% off Recommended Retail Price; brand name carpets at what they claim are highly competitive prices, as well as carpet rolls, room size ends of rolls and remnants. Free delivery inside M25 area if you spend £250 *Permanent Discount Outlet*

LITTLE STARS

33 ROYSTON PARK ROAD, HATCH END, MIDDLESEX HA5 4AA
☎ 0181-537 0980. PHONE FIRST.
LITTLE STARS, 15 SYLVIA AVENUE, HATCH END, MIDDLESEX HA5 4OW
☎ 0181-621 4378. PHONE FIRST.

Part of the Baby Equipment Hirers Association (BEHA), which has more than 100 members countrywide. A range of equipment can be hired from high chairs, cots and travel cots to baby car seats and buggies. Some members also hire out party equipment including child-sized tables and chairs. They also sell branded and unbranded equipment competitively, price list available by phone request. BEHA run an advice line which will try and answer any queries you have regarding hiring services for children. Phone the Babyline on 0831 310355. *Hire Shop*

OCEAN

ST ANN'S ROAD, HARROW, MIDDLESEX
☎ 0181-861 3554. OPEN 9 - 6 MON - SAT, 7 ON THUR, 11 - 5 SUN.
Manufacturers of ladies fashion, they sell everydaywear at very cheap price: tops, £2.50; dresses £10; suits, £20; eveningwear from £20; skirts and trousers, £10 each. *Permanent Discount Outlet*

PECO

72 STATION ROAD, HAMPTON, MIDDLESEX TW12 2BT
☎ 0181-979 8310. FAX ☎ 0181-941 3319. OPEN 8.15 - 5.15 MON - SAT.
One of the largest door and fireplace warehouse in the country with two floors of display area and three additional shops featuring at least 600 fireplaces, 100 in marble and slate. Stocks about 2,000 period doors up to 1930s as well as oak beams. Wooden beds and pot stoves from France. Stained glass studio on site. Cast-iron fireplaces and marble restoration. *Architectural Salvage*

SESSION

GARDEN ROOM, SYON PARK, BRENTFORD, MIDDLESEX
☎ 0181-994 4983.

Designer sales run by fashion trade insider and featuring big-name British and international labels, all at discounted prices. There are usually about 8 sales per year, each one featuring a variety of different names which can't be mentioned here as the designers are very sensitive about their names being used in promoting discount sales. Membership costs £29.50 a year which also entitles you to other concessions, which were being put together as we went to press. Phone for more details. Also offers exclusive one-day showroom sales for members. *Designer Sale*

SEVALS

21 GARNAULT ROAD, ENFIELD, MIDDLESEX
☎ 0181-342 1988. OPEN 9 - 6 MON - SAT.
17 SILVER STREET, ENFIELD, MIDDLESEX
(☎ 0181 363 7059. OPEN 9 - 5.30 MON - SAT.

Warehouse at Garnault Road selling mostly women's clothes, with some children's; the Silver Street branch is a shop. Most are one-off samples or bankrupt stock of well-known brand names, although some of the labels are cut out. Discounts are about 20%. *Permanent Discount Outlet*

STEWART & YOUNG

30 & 105-107 HIGH STREET, HAMPTON HILL, MIDDLESEX TW12 1NJ
☎ 0181-979 1178. OPEN 9 - 5.30 MON - FRI, 9 - 4.30 SAT.

Sells domestic household goods as well as servicing them. As they belong to the Euronics group, the biggest buying group in Europe, prices match those of big stores. Where Stewart & Young have the edge is that they include delivery, installation to existing fitting and removal of any old machine in their price. The branch at 30 High Street specialises in cookers and refrigeration. *Permanent Discount Outlets*

THE CURTAIN MILL

13-19 LONDON ROAD, ENFIELD, MIDDLESEX EN2 6BS
☎ 0181-364 6515.

Huge choice of fabrics at really low prices - from £1.99p a metre and including excellent discounts on many designer labels. A large warehouse, it stocks Warwick Fabrics, Curtina and Swatchbox, among other leading names at discount prices. *Permanent Discount Outlet*

Live Well On Less Tips
Use stale bread to make breadcrumbs - store in the freezer.

THE SALVAGE SHOP

34-40 WATLING AVENUE, BURNT OAK, MIDDLESEX HA8 OLR

☎ 0181-952 4353. OPEN 9 - 5.30 MON - SAT, 10 - 4 SUN.

An Aladdin's cave of salvaged stock for the avid bargain hunter, most of which has been the subject of bankruptcy, insurance claims, fire or flood. Regular visitors have found anything from half-price Kenwood Chefs, typewriters and telephones to furniture, kitchen items and designer clothes. Yves St Laurent, Ungaro, MaxMara, Chloe, Agnes B and Mondi are just some the labels (though they are often cut out) to appear. Discounts range from 50%-75%. Phone first to check stock. ***Permanent Discount Outlet***

WHEELHOUSE LTD

9-21 BELL ROAD, HOUNSLOW, MIDDLESEX TW3 3NS

☎ 0181-570 3501. OPEN 9 - 6 MON - SAT, 10 - 4.30 SUN.

Sells all sorts of household goods (plates, cups, cutlery, Addis bins, tea towels etc), DIY, garden equipment (flowers, plants, lawn seed), everything to do with cars, etc. There is an extensive tool section on the upper floor - everything for the DIY enthusiast. You need to visit it regularly as items change each time, but it's very cheap with easy access and helpful staff. They buy in bulk and job lots of branded products, adding new lines every week. Plenty of car parking. ***Permanent Discount Outlet***

Live Well On Less Tips

MONEY £ACTS. (01603) 476476.

Very little in this life comes free and often saving money involves spending some first. This is true in the case of Money £acts, the guide to savings, investment and mortgage rates, guaranteed income bonds, national savings and annuities, which operates an update by fax. Whether you want to find out what the interest rates are on mortgages or where to open your savings account to get the best rates, you simply dial the relevant fax number and wait for the information to appear at your end. Commercial and residential mortgage information is updated daily, as is savings information. Cost is not more than 75p per minute.

Norfolk

WOMENSWEAR ONLY Alexon Sale Shop, *Great Yarmouth*. Essential Collection, *Norwich*.
Gladrags, *Watton*. Harpers And 73 Boutique, *Great Yarmouth*.

WOMENSWEAR & MENSWEAR Bally Outlet Store, *Norwich*.
East Quay Factory Shop, *Wells Next The Sea*. Jaeger Factory Shop, *King's Lynn*.
Lathams, *Great Yarmouth*. Matalan, *King's Lynn*. Matalan, *Great Yarmouth*.
Mr Shoe's Factory Shop, *Dereham*. Rombah Wallace Factory Shop, *Hingham*.
Roys Of Wroxham Ltd, *Norwich*. Roys Variety Store, *North Walsham*. Roys Variety Store, *Dereham*.
Roys Variety Store, *Thetford*. Roys Variety Store, *Norwich*. Start-Rite, *King's Lynn*.
The Factory Shop Ltd, *East Dereham*. The Factory Shop Ltd, *Harleston*.
The Factory Shop Ltd, *Snettisham*. Vandel Factory Shoe Shop, *Norwich*.

CHILDREN Bo Peep, *Wymondham*. Lathams, *Great Yarmouth*. Matalan, *King's Lynn*.
Matalan, *Great Yarmouth*. Mr Shoe's Factory Shop, *Dereham*.
Mrs Pickering's Dolls' Clothes, *Great Yarmouth*. Norwich Camping Sports And Leisure, *Norwich*.
Roys Of Wroxham Ltd, *Norwich*. Roys Variety Store, *North Walsham*. Roys Variety Store, *Norwich*.
Roys Variety Store, *Dereham*. Roys Variety Store, *Thetford*. Start-Rite, *King's Lynn*.
The Factory Shop Ltd, *East Dereham*. The Factory Shop Ltd, *Harleston*.
The Factory Shop Ltd, *Snettisham*.

HOUSEHOLD AND GIFTWARE Caithness Crystal, *King's Lynn*.
Lathams, *Great Yarmouth*. Matalan, *King's Lynn*. Matalan, *Great Yarmouth*. Spoils, *Norwich*.
The Factory Shop Ltd, *East Dereham*. The Factory Shop Ltd, *Harleston*.
The Factory Shop Ltd, *Snettisham*.

ELECTRICAL EQUIPMENT Secondhand Land, *Norwich*.

DIY/RENOVATION Aylesham Bath & Door Centre, *Aylesham*.
Tony Hodgson & Partners, *Nr King's Lynn*.

ARCHITECTURAL SALVAGE Tony Hodgson & Partners, *Nr King's Lynn*.

FURNITURE/SOFT FURNISHINGS *Including fabrics, curtains, beds, sofas, tables, chairs, carpets*
Sue Mebbrey Fabrics, *Nr King's Lynn* The Factory Shop Ltd, *East Dereham*.
The Factory Shop Ltd, *Harleston*. The Factory Shop Ltd, *Snettisham*.

FOOD AND LEISURE Booksale, *Norwich*. Cartwright & Butler, *Holt*.
Gilchrist Confectionery Ltd, *Fakenham*.

SPORTSWEAR AND EQUIPMENT Lathams, *Great Yarmouth*.
Norwich Camping Sports And Leisure, *Norwich*.

ALEXON SALE SHOP

THEATRE PLAIN, GREAT YARMOUTH, NORFOLK
☎ (01493) 332146. OPEN 9 - 5.30 MON - SAT.
Alexon and Eastex from last season at 40% less than the original price; during
sale time in January and June, the reductions are as much as 70%. Stock
includes separates, skirts, jackets, blouses; there is no underwear or night
clothes. ***Permanent Discount Outlet***

AYLSHAM BATH & DOOR CENTRE

BURGH ROAD, AYLESHAM, NORFOLK NR11 6AR

☎ (01263) 735396. OPEN 8.30 - 5 MON - FRI, 9 - 5 SAT, 10 - 4 SUN.

Bathroom equipment, kitchen displays, all at reduced prices of at least 20%-25% less than normal retail prices. Top brands such as Dalton, Ideal Standard, Armitage, Shires and Shanks are some of the 70 bathrooms displayed here; and there are 30 display kitchens with appliances by Neff, Philips, Whirlpool and Zanussi. *Permanent Discount Outlet*

BALLY OUTLET STORE

HALL ROAD, NORWICH, NORFOLK NR4 6DP

☎ (01603) 226040. OPEN 9.30 - 5.30 MON - FRI, 9 - 5.30 SAT, 11 - 5 SUN AND MOST BANK HOLIDAYS. PHONE FIRST.

The Bally Outlet Store is located on the outskirts of Norwich, and sells women's and men's footwear, handbags, and accessories. Other items are also available such as socks, scarves, silk ties, shoe horns and shoe care products. Most of the merchandise is ex-sale, reject or substandard and is priced from £5-£400. A saving of at least one-third off the recommended retail price can usually be made. Also on the same site is a coffee shop which serves morning coffee, light lunches and afternoon teas in a pleasant and relaxing atmosphere. Toilet facilities and ample free parking are available. Coach parties are welcome by prior arrangement. *Factory Shop*

BO PEEP

28 ETHEL GOOCH ROAD, WYMONDHAM, NORFOLK NR18 0LH

☎ (01953) 608494.

Part of the Baby Equipment Hirers Association (BEHA), which has more than 100 members countrywide. BEHA run an advice line which will try and answer any queries you have regarding hiring services for children. Phone the Babyline on 0831 310355. *Hire Shop*

BOOKSALE

31 GENTLEMANS WALK, NORWICH, NORFOLK

☎ (01603) 667209. OPEN 9 - 6 MON - SAT, 8 ON THUR, 10 - 4 SUN.

Founded 15 years ago, Booksale now boasts more than 100 shops throughout the UK. It sells books, stationery, paints, tapes, videos, all at enormously discounted prices. Paperbacks from 99p, hardbacks, £2.99; story tapes, £1.99; children's books, 75p; videos 99p - £2.99; prints in clip frames, 99p - £19.95; posters, £1.50 - £6.99, and classical CDs from £2.99. *Permanent Discount Outlet*

Live Well On Less Tips
Cook complete meals in a steamer.

Live Well On Less Tips
Be vigilant - watch the shelf strips in Supermarkets even if you don't intend to buy the product that week. There may be a special promotion on that is only advertised at point of sale.

CAITHNESS CRYSTAL

11 PAXMAN ROAD, HARDWICK INDUSTRIAL ESTATE, KINGS LYNN, NORFOLK PE30 4NE
☎ (01553) 765111. OPEN 9 - 5 MON - SAT, 10.30 - 4.30 SUN.
Well stocked factory shop with many bargains all year round in glass and crystal, giftware and tableware. Also selection of Royal Doulton products and other great gift ideas to choose from. *Factory Shop*

CARTWRIGHT & BUTLER

HEMPSTEAD ROAD INDUSTRIAL ESTATE, HOLT, NORFOLK NR25 6EC
☎ (01263) 711447. OPEN 9 - 5 MON - SAT, 10 - 4 SUN.
Sells overstocks of the full range of famous Cartwright & Butler foods: preserves, pickles, chutneys, marmalades, biscuits, seasonings and spices. Also sells over-runs of own-label product which is packaged for the high street major stores. Specialises in unique and original gifts by producing hampers and baskets in a whole range of gifts to eat. *Food and Drink Discounter*

EAST QUAY FACTORY SHOP

6 STATION ROAD, CORNER OF BUTTLANDS, WELLS NEXT THE SEA, NORFOLK NR23 1AE
☎ (01328) 710308. OPEN 10 - 6 SEVEN DAYS A WEEK IN SUMMER, 10.30 - 5.30 MON - SAT, 10 - 4.30 SUN, IN WINTER. MAIL ORDER.
Men's, ladies' and children's natural fibre knitwear at prices from £20 - £70 which are either agents' samples or knitted out from the left over yarn from a production run. All are perfects. Also on sale are current lines at full price. Children's knitwear from £16. *Factory Shop*

ESSENTIAL COLLECTION

63 SUSSEX STREET, NORWICH, NORFOLK
☎ (0421) 391909. OPEN 10 - 4 MON - SAT.
Two-storey shop just out of the city centre with a marble entrance and staircase. It specialises in bridal wear, mother of the bride, evening wear and ballgowns, plus a good selection of casual daywear. Labels range from high street to designer: Frank Usher, Jacques Vert, Mark Angelo, Bianca, Wallis, Next, M&S, Monsoon as well as some one-off samples and large sizes. There is a large selection of shoes, bags, belts, scarves and jewellery. A special room is set aside with hundreds of fancy dress costumes, and there is a hat hire and seamstress service available. *Dress Agency*

GILCHRIST CONFECTIONERY LTD

UNITS 1 & 2, OXBOROUGH LANE, FAKENHAM, NORFOLK NR21 8AF

☎ (01328) 862632. OPEN 8 .30 - 4.30 MON - WED, 7.30 - 4.30 THUR, 8.30 - 4 FRI, 9 - 12 SAT

Factory shop underneath the offices sells all sorts of chocolate items - walnut whips, petit fours, mints, Thomas the Tank Engine chocolates, Christmas chocolate tree decorations - to well-known department stores. Seconds and misshapes are sold in bags for £1; overmakes at half price. Stock varies from week to week. *Food and Drink Discounter*

GLADRAGS

THE BARN, HUNTS FARM, HILLS ROAD, SAHAM TONEY, WATTON, NORFOLK

☎ (01953) 885210. OPEN 10 - 4 TUE - THUR AND SAT.

Sells women's new and nearly-new outfits, including ballgowns. Accessories also on sale range from hats and bags to shoes and belts. *Dress Agency*

HARPERS AND 73 BOUTIQUE

73 ST NICHOLAS ROAD, GREAT YARMOUTH, NORFOLK NR30 1NN

☎ (01493) 855614 OPEN 9.30 - 5 DAILY, CLOSED 4 THUR & SAT.

Designer labels at drastically reduced prices. Occasionally, clothes from High Street retailers such as Wallis can be found. Mostly current fashions and designer labels from £10 - £200. Good range of hats, shoes, costume jewellery and handbags and accessories range in price from £10-£20. Many of the items are brand new. *Dress Agency*

JAEGER FACTORY SHOP

1 HANSA ROAD, KING'S LYNN, NORFOLK PE30 4HZ

☎ (01553) 732132. OPEN 9 - 5.30 MON - SAT, 11 - 4 SUN.

Contemporary classics from Jaeger at excellent prices. Most of the merchandise is previous seasons' stock, but you might also find some special makes. The King's Lynn shop stocks tailoring and knitwear for women and men. *Factory Shop*

LATHAMS

BRIDGE STREET, POTTER HEIGHAM, GREAT YARMOUTH, NORFOLK NR29 5JE

☎ (01692) 670080. OPEN 9 - 5.30 MON - SAT, 10 - 4 SUN.

Sell a wide range of fashions, hardware, china, fishing tackle, books, gardening equipment, linen, groceries and Christmas gifts at very reasonable prices. Most of the makes are high street labels and consist of discontinued lines and seconds. Also jewellery concessions, shoes, photo developing and in-store coffee shop. *Factory Shop*

MATALAN

BLACKFRIARS ROAD, KINGS LYNN, NORFOLK PE30 1RX

☎ (01553) 765696. OPEN 10 - 8 MON - FRI, 9 - 6 SAT, 11 - 5 SUN.

SOUTHTOWN ROAD, GREAT YARMOUTH NR31 OJB

☎ (01493) 444734. OPEN 9 - 8 MON - FRI, 9 - 6, 11 - 5 SUN.

Matalan is a fashion and homewares shop giving customers what they claim to be unbeatable value for money with huge savings on a wide range of products including high quality fashionable clothing for women, women and children at up to 50% off high street prices. Matalan is situated out of town and stores are open seven days a week. *Permanent Discount Outlet*

MR SHOE'S FACTORY SHOP

YAXHAM ROAD, DEREHAM, NORFOLK NR1Q 1HD

☎ (01362) 699599. OPEN 9 - 6 MON - SAT, 10.30 - 4.30 SUN.

Shoes for all the family at discounted prices. *Permanent Discount Outlet*

MRS PICKERING'S DOLLS' CLOTHES

THE PINES, DECOY ROAD, POTTER HEIGHAM, GREAT YARMOUTH, NORFOLK NR29 5LX

☎ (01692) 670407. MAIL ORDER.

A wide selection of well-made dolls' clothes which are easy to put on and take off and, especially for smaller children, will help them learn to use various methods of fastening. All the popular dolls are catered for including Tiny Tears, Timmy, Baby Born, Katie, Action Man, Sindy, Paul, Barbie, Ken, Skipper, Stacie and Shelly as well as Teddies. Special outfits, such as school uniforms to match the child's, can be made on request. Prices range from 40p for a Barbie-sized skirt and £1.25 for a nappy to £2.25 for a Tiny Tears-sized dress and £3 for a wedding dress. Please send a stamped, self-addressed envelope for a catalogue and mention The Good Deal Directory. Website: http://freespace.virgin.net/dolls,clothes/index.html. *Permanent Discount Outlet*

NORWICH CAMPING SPORTS AND LEISURE

54-56 MAGDALEN STREET, NORWICH, NORFOLK NR3 1JE

☎ (01603) 615525. OPEN 9 - 5.45 MON - SAT.

Reductions of up to 50% on skiing jackets, one-pieces and salopettes all year round. This includes brand names such as Berghaus, O'Neill and Quicksilver, in children's sizes too. Also many ends of lines and last year's colours in fleeces, cagoules and waterproofs, as well as some reductions on ski boots and tents. *Permanent Discount Outlet*

ROMBAH WALLACE FACTORY SHOP

14-17 IRONSIDE WAY, NORWICH ROAD, HINGHAM, NORFOLK NR9 4LF
☎ (01953) 851106. OPEN 9 - 5 MON - SAT, 10 - 4 SUN.
Good selection of shoes for women and men at discount (ladies courts from
£19.95 - £65). Sandals, court shoes, smart or casual. Rombah Wallace shoes
are on sale at discounts of 30%. Also sells shirts, ties, handbags and jewellery
at competitive prices. *Factory Shop*

ROYS OF WROXHAM LTD

WROXHAM, NORWICH, NORFOLK NR12 8DB
☎ (01603) 782131. OPEN 9 - 5.30 MON, TUE, 9 - 8 WED, THUR, FRI, 9 - 6
SAT, 10.30 - 4.30 SUN.
10 YARMOUTH ROAD, NORTH WALSHAM, NORFOLK NR28 9BW
☎ (01692) 501058. OPEN 9 - 5.30 MON, TUE, 9 - 8 WED, THUR, FRI, 9 - 6
SAT, 10.30 - 4.30 SUN.
90-96 MAGDALEN STREET, NORWICH, NORFOLK NR3 1JF
☎ (01603) 761696. OPEN 9 - 5.30 MON, TUE, 9 - 8 WED, THUR, FRI, 9 - 6
SAT, 10.30 - 4.30 SUN.
YAXHAM ROAD, DEREHAM NR19 1HD
☎ (01362) 690555. OPEN 9 - 5.30 MON, TUE, 9 - 8 WED, THUR, FRI, 9 - 6
SAT, 10.30 - 4.30 SUN.
GOODALL STREET, THETFORD, NORFOLK IP24 2DP
☎ (01842) 766161. OPEN 9 - 5.30 MON, TUE, 9 - 8 WED, THUR, FRI, 9 - 6
SAT, 10.30 - 4.30 SUN.
GREAT EASTERN ROAD, SUDBURY, SUFFOLK CO10 6TJ
☎ (01787) 882800. OPEN 9 - 5.30 MON, TUE, 9 - 8 WED, THUR, FRI, 9 - 6
SAT, 10.30 - 4.30 SUN.
Reputed to be the largest village shops in the world, they sell branded house-
hold goods at what they call valued prices . The Save 'N Wear Department
deals with the cheaper end of the clothing market for men, women and children. Other departments include DIY, gardening, electrical, housewares and
gifts. There is also a pharmacy department that deals with photography,
records and toiletries, all at competitive prices, and a large food hall.
Permanent Discount Outlet

SECONDHAND LAND

113-117 MAGDALEN STREET, NORWICH, NORFOLK NR3 1LN
☎ (01603) 611922. OPEN 9 - 6 MON - SAT.
Sells tvs, videos, computers, hi-fi systems, recording equipment - all of which
are, as the name suggests, second-hand. Some are reconditioned, all come with
a six or twelve month gaurantee. A two-year-old 26-inch standard tv set with
remote control and Teletext costs between £125-£175. Also sells household
furniture and white goods. For example, reconditioned washing machine with
a 3-month guarantee, £100. Free local delivery. *Secondhand Shop*

Live Well On Less Tips
POWER PLUS DIRECT. (0700) 234 0700. MAIL ORDER ONLY.
If you're looking for a washing machine, fridge, freezer, tumble dryer, television set, hi-fi or camcorder, shop around, find the product you want and make a note of the product code. Then phone Power Plus Direct and they will usually beat the best price you have found. They can deliver countrywide, but there is a charge.

SPOILS

UNIT LS2, CASTLE MALL, ST JOHN'S WALK, NORWICH, NORFOLK NR1 3DD
☎ (01603) 762052. OPEN 9 - 5.30 MON - FRI, UNTIL 8 ON THUR, 9 - 6 SAT.
General domestic glassware, non-stick bakeware, kitchen gadgets, ceramic oven-to-tableware, textiles, cutting boards, aluminium non-stick cookware, bakeware, plastic kitchenware, plastic storage, woodware, coffee pots/makers, furniture, mirrors and picture frames. Rather than being discounted, all the merchandise is very competitively priced - in fact, the company carry out competitors' checks frequently in order to monitor pricing. With 38 branches, the company is able to buy in bulk and thus negotiate very good prices.
Permanent Discount Outlet

START-RITE

8 HIGH STREET, KING'S LYNN, NORFOLK P30 1BX
☎ (01553) 760786. OPEN 9 - 5.30 MON - SAT.
The children's shoe experts have a large factory shop selling clearance lines at discounts of one third, and rejects at discounts of 50%. They don't stock the full range - it's a matter of choosing from what's available. Rejects are sold at at least half price; end of sales stock with not quite such a high discount. There are also some senior sizes up to 9. *Factory Shop*

SUE MEBBREY FABRICS

4 POST OFFICE ROAD, DERSINGHAM, NEAR KING'S LYNN, NORFOLK PE31 6HP
☎ (01485) 541111. OPEN 9 - 5 TUE - SAT.
Sells curtain and upholstery fabrics, with a good selection of top brands, at discount prices. There is a full making-up service for curtains, blinds, valances, cushions and loose covers. Names include Crowsons, Blendworth, A & R Swaffer, Warwick, Harlequin and Fibre Naturelle. The most expensive fabric in this shop costs £17.95 a metre. *Permanent Discount Outlet*

THE FACTORY SHOP LTD

NORWICH STREET, EAST DEREHAM, NORFOLK NR19 1AD
☎ (01362) 691868. OPEN 9 - 5.30 MON - SAT, 10 - 4 SUN.
52 LONDON ROAD, HARLESTON, NORFOLK IP20 9BZ
☎ (01379) 854860. OPEN 9 - 5.30 MON - SAT, 10.30 - 4.30 SUN.
LYNN ROAD, SNETTISHAM, NORFOLK PE31 7QG
☎ (01485) 544441. OPEN 9 - 5.30 MON - SAT, 10 - 4 SUN.

Wide range on sale includes men's, ladies and children's clothing and footwear; household textiles; toiletries; hardware; luggage; lighting and bedding, most of which are chainstore and high street brands at discounts of approximately 30%-50%. There are kitchen and furniture displays and on sale is the Cape Country Furniture range with free-standing kitchens, as well as living, bedroom and dining furniture. There are weekly deliveries and brands include many major stars such as Adidas, Nike, Wrangler and Dartington, to name just a few. Lines are continually changing and few factory shops offer such a variety under one roof. This branch has food and drink facilities. *Factory Shop*

TONY HODGSON & PARTNERS

THE FORGE, 2 WESLEY ROAD, TERRINGTON ST CLEMENT, NR KING'S LYNN, NORFOLK PE34 4NG
☎ (01553) 828637. OPEN 8 - 5 MON - FRI, WEEKENDS BY APPOINTMENT.

Hand-forged wrought iron work, including restoration. Anything from fenders and fire irons to finials and gates. *Architectural Salvage*

VANDEL FACTORY SHOE SHOP

DRAYTON ROAD, NORWICH, NORFOLK NR3 2DB
☎ (01603) 493185. OPEN 10 - 4 MON - SAT.

Leather shoes for men and women, all of which are discounted by at least one third. The men's shoes are perfects while the women's selection includes some slight seconds and ends of ranges. Vandel Shoes are known for their wide fit, while the shop also sells Holmes shoes which are known for their narrow (double A) fit. A bonus scheme operates whereby if you buy five pairs of shoes in one year, you get an extra £10 discount off your sixth pair. *Factory Shop*

Live Well On Less Tips
When you're in the mood, prepare ahead casseroles and soups in quantitiy and freeze them in portions just big enough for one meal. When you don't feel like cooking after a hard day, instead of dialling the local take-away, you can just retrieve one of these from the freezer.

Northamptonshire

WOMENSWEAR ONLY Belle Of The Ball, *Kettering.*
Finedon Dress Agency, *Finedon. (Off A6)* Jane's Designer Evening Wear, *Northampton.*
Occasions, *Higham Ferrers.* Orchids, *Northampton.*
Rigby & Peller & Fantasie Factory Shop, *Desborough.*

MENSWEAR ONLY Ian M Roberts Ltd, *Kettering.*

WOMENSWEAR & MENSWEAR   Barker Shoes Ltd, *Northampton.*
Barratt's Sale Shop, *Northampton.* Big L Factory Outlet, *Northampton.* Matalan, *Northampton.*
Matalan, *Corby.* Northampton Footwear Distributors Ltd, *Moulton Park.*
Regent Belt Company, *Buckby.* T Groocock & Co Ltd, *Rothwell.* The Doc Shop, *Irthlingborough.*

CHILDREN Barratt's Sale Shop, *Northampton.* Matalan, *Northampton.* Matalan, *Corby.*
Orchids, *Northampton.* The Doc Shop, *Irthlingborough.*

HOUSEHOLD AND GIFTWARE Matalan, *Northampton.* Matalan, *Corby.*
Stuart Buglass Interior Design Ironwork, *Little Houghton.*

DIY/RENOVATION Architectural Heritage, *Nr Weedon.* Bathcraft, *Kettering.*

ARCHITECTURAL SALVAGE Architectural Heritage, *Nr Weedon.* Bathcraft, *Kettering.*

FURNITURE/SOFT FURNISHINGS Showhome Warehouse, *Rushden.*
Stuart Buglass Interior Design Ironwork, *Little Houghton.*

ARCHITECTURAL HERITAGE

HEART OF THE SHIRES, A5, NR WEEDON, NORTHAMPTONSHIRE
NN7 4LB
☎ (01327) 349249. OPEN 10 - 5 TUE - FRI.
Situated in converted farm buildings dealing in architectural antiques and
reclamation - everything from a belltower to a doorknob. Also bespoke furniture, antiques, stoves, bathroom suites and re-enamelling. There is a tea room
and gift shop on site, and a shop selling cookware. On A5, two miles north of
Weedon. *Architectural Salvage*

BARKER SHOES LTD

STATION ROAD, EARLS BARTON, NORTHAMPTON,
NORTHAMPTONSHIRE NN6 0NT
☎ (01604) 810387. OPEN 10 - 5 MON - FRI, 10 - 4 SAT, SUN.
Discontinued lines of shoes at about 30% off the retail price, and rejects at
40% off the normal retail price. Sells shoes manufactured by its own factory
which include brogues, smart day shoes for men and women, but no trainers.
There are men's high grade, traditional shoes which sell to top stores, casual
shoes and moccasins. *Factory Shop*

Live Well On Less Tips
Don't go shopping every week on the same day. Delay it by one day each week so that you're extending your shopping cycle so that instead of making 52 trips to the supermarket a year, you make 44.

BARRATT'S SALE SHOP
BARRACK ROAD, KINGSTHORPE HOLLOW, NORTHAMPTON,
NORTHAMPTONSHIRE NN2 6EL
☎ (01604) 718632. OPEN 9 - 5.30 MON - SAT.
Reject trainers and ex-window display shoes for men, women and children at factory prices among a range of perfect shoes, the latter of which are sold at sale prices. Discounts of up to at least 50% compared to normal retail prices.
Factory Shop

BATHCRAFT
4A HAVELOCK STREET, KETTERING,
NORTHAMPTONSHIRE NN16 9PZ
☎ (01536) 417009. OPEN 10 - 5.30 WED - SAT.
Old fashioned rolltop baths, taps, bath fittings, reproduction shower roses, re-enamelling. *Architectural Salvage*

BELLE OF THE BALL
42 LONDON ROAD, KETTERING, NORTHAMPTONSHIRE NN15 7QA
☎ (01536) 484949. OPEN 10 - 4 TUE - SAT.
Sells both new and secondhand clothes for women, as well as wedding dresses. Only famous name labels are stocked, from Windsmoor, Jaeger, Berkertex and Bellino to Betty Barclay, Mondi and Jacques Vert. For example, Tom Bowker three-piece suit suitable for a mother of the bride, £199, normal retail price, £499. There are usually about 1,000 outfits from which to choose including a wide range of hats. Wedding dresses include Ronald Joyce, Hilary Morgan and Dante, with head-dresses, veils and shoes. *Dress Agency*

BIG L FACTORY OUTLET
34 COMMERCIAL STREET, NORTHAMPTON,
NORTHAMPTONSHIRE NN1 1PJ
☎ (01604) 603022. OPEN 10 - 6 MON - FRI, 9 - 6 SAT, 10.30 - 4.30 SUN.
This store retails a large range of Levi jeans, shirts, jackets, sweatshirts and t-shirts, all at discounted prices. Most of the stock is seconds or end-of-line.
Factory Shop

FINEDON DRESS AGENCY

23 HIGH STREET, FINEDON, (OFF A6), NORTHAMPTONSHIRE
NN9 5JN

☎ (01933) 680080. FAX ☎ (01933) 680714. OPEN 10 - 5 MON - SAT.

Pretty shop which specialises in good quality bridal wear and brides mothers outfits, hats, smart guest wear and evening wear in sizes 8-24. Wedding dress designers include Ronald Joyce, Margaret Lee, Benjamin Roberts, Hilary Morgan, Sally Bee, Brides of Paradise and Angelo Dreammaker in sizes 8-30. Prices range form £75-£800. Also veils, headdresses, flowers and shoes, all beautifully presented and an enormous range of hats from £25-£150. Other outfits include designers such as Coterie, Hardob, and Condici up to size 24 and priced from £55-£500. There are lots of samples at good prices and lots of larger sizes. *Dress Agency*

IAN M ROBERTS LTD

57-75 ST PETER'S AVENUE, KETTERING, NORTHAMPTONSHIRE
NN16 OEL

☎ (01536) 518846. OPEN 12.30 - 4.30 TUE - FRI, 10 - 4 SAT.

Suits for all occasions: lounge suits, morning suits, dinner suits, jackets, blazers, both single and double breasted, and trousers at factory shop prices - reduced by up to 50%. Stocks up to size 58. *Factory Shop*

JANE'S DESIGNER EVENING WEAR

69 ST LEONARD'S ROAD, NORTHAMPTON, NORTHAMPTONSHIRE
NN4 8DL

☎ (01604) 705256. OPEN 11 - 2 MON - SAT OR BY APPOINTMENT.

Hire or buy evening wear from names such as House of Nicholas, Roots, Cinderella and Consortium at a cost of £40-£55 for up to six days. There are usually rails of ex-hire for sale at bargain prices as well as brand-new merchandise at competitive prices. *Hire Shop*

MATALAN

UNIT 1, WEEDON ROAD INDUSTRIAL ESTATE, TYNE ROAD,
NORTHAMPTON, NORTHAMPTONSHIRE NN5 5BE

☎ (01604) 589119. OPEN 10 - 8 MON - FRI, 9 - 6 SAT, 11 - 5 SUN.

UNIT 1, PHOENIX RETAIL PARK, PHEONIX PARKWAY, CORBY,
NORTHAMPTONSHIRE NN17 5DT

☎ (01536) 408042. OPEN 10 - 8 MON - FRI, 9 - 6 SAT, 10 - 4 SUN.

Matalan is a fashion and homewares shop giving customers what they claim to be unbeatable value for money with huge savings on a wide range of products including high quality fashionable clothing for women, women and children at up to 50% off high street prices. Matalan is situated out of town and stores are open seven days a week all year round. *Permanent Discount Outlet*

NORTHAMPTON
FOOTWEAR DISTRIBUTORS LTD

SUMMERHOUSE ROAD, MOULTON PARK, NORTHAMPTONSHIRE
NN3 1WD

☎ (01604) 790 827. OPEN 9 - 12 AND 2 - 4 MON - FRI FOR PHONE
ENQUIRIES. MAIL ORDER.

Direct mail clearance brochures featuring a wide range of footwear at incredible prices. There is no minimum order, although there is p & p for orders under £175. Size ranges are limited, but not overly so. If they don't fit you get your money refunded if returned within 10 days. *Permanent Discount Outlet*

OCCASIONS

9A HIGH STREET, HIGHAM FERRERS, NORTHAMPTONSHIRE
NN10 8BW

☎ (01933) 314970. OPEN 10 - 2 TUE, 10 - 4 WED - SAT.

Small, friendly shop selling names from BhS and Marks & Spencer to Betty Barclay, Givenchy and Jacques Vert. Good selection of bridal wear and mother of the bride outfits, as well as evening wear. Seamstress service available. *Dress Agency*

ORCHIDS

3 PARK STREET, TOWCESTER, NORTHAMPTON NH12 6DQ

☎ (01327) 358455. OPEN 9.30 - 5 MON - SAT, AND 7 - 8 WED EVENING.

Sells women's and children's new and as-new clothes. The ladies wear includes a range of good quality accessories: belts, tights and stockings, socks, scarves, costume jewellery and hair accessories. Labels sold include Marks & Spencer, Jaeger, Betty Barclay, Mondi and Alexon. Nothing is more than two years old and sizes range from 8-20. Occasionally, there are free open sessions with a colour consultant who will help to co-ordinate your wardrobe. The children's range is from birth to twelve years, with more girl's outfits than boy's, and includes snowsuits and coats, with labels from Marks & Spencer, Mothercare and Gap to Osh Kosh and Oilily. *Dress Agency*

REGENT BELT COMPANY

88, STATION ROAD, LONG BUCKBY, NORTHAMPTONSHIRE NN6 7QB

☎ (01327) 842434. OPEN 12.30 - 3.30 THUR, FRI, 10 - 2 SAT.

Leather belts, bags, luggage, hip flasks, wallets, purses, key fobs, ties and braces all at substantially reduced prices. Station Road is the main road through the village of Long Buckby, so called because it is the longest village in England. Bi-annual clearance sales offer even better value with leather belts from £5. *Factory Shop*

RIGBY & PELLER & FANTASIE FACTORY SHOP

ROTHWELL ROAD, DESBOROUGH NORTHAMPTONSHIRE

☎ (01536) 761252. OEN 10 - 4 TUE - FRI, 9 - 1 SAT.

Range of Fantasie swimwear and Rigby & Peller underwear including bras, pants, thongs, suspender belts at discounted prices. Specialises in larger cup sizes up to H cup fitting. For example Fantasie swimsuit, £15.99, usually £55; matching pareo, £15.99, usually £50. Some of the stock is made up of seconds but most is perfect, redundant stock. *Factory Shop*

SHOWHOME WAREHOUSE

12-17 FRANCIS COURT, WELLINGBOROUGH ROAD, RUSHDEN, NORTHAMPTONSHIRE, NN10 6AY

☎ (01933) 411695. OPEN 12 - 5 TUE - FRI, 10 - 5 SAT, SUN.

Weekly warehouse clearance of the contents of quality show homes via either auctions or warehouse clearance. The contents of the show houses are sold either at auction countrywide on Sundays or at this Showhome Warehouse, recently extended to 10,000 ft, on weekdays at prices which are claimed to be the average achieved at the last auction. These normally average between 50%-70% savings on the prices seen in the stores. About 50% of their stock is sold each week and different stock arrives daily. Buy a range of kitchen appliances, lounge furniture, three-piece suites, dining tables and chairs, rugs, study and bedroom furniture, oil paintings, mirrors, ornaments, TVs and videos, patio and garden furniture and gym equipment. The range is eclectic: from suits of armour to lion's heads, Tiffany lampshades to leather zebras, handpainted furniture to mahogany classics, alien-shaped CD racks to antique carts made into bookcases or sets of oars turned into coat racks. Prices exclude VAT and 10% auction commission but still represent very good value for money. For example, elaborate metal bed, £175, normally £750; dining room table and chairs, £350, normally £1,500; washer-dryer, £300, usually £500-600. *Permanent Discount Outlet*

Live Well On Less Tips

Use coupons. When you are unpacking in the kitchen, always check the backs of packets for "money off next purchase" coupons. Cut the coupon out then rather than when you have finished with the item and may throw it straight into the bin, having forgotten about it.

Live Well On Less Tips
TOLL-FREE US DIRECTORY, 00 1 800 555 1212.
If you want to buy goods from US mail order catalogues, where many of them are considerably cheaper than the British equivalent, despite the postage and duty, ring this number and they will give you the toll-free number for the particular catalogue company you are seeking. Toll-free numbers in the US and Canada cost the price of an international phone call, and you have to know the name of the company for which you are searching.

STUART BUGLASS
INTERIOR DESIGN IRONWORK

THE BUGLASS METALWORK GALLERY, CLIFFORD MILL HOUSE, LITTLE HOUGHTON, NORTHAMPTONSHIRE NN7 1AL
☎ (01604) 890366. OPEN 10 - 5 WED-SAT, 11 - 4 SUN.
26 REGENT STREET, LEAMINGTON SPA, WARWICKSHIRE CV 32 5EH
☎ (01926) 426900. OPEN 10 - 5 TUES - SAT.
Hand-crafted interior design wrought-iron work from candleholders, wine racks, electric lighting (including wall sconces and chandeliers) to curtain poles, and furniture including beds, tables, chairs and shelving, are all on sale in this converted barn at direct-to-the-public prices. The showroom was extended in 1998 and is now twice the size. There is now a high street outlet in Leamington Spa. *Factory Shop*

T GROOCOCK & CO LTD

GORDON STREET, ROTHWELL, NORTHAMPTONSHIRE NN14 6BJ
☎ (01536) 714115. OPEN 10 - 5 MON - FRI, 9 - 1 SAT.
New 3000 sq ft shop selling high quality men's and women's leather shoes. Padders and other brands stocked. Comfortable, stylish leisure walking shoes: women's sizes 3-9, men's sizes 6-14. Easy access for wheelchairs. Credit cards accepted. *Factory Shop*

THE DOC SHOP

RUSHDEN & DIAMONDS FOOTBALL CLUB, NENE PARK, STATION ROAD, IRTHLINGBOROUGH, NORTHAMPTONSHIRE NN9 5QF
☎ (01933) 652000. OPEN 9 - 5.30 MON - FRI, 9 - 5 SAT, 10 - 4 SUN.
BARN WAY, LODGE FARM INDUSTRIAL ESTATE, NORTHAMPTON
☎ (01604) 591174. OPEN 9 - 5.30 MON - FRI, 9 - 5 SAT, 10 - 4 SUN.
71 HIGH STREET, WOLLASTON, NORTHAMPTONSHIRE
☎ (01993) 666144. OPEN 9 - 5.30 MON - FRI, 9 - 5 SAT, 11 - 4 SUN.
Sells Doc Martens footwear, Mitre football boots, as well as clothing such as Umbro and a vast range of accessories, at discounted prices. For example, children's shoes and boots at £15. Nene Park is the only official outlet for Rushden & Diamonds merchandise. *Permanent Discount Outlet*

Northumberland

WOMENSWEAR ONLY   Bairdwear Ladieswear, *Haughton La Spring.*
Claremont Garments, *Blyth.*   Gladrags, *Alnwick.*   Jane Shilton, *North Shields.*
Margaret Williams Dress Agency, *Whitburn.*   Penny Plain, *Newcastle Upon Tyne.*

MENSWEAR ONLY   James Barry Menswear, *Newcastle Upon Tyne.*
Slaters Menswear, *Tyne & Wear.*   Tom Sayers Clothing Co, *Tyne & Wear.*

WOMENSWEAR & MENSWEAR   Attica, *Newcastle Upon Tyne.*   Burberry, *Blyth.*
Claremont Garments, *Blyth.*   Colours, *Newcastle.*   Dewhirst Clothing Factory Shop, *Sunderland.*
Dewhirst Clothing Factory Shop, *Ashington.*   Dewhirst Impressions Clothing Factory Shop, *Ashington.*
Discount Clothing Store, *Kingston Park.*   J Barbour & Sons Ltd, *Jarrow.*   Joe Bloggs, *North Shields.*
Mexx International, *Newcastle Upon Tyne. (Near A19)*
Royal Quays Factory Outlet Centre, *Newcastle Upon Tyne. (Near A19)*
Second Time Around, *Berwick Upon Tweed.*   Shark Group, *Morpeth.*
The Factory Shop, *Houghton Le Spring.*   TK Maxx, *Tyne & Wear.*   TK Maxx, *Newcastle*
Tog 24, *Tyne & Wear*   Tog 24, *Newcastle*   Tynedale Park, *Hexham*

CHILDREN   Burberry, *Blyth.*   Dewhirst Clothing Factory Shop, *Sunderland.*
Dewhirst Clothing Factory Shop, *Ashington.*   Dewhirst Impressions Clothing Factory Shop, *Ashington.*
Discount Clothing Store, *Kingston Park.*   J Barbour & Sons Ltd, *Jarrow.*
Joe Bloggs, *North Shields.*   Mexx International, *Newcastle Upon Tyne.*
Royal Quays Factory Outlet Centre, *Newcastle Upon Tyne.*   Shark Group, *Morpeth.*
Silvia Jeffery Ltd, *Blyth.*   The Factory Shop, *Houghton Le Spring.*   TK Maxx, *Tyne & Wear.*
TK Maxx, *Newcastle.*   Tog 24, *Tyne & Wear.*   Tog 24, *Newcastle.*
Toyworld Factory Outlets Ltd, *Newcastle Upon Tyne Marina.*

HOUSEHOLD AND GIFTWARE   Bardon Mill Pottery, *Hexham.*   Birthdays, *North Shields.*
Cramlington Textiles, *Cramlington.*   Ponden Mill Linens, *North Shields.*
Royal Quays Factory Outlet Centre, *Newcastle Upon Tyne (Near A19).*
Spoils, *Tyne & Wear.*   TK Maxx, *Tyne & Wear.*   TK Maxx, *Newcastle.*   Tynedale Park, *Hexham.*

ELECTRICAL EQUIPMENT   Remington, *Newcastle Upon Tyne.*
Royal Quays Factory Outlet Centre, *Newcastle Upon Tyne. (Near A19)*

FURNITURE/SOFT FURNISHINGS   Curtain Fabrics Factory Shop, *Blyth.*
Factory Shop Centre, *Blaydon.*   The Fabric And Tapestry Shop, *Corbridge.*   Tynedale Park, *Hexham.*

FOOD AND LEISURE   Bargain Baggage Factory Shop, *North Shields.*
Luggage & Baggage, *North Shields.*   Luggage & Bags, *North Shields.*   Thorntons, *Tyne & Wear.*
Tynedale Park, *Hexham.*

SPORTSWEAR AND EQUIPMENT
Royal Quays Factory Outlet Centre, *Newcastle Upon Tyne. (Near A19)*
Shark Group, *Morpeth.*   Vaude (UK) Ltd, *Haltwhistle.*

ATTICA
2 OLD GEORGE YARD, BIGG MARKET, NEWCASTLE-UPON-TYNE,
NORTHUMBERLAND NE1 1EZ
☎ (0191) 261 4062. OPEN 10.30 - 5.30 MON - SAT.
Two floors of vintage clothes from Twenties to Seventies with most of the
stock coming from the Sixties and Seventies. Blouses, lots of suede, Sixties
mini-skirts and dresses, jewellery, hats and shoes as well as men's formalwear
including dinner suits. Also large range of Fifties to Seventies furnishings,
lamps and decor. *Secondhand and Vintage Clothe*

BAIRDWEAR LADIESWEAR
BLOCKS 1,2,3, DUBMIRE INDUSTRIAL ESTATE, FENCEHOUSES,
HAUGHTON LA SPRING, NORTHUMBERLAND
☎ (0191) 385 8923. OPEN 9.30 - 4.30 MON - SAT, 11 - 4.30 SUN.
Manufacturers for one of the top department store chains for more than 20
years, Bairdwear has a wide selection of seconds and overmakes in its factory
shops. About 80% of the stock sold here is made by the factory itself, while
another 20% is made by other factories within the same group. *Factory Shop*

BARDON MILL POTTERY
TYNESIDE POTTERY WORKS, HEXHAM, NORTHUMBERLAND
NE47 7HU
☎ (01434) 344245. OPEN 9 - 5 MON - FRI, 10 - 5 SAT, SUN.
Large, salt-glazed garden and domestic clay pots in all sizes from £7.50. Lots
of storage pot seconds available from this supplier to garden centres from £6
to £45. *Factory Shop*

BARGAIN BAGGAGE FACTORY SHOP
BUGATTI HOUSE, NORHAM ROAD, NORTH SHIELDS,
NORTHUMBERLAND
☎ (0191) 258 4451. OPEN 10 - 2 TUES, 10 - 3 WED, THUR, FRI.
Leather goods from Pierre Cardin, Gina Ferrari, Cardin Weekender and
Executive Essentials at discounts of up to 50%. Suitcases, weekend bags,
handbags, wallets, purses, briefcases, attache cases, suiters. Situated next door
to Welch's sweet factory. *Factory Shop*

Live Well On Less Tips
Buy supermarket own-brand products which are usually cheaper than brand
name products.

> *Live Well On Less Tips*
> Buy vegetables and fruit loose rather than already wrapped. It's almost always cheaper.

BIRTHDAYS

ROYAL QUAYS FACTORY OUTLET, UNIT 55, HAYHOLE ROAD, NORTH SHIELDS, NORTHUMBERLAND NE29 6DY
☎ (0191) 2574767. OPEN 10 - 6 MON - SAT, 11 - 5 SUN.
Cards, notelets, stationery sets, colouring books, stuffed toys, photo albums, picture frames, gifts, giftwrap, tissue paper, party packs, candlesticks, christmas crackers, soft toys, string puppets, fairy lights all at discounts of up to 30%. Some are special purchases, some seconds. *Factory Shopping Village*

BURBERRY

KITTY BREWSTER INDUSTRIAL ESTATE, BLYTH, NORTHUMBERLAND NE24 4RG
☎ (01670) 352524. OPEN 10 - 4 MON, 9.30 - 4 TUE - FRI, 8.45 - 3.30 SAT.
This Burberry factory shop sells seconds and overmakes of the famous name raincoats and duffle coats as well as accessories such as the distinctive umbrellas, scarves and handbags. It also sells childrens duffle coats, knitwear and shirts, as well as some of the Burberry range of food: jams, biscuits, tea, coffee and chocolate. All carry the Burberry label and are about one third of the normal retail price. *Factory Shop*

CATALOGUE BARGAIN SHOP

51 SHIELDS ROAD, BYKER, NEWCASTLE-UPON-TYNE, NORTHUMBERLAND NE6 1DJ
☎ (0191) 265 6033. OPEN 9 - 5 MON - SAT, 10 - 4.30 SUN.
Catalogue Bargain Shop is a growing national chain of stores which obtains the majority of its goods from mail order giants Great Universal and Kays, and offers a range of clothing for all the family, a wide selection of shoes, bed linen, household goods, electrical equipment and hundreds of other catalogue items at very competitive prices. The merchandise consists of ends of ranges and previous season's stock for which there is no longer storage space when the catalogues change. *Permanent Discount Outlet*

CLAREMONT GARMENTS

ENNERDALE ROAD, KITTY BREWSTER TRADING ESTATE, BLYTH, NORTHUMBERLAND NE24 4RG
☎ (01670) 351195. OPEN 9 - 4.30 MON - FRI, 9 - 5 SAT.
Manufacturers for Marks & Spencer, this factory shop sells mainly ladies clothes from this well-known name at discounted prices of up to 50%. *Factory Shop*

CLAREMONT GARMENTS

HOWDEN GREEN ESTATE, NORMAN TERRACE, WALLSEND,
NORTHUMBERLAND NE28 6SP

☎ (0191) 263 1690. OPEN 9 - 4.30 MON - FRI, 9 - 5 SAT.

Claremont manufacture for Marks & Spencer and sell overmakes and ends of
lines here at about half price. Most of the stock is for ladies and men. *Factory
Shop*

COLOURS

3 PEPPER STREET, NEWCASTLE, NORTHUMBERLAND

☎ (01782) 714164. OPEN 9 - 5 MON - SAT.

Dress agency catering for both men and women. Men's labels include Armani,
Boss, Josef, Calvin Klein, Thomas Burberry and Ralph Lauren. Women's
labels: Armani, Betty Barclay, Paul Costelloe, Nicole Farhi, Wallis and Next.
There is always a marvellous selection of shoes in sizes 3-8. *Dress Agency*

CRAMLINGTON TEXTILES

NELSON WAY, NORTH NELSON INDUSTRIAL ESTATE, CRAMLINGTON,
NORTHUMBERLAND NE23 9JT

☎ (01670) 713434. OPEN 10 - 5 MON - FRI, 9.30 - 5 SAT.

Perfects and seconds in bedlinen, curtains and towels, bath sets, blankets, bedspreads, duvets and pillows including polycotton flat sheets, children's quilt
cover sets, curtain sets (curtains, tie backs and pelmets), valances and
throwover bedspreads. *Factory Shop*

CURTAIN FABRICS FACTORY SHOP

36 GRASSMER WAY, KITTY BREWSTER INDUSTRIAL ESTATE, BLYTH,
NORTHUMBERLAND

☎ (01670) 540240. OPEN 10 - 3 MON - SAT.

Low prices on curtains, fabrics, made-to-measure curtains or ready-made curtains. Lots of fabrics on the roll or you can order through books, though this
is not as god value as buying from the rolls. *Permanent Discount Outlet*

DEWHIRST IMPRESSIONS
CLOTHING FACTORY SHOP

NORTH SEATON INDUSTRIAL ESTATE, OFF NEWBIGGIN ROAD,
ASHINGTON, NORTHUMBERLAND NE63 OYB

☎ (01670) 813493. OPEN 10 - 8 MON - FRI, 9 - 6 SAT, 10.30 - 4.30 SUN.

Dewhirst Impressions Clothing Factory Shop sell garments from the manufacturing side of the business direct to the public and are part of the Dewhirst
Group plc which manufactures ladies, men's and childrenswear for a leading
high street retailer. Dewhurst launched its largest store in March 1999 as
Dewhirst Impressions. This flagship store offers more departments and a

wider choice of clothing than ever before. For men there is a wide range of suits, formal shirts and casual wear. For example, wool suits from £60, formal and casual shirts from £7. For ladies there's a selection of blouses, smart tailoring and casual wear that includes a denim range. You can find ladies jackets from £50, skirts, trousers and blouses from £8. Children's clothes start at £3. In addition to this they now offer a superb new ladies underwear department, men's and ladies shoe departments, plus an extensive range of men's and ladies accessories. With a coffee bar, public toilets and ample free car parking space, this is a whole new factory shopping experience. Well worth a visit.
Factory Shop

DISCOUNT CLOTHING STORE
19 KINGSTON PARK CENTRE, KINGSTON PARK, NORTHUMBERLAND NE3 2FP
☎ (0191) 271 4126. OPEN 9.30 - 5.30 MON - SAT.
Seconds and overstock in ladies, men's and childrenswear from Next and other well-known high street names. A good selection of jackets, skirts, trousers, dresses and tops for ladies with a small selection of men's trousers, jackets, shirt and ties. There are a few rails of childrenswear. All are at half price or less.
Permanent Discount Outlet

FACTORY SHOP CENTRE
CHAINBRIDGE INDUSTRIAL ESTATE, BLAYDON, NORTHUMBERLAND NE21 5SJ

UNIT 23 & 24 FACTORY FABRIC CENTRE
☎ (0191) 414 4515. OPEN 10 - 5 MON - FRI, 7 ON THUR, 9 - 5 SAT, 10 - 4 SUN.

UNIT 5 CUT PRICE WALLPAPER
☎ (0191) 414 6716. OPEN 9.30 - 5 MON - SAT, 7 ON THUR, 10 - 4 SUN.

UNIT 2 MCINTOSH FACTORY BEDDING SHOP
☎ (0191) 414 8969. OPEN 10 - 5 MON - FRI, 7 ON THUR, 9 - 5 SAT, 10 - 4 SUN.

FACTORY BEDS
☎ (0191) 414 6331. OPEN 9 - 5 MON - SAT 7 ON THUR, 10 - 4 SUN.

FACTORY CARPETS
☎ (0191) 414 5887. OPEN 9 - 5 MON - FRI, 7 ON THUR, 10 - 4 SUN.
Large industrial estate on which a variety of discount shops operate selling everything from brand-name wallpaperand paint, fire surrounds, gas fires and back boilers, curtains, bedding, towels, upholstery fabrics and textiles to Axminster and Wilton carpets, Rest Assured and Silent Night beds
Permanent Discount Outlet

Live Well On Less Tips
Shop on a full stomach, not an empty one and you'll be far less likely to buy foods impulsively.

GLADRAGS
51 BONDGATE WITHIN, ALNWICK, NORTHUMBERLAND NE66 1HZ
☎ (01665) 602396. OPEN 10 - 4 MON - SAT, CLOSED WED.
High quality nearly-new ladies clothing with labels such as Alexon, Planet and Donna Karan *Dress Agency*

J BARBOUR & SONS LTD
CUSTOMER SERVICE DEPARTMENT, MONKSWAY, JARROW, NORTHUMBERLAND NE32 3HQ
☎ (0191) 428 4707. OPEN 10 - 5 MON - THUR, 10 - 4 FRI, 10 - 2 SAT.
The famous waterproof waxed jackets and outdoor wear, all of which are seconds or discontinued lines, at discounts of up to 50%. Jackets comes in fifteen different styles from short to full-length and in various colours, but you may not find the style, colour and size you want as quantities vary. There are also quilted jackets, jumpers, hats and caps, linings for jackets, bags, Wellingtons and waders. There is also a new range of Barbour shoes. Free parking. *Factory Shop*

JAMES BARRY MENSWEAR
ROYAL QUAYS, NORTH SHIELDS, NEWCASTLE-UPON-TYNE, NORTHUMBERLAND NE29 6DW
☎ (0191) 296 4821. OPEN 10 - 6 MON - SAT, 11 - 5 SUN.
Outdoor factory shopping centre in which James Barry sells branded menswear including Double Two casual shirts, two for £20; James Barry shirts, £11.95, or two for £20; 100% cotton Savile Row shirts reduced to £20 each or two for £30; Lancers trousers, £34.95, or two for £60; jackets from £69.95; belts from £7.95 to £15.95; single breasted suits from £99; dinner suits, £139. *Factory Shop*

JANE SHILTON
ROYAL QUAYS, NORTH SHIELDS, NEAR A19, NORTH SHIELDS, NORTHUMBERLAND NE29 6DW
☎ (0191) 257 3672. OPEN 10 - 6 MON - SAT, 11 - 5 SUN.
This shop, one of up to 60 in this open-air factory shopping centre, only carries merchandise from past seasons' collections or factory seconds at discounts of at least 30% and up to 50% off the original price. There is a wide range of handbags, suitcases, women's shoes, luggage, briefcases, umbrellas, scarves and travel bags. *Factory Shopping Village*

JOE BLOGGS

ROYAL QUAYS OUTLET VILLAGE, NORTH SHIELDS,
NORTHUMBERLAND NE29 6DW

☎ (0191) 296 1999. OPEN 10 - 6 MON - SAT, 11 - 5 SUN.

Range of casual clothing for men, women, children and babies which are ends
of lines, imperfects or surplus ranges. Jeans, tops, long sleeved shirts and jackets at discounts of between 30% and70%. *Factory Shopping Village*

LUGGAGE & BAGGAGE

ROYAL QUAYS OUTLET VILLAGE, NORTH SHIELDS,
NORTHUMBERLAND NE29 6DW

☎ (0191) 257 4458. OPEN 10 - 6 MON - SAT, 11 - 5 SUN.

Luggage and travel-related products including executive cases, handbags,
umbrellas and accessories available in leading brands such as Samsonite, Brics,
Hidesign, Globe Trotter and Tula. The products also include couture and high
fashion brands such as YSl and Moschino. All products are offered at a considerably reduced price due to their being production over-runs, last season's
stock of slight seconds (ie they have minor aesthetic blemishes). *Factory
Shopping Village*

LUGGAGE & BAGS

ROYAL QUAY OUTLET VILLAGE, NORTH SHIELDS,
NORTHUMBERLAND NE29 6DW

☎ (0191) 257 4458. OPEN 10 - 6 MON - SAT, 11 - 5 SUN.

A range of travel goods and accessories from recognisable brands and high
street names including Samsonite, Delsey, Head, Studio and Taurus. Each
product is offered at a substantially reduced prices to that found on the high
street due to their being production over-runs, last season's products or having
small cosmetic faults. Discounts range from 30% to 75% off high street
prices. *Factory Shopping Village*

MARGARET WILLIAMS DRESS AGENCY

21 EAST STREET, WHITBURN, NORTHUMBERLAND SR6 7BY

☎ (0191) 529 2247 OPEN 10 - 5 MON - SAT.

Large shop selling mainly designer labels, varying from Frank Usher, Jean
Muir and Mondi to the occasional selection of Marks & Spencer, Laura Ashley
and Next. Stocks both day wear and special occasion outfits, including hats,
costume jewellery and shoes. Also holds seasonal stock such as shorts and T-
shirts, as well as antiques, prints, paintings and porcelain. *Dress Agency*

Live Well On Less Tips
Never shop without a grocery list in hand

MATALAN

UNIT 1, BELVEDERE RETAIL PARK, KINGSTON PARK, NEWCASTLE
UPON TYNE NE3 2PA

☎ (0191) 214 0352. OPEN 10 - 8 MON - FRI, 9 - 6 SAT, 11 - 5 SUN.

Matalan is a fashion and homewares shop giving customers what they claim
to be unbeatable value for money with huge savings on a wide range of products including high quality fashionable clothing for women, women and children at up to 50% off high street prices. Matalan is situated out of town and
stores are open seven days a week all year round. *Permanent Discount
Outlet*

MEXX INTERNATIONAL

ROYAL QUAYS FACTORY OUTLET CENTRE, NORTH SHIELDS,
NEWCASTLE-UPON-TYNE, NEAR A19, NORTHUMBERLAND

☎ (0191) 257 5001. OPEN 10 - 6 MON - FRI, 9 - 6 SAT, 11 - 5 SUN.

High street fashion at factory outlet prices for men, women, babies, children
and teenagers, all of which are heavily discounted by more than 30%.*Factory
Shopping Village*

PENNY PLAIN

10 MARLBOROUGH CRESCENT, NEWCASTLE UPON TYNE,
NORTHUMBERLAND NE1 4EE

☎ (0191) 232 1124. OPEN 10 - 4 FRI, SAT.

Overstocks and ends of lines from Penny Plain mail order collections; also
designer samples and slight seconds. High quality, well made clothes. Superb
savings on original prices. Ladies separates and knitwear in smart and casual,
summer and winter styles. Garments are made in colourful, luxurious fabrics,
especially natural fibres: pure cotton, linen, silk, wool, velvet and cupro. Sizes
8 - 22. *Permanent Discount Outlet*

PONDEN MILL LINENS

ROYAL QUAYS FACTORY OUTLET CENTRE, ROYAL QUAYS, NORTH
SHIELDS, NORTHUMBERLAND NE29 6DY

☎ (0191) 257 4607. OPEN 10 - 6 MON - SAT, 11 - 5 SUN.

Famous branded products at direct from the mill prices. Towels, co-ordinated
bedlinen, duvets, pillows and curtains from Crown, Coloroll, Chortex,
Rectella together with bathroom and kitchen accessories. *Factory Shopping
Village*

Live Well On Less Tips
Buy your Christmas turkey several months in advance when prices are lower
than during the festive season and freeze.

REMINGTON

ROYAL QUAYS, NORTH SHIELDS, NEWCASTLE-UPON-TYNE, NORTHUMBERLAND

☎ (0191) 258 3622. OPEN 10 - 6 MON - SAT, 11 - 5 SUN.

Lots of famous names at this outlet in the Royal Quays factory outlet village from Oneida and Monogram cutlery to Braun, Philips, Remington, Clairol, Wahl, Krups and Kenwood small kitchen equipment and grooming tools for men and women. *Factory Shopping Village*

ROYAL QUAYS
FACTORY OUTLET CENTRE

NORTH SHIELDS, NEWCASTLE-UPON-TYNE, NEAR A19, NORTH SHIELDS, NORTHUMBERLAND NE29 6DW

☎ (0191) 296 3743. OPEN 10 - 6 MON - SAT, 11 - 5 SUN.

Having opened in late October 1996, there are plans for 60 shops for phase 1, making a total of 130,000 sq ft of shops with leisure facilities nearby including a full-scale steam railway, working harbour, Roman ruins and the usual seaside attractions. Adjacent to the Wet and Wild Water Park which has 350,000 visitors a year and next door to an international ferry terminal, the village has a nautical feel to it. Shops here include: August Silk; Bed & Bath Works linen and bathroom accessories; Broughton Shoe Warehouse; Cards and Gifts selling, as their name suggests, cards, soft toys, wrapping paper and mugs; CBS for fashion for the whole family; Ciro Citterio menswear; Diamonds Direct; Direct Design womenswear (mostly knits and tops) with some children's clothes; Discount Clothing Store, which sells lots of cheaper styles for women and children; Easy Jeans for men, women and children; Honey ladieswear; James Barry men's suits, trousers, and coats; Jane Shilton shoes for women, handbags, scarves, jewellery, gloves and luggage; Joe Bloggs for men, women and children; John Jenkins crystal and porcelain; Leading Labels for men and women, a large shop with, for women, Roman Originals, Alexara, Blast leisurewear, Katherine Hamnett Denim, Cote a Cote Paris, Klass coats and jackets, Jersey Masters and Just Elegance and, for men, Pringle, Farah trousers, Kangol, Double Two shirts, Tommy Hilfiger, Calvin Klein, Ralph Lauren, Oakman, Lee Cooper, Fruit of the Loom and Wolsey; Mexx for men, women and children; Pavers Branded Shoes for men, women and children; Pilot womenswear; Ponden Mill bedlinen, duvets, towels, curtains and tea towels from Dorma, Coloroll, Horrockses, Vantona and Sheridan; Remington branded electrical goods from hairdryers to kitchen knives; Sports Mill; Sports Unlimited with Puma shoes and clothes, Head rucksacks, Le Coq Sportif clothes, Wilson, Arena ladies swimwear, Hi-Tec gym shoes, Trespass ski clothes and Fila; Tom Sayers menswear; Tog 24 outdoor clothes, shoes and equipment for men, women and children; Lee jeans for men and women, with a youth section; The Designer Room; The Suit Company (Moss Bros) for men selling Pierre Cardin suits, Moss Bros dress shirts, Baumler and Daks shirts; Suits You menswear including Van Kollem, Pierre Cardin, Pierre Balmain, Tom English, Daniel Hechter, Ralph Lauren and Ben Sherman; Luggage & Bags including Tula handbags, Samsonite, Delsey and Pierre Balmain; Thorntons chocolates; The Book Depot; Toyworld selling Matchbox, Lego, Little Tikes, Tyco, Tomy and Waddingtons; The Chainstore Outlet, which sells clothes from leading chainstores, many with their labels cut out, for men, women and children - uncut labels seen here include Next, Adams, Gossard, Farah, Wallis; The Mountain Outlet, a ski and walkers shop for men, women and children with walking boots, Nevica ski jackets, ski luggage; Warners underwear; XS music and videos. *Factory Shopping Village*

SECOND TIME AROUND

1 - 3 WOOL MARKET, BERWICK-UPON-TWEED, NORTHUMBERLAND PD15 1DH

☎ (01289) 307875 10 - 5 MON - SAT, 10 - 2 THUR.

High quality, nearly new clothes with designers ranging from Jacques Vert to Marks & Spencer and Laura Ashley. Established for more than seven years, this two-storey shop now caters for the whole family with an across the board selection of clothing from casual daywear to wedding outfits, babywear to men's outfits. There is usually a bargain rail with skirts going for as little as £4, and twice yearly sales in the summer and winter. A varied selection of clothes can be found year round as the stock is not necessarily seasonal. Accessories can be found: shoes, hats and handbags. Menswear includes Armani, Hugo Boss and other Continental designers. Childrenswear ranges from babies to teenagers and there is also a selecton of baby equipment such as high chairs and buggies as well as toys, games and books. Rest area and refreshments always available in thie friendly, spacious shop. *Dress Agency*

SHARK GROUP

NORDSTROM HOUSE, NORTH BROOMHILL, NEAR AMBLE, MORPETH, NORTHUMBERLAND NE65 9UJ

☎ (01670) 760365. OPEN 2 - 4 MON - FRI (ALL YEAR ROUND), 10 - 12 SAT (APRIL - MID-DEC).

Manufactures and sells in the factory shop wetsuits, dry suits, diving suits, cag tops, sailing suits, boots and gloves, for men, women and children at factory prices. Children's one-piece wetsuits, £42.50 - £47.50; steamers, £130 and adult two-piece wetsuits, from £80; adult one-piece wetsuits, £65. Special sales are held occasionally. The factory shop closes for the usual factory holidays in late July/early August and late October as well as bank holidays. *Factory Shop*

Live Well On Less Tips
When you make a pot of coffee, put the rest in a Thermos until you want another one.

SILVIA JEFFERY LTD

KITTY BREWSTER INDUSTRIAL ESTATE, BLYTH, NORTHUMBERLAND
☎ (01670) 365425. OPEN 9.30 - 3 MON - THUR, 9 - 12 FRI.
Mostly sells girls chainstore items excluding school uniforms, although there is some womenswear (nightdresses and dressing gowns mostly). *Factory Shop*

SLATERS MENSWEAR

10 GRAINGER STREET, NEWCASTLE-UPON-TYNE, TYNE & WEAR, NORTHUMBERLAND NE1 5EW
☎ (0191) 232 5557. OPEN 8.30 - 5.30 MON - SAT, 7.30 ON THUR.
Full range of men's clothes from underwear and shoes to casualwear, suits and dresswear and including labels such as Odermark, Bulmer, Valentino, Charlie's Co, and Charlton Gray. Men's suits from £79. *Permanent Discount Outlet*

SPOILS

17-19 WHITE ROSE WAY, ELDON SQUARE, NEWCASTLE UPON TYNE, TYNE & WEAR, NORTHUMBERLAND NE1 7XN
☎ (0191) 222 0184. OPEN 9 - 5.30 MON - SAT, 8 ON THUR, 11 - 5 SUN.
METRO CENTRE, NEWCASTLE, TYNE & WEAR
☎ (0191) 460 7573.
General domestic glassware, non-stick bakeware, kitchen gadgets, ceramic oven-to-tableware, textiles, cutting boards, aluminium non-stick cookware, bakeware, plastic kitchenware, plastic storage, woodware, coffee pots/makers, furniture, mirrors and picture frames. Rather than being discounted, all the merchandise is very competitively priced - in fact, the company carry out competitors' checks frequently in order to monitor pricing. With 38 branches, the company is able to buy in bulk and thus negotiate very good prices.*Permanent Discount Outlet*

THE FABRIC AND TAPESTRY SHOP

SYDGATE HOUSE, MIDDLE STREET, CORBRIDGE, NORTHUMBERLAND NE45 5AT
☎ (01434) 632902. OPEN 10 - 5 MON -SAT.
Designer discount fabric in two-yard lengths (fents) at £7 or £8 a fent (also 3 metre lengths on the roll) including names such as Colefax & Fowler and Ramm Son & Crocker. Also good quality secondhand curtains as well as leading brand tapestry kits, such as Elizabeth Bradley, the latter at full price. *Permanent Discount Outlet and Secondhand Shop*

Live Well On Less Tips
LONDON FOR LESS 222 KENSAL ROAD, LONDON W10 5BN.
0181-964 4242.
Anyone who likes visiting London may like to take advantage of London for Less. Usually promoted to American visitors, it has recently been launched to the domestic British market. For just £12.95, you get a package which includes a discount card providing discounts at over 250 places in central London, plus a 288-page full colour guidebook and a fold-out map. Discounts are applicable for up to four people for up to eight days. Example of discounts include: 20%-50% off 45 attractions and museums such as Madame Tussaud's; 25%-75% off ticket prices at shows, concerts, operas and ballets, such as The London Philharmonic; 20%-50% off rack rates at 42 hotels such as The Rochester Hotel; 25% off the total bill at 90 restaurants; and 20% off all goods at 50 shops. Restaurants included range from Bella Pasta for very inexpensive meals, to Cafe Lazeez for award-winning Indian food. Shops included range from Piccadilly Souvenirs, situated right next to Piccadilly Circus, to Cashmere Gallery on Brompton Road selling famous brand-name clothes. Books are also available at £5.95 for European cities: Amsterdam, Athens, Barcelona, Berlin, Bruges, Brussels, Budapest, Copenhagen, Dublin, Florence, Istanbul, Lisbon, Madrid, Prague, Rome, Venice and Vienna and for the USA guides on: California, Florida, Hawaii, Las Vegas, Los Angeles, Orlando and San Francisco. All For Less titles can be purchased at good book shops and at the British Travel Centre on Lower Regent Street or via the above telephone number.

THE FACTORY SHOP
DUBMIRE INDUSTRIAL ESTATE, FENCEHOUSES, HOUGHTON LE SPRING, NORTHUMBERLAND DH4 5RE
☎ (0191) 385 8923. OPEN 9 - 4.30 MON - FRI, 10 - 4.30 SAT, 11 - 4.30 SUN.
Discontinued lines and seconds of Marks & Spencer, BhS and Littlewoods clothes for men, women and children. *Factory Shop*

THORNTONS
SOUTH PARADE, ROYAL QUAYS SHOPPING CENTRE, COBLE DENE, NORTH SHIELDS, TYNE & WEAR, NORTHUMBERLAND NE29 6DN
☎ (0191) 258 0623. OPEN 10 - 6 MON - SAT, 11 - 5 SUN.
The UK's leading specialist confectionery retailer has more than 500 shops and franchises nationwide selling a wide range of boxed and loose, chocolate and sugar confectionery. The factory outlets sell three different categories: misshapes. discounted lines and standard lines. Misshapes are loose chocolates which are the result of new product development, product trials or end of production runs which cannot be packed as Thorntons standard lines. They are packed into assorted bags and offer a saving of 35%-55% over the recommended retail price of standard loose line products. Discounted lines are

excess to Thorntons' normal retail requirements and can be as a result of excess seasonal or export stock, discontinued lines or packaging changes. These products, when available, are offered at a discount of 25%-50% over the standard retail price. Standard lines from the full Thorntons range are also on sale at normal prices. *Factory Shopping Village*

TK MAXX

LOWER GROUND FLOOR, MONUMENT MALL SHOPPING CENTRE, NEWCASTLE-UPON-TYNE, TYNE & WEAR, NORTHUMBERLAND NE1 7AL

☎ (0191) 261 0404. OPEN 9 - 5.30 MON - SAT, UNTIL 8 ON THUR, 11 - 5 SUN.

UNIT 13A, TEAM VALLEY RETAIL WORLD, GATESHEAD, NEWCASTLE NE11 OBD

☎ (0191) 487 4468. OPEN 9 - 5.30 MON - SAT, UNTIL 8 THUR, 11 - 5 SUN.

Based on an American concept, TK Maxx is situated in easily accessible, often centrally located stores and offers famous label goods with up to 60% savings off recommended retail prices. TK Maxx has fashion for the whole family - women's, men's and childrenswear - accessories, shoes, gifts, kitchenware and home goods. Everything in the store is branded with a choice of well-known high street names to designer labels, and while a small percentage might be clearly marked past season, the great majority of items in store are current season, current stock and still with phenomenal savings. There is a huge choice with 50,000 pieces in store and up to 10,000 new items arriving a week. The stores are simple and unfussy with wide aisles, shopping trolleys and baskets, and a spacious, functional feel to them but there are individual changing rooms, ramps for buggies and wheelchairs and plenty of staff on the shop floor. Every branch accepts all major credit and debit cards and has a liberal refund and return policy. *Permanent Discount Outlet*

TOG 24

UNIT 2C, NORTHERN PARADE, ROYAL QUAYS, NORTH SHIELDS, NEAR A19, NORTH SHIELDS, TYNE & WEAR , NORTHUMBERLAND NE29 6DS

☎ (01912) 583754. OPEN 10 - 6 MON - SAT, 11 - 5 SUN.

32 HIGH FRIARS, NEWCASTLE, TYNE & WEAR NE1 7JB

TEL & FAX (01912) 602810. OPEN 9 - 5 MON, TUE, WED, FRI, 9 - 8 THUR, 9 - 6 SAT, 11 - 5 SUN.

Tog 24 are the UK's fastest growing brand name in outdoor clothing and leisurewear, with a total of three UK factories and 36 stores nationwide. They utilise the world's finest performance fabrics including Gore-Tex, Polartec and Burlington macs. Catering for all the family for all seasons, with cosy fleeces and waterproofs for the winter, and trekking ranges, shorts and t-shirts for the summer. With all prices at least 30% below the recommended retail price you can afford to enter the Tog comfort zone. *Factory Shopping Village*

TOM SAYERS CLOTHING CO

ROYAL QUAYS, NORTH SHIELDS, TYNE & WEAR, NORTHUMBERLAND
NE29 6DW

☎ (0191) 257 3369. OPEN 10 - 6 MON - SAT, 11 - 5 SUN.

Tom Sayers make sweaters for some of the top high street department stores.
Unusually for a factory shop, if they don't stock your size, they will try and order
it for you from their factory or one of their other factory outlets and send it to
you. Most of the stock here is overstock, cancelled orders or last season's and
includes jumpers, trousers and shirts at discounts of 30%. The trousers and shirts
are bought in to complement the sweaters which they make. *Factory Shopping
Village*

TOYWORLD FACTORY OUTLETS LTD

UNIT 53, ROYAL QUAYS SHOPPING OUTLET, SOUTH PARADE, NORTH
SHIELDS, NEWCASTLE-UPON-TYNE MARINA, NORTHUMBERLAND
NE29 6DW

☎ (0191) 257 3333. OPEN 10 - 6 MON - SAT, 11 - 5 SUN.

Toy World sells brand name items including a wide range of toys with well-
known brand names. For example, Barbie (Mattel), Disney, Playskool, Lego,
Sylvanian Families, Fisher-Price, Tyco, Tomy, Waddington, M&B Games,
Safe & Sound, Matchbox, and many others at very low prices. *Factory
Shopping Village*

TYNEDALE PARK

HEXHAM, NORTHUMBERLAND

☎ (01434) 607788. OPEN 10 - 6 MON - FRI, 9.30 - 6 SAT, 11 - 5 SUN.

Large discount outlet selling the overstock and clearance lines from Robbs
superb department store in the centre of Hexham. There are lots of good
names here in fashion (Windsmoor, Dannimac, Berlei, Pringle), furniture,
electrical items, toys, gifts, and diy equipment. The main section is a garden
centre and there is also a pets golf and a sports department. There is a restaurant upstairs, lifts, and lots of free parking. *Permanent Discount Outlet*

VAUDE (UK) LTD

HALTWHISTLE INDUSTRIAL ESTATE, HALTWHISTLE,
NORTHUMBERLAND NE49 9HA

☎ (01434) 320744. OPEN 4 - 7 FRI, 10 - 1 SAT.

Well-known tent and outdoor wear manufacturer, Vaude has a small factory
shop selling rucksacks, tents, winter clothing and fleece clothing, all of which are
ends of lines, seconds, or have been used for display purposes and cannot be sold
at full retail price. Vaude's tents are made for real-life situations, designed to
withstand any weather conditions. These tents are for serious camping and outdoor enthusiasts. To see the full range, send for the catalogue or call in at the
shop. Stock changes seasonally. They don't accept credit cards. *Factory Shop*

Nottinghamshire

WOMENSWEAR ONLY Change Of A Dress, *Nottingham*.
Claremont Garments Ltd, *Sutton-In-Ashfield*. Elegant Exchange, *Radcliffe-On-Trent*.
Labels Of Edwinstowe, *Edwinstowe*. Martin Lindsay Ltd, *Newark*. Westdale Textiles, *Carlton*.

MENSWEAR ONLY The Designer Warehouse, *Nottingham*.

WOMENSWEAR & MENSWEAR Broughton Shoe Warehouse, *Lenton Lane*.
Catalogue Bargain Shop, *Nottingham*. Catalogue Bargain Shop, *Mansfield*.
Clarks Factory Shop, *Arnold*. Cooper & Roe Factory Shop, *Sutton-In-Ashfield*.
Factory Shop Outlet, *Newark*. Harriets, *Newark*. Matalan, *Nottingham*.
Meridian Retail Factory Shop, *Nottingham*. Renaissance, *Nottingham*.
The Factory Shop, *Worksop*. The Factory Shop, *Sutton-In-Ashfield*.
The Shoe Factory Shop, *Nottingham*. The Shoe Shed, *Kirkby-In-Ashfield*. Tweedies, *Hucknall*.
Warners UK Ltd, *Bulwell*.

CHILDREN Absolute Beginners, *Nottingham*. Broughton Shoe Warehouse, *Nottingham*.
Catalogue Bargain Shop, *Nottingham*. Claremont Garments Ltd, *Sutton-In-Ashfield*.
Clarks Factory Shop, *Arnold*. Cooper & Roe Factory Shop, *Sutton-In-Ashfield*.
Factory Shop Outlet, *Newark*. Matalan, *Nottingham*. Meridian Retail Factory Shop, *Nottingham*.
The Factory Shop, *Worksop*. The Factory Shop, *Sutton-In-Ashfield*.
The Shoe Factory Shop, *Nottingham*. The Shoe Shed, *Kirkby-In-Ashfield*. Tweedies, *Hucknall*.

HOUSEHOLD AND GIFTWARE Catalogue Bargain Shop, *Nottingham*.
Catalogue Bargain Shop, *Mansfield*.
Cooper & Roe Factory Shop, *Sutton-In-Coppice Side Pottery, Nottingham*.
Denby Factory Shop, *Nottingham*. Labels Of Edwinstowe, *Edwinstowe*. Matalan, *Nottingham*.
Meridian Retail Factory Shop, *Nottingham*. Spoils, *Nottingham*. Tweedies, *Hucknall*.
Tweedies, *West Bridgford*. Tweedies, *Beeston*. Tweedies, *Keyworth*. Weston Mill Pottery, *Newark*.

ELECTRICAL EQUIPMENT Appliance Warehouse, *Nottingham*.
Catalogue Bargain Shop, *Nottingham*. Catalogue Bargain Shop, *Mansfield*.
Dayclear Lighting Ltd, *Nottingham*. Liquidation Supplies, *Retford*.

DIY/RENOVATION Nottingham Architectural Antiques, *Nottingham*.
Tile Clearing House, *Nottingham*.

ARCHITECTURAL SALVAGE Nottingham Architectural Antiques, *Nottingham*.

FURNITURE/SOFT FURNISHINGS Essential Items, *Nottingham*.
Just A Second Fabrics, *Mansfield*.

FOOD AND LEISURE Denby Factory Shop, *Nottingham*.
Edwardian Confectionery Ltd, *Nottingham*. Weston Mill Pottery, *Newark*.

Live Well On Less Tips
If you're not eligible to join a warehouse club, take a look locally. When the first warehouse club opened at Thurrock in Essex, Tesco had bulk-saver aisles and Savacentre opened a Bulk Saver nearby which sold supermarket own label products and which didn't require a membership fee.

APPLIANCE WAREHOUSE

UNIT 1 & 2, BUNNY TRADING ESTATE, GOTHAM LANE, BUNNY, JUNCTION 24 OF M1, NOTTINGHAM NG11 6QJ

☎ (0115) 9844357. OPEN 10 - 5 MON - FRI, 10 - 4 SAT, 11 - 3 SUN.

Large warehouse with 10,000 fitted kitchen appliances. They specialise in built-in kitchen appliances, stocking all leading brands from AEG to Zanussi at up to 60% discounts. For example, Bosch/Siemens integrated washer/dryers with a recommended retail price of £949 are sold by Appliance Warehouse for £439. There is a large showroom /warehouse displaying 90 single/double ovens in gas and electric, and 800 ceramic, halogen, gas and electric hobs are always in stock. Specialise in American fridge freezers with up to £500 off, and range cookers. *Permanent Discount Outlet*

BROUGHTON SHOE WAREHOUSE

6 QUEENS COURT, LENTON LANE, NOTTINGHAM NG7 2NR

☎ (0115) 986 6385. OPEN 10 - 6 MON - SAT, 10 - 4 SUN.

32 KING STREET, SOUTHWELL, NOTTINGHAMSHIRE

☎ (01636) 812078. OPEN 9.30 - 5 MON - SAT.

Sells ladies boots, shoes, sandals and slippers as well as men's and children's footwear. Savings can be between 20% and 50% here. Some of the boots are by Mondi, and there are shoes by Kappa, Timberalnd, Hi-Tec, Trickers, Caterpillar, Kickers and some Italian and Spanish designers. Deliveries are made every Tuesday. *Permanent Discount Outlet*

CHANGE OF A DRESS

294 BROXTOWE LANE, NOTTINGHAM NG8 5NB

☎ (0115) 929 1531. ☎ (0115) 929 6888 FAX. OPEN 9.30 - 5 MON - SAT

This must be the country's most glamorous dress agency, as its appearance on TV can testify. Where else could you find Chanel, Armani, Moschino and Escada modelled by the agency's in house mannequin, whilst accompanied by their resident pianist at a grand piano? The owner imports clothing from Hollywood and has sold garments from Joan Collins, Priscilla Presley and Zsa Zsa Gabor. The extensive salon is decorated with 15 chandeliers and ornate gilded mirrors, with a coffee lounge for customers' comfort; alterations can be undertaken on site. Clients travel far and wide to this mecca for the fashion-conscious and penny-wise. The internet address is: email:sales@coadress proweb.co.uk. *Dress Agency*

ABSOLUTE BEGINNERS
162 RADCLIFFE ROAD, WEST BRIDGFORD, NOTTINGHAM,
NOTTINGHAMSHIRE NG2 5HF
☎ (0115) 981 8135.
Part of the Baby Equipment Hirers Association (BEHA), which has more than
100 members countrywide. BEHA run an advice line which will try and
answer any queries you have regarding hiring services for children. Phone the
Babyline on 0831 310355. *Hire Shop*

CATALOGUE BARGAIN SHOP
50 MAIN STREET, BULWELL, NOTTINGHAM, NOTTINGHAMSHIRE
NG6 8EY
☎ (0115) 927 8373. OPEN 9 - 5.30 MON - SAT, 10 - 4 SUN.
24-28 LEEMING STREET, MANSFIELD, NOTTINGHAMSHIRE NG18 1NE
☎ (01623) 623353. OPEN 9 - 5.30 MON - SAT, 10 - 4 SUN.
Catalogue Bargain Shop is a growing national chain of stores which obtains
the majority of its goods from mail order giants Great Universal and Kays, and
offers a range of clothing for all the family, a wide selection of shoes, bed linen,
household goods, electrical equipment and hundreds of other catalogue items
at very competitive prices. The merchandise consists of ends of ranges and previous season's stock for which there is no longer storage space when the catalogues change. *Permanent Discount Outlet*

CLAREMONT GARMENTS LTD
BOWNE STREET, SUTTON-IN-ASHFIELD, NOTTINGHAMSHIRE
NG17 4BA
☎ (01623) 442466. OPEN 9 - 4.30 MON - SAT.
Manufacturers for Marks & Spencer, they sell seconds and overmakes of mostly womenswear including coats, dresses, skirts, lingerie, tops, leisure and
sports wear, all at discounts of up to 50%. *Factory Shop*

Live Well On Less Tips
Join the National Art Collections Fund (0171 225 4800) and get a whole host
of benefits. It costs £25 to join (£20 if you're under 25 or over 60) and you
get free admission to over 80 permanent collections including the Imperial
War Museum, The Royal Pavilion in Brighton, National Maritime Museum and
the Christ Church Picture Gallery in Oxford. You also get the Art Quarterly
and Review magazines, first choice of tours at home and abroad and talks by
artists and experts and visits to historic private houses. Your subscription will
enable you to become a patron of the arts as it is used to help galleries buy
works of art.

CLARKS FACTORY SHOP

111 FRONT STREET, ARNOLD, NOTTINGHAMSHIRE NG5 7ED

☎ (0115) 967 4212. OPEN 9 - 6 MON - SAT, 10 - 4 SUN, BANK HOLIDAYS.

Clarks International operate a chain of factory shops nationally which specialise in selling discontinued lines and slight sub-standards for children, women and men from Clarks, K Shoes and other famous brands. These shops trade under the name of K Shoes Factory shop or Clarks Factory Shop and while not all are physically attached to a shoe factory, they are treated as factory shops by the company. Customers can expect to find an extensive range of quality shoes, sandals, walking boots, slippers, trainers, handbags, accessories and gifts, while their major outlets also offer luggage, sports clothing, sports equipment and outdoor clothing. Brands stocked include Clarks, K Shoes, Springer, CICA, Hi-Tec, Puma, Mercury, Dr Martens, Nike, LA Gear, Fila, Mizuno, Slazenger, Weider, Antler and Carlton, although not all are sold in every outlet. Discounts are on average 30% off the normal high street price for perfect stock. *Factory Shop*

COOPER & ROE FACTORY SHOP

KIRKBY ROAD, SUTTON-IN-ASHFIELD, NOTTINGHAMSHIRE

☎ (01623) 554026. OPEN 9 - 5 MON - FRI, 9 - 4 SAT, 10 - 4 SUN.

Part of a larger chain of shops catering for a manufacturer for the popular high street chains, including Marks & Spencer and Next. Merchandise includes fashion for all the family, underwear, pyjamas, evening wear, coats, gifts, towels, bedding, socks. *Factory Shop*

COPPICE SIDE POTTERY

NORTH STREET, LANGLEY MILL, NOTTINGHAM, NOTTINGHAMSHIRE NG16 4DF

☎ (01773) 716854. OPEN 9 - 5 MON - FRI, 9 - 1 SAT.

Specialists in quality terracotta pots for the home and garden, the factory shop sells perfects, overstocks and seconds in wall planters, jardinieres, patio pots, window boxes and Ali Baba urns at prices which are lower than retail. Prices range from 50p to £40. Easy car parking. Staff will load your car for safe transit. *Factory Shop*

DAYCLEAR LIGHTING LTD

85A CROMFORD ROAD, LANGLEY MILL, NOTTINGHAM, NOTTINGHAMSHIRE NG16 4DP

☎ (01773) 763787. OPEN 9 - 5 MON - FRI, 9 - 4 SAT.

Lampshades, table lamps, chandeliers and decorative lighting at manufacturers prices. There are usually at least 300 lines in stock at any one time. For example, 12 table lamps with pleated shades, £6.99; three-arm solid brass chandelier, £68; standard lamp, £27.95. There is parking at the rear of the building. *Factory Shop*

DENBY FACTORY SHOP
DURY WALK, BROADMARSH SHOPPING CENTRE, NOTTINGHAM,
NOTTINGHAMSHIRE NG1 7LP
☎ (0115) 948 3932. OPEN 9 - 5.30 MON - SAT ONLY.
Denby is renowned for its striking colours and glaze effects. The Factory
Shops stock first and second quality with seconds discounts starting at 20%
off RRP. There are regular mega bargains with up to 75% off throughout the
year. *Factory Shopping Village*

EDWARDIAN CONFECTIONERY LTD
HUTHWAITE, BARKER STREET, NOTTINGHAMSHIRE NG17 2LG
☎ (01623) 554712. OPEN 8 - 6 MON - FRI, 9 - 1 SAT.
Sweets and rock sold at two-thirds of the shop price. Range includes peanut
brittle, treacle slab, caramel slab and chocolate, all of which can be bought
either whole or broken up. Approximately 70 types of boiled sweets made on
the premises. *Food and Drink Discounter*

ELEGANT EXCHANGE
24 SHELFORD ROAD, RADCLIFFE-ON-TRENT, NOTTINGHAMSHIRE
NG12 2AG
☎ (0115) 9336086. OPEN 10 - 5 MON - FRI, 9 - 4 SAT, CLOSED WED.
Sells middle to top range designer labels including names such as Escada,
Caroline Charles, Jaeger, Windsmoor, Valentino and MaxMara. Lots of hats
for special occasions and some accessories such as shoes, handbags and jewellery. *Dress Agency*

ESSENTIAL ITEMS
CHURCH HOUSE, PLUNGAR, NOTTINGHAM NG13 0JA
☎ (0194) 9861172. FAX (0194) 9861320. OPEN 8 - 8 SEVEN DAYS A WEEK.
MAIL ORDER.
Essential Items is one of the country's most established companies manufacturing and designing stools and Ottomans. Other items new to their range are
elegant window seats and bed-end stools, all made to order and covered in the
customers' own fabric. Because of their low overheads, their mail order service
offers much more competitive prices than similar items bought in department
stores. Although items can be covered in calico, most lines are covered in customers' own material at no extra charge. Now specialising in hand made curtains as well as re-upholstery. *Permanent Discount Outlet*

Live Well On Less Tips
Cut down on the cost of marinading by reducing the amount of liquid called
for and marinading in a self-closing plastic bag instead of an open dish.

FACTORY SHOP OUTLET

CV CLOTHING LADIES AND CHILDRENSWEAR, SLEAFORD ROAD,
NEWARK, NOTTINGHAMSHIRE NG24 1NG
☎ (01636) 701390. OPEN 10 - 5 MON - SAT, 10 - 4 SUN, BANK HOLS.
CV CLOTHING, HUTHWAITE ROAD, SUTTON IN ASHFIELD NG17 2PE
☎ (01623) 517954. OPEN 10 - 2.30 MON, TUE, THUR, 8.30 -2 - FRI.
Part of the Coats Viyella group, which makes quality clothing for many of the
major high street storres, overstocks and clearance lines are sold through more
than 30 of the group's factory shops. Many of you will recognise the garments
on sale, despite the lack of well-known labels. Ladieswear includes dresses,
blouses, jumpers, cardigans, trousers, nightwear, underwear, lingerie, hosiery,
coats and swimwear. Menswear includes trousers, belts, shirts, ties, pullovers,
cardigans, T-shirts, underwear, nightwear, hosiery and jackets. Childrenswear
includes jackets, trousers, T-shirts, underwear, hosiery, jumpers and babywear.
There are regular deliveries to constantly update the range. *Factory Shop*

HARRIETS

13 CARTERGATE, NEWARK, NOTTINGHAMSHIRE NG24 1VA
☎ (01636) 611715. OPEN 9 - 5 MON - SAT, 10 - 4 SUN.
Many high street chainstore over-productions at discounted prices. Clothes
which are mostly Marks & Spencer seconds and discontinued lines, but also
some from Next, Dorothy Perkins and Littlewoods. For example, a Marks &
Spencer jacket which would normally cost £85, for sale at £40; skirts less than
£20; and coats and jackets to suit everyone from teenagers upwards in sizes 8-
20. *Permanent Discount Outlet*

JUST A SECOND FABRICS

7 KIRKSTALL LODGE, HIGH ST, EDWINSTOWE, MANSFIELD,
NOTTINGHAMSHIRE NG21 9QS
☎ (01623) 825156. OPEN 9.30 - 4.30 MON - FRI, 10 - 4 SAT, CLOSED WED.
Specialists in all aspects of soft furnishings, all products (fabrics, wallpaper,
carpets, etc) are carefully sourced to provide individual designs of exceptional
quality at affordable prices. Home design service available with first class making up service, upholstery, loose covers, quilting and much more. Hand-fin-
ished poles, tassle tie-backs, fringes and braids offer the perfect finishing
touches. These are price leaders at an average of 20% off brand names.
Permanent Discount Outlet

Live Well On Less Tips
Most new films are available on video fairly soon after general release in the
cinema. Wait until the video comes out and hire it for the night, saving yourself the price of cinema tickets.

LABELS OF EDWINSTOWE

25 HIGH STREET, EDWINSTOWE, NOTTINGHAMSHIRE NG21 9QP
☎ (01623) 825479.
Friendly and accommodating shops (there are other branches at Matlock and in the Peak District, Derbyshire), concentrating on upmarket and designer labels, they stock only items in immaculate condition. Their range covers clothes for every occasion from beachwear to ballgowns as well as a comprehensive selection of leather accessories and jewellery, all at very competitive prices. They also stock a large range of the very best fragrances at prices which compete very favourably with duty-free prices. Labels of Edwinstowe also incorporates The Desired Effect, selling unusual gifts, jewellery and offering aromatherapy and a range of beauty treatments and massages. All the Labels shops are well situated in areas which offer visitors other interesting attractions. *Dress Agency*

LIQUIDATION SUPPLIES

26 LONDON ROAD, RETFORD, NOTTINGHAMSHIRE DN22 6AY
☎ (01777) 711151. OPEN 9 - 5 MON - SAT, 11 - 4 SUN.
Factory soiled, new dishwashers, cookers, fridges, washing machines and built-in ovens, all with a one-year guarantee, at discount prices. *Permanent Discount Outlet*

MARTIN LINDSAY LTD

PO BOX 126, NEWARK, NOTTINGHAMSHIRE NG23 5PZ
☎ (01949) 836936/01636 525989.
Accessories and clothing made from exquisite, hand-printed fabrics including velvets, devore, silks and satins under the Jan Lindsay label which is sold in top department stores countrywide. Annual warehouse sale, usually towards the end of November, is well worth a visit. Write or ring to put your name on the mailing list for an invitation. Frequent sales throughout the year, please phone for details. *Designer Sale*

MATALAN

CHILWELL RETAIL PARK, NOTTINGHAM,
NOTTINGHAMSHIRE N69 6DS
☎ (0115) 946 9354. OPEN 10 - 8 MON - FRI, 9 - 6 SAT, 11 - 5 SUN.
Matalan is a fashion and homewares shop giving customers what they claim to be unbeatable value for money with huge savings on a wide range of products including high quality fashionable clothing for women, women and children at up to 50% off high street prices. Matalan is situated out of town and stores are open seven days a week all year round. *Permanent Discount Outlet*

MERIDIAN RETAIL FACTORY SHOP

PO BOX 54, HAYDN ROAD, NOTTINGHAM, NOTTINGHAMSHIRE
NG5 1DH

☎ (0115) 924 6154. OPEN 9 - 5.30 MON - SAT, UNTIL 7.30 WED,
10.30 - 4.30 SUN.

RAYMOTH LANE, WORKSOP, NOTTINGHAM, NOTTINGHAMSHIRE
S81 7LT

☎ (01909) 5☎ 01716. OPEN 9 - 5.30 MON - SAT, 10.30 - 4.30 SUN.

ELLIS STREET, KIRKBY IN ASHFIELD, NOTTINGHAM,
NOTTINGHAMSHIRE NG17 7AL

☎ (01623) 754193. OPEN 9 - 5 MON - SAT, 10.30 - 4.30 SUN.

SHERWOOD DRIVE, NEW OLLERTON, NEAR NEWARK, NOTTINGHAM,
NOTTINGHAMSHIRE NG22 9PN

☎ (01623) 836335. OPEN 9 - 5 MON - SAT.

The Haydn shop sells a wide range of ladies, men's and childrens high street
fashions at between 30% and 50% below high street prices as well as a good
selection of household textiles, shoes and accessories. The Raymoth, Kirky in
Ashfield and New Ollerton shops stock family clothing and baggage but no
household goods. Sells extensive range of casual wear for girls and boys from
birth to twelve years, men's and women's clothes, as well as seconds and
bought-in stock in bedding, towels, duvets and pillows, luggage, shoes and
accessories at discounts of 30%-50%. about half the stock is perfect, the other
half seconds. *Factory Shop*

NOTTINGHAM ARCHITECTURAL ANTIQUES

531 WOODBOROUGH ROAD, NOTTINGHAM, NOTTINGHAMSHIRE
NG3 5FR

☎ (0115) 960 5665. OPEN 9 - 5 MON - SAT, CLOSED WED.

Garden ornaments, bathroom fittings, Victorian fireplaces, doors, stained and
etched glass. *Architectural Salvage*

RENAISSANCE

31 WOLLATON ROAD, BEESTON, NOTTINGHAM, NOTTINGHAMSHIRE
NG9 2NG

☎ (0115) 9220653. OPEN 9 - 5.30 MON - THUR, SAT, 9 - 7 FRI, 11 - 4 SUN.

Ever-changing stock of labels from M&S to Moschino, Next to Nicole Farhi,
Jigsaw to Jacques Vert, Laura Ashley to Ralph Lauren, Gap to Gaultier, Austin
Reed to Armani. Prices from £5 to £300. About one quarter of the space is
devoted to men's clothes including a regular stock of Paul Smith, and there is
also some secondhand jewellery. All clothes and accessories are pristine and
imaginatively presented, in delightful, relaxed surroundings. Credit/Debit
cards welcome. *Dress Agency*

SPOILS

2B HIGH STREET, NOTTINGHAM, NOTTINGHAMSHIRE NG1 2ET
☎ (0115) 958 1210. OPEN 9 - 5.30 MON - SAT.
General domestic glassware, non-stick bakeware, kitchen gadgets, ceramic oven-to-tableware, textiles, cutting boards, aluminium non-stick cookware, bakeware, plastic kitchenware, plastic storage, woodware, coffee pots/makers, furniture, mirrors and picture frames. Rather than being discounted, all the merchandise is very competitively priced - in fact, the company carry out competitors' checks frequently in order to monitor pricing. With 38 branches, the company is able to buy in bulk and thus negotiate very good prices.
Permanent Discount Outlet

THE DESIGNER WAREHOUSE

FIFTH AVENUE INTERNATIONAL, CASTLE BUILDINGS, CASTLE BOULEVARD, NOTTINGHAM, NOTTINGHAMSHIRE N97 1SA
☎ (0115) 948 0100. OPEN 9 - 6 MON - SAT, 10 - 5 SUN.
Wholesalers who buy surplus stock in a wide variety of sizes and sell it to the public at this clearance shop. Most of the stock is for men and features Ralph Lauren, Versace, Armani, Calvin Klein, Cerruti jeans, leather jackets and sweatshirts at about half price. *Permanent Discount Outlet*

CV CLOTHING

RETFORD ROAD, MANTON, WORKSOP, NOTTINGHAMSHIRE S80 2PX
☎ (01909) 483898. OPEN 10 - 5 MON - SAT.
Part of the Coats Viyella group, which makes quality clothing for many of the major high street storres, overstocks and clearance lines are sold through more than 30 of the group's factory shops. Many of you will recognise the garments on sale, despite the lack of well-known labels. Ladieswear includes dresses, blouses, jumpers, cardigans, trousers, nightwear, underwear, lingerie, hosiery, coats and swimwear. Menswear includes trousers, belts, shirts, ties, pullovers, cardigans, T-shirts, underwear, nightwear, hosiery and jackets. Childrenswear includes jackets, trousers, T-shirts, underwear, hosiery, jumpers and babywear. There are regular deliveries to constantly update the range. *Factory Shop*

THE SHOE FACTORY SHOP

20 BROAD STREET, NOTTINGHAM, NOTTINGHAMSHIRE NG1 3AL
☎ (0115) 924 2390. OPEN 10 - 5 MON - FRI, 9.30 - 5.30 SAT.
Men's, women's and children's shoes and accessories which are bought in from other manufacturers including Spanish, Portuguese and Italian companies. All are unbranded. The range covers from mocassins to dressy shoes. Ladies shoes which would cost £35 retail are £29. Children's shoes from size 6 to adult size 5 from £10 upwards. Slippers start at baby size 4 to junior size 2 from £3.50 - £6.50.
Factory Shop

Live Well On Less Tips
Shop after 4pm on a Saturday when prices are often reduced on products whose sell-by dates won't last the weekend - especially fresh meat and bread. However, if the store opens on a Sunday reductions may well be kept until the end of the weekend.

THE SHOE SHED

ELLIS STREET, KIRKBY-IN-ASHFIELD, NOTTINGHAMSHIRE NG17 7AL
☎ (01623) 723083. OPEN 9 - 5 MON - SAT, 10.30 - 4.30 SUN.
Large factory shop selling a vast range of all types of women's, men's and children's shoes, all of which are perfects, at up to 30% below normal high street prices. Ladies sandals cost from £5; ladies shoes from £7.50. Men's shoes from £10; sports shoes from £10. *Factory Shop*

TILE CLEARING HOUSE

POULTON DRIVE, OFF DALESIDE ROAD, NOTTINGHAM, NOTTINGHAMSHIRE NG4 4DH
☎ (01159) 851 921. OPEN 8 - 6 MON - FRI, 9 - 6 SAT, 10 - 4 SUN.
Over 500 ranges of top quality ceramic wall and floor tiles permanently in stock, plus a comprehensive range of grouts, adhesives, tools and accessories to complete the job. Save up to 75% on manufacturers' recommended selling prices. *Permanent Discount Outlet*

TWEEDIES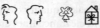

OGLE STREET, HUCKNALL, NOTTINGHAMSHIRE NG15 NFR
☎ (0115) 963 6662. OPEN 9 - 5 MON - SAT.
CENTRAL AVENUE, WEST BRIDGFORD, NOTTINGHAMSHIRE NG2 5GR
☎ (0115) 981 8752. OPEN 9 - 5.30 MON - FRI, 9 - 5 SAT.
THE SQUARE, BEESTON, NOTTINGHAMSHIRE NG9 2JH
☎ (0115) 943 0054. OPEN 9 - 5.30 MON - FRI, 9 - 5 SAT.
NOTTINGHAM ROAD, KEYWORTH, NOTTINGHAMSHIRE NG12 5GS
☎ (0115) 937 5067. OPEN 9 - 5.30 MON - FRI, 9 - 5 SAT.
Top brand names and favourite high street labels, all at discount prices of up to 50%. Family fashions plus some household goods and giftware to suit all budgets and ages. Although some of the labels are cut out, names you will recognise include Marks & Spencer, Evans, Wallis, Dorothy Perkins, Next and Etam, plus brands such as Farah, Wolsey, Fruit of the Loom, Wrangler, Nike, Adidas and Lyle & Scott. They now also have a range of top European designer labels like Steilman and Hucke. *Permanent Discount Outlet*

WARNERS UK LTD

DABELL AVENUE, BLENHEIM INDUSTRIAL PARK, BULWELL,
NOTTINGHAMSHIRE NG6 8WA

☎ (0115) 979 5796. OPEN 10 - 5 TUE - SAT.

This shop sells a wide range of women's lingerie from Leisureby, Valentino, Warners, with bras, slips, thongs, bodies and briefs at discounts from 25% to 70%. Each item is labelled with both the rrp and the discounted prices. For example, bikini brief, £6.99 reduced from £17; underwire bra, £14.99 reduced from £33; body, £24.99 reduced from £65. Slightly imperfect stock as well as perfect quality, end of season and discontinued merchandise and swimwear are also stocked. Underwear for men, including Calvin Klein briefs for £2.99, is on offer too. *Factory Shop*

WESTDALE TEXTILES

385 FOXHILL ROAD, CARLTON, NOTTINGHAMSHIRE NG4 1PZ

☎ (0115) 987 3353. OPEN 8.30 - 4 MON - FRI . MAIL ORDER.

A dream shop for dressmakers, it specialises in lace of all kinds - two-toned, coloured cotton, nylon and polyester - sold in minimum of 25 metre lengths. It also sells beads, ribbons, sequins, ribbon, ribbon roses, ribbon bows, beads on a string, dress nets and tulle, tiaras, broderie Anglaise, trimmings, bridal lace, plain satin ribbon and sewing threads. Discounts available as well as mail order, though prices are not reduced in the latter. *Factory Shop*

WESTON MILL POTTERY

NAVIGATION YARD, MILLGATE, NEWARK, NOTTINGHAMSHIRE
NG24 4TY

☎ (01636) 676835. OPEN 9 - 5 MON - SAT, 11 - 5 SUN, BANK HOLIDAYS.

Manufacturers of terracotta for home and garden, they stock garden pots, wall pots, troughs, novelty planters, kitchenware, casseroles, chicken bricks, egg racks, bread bins, mugs, perfume burners, candle pots. Garden pots are hand thrown on the premises in a variety of shapes and sizes. Made from quality clay and well-fired, they are very frost resistant. There's a wide range of kitchen and cookware on offer and quality imported flower pots, urns and small planters etc. Seconds and discontinued items at bargain prices. *Factory Shop*

Live Well On Less Tips

Stop felt pens from drying out because their caps are left off and having to be replaced. Take an old block of wood and drill holes in it. Then put the children's felt tip pens in the wood, cap side down so that the caps are permanently held in place by the holes and the children simply use the pens and then replace them in the block with the caps in.

Oxfordshire

WOMENSWEAR ONLY 🦃 Cerruti 1881-Femme Ltd, *Bicester*. Good As New, *Wantage*.
Hilary's Hat Hire, *Bodicote*. Hobbs, *Bicester*. Jane Shilton, *Bicester*. Jeffrey Rogers, *Bicester*.
Monsoon, *Bicester*. Ouiset, *Bicester*. Scoop, *Henley-On-Thames*. The Designer Room, *Bicester*.
The Pamela Howard Fashion Consultancy, *Boars Hill*. Togs, *Thame*.

MENSWEAR ONLY 👔 The Savoy Taylors Guild, *Bicester*.

WOMENSWEAR & MENSWEAR 🦃 👔 Aquascutum, *Bicester*. Benetton, *Bicester*.
Bicester Outlet Shopping Village, *Bicester*. Big Dog, *Bicester*. Burberrys Ltd, *Bicester*.
Clarks Factory Shop, *Bicester*. IMPS, *Witney*. IMPS, *Thame*. IMPS, *Bicester*.
In Wear Factory Outlet, *Bicester*. Jaeger Factory Shop, *Bicester*. Joan & David, *Bicester*.
John Partridge Outlet Store, *Bicester*. Matalan, *Oxford*. Nicole Farhi, *Bicester*.
French Connection, *Bicester Village*. Pepe Jeans London, *Bicester*.
Peruvian Connection, *Henley On Thames*. Polo Ralph Lauren Factory Store, *Bicester*.
Principles, *Bicester*. Racing Green, *Bicester*. Red/Green, *Bicester*. Revival Clothes Agency, *Oxford*.
The Ballroom, *Oxford*. TK Maxx, *Banbury*. Tog 24, *Bicester*. Top Marks, *Chipping Norton*.
Top Marks, *Banbury*. Triumph International Ltd, *Bicester*. Walton Clothing Co, *Chipping Norton*
Warners, *Bicester*

CHILDREN 🧸 Benetton, *Bicester*. Bicester Outlet Shopping Village, *Bicester*. Big Dog, *Bicester*.
Clarks Factory Shop, *Bicester*. IMPS, *Witney*. IMPS, *Thame*. IMPS, *Bicester*.
John Partridge Outlet Store, *Bicester*. Kids Play Factory, *Bicester*. Matalan, *Oxford*.
Pepe Jeans London, *Bicester*. The Red House, *Witney*. TK Maxx, *Banbury*. Tog 24, *Bicester*
Top Marks, *Chipping Norton* Top Marks, *Banbury*

HOUSEHOLD AND GIFTWARE 🏛 Bicester Outlet Shopping Village, *Bicester*.
Descamps, *Bicester Village*. Discount China, *Burford*. Early's Of Witney, *Witney*.
IMPS, *Witney*. IMPS, *Thame*. IMPS, *Bicester*. Isis Ceramics, *Oxford*.
Jane And Stephen Baughan, *Aston*. Matalan, *Oxford*. Mill Outlets Ltd, *Banbury*. Oneida, *Bicester*.
Price's Candles, *Bicester*. TK Maxx, *Banbury*. Villeroy & Boch (UK) Ltd, *Bicester*.
Woods Of Windsor, *Bicester*.

DIY/RENOVATION 🔨 Fired Earth, *Adderbury*.

FURNITURE/SOFT FURNISHINGS 🛋 Curtain World, *Oxford*. Just Fabrics, *Burford*.
Loose Ends, *Witney*. The Curtain Exchange, *Thame*.
The Lighthouse Collection, *Long Hanborough*. The Weavers Shop, *Bloxham*.

FOOD AND LEISURE 📖 Dakota Marketing, *Witney*. Sapphire Books, *Bicester*.
Travel Accessory Outlet, *Bicester*.

SPORTSWEAR AND EQUIPMENT 🎿 Bicester Outlet Shopping Village, *Bicester*
Clarks Factory Shop, *Bicester*. Fred Perry Ltd, *Bicester*. Red/Green, *Bicester*.

Live Well On Less Tips
When you're at the cinema, take your own sweets/crisps/popcorn.

AQUASCUTUM

BICESTER OUTLET SHOPPING VILLAGE, PINGLE DRIVE, BICESTER, OXFORDSHIRE OX6 7WD

☎ (01869) 325943. OPEN 10 - 6 SEVEN DAYS A WEEK.

Ends of ranges, last season's stock and cancelled export orders for women and men from the complete Aquascutum range. There is a minimum 25% discount against normal retail prices, and up to 50% on some lines. *Factory Shopping Village*

BENETTON

BICESTER OUTLET SHOPPING VILLAGE, PINGLE DRIVE, BICESTER, JUNCTION 9 OF M40, OXFORDSHIRE OX6 7WD

☎ (01869) 320030. OPEN 10 - 6 SEVEN DAYS A WEEK.

Benetton stocks a wide range of clothes for women, men and children including colourful T-shirts, sweatshirts, men's button-neck T-shirts, swimwear, jeans, children's jackets, stretch short and all-in-one shorts. Some of the stock is marked seconds, but it is often difficult to tell why. *Factory Shopping Village*

BICESTER OUTLET SHOPPING VILLAGE

PINGLE DRIVE, BICESTER, JUNCTION 9 OF M40, OXFORDSHIRE OX6 7WD

☎ (01869) 323200. OPEN 10 - 6 SEVEN DAYS A WEEK.

Described as 'Bond Street comes to Bicester', when it opened four years ago, Bicester Village has established itself as the UK's leading outlet shopping destination with by far the largest selection of international Bond Street names to choose from. Currently there are 60 shops offering quality merchandise at discounts of up to 60%, sometimes even more. The choice of famous brands at Bicester Village is second to none. International star names include a Polo Ralph Lauren store, newly enlarged to include more goods from their sport and home collections, Donna Karan, Versace, Christian Lacroix, Cerruti 1881 and TSE Cashmere. New arrivals from the international fashion scene are Escada, Gianfranco Ferre and Alta Moda, a shop which stocks Valentino among its other brands. Both of Britain's leading designers, Nicole Farhi and Paul Smith, have shops with goods from their men's and women's collections. Karen Millen and Whistles both cater for the younger set with much more women's fashion to be found in The Designer Room, Episode, Hobbs, Jigsaw and Inwear Matinique. Top high street names are also well represented by Benetton, Principles, French Connection, Monsoon, Pepe Jeans, Racing Green and Jeffery Rogers. The more classic customer also has an unequalled choice with Burberry, Aquascutum, Jaeger and the Scandinavian company Red/Green, whose yachting style of casualwear is very popular. Rugged outdoor wear can be found at Helly Hansen, Tog

24, the climbing and walking specialist and John Partridge for traditional countrywear. Active sportswear, represented by Fred Perry and Reebok, has now been joined by one of America's most famous sports shoe brands, Vans. A comprehensive collection of shoes, including many ranges for children, can be found in Clarks, with elegant high fashion styles in Charles Jourdan from Paris and Joan & David from New York. Also, for ladies shoes, handbags and accessories, there is Jane Shilton; for luggage, there is The Travel Accessory Outlet, which features much of the Samsonite range, plus the exciting new addition of the first TAG-Heuer outlet, which will stock end-of-line designer watches, all fully guaranteed, at very attractive prices. Lingerie and underwear is to be found at Warners and Triumph, with HOM, the French brand, for the men; the finest French childrenswear at Petit Bateau; English fragrances at Penhaligon's and soaps and gifts at Woods of Windsor. For the home, there are Price's candles and towels and duvets from another leading French brand, Descamps; cutlery from Oneida; china and crystal from Villeroy & Boch and Waterford Wedgwood. Another exciting addition is the Cosmetic Company, which stocks well-known skincare products, cosmetics and fragrances for men and women. Bicester Village likes to see itself as something akin to a 'one-floor department store' and menswear, which can often be found in the designer shops, is also well represented in its own right with Blazer, Savoy Taylors Guild, Jigsaw Menswear and Dockers, plus another international touch being provided by Cerruti Menswear, all offering good size ranges in a wide choice from very casual through to traditional business clothes, and even Millennium vital eveningwear from Moss Bros. To complete the day out at Bicester Village, take home some popular titles from Sapphire Books, the outlet shop of the Borders/Books etc. Group, get to know more about the location for a return visit from the Tourist Information Centre, and regain strength with top quality refreshment at Pret-A-Manger. There are cash machines, a children's play area, free parking and a shuttle bus and taxi connection to Bicester North Station, which is on the Chiltern Railways line, and runs between Marylebone and Birmingham. Bicester Village is about one hour's drive from London, two miles from Junction 9 on the M40. Take the A41and follow signs for Village Retail Park. *Factory Shopping Village*

BIG DOG

BICESTER OUTLET SHOPPING VILLAGE, PINGLE DRIVE, BICESTER, JUNCTION 9 OF M40, OXFORDSHIRE OX6 7WD

☎ (01869) 323280. OPEN 10 - 6 SEVEN DAYS A WEEK.

This is a Californian casualwear company selling a wide range of T-shirts, sweatshirts, shorts and nightwear for men, women and children. All the clothes are unisex. All the stock is available in the USA and through the UK mail order catalogue. Examples of prices include sweatshirts, £14.99, reduced from £38; T-shirts from £5.99 to £16.99; men's shorts, £24.99 reduced from £30. *Factory Shopping Village*

BURBERRYS LTD

BICESTER OUTLET SHOPPING VILLAGE, PINGLE DRIVE, BICESTER,
JUNCTION 9 OF M40, OXFORDSHIRE OX6 7WD

☎ (01869) 323522. OPEN 10 - 6 SEVEN DAYS A WEEK.

Sells a variety of Burberry and Thomas Burberry goods for men and women.
Thomas Burberry jeans and polo shirts, £19.95 reduced from £49.50; classic
men's check shirts, £41.95, reduced from £99.50; umbrellas, £26.95 reduced
from £65; a variety of purses and wallets, some reduced to £31.95 from £65.
Also handbags and travel bags; classic trench coats and overcoats reduced from
£160 to £78.95. Thomas Burberry cashmere from £21.95. *Factory
Shopping Village*

CERRUTI 1881-FEMME LTD

BICESTER OUTLET SHOPPING VILLAGE, PINGLE DRIVE, BICESTER,
JUNCTION 9 OF M40, OXFORDSHIRE OX6 7WD

☎ (01869) 325519. OPEN 10 - 6 SEVEN DAYS A WEEK.

Cerruti has a very stylish shop in this designer village, offering a range of their
women's clothes at discounts of up to 60%. Examples of prices include jackets reduced from £499 to £299; silk blouses reduced from £159 to £89; linen
dresses reduced from £229 to £115; trousers suits reduced from £625 to £339;
trousers reduced from £199 to £99. *Factory Shopping Village*

CLARKS FACTORY SHOP

BICESTER OUTLET SHOPPING VILLAGE, PINGLE DRIVE, BICESTER,
JUNCTION 9 OF M40, OXFORDSHIRE OX6 7WD

☎ (01869) 325646. OPEN 10 - 6 SEVEN DAYS A WEEK AND BANK
HOLIDAYS.

Clarks International operate a chain of factory shops nationally which specialise in selling discontinued lines and slight sub-standards for men, women
and children from Clarks, K Shoes and other famous brands. These shops
trade under the name of Crockers, K Shoes Factory shop or Clarks Factory
Shop and while not all are physically attached to a shoe factory, these shops
are treated as factory shops by the company. Customers can expect to find an
extensive range of quality shoes, sandals, walking boots, slippers, trainers,
handbags, accessories and gifts, while their major outlets also offer luggage,
sports clothing, sports equipment and outdoor clothing. Brands stocked
include Clarks, K Shoes, Springer, CICA, Hi-Tec, Puma, Mercury, Dr
Martens, Nike, LA Gear, Fila, Mizuno, Slazenger, Weider, Antler and Carlton,
although not all are sold in every outlet. Discounts are from 30% to 60% off
the normal high street price for perfect stock. *Factory Shopping Village*

Live Well On Less Tips
About to throw away your used mascara? Let it sit in hot water for half an hour and it will revive to give you another week or two of longer lashes.

CURTAIN WORLD
276 BANBURY ROAD, OXFORD, OXFORDSHIRE OX2 3TX
☎ (01865) 516181. OPEN 9.30 - 5 MON - FRI, 9.30 - 4 SAT.
Brand name fabrics at bargain prices including Osborne & Little, Next, Ametex, Sanderson and Monkwell. The average discount is between 40%-50% and they also sell a wide range of chintzes from £2.99 a yard, curtain poles and accessories. The company has been in operation for more than 20 years and can offers lots of helpful advice. Up to 900 rolls of fabric at any one time sold at about half price including lots of natural and Indian fabrics.
Permanent Discount Outlet

DAKOTA MARKETING
PO BOX 121, WITNEY, OXFORDSHIRE OX8 1YU
☎ (01865) 880024. MAIL ORDER ONLY.
Best-selling paperbacks, audio books and a few CD Roms at discounted prices. A reader who has used this service a few times tells the GDD that the books can take up to four weeks to arrive. Audiobook cassettes, from £3.50; paperbacks, from £1.95; children's books, from £1.65; CD Roms, from £2.
Permanent Discount Outlet

FACTORY SHOPPING VILLAGE

DESCAMPS
BICESTER VILLAGE, PINGLE DRIVE, JUNCTION 9 OF M40, OXFORDSHIRE OX6 7WD
☎ (01869) 323636. OPEN 10 - 6 SEVEN DAYS A WEEK.
French designer range of bedlinen, towels and dressing gowns. By using a very high cotton count (the amount of thread used per square metre), their bedlinen is very soft. The higher the density of cotton, the better the quality.
Factory Shopping Village

DISCOUNT CHINA
HIGH STREET, BURFORD, OXFORDSHIRE OX18 4QA
☎ (01993) 823452. OPEN 10 - 5 SEVEN DAYS A WEEK.
Retailers of china and cookware direct from the factories of Staffordshire. Supplies are sourced from different manufacturers so varies according to what is available at the time, but includes china fancies, beakers, cookware, planters, Portmerion cookware and dinner sets. *Permanent Discount Outlet*

EARLY'S OF WITNEY

WITNEY MILL, BURFORD ROAD, WITNEY, OXFORDSHIRE OX8 5EB
☎ (01993) 703131. OPEN 10 - 4 MON - SAT.

Having moved to a different position on the same site, the shop is now bigger and sells a wider range of stock. Blankets in pure new Merino wool, traditional cellular blankets, new designs in cotton blankets in a myriad selection of colours, economy priced acrylic blankets, baby blankets, the famous Witney Point blankets, white cotton embroidered bedlinen, pram blankets, table cloths, teacloths, at factory prices. Blanket stock is made in the next door factory and depends on what is available from there. There are also some seconds, but most of the goods are perfects. Great place to shop for new bedlinen and bedspreads. There were some exceptional bargains in clearance items when we visited. The shop also stocks Coloroll bedlinen at 20% discount; a wide range of perfect and imperfect towels from Chortex, plus towelling robes, and duvets and pillows from Polywarm, including Horrockses branded products.
Factory Shop

FIRED EARTH

TWYFORD MILL, ADDERBURY, OXFORDSHIRE OX5 3PX
☎ (01295) 814399. OPEN 9.30 - 5.30 MON - SAT, 12 - 4 SUN.

Fired Earth sell seconds and discontinued ranges of tiles, fabric and natural fibre floor coverings from their countryside venue, as well as rugs, kelims, gabbehs and other tribal weaving at full price. Terracotta and slate floor tiles are sold from around £15 a square metre upwards: some glazed tiles from around £5 a square metre. Typical bargains in fabric range from prototype tartans (unique because they have not been put into production) to slightly soiled crewel works (which simply need dry cleaning) often at less than cost price. Fired Earth also produce the V&A range of historic and traditional paints and dented paints tins are sold at a discount alongside other bruised accessories.
Factory Shop

FRED PERRY LTD

BICESTER OUTLET SHOPPING VILLAGE, PINGLE DRIVE, BICESTER, JUNCTION 9 OF M40, OXFORDSHIRE OX6 7WD
☎ (01869) 325504. OPEN 10 - 6 SEVEN DAYS A WEEK.

Sells men's and women's ranges of the famous Fred Perry active performance clothing: shorts, tennis tops, tracksuits, T-shirts. All price labels show the original and the reduced price. *Factory Shopping Village*

Live Well On Less Tips
Have a dry cut at the hairdressers or a wet cut and leave with your hair wet

GOOD AS NEW

21 NEWBURY STREET, WANTAGE, OXFORDSHIRE OX12 8BU

☎ (01235) 769526 OPEN 10 - 4 TUE - SAT.

High street, medium sized shop selling ladies designer wear ranging from Marks & Spencer to Armani, though the majority of clothes come from Jaeger, Windsmoor and Planet. All nearly-new clothes are under two years old and come in a wide range of sizes. Good selection of evening wear including Frank Usher, Jean Allen and Laura Ashley ballgowns. The full range from coats, dresses, separates, evening wear and hats to shoes and handbags are sold. *Dress Agency*

HILARY'S HAT HIRE

THE OVEN, 1 HIGH STREET, BODICOTE, OXFORDSHIRE OX15 4BZ

☎ (01295) 263880. OPEN 9.30 - 7 MON - FRI, BY APPOINTMENT ONLY.

Home-based business in a converted barn with more than 500 hats from which to choose. £25 hires a hat for a weekend. Whether you're looking for something for a wedding, funeral or graduation, regattas or race events, you'll find something suitable here, whatever your age. *Hire Shop*

HOBBS

BICESTER OUTLET SHOPPING VILLAGE, PINGLE DRIVE, BICESTER, JUNCTION 9 OF M40, OXFORDSHIRE OX6 7WD

☎ (01869) 325660. OPEN 10 - 6 SEVEN DAYS A WEEK.

Hobbs has a range of clothes for women and a large shoe selection. All carry reductions of between 30% and 70%. Styles include business suits, evening wear, and fashionable high street designs. *Factory Shopping Village*

IMPS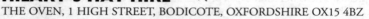

34 MARKET SQUARE, WITNEY, OXFORDSHIRE OX8 58A

☎ (01993) 779875. OPEN 9 - 5.30 MON - SAT.

40 UPPER HIGH STREET, THAME, OXFORDSHIRE OX9 3AG

☎ (01844) 212985. OPEN 9 - 5 MON - SAT.

52 SHEEP STREET, BICESTER, OXFORDSHIRE

☎ (01869) 243455. OPEN 9 - 5 MON - SAT.

High street shops selling popular chainstore seconds fashion for all the family as well as towels, china, trays and flower cachepots. For women, there are jeans, £12.99, dressing gowns, £20. For men, shirts, £8-£12, Y-fronts, £1.65, boxer shorts, £2.99, socks, 90p, pyjamas, £11.99, four-button collar T-shirts, £6.99. For children, vests and knickers, 75p, socks, 75p, jeans, £6.99, pyjamas, £6.99, smocked dresses, £6.99. There are also hand towels, £2.99, bath towels, £5.99, bath sheets, £9.99, plates, £3.50. Stock changes constantly. *Permanent Discount Outlet*

Live Well On Less Tips
If you're one of the estimated 25% who pays for their prescriptions and you need to take regular medication for a while, you can save money by buying a pre-payment certificate. A six-month certificate costs £30.80, a 12-month one £84.60 and both entitle you to as many prescriptions as you need during that period. With prescriptions costing £5.90 an item, you can save on the six-month certificate after just six items. Ask for form FP95 from your post office or local pharmacy; form EC95 if you live in Scotland.

IN WEAR FACTORY OUTLET

BICESTER VILLAGE, PINGLE DRIVE, JUNCTION 9 OF M40,
OXFORDSHIRE OX6 7WD
☎ (01869) 369415. OPEN 10 - 6 SEVEN DAYS A WEEK.
In Wear for women and Matinique for men and Part Two for both men and women at discounts of between 30%-70% for last season's stock, ends of lines and seconds. All the stock is made up of separates and tends to be stylishly casual and includes blazers, jeans, trousers, dresses, knitwear, suits and outerwear. *Factory Shopping Village*

ISIS CERAMICS

THE OLD TOFFEE FACTORY, 120A MARLBOROUGH RD,
OXFORD OX1 4LS
☎ (01865) 722729. OPEN 10 - 4 MON -FRI, SAT BY APPOINTMENT.
Makers of ceramics which are handpainted in the style of seventeenth and eighteenth century Delftware, Isis has a range of cut-price seconds on sale at its workshops and showroom set in an old toffee factory in Oxford. Their most popular seller is the flower brick followed by lamps and colander bowls, all painted in traditional colours - blue, green and plum. They also do complete dinner services, platters with tulips, birds and farmyard animals, dessert plates with scalloped edges, teapots and cream jugs, vases, baluster vases and cachepots. Seconds range from £10, high quality seconds enjoy discounts of at least 25%, and seconds in candlesticks, flower bricks and colander bowls are half price. There are twice-yearly clearance sales in January and July. Best to phone ahead for weekend opening times. *Factory Shop*

JAEGER FACTORY SHOP

BICESTER VILLAGE, 35 PINGLE DRIVE, BICESTER (JUNCTION 9 OF M40), OXFORDSHIRE OX6 7WD
☎ (01869) 369220. OPEN 10 - 6 MON - SAT, 11 - 5 SUN.
Contemporary classics from Jaeger at excellent prices. Most of the merchandise is previous seasons' stock, but you might also find some special makes. Both shops stock tailoring and knitwear for women and men. *Factory Shopping Village*

JANE AND STEPHEN BAUGHAN

THE STABLE, KINGSWAY FARM, ASTON, OXFORDSHIRE OX18 2BT

☎ (01993) 852031. OPEN 9 - 5 MON - SAT, 10.30 - 4.30 SUN, BANK HOLS.
Set in a converted barn next to their workshop, Jane and Stephen Baughan's factory shop sells seconds and overmakes of their hand decorated pottery. The pottery is made using traditional methods of slip-casting and jollying before being decorated by hand using a combination of fresh colours and a wide variety of surface designs. They have also developed their own specialised technique of hand stencilling on pottery. Designs range from Sunflower and Blue Wild Clematis to birds and animals, and all products are microwave and dishwasher safe. Stephen and Jane usually supply more than 200 shops, as well as the National Trust. There is now a visitors' centre open on weekdays from 9 to 5. Tours take place four times a day at £1.50 for adults and £1 for children, with the chance to decorate you own piece. Coffee shop and free parking for 250 cars. *Factory Shop*

JANE SHILTON

BICESTER OUTLET SHOPPING VILLAGE, BICESTER, JUNCTION 9 OF M40, OXFORDSHIRE OX6 7WD

☎ (01869) 325387. OPEN 10 - 6 SEVEN DAYS A WEEK.
This shop only carries merchandise from past seasons' collections or factory seconds at discounts of at least 30% and tup to 50%. There is a wide range of handbags, suitcases, women's shoes, luggage, briefcases, umbrellas, scarves and travel bags. *Factory Shopping Village*

JEFFREY ROGERS

BICESTER OUTLET SHOPPING VILLAGE, PINGLE DRIVE, BICESTER, JUNCTION 9 OF M40, OXFORDSHIRE OX6 7WD

☎ (01869) 323567. OPEN 10 - 6 SEVEN DAYS A WEEK.
Jeffrey Rogers stocks fashions for the younger, trendy end of the market . There is also the Rogers Plus range for sizes 16-24. Twenty five percent of the stock is discounted by 75%. *Factory Shopping Village*

JOAN & DAVID

BICESTER OUTLET SHOPPING VILLAGE, PINGLE DRIVE, BICESTER, JUNCTION 9 OF M40, OXFORDSHIRE OX6 7WD

☎ (01869) 323387. OPEN 10 - 6 SEVEN DAYS A WEEK.
This is a very stylish shop stocking about 60% footwear for men and women, 25% classic clothing for women only and 15% accessories. J & D's divine shoes are reduced by about 50%, though they are still mostly above the £60 mark. *Factory Shopping Village*

JOHN PARTRIDGE OUTLET STORE

BICESTER OUTLET VILLAGE, 32 PINGLE DRIVE, JUNCTION 9 OF M40, BICESTER, OXFORDSHIRE OX6 7WD

☎ (01869) 325332. OPEN 10 - 6 SEVEN DAYS A WEEK.

John Partridge specialises in hardwearing outdoor clothes. Ranges include waxed cotton jackets, trench coats and waistcoats; showerproof classic town coats; Gore-tex coats and tweed coats; quilted jackets and waistcoats; children's waxed jackets, quilted jackets and waistcoats; hats and caps; moleskin and cord trousers; knitwear and shirts. Discontinued lines and seconds are on sale at discounted prices - a minimum of 30% and up to 70% off during promotions. *Factory Shopping Village*

JUST FABRICS

BURFORD ANTIQUES CENTRE, CHELTENHAM ROAD, BURFORD, OXFORDSHIRE OX18 4JA

☎ (01993) 823391. OPEN 9.30 - 5.30 MON - SAT, 12 - 4 SUN.
MAIL ORDER.

Just Fabrics offers huge savings on a comprehensive selection of quality furnishing fabrics from stock. Whether choosing a leading designer name, clearance or from their own range of linen unions or checks and stripe collection, all are very competitively priced. Their telephone enquiry service is also very popular. After discussing your fabric requirements, stock fabric cuttings are then despatched. A mail order service is available. They do not order from pattern books. The enquiry line is 01993 823690, open 9 - 4 Monday to Friday with an answerphone out of hours. *Permanent Discount Outlet*

KIDS PLAY FACTORY

BICESTER OUTLET SHOPPING VILLAGE, BICESTER, JUNCTION 9 OF M40, OXFORDSHIRE OX6 7WD

☎ (01869) 323434. OPEN 10 - 6 SEVEN DAYS A WEEK.

This shop sells a wide range of well-known children's brand names: Tomy, Matchbox, Lego, The First Years, Hasbro, Disney, Playskool, Mattel and Fisher-Price at discounts of up to 50%. They also stock a wide range of soft toys including TY Beanie Babies. *Factory Shopping Village*

LOOSE ENDS

78 HIGH STREET, WITNEY, OXFORDSHIRE OX8 6HL

☎ (01993) 773508. OPEN 9.30 - 5 MON - SAT.

Selected seconds in furnishing fabrics from well-known designers. Budget ranges of first quality fabrics in cotton prints and natural fabrics. Damasks and Madras checks mostly £11.50 a metre. Medium-sized shop in busy high street with double yellow lines outside, although there is a car park nearby. Full making up service is available. *Permanent Discount Outlet*

MATALAN

UNIT 5, THE JOHN ALLEN CENTRE, COWLEY, OXFORD, OXFORDSHIRE OX4 3JP

☎ (01865) 747400. OPEN 10 - 8 MON - FRI, 9.30 - 5.30 SAT, 10 - 6 SUN.

Matalan is a fashion and homewares shop giving customers what they claim to be unbeatable value for money with huge savings on a wide range of products including high quality fashionable clothing for women, women and children at up to 50% off high street prices. Matalan is situated out of town and stores are open seven days a week all year round. *Permanent Discount Outlet*

MILL OUTLETS LTD

51 HIGH STREET, BANBURY, OXFORDSHIRE, OX16 BLA

☎ (01295) 264455. OPEN 9 - 5 MON - SAT.

Specialises in curtains, net curtains, bedding, bed linens, towels, kitchen textiles and other household textiles. They also offer ranges of hand knitting yarns, men's and ladies socks, hosiery and underwear. Merchandise comes direct from the manufacturers, often made up of clearance stock or chainstore overmakes and seconds. Prices are very competitive with savings of up to 50% and more off manufacturer's recommended prices. *Permanent Discount Outlet*

MONSOON

BICESTER VILLAGE, JUNCTION 9 OF M40, BICESTER, OXFORDSHIRE, OX6 7WD

☎ (01869) 323200. OPEN 10 - 6 SEVEN DAYS A WEEK.

Medium-sized outlet selling last year's stock and discontinued lines, including jewellery. There is also an outlet at Clarks Village in Somerset. The telephone number given here is for the village *Factory Shop*

NICOLE FARHI

BICESTER VILLAGE, JUNCTION 9 OF M40, BICESTER, OXFORDSHIRE OX6 7WD

☎ (01869) 232346. OPEN 10 - 6 SEVEN DAYS A WEEK.

FRENCH CONNECTION, BICESTER VILLAGE

☎ (01869) 369582. OPEN 10 -6 SEVEN DAYS A WEEK.

Sells previous season merchandise, samples and seconds form Nicole Farhi at 30% - 80% less than retail price. There is also a Nicole Farhi/French Connection factory shop in London *Factory Shop*

Live Well On Less Tips
Always order the house wine at restaurants.

Live Well On Less Tips

Booking a holiday through a well-known high street agent? Before you pay your deposit, phone your credit card company's holiday travel service. Because they mostly operate a phone service rather than high street retail outlets, they can pass on their cost savings to you in the form of a discount on your chosen holiday.

ONEIDA

BICESTER OUTLET SHOPPING VILLAGE, PINGLE DRIVE, BICESTER, JUNCTION 9 OF M40, OXFORDSHIRE OX6 7WD

☎ (01869) 324789. OPEN 10 - 6 SEVEN DAYS A WEEK.

Oneida is one of the world's largest cutlery companies and originates from the United States of America. In addition to cutlery, it sells silver and silver plate at discounts of between 30% and 50%, plus frames, candlesticks and trays. They now also have their own range of chinaware and glass, also sold here at discounts of 30%-50%. *Factory Shopping Village*

OUISET

BICESTER VILLAGE, BICESTER, JUNCTION 9 OF M40, OXFORDSHIRE

☎ (01869) 242402. OPEN 10 - 6 SEVEN DAYS A WEEK.

Sells clearance lines from Ouiset branches countrywide. Current season end of lines are sold off at 30%-40% discounts; last year's seasonal stock at 50% off and out of season stock at 70% reductions. There are usually also some samples to be found. Stock includes sweaters, jackets, trousers, blouses and skirts. Sizes range from 8-18. *Factory Shopping Village*

PEPE JEANS LONDON

UNIT 2, BICESTER OUTLET SHOPPING VILLAGE, PINGLE DRIVE, BICESTER, JUNCTION 9 OF M40, OXFORDSHIRE OX6 7WD

☎ (01869) 325378. OPEN 10 - 6 SEVEN DAYS A WEEK.

Pepe Jeans is a European fashion jean company stocking a wide range of casual wear including men's, women's and children's jeans, all of which are end of season or fragmented ranges. Free alteration service and full refund and exchange policy offered. There's also a postal service - phone for details. *Factory Shopping Village*

PERUVIAN CONNECTION

28 HART STREET, HENLEY ON THAMES, OXFORDSHIRE RG9 2AU

☎ (01491) 414446. OPEN 9.30 - 5.30 MON - SAT, JULY - DEC: 12 - 5 SUN.

Last season's stock from the well-known Peruvian Connection catalogue. Alpaca and cotton sweaters, lighter weight polo necks, cardigans and pullovers for men and women at discounted prices. *Permanent Discount Outlet*

POLO RALPH LAUREN FACTORY STORE

BICESTER OUTLET SHOPPING VILLAGE, PINGLE DRIVE, BICESTER, JUNCTION 9 OF M40, OXFORDSHIRE, OX6 7WD

☎ (01869) 325200. OPEN 10 - 6 MON - SAT, 12 - 6 SUN.

Polo Ralph Lauren, the largest shop in this factory shopping village with the prime spot, has discounted items by between 35% and 60% for men, women and boys. For men wool jackets, jackets, sports jackets, Polo T-shirts, rugby shirts, trousers, jeans, ties, as well as accessories. For women, outerwear, skirts, jackets, dresses, trousers, skirts, knits, T-shirts and accessories. *Factory Shopping Village*

PRICE'S CANDLES

BICESTER OUTLET SHOPPING VILLAGE, PINGLE DRIVE, BICESTER, JUNCTION 9 OF M40, OXFORDSHIRE, OX6 7WD

☎ (01869) 325520. OPEN 10 - 6 SEVEN DAYS A WEEK.

Everything sold in this shop are seconds, which may be discoloured or have a damaged pattern; discontinued sizes not available elsewhere; over-runs from the garden selection or dinner candles in old packaging that has now been replaced. There are church candles, lanterns, candles in pots and glass jars, star-shaped candles, floating candles, candlestick holders, serviettes, scented candles and garden torches. Some of the ceramic items are bought in. The village also has a cafe, children's play area and free parking. *Factory Shopping Village*

PRINCIPLES

BICESTER VILLAGE, PINGLE DRIVE, BICESTER, JUNCTION 9 OF M40, OXFORDSHIRE OX6 7WD

☎ (01869) 325300. OPEN 10 - 6 SEVEN DAYS A WEEK.

End of season lines with the normal Principles refund guarantee. The range includes, for women, dresses, blouses, coats, outerwear, knitwear, casualwear and a selection of Petite clothing for women who are 5ft 3ins and under. For men, there is formalwear, smart casualwear, knitwear, outerwear, PFM Sport, jeanswear and casualwear. *Factory Shopping Village*

RACING GREEN

BICESTER VILLAGE, BICESTER, JUNCTION 9 OF M40, OXFORDSHIRE OX6 7WD

☎ (01869) 325484. OPEN 10 - 6 SEVEN DAYS A WEEK.

Overstocks and clearance lines from this mail order catalogue are sold here at discount prices. *Factory Shopping Village*

Live Well On Less Tips
Call 151 for details of schemes for saving money on your phone bill.

RED/GREEN

UNIT 47, BICESTER OUTLET SHOPPING VILLAGE, PINGLE DRIVE,
BICESTER, JUNCTION 9 OF M40, OXFORDSHIRE OX6 7WD
☎ (01869) 323324. OPEN 10 - 6 SEVEN DAYS A WEEK.
Red/Green is a Scandinavian company which sells very stylish post sailing or
leisure wear clothes (you don't have to sail to wear them) for men and women.
All the clothes are last season's and discounts are between 25% and 70%.
There are sailing clothes, golf wear, nautical and casual wear, shirts, sweatshirts, apres ski wear, anoraks, gilets, classic sweaters, sailing shoes and soft
bags. *Factory Shopping Village*

REVIVAL CLOTHES AGENCY

60 ST CLEMENT'S, OXFORD, OXFORDSHIRE 0X4 1AH
☎ (01865) 251005, OPEN 10 - 4 TUE, WED, THUR, 10 - 5 FRI, SAT.
A large shop containing two large rooms behind a showroom. The ladies section includes labels from Wallis and Next to Whistles, Nicole Farhi, Jaeger and
Karl Lagerfeld. There are also accessories such as hats and jewellery. All prices
are well under half the original price, unless the item is brand new - Revival
does occasionally take in stock from shops that have closed down or people
bring in mistakes . Sizes range from 8 - 24. The Wedding dress section has
dresses from £90 - £600 including Ronald Joyce and Anna Belinda. The
evening dresses range from £30 - £100 and include many Monsoon ballgowns.
The menswear is not extensive but includes Armani, Next and Jaeger suits, and
Aquascutum overcoats. Hat hire now also available at £15. *Dress Agency*

SAPPHIRE BOOKS

BICESTER OUTLET SHOPPING VILLAGE, PINGLE DRIVE, BICESTER,
JUNCTION 9 OF M40, OXFORDSHIRE OX6 7WD
☎ (01869) 325417. OPEN 10 - 6 SEVEN DAYS A WEEK.
This shop sells a wide range of books, including popular paperback and hardback fiction, classics, cookery titles, children's books and reference tomes, as
well as wrapping paper and greetings cards. All books are sold at a discount of
at least 30% from the reccommended retail price and many are available at
even greater savings. *Factory Shopping Village*

SCOOP

77 BELL STREET, HENLEY-ON-THAMES, OXFORDSHIRE RG9 2BD
☎ (01491) 572962. OPEN 10 - 5 MON - SAT.
Nearly-new ladies wear from designers at the top end of the market, including Escada, Betty Barclay, Valentino, Armani, Emanuel, Louis Feraud. Often
stocks seasonal wear for Ascot and Derby Day, as well as cocktail and wedding
outfits. Also has a supply of holidaywear, shoes, hats, jewellery and other
accessories. *Dress Agency*

THE BALLROOM

5-6 THE PLAIN, OXFORD, OXFORDSHIRE OX4 1AS
☎ (01865) 241054. ☎ (01865) 202303 FOR MENSWEAR.
OPEN 9.15 - 5.45 MON - SAT.
Bridal wear, ballgowns, and formal wear for men to hire or to buy. £25-£200 to hire and £65-£800 to buy. Dinner jackets, from £12 to buy or £25 to hire a dinner suit. More than 2,000 ballgowns in stock; Also clearance short dresses from £15, long dresses from £45. *Hire Shop*

THE CURTAIN EXCHANGE

85 HIGH STREET, THAME, OXFORDSHIRE OX9 3EH
☎ (01844) 261566. OPEN 9.30 - 5.30 MON - SAT.
The Curtain Exchange is a franchised group of shops selling beautiful top quality secondhand curtains, blinds, pelmets, etc at between one-third and one half of the brand new price. Their stock comes from a variety of sources: people who are moving house and dislike the drapes in their new home; people who are moving house and want to sell their old curtains to help with the bills; show houses, where the builder wants to recoup some of his outgoings; interior designers' mistakes. Stock changes constantly and ranges from rich brocades, damasks and velvets to chintzes, linens and cottons. Designer names include Colefax & Fowler, Designers Guild, Laura Ashley, Warner, Sanderson, Osborne & Little, Fortuny and Bennison. A team of fitters and alteration experts are available if required. They offer a 24-hour availability. The Curtain Exchange also supply bespoke ranges with samples of curtains hanging. These fabrics are chosen from suppliers all over the world and are an excellent buy. *Secondhand Shop*

THE DESIGNER ROOM

BICESTER VILLAGE, BICESTER, JUNCTION 9 OF M40,
OXFORDSHIRE OX6 7WD
☎ (01869) 320052. OPEN 10 - 6 MON - SAT, 11 - 5 SUN.
Ever-changing range of top designer clothes including Jean- Paul Gaultier, Jasper Conran, Calvin Klein, Dolce e Gabanna andThe Maska Group. Discounts vary from 30%-70%. *Factory Shopping Village*

THE LIGHTHOUSE COLLECTION

UNIT 2, HANBOROUGH BUSINESS PARK, LODGE ROAD, LONG HANBOROUGH, OXFORDSHIRE OX8 8LH
☎ (01993) 880404. OPEN 8 - 5.30 SEVEN DAYS A WEEK. PLEASE PHONE BEFOREHAND.
The Lighthouse Collection of teak furniture is made from teak exclusively grown on the plantations of East Java and not in the tropical forest. These plantations are under the control of the Indonesian Government and are strictly

managed by the Forest Commission. The Lighthouse Collection currently manufactures teak garden furniture, but included in their winter collection is bedroom furniture and their own range of bed linens. They encourage price comparisons with other suppliers of teak furniture as they claim to be by far the best value for money. Phone, giving them 24 hours notice of your intention to visit the showroom in Long Hanborough, and they will arrange for more furniture to be brought from the warehouse. *Permanent Discount Outlet*

THE PAMELA HOWARD FASHION CONSULTANCY

WOODLAND, BEDWELLS HEATH, BOARS HILL, OXFORDSHIRE OX1 5JE

☎ (01865) 735735. BY APPOINTMENT ONLY.

Pamela Howard holds successful Open Days of new and nearly-new designer clothes, shoes and accessories including Armani, Valentino, Joseph, Chanel, Moschino, Nicole Farhi etc. Prices range from £25 - £400. The Open Days have become extremely popular over a number of years, and have been described as fun and a totally different concept of shopping in a relaxed and friendly atmosphere. For shopaholics it is an Aladdins Cave, but ladies who hate clothes shopping also save time and gain confidence by trying different colours and styles that are not just in the current season's fashion. The Consultancy was recently featured on Central Television in a programme on value for money designer wear and in several articles written in magazines, books and the national press. The Hire Service - Prelude - for designer evening wear, ball gowns and outfits for Ascot and Henley, is available by appointment. Write or telephone to go on the mailing list, or if you are visiting Oxford, phone and arrange to view the wide selection of clothes. *Dress Agency and Hire Shop*

THE RED HOUSE

WINDRUSH PARK, WITNEY, OXFORDSHIRE OX8 5YF

☎ (01993) 771144. MAIL ORDER.

An excellent catalogue of children's books, The Red House covers both educational matters, from reading skills to history, and practical activity books as well as fiction. The books are a mixture of hardback and paperback from a variety of different publishers, and good savings are to be made. Occasionally some CD Roms are available. They hold end of season sales about twice a year at their warehouse in Witney, Oxfordshire. Telephone for dates. *Permanent Discount Outlet*

Live Well On Less Tips
Make any directory enquiry phone calls from a public phone box where they are free.

THE SAVOY TAYLORS GUILD FACTORY OUTLET

BICESTER OUTLET SHOPPING VILLAGE, PINGLE DRIVE, BICESTER,
JUNCTION 9 OF M40, OXFORDSHIRE OX6 7WD

☎ (01689) 324321. OPEN 10 - 6 SEVEN DAYS A WEEK.

Part of the Moss Bros group, every item has a large price tag with the old and
the new price. For example, three-button T-shirts, £9.95, reduced from
£14.95; casual trousers, £14.95, reduced from £25.95; cotton shirts, £19.95
usually £25.95; YSL shirts, £22.50, usually £29.95; macs, £69.50, usually
£89.50; also leather gloves, belts, ties, work shirts, suits, jackets. *Factory
Shopping Village*

THE WEAVERS SHOP

STEELES CARPETS, BARFORD ROAD, BLOXHAM, OXFORDSHIRE
OX14 4HA

☎ (01295) 721225. OPEN 9 - 5 MON - SAT.

Makes Wilton carpets on narrow looms and offcuts are for sale at heavily discounted prices. Parent company in Kidderminster makes a wide range of
broadloom carpets for Wilton and Axminster and computer access enables
shoppers to choose from a much wider range of offcuts than the factory shop
holds. Also sells rugs, underlay and coir. Gives you name of reputable fitters
who will measure up. *Factory Shop*

TK MAXX

CALTHORPE STREET, OF HIGH STREET, BANBURY, OXFORDSHIRE

☎ (01295) 277022. OPEN 9 - 5.30 MON - WED, 9 - 7 THUR, 9 - 6 FRI,
SAT 10 - 4 SUN.

Based on an American concept, TK Maxx is situated in easily accessible, often
centrally located stores and offers famous label goods with up to 60% savings
off recommended retail prices. TK Maxx has fashion for the whole family -
women's, men's and childrenswear - accessories, shoes, gifts, kitchenware and
home goods. Everything in the store is branded with a choice of well-known
high street names to designer labels, and while a small percentage might be
clearly marked past season, the great majority of items in store are current season, current stock and still with phenomenal savings. There is a huge choice
with 50,000 pieces in store and up to 10,000 new items arriving a week. The
stores are simple and unfussy with wide aisles, shopping trolleys and baskets,
and a spacious, functional feel to them but there are individual changing
rooms, ramps for buggies and wheelchairs and plenty of staff on the shop
floor. Every branch accepts all major credit and debit cards and has a liberal
refund and return policy. *Permanent Discount Outlet*

Live Well On Less Tips

If you're single and want to go on holiday but avoid paying the single supplement, contact Travelmate. They will send you details of those wanting to go to the same area or who have the same holiday interest or wish to go on holiday and are willing to share a room with a stranger but still keep their independence. Travelmate, 52 York Place, Bournemouth, Dorset BH7 6JN; 01202 431520.

TOG 24

BICESTER OUTLET SHOPPING VILLAGE, PINGLE DRIVE, BICESTER, JUNCTION 9 OF M40, OXFORDSHIRE OX6 7WD

☎ (01869) 323278. OPEN 10 - 6 SEVEN DAYS A WEEK.

Tog 24 are the UK's fastest growing brand name in outdoor clothing and leisurewear, with a total of three UK factories and 36 stores nationwide. They utilise the world's finest performance fabrics including Gore-Tex, Polartec and Burlington macs. Catering for all the family for all seasons, with cosy fleeces and waterproofs for the winter, and trekking ranges, shorts and t-shirts for the summer. With all prices at least 30% below the recommended retail price you can afford to enter the Tog comfort zone. *Factory Shopping Village*

TOGS

13 HIGH STREET, THAME, OXFORDSHIRE OX9 2BZ

☎ (01844) 215002. OPEN 9.30 - 5 MON - SAT.

36 STERT STREET, ABINGDON, OXFORDSHIRE

☎ (01235) 524989. OPEN 9.30 - 5 MON - SAT.

Wide range of casual wear for women at competitive prices, including labels such as Viz-A-Viz, Adini and Chilli pepper. Sizes range from 10 - 18 for women. All items are perfects and current fashion. Prices start from £10. *Permanent Discount Outlet*

TOP MARKS

8 HIGH STREET, CHIPPING NORTON, OXFORDSHIRE OX7 5ND

☎ (01608) 642653. OPEN 9 - 5.30 MON - FRI, 9 - 5 SAT.

60 PARSON STREET, BANBURY, OXFORDSHIRE OX16 8NB

☎ (01295) 270530. OPEN 9 - 5.30 MON - FRI, 9 - 5 SAT.

Sells seconds from leading chain stores for all the family. Most of the stock is made up of men's and women's wear, with some childrenswear. The clothes are mainly Marks & Spencer seconds, sold at about one third cheaper than in the high street. Wide range of stock in various sizes with new stock arriving twice a week. they also stock debenhams' and Richards' stock when available. There is another branch at Moreton-in-Marsh, Gloucestershire. *Permanent Discount Outlet*

TRAVEL ACCESSORY OUTLET

UNIT 13, BICESTER OUTLET SHOPPING VILLAGE, PINGLE DRIVE, BICESTER, JUNCTION 9 OF M40, OXFORDSHIRE OX6 7WD

☎ (01869) 240444. OPEN 10 - 6 SEVEN DAYS A WEEK.

Luggage and travel-related products including executive cases, handbags, umbrellas and accessories available in leading brands such as Samsonite, Brics, Hidesign, Globe Trotter and Tula. The products also include couture and high fashion brands such as YSl and Moschino. All products are offered at a considerably reduced price due to their being production over-runs, last season's stock of slight seconds (ie they have minor aesthetic blemishes). *Factory Shopping Village*

TRIUMPH INTERNATIONAL LTD

BICESTER OUTLET SHOPPING VILLAGE, PINGLE DRIVE, BICESTER, JUNCTION 9 OF M40, OXFORDSHIRE OX6 7WD

☎ (01869) 329930. OPEN 10 - 6 SEVEN DAYS A WEEK.

This shop sells Hom swimwear and underwear for men, outerwear including shirts, trousers, jackets as well as nightwear. For women, there is the Triumph range of lingerie, swimwear and nightwear. There is also a small children's range of swimwear. *Factory Shopping Village*

VILLEROY & BOCH (UK) LIMITED

BICESTER OUTLET SHOPPING VILLAGE, PINGLE DRIVE, BICESTER, JUNCTION 9 OF M40, OXFORDSHIRE OX6 7WD

☎ (01869) 324646. OPEN 10 - 6 SEVEN DAYS A WEEK AND BANK HOLIDAYS.

This factory outlet carries an exclusive range of tableware, crystal and cutlery from Europe's largest tableware manufacturer. Convenient parking and pleasant surroundings make for a pleasurable and unhurried shopping experience. A varied and constantly changing stock, including seconds, hotelware and discontinued lines, on sale at excellent reductions, always makes for a worthwhile visit. *Factory Shopping Village*

WALTON CLOTHING CO

9 MARKET PLACE, CHIPPING NORTON, OXFORDSHIRE

☎ (01608) 642153. OPEN 9 - 6 MON - SAT, 10 - 4 SUN.

Well-known labels for men and women at very competitive, rather than discounted, prices. For women, there is Liz Claiborne, Henney, Principles. For men, Ralph Lauren, Calvin Klein. Part of a chain of twelve in the Cotswold area. *Permanent Discount Outlet*

Live Well On Less Tips
Buy your phone and after a time, you'll save the quarterly rental.

WARNERS

BICESTER OUTLET SHOPPING VILLAGE, PINGLE DRIVE, BICESTER,
JUNCTION 9 OF M40, OXFORDSHIRE OX6 7WD
☎ (01869) 324401. OPEN 10 - 6 SEVEN DAYS A WEEK.

This shop sells a wide range of women's lingerie from Leisureby, Valentino,
Warners, with bras, slips, thongs, bodies and briefs at discounts from 25% to
70%. Each item is labelled with both the rrp and the discounted prices. For
example, bikini brief, £6.99 reduced from £17; underwire bra, £14.99
reduced from £33; body, £24.99 reduced from £65. Slightly imperfect stock
as well as perfect quality, end of season and discontinued merchandise and
swimwear are also stocked. Underwear for men, including Calvin Klein briefs
for £2.99, is on offer too. The telephone number given here is for the village.
Factory Shopping Village

WOODS OF WINDSOR

BICESTER OUTLET SHOPPING VILLAGE, PINGLE DRIVE, BICESTER,
JUNCTION 9 OF M40, OXFORDSHIRE OX6 7WD
☎ (01869) 325307. OPEN 10 - 6 SEVEN DAYS A WEEK.

Sells traditional gift sets, soaps, perfume, and talc at discounts of 25% for
standard ranges and 50% for discontinued ranges. *Factory Shopping Village*

Live Well On Less Tips

BATH SHIELD BLENHEIM STUDIO, LONDON ROAD, FOREST ROW,
SUSSEX RH18 5EZ. (01342) 823243. OPEN 8.30 - 5.30 MON - FRI, 8.30 -
2 SAT. PHONE FIRST FOR AN APPOINTMENT.

If you've got a good quality bath which is looking a bit tatty, have it re-enamelled in situ or in the workshop. While it will cost from £275 plus VAT, just
think of the savings made by not having to rip out on old bath, hire a plumber,
redo tiling etc. And because the re-enamelled bath is baked with infra-red
lamps and polished, it will repel calcium and dirt and be easier to clean in the
future. Also provides traditional and Victorian bathroom equipment, taps,
shower roses and fittings and old-fashioned bathrooms. Up to 150 different
baths and accessories on display at any one time at the retail shop, Chadder
& Co. Delivers in the London area and abroad.

Rutland

WOMENSWEAR ONLY   Cottesmore Dress Agency, *Nr Oakham.*

WOMENSWEAR & MENSWEAR   Lands' End Direct Merchants, *Oakham.*
The Uppingham Dress Agency, *Uppingham.*

CHILDREN Nikki's Nursery Hire, *Oakham.* The Uppingham Dress Agency, *Uppingham.*

HOUSEHOLD AND GIFTWARE Rutland Lighting, *Oakham.*

FURNITURE/SOFT FURNISHINGS Qualitium: Oldwood Pine Furniture, *Langham.*

COTTESMORE DRESS AGENCY

MAIN STREET, COTTESMORE, NR OAKHAM, RUTLAND, LE15 7DJ
☎ (01572) 813247. OPEN 10 - 5 TUE - SAT.
Middle market to high quality designer clothes including labels such as Basler,
Escada, Bianca, Jaeger, Louis Feraud, Mansfield. Also high quality evening
wear and costume jewellery to buy, sizes 8 - 24. Please phone before making a
special journey during holiday periods. *Dress Agencies*

LANDS' END DIRECT MERCHANTS

LANDS' END WAY, OAKHAM, RUTLAND LE15 6US
☎ (01572) 722553. OPEN 10 - 6 MON - SAT, 10 - 4 SUN AND
BANK HOLIDAYS.
Lands' End, a US mail order company, moved its headquarters and factory
outlet to a larger site in summer 1998. Their factory outlet store is now 25%
larger and only a few minutes walk down the road from the old location.
Modelled on the dozen or so clearance outlets they operate in and around
their US headquarters in Dodgeville, Wisconsin, this factory shop is designed
to sell warehouse overstocks, obsolete lines and a range of not quite perfect
products. There will normally be about 3,000 items in the store from jeans to
jumpers, leggings to luggage, turtlenecks to trousers. Genuine overstocks are
priced at 25%-40% below normal catalogue prices; catalogue returns and
near-perfect seconds are reduced by between 40%-85%. All overstock items
are guaranteed, first quality Lands' End label products, all of which have been
offered previously in their catalogues at regular prices. There is ample free
parking, easy wheelchair and pushchair access and changing facilities. You
cannot buy current catalogue merchandise from the clearance outlet. *Factory
Shop*

NIKKI'S NURSERY HIRE

1 RECTORY FARM COTTAGE, ROOKERY ROAD, STRETTON, OAKHAM, RUTLAND LE15 7RA

☎ (01780) 410359.

Part of the Baby Equipment Hirers Association (BEHA), which has more than 100 members countrywide. BEHA run an advice line which will try and answer any queries you have regarding hiring services for children. Phone the Babyline on 0831 310355. *Hire Shop*

QUALITIUM: OLDWOOD PINE FURNITURE

MANOR STABLES, MANOR LANE, LANGHAM, RUTLAND LE15 7JE

☎ (01572) 771330. OPEN 9 - 5.30 SEVEN DAYS A WEEK.

Pine furniture constructed from old wood pine which has been recovered from old buildings and halls. It is dipped twice to regain its original state and then polished by hand in a mellow wax. This gives the products a warm, rustic look and the quality portrays the individual handcrafting which goes into each peice. Most pieces are custom built to the customer's specifications and design. At Langham, you can view 4,000 sq ft of standard items including wardrobes, beds, dressers, chests, tables, chairs, etc. *Permanent Discount Outlet*

RUTLAND LIGHTING

THISTLETON ROAD INDUSTRIAL ESTATE, MARKET OVERTON, OAKHAM, RUTLAND LE15 7PP

☎ (01572) 767587. OPEN 9 - 4 MON - SAT.

Sells a full range of lampshades, table and floor lamps, chandeliers, bulbs, outdoor and indoor lights, plus other manufacturers' ends of lines and chainstore seconds. Most lines have genuine reductions on normal retail prices. This shop is small and within the factory itself unlike the Grantham shop which is large and on the high street. *Permanent Discount Outlet*

THE UPPINGHAM DRESS AGENCY

2-6 ORANGE STREET, UPPINGHAM, RUTLAND LE15 9SQ

☎ (01572) 823276. OPEN 9 - 5.30 MON - SAT, 12 - 4 SUN AND BANK HOLS.

One of Britain's largest, longest established and most reputable dress agencies with ten rooms packed with over 4000 quality nearly-new and end of line garments from famous high street names to top designer labels. Featured on TV and in numberous national newspapers and magazines, this agency, situated in a picturesque market town has everything from casuals to occasion wear, evening wear, suits and separates, hats, shoes, handbags, scarves and costume jewellery. There are departments for men, women and children, seven changing rooms and a small coffee lounge where the coffee and biscuits are free. *Dress Agency*

Shropshire

WOMENSWEAR ONLY   Nightingales, *Craen Arms*.   Windsmoor Sale Shop, *Shropshire*.

MENSWEAR ONLY   Tom Sayer's Clothing Co, *Street*.

WOMENSWEAR & MENSWEAR   Catalogue Bargain Shop, *Bridgnorth*.
Catalogue Surplus Centre Ltd, *Newport*.   E Walters Factory Shop, *Ludlow*.   Fashion Factory, *Telford*.
Matalan, *Telford*.   Matalan, *Shrewsbury*.   TK Maxx, *Shrewsbury*.
Wrekin Workwear Factory Shop, *Telford*.

CHILDREN   Catalogue Bargain Shop, *Bridgnorth*.   Catalogue Surplus Centre Ltd, *Newport*.
Matalan, *Telford*.   Matalan, *Shrewsbury*.   TK Maxx, *Shrewsbury*.   Togs For Tots, *Nessdiffe*.

HOUSEHOLD AND GIFTWARE   Catalogue Bargain Shop, *Bridgnorth*.
Catalogue Surplus Centre Ltd, *Newport*.   Matalan, *Telford*.   Matalan, *Shrewsbury*.

ELECTRICAL EQUIPMENT   Catalogue Bargain Shop, *Bridgnorth*.

DIY/RENOVATION   Dickinsons Architectural Antiques, *Ludlow*.
Dunelm Mill Shops Ltd, *Shrewsbury*.   Glynn Webb, *Shrewsbury*.

ARCHITECTURAL SALVAGE   Dickinsons Architectural Antiques, *Ludlow*.

FURNITURE/SOFT FURNISHINGS   Cane And Wicker Factory Shop, *Shrewsbury*.
The Fabric Barn, *Claverley*.   The Weavers Shop, *Craven Arms*.

FOOD AND LEISURE   Barn Books, *Whitchurch*.   Classical Passions, *Oswestry*.
The Art Bookshop, *Ludlow*.

BARN BOOKS
PEAR TREE FARM, NORBURY, WHITCHURCH, SHROPSHIRE
☎ (01948) 663742. OPEN 2 - 6 FRI, 10 - 6 SAT, 2 - 6 SUN.
Remainders, publishers' returns and secondhand books of an excellent quality and range. Comprehensive gardening, architecture and countryside selection as well as children's boks. ***Permanent Discount Outlet***

CANE AND WICKER FACTORY SHOP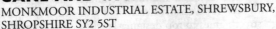
MONKMOOR INDUSTRIAL ESTATE, SHREWSBURY,
SHROPSHIRE SY2 5ST
☎ (01743) 240261. OPEN 9.30 - 5 MON - SAT.
The UK's largest importer of cane and wicker furniture has a huge factory shop with over 50 suites on display at prices starting from £199. There are more than 1,000 fabrics from which to choose. This importer and wholesaler runs two factory shops (here and a larger outlet in Walsall) to clear stock which has been returned by retailers. There may be nothing wrong with the furniture other

than a change of mind on the part of the original customer, but the furniture has probably been unwrapped, delivered and handled so cannot be sold to other retailers to sell on to full-price customers. The furniture comes in part-assembled and is finished, stuffed and upholstered on site. It comes in various finishes including light and dark antique, honey, mahogany and walnut. There is also a Mexican pine furniture range and fabric for curtains (though because the fabric is back coated for fire retardancy, it is very heavy). The cheapest cane suites cost from £150, the most expensive, £2,500. This represents a saving of about 15% - 20% on normal retail prices. There is immediate delivery for furniture in stock; orders will be fulfilled within about one week. *Factory Shop*

CATALOGUE BARGAIN SHOP

59 HIGH STREET, BRIDGNORTH, SHROPSHIRE WV16 4DX
☎ (01746) 763282. OPEN 9 - 5.30 MON - SAT, 11 - 5 SUN.
Catalogue Bargain Shop is a growing national chain of stores which obtains the majority of its goods from mail order giants Great Universal and Kays, and offers a range of clothing for all the family, a wide selection of shoes, bed linen, household goods, electrical equipment and hundreds of other catalogue items at very competitive prices. The merchandise consists of ends of ranges and previous season's stock for which there is no longer storage space when the catalogues change. *Permanent Discount Outlet*

CATALOGUE SURPLUS CENTRE LTD

28-30 ST MARY'S STREET, NEWPORT, SHROPSHIRE TF10 7AB
☎ (01952) 825889. OPEN 9 - 5 MON - SAT.
Ex-catalogue clothes for men, women and children as well as shoes and bedlinen, with occasional supplies of cookware, china and television sets - in fact some of everything a large catalogue sells, all at half price. There are other outlets at Telford, Oswestry, Shrewsbury and Stoke. *Permanent Discount Outlet*

CLASSICAL PASSIONS

PO BOX 7, OSWESTRY, SHROPSHIRE
☎ (01691) 670 750/670 747 FAX. MAIL ORDER.
Mail order company which claims to better most prices for CDs, cassettes, DVDs and videos. Rather than operating by catalogue, you simply phone up - having checked prices locally - and find out what their best price is. Their name suggests they are classical specialists, but they deal in any type of music and any video on general release. Postage free over £30. *Permanent Discount Outlet*

DICKINSONS ARCHITECTURAL ANTIQUES
140 CORVE STREET, LUDLOW, SHROPSHIRE SY8 2PG
☎ (01584) 876207. 9.30 - 5 MON - SAT.
Specialise in genuine period bathrooms, fireplaces, architectural fittings, doors, lighting and fenders. *Architectural Salvage*

DUNELM MILL SHOPS LTD
18 MARKET STREET, SHREWSBURY, SHROPSHIRE SY1 1LE
☎ (01743) 271478. OPEN 9 - 5 MON - THUR, 9 - 5.30 FRI, SAT.
BRIDGE ROAD, WELLINGTON, SHROPSHIRE TF1 1ED
☎ (01952) 245593. OPEN 9 - 5.30 MON - THUR, 9 - 8 FRI, 9 - 6 SAT, 10.30 - 4.30 SUN.
Part of a chain of shops based in the Midlands selling brand-name and chain-store curtains, masses of bedlinen, towels, wickerware, pictures and frames, all at competitive prices. *Permanent Discount Outlet*

E WALTERS FACTORY SHOP
CHAPEL WORKS, OLD STREET, LUDLOW, SHROPSHIRE SY8 1NR
☎ (01584) 875595. OPEN 9 - 5 MON - FRI, 9 - 4 SAT.
Europe's largest trouser manufacturer sells ends of lines, cancelled orders and samples of jeans, trousers and shorts for all the family at factory direct prices. Also available ancillary lines of casual wear at bargain prices. *Factory Shop*

FASHION FACTORY
THE MALTINGS, KING STREET, WELLINGTON, TELFORD, SHROPSHIRE TF1 3AE
☎ (01952) 260489. OPEN 9.30 - 5.30 MON - SAT, 11 - 5 SUN.
At the Fashion Factory stores in Cannock (see Staffordshire) and Telford, you'll find a comprehensive selection of quality branded and designer fashions for men and women, all reduced by up to 70% off the normal high street prices. Stock is made up of excess production, cancelled orders and ends of season ranges from dozens of UK and international clothing manufacturers. This means a constantly changing selection from lingerie and basic fashion essentials to dresses, suits and separates, all at a fraction of the prices you'd normally expect to pay. The boutique-style store in Telford features two floors packed with a huge variety of ladieswear, while the Cannock superstore boasts possibly one of the largest selection of discounted clothing and footwear under one roof in the Midlands, with between 50,000-60,000 garments on display in a massive 20,000 sq ft of retail space. There are four sales a year: Dec/Jan, Feb, Jun/July and August. *Permanent Discount Outlet*

Live Well On Less Tips
Pay your monthly bills by direct debit and save money.

> *Live Well On Less Tips*
> Telephone friends when you're reasonably sure they won't be there but they
> have an answer machine so you can save money on your call and they can
> spend it phoning you back

GLYNN WEBB

UNIT 3, SUNDOME RETAIL PARK, SHREWSBURY, SHROPSHIRE 5Y1 4YA
☎ (01743) 460993. OPEN 9 - 8 MON - SAT, 10 - 4 SUN AND BANK
HOLIDAYS.

Stockists of all your home improvement needs from wallpaper to paint, furniture to flooring, tiles to textiles, housewares to lighting - in fact, almost everything for your home, with 24 branches in the North-West, Midlands and Yorkshire. Specialists in discontinued mail order, slightly imperfect branded stocks as well as perfect quality superior products. They carry top brands such as Dulux, Crown Paints and Vymura and Coloroll wall coverings, Rectella and Norwood textiles and much more in store. Different branches carry different lines so if you want something specific, phone first. To find your nearest branch, phone 0161 621 4500. *Permanent Discount Outlet*

MATALAN

UNIT J, WREKIN RETAIL PARK, WELLINGTON, TELFORD, SHROPSHIRE
TF1 2DE
☎ (01952) 641080. OPEN 10 - 8 MON - FRI, 9 - 6 SAT, 10 - 4 SUN.
UNIT 1, MEOLE BRACE RETAIL PARK, HEREFORD ROAD, SHREWSBURY
SY3 9NB
☎ (01743) 363240. OPEN 10 - 8 MON - FRI, 9.30 - 5.30 SAT, 10 - 6 SUN.

Matalan is a fashion and homewares shop giving customers what they claim to be unbeatable value for money with huge savings on a wide range of products including high quality fashionable clothing for women, women and children at up to 50% off high street prices. Matalan is situated out of town and stores are open seven days a week all year round. *Permanent Discount Outlet*

NIGHTINGALES

NIGHTINGALES HOUSE, LONG LANE, CRAEN ARMS, SHROPSHIRE
☎ (01588) 673973. OPEN 93.0 - 4.30 MON - FRI.

The mail order company which sells smart but casual clothes for women - twill lined jackets in blazer stripes, button-through dresses, pinafore dresses, shirtwaisters, pure cotton blouses, lined short-sleeved jackets, polo neck sweaters, boucle jackets, blouses and skirt sets and cotton nightdresses - sells samples, ends of lines, seconds and material lengths here at discounted prices. *Factory Shop*

STANWAY FABRICS AND INTERIORS
SHIPTON HALL BARN, SHIPTON, NEAR MUCH WENLOCK,
SHROPSHIRE TF13 6JZ
☎ (01746) 785151. OPEN 10 - 4 MON - SAT.
Leading suppliers of top designer fabric seconds and clearances at prices from
as little as £3.95 per metre for fabrics which would normally retail between
£25 and £35. Thousands of metres of curtain and upholstery fabrics always in
stock, together with linings, interlinings, tape etc, at extremely competitive
prices. They stock a wide range of tassels, tie-backs, trimmings and accessories,
with many more available to order. Curtains, cushions, loose covers and headboards can be made to customers' specification by their experienced in house
team at affordable prices. They also have a swap shop where customers can
buy or sell beautiful curtains. Situated in a converted barn next to the six-
teenth century Shipton Hall in the beautiful Corvedale area of South
Shropshire, close to the historic towns of Ludlow, Much Wenlock and
Shrewsbury, there is also a coffee shop within the barn and parking is right
outside the door. *Permanent Discount Outlet*

THE ART BOOKSHOP
3 QUALITY SQUARE, LUDLOW, SHROPSHIRE SY8 1AR
☎ (01584) 872758. OPEN 10 - 5 FRI, SAT.
Superb range of specialist stock of new art, design and architecture books as
well as secondhand books. Some books are reduced by 25%-50%, while there
are bargain boxes of books at £1 and £2 each. *Permanent Discount Outlet*

THE FABRIC BARN
UPPER ASTON FARM, CLAVERLEY, SHROPSHIRE WV5 7EE
☎ (01746) 710237. OPEN 9 - 5 MON - SAT.
Sells designer curtain and upholstery fabrics from £3.50 a metre as well as linings from £2 a metre, craft poles and tracks. *Permanent Discount Outlet*

THE WEAVERS SHOP
THE MARKET HALL, CRAVEN ARMS, SHROPSHIRE SY7 9NF
☎ (01588) 673161/673162 FAX. OPEN 10 - 5 MON - FRI, 10 - 4 SAT,
CLOSED WED.
Formerly the Crucial Trading factory shop, the Weavers Shop has a wide collection of natural floor coverings and rugs at a considerable discount off high
street prices. Also now offers a large selection of tufted and Axminster plain
and patterned carpets from their factory at Kidderminster. All goods sold are
returns, discontinued, contract overmakes, ends of lines or slight seconds and
therefore represent excellent value for money. Fitters can be suggested and
delivery arranged. *Factory Shop*

TK MAXX

DARWIN SHOPPING CENTRE, SHREWSBURY, SHROPSHIRE

☎ (01743) 341370. OPEN 9 - 5.30 MON - SAT, 9 - 7 WED, 11 - 5 SUN.

Based on an American concept, TK Maxx is situated in easily accessible, often centrally located stores and offers famous label goods with up to 60% savings off recommended retail prices. TK Maxx has fashion for the whole family - women's, men's and childrenswear - accessories, shoes, gifts, kitchenware and home goods. Everything in the store is branded with a choice of well-known high street names to designer labels, and while a small percentage might be clearly marked past season, the great majority of items in store are current season, current stock and still with phenomenal savings. There is a huge choice with 50,000 pieces in store and up to 10,000 new items arriving a week. The stores are simple and unfussy with wide aisles, shopping trolleys and baskets, and a spacious, functional feel to them but there are individual changing rooms, ramps for buggies and wheelchairs and plenty of staff on the shop floor. Every branch accepts all major credit and debit cards and has a liberal refund and return policy. *Permanent Discount Outlet*

TOGS FOR TOTS

LONGACRE HOUSE, WILCOTT, NESSCLIFFE, SHROPSHIRE SY4 1BJ

☎ (01743) 741335.

Part of the Baby Equipment Hirers Association (BEHA), which has more than 100 members countrywide. A range of equipment can be hired from high chairs, cots and travel cots to baby car seats and buggies. Some members also hire out party equipment including child-sized tables and chairs. BEHA run an advice line which will try and answer any queries you have regarding hiring services for children. Phone the Babyline on 0831 310355. *Hire Shop*

WINDSMOOR SALE SHOP

16 HIGH STREET, SHREWSBURY, SHROPSHIRE SY1 1SP

☎ (01743) 244980. OPEN 9 - 5.30 MON - FRI AND 9.30 - 5.30 SAT.

Sells last year's stock including blouses, coats, knitwear, dresses, skirts, trousers, jackets, waistcoats from the Windsmoor, Planet and Precis Petite ranges at discounts averaging about 50% off the original price and sometimes up to 70%. Sizes range from 10 - 18 for the Windsmoor range, 8 - 16 for Planet and 8 - 16 for Precis Petite. *Permanent Discount Outlet*

WREKIN WORKWEAR FACTORY SHOP

UNIT 26, SNEDSHILL TRADING ESTATE, TELFORD, SHROPSHIRE
TF2 9NH

☎ (01952) 615976. OPEN 10 - 5 MON, TUE, WED, THUR, 10 - 3.30 FRI.

Fleece jackets, workwear trousers and jackets, dust coats, work shirts, dry suits, dry socks for walkers, waterproofs, Wellingtons, polo shirts, T-shirts, all at discounted prices. For example, end of line Polar fleece jacket, £19.99, originally £59.99. *Permanent Discount Outlet*

Somerset

WOMENSWEAR ONLY ♡ Browsers, *Wedmore*. Jane's Dress Agency, *Somerton*.
Laura Ashley, *Street*. Liz Claiborne, *Street*. Monsoon, *Street*. Paco Life in Colour, *Street*.
Windsmoor Sale Shop, *Street*.

WOMENSWEAR & MENSWEAR ♡ ♡ Absent Labels, *Taunton*.
Clarks Village Factory Shopping, *Street*. Clarks Shoes, *Bridgwater*. Clarks Shoes, *Burnham-on-Sea*.
Clarks Shoes, *Weston Super Mare*. Clothing World, *Weston Super Mare*. Collectable Costume, *Bath*.
Dickies UK, *Bath*. Ecco, *Street*. Fox's Mill Shop, *Wellington*. Jaeger, *Street*.
JPS Footwear Ltd, *Burnham-on-Sea*. Jumper, *Street*. Minehead Shoes Co Ltd, *Minehead*.
Morlands, *Glastonbury/Street*. Mulberry, *Shepton Mallet*. Next to Nothing, *Street*. Pennywise, *Yeovil*.
Rock-A-Bye, *Taunton*. Second To None, *Burnham-on-Sea*. The Doc Shop, *Shepton Mallett*.
The Factory Shop Ltd, *Minehead*. The Sports Factory, *Street*.
Tog 24, *Street*. Triumph International Ltd, *Street*. Viyella, *Street*.

CHILDREN ☺ Clarks Village Factory Shopping, *Street*. Clarks Shoes, *Bridgwater*.
Clarks Shoes, *Burnham-on-Sea*. Clarks Shoes, *Weston Super Mare*.
Clothing World, *Weston Super Mare*. Jokids, *Street*. Just For You, *Weston Super Mare*.
Kids Play Factory, *Street*. Next to Nothing, *Street*. Paco Life in Colour, *Street*.
Pennywise, *Yeovil*. Rock-A-Bye, *Taunton*. Roundabout, *Bath*. Second To None, *Burnham-on-Sea*.
The Doc Shop, *Shepton Mallett*. The Factory Shop Ltd, *Minehead*. The Sports Factory, *Street*.
Tog 24, *Street*.

HOUSEHOLD AND GIFTWARE ⊞ Clarks Village Factory Shopping, *Street*. Crafts, *Bath*.
Denby Factory Shop, *Street*. Mulberry, *Shepton Mallet*. Price's Candles, *Street*.
Royal Brierley Crystal, *Street*. Royal Worcester & Spode Factory Shop, *Street*. Spoils, *Bristol*.
Taylors of Taunton, *Taunton*. The Factory Shop Ltd, *Minehead*. The Linen Cupboard, *Street*.

ELECTRICAL EQUIPMENT ⊄ Remington, *Street*.

DIY/RENOVATION ☆ Black & Decker, *Street*. Bridgewater Reclamation, *Bridgewater*.
Old Harry's (Demolition) Ltd, *Street*. Screwfix Direct, *Yeovil*.
South West Architectural Salvage, *Bristol*. Wells Reclamation Co, *Coxley, Nr Wells*.

ARCHITECTURAL SALVAGE ☆ Bridgwater Reclamation, *Bridgwater*.
Old Harry's (Demolition) Ltd, *Street*. South West Architectural Salvage, *Bristol*.
Wells Reclamation Co, Coxley, *Nr Wells*.

FURNITURE/SOFT FURNISHINGS ⠶ James Gaunt, *Frome*. Knickerbean, *Bath*.
Laura Ashley, *Street*. Taunton Remnanat Shop, *Taunton*. Mulberry, *Shepton Mallet*.
Sala Design Ltd, *Martock*. Sandpits Heating Centre, *Langoport*.
Somerset Creative Products, *Wedmore*. The Curtain Exchange, *Taunton*.
The Factory Shop Ltd, *Minehead*.

FOOD AND LEISURE ⠶ Clarks Village Factory Shopping, *Street*.
Denby Factory Shop, *Street*. Hallmark, *Street*. The Pot People, *Street*. Thorntons, *Street*.

SPORTSWEAR AND EQUIPMENT ☆ Clarks Factory Shop, *Street*.
Paco Life in Colour, *Street*. The Sports Factory, *Street*.

ABSENT LABELS

51B ST JAMES' STREET, TAUNTON, SOMERSET TA1 IJH

☎ (01823) 3330242. OPEN 9.30 - 5.30 MON - FRI, SAT, 9 - 5.30 SAT.

CHURCH HOUSE, CHURCH STREET, YEOVIL BA20 1HE

☎ (01935) 78183. OPEN 9.30 - 5 MON - SAT.

Chainstore clothes, specialising in Marks & Spencer stock, for ladies and men at reduced prices. Discontinued lines and Grade A garments are reduced by about one third. There are skirts, trousers, socks, underwear, nightwear, sweaters, blouses, dressing gowns, shorts, T-shirts and swimwear. *Permanent Discount Outlet*

BLACK & DECKER

CLARKS VILLAGE, FARM ROAD, STREET, SOMERSET BA16 OBB

☎ (01458) 840205. OPEN 9 - 5.30 MON - SAT, 11 - 5 SUN. 9 - 6 MAY - OCT.

Reconditioned tools and acccessories from the famous Black & Decker range, all with full manufacturer's warranty. Often, stock consists of goods returned from the shops because of damaged packaging or are part of a line which is being discontinued. Lots of seasonal special offers. *Factory Shopping Village*

BRIDGWATER RECLAMATION

THE OLD CO-OP DAIRY, MONMOUTH STREET, BRIDGEWATER, SOMERSET TA6 5EJ

☎ (01278) 424636. OPEN 8 - 5 MON - FRI, 8 - 12 SAT.

Secondhand building materials: reclaimed bricks, Bridgwater-made clay roof and ridge tiles, natural Welsh slates, flagstones, chimney pots, doors, baths, fireplaces, reproduction furniture, purpose-made joinery from the on-site workshop - in fact everything! *Architectural Salvage*

BROWSERS

THE BOROUGH, WEDMORE, SOMERSET BS28 4EB

☎ (01934) 713663. OPEN 10 - 5 MON - SAT.

An upmarket dress agency selling nearly-new labels from Jaeger to Mondi, Viyella to Valentino. Whilst most of their range consists of designer labels, some better quality high street names are also available. This shop is renowned for brand new clearance stock, overmakes and sample sales. It has a large stock which turns over very quickly. They also stock belts, hats, handbags, jewellery and accessories. *Dress Agency*

Live Well On Less Tips

Join BT's Friends and Family Scheme when you can get five percent off the cost of your most frequently dialled numbers - you nominate 5 numbers, pay a one-off fee.

CLARKS FACTORY SHOP

UNIT 13, CLARKS VILLAGE, FARM ROAD, STREET, SOMERSET
BA16 OBB

☎ (01458) 843161. OPEN 9 - 6 MON - SAT, 9 - 5.30 WINTER, 11 - 5 SUN.

Clarks International operate a chain of factory shops nationally which specialise in selling discontinued lines and slight sub-standards for children, women and men from Clarks, K Shoes and other famous brands. These shops trade under the name of Crockers, K Shoes Factory shop or Clarks Factory Shop and while not all are physically attached to a shoe factory, these shops are treated as factory shops by the company. Customers can expect to find an extensive range of quality shoes, sandals, walking boots, slippers, trainers, handbags, accessories and gifts, while their major outlets such as at here at Clarks Village also offer luggage, sports clothing, sports equipment and outdoor clothing. Brands stocked include Clarks, K Shoes, Springer, CICA, Hi-Tec, Puma, Mercury, Dr Martens, Nike, LA Gear, Fila, Mizuno, Slazenger, Weider, Antler and Carlton, although not all are sold in every outlet. Discounts are from 30% to 60% off the normal high street price for perfect stock. This shop also incorporates Sports Factory, Baggage Factory and Gift Shop. *Factory Shopping Village*

CLARKS SHOES

2 EASTOVER, BRIDGWATER, SOMERSET TA6 5AB

☎ (01278) 452617. OPEN 9 - 5.30 MON - SAT.

10A HIGH STREET, BURNHAM-ON-SEA, SOMERSET TA8 1NX

☎ (01278) 794668. OPEN 9 - 5.30 MON - SAT, 11 - 5 SUN, 10 - 5 BANK
HOLIDAYS.

112-114 HIGH STREET, STREET, SOMERSET BA16 OEW

☎ (01458) 442055. OPEN 9 - 5.30 MON - SAT AND BANK HOLIDAYS,
11 - 5 SUN.

UNIT 2, SAINSBURYS PRECINCT, QUEENSWAY SHOPPING CENTRE,
WORLE, SOMERSET BS22 OBT

☎ (01934) 521693. OPEN 9 - 6 MON - SAT, 10.30 - 4.30 SUN,
10 - 5 BANK HOLIDAYS.

Clarks International operate a chain of factory shops nationally which specialise in selling discontinued lines and slight sub-standards for men, women and children from Clarks, K Shoes and other famous brands. These shops trade under the name of Crockers, K Shoes Factory shop or Clarks Factory Shop and while not all are physically attached to a shoe factory, these shops are treated as factory shops by the company. Customers can expect to find an extensive range of quality shoes, sandals, walking boots, slippers, trainers, handbags, accessories and gifts, while their major outlets also offer luggage, sports clothing, sports equipment and outdoor clothing. Brands stocked include Clarks, K Shoes, Springer, CICA, Hi-Tec, Puma, Mercury, Fila, Mizuno, Slazenger, Samsonite, Delsey, Antler and Carlton, although not all are sold in every outlet. Discounts are from 30% to 60% off the normal high street price for perfect stock. The Swindon branch is also a sports factory shop and baggage factory shop. *Factory Shop*

CLARKS VILLAGE
FACTORY SHOPPING

FARM ROAD, STREET, JUNCTION 23 OF M5, THEN A39, SOMERSET BA16 OBB

(01458) 840064. OPEN 9 - 6 MON - SAT, 9 - 5.30 WINTER, 11 - 5 SUN.
Purpose-built village of brick-built shops with extensive car parking facilities. Restaurant, fast food stands, carousel, indoor and outdoor play areas, and working village pottery and artists' studio. Here, there are 56 shops with more planned. Shops include: Monsoon/Accessorize, Laura Ashley, Benetton, Wrangler, The Designer Room, Jaeger, Viyella, Alexon/Eastex, Triumph/Hom, Jacques Vert, Gossard, JoKids, Clarks Factory Shop, Woolea (which also sells Aquascutum, Lyle & Scott and Barbour), Rohan, Paco, Windsmoor (which also sells Planet, Berkertex, Precis and Genesis), Liz Claiborne, Jumper, Centaur, Calvin Klein, Van Heusen, Next, Warehouse, Tom Sayers men's sweaters and trousers, Warner's lingerie, Tog 24 outerwear, Jane Shilton handbags, luggage and shoes, The Suit Company and Blazer and Event jewellery. Other shops include: Royal Brierley, Royal Worcester, Denby Pottery, Dartington Crystal, Crabtree & Evelyn, Clarks Baggage Factory, Clarks Sports Factory, The Linen Cupboard, Thorntons Chocolates, Clarks Sports Factory, Black & Decker, Hallmark Cards, Remington, Whittard of Chelsea, XS CDs and videos, Price's Candles, Cadbury's, Bookends, The Kitchen Cupboard (Cloverleaf table mats, trays and caddies, Hackman cutlery, Chasseur cookware), Stuart Crystal, Poole Pottery, Village Pottery, Waterford/Wedgwood, The Pot People, Gardeners' Gate, Michael Cooper's Studio, The National Trust Gift Shop, and Kid's Play Factory children's toys. *Factory Shopping Village*

CLOTHING WORLD

NORTH WORLE DISTRICT CENTRE, QUEENSWAY, WORLE, WESTON SUPER MARE, SOMERSET BS22 7BT

(01934) 522065. OPEN 9 - 5.30 MON - THUR, 9 - 6.30 FRI, 9 - 6 SAT, 10.30 - 4.30 SUN.
Manufacturers for Marks & Spencers, this shop sells men's, ladies and children's clothing from this high street chainstore at discounts of up to 50%. *Factory Shop*

Live Well On Less Tips
Wetproof your shoes when you first buy them: it protects them from the elements and keeps them looking good for longer

COLLECTABLE COSTUME

FOUNTAIN ANTIQUES CENTRE, 3 FOUNTAIN BUILDINGS, LANSDOWN ROAD, BATH, SOMERSET BA1 5DU

☎ (01225) 428731. OPEN 10 - 5 MON - SAT, 8 - 5 WED.

Area in Antiques Centre selling wearable early 19th century costumes, linen and lace, pre-Fifties men's and women's costumes, also accessories including costume jewellery, beaded bags, hats and fans. Quality leather suitcases can be bought for £30 upwards. *Secondhand and Vintage Clothe*

CRAFTS

16 CHEAP STREET, BATH, SOMERSET

☎ (01225) 464397. OPEN 9.30 - 5.30 MON - SAT, 11 - 4 SUN.

Crafts is a cooperative selling direct to the public at makers' direct prices. Items range from ceramics to wood, clocks, musical intruments and glassware. Everything is hand made and commissions are welcome. They also sell a small amount of English Country Pottery. *Factory Shop*

DENBY FACTORY SHOP

CLARKS VILLAGE, FARM ROAD, STREET, SOMERSET BA16 OBB

☎ (01458) 840940. OPEN 9 - 5.30 MON - SAT (WINTER), 9 - 6 MON - SAT (SUMMER), 11 - 5 SUN.

Denby is renowned for its striking colours and glaze effects. The Factory Shops stock first and second quality with seconds discounts starting at 20% off RRP. There are regular mega bargains with up to 75% off throughout the year. *Factory Shopping Village*

DICKIES UK LTD

CHARLTON LANE, MIDSOMER NORTON, NEAR BATH, SOMERSET BA3 4BH

☎ (01761) 410732. OPEN 9 - 5 MON - SAT, 10 - 4 SUN.

Casual outdoor wear, workwear, footwear and waterproof clothing: polar fleece, wax jackets, anoraks, shirts, trousers, and boots. All the products sold here are end of production and clearance lines. Examples of prices include fleece jacket, £10, padded anorak, £20, brushed cotton shirts, from £3. *Factory Shop*

ECCO

82 HIGH STREET, STREET, SOMERSET BA16 OEN

☎ (01458) 443950. 9 - 5.30 MON -SAT.

Ladies', men's and children's shoes, all discounted by at least 25%. Phone 0800 387368 for a catalogue. *Factory Shopping Village*

FOX'S MILL SHOP

TONEDALE MILLS, WELLINGTON, SOMERSET TA21 OAW

☎ (01823) 662271. OPEN 10 - 5 TUE - SAT.

Newly refurbished, this shop sells wool and cashmere fabrics for men and women made up of seconds and perfect quality but end of season lines at very low prices starting at £5 a metre for material that would normally retail at £25-£35, cashmere jumpers, silk ties, woollen scarves, umbrellas and fashion accessories. Cloth can be bought and taken away or the in-situ tailor will make up garments at a fraction of the London charges. The shop sells woollen and worsted cloth, wool and cashmere seconds and perfect quality and there's a bargain basket with fabric at silly prices. The tailor is on site one day a week and will make men's and women's suits. *Factory Shop*

HALLMARK

CLARKS VILLAGE, STREET, SOMERSET BA16 OBB

☎ (01458) 447005. OPEN 9 - 6 MON - SAT, 11 - 5 SUN SUMMER, 9 - 5.30 WINTER.

A wide range of cards to suit every occasion, as well as stuffed toys, wrapping paper, rosettes, gift cards from names such as Andrew Brownswood, Gordon Fraser and Sharpe's Classics. Almost all the stock here is ends of lines as the card business demands constant change and so there are always unsold lines. Most of the items are half price. Cafes on site as well as children's play areas; free parking. *Factory Shop*

JAEGER

UNIT 30, CLARKS VILLAGE, FARM ROAD, STREET, SOMERSET BA16 OBB

☎ (01458) 447215. OPEN 9 - 6 MON - SAT, 11 - 5 SUN.

Contemporary classics from Jaeger at excellent prices. Most of the merchandise is previous seasons' stock, but you might also find some special makes. Both shops stock tailoring and knitwear for women and men. *Factory Shopping Village*

JAMES GAUNT

1 CHURCH STREET, FROME, SOMERSET BA11 1PW

☎ (01373) 452344. OPEN 9 - 5.30 MON - SAT.

Specialist interior designers James Gaunt have a clearance fabric shop which also sells regular lines. It stocks labels such as Crowsons and Malabar. Curtain material costs from £1.99 to £30 per metre. A large selection of cotton and damask fabrics. Half price is the average discount but fabrics sold for, say £6 or £7, may well have been originally priced at £30. The emphasis is on designer stock at bargain prices. *Permanent Discount Outlet*

JANE'S DRESS AGENCY

THE TRIANGLE, SOMERTON, SOMERSET TA11 6QJ

☎ (01458) 273711. OPEN 9.30 - 5 MON - FRI, 9.30 - 4.30 SAT.

Small, well-stocked shop selling high street and designer labels, Viyella, Bianca Country Casuals, Betty Barclay, and German labels such as Escada. Also sells belts, secondhand jewellery, shoes, scarves, handbags and lots of hats. Evening wear and cruise wear stocked - will help put together outfits for weddings and special occasions. *Dress Agency*

JOKIDS

CLARKS VILLAGE, FARM ROAD, STREET, SOMERSET BA16 OBB

☎ (01458) 841909. OPEN 9 - 6 MON - SAT, 9 - 5.30 WINTER, 11 - 5 SUN.

This shop sells childrenswear for 0-10-year-olds including pretty party dresses for girls at reductions of up to 40%, all-in-one smocked playsuits, T-shirts, denim shirts, denim dresses, sunhats, shorts, and accessories. *Factory Shopping Village*

JPS FOOTWEAR LTD

2 HIGH STREET, BURNHAM-ON-SEA, SOMERSET TA8 1NX

☎ (01278) 780141. OPEN 9 - 5.30 MON - SAT, 11 - 6 SUN.

Stock over 10,000 pairs of shoes for men, women and children. The men's sizes range from 6-12; and women's from 4-9. Most of the stock consists of warehouse clearance lines and ends of lines. *Factory Shop*

JUMPER

CLARKS VILLAGE, FARM ROAD, STREET, SOMERSET BA16 OBB

☎ (01458) 840320. OPEN 9 - 6 MON - SAT, 9 - 5.30 WINTER, 11 - 5 SUN.

A wide range of Jumper label sweaters, gloves, socks, scarves, shirts and cardigans for men and women all at discount prices of up to 50% off. Prices start at £2. *Factory Shopping Village*

JUST FOR YOU

9 TREMLETT MEWS, NORTH WORLE, WESTON SUPER MARE, SOMERSET BS22 7LY

☎ (01934) 510092.

Part of the Baby Equipment Hirers Association (BEHA), which has more than 100 members countrywide. A range of equipment can be hired from high chairs, cots and travel cots to baby car seats and buggies. Some members also hire out party equipment including child-sized tables and chairs. BEHA run an advice line which will try and answer any queries you have regarding hiring services for children. Phone the Babyline on 0831 310355. *Hire Shop*

Live Well On Less Tips
If you prefer the big screen, ring your local cinema and find out if they have a reduced ticket night. Many cut the price of tickets on a Monday night when business is usually slow.

KIDS PLAY FACTORY

CLARKS VILLAGE, FARM ROAD, STREET, SOMERSET BA16 0BB

☎ (01458) 440771. OPEN 10 - 6 MON - SAT, 11 - 5 SUN. SEASONAL LATE NIGHTS, PHONE AHEAD TO CHECK.

This shop sells a wide range of well-known children's brand names: Tomy, Matchbox, Lego, The First Years, Hasbro, Disney, Playskool, Mattel and Fisher-Price at discounts of up to 50%. They also stock a wide range of soft toys including TY Beanie Babies. *Factory Shopping Village*

KNICKERBEAN

5 WALCOT STREET, BATH, SOMERSET BA1 5BN

☎ (01225) 445741. OPEN 9 - 5.30 MON - SAT.

Knickerbean is one of the few companies that continue to offer genuine top-name designer fabric bargains. . .the kind of curtain and upholstery fabrics that are found at Decorex and the Chelsea Harbour Design Centre. Their rapidly-changing stock often includes excess inventory and discontinued lines from these kinds of designers, as well as occasional slight seconds, with many sold at between 20%-50% off the regular price. They also carry a large range of top-quality fabrics in the latest styles which they buy directly from mills and man-ufacturers in the UK, Europe and North America, offering similar top quality, but at vastly reduced prices. Their attractively laid-out shops feature a vast range of different selections of curtain and upholstery fabrics. These include classic country house glazed chintzes, fresh stripes and checks, fashionable toiles de jouy, bright cotton prints and PVC-coated fabrics, a wide range of damasks and natural fabrics, sumptuous chenilles, rich kilim patterns, self-patterned dobby weaves and a fabulous selection of upholstery brocades and tapestries. Prices start from £4.95 for plain cottons and prints to £19.95 and occasional-ly more for chenilles and tapestries. Customers are encouraged to pop in regu-larly to check out the latest arrivals in their stock. The benefit here is that they are able to see entire rolls rather than just a small sample book of swatches. Their professionally trained staff are ready to advise on quality and quantity for any type of furnishing project. They extend their service to measure and quote, as they offer a complete making up service for all soft furnishings, including loose covers and upholstery. They are even prepared to bring along a few rolls to try out against a customer's own colour scheme. Twice-yearly sales are held in January and June to enable customers to snap up even bigger bargains. *Permanent Discount Outlet*

LAURA ASHLEY

CLARKS VILLAGE, FARM ROAD, STREET, SOMERSET BA16 OBB

☎ (01458) 840405. OPEN 9 - 5.30 MON - SAT, 9 - 6 SAT, 11 - 5 SUN.

Laura Ashley home furnishings and fashion at Clarks. Most of the merchandise is made up of perfect carry-overs from the high street shops around the country, though there are also some discontinued lines. Stock reflects the normal high street variety, though at least one season later and with less choice in colours and sizes. *Factory Shopping Village*

LIZ CLAIBORNE UK

CLARK'S VILLAGE, FARM ROAD, STREET, SOMERSET BA16 OBB

☎ (01458) 840912. OPEN 9 - 6 MON - SAT, 11 - 5 SUN, WINTER 9 - 5.30.

American designer Liz Claiborne's factory shop at Clarks Factory Shopping Village offers middle of the range, mid-priced smart clothes for work and casual wear. All are end of lines or styles which are at least one year old. Stock quantities and sizes vary, depending on whether there has recently been a delivery, so it's worth making frequent visits. Suited jackets start from £45; casual trousers, £15; skirts from £15. A range is available in Petite sizing and there is a good selection of discounted accessories. Most items are reduced by 50% with further reductions always on offer. *Factory Shopping Village*

TAUNTON REMNANT SHOP

9A EASTREACH, TAUNTON, SOMERSET TA1 3EN

☎ (01823) 323932. OPEN 9 - 5 MON - SAT.

Packed full of ends of lines and seconds from famous name furnishing manufacturers. Lining, £2.20 a metre, upholstery fabrics, velvet, from £3.99 a metre for seconds. Curtain fabrics stocked include those from famous names such as Hardy, Sanderson, Derby House, Prestigious, Curtaina, Crowsons and many others. Fabrics start at £2.99 a yard or £3.20 a metre. *Permanent Discount Outlet*

MINEHEAD SHOE CO LTD

1 NORTH ROAD, MINEHEAD, SOMERSET TA24 5QW

☎ (01643) 705591. OPEN 9 - 5 MON - THUR, 9 - 4 FRI, 10 - 1 SAT.

CLOSED FOR LUNCH 1 - 2 EVERYDAY.

Specialists in made-to-measure footwear, including some golf and bowling shoes. Goods are supplied by the factory next door and sold at factory prices. Mail order available. *Permanent Discount Outlet*

MONSOON

UNIT 6, CLARKS VILLAGE, FARM ROAD, STREET, SOMERSET BA16 OBB

☎ (01458) 840890. OPEN 9 - 6 MON - SAT, 9 - 5.30 WINTER, 11 - 5 SUN.

Medium-sized outlet selling last year's stock and discontinued lines, including jewellery. *Factory Shopping Village*

MORLANDS (GLASTONBURY)

NORTHOVER, BETWEEN GLASTONBURY & STREET, GLASTONBURY, SOMERSET BA6 9YA

☎ (01458) 835042. OPEN 9.30 - 5 MON - SAT AND MOST BANK HOLIDAYS.

Established in 1870, Morlands are the leading brand name in quality sheepskin garments and footwear. The Factory Shop on the A39 (just north of Clarks Village) offers the opportunity to buy both men's and women's sheepskin coats, slippers and ladies boots at attractive prices. Ranges include first quality design samples, ends of runs and overstock, together with slight seconds. There is also a wide range of rugs, hats, mitts, handbags, belts, leatherwear and gifts. *Factory Shop*

MULBERRY

THE OLD SCHOOL HOUSE, KILVER STREET ON THE A37, SHEPTON MALLET, SOMERSET BA4 5NF

☎ (01749) 340583. OPEN 10 - 6 MON - SAT, 11 - 5 SUN AND BANK HOLIDAYS.

A very popular large, attractive, factory outlet situated in an old school house with parking outside, which sells last season's and slightly substandard items from the famous Mulberry leather handbags, briefcases, filofaxes and wallets at discounted prices. The factory shop is sufficiently large also to display ends of lines from the homes range of sofas, fabrics, occasional tables, lamps, rugs, throws, cushions, china, decanters, glass. Also rails of last season's clothes including men's jackets, waxed jackets, trousers, shirts, waistcoats, braces and shoes; and women's jackets, handknitted sweaters and cardigans, jackets and coats. There are also umbrellas, pewter napkin rings, golfing and fishing gifts, shaving kits, and a skincare range. Discontinued lines are discounted from 30%; current seconds, many of which come direct from the factory, are discounted by 30%. Examples of prices include cashmere from £89, fabric clippers at £79. Small coffee shop and toilet and disabled facilities. *Factory Shop*

NEXT TO NOTHING

CLARKS VILLAGE, FARM ROAD, STREET, SOMERSET BA16 OBB

☎ (01458) 840828. OPEN 10 - 6 MON - SAT, 11 - 5 SUN.

Sells perfect surplus stock from Next stores and the Next Directory catalogue - from belts, jewellery and underwear to day and evening wear - at discounts of 50% or more. The ranges are usually last season's and overruns. Stock consists of women's, men's and children's clothing, with some homeware and shoes. Stock is replenished three times a week and there is plenty of it. *Factory Shopping Village*

OLD HARRY'S (DEMOLITION) LTD

FAIRWATER YARD, STAPLEGROVE ROAD, TAUNTON, SOMERSET TA1 1DP

☎ (01823) 337035. OPEN 9.5.30 MON - FRI, 10 - 12 SAT.

Tiles, slates, bricks, recycled timber, floorboards, fireplaces, sanitaryware, stair-cases and interesting curios discovered during demolition. *Architectural Salvage*

PACO LIFE IN COLOUR

UNIT 17, CLARKS VILLAGE, FARM ROAD, STREET, SOMERSET BA16 0BB

☎ (01458) 440222. OPEN 9 - 6 MON - SAT, 11 - 5 SUN.

Comprehensive range of casualwear clothing and accessories for women in a wide variety of colours. End-of-season lines are on sale at discounts of around 30%. Included in the range are t-shirts, sweatshirts, wool sweaters and cardigans, jeans, leggings, shorts, bags and socks, all offering outstanding value for money. *Permanent Discount Outlet*

PENNYWISE

10 WESTMINSTER STREET, YEOVIL, SOMERSET

☎ (01935) 423938. OPEN 9.15 - 5 MON - SAT.

Dress agency selling men's, women's and children's clothes, shoes and accessories. Labels include Betty Barclay, Daks, Marks & Spencer, Windsmoor and Long Tall Sally. There is no parking available but the shop is near a large Tesco car park. *Dress Agency*

PRICE'S CANDLES

CLARKS VILLAGE, FARM ROAD, STREET, SOMERSET BA16 OYL

☎ (01458) 440006. OPEN 9 - 6 MON - SAT, 9 - 5.30 WINTER, 11 - 5 SUN.

Everything sold in this shop are seconds, which may be discoloured or have a damaged pattern; discontinued sizes not available elsewhere; over-runs from the garden selection or dinner candles in old packaging that has now been replaced. There are church candles, lanterns, candles in pots and glass jars, star-shaped candles, floating candles, candlestick holders, serviettes, scented candles and garden torches. Some of the ceramic items are bought in.

REMINGTON

UNIT 33, CLARKS VILLAGE, FARM ROAD, STREET,
SOMERSET BA16 OBB

☎ (01458) 840209. OPEN 9 - 6 MON - SAT, 9 - 5.30 WINTER, 11 - 5 SUN.

Lots of famous names here from Oneida and Monogram cutlery to Braun, Philips, Remington, Clairol, Wahl, Krups and Kenwood small kitchen equip-ment. *Factory Shopping Village*

Live Well On Less Tips
Clean windscreen wipers with vinegar and water in order to get rid of the grime and dirt that accumulate.

ROCK-A-BYE

7 BOWOOD ROAD, TAUNTON, SOMERSET TAZ 7QE
☎ (01823) 254395.
Hire cots, prams, highchairs, car seats, travel cots, stairgates, moses baskets etc. In fact any equipment you could possibly need for a baby they will try to obtain for you on long hire (three months) or short hire (one day) at good prices. *Hire Shop*

ROUNDABOUT

2 PRIOR PARK ROAD, WIDCOMBE, BATH, SOMERSET BA2 4NG
☎ (01225) 316696. OPEN 9 - 5 MON - SAT.
Newly refurbished side by side shops, one selling nearly-new and sample childrenswear from Oilily to Cakewalk at discounts of about 45%, the other selling womenswear such as Gap. Roundabout has half-price brand new samples from Cakewalk and Oilily as well as nearly-new Laura Ashley, Gap, Next and Petit Bateau. *Dress Agency*

ROYAL BRIERLEY CRYSTAL

CLARKS VILLAGE, FARM ROAD, STREET, SOMERSET BA16 OBB
☎ (01458) 840039. OPEN 9 - 6 MON - SAT, 9 - 5.30 WINTER, 11 - 5 SUN.
Royal Brierley crystal seconds and Poole Pottery at very good prices, with a minimum discount of 30% off retail. Closing times are half an hour earlier on weekdays and Saturdays from November to end March. *Factory Shopping Village*

ROYAL WORCESTER & SPODE FACTORY SHOP

CLARKS VILLAGE, FARM ROAD, STREET, SOMERSET BA16 OBB
☎ (01458) 840554. OPEN 9 - 6 MON - SAT, 9 - 5.30 WINTER, 11 - 5 SUN.
Infinitesimally flawed porcelain and china seconds at 25% less than perfect prices. This outlet also sells Mayflower, Langham Glass, Clover Leaf & Pimpernel table mats, Lakeland Plaques, Leeds Display, Arthur Price cutlery, Paw Prints and Collectable World Studios. There is a vast range with special offers throughout the year on anything from crystal decanters and bowls to figurines, cookware and dinner sets. Shipping arrangements worldwide can be organised. *Factory Shopping Village*

Live Well On Less Tips
R F GREASBY LTD 211 LONGLEY ROAD, TOOTING, LONDON
SW17 9LG. 0181-672 2972/0181-682 4564. OPEN 9 - 5 MON - THUR, 9 -
4 FRI, VIEWING 4 - 8.30 MON.
Want to buy a computer for £30, a leather briefcase for £20, a dozen umbrellas for the price of one good one? R F Greasby Ltd (Public Auctioneers) deal
in goods from London Transport's and British Airways lost property offices,
Customs & Excise, among others, plus those obtained because of outstanding debt. Merchandise includes office equipment, clothing, computers, furniture, coffins, garden and agricultural equipment, television sets and hi-fis. This
is the place where dealers get great bargains, but there's still some left for
members of the public. Entry is on a first-come, first-served basis every second Tuesday. The catalogue can be obtained by annual subscription (phone
0181 672 2972 for details) or from the premises for £1.50.

SALA DESIGN LTD

THE WORKS, BOWER HINTON, MARTOCK, SOMERSET TA12 6LG
☎ (01935) 827050. OPEN 9 - 5 MON - SAT, 10 - 4 SUN.
PHONE FOR SALE DATES.
Sala supplies top London interiors shops and department stores countrywide
with imported furniture from India, rattan and wooden furniture from
Thailand and metal pieces from the Philippines, as well as furniture from
Africa, Afghanistan, Nepal and China; Aghanistan and Persian kelims; and
Persian and Belouchi carpets. Their warehouse outlet, which is open to the
public, also sells unusual ornaments, candles, rugs, glasses and cutlery, and
one-off antique pieces and artefacts. There are twice-yearly warehouse sales
where prices are cut dramatically, sometimes by up to 75%. Otherwise, prices
here represent savings of about 40-50%. *Designer Sale*

SANDPITS HEATING CENTRE

SANDPITS HILL, CURRY RIVEL, LANGPORT, SOMERSET TA10 ONG
☎ (01458) 251476. OPEN 8 - 5.30 MON - FRI, 8 - 4.30 SAT.
A Rayburn Cooking Centre specialising in new and reconditioned Rayburns
and Agas. The reconditioned models are considerably cheaper than the new
and some can incorporate a domestic heating system for hot water and radiators. They also stock Stanley, Alpha and Nobel cookers at full price and a selection of wood burning stoves. *Secondhand Shop*

Live Well On Less Tips
Use the turnovers from old worn socks as cuff protectors on children's
clothes when they are painting or messing about with glue or water.

Live Well On Less Tips
Use a shower instead of a bath at least once a week and save water.

SCREWFIX DIRECT

HOUNDSTONE BUSINESS PARK, YEOVIL, SOMERSET BA22 8RT
(0500) 414141. MAIL ORDER. SHOP: 8 - 6 MON - FRI, 8 - 4 SAT.
DIY materials by mail order - everything from nails, screws, torches and bulbs
to electric screwdrivers, plumbing materials and sealants - at prices which, one
reader claims, are lower than the local diy superstore. Send for a catalogue,
which is updated quarterly. Warehouse shop on site also sells ends of lines and
one-off samples at discounted prices. ***Permanent Discount Outlet***

SECOND TO NONE

85 HIGH STREET, BURNHAM-ON-SEA, SOMERSET TA8 1PE,
☎ (01278) 787457. OPEN 9 - 5 MON - SAT, SOME BANK HOLIDAYS.
UNIT 2, CHESTERFIELD HOUSE, HIGH STREET, MIDSOMER NORTON
BA3 2DD
☎ (01761) 415545. OPEN 9 - 5 MON - SAT.
Established in the South West for twenty-six years, this company has built a
reputation for giving excellent customer service and for selling goods which are
of a quality and value that are Second to None! This chain of shops specialise
in selling famous chainstore and branded clearing lines, which includes surplus
stocks of branded goods such as Gossard, Berlei, Zorbit, Naturana and many
more. They stock a large range of ladies and children's and baby wear (including baby bedding and accessories), some menswear, and an extensive range of
underwear and nightwear for all the family. You can save up to 75% off recommended retail prices and they offer a seven-day money back guarantee.
Permanent Discount Outlet

SOMERSET CREATIVE PRODUCTS

SOMERSET DESIGN, LAUREL FARM, WESTHAM, WEDMORE,
SOMERSET BS28 4UZ
☎ (01934) 712416. OPEN BY APPOINTMENT ONLY.
A large range of garden furniture and accessories made from reclaimed timber
furniture in ocean drift and honey finishes. The range includes coffee tables,
tall and low waisted cupboards, mirrors etc, plus a range of painted wooden
Somerset trugs, trays, food larders, egg cupboards, footstools, crockery shelves,
country cupboards and butlers' trays. Seconds are on sale here at discount
prices. Westham is about 8 miles from Clarks Village Factory Shopping
Centre in Street; telephone for directions. ***Factory Shop***

Live Well On Less Tips
Cut old towels up into washcloths which can be cut in quarters to make re-usbale handwipes or baby wipes. Store damp in a plastic bag when travelling.

SOUTH WEST ARCHITECTURAL SALVAGE

28-30 MIDLAND ROAD, ST PHILIPS, BRISTOL, SOMERSET BS2 OJY
☎ (0117) 929 9143. OPEN 10 - 5 TUE - SAT.
Established for more than 20 years, this architectural salvage specialist stocks more than 300 stripped doors and general salvage. Au Temps Perdu is also located on this site selling fireplaces, bathroom ware and general fixtures and fittings for period houses. *Architectural Salvage*

SPOILS

UNIT CG9, THE GALLERIES SHOPPING CENTRE, BROADMEAD,
BRISTOL, SOMERSET BS1 3XD
☎ (0117) 922 5955. OPEN 9 - 5.30 MON - FRI, 7 ON THUR, 9 - 6 SAT,
11 - 5 SUN.
General domestic glassware, non-stick bakeware, kitchen gadgets (but no electricals), ceramic oven-to-tableware, textiles, cutting boards, aluminium non-stick cookware, bakeware, plastic kitchenware, plastic storage, woodware, coffee pots/makers, furniture, mirrors and picture frames. Rather than being discounted, all the merchandise is very competitively priced - in fact, the company carry out competitors' checks frequently in order to monitor pricing. With 38 branches, the company is able to buy in bulk and thus negotiate very good prices. *Permanent Discount Outlet*

TAYLORS OF TAUNTON

RICHMOND ROAD, OFF STAPLEGROVE ROAD, TAUNTON,
SOMERSET TA1 1EN
☎ (01823) 272961. OPEN 9 - 5.30 MON - SAT.
Large shop with a free car park and a coffee shop which sells both perfect and seconds in a wide range of china and glassware, as well as cutlery, cooking utensils, baskets, wrapping paper, cards, napkins, table mats, garden pots, logs and pet baskets and sundials. There are always special offers in the china and glassware sections such as Denby Pottery reduced by 20%, Johnson Bros dinner services reduced by 25%, seconds of Churchill tableware; George Butler stainless steel 44-piece canteens reduced from £390 to £195, special offers on Edinburgh crystal and half-price offers on Dartington Crystal as well as run of kiln Spode Blue Italian at reductions of 30% (run of kiln means the factory hasn't checked the products - while there is certain to be a few seconds, the majority of the products are fine). *Permanent Discount Outlet*

THE CURTAIN EXCHANGE

LONGALLER MILL, BISHOP'S HULL, TAUNTON, SOMERSET TA4 1AD
☎ (01823) 326071. OPEN 10 - 4 WED - SAT OR BY APPOINTMENT.
11 WIDCOMBE PARADE, BATH BA2 4JT
☎ (01225) 422078. OPEN 9.30 - 1 MON, 10 - 4 TUE - SAT.

The Curtain Exchange is a franchised group of shops selling beautiful top quality secondhand curtains, blinds, pelmets, etc at between one-third and one half of the brand new price. Their stock comes from a variety of sources: people who are moving house and dislike the drapes in their new home; people who are moving house and want to sell their old curtains to help with the bills; show houses, where the builder wants to recoup some of his outgoings; interior designers' mistakes. Stock changes constantly and ranges from rich brocades, damasks and velvets to chintzes, linens and cottons. Designer names include Colefax & Fowler, Designers Guild, Laura Ashley, Warner, Sanderson, Osborne & Little, Fortuny and Bennison. A team of fitters and alteration experts are available if required. They offer a 24-hour availability. The Curtain Exchange also supply bespoke ranges with samples of curtains hanging. These fabrics are chosen from suppliers all over the world and are an excellent buy.
Secondhand Shop

THE DOC SHOP

TOWNSEND ROAD, SHEPTON MALLET, SOMERSET BA4 5SB
☎ (01794) 347081. OPEN 9 - 5.30 MON - FRI, 9 - 5 SAT, 10 - 4 SUN.

Sells Doc Martens shoes and boots, Mitre football boots, as well as clothing such as Umbro and a vast range of accessories at discounted prices. For example, children's shoes and boots at £15. *Permanent Discount Outlet*

THE FACTORY SHOP LTD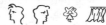

MART ROAD, MINEHEAD, SOMERSET TA24 5BJ
☎ (01643) 705911. OPEN 9.30 - 5.30 MON - SAT, 11 - 5 SUN.

Wide range on sale includes men's, ladies and children's clothing and footwear; household textiles, toiletries, hardware, luggage, lighting and bedding, most of which are chainstore and high street brands at discounts of approximately 30%-50%. There are weekly deliveries and brands include many major stars such as Adidas, Nike, Wrangler and Dartington, to name just four. Lines are continually changing and few factory shops offer such a variety under one roof. This branch also display kitchens and furniture and sells the Cape Country Furniture range. This high quality pine furniture made exclusively for The Factory Shop in South Africa is sold at factory direct prices with home delivery throughout the UK. Colour brochure and price list available. It also has its own free car park. *Factory Shop*

Live Well On Less Tips
Punch holes in the bottom of a plastic milk container to make an irrigation jug. Set into the ground near plants to be watered. This allows for slow watering without evaporation....
....Or make simple stencils from the side panels....
....Or cut off the top and handle to make a toilet brush holder....

THE LINEN CUPBOARD

CLARKS VILLAGE, FARM ROAD, STREET, SOMERSET BA16 OBD
☎ (01458) 447447. OPEN 9 - 6 MON - SAT, 9 - 5.30 WINTER, 11 - 5 SUN.
Bedlinen, sheets, valances, duvet covers, pillowcases, duvets, eiderdowns, towels and bath mats from leading brands all at discount prices. Also nursery bedding, lampshades and cushions, bean bags and sleeping bags. *Factory Shopping Village*

THE POT PEOPLE

37 CLARKS VILLAGE, STREET, SOMERSET BA16 OBB
☎ (01458) 840652. OPEN 9 - 6 MON - SAT, WINTER 9 - 5.30, 11 - 5 SUN.
A family-run business, the Pot People have years of experience producing a wide variety of pots and ornaments for garden centres and retails all round the country. In 1993, they started selling their garden stoneware directly to the public at wholesale prices, about half what you might expect to pay for similar stoneware products. When shopping at Clarks Village, they will happily deliver your purchase directly to your car, wrapped in sacking to help prevent damage en route. Ornaments include cherub bird baths, £15, normal price, £32.50; swag pots, £11, usually £22.80; plumed tubs, £11, usually £20.95; lion's head troughs, £16, usually £30.50; sundials, £33, usually £77.75. *Factory Shopping Village*

THE SPORTS FACTORY

UNIT 13, CLARKS VILLAGE, FARM ROAD, STREET,
SOMERSET BA16 OBB
☎ (01458) 843156. OPEN 9 - 6 MON - SAT, (9 - 5.30 WINTER), 11 - 5 SUN.
Wide range of sports clothes, equipment and accessories, some of which are only stocked in season (for example, cricket bats and tennis rackets in summer only). Golf equipment includes clubs, shoes, balls, bags, putters, and brands on sale include Howson, Hippo, Wilson, Penfold, Second Chance golf balls and Walrus golf waterproofs. There are also tennis rackets, cricket gear, leisure clothing (Kicker, Kangol, Timberland, Mizuno, Penn, Champion, and Reggatta). All are discontinued lines and are cheaper than in the high street by between 10% - 40%. *Factory Shopping Village*

THORNTONS

CLARKS VILLAGE, FARM ROAD, STREET, SOMERSET BA16 OBB

☎ (01458) 841553. OPEN 9 - 6 MON - SAT, 11 - 5 SUN.

The UK's leading specialist confectionery retailer has more than 500 shops and franchises nationwide selling a wide range of boxed and loose, chocolate and sugar confectionery. The factory outlets sell three different categories: misshapes. discounted lines and standard lines. Misshapes are loose chocolates which are the result of new product development, product trials or end of pro-duction runs which cannot be packed as Thorntons standard lines. They are packed into assorted bags and offer a saving of 35%-55% over the recom-mended retail price of standard loose line products. Discounted lines are excess to Thorntons' normal retail requirements and can be as a result of excess seasonal or export stock, discontinued lines or packaging changes. These prod-ucts, when available, are offered at a discount of 25%-50% over the standard retail price. Standard lines from the full Thorntons range are also on sale at normal prices. *Factory Shopping Village*

TOG 24

UNIT 44, CLARKS VILLAGE, STREET, SOMERSET BA16 OND

☎ (01458) 840468. OPEN 9 - 6 MON - SAT, 11 - 5 SUN.

Tog 24 are the UK's fastest growing brand name in outdoor clothing and leisurewear, with a total of three UK factories and 36 stores nationwide. They utilise the world's finest performance fabrics including Gore-Tex, Polartec and Burlington macs. Catering for all the family for all seasons, with cosy fleeces and waterproofs for the winter, and trekking ranges, shorts and t-shirts for the summer. With all prices at least 30% below the recommended retail price you can afford to enter the Tog comfort zone. *Factory Shopping Village*

TOM SAYERS CLOTHING CO

CLARKS VILLAGE, FARM ROAD, STREET, SOMERSET

☎ (01458) 448874. OPEN 9 - 6 MON - SAT, 11 - 5 SUN.

Tom Sayers make sweaters for some of the top high street department stores. Unusually for a factory shop, if they don't stock your size, they will try and order it for you from their factory or one of their other factory outlets and send it to you. Most of the stock here is overstock, cancelled orders or last sea-son's and includes jumpers, trousers and shirts at discounts of 30%. The trousers and shirts are bought in to complement the sweaters which they make. *Factory Shopping Village*

Live Well On Less Tips

After cleaning and drying a razor blade, coat it with Vaseline or cold cream. This keeps the air from coming into contact with the cutting edge and caus-ing rust. It also helps to lubricate the next shave.

TRIUMPH INTERNATIONAL LTD
UNIT 11, CLARKS VILLAGE, STREET, SOMERSET BA16 OBB
☎ (01458) 840700. OPEN 9 - 6 MON - SAT, 9 - 5.30 WINTER, 11 - 5 SUN.
Factory shop selling a wide and ever-changing range of Triumph lingerie, a French range: Valisere, and swimwear which are last season's stock or discontinued lines. Also stocks Sloggi underwear for men and women. The smaller department for men includes shirts, T-shirts, socks, underwear and swimwear from the Hom range. *Factory Shopping Village*

VIYELLA
CLARKS VILLAGE, STREET, SOMERSET BA16 OBB
☎ (01458) 448533. OPEN 9 - 6 MON - SAT, 9 - 5.30 WINTER, 11 - 5 SUN.
Wide range of Viyella ladieswear at discount prices of 30% from jackets and blouses to sweaters and hats. *Factory Shop*

WELLS RECLAMATION COMPANY
COXLEY, NR WELLS, SOMERSET BA5 1RQ
☎ (01749) 677087. FAX ☎ (01749) 671089. OPEN 8.30 - 5.30 MON - FRI, 9 - 4 SAT.
Reclaimed timber: pine and oak beams, pine doors, flooring; bathroom accessories, quarry tiles and flagstones (pennent and blue lias), fireplaces and bricks sold from this four-acre site. *Architectural Salvage*

WINDSMOOR SALE SHOP
CLARKS VILLAGE, STREET, SOMERSET BA16 OBB
☎ (01458) 840888. OPEN 9 - 6 MON - SAT, 11 - 5 SUN.
Previous season's stock as well as any returned merchandise and overmakes from the Windsmoor, Planet and Precis Petite ranges at discounts averaging about 50% off the original price. There is also a selection from the Baird Menswear and Outerwear range for men here. *Factory Shopping Village*

Live Well On Less Tips
Make a clove-studded orange for an air freshener. You need an orange and about 2 ounces of fresh cloves. Use a small nail to make holes in the orange and push the cloves in, packing them tightly. Allow the orange to dry for about 2 weeks. The finished orange can then be tied with a ribbon to hang in a wardrobe or put in a drawstring bag for use in a drawer.

Staffordshire

WOMENSWEAR ONLY ⬠ Alexon Sale Shop, *Tamworth*.
Beverley's Dress Agency, *Wolverhampton*.   Five Star Dress Agency, *Cannock*.
Prima, *Wolverhampton*.   Revival Bridal Agency, *Stoke-On-Trent*.   Slimma, *Leek*.   Slimma, *Cheadle*.

WOMENSWEAR & MENSWEAR ⬠ ⬡ Charles Clinkard, *Stoke-On-Trent*.
Direct Specs, *Tamworth*.   Fashion Factory, *Cannock*.   Freeport Talke Outlet Mall, *Stoke-On-Trent*.
Jaeger Factory Shop, *Tamworth*.   John Partridge Outlet Store, *Rugeley*.
Lew-Ways Factory Shop, *Cannock*.   London Leathers Direct, *Stoke-On-Trent*.   Matalan, *Wolverhampton*.
Matalan, *Tamworth*.   Matalan, *Stafford*.   Matalan, *Burton-On-Trent*.   Matalan, *Newcastle*.
New Life, *Cannock*.   Revue Dress Agency, *Stoke-On-Trent*.   T J Hughes, *Lichfield*.
The Factory Shop, *Market Drayton*.   The Shoe Shed, *Stafford*.   TK Maxx, *Stoke-On-Trent*.
Tog 24, *Stoke-On-Trent*.   Toyworld Factory Outlets Ltd, *Stoke-On-Trent*.
Webb Ivory Ltd, *Burton-On-Trent*.   Wynsor Shoes, *Stoke-On-Trent*.

CHILDREN 🎲 Charles Clinkard, *Stoke-On-Trent*.   Freeport Talke Outlet Mall, *Stoke-On-Trent*.
John Partridge Outlet Store, *Rugeley*.   Lew-Ways Factory Shop, *Cannock*.   Matalan, *Wolverhampton*.
Matalan, *Tamworth*.   Matalan, *Stafford*.   Matalan, *Burton-On-Trent*.   Matalan, *Newcastle*.
New Life, *Cannock*.   T J Hughes, *Lichfield*.   The Factory Shop, *Market Drayton*.
The Shoe Shed, *Stafford*.   TK Maxx, *Stoke-On-Trent*.   Tog 24, *Stoke-On-Trent*.
Webb Ivory Ltd, *Burton-On-Trent*.   Wynsor Shoes, *Stoke-On-Trent*.

HOUSEHOLD AND GIFTWARE 🏠 Allsorts Catalogue & Surplus Store, *Stoke-On-Trent*.
Arthur Price of England, *Lichfield*.   Aynsley China, *Stoke-On-Trent*.
Blakeney Pottery Ltd, *Stoke-On-Trent*.   Bridgewater, *Stoke-On-Trent*.
Chinacave, *Stoke-On-Trent*.   Dunelm Mill Shop, *Newcastle Under Lyme*.   Dunelm Mill Shop, *Stafford*.
Dunelm Mill Shop, *Tamworth*.   Dunelm Mill Shop, *Cannock*.   Dunelm Mill Shop, *Burton-On-Trent*.
Freeport Talke Outlet Mall, *Stoke-On-Trent*.   Georgian Crystal Factory Shop, *Burton-On-Trent*.
John Partridge Outlet Store, *Rugeley*.   Matalan, *Wolverhampton*.   Matalan, *Tamworth*.
Matalan, *Stafford*.   Matalan, *Burton-On-Trent*.   Matalan, *Newcastle*.
Minton Factory Shop, *Stoke-On-Trent*.   Moorland Pottery, *Stoke-On-Trent*.   New Life, *Cannock*.
Ponden Mill Linens, *Stoke-On-Trent*.   Portmeirion, *Stoke-On-Trent*.   Portmeirion, *Stoke*.
Portmeirion, *Longton*.   Price And Kensington Potteries, *Stoke-On-Trent*.
Royal Doulton, *Stoke-On-Trent*.   Schott Zwiesel, *Stafford*.   Spode, *Stoke-On-Trent*.
The Aynsley Factory Shop, *Hanley*.   The Factory Shop, *Market Drayton*.   The Shoe Shed, *Stafford*.
TK Maxx, *Stoke-On-Trent*.   Tutbury Crystal Factory Shop, *Burton-On-Trent*.
Waterford Wedgwood Factory Shop, *Stoke-On-Trent*.   Webb Ivory Ltd, *Burton-On-Trent*.
Webb Ivory Ltd, *Stoke-On-Trent*.   Webb Ivory Ltd, *Tamworth*.

ELECTRICAL EQUIPMENT 🔌 Russell Hobbs Factory Shop, *Wolverhampton*.
Spectrum Services, *Stoke-On-Trent*.

DIY/RENOVATION 🔨 Cawarden Brick Company, *Rugeley*.
Discount Ceramics, *Wolverhampton*.   Glynn Webb, *Stoke-On-Trent*.   Hyde Park Tiles, *Stone*.
Hyde Park Tiles, *Stoke-On-Trent*.   Topps Tiles, *Stoke-On-Trent*.

ARCHITECTURAL SALVAGE 🔨 Cawarden Brick Company, *Rugeley*.

FURNITURE/SOFT FURNISHINGS ▨
Allsorts Catalogue And Surplus Store, *Stoke-On-Trent.* British Trimmings Ltd, *Leek.*
Cannock Gates Factory Shop, *Cannock.* Carpet Mill Factory Shop, *Stoke-On-Trent.*
Dean's Furniture World, *Stoke-On-Trent.* Freeport Talke Outlet Mall, *Stoke-On-Trent.*
H L Linens Bazaars, *Wolverhampton.* New Life, *Cannock.* Suites Direct, *Stoke-On-Trent.*
Terry's Fabrics Warehouse, *Newcastle.* The Factory Shop, *Market Drayton.*
Vogue Carpets, *Newcastle Under Lyme.*

FOOD AND LEISURE ▥ Cannock Gates Ltd, *Cannock.*
Freeport Talke Outlet Mall, *Stoke-On-Trent.* Thorntons, *Stoke-On-Trent.*

SPORTSWEAR AND EQUIPMENT ⚲ Allsorts Catalogue And Surplus Store, *Stoke-On-Trent.*
Amber Leisure, *Wolverhampton.* American Discount Golf, *Stoke-On-Trent.*
Freeport Talke Outlet Mall, *Stoke-On-Trent.* John Partridge Outlet Store, *Rugeley.*
Lew-Ways Factory Shop, *Cannock.*

ALEXON SALE SHOP ⁀

34 GEORGE STREET, TAMWORTH, STAFFORDSHIRE
☎ (01827) 310041. OPEN 9 - 5.30 MON - SAT.
Alexon, Eastex and Ann Harvey from last season at 40% less than the original
price; during sale time in January and June, the reductions are as much as
70%. Stock includes separates, skirts, jackets, blouses; there is no underwear
or night clothes. *Permanent Discount Outlet*

ALLSORTS CATALOGUE ▨ ⌂ ⚲
AND SURPLUS STORE

23 HAMILL ROAD, BURSLEM, STOKE-ON-TRENT, STAFFORDSHIRE
☎ (01782) 833006. OPEN 10 - 5 MON - SAT, 11 - 4 SUN.
Household goods, furniture and exercise equipment at discounts of 40%-
60%. Furniture includes three-piece suites, pine tables and chairs, TV cabinets, nests of tables, kitchen furniture. Household goods include pots and
pans, ovenware, casserole dishes. There are also suitcases, exercise bikes, step
striders, walking and running machines, but no clothes, fabrics, eletrical items
or curtains. *Permanent Discount Outlet*

AMBER LEISURE ⚲

PEARSON STREET, WOLVERHAMPTON, STAFFORDSHIRE WV2 4HP
☎ (01902) 871301. OPEN 9 - 5 MON - FRI, 9 - 1 SAT.
Mail order company which also has a factory shop selling sunbeds and saunas
at factory prices. Delivery extra. *Factory Shop*

Live Well On Less Tips
When new envelopes have sealed closed due to moisture, heat in the
microwave for 20 seconds. This will open them all or part way.

AMERICAN DISCOUNT GOLF

75-81 NEWCASTLE ROAD, TRENT VALE, STOKE-ON-TRENT,
STAFFORDSHIRE

☎ (01782) 747787. OPEN 9.30 - 6.30 MO - SAT, 8 ON THUR, 10 - 6 SUN.

A wide selection of discounted gold equipment and apparel: sweaters, rain-suits, gloves, clubs, balls - everything you need for a golf game. Stocks all the top names including Wilson, MacGregor, Slazenger, Callaway, Serenade, Links and Mizuno. *Permanent Discount Outlet*

ARTHUR PRICE OF ENGLAND

BRITANNIA WAY, BRITTANIA ENTERPRISE PARK, LICHFIELD,
STAFFORDSHIRE WS14 9UY

☎ (01543) 257775. OPEN 9 - 5 MON - FRI, 10 - 1 SAT.

This factory shop in Lichfield sells seconds, discontinued lines and shop-soiled samples of silver-plated and stainless steel cutlery. There are sets as well as loose items on sale at half price or less. Also on sale is giftware consisting of cande-labras, cruet sets, tea services, tankards and trays, most at half price. There are usually four sales a year - in March, June, September and December - when there is up to 50% off. *Factory Shop*

AYNSLEY CHINA

SUTHERLAND ROAD, LONGTON, STOKE-ON-TRENT, STAFFORDSHIRE
ST3 1HS

☎ (01782) 593536. OPEN 9 - 5.30 MON - SAT, 11 - 4 SUN. MAIL ORDER.

UNIT 14, LOWER MALL, POTTERIES SHOPPING CENTRE, HANLEY,
STOKE-ON-TRENT, STAFFORDSHIRE ST1 1PS

☎ (01782) 204108. OPEN 9 - 5.30 MON - SAT, TILL 8 THUR.

The chance to buy beautiful china at affordable prices. All of Aynsley's gift-ware and tableware is stocked, plus there is a selection of seconds and discon-tinued lines at factory shop prices. The giftware range includes handmade china flowers and jewellery, Portland clocks, tableware, and textiles, vases, trinket boxes, table mats, trays, worktop savers, elegant lamps, Belleck Parian China, Galway Irish crystal, cutlery and crockery. *Factory Shop*

BEVERLEY'S DRESS AGENCY

211 TRYSULL ROAD, WOLVERHAMPTON, STAFFORDSHIRE

☎ (01902) 839111. OPEN 10 - 5 TUE - SAT.

Good quality designer clothes at realistic prices including Moschino jeans, Jacques Vert, Alexon, Jaeger, Versace jeans and high street labels such as Wallis and Windsmoor. Shoes, hats, bags and jewellery also stocked. *Dress Agency*

BLAKENEY POTTERY LTD

WOLFE STREET, STOKE-ON-TRENT, STAFFORDSHIRE ST4 4DA

☎ (01782) 847244. OPEN 9 - 4.30 MON - THUR, 9 - 3.30 FRI.

Large range of decorative ware, floral art, kitchenware, vases, jugs, bowls and a Victorian range, all of which are handmade and hand decorated. Because all the items are made on the premises to be sold to retail outlets, they are sold to individual customers at factory direct prices. *Factory Shop*

BRIDGEWATER

EASTWOOD WORKS, LICHFIELD STREET, HANLEY, STOKE-ON-TRENT, STAFFORDSHIRE

☎ (01782) 201328. OPEN 9.30 - 5.30 MON - SAT 11 - 5. MAIL ORDER.

Emma Bridgwater's distinctive hand decorated and sponge painted pottery, textiles and cookware ranges at discounts of 30% for seconds and discontinued lines. All the pottery on sale here has been made on site. Also on sale across the county and at Bridgewater Pastery Cafes is the equally distinctive Matthew Rice range of stationery, boxes, tins and recipe boxes, some of which are discounted, though the current range is on sale at full price. A mail order system operates for both sides of the business. *Factory Shop*

BRITISH TRIMMINGS LTD

BALL HAYE ROAD, LEEK, STAFFORDSHIRE ST13 6AU

☎ (01538) 383634. OPEN 9.30 - 4.30 MON - FRI, 10 - 2 FIRST SAT EACH MONTH (EXCL AUG).

An exciting range of trimmings, braids, tie-backs cord and fringing, all made originally for department stores with seconds reduced here by one third to one half. £1 bargain bags of oddments set out in boxes for those who like to rummage. Prices range from 25p to £11 per metre. *Factory Shop*

CANNOCK GATES FACTORY SHOP

HAWKS GREEN INDUSTRIAL ESTATE, CANNOCK, STAFFORDSHIRE WS11 2XT

☎ (01543) 462500. OPEN 9 - 5 MON - SAT, 10 - 4 SUN. MAIL ORDER.

Small shop next to the factory selling garden gates in wrought iron and timber, garden furniture, beds, furniture, gazebos, arches, gifts and accessories, all sold at direct to the public prices. Regular newsletter outlines special deals in a wide range of wrought iron and wooden gates, as well as an ever-growing selection of garden loungers, wrought iron beds, parasols, summer houses, garden arches, wooden planters, cast-iron garden furniture.*Factory Shop*

Live Well On Less Tips
Instead of redecorating a room, why not try just re-arranging the furniture instead. You'll be surprised how different a room looks with one or two major pieces moved around.

CARPET MILL FACTORY SHOP
WATERLOO ROAD, BURSLEM, STOKE-ON-TRENT, STAFFORDSHIRE
☎ (01782) 833823. OPEN 9 - 6 MON - WED, 9 - 8 THUR, FRO, 10 - 4 SUN.
The biggest carpet warehouse in Stoke-on-Trent, it usually has at least 1,000 remnants in all sizes as well as a big selection of roll stock - all one-offs and non-repeatable - and samples from which customers can order. They don't stock Axminsters, but there is a good selection of Wiltons (from £10 a yard), Berbers and Saxony, both plain and patterned. Prices are obviously cheaper for the remnants and roll stock, although carpets to order are still very competitive. *Factory Shop*

CAWARDEN BRICK COMPANY
CAWARDEN SPRINGS FARM, BLYTHBURY ROAD, BLITHBURY, RUGELEY, STAFFORDSHIRE WS15 3HL
☎ (01889) 574066. OPEN 8 - 5 MON - FRI, 8 - 4 SAT.
New showroom with fireplaces, large quantities of reclaimed handmade bricks, also tiles, flagstone and block stone. Oak flooring, doors, cupboards, garden ornaments and oak beams. *Architectural Salvage*

CHARLES CLINKARD
UNIT 42/43 FREEPORT OUTLET MALL, TALKE PITTS, STOKE ON TRENT, STAFFORDSHIRE ST7 1QE
☎ (01782) 774113. OPEN 10 - 8 MON - SAT, 11 - 4 SUN.
Footwear for the family at discounts of between 20% and 50%. Labels on sale here include Rockport, Loake, Camel, Bally, Church's, Ecco, Gabor, Rohde, Van-Dal, Kickers, Clarks, Dr Martens, K Shoes, Lotus and Renata. The telephone number given here is for the centre, not the shop. *Factory Shopping Village*

CHINACAVE
LEWIS'S ARCADE, THE POTTERIES SHOPPING CENTRE, HANLEY, STOKE-ON-TRENT, STAFFORDSHIRE ST1 1PS
☎ (01782) 204156. OPEN 9 - 5.30 MON - SAT, 8 ON THUR, 11 - 4 SUN.
This outlet sells seconds in Royal Doulton, Royal Albert crystal, Beatrix Potter figurines and Royal Minton at discounts of up to 50%. In the same complex is Royal Aynsley and the general discount shop, TK Maxx. *Factory Shop*

Live Well On Less Tips
7 ways to cut your heating costs
Turn your central heating thermostat down by just one degree - you can save
up to 10 percent of your heating bill ...
..... If you're cold, put on a sweater!
Don't waste gas on rooms you don't use. Leave the radiator on to stop
mould or condensation but at a very low level
Instal a roll of clear film from any diy shop across your window frames in winter. This keeps the heat in and the cold out.
Draught proof doors
Make sure your curtains do not cover the radiator. Heat then rises straight
up behind them and escapes out of the window instead of circulating around
the room.
Insulate all hot water pipes with pre-formed insulation from a diy shop or
builders merchant.

DEAN'S FURNITURE WORLD

LEEK ROAD, HANLEY, STOKE-ON-TRENT, STAFFORDSHIRE
☎ (01782) 286677. OPEN 9.30 - 5.30 MON - SAT, 11 - 5 SUN.
Furniture at discounted prices. They specialise in three-piece suites, beds and
dining sets, some of which are recognisable brand names. A 5 ft double divan
bed costs £250. *Permanent Discount Outlet*

DIRECT SPECS

39 LOWER GUNGATE, TAMWORTH, STAFFORDSHIRE B79 7AS
☎ (01827) 50233. OPEN 9 - 5 MON - SAT.
1 CHURCH HOUSE, OLD HALL STREET, HANLEY, STOKE-ON-TRENT,
STAFFORDSHIRE ST1 3AU
☎ (01782) 263038. OPEN 9 - 5 MON - SAT.
Spectacles and sunglasses at prices which the owner claims beat any competitor's. Most designer names are stocked at one time or another, though if you
have a favourite, check first. Bring along your prescription and glasses will be
found to suit. No eye tests conducted. *Permanent Discount Outlet*

DISCOUNT CERAMICS

7 MILLFIELDS ROAD, BILSTON, WOLVERHAMPTON, STAFFORDSHIRE
WV1 0QS
☎ (01902) 620679. OPEN 8 - 6 MON - FRI, 8 - 5.30 SAT, 10 - 4 SUN.
Stocks a vast range of imported wall and floor tiles. As they buy direct from
the importer, they can cut costs to below that of most of their competition,
though in areas with a wide selection of tile shops, prices will be on a par.
Permanent Discount Outlet

DUNELM MILL SHOP

98-104 HIGH STREET, NEWCASTLE UNDER LYME, STAFFORDSHIRE
ST5 1QQ
☎ (01782) 713400. OPEN 9 - 5.30 MON - SAT.
UNIT 3, QUEENSVILLE RETAIL PARK, SILKMORE LANE, STAFFORD
ST17 4SU
☎ (01785) 248433. OPEN 10 - 6 MON - WED, 10 - 8 THUR, FRI, 9 - 6 SAT
11 - 5 SUN.
GUNGATE PRECINCT, LOWER GUNGATE, TAMWORTH,
STAFFORDSHIRE B79 7AG
☎ (01827) 69504. OPEN 9 - 5 MON - SAT, UNTIL 5.30 ON FRI.
FABRIC SHOP, 81 HIGH GREEN, CANNOCK, STAFFORDSHIRE WS1 1BH
☎ (01543) 503437. OPEN 9 - 5 MON - FRI, 9 - 5.30 SAT, 10 - 4 SUN.
4 WORTHINGTON WALK, BURTON-ON-TRENT, STAFFORDSHIRE
DE14 1BU
☎ (01283) 512803. OPEN 9 - 5 MON - FRI, 9 - 5.30 SAT.
Part of a chain of shops based in the Midlands selling brand-name and chainstore curtains, masses of bedlinen, towels, wickerware, pictures and frames, all
at competitive prices. Some of the shops sell fabric on the roll. *Permanent
Discount Outlet*

FASHION FACTORY

WYRLEY BROOK PARK, VINE LANE, BRIDGETOWN, CANNOCK,
STAFFORDSHIRE WS11 3XF
☎ (01543) 466000. OPEN 9.30 - 5.30 MON - SAT, 11 - 5 SUN.
At the Fashion Factory stores in Cannock and Telford (see Shropshire) you'll
find a comprehensive selection of quality branded and designer fashions for
men and women, all reduced by up to 70% off the normal high street prices.
Stock is made up of excess production, cancelled orders and ends of season
ranges from dozens of UK and international clothing manufacturers. This
means a constantly changing selection from lingerie and basic fashion essentials to dresses, suits and separates, all at a fraction of the prices you'd normally expect to pay. The boutique-style store in Telford features two floors packed
with a huge variety of ladieswear, while the Cannock superstore boasts possibly one of the largest selection of discounted clothing and footwear under one
roof in the Midlands, with between 50,000-60,000 garments on display in a
massive 20,000 sq ft of retail space. There are four sales a year: Dec/Jan, Feb,
Jun/July and August. Coffee shop now open. *Permanent Discount Outlet*

Live Well On Less Tips
Use the public library instead of buying books/newspapers

Live Well On Less Tips
If your favourite tablecloth has candle wax on it, before resorting to the expensive specialists, scrape off as much as you can with a blunt knice, place clean, absorbent paper on both sides of the stain, press with a warm iron to melt remaining wax and then launder on a hot wash.

FIVE STAR DRESS AGENCY

7 - 8 BRIDGTOWN BUSINESS CENTRE, NORTH STREET, BRIDGTOWN, CANNOCK, STAFFORDSHIRE

☎ (01543) 571397. OPEN 10 - 4 MON - SAT.

Good range of designer wear as well as high street names. For example, Planet, Laura Ashley, Next, Wallis and Windsmoor to Frank Usher, Betty Barclay, Klass and Louis Feraud. Offers small selection of evening wear, mother of the bride/groom outfits including hats, also large selection of day wear. *Dress Agency*

FREEPORT TALKE OUTLET MALL

TALKE, NEAR STOKE-ON-TRENT, NEWCASTLE UNDER LYME, PIT LANE, TALKE PITS, STOKE ON TRENT, STAFFORDSHIRE ST7 1XD

☎ (01782) 774113. OPEN 10 - 8 MON - SAT, 11 - 5 SUN.

Fully covered indoor outlet mall. Ladieswear: Designer Room, Edinburgh Woollen Mill, Giorgio, Iceberg, London Leathers, Nickelbys, The Suit Company. Childrenswear: Giorgio, Used Co. Kids. Luggage and Accessories: Carlton, Claires Outlet. Footwear: Charles Clinkard, Jane Shilton, Rohde Shoes. Sports and outdoorwear: Factory Brands, Tog 24, Trespass, Streetwise Sports. Thornton's confectionery, Birthdays, Mobile Phone Shop, Book Depot, Pictureport, Ponden Mill, XS Music and Video. Three cafes and a childrens' play area. *Factory Shopping Village*

GEORGIAN CRYSTAL FACTORY SHOP

SILK MILL LANE, TUTBURY, BURTON-ON-TRENT, STAFFORDSHIRE DE13 9LE

☎ (01283) 814534. OPEN 9 - 5 MON - SAT, 10 - 4 SUN.

Good quality crystal glasses, vases and gifts, seconds of which are sold at considerable discounts. Call and see a free demonstration of glass being made on the premises - from Monday to Thursday. *Factory Shop*

GLYNN WEBB

122-126 BROAD STREET, HANLEY, STOKE-ON-TRENT,
STAFFORDSHIRE ST1 4EQ

☎ (01782) 214471. OPEN 9 - 8 MON - SAT, 10 - 4 SUN.

Stockists of all your home improvement needs from wallpaper to paint, furniture to flooring, tiles to textiles, housewares to lighting - in fact, almost everything for your home, with 24 branches in the North-West, Midlands and Yorkshire. Specialists in discontinued mail order, slightly imperfect branded stocks as well as perfect quality superior products. They carry top brands such as Dulux, Crown Paints and Vymura and Coloroll wall coverings, Rectella and Norwood textiles and much more in store. Different branches carry different lines so if you want something specific, phone first. To find your nearest branch, phone 0161 621 4500. *Permanent Discount Outlet*

H L LINEN BAZAARS

9 WULFRUN WAY, WULFRUN CENTRE, WOLVERHAMPTON,
STAFFORDSHIRE WV1 3HG

☎ (01902) 714083. OPEN 9 - 5.30 MON - SAT.

The mail order catalogue of this company which sells bedlinen, duvets, towels and sheets is very busy and hides some of the gems which are on sale, ends of lines of which can be found in their warehouse outlets both here and in Liverpool and the West Midlands. Hunt carefully at these outlets and you will find many famous brand names such as Early's of Witney, Vantona and Slumberdown. Their warehouse sells ends of lines, slight seconds and bulk purchases of duvets, pillows, cotton sheets (usually hotel over-orders) at discounts of up to 50%. *Permanent Discount Outlet*

HYDE PARK TILES

UNIT 7, EMERALD WAY, STONE BUSINESS PARK, STONE,
STAFFORDSHIRE

☎ (01785) 816161. OPEN 9 - 5.30 MON - FRI, 9 - 5 SAT.

Retail shop for Creta Ceramica, a company which imports good quality Italian and Spanish wall and floor tiles. You can find their tiles in shops countrywide, but at varying prices depending on the local competition and almost always more expensive than they are in this shop, which is on the same industrial estate as the wholesale warehouse. For the floor, they offer terracotta lookalike tiles averaging £14 a quare yard, quarry tiles, porcelain tiles, both glazed and unglazed, octagon, dot, hexagon, square and lozenge shaped. For walls, the tiles are glazed in a variety of finishes from satin and glossy to eggshell and come in sizes from four inches quare to 14 inches square by nine inches. *Permanent Discount Outlet*

HYDE PARK TILES

UNIT 6, HYDE PARK INDUSTRIAL ESTATE, CITY ROAD, STOKE-ON-TRENT, STAFFORDSHIRE

☎ (01782) 747547. OPEN 8.30 - 5.30 MON, WED, FRI, 8.30 - 8 TUE, THUR, 8.30 - 5 SAT, 10 - 2 SUN.

Part of a tile distribution company, which means that when they sell the tiles themselves, they are their own middleman and can cut out most of that cost to pass savings on to their customers. For example, they sell tiles at £16.95 a sq yard which are on sale at other tile shops for £29.50. They specialise in top Italian and Spanish companies such as Apperici, Richoti and Gomez Gomez and deal in sizes from 10cms x 10cms to 45cms x 45cms. *Permanent Discount Outlet*

JAEGER FACTORY SHOP

42-43 CHURCH STREET, TAMWORTH, STAFFORDSHIRE B79 7DE

☎ (01827) 52828. OPEN 9.30 - 5.30 MON - SAT.

Contemporary classics from Jaeger at excellent prices. Most of the merchandise is previous seasons' stock, but you might also find some special makes. Both shops stock tailoring and knitwear for women and men. *Factory Shop*

JOHN PARTRIDGE OUTLET STORE

POWER STATION ROAD, TRENT MEADOWS, RUGELEY, STAFFORDSHIRE WS15 2HS

☎ (01889) 584438. OPEN 9 - 5 MON - FRI, 9 - 4 SAT.

John Partridge specialises in hardwearing outdoor clothes. Ranges include waxed cotton jackets, trench coats and waistcoats; showerproof classic town coats; Gore-tex coats and tweed coats; quilted jackets and waistcoats; children's waxed jackets, quilted jackets and waistcoats; hats and caps; moleskin and cord trousers; knitwear and shirts. Discontinued lines and seconds are on sale at discounted prices - a minimum of 30% and up to 70% off during promotions. There's a small riding section within the shop wich stocks body protectors, skull caps, boots - jodphurs where prices are competitive rather than discounted. *Factory Shopping Village*

JOHN TAMS

SUTHERLAND ROAD, LONGTON, STOKE-ON-TRENT, STAFFORDSHIRE ST3 1JB

☎ (01782) 599667. OPEN 9 - 4.30 MON - FRI, 9 - 3 SAT. 11 - 4 SUN.

Discounted prices of between 50%-75% for seconds and discontinued lines of Royal Grafton, Duchess, John Tams and other chinaware. *Factory Shop*

LEW-WAYS FACTORY SHOP

WATLING STREET, CANNOCK, STAFFORDSHIRE WS11 3NB
☎ (01543) 363711. OPEN 9 - 5 MON - SAT, 8 - 8 THUR,10 - 4 SUN IN SUMMER, BANK HOLIDAYS.
Wide range of children's outdoor and indoor play equipment and bicycles. There are trikes from as little as £9.99, children's bicycles, scooters, as well as slides, climbing frames, play mats, sand pits, play sand, goal posts, basket ball sets and pools, baby swings, trampolines, and water trays. Adult equipment includes cycles, car roof boxes, camping trailers and garden ponds. *Factory Shop*

LONDON LEATHERS DIRECT

FREEPORT OUTLET MALL, UNIT 47, JAMADGE ROAD, TALKE, STOKE ON TRENT, STAFFORDSHIRE ST7 1QE
☎ (01782) 788288 . OPEN 10 - 8 MON - SAT, 11 - 5 SUN.
Very good quality leather and suede jackets, coats and trousers, at discounts of at least 30%, with most at 50% off in this village which features lots of restaurants and fun things for the family to take part in. *Factory Shopping Village*

MATALAN

BIRMINGHAM ROAD, HOWARD STREET, WOLVERHAMPTON, STAFFORDSHIRE WV2 2LQ
☎ (01902) 352813. OPEN 10 - 8 MON - FRI, 9.30 - 5.30 SAT, 10 - 6 SUN.
UNIT 7, VENTURA SHOPPING CENTRE, VENTURA PARK ROAD, BONE HILL DRIVE, TAMWORTH, STAFFORDSHIRE B78 3HB
☎ (01827) 50900. OPEN 10 - 8 MON - FRI, 9.30 - 5.30 SAT, 10 - 6 SUN.
UNITS 5 & 6, QUEENSVILLE RETAIL PARK, SILKMORE LANE, STAFFORD ST17 4SU
☎ (01785) 226211. OPEN 10 - 8 MON - FRI, 9.30 - 5.30 SAT, 10 - 6 SUN.
UNIT A, LICHFIELD STREET, BURTON-ON-TRENT, STAFFORDSHIRE DE14 3QZ
☎ (01283) 540856. OPEN 10 - 8 MON - FRI, 9 - 6 SAT, 11 - 5 SUN.
WOLSTANTON RETAIL PARK, WOLSTANTON, NEWCASTLE, STAFFORDSHIRE ST5 1DY
☎ (01782) 711731. OPEN 10 - 8 MON - FRI, 9 - 6 SAT, 11 - 5 SUN.
Matalan is a fashion and homewares shop giving customers what they claim to be unbeatable value for money with huge savings on a wide range of products including high quality fashionable clothing for women, women and children at up to 50% off high street prices. Matalan is situated out of town and stores are open seven days a week all year round. *Permanent Discount Outlet*

MINTON FACTORY SHOP

LONDON ROAD, STOKE-ON-TRENT, STAFFORDSHIRE ST4 7QD
☎ (01782) 292121. OPEN 9 - 5.30 MON - SAT.
Part of the Royal Doulton company which operates seven factory shops. As well as selling at normal retail prices, the factory shops also offer a variety of discontinued and slightly imperfect pieces at reduced prices. Most of the shops sell the company's other three main brands as well: Royal Crown Derby, Royal Albert and Royal Doulton itself. For a tour of china factory shops in this area, go to the railway station and take the Potteries tour. There is an information service on: 01782 292292. *Factory Shop*

MOORLAND POTTERY

CHELSEA WORKS, 72A MOORLAND ROAD, BURSLEM, STOKE-ON-TRENT, STAFFORDSHIRE ST6 1DY
☎ (01782) 834631. OPEN 9 - 5 MON - FRI, 10 -4 SAT.
The place where Susie Cooper started her business. Moorland Pottery is one of the few artware potteries still producing hand thrown, hand turned and hand painted pottery. The small factory shop selling tableware, giftware, reproduction Art Deco, reproduction Staffordshire dogs, and flatbacks and hand decorated spongeware - all manufactured at the works - at reasonable prices. *Factory Shop*

Live Well On Less Tips
CHINASEARCH P.O. BOX 1202, KENILWORTH, WARWICKSHIRE CV8 2WW. (01926) 512402, FAX: (01926) 859311. MAIL ORDER. VISITORS BY APPOINTMENT ONLY. ALL CORRESPONDENCE TO BE ACCOMPANIED BY S.A.E. PLEASE.
During the past decade, Chinasearch has built up a stock of around 1500 patterns of china and pottery which have been discontinued over the last 30 years or more. This stock changes daily, and due to ever-increasing business, they have moved to a warehouse. The manufacturers whose products they keep in stock include Royal Doulton, Minton, Crown Derby, Royal Albert, Paragon, Colclough and Booths, Wedgwood, Coalport, Susie Cooper, Adams, Johnsons, Masons, Meakin and Midwinter, Royal Worcester, Palisay and Copeland Spode, Aynsley, Denby, Hornsea, Marks & Spencer, Poole, Portmeiron and Villeroy & Boch. Friendly staff are always willing to help: If they don't have the items you require, whether it be one tea saucer, a complete dinner service, a china egg or a miniature coffee pot, they will keep details on file until they find them. They do not charge a registration fee and there is no obligation to buy. Always pleased to hear from people who wish to sell unwanted tableware or collectables and can arrange collection countrywide.

PONDEN MILL LINENS

FREEPORT OUTLET MALL, PIT LANE, TALKE PITS, STOKE-ON-TRENT, STAFFORDSHIRE ST7 1XD

☎ (01782) 787150. OPEN 10 - 8 MON - SAT, 11 - 5 SUN.

Famous branded products at direct from the mill prices. Towels, co-ordinated bedlinen, duvets, pillows and curtains from Crown, Coloroll, Chortex, Rectella together with bathroom and kitchen accessories. *Factory Shopping Village*

PORTMEIRION

SILVAN WORKS, NORMACOTT ROAD, LONGTON, STOKE-ON-TRENT, STAFFORDSHIRE ST3 1PW

☎ (01782) 326412. OPEN 9.30 - 5.30 MON - SAT, 10 - 4 SUN.
VICTORIA ROAD, FENTON, STOKE-ON-TRENT, STAFFORDSHIRE
☎ (01782) 743460. OPEN 9.30 - 5.30 MON - SAT, 10 - 4 SUN.
LONDON ROAD, STOKE, STAFFORDSHIRE
☎ (01782) 411756. OPEN 9.30 - 5.30 MON - SAT, 10 - 4 SUN.
NORMACOTT ROAD, LONGTON, STAFFORDSHIRE
☎ (01782) 326412. OPEN 9.30 - 5.30 MON - SAT, 10 - 4 SUN.

Factory shops selling Portmeirion seconds in all patterns. The selection includes tableware (tea, coffee and dinner set); giftware (vases, planters, mugs, candlesticks, salad and fruit bowls) and co-ordinating accessories (placemats, cookware, textiles, tumblers). Discounts are approximately one third but vary from item to item. *Factory Shop*

PRICE AND KENSINGTON POTTERY

TRUBSHAW CROSS, LONGPORT, STOKE-ON-TRENT, STAFFORDSHIRE ST6 4LR

☎ (01782) 838631. OPEN 9.15 - 5 MON - FRI, 9.30 - 4.30 SAT.

Renowned for its traditionally hand-decorated spongeware, novelty teapots and cottageware, Price and Kensington now also produce an extensive selection of quality earthenware items for the kitchen. The on-site factory shop boasts a wide range of selected seconds from both Price and Kensington and its parent company, Arthur Wood and Son. *Factory Shop*

PRIMA

FINCHFIELD ROAD, WOLVERHAMPTON, STAFFORDSHIRE
☎ (01902) 380398. OPEN 9.30 - 5 MON - SAT.

Elegant shop with friendly owner selling a good selection of nearly-new designer clothes for women, with a small selection for children. Accessories include shoes, handbags, hats and some jewellery. *Dress Agency*

> *Live Well On Less Tips*
> Cut rolls of paper kitchen towels in half right down to the cardboard tube so
> that a half sheet rather than a whole sheet is used most of the time.

REVIVAL BRIDAL AGENCY

10 ALBION STREET, HANLEY, STOKE-ON-TRENT, STAFFORDSHIRE
☎ (01782) 202195. OPEN 10 - 4 TUE, WED, FRI, SAT, 11.30 - 4 THUR.
More than 200 once-worn bridal gowns in stock at any one time, plus bridesmaids dresses from children's sizes to adults and some page boys outfits. There
is a dress agency downstairs, with the bridal agency upstairs. *Dress Agency*

REVUE DRESS AGENCY

12 FORSTER STREET, TUNSTALL, STOKE-ON-TRENT, STAFFORDSHIRE
☎ (01782) 813939. OPEN 10 - 4 MON, TUE, 9.30 - 4.30 WED - SAT.
A wide selection of nearly-new women's clothes with some men's casual clothes
only. The labels are middle of the market and more inclined to the high street
- names such as Laura Ashley, Morgan and Wallis - and there are also shoes,
bags, jewellery and perfume. *Dress Agency*

ROYAL DOULTON

MINTON HOUSE, LONDON ROAD, STOKE-ON-TRENT,
STAFFORDSHIRE ST4 7QD
☎ (01782) 292292. OPEN 9 - 5.30 MON - SAT, 11 - 5 SUN.
NILE STREET, BURSLEM, STOKE-ON-TRENT
OPEN 9.- 5.30 MON - SAT, 10 - 4 SUN.
LEEK NEW ROAD, BADDELEY GREEN, STOKE-ON-TRENT
☎ (01782) 291700. OPEN 9.- 5.30 MON - SAT, 11 - 5 SUN.
VICTORIA ROAD, FENTON,
☎ (01782) 291869. OPEN 9.- 5.30 MON - SAT, 10 - 4 SUN.
REGENT WORKS
LAWLEY STREET, LONGTON, STOKE-ON-TRENT, STAFFORDSHIRE
ST3 2PH
☎ (01782) 291172. OPEN 9 - 5.30 MON - SAT, 10.30 - 4.30 SUN.
BESWICK FACTORY SHOP, BARFORD STREET, STOKE-ON-TRENT
ST3 2NN
☎ (01782) 291237. OPEN 9 - 5.30 MON - SAT, 10 - 4 SUN.
Royal Doulton's factory shops which, as well as selling at normal retail prices,
also offer a variety of discontinued and slightly imperfect pieces at reduced
prices. The shops sell the company's four main brand: Royal Crown Derby,
Minton, Royal Albert and Royal Doulton itself. For a tour of china factory
shops in this area, go to the railway station and take the Potteries tour. There
is an information service on: 01782 292292. *Factory Shop*

RUSSELL HOBBS FACTORY SHOP

BRIDGNORTH ROAD, WOMBOURNE, WOLVERHAMPTON, STAFFORDSHIRE WV5 8AQ

☎ (0161) 947 3000. OPEN 9 - 4.30 TUE - FRI, 9 - 12.30 SAT.

Discontinued lines and seconds of Pifco, Carmen, Salton, Russell Hobbs, Mountain Breeze and Tower, as well as some perfect lines. For example, kettles, haircare, saucepan sets, slow cookers, mini ovens, air cleaners, ionisers and aromatherapy products. Also Christmas tree lights in season. *Factory Shop*

SCHOTT ZWIESEL

DRUMMOND ROAD, ASTONFIELDS INDUSTRIAL ESTATE, STAFFORD, STAFFORDSHIRE ST16 3EL

☎ (01785) 222707. OPEN 10 - 4.30 WED - FRI, 10 - 3 SAT. MAIL ORDER.

One of Europe's largest manufacturers of blown crystal glassware, Schott Zwiesel has been established for more than 100 years. They make fine cut crystal stemware, plain crystal stemware, crystal giftware and blown decorative crystal. The factory shop sells a variety of glassware including stemware, glass bowls, vases, sets of handmade crystal, boxed presentation sets with matching decanters and tankards. *Factory Shop*

SLIMMA

JAMES STREET, LEEK, STAFFORDSHIRE ST13 8BQ

☎ (01538) 388096. OPEN 9 - 5 MON - FRI, 9 - 3 SAT.

7 CROSS STREET, CHEADLE, STAFFORDSHIRE ST10 1NP

☎ (01538) 751455. OPEN 9 - 5 MON, TUE, THUR, FRI, 9 - 1 WED, 9 - 4 SAT.

Manufacturers for 850 independent retailers countrywide of smart, tailored clothing, the factory shops stock over-runs and seconds from the Slimma ranges as well as chainstore seconds. Examples of prices include, skirts from £4; trousers from £5; swimwear from £8. Co-ordinated ranges available. *Factory Shop*

SPECTRUM SERVICES

11-13 HIGH STREET, TUNSTALL, STOKE-ON-TRENT, STAFFORDSHIRE

☎ (01782) 826162. OPEN 9 - 5.30 MON - SAT, 9 - 3.30 SUN.

Graded electrical items which have either been returned because of a slight cosmetic mark or because the packaging is broken. Cookers, fridges, freezers, vacuum cleaners, spin dryers etc from Zanussi, Electrolux, Hoover, Creda, Hotpoint. *Permanent Discount Outlet*

Live Well On Less Tips
Re-use old wrapping paper from bouquets of flowers, wallpaper, old maps

SPODE

CHURCH STREET, STOKE-ON-TRENT, STAFFORDSHIRE ST4 1BX

☎ (01782) 744011. OPEN 9 - 5 MON - SAT, 10 - 4 SUN.

Factory shop selling Spode china and earthenware at about 25% below the normal retail price, as well as holding regular sales at which further discounts are available on some discontinued lines. All the stock, including seconds, are current patterns and include tableware, wall plaques, fine bone china dinner sets, tea and coffee sets and giftware. Also exceptional bargains in the white-ware shop. There is also a Museum and Visitor Centre which is open seven days a week with factory tours running every week day. *Factory Shop*

SUITES DIRECT

MINSTER MILLS, WALLEY STREET, BIDDULPH, STOKE-ON-TRENT, STAFFORDSHIRE

☎ (01782) 510007. OPEN 9 - 5 MON - FRI, 10 - 5 SAT, 11 - 4 SUN.

Manufacturers of three-piece suites mainly, as well as some beds, they sell to the public at excellent prices as there is no middleman. There are three show-rooms here so you can see lots of examples of their products or choose to have something unique made up - perhaps a three and a half seater sofa. Sofas can be manufactured and delivered within 10 days. Plenty of fabric from which to choose covers. *Factory Shop*

T J HUGHES

BAKERS LANE, 3 SPIRES SHOPPING CENTRE, LICHFIELD, STAFFORDSHIRE

☎ (01543) 418181. OPEN 9 - 5.30 MON - SAT.

Expanding chain of shops offering, not discounts as such, but very competi-tively priced goods from clothes for all the family to china, towels, bedlinen, duvets, pots and pans, kettles, vacuum cleaners, television sets, CDs, toasters. There are branches around the contry, mostly in the Midlands and North West. Readers have found here and at other branches Dyson vacuum cleaner, £165; Kangol stationery, Waterman pens, Polo Ralph Lauren men's shirts, £19.99; Calvin Klein jeans, £25; Ultima cosmetics. *Permanent Discount Outlet*

TERRY'S FABRICS WAREHOUSE

CARTLIDGE STREET, OFF SHELTON NEW ROAD, NEWCASTLE, STAFFORDSHIRE

☎ (01782) 710777. OPEN 9 - 5.30 MON - SAT, 11 - 5 SUN.

Fabric warehouse with thousands of rolls on sale from £1 to £17 a metre. The most popular name stocked here is Prestigious, but there is also some Sanderson and Crowson. Parking outside. *Permanent Discount Outlet*

Live Well On Less Tips

Rather than putting a brick in a toilet tank to save water (this usually just means you have to flush twice instead of once), lower the water level an inch or two. If the toilet still operates efficiently, you'll save a significant amount of water. If not, unbend the float rod a bit until it does.

THE AYNSLEY FACTORY SHOP

UNIT 14, LOWER MALL, THE POTTERY SHOPPING CENTRE, HANLEY, STAFFORDSHIRE ST5 8ET

☎ (01782) 204108. OPEN 9 - 5.30 MON - SAT, 8 ON THUR.

Next door to the Chinacare shop, this sells dinner services, gifts, perfume puffs, vases, bells mugs and clocks from the Aynsley range at discount prices. *Factory Shop*

THE FACTORY SHOP

QUEEN STREET CAR PARK, QUEEN STREET, MARKET DRAYTON, STAFFORDSHIRE TF9 1EQ

☎ (01630) 655673. OPEN 9 - 5 MON - SAT, 10 - 4 SUN.

Wide range on sale includes men's, ladies and children's clothing and footwear; household textiles; toiletries; hardware; luggage; lighting and bedding, most of which are chainstore and high street brands at discounts of approximately 30%-50%. There are weekly deliveries and brands include many major stars such as Adidas, Nike, Wrangler and Dartington, to name just a few. Now has kitchen and furniture displays with a line of Cape Country furniture on sale. Ranges are continually changing and few factory shops offer such a variety under one roof. Most of the shops have their own car parks or there are nearby car parking facilities. *Factory Shop*

THE SHOE SHED

CASTLEFIELDS, NEWPORT ROAD, STAFFORD, STAFFORDSHIRE ST16 1BQ

☎ (01785) 211311. OPEN 9 - 5.30 MON - SAT, 10 - 4 SUN.

Large factory shop selling a vast range of all types of women's, men's and children's shoes, all of which are perfects, at up to 30% below normal high street prices. Ladies sandals cost from £5; shoes from £7.50. Men's shoes cost from £10; sports shoes from £10. A large range of casualwear, including T-shirts and tracksuits for women, men and children, plus a selection of ladies underwear. Kitchenware, ceramics, household goods and giftware are also stocked at discounted prices. *Factory Shop*

THORNTONS

FREEPORT OUTLET MALL, PIT LANE, TALKE PITS, STOKE-ON-TRENT,
STAFFORDSHIRE ST7 1QE

☎   (01782) 787793. OPEN 10 - 8 MON - SAT, 11 - 5 SUN.

The UK's leading specialist confectionery retailer has more than 500 shops
and franchises nationwide selling a wide range of boxed and loose, chocolate
and sugar confectionery. The factory outlets sell three different categories:
misshapes. discounted lines and standard lines. Misshapes are loose chocolates
which are the result of new product development, product trials or end of production runs which cannot be packed as Thorntons standard lines. They are
packed into assorted bags and offer a saving of 35%-55% over the recommended retail price of standard loose line products. Discounted lines are
excess to Thorntons' normal retail requirements and can be as a result of excess
seasonal or export stock, discontinued lines or packaging changes. These products, when available, are offered at a discount of 25%-50% over the standard
retail price. Standard lines from the full Thorntons range are also on sale at
normal prices. *Factory Shopping Village*

TK MAXX

THE POTTERIES SHOPPING CENTRE, HANLEY, STOKE-ON-TRENT,
STAFFORDSHIRE ST1 1PP

☎   (01782) 207509. OPEN 9 - 5.30 MON - FRI, 9 - 6 SAT, 11 - 5 SUN, UNTIL
8 ON THUR.

Based on an American concept, TK Maxx is situated in easily accessible, often
centrally located stores and offers famous label goods with up to 60% savings
off recommended retail prices. TK Maxx has fashion for the whole family -
women's, men's and childrenswear - accessories, shoes, gifts, kitchenware and
home goods. Everything in the store is branded with a choice of well-known
high street names to designer labels, and while a small percentage might be
clearly marked past season, the great majority of items in store are current season, current stock and still with phenomenal savings. There is a huge choice
with 50,000 pieces in store and up to 10,000 new items arriving a week. The
stores are simple and unfussy with wide aisles, shopping trolleys and baskets,
and a spacious, functional feel to them but there are individual changing
rooms, ramps for buggies and wheelchairs and plenty of staff on the shop
floor. Every branch accepts all major credit and debit cards and has a liberal
refund and return policy. *Permanent Discount Outlet*

Live Well On Less Tips

Make a toilet roll last longer by kneeling on it so it's slightly squashed. You'll
find that it then winds round fewer times and tears off easily.

Live Well On Less Tips
Hang four loads of laundry a week instead of using your dryer.

TOG 24

UNIT 34, FREEPORT OUTLET CENTRE, JAMAGE ROAD, TALKE PITS, STOKE-ON-TRENT, STAFFORDSHIRE ST7 1QT
☎ (01782) 787558. OPEN 10 - 8 MON - SAT, 11 - 5 SUN.
Tog 24 are the UK's fastest growing brand name in outdoor clothing and leisurewear, with a total of three UK factories and 36 stores nationwide. They utilise the world's finest performance fabrics including Gore-Tex, Polartec and Burlington macs. Catering for all the family for all seasons, with cosy fleeces and waterproofs for the winter, and trekking ranges, shorts and t-shirts for the summer. With all prices at least 30% below the recommended retail price you can afford to enter the Tog comfort zone. *Factory Shopping Village*

TOPPS TILES

UNIT B, SCOTIA ROAD, BURSLEM, STOKE-ON-TRENT, STAFFORDSHIRE
☎ (01782) 819111. OPEN 8 - 6 MON - FRI, 8 ON THUR, 8.30 - 5.30 SAT.
Owners of the Tile Clearing House whose shops are detailed in this book, their main business also offers tiles at competitive prices. They sell wall and floor tiles from names such as Johnsons, Pilkington's and Candy as well as Spanish and Bulgarian tiles. Here, if you buy more than four square metres, you get a discount of 30%. There is a catalogue availabe on freephone 0800 783 6262. *Permanent Discount Outlet*

TOYWORLD FACTORY OUTLETS LTD

UNIT 26, FREEPORT OUTLET MALL, PIT LANE, TALKE, STOKE-ON-TRENT, STAFFORDSHIRE ST7 1QE
☎ (01782) 777744. OPEN 10 - 8 MON - SAT, 11 - 5 SUN.
Toy World sells brand name items including a wide range of toys with well-known brand names. For example, Barbie (Mattel), Disney, Playskool, Lego, Sylvanian Families, Fisher-Price, Tyco, Tomy, Waddington, M&B Games, Safe & Sound, Matchbox, and many others at very low prices. *Factory Shopping Village*

TUTBURY CRYSTAL FACTORY SHOP

BURTON STREET, TUTBURY, BURTON-ON-TRENT, STAFFORDSHIRE DE13 9NG
☎ (01283) 813281. OPEN 9 - 5 MON - SAT, 10 - 4 SUN.
Cut-glass from liqueur glasses and goblets to tumblers, jugs, decanters, rose bowls and vases, seconds of which are sold at discounts of up to 50%. *Factory Shop*

VOGUE CARPETS

11 BRUNSWICK STREET, NEWCASTLE UNDER LYME,
STAFFORDSHIRE ST5 1HF

☎ (01782) 630569. OPEN 9 - 5 MON - SAT.

All types and styles of carpets including Axminsters and Wilton at very competitive prices. Vogue work on small margins and buy direct as part of a large group from the manufacturers, thereby buying in at good prices *Factory Shop*

WATERFORD WEDGWOOD FACTORY SHOP

KING STREET, FENTON, STOKE-ON-TRENT, STAFFORDSHIRE
ST4 3DQ

☎ (01782) 316161. OPEN 9 - 5.30 MON - SAT, 11 - 5 SUN, 9 - 5.30 BANK
HOLIDAYS.

Now incorporating ranges from Wedgwood, Johnson Brothers, Dartington Crystal, Masons Ironstone, Coalport, Waterford and Dartington, and Arthur Price cutlery. Masons' decorative tableware and giftware and Stuart Crystal at factory shop prices with seconds starting at 30% off the first quality prices. There's a nursery range of Wedgwood Peter Rabbit, and a selection of Coalport figurines. The Johnson Brothers department has some imperfect china, while others are ends of lines or discontinued patterns. There is a wide variety on sale. Large car park and facilities for the disabled. *Factory Shop*

WEBB IVORY LTD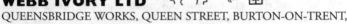

QUEENSBRIDGE WORKS, QUEEN STREET, BURTON-ON-TRENT,
STAFFORDSHIRE DE14 3LP

☎ (01283) 566371. OPEN 9 - 5 MON - FRI, 9 - 2 SAT.

POTTERIES SHOPPING CENTRE, HANLEY, STOKE-ON-TRENT,
STAFFORDSHIRE ST1 1PP

☎ (01782) 202570. OPEN 9 - 5.30 MON - SAT, 8 ON THUR.

6 MARKET STREET, TAMWORTH, STAFFORDSHIRE

☎ (01827) 60266. OPEN 9 - 5 MON - SAT.

Items from the Webb Ivory catalogue at reduced prices including cards, gifts, soft toys, books, pens, lamps, kitchenware, garden furniture and clothes. Discounts range from at least 50%. The Burton shop is the main outlet and has a large car park. *Factory Shop*

WYNSOR SHOES

151-153 MARSH STREET, HANLEY, STOKE-ON-TRENT,
STAFFORDSHIRE ST1 5HR

☎ (01782) 266660.

Stocks top brand-name shoes at less than half price. Special monthly offers always available. There are shoes, trainers, slippers, sandals and boots for all the family, with a selection of bags, cleaners and polishes available. *Permanent Discount Outlet*

Suffolk

WOMENSWEAR ONLY Dindy's, *Bury St Edmunds*. Glad Rags, *Ipswich*. Shuffles, *Newmarket*. The Dress Circle, *Ipswich*. The Dressing Room, *Bury St Edmunds*. Top Drawer, *Woodbridge*.

WOMENSWEAR & MENSWEAR Lambourne Clothing, *Ipswich*. Roys Variety Store, *Sudbury*. The Factory Shop, *Bury St Edmunds*. TK Maxx, *Ipswich*.

CHILDREN Glad Rags, *Ipswich*. Roys Variety Store, *Sudbury*. The Factory Shop, *Bury St Edmunds*. TK Maxx, *Ipswich*.

HOUSEHOLD AND GIFTWARE Spoils, *Ipswich*. The Crockery Barn, *Ipswich*. The Factory Shop, *Bury St Edmunds*. TK Maxx, *Ipswich*. Vanners Mill Shop, *Sudbury*.

DIY/RENOVATION Orwell Pine Co Ltd, *Ipswich*. Terracotta Direct, *Bury St Edmunds*. The Tool Shop, *Needham Market*.

ARCHITECTURAL SALVAGE Orwell Pine Co Ltd, *Ipswich*.

FURNITURE/SOFT FURNISHINGS Knickerbean, *Bury St Edmunds*. The Curtain Agency & Period House Interiors, *Needham Market*. The Curtain Exchange, *Bury St Edmunds*. The Curtain Exchange, *Cambridge*. The Curtain Exchange, *Oakham*. The Factory Shop, *Bury St Edmunds*. The Remnant Shop, *Felixstowe*.

FOOD AND LEISURE First Stop Discount Food Store, *Bury St Edmunds*.

DINDY'S

HAWSTEAD HOUSE, HAWSTEAD, BURY ST EDMUNDS, SUFFOLK IP29 5NL

☎ (01284) 388276. OPEN 10 - 4 TUE & THUR, 10 - 1 SAT. CLOSED DURING STATE SCHOOL HOLIDAYS.

Set in a converted stables, Dindy's sells high quality second hand clothes ranging from Marks & Spencer to Yves St Laurent, Betty Barclay, Escada, Louis Feraud, Tom Bowker, etc. Well respected for evening dresses, cocktail wear and wedding outfits, they also sell a selection of new, top label clothes at less than 50% of the normal retail price. Also a wide range of new gift items such as jewellery, handbags and belts. ***Dress Agency***

FIRST STOP DISCOUNT FOOD STORE

71 ST ANDREW'S STREET NORTH, OFF RISBEYGATE, BURY ST EDMUNDS, SUFFOLK 1P33 1TZ

☎ (01284) 754585. OPEN 9 - 5.30 MON - SAT.

Gourmet food close to its sell-by date. For example, Irish truffles, Lloyd Grossman sauces and boxed Ribena soft drinks, four for 50p. Discounted lines constantly changing. ***Permanent Discount Outlet***

> *Live Well On Less Tips*
> Re-use old winter or sports socks as dishcloths by washing them and slitting
> lengthways. Or cut a thumb hole and use as a mitten liner.

GLAD RAGS

24 HIGH STREET, HADLEIGH, IPSWICH, SUFFOLK
☎ (01473) 827768. OPEN 9.30 - 4 TUE, THUR - SAT.
Established for more than 18 years, this shop sells a range of nearly-new out-
fits including Monsoon, Gerry Weber, Viyella, Jacques Vert, Betty Barclay,
Caroline Charles, Windsmoor and Alexon as well as American, Italian and
German designers. Accessories on sale include belts, scarves, hats and shoes.
Prices vary according to design and wear. Childrenswear - both English and
Continental for 0 to 14-year-olds - is sold very quickly. *Dress Agency*

KNICKERBEAN

4 OUT NORTHGATE, BURY ST EDMUNDS, SUFFOLK IP33 1JQ
☎ (01284) 704055. OPEN 9 - 5.30 MON - SAT.
Knickerbean is one of the few companies that continue to offer genuine top-
name designer fabric bargains...the kind of curtain and upholstery fabrics that
are found at Decorex and the Chelsea Harbour Design Centre. Their rapidly-
changing stock often includes excess inventory and discontinued lines from
these kinds of designers, as well as occasional slight seconds, with many sold
at between 20%-50% off the regular price. They also carry a large range of
top-quality fabrics in the latest styles which they buy directly from mills and
manufacturers in the UK, Europe and North America, offering similar top
quality, but at vastly reduced prices. Their attractively laid-out shops feature a
vast range of different selections of curtain and upholstery fabrics. These
include classic country house glazed chintzes, fresh stripes and checks, fashionable toiles de jouy, bright cotton prints and PVC-coated fabrics, a wide
range of damasks and natural fabrics, sumptuous chenilles, rich kilim patterns,
self-patterned dobby weaves and a fabulous selection of upholstery brocades
and tapestries. Prices start from £4.95 for plain cottons and prints to £19.95
and occasionally more for chenilles and tapestries. Customers are encouraged
to pop in regularly to check out the latest arrivals in their stock. The benefit
here is that they are able to see entire rolls rather than just a small sample book
of swatches. Their professionally trained staff are ready to advise on quality
and quantity for any type of furnishing project. They extend their service to
measure and quote, as they offer a complete making up service for all soft furnishings, including loose covers and upholstery. They are even prepared to
bring along a few rolls to try out against a customer's own colour scheme.
Twice-yearly sales are held in January and June to enable customers to snap up
even bigger bargains. *Permanent Discount Outlet*

LAMBOURNE CLOTHING

15 CHRISTCHURCH STREET, IPSWICH, SUFFOLK IP4 2DP

☎ (01473) 250404. OPEN 10 - 3 TUE - FRI.

Manufactures and sells own brand, Windsmoor and Country Casuals skirts, trousers, and jackets. The clothes, for men and women, are overmakes and seconds and are usually discounted by about 50%. *Factory Shop*

ORWELL PINE CO LTD

HALIFAX MILL, 427 WHERSTEAD ROAD, IPSWICH, SUFFOLK IP2 8LH

☎ (01473) 680091. OPEN 8.30 - 5.30 MON - FRI, 8 - 4 SAT.

Buys old pine floorboards and joists to make new old pine furniture, including kitchens. It usually has 1,000 doors in stock in old pine. As its name suggests it also strips doors for £14 plus VAT a door, as well as making bedroom furniture, and selling fireplaces and restored house clearance furniture. 100-year-old pine doors cost from £35-£65. *Architectural Salvage*

ROYS VARIETY STORE

GREAT EASTERN ROAD, SUDBURY, SUFFOLK CO10 6TJ

☎ (01787) 882800. OPEN 9 - 5.30 MON, TUE, 9 - 8 WED, THUR, FRI, 9 - 6 SAT, 10.30 - 4.30 SUN.

Reputed to be the largest village shop in the world, it sells branded household goods at what it calls valued prices . The Save 'N Wear Department deals with the cheaper end of the clothing market for men, women and children. Other departments include DIY, gardening, electrical, housewares and gifts. There is also a pharmacy department that deals with photography, records and toiletries, all at competitive prices, and a large food hall. *Permanent Discount Outlet*

SHUFFLES

16 OXFORD STREET, EXNING, NEWMARKET, SUFFOLK CB8 7EW

☎ (01638) 578297. OPEN 10 - 4.30 TUE - SAT.

Friendly little shop in village location selling day dresses, suits, separates and evening gowns and a small selection of accessories. Labels include Gerry Weber, Escada, Betty Barclay, Mondi, Jaeger, Paul Costelloe and Windsmoor. *Dress Agency*

Live Well On Less Tips

Cut off the metal clip from mesh onion bags and knot. Use to store soap bits. The mesh and soap combine to form an effective cleaning agent when washing hands.

SPOILS

ST MATTHEW'S STREET, IPSWICH, SUFFOLK IP1 3EU
☎ (01473) 252020. OPEN 9 - 5.30 MON -SAT.
General domestic glassware, non-stick bakeware, kitchen gadgets, ceramic oven-to-tableware, textiles, cutting boards, aluminium non-stick cookware, bakeware, plastic kitchenware, plastic storage, woodware, coffee pots/makers, furniture, mirrors and picture frames. Rather than being discounted, all the merchandise is very competitively priced - in fact, the company carry out competitors' checks frequently in order to monitor pricing. With 38 branches, the company is able to buy in bulk and thus negotiate very good prices. *Permanent Discount Outlet*

TERRACOTTA DIRECT

PINFORD END FARM, PINFORD END, HAWSTEAD, BURY ST EDMUNDS, SUFFOLK IP29 5NU
☎ (01284) 386004. BY APPOINTMENT ONLY.
Handmade Spanish floor tiles in different shades at prices which are discounted by one third. Delivery within three days. Colour brochure available. *Permanent Discount Outlet*

THE CROCKERY BARN

ASHLEIGH FARM, ASHBOCKING, IPSWICH, SUFFOLK IP6 9JS
☎ (01473) 890123. OPEN 10 - 5 SEVEN DAYS A WEEK.
Mountains of white tableware, huge stocks of Portmerion, Spode, Emma Bridgewater and imported ceramics. New stock arrives weekly so there is always something new to see. *Permanent Discount Outlet*

THE CURTAIN AGENCY
AND PERIOD HOUSE INTERIORS

73 HIGH STREET, NEEDHAM MARKET, IPSWICH, SUFFOLK IP6 8AN
☎ (01449) 722885. OPEN 10 - 5 MON - FRI, 10 - 1 SAT.
An emporium of quality secondhand and new made-to-measure or ready-to-hang curtains. Classic fabrics by the metre include brocades, Toile de Jouy, Gainsborough silks, country house chintzes, Crewel work, Cath Kidston, Ramm Son & Crocker and Bernard Thorp hand-printed designs (half price seconds as well as affordable stock lines). A wide range of fabulous old and new continental accessories, including tie backs and trimmings. Tapestries, handmade finials, reeded, plain and antique gilt curtain poles. Elegant secondhand period lighting: crystal brass and ceramic chandeliers and pretty glass shades; new traditional fittings - switches, ceiling roses and flex complete the look. Lovely French linen, lace voiles and 19th Century tapestry curtains and textiles. Decorative furniture and original French beds - all at sensible prices. *Secondhand Shop*

> *Live Well On Less Tips*
> For a cheap Valentine's day card, get a piece of blank paper and have every-
> one put red lipstick on. Then ask them all to kiss the paper and sign it.

THE CURTAIN EXCHANGE

56 ST JOHN'S STREET, BURY ST EDMUNDS, SUFFOLK IP33 1SN
☎ (01284) 760059. OPEN 9.30 - 5 MON - SAT.
16 NORFOLK STREET, CAMBRIDGE CB1 2LF.
☎ (01223) 312500. OPEN 10 - 5 MON - SAT.
4 CROWN WALK, HIGH STREET, OAKHAM, RUTLAND.
☎ (01572) 770990. OPEN 10 - 4 MON - SAT.
The Curtain Exchange is a franchised group of shops selling beautiful top
quality secondhand curtains, blinds, pelmets, etc at between one-third and
one half of the brand new price. Their stock comes from a variety of sources:
people who are moving house and dislike the drapes in their new home; people who are moving house and want to sell their old curtains to help with the
bills; show houses, where the builder wants to recoup some of his outgoings;
interior designers' mistakes. Stock changes constantly and ranges from rich
brocades, damasks and velvets to chintzes, linens and cottons. Designer names
include Colefax & Fowler, Designers Guild, Laura Ashley, Warner, Sanderson,
Osborne & Little, Fortuny and Bennison. A team of fitters and alteration
experts are available if required. They offer a 24-hour availability. The Curtain
Exchange also supply bespoke ranges with samples of curtains hanging. These
fabrics are chosen from suppliers all over the world and are an excellent buy.
Secondhand Shop

THE DRESS CIRCLE

64 UPPER ORWELL STREET, IPSWICH, SUFFOLK IT4 1HR
☎ (01473) 258513. OPEN 10 - 5 MON - SAT.
Sells nearly-new labels from Next and Principles to Nicole Farhi and Jasper
Conran in sizes 8-20. A Caroline Charles evening dress, size 12, £75; a Jaeger
spring suit, size 18, £40; Ally Cappellino dress, size 10, £30. Evening wear is
stocked all year round. *Dress Agency*

THE DRESSING ROOM

22 ST JOHN'S STREET, BURY ST EDMUNDS, SUFFOLK 1P33 1SJ
☎ (01284) 723700. OPEN 11 - 5 MON, THUR, 10 - 5 TUE, WED, FRI, SAT.
Excellent selection of evening wear with daywear labels such as Ouiset,
Mondi, Jaeger, Windsmoor, Betty Barclay, Ara, Planet and designer names
such as Gucci, YSL, Louis Feraud. Some as new shoes, lots of hats and a few
handbags. *Dress Agency*

THE FACTORY SHOP

BARTON BUSINESS CENTRE, BARTON ROAD, BURY ST EDMUNDS, SUFFOLK IP32 7BQ

☎ (01284) 701578. OPEN 9.30 - 5 MON - FRI, 9.30 - 5.30 SAT, 10 - 4 SUN.

Wide range on sale includes men's, ladies and children's clothing and footwear; household textiles; toiletries; hardware; luggage; lighting and bedding, most of which are chainstore and high street brands at discounts of approximately 30%-50%. There are weekly deliveries and brands include many major stars such as Adidas, Nike, Wrangler and Dartington, to name just a few. Now has kitchen and furniture displays with a line of Cape Country furniture on sale. Ranges are continually changing and few factory shops offer such a variety under one roof. Most of the shops have their own car parks or there are near-by car parking facilities. *Factory Shop*

THE REMNANT SHOP

3-5 HAMILTON ROAD, FELIXSTOWE, SUFFOLK IP11 7AX

☎ (01394) 283186. OPEN 9 -5.30 MON - SAT.

Although not strictly a discount fabric shop, they sell cut-price ends of rolls and remnants in curtain materials, dressmaking fabrics (satins, silks, dupions, polyesters) and patterns. They always have a good range of curtain fabrics and hold thousands of rolls of fabric in stock. But lines change constantly so you might not always find something to suit. *Permanent Discount Outlet*

THE TOOL SHOP

78 HIGH STREET, NEEDHAM MARKET, SUFFOLK IP6 8AW

☎ (01449) 722992. FAX ☎ (01449) 722683. OPEN 10 - 5 MON - SAT. MAIL ORDER.

Specialises in antique and usable tools with a vast selection always in stock. They always have more than 1,500 carving tools (planes, chisels, gauges) at the shop as well as many tools associated with other trades. They also send tools by mail all over the world and will always try and find a specific tool. Four times a year, they hold tool auctions at the Limes Hotel, opposite the shop. Three of these auctions contain tools of mixed quality, ranging from tools in as found condition to items of collectable quality. There is also a fishing tackle section and a bygones section containing items of interest, kitchenalia, old golf clubs etc. Once a year, there is also an International Tool Sale. This comprises more than 1,500 lots of superior quality tools for the user and collector. In order to qualify for this sale, the tools have to be in superb condition and are presented in a large format colour catalogue. Also now sells a fine range of new Japanese tools and French Auriou handmade chisels. *Secondhand Shop*

Live Well On Less Tips

Don't leave gift buying until the last minute when you're tempted to pay any-thing just to turn up with something. Keep a list of everyone on your birth-day/Christmas/wedding anniversary list and take it with you whenever you go shopping. Look over it quickly before you shop in case you find something that suits someone on your list. The right gift at the right price may not be around the week before a birthday, but it might be there six months before. Remember to keep a note of what you've bought and when it has been given.

TK MAXX

BUTTERMARKET SHOPPING CENTRE, IPSWICH, SUFFOLK

☎ (01473) 226800. OPEN 9 - 5.30 MON - FRI, 9 - 6 SAT, CLOSED SUN.

Based on an American concept, TK Maxx is situated in easily accessible, often centrally located stores and offers famous label goods with up to 60% savings off recommended retail prices. TK Maxx has fashion for the whole family - women's, men's and childrenswear - accessories, shoes, gifts, kitchenware and home goods. Everything in the store is branded with a choice of well-known high street names to designer labels, and while a small percentage might be clearly marked past season, the great majority of items in store are current sea-son, current stock and still with phenomenal savings. There is a huge choice with 50,000 pieces in store and up to 10,000 new items arriving a week. The stores are simple and unfussy with wide aisles, shopping trolleys and baskets, and a spacious, functional feel to them but there are individual changing rooms, ramps for buggies and wheelchairs and plenty of staff on the shop floor. Every branch accepts all major credit and debit cards and has a liberal refund and return policy. *Permanent Discount Outlet*

TOP DRAWER

21A THORO'FARE, WOODBRIDGE, SUFFOLK

☎ (01394) 388775. OPEN 9.30 - 5 MON - SAT.

Dress agency selling a mixture of labels from high street names to Armani, Escada, Paul Costelloe and Jaeger. All the shoes are new, although there are nearly-new hats and accessories. *Dress Agency*

VANNERS MILL SHOP

GREGORY STREET, SUDBURY, SUFFOLK CO10 6BB

☎ (01787) 313933. OPEN 9 - 5 MON - FRI, 9 - 12 SAT.

Silk ties, silk fabric, purses, wallets, handbags, photo frames, silk cosmetic bags, dressing gowns and waistcoats, and seconds in scarves are all on sale here at incredibly low prices, also printed woven silks by the metre. Twice-yearly clearance sales make for even better bargains. Phone for details. *Factory Shop*

Surrey

WOMENSWEAR ONLY ⏙ Ancora Dress Agency, *Weybridge*.
Angela Marber's Private Buy, *Kingston Hill*. Apres Vous, *Chipstead*.
Browsers of Richmond, *Richmond*. Bumpsadaisy Maternity Style, *Grayshott*.
Clothes Line, Albury, *Nr Guildford*. Designer Nearly New, *South Croydon*. Encore, *Englefield Green*.
Flair of Ashstead, *Lower Ashstead*. Flair of Cobham, *Cobham*. Linda Amarnani, *Walton-on-Thames*.
Mums2Be, *Kew*. Phoenix, *Cobham*. Riche, *Ewell*. Sequel, *West Ewell*. The Dress Agency, *Ashstead*.
The Dress Circle, *Farnham*.

MENSWEAR ONLY ⏛ Dorking Exchange, *Dorking*. Kent & Curwen, *Godalming*.
Suit City, *Redhill*.

WOMENSWEAR & MENSWEAR ⏙ ⏛ Alan Paine Knitwear Ltd, *Godalming*.
Chanterelle, *Oxted*. Choice Discounts Ltd, *Redhill*. City Menswear, *Croydon*.
Designer Fashion Sale, *Epsom Downs*. Matalan, *Sutton*. Special Occasions, *West Byfleet*.
The Factory Shop Ltd, *Horsley*. TK Maxx, *Sutton*. TK Maxx, *Croydon*. TK Maxx, *Woking*.
Tog 24, *Croydon*.

CHILDREN 🧸 Ancora Bambini, *Weybridge*. Choice Discount Stores Ltd, *Redhill*.
Kid-Equip, *Coulsen*. Matalan, *Sutton*. Nippers, *Chessington*. The Factory Shop Ltd, *Horsley*.
Tinkers, *Chipstead*. TK Maxx, *Sutton*. TK Maxx, *Croydon*. TK Maxx, *Woking*. Tog 24, *Croydon*.

HOUSEHOLD AND GIFTWARE 🎁 Genevieve The Gallery, *Englefield Green*.
Habitat Outlet, *Croydon*. Matalan, *Sutton*. Spoils, *Croydon*. Spoils, *Kingston-Upon-Thames*.
Spoils, *Sutton*. The Factory Shop Ltd, *Horsley*. TK Maxx, *Sutton*.

ELECTRICAL EQUIPMENT 📻 Raff Radio, *Hinchley Wood*.
RDO Kitchen Appliances, *Reigate*.

DIY/RENOVATION 🔨 Alfred G Cawley, *Sutton Green*. Antique Buildings Ltd, *Dunsford*.
Drummonds Architectural Antiques Ltd, *Hindhead*. Pew Corner Ltd, *Guildford*.
Siesta Cork Tiles, *Croydon*. Silverland Stone, *Chertsey*. The Tap Factory Workshop, *Near Chertsey*.

ARCHITECTURAL SALVAGE 🔨 Alfred G Cawley, *Sutton Green*.
Antique Buildings Ltd, *Dunsford*. Drummonds Architectural Antiques Ltd, *Hindhead*.
Pew Corner Ltd, *Guildford*. Silverland Stone, *Chertsey*. The Tap Factory Workshop, *Near Chertsey*.

FURNITURE/SOFT FURNISHINGS 🛋 Angela Marber's Private Buy, *Kingston Hill*.
CH Furniture Ltd, *Guildford*. Corcoran & May's Fabric Warehouse, *New Malden*.
Curtain Call, *Richmond*. Fabric Warehouse, *Wallington*. Fabric World, *Sutton*.
Habitat Outlet, *Croydon*. London Curtain Agency, *Kew*. The Curtain Agency, *Camberley*.
The Curtain Agency, *Farnham*. The Factory Shop Ltd, *Horsley*.

FOOD AND LEISURE 📖 Beanos, *Croydon*. Richmond Book Shop, *Richmond*.

SPORTSWEAR AND EQUIPMENT 🏌 Golf Factory Shop, *Crawley*. Canon Golf, *Haslemere*.

ALAN PAINE KNITWEAR LTD

SCATS COUNTRY STORE, BRIGHTON ROAD, GODALMING, SURREY
GU7 1NS

☎ (01483) 419962. OPEN 9 - 5 MON - FRI, 9.30 - 4 SAT.

Knitwear, made in Derbyshire and sold here at factory shop prices. Although the majority of the jumpers and cardigans are made for men and start at size 38 inch chest, they are just as likely to be bought by women. They do also have a small selection of styles specially for women. Choose from cotton, cashmere, lambswool, camel hair, merino and merino and silk mix. The factory makes most of its stock for export, and sells to some of the top shops in London. This outlet also sells men's T-shirts. *Factory Shop*

ALFRED G. CAWLEY

HAVERING FARM, GUILDFORD ROAD, SUTTON GREEN, SURREY
GU4 7QA

☎ (01483) 232398. OPEN 8 - 5 MON - FRI, 8 - 1 SAT.

Demolition experts, they stock bathroom fittings, floorboards, roof tiles, bricks, windows, doors and beams. *Architectural Salvage*

ANCORA BAMBINI

27 CHURCH STREET, WEYBRIDGE, SURREY KT13 8DG

☎ (01932) 857665. OPEN 9.30 - 5 MON - SAT.

Up the road from the women's dress agency, Ancora, Ancora Bambini sells middle of the road to designer labels for children aged from birth to 10 years, including Next, Gap, Oilily and Jacardi. Also small selection of maternity wear. *Dress Agency*

ANCORA DRESS AGENCY

74 CHURCH STREET, WEYBRIDGE, SURREY KT13 8DL

☎ (01932) 855267. OPEN 9.30 - 5.30 MON, TUE, THUR, FRI, 9.30 - 5 WED, SAT.

Middle to upper range designer outfits from Alexon, Monsoon and Wallis to Betty Barclay, Mondi, Yarell and Frank Usher. *Dress Agency*

Live Well On Less Tips

Potato peels and chicken skin can be mixed, baked in the oven (when baking something else). It makes a great treat for dogs who need extra fat during the winter months.

ANGELA MARBER'S PRIVATE BUY

FIVEMARCH, COOMBE PARK, KINGSTON HILL, SURREY KT2 7JA

☎ 0181-549 8453.

Private Buy arranges for its club members to purchase current and next season's top label European and American samples and stock in the Agents' intimate and friendly showrooms, most of which are in London, ahead of the season at half the cost. Also available at trade prices are household linens, fabrics, wall-papers - even holidays. Usually a recommendation-only club; due to this exclusivity, some personal references may be required. Membership costs £60 a year and includes a regular newsletter informing you of future showroom visits, restaurant reviews and member-to-member recommendations. *Designer Sale*

ANTIQUE BUILDINGS LIMITED

ALFOLD ROAD, DUNSFOLD, SURREY GU8 4NP

☎ (01483) 200477. OPEN 8.15 - 4.30 MON - FRI, OR BY APPOINTMENT, CLOSED WED.

Stock an immense number of ancient oak beams, ceiling joists, bressumes, handmade clay tiles, bricks and walling stone, reclaimed handmade bricks and peg tiles. Specialises in ancient timber framed buildings, with more than thir-ty-five barns, cartsheds, hovels, granary and house frames available for re-erec-tion, each of which has been measured, drawn and photographed before being dismantled. *Architectural Salvage*

APRES VOUS

2 STATION APPROACH, CHIPSTEAD, SURREY CR3 3TD

☎ (01737) 556791. OPEN 10 - 4.30 TUE, THUR, FRI, 10 - 1 SAT.

Beautifully presented nearly-new shop with a wide selection of good quality day and evening wear in all sizes. Also hats, handbags, shoes, belts and some jewellery. Suits all budgets from high street brands to Bianco, Betty Barclay, MaxMara, Jaeger and Jacques Vert. Parking in front, and close to Chipstead station. *Dress Agency*

BEANOS

MIDDLE STREET, CROYDON, SURREY CR0 1RE,

☎ 0181-680 1202. OPEN 10 - 6 MON - FRI, 9 - 6 SAT.

The largest secondhand record store in Europe with more than two and a quarter million items on display in this three-storey shop. The three floors of nostalgia cover all formats and styles of music, a Sixties-style cafe and mini-cine on the top floor and a small stage on the middle floor with live bands per-forming every Saturday. They also run a mail order service which endeavours to search out and provide all musical requirements through the Internet (beanos@easynet,co.uk.) A GDD reader says they have a wide choice of CDs at an average price of £7. *Secondhand Shop*

Live Well On Less Tips
Money £acts is a guide to savings, investment and mortgage rates, guaranteed income bonds, national savings and annuities, which operates an update by fax. Whether you want to find out what the interest rates are on mortgates or where to open your Tessa account to get the best rates, you simply dail the relevant fax number and wait for the information to appear at your end. Commercial and residential mortgage information is updated daily, as is savings information. Cost is about 75p per minute at daytime rates; tel 01603 476476.

BROWSERS OF RICHMOND

36 FRIARS STILE ROAD, RICHMOND, SURREY TW10 6QN,
☎ 0181-332 0875. OPEN 10 - 5.30 MON - SAT.
The largest dress agency in Surrey, Browsers carries a wide range of top designer labels at realistic and irresistible prices. The owners keep up to date with fashion trends and are experienced at both pricing and merchandising their stock at a realistic level. They have a large volume of stock and a fast turnover and are therefore constantly looking for new stock. *Dress Agency*

BUMPSADAISY MATERNITY STYLE

CROSSWAYS ROAD, GRAYSHOTT, SURREY GU26 6HG
☎ (01428) 608345. OPEN 9.30 - 5.30 MON - SAT.
Franchised shops and home-based branches with large range of specialist maternity wear, from wedding outfits to ball gowns, to hire and to buy. Hire costs range from £30 to £100 for special occasion wear. To buy are lots of casual and business wear in sizes 8 - 18. For example, skirts £20-£70; dresses £40-£100. Phone ☎ 0181-789 0329 for details of your local stockist. *Hire Shop*

C H FURNITURE LTD

19-21 NORTH STREET, GUILDFORD, SURREY GU1 4TB
☎ (01483) 573405. OPEN 9 - 5.30 MON - SAT.
Privately owned by the same owner since 1932, this shop sells better end furniture of the same sort of quality as seen in Furniture Village. They stock cabinets, beds, upholstery, dining tables (both modern and traditional in glass, wicker, iron and painted), sofas, wardrobes, etc at very competitive prices. The cabinets are all imported, the upholstery English. Most of the furniture comes from Italy, Denmark and France with some from Germany, India, Belgium and Holland. There is a small section of cane conservatory furniture, while the metal tables and chairs and the Mexican mosaic range can be used outdoors as long as they're not left out in winter. *Permanent Discount Outlet*

Live Well On Less Tips
An old sock makes a good toy for a cat. Sew over any holes and stuff with leftover quilt batting. Sew over the top.

CHANTERELLE
95-99 STATION ROAD EAST, OXTED, SURREY RH8 OAX
☎ (01883) 714389. OPEN 9.30 - 5.30 MON - SAT, 11 - 5 SUN AND BANK HOLIDAYS.
At Chanterelle, you will find a huge range of famous fashion labels - all under one roof - and all with massive discounts. One of the largest ladies and men's fashion discounters in the South East, Chanterelle occupies a spacious and beautifully fitted emporium packed with bargains. Most of the stock consists of current season ranges, including well-known high street brands at excellent discounts - a bargain hunter's paradise. All the ranges are fully co-ordinated and merchandised and cover everything from casual wear, daytime, executive suits, special occasion and evening wear. New collections arrive daily. Sizes range from 10-20. Stock is sourced from all over Europe and the USA. The shop is only five minutes from junction 6 of the M25 and there is free car parking nearby. *Permanent Discount Outlet*

CHOICE DISCOUNT STORES LIMITED
1 WARWICK QUADRANT, LONDON ROAD, REDHILL, SURREY
☎ (01737) 772777. OPEN 9 - 6 MON - WED, SAT, 9 - 7 THUR, FRI.
Surplus stock including women's, men's and children's fashions from Next plc, Next Directory and other high street fashion houses, Next Interiors and footwear. You can save up to 50% off normal retail prices for first quality; up to two thirds for seconds. There are no changing rooms but the shop offers refunds if goods are returned in perfect condition within 28 days. There are special sales each January and September. Easy access for wheelchairs and pushchairs. *Permanent Discount Outlet*

CITY MENSWEAR
3-5 HIGH STREET, CROYDON, SURREY CRO 1QA,
☎ 0181-686 5047. OPEN 9 - 6 MON - SAT, 11 - 5 SUN, 8 ON THUR.
City Menswear is Moss Bros's permanent sale shop and this two-storey shop is rumoured to be the biggest quality menswear discount store in the South East . It now also has some ladieswear and perfumes for both sexes. With 5,000 square feet of space on two levels, it sells 150 suits every week in a wide range of sizes at discounts of up to 50%, as well as the full range of Moss Bros merchandise: Pierre Cardin shirts; YSL shirts; Dior shirts at half price. As well as suits, there are also jackets and blazers. *Permanent Discount Outlet*

CLOTHES LINE

KILNHANGER, FARLEY HEATH, ALBURY, NEAR GUILDFORD, SURREY
GU5 9EW

☎ (01483) 898855. BY APPOINTMENT ONLY.

Beautifully cut jackets, infinitely wearable skirts and trousers, modern tailoring from business suits to special occasion wear. Designers include Jasper Conran, Edina Ronay, Ghost, Betty Jackson and Nicole Farhi. Most are nearly new, although some are one-off samples from designer ranges. There is also an evening wear hire service from designers such as Belville Sassoon, David Fielden and Roland Klein at prices ranging from £25-£45. *Permanent Discount Outlet*

CORCORAN & MAY'S FABRIC WAREHOUSE

31-35 BLAGDON ROAD, NEW MALDEN, SURREY KT3 4AH

☎ 0181-949 0234. OPEN 9.30 - 5.30 MON - SAT, 11 - 4 SUN, BANK HOLS.

Huge fabric superstore opened this year, drawing on Corcoran & May's long years of expertise in the industry where they are known for getting the best of seconds and overstocks from a whole host of designers such as Jane Churchill, Anna French, Monkwell and the Malabar Cotton Company. They also have a vast range of repeatable designs from the brightest newcomers, as well as traditional damasks, plains and weaves. Prices start at £1.99 per metre, and there's everything in-store for the home curtain maker, plus an expert curtain making service, ready-made curtains and blinds, and plenty of friendly advice. *Permanent Discount Outlet*

CURTAIN CALL

52 FRIARS STILE ROAD, RICHMOND, SURREY TW10 6NQ

☎ 0181-332 6250. OPEN 9.30 - 5.30 MON - FRI, 10 - 6 SAT, CLOSED WED.

Curtain Call offers nearly-new curtains for at least half of their original price. The current stock of more than 300 pairs includes Colefax & Fowler, Osborne & Little and Designers Guild fabrics. They range in price from £50 to £1,250 for sets which include valances and swags and tails, etc. An alteration service is also available on the premises, as well as a making-up service using customers' own fabric. They also have a large selection of made-to-measure fabrics which can be made up in two to three weeks. This range comprises natural textured cottons through to more elaborate toiles, damasks, velvets and silks. The samples are made as curtains for customers to take home and try before ordering. New this year - a large range of textured silks in checks and stripes as well as plains in 60 colours. *Secondhand Shop*

DESIGNER FASHION SALE
79 GROSVENOR ROAD, LANGLEY VALE, EPSOM DOWNS, SURREY
KT18 6JF
☎ (01372) 278194.
British, Continental and American designer label clothes at wholesale prices or less - most items less than half the price you would pay in the shops. Established for six years, the Designer Fashion Sale allows you to buy samples, cancelled orders and current season stock at regular one, two or three-day events throughout the year. There are usually 15 to 20 designers at each womenswear sale including names such as Bruce Oldfield, Edina Ronay, Mondi, Escada, Ozbek, Joseph Ribkoff, Sara Sturgeon and Workers for Freedom. The Menswear Sales have collections from Versace, Armani, Valentino and Boss. There are also Shoe Sales and Bag and Accessory Sales where you will find top quality Italian and Spanish designer merchandise at wholesale prices. Attendance is by invitation only for which there is a £5 registration fee. For £15, you can join the Designer Fashion Sale Club which entitles you to visit the Sales on the preview day to buy the collections a day early and also to take advantage of some current season designer collections at prices which are significantly less than recommended retail. *Designer Sale*

DESIGNER NEARLY NEW
109 SANDERSTEAD ROAD, SOUTH CROYDON, SURREY CR2 OPJ,
☎ 0181-680 5734. OPEN 10 - 5.30 MON - SAT.
121 STATION ROAD EAST, OXTED, SURREY RH8 OQE
☎ (01883) 717604. OPEN 10 - 5.30 MON - SUN.
Upmarket ladies designer wear such as Escada and Laurel, as well as YSL, Chanel, Donna Karan and Nicole Farhi. The Croydon branch also offers ballgown and hat hire. *Dress Agency*

DORKING EXCHANGE
78 SOUTH STREET, DORKING, SURREY RH4 2HD
☎ (01306) 876828. OPEN 9.30 - 5.30 TUE - SAT, CLOSED MON.
New and nearly-new top label menswear and shoes from British and Italian designers. Nearly-new designers include Armani, Hugo Boss, Valentino, Jaeger, Daks and Newman. There are also some showroom samples such as Valentino three-piece suit, £60. Secondhand dinner suits cost from £30-£70. Hire of top quality formal wear. *Dress Agency and Hire Shop*

Live Well On Less Tips
Old metal bedheds and foot boards can be re-used to make gates, especially around vegetable gardens.

Live Well On Less Tips
Store leftovers in re-usable glass or plastic container. If they are sealed tightly, food will stay fresh longer and you'll cut down on your use of expensive bags. Better still, use a bowl covered with a saucer. Or an old margarine tub.

DRUMMONDS ARCHITECTURAL ANTIQUES LTD

KIRKPATRICK BUILDINGS, 25 LONDON ROAD, HINDHEAD, NEAR A3, SURREY GU26 6AB

☎ (01428) 605444. OPEN 9 - 6 MON - FRI, 10 - 5 SAT.

Now in new, larger premises, Drummonds cover the complete spectrum of architectural antiques from chimney pots to the gamekeeper's gate. Their speciality is in period bathrooms, including proper vitreous enamelling of antique baths. Also manufacture their own range of cast iron baths and accessories. *Architectural Salvage*

ENCORE

22-23 VICTORIA STREET, ENGLEFIELD GREEN, SURREY TW20 OQY

☎ (01784) 439475. OPEN 10 - 5.30 TUE, FRI, SAT 10 - 4 WED, 10 - 7 THUR.

The service is friendly and the shop is bright, giving you the impression of being in a high class dress shop. The prices are reasonable as the owner is prepared to negotiate on commission rates for more expensive items. There is a large range of end of lines and designer samples including exclusive evening and special occasion wear from Milan, as well as nearly-new. Labels include Moschino, Mondi, Betty Barclay, Armani and many more. Encore can also offer colour analysis, image consultancy and a range of beauty treatments and alternative therapies. They also offer an evening wear hire service. *Dress Agency and Hire Shop*

FABRIC WAREHOUSE

UNIT F2, FELNEX TRADING ESTATE, 190 LONDON ROAD, OFF HACKBRIDGE ROAD, WALLINGTON, NEAR SUTTON, SURREY SM6 7ED,

☎ 0181-647 3313. OPEN 9 - 5 MON - SAT, 10 - 4 SUN.

Large warehouse chain, now with 39 other outlets countrywide, selling dress and furnishing fabric, ready-made curtains and net curtains. Most of the merchandise is made up of clearance material from mills and manufacturers. Free car parking. Phone the telephone number above for details of other outlets. *Permanent Discount Outlet*

FABRIC WORLD

287-289 HIGH STREET, SUTTON, SURREY SM1 1LL
☎ 0181-643 5127.
OPEN 9 - 5.30 MON - SAT.
6-10 BRIGHTON ROAD, SOUTH CROYDON, SURREY CR2 6AA
☎ 0181-688 6282. OPEN 9 - 5.30 MON - SAT.
A family business which claims to be the largest factory warehouse of design-er curtain and upholstery fabrics in England. It stocks at least 2,000 rolls of material, most selling at between £3.30 and £14.50 a metre for fabric which would normally cost between £22 and £55 a metre. Designer names on sale include Warners and Sandersons, and stock is all perfect and includes current lines. The company imports from all over the world: tapestries, damasks, nat-ural fabrics, checks, stripes, linens, cottons and satins. There is a making-up service available. *Permanent Discount Outlet*

FLAIR OF ASHTEAD

11 CRADDOCKS PARADE, CRADDOCKS AVENUE, LOWER ASHTEAD,
SURREY KT21 1QL
☎ (01372) 277207 OPEN 9.30 - 5 MON - SAT.
Nearly new ladies wear with a wide variety of good labels to choose from. Strong on seasonal event clothing as well as wedding outfits. Friendly and well informed, will alter garments and assist in wardrobe selection, even keeping an eye out for suitable outfits for regular customers. Some costume jewellery, as well as shoes, handbags and belts. Hat hire service offering a variety of more than 150 hats at £7 to £25 per hiring. Ex-hire hats also sold at bargain prices. *Dress Agency and Hire Shop*

FLAIR OF COBHAM

15 CHURCH STREET, COBHAM, SURREY
☎ (01932) 865825 OPEN 9.30 - 5 MON - SAT
Nearly new ladies wear with a wide variety of good labels to choose from ie; Caroline Charles, Jaeger, etc. Strong on seasonal event clothing as well as wed-ding outfits. Friendly and well informed, will alter garments and assist in wardrobe selection, even keeping an eye out for suitable outfits for regular cus-tomers. Many accessories, including handbags, shoes, hats, jewellery and scarves. *Dress Agency*

GENEVIEVE THE GALLERY

13 VICTORIA STREET, ENGLEFIELD GREEN, SURREY TW20 OQY
☎ (01784) 430516. OPEN 10 - 5 TUE - SAT.
A ceramicist of handmade and handpainted items with bright floral, fruit and foliage designs, Genevieve Neilson is now manufacturing and retailing from the same outlet. At the back is the workshop; at the front, the shop where she

sells her own products at factory direct prices. Among other items on sale are mirrors, candles, candlesticks, clocks, soft toys, cards and gift wrap and a slipware range was recently introduced. Commissions taken for specific orders. *Factory Shop*

GOLF FACTORY SHOP

BRIGHTON ROAD, PEASE POTAGE, CRAWLEY, SURREY RH11 9AD
☎ (01444) 400219. OPEN 10 - 6 MON - FRI, 10 - 5 SAT, 10 - 2 SUN.
6 JUNCTION PLACE, SHOTTERS MILL, HASLEMERE, SURREY GU27 2AG
☎ (01428) 641108. OPEN 10 - 6 MON - FRI, 10 - 5 SAT, 10 - 4 SUN.
Golf clubs and full range of accessories such as trolleys and clothing. Made to measure golf clubs start at £56 per set up to £218. Left-handed sets available. Trolleys from £19.99 to £50. Canon Golf at Shotters Hill, also offers part exchange for old clubs. *Permanent Discount Outlet*

HABITAT OUTLET

1 DRURY CRESCENT, PURLEY WAY, CROYDON, SURREY CR9 4PE
☎ 0181-649 9312. OPEN 9.30 - 6 MON - SAT, 8 ON THUR, FRI, 11 - 5 SUN.
Ends of ranges and slightly damaged stock from the famous Habitat stores including sofas, tables, kitchenware, plates, glasses, upholstery and cookware, discounted by 20%-40%. Discontinued perfects also available at similarly reduced prices. *Permanent Discount Outlet*

KENT & CURWEN

8A FARNCOMBE STREET, FARNCOMBE, GODALMING, SURREY
GU7 3AY
☎ (01483) 426917. OPEN 10 - 5 FRI, SAT ONLY.
Sells high quality menswear - shirts, ties, jackets, suits, blazers and sportswear including golfwear. Samples and ends of ranges are priced at one third to one half of the london shop prices. Suits from £150, that normally retail for £400; cotton shirts from £29, usually £60; pure silk ties from £5 and pique shirts from £15 that normally retail at £40. *Factory Shop*

KID-EQUIP

187 CHIPSTEAD VALLEY ROAD, COULSDEN, SURREY CR5 3BR
☎ (01737) 552545. OPEN 9.30 - 4 MON - FRI, 10 - 2 SAT, 9.30 - 1 WED.
Sell and hire out baby and nursery equipment for periods of one day to eight months. Equipment includes travel cots, double buggies, folding high chairs, cots, stairgates, Z beds and much more. Now also sells new and nearly-new clothes and toys, and a repair service is available. *Hire Shop*

LINDA AMARNANI

21 STANLEY GARDENS, WALTON-ON-THAMES, SURREY KT12 4HB
☎ (01932) 224368. PHONE FOR APPOINTMENT.
Made to measure cashmere knitwear in a variety of colours to Linda's own designs in a choice of colourways. *Permanent Discount Outlet*

LONDON CURTAIN AGENCY

298 SANDYCOMBE ROAD, KEW, SURREY TW9 3NG,
☎ 0181-940 5959. OPEN 10 - 4 TUE - FRI 10 - 5 SAT.
A mixture of new and secondhand curtains. Reflecting the fact that the owner is the former Sales and Marketing Director of a top London hotel, some of the curtains are refurbishment stock from London's five-star hotels, others designer samples and former display stock from fabric houses and interior designers. Stock ranges from curtains for small windows for £50 up to £800 for drapes for huge bay windows with swags and tails. Designer fabrics include Designer's Guild, Osborne & Little and Colefax & Fowler. There are also curtain rails, cushions, bedheads, lamps, blinds, tie-backs and pelmets. All the curtains are lined or interlined. Fantastic bargains at approximately one third of the original cost. Their made-to-measure collection of calico and cream cotton damask curtains handmade to individual requirements, as recommended in Homes & Gardens magazine, are at competitive prices. *Secondhand Shop*

MATALAN

268-278 HIGH STREET, SUTTON, SURREY SM1 1PG
☎ 0181-652 9600. PHONE FOR OPENING TIMES.
Matalan is a fashion and homewares shop giving customers what they claim to be unbeatable value for money with huge savings on a wide range of products including high quality fashionable clothing for men, women and children at up to 50% off high street prices. Matalan is situated out of town and stores are open seven days a week all year round. *Permanent Discount Outlet*

MUMS2BE

3 MORTLAKE TERRACE, MORTLAKE ROAD, KEW, RICHMOND, SURREY TW9 3DT
☎ 0181-332 6506. OPEN 10 - 6 MON - SAT.
Offers retail and special occasion wear hire from businesswear to leisure wear during your pregnancy. Whether you want suits or trousers, dresses or skirts, blouses or jumpers, leggings or miniskirts, wedding outfits or evening gowns, Mums2Be can kit you out. Evening wear costs from £69 to buy and £40 to hire. After you have given birth, suits can be re-tailored for you for a small fee. *Permanent Discount Outlet*

NIPPERS

THE WAFFRONS, WOODSTOCK LANE SOUTH, CHESSINGTON, SURREY KT9 1UF

☎ 0181-398 3114. FAX ☎ 0181-398 7553. OPEN 10 - 4 TUE, WED, FRI, SAT, 2 - 8 THUR, 2 - 4 SUN.

Nippers, the nursery equipment and toy specialists, operate from previously redundant buildings in rural areas around the country. They offer easy parking, no queues and personal service. This is on top of competitive prices on prams, cots, pushchairs, car seats, outdoor play equipment and toys, some of which are new, some seconds or secondhand and some ends of lines. Prices are low because they avoid the high overheads of traditional retail outlets and also because the successful growth of a number of branches means they can now buy in bulk and negotiate good deals. Customers are invited to try out the merchandise while the children look at the animals, mostly sheep, chicken and pigs. Familiar brand names are on sale at all the branches, including Mamas & Papas, Britax, Maclaren and Bebe Confort, plus Fisher-Price and Little Tikes. You can try out the car seats in your car and there is usually a pram/pushchair repair service on site.

PEW CORNER LTD

ARTINGTON MANOR FARM, OLD PORTSMOUTH ROAD, GUILDFORD, SURREY GU3 1LP

☎ (01483) 533337. OPEN 10 - 5 MON - SAT.

Showroom with over 10,000 sq ft of floor space filled with scores of styles of church pew in pine, oak, elm and mahogany. Also pulpits, lecterns, fonts, panelling. Also creates fine bespoke furniture from reclaimed timber. Phone for brochure and map. *Architectural Salvage*

PHOENIX

5 CHURCH STREET, COBHAM, SURREY KT11 3EG

☎ (01932) 862147. OPEN 9.30 - 5 MON - SAT.

This black and pink cottage devotes two floors and four rooms to middle to upmarket labels, usually no more than two years old, from Marks & Spencer to Escada, Laurel, Mondi, Simon Ellis and Parigi. One whole floor is devoted to evening wear. There's also plenty of accessories from jewellery and hats to belts and shoes, as well as a bargain rail. *Dress Agency*

Live Well On Less Tips

Cut up your old Christmas tree and store in boxes or bags for later use as a charcoal starter when barbecuing out of doors.

Live Well On Less Tips
Make fire starters by dipping pine cones in hot wax.

RAFF RADIO
1 STATION APPROACH, HINCHLEY WOOD, SURREY KT10 OSR,
☎ 0181-398 0987. OPEN 9.15 - 5.30 MON - SAT, CLOSED WED.
Kitchen appliances from leading brand names at prices which are cheaper than
most other white goods retailers. Fridges, freezers, washing machines, etc from
AEG, Electrolux, Hotpoint, Creda, Neff, Bosch. Stainless steel specialists, they
also offer a good selection of range-style cookers from Baumatic, Stoves,
Leisure, Britannia and Belling, and US-style fridges from Admiral and Amana.
Permanent Discount Outlet

RDO KITCHEN APPLIANCES
BANCROFT ROAD, REIGATE, SURREY RH2 7RP
☎ (01737) 240403. OPEN 9 - 5.30 MON - FRI, 9 - 4.30 SAT.
Any kitchen appliance you can think of with up to 6,000 items to choose
from. Specialises in British, French and German brand names - Gaggenau,
Zanussi, De Dietrich, Britannia, Neff, Bosch, AEG, Creda - at trade prices.
There are continuous special offers - phone for details. Delivery nationwide.
Range of more than 300 appliances constantly on show, including built-in
and freestanding appliances. Access/Visa phone orders accepted. Huge dis-
counts available.*Permanent Discount Outlet*

RICHE
87 HIGH STREET, EWELL, SURREY KT17 1RX,
☎ 0181-393 2256. OPEN 9.30 - 5 MON - SAT.
Riche has made its name selling current top quality designer wear at much
reduced prices. The owner is a former model and fashion buyer and has brought
a wealth of experience to this small high street shop, making it more than just
another nearly-new agency. Escada, Yves St Laurent, Mondi, Gucci, Chanel and
Krizia are just a few of the regular labels. While most of the stock is nearly-new,
some is ex-fashion show samples and ends of lines. There's an extensive range of
new accessories such as jewellery and hats at reasonable prices. *Dress Agency*

RICHMOND BOOK SHOP
20 RED LION STREET, RICHMOND, SURREY TW9 1RW,
☎ 0181-940 5512. OPEN 10 - 5.30 WED, THUR, BANK HOLIDAY
MONDAY.
Modern secondhand books which are mostly reps' copies and review copies of
recently published books. Discounts are at least 25%, although most of the
fiction is reduced by two thirds. The shop is situated opposite the back
entrance to Marks & Spencer. *Permanent Discount Outlet*

SEQUEL

181 CHESSINGTON ROAD, WEST EWELL, SURREY KT19 9XE,
☎ 0181-786 7552. OPEN 10 - 5 MON- SAT, CLOSED WED.

Sells new and nearly-new womenswear including ends of lines and samples in sizes 8-16. There is always a good cross-section of garments to be found on the rails with labels such as Jaeger, Betty Barclay, Jigsaw, DKNY, Karen Millen and Gerry Weber complemented by a wide range of hats, handbags, scarves and jewellery. Covering a wide range of labels from well-known high street names to Armani, Moschino, Escada, Mondi, Betty Barclay and Gerry Weber. Many outfits are current designer samples. Nothing is more than two seasons old. At time of going to press they were selling a Cerruti suit for £89, as new £450; a Karl Lagerfeld navy jacket, £79, usual retail price price £289. Sizes range from 8-18. They also stock hats, new scarves, bags, new jewellery and shoes. *Dress Agency*

SIESTA CORK TILES

UNIT 21, TAIT ROAD, CROYDON, SURREY CRO 2DP,
☎ 0181- 683 4055. FAX: ☎ 0181-683 4480. OPEN 9 - 5 MON - FRI. MAIL ORDER

Cork importers, who supply on a mail order basis, a complete range of cork floor tiles in all thicknesses - unsealed, acrylic varnished, hard wax or PVC surfaced, plus a coloured range. Special offers usually available. Details and samples sent on request. They also sell cork for walls and ceilings, decoration, insulation and for noticeboards. Large range tiles are stocked in thicknesses of 3mm, 6mm, 8mm and 10mm and in sizes 300x300mm and 600x300mm. Composition cork (fine grain) comes in rolls up to 1.22mx5m in a variety of thicknesses: 2mm, 3mm and 6mm, ideal for large noticeboards. Remember that unsealed floor cork can be coloured using diluted water-based paints then clear varnish when laid with quick-dry water-based floor sealant. *Permanent Discount Outlet*

SILVERLAND STONE

HOLLOWAY HILL, CHERTSEY, SURREY KT16 0AE
☎ (01932) 569277. OPEN 8 - 5 MON - FRI, 9 - 1 SAT, 9 - 1 SUN IN SUMMER ONLY.

Natural stone floors for both interior and exterior and fireplaces. Extensive range of hard landscaping materials sold including rockery and pebbles. *Architectural Salvage*

Live Well On Less Tips
Get rid of unpleasant smells without the expense of air fresheners. Just light a match.

SPECIAL OCCASIONS
1 OLD WOKING ROAD, WEST BYFLEET, SURREY KT14 6LW
☎ (019323) 54907. OPEN 9.30 - 5.30 MON - SAT EVENINGS AND IN AUGUST BY APPOINTMENT.
Established for more than 12 years, Special Occasions has more than 400 evening dresses for hire. Also agents for men's dress hire. *Hire Shop*

SPOILS
UNIT 17, THE DRUMMOND CENTRE, CROYDON, SURREY CRO 1TQ
☎ 0181- 688 8717. OPEN 9.30 - 6 MON - SAT, 9 ON THUR, 1 - 6 SUN.
UNIT S12, THE BENTALL CENTRE, KINGSTON-UPON-THAMES, SURREY KT1 1TP
☎ 0181-974 9303. OPEN 9 - 6 MON - WED & FRI, SAT, 9 - 9 THUR, 11 - 5 SUN.
UNITS 9-11, ST NICHOLAS CENTRE, SUTTON, SURREY SM1 1AW
☎ 0181-642 4450. OPEN 9 - 5.30 MON - FRI, 8 ON THUR, 9 - 6 SAT, 10.30 - 4.30 SUN.
General domestic glassware, non-stick bakeware, kitchen gadgets, ceramic oven-to-tableware, textiles, cutting boards, aluminium non-stick cookware, bakeware, plastic kitchenware, plastic storage, woodware, coffee pots/makers, furniture, mirrors and picture frames. Rather than being discounted, all the merchandise is very competitively priced - in fact, the company carry out competitors' checks frequently in order to monitor pricing. With 38 branches, the company is able to buy in bulk and thus negotiate very good prices. *Permanent Discount Outlet*

SUIT CITY
15 HOLMETHORPE AVENUE, HOLMETHORPE INDUSTRIAL ESTATE, REDHILL, SURREY RH1 2NB
☎ (0173) 778 9963. OPEN 11 - 3 FRI, 10 - 4 SAT, SUN.
Quality menswear at discounts of up to 65%. For example, 100% wool suits from £69.95 to £129.95. Sizes to fit 36 inch to 60 inch chest. *Permanent Discount Outlet*

THE CURTAIN AGENCY
231 LONDON ROAD, CAMBERLEY, SURREY GU15 3EY
☎ (01276) 671672. OPEN 10 - 5 MON - SAT.
103 WEST STREET, FARNHAM, SURREY GU9 7EN
☎ (01252) 714711. OPEN 10 - 5 MON - SAT.
Two shops in Surrey offering a wide range of quality secondhand curtains from designer elegance to practical and functional. Many are from shops' display stock and executive home relocations. All the curtains are ready to hang, but if alterations are needed an excellent service is available and a 24 hour sale or return option can be requested at both shops. A good range of quality fab-

rics is stocked for making up to customers' own requirements, with a delivery time of five weeks. A unique selection of antique and decorative lighting has increased to include a selection of top brand lighting seconds. Poles and rings, antique or new, metal or wood, tiebacks and holdbacks, door furnishing knobs and knockers, shades and carriers, cushions and kilims are all found here under one roof. *Secondhand Shop*

THE DRESS AGENCY

5B RECTORY LANE, ASHTEAD, SURREY KT21 2BA
☎ (01372) 271677. OPEN 9 - 5 MON - FRI, 9 - 3 WED, 9 - 4 SAT.
Double-fronted shop, half of which is devoted to daywear, the other of which has nearly-new bridal outfits. The daywear includes good quality names such as Planet, Basler, Jaeger, Jigsaw, Mondi, Frank Usher, Betty Barclay and Episode. The bridal section has about 50 wedding dresses at any one time from £100-£600, plus veils. They also have a large range of evening wear sizes 8-22 for hire. *Dress Agency*

THE DRESS CIRCLE

6 WOOLMEAD WALK, FARNHAM, SURREY GU9 7SH
☎ (01252) 716540 OPEN 9.30 - 4.30 MON - SAT.
Renowned designer labels in good condition - Parigi, Betty Barclay, Louis Feraud - as well as good high street names such as Marks & Spencer, Laura Ashley, Next and Benetton. Caters for seasonal events such as Ascot and towards Christmas supplies a wide variety of good evening wear. also stocks hats and some shoes but no jewellery. *Dress Agency*

THE FACTORY SHOP LTD

THE ENGINE SHED, CONSORT WAY, EAST, HORSLEY, SURREY RH6 7AU
☎ (01293) 823883. OPEN 9 - 5.30 MON - SAT, 10 - 4 SUN.
High street chainstore seconds and ends of ranges from clothes for all the family, bedding, toiletries, kitchenware, glassware, footwear, lighting, cosmetics, jewellery, and luggage at discounts of approximately 30%-50%. There are weekly deliveries and brands include many major stars: Wrangler, Nike, Adidas and Dartington, to name just four. Lines are continually changing and few factory shops offer such a variety under one roof. There are kitchen and furniture displays and a new line of Cape Country Furniture has recently been introduced. This high quality pine furniture made exclusively for The Factory Shop in South Africa is sold at factory direct prices with home delivery throughout the UK. Colour brochure and price list available. *Factory Shop*

Live Well On Less Tips
Use tumble dryer lint for garden compost.

Live Well On Less Tips
Cut the tips off the fingers of old rubber gloves which have a hole in and use for picking fruit. The gloves prevent your hands and arms from being scratched but you can still pick berries with your fingertips.

THE TAP FACTORY WORKSHOP

RANDALLS NURSERY, LYNE LANE, LYNE, NEAR CHERTSEY, SURREY KT16 OAW

☎ (01932) 566106. OPEN 10 - 6.30 MON - FRI, 9.30 - 5 SAT. PLEASE PHONE FIRST.

Specialises in the supply and restoration of original period bathroom fittings in a variety of finishes including brass, chrome, lacquer and and nickel. Also metal polishing services for general antiques. *Architectural Salvage*

TINKERS

17 OLD OAK AVENUE, CHIPSTEAD, SURREY CR5 3PG

☎ (01737) 553761. PHONE FIRST.

ABACUS BABY HIRE, LONG LODGE, NIGHTINGALE AVENUE, WEST HORSLEY, SURREY KT24 6PA

☎ (01483) 285142. PHONE FIRST.

Part of the Baby Equipment Hirers Association (BEHA), which has more than 100 members countrywide. A range of equipment can be hired from high chairs, cots and travel cots to baby car seats and buggies. Some members also hire out party equipment including child-sized tables and chairs. BEHA run an advice line which will try and answer any queries you have regarding hiring services for children. Phone the Babyline on 0831 310355. *Hire Shop*

TK MAXX

TIMES SQUARE SHOPPING CENTRE, HIGH STREET, SUTTON, SURREY SM1 1LF

☎ 0181-770 7786. OPEN 9 - 5.30 MON - FRI, 9 - 6 SAT, 11 - 5 SUN, UNTIL 8 ON THUR.

THE DRUMMOND CENTRE, CROYDON, SURREY CR0 1TY

☎ 0181-686 9753. OPEN 9 - 6 MON - WED, SAT, 9 - 9 THUR, 9 - 7 FRI, 11 - 5 SUN.

THE PEACOCKS CENTRE, WOKING, SURREY

☎ (01483) 771660. OPEN 9.30 - 5 MON - FRI, 9.30 - 8 THUR, 9 - 6 SAT, 11 - 5 SUN.

Based on an American concept, TK Maxx is situated in easily accessible, often centrally located stores and offers famous label goods with up to 60% savings off recommended retail prices. TK Maxx has fashion for the whole family - women's, men's and childrenswear - accessories, shoes, gifts, kitchenware and

home goods. Everything in the store is branded with a choice of well-known high street names to designer labels, and while a small percentage might be clearly marked past season, the great majority of items in store are current season, current stock and still with phenomenal savings. There is a huge choice with 50,000 pieces in store and up to 10,000 new items arriving a week. The stores are simple and unfussy with wide aisles, shopping trolleys and baskets, and a spacious, functional feel to them but there are individual changing rooms, ramps for buggies and wheelchairs and plenty of staff on the shop floor. Every branch accepts all major credit and debit cards and has a liberal refund and return policy. *Permanent Discount Outlet*

TOG 24

UNIT 11, WHITGIFT CENTRE, CROYDON, SURREY CRO 1UP
(☎ 01816) 807902. OPEN 9 - 6 SEVEN DAYS A WEEK, 11 - 5 BANK HOLIDAYS.

Tog 24 are the UK's fastest growing brand name in outdoor clothing and leisurewear, with a total of three UK factories and 36 stores nationwide. They utilise the world's finest performance fabrics including Gore-Tex, Polartec and Burlington macs. Catering for all the family for all seasons, with cosy fleeces and waterproofs for the winter, and trekking ranges, shorts and t-shirts for the summer. With all prices at least 30% below the recommended retail price you can afford to enter the Tog comfort zone. *Factory Shopping Village*

Live Well On Less Tips

CHINA CHASE LONG BYRE, BORRAS, NEAR CHESTER, WALES LL13 9TL. (01978) 856400. CALL OR SEND LETTER AND S.A.E. FOR DETAILS OR CONTACT MOBILE NUMBER 0370 837137.

Rather like a marriage agency, China Chase matches up those who've lost or broken an item of china with those who've got one to sell. They can help if you need to replace a piece or pieces of tableware, wish to increase your service even though it is no longer available from the manufacturer, want to increase the number of place settings, or would like to build up stock against future breakages. They also search for china at auctions and antique shops. There is a one-off registration fee of £6 but no commission on matching pieces as buyers and sellers work that out for themselves. Stocks of obsolete china are held.

Sussex *(East and West)*
East Sussex

WOMENSWEAR ONLY   Cancer Research Campaign, *Eastbourne*.   Napier, *Eastbourne*.
Panache, *Worthing*.   Quantum, *Brighton*.   Revival Dress Agency, *Eastbourne*.   Roundabout, *Lewes*.
Snips In Fashion, *Hove*.   Something Special, *Worthing*.

WOMENSWEAR & MENSWEAR   Matalan, *Eastbourne*.   Matalan, *Brighton*.
Village Square, *Brighton*.

CHILDREN   Daisy Daisy, *Brighton*.   Gooseberry Bush, *Nr Bognor*.   Matalan, *Eastbourne*.
Matalan, *Brighton*.   Panache, *Worthing*.   Second Look, *Uckfield*.   Village Square, *Brighton*.

HOUSEHOLD AND GIFTWARE   Edinburgh Crystal, *Brighton*.   Hornsea Pottery, *Brighton*.
Matalan, *Eastbourne*.   Matalan, *Brighton*.   Rye Pottery Ltd, *Rye*.   Village Square, *Brighton*.

DIY/RENOVATION   Brighton Architectural Salvage, *Brighton*.

ARCHITECTURAL SALVAGE   Brighton Architectural Salvage, *Brighton*.

FURNITURE/SOFT FURNISHINGS   Ansell's Warehouse, *Wisborough Green*.
Collins And Hayes, *Hastings*.   Furniture Warehouse, *Brighton*.

FOOD AND LEISURE   Not Just Books, *Brighton*.   Village Square, *Brighton*.

SPORTSWEAR AND EQUIPMENT   Village Square, *Brighton*.

ANSELL'S WAREHOUSE

KIRDFORD ROAD, WISBOROUGH GREEN, SUSSEX
☎ (01403) 700359. OPEN 10 - 4 SAT.
Specialises in three-piece suites and beds from most of the leading brand
names such as Collins & Hayes, Heirloom Wade, G-Plan, Peter Guild,
Derwent and beds from Rest Assured, Reylon, Stuart Jones and Sprung
Slumber. There are ten big buildings full of sofas and beds so come prepared
to spend some time walking round. Offers excellent value for money all year
round. ***Permanent Discount Outlet***

Live Well On Less Tips
Old roll-on deodorants bottles can be re-used by prying off the cap, rinsing,
and filling with powder or poster paint thinned with water. Replace the top
and let the children paint with it.

Live Well On Less Tips
Re-use a paint roller by covering it, putting it in the freezer overnight and thawing.

BRIGHTON ARCHITECTURAL SALVAGE

33-34 GLOUCESTER ROAD, BRIGHTON, SUSSEX BN1 4AQ

☎ (01273) 681656. OPEN 10 - 5 MON - SAT.

Lots of fireplaces including marble, cast iron and wood surrounds; reclaimed flooring; cast-iron inserts from Regency to Art Nouveau; doors, pine furniture, columns, stained and etched glass, panelling, railings and garden ornaments. *Architectural Salvage*

CANCER RESEARCH CAMPAIGN

172 TERMINUS ROAD, EASTBOURNE, EAST SUSSEX BN21 3BB

☎ (01323) 739703. OPEN 9 - 5 MON - SAT, 9.30 - 4 SUN (EASTER TO CHRISTMAS ONLY).

Shop with a department specifically aimed at the bridal market which sells or hires wedding dresses, bridesmaids dresses and pageboy outfits, with accessories. Most of the stock is either donated or straight from the manufacturer. *Dress Agency*

COLLINS AND HAYES

PONSWOOD INDUSTRIAL ESTATE, MENZIES ROAD, ST LEONARDS, HASTINGS, EAST SUSSEX TN34 1XF

☎ (01424) 443834. OPEN 9 - 5 MON - SAT.

Manufacturers of upholstered furniture and with their own collection of fabrics, this is Collins and Hayes only factory shop. Here, they sell ends of lines, discontinued models and cancelled orders of sofas and chairs, as well as fabrics, at half price or less. Upholstered furniture is a fashion industry and accordingly new collections are brought out once or twice a year, so there is a steady supply of ends of lines. *Factory Shop*

DAISY DAISY

33 NORTH ROAD, BRIGHTON, EAST SUSSEX BN11YB

☎ (01273) 689108. OPEN 10.30 - 5 MON - SAT.

Only the best quality secondhand children's clothes are sold here: both designer and high street names including Oilily, Jean Bourget, Osh Kosh and Nipper alongside Baby Gap, Next, Laura Ashley and Hennes. All are priced at between one quarter and one half of the original price. There are also plenty of accessories including shoes, hats, socks, tights and swimwear. They now also stock a selection of new wooden toys and dolls houses. As there's so much to choose from, toys are provided to keep the children amused while parents browse. There's also a toilet if needed. *Dress Agency*

EDINBURGH CRYSTAL

UNIT 5, THE VILLAGE SQUARE, MERCHANTS QUAY, BRIGHTON
MARINA, BRIGHTON, EAST SUSSEX BN2 5WA

☎ (01273) 818702. OPEN 10 - 5.30 MON - SAT, 10 - 5 SUN.

Edinburgh Crystal's seconds stock is clearly marked with wine glasses and
decanters at discounts from 30% up to 50%. There is also Arthur Price silverware, Royal Grafton china, and Scott cutlery. *Factory Shop*

FURNITURE WAREHOUSE

HOVE SEAFRONT, NEAR LAGOON, HOVE, BRIGHTON, EAST SUSSEX
BN41 1NS

☎ (01273) 273890. OPEN 9 - 6 MON - SAT, 10 - 5 SUN.

UNIT 1, QUAY SIDE, BASIN ROAD SOUTH, PORTSLADE, HOVE,
BRIGHTON BN41 1NF

High street quality furniture at warehouse prices. Three-piece suites from
£299-£2,000; sofa beds from £89-£699; sofas from £129-£799; beds from
£89 upwards. Also antique pine furniture, wardrobes, chests of drawers and a
range of repro furniture. Local delivery *Permanent Discount Outlet*

GOOSEBERRY BUSH

2 BARNHAM ROAD, BARNHAM, NR BOGNOR, SUSSEX PO22 OES

☎ (01243) 554552 OPEN 10 - 4 MON - SAT

Nearly-new largely high street fashions for children ie Next, Gap, Osh Kosh.
Stock ranges from a good selection of maternity wear and toys to all baby
equipment including cots, pushchairs and stairgates. Stock changes daily. New
items at reasonable prices. *Dress Agency*

HORNSEA POTTERY

THE VILLAGE SQUARE, MERCHANTS QUAY, BRIGHTON MARINA,
BRIGHTON, EAST SUSSEX BN2 5UF

☎ (01273) 818444. OPEN 10 - 5.30 SEVEN DAYS A WEEK.

Sells table cloths, mugs, mug racks, aprons, bowls, cafetieres, storage jars and
plates at discount prices, with a minimum 30% discount on selected seconds
compared with the retail price. *Factory Shopping Village*

Live Well On Less Tips

Join the National Society of Allotment and Leisure Gardeners Ltd and save
on everyday gardening products. Join by either visiting the hut on your nearest gardening allotment at the weekend between 9.30 and 11.30 or phone
01536 266576 for an application form. Association membership costs £1 per
member per year; single membership £6.70 a year or £67 for life. After
you've joined you can then make purchases which will save you money such
as the seed scheme in which seeds are discounted by 50%.

MATALAN

UNIT 4, THE CRUMBLES RETAIL PARK, PEVENSEY BAY ROAD, EASTBOURNE, SUSSEX BN23 6JH

☎ (01323) 470347. OPEN 10 - 8 MON - FRI, 9 - 6 SAT, 10.30 - 4.30 SUN.

CARDEN AVENUE, HOLLINGBURY, BRIGHTON BN1 8NS

NO TELEPHONE NUMBER AS WE WENT TO PRESS.

Matalan is a fashion and homewares shop giving customers what they claim to be unbeatable value for money with huge savings on a wide range of products including high quality fashionable clothing for women, women and children at up to 50% off high street prices. Matalan is situated out of town and stores are open seven days a week all year round. *Permanent Discount Outlet*

NAPIER

3 COURTLANDS ROAD, EASTBOURNE, SUSSEX BN22 8SW

☎ (01323) 644511. OPEN 9.30 - 5.30 MON - FRO, 10 - 6 SAT, 10 - 4 SUN.

Ends of lines and limited edition designer fashion jewellery in classic and contemporary styles direct from US manufacturers. Stock includes classic chains, necklaces, brooches, earrings, rings, chokers and bracelets at up to 75% discount. Prices range from £2.50 to £500. Parking available. *Permanent Discount Outlet*

NOT JUST BOOKS

THE VILLAGE SQUARE, MERCHANTS QUAY, BRIGHTON MARINA, BRIGHTON, EAST SUSSEX BN2 5UF

☎ (01273) 818719. OPEN 10 - 6 SEVEN DAYS A WEEK, SUMMER HOLIDAYS FRI, SAT, SUN 10 - 10,

Not Just Books sells a wide range of books, many at half price, from fiction to health, sport to children, cookbooks to biographies. There are also jigsaws, posters and stationery and a new range of discount cds. *Factory Shopping Village*

PANACHE

5 STANFORD SQUARE, WARWICK ST, WORTHING, SUSSEX BN11 3EZ

☎ (01903) 212503. OPEN 10 - 5 MON - SAT.

Two shops in one: Panache sells women's nearly-new at savings of up to 50% on high street prices; Smarties sells childrenswear up to the age of nine. The children's selection ranges from Petite Bateau, Laura Ashley and Oilily to Matrise and Osh Kosh. They do not stock children's sleepwear or underwear. The adult dress agency stocks a wide range of labels from Marks and Spencer and Viyella to Jacques Vert, MaxMara and Escada. They also sell hats, evening wear, coats, shoes, jackets, handbags and belts. *Dress Agency*

QUONTUM

UNIT 3, NILE PAVILIONS, 10 NILE STREET, BRIGHTON, SUSSEX BN1

☎ (01273) 321509. OPEN 10 - 6 MON - SAT, 12 - 5 SUN.

Original own-label designs and secondhand clothing together, with the emphasis on a directional look. Prices are very reasonable: a cashmere jumper for £35 which would cost £250 new. Also sell shoes. *Secondhand and Vintage Clothe*

REVIVAL DRESS AGENCY

24 GROVE ROAD, EASTBOURNE, EAST SUSSEX BN21 4TR

☎ (01323) 649552. OPEN 9 - 5.30 MON - SAT.

Excellent selection of good chainstore labels such as Principles, Monsoon, Wallis, Jaeger, Country Casuals and some designer stock such as Giorgio Armani, Calvin Klein and Nicole Farhi. The majority of items are less than two years old. Shoes and accessories are also available. A relaxed and comfortable environment with friendly staff. Browsers are more than welcome. *Dress Agency*

ROUNDABOUT

31 CLIFFE HIGH STREET, LEWES, EAST SUSSEX BN7 2DN

☎ (01273) 471325. OPEN 9.30 - 4.30 MON, TUE, THUR, FRI, SAT.

Good quality Jaeger, Marks & Spencer, Windsmoor, Principles, Paul Costelloe and MaxMara. Also small selection of hats, some jewellery, shoes and handbags. *Dress Agency*

RYE POTTERY LTD

77 FERRY ROAD, RYE, EAST SUSSEX TN31 7DJ

☎ (01797) 223363. OPEN 9 - 5 MON - FRI, 10.30 - 1 AND 2.15 - 4.30 SAT.

There is always a selection of seconds available in distinctive, hand-decorated designs. No two items of this 'majolica' or 'delft' decorated pottery are the same, which is why it is still popular with the Royal Family. Choose from Chaucer figures, American folk heroes or Pastoral Primitives; seconds are usually two-thirds of retail price. *Factory Shop*

SECOND LOOK

166 HIGH STREET, UCKFIELD, EAST SUSSEX TN22 1AT

☎ (01825) 768622. OPEN 9.30 - 4.30 MON - SAT.

Children's nearly-new dress and equipment shop, selling clothes for 0-12 year olds, prams, pushchairs, car seats and toys, as well as maternity wear. Also stocks new prams and strollers at very competitive prices - you can pay by instalment or credit card. *Dress Agency*

SNIPS IN FASHION

40 CHURCH ROAD, HOVE, SUSSEX BN3 2NF

☎ (01273) 729059. OPEN 9.30 - 5.30 TUE - SAT.

Clearance outlet featuring labels such as Olsen, Fink, Michelle, Dolores and Apsa at less than half the original price. Some are current stock, others samples from showrooms, yet others discontinued lines, seconds or late deliveries. The whole range of clothing is stocked from ballgowns and coats to jeans and beach wear, but no accessories. *Permanent Discount Outlet*

SOMETHING SPECIAL

15 ARDSHEAL ROAD, BROADWATER GREEN, WORTHING, SUSSEX BN14 7RN

☎ (01903) 217317. OPEN 9.30 - 5 MON - SAT.

Sells good-as-new clothes for women at discount prices from Marks & Spencer to designer labels, as well as manufacturers' samples, once-worn bridal gowns and hats. The shop also hires out bridesmaids dresses and evening wear. *Dress Agency*

THE FACTORY SHOP LTD

UNITS 15a-c, THE VILLAGE SQUARE, BRIGHTON MARINA, BRIGHTON, SUSSEX BN2 5WA

☎ (01273) 818590. OPEN 10 - 5.30 MON - FRI, 10 - 6 SAT, 10.30 - 4.30 SUN.

High street chainstore seconds and ends of ranges from clothes for all the family, bedding, toiletries, kitchenware, glassware, footwear, lighting, cosmetics, jewellery, and luggage at discounts of approximately 30%-50%. There are weekly deliveries and brands include many major stars: Wrangler, Nike, Adidas and Dartington, to name just four. Lines are continually changing and few factory shops offer such a variety under one roof, with at this branch, a large number of clothing concessions in addition to The Factory Shop range. There are furniture displays and a line of Cape Country Furniture is on sale. This high quality pine furniture made exclusively for The Factory Shop in the new South Africa is sold at factory direct prices with home delivery throughout the UK. Colour brochure and price list available. This branch is part of the Merchants Quay Factory Outlet centre with several other high street brands' clearance shops, leisure facilities and many restaurants. *Factory Shopping Village*

THE FABRIC WAREHOUSE

42 GEORGE STREET, BRIGHTON, EAST SUSSEX BN2 1RJ

☎ (01273) 620744. OPEN 9.30 - 5 MON - SAT.

Curtain and upholstery fabric including names such as Designers Guild, Monkwell, Sanderson, Gp & J Baker, Ramm Son & Crocker, Anna French and Jane Churchill. Stock depends on what is available on the end of line market so changes constantly. If you are particularly interested in one label, phone first to check they have it in stock. *Permanent Discount Outlet*

Live Well On Less Tips
Re-use plastic milk jug cartons by cutting off the bottom at an angle to make a pooper scooper or a dust pan.

THE OLD LOOM MILL

MULBROOKS FARM, ERSHAM ROAD, HAILSHAM, EAST SUSSEX
BN27 2RH
☎ (01323) 848007. OPEN 9 - 5 MON - SAT, 10 - 5 SUN & BANK
HOLIDAYS.
Sells fabric and wool, curtaining, sheeting, lining and dress fabric by the
weight. Curtaining ranges from £2.50-£5 per meter; sheeting is £6 per kilo,
£1.50 per metre; 54 wide lining £2.22 per metre; dress fabrics are £2.50 a yard
for end of rolls. All the material here is sold as seconds, although 90% of it is
perfect. There are lots of well-known brands here, adding up to savings of
about 60% on the high street. The outlet also offers a curtain-making service,
a tea room and a craft hall. *Factory Shop*

THE TRUGGERY

COOPERS CROFT, HERSTMONCEUX, EAST SUSSEX BN27 1QL
☎ (01323) 832314. OPEN 10 - 5 TUE - SAT.
Manufacturers of Sussex trugs, shallow wooden gardening baskets made from
sweet chestnut and willow and particular to the region. Prices range from
£13.50 to £45. Also English willow baskets, all shapes and sizes from £15 -
£40. Parking provided. *Factory Shop*

TK MAXX

36/37 NORTH STREET, BRIGHTON, EAST SUSSEX , BN1 1EB
☎ (01273) 727483. OPEN 9 - 6 MON - SAT, 8 ON THUR, 11 - 5 SUN.
Based on an American concept, TK Maxx is situated in easily accessible, often
centrally located stores and offers famous label goods with up to 60% savings
off recommended retail prices. TK Maxx has fashion for the whole family -
women's, men's and childrenswear - accessories, shoes, gifts, kitchenware and
home goods. Everything in the store is branded with a choice of well-known
high street names to designer labels, and while a small percentage might be
clearly marked past season, the great majority of items in store are current season, current stock and still with phenomenal savings. There is a huge choice
with 50,000 pieces in store and up to 10,000 new items arriving a week. The
stores are simple and unfussy with wide aisles, shopping trolleys and baskets,
and a spacious, functional feel to them but there are individual changing
rooms, ramps for buggies and wheelchairs and plenty of staff on the shop
floor. Every branch accepts all major credit and debit cards and has a liberal
refund and return policy. *Permanent Discount Outlet*

TOG 24

UNIT 13, THE VILLAGE SQUARE, MERCHANTS QUAY, BRIGHTON MARINA, BRIGHTON, EAST SUSSEX BN2 5UF

☎ (01273) 818759. OPEN 10 - 5.30 SEVEN DAYS A WEEK.

UNIT 24, CHURCHILL SQUARE SHOPPING CENTRE, BRIGHTON BN1 2EP

☎ (01273) 737090. OPEN 9 - 6 MON - SAT, 9 - 8 THUR, 11 - 5 SUN.

Tog 24 are the UK's fastest growing brand name in outdoor clothing and leisurewear, with a total of three UK factories and 36 stores nationwide. They utilise the world's finest performance fabrics including Gore-Tex, Polartec and Burlington mcs. Catering for all the family for all seasons, with cosy fleeces and waterproofs for the winter, and trekking ranges, shorts and T-shirts for the summer. With all prices at least 30% below the recommended retail price you can afford to enter the Tog comfort zone. *Factory Shopping Village*

TOM SAYERS CLOTHING CO

THE VILLAGE SQUARE, MERCHANTS QUAY, BRIGHTON MARINA, BRIGHTON, EAST SUSSEX BN2 5UA

☎ (01273) 818705. OPEN 10 - 5.30 MON - SAT, 10 - 5 SUN.

Tom Sayers make sweaters for some of the top high street department stores. Unusually for a factory shop, if they don't stock your size, they will try and order it for you from their factory or one of their other factory outlets and send it to you. Most of the stock here is overstock, cancelled orders or last season's and includes jumpers, trousers, jackets and shirts. The trousers and shirts are bought in to complement the sweaters which they make. *Factory Shopping Village*

VILLAGE SQUARE

BRIGHTON MARINA VILLAGE, BRIGHTON, EAST SUSSEX BN2 5WB

☎ (01273) 693636. FAX ☎ (01273) 818701. OPEN 10 - 5.30 SEVEN DAYS A WEEK.

Twelve main factory shops including Leading Labels, The Factory Shop, Edinburgh Crystal, Hornsea Pottery, Not Just Books, Toorak, Tog 24 outdoor wear and Tom Sayers. There are also pubs and restaurants, most offering al fresco eating, and a selection of specialists yachting shops, gifts shops and boutiques. There is a small children's playground, an ASDA superstore, an 8-screen Virgin cinema complex, a 26-lane Bowlplex bowling alley and a David Lloyd health and fitness centre. All this is based around the working marina and picturesque village square. There are 1,600 free parking spaces in the multi-storey car park. Further developments are planned for opening in the year 2000 including more factory outlet shops, nightclub, casino, 100-room hotel, pubs and restaurants. *Factory Shopping Village*

West Sussex

WOMENSWEAR ONLY　Always In Vogue, *Arundel*.　Browns, *Haywards Heath*.
Diamonds Dress Agency, *Storrington*.　M & G Designer Fashions, *Near Hickstead Village*.

MENSWEAR ONLY　Tom Sayers Clothing Co, *Brighton*.

WOMENSWEAR & MENSWEAR　TK Maxx, *Brighton*.　Tog 24, *Brighton*.
Impulse, *Hickstead*.　Jaeger Factory Shop, *Burgess Hill*.　Ricara Factory Shop, *Littlehampton*.
Stockley Trading, *Littlehampton*.　The Shoe Shed, *Bognor Regis*.

CHILDREN　Baby Things, *Horsham*.　Baby Things, *Shoreham-By-Sea*.　TK Maxx, *Brighton*.
Tog 24, *Brighton*.　Gooseberry Bush, *Chichester*.　Ricara Factory Shop, *Littlehampton*.
Stockley Trading, *Littlehampton*.　The Shoe Shed, *Bognor Regis*.

HOUSEHOLD AND GIFTWARE　Country Traditionals, *Ashurst Wood*.
Dexam International Ltd, *Midhurst*.　The Truggery, *Herstmonceux*.　TK Maxx, *Brighton*.
Heirlooms Ltd, *Bognor Regis*.　Second Edition, *Worthing*.　Second Edition, *Bognor Regis*.
Spoils, *Crawley*.　Spoils, *Brighton*.

ELECTRICAL EQUIPMENT　Power Warehouse, *East Grinstead*.

DIY/RENOVATION　The West Sussex Antique Timber Company Ltd, *Wisborough Green*.

ARCHITECTURAL SALVAGE
The West Sussex Antique Timber Company Ltd, *Wisborough Green*

FURNITURE/SOFT FURNISHINGS　The Fabric Warehouse, *Brighton*.
The Old Loom Mill, *Hailsham*.　The Curtain Exchange, *Cuckfield*.

FOOD AND LEISURE　The Factory Shop Ltd, *Brighton*.

SPORTSWEAR AND EQUIPMENT　Ricara Factory Shop, *Littlehampton*.
Stockley Trading, *Littlehampton*.

ALWAYS IN VOGUE

1 THE OLD MILL, RIVER ROAD, ARUNDEL, WEST SUSSEX BN18 9DH
☎ (01903) 883192. OPEN 10 - 5 MON - SAT, 10 - 4 WINTER.
Founded in 1993 by former model, Lisa Knight, Always in Vogue now has a
reputation for being one of the best dress agencies in the south. No high street
labels are taken and all garments must be dry cleaned and no more than three
years old. Planet, Jacques Vert and Country Casuals form the bottom line of
the stock, and you can generally find Jaeger, Windsmoor, Alexon, Condici,
Nicole Farhi, Louis Feraud, Chanel, Karl Lagerfeld, Armani, Thierry Mugler,
Escada, Gaultier, Ralph Lauren, Frank Usher and Gina Bacconi at between
one quarter and one half of the as-new price. There is also new Gottex at
about half price. Such is the quality of the merchandise, much of it unworn

and still carrying the original price labels, that customers come here for out-fits and accessories for Ascot, Goodwood, Henley, polo matches, weddings or simply for a blouse and skirt. Because the client base covers ten counties, cus-tomers are unlikely to buy an item that originated from their next door neigh-bour. Now also offering brand new end of line garments from top British designers at 50% discounts. Always in Vogue continues to set new standards both in the stock it carries and its service to clients. *Dress Agency*

BABY THINGS

111 LONGFIELD ROAD, HORSHAM, WEST SUSSEX RH12 1LE
☎ (01403) 261605. PHONE FIRST.
ROBINA BABY & NEH, 10 DOWNSWAY, SHOREHAM-BY-SEA, WEST SUSSEX BN43 5GH
☎ (01273) 453548. PHONE FIRST.
Part of the Baby Equipment Hirers Association (BEHA), which has more than 100 members countrywide. A range of equipment can be hired from high chairs, cots and travel cots to baby car seats and buggies. Some members also hire out party equipment including child-sized tables and chairs. BEHA run an advice line which will try and answer any queries you have regarding hir-ing services for children. Phone the Babyline on 0831 310355. *Hire Shop*

BROWNS

SUSSEX ROAD, HAYWARDS HEATH, WEST SUSSEX
☎ (01444) 458295. OPEN 10 - 4.30 MON - SAT, 10 - 4 THUR.
32 EAST STREET, HORSHAM, WEST SUSSEX
☎ (01403) 259 711. OPEN 10 - 4.30 MON - SAT.
Sell everything from T-shirts to ballgowns from high street names to designer label. Sizes range from 8-20. Designs by Jaeger, Country Casuals, Betty Barclay, Yarell and Gerry Weber. *Dress Agency*

COUNTRY TRADITIONALS

BRAMBLEHURST HOUSE, WELL HILL, ASHURST WOOD, WEST SUSSEX RH19 3TQ
☎ (01342) 822622. OPEN 9 - 12 FIRST SAT EACH MONTH.
Original Bunzlau ceramics from Poland are sold at shows countrywide or at monthly warehouse sales. Phone 01342 822622 for a catalogue and direc-tions. *Designer Sale*

DEXAM INTERNATIONAL LTD

HOLMBUSH WAY, MIDHURST, WEST SUSSEX GU29 9HX
☎ (01730) 814188. OPEN 10 - 3 MON - FRI, 10 - 1 SAT.
Sells figurines, glass, china, gifts and housewares at well below normal retail prices.. *Factory Shop*

DIAMONDS DRESS AGENCY
4 SCHOOL HILL, STORRINGTON, WEST SUSSEX RH20 4NB
☎ (01903) 746824. OPEN 10 - 5 MON - SAT.
Ground floor shop in the middle of the village selling everything from day-wear to, in the winter, ballgowns. Designer labels such as MaxMara, Yves St Laurent, Valentino, Escada, Mondi, Betty Barclay, as well as good high street names, and accessories: belts, shoes and bags. *Dress Agency*

FOOD AND DRINK DISCOUNTERS

EDGCUMBE TEA AND COFFEE
WICKS HOUSE, FORD LANE, FORD, ARUNDEL, WEST SUSSEX
BN18 ODF
☎ (01243) 555775. OPEN 9 - 6 MONDAY TO FRIDAY. MAIL ORDER.
Primarily trade suppliers, Edgcumbe sell direct to personal shoppers and have some very good bargains in ends of lines. They offer top quality tea blends in tea bag or loose form and a roast and post coffee service by mail order - within 24 hours of ordering, you will find fresh coffee on your doorstep. They roast and blend their own coffee on site to order, and you can enjoy a range of flavoured coffee from amaretto to choc-mint. Because of their low over-heads, the prices are very competitive. For example, £25 for 3,000 tea bags of English Breakfast blend. They also sell Cobra Indian Beer and premium bot-tled lager in ½ pint and pint measures. Van delivery service to local areas.
Food and Drink Discounter

GOOSEBERRY BUSH
SALTHAM LANE, RUNCTON, CHICHESTER, WEST SUSSEX
☎ (01243) 538060. OPEN 10 - 4 MON - SAT.
Babies and children's new and nearly-new clothes, equipment and small toys. The shop is up a concrete slope in the industrial area. *Dress Agency*

HEIRLOOMS LTD
2 ARUN BUSINESS PARK, BOGNOR REGIS, WEST SUSSEX PO22 9SX
☎ (01243) 820252. OPEN 10 - 4 ALMOST EVERY FRIDAY AND SOME SATS.
Sleep like a king, dine like a lord or lounge like a lady. . . .the Heirlooms fac-tory shop is brimming with luxury at affordable prices, the majority of which are made on the premises. Elegant and exceptionally high quality bed linens in Egyptian cotton, pure linen and the finest polycotton percale, in four sizes up to super-king are sold in this 1,200 sq ft outlet. There's also table linens using classic hem stitching or handmade laces, a cornucopia of gifts with exquisite laces and embroideries, and handmade christening and baby wear. Also seconds in sterling silver and silverplated frames and sterling silver clocks,

all in boxes. Normally only found in the most exclusive shops, homes and palaces all over the world, here you can buy ends of lines and slight seconds at between 30% and 65% off the recommended retail price. This busy exporting company only opens the factory shop about once a week, so check before making what will be a worthwhile journey. Free parking. May be relocating in 2000, so please phone first before visiting. *Factory Shop*

IMPULSE

LONDON ROAD, HICKSTEAD, WEST SUSSEX RH17 5RL
☎ (01444) 881255. OPEN 10 - 5 MON - SAT.
Men's trousers, jackets and shoes and a large selection of ladies shoes, handbags and belts - all at up to 50% discount. Next door to the ladies designer fashion warehouse, M & G Designer Fashions. *Permanent Discount Outlet*

JAEGER FACTORY SHOP

UNIT B, 208-216 LONDON ROAD, BURGESS HILL, WEST SUSSEX RH15 9NF
☎ (01444) 333100. OPEN 10 - 6 MON - FRI, 9 - 6 SAT, 11 - 5 SUN.
New, purpose-built factory shops selling contemporary classics from Jaeger at excellent prices. Most of the merchandise is previous seasons' stock, but you might also find some special makes. This shop stocks tailoring and knitwear for women and men. *Factory Shop*

M & G DESIGNER FASHIONS

OLD LONDON ROAD (OLD A23), NEAR HICKSTEAD VILLAGE, WEST SUSSEX RH17 5 RL
☎ (01444) 881511. OPEN 10 - 5 MON - SAT.
A large fashion warehouse selling designer and famous high-street name clothes at discounted prices from 20% to 80% less than the normal retail price. Because they carry many famous high street and designer labels in the 3,400 sq ft outlet, they are unable to advertise these names. Many of the clothes are the current season's fashions, discontinued lines, late deliveries, bankrupt stock and cancelled orders. Twice a year, they hold Silly sales where no garment is over £30. They also hold winter and summer clearance sales. Their range covers everything from T-shirts to ballgowns in sizes 10-24. There is ample parking, free coffee or tea, easy access for wheelchairs and individual changing rooms. They have recently started selling menswear, millinery and ladies shoes in the next door shop. (Follow the signs to Ricebridge and Hickstead Village.) Please phone for Christmas and bank holiday hours. Amex, Mastercard, Switch and Visa cards accepted. *Permanent Discount Outlet*

Live Well On Less Tips,
ANTIQUE BATH AND TAP STUDIO CHAPEL COURT, 70 HOSPITAL STREET, NANTWICH, CHESHIRE CW5 5RF. (01270) 626554. OPEN 9 - 5 MON, TUE, THUR, FRI, 9 - 1 SAT.
Bath re-enamelling carried out by fully trained operatives in your home for £178 or baths can be collected for stove enamelling or vitreous enamelling at 1100 degrees Centigrade. Examples can be seen in the showroom here together with stimulating ideas for creating period bathrooms. Reclaimed baths for sale.

POWER WAREHOUSE

53-59 LINGFIELD ROAD, EAST GRINSTEAD, WEST SUSSEX RH19 2EU
☎ (01342) 410444. OPEN 9 - 5.30 MON - SAT.
Small showroom displaying all major domestic kitchen appliances (from fridges and washing machines to hobs and ovens and including American washing and refrigeration units) from Creda, Neff, Bosch, Miele, AEG, Hotpoint, Zanussi, Siemens, De Dietrich, Smeg, etc, both free-standing and built-in appliances. They claim to be able to beat any competitor's price. Offer a phone service whereby you can ring them with the make and model number of your chosen piece of equipment and they will quote you a more competitive price. Small charge for UK delivery may apply. ***Permanent Discount Outlet***

RICARA FACTORY SHOP

RIVER ROAD, LITTLEHAMPTON, WEST SUSSEX BN17 5BZ
☎ (01903) 723843. OPEN 9.30 - 5 MON - FRI, 9 - 5 SAT, 10 - 4 SUN.
Sells mainly schoolwear and men's casualwear, and branded sportswear such as unisex cycling shorts, track suits and leggings at very reasonable prices. ***Factory Shop***

SECOND EDITION

MONTAGUE STREET, WORTHING, WEST SUSSEX BN11 3BP
☎ (01903) 823163. OPEN 9.30 - 5 MON - SAT.
46-48 HIGH STREET, BOGNOR REGIS, WEST SUSSEX PO21 1SP
☎ (01243) 868319. OPEN 9.30 - 5 MON - SAT.
Second Edition sells a wide range of household goods from children's bedding to lamps, china ornaments, tablecloths, giftware, garden ornaments, cushion covers, duvets, pillows and kitchenware. Some are seconds, some perfects and discounts range from 25%-50%. They have been known to sell perfect Caroline Charles bedding at seconds prices, as well as a wide range of high street and chainstore brand names. Kitchenware includes storage jars, assorted mugs, assorted melamine and various designs in kitchen linens. ***Permanent Discount Outlet***

SPOILS

85, 86 & PART 87, COUNTY MALL, CRAWLEY, WEST SUSSEX RH10 1FD
☎ (01293) 539941. OPEN 9 - 5.30 MON - WED, 9 - 8 THUR, 9 - 6 FRI, SAT.
UNITS 88-90 CHURCHILL SQUARE, BRIGHTON
☎ (01273) 735 097. OPEN 9 - 6 MON - SAT, 8 ON THUR, 11 - 5 SUN
General domestic glassware, non-stick bakeware, kitchen gadgets, ceramic
oven-to-tableware, textiles, cutting boards, aluminium non-stick cookware,
bakeware, plastic kitchenware, plastic storage, woodware, coffee pots/makers,
furniture, mirrors and picture frames. Rather than being discounted, all the
merchandise is very competitively priced - in fact, the company carry out
competitors' checks frequently in order to monitor pricing. With 38 branches, the company is able to buy in bulk and thus negotiate very good prices.
Permanent Discount Outlet

STOCKLEY TRADING

UNIT N10/11, RIVERSIDE INDUSTRIAL ESTATE, LITTLEHAMPTON,
WEST SUSSEX BN17 5DF
☎ (01903) 732392. OPEN 9 - 6 TUE - FRI, 9.30 - 5 SAT, 10 - 4 SUN.
Warehouse shop which operates as a wholesaler and retailer, but which is open
to members of the public. The outlet sells a range of sportswear which changes
depending on what they are able to buy in at good prices. There is a good
selection of trainers, including brand names Adidas, Nike and Reebok, tracksuits, toys and equestrian leisurewear, boots for riders, and saddles for horses.
Permanent Discount Outlet

THE CURTAIN EXCHANGE

45 HIGH STREET, CUCKFIELD, WEST SUSSEX RH17 5JU
☎ (01444) 417000. OPEN 10 - 4 MON - SAT
The Curtain Exchange is a franchised group of shops selling beautiful top
quality secondhand curtains, blinds, pelmets, etc at between one-third and
one half of the brand new price. Their stock comes from a variety of sources:
people who are moving house and dislike the drapes in their new home; people who are moving house and want to sell their old curtains to help with the
bills; show houses, where the builder wants to recoup some of his outgoings;
interior designers' mistakes. Stock changes constantly and ranges from rich
brocades, damasks and velvets to chintzes, linens and cottons. Designer names
include Colefax & Fowler, Designers Guild, Laura Ashley, Warner, Sanderson,
Osborne & Little, Fortuny and Bennison. A team of fitters and alteration
experts are available if required. They offer a 24-hour availability. The Curtain
Exchange also supply bespoke ranges with samples of curtains hanging. These
fabrics are chosen from suppliers all over the world and are an excellent buy.
Secondhand Shop

Live Well On Less Tips
WORLDWIDE HOME EXCHANGE CLUB 18 - 20 LONDON ROAD, TUNBRIDGE WELLS, KENT, TN11 DA. (01892) 619300. FAX 01892 619311.

Home exchange and rental is a great way to see the world at a fraction of the cost. Mainly aimed at seasoned travellers who eschew package holidays and prefer to stay in a private home rather than a hotel room or bleak apartment, you pay for travel, food and holiday spending only and you get to taste some-one else's lifestyle! They have 450 quality homes on their books in places as diverse as Vanuatu, Zimbabwe and Alaska, as well as properties in Europe, the USA and worldwide. Exchange guidelines are provided, sample agreements and general useful information. They publish an annual directory at the end of January with a supplement in April. Phone them for more details or e-mail: david.gurdon@btinternet.com or visit www.wwhec.com.

THE SHOE SHED

3 THE ARCADE, BOGNOR REGIS, WEST SUSSEX PO21 1LH
☎ (01243) 829600. OPEN 9 - 5.30 MON - SAT, 10 - 4 SUN.
Large factory shop selling a vast range of all types of men's, women's and children's shoes, all of which are perfects, at up to 30% below normal high street prices. Men's shoes from £10; sports shoes from £10. Ladies sandals cost from £5; ladies shoes from £7.50. *Factory Shop*

THE WEST SUSSEX
ANTIQUE TIMBER COMPANY LTD

RELIANCE WORKS, NEWPOUND, WISBOROUGH GREEN, WEST SUSSEX RH14 0AZ
☎ (01403) 700139. ☎ (01403) 700936 FAX. OPEN 8.30 - 5 MON - FRI, 9 - 1 SAT.
Specialists in old pine, oak beams, oak flooring and mouldings (the oak flooring is supplied and laid). Also sells pine and oak doors and old timber furniture. Kit form pine door, £95, made up doors, £185; oak doors, £250 plus VAT. Undertakes barn restoration and conversion too. *Architectural Salvage*

Warwickshire

(Including West Midlands)

WOMENSWEAR ONLY Forget-Me-Not Designer Bridal Wear, *Nuneaton.*
Into Clothing, *Leamington Spa.* The Cuckoo's Nest, *Warwick.*
Top Drawer As New, *Stratford-Upon-Avon.*

WOMENSWEAR & MENSWEAR   Arkwrights Mill, *Near Warwick.*
Littlewoods Catalogue Discount Store, *Rugby.* Matalan, *Stratford-Upon-Avon.* Scoops, *Warley.*
The Factory Shop, *Nuneaton.*

CHILDREN Games Carousel, *Leamington Spa.* Lilliput, *Stratford-Upon-Avon.*
Littlewoods Catalogue Discount Store, *Rugby.* Matalan, *Stratford-Upon-Avon.*
Mercia Safety, *Near Warwick.* Nippers, *Near Rugby.* Scoops, *Warley.*
The Factory Shop, *Near Nuneaton.* Yews Farm Baby Equipment, *Rugby.*

HOUSEHOLD AND GIFTWARE Alison's Shepherd's Craft Company, *Warwick.*
Dunelm Mill Shop, *Rugby.* Hatton Country World, *Warwick.* Maid Of China, *Near Warwick.*
Matalan, *Stratford-Upon-Avon.* Mesdame's Collection, *Near Warwick.* Mill Outlets Ltd, *Rugby.*
Scoops, *Warley.*

ELECTRICAL EQUIPMENT Littlewoods Catalogue Discount Store, *Rugby.*
Scoops, *Warley.*

DIY/RENOVATION Robertson & Partners Ltd, *Nuneaton.*
The Original Choice Ltd, *Gaydon.*

ARCHITECTURAL SALVAGE Robertson & Partners Ltd, *Nuneaton.*
The Original Choice Ltd, *Gaydon.*

FURNITURE/SOFT FURNISHINGS Top Service, *Shipston On Stour.*

FOOD AND LEISURE Mesdame's Collection, *Near Warwick.* Renahall Ltd, *Rugby.*

ALISON'S SHEPHERD'S CRAFT COMPANY

23 COTEN END, WARWICK, WARWICKSHIRE CV34 4NT
☎ (01926) 492505. OPEN 9 - 5.30 MON - SAT. MAIL ORDER ALSO.
Needlecraft warehouse which also operates a mail order leaflet. There are every type of thread, tapestry wool, stranded cotton, shade cards, metallic threads, crochet cotton, flexi-hoops, needles, tapestry frames, scissors, beads, anchor accessories such as organiser boxes, as well as fabrics (Aida, Evenweave and Sweigart linens). ***Permanent Discount Outlet***

Live Well On Less Tips,
ANTIQUE BATH AND TAP STUDIO CHAPEL COURT, 70 HOSPITAL STREET, NANTWICH, CHESHIRE CW5 5RF. (01270) 626554. OPEN 9 - 5 MON, TUE, THUR, FRI, 9 - 1 SAT.
Bath re-enamelling carried out by fully trained operatives in your home for £178 or baths can be collected for stove enamelling or vitreous enamelling at 1100 degrees Centigrade. Examples can be seen in the showroom here together with stimulating ideas for creating period bathrooms. Reclaimed baths for sale.

ARKWRIGHTS MILL

HATTON COUNTRY WORLD, DARK LANE, HATTON, NEAR WARWICK, WARWICKSHIRE CV35 8XA
☎ (01926) 842761. OPEN 10 - 5 SEVEN DAYS A WEEK (NOT CHRISTMAS DAY AND BOXING DAY).
Claims to be the most interesting clothes store in the Midlands. Where else can you find factory discount bargains in men's and women's clothing mixed with some of the finest fabric services available? There are in-store seamstresses ready and waiting to do instant alterations, commissions and all sorts of dressmaking services, often whilst you wait and look around. Brand names available direct from the factories at big discounts incude: Alexara, Hyde Park Leathers, Klasse, Double Two, Jordana, Just Elegance, Aristoc, Wolsey, Woodville and a whole host of others. Hatton Country World is home to the biggest Craft Centre in the UK and provides plenty to amuse both adults and children alike, including more than 30 craft and discount shops, rare farm animals, pets' corner, large antiques' centre, cafe/bar and free car parking. *Factory Shop*

DUNELM MILL SHOP

CLOCK TOWERS CENTRE, MANNINGS WALK, RUGBY, WARWICKSHIRE CV21 2JT
☎ (01788) 541171. OPEN 9 - 5 MON - SAT.
20 QUEENS ROAD, NUNEATON, WARWICKSHIRE CV11 5JW
☎ (01203) 344711. OPEN 9 - 5 MON - SAT, UNTIL 5.30 ON FRI.
Part of a chain of shops based in the Midlands selling brand-name and chain-store curtains, masses of bedlinen, towels, wickerware, pictures and frames, all at competitive prices. *Permanent Discount Outlet*

E WALTERS FACTORY SHOP

42 HIGH STREET, BLACKHEATH, ROWLEY REGIS, WEST MIDLANDS
OPEN 9 - 5 MON - FRI, 9 - 4 SAT,
Europe's largest trouser manufacturer sells ends of lines, cancelled orders and samples of jeans, trousers and shorts for all the family at factory direct prices. Also available ancillary lines of casual wear at bargain prices. *Factory Shop*

FORGET-ME-NOT DESIGNER BRIDAL WEAR
THE WEDDING CENTRE, 5 - 7 LUTTERWORTH ROAD,
ATTLEBOROUGH GREEN, NUNEATON, 3 MILES EAST OF JUNCTION 3
ON THE M6, WARWICKSHIRE CV11 4LD
☎ (01203) 375555. FAX ☎ (01203) 374455. OPEN 9.30 - 5 MON - FRI, 9.30
- 5 SAT OR BY APPOINTMENT.
The complete wedding shop. Forget-Me-Not Designer Bridalwear operates
from a dedicated Wedding Centre where, as well as being able to choose from
a stunning collection of both new and immaculate once-worn wedding dresses
(mainly to buy but also to hire) there are also some designers' samples at very
affordable prices. There is a gent's formal wear hire service with a massive selection of frock coats in brocade velvets and silks, highland wear and a choice of
100 waistcoats; wedding florist specialist, photographic studio, on-site beauti-
cian, wedding stationers and wedding cake business. You can find tiaras, balloons and a bridal register of caterers, musicians, pipers, vocalists and video specialists. There are more than 200 dresses on display at any one time, with 600
more on computer, many of which are in larger sizes. Designers on sale here
include Catherine Rayner, Tracy Connop, Jasper Conran, Neil Cunningham,
Beverley Summers, Donna Salado, David Fielden, Ritva Westinius, Philipa
Lepley, Ave Maria, Beverley Lister, Alfred Angelo, Pretty Maids, Ellis, Kelsey
Rose, Pronovias, Hilary Morgan, Mon Cheri, Ronald Joyce and Sassi Holford
among a host of about 30 top designers. If bridesmaids' dresses need sorting
out, too, there is a made-to-measure service with such leading firms as
Prettymades and Catherine Jane. Forget-Me-Not can also make bridesmaids
dresses themselves in a choice of over 100 silks and fabrics, provide accessories
including shoes and hats and even personalised wedding wines and champagne.
Permanent Discount Shop, Dress Agency and Hire Shop

GAMES CAROUSEL
129 REGENT STREET, LEAMINGTON SPA, WARWICKSHIRE CV32 4NX
☎ (01926) 335600. OPEN 10 - 5.30 MON - SAT.
Offer part-exchange deals and sells both new and used computer leisure and
games software. All are in their original boxes with the original manuals and
in good condition and savings of over half price are available. These include
PCs, Play Station, Dreamcast and Nintendo entertainment. *Permanent
Discount Outlet*

Live Well On Less Tips
Use old tights and stockings to make tiny pouches for fish bait. They help to
keep the bait on the hook.

HATTON COUNTRY WORLD

DARK LANE, HATTON, WARWICK, WARWICKSHIRE CV35 8XA

☎ (01926) 843411. OPEN 10 - 6 SEVEN DAYS A WEEK.

The biggest craft centre in the country, Hatton Country World is also host to three large factory shops: The Maid of China selling cut-price china and glass, Arkwright's Mill, a 5,000 sq ft discount fashion centre, and Mesdames Collection, a discount book and card shop. As well as this, there are a range of craft shops, candle shop, stencil shop, antiques centre, fragrance room, garden centre, garden pottery, farm shop, butcher's, sweets shop, rare breeds farm, pets corner, guinea pig village, restaurant, cafe and free parking. *Factory Shop*

INTO CLOTHING

144 THE PARADE, LEAMINGTON SPA, WARWICKSHIRE CB32 0AG

☎ (01926) 430407. OPEN 9 - 5 MON - SAT, AND BANK HOLIDAYS.

Sells ladies clothing, cotton knitwear, separates and jackets at factory direct prices, which can be as much as 70% off the normal retail prices. The shop is small but well stocked and organised to make the maximum use of the space. Most of the stock is leading chainstore makes and includes dresses, jackets, rainwear, shoes, underwear, tights, suits, blouses, sweaters, nightwear, leggings, trousers, jeans, anoraks, with dressing gowns and eveningwear at Christmas only. There is another branch at Hinckley, Leicestershire. *Permanent Discount Outlet*

Live Well On Less Tips

HI-LIFE DINERS CLUB THE EPICENTRE, 5 HARDHORN ROAD, POULTON, NEAR BLACKPOOL, LANCASHIRE FY6 7SR. (01253) 884477. 24-HOUR MEMBERSHIP LINE.

The Hi-Life Club has been operating for more than 15 years in the north-west of England and is the biggest diners' club of its type, with more than 25,000 members. Members can choose from among 600 Lancashire restaurants, most of which now give two meals for the price of one. Restaurants included vary and include Nico Central, Gary Rhodes & Co, Mash & Air, Cafe Rouge, Henry's table, Beefeaters, Brewers' Fare, Millers' Kitchen, TGI Fridays etc. Every cuisine is covered form French to Indian, English or Mexican. The club literature says that most people save £100s or even £1000s per year and there's a no-quibbble money back guarantee if you're not delighted with your membership. Membership costs £31.95 per annum.

Live Well On Less Tips

HENRY BUTCHER INTERNATIONAL LTD BROWNLOW HOUSE, 50-51 HIGH HOLBORN, LONDON WC1V 6EG. 0171-405 8411. OPEN 9 - 5 MON - FRI.

Established more than 100 years ago, Henry Butcher International are global auctioneers and valuers, dealing with all types of industrial plant, machinery and equipment. They have a mailing list of some 30,000 names under the categories of equipment which they are looking for from heavy engineering to office furniture and computers. They sell anything from boardroom tables to typists' chairs, computers to manufacturing plants. Put your name on their mailing list for a colour flysheet of sales which you might be interested in.

LILLIPUT

63 AVON CRESCENT, STRATFORD-UPON-AVON, WARWICKSHIRE CV37 7EZ

☎ (01789) 267991. OPEN 10 - 4.30 TUE - SAT.

Children's toys, secondhand clothes, and secondhand baby equipment from 0 - 10 years as well as some maternity wear. Most of the children's merchandise is baby and toddler equipment and toys, though there is some end of line branded clothing and equipment, including quality secondhand and shop seconds. Beebop and Chicco equipment stocked with some slight seconds at discount. Short term hire is available on most equipment. *Dress Agencies, Hire Shop*

LITTLEWOODS
CATALOGUE DISCOUNT STORE

14-16 NORTH STREET, RUGBY, WARWICKSHIRE CV21 2AF

☎ (01788) 565116. OPEN 9.30 - 5.30 MON - WED, 9 - 5.30 THUR - SAT.

Littlewoods clearance shops offering up to 50% off the catalogue price for clothing and between 50% and 60% off for electrical goods. Stock changes constantly and varies from day to day but can include well-known brand names such as Berlei and Gossard lingerie, Vivienne Westwood, Pamplemousse leisure wear, Nike and Adidas sports shoes, Workers For Freedom, and Timberland and Caterpillar footwear. Stock depends on the size and location of the shop, so larger shops will get the longer discontinued runs and smaller shops over-runs with only a small amount of colour and size variations left. Littlewoods also run a mobile shop which operates in cities where they don't have a sale shop. For details of further venues for the sales, which usually take place once a month, contact Melanie Lamb, c/o Crosby DC, Kershaw Avenue, Endbutt Lane, Crosby, Merseyside L70 1AH. *Permanent Discount Outlet*

MAID OF CHINA

HATTON COUNTRY WORLD, DARK LANE, HATTON, NEAR WARWICK, WARWICKSHIRE CV35 8XA

☎ (01926) 842789. OPEN 9 - 5 SEVEN DAYS A WEEK (NOT CHRISTMAS OR BOXING DAY).

Set in the centre of the shopping village and leisure complex, these rambling 19th century farm buildings are full of character, as well as great bargains in china and glassware from famous names. The 3,000 sq ft premises offer first-quality, select seconds and ends of lines at 30% or more off list price as well as a fabulous cookshop stuffed full of those hard-to-find gadgets you thought had disappeared years ago. Look out for bargains from Arthur Price International, Gleneagles Crystal, Hornsea, Royal Stafford, Henry Watson, Mondian, Poole Pottery, Cloverleaf, T&G Green, and many more. Hatton Country World is home to the biggest craft centre in the UK and provides plenty to amuse both adults and children, including more than 30 craft and discount shops, rare farm animals, pets' corner, large antiques' centre, cafe, bar and free car parking. *Factory Shop*

MATALAN

UNIT E, MAYBIRD CENTRE, BIRMINGHAM ROAD, STRATFORD-UPON-AVON, WARWICKSHIRE CV37 OHZ

☎ (01789) 262223. OPEN 10 - 8 MON - FRI, 10 - 5.30 SAT, 10 - 6 SUN.

Matalan is a fashion and homewares shop giving customers what they claim to be unbeatable value for money with huge savings on a wide range of products including high quality fashionable clothing for women, women and children at up to 50% off high street prices. Matalan is situated out of town and stores are open seven days a week all year round. *Permanent Discount Outlet*

MERCIA SAFETY

WARBORO FARM, HENLEY ROAD, NEAR WARWICK, WARWICKSHIRE CV38 8QX

☎ (01926) 411388.

Part of the Baby Equipment Hirers Association (BEHA), which has more than 100 members countrywide. A range of equipment can be hired from high chairs, cots and travel cots to baby car seats and buggies. Some members also hire out party equipment including child-sized tables and chairs. BEHA run an advice line which will try and answer any queries you have regarding hiring services for children. Phone the Babyline on 0831 310355. *Hire Shop*

Live Well On Less Tips

If you work and buy your lunch locally each day, take a pre-packed lunch with you instead as well as tea bags or juice and save money.

Live Well On Less Tips
REMARK 103 WALGRAVE, ORTON MALBORNE, PETERBOROUGH,
CAMBRIDGESHIRE, PE2 5NS. (01832) 274900. OPEN 9 - 5 MON - FRI.
25 TRESHAM ROAD, ORTON, SOUTHGATE, PETERBOROUGH PE2
6SG
(01733) 231639. OPEN 8 - 6 MON - FRI.
Acts on behalf of liquidators, selling repossessed telephone systems and fax
machines. Faxes have been sold for about £200, telephones for £8, but the
normal price is at least half the as-new price. Can install equipment, voice
and data networks, arrange service and supply maintenance.

MESDAME'S COLLECTION
HATTON COUNTRY WORLD, DARK LANE, HATTON, NEAR WARWICK,
WARWICKSHIRE CV35 8XA
☎ (01926) 842021. OPEN 10 - 5.30 SEVEN DAYS A WEEK (NOT
CHRISTMAS DAY AND BOXING DAY).
A large range of discount books (many at less than half price) are tucked discreetly into this converted barn cheek by jowl with a full range of picture
framing services and supplies and a huge selection of greetings cards. Hatton
Country World is home to the biggest Craft Centre in the UK and provides
plenty to amuse both adults and children alike, including more than 30 craft
and discount shops, rare farm animals, pets' corner, large antiques' centre,
cafe/bar and free car parking. *Factory Shop*

MILL OUTLETS LTD
33 SOUTHAM ROAD, DUNCHURCH, RUGBY,
WARWICKSHIRE CV22 6NL
☎ (01788) 816008. OPEN 9 - 5 MON - SAT, 10 - 4 SUN.
3 ALBERT STREET, RUGBY, WARWICKSHIRE CV21 2R7
☎ (01788) 542947. OPEN 9 - 5 MON - SAT.
2 CANNON PARK CENTRE, CANLEY, COVENTRY CV4 7AY
☎ (01203) 418441. OPEN 9 - 5.30 MON - WED, 9 - 6 THUR,
FRI, 8.30 - 5 SAT, 10 - 4 SUN.
14 FAIRFAX STREET, COVENTRY CV1 5RY
☎ (01203) 223508. OPEN 9 - 5.30 MON - SAT.
134 THE PARADE, LEAMINGTON SPA, WARWICKSHIRE CV32 4AG
☎ (01926) 470015. OPEN 9 - 5.30 MON - SAT.
Specialises in curtains, net curtains, bedding, bed linens, towels, kitchen textiles
and other household textiles. They also offer ranges of hand knitting yarns,
men's and ladies socks, hosiery and underwear. Merchandise comes direct from
the manufacturers, often made up of clearance stock or chainstore overmakes
and seconds. Prices are very competitive with savings of up to 50% and more
off manufacturer's recommended prices. *Permanent Discount Outlet*

NIPPERS

FIELDS FARM, MARTON, NEAR RUGBY, WARWICKSHIRE CV23 9RS
☎ (01926) 633100. FAX ☎ (01926) 633007. OPENING HOURS VARY
SO PHONE FIRST.

Nippers, the nursery equipment and toy specialists, operate from previously redundant buildings in rural areas around the country. They offer easy parking, no queues and personal service. This is on top of competitive prices on prams, cots, pushchairs, car seats, outdoor play equipment and toys, some of which are new, some seconds or secondhand and some ends of lines. Prices are low because they avoid the high overheads of traditional retail outlets and also because the successful growth of a number of branches means they can now buy in bulk and negotiate good deals. Customers are invited to try out the merchandise while the children look at the animals, mostly sheep, chicken and pigs. Familiar brand names are on sale at all the branches, including Mamas & Papas, Britax, Maclaren and Bebe Confort, plus Fisher-Price and Little Tikes. You can try out the car seats in your car and there is usually a pram/pushchair repair service on site. *Permanent Discount Outlet*

RENAHALL LTD

61 LIMETREE AVENUE, BILTON, RUGBY, WARWICKSHIRE CV22 7QT
☎ (01788) 811454. MAIL ORDER ONLY.

Vitamins and similar products such as evening primrose oil, fish oil are sold by mail order only (post paid) usually within 48 hours of receipt of order. Vitamin C is sold in powder form (also as Calcium Ascorbate) to avoid unwanted fillers and binders (and the cost of tabletting) in packs of 240 grams. It is pure ascorbic acid and costs £9.25 for 240 grams compared with £7 for 60 grams at a high street chain chemist. Vitamin E is sold in both powder and capsule form, from d-alpha tocopheryl ex soya beans and other vegetable oils. Send for price list by return. Telephone orders are accepted from established customers. *Permanent Discount Outlet*

ROBERTSON & PARTNERS LTD

JODRELL STREET, NUNEATON, WARWICKSHIRE CV11 5EH
☎ (01203) 384110. FAX 01203 642403. OPEN 9 - 5 MON - FRI, 9 - 1 SAT.

Reclaimed materials from demolition sites, including doors, chimney pots, staircase parts, baths, reclaimed timber, reinforced steel joists, roof tiles and slates. *Architectural Salvage*

Live Well On Less Tips

Save aquarium water to feed your plants with. It is tepid and contains algae and other organic waste which is nourishing for both house and garden plants.

SCOOPS

567-569 BEARWOOD ROAD, SMETHWICK, WARLEY,
WARWICKSHIRE BA1 1DA

☎ (0121) 434 3086. OPEN 9 - 5.30 MON - SAT.

Grattan catalogue shop. There is a selection of items from those featured in the catalogue, which can consist of anything from children's clothes and toys to bedding, electrical equipment and nursery accessories. Each shop sells a slightly different range, so always ring first to check they stock what you want. All items are discounted by up to 50%. *Permanent Discount Outlet*

THE CUCKOO'S NEST

70 SMITH STREET, WARWICK, WARWICKSHIRE CV34 4HU

☎ (01926) 496804. OPEN 9.30 - 5 TUE - SAT.

Wide range of ladies clothing from Marks & Spencer to Margaret Howell, Workers for Freedom and John Rocha. Prices equally variable, anything from £8 to £250. For example, a Margaret Howell suit retailing at £600 was sold for £210. Limited stock of evening wear, although there are usually some special occasion outfits including once-worn mother-of-the-bride outfits. A lot of casual wear, suits and jackets, as well as classical tailored wear. The varied contents of the shop is reflected in the rapid turnover and age range - between 14 and 95 - of those who visit. No garment is more than two years old. *Dress Agency*

THE FACTORY SHOP

CV CLOTHING LADIES AND CHILDRENSWEAR, BOSWORTH ROAD,
BARLESTONE, NEAR NUNEATON, WARWICKSHIRE CV13 OEL

☎ (01455) 290685. OPEN 10 - 4 MON - SAT.

Part of the Coats Viyella group, which makes quality clothing for many of the major high street storres, overstocks and clearance lines are sold through more than 30 of the group's factory shops. Many of you will recognise the garments on sale, despite the lack of well-known labels. Ladieswear includes dresses, blouses, jumpers, cardigans, trousers, nightwear, underwear, lingerie, hosiery, coats and swimwear. Menswear includes trousers, belts, shirts, ties, pullovers, cardigans, T-shirts, underwear, nightwear, hosiery and jackets. Childrenswear includes jackets, trousers, T-shirts, underwear, hosiery, jumpers and babywear. There are regular deliveries to constantly update the range. *Factory Shop*

THE ORIGINAL CHOICE LTD

ANTIQUE FIREPLACE WORKSHOP, CASTLE FARM, GAYDON,
WARWICKSHIRE CV35 OHE

☎ (01926) 641411. OPEN BY APPOINTMENT ONLY.

Specialist in restoring and supplying top quality Edwardian and Victorian fireplaces and stained glass windows from 1750 to 1930. *Architectural Salvage*

Live Well On Less Tips
LLOYDS INTERNATIONAL AUCTION GALLERIES 118 PUTNEY
BRIDGE ROAD, LONDON SW15 2NQ. 0181-788 7777. TIMES VARY,
PHONE FIRST.
Auctioneers which specialise in Victorian and Edwardian furniture and carpets
as well as china, glass, art and collectables, also offer unclaimed goods from
the Customs department and lost property which are sold here by auction.
Usually new goods range from jewellery to clothing, lap tops, cameras, CDs,
videos, cups and saucers and double beds. Auctions are usually held monthly
on a Wednesday and there is a minimum of 500 lots. Viewing is from 10.30am
to 6pm and sales start at 6.30pm. No reserves are allowed and all lots must
be sold on the day. Telephone beforehand to find out date of next auction.

TOP DRAWER AS NEW

19-20 WOOD STREET, STRATFORD-UPON-AVON,
WARWICKSHIRE CV37 6JF
☎ (01789) 269766. OPEN 10 - 4.30 TUE - SAT
Clothes and acccesories for the discerning woman. Top Drawer, established in
1978, has hundreds of gently 1-12 used top quality and designer ladies wear.
Proprietor Joanne Hastie carefully selects her collection which boasts amongst
others, labels such Valentino and Escada. It's an adventure in itself setting out
ot find this pretty shop with its Tudor beams and friendly atmosphere, discreetly tucked away above Bottoms Up. *Dress Agency*

TOP SERVICE

CHURCH END HOUSE, WHICHFORD, SHIPSTON ON STOUR,
WARWICKSHIRE CV36 5PG
☎ (01608) 684829. OPEN 9 - 5 MON - FRI.
An extensive interiors showroom supplying many manufacturers and designers products at very competitive prices. The larger the order, the bigger the discount. Customers order through pattern books. *Permanent Discount
Outlet*

YEWS FARM BABY EQUIPMENT

RUGBY ROAD, PAILTON, RUGBY, WARWICKSHIRE CV23 OQH
☎ (01788) 832219. OPEN 9 - 5.30 MON - SAT, CLOSED WED.
Sells a wide variety of equipment for babies' needs including all leading makes
of pushchairs, prams, cots, cot beds, and toys, as well as new clothes, all at
much discounted prices. They also carry out repairs to most makes of buggies.
The shop is situated in a small village outside Rugby on a deer farm, where
you can also buy country fresh produce such as duck's eggs. There is car parking, a cafe, public toilets and baby changing facilities. *Permanent Discount
Outlet*

West Midlands

WOMENSWEAR ONLY   ⑂ Bags By Anne Marie Direct, *Birmingham.*   Cambio, *Stourbridge.*
Deja Vu, *Sutton Coldfield.*   Dress Exchange, *Birmingham.*   Eliza's Dress Agency, *Kingswimford.*
Gowns Galore, *Solihull.*   PJ Gold Depot Ltd, *Birmingham.*   The Changing Room At Four Oaks,
Sutton Coldfield.   The Dress Exchange, *Birmingham.*   V & F Parker Ltd, *Birmingham.*
MENSWEAR ONLY   ⑂ Bairdwear Menswear, *Brierley Hill.*
Slaters Menswear, *Birmingham.*

WOMENSWEAR & MENSWEAR   ⑂ ⑂ Catalogue Bargain Shop, *Bilston.*
Catalogue Bargain Shop, *Stourbridge.*   Catalogue Bargain Shop, *Sutton Coldfield.*
Catalogue Bargain Shop, *Walsall.*   Encore, *Birmingham.*   International Stock Ltd, *Birmingham.*
Littlewoods Catalogue Discount Store, *Birmingham.*   M Latif & Sons, *Birmingham.*
Matalan, *Walsall.*   Matalan, *Coventry.*   Matalan, *Oldbury.*   Matalan, Stechford, *Birmingham.*
Next To Nothing, *Birmingham.*   Scoops, *Brownhills.*   Stage 2, *Coventry.*   TK Maxx, *Dudley.*

CHILDREN   ⑆ Catalogue Bargain Shop, *Bilston.*   Catalogue Bargain Shop, *Stourbridge.*
Catalogue Bargain Shop, *Sutton Coldfield.*   Catalogue Bargain Shop, *Walsall.*
Hawk Factory Cycle Stores, *Heath.*   International Stock Ltd, *Birmingham.*
Littlewoods Catalogue Discount Store, *Birmingham.*   M Latif & Sons, *Birmingham.*
Matalan, *Walsall.*   Matalan, *Coventry.*   Matalan, *Oldbury.*   Matalan, Stechford, *Birmingham.*
Minor Matters, *Birmingham.*   Next To Nothing, *Birmingham.*   Nursery To Leisure, *West Bromwich.*
Scoops, *Brownhills.*   Stage 2, *Coventry.*   TK Maxx, *Dudley.*

HOUSEHOLD AND GIFTWARE   ⌂ Catalogue Bargain Shop, *Bilston.*
Catalogue Bargain Shop, *Stourbridge.*   Catalogue Bargain Shop, *Sutton Coldfield.*
Catalogue Bargain Shop, *Walsall.*   H L Linen Bazaars, *Oldbury.*   H L Linen Bazaars, *Cradley Heath.*
H L Linen Bazaars, *Dudley.*   International Stock Ltd, *Birmingham.*   M Latif & Sons, *Birmingham.*
Matalan, *Walsall.*   Matalan, *Coventry.*   Matalan, *Oldbury.*   Matalan, Stechford, *Birmingham.*
Royal Brierley Crystal, *Brierley Hill.*   Royal Worcester & Spode Factory Shop, *Brierley Hill.*
Scoops, *Brownhills.*   Spoils, *Dudley.*   Stuart Crystal, *Stourbridge.*   TK Maxx, *Dudley.*
Whitehouse Cox Factory Shop, *Walsall.*

ELECTRICAL EQUIPMENT   ⌁ Borshch Electric, *Birmingham.*
Catalogue Bargain Shop, *Bilston.*   Catalogue Bargain Shop, *Stourbridge.*
Catalogue Bargain Shop, *Sutton Coldfield.*   Catalogue Bargain Shop, *Walsall.*
International Stock Ltd, *Birmingham.*   Littlewoods Catalogue Discount Store, *Birmingham.*
Scoops, *Brownhills.*   Stage 2, *Coventry.*   The Moulinex Swan Factory Shop, *Birmingham.*

DIY/RENOVATION   ⚒ BMJ Power, *Birmingham.*
Conservation Building Products Ltd, *Warley.*   International Stock Ltd, *Birmingham.*
Tile Clearing House, *Birmingham.*
ARCHITECTURAL SALVAGE   ⚒ Conservation Building Products Ltd, *Warley.*

FURNITURE/SOFT FURNISHINGS   ▦ Cane And Wicker Factory Shop, *Walsall.*
H L Linen Bazaars, *Oldbury.*   International Stock Ltd, *Birmingham.*
Magnet Ltd Clearance Centre, *Birmingham.*   RMJ (Alloys) Ltd, *Coventry.*
FOOD AND LEISURE   ▥ Bookends, *Birmingham.*

SPORTSWEAR AND EQUIPMENT   ⚔ E Walters Factory Shop, *Rowley Regis.*
Harold Bird & Son, *Walsall.*   Hawk Factory Cycle Stores, *Cradley Heath.*

BAGS BY ANNE MARIE DIRECT

133 HIGH STREET, ERDINGTON, BIRMINGHAM,
WEST MIDLANDS, B23 6FA

☎ (0121) 3377 6916. OPEN 10 - 4 SEVEN DAYS A WEEK.

Bags by Anne Marie started as small high street shops around the Midlands
with keenly priced branded lines. This is a discount showroom-type outlet situated next door to Littlewoods. They stock big brand names like Elle,
Morgan, Kangol at very good prices, as well as bags featuring characters like
Wallace and Gromit and luggage. *Permanent Discount Outlet*

BAIRDWEAR MENSWEAR

LEVEL STREET, BRIERLEY HILL, WEST MIDLANDS DY5 1UB

☎ (01384) 77102. OPEN 10 - 4 MON - SAT.

HALESFIELD 13, TELFORD, SHROPSHIRE TF7 4PL

☎ (01952) 683729. OPEN 9 - 4.30 MON - FRI, 9 - 3 SAT, SUN.

Manufactures men's casualwear and separates for a well-known high street
chain store, the factory shops sell seconds and overmakes at as little as one-
third of their normal retail price. About 60% of the merchandise sold here is
made by the factory, with a further 40% manufactured within the company.
Factory Shop

BMJ POWER

LONG ACRE, BIRMINGHAM, WEST MIDLANDS B7 5SL

☎ (0121) 327 3411. OPEN 8 - 5.30 MON - FRI, 8.30 - 5 SAT.

Reconditioned tools and accessories from the famous Black & Decker range,
as well as other power tools from well-known brands such as Makita, Flymo
and Kress, all with full manufacturer's warranty. This is essentially an after-
sales service with a retail outlet. Often, stock consists of goods returned from
the shops because of damaged packaging or are part of a line which is being
discontinued. Lots of seasonal special offers. There are more than three dozen
BMJ service outlets countrywide. Phone 0345 230230 and you can find out
where your nearest outlet is. *Factory Shop*

BOOKENDS

134 NEW STREET, BIRMINGHAM, WEST MIDLANDS B2 4QJ

☎ (0121) 643 8739. OPEN 9 - 5.30 MON - SAT, 11 - 4 SUN.

114-118 HIGH STREET, ERDINGTON, BIRMINGHAM B23 6RS

☎ (0121) 373 9111. OPEN 9 - 5.30 MON - SAT.

Secondhand and damaged books and publishers' returns, as well as new and
review copies, including recently published books, usually one-third off and
sometimes half price. *Secondhand Shop*

Live Well On Less Tips
BCP AIRPORT PARKING AND CHAUFFEUR-DRIVEN CARS
(01293) 594500. 7AM - 10.30 PM, 7 DAYS A WEEK.
BCP provides secure, value-for-money car parking at Gatwick, Heathrow, Manchester, Glasgow, and all other major UK airports, with prices from just £2.60 NET per day. For an extra £24.95, you can save time by being met at the airport terminal on your departure and return as part of BCP's Meet and Greet Parking service. Your car is then taken to the BCP secure car park nearby. Or you can pre-book a chauffeur-driven airport car to and from the airport. This service is ideal if you live within 30 miles of your departure airport, where the cost will be about £60 return. To book and save up to 20% on the gate price, phone the BCP reservations line above quoting reference 'GOOD.' BCP will confirm your booking by post with directions to your car park or details of the pick-up or meeting arrangements as appropriate.

BORSHCH ELECTRIC

NEPTUNE HOUSE, UPPER TRINITY STREET, BORDESLEY,
BIRMINGHAM, WEST MIDLANDS B9 4EG
☎ (0121) 773 6361/771 0453 FAX. OPEN 9 - 5.30 MON - SAT, 10 - 4 SUN.
Sells gas and electric items which include fridges, freezers, fridge/freezers, washing machines, microwaves, dishwashers, ovens, vacuum cleaners and a small selection of smaller electrical items for the kitchen such as toasters and kettles which are manufacturers' new graded returns from this 10,000 sq ft showroom. These are not A grade and therefore cannot be sold in high street stores. All are guaranteed for parts and service. Examples of prices include fridges, from £99; cookers, from £159; microwaves from £69; washing machines from £169; fridge/freezers from £139; gas fires, £159; tumble dryers, from £99; built-in ovens, £109. Manufacturers on sale include Zanussi, Panasonic, Candy, Servis, Hotpoint, Bosch, Leisure, Canon, White Knight. Full delivery service is available, which is free to pensioners. *Permanent Discount Outlet*

CAMBIO

168A LOWER HIGH STREET, STOURBRIDGE, WEST MIDLANDS
DY8 1TT
☎ (01384) 371600. OPEN 9.30 - 5 MON - SAT.
Nearly-new designer wear, as well as some new clothes which are new ends of lines from boutiques and samples, all at greatly reduced prices. Designers for the brand new range include Rifat Ozbek, Louis Feraud, Tomasz Starzewski and Betty Barclay. Evening wear is sold all year round in sizes ranging from 8-16. Evening wear tops cost from £65, long dresses from £95, suits, £175 which originally cost £600; Escada blouses, £45 which were £300 new. There is also a hire service for hats from £15 per day. *Dress Agency and Hire Shop*

CANE AND WICKER FACTORY SHOP

TAME BRIDGE, WEST BROMWICH ROAD, WALSALL, WEST MIDLANDS
☎ (01922) 636364. OPEN 10 - 5 MON - SAT, 11 - 4 SUN.

The largest cane and wicker furniture showroom in the country, with up to 80 suites on display at any one time. This importer and wholesaler runs two factory shops (here and a smaller outlet in Shrewsbury) to clear stock which has been returned by retailers. There may be nothing wrong with the furniture other than a change of mind on the part of the original customer, but the furniture has probably been unwrapped, delivered and handled so cannot be sold to other retailers to sell on to full-price customers. The furniture comes in part-assembled and is finished, stuffed and upholstered on site. It comes in various finishes including light and dark antique, honey, mahogany and walnut. There is also a Mexican pine furniture range and fabric for curtains (though because the fabric is back coated for fire retardancy, it is very heavy). The cheapest cane suites cost from £150, the most expensive, £2,500. This represents a saving of about 15% - 20% on normal retail prices. There is immediate delivery for furniture in stock; orders will be fulfilled within about one week. *Factory Shop*

CATALOGUE BARGAIN SHOP

95 CHURCH STREET, BILSTON, WEST MIDLANDS WV14 OBJ
☎ (01902) 353624. OPEN 9 - 5.30 MON - SAT, 9.30 - 3.30 SUN.
78 HIGH STREET, STOURBRIDGE, WEST MIDLANDS DY8 1DX
☎ (01384) 374544. OPEN 9 - 5.30 MON - SAT, 10.30 - 4.30 SUN.
182 THE PARADE, SUTTON COLDFIELD, WEST MIDLANDS B72 1PA
☎ (0121) 321 3889. OPEN 9 - 5.30 MON - SAT, 11 - 5 SUN.
17 BRADFORD STREET, WALSALL, WEST MIDLANDS WS1 1PB
☎ (01922) 722286. OPEN 9 - 5.30 MON - SAT, 10.30 - 4.30 SUN.

Catalogue Bargain Shop is a growing national chain of stores which obtains the majority of its goods from mail order giants Great Universal and Kays, and offers a range of clothing for all the family, a wide selection of shoes, bed linen, household goods, electrical equipment and hundreds of other catalogue items at very competitive prices. The merchandise consists of ends of ranges and previous season's stock for which there is no longer storage space when the catalogues change. *Permanent Discount Outlet*

CONSERVATION BUILDING PRODUCTS LTD

FORGE WORKS, FORGE LANE, CRADLEY HEATH, WARLEY, WEST MIDLANDS B64 5AL
☎ (01384) 564219. 8 - 4 MON - FRI, 8 - 12 SAT.

Bricks, roof tiles, slates, quarry tiles, flooring beams, decorative ironwork, staircase parts, complete oak-framed buildings, garden statuary and interesting artefacts. *Architectural Salvage*

Live Well On Less Tips
Six or seven times a year, pull your fridge away from the wall, unplug it and
vacuum or brush off the coils at the back. The dust and dirt that collect there
seriously reduce its operating efficiency, thus costing you more.

DEJA VU

5 BOLDMERE ROAD, SUTTON COLDFIELD, WEST MIDLANDS B73 5UY
☎ (0121) 321 3110. OPEN 10 - 5 MON - SAT, CLOSED WED.
Stock anything from Marks & Spencer to top designer labels, all at very reasonable prices. Names include Mondi, Escada, Windsmoor and Country
Casuals. All sizes from 10-22. Also offers ranges of new samples at discounts
of one third and has 150 pairs of good quality shoes, as well as belts, handbags, hats and costume jewellery. *Dress Agency*

DRESS EXCHANGE

1003 ALCESTER ROAD (ABOVE THREE COOKS), THE MAYPOLE,
BIRMINGHAM, WEST MIDLANDS B14 5JA
☎ (0121) 474 5707. OPEN 10 - 5 MON - SAT
Middle to up-market designer wear, with accessories to match, at prices rang-
ing from £10-£200. Designers range from Marks & Spencer upwards and
include MaxMara, Escada, Ghost, Jasper Conran, Moschino, Armani and
Valentino. Occasionally stocks wedding outfits, as well as seasonal event wear.
Casual wear is stocked. *Dress Agency*

E WALTERS FACTORY SHOP

42 HIGH STREET, BLACKHEATH, ROWLEY REGIS,
WEST MIDLANDS B65 0DR
☎ (0121) 559 0774. OPEN 9 - 5 MON - FRI, 9 - 4 SAT.
Europe's largest trouser manufacturer sells ends of lines, cancelled orders and
samples of jeans, trousers and shorts for all the family at factory direct prices.
Also available: ancillary lines of casual wear at bargain prices. *Factory Shop*

ELIZA'S DRESS AGENCY

18 PARK STREET, KINGSWIMFORD, WEST MIDLANDS
☎ (01384) 402638. OPEN 9.30 - 5 MON - WED, FRI, 9.30 - 1 THUR,
10 - 4.30 SAT.
Designer nearly-new clothes as well as high street names from Marks &
Spencer to Jean Muir, Versace, Condicci and Cara. Also evening wear, wedding outfits, shoes, handbags and jewellery. *Dress Agency*

ENCORE

48-52A ST MARY'S ROW, MOSELEY, BIRMINGHAM,
WEST MIDLANDS B13 8JG

☎ (0121) 442 4888. OPEN 9.30 - 5 MON - FRI, 9.30 - 4.45 SAT

Middle to up market designer wear and accessories for both men and women with formal and casual clothing for all occasions. Labels include Armani, Max Mara, Ferretti, Hugo Boss, Moschino, Calvin Klein, alongside High Street names like Mondi, Betty Barclay, Windsmoor, Principles and Next. New stock arrives daily. Prices range from £5 to £200. The shop welcomes customers wishing to sell their own quality clothing. *Dress Agency*

GOWNS GALORE

1 OLD WARWICK ROAD, HOCKLEY HEATH, SOLIHULL,
WEST MIDLANDS B94 6HH

☎ (01564) 783003. OPEN 9 - 5 MON - SAT, UNTIL 8 ON TUE.

Specialises in the hire of designer ball gowns, cocktail wear and accessories. A three-day hire, including alterations and VAT, costs from £39. *Hire Shop*

H L LINEN BAZAARS

CHURCHBRIDGE, OLDBURY, WEST MIDLANDS B69 2AS

☎ (0121) 541 1918. OPEN 9 - 5 MON - FRI, RING FOR SAT OPENING.

14 MARKET SQUARE, CRADLEY HEATH, WEST MIDLANDS B64 5HH

☎ (01384) 565548. OPEN 9 - 5.30 MON - SAT.

225 MARKET PLACE, DUDLEY, WEST MIDLANDS

☎ (01384) 239776. OPEN 9 - 5.30 MON - SAT.

The mail order catalogue of this company which sells bedlinen, duvets, towels and sheets is very busy and hides some of the gems which are on sale, ends of lines of which can be found in their warehouse outlets both here and in Liverpool and Staffordshire. Hunt carefully at these outlets and you will find many famous brand names such as Early's of Witney, Vantona and Slumberdown. Their warehouse sells ends of lines, slight seconds and bulk purchases of duvets, pillows, cotton sheets (usually hotel over-orders) at discounts of up to 50%. *Permanent Discount Outlet*

HAROLD BIRD & SON

NORTHGATE, ALDRIDGE, WALSALL, WEST MIDLANDS WS9 8UB

☎ (01922) 451444. OPEN 8 - 5 MON - THUR, 8 - 3.45 FRI, 9 - 12 SAT.

Golf club manufacturers for some of the mail order catalogues such as Kays and Littlewoods, the brands sold in the factory shop here aren't well known but the prices are very keen indeed. They also sell waterproofs. Free parking. *Factory Shop*

HAWK FACTORY CYCLE STORES

FORGE LANE, CRADLEY HEATH, WEST MIDLANDS B64 5AL

☎ (01384) 636535. OPEN 9 - 6 MON - SAT, 9 - 4.30 SUN.

Sells all types of adult's and children's bikes direct to the public at factory prices. Children's trikes start at £26.99, adult mountain bikes at £99.99, normally £159.99. There are also clearance shops in South Yardley, Birmingham ☎ (0121 742 3332) and Nottingham ☎ (0115 958 5900). *Factory Shop*

INTERNATIONAL STOCK LTD

1-17 SILVER STREET, KINGS HEATH, BIRMINGHAM, WEST MIDLANDS B14 7QX

☎ (0121) 443 3232. OPEN 9 - 6 MON - SAT, CLOSED 1 ON WED.

95 - 100 REA STREET, DIGBETH, BIRMINGHAM B5 6HA

☎ (0121) 6223232. OPEN 9 - 5 MON - SAT, CLOSED 1 ON WED.

Bankrupt, fire and flood damaged articles from CDs and videos, household goods and clothes to diy tools and television sets, carpets and cokers. Two-storey warehouse with ever-changing stock. The upper floor is devoted to electrical goods, some marked down to 30% of their normal retail cost. The Digbeth branch sells bigger items such as kitchens, flooring, tiles, dining room and lounge furniture, central heating radiators and clothing for all the family, at wholesale or even below manufacturers' cost price. Top brand name kitrchens, when in stock, are discounted by 75%. *Permanent Discount Outlet*

LITTLEWOODS CATALOGUE DISCOUNT STORE

299-303 COVENTRY ROAD, BIRMINGHAM, WEST MIDLANDS B10 0RA

☎ (0121) 772 1637. OPEN 9.30 - 5.30 MON - SAT, 11 - 4 SUN.

236 HAWTHORN ROAD, KINGSTANDING, BIRMINGHAM, WEST MIDLANDS B44 8PP

☎ (0121) 373 1276. OPEN 9.15 - 5.30 MON - SAT.

Littlewoods clearance shops offering up to 50% off the catalogue price for clothing and between 50% and 60% off for electrical goods. Stock changes constantly and varies from day to day but can include well-known brand names such as Berlei and Gossard lingerie, Vivienne Westwood, Pamplemousse leisure wear, Nike and Adidas sports shoes, Workers For Freedom, and Timberland and Caterpillar footwear. Stock depends on the size and location of the shop, so larger shops will get the longer discontinued runs and smaller shops over-runs with only a small amount of colour and size variations left. Littlewoods also run a mobile shop which operates in cities where they don't have a sale shop. For details of further venues for the sales, which usually take place once a month, contact Melanie Lamb, c/o Crosby DC, Kershaw Avenue, Endbutt Lane, Crosby, Merseyside L70 1AH. *Permanent Discount Outlet*

Live Well On Less Tips

If you have an electric cooker, turn the ring off a couple of minutes before
the meal is cooked. The heating element stays hot for at least that long after
it has been turned off and over a year you will save money.

M LATIF & SONS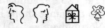

NEW CANAL STREET, DIGBETH, BIRMINGHAM,
WEST MIDLANDS B5 5PL

☎ (0121) 643 2822. OPEN 9.30 - 5.30 MON - SAT, 8 ON THUR, 10 - 2.30
SUN.

Household and electrical goods, bedding, linens, ready-made curtains, clothes
for all the family, pictures, garden equipment, toys, gifts and silk flowers,
which are ex-catalogue and department store seconds from shops such as
Marks & Spencer. *Permanent Discount Outlet*

MAGNET LTD CLEARANCE CENTRE

CHESTON ROAD, ASTON, BIRMINGHAM, WEST MIDLANDS B7 5EL

☎ (0121) 327 3201. OPEN 8 - 5 MON - FRI, 9 - 1 SAT.

With more than 200 branches countrywide, when Magnet Kitchens discon-
tinue one of their ranges, there are always some shops with spare stock they
can no longer sell. This applies to equipment such as ovens, hob, hoods, washing machines, tumble dryers and fridges, too. When manufacturers upgrade
their ranges, Magnet customers don't want to buy the old model currently in
situ in the showroom. Old stock is sent to two sites in Aston, Birmingham and
the head office factory site in Keighley, West Yorkshire. Earlier this year, customers could choose entire kitchens from two discontinued ranges -
Churchwood and Traditional White - and units and smaller entire kitchens
from three other ranges. Minster, a light oak kitchen, and Traditional Oak, a
limed oak range are due in the near future. Prices on average are about 75%
less than the high street price - they recently kitted out a large kitchen, including all appliances, for £2,5000. Equipment is all top brands - Neff and Smeg
ovens, as well as Magnet's own brand range which is made by Whirlpool.
Some is ex-display, some discontinued models, some just overstock which is
still boxed. A brand new Smeg stainless steel fridge/freezer which would normally cost £900 was sold recently for £250 while ovens cost from £125-£500.
There are also wood and PVC glazed window frames, conservatory panels
(from £25 for panels which normally cost £100), patio doors and French
doors. Magnet is about to standardise all its ranges from three carcass sizes so
there will be lots of discontinued stock due in to the clearance centres.
Factory Shop

MATALAN

UNIT 9, BROADWAY RETAIL PARK, BESCOT CRESCENT, WALSALL, WEST MIDLANDS WS1 4DK

☎ (01922) 615188. TELEPHONE FOR OPENING HOURS.

GALLAGHER RETAIL PARK, STONEY STANTON ROAD, COVENTRY, WEST MIDLANDS CV6 5QQ.

☎ (01203) 637320. TELEPHONE FOR OPENING HOURS.

PORTWAY ROAD, PORTWAY GREEN, OLDBURY, WEST MIDLANDS B69 2BZ

☎ (0121) 544 4899. OPEN 10 - 8 MON - FRI, 9 - 6 SAT, 11 - 5 SUN.

UNIT A, STECHFORD RETAIL PARK, STATION ROAD, STECHFORD, BIRMINGHAM B33 8BB

☎ (0121) 789 5950. PHONE FOR OPENING TIMES.

Matalan is a fashion and homewares shop giving customers what they claim to be unbeatable value for money with huge savings on a wide range of products including high quality fashionable clothing for women, women and children at up to 50% off high street prices. Matalan is situated out of town and stores are open seven days a week all year round. *Permanent Discount Outlet*

MINOR MATTERS

54 ST MARY'S ROW, MOSELEY, BIRMINGHAM, WEST MIDLANDS B13 8JG

☎ (0121) 449 3553. OPEN 9.30 - 5 MON - SAT.

Good quality childrenswear from birth to pre-teens. Labels include Oilily and Osh Kosh as well as high street names, equipment such as prams, cots and pushchairs, books, toys, games and maternity wear. This shop is next door to Encore ladies and men's dress agency. *Dress Agency*

NEXT TO NOTHING

104 CORPORATION STREET, BIRMINGHAM, WEST MIDLANDS

☎ (0121) 233 0022. OPEN 10 - 5.30 MON - FR, 11 - 5 SAT.

Sells perfect surplus stock from Next stores and the Next Directory catalogue - from belts, jewellery and underwear to day and evening wear - at discounts of 50% or more. The ranges are usually last season's and overruns but there is the odd current item if you look carefully. Stock, which consists of men's, women's and children's clothing, some homeware and shoes, is replenished three times a week and there is plenty of it. *Permanent Discount Outlet*

Live Well On Less Tips
Buy heating oil in the summer when it is cheaper.

NURSERY TO LEISURE

35 SANDWELL CENTRE, QUEENS SQUARE, WEST BROMWICH, WEST MIDLANDS B70 7NG

☎ (0121) 525 5162. OPEN 9 - 5.30 MON - SAT, CLOSED WED.

Has a shop and a mail order arm called prams direct. The shop sells reconditioned prams and pushchairs, as well as ends of lines which are particularly prevalent around the end of October after the nursery trade fair when fabric designs change. It also sells baby monitors, Zorbit baby cot linen; and cots and mattresses. *Permanent Discount Outlet*

PJ GOLD DEPOT LTD

37 VYSE STREET, BIRMINGHAM, WEST MIDLANDS B18 6JY

☎ (0121) 554 6165/2438 FAX. OPEN 9 - 4 MON - SAT, SUN BEFORE CHRISTMAS ONLY.

Manufacturers of wedding rings, engagement rings, bracelets and necklets, which are sold here at savings of about 30% compared with high street prices. Gold jewellery can be made to customer's own design with any gem stones. Also sells glassware and pewter items. *Permanent Discount Outlet*

RMJ (ALLOYS) LTD

46-48 BAYTON ROAD, COVENTRY, WEST MIDLANDS CV7 9EJ

☎ (01203) 367508. OPEN 9 - 4.30 MON - THUR, 9 - 3.30 FRI.

Made to measure staircases in metal or wood for indoors or outdoors - spiral, straight or fire escapes - at factory prices. *Factory Shop*

ROYAL BRIERLEY CRYSTAL

MOOR STREET, OFF NORTH STREET, BRIERLEY HILL, WEST MIDLANDS DY5 3SJ

☎ (01384) 573580. OPEN 9 - 5 MON - SAT, 10 - 4 SUN.

Sells seconds of Royal Brierley crystal at 30%-50% off retail price, with two special sales. Also Royal Worcester porcelain available at seconds prices. *Factory Shop*

ROYAL WORCESTER & SPODE FACTORY SHOP

ROYAL BRIERLEY CRYSTAL, NORTH STREET, BRIERLEY HILL, WEST MIDLANDS DY5 3SJ

☎ (01384) 573580. OPEN 9 - 5 MON - SAT, 10 - 4 SUN.

Infinitesimally flawed porcelain and china seconds at 25% less than perfect prices. This outlet also sells Crummles, Country Artists, Clover Leaf, Lakeland Plaques, Fo-Frame, Leeds Display, Paw Prints and Collectable World Studios. There is a vast range with special offers throughout the year on anything from crystal decanters and bowls to figurines, cookware and dinner sets. Shipping arrangements worldwide can be organised. *Factory Shop*

SCOOPS

63 HIGH STREET, BROWNHILLS, WEST MIDLANDS WS8 6HH
☎ (01543) 372933. OPEN 9 - 5.30 MON - SAT.
Grattan catalogue shop. There is a selection of items from those featured in the catalogue, which can consist of anything from children's clothes and toys to bedding, electrical equipment and nursery accessories. Each shop sells a slightly different range, so always ring first to check they stock what you want. All items are discounted by up to 50%. *Permanent Discount Outlet*

SLATERS MENSWEAR

3 CANNON STREET, BIRMINGHAM, WEST MIDLANDS B2 5EP
☎ (0121) 633 3855. OPEN 8.30 - 5.30 MON - SAT, 7.30 ON THUR.
Full range of men's clothes from underwear and shoes to casualwear, suits and dresswear and including labels such as Odermark, Bulmer, Valentino, Charlie's Co, and Charlton Gray. Men's suits from £79. *Permanent Discount Outlet*

SPOILS

UNIT U56B/C, U57, PHASE V, MERRY HILL CENTRE, PEDMORE ROAD, BRIERLEY HILL, DUDLEY, WEST MIDLANDS DY5 1SR
☎ (01384) 76969. OPEN 10 - 8 MON - FRI, 9 ON THUR, 9 - 7 SAT, 11 - 5 SUN.
UNIT 41, WEST TERRACE, THE PALLASADES, BIRMINGHAM B2 4XD
☎ (0121) 633 8234. OPEN 9 - 5.30 MON - SAT, 11 - 5 SUN.
General domestic glassware, non-stick bakeware, kitchen gadgets (but no electricals), ceramic oven-to-tableware, textiles, cutting boards, aluminium non-stick cookware, bakeware, plastic kitchenware, plastic storage, woodware, coffee pots/makers, furniture, mirrors and picture frames. Rather than being discounted, all the merchandise is very competitively priced - in fact, the company carry out competitors' checks frequently in order to monitor pricing. With 38 branches, the company is able to buy in bulk and thus negotiate very good prices. *Permanent Discount Outlet*

STAGE 2

AUSTIN DRIVE, COURTHOUSE GREEN, COVENTRY, WEST MIDLANDS CB6 7NS
☎ (01203) 681520. OPEN 10 - 8 MON - FRI, 9 - 6 SAT, 11 - 5 SUN.
Sells discontinued lines from Freeman's catalogues. The full range is carried, but stock depends on what has not been sold at full price from the catalogue itself, or has been returned or the packaging is damaged or soiled. Clothing discounts range from about 50% - 65%. There are also household items and electrical equipment. *Permanent Discount Outlet*

STUART CRYSTAL

RED HOUSE GLASSWORKS, WORDSLEY, STOURBRIDGE, WEST
MIDLANDS DY8 4AA

☎ (01384) 261777. OPEN 9 - 5 MON - SAT, BANK HOLS, 10 - 4 SUN.

Seconds of Stuart Crystal at about 30% discount. The selection includes wine glasses, flower holders, perfume holders, everyday tableware, salt and pepper sets, ice buckets, wine coolers, cutlery and candle lamps. Also seasonal special offers. First quality is also for sale at the appropriate price. *Factory Shop*

THE CHANGING ROOM AT FOUR OAKS

11 MERE GREEN RD, FOUR OAKS, SUTTON COLDFIELD, WEST
MIDLANDS B75 5BL

☎ (0121) 308 1848. OPEN 10 - 5 MON - SAT.

A very exclusive dress agency selling such labels as Versace, Moschino, Armani, Prada, George Rech, Louis Feraud and Christian Dior. The shop itself occupies two floors and is full to the brim with constantly changing stock including accessories such as jewellery, belts, shoes, hats and handbags. Also hats to hire. *Dress Agencies and Hire Shop*

THE DRESS EXCHANGE

1003 ALCESTER ROAD, MAYPOLE, BIRMINGHAM, WEST MIDLANDS B14
5JA

☎ (0121) 474 5707. OPEN 10 - 5 MON - SAT.

New and nearly-new from Marks & Spencer to Valentino. Labels on sale in the past have included Maxmara, Reldan, Jaeger, Betty Barclay, Yarell, Mani and Mondi. *Dress Agency*

THE MOULINEX SWAN FACTORY SHOP

35 ROCKY LANE, ASTON, BIRMINGHAM, WEST MIDLANDS B6 5RQ

☎ (0121) 380 0635. OPEN 10 - 4 MON - FRI, 9 - 1 SAT.

Moulinex, Swan and Krups kitchen appliances including microwaves, kettles, toasters, electric knives, irons, saucepans and frying pans. All are seconds or discontinued items with some slight imperfections but electrically sound. An Ovatio food processor which would cost £83.99 in department stores sells for £46.99 here; kettles, from £9.99; toasters from £7.99. All come with a one-year guarantee. *Factory Shop*

TILE CLEARING HOUSE, UNIT I

OLD WALLSHAL ROAD, GREAT BARR, BIRMINGHAM, WEST MIDLANDS
B42 1EA

☎ (0121) 357 1247. OPEN 8 - 6 MON - FRI, 9 - 6 SAT, 10 - 4 SUN.

Over 500 ranges of top quality ceramic wall and floor tiles permanently in stock, plus a comprehensive range of grouts, adhesives, tools and accessories to complete the job. Save up to 75% on manufacturers' recommended selling prices. *Permanent Discount Outlet*

TK MAXX

UPPER MALL, MERRYHILL SHOPPING CENTRE, DUDLEY, WEST MIDLANDS

☎ (01384) 77878. OPEN 10 - 8 MON - FRI, 10 - 9 THUR, 9 - 7 SAT, 11 - 5 SUN.

Based on an American concept, TK Maxx is situated in easily accessible, often centrally located stores and offers famous label goods with up to 60% savings off recommended retail prices. TK Maxx has fashion for the whole family - women's, men's and childrenswear - accessories, shoes, gifts, kitchenware and home goods. Everything in the store is branded with a choice of well-known high street names to designer labels, and while a small percentage might be clearly marked past season, the great majority of items in store are current season, current stock and still with phenomenal savings. There is a huge choice with 50,000 pieces in store and up to 10,000 new items arriving a week. The stores are simple and unfussy with wide aisles, shopping trolleys and baskets, and a spacious, functional feel to them but there are individual changing rooms, ramps for buggies and wheelchairs and plenty of staff on the shop floor. Every branch accepts all major credit and debit cards and has a liberal refund and return policy. *Permanent Discount Outlet*

V & F PARKER LTD

(ARDEN JEWELLERY), 51 VYSE STREET, OFF GREAT HAMPTON STREET, BIRMINGHAM, WEST MIDLANDS B18 6HS

☎ (0121) 554 3587. OPEN 9 - 4.30 MON - FRI, 9.30 - 2 SAT.

Part of Birmingham's famous jewellery quarter, V & F Parker are specialists in making rings, bangles and earrings. They are suppliers to jewellers, stocking more than 3,000 lines and hold stocks of major patterns enabling them to make or remake old rings. As manufacturers with a small showroom, personal customers obviously miss out on the middleman's cut. They have a small range of lockets and silver and gold chains which are not made on the premises. They also sell loose stones. They claim to be able to sell at best prices available *Factory Shop*

WHITEHOUSE COX FACTORY SHOP

MARSH STREET, OFF LITTLE STATION STREET, WALSALL, WEST MIDLANDS WS2 9LF

☎ (01922) 631259. OPEN 9.30 - 5 MON - THUR, 9.30 - 4 FRI.

Smart shop attached to this factory which has been making leather goods since 1875. There are leather handbags, belts and other fancy goods on sale here at very good prices. *Factory Shop*

Wiltshire

WOMENSWEAR ONLY   Designer Room, *Swindon*. Dorothy Perkins, *Swindon*.
Encore, *Warminster*. Jane Shilton, *Swindon*. Karalyne's, *Wilton*. Paco Life In Colour, *Swindon*.
Pied A Terre Sale Shop, *Swindon*. Sequel, *Bradford-On-Avon*. The Designer Store, *Swindon*.
The Shoestring, *Swindon*. Wear It Well, *Swindon*. Windsmoor, *Swindon*.

MENSWEAR ONLY   Tie Rack, *Swindon*. Tom Sayers Clothing Co, *Near Salisbury*.

WOMENSWEAR & MENSWEAR   Big L Factory Outlet, *Swindon*.
Burberrys Ltd, *Swindon*. Clarks Shoes, *Swindon*. Daks Simpson, *Churchward Village*.
Dents, *Warminster*. Ecco, *Swindon*. Georgina Von Etzdorf, *Near Salisbury*.
Hanro Of Switzerland, *Swindon*. Jaeger, *Swindon*. Joe Bloggs, *Swindon*. Matalan, *Swindon*.
McArthurglen Designer Outlet Great Western, *Swindon*. Mexx International, *Swindon*.
Next To Nothing, *Swindon*. Old Dairy Saddlery Ltd, *Swindon*. Principles, *Swindon*.
Second To None, *Chippenham*. Timberland, *Swindon*. TK Maxx, *Salisbury*.
Tog 24, *Swindon*. Triumph International Ltd, *Swindon*. United Footwear, *Swindon*. Viyella, *Swindon*.
Walton Clothing Co, *Marlborough*. Wilton Shopping Village, *Salisbury*.

CHILDREN   Clarks Shoes, *Swindon*. Ecco, *Swindon*. Joe Bloggs, *Swindon*.
Jokids Ltd, *Swindon*. Kids Play Factory, *Swindon*. Matalan, *Swindon*.
McArthurglen Designer Outlet Great Western, *Swindon*. Mexx International, *Swindon*.
Mums And Tots, *Near Salisbury*. Next To Nothing, *Swindon*. Nike Factory Store, *Swindon*.
Paco Life In Colour, *Swindon*. TK Maxx, *Salisbury*. Tog 24, *Swindon*. United Footwear, *Swindon*.

HOUSEHOLD AND GIFTWARE   Birthdays, *Swindon*. Clover Leaf, *Swindon*.
Le Creuset, *Swindon*. Matalan, *Swindon*. McArthurglen Designer Outlet Great Western, *Swindon*.
Oneida, *Swindon*. Ponden Mill Linens, *Near Salisbury*. Price's Candles, *Swindon*.
The Downton Trading Company, *Nr Salisbury*. The Factory Shop Ltd, *Trowbridge*.
The Factory Shop Ltd, *Warminster*. The Factory Shop Ltd, *Corsham*. TK Maxx, *Salisbury*.
United Footwear, *Swindon*. Villeroy & Boch (UK) Ltd, *Swindon*.

ELECTRICAL EQUIPMENT   McArthurglen Designer Outlet Great Western, *Swindon*.
Remington, *Swindon*. Thorn Outlet, *Swindon*.

DIY/RENOVATION   Marlborough Tiles Factory Shop, *Marlborough*.

FURNITURE/SOFT FURNISHINGS   Loose Ends, *Chippenham*.
McArthurglen Designer Outlet Great Western, *Swindon*. Off The Rails, *Wilton*.
The Curtain Company, *Marlborough*. The Magnificent Material Company, *Warminster*.

FOOD AND LEISURE   Blackwell Bros International Plants Ltd, *Swindon*.
McArthurglen Designer Outlet Great Western, *Swindon*. Thorntons, *Swindon*.

SPORTSWEAR AND EQUIPMENT   Fred Perry Ltd, *Swindon*.
McArthurglen Designer Outlet Great Western, *Swindon*. Nike Factory Store, *Swindon*.
Old Dairy Saddlery Ltd, *Swindon*.

BIG L FACTORY OUTLET

UNIT 61-3, MACARTHUR GLEN DESIGNER OUTLET, GREAT WESTERN, KEMBLE DRIVE, JUNCTION 16 OF M4, SWINDON, WILTSHIRE SN2 2DZ
☎ (01793) 693339. OPEN 10 - 6 MON - FRI, 8 ON THUR, 9 - 6 SAT, 11 - 5 SUN, BANK HOLS.

Men's and women's Levi jeans, jackets, cord and Sherpa fleece jackets, T-shirts and shirts but no children's, all at discount prices. *Factory Shopping Village*

BIRTHDAYS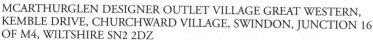

MCARTHURGLEN DESIGNER OUTLET VILLAGE GREAT WESTERN, KEMBLE DRIVE, CHURCHWARD VILLAGE, SWINDON, JUNCTION 16 OF M4, WILTSHIRE SN2 2DZ
☎ (01793) 693535. OPEN 10 - 6 MON - FRI, 8 ON THUR, 9 - 6 SAT, 11 - 5 SUN.

Cards, notelets, stationery sets, colouring books, stuffed toys, photo albums, picture frames, gifts, giftwrap, tissue paper, party packs, candles, candlesticks, vases, christmas crackers, string puppets, fairy lights all at discounts of up to 30%. Some are special purchases, some seconds. *Factory Shopping Village*

BLACKWELL BROS
INTERNATIONAL PLANTS LTD

STEPHENSON ROAD, GROUNDWELL INDUSTRIAL ESTATE, SWINDON, WILTSHIRE SN2 5AX
☎ (01793) 706275. OPEN 10 - 4 MON - SAT.

Reasonably priced plants, plant pots, terracotta ware and plant giftware of good quality. The company's core business is house plants and planted arrangements which they supply to the high street and grocery chains and sell in this retail shop at factory prices. Terracotta pots start at £1.99, bulbs, bedding plants and shrubs sold at great reductions on the high street prices. Planted arrangements can be made up on request. *Factory Shop*

BURBERRYS LTD

GREAT WESTERN OUTLET VILLAGE, CHURCHWARD VILLAGE, JUNCTION 16 OF M4, SWINDON, WILTSHIRE SN2 2DY
☎ (01793) 507600. OPEN 10 - 6 MON - FRI, 8 ON THUR, 9 - 6 SAT, 11 - 5 SUN.

Sells a variety of Burberry and Thomas Burberry goods for men and women. Thomas Burberry jeans and polo shirts, £19.95 reduced from £49.50; classic men's check shirts, £41.95, reduced from £99.50; umbrellas, £26.95 reduced from £65; a variety of purses and wallets, some reduced to £31.95 from £65. Also handbags and travel bags; classic trench coats and overcoats reduced from £160 to £78.95. Thomas Burberry cashmere from £21.95. The telephone number given here is for the village. *Factory Shopping Village*

CLARKS SHOES

GREAT WESTERN OUTLET VILLAGE, CHURCHWARD VILLAGE,
JUNCTION 16 OF M4, SWINDON, WILTSHIRE SN2 2DY
☎ (01793) 507600. OPEN 10 - 6 MON - FRI, 8 ON THUR, 9 - 6 SAT, 11 - 5
SUN.
Clarks International operate a chain of factory shops nationally which specialise in selling discontinued lines and slight sub-standards for men, women
and children from Clarks, K Shoes and other famous brands. These shops
trade under the name of Crockers, K Shoes Factory shop or Clarks Factory
Shop and while not all are physically attached to a shoe factory, these shops
are treated as factory shops by the company. Customers can expect to find an
extensive range of quality shoes, sandals, walking boots, slippers, trainers,
handbags, accessories and gifts, while their major outlets also offer luggage,
sports clothing, sports equipment and outdoor clothing. Brands stocked
include Clarks, K Shoes, Springer, CICA, Hi-Tec, Puma, Mercury, Fila,
Mizuno, Slazenger, Samsonite, Delsey, Antler and Carlton, although not all
are sold in every outlet. Discounts are from 30% to 60% off the normal high
street price for perfect stock. The Swindon branch is also a sports factory shop
and baggage factory shop The telephone number is for the centre, not the
shop. *Factory Shop*

CLOVER LEAF

ARKWRIGHT ROAD, GROUNDWELL INDUSTRIAL ESTATE, SWINDON,
WILTSHIRE SN2 5BB
☎ (01793) 720709. OPEN 9.30 - 4.30 MON - SAT, 10 - 4 SUN.
Makes coasters, trays, chopping boards, melamine oven to tableware, and
bathroom accessories. Seconds and discontinued lines are sold here at discounted prices. There are sales in January and July. *Factory Shop*

DAKS SIMPSON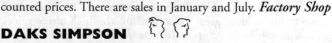

MACARTHUR GLEN DESIGNER OUTLET, GREAT WESTERN, KEMBLE
DRIVE, CHURCHWARD VILLAGE, JUNCTION 16 OF M4, WILTSHIRE
SN2 2DY
☎ (01793) 507600. OPEN 10 - 6 MON - FRI, TILL 8 ON THUR, 9 - 6 SAT,
11 - 5 SUN, BANK HOLS.
Sells previous season's stock for women and men as well as any returned merchandise and overmakes in duffle coats, belts, gloves, handbags, sweaters,
men's suits, Simpson shirts, socks, silk ties and scarves. There are good bargains to be had, but stock is very much dependent on what has not sold in the
shops. Sizes vary but tend towards the two extremes: 6s, 8s and 10s on the one
hand, and 20s and 22s on the other. Ladies jackets, £99, originally £279. Daks
Simpson was founded in 1894 by Simeon Simpson and produced quality
English tailoring for more than 100 years. His son created the Simpson store

in Piccadilly in 1936 which housed the Daks range, most of which was made in Scotland. The telephone number given here is for the centre. *Factory Shopping Village*

DENTS

FAIRFIELD ROAD, WARMINSTER, WILTSHIRE BA12 9DL
☎ (01985) 212291. OPEN 9.30 - 5 TUE - SAT.

The accessories company which produces covetable gloves, belts, handbags, leather wallets and purses for most of the big department stores has a factory outlet near Salisbury. Most of the stock in this reasonably-sized warehouse shop consists of gloves, sold at at least 50% discount, but there is also a wonderful selection of leather briefcases, handbags, silk ties, leather belts, leather card holders and key fobs. The range of handbags come from three sources: ends of ranges from last season and discontinued ranges; returned sample stock for the current season from their two dozen agents; and prototypes for next season. Some of the briefcases are in English bridle leather, full hide or split hide. Stock from the discontinued and end of ranges changes constantly. *Factory Shop*

DESIGNER ROOM

MCARTHURGLEN DESIGNER OUTLET, GREAT WESTERN, KEMBLE DRIVE, SWINDON, JUNCTION 16 OF M4, WILTSHIRE SN2 2DZ
☎ (01793) 436941. OPEN 10 - 6 MON - FRI, 8 ON THUR, 9 - 6 SAT, 11 - 5 SUN.

Sells international designers such as Moschino, Armani, Cerruti, Dolce e Gabanna, Yves St Laurent, Byblos, Gucci and Louis Feraud. Designers vary according to how much overstock or ends of line they have; don't expect to find your favourites here every visit. *Factory Shopping Village*

DOROTHY PERKINS

MCARTHURGLEN GREAT WESTERN DESIGNER OUTLET VILLAGE, CHURCHWARD VILLAGE, SWINDON, JUNCTION 16 OF M4, WILTSHIRE SN2 2DY
☎ (01793) 693796. OPEN 10 - 6 MON - FRI, 8 ON THUR, 9 - 6 SAT, 11 - 5 SUN.

End of season lines with the normal Dorothy Perkins refund guarantee. The range includes knickers, scarves, suits, blouses, sweaters, coats, jackets, dresses and jewellery. *Factory Shopping Village*

Live Well On Less Tips
Old breakfast cereal boxes make magazine holders for those you save. Cut diagonally along the widest part and horizontally along the narrowest.

ECCO

MCARTHURGLEN DESIGNER OUTLET, GREAT WESTERN, SWINDON, JUNCTION 16 OF M4, WILTSHIRE SN2 2DZ

☎ (01793) 422240. OPEN 10 - 6 MON - FRI, 8 ON THUR, 9 - 6 SAT, 11 - 5 SUN.

Ladies, men's and children's shoes, all discounted by at least 25%. Phone 0800 387368 for a catalogue. *Factory Shopping Village*

ENCORE

42 GEORGE STREET, WARMINSTER, WILTSHIRE BA12 8QB

☎ (01985) 846022. OPEN 9.30 - 5 MON - SAT.

Sells nearly-new ballgowns, wedding dresses and bridesmaids dresses, handbags, shoes, hats, accessories and many Italian designer labels. Labels on sale include Liz Claiborne, Country Casuals, Mondi, Windsmoor, Jacques Vert and Jaeger. At Christmas, there is evening wear and for the New Year and summer ball season, ballgowns and cocktail wear. Examples of prices include Laura Ashley two-piece, £30; evening wear from £20-£200; wedding dresses from £40-£450. Sizes range from 8-26. *Dress Agency*

FRED PERRY LTD

UNIT 75, MCARTHURGLEN DESIGNER OUTLET GREAT WESTERN, KEMBLE DRIVE, SWINDON, JUNCTION 16 OF M4, WILTSHIRE SN2 2DY

☎ (01793) 481900 OPEN 10 - 6 MON - FRI, 8 ON THUR, 10 - 6 SAT, 11 - 5 SUN.

Men's, women's and children's ranges of the famous Fred Perry active performance clothing: shorts, tennis tops, tracksuits, T-shirts. All price labels show the original and the reduced price, which usually amount to a 30% discount. *Factory Shopping Village*

GEORGINA VON ETZDORF

THE AVENUE, ODSTOCK, NEAR SALISBURY, WILTSHIRE

☎ (01722) 415969. OPEN 10 - 5 MON - SAT (CLOSED 1- 2 FOR LUNCH DAILY), 12 - 5 SUN.

Based in the sleepy village of Odstock, outside Salisbury, lies the Georgina von Etzdorf factory shop. Sandwiched between workrooms, it has a limited but exciting range of clothes and lots of wonderful accessories. Her products are not cheap, but the Jacquard scarves, squares and shawls are affordable at prices ranging from £20. Everything is half price. The price tag also tells you which season the outfit is from and whether it is a second. There are men's and ladies silk dressing gowns, velvet and silk long and short dresses, wool crepe long gloves, ladies scarves, Jacquard print waistcoats, silk ties and oddments of fabric. Put your name down for the twice-yearly sales: two fabric and two general. *Factory Shop*

HANRO OF SWITZERLAND

GREAT WESTERN DESIGNER OUTLET VILLAGE, CHURCHWARD
VILLAGE, SWINDON, WILTSHIRE

☎ (01793) 480118. OPEN 10 - 6 MON - FRI, UNTIL 8 ON THUR, 9 - 6 SAT,
11 - 5 SUN.

Luxury lingerie for men and women which is normally sold through Harvey
Nichols, Harrods and Selfridges is available here at reduced prices. For example, a bra which normally retails for £100 would be reduced by 35% - 50%.
Sizes range from extra small to extra large and the company specialises in garments for smaller busts, although D-cups are also stocked. Very well known
for their mercerised cottons which never fade or shrink. *Factory Shopping
Village*

JAEGER

MCARTHURGLEN DESIGNER OUTLET, GREAT WESTERN, KEMBLE
DRIVE, SWINDON, JUNCTION 16 FROM M4 WILTSHIRE SN2 7AA

☎ (01793) 484660. OPEN 10 - 6 MON - FRI, UNTIL 8 ON THUR, 9 - 6 SAT,
11 - 5 SUN AND BANK HOLIDAYS.

Contemporary classics from Jaeger at excellent prices. Most of the merchan-
dise is previous seasons' stock, but you might also find some special makes.
Both shops stock tailoring and knitwear for women and men. *Factory
Shopping Village*

JANE SHILTON

GREAT WESTERN DESIGNER OUTLET VILLAGE, KEMBLE DRIVE,
CHURCHWARD VILLAGE, JUNCTION 16 OF M4, SWINDON, WILTSHIRE
SN2 2DY

☎ (01793) 430356. OPEN 10 - 6 MON - FRI, UNTIL 8 ON THUR, 9 - 6 SAT,
11 - 5 SUN AND BANK HOLIDAYS.

Merchandise from past seasons' collections or factory seconds at discounts of
at least 30% and up to 70% off the original price. There is a wide range of
handbags, suitcases, women's shoes, luggage, briefcases, umbrellas, scarves and
travel bags. Examples of prices include handbags, £23.99 reduced from £35;
scarves, £4.99 reduced from £9.99; belts, £4.99 from £19.99; briefcases,
£34.99 from £50.99. *Factory Shopping Village*

JOE BLOGGS

MCARTHURGLEN DESIGNER OUTLET GREAT WESTERN, KEMBLE
DRIVE, SWINDON, JUNCTION 16 OF M4, WILTSHIRE SN2 2DY

☎ (01793) 435543. OPEN 10 - 6 MON - SAT, 11 - 5 SUN.

Range of casual clothing for men, women, children and babies which are ends
of lines, imperfects or surplus ranges. Jeans, tops, long sleeved shirts and jackets at discounts of between 30% and70%.

JOKIDS LTD

UNIT 48, MACARTHURGLEN DESIGNER OUTLET, GREAT WESTERN, KEMBLE DRIVE, SWINDON, JUNCTION 16 OF M4, WILTSHIRE SN2 7AA

☎ (01793) 436944. OPEN 10 -6 MON - SAT, 10 - 8 THUR, 11 - 5 SUN.

JoKids is the factory shop trading name for Jeffrey Ohrenstein which sells unusual and attractive clothes for children aged from birth to ten years. This includes pretty party dresses for girls at reductions of up to 40%, all-in-one smocked playsuits, T-shirts, denim shirts, denim dresses, sunhats, shorts, and accessories. *Factory Shopping Village*

KARALYNE'S

20 WEST STREET, WILTON, WILTSHIRE SP2 ODF

☎ (01722) 742802. OPEN 9.30 - 4 TUE, THUR - SAT.

Established for 12 years, this tiny but full shop sells nearly-new clothing and accessories for women at bargain prices, including evening wear. Stocks more than 1,000 items at a time with top designer labels and a constant flow of new arrivals and very popular special rails selling top makes including shoes, handbags, hats and belts. Permanent half-price rails added to weekly, plus two everything half price sales each year in February and August. If required, they will help to put together a special outfit or keep an eye out for something specific. They cater for all ages and sizes from 8 to 20+. Useful children's play corner for hassle-free browsing. *Dress Agency*

KIDS PLAY FACTORY

MCARTHURGLEN DESIGNER OUTLET GREAT WESTERN, KEMBLE DRIVE, JUNCTION 16 OF M4, SWINDON, WILTSHIRE SN9 2DY

☎ (01793) 695550. OPEN 10 - 6 MON - FRI, 8 ON THUR, 9 - 6 SAT, 11 - 5 SUN.

This shop sells a wide range of well-known children's brand names: Tomy, Matchbox, Lego, The First Years, Hasbro, Disney, Playskool, Mattel and Fisher-Price at discounts of up to 50%. They also stock a wide range of soft toys including TY Beanie Babies. *Factory Shopping Village*

LE CREUSET

UNIT 53, NORTH MALL, MCARTHURGLEN DESIGNER OUTLET, GREAT WESTERN, KEMBLE DRIVE, SWINDON, JUNCTION 16 OFF M4, WILTSHIRE SN2 2DZ

☎ (01793) 641587. OPEN 10 - 6 MON - FRI, 8 ON THUR, 9 - 6 SAT, 11 - 5 SUN.

Items from the famous Le Creuset range - casseroles, saucepans, fry pans etc - plus their pottery collection at discounts of at least 30%. *Factory Shopping Village*

Live Well On Less Tips
GEORGIANA GRIMSTON 18 EDNA STREET, LONDON SW11 3DP.
0171-978 6161. BY APPOINTMENT ONLY.
Georgiana Grimston bespoke tailoring service is perfectly suited to worka-
holic men and women who barely have time to go home, let alone to the tailor. She and her team of Savile Row cutters produce high quality clothes at
prices considerably lower than Savile Row (starting at £675) and conduct fittings almost anywhere: at the office, at home or in Savile Row. All patterns
are individually designed, cut in the traditional method and are 100% handmade and hand-stitched. Ring for an appointment.

LOOSE ENDS
GILES GREEN, BRINKWORTH, CHIPPENHAM, WILTSHIRE SN15 5DQ
☎ (01666) 510685. OPEN 9 - 1 MON - SAT OR BY APPOINTMENT.
Operating from two large converted barns in the grounds of the proprietor's
house, Loose Ends offers top quality discontinued lines of fabric and textured
and plain upholstery fabrics which they obtain from the best manufacturers in
England and sell at about one third of the normal price. They hold very large
stocks of all types of furnishing fabrics including lining, interlining and wallpapers which you can buy on the spot. *Permanent Discount Outlet*

MARLBOROUGH TILES FACTORY SHOP
16 HIGH STREET, MARLBOROUGH, WILTSHIRE SN8 1AA
☎ (01672) 515287. OPEN 9.30 -5 MON - SAT.
MARLBOROUGH TILES 13 MILFORD STREET, SALISBURY,
WILTSHIRE SP1 2AJ
☎ (01722) 328010. OPEN 9.30 - 5 MON - SAT.
Wall and floor tiles from Marlborough and other top quality, specialist manufacturers. Seconds come mostly from Marlborough's own factory with discounts of up to 50% on first quality prices. *Permanent Discount Outlet*

MATALAN
UNIT 2B, MANNINGTON RETAIL PARK, WOOTTON BASSETT ROAD,
SWINDON, WILTSHIRE SN5 9NP
☎ (01793) 649500. OPEN 10 - 8 MON - FRI, 9 - 6 SAT, 10 - 4 SUN.
Matalan is a fashion and homewares shop giving customers what they claim
to be unbeatable value for money with huge savings on a wide range of products including high quality fashionable clothing for women, women and children at up to 50% off high street prices. Matalan is situated out of town and
stores are open seven days a week all year round. *Permanent Discount
Outlet*

MCARTHURGLEN DESIGNER OUTLET GREAT WESTERN

KEMBLE DRIVE, CHURCHWARD VILLAGE, (JUNCTION 16 OF M4)
SWINDON, WILTSHIRE SN2 2DY

☎ (01793) 507600. OPEN 10 - 6 MON - FRI, UNTIL 8 ON THUR, 9 - 6 SAT, 11 - 5 SUN AND BANK HOLIDAYS.

More than 100 individual factory shops, a themed food court, creche, indoor and outdoor play area, a forthcoming Railway Heritage Museum, and parking for 1,900 cars. Shops here include Antler, Aqascutum, Austin Reed, Baron Jon menswear (Moschino, Versace, Romeo Gigli, Polo Ralph Lauren, Calvin Klein jeans, Kenzo), Benetton, Ben Sherman, Bookends, Burberrys, Cap It All, Card and Gift, Ciro Pearls, Ciro Citterio, Clarks Shoes, Daks Simpson, Dorothy Perkins, Easy Jeans, Ecco shoes, Edinburgh Crystal, Faith shoes, Fred Perry, French Connection, Gap selling Gap and Gapkids, Hanro lingerie, Henri Lloyd, Iceberg (children's designerwear), Jacques Vert, Jaeger, James Barry, Jane Shilton, Jigsaw, Joe Bloggs, Jokids, Just Sweets, Kids Play Factory, Le Creuset, Levi's The Big L, Liz Claiborne, Mexx, Mondian glass and gifts, Next to Nothing, Nike, Olsen ladies fashion, Oneida cutlery, Osh Kosh, Overland, Paco, Pied a Terre, Pilot womenswear, Ponden Mill, Price's Candles, Principles for men and women, Quiksilver beach and casualwear, Remington small electrical appliances and cutlery, Sia vases and ceramics, Soled Out footwear, Spiegelau glass, Suit Co, Suits You, Swatch selling watches, telephones, pagers and the FlikFlak children's range; Ted Baker selling men's and womenswear, Vecopri; The Designers store selling top British designer labels and featuring Amanda Wakeley, N Peal, Paddy Campbell, David Fielden, Sally Gissing, Wonderful Wraps, Orford & Swan, Apara and Krizia, though stock changes all the time so the aforementioned designers are not guaranteed to be on sale when you visit; a second Designer Room selling international designers such as Moschino, Armani, Cerruti, Dolce & Gabanna, Yves St Laurent, Gucci, Jasper Conran and Louis Feraud; Thomas Pink men's shirts, The Karrimor Store, Thorn (selling televisions, Scalextric, sound systems and small domestic equipment) Thorntons, Tie Rack, Timberland, Tog 24 outerwear, Travel Accessory (Samsonite, Fiorelli, Delsey, Tula bags, Gucci handbags, Valentino bags), Triumph/Hom swimwear and underwear for men and women, Van Heusen, Villeroy & Boch, Vitamin World, Viyella, Walker & Hall jewellery, Warners lingerie, Whittard of Chelsea, Windsmoor, Woods of Windsor, XS music and video (CDs and videos). Shops here selling items for children include Benetton, Bookends, Card and Gift, Easy Jeans, Ecco shoes, Joe Bloggs, Jokids, Just Sweets, Kids Play Factory, Mexx, Next to Nothing, Osh Kosh, Principles, Soled Out footwear, Sportsystem (Benetton-owned sports equipment), Swatch's FlikFlak range, Thorntons. Shops here for the home include Bookends, Card and Gift, Edinburgh Crystal, John Jenkins china and glass, Laura Ashley wallpaper, furniture and fabric, Le Creuset, Mondian glass and gifts, Oneida cutlery, Ponden Mill duvets, towels and bedlinen, Price's

Candles, Sia vases and ceramics, Spiegelau glass, Villeroy & Boch, Whittard of Chelsea. Shops here selling electrical equipment include Remington which has everything from hairdryers to kitchen knives, foot spas to kettles, and Thorn Electricals, which sells Russell Hobbs kettles, Philips toasters, Sony and Sanyo sound systems, Ferguson tvs and video recorders, Scalextric sets, Sony Walkmans, and video tapes, although stock changes constantly. Sports shops here include Fred Perry, Nike, Sportsystem (Benetton-owned sports equipment), The Karrimor Store, Tog 24 outerwear, Triumph/Hom swimwear and underwear. Leisure shops include Antler luggage, Jane Shilton luggage and handbags and Travel Accessory brand-name luggage and travel accessories. Restaurants include McDonalds, Villa Pizza, Singapore Sam, Fat Jackets, Harry Ramsdens, Nana Massarella's, Starbucks Coffee and the Great Western Restaurant. *Factory Shopping Village*

MEXX INTERNATIONAL

MCARTHURGLEN DESIGNER OUTLET GREAT WESTERN, SWINDON, JUNCTION 16 OF M4, WILTSHIRE SN2 2DY
☎ (01793) 692205. OPEN 10 - 6 MON - FRI, 8 ON THUR, 9 - 6 SAT, 11 - 5 SUN.

High street fashion at factory outlet prices for men, women, babies, children and teenagers, all of which are heavily discounted by more than 30%. *Factory Shopping Village*

MUMS AND TOTS

2 & 4 SOUTH STREET, WILTON, NEAR SALISBURY, WILTSHIRE SP2 OJS
☎ (01722) 744582. OPEN 9.30 - 5 MON - FRI, 9.30 - 2 SAT.

Factory seconds and new nursery equipment and bedding including prams and pushchairs are sold and hired out in this shop which also sells children's clothes and soft toys. *Dress Agency, Hire Shop*

NEXT TO NOTHING

MCARTHUR GLEN DESIGNER OUTLET, GREAT WESTERN, KEMBLE DRIVE, SWINDON, WILTSHIRE SN2 7AA
☎ (01793) 525555. OPEN 10 - 6 NON - FRI, 10 - 8 THUR, 11 - 5 SUN.

Sells perfect surplus stock from Next stores and the Next Directory catalogue - from belts, jewellery and underwear to day and evening wear - at discounts of 50% or more. The ranges are usually last season's and overruns. Stock consists of women's, men's and children's clothing, with some homeware and shoes. Stock is replenished three times a week and there is plenty of it. *Factory Shopping Village*

Live Well On Less Tips
A coat hanger makes a great toilet paper holder.

Live Well On Less Tips
Don't let the water run while brushing your teeth. Wet the brush, turn off
the water, brush your teeth and then turn it back on to rinse.

NIKE FACTORY STORE

MCARTHURGLEN DESIGNER OUTLET, GREAT WESTERN, KEMBLE
DRIVE, SWINDON, JUNCTION 16 OF M4, WILTSHIRE SN2 2DZ
☎ (01793) 484440. OPEN 10 - 6 MON - FRI, 8 ON THUR, 9 - 6 SAT, 11 - 5
SUN.
Men's, women's and children's trainers, jackets, T-shirts, sports shirts, shorts,
sleeveless T-shirts and tracksuits. Nike has been making clothes for people who
live and play outdoors since 1972. This factory shop sells unsold items from
previous seasons. The selection represents their worldwide collection, which
means that some garments may not have been offered for sale in the UK. As
ranges tend to be incomplete, they are offered at up to 30% off the recommended retail price or the price they would have commanded in the UK.
Occasionally, there are some slight seconds on sale, which are always marked
as such. *Factory Shopping Village*

OFF THE RAILS

15 NORTH STREET, WILTON, WILTSHIRE SP2 0HA
☎ (01722) 744966. OPEN 10 - 4 TUE - SAT.
Secondhand curtain shop which sells drapes made from fabric by Designers
Guild, Colefax & Fowler, Osborne & Little, etc, allowing you to take them
home and try before buying. Quality is Marks & Spencer upwards with curtains at £2 to £685. Alterations can be undertaken and curtains are made up
at very good prices. Also sells anything to do with furnishing fabrics, including lampshades from £4 for pleated ones to £59 for silk ones, cushions, curtain poles, cut-price fabric, Indian crewel work. The poles selection covers
everything from plain natural untreated wooden ones to antique gilt poles.
There are also baskets of finials, and bundles of secondhand tie-backs in all
shapes and sizes. *Secondhand Shop*

OLD DAIRY SADDLERY LTD

GREENWAY FARM, TOCKENHAM, SWINDON, WILTSHIRE SN4 7PP
☎ (01793) 849284. OPEN 10 - 5 MON - SAT, 10 - 1 SUN.
Normal priced large shop on a farm selling outdoor wear, horse blankets,
country clothing etc at competitive prices. Cliff Barnsby saddlewear is also
sold. Phone first to check stock levels. *Permanent Discount Outlet*

ONEIDA

GREAT WESTERN DESIGNER OUTLET VILLAGE, 93 KEMBLE DRIVE, CHURCHWARD VILLAGE, SWINDON, JUNCTION 16 OF M4, WILTSHIRE SN2 2NZ

☎ (01793) 514103. OPEN 10 - 6 MON - FRI, 8 ON THUR, 9 - 6 SAT, 11 - 5 SUN.

Oneida is the world's largest cutlery company and originates from the United States of America. In addition to cutlery, it sells silver and silver plate at discounts of between 30% and 50%, plus frames, candlesticks and trays. They now also have their own range of chinaware and glass, also sold here at discounts of 30%-50%. *Factory Shopping Village*

PACO LIFE IN COLOUR

UNIT 107, MCARTHURGLEN DESIGNER OUTLET, GREAT WESTERN, KEMBLE DRIVE, CHURCHWARD PARK, SWINDON, WILTSHIRE SN2 2DY

☎ (01793) 536936. OPEN 10 - 6 MON - SAT, 11 - 5 SUN, UNTIL 8 ON THUR.

Comprehensive range of casualwear clothing and accessories for women in a wide variety of colours. End-of-season lines are on sale at discounts of around 30%. Included in the range are t-shirts, sweatshirts, wool sweaters and cardigans, jeans, leggings, shorts, bags and socks, all offering outstanding value for money. *Permanent Discount Outlet*

PIED A TERRE SALE SHOP

MCARTHUR GLEN DESIGNER OUTLET GREAT WESTERN, KEMBLE DRIVE, SWINDON, JUNCTION 16 OF M4, WILTSHIRE SN2 2DZ

☎ (01793) 695774. OPEN 10 - 6 MON - FRI, 8 ON THUR, 9 - 6 SAT, 11 - 5 SUN.

Pied a Terre shoes, clothing and accessories, including suits and high fashion wear, which are made up of former samples and ex-sale stock or previous season's stock from London stores at discounts of up to 70%. *Factory Shopping Village*

Live Well On Less Tips

HALF-PRICE TICKET BOOTH LEICESTER SQUARE, LONDON WC2

Half-price tickets for most musicals and plays on the day of the show only. It's usually not possible to buy tickets for the top-rated shows, but great for those which have been on for some time. Turn up in person to buy tickets. There is a smaller outlet run by a ticket agency inside the Criterion Theatre at Piccadilly Circus which has half-price tickets for a limited number of shows.

PONDEN MILL LINENS

WILTON SHOPPING VILLAGE, KING STREET, WILTON, NEAR
SALISBURY, WILTSHIRE SP2 0RS

☎ (01722) 741271. OPEN 9.30 - 5.30 MON - SAT, 11 - 5 SUN.
MCARTHURGLEN DESIGNER OUTLET VILLAGE, KEMBLE DRIVE,
SWINDON SN2 2DZ

☎ (01793) 531880. OPEN 10 - 6 MON - FRI, 8 ON THUR,
9 - 6 SAT, 11 - 5 SUN.

Famous branded products at direct from the mill prices. Towels, co-ordinated
bedlinen, duvets, pillows and curtains from Crown, Coloroll, Chortex,
Rectella together with bathroom and kitchen accessories. *Factory Shopping
Village*

PRICE'S CANDLES

GREAT WESTERN DESIGNER OUTLET VILLAGE, KEMBLE DRIVE,
CHURCHWARD VILLAGE, SWINDON, JUNCTION 16 OF M4, WILTSHIRE
SN2 2DY

☎ (01793) 693745. OPEN 10 - 6 MON - FRI, 8 ON THUR, 9 - 6 SAT, 11 - 5
SUN.

Everything sold in this shop are seconds, which may be discoloured or have a
damaged pattern; discontinued sizes not available elsewhere; over-runs from
the garden selection or dinner candles in old packaging that has now been
replaced. There are church candles, lanterns, candles in pots and glass jars,
star-shaped candles, floating candles, candlestick holders, serviettes, scented
candles and garden torches. Some of the ceramic items are bought in. Both villages also have restaurants, a children's play area and parking. *Factory
Shopping Village*

PRINCIPLES

MCARTHURGLEN DESIGNER OUTLET, GREAT WESTERN, KEMBLE
DRIVE, SWINDON, JUNCTION 16 OF M4, WILTSHIRE SN2 2DY

☎ (01793) 693890. OPEN 10 - 6 MON - FRI, 8 ON THUR, 9 - 6 SAT, 11 - 5
SUN.

End of season lines with the normal Principles refund guarantee. The range
includes, for women, dresses, blouses, coats, outerwear, knitwear, casualwear
and a selection of Petite clothing for women who are 5ft 3ins and under. For
men, there is formalwear, smart casualwear, knitwear, outerwear, PFM Sport,
jeanswear and casualwear. *Factory Shopping Village*

Live Well On Less Tips
Wait until your dishwasher is full before turning it on. One load less a week
can save you quite a lot over a year.

Live Well On Less Tips

Re-examine your regular expenses. For example, if you have your hair cut every six weeks, lengthening the time to six and a half or even seven weeks will cut one visit to the hairdressers a year.

REMINGTON

GREAT WESTERN DESIGNER OUTLET VILLAGE, KEMBLE DRIVE, SWINDON, JCT 16 OF M4, WILTSHIRE DN4 5JH

☎ (01793) 430515. OPEN 10 - 6 MON - FRI, 8 ON THUR, 9 - 6 SAT, 11 - 5 SUN.

Lots of famous names here from Oneida and Monogram cutlery to Braun, Philips, Remington, Clairol, Wahl, Krups, Swan and Kenwood small kitchen equipment. There are usually hair, beauty and male grooming accessories as well as kitchen equipment, all at reduced prices. A great place to buy gifts or replenish the kitchen equipment with combi stylers, turbo travel plus hairdryers, air purifiers, liquidisers; food processors; batteries; clocks; and cutlery. Some of the packaging may be damaged but the products are in perfect working order. *Factory Shopping Village*

SECOND TO NONE

13 THE BRIDGE, CHIPPENHAM, WILTSHIRE SN15 1HA

☎ (01249) 656456. OPEN 9 - 5 MON - SAT.

Established in the South West for twenty-six years, this company has built a reputation for giving excellent customer service and for selling goods which are of a quality and value that are Second to None! This chain of shops specialise in selling famous chainstore and branded clearing lines, which includes surplus stocks of branded goods such as Gossard, Berlei, Zorbit, Naturana and many more. They stock a large range of ladies and children's and baby wear (including baby bedding and accessories), some menswear, and an extensive range of underwear and nightwear for all the family. You can save up to 75% off recommended retail prices and they offer a seven-day money back guarantee. *Permanent Discount Outlet*

SEQUEL

28 SILVER STREET, BRADFORD-ON-AVON, WILTSHIRE

☎ (01225) 868616. OPEN 10 - 4 TUE, THUR, FRI, 10 - 1 WED, 10 - 5 SAT.

Dress agency on three floors selling a fascinating selection of clothing to suit all ages and sizes. Excellent selection of evening dresses as well as wedding dresses, jewellery and some collectables. *Dress Agency*

Live Well On Less Tips
CHINAMATCHING 23 KILN ROAD, FAREHAM, HAMPSHIRE PO16
7UA. (01329) 282785. OPEN 8 - 8 SEVEN DAYS A WEEK.
Stocks and searches for English and some European patterns from the 1940s
to the present. Brands stocked include Wedgwood, Colclough, Denby, Royal
Doulton, Royal Worcester and Hornsea. There is no registration fee. E-mail:
china.matching@BTinternet.com.

THE CURTAIN COMPANY

123 HIGH STREET, MARLBOROUGH, WILTSHIRE SN8 1LZ
☎ (01672) 516994. FAX ☎ (017939) 731949. OPEN 10 - 4.30 MON - FRI,
10 - 2.30 SAT.
The Curtain Company specialises in value for money, selling high quality, pre-
loved curtains and accessories at rock-bottom prices as well as a vast range of
flat fabrics including ends of roll and seconds at silly prices. With two floors
of constantly-changing stock, they offer an extensive variety to suit most tastes
and needs. They stock many designer names such as Osborne & Little,
Colefax & Fowler, Sanderson, Warner and Designers Guild in natural linens,
cottons, damasks, brocades, designer chintzes and velvets. They have extended their range of services to provide a fast make-up, alterations and fitting
team and can source most materials. They also offer a helping hand design service without paying expensive interior design prices. *Secondhand Shop*

THE DESIGNERS STORE

MCARTHUR GLEN DESIGNER OUTLET, GREAT WESTERN, KEMBLE
DRIVE, SWINDON, JUNCTION 16 OF M4, WILTSHIRE SN2 2DY
☎ (01793) 486161. OPEN 10 - 6 MON - FRI, 9 - 6 SAT, 11 - 5 SUN.
Sells British catwalk designers such as Paddy Campbell, N Peal, Roland Klein,
Camilla Paul, Marilyn MooreDavid Fielden, and many more depending on
the designers' overstock levels. *Factory Shopping Village*

THE DOWNTON TRADING COMPANY

THE OLD MANSION HOUSE, 3 THE HIGH STREET, DOWNTON,
NR SALISBURY, WILTSHIRE SP5 3PG
☎ (01725) 510676. OPEN 10 - 5 MON - SAT.
The DTC is the outlet shop for Bryn Parry Studios and stocks a wide range
of quality seconds and ends of lines of photographic frames, clocks, desk
accessories and cards. New stock is also available, including mugs, tea towels
and travel journals. Other gift lines vary continuously, but popular items
include tapestry stools, designer fabric nursery bags, candles, leather goods,
glass and Christmas decorations (in season). A small selection of furniture is
sometimes available. *Permanent Discount Outlet*

THE FACTORY SHOP LTD

36-37 ROUNDSTONE STREET, TROWBRIDGE, WILTSHIRE BA14 8DE
☎ (01225) 751399. OPEN 9 - 5 MON - SAT.
24 MARKET PLACE, WARMINSTER, WILTSHIRE BA12 9AN
☎ (01985) 217532. OPEN 9 - 5.30 MON - SAT.
23-25 NEW PLACE, CORSHAM, WILTSHIRE SN13 OHL
☎ (01249) 712160. OPEN 9 - 5.30 MON - SAT, 10 - 4 SUN.
Wide range on sale includes men's, ladies and children's clothing and footwear; household textiles, toiletries, hardware, luggage, lighting and bedding, most of which are chainstore and high street brands at discounts of approximately 30%-50%. There are weekly deliveries and brands include many major stars such as Adidas, Nike, Wrangler and Dartington, to name just four. Lines are continually changing and few factory shops offer such a variety under one roof. The Trowbridge branch also sells the Cape Country Furniture range. This high quality pine furniture made exclusively for The Factory Shop in South Africa is sold at factory direct prices with home delivery throughout the UK. Colour brochure and price list available. *Factory Shop*

THE MAGNIFICENT MATERIAL COMPANY

CHITTERNE LODGE, CHITTERNE, WARMINSTER,
WILTSHIRE BA12 OLQ
☎ (01985) 850501. OPEN 9.30 - 12.30 MON, THUR AND BY APPOINTMENT.
Sells a wide variety of discontinued lines, overstocks, first and seconds, including traditional chintzes, linens, damasks, checks and upholstery, and a small selection of wallpaper. These fabrics come from many of the top designer warehouse and are sold at less than half the retail price. *Permanent Discount Outlet*

THE SHOESTRING

5 APSLEY HOUSE ARCADE, WOOTTON BASSETT, SWINDON,
WILTSHIRE SN4 7AQ
☎ (01793) 850106. OPEN 9.30 - 4.30 MON - WED, FRI, SAT.
Small shop full of clothes which are a mixture of high street and designer labels. Also sells accessories such as bags, belts and shoes. *Dress Agency*

Live Well On Less Tips

Fly as a courier - if you can travel alone on a flexible schedule. You have to make do with carry-on luggage since check-in baggage is supplied by a courier company. Look them up in yellow pages.

THORN OUTLET

MCARTHURGLEN DESIGNER OUTLET VILLAGE, GREAT WESTERN,
KEMBLE DRIVE, SWINDON, JUNCTION 16 OF M4,
WILTSHIRE SN2 2DY

☎ (01793) 434787. OPEN 10 - 6 MON - FRI, 8 ON THUR, 9 - 6 SAT, 11 - 5
SUN AND BANK HOLIDAYS.

Sells Russell Hobbs kettles, Philips toasters, Sony and Sanyo sound systems,
Ferguson TVs and video recorders, Scalextric sets and video tapes. All products are sold at a minimum of 30% off high street prices. For example, ex-
rental TVs and video recorders can be bought for as little as £69; new 21-inch
sets, £189, compared with high street price of £270. Stock changes constantly with new ranges being added. *Factory Shopping Village*

THORNTONS

MCARTHURGLEN FACTORY VILLAGE GREAT WESTERN, SWINDON,
WILTSHIRE SN2 7AA

☎ (01793) 692438. OPEN 10 - 6 MON - FRI, 8 ON THUR, 9 - 6 SAT, 11 - 5
SUN, BANK HOLS.

The UK's leading specialist confectionery retailer has more than 500 shops and
franchises nationwide selling a wide range of boxed and loose, chocolate and
sugar confectionery. The factory outlets sell three different categories: misshapes.
discounted lines and standard lines. Misshapes are loose chocolates which are
the result of new product development, product trials or end of production runs
which cannot be packed as Thorntons standard lines. They are packed into
assorted bags and offer a saving of 35%-55% over the recommended retail price
of standard loose line products. Discounted lines are excess to Thorntons' normal retail requirements and can be as a result of excess seasonal or export stock,
discontinued lines or packaging changes. These products, when available, are
offered at a discount of 25%-50% over the standard retail price. Standard lines
from the full Thorntons range are also on sale at normal prices. *Factory
Shopping Village*

TIE RACK

MCARTHURGLEN DESIGNER OUTLET, GREAT WESTERN, JUNCTION
16 FROM M4, WILTSHIRE SN2 2DY

☎ (01793) 531070. OPEN 10 - 6 MON - FRI, UNTIL 8 ON THUR,
9 - 6 SAT, 11 - 5 SUN.

Usual range of Tie Rack items including boxer shorts, silk ties, socks, silk scarves
and waistcoats, all at 50% reductions. Customer Careline: ☎ 0181 230 2333.
Factory Shopping Village

TIMBERLAND

MCARTHURGLEN DESIGNER OUTLET, GREAT WESTERN, JUNCTION 16 OF M4, SWINDON, WILTSHIRE SN2 2DY

☎ (01793) 480156. OPEN 10 - 6 MON - FRI, UNTIL 8 ON THUR, 9 - 6 SAT, 11 - 5 SUN.

Footwear, clothing and outdoor gear from the well-known Timberland range at discounts of 30% or more. All stock is last season's excess stock in limited ranges and sizes. As most of Timberland's stock is from a core range which rarely changes, there are few discontinued lines. *Factory Shopping Village*

TK MAXX

CROSS KEYS SHOPPING CENTRE, SALISBURY, WILTSHIRE

☎ (01722) 320644. OPEN 9 - 5.30 MON - FRI, 9 - 8 THUR, 9 - 6 SAT, 10 - 4 SUN.

Based on an American concept, TK Maxx is situated in easily accessible, often centrally located stores and offers famous label goods with up to 60% savings off recommended retail prices. TK Maxx has fashion for the whole family - women's, men's and childrenswear - accessories, shoes, gifts, kitchenware and home goods. Everything in the store is branded with a choice of well-known high street names to designer labels, and while a small percentage might be clearly marked past season, the great majority of items in store are current season, current stock and still with phenomenal savings. There is a huge choice with 50,000 pieces in store and up to 10,000 new items arriving a week. The stores are simple and unfussy with wide aisles, shopping trolleys and baskets, and a spacious, functional feel to them but there are individual changing rooms, ramps for buggies and wheelchairs and plenty of staff on the shop floor. Every branch accepts all major credit and debit cards and has a liberal refund and return policy. *Permanent Discount Outlet*

TOG 24

MCARTHURGLEN DESIGNER OUTLET, GREAT WESTERN, JUNCTION 16 OF M4, SWINDON, WILTSHIRE SN2 2DY

☎ (01793) 695966. OPEN 10 - 6 MON, TUE, WED, FRI, 10 - 8 THUR, 9 - 6 SAT, 11 - 5 SUN.

Tog 24 are the UK's fastest growing brand name in outdoor clothing and leisurewear, with a total of three UK factories and 36 stores nationwide. They utilise the world's finest performance fabrics including Gore-Tex, Polartec and Burlington macs. Catering for all the family for all seasons, with cosy fleeces and waterproofs for the winter, and trekking ranges, shorts and t-shirts for the summer. With all prices at least 30% below the recommended retail price you can afford to enter the Tog comfort zone. *Factory Shopping Village*

Live Well On Less Tips,
TRAVELMATE 52 YORK PLACE, BOURNEMOUTH, DORSET BH7 6JN.
(01202) 431520.
This company keeps a database of people looking for travel companions and wishing to avoid single supplements. They will send you details of those wanting to go to the same area or who have the same holiday interest or wish to go on holiday and are willing to share a room with a stranger but still keep their independence. Golden Friends is a new service for the over-50s to introduce prospective travelling companions or simply those looking for friendship.

TOM SAYERS CLOTHING CO

WILTON FACTORY SHOPPING VILLAGE, KING STREET, WILTON, NEAR SALISBURY, WILTSHIRE SP2 ORS
☎ (01722) 741257. OPEN 9.30 - 5.30 MON - SAT, 11 - 5 SUN.
Tom Sayers make sweaters for some of the top high street department stores. Unusually for a factory shop, if they don't stock your size, they will try and order it for you from their factory or one of their other factory outlets and send it to you. Most of the stock here is overstock, cancelled orders or last season's and includes jumpers, trousers and shirts at discounts of 30%. The trousers and shirts are bought in to complement the sweaters which they make. *Factory Shopping Village*

TRIUMPH INTERNATIONAL LTD

MCARTHURGLEN DESIGNER OUTLET, GREAT WESTERN, KEMBLE DRIVE, SWINDON, JUNCTION 16 OF M4, WILTSHIRE SN2 7AA
☎ (01793) 480892. OPEN 10 - 6 MON - FRI, 8 ON THUR, 9 - 6 SAT, 11 - 5 SUN.
Factory shop selling a wide and ever-changing range of Triumph lingerie, a French range, Valisere, and swimwear which are last season's stock or discontinued lines. Also women's and men's Sloggi underwear and underwear and swimwear from the Hom range for men. *Factory Shopping Village*

UNITED FOOTWEAR

HORHAM CRESCENT, PARK SOUTH, SWINDON, WILTSHIRE SN3 2LX
☎ (01793) 435238. OPEN 9 - 5.30 MON - SAT, 10 - 4 SUN.
Shoes for all the family as well as clothes, handbags, sports shoes, boots, giftware and household goods, all at discounted prices. Famous brands including Clarks, K Shoes and Elmdale. Part of a national chain which covers Cardiff, Worcester, Walsall, Kettering, Bradford, St Helen's, Manchester, Chester, Dudley, Leigh, Newbold Verdon, Preston, Coventry, Nottingham and Birmingham. Large car park and nearby shopping centre. Coaches welcome. *Permanent Discount Outlet*

Live Well On Less Tips

TABLEWHERE? 4 QUEEN'S PARADE CLOSE, FRIERN BARNET, LON-DON N11 3FY. 0181 361 6111. MAIL ORDER.

The UK's largest china matching service, they stock thousands of patterns from the world's leading manufacturers including Wedgwood, Royal Doulton, Spode, Denby, Minton, Royal Albert, Johnson Bros., Royal Worcester and Aynsley, some of which go back 40 or 50 years. By buying up discontinued lines from all over the country, Tablewhere? has built up a stock of over one million pieces which are available through the London-based mail order service. Specialist staff maintain detailed computer and photographic records of all the patterns and shapes in stock so that they can locate any replacement pieces from egg cups to soup tureens, although tea cups and dinner plates are in most demand. Replacement pieces usually cost around the equivalent of today's retail prices. There is no charge to register requirements - phone or write with details of the manufacturer, pattern name and the replacement pieces needed. If there is no pattern name on the service, then a photograph showing both sides of a dinner plate with a colour description will help iden-tification. You can also visit their website: http://www.tablewhere.co.uk or e mail them at tablewhere@globalnet.co.uk

VILLEROY & BOCH (UK) LIMITED

UNIT 31, MCARTHURGLEN GREAT WESTERN DESIGNER OUTLET, SWINDON, WILTSHIRE SN2 2DY

☎ (01793) 480944. OPEN 10 - 6 MON - FRI, UNTIL 8 ON THUR, 9 - 6 SAT, 11 - 5 SUN.

One of four factory outlets for Villeroy & Boch, this shop carries an exclusive range of tableware, crystal and cutlery from Europe's largest tableware manu-facturer. A varied and constantly changing stock, including seconds, hotelware and discontinued lines, on sale at excellent reductions, always makes for a worthwhile visit. *Factory Shopping Village*

VIYELLA

GREAT WESTERN DESIGNER VILLAGE, CHURCHWARD VILLAGE, SWINDON, WILTSHIRE SN2 7AR

☎ (01793) 484450. OPEN 10 - 6 MON - SAT, 8 ON THUR, 9 - 6 SAT, 11 - 5 SUN.

Wide range of Viyella ladieswear at discount prices of 30% from jackets and blouses to sweaters and hats. *Factory Shop*

WALTON CLOTHING CO

119 HIGH STREET, MARLBOROUGH, WILTSHIRE

☎ (01672) 516954. OPEN 9 - 6 MON - SAT, 9 - 5 SUN.

Well-known labels for men and women at very competitive, rather than discounted, prices. For women, there is Liz Claiborne, Henney, Principles. For men, Ralph Lauren, Calvin Klein. Part of a chain of twelve in the Cotswold area. *Permanent Discount Outlet*

WEAR IT WELL

59 NORTH STREET, OFF EASTCOTT HILL, OLD TOWN, SWINDON, WILTSHIRE SN1 3JY

☎ (01793) 695223. OPEN 10 - 4.30 TUE, THUR, FRI, SAT.

Two-storey shop selling many high street labels in as new condition, including Wallis, Principles, as well as Precis, Windsmoor, Alexon, Louis Feraud, Betty Barclay and Rodier. There is also a selection of bridal wear, £900 down to £300, often ex-exhibition, maternity wear, evening wear and hats. *Dress Agency*

WILTON SHOPPING VILLAGE

MINSTER STREET, WILTON, SALISBURY, WILTSHIRE SP2 ORS

☎ (01722) 741 211. OPEN 9.30 - 5.30 MON - SAT, 11 - 5 SUN.

On the former site of the Royal Wilton Carpet Factory, this village uses the refurbished original factory dye houses and 300-year old listed historic courtyard buildings to house a variety of factory shops selling fashion and homewares at discounted prices. It includes shops such as Cotton Traders, Edinburgh Woollen Mill, Event Jewellery, James Barry, Julian Graves, Old Traditions, Planet Outlet, Ponden Mill, Roman Originals, Tom Sayers and the Wilton Carpet Factory Shop. *Factory Shopping Village*

WINDSMOOR SALE SHOP

GREAT WESTERN DESIGNER OUTLET VILLAGE, CHURCHWARD VILLAGE, SWINDON, WILTSHIRE SN2 2DZ

☎ (01793) 507600. OPEN 10 - 6 MON - FRI, 8 ON THUR, 9 - 6 SAT, 11 - 5 SUN.

Previous season's stock as well as any returned merchandise and overmakes from the Windsmoor, Planet and Precis Petite ranges at discounts averaging about 50% off the original price. The telephone number is for the centre and not the shop. *Factory Shopping Village*

Live Well On Less Tips

If you're going to be away for two weeks, clean out and turn off the fridge. Leave the doors open a bit to prevent mould and leave an open box of baking soda inside.

Worcestershire

WOMENSWEAR ONLY   Bumpsadaisy Maternity Style, *Worcester.*
Continental Collection, *Barnt Green.*   Designer Depot, *Worcester.*   Exchange & Smart, *Worcester.*
Studio, *Malvern.*   The Designer Agency, *Worcester.*   The House Of Beautiful Clothes, *Pershore.*
Top Drawer, *Chaddesley Corbet.*

WOMENSWEAR & MENSWEAR   Catalogue Bargain Shop, *Droitwich.*
Catalogue Bargain Shop, *Malvern.*   Catalogue Bargain Shop, *Worcester.*
Evesham Country Park Shopping And Gardening Centre, *Evesham.*   The Factory Shop Ltd, *Pershore.*

CHILDREN   Catalogue Bargain Shop, *Droitwich.*   Catalogue Bargain Shop, *Malvern.*
Catalogue Bargain Shop, *Worcester.*   Home & Away, *Redditch.*   Home & Away, *Malvern.*
Nippers, *Worcester.*   The Factory Shop Ltd, *Pershore.*   TP Activity Toys Factory Shop, *Worcester.*

HOUSEHOLD AND GIFTWARE   Ponden Mill Linens, *Evesham.*
G R Pratley & Sons, *The Shambles.*   Catalogue Bargain Shop, *Droitwich.*
Catalogue Bargain Shop, *Malvern.*   Catalogue Bargain Shop, *Worcester.*
Dunelm Mill Shops Ltd, *Worcester.*   Royal Worcester Porcelain, *Worcester.*
The Factory Shop Ltd, *Pershore.*   The Linen Cupboard, *Worcester.*   The Weavers Shop, *Kidderminster.*

ELECTRICAL EQUIPMENT   Catalogue Bargain Shop, *Droitwich.*
Catalogue Bargain Shop, *Malvern.*   Catalogue Bargain Shop, *Worcester.*

DIY/RENOVATION   Holloways, *Suckley.*   Posterity Architectural Antiques, *Little Malvern.*

ARCHITECTURAL SALVAGE   Holloways, *Suckley.*
Posterity Architectural Antiques, *Little Malvern.*

FURNITURE/SOFT FURNISHINGS   Gandolfi House, *Worcester.*
Carpets Of Worth Ltd, *Stourport-On-Severn.*
Evesham Country Park Shopping And Gardening Centre, *Evesham.*   The Curtain Rack, *Pershore.*
The Factory Shop Ltd, *Pershore.*   The Weavers Shop, *Kidderminster.*
Victoria Carpet Weavers Shop, *Kidderminster.*

FOOD AND LEISURE   Evesham Country Park Shopping And Gardening Centre, *Evesham.*

SPORTSWEAR AND EQUIPMENT
Evesham Country Park Shopping And Gardening Centre, *Evesham*

PONDEN MILL LINENS

EVESHAM COUNTRY PARK, EVESHAM, WORCESTERSHIRE WR11 4TP
☎ (01386) 45530. OPEN 9 - 6 MON - SAT, 10.30 - 4.30 SUN.
Famous branded products at direct from the mill prices. Towels, co-ordinated bedlinen, duvets, pillows and curtains from Crown, Coloroll, Chortex, Rectella together with bathroom and kitchen accessories. *Factory Shopping Village*

Live Well On Less Tips
Remove your roof rack if you're not using it regularly to reduce both drag and the car's total weight....
.... Clear out your boot, too, as extra weight reduces petrol mileage.

BUMPSADAISY MATERNITY STYLE

25 FRIARS STREET, WORCESTER
☎ (01905) 28993. OPEN 10 - 5.30 MON - SAT.
Franchised shops and home-based branches with large range of specialist maternity wear, from wedding outfits to ball gowns, to hire and to buy. Hire costs range from £30 to £100 for special occasion wear. To buy are lots of casual and business wear in sizes 8 - 18. For example, skirts £20-£70; dresses £40-£100. Phone ☎ 0181-789 0329 for details of your local stockist. *Hire Shop*

G R PRATLEY & SONS

THE SHAMBLES, WORCESTER WR1 2RG
☎ (01905) 22678/28642. FAX: 745031. OPEN 9 - 5.30 MON - SAT,
CLOSES AT 1 ON THUR.
A family business which specialises in bone china and earthenware, selling famous designer names at 15% lower than normal retail prices. Manufacturers include Royal Worcester, Spode, Royal Doulton, Wedgwood, Johnsons and many others, and individual pieces as well as sets can be bought. Good country furniture, oriental rugs and carpet specialists *Permanent Discount Outlet*

GANDOLFI HOUSE

211-213 WELLS ROAD, MALVERN WELLS, WORCESTER WR14 4HF
☎ (01684) 569747. OPEN 10 - 5.30 TUE - SAT.
Victorian Gothic house built into the Malvern Hills, where even the conservatory and the terrace are part of the shop. There are 12 rooms of room settings containing quality antiques, good repro furniture, Victorian watercolours and paintings, rocking horses, conservatory and garden furniture, and one room specialising in dolls house and furnishings. Prices vary from low average to very reasonable compared with competitors. *Secondhand Shop*

CARPETS OF WORTH LTD

SEVERN VALLEY MILLS, SEVERN ROAD, STOURPORT-ON-SEVERN,
WORCESTERSHIRE, DY13 9HA
☎ (01299) 827222. OPEN 8.30 - 5 MON - FRI, 8 - 12 SAT.
Sells Axminster carpets and rugs, both patterned or plain, and rugs. These are usually seconds or overmakes, discontinued lines or end of contract rolls. *Factory Shop*

CATALOGUE BARGAIN SHOP

WEST BANK, BERRY HILL INDUSTRIAL ESTATE, DROITWICH,
WORCESTERSHIRE, WR9 9AP
☎ (01905) 779850. OPEN 9 - 8 MON - FRI, 9 - 5.30 SAT, 10.30 - 4.30 SUN.
233 WORCESTER ROAD, MALVERN LINK, MALVERN WR14 1SY
☎ (01684) 893062. OPEN 9 - 5.30 MON - SAT, 10.30 - 4.30 SUN.
15 PUMP STREET, WORCESTER WORCESTERSHIRE WR1 2QX
☎ (01905) 617211. OPEN 9 - 5.30 MON - SAT, 10.30 - 4.30 SUN.
Catalogue Bargain Shop is a growing national chain of stores which obtains
the majority of its goods from mail order giants Great Universal and Kays, and
offers a range of clothing for all the family, a wide selection of shoes, bed linen,
household goods, electrical equipment and hundreds of other catalogue items
at very competitive prices. The merchandise consists of ends of ranges and previous season's stock for which there is no longer storage space when the catalogues change. *Permanent Discount Outlet*

CONTINENTAL COLLECTION

48 HEWELL ROAD, BARNT GREEN, WORCESTERSHIRE, B45 8NF
☎ (0121) 447 7544. OPEN 10 - 5 TUE - SAT.
The owner of this shop always endeavours to have at least one Chanel suit on
sale! The huge stock list includes everything from Marks & Spencer upwards,
including some designer samples, evening wear, wedding outfits, ball gowns,
hats and accessories, though the shop specialises in cocktail wear, ballgowns, hats
and wedding outfits. Examples of recent prices include a Simon Ellis wedding
outfit, £220, original price, £595; Mansfield suit, £160, original price £370.
Dress Agency

DESIGNER DEPOT

UNIT 5, CHARLES HOUSE, CHARLES STREET, WORCESTER
WORCESTERSHIRE, WR1 2AQ
☎ (01905) 611568. OPEN 9 - 5.30 MON - SAT.
At Designer Depot, you'll find one of the best selections of top quality branded fashions for women anywhere with amazing discounts of up to 50% off the
normal retail price. With new stock arriving weekly, you'll always find something special here. *Permanent Discount Outlet*

DUNELM MILL SHOPS LTD

F17 CROWNGATE SHOPPING CENTRE, FRIARY WALK, WORCESTER
WORCESTERSHIRE, WR1 3LE
☎ (01905) 611159. OPEN 9 - 5 MON - SAT.
Part of a chain of shops based in the Midlands selling brand-name and chainstore curtains, masses of bedlinen, towels, wickerware, pictures and frames, all
at competitive prices. *Permanent Discount Outlet*

EVESHAM COUNTRY PARK SHOPPING AND GARDENING CENTRE

COUNTRY PARK MANAGEMENT, EVESHAM, AT THE NORTHERN END OF THE EVESHAM BY-PASS AT ITS JUNCTION WITH THE STRATFORD ROAD, WORCESTERSHIRE, WR11 4TP

☎ (01386) 41661

SHOPPING & GARDEN CENTRE

☎ (01386) 761888. OPEN 9 - 6 MON - SAT (WINTER 5.30), 10.30 - 4.30 SUN.

APPLE BARN RESTAURANT

☎ (01386) 761333

VALE WILDLIFE VISITOR CENTRE

☎ (01386) 443348

COARSE FISHING/GOTTFRIED

☎ (0973) 147323

Courtyard shops and garden centre providing a wide variety of goods at bargain prices. Designer and brand name men's and women's fashions, leisurewear from Cotton Traders, co-ordinated soft furnishings, an extensive range of books from The Book Depot, quality plants, kitchen shop, colourful pots, garden equipment, pets and fish. Also restaurant, wildlife centre and coarse fishing on the River Avon for a real country day out. *Factory Shopping Village*

EXCHANGE & SMART

45 NEW STREET, WORCESTER WORCESTERSHIRE, WR1 2DL

☎ (01905) 611522. OPEN 10 - 4.30 MON - FRI, 10 - 5 SAT.

Huge amount of stock on two floors of excellent quality clothing, bags and shoes. The stock includes designer labels such as Nicole Farhi, MaxMara, Mani, and high street labels such as Marks & Spencer, Jaeger and Principles. Examples of prices include Bianca jacket, £45; Mondi suit, £65. There are lots of jackets and coats and a large stock of evening wear. *Dress Agency*

HOLLOWAYS

LOWER COURT, SUCKLEY, WORCESTERSHIRE, WR6 5DE

☎ (01886) 884665. OPEN 9.30 - 5 MON - SAT.

Conservatory furniture specialists, with perhaps the best range of furniture and garden furniture in the country, they also sell antique and reproduction garden statuary, urns, troughs, gates, old and new Coalbrookdale benches, cider mills, staddle stones. The conservatory furniture includes a wide selection of cane, willow and rattan. The rattan range includes elegant, driftwood-coloured frames, bound with leather and with woven banana fibre panels, as well as the more traditional woven rattan; the cane range includes an unpeeled cane waxed to a deep patina, while the willow range includes traditional and

Berrington willow, the latter with scrolled arms and webbed seats. They also sell a range of teak garden furniture - steamer chairs, folding chairs, loungers, benches, rectangular and round tables - conservatory fans, and outdoor ornaments. Among the antique and reproduction garden garden items are antique stone benches, sundials, urns and figures; 19th century Coalbrookdale cast iron seats and old farm artefacts such as stone troughs, staddle stones and cider mills. Other ornaments such as stone vases, urns, birdbaths and statues, are made from reconstituted limestone with a surface texture like Portland stone and coloured to resemble Portland, Bath or Cotswold stone or terracotta. This stone soon develops a covering of moss and lichen to look genuinely old. Original Coalbrookdale benches cost from £1,250, repro ones from £300; antique cider mills from £1,200. *Architectural Salvage*

HOME & AWAY

10 MILFORD CLOSE, WALKWOOD, REDDITCH, WORCESTERSHIRE
B97 5PZ
☎ (01527) 401668.
CHUCKLES, THE GRANARY, HALF KEY LANE, MALVERN,
WORCESTERSHIRE WR14 1UP
☎ (01886) 833594.
Part of the Baby Equipment Hirers Association (BEHA), which has more than 100 members countrywide. A range of equipment can be hired from high chairs, cots and travel cots to baby car seats and buggies. Some members also hire out party equipment including child-sized tables and chairs. BEHA run an advice line which will try and answer any queries you have regarding hiring services for children. Phone the Babyline on 0831 310355. *Hire Shop*

NIPPERS

ORCHARD COTTAGE FARM, CROOME ROAD, DEFFORD, WORCESTER,
WORCESTERSHIRE WR8 9AS
☎ (01386) 750888. FAX ☎ (01386) 750333.
Nippers, the nursery equipment and toy specialists, operate from previously redundant buildings in rural areas around the country. They offer easy parking, no queues and personal service. This is on top of competitive prices on prams, cots, pushchairs, car seats, outdoor play equipment and toys, some of which are new, some seconds or secondhand and some ends of lines. Prices are low because they avoid the high overheads of traditional retail outlets and also because the successful growth of a number of branches means they can now buy in bulk and negotiate good deals. Customers are invited to try out the merchandise while the children look at the animals, mostly sheep, chicken and pigs. Familiar brand names are on sale at all the branches, including Mamas & Papas, Britax, Maclaren and Bebe Confort, plus Fisher-Price and Little Tikes. You can try out the car seats in your car and there is usually a pram/pushchair repair service on site. *Permanent Discount Outlet*

POSTERITY ARCHITECTURAL ANTIQUES

UNDERHILL FARM, LITTLE MALVERN, WORCESTERSHIRE WR14 4JN
☎ (01684) 541254. OPEN 9 - 5 MON - SAT.

Sells all types of old building materials and artefacts, internal fittings, bathrooms, fireplaces, kitchen church pews, stained glass, doors, lighting, garden urns, benches, mouldings and radiators. Whether it's a lamp post for the garden, a butler's sink, a 17th century doorway or a pile of handmade bricks, you're bound to find what you're looking for here. *Architectural Salvage*

ROYAL WORCESTER PORCELAIN

SEVERN STREET, WORCESTER WORCESTERSHIRE WR1 2NE
☎ (01905) 23221. OPEN 9 - 5.30 MON - SAT, 11 - 5 SUN. MAIL ORDER.

Infitesimally flawed porcelain and china seconds at 25% less than perfect prices. Also sells Crummies, Country Artists, Clover Leaf & Pimpernel table mats, as wel as Lakeland Plaques, Fo-Frame, Leeds Display and Paw Prints. There is a vast range with special offers throughout the year on anything from crystal decanters and bowls to figurines, cookware and dinner sets. Shipping arrangements worldwide can be organised. A new attraction is Wignornia Court, incorporating several new shops selling candles, cutlery, linen, china and cookware. Sales in January and July. *Factory Shop*

STUDIO

11 ABBEY ROAD, MALVERN, WORCESTERSHIRE WR14 3ES
☎ (01684) 576253. OPEN 9 - 5.30 MON - SAT.

Finest designer clothes from the Continent (mostly Germany) at discounts of 50%. The company's team of buyers search out and secure considerable discounts on top European name ranges which include both this season's stock and next. The names are well-known but they cannot be divulged here - suffice it to say that they are excellent labels. All stock is perfect, and the vast range covers from casual wear to special occasion outfits. *Permanent Discount Outlet*

Live Well On Less Tips

NORTON & TOWNSEND 71 BONDWAY, LONDON SW8 1SQ.
0171-735 4701.

Norton & Townsend offer bespoke tailoring at off-the-peg prices with all the traditional hand-finishing and attention to detail that you expect from a quality tailor. You can buy a hand cut and finished, perfectly fitting, 100% wool/worsted suit in four to six weeks for as little as £395. The tailor will visit you at home or at work to help you choose from a range of hundreds of cloths. They carry a range of cloths that are bought straight from mills as well as well known merchants such as Dormeuil and Holland & Sherry. They will also tailor suits or jackets using the customer's own fabric. Phone the above telephone number for a list of their regional offices.

THE CURTAIN RACK

25 HIGH STREET, PERSHORE, WORCESTERSHIRE WR10 1AA

☎ (01386) 556105. OPEN 10 - 5 MON - FRI, 9.30 - 5.30 SAT.

Three large showrooms specialising in good quality secondhand curtains, readymades and fabrics. The curtains vary from some cheap and cheerful through to lined curtains, some with matching valances, cushion covers etc. One section of the shop has a large variety of brocades and damask fabrics sold by the metre or they tailor at very competitive prices. They also offer a choice of three companies for a selection of top quality ready-made lined curtains, all of which have optional accessories. There is also a large showroom, packed with sumptuous designer curtains, some interlined, some with swags, tails, tiebacks and others beautifully fringed. They can cater for extremely large windows, all at unbeatable prices. *Secondhand Shop*

THE DESIGNER AGENCY

31 PUMP STREET, WORCESTER WORCESTERSHIRE WR1 2QX

☎ (01905) 21414. OPEN 9.30 - 5 MON - SAT.

Stocks a comprehensive selection of as-new designer ladieswear including Armani jeans; suits by Joseph Janard, Escada and MaxMara; as well as a seasonal range of jackets, coats, raincoats, skirts, dresses and blouses. Also new Italian designer ladieswear by Persona and Marina Rinaldi, sizes 16 - 22, and designer childrenswear from birth - eight years, Miniman, Marese, Jean Bourget and OshKosh. *Dress Agency*

THE FACTORY SHOP LTD

NEW ROAD, PERSHORE, WORCESTERSHIRE WR10 1BY

☎ (01386) 556467. OPEN 9 - 5 MON - SAT, 10.30 - 4.30 SUN.

Wide range on sale includes men's, ladies and children's clothing and footwear; household textiles, toiletries, hardware, luggage, lighting and bedding, most of which are chainstore and high street brands at discounts of approximately 30%-50%. There are weekly deliveries and brands include many of the major stars such as Adidas, Nike, Wrangler and Dartington, to name just four. There are also kitchen and furniture displays and a line of Cape Country furniture on sale. Ranges are continually changing and few factory shops offer such a variety under one roof. Excellent tea rooms offer hot and cold freshly-prepared homemade food and drinks and has its own free car park. *Factory Shop*

THE HOUSE OF BEAUTIFUL CLOTHES

18 BRIDGE ST, PERSHORE, WORCESTERSHIRE WR10 1AT

☎ (01386) 552121. OPEN 10 - 4.30 MON - SAT, CLOSED THUR.

High class, pristine condition and seasonal garments. Some of the stock is designer label - Basler, Windsmoor, Jaeger, Eastex, Jacques Vert, Country Casuals - and nothing costs over £85. there are also hats, new jewellery and handbags. *Dress Agency*

THE LINEN CUPBOARD

OYAL WORCESTER FACTORY SHOP, SEVERN STREET, WORCESTER
WORCESTERSHIRE WR1 2NE

☎ (01905) 726708. OPEN 9 - 5.30 MON - SAT, 11 - 5 SUN.

Bedlinen, sheets, valances, duvet covers, pillowcases, duvets, eiderdowns, towels and bath mats from leading brands all at discount prices. Also nursery bedding, lampshades and cushions, bean bags and sleeping bags. *Factory Shop*

THE WEAVERS SHOP

DUKE PLACE, KIDDERMINSTER, WORCESTERSHIRE DY10 9HB

☎ (01562) 820680/820030 FAX. OPEN 9 - 5 MON - FRI, 9 - 12.30 SAT.

Offers a large selection of tufted and Axminster plain and patterned carpets from the factory. Also now has a wide collection of natural floor coverings and rugs at a considerable discount off high street prices. All goods sold here are returns, discontinued, contract overmakes, ends or slight seconds and therefore represent excellent value for money. Fitters can be suggested and delivery arranged. *Factory Shop*

TOP DRAWER

THE OLD MALT HOUSE, CHADDESLEY CORBET,
WORCESTERSHIRE DY10 4FD

☎ (01562) 777808. OPEN 10 - 4 TUE - FRI, 10 - 1 SAT.

Upmarket dress agency whose labels include Workers for Freedom, Amanda Wakeley, Bed de Lisi, MaxMara, Betty Jackson, Paul Costelloe, Nicole Farhi. Situated in a very pretty village in a delightful old building. *Dress Agency*

TP ACTIVITY TOYS FACTORY SHOP

SEVERN ROAD, STOURPORT-ON-SEVERN,
WORCESTER,WORCESTERSHIRE DY13 9EX

☎ (01299) 872872. 9 - 5 MON - FRI, 9 - 4.30 SAT.

A full range of outdoor and indoor play equipment from swings and climbing frames to sand trays, some of which are discounted at certain times of the year as they are used as display items and aren't as pristine. There is usually one big factory site sale every year as well, which is well worth going to. This usually takes place in April. Discounts for seconds are 20% on outdoor items only. Site shop has Lego, Playmobil and Brio at competitive prices. *Factory Shop*

VICTORIA CARPET WEAVERS SHOP

GREEN STREET, KIDDERMINSTER, WORCESTERSHIRE DY10 1HL

☎ (01562) 754055. OPEN 10 - 5.30 MON - FRI, 9 - 5 SAT.

Large range of Axminsters and Wilton manufactured in own factories, as well as tufted carpets. Roll ends and slight seconds are 25-30% cheaper than normal retail prices. Twelve to fourteen tufted ranges; four Axminster ranges; and one Wilton range. The factory shop does not stock carpets on the roll or large quantities of any one carpet. *Factory Shop*

Yorkshire

WOMENSWEAR ONLY ✄ Aladdin's Cave, *Leeds.* Alexon Sale Shop, *Hornsea.*
Bumpsadaisy Maternity Style, *Leeds.* Claremont Garments, *Rotherham.* Coldspring Mill, *Bradford.*
Denholme Velvets Mill Shop, *Bradford.* Discount Dressing, *Hornsea.* Dorothy Perkins, *Doncaster.*
Eleanor, *Harrogate.* High Society, *York.* Honey, *Hornsea.* Jane Shilton, *Doncaster.*
Jeffrey Rogers, *Leeds.* Labels, *Northallerton.* Laura Ashley, *Hornsea.* Midas Clothes, *York.*
Nightingales Factory Shop, *Sheffield.* Opportunities, *Wakefield.* Phase Eight, *Doncaster.*
Postoptics, *York.* Sarrouche, Rawdon, *Nr Leeds.* Sophie's Choice, *Leeds.*
Taylor's Mill Factory Shop Outlet, Scissett, *Nr Huddersfield.* The Boston Dresser, *Wetherby.*
The Ilkley Dress Agency, *Ilkley.* The Really Good Deal Fashion Sale, *Ripley.*
Windsmoor Sale Shop, *Hornsea.* Wolford, *York.*

MENSWEAR ONLY ✄ Baird Menswear Brands, *Goole.* Dunsford Wesley Menswear, *Castleford.*
Greenwoods White Cross Discount Shopping, *Leeds.* James Barry Menswear, *Doncaster.*
Spencers Trousers, *Sowerby Bridge.* Tie Rack, *Fulford.* Tom Sayers Clothing Co, *Doncaster.*

WOMENSWEAR & MENSWEAR ✄ ✄ Allders at Home, *Leeds.* As New fashions, *Halifax.*
Bargain Street, *Wetherby.* Bargain Street, *Huddersfield.* Bargain Street, *Bradford.*
Bargain Street, *Pontefract.* Bargain Street, *Wakefield.* Best for Less Fashions, *Batley.*
Big L Factory Outlet, *Doncaster.* Black Dyke Mill Shop, *Bradford.* British Mohair Spinners, *Shipley.*
Brooks Factory Outlet Stores, Elland, *Nr Halifax.* Burberry, Cross Hills, *Nr Keighley.*
Catalogue Bargain Shop, *Leeds.* Catalogue Bargain Shop, *Heckmondwike.*
Catalogue Bargain Shop, *Goole.* Catalogue Bargain Shop, *Scarborough.*
Catalogue Bargain Shop, *Middlesbrough.* Clarks Factory Shop, *Doncaster.*
Converse Emea Ltd, *Doncaster.* Cosalt International Ltd, *Wakefield.* Cotton Traders, *York.*
Cream, *Halifax.* Dalesox, *Skipton.* Daleswear Factory Outlet, *Ingleton.* Damart, *Hornsea.*
Deja Vu, *Harrogate.* Designer Shades, *York.* Designer Warehouse, *Middlesbrough.*
Dewhirst Clothing Factory Shop, *Driffield.* Double Two, *Batley.* Famous Footwear, *York.*
Famous Footwear, *Hornsea.* Freeport Castle Designer Outlet Village, *Castleford.*
Glenmatch, *Harrogate.* Golden Shuttle Mill Shop, *Bradford.* Grattan Plc Retail Division, *Doncaster.*
Harriets, *Knaresborough.* Harriets, *Otley.* Harriets, *Thirsk.* Harriets, *Keighley.* Harriets, *Leeds.*
Hornsea Freeport Outlet Village, *Hornsea.* Jaeger Factory Shop, *Cleckheaton.* Joe Bloggs, *Doncaster.*
John Smedley, *Doncaster.* Kastix Mill Shop, *Huddersfield.* La Redoubte Advantages, *Huddersfield.*
Labels for Less, *Bradford.* Lightwater Village & Factory Shopping, *Ripon.*
Littlewoods Catalogue Discount Store, *Sheffield.* Littlewoods Catalogue Discount Store, *Castleford.*
London Leathers Direct, *Hornsea.* Manorgrove, *Bingley.* Mary Cooper, *Harrogate.*
Matalan, *Doncaster.* Matalan, *Rotherham.* Matalan, *York.* Matalan, *Halifax.* Matalan, *Hull.*
Matalan, *Barnsley.* Matalan, *Wakefield.* Matalan, *Bradford.* Matalan, *Leeds.* Matalan, *Sheffield.*
McArthurglen Designer Outlet, *York.* Mexx International, *Hornsea.* Mr Value, *Bradford.*
Orvis Factory Shop, *Harrogate.* Premier & Carousel, *Leeds.* Priestley's, *York.*
Rawhide Store, *Hornsea.* Readmans, *Leeds.* Ripon Revival, *Ripon.* Second Glance, *Huddersfield.*
Shepherds Factory Shop, *Sheffield.* Shirts to Suit, *York.* Springfield Clothing, *Huddersfield.*
The Clothes Rack, *Leeds.* The Clothes Shop, *Bridlington.* The Clothes Shop, *Ilkley.*
The Factory Shop, *Doncaster.* The Factory Shop, *Keighley.* The Factory Shop, *Hornsea.*
The Factory Shop, *Leeds.* The Factory Shop, *Ripon.* The Great Clothes Fashion Store, *Leeds.*
The Harrogate Dress Agency, *Harrogate.* The Shoe Factory Shop, *Hull.*
The Shoe Shelter, *Huddersfield.* The Sports Factory, *Batley.* The Sports Factory, *Doncaster.*
The Sports Factory, *Heckmondwike.* The Sports Factory, *Hornsea.* The Sports Factory, *Ripon.*
The Yorkshire Outlet, *Doncaster.* TK Maxx, *Harrogate.* Tog 24, *Doncaster.* Tog 24, *Hornsea.*
Tog 24, *Ripon.* Tog 24, *Scarborough.* Tog 24, *Whitby.* Tradex, *Pudsey.* Tradex, *Leeds.*
United Footwear, *Bradford.* USC Branded Clothing, *York.* VF Outlets, *Doncaster.*
Warners UK Ltd, *Hornsea.* Wrangler, *Hornsea.* Wynsors World of Shoes, *York, Bradford, Thurcroft,*
Nr Rotherham, Leeds, Cleckheaton, Sheffield, York, Castleford, Hull. You & Yours, *Huddersfield.*

CHILDREN 🦃 Allders at Home, *Leeds*, As New fashions, *Halifax*.
B-Line Clothing Ltd, *Rotherham*. Baby Hire, *Bradford*. Bargain Street, *Wetherby*.
Bargain Street, *Huddersfield*. Bargain Street, *Bradford*. Bargain Street, *Pontefract*.
Bargain Street, *Wakefield*. Brooks Factory Outlet Stores, *Elland, Nr Halifax*.
Burberry, *Cross Hills, Nr Keighley*. Catalogue Bargain Shop, *Leeds*.
Catalogue Bargain Shop, *Heckmondwike*. Catalogue Bargain Shop, *Goole*.
Catalogue Bargain Shop, *Scarborough*. Catalogue Bargain Shop, *Middlesbrough*.
Clarks Factory Shop, *Doncaster*. Dalesox, *Skipton*. Daleswear Factory Outlet, *Ingleton*.
Designer Shades, *York*. Dewhirst Clothing Factory Shop, *Driffield*.
Everything But The Baby, *Knaresborough*. Freeport Castle Designer Outlet Village, *Castleford*.
Golden Shuttle Mill Shop, *Bradford*. Grattan Plc Retail Division, *Doncaster*.
Hornsea Freeport Outlet Village, *Hornsea*. Jokids Ltd, *Doncaster*.
Kastix Mill Shop, *Huddersfield*. La Redoubte Advantages, *Huddersfield*.
Lightwater Village & Factory Shopping, *Ripon*. Littlewoods Catalogue Discount Store, *Sheffield*.
Littlewoods Catalogue Discount Store, *Castleford*. Manorgrove, *Bingley*.
Mary Cooper, *Harrogate*. Matalan, *Doncaster*. Matalan, *Rotherham*. Matalan, *York*.
Matalan, *Halifax*. Matalan, *Hull*. Matalan, *Barnsley*. Matalan, *Wakefield*. Matalan, *Bradford*.
Matalan, *Leeds*. Matalan, *Sheffield*. McArthurglen Designer Outlet, *York*.
Mexx International, *Hornsea*. Mr Baby, *Huddersfield*. Nursery Needs, *Richmond*.
Opportunities, *Wakefield*. Praxis Tailoring, *Shipley*. Premier & Carousel, *Leeds*.
Rainbow, *Keighley*. Readmans, *Leeds*. Second Glance, *Huddersfield*.
Shepherds Factory Shop, *Sheffield*. Sophie's Choice, *Leeds*. Springfield Clothing, *Huddersfield*.
Taylor's Mill Factory Shop Outlet, *Scissett*. The Factory Shop, *Doncaster*.
The Factory Shop, *Keighley*. The Factory Shop, *Hornsea*. The Factory Shop, *Leeds*.
The Factory Shop, *Ripon*. The Great Clothes Fashion Store, *Leeds*. The Shoe Factory Shop, *Hull*.
The Shoe Shelter, *Huddersfield*. The Sports Factory, *Batley*. The Sports Factory, *Doncaster*.
The Sports Factory, *Heckmondwike*. The Sports Factory, *Hornsea*. The Sports Factory, *Ripon*.
The Yorkshire Outlet, *Doncaster*. TK Maxx, *Harrogate*. Tog 24, *Doncaster*. Tog 24, *Hornsea*.
Tog 24, *Ripon*. Tog 24, *Scarborough*. Tog 24, *Whitby*. Toymaster Factory Outlets, *Darlington*.
Toyworld, *Leeds*. Tradex, *Pudsey*. Tradex, *Leeds*. Travelling Tots, *Middlesbrough*.
United Footwear, *Bradford*. VF Outlets, *Doncaster*. Wynsors World of Shoes, *York*.
Wynsors World of Shoes, *Bradford*. Wynsors World of Shoes, *Thurcroft, Nr Rotherham*.
Wynsors World of Shoes, *Leeds*. Wynsors World of Shoes, *Cleckheaton*.
Wynsors World of Shoes, *Sheffield*. Wynsors World of Shoes, *York*.
Wynsors World of Shoes, *Castleford*. Wynsors World of Shoes, *Hull*. You & Yours, *Huddersfield*.
YoYo, *Beverley*.

HOUSEHOLD AND GIFTWARE 🏛 Bargain Street, *Wetherby*. Bargain Street, *Huddersfield*.
Bargain Street, *Bradford*. Bargain Street, *Pontefract*. Bargain Street, *Wakefield*. Birthdays, *Doncaster*.
Brooks Factory Outlet Stores, *Elland, Nr Halifax*. Cape Country, *Morley*. Card & Gift, *Bradford*.
Catalogue Bargain Shop, *Leeds*. Catalogue Bargain Shop, *Heckmondwike*.
Catalogue Bargain Shop, *Goole*. Catalogue Bargain Shop, *Scarborough*.
Catalogue Bargain Shop, *Middlesbrough*. Clover Leaf, *Doncaster*. Dunelm Mill Shop, *Sheffield*.
Edinburgh Crystal, *Hornsea*. Freeport Castle Designer Outlet Village, *Castleford*.
Homes & Gardens Summer Grand Sale, *Ripley*. Hornsea Freeport Outlet Village, *Hornsea*.
Le Creuset, *York*. Lightwater Village & Factory Shopping, *Ripon*. Matalan, *Doncaster*.
Matalan, *Rotherham*. Matalan, *York*. Matalan, *Halifax*. Matalan, *Hull*. Matalan, *Barnsley*.
Matalan, *Wakefield*. Matalan, *Bradford*. Matalan, *Leeds*. Matalan, *Sheffield*.
McArthurglen Designer Outlet, *York*. Mr Value, *Bradford*. Mulberry Clearance Shop, *York*.
Oneida, *York*. Osborne, *Sheffield*. Ponden Mill, *Stanbury, Nr Haworth*. Ponden Mill Linens, *Batley*.
Ponden Mill Linens, *Hornsea*. Price's Candles, *Doncaster*. Readmans, *Leeds*.
Royal Brierley Crystal, *Hornsea*. Shepherds Factory Shop, *Sheffield*. Spoils, *Hull*. Spoils, *Leeds*.
The China Ladies, *Huddersfield*. The David Mellor Factory Shop, *Sheffield*.
The Darley Mill Centre, *Darley*. The Factory Shop, *Doncaster*. The Factory Shop, *Keighley*.
The Factory Shop, *Hornsea*. The Factory Shop, *Leeds*. The Factory Shop, *Ripon*.
The Linen Cupboard, *Doncaster*. The Tea Pottery, *Wensleydale*. The Yorkshire Outlet, *Doncaster*.
TK Maxx, *Harrogate*. Tradex, *Pudsey*. Tradex, *Leeds*.
White Rose Candles Workshop, *Leyburn*. You & Yours, *Huddersfield*.

ELECTRICAL EQUIPMENT ~ Bargain Street, *Wetherby*. Bargain Street, *Huddersfield*. Bargain Street, *Bradford*. Bargain Street, *Pontefract*. Bargain Street, *Wakefield*. Catalogue Bargain Shop, *Leeds*. Catalogue Bargain Shop, *Heckmondwike*. Catalogue Bargain Shop, *Goole*. Catalogue Bargain Shop, *Scarborough*. Catalogue Bargain Shop, *Middlesbrough*. Freeport Castle Designer Outlet Village, *Castleford*. Grattan Plc Retail Division, *Doncaster*. Littlewoods Catalogue Discount Store, *Sheffield*. Littlewoods Catalogue Discount Store, *Castleford*. McArthurglen Designer Outlet, *York*. Remington, *Doncaster*. The Lighting Factory Shop, *Leeds*. You & Yours, *Huddersfield*.

DIY/RENOVATION ~ Andy Thornton Architectural Antiques Ltd, *Halifax*. Black & Decker, *Doncaster*. Chapel House Fireplaces, *Huddersfield*. Dolmens, *Cleckheaton*. Glynn Webb, *Bradford*. Glynn Webb, *Doncaster*. Glynn Webb, *Halifax*. Glynn Webb, *Huddersfield*. Glynn Webb, *Hull*. Glynn Webb, *Sheffield*. Glynn Webb, *Wakefield*. Glynn Webb, *Stockton-on-Tees*. Havenplan Ltd, *Sheffield*. Tile Clearing House, *Hull*. Tile Clearing House, *Bradford*. Tile Clearing House, *Sheffield*. W Machell & Sons Ltd, *Leeds*. York Handmade Bricks Ltd, *York*.

ARCHITECTURAL SALVAGE ~ Andy Thornton Architectural Antiques Ltd, *Halifax* Black & Decker, *Doncaster*. Chapel House Fireplaces, *Huddersfield*. Dolmens, *Cleckheaton*. Havenplan Ltd, *Sheffield*. W Machell & Sons Ltd, *Leeds*. York Handmade Bricks Ltd, *York*.

FURNITURE/SOFT FURNISHINGS ~ Burmatex Ltd, *Ossett*. Byworth Fabric Warehouse, *Bradford*. Cape Country Furniture, *Morley* Curtain Transfer, *Harrogate*. EG Interior Fabrics, *Leeds*. East Ardsley Household Textiles, *Wakefield*. Fabrics From The Mills, *Huddersfield*. Freeport Castle Designer Outlet Village, *Castleford*. House of Fabrics, *Shipley*. Howkel Rugs, *Huddersfield*. Laura Ashley, *Hornsea*. Magnet Ltd Clearance Centre, *Keighley*. RL & CM Bond Ltd, *Pudsey*. Skopos Mills, *Batley*. Skopos Mills, *Shipley*. Smith's Mill Shop, *Halifax*. Staples, *Leeds*. The Curtain Exchange, *Boston Spa*. The Fabric Emporium, Leeds The Fabric Shop, Addingham, *Nr Ilkley*. The Fabric Shop, *Keighley*. The Factory Shop, *Hornsea*. The Factory Shop, *Ripon*. The Fine Furniture Club, *Tockwith/Cowthorpe*. The Shuttle Fabric Shop, *Shipley*. Waltons Mill Shop, *Harrogate*.

FOOD AND LEISURE ~ Coldspring Mill, *Bradford*. Freeport Castle Designer Outlet Village, *Castleford*. Hallmark, *Hornsea*. Luggage & Baggage, *Hornsea*. Luggage & Bags, *Hornsea*. Mr Value, *Bradford*. The Body Shop Depot, *York*. Thorntons, *Doncaster*. Thorntons, *Fulford*. Travel Accessory Outlet, *Fulford*.

SPORTSWEAR AND EQUIPMENT ~ B-Line Clothing Ltd, *Rotherham*. Brett Harris Ltd, *Silsden*. Clarks Factory Shop, *Doncaster*. Freeport Castle Designer Outlet Village, *Castleford*. Hornsea Freeport Outlet Village, *Hornsea*. Mileta, *Heckmondwike*. The Sports Factory, *Doncaster*. United Footwear, *Bradford*.

ALADDIN'S CAVE

19 QUEEN'S ARCADE, LEEDS, YORKSHIRE LS1 6LF
☎ (0113) 245 7903. OPEN 10 - 5 MON - SAT.
Two-storey shop with a dress agency downstairs, and an array of antique jewellery, silver, and teddy bears on the ground floor. The nearly-new department sells everything from Marks & Spencer to designers such as Dolce & Gabbanna. *Dress Agency*

ALEXON SALE SHOP

HORNSEA FREEPORT SHOPPING VILLAGE, HORNSEA,
YORKSHIRE HU18 1UJ
☎ (01964) 535441. OPEN 9.30 - 6 SEVEN DAYS A WEEK.
10-14 BRIDGEGATE, ROTHERHAM, SOUTH YORKSHIRE S60 1PQ
☎ (01709) 382491. OPEN 9 - 5.30 MON - SAT.

Alexon and Eastex from last season at 40% less than the original price; during
sale time in January and June, the reductions are 70%. Stock includes separates,
skirts, jackets, blouses; there is no underwear or night clothes. The Hornsea
shop also sells the Dash and Calico ranges. *Permanent Discount Outlet*

ALLDERS AT HOME

2 BRIDGE ROAD, KIRKSTALL, LEEDS, YORKSHIRE LS5 3BL
☎ (0113) 230 5800. OPEN 10 - 5.30 MON - WED, 10 - 8 THUR, FRI,
9.30 - 5.30 SAT, 10.30 - 4.30 SUN.
Clearance outlet for Allders department stores selling men's, ladies and children's reduced stock. Famous names include Morgan, Benetton, Planet, Precis,
Windsmoor, Frank Usher, Jumper, Dannimac, Fenn Wright & Manson,
French Connection, Gabicci, O'Neil, Matinique, YSL, Shoe Studio. Samples
are also available at competitive prices twice a year from Gerry Webber, Taifun,
She, Ravens, Sigrid Olsen, Erfo and Samoon. The Sports Department sells a
mix of reduced and full price stock. *Permanent Discount Outlet*

ANDY THORNTON
ARCHITECTURAL ANTIQUES LTD

VICTORIA MILLS, STAINLAND ROAD, GREETLAND, HALIFAX,
YORKSHIRE HX4 8AD
☎ (01422) 377314. OPEN 8.30 - 5.30 MON - FRI, 9 - 5 SAT, 10 - 4.30 SUN.
Doors, fireplaces, panelled rooms, church interiors, bathroom fittings, radiators, balustrades, chandeliers, stained glass, marble, pews and light-fittings all
situated in an enormous converted mill. If you can't find the original piece you
want, they will make you a reproduction. One of the five floors is devoted to
reproductions with a huge range of Tiffany lamps. The top floor houses
Americana and outside are plenty of garden urns, statuary and cast-iron gates
Architectural Salvage

AS NEW FASHIONS

1 EMSCOTE GROVE, HAUGH SHAW ROAD, HALIFAX, YORKSHIRE
☎ (01422) 365379. OPEN 9.30 - 4.30 MON - SAT.
Ladies, men's and children's nearly-new clothes all available. Men's suits are
generally Marks & Spencer, although Simon suits, among others, are occasionally stocked, as well as dinner suits at Christmas time. For women there is

a rail exclusively for Jaeger and Jacques Vert. There is usually a selection of seasonal and sports wear, including ski clothes, as well as children's school uniforms and accessories. *Dress Agency*

B-LINE CLOTHING LTD

19 MOOR ROAD, WATH-UPON-DEARNE, ROTHERHAM, YORKSHIRE S63 7RS

☎ (01709) 878364. OPEN 9 - 5 MON - THUR, 9 - 12 FRI, 10 - 1 SAT.

Sells mostly Pulse 8 brand-name fleece jackets at half-price and also stocks some sweatshirts, waterproof jackets, chef's trousers and jackets. All are current season perfects offered at 50% discounts to men, women and children. *Factory Shop*

BAIRD MENSWEAR BRANDS

RAWCLIFFE ROAD, GOOLE, YORKSHIRE DN14 6VA

☎ (01405) 760801. OPEN 9.30 - 4.30 MON - SAT, 10 - 4 BANK HOLIDAYS.

Manufactures men's suits, jackets and trousers for a well-known high street chain store, the factory shops sell seconds and overmakes at as little as one-third of their normal retail price. About 40% percent of the merchandise sold here is made by the factory, with a further 60% manufactured within the company. *Factory Shop*

BARGAIN STREET

BUY WELL SHOPPING CENTRE, THORPE ARCH TRADING ESTATE, WETHERBY, YORKSHIRE LS22 6NF

☎ (01937) 845650. OPEN 9.30 - 5.30 MON - SAT, 10.30 - 4.30 SUN.

19-23 MARKET STREET, HUDDERSFIELD HD1 2HL

☎ (01484) 421969. OPEN 9.30 - 5.30 MON - SAT.

UNIT D, WEAVERTHORPE RETAIL PARK, TONG STREET, BRADFORD

☎ (01274) 688118. OPEN 9.30 - 5.30 MON - SAT, 8 ON THUR.

5 HORSEFAIR, PONTEFRACT, WEST YORKSHIRE WF8 1PE

☎ (01977) 690921. OPEN 9.30 - 5.30 MON - SAT.

12 PROVIDENCE STREET, WAKEFIELD, WEST YORKSHIRE WF1 3BG

☎ (01924) 29☎ 0181. OPEN 9 - 5 MON - SAT.

Offers a wide range of clothing for all the family, a large selection of footwear, household textiles, hardware, electrical equipment and hundreds of others items at very attractive prices. All the items are surplus stock from the Empire range of mail order catalogues, including famous brand names, and are offered with huge discounts from the original catalogue prices. Stock changes on a weekly basis and there are regular sales promotions offering even better value. *Permanent Discount Outlet*

Live Well On Less Tips
Use your radio on mains rather than battery - it's cheaper.

BEST FOR LESS FASHIONS

SKOPOS MILLS, BRADFORD ROAD, BATLEY, YORKSHIRE

☎ (01924) 359090. OPEN 10 - 5 MON - SAT, 11 - 5 SUN.

End of season fashion for men and women which consists of well-known brand names and sportswear. Labels include, for women, Alice Collins, J J Sloane, Ladies Pride, Jamie Oliver, Frank Eden and the Hucke range; for men, Pierre Cardin, Woodville trousers and Oakman. *Permanent Discount Outlet*

BIG L FACTORY OUTLET

UNIT 19, THE YORKSHIRE OUTLET, WHITE ROSE WAY, DONCASTER LAKESIDE, YORKSHIRE DN4 5JH

☎ (01302) 367043. OPEN 10 - 6 MON - SAT, 11 - 5 SUN.

Men's and women's Levi jeans, jackets, cord and Sherpa fleece jackets, T-shirts and shirts but no children's, all at discount prices. *Factory Shopping Village*

BIRTHDAYS

THE YORKSHIRE OUTLET, WHITE ROSE WAY, DONCASTER, SOUTH YORKSHIRE

☎ (01302) 325803. OPEN 10 - 6 MON - SAT, 11 - 5 SUN.

Cards, notelets, stationery sets, colouring books, stuffed toys, photo albums, picture frames, gifts, giftwrap, tissue paper, party packs, candlesticks, Christmas crackers, string puppets, fairy lights all at discounts of up to 30%. Some are special purchases, some seconds. *Factory Shopping Village*

BLACK & DECKER

THE YORKSHIRE OUTLET, WHITE ROSE WAY, DONCASTER, YORKSHIREDN4 5JH

☎ (01302) 344488. OPEN 10 - 6 MON - SAT, 11 - 5 SUN.

Reconditioned tools and accessories from the famous Black & Decker range, all with full manufacturer's warranty. Often, stock consists of goods returned from the shops because of damaged packaging or are part of a line which is being discontinued. Lots of seasonal special offers. *Factory Shopping Village*

BLACK DYKE MILL SHOP

BLACK DYKE MILLS COMPLEX, QUEENSBURY, BRADFORD, YORKSHIRE BD13 1QA

☎ (01274) 882271. OPEN 8.30 - 12.30, 1.30 - 4.30 MON, TUE, THUR, FRI, 9 - 12 WED, CLOSED SAT, SUN.

Manufactures men's suitings and a small selection of ladies fabric. Seconds, quality worsted and mohair suit lengths, trouser lengths and one metre fents. Suit lengths from £15-£45. Trousers lengths from £6; skirt lengths from £2.50. Closed Bank and Mill holidays so please ring before travelling far. Call in at the Mill's reception and they will open up the factory shop. *Factory Shop*

Live Well On Less Tips

Freeze candles before using as they will burn more slowly and also more evenly and with minimal wax dripping.

BRETT HARRIS LTD

WATERLOO MILLS, HOWDEN ROAD, SILSDEN, YORKSHIRE BD20 OHA
☎ (01535) 654479.

Manufacturers of sleeping bags, cold weather clothing, camping accessories, compression sacks and outdoor accessories, most of which are exported, they sell discontinued lines, demo models and slight seconds at occasional sales. These sales, which are usually held on Saturday mornings, offer stock discounted by up to 50%. Phone for the date of their next sale. *Factory Shop*

BRITISH MOHAIR SPINNERS

LOWER HOLME MILLS, SHIPLEY, YORKSHIRE BD17 7EU
☎ (01274) 583111. OPEN 9 - 4 MON - FRI.

Hand knitting yarns in mohair, British wool, arrans, as well as a small selection of quality knitwear. Knitting service allows you to choose the yarn and have an item knitted up to your pattern. *Factory Shop*

BROOKS FACTORY OUTLET STORES

SOUTH LANE, ELLAND, NEAR HALIFAX, YORKSHIRE HX5 OHQ
☎ (01422) 377337. OPEN 9.30 - 5.30 MON - SAT, 8 ON THUR, 11 - 5 SUN AND BANK HOLIDAYS.
BUYWELL RETAIL PARK, THORPE ARCH, WETHERBY, NORTH YORKSHIRE LS23 7BJ
☎ (01937) 541895. OPEN 9.30 - 5.30 MON - SAT, 11 - 5 SUN AND BANK HOLIDAYS.

Walk through the store and you will find names you recognise at prices you want. There are literally thousands of bargains with new stock arriving daily from well-known names such as Nike, Reebok, Antler, Gabicci, Gossard, Tommy Hilfiger and Ralph Lauren. Specialist departments include sportswear, menswear, linens, lingerie, accessories, womenswear and luggge. In the Ponden Mill Linen department, there are towels, co-ordinated bed linen, household textiles, duvets, pillows and lots more from names such as Vantona, Hamilton McBride, Helena Springfield, Broomhill, Monogram, Chortex, Zorbit and Christy. Other brand names in the fashion sections include Principles, Reebok, Roman, Selfridges, Tog 24, Calvin Klein and Wolsey. *Permanent Discount Outlet*

BUMPSADAISY MATERNITY STYLE

14 BANK STREET, WETHERBY, LEEDS, YORKSHIRE LS22 6NQ

☎ (01937) 580641. OPEN 9.30 - 5.30 MON - SAT, 9.30 - 1 WED.

Franchised shops and home-based branches with large range of specialist maternity wear, from wedding outfits to ball gowns, to hire and to buy. Hire costs range from £30 to £100 for special occasion wear. To buy are lots of casual and business wear in sizes 8 - 18. For example, skirts £20-£70; dresses £40-£100. Phone ☎ 0181-789 0329 for details of your local stockist. *Hire Shop*

BURBERRY, WOODROW UNIVERSAL

JUNCTION MILLS, CROSS HILLS, NEAR KEIGHLEY, YORKSHIRE BD20 7SE

☎ (01535) 633364. OPEN 10 - 4 MON - SAT.

CORONATION MILLS, ALBION STREET, CASTLEFORD, WEST YORKSHIRE

☎ (01977) 554411. OPEN 10.15 - 4.15 MON - FRI, 9.30 - 4 SAT.

MIDLAND ROAD, ROYSTON, NEAR BARNSLEY, SOUTH YORKSHIRE

☎ (01226) 728030. OPEN 9.30 - 3.30 MON - SAT.

OLD MARKET TAVERN, MARKET PLACE, WHITBY, NORTH YORKSHIRE

☎ (01947) 606161. OPEN 9.30 - 4.30 MON - SAT, 11 - 4 SUN.

These Burberry factory shops sell seconds and overmakes of the famous name raincoats and duffle coats as well as accessories such as the distinctive umbrellas, scarves and handbags. They also sell children's duffle coats, knitwear and shirts and the Castleford branch sells some of the Burberry range of food: jams, biscuits, tea and chocolate. All carry the Burberry label and are about one third of the normal retail price. *Factory Shop*

BURMATEX LTD

VICTORIA MILLS, THE GREEN, OSSETT, YORKSHIRE WF5 OAN

☎ (01924) 276 333. OPEN 9.30 - 4 MON - FRI. 8 - 11.45 SAT.

A factory shop selling B quality carpet tiles at prices that are 50% less than the high street prices and which range from £1.65 to £2. *Factory Shop*

BYWORTH FABRIC WAREHOUSE

36 CEMETERY ROAD, 4 LANE ENDS, BRADFORD, YORKSHIRE BD8 9RY

☎ (01274) 481800. OPEN 9 - 5 MON - SAT, UNTIL 7 THUR, 10 - 4 SUN.

Stocks over 6,000 rolls of curtain and furnishing fabrics in its 14,000 sq ft outlet, including muslins, linings and all accessories - tracks, poles and brassware. Most are department store brands, but at warehouse prices. Soft furnishing fabric costs from £1.99 a metre, lining from £1.99; upholstery fabrics from £4.99 a metre. There is free on-site parking and easy access for the disabled. Professional staff are on hand with advice. *Permanent Discount Outlet*

CARD & GIFT

DAWSON LANE, DUDLEY HILL, BRADFORD, YORKSHIRE BD4 6HW
☎ (01274) 689399. OPEN 10 - 5.30 MON - FRI, 10 - 5 SAT.
Wedding novelties, cards, gift wrap, toys, soft toys, banners, balloons, badges, candle sticks, stationery, all of which is perfect stock at reduced prices. *Factory Shop*

CATALOGUE BARGAIN SHOP

28 NEW BRIGGATE, BRIGGATE, LEEDS, YORKSHIRE LS1 6NU
☎ (0113) 243 6425. OPEN 9 - 5.30 MON - SAT, 11 - 5 SUN.
57-59 MARKET PLACE, HECKMONDWIKE, WEST YORKSHIRE WF16 0EZ
☎ (01924) 402674. OPEN 9 - 5.30 MON - SAT, 10 - 4 SUN.
42 JOHN WILLIAM STREET, HUDDERSFIELD, WEST YORKSHIRE HD1 1ER
☎ (01484) 535112. OPEN 9 - 5.30 MON - SAT, 10.30 - 4.30 SUN.
BOOTHFERRY ROAD, GOOLE, HUMBERSIDE DN14 6BB
☎ (01405) 765138. OPEN 8 - 8 MON - SAT, 10 - 4 SUN.
20 ST THOMAS STREET, SCARBOROUGH YO11 1DR
☎ (01723) 371733. OPEN 9 - 5.30 MON - SAT, 10.30 - 4.30 SUN.
51 ACKLAM ROAD, MIDDLESBROUGH, YORKSHIRE TS5 5HA
☎ (01642) 825925. OPEN 9 - 5 MON - SAT, 10.30 - 4.30 SUN.
Catalogue Bargain Shop is a growing national chain of stores which obtains the majority of its goods from mail order giants Great Universal and Kays, and offers a range of clothing for all the family, a wide selection of shoes, bed linen, household goods, electrical equipment and hundreds of other catalogue items at very competitive prices. The merchandise consists of ends of ranges and previous season's stock for which there is no longer storage space when the catalogues change. *Permanent Discount Outlet*

CHAPEL HOUSE FIREPLACES

ST GEORGE'S ROAD, SCHOLES, HOLMFIRTH, HUDDERSFIELD, YORKSHIRE HD7 1UH
☎ (01484) 682275. OPEN TUE - SAT BY APPOINTMENT ONLY.
Period fireplaces with correct grates, baskets and inserts, including French fireplaces dating from 1750-1910. *Architectural Salvage*

CLAREMONT GARMENTS

TENFER STREET, ROTHERHAM, YORKSHIRE S60 1LB
☎ (01709) 830575. OPEN 9 - 4.30 MON - FRI, 9 - 2.30 SAT.
Sells a wide range of ladies high street fashions at between 30% and 50% below high street prices. *Factory Shop*

CLARKS FACTORY SHOP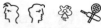

THE YORKSHIRE OUTLET, WHITE ROSE WAY, DONCASTER,
YORKSHIRE DN4 5JH

☎ (01302) 322663. OPEN 10 - 6 MON - SAT, 11 - 5 SUN.

Clarks International operate a chain of factory shops nationally which specialise in selling discontinued lines and slight sub-standards for men, women and children from Clarks, K Shoes and other famous brands. These shops trade under the name of Crockers, K Shoes Factory shop or Clarks Factory Shop and while not all are physically attached to a shoe factory, these shops are treated as factory shops by the company. Customers can expect to find an extensive range of quality shoes, sandals, walking boots, slippers, trainers, handbags, accessories and gifts, while their major outlets such as here also offer luggage, sports clothing, sports equipment and outdoor clothing. Brands stocked include Clarks, K Shoes, Springer, CICA, Hi-Tec, Puma, Mercury, Dr Martens, Nike, LA Gear, Fila, Mizuno, Slazenger, Weider, Antler and Carlton, although not all are sold in every outlet. Discounts are from 30% to 60% off the normal high street price for perfect stock. This shop also incorporates Sports Factory and Baggage Factory. *Factory Shopping Village*

CLOVER LEAF

THE YORKSHIRE OUTLET, WHITE ROSE WAY, DONCASTER,
YORKSHIRE DN4 5JH

☎ (01302) 367021. OPEN 10 - 6 MON - SAT, 11 - 5 SUN.

Sells a good range of kitchen and oven to tableware, place mats, teapot stands, teabag tidies, chopping bords, ceramic pottery, beech trays, kitchen clocks and coasters. There are usually about 48 different designs of table mat in stock at any one time. Seconds and discontinued lines are sold here at reduced prices. *Factory Shopping Village*

COLDSPRING MILL

HAWORTH ROAD, CULLINGWORTH, BRADFORD
(NEAR HAWORTH), YORKSHIRE BD13 5EE

☎ (01535) 275646. OPEN 10 - 4 SEVEN DAYS A WEEK.

Sells high quality branded knitting wool and mohair from local manufacturers at vastly discounted prices. As the yarns come direct from the spinner, Coldspring always has the latest shades. Also Yorkshire tweed skirt lengths at very good prices. There are bargain packs of knitting wools and shoppers receive 10 free patterns of their choice with their purchase. Examples of prices include 1,000 grams of Arran wool, £7.99; skirt lengths, £7.99. Situated in Emily Bronte country, it makes a marvellous day out as you drive over the bleak heights near Haworth. There is a tea room and plenty of parking. Just ten minutes away is the Denholme Velvets Factory Shop with Ponden Mill nearby, too. *Food and Leisure Factory Shop*

Live Well On Less Tips
Let hot foods cool off before putting them in the fridge or freezer to avoid releasing moisture and raising the temperature.

CONVERSE EMEA LTD

THE YORKSHIRE OUTLET, WHITE ROSE WAY, DONCASTER, YORKSHIRE DN4 5JH

☎ (01302) 367088. OPEN 10 - 6 MON - SAT, 11 - 5 SUN.

Founded in 1908, Converse is the largest manufacturer of sports footwear in the U.S. They are a leading designer, manufacturer and marketer of high quality athletic footwear and clothing, specialising in Baseball, Action Sports and Athletic Originals. Stock is sold with a minimum discount of 25% for ends of lines and discounted ranges. For example, Canvas All Star Chuck Taylor, £19.99, reduced from £29.99. *Factory Shopping Village*

COSALT INTERNATIONAL LTD

UNIT 10, HEADWAY BUSINESS PARK, DENBY DALE ROAD, WAKEFIELD, YORKSHIRE WF2 7AZ

☎ (01924) 880770 . OPEN 8.30 - 5 MON - FRI.

The company specialises in workwear, safety clothing and marine wear but some of the merchandise is eminently wearable for everyday and is sold at very reasonable prices. This particular outlet specialises in tarpaulins, ropes, ratchet straps, overalls, workwear, fleeces and T-shirts. VAT has to be added to prices. There are catalogues available for you to order from if what you want isn't in stock. They also provide marine safety and life-raft servicing. *Permanent Discount Outlet*

COTTON TRADERS

UNIT 74, MCARTHURGLEN DESIGNER OUTLET CENTRE, OLD NABURN HOSPITAL SITE, FULFORD, YORK, YORKSHIRE Y01 4RE

☎ (01904) 625490. OPEN 10 - 6 MON - SAT, TILL 8 THUR, 11 - 5 SUN.

Sells own label leisurewear for men, women and children. *Factory Shopping Village*

CREAM

27 HALIFAX ROAD, HIPPERHOLME, HALIFAX, YORKSHIRE HX3 8HQ

☎ (01422) 205080. OPEN 9 - 5.30 MON - SAT.

Three-storey shop selling a large selection of constantly changing stock: ladies daywear, evening wear, accessories and menswear. Labels on sale include Moschino, Frank Usher, Rifat Ozbek, Betty Barclay and Romeo Gigli. Examples of prices include a Romeo Gigli three-quarter length coat, £100. Menswear includes labels such as Armani and Boss. *Dress Agency*

CURTAIN TRANSFER

THE OLD STABLE, BACK TEWIT WELL ROAD, OFF SOUTH DRIVE,
HARROGATE, YORKSHIRE HG2 8JF

☎ (01423) 505520. OPEN 10 - 6 TUE - SAT, SAT BY APPOINTMENT.

Curtain Transfer opened in Harrogate in 1992. The showroom in a converted
stable in a courtyard opposite the owner's own home is a treasure trove of secondhand curtains, blinds, bedcovers and all kinds of upmarket furnishing accessories - pictures, lamps and lampshades, cushions and rugs. Goods are taken in
on sale-or-return agency terms. There is always a good selection of long lined or
interlined curtains - from Liberty, Sanderson, G P & J Baker and Laura Ashley,
as well as current designer names. Buyers can take goods home overnight on
approval. Parking is in the courtyard and children are welcome. To get there
from Leeds going towards the town centre, take a right at St George's
Roundabout on South Drive, over Tewit Well Road, left by railway bridge. From
the by-pass, go into Harrogate to the big roundabout, turn left on York Place,
left again on Stray Rein to just over the railway bridge on the right.
Secondhand Shop

DALESOX

6 SWADFORD STREET, SKIPTON, YORKSHIRE BD23 1JA

☎ (01756) 796509. OPEN 9 - 5 SEVEN DAYS A WEEK.

Based in Skipton's main shopping area, Dalesox sells quality hosiery and accessories. Most are perfect ladies, men's and children's socks made for the best
high street chainstores and cost about £1-£2.99 a pair, normal retail price up
to £4.99. There is lots of design choice from Disney character socks to
Christmas character socks. There are also ties, ski socks made for famous
department stores, unusual design Swedish polyester ties, knickers, boxer
shorts, pyjamas and nightshirts. Most of the stock is bought in from other
manufacturers, cutting out the middleman. *Factory Shop*

DALESWEAR FACTORY OUTLET

LAUNDRY LANE, INGLETON, YORKSHIRE

☎ (0154242) 42373. OPEN 9 - 5 MON - SAT, 9.30 - 5 SUN.

Manufacturer of fleeces and waterproofs using Polartec. They sell breathable
waterproof trousers and jackets and a vast range of fleece pullovers and tops.
Also a small selection of Rohan socks and hats. Thre are two shops in Ingleton,
here and in the high street. *Factory Shop*

Live Well On Less Tips

Eat your big meal at lunch time rather than dinner. The menus may be exactly the same but the price of lunch at most restaurants is invariably cheaper
than dinner

DAMART

BOWLING GREEN MILLS, BINGLEY, YORKSHIRE BD16 4BH
☎ (01274) 567152. OPEN 9.30 - 5 MON - SAT.
HORNSEA FREEPORT SHOPPING VILLAGE, HORNSEA, EAST YORKSHIRE
☎ (01964) 536581. OPEN 10 - 5 MON - SAT, 10 - 6 SUN.
Damart underwear and merchandise - anything from tights, socks and gloves to dresses, coats, cardigans and jumpers - some of which is current stock sold at full price, some discontinued and ends of lines sold at discount. There several shops selling some discounted stock from the Damart range, known as Damart Extra. *Factory Shop*

DEJA VU

8 BOWER ROAD, HARROGATE, YORKSHIRE
☎ (01423) 503535. OPEN 10.30 - 4 MON - SAT.
Two roomed shop full of good quality men's and women's clothes from sweaters to coats, scarves to costume jewellery with a large selection of evening wear. Labels on sale include Paul Costelloe, Betty Barclay and Nicole Farhi. *Dress Agency*

DENHOLME VELVETS MILL SHOP

HALIFAX ROAD, DENHOLME, BRADFORD, YORKSHIRE BD13 4EZ
☎ (01274) 832185. OPEN 1 - 5 MON - FRI, 9.30 - 4.30 SAT.
Claims to be the only factory producing dress velvet in Britain, most of which is for export. Lots of remnants as well as slight seconds in embossed velvet on silk. They also sell rayon and cotton, all at huge savings. Opening hours may vary during the summer holidays. Free parking. Just ten minutes away is Coldspring Mill, which sells knitting wools. *Factory Shop*

DESIGNER SHADES

MCARTHURGLEN DESIGNER OUTLET, FULFORD, YORK, YORKSHIRE YO19 4TA
☎ (01904) 679007. OPEN 10 - 6 MON - SAT, 11 - 5 SUN.
Sunglasses at more than 30% off manufacturers recommended prices at this designer-orientated outlet. They offer top of the range designer frames (Gucci, Diesel, Jean-Paul Gaultier, Ralph Lauren, Dior etc) as a fashion accessory must. The bright display on back-lit columns is in an inviting step-in-and-try-me-on kiosk. There is also a small selection of children's frames, unusual cases and chains. Designer shades ensure that all their stock has quality lenses which protect against UVA and UVB rays as well as filtering out damaging reflective blue light. *Permanent Discount Outlet*

DESIGNER WAREHOUSE

20 CUMBERLAND ROAD, MIDDLESBROUGH, YORKSHIRE TS5 6HZ

☎ (01642) 850651. OPEN 9 - 5 MON - WED, SAT, 9 - 7 THUR, FRI, 11 - 5 SUN,

Brand new top designer labels for men and women including Armani men's suits, £499 instead of £1,200; Versace dresses, £49.99 instead of £200; Calvin klein jeans, £29.99 instead of £69; Armani PK T-shirts, £19 instead of £45. Entrance by membership only which can be obtained, free, on entry. *Permanent Discount Outlet*

DEWHIRST CLOTHING FACTORY SHOP

,42 MIDDLE STREET NORTH, DRIFFIELD, YORKSHIRE YO25 7SS

☎ (01377) 256209. OPEN 9 - 5.30 MON - SAT.

5 WELHAM ROAD, MALTON YO10 9DP

☎ (01653) 690141. OPEN 9 - 5.30 MON - SAT, 11 - 5 SUN.

AMSTERDAM ROAD, SUTTON FIELD INDUSTRIAL ESTATE, HULL HU8 OXF

☎ (01482) 820166. OPEN 9 - 5.30 MON - WED, 9 - 7.30 THUR, 9 - 6 FRI, 9 - 6 SAT, 11 - 5 SUN.

WEST COTHAM LANE, DORMANSTOWN INDUSTRIAL ESTATE, DORMANSTOWN, REDCAR, YORKSHIRE TS10 5QD

☎ (01642) 474210. OPEN 9 - 5.30 MON - SAT, 10.30 - 4.30 SUN.

Dewhirst Clothing Factory Shops sell garments from the manufacturing side of the business direct to the public and are part of the Dewhirst Group plc which manufactures ladies, men's and childrenswear for a leading high street retailer. You can choose from a huge selection of surplus production and slight seconds at bargain prices, making savings of more than 50% of the normal retail cost. For men there is a wide range of suits, formal shirts and casual wear. For example, wool suits from £60, formal and casual shirts from £7. For ladies there's a selection of blouses, smart tailoring and casual wear that includes a denim range. You can find ladies jackets from £50, skirts, trousers and blouses from £8. Children's clothes start at £3. High street quality and style at wholesale prices. *Factory Shop*

Live Well On Less Tips
WILLIS OWEN LTD THE BUILDING SOCIETY SHOP, 98 MANSFIELD ROAD, NOTTINGHAM, NOTTINGHAMSHIRE NG1 3HD. (0115) 947 2595.

They will send you free guides to investing in PEPs (for transfers), ISAs, With Profit Bonds, Investment Bonds etc. Top discounts available on all investments. Fully independent recommendations.

DISCOUNT DRESSING

HORNSEA FREEPORT SHOPPING VILLAGE, HORNSEA, YORKSHIRE
HU18 1UT

☎ (01964) 537538. OPEN 9.30 - 6 SEVEN DAYS A WEEK.

A veritable Aladdin's Cave of designer bargains, Discount Dressing sells mostly German, Italian and French designer labels at prices at least 50% and up to
90% below those in normal retail outlets. All items are brand new and perfect.
A team of buyers all over Europe purchase stock directly from the manufacturer for this growing chain of discount shops. This enables Discount Dressing
to by-pass the importers and wholesalers and, of course, their mark-up. They
also buy bankrupt stock in this country. Their agreement with their suppliers
means that they are not able to advertise brand names for obvious reasons, but
they are all well-known for their top quality and style. So confident is
Discount Dressing that you will be unable to find the same item cheaper elsewhere, that they guarantee to give the outfit to you free of charge should you
perform this miracle. Merchandise includes raincoats, dresses, suits, trousers,
blouses, evening wear, special occasion outfits and jackets, in sizes 6-24 and in
some cases larger. GDD readers can obtain a further 10% discount if they visit
the shop taking a copy of this book with them. There are other branches in
Lincolnshire, Northern Ireland, Hertfordshire, London and Derbyshire.
Permanent Discount Outlet

DOLMENS

79 LATHAM LANE, GOMERSAL, CLECK HEATON, YORKSHIRE
BD19 4AP,

☎ (01274) 872368. FAX ☎ (01274) 869953. BY APPOINTMENT ONLY.

Old and new York stone paving flags. Various prices and quality. Worldwide
delivery. *Architectural Salvage*

DOROTHY PERKINS

YORKSHIRE OUTLET, WHITE ROSE WAY, DONCASTER, YORKSHIRE
DN4 5JH

☎ (01302) 367082. OPEN 10 - 6 MON - SAT, 11 - 5 SUN.

End of season lines with the normal Dorothy Perkins refund guarantee. The
range includes knickers, scarves, suits, blouses, sweaters, coats, jackets, dresses
and jewellery. *Factory Shopping Village*

DOUBLE TWO

BRADFORD ROAD, BATLEY, YORKSHIRE WF17 6LZ
☎ (01924) 441969. OPEN 9.30 - 5.30 MON - SAT, 11 - 5 SUN.
HORNSEA FREEPORT SHOPPING VILLAGE, ROLSTON ROAD,
HORNSEA, EAST YORKSHIRE HU18 1UT
☎ (01964) 533339. OPEN 9.30 - 6 SEVEN DAYS A WEEK.
THE YORKSHIRE OUTLET
WHITE ROSE WAY, DONCASTER, SOUTH YORKSHIRE DN4 5PH
☎ (01302) 367156. OPEN 10 - 6 MON - SAT, 11 - 5 SUN.
Men's shirts (both casual and formal), belts, ties, jeans and dress shirts and women's blouses, co-ordinates, dresses, trousers, skirts and waistcoats at discount prices of about 20%-50%. The Batley shop has particularly low prices. *Factory Shop*

DUNELM MILL SHOP

151 BRADFIELD ROAD, HILLSBOROUGH, SHEFFIELD, YORKSHIRE
S6 2BY
☎ (01142) 315600. OPEN 9 - 5 MON - SAT, 10 - 4 SUN.
UNIT 3, CANKLOW MEADOWS, WEST BAWTRY ROAD, ROTHERHAM,
SOUTH YORKSHIRE S60 2XL
☎ (01709) 820374. OPEN 10 - 8 MON - FRI, 9 - 6 SAT, 11 - 5 SUN.
Part of a chain of shops based in the Midlands selling brand-name and chain-store curtains, masses of bedlinen, towels, wickerware, pictures and frames, all at competitive prices. *Permanent Discount Outlet*

DUNSFORD WELSEY MENSWEAR

OXFORD STREET, CASTLEFORD, YORKSHIRE WF10 5SZ
☎ (01977) 710200. OPEN 10 - 5 WED, THUR, 10 - 6 FRI, 10 - 4 SAT.
Sells suits, shirts, sweaters, and a few ladies oddments as well as leather handbags and small leather goods. The garments are good quality at affordable prices. Suits from £50 to £95; leather belts, £6.99-£9.99; shirts from £10 to £20; sweaters from £15-£20; leather handbags from £5 upwards; purses and wallets from £5. *Factory Shop*

E G INTERIOR

FABRICS, 226 HARROGATE ROAD, CHAPEL ALLERTON, LEEDS,
YORKSHIRE LS7 4QD
☎ (0113) 2370447. OPEN 10 - 5 MON - SAT, CLOSED WED.
Sell curtaining and sheeting fabrics and curtain linings, specialising in wider widths. They also sell ends of lines and seconds of well-known chain store designs at savings of up to 50% and have a small haberdashery section at competitive prices. Offers a making up service. *Permanent Discount Outlet*

EAST ARDSLEY HOUSEHOLD TEXTILES

89 BRADFORD ROAD, EAST ARDSLEY, WAKEFIELD, YORKSHIRE
WF3 2JD

☎ (01924) 820593. OPEN OPEN 10 - 5 MON - SAT, CLOSED WED.

Sell curtaining and sheeting fabrics and curtain linings, specialising in wider widths. They also sell ends of lines and seconds of well-known chain store designs at savings of up to 50% and have a small haberdashery section at competitive prices. Offers a making up service. ***Permanent Discount Outlet***

EDINBURGH CRYSTAL

HORNSEA FREEPORT SHOPPING VILLAGE, HORNSEA, HU18 1UT, YORKSHIRE HU18 1UT

☎ (01964) 534260. OPEN 9.30 - 6 SEVEN DAYS A WEEK.

Wide range of crystalware from glasses and vases to tumblers and bowls at discounts of between 33% - 50%. The shop sells firsts and seconds of crystal from one third off the normal price. There are also special promotional lines at discount prices up to 70% off seconds. Hornsea has plenty to entertain the family with an adventure playgrounds, an indoor play centre, restaurants, a vintage car collection and butterfly world. ***Factory Shopping Village***

ELEANOR

14 CHELTENHAM MOUNT, HARROGATE, YORKSHIRE

☎ (01423) 524787. OPEN 10 - 2 AND 2.30 - 4.30 TUE - SAT.

Dress agency selling only the top end of the market women's fashions including Armani, Jill Sanders, Caroline Charles, Louis Feraud, Escada. ***Dress Agency***

EVERYTHING BUT THE BABY

9 KNARESBOROUGH RD, HARROGATE, YORKSHIRE HG2 7SR

☎ (01423) 888292. OPEN 10 - 4 MON - SAT, 10 - 1 WED.

Sells a wide range of nearly-new babywear from birth to ten years, as well as baby equipment, bedding, toys and maternity wear. There is an extensive range of pushchairs. All the equipment is fully checked and the clothes range from Mothercare and Ladybird to Oshkosh, Oilily and some French designers. ***Dress Agency***

FABRICS FROM THE MILLS

ARCH 9, VIADUCT STREET, HUDDERSFIELD, YORKSHIRE HD1 5DL

☎ (01484) 450509. OPEN 9.30 - 6 MON - SAT, 9.30 - 5.30 WED.

A place where you can change that room without breaking the bank! There's a huge choice of quality curtain and upholstery fabric in as many designs and colours. The stock is mainly first quality, but there are clearances and seconds of famous labels such as Next, Marks & Spencer, Prestigious, Matthew Stevens, etc: all at a fraction of their original price. There's also a speedy, professional made to measure service. ***Permanent Discount Outlet***

Live Well On Less Tips
Instal an insulation jacket on your water heater which could save you 10% on
your water heating bills.

FAMOUS FOOTWEAR

UNIT 73, DESIGNER OUTLET VILLAGE, SELBY ROAD, NABURN, YORK,
YORKSHIRE YO19 4TA
☎ (01904) 678997. OPEN 10 - 6 MON, TUE, WED, FRI, SAT,
10 - 8 THUR, 11 - 5 SUN.
UNIT 423, HORNSEA FREEPORT, ROLSTON ROAD, HORNSEA,
YORKSHIRE HU18 1UT
☎ (01964) 536503. OPEN 10 - 5 SEVEN DAYS A WEEK (WINTER),
10 - 5 MON - FRI, 10 - 6 SAT, SUN (SUMMER).
Wide range of brand names including Stead & Simpson, Lilley & Skinner,
Hobos, Hush Puppies, Lotus, Sterling & Hunt, Richleigh, Scholl, Red Tape,
Flexi Country, Padders, Canaletto, Bronx, Frank Wright, Brevitt, Romba
Wallace, Rieker, all at discount prices of up to 50%. *Factory Shopping
Village*

FREEPORT CASTLEFORD
DESIGNER
OUTLET VILLAGE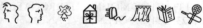

CASTLEFORD, NEAR JUNCTION 32 OF M62, YORKSHIRE
NO TELEPHONE NUMBER OR OPENING HOURS AS WE WENT TO PRESS.
Factory shop village opening in August 1999, with 150 shops and an indoor
and outdoor children's play area, restaurants, classic cars, wildlife displays.
Factory Shopping Village

FROCKS DRESS AGENCY

16 DENHOLME GATE ROAD, HIPPERHOLME, HALIFAX, YORKSHIRE
☎ (01422) 202085. OPEN 10 - 4 TUE - SAT.
Day and evening wear with designer labels. Constantly changing stock. *Dress
Agency*

GLENMATCH

20 MONTPELLIER PARADE, HARROGATE, YORKSHIRE HG1 2TG
☎ (01423) 502519. OPEN 9.30 - 5.30 MON - SAT.
Glenmatch offers you the luxury of Scottish knitwear direct from the Scottish
borders at prices which are approximately 30%-40% below normal retail
prices. You can choose from cashmere, cashmere/silk, merino and lambswool
for men and women.Also some trousers, gloves, scarves and handbags.
Factory Shop

GLYNN WEBB

KINGS ROAD, BRADFORD, WEST YORKSHIRE BD1 1EX
☎ (01274) 722 122. OPEN 9 - 8 MON - SAT, 10 - 4 SUN AND BANK HOLIDAYS.
UNIT 2, THORNE RETAIL PARK, OBDEN ROAD, DONCASTER, YORKSHIRE DN2 4SG
☎ (01302) 556556. OPEN 9 - 8 MON - SAT, 10 - 4 SUN AND BANK HOLIDAYS.
SHAY SYKE, HALIFAX, YORKSHIRE HX1 2ND
☎ (01422) 349249. OPEN 9 - 8 MON - SAT, 10 - 4 SUN AND BANK HOLIDAYS.
100 WAKEFIELD ROAD, HUDDERSFIELD, WEST YORKSHIRE HD1 3PD
☎ (01484) 539330. OPEN 9 - 8 MON - SAT, 10 - 4 SUN AND BANK HOLIDAYS.
OSLO ROAD, SUTTON FIELDS, HULL, YORKSHIRE HU8 OJY
☎ (01482) 836344. OPEN 9 - 8 MON - SAT, 10 - 4 SUN AND BANK HOLIDAYS.
UNIT C KILNER WAY, OFF HALIFAX ROAD, SHEFFIELD, SOUTH YORKSHIRE S6 1NN
☎ (0114) 2312665. OPEN 9 - 8 MON - SAT, 10 - 4 SUN. AND BANK HOLIDAYS.
INGS ROAD, WAKEFIELD, WEST YORKSHIRE WF1 1RN
☎ (01924) 298600. OPEN 9 - 8 MON - SAT, 10 - 4 SUN AND BANK HOLIDAYS.
BRIDGE ROAD, CHANDLERS WHARF, STOCKTON ON TEES, NORTH YORKSHIRE TS18 3BA
☎ (01642) 606699. OPEN 9 - 8 MON - SAT, 10 - 4 SUN AND BANK HOLIDAYS.
Stockists of all your home improvement needs from wallpaper to paint, furniture to flooring, tiles to textiles, housewares to lighting - in fact, almost everything for your home, with 24 branches in the North-West, Midlands and Yorkshire. Specialists in discontinued mail order, slightly imperfect branded stocks as well as perfect quality superior products. They carry top brands such as Dulux, Crown Paints and Vymura and Coloroll wall coverings, Rectella and Norwood textiles and much more in store. Different branches carry different lines so if you want something specific, phone first. To find your nearest branch, phone 0161 621 4500. *Permanent Discount Outlet*

Live Well On Less Tips
Share your lawn mower with your next door neighbour, reducing your costs by 50%. Other items can also be shared such as sewing machines, indoor power tools, magazine subscriptions.

> *Live Well On Less Tips*
> Water your lawn at night - at noon on a sunny summer day, probably half the
> water a lawn sprinkler throws on your lawn evaporates before it does any
> good.

GOLDEN SHUTTLE MILL SHOP

ALBION ROAD, GREENGATES, BRADFORD, YORKSHIRE BD10 9TQ
☎ (01274) 623450. OPEN 9.30 - 5 MON - SAT, MOST BANK HOLIDAYS.
Men's, women's and children's fashion at discount prices. Ladies anoraks,
coats, jackets, dresses, suits, blouses. Men's suits, blazers, sports jackets, shirts.
Childrenswear from famous name continental designer samples for babies to
10 year olds. Cloth from the mill, such as wool and polywool is also for sale,
as are handbags and luggage. There are sales twice a year in July and January.
Permanent Discount Outlet

GRATTAN PLC RETAIL DIVISION

THE YORKSHIRE OUTLET, WHITE ROSE WAY, DONCASTER,
YORKSHIRE DN14 5JH,
☎ (01302) 340747. OPEN 10 - 6 MON - SAT, 11 - 5 SUN.
Mostly consisting of unsold lines through the Grattan mail order catalogues at
the end of the season, but there is also some current season stock. There are
women's, men's and children's clothing, although the majority is women's fashion, including many famous high street labels. All items in the store retail at a
minimum of 25% off the catalogue price, with some items discounted by up
to 50%. They also have regular special offers such as receiving a £10 voucher
when you spend £25. *Factory Shop*

GREENWOODS WHITE
CROSS DISCOUNT SHOPPING

WHITE CROSS, GUISELEY, LEEDS, YORKSHIRE LS20 8ND
☎ (01943) 875414. VISITOR CENTRE OPEN 9 - 5.30 MON - SAT, 11 - 5
SUN, BANK HOLS, CLUB OPEN 9 - 5 THUR, FRI, 11 - 5 SAT,
SUN AND BANK HOLS.
Specialists in menswear, the Visitor Centre and Warehouse Club within 150
yards of each other both stock what one reader calls the best men's clothing in
the area. There are shirts from £5, jackets from £20, trousers, from £10;
knitwear from £12; suits from £40; casuals, £20; socks and briefs. Sizes range
from 38-54 inch chest and 32-52 inch waist. Wedding and evening wear hire
service available here plus famous brands. Now also have Yorkshire Linen Co,
Designer Warehouse and sports shoe warehouse within the Club. Combine
this with a trip to Harry Ramsden's Fish Shop, only 100 yards away. *Factory
Shop*

HALLMARK

HORNSEA FREEPORT, HORNSEA, YORKSHIRE HU18 1UT

☎ (01964) 533080. OPEN 9.30 - 6 SEVEN DAYS A WEEK.

A wide range of cards to suit every occasion, as well as stuffed toys, wrapping paper, rosettes, gift cards from names such as Andrew Brownswood, Gordon Fraser and Sharpe's Classics. Almost all the stock here is ends of lines as the card business demands constant change and so there are always unsold lines. Most of the items are half price. Cafes on site as well as children's play areas; free parking. *Factory Shop*

HARRIETS

11 MARKET PLACE, KNARESBOROUGH, YORKSHIRE HG5 8AL

☎ (01423) 863375. OPEN 9 - 5 MON, TUE, WED, THUR, 9 - 5.30 FRI, SAT, 1 - 5 SUN.

16 WESTGATE, OTLEY, WEST YORKSHIRE LS29 6HY

☎ (01943) 465258. OPEN 9 - 5 MON - SAT, 10 - 4 SUN.

2 KIRKGATE, THIRSK YO7 1PQ

☎ (01845) 522079. OPEN 9 - 5 MON - SAT, 10 - 4 SUN.

11 CAVENDISH STREET, KEIGHLEY BD21 3RB

☎ (01535) 611198. OPEN 9 - 5 MON - SAT, 10 - 4 SUN.

75B NEW ROAD SIDE, HORSFORTH, LEEDS, WEST YORKSHIRE LS18 4QD

☎ (0113) 239 0399. OPEN 9 - 5 MON - SAT, 10 - 4 SUN.

Many high street chainstore over-productions at discounted prices. Clothes which are mostly Marks & Spencer seconds and discontinued lines, but also some from Next, Dorothy Perkins and Littlewoods. For example, a Marks & Spencer jacket which would normally cost £85, for sale at £40; skirts less than £20; and coats and jackets to suit everyone from teenagers upwards in sizes 8-20. *Permanent Discount Outlet*

HAVENPLAN LTD

THE OLD STATION, STATION ROAD, KILLARMARSH, SHEFFIELD, YORKSHIRE S21 1EN

☎ (0114) 2489972. OPEN 10 - 4 TUE - SAT.

Very large stock of architectural antiques, bygones, decorative items ideal for the home and garden, stained glass, doors, lighting, fireplaces, church pews, kitchenalia, stone troughs. *Architectural Salvage*

Live Well On Less Tips

CHINA MATCHING SERVICE 4 QUEEN'S PARADE CLOSE, FRIEW BARNETT, LONDON N11 3FY. 0181-361 6111. OPEN 9 - 5.30 MON - FRI, 9 - 5 SAT.

Discontinued china.

HIGH SOCIETY

THE MARKET PLACE, EASINGWOLD, YORK, YORKSHIRE YO61 3AD

☎ (01347) 822668. OPEN 9 - 5 MON - SAT.

Up to 300 new evening dresses to buy or to hire by After Six, John Charles, Serenade, Simon Ellis, etc. Sale rail with new and ex-hire frocks from £20. Clearance sales take place in January and July to make way for new stock. The dress agency sells secondhand daywear and accessories, from Marks & Spencer to top designers - all in perfect condition, freshly laundered and less than three years old. Stock might include Moschino top from £20, Moschino jacket, £65, Valentino jacket, £45, David & Joan shoes, £29. *Dress Agency*

SUMMER GRAND SALE

RIPLEY CASTLE, RIPLEY, NEAR HARROGATE, YORKSHIRE ORGANISER: ROBERT TORRANCE, PO BOX 427, LONDON SW10 9QE.

☎ 0171-351 3088.

There are now three annual Grand Sales taking place countrywide. The Christmas Grand Sale in London, with over 120 different small companies selling their gifts and upmarket homes accessories to the public, is the largest. This takes place in mid-November each year (17th-20th November 1999). Quality is high and covers everything from dried flowers to bath accessories, Amish quilts to silverware, wooden toys to hand-painted kitchenware, often at discount because they are ends of lines. There is a Spring Grand Sale at Sudeley Castle, Winchcombe, near Cheltenham, Glos every April/May (11th-13th May 2000) nd a Summer Grand Sale at Ripley Castle, near Harrogate, North Yorkshire, in June (8th-11th June 2000) both of which feature gardening equipment as well as decorative homes accessories. *Designer Sale*

HONEY

HORNSEA FREEPORT, POTTERS WAY, ROLSTON ROAD, HORNSEA, YORKSHIRE HU18 1UT,

☎ 01964 537394. OPEN 10 - 6 (5 IN WINTER) MON - FRI, 11 - 5 SUN,

Leisure-oriented women's T-shirts, leggings and sweaters at discounts of mostly 30% or more. *Factory Shopping Village*

HORNSEA FREEPORT OUTLET VILLAGE

ROLSTON ROAD, HORNSEA, YORKSHIRE HU18 1UT

☎ (01964) 534211. OPEN 10 - 5 SEVEN DAYS A WEEK (WINTER), 10 - 5 MON - FRI (SUMMER) 10 - 6 SAT, SUN, BANK AND SCHOOL HOLIDAYS.

The original British factory shopping village with up to 50 shops offering discounts of 30% and more below high street prices, plenty of places to eat in a relaxed rural setting with free parking and entry. Womenswear labels include

Alexon, Dash, Damart, Double Two, The Factory Shop, Honey, Laura Ashley, London Leathers, Warner's, Windsmoor and Wrangler. Menswear includes Damart, Double Two, The Factory Shop, London Leathers, Mexx, Rawhide, Tom Sayers and Wrangler, with Tog 24, Sports Unlimited and Planet Outlet offering family outdoor/sports clothing. Footwear and accessories are sold by Shoe Sellers and the Factory Shop, while Woods of Windsor stocks traditional English fragrances and Evans the Jeweller stocks a range of jewellery. Shops selling childrenswear include The Factory Shop, Laura Ashley, Rawhide, Wrangler, Mexx, Sweater Shop and Shoe Sellers which, between them, offer a full range of children's clothes for all ages from formal to casual. Tog 24, Planet Outlet and Sports Unlimited carry children's sports and outdoor wear, including trainers, waterproofs and fleeces. Shops selling household goods include Churchill China, Edinburgh Crystal, Ponden Mill, Dartington Crystal, The Factory Shop, Hornsea Pottery, Laura Ashley and Woods of Windsor which, between them sell homewares ranging from linens, quilts, cushions, china, pottery, glass gift and tableware, dried and silk flowers, pot pourri, soaps etc. Shops selling sports goods include Planet Outlet and Sports Unlimited offering a wide range of branded sports shoes, clothes and equipment for all ages. Tog 24 specialises in outdoor wear for all the family; Luggage & Bags stocks an extensive range of luggage and travel accessories; Not Just Books and the Gadget Shop selling pens, lighters, lava lamps, watches, Wallace & Grommet goods and key rings. To keep the children amused there's a model village, Butterfly World, adventure playground and an indoor soft play area. *Factory Shopping Village*

HOUSE OF FABRICS

HIRST LANE, SALTAIRE, SHIPLEY, YORKSHIRE BD18 4ND
☎ (01274) 595952. OPEN 9 - 5 MON - SAT, 10 - 4 SUN.
Curtaining and upholstery fabrics from a range which includes plain cotton, chintz, damasks and heavy upholstery fabric. Prices from 99p a metre. The upholstery fabric is sold at wholesale prices. Labels include Rectella, Curtina and Wilson Wilcox. They can supply all accessories too, like braid, tiebacks and brassware and offer a complete measure, make-up and fitting service, including upholstery. *Permanent Discount Outlet*

HOWKEL RUGS

60 LOWER VIADUCT STREET, HUDDERSFIELD, YORKSHIRE
☎ (01484) 425422. OPEN 9 - 5 MON - FRI, 9 - 4.30 SAT.
Warehouse type building on three floors stacked with quality carpets and ends of lines, they specialise in 80% wool twist pile carpets. For example 40 oz wool twist off the roll costs £10 a sq yard. There is a small offshoot shop selling their seconds and offcuts at Blackmoorfoot Road. *Factory Shop*

JAEGER FACTORY SHOP

C/O THOMAS BURNLEY, GOMERSAL MILLS, CLECKHEATON,
YORKSHIRE BD19 4LU
☎ (01274) 852292. OPEN 9 - 5 MON - SAT.
MCARTHURGLEN DESIGNER OUTLET VILLAGE, ST NICHOLAS
AVENUE, FULFORD, YORK YO19 4TA
☎ (01904) 682700. OPEN 10 - 6 MON - SAT. 8 ON THU, 11 - 5 SUN.
Contemporary classics from Jaeger at excellent prices. Most of the
merchandise is previous seasons' stock, but you might also find some special
makes. All shops stock tailoring and knitwear for women and men. The
telephone number for the York outlet is for the centre, not the shop.
Factory Shop

JAMES BARRY MENSWEAR

THE YORKSHIRE OUTLET, WHITE ROSE WAY, DONCASTER,
YORKSHIRE DN4 5JU
☎ (01302) 361127. OPEN 10 - 6 MON - SAT, 11 - 5 SUN.
Range of men's suits, jackets, trousers, socks, belts, briefs and shirts from
James Barry, Pierre Cardin, Haggar and Wolsey. Some of the factory shops also
stock the Double Two range of brand names. Suits reduced from £175 to
£115; casual shirts, £11.95 or two for £20; trousers reduced from £44.95 to
£29.95; Pierre Cardin casual and business shirts, knitwear and trouser are
available, too. *Factory Shopping Village*

JANE SHILTON

THE YORKSHIRE OUTLET, WHITE ROSE WAY, DONCASTER,
YORKSHIRE DN4 5JH
☎ (01302) 320035. OPEN 10 - 6 MON - SAT, 11 - 5 SUN.
Merchandise from past seasons' collections or factory seconds at discounts of
at least 30% off the original price. There is a wide range of handbags, suitcases, women's shoes, luggage, briefcases, umbrellas, scarves and travel bags.
Factory Shopping Village

JEFFREY ROGERS

UNIT 42, THE WHITE ROSE CENTRE, DEWSBURY, LEEDS, YORKSHIRE
LS1 8LL
☎ (01302) 325262. OPEN 10 - 6 MON - SAT, 11 - 5 SUN.
Factory outlet with the emphasis on young street style: from sleeveless mini
dresses to drawstring waist trousers, T-shirts, sweaters and skirts though there
is also the Roger Plus range for sizes 16-24. Twenty-five percent of the stock
is sold at a discount of 75%. *Factory Shopping Village*

Live Well On Less Tips
CHINA MATCHING REPLACEMENTS 29 GREENHILL ROAD, CAMBERLEY, SURREY, GU15 1HE. (01276) 64587. OPEN 9 - 1 MON - FRI, THEN ON ANSWERPHONE AND FAX. MAIL ORDER.
Specialist stockists and finders of discontinued English twentieth century tableware such as Royal Doulton, Wedgwood, Royal Worcester, Spode, Denby etc. Single or multiple pieces bought and sold. Mail order or collections/deliveries from an antiques and garden centre in Bracknell which closes on Sundays. Don't buy an entire new service when you can replenish your treasured collection.

JOE BLOGGS

THE YORKSHIRE OUTLET, WHITE ROSE WAY, DONCASTER, YORKSHIRE DH14 5JH
☎ (01302) 325091. OPEN 10 - 6 MON - SAT, 11 - 5 SUN.
Range of casual clothing for men, women, children and babies which are ends of lines, imperfects or surplus ranges. Jeans, tops, long sleeved shirts and jackets at discounts of between 30% and 70%. *Factory Shopping Village*

JOHN SMEDLEY LTD

RANDS LANE, ARMTHORPE, DONCASTER, YORKSHIRE DN3 3DY
☎ (01302) 832346. OPEN 11 - 3.30 MON - FRI, 10 - 3 SAT.
John Smedley knitwear for men and women in lambswool, cotton sportswear and casual ranges and wool and cotton underwear, all at reduced prices. There is another, much larger outlet in Derbyshire. *Factory Shop*

JOKIDS LTD

THE YORKSHIRE OUTLET, WHITE ROSE WAY, DONCASTER, YORKSHIRE DN4 5JH
☎ (01302) 760137. OPEN 10 - 6 MON - SAT, 11 - 5 SUN.
JoKids is the factory shop trading name for Jeffrey Ohrenstein which sells unusual and attractive clothes for children aged from birth to ten years. This includes pretty party dresses for girls at reductions of up to 40%, all-in-one smocked playsuits, T-shirts, denim shirts, denim dresses, sunhats, shorts, and accessories. *Factory Shopping Village*

KASTIX MILL SHOP

11 UPPER BRIDGE, WOODHEAD ROAD, HOLMFIRTH, HUDDERSFIELD, YORKSHIRE
☎ (01484) 681797. OPEN 9 - 5 MON - SAT.
Kastix manufacture everything on the premises, mostly for the catalogue business, selling an ever-changing mix of short, Capril trousers, clam diggers, jumpers, T-shirts, jackets, fleeces at discounted prices. *Factory Shop*

LA REDOUTE LES AVANTAGES

91 THE HEADROW, LEEDS, YORKSHIRE LS1 6LJ

☎ (0113) 243 6833. OPEN 9.30 - 5.30 MON - FRI, 9.30 - 7 THUR, 9 - 6 SAT.
Clearance lines from the famous La Redoute catalogue providing stylish fashion with French flair for all the family. Selling overstocks of menswear and childrenswear at discounts of up to 50% off the original price (and up to 70% at sales times), there are always great bargains to be found and with over 10,000 items on display and sizes ranging from 6 - 30, there is plenty to choose from. Speciality catalogues Anne Weyburn, providing a more classic look for women, and Taillissime, for both men and women with a tall and fuller figure, add to the variety available in the store. As well as La Redoute's own brand clothes, JPG by Gaultier, Joseph, Adidas, Levis, DKNY and Diesel are just a few of the famous names that have appeared in the pages of the La Redoute catalogue. If you live nearby drop in frequently as new stock arrives every day. A three for two offer runs during Happy Hours from 12 - 2 on weekdays, with special offers every Saturday. *Permanent Discount Outlet*

LABELS

1 MARKET ROW, BARKERS ARCADE, NORTHALLERTON, YORKSHIRE DL7 8LN

☎ (01609) 779483. OPEN 9.30 - 5 MON - SAT.
Two-storey shop selling designer nearly-new wear from Pangi, Droopy & Browns, Jaeger, Escada and Windsmoor to Cache D'Or at about half the initial shop price. Two-piece suits, wedding outfits, holiday wear, blazers, evening wear cocktail dresses. Up to 50 hats to buy and to hire from £10. *Dress Agency*

LABELS FOR LESS

ALLERTON ROAD, BRADFORD,YORKSHIRE BD15 7AB
(O1274) 491311. OPEN 9 - 5.30 MON - SAT.
Designer shopping outlet within the elegant department store surroundings of the former Hoopers store. Stocks a wide selection of well-known contemporary designer and classic fashion labels for men and women at prices at least 50% below the original selling price. Seen here in the past have been Moschino, Hugo Boss, Christian Lacroix. There is a hair and beauty salon on site and easy parking. *Permanent Discount Outlet*

Live Well On Less Tips

To scour copper pans, mix half a tablespoon salt with one quarter cup of vinegar. Scrub on, remove with water, then wipe dry to shine.

Live Well On Less Tips

TIMOTHY EVEREST 32 ELDER STREET, LONDON E1 6BT. 0171-377 5770. OPEN 9 - 5.30 MON - FRI, 9 - 4 SAT. PHONE FOR AN APPOINTMENT.

Having trained at Tommy Nutter in Savile Row, Timothy now offers bespoke tailoring at accessible prices. A suit selling in Savile Row for £2,000 can be made from £995 for full bespoke, £875 for semi-bespoke. Jackets, trousers, shirts, overcoats and silk ties can also be bought. Everything is made on the premises of this unusual eighteenth century building.

LAURA ASHLEY

HORNSEA FREEPORT SHOPPING VILLAGE, HORNSEA, YORKSHIRE HU18 1UT

☎ (01964) 536503. OPEN 10 - 5 SEVEN DAYS A WEEK (WINTER), 10 - 5 MON - FRI, 10 - 6 SAT, SUN (SUMMER).

At Hornsea, Laura Ashley fashion is on the ground floor and home furnishings on the first floor. Most of the merchandise is made up of perfect carry-overs from the high street shops around the country, though there are also some discontinued lines. Stock reflects the normal high street variety, though at least one season later and with less choice in colours and sizes. *Factory Shopping Village*

LE CREUSET

MCARTHURGLEN DESIGNER OUTLET VILLAGE, ST NICHOLAS AVENUE, NABURN, YORK, YORKSHIRE YO19 4TA

☎ (01904) 630485. OPEN 10 - 6 MON - SAT, 11 - 5 SUN.

Items from the famous Le Creuset range - casseroles, saucepans, fry pans etc - plus their pottery collection at discounts of at least 30%. There is another discount outlet in Swindon. *Household Factory Shopping Village*

LIGHTWATER VILLAGE AND FACTORY SHOPPING

NORTH STAINLEY, RIPON, YORKSHIRE HG4 3HT

☎ (01765) 635321. OPEN 10 - 5 SEVEN DAYS A WEEK. OPENING TIMES VARY SEASONALLY.

Large complex of retail and factory outlets with a wide range of branded ladies' wear including blouses, skirts, suits, dresses, lingerie, outerwear, shoes and accessories as well as menswear from jeans and outdoor wear (from Tog 24) to formal wear. Shoes, jewellery, perfumery, home furnishings, crystal and glass, a large range of pottery as well as a seasonal shop, garden centre, toys, a bakery, cheese and confectionery. Old Macdonald's farm is open to shoppers all year free of charge. There is a restaurant and coffee shop serving snacks and refreshments. *Factory Shop*

LITTLEWOODS
CATALOGUE DISCOUNT STORE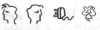

602-608 ATTERCLIFFE ROAD, SHEFFIELD, YORKSHIRE S9 3QS

☎ (0114) 244 1611. OPEN 9 - 5.30 TUE - SAT.

FREEPORT CASTLEFORD, CASTLEFORD, NEAR JUNCTION 32 OF M62, WEST YORKSHIRE

NO TELEPHONE NUMBER AS WE WENT TO PRESS.

Littlewoods clearance shops offering up to 50% off the catalogue price for clothing and between 50% and 60% off for electrical goods. Stock changes constantly and varies from day to day but can include well-known brand names such as Berlei and Gossard lingerie, Vivienne Westwood, Pamplemousse leisure wear, Nike and Adidas sports shoes, Workers For Freedom, and Timberland and Caterpillar footwear. Stock depends on the size and location of the shop, so larger shops will get the longer discontinued runs and smaller shops over-runs with only a small amount of colour and size variations left. Littlewoods also run a mobile shop which operates in cities where they don't have a sale shop. For details of further venues for the sales, which usually take place once a month, contact Melanie Lamb, c/o Crosby DC, Kershaw Avenue, Endbutt Lane, Crosby, Merseyside L70 1AH. *Permanent Discount Outlet*

LONDON LEATHERS DIRECT

FREEPORT VILLAGE, ROLSTON ROAD, HORNSEY, YORKSHIRE HU18 1UT

☎ (01964) 535432 . OPEN 10 - 6 SEVEN DAYS A WEEK.

Very good quality leather and suede jackets, coats and trousers, at discounts of at least 30%, with most at 50% off in this village which features lots of restaurants and fun things for the family to take part in. *Factory Shopping Village*

LUGGAGE & BAGGAGE

UNIT 15, FREEPORT LEISURE VILLAGE, FALSTON ROAD, HORNSEA, YORKSHIRE HU18 1UT

☎ (01964) 535651. OPEN 9.30 - 6 EVERY DAY.

Luggage and travel-related products including executive cases, handbags, umbrellas and accessories available in leading brands such as Samsonite, Brics, Hidesign, Globe Trotter and Tula. The products also include couture and high fashion brands such as YSl and Moschino. All products are offered at a considerably reduced price due to their being production over-runs, last season's stock of slight seconds (ie they have minor aesthetic blemishes). *Factory Shopping Village*

LUGGAGE & BAGS

UNIT 15, FREEPORT LEISURE VILLAGE, ROLSTON ROAD,
HORNSEA, YORKSHIRE HU18 1UT

☎ (01964) 535 651. OPEN 10 - 5 MON - FRI (WINTER), 10 - 6 MON - FRI
(SUMMER) 10 - 6 SAT, SUN, BANK HOLIDAYS.

A range of travel goods and accessories from recognisable brands and high
street names including Samsonite, Delsey, Head, Studio and Taurus. Each
product is offered at a substantially reduced prices to that found on the high
street due to their being production over-runs, last season's products or having
small cosmetic faults. Discounts range from 30% to 75% off high street prices.
Factory Shopping Village

MAGNET LTD CLEARANCE CENTRE

ROYDINGS AVENUE, KEIGHLEY, YORKSHIRE BD21 4BY

☎ (01535) 680461. OPEN 8 - 5 MON - FRI, 9 - 1 SAT.

With more than 200 branches countrywide, when Magnet Kitchens discon-
tinue one of their ranges, there are always some shops with spare stock they can
no longer sell. This applies to equipment such as ovens, hob, hoods, washing
machines, tumble dryers and fridges, too. When manufacturers upgrade their
ranges, Magnet customers don't want to buy the old model currently in situ in
the showroom. Old stock is sent to two sites in Aston, Birmingham and the
head office factory site in Keighley, West Yorkshire. For example last year, customers could choose entire kitchens from two discontinued ranges -
Churchwood and Traditional White - and units and smaller entire kitchens
from three other ranges. Prices on average are about 75% less than the high
street price - they recently kitted out a large kitchen, including all appliances,
for £2,500. Equipment is all top brands - Neff and Smeg ovens, as well as
Magnet's own brand range which is made by Whirlpool. Some is ex-display,
some discontinued models, some just overstock which is still boxed. A brand
new Smeg stainless steel fridge/freezer which would normally cost £900 was
sold recently for £250 while ovens cost from £125-£500. There are also wood
and PVC glazed window frames, conservatory panels (from £25 for panels
which normally cost £100), patio doors and French doors. *Factory Shop*

Live Well On Less Tips

CHINA TIME FENWICK STEAD, BELFORD, NORTHUMBERLAND
NE70 7PL. (01289) 381363.

China Search Agency which specialises in fine bone china as individual pieces
or complete antique tea and coffee sets.

MANORGROVE

121-123 MAIN STREET, BINGLEY, YORKSHIRE BD16 2ND

☎ (01274) 561933. OPEN 9 - 5.30 MON - SAT.

105-109 WESTGATE, HECKMONDWIKE WF16 OEW

☎ (01924) 410734. OPEN 9 - 5.30 MON - SAT.

A selection of clearance items from those featured in the Grattan catalogue, which can consist of anything from children's clothes and toys to bedding, electrical equipment and nursery accessories. Each shop sells a slightly different range, so always ring first to check they stock what you want. All items are discounted by up to 50%. *Permanent Discount Outlet*

MARY COOPER

GINNEL ANTIQUES CENTRE, OFF PARLIAMENT STREET, HARROGATE, YORKSHIRE HG1 1DH

☎ (01765) 677483. OPEN 9.30 - 5.30 MON - SAT.

Mainly sells fans and lace but also stocks vintage clothes up to 1935, with Twenties underwear, beaded dresses, accessories and shawls. Also quilts, sheets, pillowcases, tablecloths, hats, men's hats, waistcoats and shirts. For men, there are only hats and waistcoats; for children, christening gowns. Beaded dresses, £200-£300. Discounts for cash purchases. Phone before visiting if you have a specific request and Mary will try to get it for you. *Secondhand and Vintage Clothe*

MATALAN

UNIT 13, THE WHEATLEY CENTRE, WHEATLEY HALL ROAD, DONCASTER, YORKSHIRE DN2 4PE

☎ (01302) 760444. OPEN 10 - 8 MON - FRI, 9 - 6 SAT, 11 - 5 SUN.

UNIT 4B, STADIUM WAY RETAIL PARK, PARKGATE, ROTHERHAM S60 1TG

☎ (01709) 780173. OPEN 10 - 8 MON - FRI, 9 - 6 SAT, 11 - 5 SUN.

UNIT 10 & 11, CLIFTON MOORE CENTRE, YORK YO3 4WZ

☎ (01904) 693080. OPEN 10 - 8 MON - FRI, 9 - 6 SAT, 11 - 5 SUN.

UNIT 1, GREENMOUNT RETAIL PARK, PELLON LANE, HALIFAX HX1 5QN

☎ (01422) 383051. OPEN 10 - 8 MON - FRI, 9 - 6 SAT, 11 - 5 SUN.

UNIT 2, KINGSTON RETAIL PARK, HULL HU2 2TX

☎ (01482) 586184. OPEN 10 - 8 MON - FRI, 9 - 6 SAT 11 - 5 SUN.

1 WOMBWELL LANE, STAIRFOOT, BARNSLEY S70 3NS

☎ (01226) 733372. TELEPHONE FOR OPENING HOURS.

INGS ROAD RETAIL PARK, INGS ROAD, WAKEFIELD WF1 1RF

☎ (01924) 367395. TELEPHONE FOR OPENING HOURS.

UNIT 9, FORSTER SQUARE RETAIL PARK, 53 VALLEY ROAD, BRADFORD BD1 4RN

☎ (01274) 381000. PHONE FOR OPENING TIMES.

WORTLEY RING ROAD, LEEDS LE35
NO TELEPHONE NUMBER AS WE WENT TO PRESS.
UNIT 1 HEELEY RETAIL PARK, CHESTERFIELD ROAD, SHEFFIELD
S8 ORG
☎ (01142(629400. PHONE FOR OPENING TIMES.
Matalan is a fashion and homewares shop giving customers what they claim to be unbeatable value for money with huge savings on a wide range of products including high quality fashionable clothing for women, women and children at up to 50% off high street prices. Matalan is situated out of town and stores are open seven days a week all year round. ***Permanent Discount Outlet***

MCARTHURGLEN DESIGNER OUTLET YORK

ST NICHOLAS AVENUE, FULFORD, JUNCTION OF A19 AND A64, YORK, YORKSHIRE YO19 4TA
☎ (01904) 682700. OPEN 10 - 6 MON - SAT, 8 ON THUR, 11 - 5 SUN.
This indoor centre three miles outside York will have more than 150 stores eventually. Designers on sale here include Giorgio Armani, Guess, as well as Adidas, the Body Shop, Burberry, Calvin Klein Jeans, Cerruti, Daniel Shoes, Descamps, Dunhill, Episode, Escada Sport, Flannels, Franchetti Bond, Levi's, Margaret Howell, China, China china and glassware, Hanro, Iceberg, Jacques Vert, Jaeger, Joan & David, Mulberry, Nine West, Oneida, Paul Smith, Pilot, Proibito, Reebok, Rockport, Sense, Ted Baker, Thomas Pink, Tie Rack, USC - stocking well-known designer brands, Van Heusen, Vans, Virgin, Viyella, Warners Brothers, Wolford, Woods of Windsor. Household names include China, China, famous for their twice-yearly china and glass sales in York and now offering a permanent opportunity to buy a huge range of famous-name china and glass at discount prices, Descamps, Le Creuset, Oneida, Remington and Whittard Kitchen. ***Factory Shopping Village***

MEXX INTERNATIONAL

HORNSEA FREEPORT VILLAGE, HORNSEA, YORKSHIRE HU18 1UT
☎ (01964) 537401. OPEN 9 - 6.30 MON - SAT, 11 - 5 SUN.
High street fashion at factory outlet prices for men, women, babies, children and teenagers, all of which are heavily discounted by more than 30%. ***Factory Shopping Village***

MIDAS CLOTHES

10 LITTLE STONEGATE, YORK, YORKSHIRE
☎ (01904) 625870. OPEN 10 - 4 MON - WED, 10 - 5 THUR - SAT.
Nearly-new shop selling designer labels and high street names, shoes, hats, handbags and a small selection of jewellery. The shop is on one level, with car parking in The Shambles. ***Dress Agency***

MILETA

STATION LANE, HECKMONDWIKE, YORKSHIRE WF16 ONQ

☎ (01924) 409314. OPEN 10 - 5 MON - SAT, 11 - 5 SUN.

Manufacturer of specialist outdoor clothing with lots of seconds and overmakes: golf suits, golf gilets, T-shirts, waterproof breathable jackets, weatherproof anoraks, marginal seconds in jackets and hiking boots. Has now spawned a host of factory shops called Tog 24, of which there are more than 30 countrywide. *Factory Shop*

MR BABY

4 ST JOHN'S ROAD, HUDDERSFIELD, YORKSHIRE HD1 5AT

☎ (01484) 515381. OPEN 9 - 5.30 MON - SAT.

Sells reconditioned, seconds and former showroom models of the Mamas & Papas range and their nursery equipment, as well as everything for the nursery. *Permanent Discount Outlet*

MR VALUE

KILLINGHALL ROAD, BRADFORD, YORKSHIRE

☎ (01274) 669674. OPEN 9 - 8 MON - FRI, 9 - 5.30 SAT, 10 - 4 SUN.

A wide selection of goods which are factory rejects, seconds and ends of lines - everything from clothes with the labels cut out to tapes, kettles, TVs, toasters, bedlinen, towels, sweets, artificial floers, batteries, toiletires, crockery, glass, stationery, pots and pans, toys and bins. *Permanent Discount Outlet*

MULBERRY CLEARANCE SHOP

23 SWINEGATE, YORK, YORKSHIRE

☎ (01904) 611055. OPEN 10 - 6 MON - SAT.

Clearance shop for the famous Mulberry brands with some full-price goods also on sale. There's a smaller selection of the goods on sale at the larger Mulberry factory shop in Somerset including leather goods, handbags, filofaxes, walles, last season's clothes for men and women, cushions, lamps, china, throws, fabric. The shop is small and on one level. *Permanent Discount Outlet*

MULBERRY HALL

STONEGATE, YORK, YORKSHIRE YO1 8ZW

☎ (01904) 620736. OPEN 10 - 6 MON - SAT, 11 - 4 BANK HOLIDAYS,

Mulberry Hall's once a year only, January sale is the greatest sale of top quality china and crystal in the north of England. Held in Mulberry Hall's superb premises in Swinegate, there are reductions of between 25% and 50% on many thousands of items of tableware including hundreds of dinner and tea services, giftware from leading British manufacturers including Royal Crown Derby, Royal Doulton, Royal Worcester, Spode, Wedgwood, Royal Brierley, Edinburgh Crystal and Stuart Crystal. Phone and put your name on the mailing list. *Designer Sale*

NIGHTINGALES FACTORY SHOP

13 CHESTERFIELD ROAD, SHEFFIELD, YORKSHIRE S8 ORL
☎ (0114) 255 4623. OPEN 10 - 5 MON - SAT.
The mail order company which sells smart but casual clothes for women has a factory shop above their shop in Sheffield. Their catalogue features button-through dresses for about £28.99; mix and match two-pieces, £39.50, cotton camisoles, £17.99; and tucked cotton shirts, £14.99. The factory shop sells a selection of seconds and some returns. *Factory Shop*

NURSERY NEEDS

43 PIKEPURSE LANE, RICHMOND, YORKSHIRE DL10 4PS
☎ (01748) 824524.

JACK & JILL

1 WEST PARK DRIVE, WEST PARK, LEEDS, WEST YORKSHIRE LS16 5AS
☎ (0113) 278 5560.

BABY HIRE

25 FARLEA DRIVE, ECCLESHILL, BRADFORD, WEST YORKSHIRE BD2 3RJ
☎ (01274) 642140.
Part of the Baby Equipment Hirers Association (BEHA), which has more than 100 members countrywide. A range of equipment can be hired from high chairs, cots and travel cots to baby car seats and buggies. Some members also hire out party equipment including child-sized tables and chairs. BEHA run an advice line which will try and answer any queries you have regarding hiring services for children. Phone the Babyline on 0831 310355 for your nearest BEHA shop. *Hire Shop*

ONEIDA

MCARTHURGLEN DESIGNER OUTLET CENTRE, ST NICHOLAS AVENUE, FULFORD, YORK, YORKSHIRE YO1 4RE
☎ (01904) 610675. OPEN 10 - 6 MON, TUE, WED, FRI, SAT, 10 - 8 THUR, 11 - 5 SUN.
Oneida is the world's largest cutlery company and originates from the United States of America. In addition to cutlery, it sells silver and silver plate at discounts of between 30% and 50%, plus frames, candlesticks and trays. They now also have their own range of chinaware and glass, also sold here at discounts of 30%-50%. *Factory Shopping Village*

OPPORTUNITIES

13 PROVIDENCE STREET, WAKEFIELD, YORKSHIRE WF1 3BG
☎ (01924) 290310 OPEN 10 - 5.30 MON - SAT, EVENINGS BY
APPOINTMENT.
Two floors of nearly-new outfits, from wedding outfits, evening wear and
cruise wear to suits and separates for daywear. Larger sizes always in stock.
Anything from Louis Feraud and Calvin Klein to Next and Principles.
Childrenswear includes Osh Kosh, Oilily, Gap and Mothercare. New and gen-
tly-worn jewellery. A large selection of designer shoes, handbags and belts.
Free parking. Easy sofas. Coffee and tea. *Dress Agency*

ORVIS FACTORY SHOP

17 PARLIAMENT STREET, HARROGATE, YORKSHIRE
☎ (01423) 561354. OPEN 9.30 - 5.30 MON - SAT.
Factory shop above the normal retail shop selling previous season's overstock
from their catalogue at much reduced prices. Merchandise includes clothing
for a country lifestyle, fly fishing equipment, waders, waxed jackets, gardening shoes, waterproofs, Wellingtons etc. Previous good deals have included a
hacking jacket for £29.99 reduced from £129.99; windcheater jacket for
£14.99 from £59. *Factory Shop*

OSBORNE SILVERSMITHS LTD

WESTWICK WORKS, SOLLY STREET, WEST BAR, SHEFFIELD,
YORKSHIRE S1 4BA
☎ (0114) 272 4929. OPEN 9.30 - 4 TUE - FRI, SAT BY PRIOR
ARRANGEMENT; CLOSED END JULY/BEGINNING AUGUST.
For almost 300 years, the Osborne family have been Sheffield craftsmen, and
now is one of Britain's leading cutlery manufacturers, supplying many of the
top stores in London's West End. The factory shop sells slightly blemished or
surplus perfect items of cutlery at special prices direct to the public. Their
extensive ranges cover both English and Continental patterns in sterling silver,
silver plate and stainless steel. In addition to canteens, place sets or individual
pieces, they also manufacture an extensive selection of servicing and accessory
items often difficult to find elsewhere. *Factory Shop*

PHASE EIGHT

THREE COUNTIES ARCADE, BAWTRY, DONCASTER, YORKSHIRE
DN10 6JG
☎ (01302) 271172. OPEN 9.30 - 5.30 MON - SAT, 10 - 4 SUN.
Phase Eight, the 24-strong chain which sells smart workwear and wearable
special occasion outfits, has a Sale Shop where end of season merchandise,
samples and seconds are sold at discount prices, including tailored trouser
suits, dresses, skirts, knitwear and tops as well as more formal outfits for special occasions and casual weekend wear. *Permanent Discount Outlet*

PONDEN MILL

COLNE ROAD, STANBURY, NEAR HAWORTH, YORKSHIRE
☎ (01535) 643500.
You'll find it piled high with thousands of linen bargains. Low prices on ends of ranges from local manufacturers and tremendous reductions on top name brands such as Crown and Coloroll. A Craft and Gift Shop sells interesting gifts and pottery items and the centre also has a restaurant and coffee shop.

PONDEN MILL LINENS

SKOPOS MILLS, CHEAPSIDE MILLS, BRADFORD ROAD, BATLEY,
YORKSHIRE WF17 6LZ
☎ (01924) 444948. OPEN 9.30 - 5.30 MON - FRI, 9 - 5.30 SAT, 11 - 5 SUN.
HORNSEA FREEPORT VILLAGE, ROLSTON ROAD, HORNSEA, EAST
YORKSHIRE HU18 1UT
☎ (01964) 535054. OPEN 10 - 5 SEVEN DAYS A WEEK.
FIRST FLOOR, DECK 3, UNIT 4, PRINCES QUAY, HULL HU1 2PQ
☎ (01302) 360117. OPEN 10 - 6 MON - SAT, 11 - 5 SUN.
☎ (01482) 210230.
THE YORKSHIRE OUTLET, WHITE ROSE WAY, DONCASTER, SOUTH
YORKSHIRE DN4 5PH
☎ (01302) 366444. OPEN 10 - 6 MON - SAT, 11 - 5 SUN.
Famous branded products at direct from the mill prices. Towels, co-ordinated bedlinen, duvets, pillows and curtains from Crown, Coloroll, Chortex, Rectella together with bathroom and kitchen accessories. The telephone number for the Doncaster shop is for the centre. *Factory Shopping Village*

POSTOPTICS

ORDER DEPT, FREEPOST, YORK, YORKSHIRE YO1 8GX
(0800) 038 3333. MAIL ORDER.
PostOptics is a division of Viewpoint, one of the largest contact lens practices in the UK. Using their massive purchasing power, they are able to offer dramatic savings of up to 33% on contact lens solutions. Their products are supplied by post in three-month packs which are significantly cheaper than the smaller sizes normally found on sale. £2.50 p&p is added to single orders, six month packs are supplied post free. *Permanent Discount Outlet*

Live Well On Less Tips
Open a window near your fireplace. Air needed by the fire will be drawn from the outside instead of from the expensive heated air in the house.

PRAXIS TAILORING LTD

31 SALTAIRE ROAD, SHIPLEY, YORKSHIRE BD18 3HH

☎ (01274) 531919. OPEN 11 - 3 TUE - FRI, 10 - 4 SAT.
CLOSED PART OF SUMMER HOLIDAYS.

Sells high quality high street brand name clothes (Next, Laura Ashley, BHS, Active Sportswear) for women. There are jackets, skirts, trousers and suits, tailored trousers, perfect blazers at half the retail price; jackets, kilts, stretch bodies and tops, raincoats, luxury lingerie, nightwear, and a small selection of both bedding and schoolwear. Sizes range from 8-20. *Factory Shop*

PREMIER & CAROUSEL

78 STREET LANE, LEEDS, YORKSHIRE LS8 2AL

☎ (0113) 266 6680. OPEN 11 - 5 TUE - FRI, 10 - 5 SAT.

Premier & Carousel has an extensive range of nearly-new designer and high street fashion for all seasons and occasions at a fraction of the original cost. They stock evening wear, daywear, smart casuals, special occasion outfits, costume jewellery, accessories for men and women. *Dress Agency*

PRICE'S CANDLES

THE YORKSHIRE OUTLET, WHITE ROSE WAY, DONCASTER, YORKSHIRE DN4 5JH

☎ (01302) 325362. OPEN 10 - 6 MON - SAT, 11 - 5 SUN.
MCARTHURGLEN DESIGNER OUTLET CENTRE
ST NICHOLAS AVENUE, FULFORD, JUNCTION OF A19 AND A64, YORK YO1 3RE

☎ (01904) 677997. OPEN 10 - 6 MON - SAT, UNTIL 8 ON THUR, 11 - 5 SUN.

Everything sold in this shop are seconds, which may be discoloured or have a damaged pattern; discontinued sizes not available elsewhere; over-runs from the garden selection or dinner candles in old packaging that has now been replaced. There are church candles, lanterns, candles in pots and glass jars, star-shaped candles, floating candles, candlestick holders, serviettes, scented candles and garden torches. Some of the ceramic items are bought in. *Factory Shopping Village*

PRIESTLEY'S

1 NORMAN COURT, 11 GRAPE LANE, YORK, YORKSHIRE YO1 2HU

☎ (01904) 623114. OPEN 11 - 5 MON - FRI, 9.30 - 5 SAT.

Period clothing from the 1930s-1970s, particularly tailored clothing, men's and women's tailored jackets, tweeds, blazers, dresses and waistcoats, hats and scarves. Prices from £12 for a tailored blouses, £50 for dinner suits, £25 for 1940s ladies jackets. *Secondhand and Vintage Clothes*

RAINBOW

STATION ROAD, OAKWORTH, KEIGHLEY, YORKSHIRE BD22 ODU
☎ (01535) 644433. OPEN 9 - 5 MON - FRI, 10 - 5 SAT.

Retail shop which also hires out baby equipment from wooden cots and car seats to pushchairs, bouncy castles and baby monitors. A wooden cot costs £15 to hire for 1 month, plus a £10 refundable deposit. There is no minimum time limit. *Hire Shop*

RAWHIDE STORE

FREEPORT HORNSEA SHOPPING VILLAGE, ROLSTON ROAD, HORNSEA, YORKSHIRE HU18 1UT
☎ (01964) 535053. OPEN 9.30 - 6 SEVEN DAYS A WEEK.

Small shop as you enter this waterfront shopping village. It sells leather belts, fashion bags (eg Fiorelli), all at least 30% below recommended retail price. The belts on sale here are made in their factory on the East coast and are slight seconds or discontinued lines. *Factory Shopping Village*

READMANS LTD

ALFRED HOUSE, SPENCE LANE, HOLBECK, LEEDS, YORKSHIRE LS12 1EF
☎ (0113) 243 6355 CASH AND CARRY. OPEN 9 - 9 MON - FRI, 8.30 - 5.30 SAT, 10 - 4 SUN.

Mainly women's, men's and children's clothing as well as bedding, textiles, toiletries, footwear, toys, children's books, shoes and towels at prices which are cheaper than the high street. Most of the stock is from Marks & Spencer, but they also sell Calvin Klein, Italian leather shoes, Playtex and Gossard underwear, Dorma bedding. Members of the public can enter with admission card, obtainable on application on a day basis. Cafe on second floor. *Permanent Discount Outlet*

REMINGTON

THE YORKSHIRE OUTLET, WHITE ROSE WAY, DONCASTER, YORKSHIRE DN4 5JH
☎ (01302) 366434. OPEN 10 - 6 MON - SAT, 11 - 5 SUN.
MCARTHURGLEN DESIGNER OUTLET CENTRE YORK.
☎ (01904) 677899. OPEN 10 - 6 MON - SAT, 8 ON THUR, 11 - 5 SUN.

Lots of famous names here from Oneida and Monogram cutlery to Braun, Philips, Remington, Clairol, Silencio, Wahl, Krups, Swan and Kenwood small kitchen equipment. There are usually hair, beauty and male grooming accessories as well as kitchen equipment, all at reduced prices. A great place to buy gifts or replenish the kitchen equipment with combi stylers, turbo travel plus hairdryers, air purifiers, liquidisers; food processors; batteries; clocks; and cutlery. Some of the packaging may be damaged but the products are in perfect working order. *Factory Shopping Village*

RIPON REVIVAL

6 KIRKGATE, RIPON, YORKSHIRE

☎ (01765) 604007. OPEN 10 - 5 MON - SAT.

Nearly-new clothes for men and women including MaxMara, Basler, Penny Black, Armani, Escada, Louis Feraud, Betty Barclay, Jaeger, Aquascutum. There is a mix of high street and designer wear as well as shoes, bags and accessories. *Dress Agency*

RL & CM BOND LTD

93 TOWN STREET, FARSLEY, PUDSEY, NEAR LEEDS, YORKSHIRE
LS28 5HX

☎ (0113) 257 4905. OPEN 9 - 4.30 WED - SAT.

Two-storey shop selling everything for the needlecraft and cross stitch enthusiast at very competitive prices. There are tapestry kits, silks, zips, threads, buttons, ribbons, cross stitch books galore, as well as rufflette tape, braid, trimmings, fringing and tie-backs. All sewing supplies and haberdashery at unbelievable prices. *Permanent Discount Outlet*

ROYAL BRIERLEY CRYSTAL

HORNSEA FREEPORT VILLAGE, ROLSTON ROAD, HORNSEA, YORKSHIRE HU18 1UT

☎ (01964) 532928. OPEN 9.30 - 6 SEVEN DAYS A WEEK.

Sells seconds of Royal Brierley crystal at 30%-50% off retail price, with two special sales. Also Royal Worcester porcelain available at seconds prices. *Factory Shop*

SARROUCHE

28 HARROGATE ROAD, RAWDON, NEAR LEEDS, YORKSHIRE LS19 6HJ

☎ (0113) 250 9990. OPEN 10 - 5 MON - SAT.

Discount outlet selling Italian and French designers including Gina, Sarrouche, Tricot Lorrain and Ronald Joyce evening wear. Wedding outfits, shoes and evening wear is stocked and jewellery are also sold. *Permanent Discount Outlet*

SECOND GLANCE

STABLE COURT, HUDDERSFIELD ROAD, HOLMFIRTH, HUDDERSFIELD, YORKSHIRE

☎ (01484) 684521. OPEN 9 - 5 MON - SAT.

Quality chainstore seconds from M&S and BhS for men, women and children. The labels are cut out, however. *Permanent Discount Outlet*

Live Well On Less Tips

INTERVAC INTERNATIONAL HOME EXCHANGE 3 ORCHARD COURT, NORTH WRAXALL, WILTSHIRE SN14 7AD. (01225) 892208. FAX (01225) 892011.

Home exchange is a great way to see the world, have a holiday and save money. You pay for travel, food and holiday spending only and make hotel bills a thing of the past! You also take on a home that has all the facilities and comforts you take for granted and sample another lifestyle and region from a better perspective: not as a tourist, but as part of the community. Subscribe at £80 per annum to receive an up-to-date directory of 11,500 homes in 67 countries, including your own personal listing. The directory is updated five times a year. Information is also published on the Internet or e-mail: intervac-gb@msn.com.

SHEPHERDS FACTORY SHOP

643 CHESTERFIELD ROAD, WOODSEATS, SHEFFIELD, YORKSHIRE
☎ (0114) 255 8418. OPEN 9 - 5 MON - SAT.

Good quality ex-chainstore merchandise from shops such as Marks & Spencer and Next, although all the labels are cut out. As well as knitwear, dresses, suits, blouses, skirts, sportswear, nightwear and trousers for ladies, there are shirts, trousers, underwear, swimwear, outdoor quilted jackets, reefer jackets, sportswear and T-shirts for men and childrenswear. Also some household goods such as towels. Discounts range up to 50%. There are other branches in Derby, Ilkeston and Lichfield. *Factory Shop*

SHIRTS TO SUIT

3 MAIN STREET, FULFORD, YORK, YORKSHIRE YO1 4HJ
☎ (01904) 634508. OPEN 8.30 - 5 MON - THUR, 8.30 - 4.30 FRI, 9.30 - 4 SAT.

Makes shirts and blouses for many of the high street department stores, as well as its own range of perfects which it sells in the factory shop at discounts of 30%. Cotton and polycotton blouses cost from £13.95, Viyella ones, £32.95. Also makes extra long sleeved shirts for the taller man from £17.95 and sells socks and ties.

SKOPOS MILLS

COLBECK HOUSE, CHEAPSIDE MILLS, BRADFORD ROAD, BATLEY, YORKSHIRE WF17 6LZ
☎ (01924) 475756. OPEN 9.30 - 5.30 MON - FRI, 9 - 5.30 SAT, 11 - 5 SUN.

SALTS MILL

VICTORIA ROAD, SALTAIRE, SHIPLEY, WEST YORKSHIRE BD18 3LB
☎ (01274) 581121. OPEN 10 - 6 SEVEN DAYS A WEEK.
One of the world's leading designers and manufacturers of furnishing fabrics, you can now buy many of these superb ranges at substantial savings. At their Yorkshire mill, they design and manufacture flame retardant fabrics for leading international hotel groups and interior designers. They now offer end of contract runs, specials and quality seconds direct to the public. Ends of rolls are half price, plus there are 100% cotton furnishing fabrics, sheers, voiles and linings, ex-contract and ex-display curtains, quilted bedspreads, quilted pieces, polycotton duvets and sheets, cushions, haberdashery and remnants. There is also a wide range of gifts including lamps, candlesticks, bowls, vases, mirrors and pictures, some at normal retail price, some reduced. The furniture showroom on the second floor of the Batley outlet also sells ex-display and prototype sofas and armchairs at greatly reduced prices. The top two floors at Batley sell the furnishing fabrics, cushions, throws and a large range of finished curtains at amazingly reasonable prices. Bring your measurements and forget about making them up yourself. There is also ex-display furniture at the Shipley branch. The Skopos Mill complex also includes Ponden Mills (bedlinen and towels), Edinburgh Woollen Mills and Armstrong's Mill selling a variety of men's formal and leisure wear. There are other factory shops on site with a variety of goods including glass, china and cookware and exciting new developments were being planned as went to press. *Factory Shop*

SMITH'S MILL SHOP

THOMAS STREET, HALIFAX, YORKSHIRE HX1 1QX
☎ (01422) 343432. OPEN 9 - 5 MON - SAT.
Mostly seconds in a wide range of curtain fabrics at discounts of 50%, as well as tracks, poles and haberdashery. Laura Ashley and Liberty are among the labels stocked in the past. The most expensive fabric in the shop is £9 a square yard; the cheapest £1. *Permanent Discount Outlet*

SOPHIE'S CHOICE

27 NORTH LANE, HEADINGLEY, LEEDS, YORKSHIRE LS6 3HW
☎ (0113) 2743913. OPEN 10 - 5 MON - SAT.
Nearly-new ladies and children's clothes which caters for middle to upmarket labels. Also sells shoes, handbags, hats and children's accessories. Navy blue blazers, £35, originally £200; designer shirts, £14.50, usually £80. Recently moved into large premises. *Dress Agency*

SPENCERS TROUSERS

FRIENDLY WORKS, BURNLEY ROAD, SOWERBY BRIDGE, YORKSHIRE HX6 2TL

☎ (01422) 833020. OPEN 9 - 5 MON - SAT, 10 - 4 SOME SUNS (PHONE FIRST)

Spencers Trousers manufacture better quality trousers in traditional fabrics (cords, moleskin, worsteds) and sell seconds, overstocks, returns and ends of lines at marvellous savings. The shop is situated on the A646 in West Yorkshire and is a traditional factory shop. It also offers a made-to-measure service with next-day delivery on some materials. *Factory Shop*

SPOILS

UNIT LG9, LG22, PART LG21, PRINCES QUAY, HULL, YORKSHIRE HU1 2PQ

☎ (01482) 327102. OPEN 9 - 5.30 MON - SAT, 10.30 - 4 SUN.

UNIT 5, ST JOHN'S CENTRE, MERRION STREET, LEEDS LS2 8LQ

☎ (0113) 244 8187. OPEN 9 - 5.30 MON - SAT, 11 - 5 SUN.

UNIT M8U7, WHITE ROSE SHOPPING CENTRE, DEWSBURY ROAD, LEEDS LS11 8LU

☎ (0113) 271 1433. OPEN 9.30 - 6 MON - FRI, 8 ON WED, 9 - 6 SAT, 11 - 5 SUN.

General domestic glassware, non-stick bakeware, non-electrical kitchen gadgets, ceramic oven-to-tableware, textiles, cutting boards, aluminium non-stick cookware, bakeware, plastic kitchenware, plastic storage, woodware, coffee pots/makers, furniture, mirrors and picture frames. Rather than being discounted, all the merchandise is very competitively priced - in fact, the company carry out competitors' checks frequently in order to monitor pricing. With 38 branches, the company is able to buy in bulk and thus negotiate very good prices. *Permanent Discount Outlet*

SPRINGFIELD CLOTHING

THE MILL SHOP, NORMAN ROAD, DENBY DALE, HUDDERSFIELD, YORKSHIRE HD8 8TH

☎ (01484 865082). OPEN 9 - 5 MON - WED, SAT, 9 - 6 THUR, FRI, 10 - 5 SUN.

Located in newly-refurbished premises, Springfield Clothing sells clothes for all the family from high street stores such as Marks & Spencer, Principles, Next, Monsoon and Dorothy Perkins. For example, M&S blouse, £12.99, normal retail price, £24; M&S men's jeans, £12.99; a selection of men's shorts, £5.99, original price, £12.99; children's shorts and T-shirts from £3.99; ladies nightshirts, from £2.99. Also stocks men's and women's underwear. They have recently added a selection of basic bedding, duvets, sheets, pillows, pillow cases as well as tea towels and table cloths, all at discounted prices. *Permanent Discount Outlet*

STAPLES

UNIT 11B, JUNCTION STREET, CROWN POINT RETAIL PARK, HUNSLET LANE, LEEDS, YORKSHIRE LS10 1ET

☎ (0113) 2421061. OPEN 8 - 8 MON - FRI, 9 - 6 SAT, 11 - 5 SUN. MAIL ORDER ALSO.

Office equipment and furniture supplier which is aimed at businesses, but is also open to the public. The owner buys in bulk and so is able to sell at very competitive prices a range of goods from paper clips to personal computers. Customers do not have to buy in bulk to make savings. A mail order catalogue is available and delivery is free on purchases over £30 (area permitting). *Permanent Discount Outlet*

TAYLOR'S MILL SHOP FACTORY OUTLET

NORTONTHORPE MILL, WAKEFIELD ROAD, SCISSETT, NEAR HUDDERSFIELD, YORKSHIRE HD8 9FB

☎ (01484) 861442. OPEN 10 - 5 MON - SAT, 11 - 5 SUN.

Quality chainstore and well-known label women's and children's clothing. On sale are suits, casualwear, evening wear, raincoats at appropriate times of year, accessories such as handbags, purses and scarves, underwear and hosiery. Also men's sweaters, underwear and socks. *Factory Shop*

THE BODY SHOP DEPOT

MCARTHURGLEN DESIGNER OUTLET, ST NICHOLAS AVENUE, FULFORD, YORK, YORKSHIRE YO19 4TA

☎ (01904) 613873. OPEN 10 - 6 MON - SAT, 10 - 8 THUR, 11 - 5 SUN.

Popular lines from a range of toiletries, The Body Shop Colourings make-up, gifts and accessories, bath, sun and skincare products, all of which are ends of lines sold at 50% less than its high street sites. *Factory Shopping Village*

THE BOSTON DRESSER

154 HIGH STREET, BOSTON SPA, WETHERBY, YORKSHIRE

☎ (01937) 844944. OPEN 10 - 5 TUE - SAT.

New and nearly-new top quality ladieswear including names such as, Max Mara, Viyella, Yarell, Mondi and Dolce & Gabbana as well as Marks & Spencer. *Dress Agency*

CAPE COUNTRY FURNITURE

COMMERCIAL STREET, MORLEY, YORKSHIRE LS27 8HN

☎ (0113) 2531024. OPEN 9 - 5 MON - SAT.

High quality, high density pine furniture made in South Africa from trees grown in managed forests, is sold at factory direct prices with home delivery throughout the UK. The range includes beds, wardrobes, blanket boxes, chests of drawers, tallboys, dressing tables, cheval mirrors, headboards, mattresses, a kitchen range, dining room tables, Welsh dressers, hi-fi units, bookcases. Also on sale in this shops is a range of African accessories and artefacts from Zimbabwe encompassing mirrors, prints, serpentine (stone) ornaments, recylced stationery, handmade wirework, candles and other ethnic and traditional gifts. Colour brochure and price list available on 01535 600483. *Factory Shop*

THE CHINA LADIES

78 HUDDERSFIELD ROAD, HOLMFIRTH, HUDDERSFIELD, YORKSHIRE
☎ (01484) 687294. OPEN 9.30 - 4.45 MON - SAT, 11.30 - 4.30 SUN.
Staffordshire bone china seconds (cups and saucers, plates, beakers, jugs, bowls, ornaments and picture plates), imported porcelain (planters, jardinieres, vases, jugs and lamp bases), and bed and nursery line seconds (sheets, duvets, pillows, cushions and cot sets). *Permanent Discount Outlet*

THE CLOTHES RACK

249 LOW LANE, HORSFORTH, LEEDS, YORKSHIRE LS18 5NY
☎ (0113) 258 2961. OPEN 9 - 8 MON - FRI, 9 - 5 SAT, 10 - 5 SUN.
Men's and women's clothes sizes 8-30. Stock comes from a variety of different high street outlets including Dorothy Perkins, Wallis, Richards, Top Shop and Evans and the turnover is very fast. Shoes are not stocked. *Permanent Discount Outlet*

THE CURTAIN EXCHANGE

162 HIGH STREET, BOSTON SPA, WEST YORKSHIRE LS23 6BW.
☎ (01937) 849755.
The Curtain Exchange is a franchised group of shops selling beautiful top quality secondhand curtains, blinds, pelmets, etc at between one-third and one half of the brand new price. Their stock comes from a variety of sources: people who are moving house and dislike the drapes in their new home; people who are moving house and want to sell their old curtains to help with the bills; show houses, where the builder wants to recoup some of his outgoings; interior designers' mistakes. Stock changes constantly and ranges from rich brocades, damasks and velvets to chintzes, linens and cottons. Designer names include Colefax & Fowler, Designers Guild, Laura Ashley, Warner, Sanderson, Osborne & Little, Fortuny and Bennison. A team of fitters and alteration experts are available if required. They offer a 24-hour availability. The Curtain Exchange also supply bespoke ranges with samples of curtains hanging. These fabrics are chosen from suppliers all over the world and are an excellent buy. *Secondhand Shop*

THE DAVID MELLOR FACTORY SHOP

THE ROUND BUILDING, HATHERSAGE, SHEFFIELD, YORKSHIRE
S32 1BA

☎ (01433) 650220. OPEN 10 - 5 MON - SAT, 11- 5 SUN.

David Mellor's classic cutlery at discounts of 15% to personal shoppers. The shop, situated in a former industrial workshop at an old gasworks in the Peak District, also sells handthrown pottery with which David Mellor has been involved in design or development at normal prices, as well as kitchen racks, cutlery boxes. Lots of wooden utensils and good quality kitchenware. *Factory Shop*

THE DARLEY MILL CENTRE

DARLEY, NR HARROGATE, YORKSHIRE HG3 2QQ

☎ (01423) 780857.

The Centre offers a great day out for the whole family, combining great mill shopping from linens, crafts and exclusive gifts to lots for children to see and do. This 17th century corn mill has one of the largest working water wheels in Yorkshire. *Permanent Discount Outlet*

THE FABRIC EMPORIUM

KIDD HOUSE, WHITEHALL ROAD, LEEDS, YORKSHIRE LS12 1AP

☎ (0113) 2458601. OPEN 9.30 - 6 MON - SAT, 10 - 4 SUN.

Curtain and upholstery own brand fabrics and those from many well-known high street brands such as Laura Ashley, Next and Marks & Spencer. Because they buy job lots from the USA, Europe and the UK, prices range from £2.99 a metre to £12.99 a metre although the normal recommended retail price of many items ranges from £16 to £30 a metre. Most goods are first quality. The majority of goods are priced in the range of £3.99 to £7.99 a metre. Stock is continually changing and brands include Crowson, Blendworth, Moggashel, Monkwell, and Matthew Stevens. *Permanent Discount Outlet*

THE FABRIC SHOP

82 MAIN STREET, ADDINGHAM, NEAR ILKLEY, YORKSHIRE LS29 OPL

☎ (01943) 830982. OPEN 9 - 5 MON - SAT.

Great fabric bargains in this rabbit warren of interconnecting rooms, stacked high to the ceiling with bolts of perfects and seconds of furnishing fabrics. Brands include Moygashel and Harmony. Most of the fabric, tapestries and damasks are from Italian and US manufacturers. Prints on the roll cost no more than £6.60 per metre, upholstery fabric costs no more than £15 per metre. Fabrics range from £3-£13 a metre, curtain lining from £2.40 - £3 a metre, tapes from 45p a metre and interlining from £3 a metre. No making up service; telephone orders taken. They also stock seconds of basics such as lining fabrics, muslin and 90 wide sheeting. The staff are very helpful and knowledgeable and there is parking directly outside or in the next side street at the village car park. You can also find the merchandise at York market on a Tuesday and Ripon market on a Thursday. *Permanent Discount Outlet*

THE FACTORY SHOP

LAWKHOLME LANE, KEIGHLEY, YORKSHIRE BD21 3JQ

☎ (01535) 611703. OPEN 9.30 - 5 MON - SAT, 10.30 - 4.30 SUN.

HORNSEA FREEPORT & SHOPPING VILLAGE, HORNSEA, YORKSHIRE HU18 1UD

☎ (01964) 535808. OPEN 9.30 - 6 MON - SAT, 11 - 5 SUN.

5 NORTH STREET, RIPON, NORTH YORKSHIRE HG4 1JY

☎ (01765) 601156. OPEN 9 - 5 MON - SAT.

LIGHTWATER VALLEY SHOPPING VILLAGE, NORTH STAINLEY, RIPON, NORTH YORKSHIRE HG4 3HT

☎ (01765) 635438. OPEN 9 - 5.30 MON -FRI, 10 - 5 SAT, 11 - 5 SUN.

THE CLOTHES SHOP, PARK ROSE LTD, CARNABY COVERT LANE, CARNABY, BRIDLINGTON, NORTH YORKSHIRE YO15 3QF

☎ (01262) 603518. OPEN 10 - 5 MON - SUN.

WHEATLEY LANE, LEEDS ROAD, ILKLEY, WEST YORKSHIRE LS29 8BS

☎ (01943) 604514. OPEN 9 - 5.30 MON - SAT, 10.30 - 4.30 SUN.

Wide range on sale includes men's, ladies and children's clothing and footwear; household textiles; toiletries; hardware; luggage; lighting and bedding, most of which are chainstore and high street brands at discounts of approximately 30%-50%. There are weekly deliveries and brands include many major stars such as Adidas, Nike, Wrangler and Dartington, to name just a few. There are kitchen and furniture displays and a new line in Cape Country furniture on sale. Ranges are continually changing and few factory shops offer such a variety under one roof. Most of the shops have their own car parks or there are nearby car parking facilities. *Factory Shop*

THE FACTORY SHOP

NAYLOR JENNINGS, GREEN LANE DYEWORKS, GREEN LANE, YEADON, LEEDS,YORKSHIRE LS19 7XP

☎ (0113) 250 2933. OPEN 9.30 - 4.30 MON - FRI, 10 - 4 SAT, 11 - 4 SUN.

CV CLOTHING, BANKWOOD LANE, ROSSINGTON, DONCASTER,YORKSHIRE DN11 OPS

☎ (01302) 867330. OPEN 10 - 5 MON - SAT.

Part of the Coats Viyella group, which makes quality clothing for many of the major high street storres, overstocks and clearance lines are sold through more than 30 of the group's factory shops. Many of you will recognise the garments on sale, despite the lack of well-known labels. Ladieswear includes dresses, blouses, jumpers, cardigans, trousers, nightwear, underwear, lingerie, hosiery, coats and swimwear. Menswear includes trousers, belts, shirts, ties, pullovers, cardigans, T-shirts, underwear, nightwear, hosiery and jackets. Childrenswear includes jackets, trousers, T-shirts, underwear, hosiery, jumpers and babywear. Although predominantly fashion, there are also curtain linings, cotton chintz and towels on sale. There are regular deliveries to constantly update the range. *Factory Shop*

THE FINE FURNITURE CLUB

TOMLINSON FURNITURE GROUP, MOORSIDE, BETWEEN TOCKWITH
AND COWTHORPE, NEAR YORK, YORKSHIRE YO26 7QG
☎ (01423) 358833. OPEN 9 - 4.30 SAT ONLY.
One of the North's leading wholesalers and exporters of antique and reproduction furniture and artefacts with over 5,000 items of antique furniture
under one roof. They are open to the public on Saturdays only. Membership
is free and instant to this huge emporium selling everything from antique
china services, some a little the worse for wear, to original and reproduction
nests of tables, rocking horses, dining tables, beds, sideboards and wardrobes.
If you see something you like but it needs restoration work, this can be quoted for on site. *Secondhand Shop*

THE GREAT CLOTHES
FASHION STORE

84 YORK ROAD, LEEDS, YORKSHIRE LS9 9AA
☎ (0113) 2350303. OPEN 9.30 - 9 MON - FRI, 9.30 - 6 SAT, 11 - 5 SUN.
Clothes for men, women and children from French Connection, Adidas,
Berghans, Pringle, Wolsey, Puma, Nike, Christian Dior to Sonnetti, and
including all brands of jeans. There are also accessories such as socks, shoes,
hats, scarves and underwear. They also sell bridalwear and hire out ballgowns,
formal men's and boyswear. Everything from outfits for two year olds to men
with a 54 chest. All stock is current season and is discounted by 20%.
Permanent Discount Outlets, Hire Shop

THE HARROGATE DRESS AGENCY

3 JOHN STREET, OFF JAMES STREET, HARROGATE, YORKSHIRE
☎ (01423) 521344. OPEN 9.30 - 5 MON - FRI, 10 - 5 SAT.
Two-storey shop with men's and women's good quality labels such as Georges
Rech, Jaeger, Daks, Boss, Armani as well as some high street names. Also jewellery, shoes and handbags. *Dress Agency*

THE ILKLEY DRESS AGENCY

THE ALPACA STUDIO, VICTORIAN ARCADE, HAWKSWORTH STREET,
ILKLEY, YORKSHIRE
01943) 600732. OPEN 10 - 4.30 MON - FRI, 10 - 5.30 SAT
Ever-changing stock of womenswear by MaxMara, Paul Costelloe, Monsoon,
Marks and Spencers etc to sell to you or for you. Stylishly refurbished premis-
es. Also luxurious Alpaca knitwear by Spirit of the Andes for sale. *Dress
Agency*

THE LIGHTING FACTORY SHOP

GELDERD ROAD, LEEDS, YORKSHIRE LS12 6NB

☎ (0113) 276 7491. OPEN 9 - 5 MON - SAT, 10 - 4 SUN.

First quality seconds and end of line lighting for the house and garden at very competitive prices. Large range includes wall lights, spots, fluorescents, table lamps, student and children's lamps, glass shades, party and garden lighting. Also bulbs and fluorescent tubes. *Factory Shop*

THE LINEN CUPBOARD

THE YORKSHIRE OUTLET, WHITE ROSE WAY, DONCASTER, YORKSHIRE DN4 5JH

☎ (01302) 323201. OPEN 10 - 6 MON - SAT, 11 - 5 SUN.

Bedlinen, sheets, valances, duvet covers, pillowcases, duvets, eiderdowns, towels and bath mats from leading brands all at discount prices. *Factory Shopping Village*

THE REALLY GOOD DEAL FASHION SALE

RIPLEY CASTLE, RIPLEY, NEAR HARROGATE, NORTH YORKSHIRE

☎ (01367) 860017 TICKET ENQUIRIES. OPEN 10 - 6, FRI 7TH & SAT 8TH APRIL 2000.

One of six countrywide fashion sales run by the team behind The Good Deal Directory. Each one features between 50 and 90 top quality fashion houses and well-known brand names selling their ends of lines, discounted stock and last season's merchandise at discount prices. Exhibitors usually include top catwalk names, middle market companies, some retailers clearing excess stock, a few manufacturers and and some entrepreneurs selling top Continental designer names. There are clothes for all occasions, knitwear, scarves, shawls, pashmina, shoes, jewellery, some gifts, a few childrenswear companies, and some men's gift fashion lines such as ties and shirts. Quality is middle to upper market, aimed at 25-50 year olds. *Designer Sale*

THE SHOE FACTORY SHOP

6/7 OSLO ROAD, SUTTON FIELDS, HULL, YORKSHIRE HU7 OYN

☎ (01482) 839292. OPEN 9 - 5 MON - WED, SAT, 9 - 7 THUR, FRI, 10 -4 SUN.

Men's, women's and children's shoes and accessories which are bought in from other manufacturers including Spanish, Portuguese and Italian companies. All are unbranded. The range covers from mocassins to dressy shoes. Ladies shoes which would cost £35 retail are £29. Children's shoes from size 6 to adult size 5 from £10 upwards. Slippers start at baby size 4 to junior size 2 from £3.50 - £6.50. *Factory Shop*

THE SHOE SHELTER

UNIT 25, 16A SPRINGFIELD MILLS, DENBY-DALE, HUDDERSFIELD,
YORKSHIRE HD8 9TH

☎ (01484) 866221. OPEN 10 - 5 MON - SUN.

Wide range of men's, women's and children's shoes with labels such as Ecco,
Loake, Gabor, Start-Rite, Elefanten, Lotus and LA Gear trainers, usually sold
at less than 50% of normal high street prices. *Permanent Discount Outlet*

THE SHUTTLE FABRIC SHOP

BAILDON BRIDGE, OTLEY ROAD, SHIPLEY, YORKSHIRE BD17 7AA

☎ (01274) 587171. OPEN 9 - 5.30 MON - SAT.

Sells discounted dress fabrics and some furnishing fabrics from well-known
designers as well as furnishing sheeting, quilting, curtain lining, plastic fabrics
for tablecloths, wadding, patterns and general haberdashery. Many are ends of
lines and there are always special offers. *Permanent Discount Outlet*

THE SPORTS FACTORY

THE YORKSHIRE OUTLET, WHITE ROSE WAY, DONCASTER,
YORKSHIRE DN4 5JH

☎ (01302) 322 663. OPEN 10 - 6 MON - SAT, 11 - 5 SUN.

Wide range of sports clothes, equipment and accessories, some of which are
only stocked in season (for example, cricket bats and tennis rackets in summer
only). Golf equipment includes clubs, shoes, balls, bags, putters, and brands
on sale include Phoenix, Howson, Slazenger, Second Chance golf balls,
Mizuno and Wilsons. There are also tennis rackets and cricket gear. All are discontinued lines and are cheaper than in the high street by between 10%-40%.
Factory Shopping Village

THE TEAPOTTERY

BUSINESS PARK, HARMBY ROAD, LEYBURN, WENSLEYDALE,
YORKSHIRE DL8 5QA

☎ (01969) 623839. OPEN 9 - 5 SEVEN DAYS A WEEK.

A boon for collectors of novelty teapots, all of which are manufactured on site
in up to 57 different designs and in sizes from one cup to five cups. Designs
include Welsh dressers, caravans, Agas, cookers, bellboys with luggage, can-
can girls, washbasins and a host of others, many of which are collectors' items.
Prices range from £9.95 - £45 for perfects, which represents a 10% - 20% savings on retail prices, and up to 50% discounts on seconds. This factory shop
has refreshments, a large free car park and access for the disabled, while its sister shop in Keswick, Cumbria is smaller and has no refreshments. *Factory
Shop*

THE YORKSHIRE OUTLET

WHITE ROSE WAY, JUNCTION 3 OF M18, DONCASTER LAKESIDE, YORKSHIRE DN4 5JH

☎ (01302) 366444. OPEN 10 - 6 MON - SAT, 11 - 5 SUN.

Forty factory shops, two thirds of which are fashion oriented. Built in an E shape without the middle branch, free parking is in front of the centre. Shops include: Clarks (now incorporating Ravel), Sports Factory, Baggage Factory, The Designer Room (stocking Versace, Armani, Calvin Klein), Black & Decker for electrical, gardening and household tools, Tog 24 outdoor wear, James Barry, Cloverleaf for tablemats and tablelinen; Price's Candles; Jane Shilton, Jokids, Remington, Ciro Citterio, Windsmoor/Planet/Precis, Toyworld, Birthdays, Bookends, The Suit Company (Moss Bros), Tom Sayer, Linen Cupboard, VF Corp. for casual wear and lingerie, Levi's, Ravel, Pilot, Converse, Event jewellery, Grattan, Cook 'n' Dine (Poole Pottery, Dartington Glass, Johnson Bros ceramics, Wedgwood ceramic gifts), The Garden and Christmas Outlet, Thornton's, Woods of Windsor, XS for CDs, videos and tapes, Ponden Mill for bedlinen and towels, Whittards of Chelsea, Double Two for men's shirts and trousers, Falmers, Warners Lingerie and Overland selling Caterpillar clothing and footwear. Free parking. *Factory Shopping Village*

THORNTONS

THE YORKSHIRE OUTLET, DONCASTER, YORKSHIRE DN4 5PH

☎ (01302) 320206. OPEN 10 - 6 MON - SAT, 11 - 5 SUN.

MCARTHURGLEN DESIGNER OUTLET VILLAGE, NABURN RETAIL PARK, FULFORD, YORK, YO19 4TA

☎ (01904) 679227. OPEN 10 - 6 MON - SAT, 8 ON THUR, 11 - 5 SUN.

The UK's leading specialist confectionery retailer has more than 500 shops and franchises nationwide selling a wide range of boxed and loose, chocolate and sugar confectionery. The factory outlets sell three different categories: misshapes. discounted lines and standard lines. Misshapes are loose chocolates which are the result of new product development, product trials or end of production runs which cannot be packed as Thorntons standard lines. They are packed into assorted bags and offer a saving of 35%-55% over the recommended retail price of standard loose line products. Discounted lines are excess to Thorntons' normal retail requirements and can be as a result of excess seasonal or export stock, discontinued lines or packaging changes. These products, when available, are offered at a discount of 25%-50% over the standard retail price. Standard lines from the full Thorntons range are also on sale at normal prices. *Factory Shopping Village*

TIE RACK

UNIT 66, MCARTHURGLEN DESIGNER OUTLET, ST NICHOLAS
AVENUE, FULFORD, YORK, YORKSHIRE YO19 4TA
☎ (01904) 624431. OPEN 10 - 6 MON, TUE, WED, FRI, SAT, 10 - 8 THUR,
11 - 5 SUN.
Usual range of Tie Rack items including boxer shorts, silk ties, socks, silk scarves
and waistcoats, all at 50% reductions. Customer Careline: ☎ 0181 230 2333.
Factory Shopping Village

TILE CLEARING HOUSE

149-150 CLOUGH ROAD, HULL HU5 1SW
☎ (01482) 470 711. OPEN 8 - 6 MON - FRI, 9 - 6 SAT, 10 - 4 SUN.
PEEL RETAIL PARK, CANAL ROAD, BRADFORD, WEST YORKSHIRE
BD1 4RB
☎ (01274) 741 207. OPEN 8 - 6 MON - FRI, 9 - 6 SAT, 10 - 4 SUN.
107 MEADOWHALL ROAD, MEADOWHALL, SHEFFIELD S9 1HE
☎ (01142) 432 444. OPEN 8 - 6 MON - FRI, 9 - 6 SAT, 10 - 4 SUN.
Over 500 ranges of top quality ceramic wall and floor tiles permanently in stock,
plus a comprehensive range of grouts, adhesives, tools and accessories to complete the job. Save up to 75% on manufacturers' recommended selling prices.
Permanent Discount Outlet

TK MAXX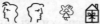

PRINCES QUAY, HULL, YORKSHIRE HU1 2PQ
☎ (01482) 223202.
THE VICTORIA SHOPPING CENTRE, HARROGATE, NORTH YORKSHIRE
☎ (01423) 536636. OPEN 9 - 5.30 MON - SAT.
LEEDS SHOPPING PLAZA, 27 ALBION ARCADE, LEEDS, WEST
YORKSHIRE LS1 5ER
☎ (0113) 246 7990. OPEN 9 - 5.30 MON - WED, 9 - 6 FRI, SAT, 11 - 5 SUN.
ORCHARD SQUARE SHOPPING CENTRE, FARGATE, SHEFFIELD, SOUTH
YORKSHIRE S1 2FB
☎ (0114) 275 1751. OPEN 9 - 6 MON - SAT, UNTIL 7 ON WED,
11 - 5 SUN.
Based on an American concept, TK Maxx is situated in easily accessible, often
centrally located stores and offers famous label goods with up to 60% savings
off recommended retail prices. TK Maxx has fashion for the whole family -
women's, men's and childrenswear - accessories, shoes, gifts, kitchenware and
home goods. Everything in the store is branded with a choice of well-known
high street names to designer labels, and while a small percentage might be
clearly marked past season, the great majority of items in store are current season, current stock and still with phenomenal savings. There is a huge choice
with 50,000 pieces in store and up to 10,000 new items arriving a week. The

stores are simple and unfussy with wide aisles, shopping trolleys and baskets, and a spacious, functional feel to them but there are individual changing rooms, ramps for buggies and wheelchairs and plenty of staff on the shop floor. Every branch accepts all major credit and debit cards and has a liberal refund and return policy. *Permanent Discount Outlet*

TOG 24

UNIT 8, THE YORKSHIRE OUTLET STORE, WHITE ROSE WAY, DONCASTER LAKESIDE, DONCASTER, YORKSHIRE DN4 5LH

☎ (01302) 364123. OPEN 10 - 6 MON - SAT, 11 - 5 SUN.

HORNSEA FREEPORT SHOPPING VILLAGE, HORNSEA, EAST YORKSHIRE HU18 1UT

☎ (01964) 535308. OPEN 10 - 5 SEVEN DAYS A WEEK (WINTER), 10 - 5 MON - FRI, 10 - 6 SAT, SUN (SUMMER).

LIGHTWATER VALLEY FACTORY SHOPPING, RIPON, NORTH YORKSHIRE

☎ (01765) 635338. OPEN 10 - 5.30 SEVEN DAYS A WEEK.

THE SPORTS FACTORY, BATLEY, YORKSHIRE WF17 5LZ

☎ (01924) 477363. OPEN 10 - 6 MON - FRI, 10 - 5 SAT, 11 - 5 SUN.

SPEN VALE MILLS, STATION LANE, HECKMONWIKE, WEST YORKSHIRE WF16 0NQ

☎ (01924) 409314. OPEN 10 - 5 MON - SAT, 11 - 5 SUN .

UNIT 23, BRUNSWICK PAVILION, SOMERSET TERRACE, SCARBOROUGH, YORKSHIRE YO11 2PA

☎ (01723) 377760. OPEN 9 - 5.30 MON - THUR, 9 - 6 FRI, SAT.

93/94 CHURCH STREET, WHITBY, YORKSHIRE YO22 4BH

☎ (01947) 820456. OPEN 10 - 5 EVERY DAY.

UNIT 54, DESIGNER OUTLET VILLAGE, NABURN, YORK YO14 4RE

☎ (01904) 677814. OPEN 10 - 6 MON, TUE, WED, FRI, SAT, 10 - 8 THUR, 11 - 5 SUN.

Tog 24 are the UK's fastest growing brand name in outdoor clothing and leisurewear, with a total of three UK factories and 36 stores nationwide. They utilise the world's finest performance fabrics including Gore-Tex, Polartec and Burlington macs. Catering for all the family for all seasons, with cosy fleeces and waterproofs for the winter, and trekking ranges, shorts and t-shirts for the summer. With all prices at least 30% below the recommended retail price you can afford to enter the Tog comfort zone. *Factory Shopping Village*

TOM SAYERS CLOTHING CO

THE YORKSHIRE OUTLET, WHITE ROSE WAY, DONCASTER,
YORKSHIRE DN4 5JH

☎ (01302) 364912. OPEN 10 - 6 MON - SAT, 11 - 5 SUN.

Tom Sayers make sweaters for some of the top high street department stores. Unusually for a factory shop, if they don't stock your size, they will try and order it for you from their factory or one of their other factory outlets and send it to you. Most of the stock here is overstock, cancelled orders or last season's and includes jumpers, trousers and shirts at discounts of 30%. The trousers and shirts are bought in to complement the sweaters which they make. *Factory Shopping Village*

TOYMASTER

FACTORY OUTLETS, 50 - 51 THE CORNMILL SHOPPING CENTRES, DARLINGTON, YORKSHIRE DL1 1LT

☎ (01325) 363 222. OPEN 9- 5.3- MON - SAT.

A large range of the very latest toys at competitive prices plus a massive range of discontinued toys, manufacturers overruns and excess stocks from many famous brand names such as Barbie, Action Man, Lego, Tomy, Fisher Price and many more, at least 30% to 70% off normal high street prices. Also available is a full range of T.P. outdoor activity toys. *Factory Shop*

TOYWORLD FACTORY OUTLETS LTD

UNIT 28, NORTH POINT SHOPPING CENTRE, BRANSHOLME, HULL, YORKSHIRE HU7 4EE

☎ (01482) 833540. OPEN 9 - 5.30 MON - SAT.

THE YORKSHIRE OUTLET, WHITE ROSE WAY, DONCASTER, SOUTH YORKSHIRE DN14 5JH

☎ (01302) 365511. OPEN 10 - 6 MON - SAT, 11 - 5 SUN.

UNIT 63, MCARTHURGLEN DESIGNER OUTLET VILLAGE, SELBY ROAD, NABURN, YORK, JUNCTION OF A19 AND A64, NORTH YORKSHIRE YO19 4TA

☎ (01904) 639 333. OPEN 10 - 6 MON - SAT, UNTIL 8 ON THUR, 11 - 5 SUN.

CROWN POINT HOUSE, BUTTERFLY STREET, LEEDS LS10 1ES

☎ (0113) 234 2221. OPEN WEEKENDS AND BANK HOLIDAYS ONLY, 10 - 5 SAT, 11 - 5 SUN AND BANK HOLIDAYS.

ToyWorld sells brand name items including a wide range of toys with well-known brand names. For example, Barbie (Mattel), Disney, Playskool, Lego, Sylvanian Families, Fisher-Price, Tyco, Tomy, Waddington, M&B Games, Safe & Sound, Matchbox, and many others at very low prices. *Factory Shopping Village*

> *Live Well On Less Tips*
> Eat dinner early when there may be a happy hour reduction.

TRADEX

BRADFORD ROAD, PUDSEY, YORKSHIRE LS28 5AS

☎ (0113) 239 3377. OPEN 9.30 - 8.30 MON - FRI, 9 - 5.30 SAT, 10.30 - 4.30 SUN.

CHATSWORTH ROAD, OFF HAREHILLS LANE, HAREHILLS, LEEDS, WEST YORKSHIRE LS8 1QW

☎ (0113) 240 7407. OPEN 9.30 - 8.30 MON - FRI, 9 - 5.30 SAT, 10.30 - 4.30 SUN.

Household goods, clothes for all the family, shoes, foodstuffs, costume jewellery, furniture and alcohol at very competitive prices. You have to be a member - bring two forms of ID including address - you can join instantly for £2. There is a coffee shop on site. *Permanent Discount Outlet*

TRAVEL ACCESSORY OUTLET

UNIT 75, MCARTHURGLEN DESIGNER OUTLET, ST NICHOLAS AVENUE, FULFORD, YORK, YORKSHIRE YO19 4TA

☎ (01904) 629978. OPEN 10 - 6 MON - SAT, UNTIL 8 THUR, 11 - 5 SUN.

Luggage and travel-related products including executive cases, handbags, umbrellas and accessories available in leading brands such as Samsonite, Brics, Hidesign, Globe Trotter and Tula. The products also include couture and high fashion brands such as YSL and Moschino. All products are offered at a considerably reduced price due to their being production over-runs, last season's stock of slight seconds (ie they have minor aesthetic blemishes). *Factory Shopping Village*

TRAVELLING TOTS

28 ALDRIDGE ROAD, PARK END, MIDDLESBROUGH, YORKSHIRE TS3 7HS

☎ (01642) 323835.

Part of the Baby Equipment Hirers Association (BEHA), which has more than 100 members countrywide. A range of equipment can be hired from high chairs, cots and travel cots to baby car seats and buggies. Some members also hire out party equipment including child-sized tables and chairs. BEHA run an advice line which will try and answer any queries you have regarding hiring services for children. Phone the Babyline on 0831 310355. Rock-a-Bye Baby specialises in christening wear for hire from £8-£25. They also have a full range of buggies, cots, high chairs, travel cots, car seats, stair gates, fire guards, bed guards, wind-up swings, exercisers, activity centres and door bouncers. *Hire Shop*

UNITED FOOTWEAR

ROOLEY LANE, DUDLEY ROUNDABOUT, BRADFORD, YORKSHIRE
☎ (01274) 680322. OPEN 9 - 8 MON - FRI, 9 - 5.30 SAT, 10 - 4 SUN.
Shoes for all the family as well as clothes, handbags, sports shoes, boots, all discontinued lines, broken ranges and oddments. Famous brands including Clarks, K Shoes and Elmdale. Part of a national chain which covers Cardiff, Worcester, Walsall, Kettering, St Helen's, Manchester, Chester, Dudley, Leigh, Newbold Verdon, Preston, Coventry, Nottingham and Birmingham. *Permanent Discount Outlet*

USC BRANDED CLOTHING

MCARTHURGLEN DESIGNER OUTLET CENTRE, ST NICHOLAS
AVENUE, FULFORD, JUNCTION OF A19 AND A64, YORK, YORKSHIRE
YO10 4RE
☎ (01904) 676 040. OPEN 10 - 6 MON - SAT, UNTIL 8 ON THUR, 11 - 5 SUN.
A variety of different designer labels including Tommy Hilfiger, Henri Lloyd, Yves St Laurent, Firetrap, Polo Jeans Co and Nautica. *Factory Shopping Village*

VF OUTLETS

THE YORKSHIRE OUTLET, WHITE ROSE WAY, DONCASTER,
YORKSHIRE DN4 5JH
☎ (01302) 325593. OPEN 10 - 6 MON - SAT, 11 - 5 SUN.
Men's, women's and children's denim jeans and jackets, cords, T-shirts, shirts, most of which are irregular (ie seconds). T-shirts and shirts are all perfects, as are some jeans. Discounts are about one-third off the normal price. Brand names on sale include Lee, Wrangler and Maverick. Children's range starts at two years. Also sells French underwear by Variance, Jan Sport bags, caps and hats. *Factory Shopping Village*

W MACHELL & SONS LTD

LOW MILLS, GUISELEY, LEEDS, YORKSHIRE LS20 9LT
☎ (0113) 2505043. OPEN 8 - 5 MON - FRI, 8 - 12 SAT.
One of the country's largest stocks of reclaimed building materials, including recycled oak and pine beams and period reclaimed flooring. Six full-time stone masons handcrafting genuine period stone fireplaces, mullioned window sets, stone doorways, all tailor-made to individual specifications. Period joinery work, including panelling, doors, etc, also undertaken. *Architectural Salvage*

Live Well On Less Tips
When shopping for a specific or unusual item, phone ahead to see if the store has it and perhaps save yourself a wasted journey.

WALTONS MILL SHOP

41 TOWER STREET, HARROGATE, YORKSHIRE HG1 1HS
☎ (01423) 520980. FAX: ☎ (01423) 520920. OPEN 10 - 5 MON - SAT.
THIRTY SIX, PIERCY END, KIRKBYMOORSIDE, YORK, NORTH
YORKSHIRE YO62 6DF
☎ (01751) 433253. OPEN 10 - 5 TUE, WED, FRI, SAT.
The Harrogate shop is a high street retail outlet which sells international designer fabrics with the emphasis on high class designs with a difference. More unusually, they also stock a vast range of quality trimmings, cords, bullions, tassels, tie-backs, etc. Regular customers really do describe the shop as an Aladdin's Cave, with its tapestries, handmade quilts, Egyptian cotton bedding, throws, cushions and traditional household textiles. Those who have tried the famous Knaresborough linen dishcloth vow never to use anything else again. Most of the stock is overmakes, bankrupt merchandise, bought from the US or imported from all over the world. Tucked away, you have to take the A61 Leeds road into Harrogate, and take the first right hand turn after the Prince of Wales roundabout at the longterm car park sign. The shop is 200 yards up on the left hand side. The Kirkbymoorside shop is small but bursting with incredible soft furnishing bargains, including fabric from as little as £1 a metre and a good selection of trimmings and accessories at budget prices. Making up service available. Kirkbymoorside is a picturesque market town, well served with restaurants and cafes, and perfect for a day out in the North York moors countryside. *Permanent Discount Outlet*

WARNERS UK LTD

HORNSEA FREEPORT, ROLSTON ROAD, HORNSEA, YORKSHIRE
HU18 1UT
☎ (01964) 536996. OPEN 9.30 - 6 MON - SUN.
This shop sells a wide range of women's lingerie from Leisureby, Valentino, Warners, with bras, slips, thongs, bodies and briefs at discounts from 25% to 70%. Each item is labelled with both the rrp and the discounted prices. For example, bikini brief, £6.99 reduced from £17; underwire bra, £14.99 reduced from £33; body, £24.99 reduced from £65. Slightly imperfect stock as well as perfect quality, end of season and discontinued merchandise and swimwear are also stocked. Underwear for men, including Calvin Klein briefs for £2.99, is on offer too. *Factory Shopping Village*

WHITE ROSE CANDLES WORKSHOP

WENSLEY MILL, WENSLEY, LEYBURN, YORKSHIRE DL8 4HR

☎ (01969) 623544. OPEN 10 - 5 MON, TUE, THUR, FRI, SUN JUNE-NOVEMBER. MAIL ORDER.

Based in an old watermill, this candle workshop has been selling direct to the public for the past 26 years. All types of candles are made in simple shapes from hand-dipped and cast dinner table candles to church candles. Sizes range up to 5 feet high x 4 inches in diameter. There are also aromatherapy candles. *Factory Shop*

WINDSMOOR SALE SHOP

HORNSEA FREEPORT SHOPPING VILLAGE, HORNSEA, YORKSHIRE HU18 1UT

☎ (01964) 536517. OPEN 9.30 - 6 SEVEN DAYS A WEEK.

THE YORKSHIRE OUTLET, WHITE ROSE WAY, DONCASTER, SOUTH YORKSHIRE DN4 5JH

☎ (01302) 320531. OPEN 10 - 6 MON - SAT, 11 - 5 SUN.

Previous season's stock as well as any returned merchandise and overmakes from the Windsmoor, Planet and Precis ranges at discounts averaging about 50% off the original price. The Hornsea outlet has plenty to entertain the family with playgrounds, an indoor play centre, restaurants, a vintage car collection and butterfly world. *Factory Shopping Village*

WOLFORD

MCARTHURGLEN DESIGNER OUTLET CENTRE, ST NICHOLAS AVENUE, FULFORD, YORK, YORKSHIRE YO19 4TA

☎ (01904) 613877. OPEN 10 - 6 MON - SAT, UNTIL 8 ON THUR, 11 - 5 SUN AND BANK HOLIDAYS.

The first factory shop for this Austrian luxury hosiery brand sells discontinued lines and seconds. Previously, these have only been on sale at Wolford's on-site factory shop in Bregenz, Austria, where the brand manufactures and houses its entire range for worldwide distribution and for special purchase sales to retailers twice a year. This factory shop stocks merchandise from Bregenz and not from Wolford's UK shops. There are bodies, swimwear, luxury tights, hold-ups at discounts of up to 60%. You can join the mailing list and order goods by phone with next day delivery. *Factory Shopping Village*

WRANGLER

HORNSEA FREEPORT SHOPPING VILLAGE, HORNSEA, YORKSHIRE
HU18 1UT
☎ (01964) 532979. OPEN 10 - 5 SEVEN DAYS A WEEK (WINTER), 9.30 - 6
MON - SAT, 11 - 5 SUN (SUMMER).
Previous season's stock as well as any seconds and overmakes. Men's and
women's jeans from £18, youths from £12. The Shopping Village has plenty
to entertain the family with playgrounds, an indoor play centre, restaurants
and butterfly world. *Factory Shop*

WYNSORS WORLD OF SHOES

CLARENCE STREET, YORK, YORKSHIRE YO3 7EW
☎ (01904) 637611. OPENING HOURS FOR ALL BRANCHES, 9 - 5.30
MON, TUE, WED, SAT, 9 - 8 THUR, FRI, 10 - 4 SUN AND BANK
HOLIDAYS.
THORNTON ROAD, BRADFORD, WEST YORKSHIRE
☎ (01274) 495016.
THURCROFT, NEAR ROTHERHAM, SOUTH YORKSHIRE
☎ (01709) 540876.
MIDDLETON SHOPPING CENTRE, LEEDS, WEST YORKSHIRE
☎ (0113) 2710849.
HORNCASTLE STREET, CLECKHEATON, WEST YORKSHIRE
☎ (01274) 851366.
INFIRMARY ROAD, SHEFFIELD, SOUTH YORKSHIRE
☎ (0114) 2737903.
CLARENCE STREET, YORK, NORTH YORKSHIRE
☎ (01904) 637611.
ENTERPRISE WAY, CASTLEFORD, WEST YORKSHIRE
☎ (01977) 514774.
HESSEL ROAD, HULL, YORKSHIRE
☎ (01482) 223585.
Stocks top brand-name shoes at less than half price. Special monthly offers
always available. There are shoes, trainers, slippers, sandals and boots for all
the family, with a selection of bags, cleaners and polishes available.
Permanent Discount Outlet

YORK HANDMADE BRICK CO LTD

FOREST LANE, ALNE, YORK, YORKSHIRE YO61 12U,
☎ (01347) 838881. OPEN 8.30 - 4.30 MON - FRI, 9 - 12 SAT.
One of the few businesses still producing handmade bricks, as well as pavers
and terracotta floor tiles. They can provide bricks for archways, slopes, edges,
ledges and corners and do all the British Standards specials as well as taking
special orders. www.yorkhandmade.co.uk. sales@yorkhandmade.co.uk
Architectural Salvage

YOU & YOURS

98-100 NEW STREET, HUDDERSFIELD, YORKSHIRE HD1 2UD

☎ (01484) 543301. OPEN 9 - 5.30 MON - SAT.

INGLEBY ROAD (OPPOSITE GRATTAN), BRADFORD BD99 2XE

☎ (01274) 624611. OPEN 9.30 - 5.30 MON, SAT, 9.30 - 8 TUE - FRI, 11 - 5 SUN.

UNIT 9, CROWN POINT, CROWN POINT RETAIL PARK, HUNSLET ROAD, LEEDS

☎ (0113) 2341924. OPEN 10 - 5 MON, 10 - 7 TUE - FRI, 9.30 - 6 SAT, 11 - 5 SUN.

SCOOPS, SHIRETHORNE CENTRE, 34-43 PROSPECT STREET, HULL HU2 8PX

☎ (01482) 224354. OPEN 9 - 5.30 MON - SAT.
SUN.

25 TOWN STREET, ARMLEY, LEEDS, WEST YORKSHIRE LS12 1UX

☎ (0113) 2631825. OPEN 9.30 - 5.30 MON - SAT.

41 BARNSLEY ROAD, SOUTH ELMSALL WF9 2RN

☎ (01977) 642256. OPEN 9 - 5.30 MON - SAT.

Grattan catalogue shops. There is a selection of items from those featured in the catalogue, which can consist of anything from children's clothes and toys to bedding, electrical equipment and nursery accessories. Each shop sells a slightly different range, so always ring first to check they stock what you want. All items are discounted by up to 50%. *Permanent Discount Outlet*

YOYO

61 EASTGATE, BEVERLEY, YORKSHIRE HU17 0DR

☎ (01482) 861713. OPEN 10.30 - 3 MON, TUE, 10 - 3 WED - SAT.

YoYo sell good quality, nearly-new childrenswear at prices from one quarter to one third of the original cost. The labels range from Marks & Spencer, Debenhams and BhS to Oilily, Patrizia Wigan, Tick Tock, Babi-Mini, Clayeaux and Absorba. Most items are under £10 and generally you can clothe a child for the price of one week's family allowance. Age range from birth to about 10 years. They also sell maternity wear and children's dance wear. *Dress Agency*

Scotland

WOMENSWEAR ONLY 🕅 Anne Thomas Natural Fibre Fabrics, *Berwickshire*.
Bairdwear Ladieswear, *Grangemouth*. Bee-Line, *Dumbarton*. Blue Moon, *Glasgow*.
Dorothy perkins, *West Calder*. Dress Sense, *Edinburgh*. Elysees Dress Agency, *Aberdeen*.
Ancore, *Strathaven*. Evans, *West Calder*. Gladrags, *Edinburgh*. Hermione Spencer, *Alexandria*.
Honey, *Alexandria*. Innovations, *Perth*. Jane Shilton, *West Calder*. Labels, *Aberdeen*.
Labels for Less, *Auchterarder*. Orchid, *Fife*. Paco Life in Colour, *Tillicoultry*. Pandora's, *Glasgow*.
Redress, *Perth*. Redress, *Glasgow*. Redress, *Bridge of Weir*. Redress, *North Berwick*.
Rummage, *Milngavie*. Saratoga Trunk, *Glasgow*. Scent To You, *Aberdeen*. Sellers, *Aberdeen*.
Shelagh Buchanan, *Glasgow*. The Address Designer Exchange, *Glasgow*. The Mad Hatter, *Glasgow*.
The Mad Hatter, *Edinburgh*.

MENSWEAR ONLY 🕅 Burtons, *West Calder*. McCalls of the Royal Mile, *Edinburgh*.
Slaters Menswear, *Glasgow*. Slaters Menswear, *Ayr*. Slaters Menswear, *Aberdeen*.
Tom Sayers, *Alexandria*.

WOMENSWEAR & MENSWEAR 🕅 🕅 A & K Clothing Ltd Andrew Elliot Ltd, *Selkirk*
Antratex Village Visitor Centre, *Alexandria*. Anthony Haines Mill Shop, *Selkirk*.
Balmoral Mill Shop, *Galston*. Belinda Robertson Cashmere, *Edinburgh*.
Cashmere at Lochleven, *Kinross*. Catalogue Bargain Shop, *Fife*. Catalogue Bargain Shop, *Glasgow*.
Catalogue Bargain Shop, *Hamilton*. Claremont Garments, *Glasgow*. Clarks Factory Shop, *Glasgow*.
Corston Sinclair Ltd, *East Kilbride*. Cosalt International Ltd, *Edinburgh*. DG Dagleish, *Selkirk*.
Damart, *Edinburgh*. Footwear Discount Centre, *Oban*. Freeport Scotland Outlet Village, *West Calder*.
Gleneagles Knitwear Co, *Tayside*. Glenmatch, *Tayside*. Gretna Gateway, *Gretna*.
Haven, *Glasgow*. Hawick, *Hawick*. Hawick Cashmere Co Ltd, *Hawick*. Jaeger Factory Shop, *Alloa*.
John Moody, *Kelso*. Johnstons of Elgin, *Elgin*. Jumper, *West Calder*. Leith Mills, *Edinburgh*.
Loch Lomond Factory Outlets, *Alexandria*. London Leathers Direct, *West Calder*.
MacGillivray & Co, Benbecula, *Western Isles*. Matalan, *Edinburgh*.
Matalan, *Wishaw*. Matalan, *Kilmarnock*. Matalan, *Aberdeen*. Matalan, *Renfrew*. Matalan, *Falkirk*.
Matalan, *Glasgow*. McArthurglen Designer Outlet, *Livingston*. Meridian Retail Factory Shop, *Wishaw*.
Mexx International, *West Calder*. Next To Nothing, *West Lothian*.
North Face Outlet Store, *East Kilbride*. Paton & Baldwins Ltd, *Alloa*. Peter Scott Factory Shop, *Hawick*.
Principles, *West Calder*. Q Mark Warehouse, *Glasgow*. Q Mark Warehouse, *Edinburgh*.
Q Mark Warehouse, *Stirling*. Starry Starry Night, *Glasgow*.
Stirling Mills Designer Outlet Village, *Tillicoultry*. The Factory Shop, *Alloa*.
The Factory Shop Ltd, *Dalry*. The Factory Shop Ltd, *Dumfries*. The Factory Shop Ltd, *Kilmarnock*.
The Great Escape, *Edinburgh*. The Mill Trail, *Clackmannanshire*. TK Maxx, *Alexandria*.
TK Maxx, *Edinburgh*. TK Maxx, *Falkirk*. Tog 24, *Alexandria*. Tog 24, *Tillicoultry*. Tog 24, *Glasgow*.
Tog 24, *West Calder*. Tom Scott Knitwear, *Hawick*. White of Hawick, *Hawick*.

CHILDREN 🐾 A & K Clothing Ltd ABC Babyhire, *Kilwinning*.
Antratex Village Visitor Centre, *Alexandria*. Baby Baby Equipment Hire, *Edinburgh*.
Babygro Ltd, *Fife*. Babyworld, *Bathgate*. Baby To Go, *Bo'Ness*. Balmoral Mill Shop, *Galston*.
Bee-Line, *Dumbarton*. Bobtails, *Inverness*. Catalogue Bargain Shop, *Fife*.
Catalogue Bargain Shop, *Glasgow*. Catalogue Bargain Shop, *Hamilton*.
Claremont Garments, *Glasgow*. Clarks Factory Shop, *Glasgow*. Dress Sense, *Edinburgh*.
Footwear Discount Centre, *Oban*. Freeport Scotland Outlet Village, *West Calder*.
Gretna Gateway, *Gretna*. Haven, *Glasgow*. Loch Lomond Factory Outlets, *Alexandria*.
Matalan, *Edinburgh*. Matalan, *Wishaw*. Matalan, *Kilmarnock*. Matalan, *Aberdeen*. Matalan, *Renfrew*.
Matalan, *Falkirk*. Matalan, *Glasgow*. McArthurglen Designer Outlet, *Livingston*.
Meridian Retail Factory Shop, *Wishaw*. Mexx International, *West Calder*.
Next To Nothing, *West Lothian*. Paco Life in Colour, *Tillicoultry*. Paton & Baldwins Ltd, *Alloa*.
Q Mark Warehouse, *Glasgow*. Q Mark Warehouse, *Edinburgh*. Q Mark Warehouse, *Stirling*.

Stirling Mills Designer Outlet Village, *Tillicoultry.*   The Factory Shop, *Alloa.*
The Factory Shop Ltd, *Dalry.*   The Factory Shop Ltd, *Dumfries.*   The Factory Shop Ltd, *Kilmarnock.*
The Great Escape, *Edinburgh.*   TK Maxx, *Alexandria.*   TK Maxx, *Edinburgh.*   TK Maxx, *Falkirk.*
Tog 24, *Alexandria.*   Tog 24, *Tillicoultry.*   Tog 24, *Glasgow.*   Tog 24, *West Calder.*
Wellowear Ltd, *Alexandria.*

HOUSEHOLD AND GIFTWARE   🎁 Birthdays, *West Calder.*
Caithness Glass Visitor Centre, *Perth.*   Caithness Glass Visitor Centre, *Caithness.*
Caithness Glass Visitor Centre, *Oban.*   Denby Factory Shop, *Tillicoultry.*   Edinburgh Crystal, *Lothian.*
Freeport Scotland Outlet Village, *West Calder.*   Gleneagles Crystal, *Broxburn.*
Gretna Gateway, *Gretna.*   Loch Lomond Factory Outlets, *Alexandria.*   Matalan, *Edinburgh.*
Matalan, *Wishaw.*   Matalan, *Kilmarnock.*   Matalan, *Aberdeen.*   Matalan, *Renfrew.*   Matalan, *Falkirk.*
Matalan, *Glasgow.*   McArthurglen Designer Outlet, *Livingston.*
Meridian Retail Factory Shop, *Wishaw.*   Ponden Mill Linens, *West Calder.*   Price's Candles, *Gretna.*
Scottish Fine Soaps Factory Shop, *Falkirk.*   Spoils, *Glasgow.*   Stuart Crystal, *Crieff.*
The Factory Shop, *Alloa.*   The Factory Shop Ltd, *Dalry.*   The Factory Shop Ltd, *Dumfries.*
The Factory Shop Ltd, *Kilmarnock.*   TK Maxx, *Alexandria.*   TK Maxx, *Edinburgh.*
TK Maxx, *Falkirk.*   Wild Rose, *Edinburgh.*

ELECTRICAL EQUIPMENT   ⚡ Freeport Scotland Outlet Village, *West Calder.*

DIY/RENOVATION   🔨 BMJ Power, *Glasgow.*   Burnthill Demolition Ltd, *Johnstone.*
Capones, *Glasgow.*   Edinburgh Architectural Salvage Yard (EASY), *Edinburgh.*
Henderson Roofing Supplies Ltd, *Glasgow.*

ARCHITECTURAL SALVAGE   🔨 Burnthill Demolition Ltd, *Johnstone.*
Edinburgh Architectural Salvage Yard (EASY), *Edinburgh.*   Henderson Roofing Supplies Ltd, *Glasgow.*

FURNITURE/SOFT FURNISHINGS   🛋 Anta Scotland Ltd, *Ross-Shire.*   J & W Carpets, *Ayr.*
J & W Carpets, *Kilmarnock.*   J & W Carpets, *Irvine.*   J & W Carpets, *Rutherglen.*
J & W Carpets, *Coatbridge.*   J & W Carpets, *Glasgow.*   J & W Carpets, *Falkirk.*
John Baillie Carpets, *Paisley.*   Outlines, *Auchterarder.*   Rejects, *Fife.*
The Cotton Print Factory Shop, *Glasgow.*   The Curtain Exchange, *Glasgow.*
The Factory Shop Ltd, *Dalry.*   The Factory Shop Ltd, *Dumfries.*   The Factory Shop Ltd, *Kilmarnock.*
Valley Textiles, *Darvel, Nr Kilmarnock.*

FOOD AND LEISURE   🍴 Denby Factory Shop, *Tillicoultry.*   Luggage & Baggage, *West Calder.*
Marshalls Chunky Chicken Shop, *Midlothian.*   Royal Lochnagar Distillery, *Ballater.*
Shaw's Dundee Sweet Factory, *Dundee.*   Thorntons, *Alexandria.*
Travel Accessory Outlet, *Tillicoultry.*   Walker's Shortbread Factory Shop, *Moray.*

SPORTSWEAR AND EQUIPMENT   ⛷ Cashmere of Lochleven, *Kinross.*
Corston Sinclair Ltd, *East Kilbride.*   Freeport Scotland Outlet Village, *West Calder.*
North Cape Ltd, *Throsk.*   Paco Life in Colour, *Tillicoultry.*   Snow Sense, *Edinburgh.*
The Great Escape, *Edinburgh.*

A & K CLOTHING LTD

45 ETNA ROAD, FALKIRK, SCOTLAND

☎ (01324) 622181. OPEN 10 - 5 MON - SAT, 11 - 5 SUN.

Mostly ladies wear, with some men's and children's clothes which is made up of surplus stock from Marks & Spencer and other high street names such as Principles. There are also vases, teapots, trainers, underwear and shoes. ***Permanent Discount Outlet***

ABC BABYHIRE

9 WOODBURN AVENUE, KILWINNING, AYRSHIRE SCOTLAND KA13 7DB

☎ (01294) 552549.

BOBTAILS

20 OLD MILL ROAD, INVERNESS, INVERNESSHIRE IV2 3HR

☎ (01463) 242123.

BABY BABY EQUIPMENT HIRE

45 GLENDEVON PLACE, EDINBURGH, MIDLOTHIAN EH12 5UH

☎ (0131) 337 7016.

BABY BABY EQUIPMENT HIRE

5 CAMMO BRAE, EDINBURGH, MIDLOTHIAN EH4 8ET

☎ (0131) 339 5215.

BABYWORLD

29 CROSSHILL DRIVE, BATHGATE, WEST LOTHIAN EH48 1DE

☎ (01506) 653506.

BABY TO GO

39 GREEN TREE LANE, BO'NESS, WEST LOTHIAN EH51 OPH

☎ (01506) 824134.

Part of the Baby Equipment Hirers Association (BEHA), which has more than 100 members countrywide. A range of equipment can be hired from high chairs, cots and travel cots to baby car seats and buggies. Some members also hire out party equipment including child-sized tables and chairs. BEHA run an advice line which will try and answer any queries you have regarding hiring services for children. Phone the Babyline on 0831 310355. ***Hire Shop***

ANDREW ELLIOT LTD

DUNSDALE ROAD, FOREST MILL, SELKIRK, SCOTLAND TD7 5EA

☎ (01750) 20412. OPEN 9 - 4.30 MON - THUR, 9 - 3 FRI.

Manufactures short cloth runs for UK clients and here sells tweed fabric by the metre. The factory shop comprises two rooms above the working mill, one set out with lengths of cloth, the other with finished rugs, serapes and shawls. They also make their own range of rugs, fabric, gloves and scarves. This is the place to come if you're handy with a sewing machine as their shooting jacket material and fine lightweight lambswool is excellent quality. ***Factory Shop***

ANTARTEX VILLAGE VISITOR CENTRE

LOMOND INDUSTRIAL ESTATE, ALEXANDRIA, DUNBARTONSHIRE, SCOTLANDG83 OTP

☎ (01389) 752393. OPEN 10 - 6 MON - SUN.

Large, rambling building, well signposted off the A82, which has a vast retail area and then lots of small workshops where you can watch sheepskin jackets being made, or even whisky tasting. It's difficult to tell how good the prices are as most are not double ticketed to show the original and sale price, but there are bargain sections and lots of baskets of bargains. Edinburgh Woollen Mill has a large area, and other labels on sale include Telemac, Pitlochry, Country Rose and Regatta. As well as clothes for men (new One Valley range of waterproof jackets, Hippo and Progen) and women and children, there are tea towels, toys, books, food, gifts, blankets, mugs, candles, CDs and tapes, table mats, sports equipment and countrywear. There is a big golf department selling Wilson, Spalding and Arnold Palmer equipment at discounts of 20%-30% and lots of different workshops. The Loch Lomand factory shopping village is nearby. *Factory Shop*

ANNE THOMAS NATURAL FIBRE FABRICS

MAINHILL, 43 BRIDGEND, DUNS, BERWICKSHIRE, SCOTLAND TD11 3ES

☎ (01361) 883030/882633 FAX. OPEN 9 - 5 MON - FRI. MAIL ORDER ONLY.

Designer and high quality dress fabrics from well-known British manufacturers, all sold by the metre from £7 per metre. Specialises in natural fibre fabrics. No minimum purchase. The Fabric Club allows you to receive four collections of outstanding quality dressmaking fabrics throughout the year for £16, enabling you to purchase top quality fabrics at very low prices. Customers can receive up to 50 samples in each batch. Most of the fabrics are suited to smart daywear, although there are some eveningwear fabrics at Christmas. *Permanent Discount Outlet*

ANTA SCOTLAND LTD

FEARN, TAIN, ROSS-SHIRE, SCOTLAND IV20 1XW

☎ (0186) 283 2477. OPEN 10 - 5 MON - SAT. ALSO MAIL ORDER.

Anta design everything on site, using tartan check designs in traditional Scottish landscape colours and there are usually seconds and ends of lines available at discounted prices. There are jazzy check woollen rugs, carpets, fabrics, throws, blankets and ceramics (also made on site) on sale at greatly discounted prices. Mail order is not at discount prices. *Factory Shop*

Live Well On Less Tips
If you haven't got children and have to work to school holiday timetables, choose out-of-season holidays.

ANTHONY HAINES MILL SHOP

UNIT 1, DUNSDALE ROAD, SELKIRK, SCOTLAND TD7 5EA
☎ (01750) 20046. OPEN 9 - 5.30 MON - FRI.
Family-run company specialising in producing quality wool ties from fabric designed and woven in their own mill. Tiny factory shop at the front of the factory selling tartan kilts, skirts, stoles, scarves, rugs, cloth and wool ties. *Factory Shop*

BABYGRO LTD

HAYFIELD INDUSTRIAL ESTATE, KIRKCALDY, FIFE, SCOTLAND KY2 5DN
☎ (01592) 647800. OPEN 10.30 - 4.30 MON, 9.30 - 4.30 TUE - SAT, 12.30 - 4.30 SUN.
GATESIDE INDUSTRIAL ESTATE, OLD PERTH ROAD, COWDEN BEATH
☎ (01383) 511105. OPEN 11 - 4.30 MON, 9.30 - 4.30 TUE, WED, THUR, 9.30 - 12.30 FRI, CLOSED 1.30-2.30 DAILY.
Babywear for 0-5 year olds at discounts of up to 50%: all-in-ones, playsuits, shorts, t-shirts, vests, shirts, pyjamas, and rompers at factory shop prices. Pyjamas upwards of £3 - a pair for a 4-year-old cost £6.99 compared with £12.99 for the same make in a high street store. Also does a line of adult leisurewear. Factory sales take place throughout the year and are advertised locally. *Factory Shop*

BAIRDWEAR

LADIESWEAR, UNIT 6C, WEST MAINS INDUSTRIAL ESTATE, GRANGEMOUTH, SCOTLAND FX3 9XB
☎ (01324) 665587. OPEN 9.30 - 4.30 MON - SAT, 11 - 4.30 SUN.
24 ROSYTH ROAD, POLMADIE, GLASGOW G5 OYB
☎ (0141) 429 6611. OPEN 10 - 4 MON - THUR, 9.30 - 12.30 FRI.
ABBOTSBURN INCHINNAN INDUSTRIAL ESTATE, INCHINNAN, RENFREWSHIRE PA94 9RP
☎ (0141) 812 6388. OPEN 9.30 - 4.30 MON, TUE, WED, 9.30 - 2 THUR.
Manufacturers for one of the top department store chains for more than 20 years, Bairdwear has a wide selection of seconds and overmakes in its factory shops. About 80% of the stock sold here is made by the factory itself, while another 20% is made by other factories within the same group. *Factory Shop*

BALMORAL MILL SHOP

16 CHURCH LANE, GALSTON, AYRSHIRE, SCOTLAND KA4 8HF

☎ (01563) 820213/821740 FAX. OPEN 9 - 5 MON - SAT, 12 - 5 SUN.

Sells cashmere and lambswool knitwear, embroidered knitwear, sweatshirts, polo shirts, bowling and golf attire, some of which is brand name and some own label, but all sold at factory direct prices. Ladies, men's, children's and babywear are all stocked. Popular ranges are Alice Collins, Emreco, Lyle and Scott, Farah, Hodgsons and Poppy. Examples of prices include cotton sweatshirts, £9.95, polo shirts, £8.95, lambswool jumpers, £22.95, Seconds, from £4.95. Telephone orders welcome. *Factory Shop*

BEE LINE, NO 6

DARLIETH ROAD, LOMOND INDUSTRIAL ESTATE, ALEXANDRIA, DUMBARTON, SCOTLAND G83 0TL

☎ (01389) 756161. OPEN 10 - 5 MON - SAT, 12 - 5 SUN.

Major chainstore overmakes for women and children. Stock depends on the time of year but includes shorts, T-shirts, jogging pants, dresses, skirts and sweaters, smart separates, some underwear, branded sportswear and bags, all sold at 30% less than normal retail prices. Stock is current and last season's. *Factory Shop*

BELINDA ROBERTSON CASHMERE

22 PALMERSTON PLACE, EDINBURGH, SCOTLAND EH12 5AL

☎ (0131) 225 1057. OPEN 9 - 5.30 MON - FRI, 10 - 4 SAT, OR BY APPOINTMENT.

Belinda Robertson is an award-winning designer of ladies fashion and classic knitwear in 100% cashmere. The collection is designed and manufactured in Scotland and is sold in boutiques and leading department stores throughout the world. Focusing on the working woman of the Nineties, the designs range from essential pieces to high fashion and can be worn for day and evening. Her showroom in Edinburgh carries ends of ranges, samples and over-runs, all sold at discounted prices, usually between 25%-75% less than retail, and many styles can be ordered on request in a wide range of colours and sizes. There is also a small range of men's classic and handknit sweaters available. *Factory Shop*

BIRTHDAYS

FIVE SISTERS, FREEPORT VILLAGE, WESTWOOD, WEST CALDER, WEST LOTHIAN, SCOTLAND EH55 8PN

☎ (01501) 762030. OPEN 10 - 6 MON - SAT, 8 ON THUR, 10 - 6 SUN.

Cards, notelets, stationery sets, colouring books, stuffed toys, photo albums, picture frames, gifts, giftwrap, tissue paper, party packs, candlesticks, Christmas crackers, string puppets, fairy lights all at discounts of up to 30%. Some are special purchases, some seconds. *Factory Shopping Village*

> *Live Well On Less Tips*
> Grow your own plants and flowers from cuttings.

BLUE MOON

GORDON CHAMBERS, 90 MITCHELL STREET, GLASGOW, SCOTLAND
G1 3NQ
☎ (0141) 248 4983. OPEN 9.30 - 5 MON - FRI, 9.30 - 3 SAT.
SECOND FLOOR, 11 BELMONT STREET, ABERDEEN AB10 1JR.
☎ (01224) 641741. OPEN 9.30 - 5 TUE - SAT, 9.30 - 7 THUR.
Dress agency specialising in wedding dresses and accessories. Up to 200 dress-
es at any one time ranging in price from £300-£1,000 and with labels such as
Alison Blake, Catherine Rayner, Tracy Connop, Dizzy Lizzy, Pretty Maids and
Andrea Wilkin. Also sells bridesmaids dresses, veils, shoes. It's advisable to
book an appointment before visiting. *Dress Agency*

BMJ POWER

280 GREAT WESTERN ROAD, ST GEORGE'S CROSS, GLASGOW,
SCOTLAND G4 9EJ
☎ (0141) 332 8000. OPEN 8 - 5.30 MON, TUE, THUR, FRI, 8 - 9 WED,
9 - 4 SAT.
Reconditioned tools and acccessories from the famous Black & Decker range,
as well as other power tools from brands such as Matabo, Makito, Flymo and
Kress, all with full manufacturer's warranty. This is essentially an after-sales
service with a retail outlet. Often, stock consists of goods returned from the
shops because of damaged packaging or are part of a line which is being discontinued. Lots of seasonal special offers. There are more than three dozen
BMJ service outlets countrywide. Phone 0345 230230 and you can find out
where your nearest outlet is. *Factory Shop*

BURNTHILL DEMOLITION LTD

FLOORS STREET, JOHNSTONE, RENFREWSHIRE, SCOTLAND PA5 8QS
☎ (01505) 329644. OPEN 8 - 6 MON - FRI, 8 - 12 SAT.
Secondhand timber, roofing tiles, slates, steel and wooden beams and a selection of other reclaimed items. *Architectural Salvage*

BURTONS

FREEPORT VILLAGE FIVE SISTERS, WESTWOOD, WEST CALDER,
JUNCTION 4 OF M8, WEST LOTHIAN, SCOTLAND EH55 8QB
☎ (01501) 762439. OPEN 10 - 6 SEVEN DAYS A WEEK 8 ON THUR.
Burton menswear end of season lines with the normal refund guarantee. The
range includes suits, formal shirts, ties, trousers, jackets, casual shirts, T-shirts,
sweatshirts, knitwear, shoes, jeans, socks and underwear. *Factory Shop*

CAITHNESS GLASS VISITOR

CENTRE, INVERALMOND INUSTRIAL ESTATE, PERTH, SCOTLAND
PH1 3TZ
☎ (01738) 637373. OPEN 9 - 5 MON - SAT, 10 - 5 SUN IN SUMMER, 12 - 5
WINTER.
VISITORS CENTRE, AIRPORT INDUSTRIAL ESTATE, WICK, CAITHNESS
KW1 5BP
☎ (01955) 602286. OPEN 9 - 5 MON - SAT, 11 - 5 SUN EASTER-
DECEMBER.
VISITORS CENTRE, THE WATERFRONT CENTRE, RAILWAY PIER, OBAN,
ARGYLL PA34 4LW
☎ (01631) 563386. OPEN 9 - 5 MON - SAT MARCH - OCTOBER,
9 - 7.30 MAY - OCTOBER, 11 - 5 SUN APRIL - OCTOBER,
Well stocked factory shop with many bargains all year round in glass and crys-
tal, giftware and tableware. Also selection of Royal Doulton products and
other great gift ideas to choose from. Special offers throughout the year.
Factory Shop

CAPONES

1- 7 MOLENDINAR STREET, GLASGOW, SCOTLAND G1 5AT
☎ (0141) 552 4399. OPEN 9 - 5.30 MON - SAT, 10 - 5.30 SUN.
Wallpaper and paint clearance warehouse which also sells paste, borders, tiles,
brushes, rollers. Paste free when you buy three rolls of wallpaper. Stocks
Valspar, Crown and Norvar paints; Vymura and Coloroll wallpaper with thousands of rolls in stock at any one time. *Permanent Discount Outlet*

CASHMERE AT LOCHLEVEN

LOCHLEVEN MILLS, KINROSS, SCOTLAND KY13 8DH
☎ (01577) 863521. OPEN 9 - 5.30 MON - SAT.
For over 100 years Todd & Duncan have been spinning finest cashmere yarn
by the side of picturesque Loch Leven in Kinross. Their adjacent factory shop
acts as an ideal focal point for those eager to purchase sophisticated cashmere
lines at affordable prices. Visitors will be captivated by The Cashmere Story, a
visually stimulating pictorial history of the journey taken by cashmere from
the barren plains of Mongolia, through the traditional Scottish yarn spinning
processes, and on to its final destination - the catwalks of the world's leading
fashion designers. The shop provides a terrific selection of clothing of perfect
quality, with no damaged goods or seconds. Labels stocked include their own
popular Kinross Cashmere label, as well as complementary classics from famed
collections such as Daks, Henri White, Barrie etc. and the full Pringle range
of both men and women's fashion sportswear. The shop and visitors' centre is
located about half an hour's drive from Edinburgh and just five minutes from
the M90 motorway. *Factory Shop*

CATALOGUE BARGAIN SHOP

315-317 HIGH STREET, COWDENBEATH, FIFE, SCOTLAND KY4 9QJ
☎ (01383) 611054. OPEN 9 - 5.30 MON - SAT, 11 - 4 SUN.
36-38 QUEEN STREET, GLASGOW G1 3LU
☎ (0141) 204 5696. OPEN 9 - 5 MON - SAT, 12 - 5 SUN.
THE FORGE SHOPPING CENTRE, PARKHEAD, GLASGOW
☎ (0141) 556 5352. OPEN 9 - 6 MON - SAT, 8 ON THUR, 11 - 5 SUN.
12-16 CADZOW STREET, HAMILTON, LANARKSHIRE ML3 6DG
☎ (01698) 421112. OPEN 9 - 5.30 MON - SAT, 12 - 4 SUN.
Catalogue Bargain Shop is a growing national chain of stores which obtains
the majority of its goods from mail order giants Great Universal and Kays, and
offers a range of clothing for all the family, a wide selection of shoes, bed linen,
household goods, electrical equipment and hundreds of other catalogue items
at very competitive prices. The merchandise consists of ends of ranges and previous season's stock for which there is no longer storage space when the catalogues change. The Queen Street shop is on the first floor of an office block.
The Parkhead branch has a new section selling different types of furniture.
Permanent Discount Outlet

CLAREMONT GARMENTS

2 COUSTENHOLM ROAD, POLLOCKSHAWS, GLASGOW,
SCOTLAND G43 1UE
☎ (0141) 649 7080. OPEN 10 - 4.30 MON - SAT.
Sells a wide range of ladies, men's and childrens high street fashions at discounts of up to 50% from high street prices. *Factory Shop*

CLARKS FACTORY SHOP

UNIT 26, THE FORGE SHOPPING CENTRE, PARKHEAD, GLASGOW,
SCOTLAND G31 4EB
☎ (0141) 556 5290. OPEN 9.30 - 5.30 MON - SAT, 12 - 4.30 SUN AND
BANK HOLIDAYS.
Clarks International operate a chain of factory shops nationally which specialise in selling discontinued lines and slight sub-standards for children,
women and men from Clarks, K Shoes and other famous brands. These shops
trade under the name of K Shoes Factory shop or Clarks Factory Shop and
while not all are physically attached to a shoe factory, they are treated as factory shops by the company. Customers can expect to find an extensive range
of quality shoes, sandals, walking boots, slippers, trainers, handbags, accessories and gifts, while their major outlets also offer luggage, sports clothing,
sports equipment and outdoor clothing. Brands stocked include Clarks, K
Shoes, Springer, CICA, Hi-Tec, Puma, Mercury, Dr Martens, Nike, LA Gear,
Fila, Mizuno, Slazenger, Weider, Antler and Carlton, although not all are sold
in every outlet. Discounts are on average 30% off the normal high street price
for perfect stock. *Factory Shop*

CORSTON SINCLAIR LTD

INDUSTRIAL PROTECTIVE CLOTHING, 36 GLENBURN ROAD,
COLLEGE MILTON NORTH, EAST KILBRIDE, SCOTLAND G74 5BA

☎ (01355) 222273. OPEN 8.30 - 4.30 MON - THUR, 8.30 - 4 FRI.

Designer trainers from Reebok, Nike, Dunlop and Inter trainers as well as
protective clothing (safety helmets, safety footwear, overalls), sports and leisure
items: jeans, shorts, sweatshirts, socks and underwear at discounts of between
20% and 30% off normal retail prices. *Permanent Discount Outlet*

COSALT INTERNATIONAL LTD

UNIT 7, WEST SHORE TRADING ESTATE, WEST SHORE ROAD,
GRANTON, EDINBURGH, SCOTLAND EH5 1QF

☎ (0131) 552 0011. OPEN 8 - 5 MON - FRI.

The company specialises in workwear, safety clothing and marine wear but
some of the merchandise is eminently wearable for everyday and is sold at very
reasonable prices. They have a wide selection of leisure and outdoor clothes
from Doc Martens to padded jackets and denim shirts, dungarees and donkey
jackets, safety footwear and hard hats, protective clothing and boiler suits.
VAT has to be added to prices. There are catalogues available for you to order
from if what you want isn't in stock. They also provide marine safety and life-
raft servicing. *Permanent Discount Outlet*

D C DAGLEISH LTD

DUNSDALE MILL, SELKIRK, SCOTLAND TD7 5EQ

☎ (01750) 20781. OPEN 9 - 12 AND 1 - 4 MON - FRI.

Small shop to the side of the factory which specialises in tartan manufacture.
Pure wool headsquares, £3.50; tartan braces; tartan dolls; tartan scarves; Celtic
brooches; tartan kilts and waistcoats; knee rugs and woollen rugs. *Factory
Shop*

DAMART

32-33 NEW KIRKGATE, LEITH, EDINBURGH, SCOTLAND

☎ (0131) 553 3073. OPEN 9.30 - 5 MON - SAT.

36-40 MARKET STREET, ABERDEEN, SCOTLAND

☎ (01124) 571146. OPEN 9.30 - 5 MON - SAT.

Damart underwear and merchandise - anything from tights, socks and gloves
to dresses, coats, cardigans and jumpers - some of which is current stock sold
at full price, some discontinued and ends of lines sold at discount. There several shops selling some discounted stock from the Damart range, known as
Damart Extra. *Factory Shop*

DENBY FACTORY SHOP

STERLING MILLS DESIGNER OUTLET VILLAGE, MOSS ROAD,
TILLICOULTRY, CLACKMANNANSHIRE, SCOTLAND , FK13 6HN

☎ (01259) 753 939. OPEN 9 - 5.30 MON - SAT (WINTER), 9 - 6 MON - SAT
(SUMMER), 11 - 5 SUN.

Denby is renowned for its striking colours and glaze effects. The Factory Shops
stock first and second quality with seconds discounts starting at 20% off RRP.
There are regular mega bargains with up to 75% off throughout the year.
Factory Shopping Village

DOROTHY PERKINS

FREEPORT LEISURE VILLAGE, WESTWOOD, WEST CALDER,
SCOTLAND EH55 8OB

☎ (01501) 763386. OPEN 10 - 6 SEVEN DAYS A WEEK, 8 ON THUR.

End of season lines with the normal Dorothy Perkins refund guarantee. The
range includes knickers, scarves, suits, blouses, sweaters, coats, jackets, dresses
and jewellery. *Factory Shop*

DRESS SENSE

44 HANOVER STREET, EDINBURGH, SCOTLAND EH2 2DR

☎ (0131) 220 1298. OPEN 10.30 - 4.30 TUE - SAT.

In operation for 25 years, Dress Sense is run by a mother and daughter team.
Occupying a three-room suite on the top floor of a building in central
Edinburgh, it deals mainly in designer labels, wedding outfits and evening
gowns, with some childrenswear for 3-8-year-olds. Labels stocked include
Basler, Jaeger, Escada and the ubiquitous M&S. The non-designer clothes are all
under £60. Lots of cruise wear and holiday wear as well as handbags and hats.
Dress Agency

EDINBURGH ARCHITECTURAL
SALVAGE YARD (E.A.S.Y.)

UNIT 6, COUPER STREET, OFF COBURG STREET, LEITH, EDINBURGH,
SCOTLAND EH6 6HH

☎ (0131) 554 7077. OPEN 9 - 5 MON - SAT.

Fire surrounds, fire inserts, wooden doors, cast iron spiral staircases, original
fixtures and fittings, panelled doors, shutters, baths, sinks, radiators, and general architectural salvage. *Architectural Salvage*

EDINBURGH CRYSTAL

EASTFIELD, PENICUIK, LOTHIAN, SCOTLAND EH26 8HB

☎ (01968) 675128. OPEN 9 - 5 MON - SAT, 11 - 5 SUN.

Home to the world's largest collection of Edinburgh crystal, wine glasses, vases
and decanters, both perfects and seconds with discounts of up to 75% off normal shop prices. There is a Visitor Centre and tea room on site. *Factory Shop*

Live Well On Less Tips
Set up an exchange cutting service with friends and neighbours for favourites
of theirs which you would like.

ELYSEES DRESS AGENCY

4 HOWBURN PLACE, ABERDEEN, SCOTLAND AB1 2XX
☎ (01224) 582257. OPEN 10.30 - 4.30 MON - WED, FRI,
10.30 - 6.30 THUR, 10.30 - 5 SAT.
New and nearly-new clothes including ends of ranges and designer samples as
well as a few high street names. Daywear, evening wear and accessories and
very extensive 'Mother of the Bride' and hat selection. *Dress Agency*

ENCORE

48 WATERSIDE STREET, STRATHAVEN, LANARKSHIRE, SCOTLAND
ML10 6AW
☎ (01357) 529779. OPEN 10 - 5 MON - SAT, CLOSED WED.
Encore has a large stock of nearly-new outfits from designers such as Frank
Usher, Condici, Basler, Jacques Vert, Escada, Mondi, Tom Bowker, Mansfield
and Alexon. Clothes range from daywear and suits to coats and evening wear
and there is a large number from which to choose. Good place to find mother
of the bride and groom outfits as well as accessories such as hats, bags and shoes.
Dress Agency

EVANS

FREEPORT VILLAGE FIVE SISTERS, WESTWOOD, WEST CALDER,
JUNCTION 4 OF M8, WEST LOTHIAN, SCOTLAND EH55 8QB
☎ (01501) 763473. OPEN 10 - 6 SEVEN DAYS A WEEK, 8 ON THUR.
End of season lines with the normal Evans refund guarantee. The range
includes tailoring, soft dressing, dresses, Profile, knitwear, East Coast
(denim/jeans), lingerie/nightwear, blouses, coats, outerwear and accessories.
Factory Shop

FOOTWEAR DISCOUNT CENTRE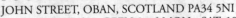

JOHN STREET, OBAN, SCOTLAND PA34 5NI
☎ (01631) 563633. OPEN 9 - 6 MON - SAT, 10 - 5 SUN.
Two floors of more than 10,000 pairs of quality branded footwear such as
Lotus, Nil Simile and Equity, which are seconds, discontinued lines, factory
directs and Italian imports. Ladies shoes, fashion courts to leather walking
shoes, from size 2 to 9. Men's leather shoes in sizes 5-13, including walking
boots, trainers, work boots and safety boots. Children's shoes and Wellingtons.
Permanent Discount Outlet

FREEPORT SCOTLAND OUTLET VILLAGE

FIVE SISTERS, WESTWOOD, WEST CALDER, NEAR JUNCTION 4 OF
THE M8, WEST LOTHIAN, SCOTLAND EH55 8QB
☎ (01501) 763488. OPEN 10 - 6 SEVEN DAYS A WEEK,
UNTIL 8 THUR APRIL - DEC.

Scottish heritage themed village with portcullis, grass moat and castellated
buildings. More than 40 outlets offering discounts of 30% and more below
high street prices, as well as restaurants, family attractions, free parking and
entry. Outlets for women include The Designer Room selling Donna Karan,
Christian Lacroix, Versace, Armani and Kenzo; Principles, Mexx, Next to
Nothing, Dorothy Perkins, Leather Direct, Honey Fashion and Evans offering
formal and casual clothes and accessories; Jane Shilton with shoes and handbags and Luggage & Bags with bags, while The Perfume Shop sells top name
fragrances. Men's outlets include the Suit Company, Jeanscene, Principles,
Burtons, Next to Nothing and London Leather. Sportswear outlets include
Russell Athletic, Tog 24 and Sports Unlimited while footwear is covered by
Branded Shoe Warehouse (Ecco, Lotus, Gabor, Loake, Van-Dal and
Salamander) and Sports Unlimited. Sweet-toothed visitors can savour the
chocolates at Thornton's. Shops which stock items for children include
Principles, Next to Nothing, Russell Athletic, Sports Unlimited, Tog 24, The
Toy Shop, Card & Gift, Thornton's, Book Depot, while for teenage girls, there
is Dorothy Perkins and for boys, Burtons and Jean Scene. Shoes and trainers
are catered for by Branded Shoe Warehouse, Foothold and Sports Unlimited.
There is plenty to keep the children amused with Tropical Rainforest World,
Frontierland, Go-Kart track, Monster Trucks, Cheeky Chimp's soft-play jungle and lots of places to eat. There is with a good selection of homeware shops
offering a wide variety of products including mirrors, picture frames, framed
prints, lamps, linens, cushions, rugs, quilts, glass and china gift and tableware
as well as soaps, dried flowers, pot pourri etc. These shops include Beautiful
Homes, John Jenkins, Ponden Mill, Spiegelau Crystal. Electrical goods are
supplied by Beautiful Homes, which sells an extensive range of household
lamps along with other homewares such as mirrors and framed prints; DX
Communications, which specialises in mobile telephones and offers comprehensive service and advice regarding networks and air-time agreements as well
as a wide choice of mobile phones. Sports and leisure outlets comprise Russell
Athletic and Sports Unlimited which carry a wide range of sports clothes,
shoes and equipment for all the family. Tog 24 has golf, walking and hiking
gear for men and women such as waterproofs, day packs and boots as well as
fleeces and waterproofs for children. Luggage & Bag stocks a wide selection of
luggage and travel accessories. *Factory Shopping Village*

GLADRAGS

17 HENDERSON ROW, EDINBURGH, SCOTLAND EH3 5DH

☎ (0131) 557 1916. OPEN 10.30 - 6 TUE - SAT.

Exquisite collecton of period clothes, accessories and costume jewellery. Victorian linen and whites to mid Sixties and some Seventies clothes with Twenties accessories and hats. *Secondhand and Vintage Clothe*

GLENEAGLES CRYSTAL

9 SIMPSON ROAD, EAST MAIN INDUSTRIAL ESTATE, BROXBURN, LOTHIAN, SCOTLAND EH52 5NP

☎ (01506) 852566. OPEN 10 - 5 MON - SAT, 11 - 4 SUN.

Hand-cut crystal, wine glasses, tumblers, ornaments, giftware, china and ceramics at discounts of about 15% for seconds. Tableware, dinner sets, complete china range from names such as Villeroy-Boch, Wedgwood, Royal Doulton, Royal Worcester, Spode, Denby, PortMerion and Arthur Price cutlery. *Factory Shop*

GLENEAGLES KNITWEAR COMPANY

ABBEY ROAD, AUCHTERARDER, TAYSIDE, SCOTLAND PH3 1DP

☎ (01764) 662112. OPEN 9 - 5 MON - SAT.

Perfect knitwear for women and men including cardigans, jumpers, socks and some merchandise made of 80% pure cashmere. Also stocks coats and jackets by Burberry and Daks; sweaters by Jaeger and cashmere made to order. *Factory Shop*

GLENMATCH

20 BRIDGE STREET, KELSO, SCOTTISH BORDERS, SCOTLAND TD5 7JD

☎ (01573) 226776. OPEN 9.30 - 5.30 MON - FRI, 9.30 - 5 SAT, 9 - 1 WED.

Glenmatch offers you the luxury of Scottish knitwear direct from the Scottish borders at prices which are approximately 30%-40% below normal retail prices. You can choose from cashmere, cashmere/silk, merino and lambswool for men and women. Also some trousers, gloves, scarves and handbags. *Factory Shop*

GRETNA GATEWAY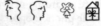

GLASGOW ROAD, GRETNA, SCOTLAND DG16 6GG

(07771) 658343. OPEN 10 - 6 SEVEN DAYS A WEEK EXCEPT CHRISTMAS AND NEW YEAR'S DAY.

One of the latest factory shopping villages to open (in summer 1999) there are more than 30 different outlets and a planned second phase of 30 shops. Includes Designer Room, Edinburgh Woollen Mill, Jane Shilton, Leather Rat (for leather clothing and footwear), LMI baggage, John Partridge, Price's Candles, the largest Polo Ralph Lauren factory shop in Europe (stocking clothes for men, women and children as well as homewares), Reebok, Tog 24, Tommy Hilfiger, Whittards, a specialist golf shop and several more international fashion and sports names due to commit at the time of going to press. There are restaurants, a children's play area and a themed visitor centre. *Factory Shopping Village*

HAVEN

473 HILLINGTON ROAD, HILLINGTON INDUSTRIAL ESTATE, GLASGOW, DUNBARTONSHIRE, SCOTLAND G52 4QX
☎ (0141) 883 4801. OPEN 8 - 4.20 MON - THUR, 8 - 3 FRI.
A sheltered workshop owned by the Haven Products Trust to whom all the profits go. It sells women's, men's and children's knitwear, many of them high street and brand names such as Burberry, Etienne Aigner and Laura Ashley, at reduced prices. *Permanent Discount Outlet*

HAWICK, SCOTLAND

Renowned for knitwear, Hawick is a cashmere buyer's dream town with four or five shops selling a wide variety of knits at bargain prices. As well as White of Hawick, there's the Cashmere Sweater Store which sells Chas N Whillans, Pringle, Alice Collins leisure wear, Tulchan hand embroidered knitwear, Cross Creek sports hats, rugs and socks. In the high street, there's Peter Scott selling cashmere and lambswool/merini wool for men and women. The Hawick Cashmere Co sells cashmere, lambswool, jackets and cardigans for men and women. Walk around the town and you'll find other knitwear treasures. *Factory Shop*

HAWICK CASHMERE CO LTD

TRINITY MILLS, DUKE STREET, HAWICK, SCOTLAND TD9 9QA
☎ (01450) 372510. OPEN 9.30 - 5 MON - FRI, 11 - 4 SUN.
Manufactures high quality ladies and men's knitwear for top department stores and sells ends of lines here at below retail prices. Specialises in such luxury fibres as cashmere and cashmere silk and lambswool and merino in a range which comprises sweaters, capes, cardigans, dresses, skirts and gloves. Visitor Centre on site. *Factory Shop*

HENDERSON ROOFING SUPPLIES LTD

31 WESTERBURN STREET, CARNTYNE, GLASGOW, SCOTLAND G32 6AT
☎ (0141)778 3602. OPEN 8 - 4.30 MON - THUR, 8 - 3.30 FRI.
Dealers in slate and accessories. Suppliers of Caborco Spanish slate and specialists in new and secondhand slates. Free car park. *Architectural Salvage*

HERMIONE SPENCER

UNIT 15, LOMOND TRADE CENTRE, ALEXANDRIA,
DUNBARTONSHIRE, SCOTLAND G83 OTL
☎ (01389) 721542. OPEN 9 - 4 MON - FRI.

Designer knitwear, including cashmere, as well as wool for knitting in this factory which manufactures for N Peal. Everything on sale here has been manufactured on site, mostly for export to the United States. Phone first to check stock levels. *Factory Shop*

HONEY

LOCH LOMOND FACTORY OUTLET, ALEXANDRIA,
DUNBARTONSHIRE, SCOTLAND G83 ODG
☎ (013890) 607268. OPEN 10 - 6 MON - SAT, 11 - 5 SUN.
FREEPORT VILLAGE WESTWOOD, WEST CALDER, SCOTLAND
EH55 8PW
☎ (015010) 763222. OPEN 10 - 6 MON - SAT, 10 - 8 THUR, 11 - 5 SUN.

Leisure-oriented women's T-shirts, leggings and sweaters at discounts of mostly 30% or more. *Factory Shopping Village*

INNOVATIONS

5 ABBOT STREET, PERTH, SCOTLAND PH2 OEB
☎ (01738) 638568. OPEN 10 - 4 MON - SAT.

Small, friendly shop where customers speak to each other over countless cups of coffee sipped by ladies who come from afar to snap up some of the wonderful clothes which come and go on a daily basis. Prices are kept low to maintain a high turnover. Stocks ballgowns, wedding outfits, business suits and casual/holiday wear, all at less than one third of the original price. Examples of prices include Weill suit for £120, originally £425, Cerruti suit £130, origianlly £700, wolford Boday £18, originally £79 . There are usually hundreds of different outfits in stock in sizes 8-24, plus lots of costume jewellery, scarves, handbags, and some shoes. Half-price sales take place in January and July. *Dress Agency*

Live Well On Less Tips

REAL NAPPY ASSOCIATION PO BOX 3704, LONDON SE26 4RX.
WEBSITE www.realnappy.com.
Encourages the use of real nappies which, compared to disposable ones, are much cheaper. Plus, they argue, your baby stays comfortable and healthy and you save resources and minimise pollution. Over two and a half years, or 5,020 nappy changes, disposables cost from £645 whereas real nappies can cost from £250 including all accessories, washing agents, energy and £150 wear and tear on a washing machine. Nappy washing services are especially good value for families with two or more children in nappies. Send large SAE for free information pack.

J & W CARPETS

24 BACK MAIN STREET, AYR, SCOTLAND KA8 8BZ
☎ (01292) 265539. OPEN 9 - 8 MON - FRI, 9 - 5.30 SAT, 12 - 5 SUN.
UNIT 1, FORGE INDUSTRIAL ESTATE, BONNYTON ROAD,
KILMARNOCK
☎ (01563) 535397. OPEN 9 - 8 MON - FRI, 9 - 5.30 SAT, 12 - 5 SUN.
9 PORTLAND ROAD, IRVINE, SCOTLAND KA12 8HY
☎ (01294) 274724. OPEN 9 - 8 MON - FRI, 9 - 5.30 SAT, 12 - 5 SUN.
3 RUTHERGLEN ROAD, RUTHERGLEN G73 1SX
☎ (0141) 647 9442. OPEN 9 - 8 MON - FRI, 9 - 5.30 SAT, 12 - 5 SUN.
WAREHOUSE 1, LOCH STREET, COATBRIDGE ML5 3RT
☎ (01236) 440090. OPEN 9 - 8 MON - FRI, 9 - 5.30 SAT, 12 - 5 SUN.
32 POSSIL ROAD, GLASGOW G4 9SR
☎ (0141) 333 1212. OPEN 9 - 8 MON - FRI, 9 - 5.30 SAT, 12 - 5 SUN
WAREHOUSE 1, CARRON ROAD, FALKIRK FK2 7RR
☎ (01324) 610210. OPEN 9 - 8 MON - FRI, 9 - 5.30 SAT, 12 - 5 SUN
Sells carpets from polyproplene and wool twists to Axminsters at discounts of
up to 50%. They also sell Chinese rugs from £20-£175, representing discounts of 20%-30% on the high street. Carpets range from £1.50 a square
yard to £20. *Permanent Discount Outlet*

JAEGER FACTORY SHOP

TULLIBODY ROAD, LORNSHILL, ALLOA, SCOTLAND FK10 2EZ
☎ (01259) 218985. OPEN 9 - 5 MON - SAT, 10 - 4 SUN.
15 MUNRO PLACE, BONNYTON INDUSTRIAL ESTATE, KILMARNOCK
KA1 2NP
☎ (01563) 526511. OPEN 9 - 12 AND 2 - 4 MON, THUR, 9 - 4 TUE, WED,
FRI, 10 - 4 SAT, SUN.
Contemporary classics from Jaeger at excellent prices. Most of the merchandise is previous seasons' stock, but you might also find some special makes.
Both shops stock tailoring and knitwear for women and men *Factory Shop*

JANE SHILTON

FREEPORT VILLAGE, FIVE SISTERS, WESTWOOD, WEST CALDER, WEST
LOTHIAN, SCOTLAND EH55 8QB
☎ (01501) 762985. OPEN 10 - 6 SEVEN DAYS A WEEK, UNTIL 8 THUR.
This shop only carries merchandise from past seasons' collections or factory
seconds at discounts of at least 30% off the original price. There is a wide
range of handbags, suitcases, women's shoes, luggage, briefcases, umbrellas,
scarves and travel bags. *Factory Shop*

JOHN BAILLIE CARPETS

22 GREENHILL ROAD, PAISLEY, SCOTLAND PA3 1RN

☎ (0141) 848 5502. OPEN 9 - 8 MON - FRI, 9 - 5.30 SAT, 11 - 5 SUN.

Sells carpets from polyproplene and wool twists to Axminsters at discounts of up to 50%. Carpets range from £1.50 a square yard to £20. Hardwood flooring also available at discounts of up to 20%. *Permanent Discount Outlet*

JOHN MOODY

38 THE SQUARE, KELSO, SCOTTISH BORDERS, SCOTLAND

☎ (01573) 224400. OPEN 10 - 5 MON - SAT, CLOSED 1.30 - 2 DAILY.

Cashmere and lambswool sweaters and cardigans for men and women at factory shop prices. *Permanent Discount Outlet*

JOHNSTONS OF ELGIN

CASHMERE VISITORS CENTRE, NEW MILL, ELGIN, SCOTLAND 1V30 2AF

☎ (01343) 554099. OPEN 9 - 5.30 MON - SAT, 11 - 5 SUN JUNE - SEPTEMBER.

A factory shop with an on-site visitors mill, where you can watch raw wool being made into luxurious cashmere from the dyeing and blending through to the spinning, winding and weaving. Cashmere sweaters sold from £75 - £250, plus regular bargain baskets. *Factory Shop*

JUMPER

UNIT B9, FREEPORT SHOPPING AND LEISURE VILLAGE, WESTWOO, WEST CALDER, WEST LOTHIAN, SCOTLAND EH55 8QB

☎ (01501) 763203. OPEN 9.30 - 5.30 MON - SAT, 11 - 5 SUN.

A wide range of Jumper label sweaters, gloves, scarves, shirts and cardigans for men and women all at discount prices of up to 50% off. Prices start at £2. *Factory Shopping Village*

LABELS

36 BROOMHILL ROAD, ABERDEEN, SCOTLAND AB1 6HT

☎ (01224) 213345. OPEN 10 - 5 WED - SAT.

Small but interesting shop which stocks both high street and designer names including Versace, Moschino, Jasper Conran, Country Casuals, Principles, Wallis, Next and Jaeger. Stock is constantly changing and there is always something different to see on each visit. There are also shoes, handbags, hats and jewellery. Clothes range from daywear and holiday wear to ballgowns, evening wear and business outfits. Coffee always available! *Dress Agency*

LABELS FOR LESS

78 HIGH STREET, AUCHTERARDER, PERTHSHIRE, SCOTLAND PH3 18J
☎ (01764) 664482. OPEN 10 - 5 MON - SAT, WED 10 - 4.30.
Top quality labels such as Mondi, Escada and Betty Barclay in daywear, cocktail and evening wear. New and nearly new garments in pristine condition are accepted daily. *Dress Agency*

LEITH MILLS

70 - 74 BANGOR ROAD, OFF GREAT JUNCTION STREET, LEITH, EDINBURGH, SCOTLAND EH6 5JU
☎ (0131) 553 5161. OPEN SUMMER: 9 - 5.30 MON - SAT, 10 - 5 SUN, WINTER 10 - 5 MON - SAT, 11 - 5 SUN.
Leith Mills is one of those places I find hard to place among discounters and factory shops. It's not really a factory shop as the stock is not made on site but bought in from all over Scotland, but it does claim to be very competitively priced. The only time prices may be equal with those in the high street is when the latter is on sale. As I'm not familiar with prices in Edinburgh, I couldn't tell how much of a good deal they were. Leith Mills is a very big outlet with plenty of car parking. It houses the Edinburgh Woollen Mill, James Pringle and the Clan Tartan Centre. The men's department houses Antartex sweaters, Pitlochry countrywear, Pringle, Clan Royal sweaters, Tulchan knitwear, golf balls and golfing gifts, golf clubs, T-shirts, jeans, and trousers. The women's department has Country Rose knitwear, blouses, shawls, pleated tartan skirts, Arran knits, gloves, scarves, hats, and cashmere. There is a very small children's clothing section and also a department selling tapes, teddies, cushions, books, silver spoons, Edinburgh and Stuart Crystal, Portmeirion china and Caithness giftware but at the normal shop prices. There is a coffee shop on site and a small food gift area. *Permanent Discount Outlet*

LOCH LOMOND
FACTORY OUTLETS

MAIN STREET, ALEXANDRIA, JUNCTION 17 OF M8 THEN A82, LOCH LOMOND, SCOTLAND G83 0UG
☎ (01389) 710077. OPEN 10 - 6 SEVEN DAYS A WEEK.
Just off the A82, the main route between Glasgow and the West Highlands and Islands, and only one mile from Loch Lomond, this factory outlet centre combines history, heritage, adventure and shopping under one roof. Shops include Benetton, Book Depot, Designer Room (Christian Lacroix, Louis Feraud, Mondi and Maska), G2 Fashion, Honey, Hornsea Pottery, Jean Scene, Leading Labels, Luggage & Bags (which as well as selling luggage also carries Mulberry bags), Original Shoes, Pavers Shoes, Ponden Mill, Russell Athletic, Stuart Crystal, The Sports Mill, The Toy Shop, Thorntons, Tog 24, Tom Sayers, Versace, and XS Music. There is also a Motor Heritage Centre telling the history of the Scottish Motor Car industry. *Factory Shopping Village*

LONDON LEATHERS DIRECT

FREEPORT VILLAGE, WEST CALDER, WEST LOTHIAN, SCOTLAND EH55 8QB

☎ (01501) 762405. OPEN 10 - 6 SEVEN DAYS A WEEK.

Very good quality leather and suede jackets, coats and trousers, at discounts of at least 30%, with most at 50% off in this village which features lots of restaurants and fun things for the family to take part in. *Factory Shopping Village*

LUGGAGE & BAGGAGE

UNIT E4 - E5, FIVE SISTERS, WESTWOOD, WEST CALDER, WEST LOTHIAN, SCOTLAND EH55 8QB

☎ (01501) 763443. OPEN 10 - 6 EVERY DAY.

UNIT 2B, LOCH LOMOND FACTORY OUTLET, MAIN STREET, ALEXANDRIA, STRATHCLYDE, SCOTLAND G83 OUG

☎ (01389) 607251. OPEN 10 - 6 EVERY DAY.

Luggage and travel-related products including executive cases, handbags, umbrellas and accessories available in leading brands such as Samsonite, Brics, Hidesign, Globe Trotter and Tula. The products also include couture and high fashion brands such as YSl and Moschino. All products are offered at a considerably reduced price due to their being production over-runs, last season's stock of slight seconds (ie they have minor aesthetic blemishes). *Factory Shopping Village*

MACGILLIVRAY & CO

BALIVANICH, BENBECULA, WESTERN ISLES, SCOTLAND HS7 5LA

☎ (01870) 602525. OPEN 9.30 - 5 MON - FRI, CLOSED 1 - 2, 9.30 - 4 SAT. MAIL ORDER.

The MacGillivray Company has been selling handwoven Harris tweed and hand-knitted sweaters all over the world since 1941. Usually hand-knitted sweaters in pure new wool cost from £49.50 and 72cm (28) wide Harris tweed costs £11.55 a metre (£10.50 a yard). They sometimes hold a stock of special offer fabrics, which they obtain from various mills throughout Britain. Because these are surplus stock, cancelled export orders or out of season fabrics, they can be sold at less than half the original selling price. These can range from Scottish tweeds, Shetlands, Donegals, dress and fancy fabrics, suitings and coatings. Send for a brochure. *Factory Shop*

MARSHALLS CHUNKY CHICKEN SHOP

NEWBRIDGE, MIDLOTHIAN, SCOTLAND EH28 8SW

☎ (0131) 333 3341. OPEN 8.30-5 MON - THUR, 8.30-4.30 FRI. 8.30-12 SAT.

Sells whole fresh chickens, minimum four and a half pounds in weight, bags of about two dozen cooked drumsticks; bags of ten cooked thighs and chicken breast fillets. The company supply Marks & Spencer, Tesco and Asda. *Food and Drink Discounter*

MATALAN

SEAFIELD WAY, SEAFIELD ROAD, EDINBURGH, SCOTLAND EH15 1TB
☎ (0131) 657 5045. OPEN 10 - 8 MON - FRI, 9.30 - 5.30 SAT, 10 - 6 SUN.
UNIT 5, CALEDONIAN CENTRE, NEW ASHTREE STREET, WISHAW
ML2 7UR
☎ (01698) 357075. OPEN 10 - 8 MON - FRI, 9.30 - 5.30 SAT, 10 - 6 SUN.
UNIT 7, GLENCAIRN RETAIL PARK, KILMARNOCK KA1 4AY
☎ (01563) 573892. OPEN 10 - 8 MON - FRI, 9.30 - 5.30 SAT, 10 - 6 SUN.
155 SLATEFORD ROAD, EDINBURGH EH14 1NZ
☎ (0131) 455 7224. OPEN 10 - 8 MON - FRI, 9.30 - 5.30 SAT, 10 - 6 SUN.
CONSTITUTION STREET, ABERDEEN AB24 5 ET
☎ (01224) 650690.
UNIT 13A BLYTHSWOOD RETAIL PARK, WESTLODGE ROAD, RENFREW
PA4 9EN
☎ (0141) 886 8050.
CARRON ROAD, FALKIRK FK1
☎ NO TELEPHONE NUMBER AS WE WENT TO PRESS.
CLYDE RETAIL PARK, LIVINGSTONE STREET, CLYDEBANK, GLASGOW
G81 2XA
☎ (0141) 435 7450.
NITSHILL ROAD, DARNLEY, GLASGOW G53 7BW
☎ (0141) 880 3900. PHONE FOR OPENING TIMES.

Matalan is a fashion and homewares shop giving customers what they claim to be unbeatable value for money with huge savings on a wide range of products including high quality fashionable clothing for women, women and children at up to 50% off high street prices. Matalan is situated out of town and stores are open seven days a week all year round. *Permanent Discount Outlet*

MCARTHURGLEN
DESIGNER OUTLET LIVINGSTON

ALMONDVALE BOULEVARD, LIVINGSTON, WEST LOTHIAN,
SCOTLAND

Scheduled to open in August 2000, there will be 100 factory shops all selling last season's or excess stock at 30%-50% below usual prices, a food court, cafes and restaurants. There will also be an 8-screen licensed cinema plus other leisure outlets, a children's play area and parking for 2,500 cars. *Factory Shopping Village*

McCALLS OF THE ROYAL MILE

11 THE HIGH STREET, EDINBURGH, SCOTLAND EH1 1SR

☎ (0131) 557 3979. OPEN 9 - 5.30 MON - SAT, UNTIL 7.30 ON THUR, 12 - 4 SUN.

Hire and sell men's formal wear, whether a dinner suit or the full regalia. Kilt, shoes, bow tie, socks, sporran costs £29.50 plus £5 for the shirt; men's formal dinner suit, £20. Also hires morning suits, jackets, waistcoats, trousers, shirts and cravat or tie, £40; boys outfits, £28.50, but not girls or ladies. However, does sell women's outfits at full retail price. *Hire Shop*

MERIDIAN RETAIL FACTORY SHOP

GRANBY GARMENTS, EXCELSIOR PARK, WISHAW, LANARKSHIRE, SCOTLAND ML2 OER

☎ (01698) 375745. OPEN 9 - 5 MON - SAT, 10 - 4 SUN.

Part of the Courtaulds Textiles Group, this shop sells clothes for men, women, girls and boys at discounts of 30%-50%. A majority of stock is perfect with a limited amount of seconds and there's a large selection of casual and formal wear for the whole family. *Factory Shop*

MEXX INTERNATIONAL

FREEPORT VILLAGE, SCOTLAND, FIVE SISTERS, WESTWOOD, WEST CALDER, NEAR JUNCTION 4 OF THE M8, WEST LOTHIAN, SCOTLAND EH55 8QB

☎ (01501) 763488. OPEN 10 - 6 SEVEN DAYS A WEEK, UNTIL 8 THUR.

High street fashion at factory outlet prices for men, women, babies, children and teenagers, all of which are heavily discounted by more than 30%. The telephone number given here is for the centre. *Factory Shop*

NEXT TO NOTHING

UNIT D9-12, FREEPORT VILLAGE SCOTLAND FIVE SISTERS, WEST LOTHIAN, SCOTLAND

☎ (01501) 763263. OPEN 10 - 6 SEVEN DAYS A WEEK, 8 ON THUR.

Sells perfect surplus stock from Next stores and the Next Directory catalogue - from belts, jewellery and underwear to day and evening wear - at discounts of 50% or more. The ranges are usually last season's and overruns. Stock consists of women's, men's and children's clothing, with some homeware and shoes. Stock is replenished three times a week and there is plenty of it. *Factory Shopping Village*

NORTH CAPE (SCOTLAND) LTD

ROYAL SCOT LTD, BANDEATH ESTATE, THROSK, NEAR STIRLING,
SCOTLAND FK7 7NP

☎ (01786) 815349. OPEN 12 - 4 MON - SAT.

North Cape manufacture a leading range of outdoor clothing, including
Rhovyl thermal underwear, silk underwear, Coolmax underwear, Polartec
fleece ranges and Cyclone waterproofs as well as making North Cape own-
label outdoor wear. The factory shop sells seconds, surplus stock and discontinued lines at discounts of 50% and more. *Factory Shop*

NORTH FACE OUTLET STORE

53 THE PLAZA, TOWN CENTRE, EAST KILBRIDE, SCOTLAND G74 1LW,

☎ (01355) 238 383. OPEN 9.30 - 5.30 MON - SAT.

Sells first quality discounted North Face clothing and equipment up to 40% off.
Permanent Discount Outlet

ORCHID

110 ST CLAIR'S STREET, KIRKCALDY, FIFE, SCOTLAND KY1 2BZ

☎ (01592) 655364. OPEN 10 - 5 MON - SAT.

Samples and cancelled orders of a wide range of German, Italian, French, Irish
and British designers at reduced prices. Names cannot be mentioned here as
confidentiality is demanded by the suppliers to this shop. Day and evening
wear is stocked in sizes 10-22. Also samples and cancelled orders of top quality Spanish shoes and boots at reduced prices. *Permanent Discount Outlet*

OUTLINES

TRINITY GASK, AUCHTERARDER, PERTHSHIRE, SCOTLAND PH3 1LG

☎ (01764) 683733. FAX ☎ (01764) 683462. OPEN 9.30 - 5 MON - FRI, 9 - 1
SAT.

Two businesses, one selling current ranges of furnishing fabrics and
wallpapers to order, while the one next door stocks discontinued fabrics and
wallpapers from £1.99 a metre or £5 a roll. Fabric names include Designers
Guild, Osborne & Little, Baker's, Zoffany, Marvic, Titley & Marr, Warner's,
etc. There are also linings, cushions, heading tapes, remnants and
accessories. Prices are about one half to one third of the normal price. Many
of the fabrics are flameproofed and are suitable for hotels as well as for
private houses. The shop will deliver in the UK by carrier and can arrange
for making up. There is a vast amount of stock in the shop, which is well
worth a visit. Telephone for directions. Parking facilities are available. E-mail
northwood@mcmail.com. *Permanent Discount Outlet*

PACO LIFE IN COLOUR

UNIT 27, STERLING MILLS, MOSS ROAD, TILLICOULTRY,
CLACKMANNANSHIRE, SCOTLAND FK13 6HN

☎ (01259) 753933. OPEN 10 - 6 MON - SAT, 11 - 5 SUN.

Comprehensive range of casualwear clothing and accessories for women in a
wide variety of colours. End-of-season lines are on sale at discounts of around
30%. Included in the range are t-shirts, sweatshirts, wool sweaters and cardigans, jeans, leggings, shorts, bags and socks, all offering outstanding value for
money. *Permanent Discount Outlet*

PANDORA'S

5 SINCLAIR DRIVE, LANGSIDE, GLASGOW, SCOTLAND G42 9PR

☎ (0141) 649 7714. OPEN 10 - 6 MON - SAT, 7 ON THUR.

According to one reader, this is the best nearly-new mother of the bride shop
in Scotland. There are more than 1,000 designer hats in stock at any one time
by Genevieve Louis, Philip Somerville and Hazel Kettles, which can be hired
for £25. Outfits feature labels such as Frank Usher, Escada and MaxMara.
Famous items include a dress worn by Rita Hayworth and a hat worn by
Andie McDowell in Four Weddings and a Funeral, as well as dresses from the
television series House of Eliot. *Dress Agency*

PATON & BALDWINS LTD

MILL STREET, ALLOA, SCOTLAND SK10 1EG

☎ (01259) 211678. OPEN 10 - 4.30 MON - FRI, 10 - 4 SAT, 12 - 4 SUN.

Sells a range of Patons wool and discontinued yarns: mohair wool at £8 per
bag, double knitting wool from £5 per bag. It also sells chainstore seconds for
all the family at less than the normal retail price. This is a working mill with
an on-site factory shop. *Factory Shop*

PETER SCOTT FACTORY SHOP

11 BUCCLEUCH STREET, HAWICK, SCOTLAND TD9 OHJ

☎ (01450) 372311. OPEN 10 - 5 MON - FRI, 10 - 4 SAT.

Peter Scott is one of the oldest woollen factories in the country. It stocks
sweaters for women and men in almost every conceivable material from cotton and merino wool to cashmere and silk. Some of the stock is current season, some discontinued, but there are no seconds. Visit on a weekday and if
they haven't got what you want in stock, they can phone up to the factory for
it. Opening times are shorter in the winter time so ring first. *Factory Shop*

Live Well On Less Tips
CHINA TABLEWARE BROWNINGS FARM, BLACKBOYS, UCKFIELD, EAST SUSSEX. (01825) 890 664. OPEN 10 - 1 SAT.
Buys and sells discontinued tableware from Denby, Poole and Marks & Spencer, among others, as well as garden furniture. Phone for an appointment.

PONDEN MILL LINENS

FREEPORT SHOPPING VILLAGE, FIVE SISTERS, WESTWOOD, WEST CALDER, WEST LOTHIAN, SCOTLAND EH55 8QB
☎ (01501) 763053. OPEN 10 - 6 SEVEN DAYS A WEEK, UNTIL 8 ON THUR APRIL - DEC.
LOCH LOMOND FACTORY OUTLET, ARGYLE WORKS, MAIN STREET, ALEXANDRIA, LOCH LOMOND G83 OUG
☎ (01389) 607200. OPEN 10 - 6 SEVEN DAYS A WEEK.
Famous branded products at direct from the mill prices. Towels, co-ordinated bedlinen, duvets, pillows and curtains from Crown, Coloroll, Chortex, Rectella together with bathroom and kitchen accessories. *Factory Shopping Village*

PRICE'S CANDLES

GRETNA GATEWAY OUTLET VILLAGE, JUNCTION 22 OF A74, SCOTLAND
☎ (01461) 339028 (CENTRE INFORMATION LINE).
Everything sold in this shop are seconds, which may be discoloured or have a damaged pattern; discontinued sizes not available elsewhere; over-runs from the garden selection or dinner candles in old packaging that has now been replaced. There are church candles, lanterns, candles in pots and glass jars, star-shaped candles, floating candles, candlestick holders, serviettes, scented candles and garden torches. Some of the ceramic items are bought in. Both villages also have restaurants, a children's play area and parking. *Factory Shopping Village*

PRINCIPLES

FREEPORT VILLAGE FIVE SISTERS, WESTWOOD, WEST CALDER, JUNCTION 4 OF M8, WEST LOTHIAN, SCOTLAND EH55 8QB
☎ (01501) 763358. OPEN 10 - 6 SEVEN DAYS A WEEK, 8 ON THUR.
End of season lines with the normal Principles refund guarantee. The range includes, for women, dresses, blouses, coats, outerwear, knitwear, casualwear and a selection of Petite clothing for women who are 5ft 3ins and under. For men, there is formalwear, smart casualwear, knitwear, outerwear, PFM Sport, jeanswear and casualwear. *Factory Shop*

PUTTING ON THE RITZ

THE VICTORIAN VILLAGE, 93 WEST REGENT STREET, GLASGOW,
SCOTLAND G2 2BA

☎ (0141) 332 9808. OPEN 10 - 5 MON - SAT.

Retro jewellery, marcasite and Fifties silver, nightwear, Paisley shawls, vintage
dinner suits and tuxedos, Thirties and Forties sportswear, riding boots, stet-
sons, 1930s USA football outfits. Jewellery from £5, dinner suits from £15.
Unusual gifts, exciting decorative items, interior furnishings, small pieces of
furniture, also stocked. ***Secondhand and Vintage Clothes***

Q MARK WAREHOUSE

CROW ROAD, GLASGOW, SCOTLAND G11 7DN

☎ (0141) 954 0000. OPEN 9.30 - 6 MON - SAT, UNTIL 7 ON THUR,
12 - 5 SUN.

56 BELFORD ROAD, EDINBURGH EH4 3BR

☎ (0131) 225 6861. OPEN 9 - 5.30 MON - SAT, 12 - 5 SUN.

BRAIDHOLM ROAD, GIFFNOCK, GLASGOW, SCOTLAND G46 6EB

☎ (0141) 633 3636. OPEN 9 - 6 MON - SAT, UNTIL 8 ON THUR, 12 - 5
SUN.

KERSE ROAD INDUSTRIAL ESTATE, KERSE ROAD, STIRLING

☎ (01786) 474747. OPEN 9 - 6 MON- SAT, 8 ON THUR, 12 - 5 SUN.

Scotland's biggest discount clothing warehouse for women, men and children
offers top quality fashions at up to 50% off normal high street prices as well
as designerwear and homewares. All garments are good quality seconds, overmakes or cancelled contracts but with their labels cut. Regular stock deliveries
ensure a constant selection of new styles - often recognised in famous chain
stores, but always at ridiculously low prices. For example, Armani, Valentino,
Timberland, Helly Hansen, Principles, Next, Wallis and Marks & Spencer. Q
Mark operate a once-a-year membership fee of £5. All prices are subject to
VAT, charged at point of sale. The Crow Road, Glasgow, store is the latest and
largest at up to 20,000 sq ft. ***Permanent Discount Outlet***

RE-DRESS

43 NEW ROW, OFF GLASGOW ROAD, PERTH, SCOTLAND PH1 5QA

☎ (01738) 444447. OPEN 10 - 4.30 MON - SAT.

Situated in a discreet area in the town of Perth, Re-dress stocks a range of middle to top name nearly-new designer labels and some new clothes. There are
wedding outfits and matching accessories at about one third of the original
price, as well as evening wear, and a large selection of daywear, shoes and hats.
You can choose from labels such as Laurel, Mondi, Louis Feraud, Escada,
MaxMara, Paul Costelloe, Caroline Charles, Basler, Geiger, Oui Set, Betty
Barclay and Austin Reed. Clearance sales are usually held twice a year. Stock
changes constantly. ***Dress Agency***

RE-DRESS

51 EASTWOODMAINS ROAD, GIFFNOCK, GLASGOW, SCOTLAND

☎ (0141) 638 5090. OPEN 9.30 - 5.30 MON -SAT.

Designer labels on sale here include Escada, Armani, Mondi and Betty Barclay. Day and eveningwear is sold, as well as handbags, shoes, hats, and costume jewellery. *Dress Agency*

REDRESS

1 PRIESTON ROAD, BRIDGE OF WEIR, SCOTLAND PA11 3AJ

☎ (01505) 615151. OPEN 9.30 - 5.30 MON - SAT.

Sells both new and nearly-new fashion items at bargain prices in the 400 square feet shop. The designers range from high street to top designers, and often feature Parigi, Armani, Versace, Betty Barclay, Puccini, and Jacques Vert. Sells everything from blouses, shirts, suits and dresses to beads, shoes, hats, bags, belts and jewellery. Prices range from £10 upwards and sizes from 8-18. *Dress Agency*

REDRESS

7 HIGH STREET, NORTH BERWICK, EAST LOTHIAN, SCOTLAND EH39 4HH

☎ (01620) 895633. OPEN 10 - 4.30 MON - SAT, CLOSED THUR DURING WINTER.

Shop with a friendly atmosphere stocking Jaeger, Country Casuals, Frank Usher, Jacques Vert, Laura Ashley, Next, After Six, Bally, Russell & Bromley in sizes 8-30. When available, there is also Hardob, Planet, Wallis, Eastex, Windsmoor, Yarrell, Peter Barron, Parigi, Viyella, Bally, Van Dal, FinnKarelia and many more. There are good prices for quality names and reductions are always available. The shop also sells handbags, shoes, jumpers, evening gowns and a selection of special occasion hats. *Dress Agency*

REJECTS

123 ST CLAIR STREET, KIRKCALDY, FIFE, SCOTLAND KY1 2BS

☎ (01592) 655955. OPEN 9 - 5.30 MON - SAT, 12.30 - 4.30 SUN.

Rejects Department Store sells curtain and dress fabric, china, pottery, carpets, silk flower, glassware, home decoration equipment and materials, lighting, basketware, carpet and flooring and has a cookshop. The shop is 100,000 sq feet and claims to be the best value department store in the UK, although it isn't a discount store as such. For example, in the curtain shop, which is larger than Harrods curtain department with thousands of rolls of material, fabric costs from £10.99 to £29.95 a metre. There is a particularly large selection of pottery and china seconds, bedding, cushions, pictures, mirrors, wallpaper, paint, hardware and garden tools. The shop also has a self-service cafe. *Permanent Discount Outlet*

ROYAL LOCHNAGAR DISTILLERY

CRATHIE, BALLATER, ABERDEENSHIRE, SCOTLAND AB35 5TB

☎ (013397) 42273. OPEN 10 - 5 MON - SAT, 12 - 4 SUN IN SUMMER. MAIL ORDER.

Spend £3 on a distillery tour and you get a £4 voucher to spend against any 70cl bottle of malt whisky at the shop attached to the distillery. While prices for these classic malts - sixty of Scotland's finest - aren't rock bottom, they are likely to be cheaper than you'll find elsewhere. *Factory Shop*

RUMMAGE

5 STEWART STREET, MILNGAVIE, SCOTLAND J62 6BW

☎ (0141) 956 2333. OPEN 10 - 5 MON - SAT.

New and nearly-new designer clothes from Lagerfeld and Dior to Givenchy as well as items from high street chain stores. There are usually at least 200 special occasion outfits available as well as handbags, shoes and costume jewellery. There's also evening wear, ballgowns, bric a brac, china, ornaments, glassware and hat boxes. *Dress Agency*

SARATOGA TRUNK

TOP FLOOR, 93 WEST REGENT STREET, GLASGOW, SCOTLAND G2 2BA

☎ (0141) 331 2707. OPEN 10.30 - 5 MON - FRI, 10.30 - 5 SAT.

Old-fashioned and antique clothing, Paisley shawls, embroidered shawls, wedding dresses from the Forties and Fifties, and Christening robes. Victorian to 1950s daywear, evening wear and underwear. Accessories including costume jewellery. Patchwork, lace curtains, bedlinen, table covers and collectibles including dolls and teddy bears. *Secondhand and Vintage Clothes*

SCENT TO YOU

UNIT 12A, BON ACCORD CENTRE, GEORGE STREET, ABERDEEN, SCOTLAND AB25 1HZ

☎ (01224) 625340. OPEN 9 - 5.30 MON - SAT, 8 ON THUR, 12 - 4 SUN.

Discounted perfume and accessories including body lotions and gels. The company, buys in bulk and sells more cheaply, relying on a high turnover for profit. Discounts range from 5% to 60%, with greater savings during their twice-yearly sales (phone for details). Most of the leading brand names are stocked including Christian Lacroix, Armani, Givenchy, Anais Anais from Cacherel, Charlie from Revlon, Coco Chanel, Christian Dior, Elizabeth Taylor, Blue Grass from Elizabeth Arden, Aramis, Lagerfeld. Occasionally, they also buy in a limited range of skincare lines. Stock varies greatly due to the fast turnover and varying supplies so more than one visit may be necessary to obtain the scent of your choice. Or phone first to avoid disappointment. *Permanent Discount Outlet*

SCOTTISH FINE SOAPS FACTORY SHOP

UNIT 2, OCHILTERRACE, CARRON, FALKIRK, SCOTLAND FK2 8DZ

☎ (01324) 551377. OPEN 1 - 4 MON -THUR, 1 - 3.30 FRI.

Makes soap, pot pourri, bubble bath and a novelty range of soaps in the shape of cats, pigs, elephants and dogs. Prices are half that of the high street for discontinued lines in soaps which are made for many of the major department stores from 5p to 50p for a bar of soap. *Factory Shop*

SELLERS

2 CROWN LANE, OFF CROWN TERRACE, ABERDEEN, SCOTLAND AB1 2HF

☎ (01224) 582528. OPEN 10.30 - 5 TUE - SAT, UNTIL 6 ON THUR.

Run by a mother and daughter team, this dress agency has been operating for more than 12 years. It sells a wide selection of day and evening wear from Louis Feraud and Paul Costelloe to Mondi and Jaeger at between one third and one half of the original price as well as hats, jewellery, accessories and some shoes. Wide selection of special occasion wear. Stock is a mixture of new and nearly-new as some designer merchandise is bought in from boutiques' ends of ranges. *Dress Agency*

SHAW'S DUNDEE SWEET FACTORY

THE KEILLERS BUILDING, MAINS LOAN, DUNDEE, SCOTLAND DD4 7BT

☎ (01382) 461435. OPENING TIMES VARY. PHONE FIRST.

Specialises in fudge, toffees and boiled sweets, and Scottish Tablet. Live demos take place with tasting while sweets are still hot. Special offers always available. Free car and coach park, disabled facilities. Entrance £1 or 50p for children and concessions; free for under threes. *Food and Drink Discounter*

SHELAGH BUCHANAN

65 BATH STREET, GLASGOW, SCOTLAND G2 2BX

☎ (0141) 331 1862. OPEN 9 - 5 MON - FRI, 9 - 12 SAT.

Sells anything from shoes to ballgowns, including cocktail dresses, evening wear, suits and outfits, bags and accessories. Designer labels in this outlet can be found on the second floor and include Armani, Versace, Country Casuals, Jaeger, Mondi, Escada, Jean Muir, Jobis and Basler. There is a tailoring alterations service on the premises. Situated near to the bus and train station as well as Buchanan Galleries Shopping Mall. *Dress Agency*

SLATERS MENSWEAR
165 HOWARD STREET, GLASGOW, SCOTLAND G1 4HF
☎ (0141) 552 7171. OPEN 8.30 - 5.30 MON - SAT, 7.30 ON THUR.
184 HIGH STREET, AYR, AYRSHIRE KA7 1RQ
☎ (01292) 261730. OPEN 8.30 - 5.30 MON - SAT, 7.30 ON THUR.
10 BON ACCORD STREET, ABERDEEN AB11 6EL
☎ (01224) 212334. OPEN 8.30 - 5.30 MON - SAT, 7.30 ON THUR.
Full range of men's clothes from underwear and shoes to casualwear, suits and
dresswear and including labels such as Odermark, Bulmer, Valentino, Charlie's
Co, and Charlton Gray. Men's suits from £79. *Permanent Discount Outlet*

SNOW SENSE
2 HOWE STREET, EDINBURGH, SCOTLAND EH3 6TD
☎ (0131) 662 4487. OPEN 5.30 - 7.30 TUE - THUR (MID OCT - END
MAR), 10.30 - 5.30 SAT, SUN DURING HIGH SEASON ONLY.
Open only during the ski season, there is everything here that the enthusiastic
skier could want from nearly-new salopettes and ski jackets to gloves, goggles and
other accessories as well as the hardware: boots, skis and poles. They also stock
high quality snowboards and some nearly-new equipment. *Dress Agency*

SPOILS
UNIT 6/7 RIGHEAD GATE, TOWN CENTRE, EAST KILBRIDE, GLASGOW,
SCOTLAND G74 1LS
☎ (01355) 579224. OPEN 9 - 5.30 MON - SAT, 12 - 5 SUN.
UNIT MSU2, ST ENOCH CENTRE, GLASGOW
TELEPHONE NUMBER NOT KNOWN AS WE WENT TO PRESS.
General domestic glassware, non-stick bakeware, kitchen gadgets, ceramic
oven-to-tableware, textiles, cutting boards, aluminium non-stick cookware,
bakeware, plastic kitchenware, plastic storage, woodware, coffee pots/makers,
furniture, mirrors and picture frames. Rather than being discounted, all the
merchandise is very competitively priced - in fact, the company carry out
competitors' checks frequently in order to monitor pricing. With 38 branches, the company is able to buy in bulk and thus negotiate very good prices.
Permanent Discount Outlet

STARRY STARRY NIGHT
19 DOWNSIDE LANE, GLASGOW, SCOTLAND G12 9BZ
☎ (0141) 337 1837. OPEN 10 - 5.30 MON - SAT.
Retro gear, especially evening gowns, menswear, including morning coats, tails
and striped blazers from Victorian through the Twenties and Thirties to Sixties
and Seventies gear. Morning suits, £35, dinner suits, £30, leather jackets, £15-
£20, evening gowns, £10 upwards, waistcoats, collarless shirts and bow ties.
Also Levi 501s and all types of Levis, £10. *Secondhand and Vintage
Clothes*

STIRLING MILLS
DESIGNER OUTLET VILLAGE

TILLICOULTRY, NEAR STIRLING, MIDWAY BETWEEN M9 AND M90, SCOTLAND FK13 6HQ

☎ (01259) 752100. OPEN 10 - 6 SEVEN DAYS A WEEK, 8 ON THUR.

This new factory shopping centre in Scotland guarantees prices of at least 30% off typical high street prices and sometimes as much as 70%. Outlets so far include Because It's There, clothes for outdoor pursuits; Bed & Bath Works; Book Depot; Claire's Accessories; D2, men and women's fashion; Denby Pottery; Designer Room; Double Two shirts; Jacques Heim, featuring Whitbread, Jules Verne and men's formal wear; Julian Graves, herbs, spices and nuts; Nike; Nickelbys menswear; Paco for adults and children; Pavers Shoes; Roman Originals; Thorntons; Tog 24 outdoor wear; The Toy Shop; Travel Accessory Outlet; VF Corporation Factory Store; Winning Line ladieswear and XS Music and more are planned. There's also a restaurant and coffee shop. *Factory Shopping Village*

STUART CRYSTAL

MUTHILL ROAD, CRIEFF, PERTHSHIRE, SCOTLAND PH7 4HQ

☎ (01764) 654004. OPEN 10 - 6 SEVEN DAYS A WEEK JUNE-SEPT, 10 - 5 OTHERWISE.

Seconds of Stuart Crystal at about 30% discount. The selection includes wine glasses, flower holders, perfume holders, everyday tableware, salt and pepper sets, ice buckets, wine coolers, and candle lamps. Also seasonal special offers. First quality is also for sale at the appropriate price. *Factory Shop*

THE ADDRESS DESIGNER EXCHANGE

3 ROYAL EXCHANGE COURT, OFF 17 ROYAL EXCHANGE SQUARE, GLASGOW, SCOTLAND G1 3DB

☎ (0141) 221 6898. OPEN 10 - 5.30 TUE - SAT.

A warm, inviting shop tucked away, yet in the heart of the city centre, which is about to celebrate ten years in business. Sharp-eyed lovers of style travel from afar to this exciting shop which is full of new and nearly-new designer clothes and accessories ranging from Chanel, Armani, Versace and Moschino to high-fashion high street names such as Whistles, Jigsaw, Kookai and Morgan. Stock turns around quickly with new items arriving daily, all of which are personally selected by the owners. Items come from all over the UK, many from well-known celebrities. Customers can browse in a relaxed, fun and low-pressure environment, where an honest opinion is always given. *Dress Agency*

THE COTTON PRINT FACTORY SHOP

58 ADMIRAL STREET, GLASGOW, SCOTLAND G41 1HU

☎ (0141) 420 1855. OPEN 9 - 5.30 MON - SAT, 10 - 5 SUN.

Offers the largest selection of top quality curtain fabric at discount prices in Scotland as well as wallpaper and borders. There are up to 6,000 rolls of curtaining fabric from names such as Ashley Wilde and Leon, heading tapes, tiebacks, curtain pulls, cushion pads, track fabrics. They claim no one in Scotland can beat their prices. *Factory Shop*

THE CURTAIN EXCHANGE

1ST FLOOR, 30 JAMAICA STREET, GLASGOW, SCOTLAND G1 4QD

☎ (0141) 2211070. OPEN 10 - 5 TUE - SAT.

The Curtain Exchange is a franchised group of shops selling beautiful top quality secondhand curtains, blinds, pelmets, etc at between one-third and one half of the brand new price. Their stock comes from a variety of sources: people who are moving house and dislike the drapes in their new home; people who are moving house and want to sell their old curtains to help with the bills; show houses, where the builder wants to recoup some of his outgoings; interior designers' mistakes. Stock changes constantly and ranges from rich brocades, damasks and velvets to chintzes, linens and cottons. Designer names include Colefax & Fowler, Designers Guild, Laura Ashley, Warner, Sanderson, Osborne & Little, Fortuny and Bennison. A team of fitters and alteration experts are available if required. They offer a 24-hour availability. The Curtain Exchange also supply bespoke ranges with samples of curtains hanging. These fabrics are chosen from suppliers all over the world and are an excellent buy. *Secondhand Shop*

THE FACTORY SHOP

COATS PATONS CRAFTS, KILNCRAIGS MILL, ALLOA, CLACKMANNANSHIRE, SCOTLAND FK10 1EG

☎ (01259) 211678. OPEN 9.30 - 4.30 MON - FRI, 10 - 4 SAT, 12 - 4 SUN.

Part of the Coats Viyella group, which makes quality clothing for many of the major high street storres, overstocks and clearance lines are sold through more than 30 of the group's factory shops. Many of you will recognise the garments on sale, despite the lack of well-known labels. Ladieswear includes dresses, blouses, jumpers, cardigans, trousers, nightwear, underwear, lingerie, hosiery, coats and swimwear. Menswear includes trousers, belts, shirts, ties, pullovers, cardigans, T-shirts, underwear, nightwear, hosiery and jackets. Childrenswear includes jackets, trousers, T-shirts, underwear, hosiery, jumpers and babywear. There are regular deliveries to constantly update the range. *Factory Shop*

THE FACTORY SHOP LTD

DRAKEMYRE, DALRY, AYRSHIRE, SCOTLAND KA24 5JD
☎ (01294) 832791. OPEN 10 - 5 MON - SAT, 11 - 5 SUN.
54 - 60 HIGH STREET, ANNAN, DUMFRIES DG12 6AJ
☎ (01461) 207687. OPEN 9 - 5.30 MON - SAT, 10.30 - 4.30 SUN.
STANDALANE STREET, GALSTON, KILMARNOCK KA4 8AY
☎ (01563) 820320. OPEN 9 - 5.30 MON - SAT, 11 - 5 SUN.
Wide range on sale includes men's, ladies and children's clothing and footwear; household textiles; toiletries; hardware; luggage; lighting and bedding, most of which are chainstore and high street brands at discounts of approximately 30%-50%. There are weekly deliveries and brands include many major stars such as Adidas, Nike, Wrangler and Dartington, to name just a few. Lines are continually changing and few factory shops offer such a variety under one roof. The Factory Shop also has kitchen and furniture displays and sells Cape Country Furniture, highest quality pine furniture made exclusively for The Factory Shop Ltd in South Africa. Prices are direct from the factory and there is home delivery service throughout the UK. A colour brochure and price list is available. Tea room with home prepared food and free car park. *Factory Shop*

THE GREAT ESCAPE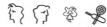

MEADOWBANK RETAIL PARK, EDINBURGH, SCOTLAND
☎ (0131) 661 8855. OPEN 10 - 6 MON - WED, 10 - 8 THUR, 10 - 6.30 FRI, 9 - 6 SAT, 11 - 5 SUN.
Competitively priced bikes and biking accessories for adults and children, as well as outdoor clothing and tents. For adults, there are touring and racing bikes from Falcon, Claude Butler and Universal at prices which, they claim, can't be beaten. For children, there are BMX bikes, plus accessories such as drink cages, bells, halogen lights and mudguards. The clothes range includes fleeces, waterproofs and sportswear from Regatta, Berghaus, Helly Hansen and Russell Athletic. Tents range from one-person tents to 8-person ones. *Permanent Discount Outlet*

THE MAD HATTER

6 CANNIESBURN TOLL, BEARSDEN, GLASGOW, SCOTLAND G61 2QU
☎ (0141) 942 1711. OPEN 10 - 5 MON - SAT.
COMMLEYBANK AVENUE, COMMLEYBANK, EDINBURGH
☎ (0131) 315 4111. OPEN 10 - 5 MON - SAT.
Hats hired out from a superb selection of 500. Top-name designer hats for Ascot and garden parties. Hire charges from £15 to £75. The Glasgow shop also sells shoes and handbags. *Hire Shop*

THE MILL TRAIL

CLACKMANNANSHIRE, SCOTLAND

Follow the mill trail and you're guaranteed a great shopping experience. You can pick up Mill Trail leaflets at tourist information centres in Clackmannanshire and the different shops are also signposted. Some of the mill shops are modern tourist centres, others cordonned-off parts of the actual working mill. In one such old-fashioned factory shop (the type I love), I bought an Arran sweater for £5; in its more modern counterpart, I bought a pure wool serape for £49 which I'm sure would have cost me twice as much down south. *Factory Shop*

THE REALLY GOOD DEAL FASHION SALE

THE ASSEMBLY ROOMS, GEORGE STREET, EDINBURGH

☎ (01367) 860071 TICKET ENQUIRIES. OPEN 10 - 6, THURS 28TH & FRI 29TH SEPTEMBER 2000.

One of six countrywide fashion sales run by the team behind The Good Deal Directory. Each one features between 40 and 50 top quality fashion houses and well-known brand names selling their ends of lines, discounted stock and last season's merchandise at discount prices. Exhibitors usually include top catwalk names, middle market companies, some retailers clearing excess stock, a few manufacturers and and some entrepreneurs selling top Continental designer names. There are clothes for all occasions, knitwear, scarves, shawls, pashmina, shoes, jewellery, some gifts, a few childrenswear companies, and some men's gift fashion lines such as ties and shirts. Quality is middle to upper market, aimed at 25-50 year olds. *Designer Sale*

THORNTONS

LOCH LOMOND FACTORY OUTLET CENTRE, MAIN STREET, ALEXANDRIA, STRATHCLYDE, SCOTLAND G83 OUG

☎ (01389) 729994. OPEN 10 - 6 SEVEN DAYS A WEEK.

FREEPORT VILLAGE FIVE SISTERS, WESTWOOD, WEST CALDER EH55

☎ (01501) 762271. OPEN 10 - 6 SEVEN DAYS A WEEK, 8 ON THUR.

The UK's leading specialist confectionery retailer has more than 500 shops and franchises nationwide selling a wide range of boxed and loose, chocolate and sugar confectionery. The factory outlets sell three different categories: misshapes. discounted lines and standard lines. Misshapes are loose chocolates which are the result of new product development, product trials or end of production runs which cannot be packed as Thorntons standard lines. They are packed into assorted bags and offer a saving of 35%-55% over the recommended retail price of standard loose line products. Discounted lines are excess to Thorntons' normal retail requirements and can be as a result of excess seasonal or export stock, discontinued lines or packaging changes. These products, when available, are offered at a discount of 25%-50% over the standard retail price. Standard lines from the full Thorntons range are also on sale at normal prices. *Factory Shopping Village*

TK MAXX

THE SAUCHIEHALL CENTRE, GLASGOW, SCOTLAND G2 3ER
☎ (0141) 331 0411. OPEN 9 - 5.30 MON - FRI, 9 - 7 THUR, 9 - 6 SAT,
12 - 5 SUN.
MEADOW BANK RETAIL PARK, EDINBURGH EH17 5TS
☎ (0131) 661 6611. OPEN 9 - 5.30 MON - FRI, UNTIL 7 ON THUR,
9 - 6 SAT, 12 - 5 SUN.
CALLENDER SQUARE SHOPPING CENTRE, FALKIRK
☎ (01324) 619881. OPEN 9 - 5.30 MON - WED, 9 - 7 THUR, 9 - 6 FRI,
SAT, 12 - 4 SUN.

Based on an American concept, TK Maxx is situated in easily accessible, often centrally located stores and offers famous label goods with up to 60% savings off recommended retail prices. TK Maxx has fashion for the whole family - women's, men's and childrenswear - accessories, shoes, gifts, kitchenware and home goods. Everything in the store is branded with a choice of well-known high street names to designer labels, and while a small percentage might be clearly marked past season, the great majority of items in store are current season, current stock and still with phenomenal savings. There is a huge choice with 50,000 pieces in store and up to 10,000 new items arriving a week. The stores are simple and unfussy with wide aisles, shopping trolleys and baskets, and a spacious, functional feel to them but there are individual changing rooms, ramps for buggies and wheelchairs and plenty of staff on the shop floor. Every branch accepts all major credit and debit cards and has a liberal refund and return policy. ***Permanent Discount Outlet***

TOG 24

UNIT 15, LOCH LOMOND FACTORY OUTLETS, MAIN STREET,
ALEXANDRIA, STRATHCLYDE, SCOTLAND G83 OUG
☎ (01389) 607175. OPEN 10 - 6 SEVEN DAYS A WEEK.
UNIT 23, STERLING MILLS DESIGNER OUTLET, MOSS ROAD,
TILLICOULTRY, CLACKMANNANSHIRE, SCOTLAND FK13 6HN
☎ (01259) 753911. OPEN 10 - 6 MON - SAT, 11 - 5 SUN .
UNIT 5, LEVEL 3, BUCHANAN GALLERIES SHOPPING CENTRE, 6
SAUCHIEHALL STREET, GLASCOW, STRATHCLYDE, SCOTLAND G2 3GF
☎ (01413) 339377. OPEN 9 - 6 MON - SAT, 11 - 5 SUN.
UNIT II1/2, FIVE SISTERS FREEPORT, WEST CALDER, LOTHIANS,
SCOTLAND EH55 8QB
☎ (01501) 762823. OPEN 10 - 6 EVERY DAY EXCEPT 10 - 8 THURS.

Tog 24 are the UK's fastest growing brand name in outdoor clothing and leisurewear, with a total of three UK factories and 36 stores nationwide. They utilise the world's finest performance fabrics including Gore-Tex, Polartec and Burlington macs. Catering for all the family for all seasons, with cosy fleeces and waterproofs for the winter, and trekking ranges, shorts and t-shirts for the summer. With all prices at least 30% below the recommended retail price you can afford to enter the Tog comfort zone. ***Factory Shopping Village***

TOM SAYERS CLOTHING CO

LOCH LOMOND FACTORY OUTLTS, MAIN STREET, ALEXANDRIA,
SCOTLAND G83 OUG

☎ (01389) 607617. OPEN 10 - 6 SEVEN DAYS A WEEK.

Tom Sayers make sweaters for some of the top high street department stores. Unusually for a factory shop, if they don't stock your size, they will try and order it for you from their factory or one of their other factory outlets and send it to you. Most of the stock here is overstock, cancelled orders or last season's and includes jumpers, trousers and shirts at discounts of 30%. The trousers and shirts are bought in to complement the sweaters which they make. *Factory Shop*

TOM SCOTT KNITWEAR

DENHOLM, HAWICK, SCOTLAND TD9 8NJ

☎ (01450) 870531. OPEN 10 - 12 AND 2 - 4.30 MON, TUE, WED, FRI,
2 - 4.30 THUR, SAT.

Overmakes, samples and prototypes from this mill shop which operates just a few hundred yards from the factory where the garments are made, about five miles from Hawick. Most of the stock has been made for some of the top designers and couture houses in the world. The shop is crammed with stock so you have to be good at rummaging. *Factory Shop*

TRAVEL ACCESSORY OUTLET

UNIT 13, STIRLING MILLS DESIGNER OUTLET VILLAGE, MOSS ROAD,
TILLICOULTRY, CLACKMANNANSHIRE , SCOTLAND FK1 36HN

☎ (01259) 753884. OPEN 10 - 6 EVERY DAY, 10 - 8 THUR.

Luggage and travel-related products including executive cases, handbags, umbrellas and accessories available in leading brands such as Samsonite, Brics, Hidesign, Globe Trotter and Tula. The products also include couture and high fashion brands such as YSl and Moschino. All products are offered at a considerably reduced price due to their being production over-runs, last season's stock of slight seconds (ie they have minor aesthetic blemishes). *Factory Shopping Village*

VALLEY TEXTILES

1 CAMPBELL STREET, DARVEL, NEAR KILMARNOCK, SCOTLAND
KA17 OBZ

☎ (01560) 320140. OPEN 8.30 - 5 MON - THUR, 8.30 - 1 FRI.

All types of curtaining materials from lace and cotton to voiles, satins and Terylene, as well as a making-up service on site. Fabric costs from £2 - £25 a metre, at least half the normal retail price. They also sell table linens, bedcovers and bed canopies from £25 - £50, as well as swags and tails. *Factory Shop*

WALKER'S SHORTBREAD FACTORY SHOP

ABERLOUR-ON-SPEY, OFF A95, MORAY, SCOTLAND AB38 9PD

☎ (01340) 871555. OPEN 8.30 - 5 MON - THUR, 8.30 - 4.30 FRI, 9 - 2 SAT.

Misshapes and ends of lines of these famous shortbread biscuits and Scotch oatcakes, plus a wide variety of other tasty cakes and biscuits. Many of the products are in presentation boxes and packs and make excellent gifts. The factory shop is on the banks of the River Spey and on the well publicised Malt Whisky trail. Joseph Walker's original bakery shop is further along the high street in Aberlour and this, along with other bakery shops in Elgin and Grantown on Spey also carry a reduced range of factory shop products. *Factory Shop*

WELLOWEAR LTD

BLOCK 2, UNITS 4 & 5, LOMOND INDUSTRIAL ESTATE, ALEXANDRIA, SCOTLAND G83 OTP

☎ (01389) 757450. OPEN 9 - 4.30 MON - FRI, 12.30 - 4.30 SAT (PHONE FIRST).

Babywear for under two-year-olds. Baby pants, dresses and underskirts for girls; sleep suits for boys. *Factory Shop*

WHITE OF HAWICK

VICTORIA ROAD, HAWICK, SCOTLAND TD9 7AH

☎ (01450) 373206. FAX: ☎ (01450) 371900. OPEN 9 - 5.15 MON - FRI, 9.30 - 5.30 SAT. MAIL ORDER ALSO.

White of Hawick is a privately owned family-run business selling the highest quality cashmere and lambswool at the keenest prices in the UK, including garments manufactured by top names such as Lyle & Scott, Peter Scott, Johnstons and White of Hawick. While their shop is not a discount shop as such, everything there is very competitively priced with many items sold at up to one third of the price of the same merchandise in top London department stores. For example, ladies round-neck, long-sleeved pullover in 100% single cashmere, from £79; ladies high button, long-sleeved cashmere cardigan with contrast trimming, £99; classic long-sleeved turtle neck pullover in 100% single cashmere, from £79; men's long-sleeved, V-neck pullover with saddle shoulders in 100% double cashmere, from £99. Round neck, long-sleeved ladies pullover in 100% shrink resistant single geelong lambswool, £35.95; men's long-sleeved V-neck cardigan with two pockets and saddle shoulders in 100% double lambswool, £39.95. Ladies fringed cape in 100% woven double lambswool, £26.95. The shop also sells cashmere scarves from £15.95 and lambswool scarves from £2, cashmere and lambswool gloves and all-wool rugs. Also available is four-ply chunky cashmere and factory seconds at unbeatable prices. Mail order brochure available. *Permanent Discount Outlet*

WILD ROSE

15 HENDERSON ROW, EDINBURGH, SCOTLAND EH3 5DH
☎ (0131) 557 1916. OPEN 10.30 - 6 TUE - SAT.
Established over 20 years, this distinctive specialist shop sells decorative functional silver ladies and men's jewellery, porcelain, pottery, glass, metalware,
prints and paintings. Next door at number 17 is Gladrags which has a unique
selection of exquisite period clothes, accessories and costume jewellery, lace-
edged table and bed linen, paisley shawls. *Secondhand Shop*

Live Well On Less Tips
KEYSTONES PO BOX 387, STAFFORD, STAFFORDSHIRE ST16 3FG.
(01785) 256648. MAIL ORDER.
Specialist dealers in 19th and 20th century decorative Denby and other
stonewares and salt-glaze, they offer a matching service for discontinued
Denby tableware. All pottery supplied by them is in nearly new condition,
unless otherwise stated, and they have available at least 50 different patterns
as well as operating a free search service for items not in stock. They have
shops at the Gloucester Antiques Centre in Gloucester Docks and Stables
Antiques' Centre, Hatton Country World near Warwick, as well as operating a postal service.

Wales

WOMENSWEAR ONLY 🐾 Alexon Sale Shop, *Pontypridd.* Bairdwear Lingerie, *Merthyr Tydfil.*
Bairdwear Lingerie, *Port Talbot.* Bairdwear Lingerie, *Caerphilly.* Bairdwear Lingerie, *Pyle.*
Bairdwear Lingerie, *Pontardawe.* Bairdwear Lingerie, *Bargoed.* Beulah Dress Agency, *Cardiff.*
Changes Dress Agency, *Cowbridge.* Elle, *Cowbridge.* Gainsborough, *Swansea.*
Gossard Factory Shop, *Blackwood.* Honey, *Ebbw Vale.* Jane Shilton, *Ebbw Vale.*
Laura Ashley Sale Shop, *Newtown.* Phoebe's Dress Agency, *Anglesey.* Togs, *Bridgend.*
Velmore Ltd, *Wrexham.*

MENSWEAR ONLY 🐾 Slaters Menswear, *Cardiff.* Tom Sayers, *Ebbw Vale.*

WOMENSWEAR & MENSWEAR 🐾 🐾 Big L Factory Outlet, *Bridgend.* Burberry, *Rhondda.*
Catalogue Bargain Shop, *Ebbw Vale.* Catalogue Bargain Shop, *Llandudno.*
Catalogue Bargain Shop, *Merthyr Tydfil.* Catalogue Bargain Shop, *Newtown.*
Catalogue Bargain Shop, *Pontypridd.* Catalogue Bargain Shop, *Port Talbot.*
Catalogue Bargain Shop, *Pyle.* Catalogue Bargain Shop, *Swansea.* Cosalt International Ltd, *Haven.*
Dewhirst Clothing Factory Shop, *Swansea.* Ecco, *Bridgend.* Famous Footwear, *Bridgend.*
Festival Park Factory Outlet Shopping Village, *Ebbw Vale.* Jaeger Factory Shop, *Bridgend.*
John Patridge Outlet Store, *Ebbw Vale.* Littlewoods Catalogue Discount Store, *Bridgend.*
Matalan, *Llantrisant.* Matalan, *Swansea.* Matalan, *Cwnbran.* Matalan, *Bangor.* Matalan, *Cardiff.*
Matalan, *Wrexham.* McArthurglen Designer Outlet, *Bridgend.* Mexx International, *Bridgend.*
Next To Nothing, *Bridgend.* Peggy Sue Dress Agency, *Usk.* Pendor Factory Shop, *Merthyr Tydfil.*
Second To None, *Chepstow.* Seconds Ahead, *Cardigan.* Seconds Out, *Aberystwyth.*
Stewart's, *Aberystwyth.* Stewart's, *Camarthen.* Stewart's, *Lampeter.* Stewart's, *Llanelli.*
Stewart's, *Pwllheli.* Stewart's, *New Quay.* Stewart's, *Saudersfoot.* Stewart's, *Tenby.*
Stewart's, *Porthmadog.* Stewart's, *Swansea.* Stewart's, *Monmouth.* Stewart's, *Pontypridd.*
Stewart's, *Llandudno.* Stewart's, *Caerphilly.* Stewart's, *Pylecross.* The Factory Shop Ltd, *Ebbw Vale.*
The Factory Shop Ltd, *Haversfordwest.* TK Maxx, *Carmarthen.* TK Maxx, *Cardiff.* Tog 24, *Bridgend.*
Tog 24, *Ebbw Vale.* Tweedmill Factory Shopping Ltd, *St Asaph.* Viyella, *Bridgend.*

CHILDREN 🐾 ABC2, *Cardiff.* Anglesey Nursery Hire, *Anglesey.* Babyland, *Ammanford.*
Burberry, *Rhondda.* Catalogue Bargain Shop, *Ebbw Vale.* Catalogue Bargain Shop, *Llandudno.*
Catalogue Bargain Shop, *Merthyr Tydfil.* Catalogue Bargain Shop, *Newtown.*
Catalogue Bargain Shop, *Pontypridd.* Catalogue Bargain Shop, *Port Talbot.*
Catalogue Bargain Shop, *Pyle.* Catalogue Bargain Shop, *Swansea.*
Dewhirst Clothing Factory Shop, *Swansea.* Ecco, *Bridgend.*
Festival Park Factory Outlet Shopping Village, *Ebbw Vale.* John Patridge Outlet Store, *Ebbw Vale.*
Kids Play Factory, *Bridgend.* Kids Stock & Exchange, *Rhyl.*
Littlewoods Catalogue Discount Store, *Bridgend.* Matalan, *Llantrisant.* Matalan, *Swansea.*
Matalan, *Cwnbran.* Matalan, *Bangor.* Matalan, *Cardiff.* Matalan, *Wrexham.*
McArthurglen Designer Outlet, *Bridgend.* Mexx International, *Bridgend.*
Next To Nothing, *Bridgend.* Now & Then, *Rhyl.* Pendor Factory Shop, *Merthyr Tydfil.*
Pyjama Tops, *Bala.* Second To None, *Chepstow.* Seconds Ahead, *Cardigan.*
Seconds Out, *Aberystwyth.* Stewart's, *Aberystwyth.* Stewart's, *Camarthen.* Stewart's, *Lampeter.*
Stewart's, *Llanelli.* Stewart's, *Pwllheli.* Stewart's, *New Quay.* Stewart's, *Saudersfoot.*
Stewart's, *Tenby.* Stewart's, *Porthmadog.* Stewart's, *Swansea.* Stewart's, *Monmouth.*
Stewart's, *Pontypridd.* Stewart's, *Llandudno.* Stewart's, *Caerphilly.* Stewart's, *Pylecross.*
The Factory Shop Ltd, *Ebbw Vale.* The Factory Shop Ltd, *Haversfordwest.* TK Maxx, *Carmarthen.*
TK Maxx, *Cardiff.* Tog 24, *Bridgend.* Tog 24, *Ebbw Vale.*

HOUSEHOLD AND GIFTWARE 🏠 Catalogue Bargain Shop, *Ebbw Vale*.
Catalogue Bargain Shop, *Llandudno*. Catalogue Bargain Shop, *Merthyr Tydfil*.
Catalogue Bargain Shop, *Newtown*. Catalogue Bargain Shop, *Pontypridd*.
Catalogue Bargain Shop, *Port Talbot*. Catalogue Bargain Shop, *Pyle*.
Catalogue Bargain Shop, *Swansea*. Dartington Crystal, *Anglesey*.
Festival Park Factory Outlet Shopping Village, *Ebbw Vale*. Glamourline Blinds, *Tonypandy*.
Hyper Value Holdings Ltd, *Pontypridd*. Matalan, *Llantrisant*. Matalan, *Swansea*. Matalan, *Cwnbran*.
Matalan, *Bangor*. Matalan, *Cardiff*. Matalan, *Wrexham*. McArthurglen Designer Outlet, *Bridgend*.
Mexx International, *Bridgend*. Pendor Factory Shop, *Merthyr Tydfil*. Ponden Mill Linens, *Ebbw Vale*.
Price's Candles, *Bridgend*. Royal Worcester & Spode Factory Shop, *Ebbw Vale*.
Royal Worcester & Spode Factory Shop, *Bridgend*. Stewart's, *Aberystwyth*. Stewart's, *Camarthen*.
Stewart's, *Lampeter*. Stewart's, *Llanelli*. Stewart's, *Pwllheli*. Stewart's, *New Quay*.
Stewart's, *Saudersfoot*. Stewart's, *Tenby*. Stewart's, *Porthmadog*. Stewart's, *Swansea*.
Stewart's, *Monmouth*. Stewart's, *Pontypridd*. Stewart's, *Llandudno*. Stewart's, *Caerphilly*.
Stewart's, *Pylecross*. Stuart Crystal, *Chepstow*. The Abbey Woollen Mills, *Swansea*.
The Factory Shop Ltd, *Ebbw Vale*. The Factory Shop Ltd, *Haversfordwest*. TK Maxx, *Carmarthen*.
TK Maxx, *Cardiff*. Whittard, *Bridgend*.

ELECTRICAL EQUIPMENT 🔌 Catalogue Bargain Shop, *Ebbw Vale*.
Catalogue Bargain Shop, *Llandudno*. Catalogue Bargain Shop, *Merthyr Tydfil*.
Catalogue Bargain Shop, *Newtown*. Catalogue Bargain Shop, *Pontypridd*.
Catalogue Bargain Shop, *Port Talbot*. Catalogue Bargain Shop, *Pyle*.
Catalogue Bargain Shop, *Swansea*. Littlewoods Catalogue Discount Store, *Bridgend*.
McArthurglen Designer Outlet, *Bridgend*. Remington, *Bridgend*. Thorn Outlet, *Bridgend*.

DIY/RENOVATION 🔨 Adferiad Gwent of Monmouthshire, *Gwent*.
Cardiff Reclamation, *Cardiff*. Dyfed Antiques & Architectural Salvage, *Haverfordwest*.
Glynn Webb, *Swansea*.

ARCHITECTURAL SALVAGE 🔨 Adferiad Gwent of Monmouthshire, *Gwent*.
Cardiff Reclamation, *Cardiff*. Dyfed Antiques & Architectural Salvage, *Haverfordwest*.

FURNITURE/SOFT FURNISHINGS 🪑 Abakhan Fabrics, *Mostyn*.
Classic Choice Furnishings Ltd, *Bridgend*. Deeside Furniture Ltd, *Holywell*.
Laura Ashley Sale Shop, *Newtown*. The Curtain Exchange, *Llandudno*.
The Factory Shop Ltd, *Ebbw Vale*. The Factory Shop Ltd, *Haversfordwest*.
Trefriw Woollen Mills Ltd, *Conway County*.

FOOD AND LEISURE 🍴 Bookends, *Ebbw Vale*. Harry Tuffins Supermarket, *Nighton, Powys*.
McArthurglen Designer Outlet, *Bridgend*. Thorntons, *Bridgend*. Thorntons, *Ebbw Vale*.
Travel Accessory Outlet, *Bridgend*.

SPORTSWEAR AND EQUIPMENT 🎿 McArthurglen Designer Outlet, *Bridgend*.
Pendor Factory Shop, *Merthyr Tydfil*. Stewart's, *Aberystwyth*. Stewart's, *Camarthen*.
Stewart's, *Lampeter*. Stewart's, *Llanelli*. Stewart's, *Pwllheli*. Stewart's, *New Quay*.
Stewart's, *Saudersfoot*. Stewart's, *Tenby*. Stewart's, *Porthmadog*. Stewart's, *Swansea*.
Stewart's, *Monmouth*. Stewart's, *Pontypridd*. Stewart's, *Llandudno*. Stewart's, *Caerphilly*.
Stewart's, *Pylecross*.

ABAKHAN FABRICS

LLANERCH-Y-MOR, COAST ROAD, MOSTYN, FLINTSHIRE,
WALES CH8 9DX

☎ (01745) 562100. OPEN 9 - 5.15 MON - SAT, 8 ON THUR,
10.30 - 4.30 SUN.

With five outlets in the North West, Abakhan Fabrics are as well known for
the emphasis they put on value for money as they are for the huge variety of
fabrics, needlecrafts, haberdashery, gifts and knitting yarns that they have
gathered from all around the world. The large mill shop complex has baskets
of remnant fabrics, wools, yarns and unrivalled selections of fabrics sold by the
metre from evening wear, bridal wear and crepe de Chine to curtaining, nets
and velvets. Here in this historic building, there are more than ten tonnes of
remnant fabrics and 10,000 rolls, all at mill shop prices. Abakhan is able to
offer such bargains through bulk buying, or selling clearance lines, job lots and
seconds. There is a coffee shop and free parking and coach parties are welcome
provided they pre-book. Free information pack available: ring 01745 562100.
Factory Shop

ADFERIAD GWENT OF MONMOUTHSHIRE

MONMOUTHSHIRE, WALES

☎ (01291) 690709. RING FOR APPOINTMENT.

Original Victorian pitch pine and pine floorboards, panelling, doors and
beams. Ancient oak timbers and floorboards and other original re-claimed
flooring. There isn't really a showroom and the barns are hard to find so it's
best to ring up first to get directions and make sure someone will be there. The
outlet is near Monmouth. *Architectural Salvage*

ALEXON SALE SHOP

CARDIFF ROAD, HAWTHORN, PONTYPRIDD,
MID GLAMORGAN, WALES
01443 480673. OPEN 10 - 5 MON - SAT.

Alexon, Eastex, Ann Harvey and Calico from last season at 40% less than the
original price; during sale time in January and June, the reductions are as
much as 70%. Stock includes separates, skirts, jackets, blouses; there is no
underwear or night clothes. This branch is situated at the back of the factory
itself. *Permanent Discount Outlet*

Live Well On Less Tips

Buy dry staples in bulk and save money, as long as you've got the storage
space. Properly stored dried spaghetti, for instance, lasts at least two years.

ANGLESEY NURSERY HIRE

10 GORWEL DEG, RHOSTREHWFA, LLANGEFNI,
ANGLESEY, WALES LL77 7JR
☎ (01248) 723181.
NOW & THEN, 101 DYSERTH ROAD, RHYL,
DENBIGHSHIRE LL18 4DU
☎ (01754) 343983.
ABC2, 16 PENNSYLVANIA, LLANDEYRN, CARDIFF,
SOUTH GLAMORGAN CF23 9LN
☎ (01222) 316894.
BABYLAND, 21-23 LLOYD STREET, AMMANFORD,
CARMARTHENSHIRE SA18 3BY
☎ (01269) 595200.
NOW & THEN, 1 LLYS TUDUR, PARK VIEW, RHYL,
DENBIGHSHIRE
LL18 4AX
☎ (01745) 332530.
Part of the Baby Equipment Hirers Association (BEHA), which has more than
100 members countrywide. A range of equipment can be hired from high
chairs, cots and travel cots to baby car seats and buggies. Some members also
hire out party equipment including child-sized tables and chairs. BEHA run
an advice line which will try and answer any queries you have regarding hiring services for children. Phone the Babyline on 0831 310355. *Hire Shop*

Live Well On Less Tips

VIDAL SASSOON SCHOOL OF HAIRDRESSING 56 DAVIES
MEWS, LONDON W1Y 1AS. 0171-318 5205. OPEN 10 - 3 MON - FRI.
VIDAL SASSOON STAFF TRAINING, WHITELEYS OF BAYSWATER, 151
QUEENSWAY LONDON W2 4SB
0171-792 5540. OPEN 10 - 3 MON - SAT.
Cuts and styles undertaken by students at the School of Hairdressing for
£16.50 or £8.25 if you're a student or OAP. Appointment must be made at
least one week in advance. At the Staff Training School in Bayswater, you can
pay between £15 and £29, depending on the level of experience of the staff.
Again, appointments must be made.

BAIRDWEAR LINGERIE

CYFARTHA INDUSTRIAL ESTATE, MERTHYR TYDFIL, MID
GLAMORGAN, WALES CF47 8PE

☎ (01685) 383837. OPEN 10 - 4.30 MON - SAT.
SANDFIELDS ESTATE, PURCELL AVENUE, SANDFIELDS, PORT TALBOT,
WEST GLAMORGAN, WALES SA12 7UF

☎ (01639) 895038. OPEN 9.30 - 4 MON - THUR, 9 - 4 FRI.
UNIT 5, BEDWAS BUSINESS PARK, BEDWAS, CAERPHILLY, GWENT
NP1 6XH

☎ (01222) 864699. OPEN 10 - 4 MON - SAT.
VILLAGE FARM INDUSTRIAL ESTATE, PYLE WEST GLAMORGAN
CF33 6NU

☎ (01656) 742511. OPEN 9.30 - 4.30 MON - SAT.
CHURCH STREET, PONTARDAWE, WEST GLAMORGAN SA8 4JB

☎ (01792) 830490. OPEN 9 - 4 MON - FRI, 9 - 12 SAT.
UNIT 11, SYMONDSCLIFF WAY, SEVERN BRIDGE INDUSTRIAL ESTATE,
CALDICOT NP6 4TH

☎ (01291) 421551. OPEN 9.30 - 4.30 MON - SAT.
ST DAVIDS INDUSTRIAL ESTATE, PENGAM, BARGOED, GWENT
NP2 1SW

☎ (01443) 821430. OPEN 9.30 - 4.30 MON - FRI, 9 - 1 SAT.
Manufactures underwear for a well-known high street chain store, the factory
shops sell seconds and overmakes at as little as one-third of their normal retail
price. Stock includes designer wraps, waist slips, full slips, camisoles, bras,
French knickers, crop tops and designer nightwear in a wide choice of colours,
fabrics and sizes. The staff are friendly and helpful. *Factory Shop*

BEULAH DRESS AGENCY

3B BEULAH ROAD, RHIWBINA, CARDIFF, CF4 6EF
☎ (01222) 691039
Sells nearly new high quality designer ladieswear. *Secondhand and Vintage Clothes*

BIG L FACTORY OUTLET

MCARTHURGLEN DESIGNER OUTLET VILLAGE, THE DERWEN,
BRIDGEND, JUNCTION 35 OF M4, WALES CF32 9FU
☎ (01656) 767335. OPEN 10 - 6 MON -SAT, 8 ON THUR, 11 - 5 SUN.
Men's and women's Levi jeans, jackets, cord and Sherpa fleece jackets, T-shirts
and shirts but no children's, all at discount prices. *Factory Shopping Village*

BIRTHDAYS

FESTIVAL PARK, VICTORIA, EBBW VALE, GWENT

☎ (01495) 306434. OPEN 9.30 - 5.30 MON - SAT, 11 - 5 SUN.

Cards, notelets, stationery sets, colouring books, stuffed toys, photo albums, picture frames, gifts, giftwrap, tissue paper, party packs, candlesticks, Christmas crackers, string puppets, fairy lights all at discounts of up to 30%. Some are special purchases, some seconds. *Factory Shopping Village*

BOOKENDS

DOCK STREET, NEWPORT, MONMOUTHSHIRE, WALES NP9 1FU

☎ (01633) 222086. OPEN 9 - 5.30 MON - SAT.

Secondhand and damaged books and publishers' returns, as well as new and review copies, including recently published books, usually one-third off and sometimes half price. *Secondhand Shop*

BURBERRY

YNYSWEN ROAD, TREOCHY, RHONDDA, MID GLAMORGAN, WALES

☎ (01443) 772020. OPEN 9 - 4 MON - THUR, 9 - 2 FRI, 9 - 1.30 SAT.

This Burberry factory shop is quite difficult to find as it is some way up the Rhondda Valley. However, GDD readers have written to tell me it is definitely worth the trip - although rather olde world, it has some good merchandise at extremely good prices. It sells seconds and overmakes of the famous name raincoats and duffle coats as well as accessories such as the distinctive umbrellas, scarves and handbags. All carry the Burberrys label and are about one third of the normal retail price. For example, trench coats, £189.95; classic coats, £159.95 which amount to a reduction of two thirds. Childrenswear tends to be thin on the ground, but there are plenty of gift items such as Burberrys brand name teas, coffees and marmalade. The shop is midway between Treochy and Treherbert - phone for directions. *Factory Shop*

CARDIFF RECLAMATION

SITE 7, TREMORFA INDUSTRIAL ESTATE, CARDIFF, WALES CF2 2SD

☎ (01222) 458995. OPEN 9 - 5 MON - FRI, 9 - 1 SUN.

Flagstones, Victorian fireplaces, pine doors, church pews, handrails, chimney pots, quarry tiles, oak beams and lots more. *Architectural Salvage*

CATALOGUE BARGAIN SHOP

BRYN FERTH ROAD, RHY-Y-BLEW, EBBW VALE, GWENT, WALES NP3 5YD

☎ (01495) 309297. OPEN 9 - 8 MON - THUR, SAT, 9 - 9 FRI, 10 - 4 SUN.

6-8 MADOC STREET, LLANDUDNO, GWYNEDD LL30 2TP

☎ (01492) 877561. OPEN 9 - 5 MON - SAT, 10.30 - 4.30 SUN.

61 HIGH STREET, MERTHYR TYDFIL, MID GLAMORGAN CF47 8DE

☎ (01685) 385653. OPEN 9 - 5.30 MON - SAT, 10,30 - 4.30 SUN.

OLD KERRY ROAD, NEWTOWN, POWYS SY16 1BJ
☎ (01686) 628283. OPEN 9 - 5 MON - SAT, 10 - 4 SUN.
5 HIGH STREET, PONTYPRIDD, MID GLAMORGAN CF37 1QJ
☎ (01443) 486156. OPEN 9 - 5 MON - SAT, 10,30 - 4.30 SUN.
31 STATION ROAD, PORT TALBOT, WEST GLAMORGAN SA13 1NN
☎ (01639) 899419. OPEN 9 - 5 MON - SAT.
FFALDS ROAD SHOPPING CENTRE, PYLE CROSS, PYLE,
BRIDGEND CF33 6BH
☎ (01656) 746426. OPEN 9 - 8 MON - SAT, 10.30 - 4.30 SUN.
229-230 HIGH STREET, SWANSEA, WEST GLAMORGAN SA1 ANY
☎ (01792) 456748. OPEN 9 - 5.30 MON - SAT, 10.30 - 4.30 SUN.
Catalogue Bargain Shop is a growing national chain of stores which obtains
the majority of its goods from mail order giants Great Universal and Kays, and
offers a range of clothing for all the family, a wide selection of shoes, bed linen,
household goods, electrical equipment and hundreds of other catalogue items
at very competitive prices. For example, a three-piece leather suite, £899,
reduced from £1,600. The merchandise consists of ends of ranges and previous season's stock for which there is no longer storage space when the catalogues change. *Permanent Discount Outlet*

CHANGES DRESS AGENCY

27A HIGH STREET, COWBRIDGE, SOUTH GLAMORGAN,
WALES CF71 7AG
☎ (01446) 772184. OPEN 10 - 5 TUE - SAT. CLOSED MON.
Designer and high quality labels such as MaxMara, Cerruti, Mani, Jaeger,
Frank Usher, Nicole Farhi, Karen Millen, Jobis and Basler. All the outfits are
bought and sold on a commission basis at a fraction of the original price.
Dress Agency

CLASSIC CHOICE FURNISHINGS LIMITED

BRYNMENYN INDUSTRIAL ESTATE, BRYNMENYN, BRIDGEND,
GLAMORGAN, WALES CF32 9TD
☎ (01656) 725111. SHOWROOM: OPEN 10 - 4 SEVEN DAYS A WEEK.
MAIL ORDER.
Save money on high quality furniture by purchasing direct. Choose from
modern and traditional designs in suites or separates - all fully guaranteed for
quality and supplied with a twenty-one day, full refund, no-quibble guarantee. There is an excellent choice of fabric and leather furniture in a wide choice
of covers. Phone or write for free catalogue. Once a month, a selection of furniture is set out in hotels countrywide for customers to try out. *Permanent
Discount Outlet*

COSALT INTERNATIONAL LTD

THE DOCKS, MILFORD HAVEN, PEMBROKESHIRE, WALES SA73 3AF
☎ (01646) 692032. OPEN 8 - 5 MON-FRI SAT 9 - 12.

The company specialises in workwear, safety clothing and marine wear but some of the merchandise is eminently wearable for everyday and is sold at very reasonable prices. This particular outlet specialises in guy cotton French wet weather clothing, fishermen's gear (bib and brace trousers and smocks) and safety footwear, although there is a limited amount of donket jackets and dungarees. VAT has to be added to prices. There are catalogues available for you to order from if what you want isn't in stock. They also provide marine safety and life-raft servicing. *Permanent Discount Outlet*

DARTINGTON CRYSTAL

C/O JAMES PRINGLE WEAVERS, HOLYHEAD ROAD,
LLANFAIRPWLLGWYNGYLL, ANGLESEY, WALES LL61 5UJ
☎ (01248) 715255. OPEN 9 - 5.30 MON - SAT, 11 - 5 SUN.

An extensive range of Dartington Crystal seconds at greatly reduced prices as well as some perfect crystal at full price. Range includes wine suites, sherry glasses, tankards, decanters, rippled glass, fruit and salad bowls. Denby Pottery is also available. *Factory Shop*

DEESIDE FURNITURE LTD

GREENFIELD BUSINESS PARK, BAGILLT ROAD, HOLYWELL,
FLINTSHIRE, WALES CH8 7HJ
☎ (01352) 711196. OPEN 7.30 - 4.30 TUE - THUR, 7.30 - 12.30 FRI,
9 - 2 SAT, 10 - 2 SUN.

Large furniture warehouse selling sofas, curtains and soft furnishings at factory direct prices. Many of the sofas are made for top high street stores. *Permanent Discount Outlet*

DEWHIRST CLOTHING FACTORY SHOP

UNIT 22, THE KINGSWAY, FFORESTFACH INDUSTRIAL ESTATE,
FFORESTFACH, SWANSEA, WALES SA5 4HY
☎ (01792) 584621. OPEN 9 - 5.30 MON - SAT, 11 - 5 SUN.

Dewhirst Clothing Factory Shops sell garments from the manufacturing side of the business direct to the public and are part of the Dewhirst Group plc which manufactures ladies', men's and childrenswear for a leading high street retailer. You can choose from a huge selection of surplus production and slight seconds at bargain prices, making savings of more than 50% of the normal retail cost. For men there is a wide range of suits, formal shirts and casual wear. For example, wool suits from £60, formal and casual shirts from £7. For ladies there's a selection of blouses, smart tailoring and casual wear that includes a denim range. You can find ladies jackets from £50, skirts, trousers and blouses from £8. Children's clothes start at £3. High street quality and style at wholesale prices. *Factory Shop*

DYFED ANTIQUES & ARCHITECTURAL SALVAGE

WESLEYAN CHAPEL, PERROTS ROAD, HAVERFORDWEST,
PEMBROKESHIRE, WALES

☎ (01437) 760496. OPEN 10 - 5 MON - SAT.
Slate slabs, quarry tiles, oak beams and flooring, doors, Victorian fireplaces, tiled insets, surrounds in wood, marble and cast iron, antique furniture, many huge dressers and curios, gardenware including urns. Furniture and fire surrounds made to measure in new or old wood. *Architectural Salvage*

ECCO

MACARTHURGLEN DESIGNER OUTLET WALES THE DERWEN,
BRIDGEND, WALES CF32 3SU

☎ (01656) 767202. OPEN 10 - 6 MON - SAT 8 ON THUR, 11 - 5 SUN.
Ladies', men's and children's shoes, all discounted by at least 25%. Phone 0800 387368 for a catalogue. Other outlets in Wiltshire, Somerset and Cheshire. *Factory Shopping Village*

ELLE

41A HIGH STREET, COWBRIDGE, VALE OF GLAMORGAN,
WALES CF7 7AE

☎ (01446) 775687. OPEN 10.30 - 5.30 MON - SAT
Nearly-new Jasper Conran, Escada, Laurel, Mondi, Christian Dior and occasionally Louis Feraud, Jean Paul Gaultier and Armani are on sale at this centrally located shop. There are a lot of separates and good office wear and half-price sales in January and July. Also mother of the bride outfits and hats to buy. Prices tend to be below £100. *Dress Agency*

FAMOUS FOOTWEAR

DESIGNER OUTLET VILLAGE, BRIDGEND, JUNCTION 35 OF M4,
WALES

☎ (01656) 657779. OPEN 10 - 6 MON, TUE, WED, FRI, SAT,
10 - 8 THUR, 11 - 5 SUN.
Wide range of brand names including Stead & Simpson, Lilley & Skinner, Hobos, Hush Puppies, Lotus, Sterling & Hunt, Richleigh, Scholl, Red Tape, Flexi Country, Padders, Canaletto, Bronx, Frank Wright, Brevitt, Romba Wallace, Rieker, all at discount prices of up to 50%. *Factory Shopping Village*

FESTIVAL PARK FACTORY
OUTLET SHOPPING VILLAGE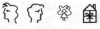
FESTIVAL PARK, VICTORIA, EBBW VALE, GWENT, WALES NP23 6FP
☎ (01495) 350010. OPEN 9.30 - 5.30 MON - SAT, 11 - 5 SUN.
Set on a former site for the Welsh National Garden Festival, with seventy acres of stunning scenery, Festival Park Outlet Shopping Centre offers 38 discount retail outlets selling a feast of end of season lines, manufacturing over-runs and excess stock at bargain prices. The shops are packed with well-known brands ensuring that you can save up to 50% off high street prices on a range which includes ladies, men's and children's fashions, leatherwear, gifts, jewellery, china, glassware, soft furnishings, books, luggage and much more. When not shopping, you can take a woodland walk, visit the tropical plants house, see all the attractions by taking the land train, or walk round the ornamental gardens. Open seven days a week, there is disabled car parking, wheelchair access, wide shop entrances, toilets and baby changing facilities. More outlets and restaurants are planned, and even more parking spaces. Factory shops include fashion from Edinburgh Woollen Mill; greetings cards from Birthdays; end of line books from Bookends; wholesale jewellery and watches from Event Jewellery; sportswear from Sports Mill; handbags and shoes from Jane Shilton; men's and ladies fashions from Leading Labels; outerwear from Mileta Tog 24; ceramics, pottery, terracotta and glass from Mondian; ladieswear from Pilot; soft furnishings and textiles from Ponden Mill; shoes from Start-Rite; lingerie from Baird Clothing; discount department store, The Factory Shop; Royal Worcester and Edinburgh Crystal from the Porcelain and Fine China Company; chocolates from Thornton's; toys and games from The Toy Shop; menswear from Tom Sayer; ladies fashion from Windsmoor and dried fruit and nuts, spices and pasta from Julian Graves. *Factory Shopping Village*

GAINSBOROUGH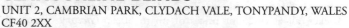
12 SWANSEA ROAD, LLANGYFELACH, SWANSEA, WALES SA5 7JD
☎ (01792) 790922. OPEN 10 - 5 MON - SAT.
This shop stocks currently fashionable flawless outfits from top labels such as Frank Usher, Jacques Vert, Kasper, Betty Barclay, Condici, Tom Bowker, Mani and Louis Feraud, all at savings of between 55% and 80% off the original price. There is plenty of day and evening wear and special occasion wear, including ballgowns and hats and more than 200 wedding outfits. Stock changes constantly. There is also an alteration service. *Dress Agency*

GLAMOURLINE BLINDS
UNIT 2, CAMBRIAN PARK, CLYDACH VALE, TONYPANDY, WALES
CF40 2XX
☎ (01443) 433232. OPEN 9 - 5 MON - THUR, 9 - 2 FRI,
CLOSED 1 - 1.30 DAILY, 9 - 12.30 SAT.
Specialise in blinds of all types - venetian, roller, vertical, austrian and conser-

vatory - as well as awnings which are sold by mail order and to high street department stores, as well as some curtains. Made to measure vertical blinds are available at up to 50% less than normal retail prices. Catalogue returns are also sometimes available. Operates a home visit and fitting service. *Factory Shop*

GLYNN WEBB

PONTARDULAIS ROAD, CADLE, SWANSEA, WALES SA5 4BA
☎ (01792) 579955. OPEN 9 - 8 MON - SAT, 10 - 4 SUN AND BANK HOLIDAYS.
Stockists of all your home improvement needs from wallpaper to paint, furniture to flooring, tiles to textiles, housewares to lighting - in fact, almost everything for your home, with 24 branches in the North-West, Midlands and Yorkshire. Specialists in discontinued mail order, slightly imperfect branded stocks as well as perfect quality superior products. They carry top brands such as Dulux, Crown Paints and Vymura and Coloroll wall coverings, Rectella and Norwood textiles and much more in store. Different branches carry different lines so if you want something specific, phone first. To find your nearest branch, phone 0161 621 4500. *Permanent Discount Outlet*

GOSSARD FACTORY SHOP

PENMAEN ROAD, PONTLLANFRAITH, BLACKWOOD, GWENT, WALES NP2 2DL
☎ (01495) 221103. OPEN 9.30 - 5.30 MON - SAT.
Factory shop sells seconds and discontinued ranges of Gossard and Berlei underwear including bras, briefs, suspender belts and bodies at discounted prices (no nightwear or long-line slips) . Most of the stock is last year's trade catalogue styles at discounts of between 25%-75%. Free parking; ramp for wheelchairs. *Factory Shop*

HARRY TUFFINS SUPERMARKET

NIGHTON, NEAR SHELL GARAGE, POWYS, WALES
☎ (01547)528645. OPEN 8.30 - 5.30 MON, TUE, WED, SAT, 8.30 - 8 THUR, FRI, 10 - 4 SUN.
Supermarket selling foodstuffs, garden furniture, household goods at incredibly competitive prices. Don't expect the looks and service of a Sainsbury's though the prices are better. There's a vast range of tinned food, pickles, sauces, dried foods, soups, cereals, household cleaning products, kitchen equipment, stationery and diy. You may decide to ignore the wine department and please note that the fruit and veg sections outside the main shop are not run by Tuffins and are not always a bargain. *Permanent Discount Outlet*

HONEY

FESTIVAL PARK, VICTORIA, EBBWVALE, GWENT NP3 6FP

☎ (01495) 309881. OPEN 10 - 5.30 MON - SUN.

Leisure-oriented women's T-shirts, leggings and sweaters at discounts of mostly 30% or more. *Factory Shopping Village*

HYPER VALUE HOLDINGS LTD

BROWN LENNOX RETAIL PARK, YUYSANGHARAD ROAD,
PONTYPRIDD, WALES CF37 4DA

☎ (01443) 480115. OPEN 8.30 - 6 SEVEN DAYS A WEEK.

Housed in old supermarket premises, this Aladdin's cave holds a huge array of just about everything, some of which is tat, some great value finds. Dig around among the frames, mirror, socks, tights, toiletries, tools, carpets, stationery, shirts, ornaments, paint, wallpaper borders and garden furniture and you may find the odd gem such as the natural canvas parasol, Habitat-style, £20, or the Christian Dior tights, 40p. There are 20 branches in South Wales, some in retail parks, others in stand-alone shops. Phone 01446 721200 for details of your nearest outlet. *Permanent Discount Outlet*

JAEGER FACTORY SHOP

MCARTHURGLEN DESIGNER OUTLET VILLAGE, THE DERWEN,
BRIDGEND, JUNCTION 35 OF M4, WALES CF32 95U

☎ (01656) 665700. OPEN 10 - 6 MON - FRI, 10 - 8 THUR, 11 - 5 SUN.

Contemporary classics from Jaeger at excellent prices. Most of the merchandise is previous seasons' stock, but you might also find some special makes. The telephone number given here is for the centre, not the shop. *Factory Shopping Village*

JANE SHILTON

FESTIVAL PARK SHOPPING CENTRE, VICTORIA ROAD, EBBW VALE,
MID-GLAMORGAN, WALES NP3 6OH

☎ (01495) 302216. OPEN 10 - 6 MON - SAT, 11 - 5 SUN.

Merchandise from past seasons' collections or factory seconds at discounts of at least 30% off the original price. There is a wide range of handbags, suitcases, women's shoes, luggage, briefcases, umbrellas, scarves and travel bags. *Factory Shop*

JOHN PARTRIDGE OUTLET STORE

FESTIVAL PARK, VICTORIA, EBBW VALE, GWENT, WALES

☎ (01495) 352643. OPEN 9.30 - 5.30 MON - SAT, 11 - 5 SUN.

DESIGNER OUTLET CENTRE, DERWEN, BRIDGEND, SOUTH WALES

☎ (01656) 667461.

John Partridge specialises in hardwearing outdoor clothes. Ranges include waxed cotton jackets, trench coats and waistcoats; showerproof classic town coats; Gore-tex coats and tweed coats; quilted jackets and waistcoats; children's waxed jackets, quilted jackets and waistcoats; hats and caps; moleskin and cord trousers; knitwear and shirts. Discontinued lines and seconds are on sale at discounted prices - a minimum of 30% and up to 70% off during promotions. *Factory Shopping Village*

KIDS PLAY FACTORY

WALES DESIGNER OUTLET VILLAGE, BRIDGEND
JUNCTION 35 OF M4, MID-GLAMORGAN, WALES
☎ (01656) 652265. OPEN 10 - 6 MON - FRI, 8 ON THUR, 9 - 6 SAT
11 - 5 SUN.
This shop sells a wide range of well-known children's brand names: Tomy, Matchbox, Lego, The First Years, Hasbro, Disney, Playskool, Mattel and Fisher-Price at discounts of up to 50%. They also stock a wide range of soft toys including TY Beanie Babies. *Factory Shopping Village*

KIDS STOCK AND EXCHANGE

UNIT 2, WELLINGTON ROAD, RHYL, CLWYD, WALES LL18 1BD
☎ (01745) 330115. OPEN 10 - 5 MON - SAT.
Sells nearly-new baby equipment and also hires out. There are buggies, stair gates, parasols, raincovers, cots, prams, Moses baskets - and everything parents of young children could want, including items with famous brand names such as Cosatto. Old prams are exchanged for nearly-new or new. Hire charges start at £1.50 per day for a baby walker, £2.50 for a pushchair. No children's clothes are stocked. *Secondhand Shop*

LAURA ASHLEY SALE SHOP

BEAR LANE, NEWTOWN, POWYS, WALES
☎ (01686) 626549. OPEN 9.30 - 5.30 MON - FRI, 9 - 5.30 SAT.
Laura Ashley fashion and home furnishings. The garments are made up of discontinued, past season lines and specially-produced lines reflecting a large choice of colours and styles. The home furnishings is second quality fabrics and wallpaper at vastly reduced prices. *Factory Shop*

Live Well On Less Tips
BABY EQUIPMENT HIRERS ASSOCIATION
(0831) 310355.
Expecting a visit from grandchildren or friends with young babies? Save them the bother of bringing cots and high chairs with them - hire the equipment instead. The BEHA has more than 100 members countrywide who can provide you with a travel cot, high chair, buggy, back pack or almost anything a parent of young children might want. Phone (tel no above) to find your nearest BEHA member.

LITTLEWOODS
CATALOGUE DISCOUNT STORE

MCARTHURGLEN DESIGNER OUTLET WALES THE DERWEN,
BRIDGEND, WALES CF32 9SU

☎ (01656) 665700. OPEN 10 - 6 MON - SAT, UNTIL 8 ON THUR,
11 - 5 SUN.

Littlewoods clearance shops offering up to 50% off the catalogue price for
clothing and between 50% and 60% off for electrical goods. Stock changes
constantly and varies from day to day but can include well-known brand
names such as Berlei and Gossard lingerie, Vivienne Westwood,
Pamplemousse leisure wear, Nike and Adidas sports shoes, Workers For
Freedom, and Timberland and Caterpillar footwear. Stock depends on the size
and location of the shop, so larger shops will get the longer discontinued runs
and smaller shops over-runs with only a small amount of colour and size variations left. Littlewoods also run a mobile shop which operates in cities where
they don't have a sale shop. For details of further venues for the sales, which
usually take place once a month, contact Melanie Lamb, c/o Crosby DC,
Kershaw Avenue, Endbutt Lane, Crosby, Merseyside L70 1AH. *Factory
Shop*

MATALAN

UNIT 8, GLAMORGAN VALE RETAIL PARK, LLANTRISANT, MID-
GLAMORGAN, WALES CF7 8RP

☎ (01443) 224854. OPEN 10 - 8 MON - FRI, 9 - 6 SAT, 11 - 5 SUN.
FOUNDRY ROAD, MORRISTON, SWANSEA SA6 8DU

☎ (01792) 792229. OPEN 10 - 8 MON - FRI, 9 - 6 SAT, 11 - 5 SUN.
UNIT 4B, CWMBRAN RETAIL PARK CWNBRAN DRIVE, CWNBRAN,
GWENT NP44 3JQ

☎ (01633) 866944. OPEN 10 - 8 MON - FRI, 9 - 6 SAT, 11 - 5 SUN.
UNIT 1A & 1B, CAENARFON ROAD, BANGOR LL57 4SU.

☎ (01248) 362778. OPEN 10 - 8 MON - FRI, 9 - 6 SAT, 11 - 5 SUN.
UNIT 2, 382-384 NEWPORT ROAD, CARDIFF CF3 7AE

☎ (01222) 491781. OPEN 10 - 8 MON - FRI, 9 - 6 SAT, 11 - 5 SUN.
UNITS E-F, PLAS COCH RETAIL PARK, WREXHAM LL1 2BA

☎ (01978) 340900. OPEN 10 - 8 MON - FRI, 9 - 6 SAT, 11 - 5 SUN.

Matalan is a fashion and homewares shop giving customers what they claim
to be unbeatable value for money with huge savings on a wide range of products including high quality fashionable clothing for women, women and children at up to 50% off high street prices. Matalan is situated out of town and
stores are open seven days a week all year round *Permanent Discount
Outlet*

MCARTHURGLEN DESIGNER OUTLET WALES

THE DERWEN, BRIDGEND, WALES CF32 9SU

☎ (01656) 665700. OPEN 10 - 6 MON - SAT, 8 ON THUR, 11 - 5 SUN.

Ninety-four shops offering discounts of 30%-50% with an Odeon multi-screen cinema and food court as part of the centre. Shops for women include Big L (Levi's), Birthdays, Calvin Klein, Chilli Pepper, Ciro accessories, Cotton Traders leisurewear, Ecco, Elle, Famous Footwear, Jaeger, John Partridge countrywear, Mexx, Pepe Jeans, Monet jewellery, Next, Nike, Pilot, Reebok, Soled Out, The Designer Room (top designer labels), Tog 24 outdoor and walking wear, U Wear I Wear sunglasses, Viyella, Walker & Hall jewellery and watches, Warners and Winning Line. For men, Big L, Calvin Klein, Cap It All, Ciro Citterio suits, Ecco, Famous Footwear, Jaeger, John Partridge countrywear, Mexx, Nickelbys, Nike, Pepe Jeans, Red/Green everyday sailing wear, Reebok, Soled Out, Suits You, The Suit Company, Tie Rack, Tog 24 outdoorwear and Van Heusen. Shops for children include Big L (Levi's), Cap It All, Ecco, Kids Play Factory, Mexx, Next to Nothing, Pepe Jeans, Nike, Reebok, Sidoli's confectionery, Soled Out footwear, Thorntons, Tog 24 outdoor and walking wear. Shops for the home include Bed & Bath Works towels and bedlinen; Birthdays cards and small gifts; Clover House tablemats and kitchenware; Mondian glass; Price's Candles; Royal Doulton; Royal Worcester; Thorn electricals such as TVs, videos and CD players; and Whittard of Chelsea's wide range of colourful kitchenware and china. Electrical shops include Remington selling everything from knives and saucepans to hairdryers and shavers and Thorn selling videos, TVs, VD players, video tapes and small electrical goods. Leisure shops include Bookends; Carphone Warehouse; Travel Accessory and XS Music and Video selling CDs and tapes. Sports shops include Elle, Nike, Red/Green everyday sailing wear, Reebok, Soled Out and Tog 24 outdoor and walking wear. *Factory Shopping Village*

MEXX INTERNATIONAL

MCARTHURGLEN DESIGNER OUTLET, THE DERWEN, BRIDGEND, WALES CF32 9SU

☎ (01656) 766870. OPEN 10 - 6 MON - SAT, 10 - 8 THUR, 11 - 5 SUN.

High street fashion at factory outlet prices for men, women, babies, children and teenagers, all of which are heavily discounted by more than 30%. *Factory Shopping Village*

Live Well On Less Tips

In many restaurants, one salad order or one veg order is more than enough for two.

NEXT TO NOTHING

MCARTHURGLEN DESIGNER OUTLET VILLAGE, BRIDGEND, WALES
CF32 95U

☎ (01656) 641950. OPEN 10 - 6 MON - FRI, 10 - 8 THUR, 11 - 5 SUN.
Sells perfect surplus stock from Next stores and the Next Directory catalogue
- from belts, jewellery and underwear to day and evening wear - at discounts
of 50% or more. The ranges are usually last season's and overruns. Stock consists of women's, men's and children's clothing, with some homeware and
shoes. Stock is replenished three times a week and there is plenty of it.
Factory Shopping Village

PEGGY SUE DRESS AGENCY

28 BRIDGE STREET, USK, GWENT, WALES NP15 1BG
☎ (01291) 673309. OPEN 10 - 5 MON - SAT, CLOSED 1 WED.
Popular labels here include Escada, Jacques Vert and Windsmoor, although
they also stock Marks & Spencer. As well as ballgowns, jewellery and hats,
there is some childrenswear and a rail of menswear. *Dress Agency*

PENDOR FACTORY SHOP LTD

DOWLAIS INDUSTRIAL ESTATE, MERTHYR TYDFIL, WALES CF48 3TD
☎ (01685) 722681. OPEN 9.30 - 6 MON - SAT, 10 - 4 SUN.
Clothing for the whole family, including sportswear at discounts of 30%-
60%. The range includes everything from underwear and night clothes to daywear and some coats and jackets. Some of the brands are department store
high street names, others include Reebok, Nike and Adidas. Pendor promise
that if you can buy their merchandise cheaper anywhere in the UK, they will
refund the difference. *Factory Shop*

PHOEBE'S DRESS AGENCY

BANGOR ROAD, BENLLECH, ANGLESEY, WALES
☎ (01248) 852756. OPEN 10 - 1 AND 2 - 5.30 TUE, WED, FRI, 11 - 3.30 SAT.
Nearly-new shop selling high quality designer labels such as Basler, Armani,
Alexon, Louis Feraud, Jaeger, Jobis and Dolce & Gabanna. Parking in layby
outside shop. *Dress Agency*

PONDEN MILL LINENS

FESTIVAL PARK SHOPPING VILLAGE, VICTORIA, EBBW VALE, WALES
NP3 6FP
☎ (01495) 302 765. OPEN 9.30 - 5.30 MON -S AT, 11 - 5 SUN.
Famous branded products at direct from the mill prices. Towels, co-ordinated
bedlinen, duvets, pillows and curtains from Crown, Coloroll, Chortex,
Rectella together with bathroom and kitchen accessories. *Factory Shopping
Village*

PRICE'S CANDLES

MCARTHURGLEN DESIGNER OUTLET WALES THE DERWEN,
BRIDGEND, JUNCTION 35 OF M4, WALES CF31 1PF
☎ (01656) 767001. OPEN 10 - 6 MON - SAT, 8 ON THUR, 11 - 5 SUN.
Everything sold in this shop are seconds, which may be discoloured or have a
damaged pattern; discontinued sizes not available elsewhere; over-runs from
the garden selection or dinner candles in old packaging that has now been
replaced. There are church candles, lanterns, candles in pots and glass jars,
star-shaped candles, floating candles, candlestick holders, serviettes, scented
candles and garden torches. Some of the ceramic items are bought in. The village also has two restaurants, a small children's play area and free parking.
Factory Shopping Village

PYJAMA TOPS

HIGH STREET, BALA, WALES LL23 7AD
☎ (01678) 520348. OPEN 10.30 - 4.30 MON - SAT, EASTER TO OCTOBER.
Excellent selection of children's pyjamas, most of which are ends of lines from
shops such as BhS, Mothercare, Tesco, Woolworth's and Littlewoods, at savings of about 50%. Sizes range from six months to 13 years. Many of the pyjamas are character PJs with, for example, Postman Pat and Toy Story and
Barbie designs. *Permanent Discount Outlet*

REMINGTON

MCARTHURGLEN OUTLET VILLAGE, BRIDGEND, WALES CF32 9SU
☎ (01656) 766722. OPEN 10 - 6 MON - SAT, 8 ON THUR, 11 - 5 SUN.
Lots of famous names here from Oneida and Monogram cutlery to Braun,
Philips, Remington, Clairol, Wahl, Krups and Kenwood small kitchen equipment. It's a great place to buy gifts or replenish the kitchen equipment with
combi stylers, turbo travel plus hairdryers, air purifiers, liquidisers; food processors; batteries; clocks; and cutlery. Some of the packaging may be damaged but
the products are in perfect working order. For example, Silencio 1200 hairdryer, £11.99; Remington beard and moustache trimmer, £12.99; Oneida cutlery
44-piece set, £39.99; Braun Multi-mix, £42.99; Remington deep heat massager with infra red, £14.49; Wahl Compact comfort massager, £17.99.
Factory Shopping Village

Live Well On Less Tips
Buy cheaper cuts of meat and marinate them - just lengthen the amount of
time of marinating.

ROYAL WORCESTER & SPODE FACTORY SHOP

FESTIVAL PARK FACTORY OUTLET CENTRE, VICTORIA, EBBW VALE, GWENT WALES NP3 6FP

☎ (01495) 308155. OPEN 9.30 - 5.30 MON - SAT, 11 - 5 SUN.

THE MCARTHURGLEN DESIGNER OUTLET, THE DERWEN, BRIDGEND, WALES CF32 9SU

☎ FREEFONE 0800 171 800. OPEN 10 - 6 MON - WED, TILL 8 ON THUR, 10 - 6 FRI - SAT, 11 - 5 SUN.

Infinitesimally flawed porcelain and china seconds at 25% less than perfect prices. The Festival Park outlet stocks Mayflower, Langham Glass, Clover Leaf and Pimpernel table mats, Lakeland Plaques, Leeds Display and Paw Prints. There is a vast range with special offers throughout the year on anything from crystal decanters and bowls to figurines, cookware and dinner sets. Shipping arrangements worldwide can be organised. *Factory Shopping Village*

SECOND TO NONE

17 HIGH STREET, CHEPSTOW, MONMOUTHSHIRE, WALES NP6 5LG

☎ (01291) 622424. OPEN 9 - 5 MON - SAT, SOME BANK HOLS.

Established in the South West for twenty-six years, this company has built a reputation for giving excellent customer service and for selling goods which are of a quality and value that are Second to None! This chain of shops specialise in selling famous chainstore and branded clearing lines, which includes surplus stocks of branded goods such as Gossard, Berlei, Zorbit, Naturana and many more. They stock a large range of ladies and children's and baby wear (including baby bedding and accessories), some menswear, and an extensive range of underwear and nightwear for all the family. You can save up to 75% off recommended retail prices and they offer a seven-day money back guarantee. *Permanent Discount Outlet*

SECONDS AHEAD

19 PENDRE, CARDIGAN, CEREDIGION, WALES SA43 1DT

☎ (01239) 612721. OPEN 9.30 - 5.30 MON - FRI, 9 - 5.30 SAT.

Sells chainstore seconds in ladies, men's and childrenswear at discounted prices at ten shops throughout Wales. If you phone ☎ (01239) 621867, they will give you the address of your nearest branch. There are other branches in Wales at Haverford West, Milford Haven, Pembroke, Fishguard, Barry, Bridgend, Maesteg, Newtown, Newcastle Emlyn, Abergavenny, Welsh Pool, Leominster, Aberdere and Newport. Also at Shrewsbury, Gloucester, Street, Wellington and Ludlow. *Permanent Discount Outlet*

SECONDS OUT

58 GREAT DARKGATE STREET, ABERYSTWYTH, DYFED, WALES
☎ (01970) 611897. OPEN 9 - 5 MON - FRI, 9 - 4 SAT.
21 BROAD STREET, NEWTOWN, POWYS
☎ (01686) 624388. OPEN 9 - 5 MON - FRI, 9 - 4 SAT.
22 BROAD STREET, KNIGHTON, POWYS
☎ (01547) 520649. OPEN 9 - 5 MON - FRI, 9 - 4 SAT.
HIGH STREET, BUITH WELLS, POWYS
☎ (01982) 551043. OPEN 9 - 5 MON - FRI, 9 - 4 SAT.
Makes clothes - mainly trousers - for women, men and children, mostly for
department stores. The factory shop sells everything from jeans, £9-£13, to
school uniform items. Ladies summer trousers, £8.50; ladies and men's shorts,
from £8.50; mini Chinos, from £35; denim jackets, £16, usually £33.99;
men's sweaters from £12. *Factory Shop*

SLATERS MENSWEAR

116 ST MARY'S STREET, CARDIFF, WALES CF1 1DY
☎ (01222) 384186. OPEN 8.30 - 5.30 MON - SAT, 7.30 ON THUR.
Full range of men's clothes from underwear and shoes to casualwear, suits and
dresswear and including labels such as Odermark, Bulmer, Valentino, Charlie's
Co, and Charlton Gray. Men's suits from £79. *Permanent Discount Outlet*

STEWART'S

12 PIER STREET, ABERSTWYTH, CEREDIGION, WALES SY23 2LJ
☎ (01970) 611437. OPEN 9 - 5.30 MON - SAT, 10.30 - 4.30 SUN IN
SUMMER.
14 NOTTS SQUARE, CAMARTHEN, CAMARTHENSHIRE SA31 3PQ
☎ (01267) 222294. OPEN 9 - 5.30 MON - SAT.
HARFORD SQUARE, LAMPETER, CEREDIGION SA48 7HD
☎ (01570) 422205. OPEN 9.30 - 5.30 MON - SAT.
52 STEPNEY STREET, LLANELLI, CAMARTHENSHIRE SA15 3TR
☎ (01554) 776957. OPEN 9 - 5 MON - SAT.
Y MAES, PWLLHELI, GWYNEDD LL53 5HG
☎ (01758) 701130. OPEN 9 - 5.30 MON - SAT.
UNIT 4, BETHEL SQUARE SHOPPING CENTRE, BRECON, POWYS
LD3 7HU
☎ (01874) 610260. OPEN 9 - 6 MON - SAT.
GLAMORE TERRACE, NEW QUAY, CEREDIGION SA45 9PL
☎ (01545) 560740. OPEN 9.30 - 5.30 MON - SAT, 10 - 5.30 SUN.
THE STRAND, SAUNDERSFOOT, PEMBROKESHIRE SA69 9GE.
☎ (01834) 812579. OPEN 9 - 5.30 MON - SAT, 10 - 5.30 SUN.
THE HIGH STREET, TENBY, PEMBROKESHIRE SA70 7EW
☎ (01834) 844621. OPEN 9.30 - 5.30 MON - SAT, 10 - 5.30 SUN.
BREWERY TERRACE, SAUNDERSFOOT, DYFED SA69 9HG.
☎ (01834) 812579. OPEN 9.30 - 5.30 SEVEN DAYS A WEEK.

144 HIGH STREET, PORTHMADOG, GWYNEDD LL49 9NU

☎ (01766) 514166. OPEN 9 - 5.30 MON - SAT, 11 - 4 SUN.

228-230 OXFORD STREET, SWANSEA

☎ (01792) 410906. OPEN 9.30 - 5.30 MON - SAT.

7-11 MONNOW STREET, MONMOUTH, MONMOUTHSIRE

☎ (01600) 716926. OPEN 9.30 - 5.30 MON - SAT.

79A TAFF STREET, PONTYPRIDD, MID GLAMORGAN CF37 4SU

☎ (01443) 402225. OPEN 9.30 - 5.30 MON - SAT.

23 MOSTYN STREET, LLANDUDNO, GWYNEDD LL30 2NL

☎ (01492) 870733. OPEN 9.30 - 5.30 MON - SAT.

4 CARDIFF ROD, Y TWYN, CAERPHILLY, MID GLAMORGAN CF8 1JN

☎ (01222) 888054. OPEN 9.30 - 5.30 MON - SAT.

12 PIER STREET, ABERYSTWYTH, CEREDIGION SY23 2LJ.

☎ (01970) 611437. OPEN 9.30 - 5.30 MON - SAT.

MARLAS ROAD, PYLECROSS, NR BRIDGEND CF 33 6AY.

☎ (01656) 744988. OPEN 9.30 - 5.30 MON - SAT.

Branded merchandise from most of the major UK chain stores, all well-known high street department store names, offered at a discount of 40%-70% off normal high street prices. The garments are selected with great care by experienced buyers direct from factories worldwide to bring customers top quality merchandise at highly competitive prices. *Factory Shop*

STUART CRYSTAL

BRIDGE STREET, CHEPSTOW, MONMOUTHSIRE, WALES NP16 5EZ

☎ (01291) 620135. OPEN 9 - 5 MON - SAT APRIL - SEPTEMBER, 10 - 5 OCTOBER - MARCH, 11 - 5 SUN.

Opposite the castle with its handy car park, this large factory shop also has a coffee shop on site. It sells Waterford crystal and Arthur Price cutlery and giftware. There is a crystal gift engraving service and chip repair service, display of old china and picnic area. *Factory Shop*

THE ABBEY WOOLLEN MILLS

MUSEUM SQUARE, MARITIME QUARTER, SWANSEA, WALES SA1 1SN

☎ (01792) 650351. OPEN 10 - 5 TUE - SUN, CLOSED MON EXCEPT FOR BANK HOLIDAYS.

Housed in the Swansea maritime and industrial museum because its products are woven on the restored nineteenth century looms housed in the museum. The mills specialise in pure wool shawls, rugs and blankets, which are sold at discounts of one third off the normal retail price, with occasional seconds selling at half price. Scarves start at £4.99, picnic rugs from £14-£20, large throwS 100 x 70, £35 in various colours and patterns. Savings can be as much as 50% off retail price. There is a small tea room open from Easter to the end of September. *Permanent Discount Outlet*

THE CURTAIN EXCHANGE

17 MOSTYN AVENUE, CRAIG-Y-DON, LLANDUDNO, WALES LL30 1YS
☎ (01492) 875532. OPEN 10 - 5 MON - SAT, CLOSED EARLY WED.

The Curtain Exchange is a franchised group of shops selling beautiful top quality secondhand curtains, blinds, pelmets, etc at between one-third and one half of the brand new price. Their stock comes from a variety of sources: people who are moving house and dislike the drapes in their new home; people who are moving house and want to sell their old curtains to help with the bills; show houses, where the builder wants to recoup some of his outgoings; interior designers' mistakes. Stock changes constantly and ranges from rich brocades, damasks and velvets to chintzes, linens and cottons. Designer names include Colefax & Fowler, Designers Guild, Laura Ashley, Warner, Sanderson, Osborne & Little, Fortuny and Bennison. A team of fitters and alteration experts are available if required. They offer a 24-hour availability. The Curtain Exchange also supply bespoke ranges with samples of curtains hanging. These fabrics are chosen from suppliers all over the world and are an excellent buy. *Secondhand Shop*

THE FACTORY SHOP LTD

UNIT 30, FESTIVAL PARK FACTORY OUTLET SHOPPING CENTRE, VICTORIA, EBBW VALE, GWENT, WALES NP3 6FP
☎ (01495) 352533. OPEN 10 - 6 MON - SAT, 10 - 4 SUN.
SNOWDROP LANE, HAVERFORDWEST, PEMBROKESHIRE, WALES SA61 1ET
☎ (01437) 766000. OPEN 9 - 5.30 MON - SAT, 10.30 - 4.30 SUN.

Wide range on sale includes men's, ladies and children's clothing and footwear; household textiles; electricals; toiletries; hardware; luggage; lighting, Cape Country Furniture and bedding, most of which are chainstore and high street brands at discounts of approximately 30%-50%. There are weekly deliveries and brands include many major stars such as Adidas, Nike, Wrangler and Dartington, to name just a few. There are kitchen and furniture displays and a new line in Cape Country furniture on sale. Ranges are continually changing and few factory shops offer such a variety under one roof. There is a free car park. The Ebbw Vale shop is part of Wales first factory outlet centre with a host of brand concessions in clothing and homeware plus restaurants. The telephone number given here is for the centre. *Factory Shopping Village*

Live Well On Less Tips

When travelling in the UK, instead of spending a fortune on a hotel room, check out the local university accommodation during holiday time. It's usually self catering and incredibly cheap.

THORN OUTLET

MCARTHURGLEN DESIGNER OUTLET WALES THE DERWEN,
BRIDGEND, JUNCTION 35 OF M4, WALES CF32 9SU

☎ (01656) 655686. OPEN 10 - 6 MON - SAT, 8 ON THUR, 11 - 5 SUN.

Sells Russell Hobbs kettles, Philips toasters, Sony and Sanyo sound systems,
Ferguson tvs and video recorders, Scalextric sets, Sony Walkmans and video
tapes. All products are sold at a minimum of 30% off high street prices. For
example, ex-rental TVs and video recorders can be bought for as little as £69;
new 21-inch sets, £189, compared with high street price of £270. Stock
changes constantly with new ranges being added. *Factory Shopping Village*

THORNTONS

MCARTHURGLEN OUTLET CENTRE, BRIDGEND, GLAMORGAN, WALES
CF32 9BU

☎ (01656) 657104. OPEN 10 - 6 MON - SAT, 8 ON THUR, 11 - 5 SUN.

FESTIVAL PARK FACTORY SHOPPING CENTRE, VICTORIA, EBBW VALE,
GWENT NP3 6FP

☎ (01495) 305099. OPEN 10 - 6 MON - SAT, 11 - 5 SUN.

The UK's leading specialist confectionery retailer has more than 500 shops and
franchises nationwide selling a wide range of boxed and loose, chocolate and
sugar confectionery. The factory outlets sell three different categories: misshapes.
discounted lines and standard lines. Misshapes are loose chocolates which are
the result of new product development, product trials or end of production runs
which cannot be packed as Thorntons standard lines. They are packed into
assorted bags and offer a saving of 35%-55% over the recommended retail price
of standard loose line products. Discounted lines are excess to Thorntons' normal retail requirements and can be as a result of excess seasonal or export stock,
discontinued lines or packaging changes. These products, when available, are
offered at a discount of 25%-50% over the standard retail price. Standard lines
from the full Thorntons range are also on sale at normal prices. *Factory
Shopping Village*

TK MAXX

UNIT 25, GREYFRIARS SHOPPING CENTRE, BLUE STREET,
CARMARTHEN, WALES

☎ (01267) 220934. OPEN 9 - 5.30 MON, TUE, 9 - 6 WED, FRI, SAT, 9 - 8
THUR, 10 - 4 SUN.

QUEENS WEST SHOPPING CENTRE, CARDIFF

☎ (01222) 341290. OPEN 9 - 5.30 MON, TUE, 9 - 6 WED, FRI, SAT,
9 - 8 THUR, 11 - 5 SUN.

Based on an American concept, TK Maxx is situated in easily accessible, often
centrally located stores and offers famous label goods with up to 60% savings
off recommended retail prices. TK Maxx has fashion for the whole family -
women's, men's and childrenswear - accessories, shoes, gifts, kitchenware and

home goods. Everything in the store is branded with a choice of well-known high street names to designer labels, and while a small percentage might be clearly marked past season, the great majority of items in store are current season, current stock and still with phenomenal savings. There is a huge choice with 50,000 pieces in store and up to 10,000 new items arriving a week. The stores are simple and unfussy with wide aisles, shopping trolleys and baskets, and a spacious, functional feel to them but there are individual changing rooms, ramps for buggies and wheelchairs and plenty of staff on the shop floor. Every branch accepts all major credit and debit cards and has a liberal refund and return policy. *Permanent Discount Outlet*

TOG 24

UNIT 87, MCARTHURGLEN DESIGNER OUTLET VILLAGE, BRIDGEND, JUNCTION 35 OF M4, MID GLAMORGAN, WALES CF32 9SU
☎ (01656) 767033. OPEN 10 - 6 MON - FRI, 8 ON THUR, 9 - 6 SAT, 11 - 5 SUN.
FESTIVAL PARK OUTLET CENTRE, VICTORIA, EBBW VALE, GWENT
☎ (01495) 301902. OPEN 10 - 6 MON - SAT, 11 - 5 SUN.
Tog 24 are the UK's fastest growing brand name in outdoor clothing and leisurewear, with a total of three UK factories and 36 stores nationwide. They utilise the world's finest performance fabrics including Gore-Tex, Polartec and Burlington macs. Catering for all the family for all seasons, with cosy fleeces and waterproofs for the winter, and trekking ranges, shorts and t-shirts for the summer. With all prices at least 30% below the recommended retail price you can afford to enter the Tog comfort zone. *Factory Shopping Village*

TOGS

6 MONNOW STREET, MONMOUTH, WALES NP25 3EE
☎ (01600) 772629. OPEN 9.30 - 5 MON - SAT.
Wide range of casual wear for women at competitive prices, including labels such as Viz-A-Viz, Adini and Chilli Pepper. Sizes range from 10 - 18 for women. All items are perfects and current fashion. Prices start from £10. *Permanent Discount Outlet*

TOM SAYERS CLOTHING CO

FESTIVAL SHOPPING CENTRE, VICTORIA ROAD, EBBW VALE, WALES NP3 6AU
☎ (01495) 301414. OPEN 9.30 - 5.30 MON - SAT, 11 - 5 SUN.
Tom Sayers make sweaters for some of the top high street department stores. Unusually for a factory shop, if they don't stock your size, they will try and order it for you from their factory or one of their other factory outlets and send it to you. Most of the stock here is overstock, cancelled orders or last season's and includes jumpers, trousers and shirts at discounts of 30%. The trousers and shirts are bought in to complement the sweaters which they make. *Factory Shop*

TRAVEL ACCESSORY OUTLET

UNIT 23, WELSH DESIGNER OUTLET VILLAGE, PEN-Y-CAE, BRIDGEND, WALES CF32 9ST

☎ (01656) 767770.

Luggage and travel-related products including executive cases, handbags, umbrellas and accessories available in leading brands such as Samsonite, Brics, Hidesign, Globe Trotter and Tula. The products also include couture and high fashion brands such as YSL and Moschino. All products are offered at a considerably reduced price due to their being production over-runs, last season's stock of slight seconds (ie they have minor aesthetic blemishes). *Factory Shopping Village*

TREFRIW WOOLLEN MILLS LTD

TREFRIW, CONWAY COUNTY, WALES LL27 ONQ

☎ (01492) 640462. OPEN 9.30 - 5 MON - FRI, 10 - 5 SAT.

Sells products manufactured on the premises: traditional Welsh tapestry bedspreads from £78, travel rugs, mohair rugs, wool, tweed fabrics from £14.45 a metre, tapestries, mohair coats; tweed sports jackets, ruanas and knitting wool at £2.80 per 100g. *Factory Shop*

TWEEDMILL FACTORY SHOPPING LTD

LLANNERCH PARK, ST ASAPH, DENBIGHSHIRE, (OFF A55), WALES LL17 OUY

☎ (01745) 730072. OPEN 9.30 - 6 MON - SAT, 11 - 5 SUN.

HAS A WIDE RANGE OF CLOTHES for both men and women with savings of up to 50% off normal high street prices. Selling directly to the public from the manufacturers, there are always at least, 30,000 garments in stock. Labels for men include James Barry, Wolsey, Double Two, Ralph Lauren and Hyde Park Leathers. For women, there is Feminella, Roman Originals, Silhouette and Klass. Everything has the original retail price on it so you can see the discounts of up to 50%. *Factory Shop*

VELMORE LTD

1-2 JAEGER HOUSE, 141 HOLT ROAD, WREXHAM, CLWYD, WALES LL13 9DY

☎ (01978) 363456. OPEN 10.30 - 3 MON, WED, FRI.

Overmakes and seconds of skirts, dresses, suits, jackets and trousers originally made for the most famous high street name at very cheap prices. *Factory Shop*

VIYELLA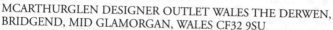

MCARTHURGLEN WELSH DESIGNER OUTLET VILLAGE, PEN-Y-CAR
LANE, BRIDGEND, JUNCTION 35 OF M4, WALES CF32 9ST
☎ (01656) 648660. OPEN 10 - 6 MON FRI, 8 THUR, FRI, 9 - 6 SAT, 11 - 5
SUN.
Wide range of Viyella ladieswear at discount prices of 30% from jackets and
blouses to sweaters and hats. *Factory Shopping Village*

WHITTARD

MCARTHURGLEN DESIGNER OUTLET WALES THE DERWEN,
BRIDGEND, MID GLAMORGAN, WALES CF32 9SU
☎ (01656) 658434. OPEN 10 - 6 MON - SAT, 8 ON THUR, 11 - 5 SUN.
Sells tea, coffee, coffee-making equipment (cafetieres and stove-top espressos),
wide range of china, colourful tableware, corkscrews, cutlery, trays, bins,
kitchen containers at discount prices. *Factory Shopping Village*

Live Well On Less Tips
Get free contraception from your family planning clinic rather than paying for
it over the counter at the chemist.

Northern Ireland

WOMENSWEAR ONLY Bairdwear Ladieswear, *Bangor.*
Cancer Research Campaign, *Newtownards.* Discount Dressing, *Belfast.*
Jeremiah Ambler (Ulster) Ltd, *Carrickfergus.* The Elliott Designer Sale Store, *Hillsborough.*

WOMENSWEAR & MENSWEAR   Adria Ltd, *Strabane.*
Desmond & Son Ltd, *Londonderry.* Hawks Bay Apparel, *Newtownards.* Linian Knitwear, *Castlederg.*
Lotus Ltd, *Banbridge.* Paul Costelloe Factory Store, *Dungannon.*
The Courtaulds Factory Shop, *Lurgan.* The Factory Shop, *Craigavon.*
The Factory Shop Outlet, *Randalstown.* The Factory Shop Outlet, *Craigavon.*
The Factory Shop Outlet, *Maydown.* TK Maxx, *Belfast.*

CHILDREN Adria Ltd, *Strabane.* Cancer Research Campaign, *Newtownards.*
Desmond & Son Ltd, *Londonderry.* Hawks Bay Apparel, *Newtownards.* Linian Knitwear, *Castlederg.*
The Courtaulds Factory Shop, *Lurgan.* The Factory Shop, *Craigavon.*
The Factory Shop Outlet, *Randalstown.* The Factory Shop Outlet, *Craigavon.*
The Factory Shop Outlet, *Maydown.* TK Maxx, *Belfast.*

HOUSEHOLD AND GIFTWARE Desmond & Son Ltd, *Londonderry.*
Oneida, *Bangor.* Spoils, *Belfast.* The Courtaulds Factory Shop, *Lurgan.*
The Factory Shop, *Craigavon.* The Factory Shop Outlet, *Randalstown.*
The Factory Shop Outlet, *Craigavon.* The Factory Shop Outlet, *Maydown.* TK Maxx, *Belfast.*
Tyrone Crystal Ltd, *Dungannon.* Ulster Weavers, *Belfast.*

DIY/RENOVATION Alexander the Grate, *Belfast.*
Wilsons Conservation Buildings Products Ireland, *Dromore.*

ARCHITECTURAL SALVAGE Alexander the Grate, *Belfast.*
Wilsons Conservation Buildings Products Ireland, *Dromore.*

SPORTSWEAR AND EQUIPMENT Octopus Sportswear MFG Ltd, *Strabane.*

ADRIA LTD
BEECHMOUNT AVENUE, MELMONT ROAD, STRABANE, COUNTY
TYRONE
☎ (01504) 382568. OPEN 9 - 5 MON - FRI, 9 - 2 SAT.
CARNBANE INDUSTRIAL ESTATE, NEWRY, CO DOWN,
☎ (01693) 254448
Manufacturer of tights and socks for Marks & Spencer, this shop sells hosiery
which consists of Marks & Spencer seconds, Charnos lingerie, seconds in
menswear, children's and women's clothes. Seconds in tights cost 45p.
Factory Shop

ALEXANDER THE GRATE
126-128 DONEGAL PASS, BELFAST, NORTHERN IRELAND BT7 1BZ
☎ (01232) 232041. OPEN 10 - 5 MON - SAT.
A specialist in antique fireplaces, as well as leaded windows, doors and general architectural salvage. There is also garden furniture in the spring and summer. The owner also runs an antiques market on the first floor of the same premises every Saturday from 9.30 - 5 with 16 different stallholders.
Architectural Salvage

BAIRDWEAR LADIESWEAR

CLANDEBOYE ROAD, BANGOR, COUNTY DOWN, NORTHERN IRELAND BT20 3JJ

☎ (01247) 270415. OPEN 9.30 - 4.30 MON - FRI, 9 - 12.30 SAT.

ANN STREET, NEWTOWNARDS, COUNTY DOWN, NORTHERN IRELAND BT23 3AQ

☎ (01247) 819502. OPEN 10 - 4.15 MON - SAT.

Manufacturers for well-known high street chainstores for more than 20 years, Bairdwear has a wide selection of seconds and overmakes in its factory shops for women. This can cover anything from underwear and lingerie to jackets, suits, coats and blouses but stock changes constantly. Most shops carry about 80% of stock manufactured on the premises and 20% of other products manufactured within the group. *Factory Shop*

CANCER RESEARCH CAMPAIGN

50 HIGH STREET, NEWTOWNARDS, COUNTY DOWN, NORTHERN IRELAND BT23 3HZ

☎ (01247) 820268. OPEN 9 - 5 MON - SAT.

Charity shop with a difference. Ground floor sells everything that you would expect to find in aush a shop. The first floor caters specifically for the bridal market and sells or hires wedding dresses, bridesmaids dresses and pageboy outfits, with accessories. All of the stock is donated by the public or the manufacturers. *Dress Agency*

DESMOND & SONS LTD

THE MAIN STREET, CLAUDY, LONDONDERRY, NORTHERN IRELAND BT47 3SD

☎ (01504) 338441. OPEN 10 - 5 MON - SAT.

KEVLIN ROAD, OMAGH

☎ (01662) 241560. OPEN 10 - 5 MON - SAT.

MILL STREET, ENNISKILLEN

☎ (01365) 325467. OPEN 10 - 5 MON - SAT.

BALLYQUINN ROAD, DUNGIVEN

☎ (01504) 742068. OPEN 10 - 5 MON - SAT.

31 GARVAGH ROAD, SWATRAGH

☎ (01648) 401639. OPEN 10 - 5 MON - SAT.

Large range of men's, women's and childrenswear including trousers, jeans, plain and round-neck lambswool and cotton sweaters, nightwear and knitwear. Most of the stock is seconds and is sold at discounts of one third. They also buy in some imperfects of household items such as handtowels and bath towels which are sold at competitive prices. *Factory Shop*

DISCOUNT DRESSING

70 BLOOMFIELD AVENUE, BELFAST, NORTHERN IRELAND BT5 5AE

☎ (01232) 738853. OPEN 9.30 - 5.30 MON - SAT.

A veritable Aladdin's Cave of designer bargains, Discount Dressing sells mostly German, Italian and French designer labels at prices at least 50% and up to 90% below those in normal retail outlets. All items are brand new and perfect. A team of buyers all over Europe purchase stock directly from the manufacturer for this growing chain of discount shops. This enables Discount Dressing to by-pass the importers and wholesalers and, of course, their mark-up. They also buy bankrupt stock in this country. Their agreement with their suppliers means that they are not able to advertise brand names for obvious reasons, but they are all well-known for their top quality and style. So confident is Discount Dressing that you will be unable to find the same item cheaper elsewhere, that they guarantee to give the outfit to you free of charge should you perform this miracle. Merchandise includes raincoats, dresses, suits, trousers, blouses, evening wear, special occasion outfits and jackets, in sizes 6-24 and in some cases larger. GDD readers can obtain a further 10% discount if they visit the shop taking a copy of this book with them. There are other branches in Lincolnshire, London, Hertfordshire, East Yorkshire and Derbyshire. *Permanent Discount Outlet*

HAWKES BAY APPAREL

16 COMBER ROAD, NEWTOWNARDS, COUNTY DOWN, NORTHERN IRELAND BT23 4HY

☎ (01247) 800200. OPEN 9.30 - 5.30 MON, TUE, WED, 9.30 - 8.30 THUR, FRI, 9.30 - 5.30 SAT.

Men's, women's and children's own-brand jeans, jackets, T-shirts, hats, and sweatshirts at 30%-50% savings. Also childrenswear, Adidas sportswear and casual men's and ladieswear at competitive prices from designers such as Calvin Klein, Versace and Armani. *Factory Shop*

JEREMIAH AMBLER (ULSTER) LTD

BARN MILLS, TAYLOR AVENUE, CARRICKFERGUS, COUNTY ANTRIM, NORTHERN IRELAND BT38 7HQ

☎ (019603) 61011. OPEN 11 - 1 AND 2 - 4 MON - FRI. ALSO MAIL ORDER.

Hand-knitting wools, especially mohair at 30%- 50% less than retail. Also wool fabric and accessories including rugs, and travel rugs. *Factory Shop*

LINIAN KNITWEAR

SPAMOUNT MILLS, CASTLEDERG, CO TYRONE, NORTHERN IRELAND BT81 7NB

☎ (016626) 71181. OPEN 9.30 - 5 MON - SAT.

Irish woollens, knitted on the premises, seconds of which are sold in the factory shop. Ends of lines and last season's garments are sold at up to 50% dis-

> *Live Well On Less Tips*
> Shop on a full stomach, not an empty one and you'll be far less likely to buy foods impulsively.

counts against normal prices. *Factory Shop*

LOTUS LTD

34 BRIDGE STREET, BANBRIDGE, COUNTY DOWN.
NORTHERN IRELAND BT32 3JL
☎ (018206) 22480. OPEN 9 - 5.30 MON - SAT.
This manufacturer for well-known chainstores sells all sizes and styles of Lotus shoes - from smart fashion shoes to walking shoes - at discounted prices for discontinued lines and rejects. Prices from £20 - £50 for men's shoes and from £12 - £35 for women's shoes. They also have a bridal shoe department with prices from £25 and a range of matching handbags. *Factory Shop*

OCTOPUS SPORTSWEAR MFG LTD

UNIT 1, DUBLIN ROAD INDUSTRIAL ESTATE, STRABANE, COUNTY TRYONE, NORTHERN IRELAND BT82 9EA
☎ (01504) 882320. OPEN 8.30 - 5.30 MON - FRI.
Manufactures own-brand sportswear: shorts, jerseys, socks, pants, hooded tops, sweatshirts and sell seconds and clearance lines at discounts of up 50%-75%. *Factory Shop*

ONEIDA

BALLOO SOUTH INDUSTRIAL ESTATE, ENTERPRISE ROAD, BANGOR, COUNTY DOWN
NORTHERN IRELAND BT19 7TA
☎ (01247) 474747. OPEN 10 - 5 MON - FRI.
Oneida is the world's largest cutlery company and originates from the United States of America. This shop is attached to the warehouse and sells ends of ranges and discontinued lines as well as cancelled orders of cutlery, silver and silver plate at discounts of between 30% and 75%. *Factory Shopping Village*

PAUL COSTELLOE FACTORY STORE

THE WORKSHOP, 9 LINEN GREEN, MAIN ROAD, MOYGASHEL, DUNGANNON, COUNTY TYRONE, NORTHERN IRELAND BT71 7HB
☎ (01868) 753867. OPEN 9.30 - 5.30 MON - SAT.
A wide range of 1,500 garments, consisting of special purchases, seconds, samples and past season stocks at substantial savings on original prices. The comprehensive selection encompasses business and special occasion designs and menswear as well as a more casual range for relaxed weekend wear. *Factory Shop*

SPOILS

UNITS 55, 56, 57, CASTLE COURT SHOPPING CENTRE, BELFAST, NORTHERN IRELAND BT1 1DD

☎ (01232) 328512. OPEN 9.30 - 6 MON - SAT, 9 ON THUR, 1 - 6 SUN.

General domestic glassware, non-stick bakeware, kitchen gadgets, ceramic oven-to-tableware, textiles, cutting boards, aluminium non-stick cookware, bakeware, plastic kitchenware, plastic storage, woodware, coffee pots/makers, furniture, mirrors and picture frames. Rather than being discounted, all the merchandise is very competitively priced - in fact, the company carry out competitors' checks frequently in order to monitor pricing. With 38 branches, the company is able to buy in bulk and thus negotiate very good prices. *Permanent Discount Outlet*

THE COURTAULDS FACTORY SHOP

PORTADOWN ROAD, LURGAN, COUNTY ARMAGH, NORTHERN IRELAND BT66 8RB

☎ (01762) 316747. OPEN 9.30 - 6 MON - FRI, UNTIL 8 ON THUR, 9 - 6 SAT, 12 - 6 SUN.

Sells a wide range of ladies, men's and childrens high street fashions at between 30% and 50% below high street prices. Also stocks a wide range of household textiles, shoes and accessories. *Factory Shop*

THE ELLIOTT DESIGNER SALE STORE

10 MAIN STREET, HILLSBOROUGH, COUNTY DOWN, NORTHERN IRELAND BT26 6AE

☎ (01846) 689992. OPEN 10 - 5 MON - SAT.

Sells brand new designer clothes from some of the best known names at very competitive prices. Labels include Ramsay of Dublin, Gerard Darel, Philippe Adec, Caractere, Anne Storey, as well as other designers from time to time. There are skirts, blouses, dresses, sweaters, waistcoats, coats and jackets, and traditional knitwear, including Arran and some jewellery. Sizes range from 8-18. Also stocks, in nearby premises, Egyptian cotton bedlinen, towels, cushions, bedroom and bathroom accessories and gift items. *Permanent Discount Outlet*

THE FACTORY SHOP

EWART LIDDELL, CV HOME FURNISHINGS LTD, 53 MAIN STREET, CRAIGAVON, DONAGHCLONEY, CRAIGAVON, COUNTY ARMAGH, NORTHERN IRELAND BT66 7LX

☎ (01762) 882923. OPEN 10 - 4.30 M ON - SAT, 1 - 6 SUN, 10 - 4 BANK HOLS.

Part of the Coats Viyella group, which makes quality clothing for many of the major high street storres, overstocks and clearance lines are sold through more than 30 of the group's factory shops. Many of you will recognise the garments on sale, despite the lack of well-known labels. Ladieswear includes dresses, blouses, jumpers, cardigans, trousers, nightwear, underwear, lingerie, hosiery, coats and swimwear. Menswear includes trousers, belts, shirts, ties, pullovers, cardigans, T-shirts, underwear, nightwear, hosiery and jackets. Childrenswear includes jackets, trousers, T-shirts, underwear, hosiery, jumpers and babywear. Also superb quality table linen and towels. There are regular deliveries to constantly update the range *Factory Shop*

THE FACTORY SHOP OUTLET

CV HOME FURNISHINGS, 36 MAGHERALANE ROAD, RANDALSTOWN, COUNTY ANTRIM, NORTHERN IRELAND BT41 2NT

☎ (01849) 444102. OPEN 9 - 4.30 MON - SAT.
53 MAIN STREET, DONAGHCLONEY, CRAIGAVON,
CO ARMAGH BT66 7LX

☎ (01762) 882923. OPEN 10 - 4.30 MON - SAT.
CV HOME FURNISHINGS, MAYDOWN INDUSTRIAL ESTATE, CARROWKEEL DRIVE, MAYDOWN, LONDONDERRY BT47 6UQ

☎ (01504) 852108. OPEN 9 - 4.30 MON - SAT, 1 - 5 SUN.
CV CLOTHING, GLENADEN FACTORY, TRENCH ROAD,
LONDONDERRY BT47 2US

☎ (01504) 311529. OPEN 12.30 - 2.30 MON - THURS, 10.15 - 1 FRI.
Part of the Coats Viyella group, which makes quality clothing for many of the major high street storres, overstocks and clearance lines are sold through more than 30 of the group's factory shops. Many of you will recognise the garments on sale, despite the lack of well-known labels. Ladieswear includes dresses, blouses, jumpers, cardigans, trousers, nightwear, underwear, lingerie, hosiery, coats and swimwear. Menswear includes trousers, belts, shirts, ties, pullovers, cardigans, T-shirts, underwear, nightwear, hosiery and jackets. Childrenswear includes jackets, trousers, T-shirts, underwear, hosiery, jumpers and babywear. There is also a range of quality towels. There are regular deliveries to constantly update the range. *Factory Shop*

Live Well On Less Tips
Grow your own herbs rather than buying from supermarkets. If you haven't got a garden, grow in pots on the windowsill.

TK MAXX

FIRST FLOOR, CASTLECOURT SHOPPING CENTRE, BELFAST,
NORTHERN IRELAND BT1 1DD

☎ (01232) 331151. OPEN 9 - 5.30 MON - SAT, 1 - 6 SUN.

Based on an American concept, TK Maxx is situated in easily accessible, often centrally located stores and offers famous label goods with up to 60% savings off recommended retail prices. TK Maxx has fashion for the whole family - women's, men's and childrenswear - accessories, shoes, gifts, kitchenware and home goods. Everything in the store is branded with a choice of well-known high street names to designer labels, and while a small percentage might be clearly marked past season, the great majority of items in store are current season, current stock and still with phenomenal savings. There is a huge choice with 50,000 pieces in store and up to 10,000 new items arriving a week. The stores are simple and unfussy with wide aisles, shopping trolleys and baskets, and a spacious, functional feel to them but there are individual changing rooms, ramps for buggies and wheelchairs and plenty of staff on the shop floor. Every branch accepts all major credit and debit cards and has a liberal refund and return policy. *Permanent Discount Outlet*

TYRONE CRYSTAL LTD

KILLYBRACKEY, DUNGANNON, COUNTY TYRONE, NORTHERN
IRELAND BT71 6TT

☎ (018687) 25335. OPEN 9 - 5 MON - SAT. MAIL ORDER.

Factory shop selling the full range of Tyrone crystal including non-current range items discounted by up to thirty percent off normal retail prices and slight imperfects discounted by up to forty percent. *Factory Shop*

ULSTER WEAVERS

44 MONTGOMERY ROAD, CASTLEREAGH, BELFAST, NORTHERN
IRELAND BT6 9QZ

☎ (01232) 404236. OPEN 9.30 - 5 MON - SAT.

Ulster Weaver products at discounts of 20% as well as quality giftware from all corners of Ireland. *Factory Shop*

WILSONS CONSERVATION
BUILDINGS PRODUCTS IRELAND

123 HILLSBOROUGH ROAD, DROMORE, COUNTY DOWN, NORTHERN
IRELAND BT25 1QW

☎ (01846) 692304. OPEN 8 - 5 MON - FRI, 8 - 12 SAT.

Reclaimed timber, slates, pine beams, radiators, cast iron fireplaces with pine and marble surrounds, chimney pots, quarry tiles and bricks. *Architectural Salvage*

Channel Islands

WOMENSWEAR ONLY Cinderella's Wardrobe, St Helier, Jersey. Stonelake Ltd, St Peter Port, Guernsey. The Frock Exchange, St Helier, Jersey.

WOMENSWEAR & MENSWEAR Cameleon, St Helier, Jersey.

CHILDREN Summerland Factory Shop, St Helier, Jersey. Summerland Factory Shop, Gorey, Jersey. Summerland Factory Shop, Guernsey.

HOUSEHOLD AND GIFTWARE Stonelake Ltd, St Peter Port, Guernsey.

FURNITURE/SOFT FURNISHINGS Cameleon, St Helier, Jersey. The Fabric Factory, St Helier, Jersey.

CAMELEON

65 NEW ST, ST HELIER, JERSEY, CHANNEL ISLANDS JE2 3RA
☎ (01534) 722438. OPEN 10 - 5 TUE - SAT.
An interesting fashion agency for men and women covering high street and designer labels, including accessories. A blend of old and new, Cameleon also stocks vintage clothing and collectables, and a curtain agency has now been started. Madhatters new hats are available in stock and to order. *Dress Agency*

CINDERELLA'S WARDROBE

10 CONWAY ST, ST HELIER, JERSEY, CHANNEL ISLANDS JE2 3NT
☎ (01534) 618545. OPEN 10 - 5.30 MON - SAT.
Sells nearly-new and new designer outfits, shoes, hats and accessories. Labels are top quality: Maxmara, Ralph Lauren, Louis Feraud, Escada, Chanel, Byblos and Krizia. *Dress Agency*

STONELAKE LTD

5 SMITH STREET, ST PETER PORT, GUERNSEY, CHANNEL ISLANDS GY1 2JN
☎ (01481) 720053. FAX 0148 713808. OPEN 9 - 5.15 MON - SAT. MAIL ORDER AVAILABLE.
Family-run business which has operated in Guernsey for more than 80 years serving both locals and tourists alike. In recent years, they have added a mail order service. They have two shops - one a pharmacy and perfumery, the other selling perfumery and cosmetics - and specialise in fragrance bargains from UK and French companies, in aftershaves, cosmetics, perfumes, toilet waters, soaps, and talcs. Being duty-free, and with no VAT, they have competitive prices on standard ranges and by buying excess stocks and ends of lines, they have a large list of extra special offers including ranges no longer sold in the UK. Brand names stocked include YSL, Elizabeth Taylor, Paloma Picasso,

Cacharel, Boss, Georgio, Paco Rabanne, Gucci, Safari, Elizabeth Arden, Givenchy, Oscar de la Renta, Nina Ricci, and Roc cosmetics. Free postage and packaging on mail orders over £40. *Permanent Discount Outlet*

SUMMERLAND FACTORY SHOP

GOREY WOOLLEN MILL, GOREY, JERSEY, CHANNEL ISLANDS
☎ (01534) 858024. OPEN 9 - 5.30 MON - FRI, 9.30 - 4.30 SAT, 10 - 5 SUN IN SUMMER.
ST AUBINS WOOLLEN MILL, JERSEY
☎ (01534) 445043. OPEN 9 - 5.30 MON - FRI, 9 - 4.30 SAT, 10 - 5 SUN.
INTERNATIONAL HOUSE, THE PARADE, ST HELIER, JERSEY
☎ (01534) 625698. OPEN 9 - 5.30 MON - SAT, IN SUMMER WEEKDAY EVENINGS 7.30 - 9.30.
NORTH ESPLANADE, GUERNSEY
☎ (01481) 701336. OPEN 9 - 5.30 MON - SAT.
Sells a large range of men's and ladies wear at factory direct prices. The ladies range includes underwear, skirts, blouses, classic and fashon knitwear and footwear. The men's range includes underwear, shirts, silk ties, trousers, knitwear, casual shirts and footwear. Labels sold include Wolsey, Jockey, Baumler, Peter England, Pierre Balmain and Pierre Cardin at discounts of up to 50%. *Factory Shop*

THE FABRIC FACTORY

35 HILGROVE STREET, ST HELIER, JERSEY, CHANNEL ISLANDS JE2 4SL
☎ (01534) 39551. OPEN 9 - 5.30 MON - SAT.
The Fabric Factory sells dress and furnishing fabrics at discounted prices. All stock is regular, not ends of lines, and they also sell tracks, poles, and offer a made-to-measure service. *Factory Shop*

THE FROCK EXCHANGE

CHEAPSIDE, ST HELIER, JERSEY, CHANNEL ISLANDS JE2 3PG
☎ (01534) 68324. OPEN 10 - 5 MON - SAT.
Sells everything from blouses and skirts to ballgowns (at christmas) and bikinis. Labels range from high street to good quality middle market names such as Jaeger and Jacques Vert. When we visited, we saw a Jaeger wool two-piece, £38, a Jacques Vert blouse and skirt, £24 and blouses from £6-£18. Please phone before making a special journey during holiday periods. *Dress Agency*

EUROPE
and Overseas

Austria

WOMENSWEAR & MENSWEAR McArthurglen Designer Outlet Village, *Parndorf.*

CHILDREN McArthurglen Designer Outlet Village, *Parndorf.*

HOUSEHOLD AND GIFTWARE McArthurglen Designer Outlet Village, *Parndorf.*

FOOD AND LEISURE Travel Accessory Outlet Unit, *Parndorf.*

MCARTHURGLEN
DESIGNER OUTLET VILLAGE

INDUSTRIE & GEWERBEZENTRUM, PARNDORF, AUSTRIA
☎ 43 21 66 36 14. OPEN 9.30 - 7 MON - FRI, 9 - 5 SAT.
Among the 50 shops here near the tourist resort of Neusiedler See, 45 milometres east of Vienna, is Villeroy & Boch and Tool Man. Other brands on sale here include Cerruti, DKNY, Nike, Chevignon, Reebok, Mexx, Designer Room, Red/Green, In Wear, Aigner, Karrimor, DKNY for children, Timberland, Kanzo Jungle, Nike, Reebok, Travel Accessory Outlet. *Factory Shopping Village*

TRAVEL ACCESSORY OUTLET

UNIT 16, PARNDORF GMBH, INDUSTRIE UND GEWERBEGEBIET, 7111 PARNDORF, AUSTRIA, EUROPE
☎ 00432 1662634.
Luggage and travel-related products including executive cases, handbags, umbrellas and accessories available in leading brands such as Samsonite, Brics, Hidesign, Globe Trotter and Tula. The products also include couture and high fashion brands such as YSl and Moschino. All products are offered at a considerably reduced price due to their being production over-runs, last season's stock of slight seconds (ie they have minor aesthetic blemishes). *Factory Shopping Village*

Live Well On Less Tips
Eat out in unlicensed restaurants where you can take your own bottle. Check if they charge corkage first.

France

WOMENSWEAR & MENSWEAR
McArthurglen Designer Outlet Village, *Roubaix, Nr Lille*.
McArthurglen Designer Outlet Village, *Troyes*.

CHILDREN McArthurglen Designer Outlet Village, *Roubaix, Nr Lille*.
McArthurglen Designer Outlet Village, *Troyes*.

HOUSEHOLD AND GIFTWARE McArthurglen Designer Outlet Village, *Roubaix, Nr Lille*.
McArthurglen Designer Outlet Village, *Troyes*.

SPORTSWEAR AND EQUIPMENT McArthurglen Designer Outlet Village, *Troyes*.

MCARTHURGLEN DESIGNER OUTLET VILLAGE: BOUTIQUE DE FABRICANTS

ROUBAIX, NEAR LILLE, FRANCE
☎ 0033 + (0)320730044.
Due to open in the summer of 1999 in a town centre location, this factory shopping village will have 85 factory shops including Adidas and Blanc Blue. *Factory Shopping Village*

MCARTHURGLEN DESIGNER OUTLET VILLAGE: BOUTIQUES DE FABRICANTS

TROYES, JUNCTION 20 OF A5, EXIT PONT-STE-MARIE. FROM CALAIS JUNCTION 31 OF THE A26, FRANCE
This area is well known for its factory shops, being in the Zone des Magazins d'Usine Nord. As you'd expect from a French site, most of the big bargains in this 60-shop village are fashion companies - Polo Ralph Lauren, Timberland, Naf Naf, Kookai, Damart, Calvin Klein Jeans, Jean Bourget, Petit Bateau. However, Francoise Saget and Jalla offer own brand and designer name linen and soft furnishings in inimitable French style. For example, Jalla sell Yves St Laurent double duvets for 279 FF, usual price 550 FF; Christian Dior bath towels, 100FF, usually 179 FF. Francoise Saget offer bath towels, 25FF, instead of 69FF and double bedsheets, 99FF instead of 189FF. Having opened in 1995, it boasts the first Disney outlet in Europe, the first Nike outlet in France as well as names such as Armani, Bally, Calvin Klein, Guess, LaCoste, Marlborough Classics and Versace. *Factory Shopping Village*

Live Well On Less Tips
Buy seasonally for your freezer

Germany

WOMENSWEAR & MENSWEAR    B5 Designer Outlet Centre, *Berlin.*
Villingen Outlet Centre, *The Black Forest.*   Zweibrucken Outlet Village Centre

CHILDREN   Villingen Outlet Centre, *The Black Forest.*
Zweibrucken Outlet Village Centre

HOUSEHOLD AND GIFTWARE   B5 Designer Outlet Centre, *Berlin.*
Villingen Outlet Centre, *The Black Forest.*   Zweibrucken Outlet Village Centre

SPORTSWEAR AND EQUIPMENT   B5 Designer Outlet Centre, *Berlin.*
Villingen Outlet Centre, *The Black Forest.*   Zweibrucken Outlet Village Centre

B5 DESIGNER OUTLET CENTRE
BERLIN, GERMANY.
DUE TO OPEN IN 2000.

VILLINGEN OUTLET CENTRE
THE BLACK FOREST, GERMANY.
DUE TO OPEN IN 2001.

ZWEIBRUCKEN OUTLET VILLAGE GERMANY
CURRENTLY BEING BUILT.
Mixture of factory shops, cafes, bars and restaurants.

Italy

WOMENSWEAR & MENSWEAR   McArthurglen Designer Outlet Village, *Serravale.*

CHILDREN   McArthurglen Designer Outlet Village, *Serravalle.*

MCARTHURGLEN DESIGNER OUTLET VILLAGE
SERRAVALLE, NORTHERN ITALY
DUE TO OPEN SUMMER 2000.
The first designer outlet village in Italy, this is an easy drive from Genoa, Milan and Turin and located in the wine region above Portofino and Rapallo. There will eventually be 180 factory shops here, a spectacular circular food court with bars and restaurants, coach parking and over 3,000 car parking spaces. *Factory Shopping Village*

Spain

WOMENSWEAR & MENSWEAR   La Roca, *Nr Barcelona.*

CHILDREN   La Roca, *Nr Barcelona.*

HOUSEHOLD AND GIFTWARE   La Roca, *Nr Barcelona.*

FOOD AND LEISURE   Travel Accessory Outlet, *Barcelona.*

SPORTSWEAR AND EQUIPMENT   La Roca, *Nr Barcelona.*

LA ROCA

30KM FROM BARCELONA, OFF EXIT 12 OF THE A7, SPAIN

☎ 34 93 842 39 39. OPEN 11 - 8.30 MON - FRI, 10 - 9 SAT.

35 shops selling a wide range of local and global brands at discount prices. For the home, Cotton Corner offers Catalan quality towels and sheets in vivid colours while established names such as Descamps and Price's Candles provide familiar products in an unfamiliar setting. Other shops here include Cacharel French clothing for men and women; Catimini quality French chiildrenswear; Champion, the US sportswear comany; Dockers; Eleonora Silvestri's quality leather goods, knitwear and accessories; Espacio de Creadores offering a selection of top Spanish designer labels; Farrutx's Spanish designer shoes for women; Gianfranco Ferre; Globe which offers contemporary Spanish fashion for women; IKKS Compagnie for quality childrens sportswear; John Partridge's traditional British country clothing for men, women and children; K&E Factory Store with classic Spanish designer clothes for men and women; Levi's; Old Ridel fashion for men and women; Nike; Pepe Jeans; Petit Bateau French childrenswear; Ray Ban sunglasses; Red/Green nautical-style casualwear; Sergio Tacchini sportswear; The Designer Room; Timberland; Travel Accessory Outlet; Vans famous American skate, surf and snowboard gear; Versace; Warner's lingerie and Yanko handmade shoes. *Factory Shopping Village*

TRAVEL ACCESSORY OUTLET UNIT 30

LA ROCA COMPANY STORES, SANTA AGNES DE MALANYANES 08430, LA ROCA, DEL VALLES, BARCELONA, SPAIN, EUROPE

☎   00349 38 45 60 61. OPEN 11 - 8.30 MON - FRI, 10 - 9 SAT.

Luggage and travel-related products including executive cases, handbags, umbrellas and accessories available in leading brands such as Samsonite, Brics, Hidesign, Globe Trotter and Tula. The products also include couture and high fashion brands such as YSl and Moschino. All products are offered at a considerably reduced price due to their being production over-runs, last season's stock of slight seconds (ie they have minor aesthetic blemishes). *Factory Shopping Village*

Sweden

WOMENSWEAR & MENSWEAR  Arlandastad Outlet Village, *Nr Sigtuna.*

CHILDREN Arlandastad Outlet Village, *Nr Sigtuna.*

HOUSEHOLD AND GIFTWARE Arlandastad Outlet Village, *Nr Sigtuna.*

FOOD AND LEISURE Travel Accessory Outlet, Jarfalla, *Stockholm.*

SPORTSWEAR AND EQUIPMENT Arlandastad Outlet Village, *Nr Sigtuna.*

ARLANDASTAD
OUTLET VILLAGE

NEAR SIGTUNA, ON ROAD BETWEEN STOCKHOLM CITY CENTRE
AND THE AIRPORT, SWEDEN
NO TELEPHONE NUMBER AS WE WENT TO PRESS.
Among the companies here at Sweden's first factory outlet centre are Nike and
Vanity Fair, manufacturer of Wrangler, Lee and JanSport. *Factory Shopping
Village*

TRAVEL ACCESSORY OUTLET

UNIT 20, BARKERBY OUTLET VILLAGE, MAJORSVAGEN 2-4, S- 17738,
JARFALLA, STOCKHOLM, SWEDEN, EUROPE
☎ 0046 870 842 6875.
Luggage and travel-related products including executive cases, handbags,
umbrellas and accessories available in leading brands such as Samsonite, Brics,
Hidesign, Globe Trotter and Tula. The products also include couture and high
fashion brands such as YSl and Moschino. All products are offered at a considerably reduced price due to their being production over-runs, last season's
stock of slight seconds (ie they have minor aesthetic blemishes). *Factory
Shopping Village*

Index of
Mail Order Discounters

Index of
Brand Names

Well-known brand names and some factory shops and permanent discount shops which are known by well-known brand names, such as Timberland, Levi's and Paul Costelloe, are listed below with the pages on which they appear. Brand names with two words to their name such as Paul Costelloe are listed under P for Paul and not C for Costelloe; those with the word The in front of them are listed under their second word. Bear in mind that if these names appear in dress agencies, the shop may not carry them all year round as it depends on whether clients bring in these particular brands. The same is true of secondhand curtain shops.

THANKS TO GOOD DEAL DIRECTORY READERS

My grateful thanks to the following readers who all contributed information about discount shops they have visited which has helped to make the Millennium edition of this book the definitive guide to bargain shopping.

Linda Arnold, *Shipley*

Kathleen Bean, *Huddersfield*

Rita Berger, *Leeds*

Ruth Bicknell, *Essex*

Brenda Bowler, *Norwich*

J D Bridges, *Kennett*

Mrs K Brown, *Wetherby*

Y M Cartwright, *Bingham*

Mary D Childs, *Yarmouth*

Mrs M D Clayson, *Richmond, Yorkshire*

Trevor Copestake, *Stoke-on-Trent*

Helen Cunningham, *Sunningdale*

Mrs B A Dunwell, *Stockton*

Miss J Franks, *Darlington*

Susan Gray, *Hampshire*

Margaret Hardy, *Herefordshire*

Nick Hillman, *Romford*

C Holdcroft, *Walsall*

Mrs Marina Hughes, *Anglesey*

Helen Lavell, *Kettering*

Marni L Lonnon, *South-west London*

Denise McLaughlin, *Halifax*

Mrs G Milden, *Essex*

Maureen Moody, *Royston*

Karen Nash, *Surrey*

Carol Partington, *York*

Mrs C F Redman, *Bradford*

S Reece, *North London*

J M Reynolds, *Chandler's Ford*

E Rutherford, *Reading*

Debra See, *North London*

Will Sharpe, *Norfolk*

Diana Stainforth, *Powys*

Mrs Denise Strang, *Glasgow*

Vicky Sweetlove, *Essex*

Helen Thomas, *Shrewsbury*

L Valentine, *Herefordshire*

Mrs C A Wilkinson, *Walsall*

S Wood, *Morpeth*

REPORT FORM
EARN £10

Write and tell us about a Good Deal shop you have visited and, if we publish details based on your information, we'll send you a cheque for £10.

TO: **The Good Deal Directory**
      PO Box 4, Lechlade, Glos GL7 3YB

Name of Outlet ....

....

Address ....

....

....

Telephone number ....

Type of Merchandise ....

....

....

Comments
(please write as much as possible, explaining in detail the type of goods sold, quality, any brand names, whether labels are cut out, discounts, car parking facilities etc)

Please continue overleaf

Signed ....

Name (capitals please) ....

Address ....

....

Tel No. ....

Date ....

REPORT FORM
EARN £10

Write and tell us about a Good Deal shop you have visited and, if we publish details based on your information, we'll send you a cheque for £10.

TO: **The Good Deal Directory
PO Box 4, Lechlade, Glos GL7 3YB**

Name of Outlet ....

....

Address ....

....

....

Telephone number ....

Type of Merchandise ....

....

....

Comments
(please write as much as possible, explaining in detail the type of goods sold, quality, any brand names, whether labels are cut out, discounts, car parking facilities etc)

Please continue overleaf

Signed ....

Name (capitals please) ....

Address ....

....

Tel No. ....

Date ....

REPORT FORM
EARN £10

Write and tell us about a Good Deal shop you have visited and, if we publish details based on your information, we'll send you a cheque for £10.

TO: **The Good Deal Directory**
       PO Box 4, Lechlade, Glos GL7 3YB

Name of Outlet ....

....

Address ....

....

....

Telephone number ....

Type of Merchandise ....

....

....

Comments

(please write as much as possible, explaining in detail the type of goods sold, quality, any brand names, whether labels are cut out, discounts, car parking facilities etc)

Please continue overleaf

Signed ....

Name (capitals please) ....

Address ....

....

Tel No. ....

Date ....